D1133553

RUSSIA AT WAR

1941-1945

RUSSIA AT WAR

1941-1945

ALEXANDER WERTH

Carroll & Graf Publishers, Inc.
New York

Reprinted by arrangement with E.P. Dutton, Inc.

First Carroll & Graf edition 1984.

ISBN: 0-88184-084-X

Carroll & Graf Publishers, Inc.
260 Fifth Avenue
New York, N.Y. 10001

Manufactured in the United States of America

To the Memory of
MITYA KHLUDOV
aged 19
Killed in Action
in Belorussia
July 1944

CONTENTS

Contents   vii

MAPS

INTRODUCTION

In his speech before the American University in Washington on June 10, 1963—a speech that foreshadowed the Moscow test-ban treaty two months later—the late President Kennedy said:

> Among the many traits the peoples of our two countries (the USA and the Soviet Union) have in common, none is stronger than the mutual abhorrence of war. Almost unique among the major world powers, we have never been at war with each other. And no nation in the history of battle ever suffered more than the Russians suffered in the course of the Second World War.

And he went on to say:

> At least twenty million lost their lives. Countless millions of homes and farms were burned or sacked. A third of the nation's [European] territory, including nearly two-thirds of its industrial base, were turned into a waste-land.

Some six months later, in a less conciliatory-sounding speech at Kalinin, delivered in the presence of Fidel Castro, Khrushchev thundered against the "imperialists", urged them to clear out of Panama "before they got kicked out", swore that the Soviet Union could defend Cuba from rocket sites on Russian territory, and, with more than usual truculence, declared:

> We are building communism in our country; but that does not mean that we are building it only within the framework of the Soviet borders

and of our own economy. No, we are pointing the road to the rest of humanity. Communism is being built not only inside the Soviet borders, and we are doing everything to secure the victory of communism throughout the world.

But, having got that *chinoiserie* off his chest, he then declared, with a nod at Peking:

> Some comrades abroad claim that Khrushchev is making a mess of things, and is afraid of war. Let me say once again that I should like to see the kind of bloody fool who is genuinely not afraid of war. Only a small child is afraid of nothing, because he doesn't understand; and only bloody fools.

He then recalled that his son, an airman, was killed in World War II, and that millions of other Russians had lost their sons, and brothers, and fathers, and mothers and sisters.

True, for Castro's benefit, he ended on an unusual note of bravado, saying that, although Russia did not want war, she would "smash the enemy" with her wonderful new rockets if war were to be inflicted on the Soviet people.* Which has, of course, to be read in the light of his usual line that it is no use trying to build socialism or communism "on the ruins of a thermo-nuclear war".

In all this there was much play-acting. Significantly, the passage in his speech which the Kalinin textile workers cheered more loudly and wholeheartedly than any other was that about the "bloody fools" who were not afraid of war. Kalinin, the ancient Russian city of Tver, only a short distance from Moscow, had been occupied by the Germans in 1941, and its older people remembered only too well what it had been like.

Kennedy had spoken of the twenty million Russian dead of World War II. Officially, the Russians have been chary about mentioning this figure; when a speaker mentioned it at a meeting of the Supreme Soviet in October 1959, *Pravda* omitted it in reporting his speech the next day.† But whether the exact number of casualties that Russia suffered in the last war was twenty million, or a little more or a little less, these appalling losses have left a deep mark on the

---

* *Izvestia,* January 18, 1964.
† See the author's *The Khrushchev Phase* (London, 1961), p. 161.

Russian character, and have, whether we like it or not, been at the root of Soviet foreign policy since the war, both before and after Stalin's death. The Russian distrust of Germany, and of anyone helping Germany to become a great military power again, remains acute. There is scarcely a Russian family which the German invasion did not affect directly, and usually in the most tragic way, and if Germany remains divided in two, and we still have trouble over Berlin, it is partly due to the memories of 1941–5. These are still fresh in every older Russian mind, and the young generation of Russians are constantly reminded by books, films, broadcasts and television shows of what Russia suffered and of how she had to fight, first for her survival, and then for victory.

It would be idle to speculate on what would have happened to Russia, Britain and the United States in 1941–5, if they had not been united in their determination to crush Nazi Germany. It may well have been a "strange alliance" (as it was described by General John R. Deane, head of the American Military Mission in Moscow towards the end of the war), and its breakdown after the job was done may have been inevitable, despite the formal twenty-year alliance that Russia and Britain had signed in 1942, and other good wartime resolutions. Whatever members of the John Birch Society and other politically certifiable people (to use my friend Sir Denis Brogan's phrase) may say today about our having fought "on the wrong side", we must still say "Thank God for the Strange Alliance".

For a year, in 1940–1, Britain fought Hitler almost single-handed; and so, in a very large measure, did Russia between June 1941 and the end of 1942; and in both cases the danger of being destroyed by the Nazis was immense. Britain held out in 1940–1; Russia held out in 1941–2. But even several months after Stalingrad Stalin still declared that Nazi Germany could not be defeated except by the joint effort of the Big Three.

Perhaps the young generation in the West knows very little about those days. The French radio recently questioned some young people about World War II, and quite a number of them said: "*Hitler? connais pas.*" When I taught at an American university a few years ago I found that many young students had only the haziest notion

of Hitler, Stalin and even Winston Churchill. But do even most
adults in the West have a clear idea of how victory over Nazi
Germany was achieved? Not unnaturally, Britons have been interested chiefly in the British war effort, and Americans in the American
war effort, and this interest has been kept up by the plethora of
memoirs by British and American generals. But these memoirs have,
on the whole, tended to obscure the important fact that, in Churchill's 1944 phrase, it was the Russians who "tore the guts out of
the German Army". It so happened, for historical and geographical
reasons, that it was, indeed, the Russians who bore the main brunt
of the fighting against Nazi Germany, and that it was thanks to this
that millions of British and American lives were saved. Not that the
Russians *chose* to save these lives, and to sacrifice millions of their
own people. But that is how it happened and, during the war, both
America and Britain were acutely conscious of it. "A wave of
national gratitude is sweeping England", Sir Bernard Pares said in
1942; and, even on the more official level, similar sentiments were
freely expressed. Thus Ernest Bevin said on June 21, 1942:

> All the aid we have been able to give has been small compared with
> the tremendous efforts of the Soviet people. Our children's children
> will look back, through their history books, with admiration and
> thanks for the heroism of the great Russian people.

I doubt whether the children of Ernest Bevin's contemporaries,
let alone the children's children, have any such feelings today; and I
hope that this "history book" will remind them of a few of the
things Ernest Bevin had in mind.

It should, of course, be added that the Russians were acutely
conscious, throughout the war, of the "unequal sacrifices" made by
the Big Three. The "little Second Front" (the landings in North
Africa) did not materialise until the end of 1942, and the "big
Second Front" not till the summer of 1944. The strangely mixed
feelings towards the Allies among the Russian people during the war
years are one of the recurring themes of this book.

What kind of book is this? It is least of all a formal history of the
war. The very scale of the Soviet-German war of 1941–5, directly

involving tens of millions and, indirectly, hundreds of millions of people, was so vast that any attempt to write a "complete" history of it is out of the question in one volume written by one man. A number of military histories of this war have been written by both Russians and Germans; but even the longest of them, the vast six-volume Russian *History of the Great Patriotic War of the Soviet Union* running to over two million words, and trying to cover not only the military operations, but "everything", is singularly unsatisfactory in many ways. It contains an immense amount of valuable information which was not available under Stalin; but it is over-burdened with names of persons, regiments and divisions and an endless variety of military and economic details. It is full of ever-recurring "heroic" clichés; and yet fails completely, in my view, to tell the story of that immense nation-wide drama in purely human terms. It has the failing common to much, though not all, Soviet writing on the war of making practically all Russians look exactly alike.

Since this book is about the war in Russia, it contains, of course, numerous chapters on the main military operations. But, in dealing with these, I have, as far as possible, avoided entering into any minute technical details of the fighting, which only interest military specialists, and have tried to portray the dramatic sweep of military events, often concentrating on those details—such as the immense German air superiority in 1941-2, or the Russian superiority in artillery at Stalingrad, or the hundreds of thousands of American lorries in the Red Army after the middle of 1943—which had a direct bearing on the soldiers' morale on both sides. Further, I have tried to treat all the main military events in Russia in their national and, often, international context: for both the morale in the country and inter-allied relations were very noticeably affected by the progress of the war itself. There is, for instance, nothing fortuitous in the intensified activity of Soviet foreign policy after Stalingrad, or in the fact that the Teheran Conference should have taken place not before, but after the Russian victory of Kursk—which was the real military turning-point of the war: more so than Stalingrad which, in the words of the German historian, Walter Goerlitz, was more in the nature of a "politico-psychological turning-point".

This book, therefore, is much less a military story of the war than its human story and, to a lesser extent, its political story. I think I may say that one of my chief qualifications for writing this story of the war years in Russia is that I was there. Except for the first few months of 1942, I was in Russia right through the war—and for three years after it—and what interested me most of all were the behaviour and the reactions of the Russian people in the face of both calamity and victory. In the fearful days of 1941–2 and in the next two-and-a-half years of hard and costly victories, I never lost the feeling that this was a genuine People's War; first, a war waged by a people fighting for their life against terrible odds, and later a war fought by a fundamentally unaggressive people, now roused to anger and determined to demonstrate their own military superiority. The thought that this was *their* war was, in the main, as strong among the civilians as among the soldiers; although living conditions were very hard almost everywhere throughout the war, and truly fearful during some periods—people went on working as they had never worked before, sometimes to the point of collapse and death. No doubt there were moments of panic and demoralisation both in the Army and among civilians—and I deal with these, too, in the course of my narrative: nevertheless, the spirit of genuine patriotic devotion and self-sacrifice shown by the Russian people during those four years has few parallels in human history, and the story of the siege of Leningrad is altogether unique.

It may seem strange today to think that this immense People's War was successfully fought under the barbarous Stalin régime. But the people fought, and fought, above all, for "themselves", that is, for Russia; and Stalin had the good sense to realise this almost at once. In the dark days of 1941 he not only explicitly proclaimed that the people were fighting this war for Russia and for "the Russian heritage", thus stimulating Russian national pride, and the national sense of injury to the utmost, but he succeeded in getting himself almost universally accepted as Russia's *national* leader. Even the Church was roped in. Later, he even deliberately singled out the Russians for special praise, rather at the expense of the other nationalities of the Soviet Union, for having shown the greatest power of endurance, and the greatest patience and for never having lost faith in the Soviet régime—and, by implication, in Stalin himself. This was one way of saying that, in fighting for Russia, the Russian people also fought for the Soviet system, which is at least partly true, especially if one considers that, practically throughout the war, the two became extraordinarily closely identified, not only in propaganda, but also in people's minds. Similarly, the Party did everything to identify itself with the Army—except on one occasion, in 1942, when an attempt was made to blame the insufficiently equipped Army for some grave military reverses.

This is not to say that the régime had no major share in the credit for Russia's ultimate victory: but for the vast industrialisation effort that had gone on since 1928, and the tremendous organisational feat of evacuating a large part of industry to the east at the height of the German invasion, Russia would have been destroyed. All the same, many fearful mistakes had been made, both before the war and at the beginning of the war; and even Stalin admitted it.

In this book, I trace the varying attitudes of the Russian people to Russia, to the régime, and to Stalin himself. Marshal Zhukov, who did not like Stalin, nevertheless paid him this tribute: "You can say what you like, but that man has got nerves of iron." Among the rank-and-file Russian soldiers, Stalin was popular: as Ehrenburg recently put it, "they had absolute confidence in him." A father-figure or, shall we say, a Churchill-figure was badly needed in wartime and, in spite of everything, Stalin provided it remarkably successfully. All the same, as will be seen, his standing during the war had a great many ups and downs.

The popular reactions to the régime and to Stalin during the war are, of course, only one of the many aspects of Russian wartime mentality with which I deal in this book. I was also careful to watch people's reactions to the Germans and to the Western Allies. The attitude to the Germans was determined partly by direct experience, and partly by propaganda lines—often seemingly contradictory lines—adopted by the Party and the government at different stages of the war. In the course of my story I report on the mounting Russian anger against the Nazis, the near-racialist anti-German propaganda of Ehrenburg and others (a propaganda which was suddenly stopped in April 1945, with the Russians well inside Germany), and the effect of the German occupation on both the local inhabitants and, later, the victorious Red Army. It is scarcely surprising that many of the Russian soldiers ran wild in Germany after all that the Germans had done in the Soviet Union. And yet the Russians' attitude to individual Germans at various stages of the war was often very far from following the "Ehrenburg" pattern.

Feelings about the Western Allies also varied considerably. The distrust of the West had been so great that the Russians heaved a real sigh of relief in 1941 when they found that Britain had not ganged up with Hitler. But, with things going from bad to worse on the Russian front, the clamour for the Second Front soon started— a clamour which became strident and abusive in the summer and autumn of 1942. Much of this anger was worked up by the Soviet press; but it would have been there, anyway; the Russians were suffering fearful reverses and the Allies "were doing nothing." By the middle of 1943, especially with considerable quantities of Lend-Lease deliveries arriving at the Russian Front, the attitude perceptibly changed, and in the Soviet air force in particular, the Western allies were distinctly popular. Russian airmen were, for instance, greatly impressed by the Anglo-American bombings of Germany. All the same, the "unequal sacrifices" were something of which the Russians were acutely conscious even at the best of times. . .

Close on twenty years have passed since the end of the war in Russia, and I am perhaps the only surviving Westerner to have lived in Russia right through the war years and to have kept an almost day-to-day record of everything I saw and heard there. Paradoxically, as far as foreigners were concerned, the war years were by far the most "liberal" of all the Stalin era. We ranked as Allies, and were treated accordingly—on the whole, very well. In the circumstances, and especially as I speak Russian as a native (I was born in old St Petersburg), I was able to speak freely and informally to thousands of soldiers and civilians. Moreover, as the correspondent of the *Sunday Times* and the writer of the "Russian Commentaries" for the BBC, read by Joseph McLeod, I was given some exceptional opportunities for travelling about the country and visiting the Front. Some of these trips were made by small groups of about five or six correspondents, but I also often went on solo trips; among the most memorable of these were my stay in blockaded Leningrad, and the ten days spent in the Ukraine at the height of the Konev offensive in March 1944 which swept the Red Army right into Rumania. On all these trips I took every opportunity of talking to all and sundry; and Russian soldiers and officers, I soon found, were among the most candid and uninhibited talkers in the world. They were human beings, each with marked individual traits of his own, and were quite unlike the uniform heroic robots that they are often made to look in some of the more official Soviet books on the war. During those trips I also had the opportunity of meeting many famous generals—among them General Sokolovsky at Viazma in the tragic autumn of 1941; Chuikov and Malinovsky in the Stalingrad area; Rokossovsky in Poland; and, finally, Marshal Zhukov in Berlin.

In Moscow I got to know personally some of the top Soviet political leaders, particularly Molotov, Vyshinsky and Shcherbakov, but I cannot say that I attempted any serious Kremlinological studies during the war. At the time all seemed to be going reasonably smoothly inside the Kremlin, especially after Stalin had given the necessary weight and authority to the "new" generals in the autumn of 1941. What we know about Stalin and his immediate entourage during the war comes chiefly from what a few Russians, such as Marshal Yeremenko, and some distinguished foreign visitors, such as Churchill, Hopkins, Deane and Stettinius, have published since the war. There are also the entertaining Russian minutes of the Stalin-de Gaulle and Bidault-Molotov talks in December 1944. A more sordid picture is provided by some (inevitably hostile) Poles like Anders and Mikolajczyk. Though this evidence gives us a general idea of how the Russian leadership worked, a detailed account of the inner workings of the Kremlin during the war will not be possible until all the documents and records become available —if they ever do.* It is most unlikely that they will, because they

* The goings on among the Nazi hierarchy have become public property only because Germany was defeated and countless documents were captured. This has had, I feel, one bad effect on books

would show how great was the part played by people whose names
are now taboo. But while we do not usually know exactly how certain far-reaching decisions were taken by the Kremlin, we do know
what their effects were.

   While I made no attempt to spy on high government spheres,
I was, on the other hand, able to observe, day after day, everyday
life among Russian workers and other civilians, and the changes of
mood among them from the consternation of 1941–2 to the
optimism and elation of 1943 onward—despite countless personal
losses and the great hardships that most, though not all, continued
to suffer. (The inequality, especially in food rationing, was one of
the most unpleasant aspects of ordinary life in Russia during the
war—and, indeed, long after.) I also saw a great deal of writers,
artists and other intellectuals—Pasternak, Prokofiev and Eisenstein
among them—and also some very queer political animals, such as
the members of the "Union of Polish Patriots", that foetus which
soon emerged from the womb of Mother Russia as the Lublin Committee.

   All these contacts with both "important" and "unimportant"
people gave me a good cross-section of Russian opinion, with its
many *nuances*, during the various stages of the war—whether in
Moscow, or at the Front, or in the newly-liberated areas—and I do
not think it necessary to apologise for having devoted a substantial
part of this book to personal observations of the life and moods in
the Soviet Union during the war years.* I even venture to think that
they will fill a substantial gap in so much of the more-or-less official
Soviet writing on the war.

   It would, however, have been quite insufficient to rely entirely on my
own observations, however numerous, and on contemporary press

---

on Germany during the war: they have concentrated on the actions
of the Nazi thugs, and have told us too little about the reactions of
the German people.

* In the earlier part of this book I have used some of the descriptive
material from my earlier books on Russia, particularly *The Year of
Stalingrad*, which are now out of print.

accounts, in writing this account of the war years in Russia. During
the first few months of the Invasion it was possible to *guess* a great
many things, but it was virtually impossible to explain with any
accuracy just why, within two months, the Germans reached the
outskirts of Leningrad and, within three-and-a-half months, the outskirts of Moscow. During those months when, in Pasternak's phrase,
autumn was advancing in steps of calamity, I shared the general
bewilderment and consternation of the Russian people. Much else
remained obscure during the war. Many such obscure points have
been clarified by the enormous amount of literature published in
Russia in recent years—since the XXth Congress of 1956 and, more
particularly, since 1959 60 of which I have made a careful study,
and which has helped me greatly. Thus, the first volume of the
official History of the War, already mentioned, contains, for all its
shortcomings, some amazing facts to explain the many military,
economic, political and psychological reasons for the unpreparedness of the Red Army to meet the German onslaught. I have also
drawn on some remarkable personal reminiscences by Russian
soldiers, such as Generals Boldin and Fedyuninsky, describing the
first days of the war in the Invasion areas. The silence and discretion
with which all this was treated in the Stalin days is now at an end.
Whether in war histories, memoirs, novels, or even poetry, more perhaps has been written in recent years about those fearful first months
of the war than about any other. A novel like Konstantin Simonov's
*The Living and the Dead** is, in fact, the best, though belated, piece
of reporting there is on these months between the Invasion and the
Battle of Moscow. Recent Russian books, included in the bibliography at the end of this volume, throw light on many other 1941
disasters, such as the Kiev encirclement, in which the Germans
claimed 660,000 prisoners, or the early stages of the Battle of
Moscow, including the equally disastrous Viazma encirclement.

Or take Leningrad, that unique story of a city of three million
people, of whom nearly one-third died of hunger, but would not
surrender. In *Leningrad*, a book I published in 1944, I gave, in
human terms, a full and accurate account of what had happened

* Published in the United States by Doubleday in 1962.

there during the famine. But I obviously could not, at the time, obtain statistical data, for instance, on the exact amount of food available in the city when the German ring closed round it, or on the exact quantities delivered at various periods across the ice of Lake Ladoga. Today the precise facts are to be found in such invaluable recent books as D. V. Pavlov's and A. V. Karasev's on the Leningrad Blockade. These are first-class historical documents by any standard.

I have also used dozens of other books recently published on other important episodes of the war—the grim summer of 1942, the tragedy of Sebastopol, the Stalingrad story, Partisan warfare during the different stages of the war, and so on.

I have also dealt in some detail with the diplomatic story of the war, some of the episodes on which I was able to observe closely. My many talks with Sir Stafford Cripps in 1941, and with Sir Archibald Clark Kerr later in the war, were of great value in throwing light on Anglo-Soviet relations. I also kept in close touch with the U.S. Embassy, and one of my most valuable contacts was the very shrewd M. Roger Garreau, General de Gaulle's representative in Moscow.

Politically, one of the main strands in this book is the story of Soviet-Polish relations, which were in the very centre of Stalin's preoccupations, and which had important effects on his relations with his allies: first, the crisis culminating in the breach of diplomatic relations with the Polish Government in London in April 1943; then the formation of a Polish Army on Russian soil; the whole lurid Katyn business, then the setting up of the Lublin Committee and the tragedy of Warsaw in the autumn of 1944. It will be seen that, with a few important reservations, and after careful reflection, I tend to agree with the Russian version of Warsaw, but not at all with the Russian version of Katyn—at least pending further information, which is remarkably slow in appearing. Mr Khrushchev has done nothing to clear *that* matter up.

In short, I have made extensive use of recent Russian books on the war—most of which might be classified as "Khrushchevite", and *ipso facto* anti-Stalinite. There is, however, a danger in taking all these as gospel truth merely because they are anti-Stalinite. Stalinite history was notorious for its lack of "objectivity", and for its shameless suppression and distortion of historical facts. But the same, to a lesser extent, is often also true of Khrushchevite history. To give a small example. When I saw General Chuikov at Stalingrad in February 1943, he declared that two members of the hierarchy had been on the Stalingrad Front almost all through the battle—Khrushchev and Malenkov. One would look in vain in any recent book, even in Chuikov's own extremely candid story, for any mention of Malenkov. Khrushchev's role is greatly magnified in recent histories of the war and much is made of two particular instances (Kiev in 1941 and Kharkov in 1942) when disaster could, allegedly, have been averted if only Stalin had followed Khrushchev's advice.

Khrushchevite history, like Stalinite history in the past, suffers from sins of omission. As Molotov, Malenkov and Beria were Stalin's closest associates on the State Defence Committee (i.e. the War Cabinet, as it were), one would correctly assume that they played a role of the utmost importance in the conduct of the war and the organisation of the war economy; but, except for a few rare references to Molotov as Foreign Commissar and to Beria's "treasonable activities", these names are not mentioned in recent accounts of the war. Similarly, the role of some generals, now in high favour, is magnified, and that of others, notably Zhukov, greatly minimised. In the official History, the fact that Zhukov had anything to do with the defence of Leningrad (which in reality he saved) is merely mentioned in a perfunctory one-line footnote. There are some other flaws in Khrushchevite history: some crucial landmarks—such as the far-reaching reforms in the Red Army in the summer and autumn of 1942 after the fall of Rostov—are glossed over completely, though General Malinovsky, whom I saw soon afterwards, attached the greatest importance to them.

The various changes in the propaganda line, the attitude of the people to Stalin and the Party and the relations between the Party and the Red Army are other topics which (perhaps not surprisingly) are rarely touched upon in Soviet writings on the war.

Much of the more or less official "Khrushchevite" writing also fails to render the real atmosphere of the war years. Thus, I find that not only my personal notes but also the Soviet press of the Black Summer of 1942, when the Germans were crashing ahead towards Stalingrad and into the Caucasus, render much more accurately than any official history written today the intense anxiety and exasperation that swept the country. There were days when the tone of the press was frantic and almost hysterical with *patrie-en-danger* propaganda and, a little later, in its outcry against cowardice, disobedience and incompetence in the Army. (This, as we shall see, was at least partly designed to divert the dismay in the country from Stalin and the government to the Army.)

Despite these shortcomings, recent Soviet books on the war still contain an enormous amount of valuable factual material. I have used this extensively, but not uncritically, and not without a great deal of laborious cross-checking. In many cases I have had to compare Russian statements and figures with their German counterparts.

Though my story is chiefly concerned with the war years in the Soviet Union, I thought it necessary to deal briefly, in an introductory part, with the 1939-41 period in Russia. After going through the Soviet press of the time and questioning scores of Russians on that period, I have tried to show in these chapters how the post-Munich developments—the Anglo-Franco-Soviet negotiations in the spring and summer of 1939, the Soviet-German Pact, the partition of Poland, the war with Finland, the fall of France, the Battle of Britain and the rapid deterioration of Soviet-Nazi relations after Molotov's Berlin visit at the end of 1940 were presented to the Soviet people in their press, and also what a very large number of Soviet people privately felt about it all. I think readers will find some interesting new facts in this story: the mixed feelings produced by the Soviet-German pact, the great anxiety caused in Russia by the rapid collapse of France, the sneaking sympathy and admiration for Britain (especially among Soviet intellectuals) during the blitz winter of 1940-1, and the great relief, reflected even in *Pravda* editorials and in Molotov's speeches, at the thought that, after the fall of France, Britain was, with American support, continuing the war and that a German victory was still very far from being a foregone conclusion! Regardless of all the official bluster about the invincibility of the Red Army, anxiety in the country grew very rapidly during the first half of 1941. Despite all Stalin's and Molotov's absurd attempts after the fall of Yugoslavia and Greece to put off the evil hour by at least a few months or even weeks, they both knew that a showdown with Germany was now inevitable, as seems apparent from Stalin's "secret" talk to the military academy graduates at the beginning of May 1941. His only hope now was to gain just a little more time. There also seems little doubt that some of the more clear-sighted Russian soldiers already had the possibility—and desirability—of an Anglo-Soviet alliance at the back of their minds.

In conclusion I wish to express my deepest appreciation to the Louis M. Rabinowitz Foundation of New York for their generous grant which has helped to meet so many of the expenses connected with the writing of this book.

My warmest thanks also go to my friend Bobby Ullstein for her frequent good advice and her untiring work on the proofs—which is far more than one normally expects from one's publisher's wife! I also thank my friend John G. Pattisson for his great help in seeing the book through the press.

Finally, I wish to record my special gratitude to John Erickson of Manchester University, our leading authority on the Red Army and author of the admirable *Soviet High Command*, for reading the greater part of the manuscript and for making many valuable and helpful criticisms and observations.

A.W.

PART ONE

Prelude to War

Chapter I

RUSSIA'S 1939 DILEMMA

On May 4, 1939 there appeared in *Pravda* and in all other Soviet papers a small paragraph entitled:

UKASE OF THE PRESIDIUM OF THE SUPREME SOVIET
ON THE APPOINTMENT OF V. M. MOLOTOV AS PEOPLE'S
COMMISSAR OF FOREIGN AFFAIRS OF THE USSR.

It read:

The Chairman of the Council of People's Commissars of the USSR V. M. Molotov is appointed People's Commissar of Foreign Affairs. The two functions are to be exercised concurrently.

Chairman of the Presidium of the Supreme Soviet of the USSR:
M. Kalinin
Secretary of the Presidium of the Supreme Soviet of the USSR:
A. Gorkin

There was no mention of Maxim Litvinov, who had resigned on the previous day "at his own request" and whom Molotov had so abruptly replaced at the head of Soviet diplomacy, or of any other post he had been given instead. The small news item caused a sensation throughout the world, where it was interpreted as the end of an epoch.

Hitler himself, at the famous military conference of August 22, 1939—the day before the signing of the German-Soviet non-aggression pact and barely ten days before the invasion of Poland—

3

declared to his generals: "Litvinov's dismissal was decisive. It came to me like a cannon shot, like a sign that the attitude of Moscow towards the Western Powers had changed."

This, like countless other statements to the effect that the dismissal of Litvinov and his replacement by Molotov meant a "decisive" change in Soviet foreign policy, is much too simple. The most that can be said is that the *ukase* of the Supreme Soviet of May 3 marked the official end of the "Litvinov epoch"; but this had, in fact, been petering out over a very long period, especially since Munich in September 1938, a settlement from which the Russians had been ostentatiously excluded.

The gravest doubts about the success of Litvinov's collective security and League of Nations policy existed in Russia for a long time. In fact, it is wrong to describe this policy as "Litvinov's" policy. He was pursuing a policy laid down and approved by the Soviet Government and the Party, and the personal factor mattered only in so far as he pursued this policy with great conviction, enthusiasm and determination. But, all along, he had found the results deeply disappointing and frustrating. For only a short period in 1934 did the French think in terms of a Grand Alliance against Nazi Germany, comprising France's allies (Poland, Czechoslovakia, Rumania, Yugoslavia), Britain and the Soviet Union. This was when Louis Barthou was Foreign Minister. Britain was, however, less than lukewarm towards the Barthou plan, and so was Poland.

After Barthou's assassination in October 1934 he was replaced at the Quai d'Orsay by Pierre Laval, whose greatest ambition was an alliance with Mussolini's Italy and some kind of agreement with Nazi Germany. If, in 1935, he signed a mutual assistance pact with the Soviet Union, it was chiefly for tactical and domestic reasons, and the practical value of this pact was not rated highly either in France or in Russia. For one thing the French were reluctant to follow up the pact with a military convention.

In March 1936 came Hitler's reoccupation of the Rhineland; and France's failure to react clearly suggested to the Russians that France could scarcely be depended upon to abide by her alliances with Poland and the Little Entente countries. There was going to be a widening gulf between France's official foreign policy and her military possibilities once the Rhineland had been occupied and fortified by Hitler.

And who, during those years, had been the men in charge of British policy? Ramsay MacDonald, Sir John Simon, who gave Mussolini a free hand in Abyssinia at the Stresa conference in 1935; then Baldwin and Simon who had discouraged any French action in response to the Rhineland *coup*; then Samuel Hoare of the Hoare-Laval Plan; then Chamberlain and Halifax. Appeasement had, in varying degrees, become the official policy of both Britain and France—appeasement over the Rhineland *coup*, appeasement over Spain, appeasement over Austria and Czechoslovakia. Munich had been the ultimate triumph of the appeasement policy. In Britain, the few sincere critics of this policy—notably Anthony Eden—had been swept aside, and Churchill was little more than a voice crying in the wilderness. In France things were no better. At the end of 1937, the well-meaning but wholly ineffectual Yvon Delbos, who had been Foreign Minister since the formation of Léon Blum's Popular Front Government in June 1936, went on a long tour through Eastern Europe—he visited Warsaw, Belgrade, Bucharest and Prague—but only to find that France's system of alliances had fallen to ruins since the Rhineland *coup*, with the Czechs alone still pathetically believing that France would come to their help if Germany attacked them. Significantly Delbos failed to include Moscow in his tour. Before long the arch-appeaser Georges Bonnet became the head of French diplomacy.

When after Munich Bonnet welcomed Ribbentrop to Paris in December 1938, he did not officially (as has sometimes erroneously been suggested) give Germany "a free hand in the East". Nevertheless the half-heartedness with which France's "special relations with third powers" were referred to, the extremely ambiguous statements Bonnet made a week later before the Foreign Affairs committee of the Chamber about France's commitments *vis-à-vis* Poland, Rumania or the Soviet Union, and above all, the press campaign launched with official blessing, in influential papers like *Le Matin* and *Le Temps*, in favour of lunatic schemes such as the

formation of a "Greater Ukraine" under the rule of German stooges
like Biskupsky and Skoropadsky, left very little doubt about the
overtones of the Bonnet-Ribbentrop "friendship talks".* When,
during the following summer, Bonnet proceeded to "warn"
Germany, Ribbentrop did not fail to point out that in December
1938 Bonnet had shown no desire to interfere with either German
designs on Danzig or with German interests in the East generally.

The idea of a "Greater Ukraine" had certainly not been a brain-
wave of the French or British "appeasers". Hitler had been playing
with this idea for some weeks after Munich; soon, however, he
realised that if his plans for a "Greater Ukraine" were to be pursued
further at this stage it might result in a *rapprochement* between
Russia, Poland and Rumania.† In January 1939 he told Beck that
he had lost interest in the Ukraine. But the very fact that such a
scheme had been considered and applauded by influential sections
of the French (and British) press, was, of course, not lost on Stalin,
and his suspicions of some deal between London, Paris and Berlin
inevitably grew during the winter of 1938–9.

Even at this stage, however, Stalin continued to distinguish carefully
between the "aggressive" powers (Germany, Italy, Japan) and the
"non-aggressive" powers (France, Britain, USA), although he
deplored the latters' weakness and gutlessness—as he was to make
very clear in his Report to the 18th Congress of the Communist
Party on March 10, that is, five days before the German march into
Prague, which put an end to the precarious "peace in our time"
after barely six months.

That winter of 1938–9 was an uneasy winter in Russia. True, the
Purges had been largely discontinued by the end of 1938, but
thousands had been sent to exile or to labour camps; and many—
no one could tell how many—had been shot. At the Lenin

* See the author's *France and Munich: Before and After the
Surrender* (London, 1939), pp. 384–91.
† Robert Coulondre, *De Staline à Hitler* (Paris, 1950), pp. 251–3.

Commemorative Ceremony at the Bolshoi Theatre on January 21, 1939, Yezhov, Stalin's No. 1 executioner, was still to be seen amongst the top Party and Army leaders—Stalin, Beria, Mikoyan, Kaganovich, Shcherbakov, Andreyev, Kalinin, Shkiriatov, Malenkov, Molotov, Budienny, Mekhlis, Zhdanov, Voroshilov, and Badayev. It was to be Yezhov's last public appearance.

Now, at the end of the Second Five-Year Plan, living—though not housing—conditions in Russia, and particularly in Moscow, had greatly improved. Stalin's *zhit' stalo legche, zhit' stalo veselei*—"life has become easier, life has become more cheerful"—had become the country's official slogan. Trivial musical comedies, operettas and comic films were in vogue. Popular song writers like Pokras, Blanter and Dunaevsky were at the height of their fame; Blanter had just composed his famous *Katyusha* (which was, alas, to become one of the favourite soldiers' marching songs in 1941) and Dunaevsky his *Shiroka strana moya rodnaya* (Vast is my Country) with the more than incongruous line "I know of no other country where man breathes so freely". (This at the height of the Purges!) Alongside popular slapstick comic films like *Volga-Volga* starring Lubov Orlova, a sort of Soviet Gracie Fields, and illustrating how cheerful life had become in the Soviet Union under the "Sun of the Stalin Constitution", there were the patriotic films, among them Eisenstein's *Alexander Nevsky*—showing what would happen to the descendants of the villainous Teutonic Knights if they ever dared invade Holy Russia. Another famous film, *Doctor Mamlock*, denounced Hitler's persecution of the Jews.

More or less consciously everybody was aware of the Nazi danger. There was an uneasy feeling that everywhere in the world the "aggressors" were having it their own way—except where they dared touch the Soviet Union and her Mongolian ally, as Japan had done at Lake Hassan only a few months before. But Japan, Italy and Germany were becoming increasingly arrogant, and throughout that winter the news from Spain was more and more depressing despite the meaningless assurances in *Pravda* that "the Spanish people would not lay down their arms until final victory". At the beginning

of January, Colonel Beck, Poland's strong man, was on his way to
Berchtesgaden to see Hitler. Had Russia *any* friends, a few wondered
on the quiet—except, of course, gallant little Mongolia?

No wonder that in those days people looked to the Army for protection and that for example some women ace-fliers like Valentina
Grizodubova, Polina Osipenko and Marina Raskova became popular idols. When in May 1939 one of them, Polina Osipenko, and the
ace-flier Serov were killed in an air-crash, it was like a day of
national mourning; they were given a public funeral in Red Square,
and the pall-bearers included Stalin, Molotov, Beria and other
leaders.

Every opportunity was taken to glorify the Armed Forces of the
Soviet homeland, though, as some observers later recalled, all this
was a little like whistling in the dark; below all the bluster about the
invincibility of the Red Army there was a good deal of anxiety. On
January 1, 1939, in its New Year's Day editorial, *Pravda* recalled a
recent warning by Stalin himself: "We must be ready at any moment
to repel an armed attack on our country, and to smash and finish off
the enemy on his own territory."

Significantly, at the Lenin Commemorative Ceremony on
January 21, 1939, a large part of the long address delivered by
Shcherbakov was devoted to the Red Army:

> The Socialist Revolution has triumphed in one country. The Socialist
> State is encircled by the capitalist world, and this encirclement is only
> waiting for an opportunity to attack our state. In such conditions there
> can, of course, be no question of any withering-away of the State . . .
> In 1919 our Party programme provided for the transformation of the
> Red Army into a People's Militia. But conditions have changed, and
> we cannot build up a mighty army on a militia basis.
>
> In these conditions our Party and our Government have built up a
> mighty Red Army and Red Navy, and a mighty armaments industry,
> and have lined with steel and concrete the frontiers of this land of
> triumphant socialism. The Soviet Union, which was weak and un-
> prepared for defence, is now ready for all emergencies; it is capable,
> as Comrade Stalin said, of producing modern weapons of defence on a
> mass scale, and of supplying our Army with them in the event of a

foreign attack. The Party and the Government are maintaining our people in a state of military preparedness, and no enemy can catch us unawares.

Shcherbakov recalled how, only a few months before, "the Japanese Samurai had felt on their own skin the might of Soviet arms; there, at Lake Hassan, where the Japanese militarists had tried to provoke us into war, our air force and artillery turned the Japanese guns into litter and their pillboxes into dust".

This clash with the Japanese had, in fact, been the Red Army's only real experience of war for many years past, and it was, a little rashly, being held up as a stern warning to all other aggressors. At the same time, there still seemed to be a certain muddleheadedness about modern warfare—an attitude curiously reminiscent of certain French military theorists at the time, who pooh-poohed the concept of the *blitzkrieg*. Thus *Pravda* wrote on February 6, 1939, in connection with the twentieth birthday of the Frunze Military Academy:

> In the land of triumphant socialism, the working class, under the leadership of the Party of Lenin and Stalin, is building up new military concepts. Following the directives of the Party and Comrade Stalin, the Frunze Academy has discarded a good number of old fetishes, cast aside quite a few mouldy traditions, and liquidated the enemies of the people who had tried to interfere with the training of Bolshevik military *cadres* devoted to the Party.

Was this intended as a nebulous reference to Tukhachevsky and the thousands of other purgees of the Red Army? Anyway, Stalin and the present Red Army leadership knew best:

> Military thought in the capitalist world has got into a blind alley. The dashing "theories" about a lightning war (*blitzkrieg*), or about small select armies of technicians, or about the air war which can replace all other military operations—all these theories arise from the bourgeoisie's deathly fear of the proletarian revolution. In its mechanical way, the imperialist bourgeoisie overrates equipment and underrates man.

This debunking of the *blitzkrieg* and the primary reliance on "man" seems, looking back on it, about as incongruous as the alleged deadly fear of the "proletarian revolution" by which Hitler in particular was supposed to be obsessed.

*

It went on like this almost day after day during that winter of
1938–9. "The Red Army is Invincible," *Pravda* wrote on Red Army
Day, February 23, 1939, and E. Shchadenko, Deputy Commissar for
Defence, declared that, under the leadership of Comrade Voroshilov,
the Red Army was ready to "answer any attack by the militarists
with a smashing blow of treble force". N. S. Khrushchev also joined
in this chorus exalting the invincibility of the Red Army. Below a
large picture of Khrushchev, Secretary of the Central Committee of
the Ukrainian Communist Party, *Pravda* of March 4, 1939 published
this message to Stalin from the Party Conference of the Kiev
province:

> The Kiev Party Organisation has spared no effort to turn the
> province of Kiev into an impregnable advance post of Soviet Ukraine.
> We are living here in a frontier zone, on the border of two worlds. . .
> The Fascist warmongers have not ceased to think of attacking Soviet
> Ukraine. We swear to you, dear Comrade Stalin, that we shall always
> be in a state of military preparedness, and shall be fully capable, with
> all the strength of Soviet patriotism, of dealing with any enemies and
> of wiping them off the face of the earth. . . Under the guidance of
> your closest brother-in-arms, N. S. Khrushchev, the Bolsheviks of the
> Kiev Zone will carry out with honour the tasks with which they have
> been entrusted. . . Long live our wise leader and teacher, the genius
> of mankind, the best friend and father of the Soviet people, great
> Stalin!

Only a few days later a patriotic speech on the same lines was
made by Khrushchev at the unveiling of the Kiev monument of
Shevchenko, the Ukraine's national poet, ending with "Long live he
who is leading us from victory to victory, our dearly beloved friend
and teacher, the great Stalin."*

The references to Kiev, both in the Kiev Party Organisation's
address to Stalin and in Khrushchev's speech, as a "frontier zone"
threatened by the "Fascists" are typical of the nervousness that
existed in Russia at the time about Hitler's designs, despite all the
bluster about "invincibility." and "impregnability". The press campaigns in the West (especially in France) about a "Greater Ukraine"
which was to be detached from the Soviet Union and was to provide
Germany with her much-needed *Lebensraum*, had clearly caused a

* *Pravda*, March 7, 1939.

profound impression in Russia. It was to be one of the principal
themes in Stalin's survey of the international situation in his Report
to the 18th Congress of the Communist Party which opened in
Moscow on March 10.

The "personality cult", as we would now say, was at its height. On
the opening day of the Congress, *Pravda* published a poem by
Djambul, the veteran Kazakh bard, aged nearly a hundred:

> Tenderly the sun is shining from above,
> And who cannot but know that this sun is—you?
> The lapping waves of the lake are singing the praises of Stalin,
> The dazzling snowy peaks are singing the praises of Stalin,
> The meadow's million flowers are thanking, thanking you;
> The well-laden table is thanking, thanking you.
> The humming swarm of bees is thanking, thanking you,
> All fathers of young heroes, they thank you, Stalin, too;
> Oh heir of Lenin, to us you are Lenin himself;
> Beware, you Samurai, keep out of our Soviet heaven!

Perhaps the only excuse for publishing this rubbish was that it
had a "folklorish" and "exotic" flavour, and was the work of an
illiterate old Asiatic. Even so, many members of the Congress must,
on the quiet, have thought it frivolous and inappropriate to splash
this kind of thing over the front page of *Pravda* on so solemn and
serious an occasion. For Stalin's foreign policy statement was
awaited with both eagerness and a touch of anxiety. It should be
remembered that Europe was already full of danger signals and that
the Congress opened, and that Stalin's report was delivered, five
days before the German march into Prague.

Stalin divided the capitalist powers into "aggressive" powers and
"non-aggressive" powers, but suspected the latter of wanting "others
to pull the chestnuts out of the fire for them", suggesting that they
might not be averse to seeing the Soviet Union involved in a war
with the "aggressors". He dealt in some detail with the economic
crisis in the capitalist world, a crisis which had begun in 1929, and
which, since then, had only been partly overcome by the armaments
race. Stalin said that the grabbing of Manchuria and Northern China

by Japan and the Italian invasion of Abyssinia already pointed to the acute struggle among the Powers. With the new economic crisis (since 1937), this imperialist conflict could not but grow in intensity. It was no longer a case of competition for markets, trade war or dumping. These weapons were no longer considered sufficient. What Russia was now facing was a redistribution of the world, of spheres of influence and colonies by means of war.

The "have-nots" were now attacking the "haves". Japan now claimed to have been tied hand-and-foot by the Nine-Power Treaty; this had prevented her from enlarging her territory at China's expense, while Britain and France possessed vast colonial territories; Italy had recalled that she also had been cheated of her share after the first imperialist war, whereas Germany was now demanding a return of her colonies and an extension of her territory in Europe. In this way a bloc had been formed among the three aggressive powers, and now the question had arisen of a new share-out of the world by military means.

The new imperialist war, Stalin said, had already begun. Since Italy's capture of Abyssinia, both she and Germany had organised their military intervention in Spain. In 1937, after grabbing Manchuria, Japan had invaded Northern and Central China, and had driven its foreign competitors out of these new occupied zones; in 1938 Germany had grabbed first Austria and then the Sudetenland, while Japan had occupied Canton, and, more recently still, Hainan.

After the first imperialist war, Stalin recalled, the victorious powers had created a new international régime of peace; this was based on the Nine-Power Treaty in the Far East and on the Treaty of Versailles and other agreements in Europe. The League of Nations was expected to regulate international relations on a basis of collective security... To give themselves a completely free hand, the three aggressor states had left the League. To cover up their treaty violations, the three aggressor states had proceeded to work on public opinion with the help of devices like the Anti-Comintern Pact. "It was a clumsy game, because it seems a bit absurd to look for Comintern breeding-grounds in the deserts of Mongolia, the mountains of Abyssinia or in the wilds of Spanish Morocco."

All these conquests were made by the aggressor states, quite regardless of the interests of the non-aggressor states. "This new imperialist war has not yet become a general world war. It is being conducted by the aggressor states against the interest of the non-aggressor states, but these, believe it or not, are not only retreating, but to some extent conniving in this aggression."

It was not, Stalin said, that the non-aggressive, democratic countries were weak; both economically and militarily these countries, taken together, were stronger than the Fascist countries; why then were they behaving in this odd way? It might, of course, be argued that they were afraid of the revolution that would follow a new war; but this was by no means the chief reason for their behaviour:

> The real reason is this: the majority of the non-aggressive states, and in the first place Britain and France, have given up the policy of collective security, and have changed over, instead, to a policy of non-intervention, to a position of "neutrality". On the face of it, this non-intervention policy may be described as follows: "Let every country defend itself against aggressors any way it can or likes; it's got nothing to do with us, and we shall go on trading with both the aggressors and their victims." But in actual practice non-intervention means connivance in aggression, and encouragement to the aggressors to turn their aggression into a world war... There is a clear desire there to let the aggressors do their dirty and criminal work—to let Japan become involved in war with China or, better still, with the Soviet Union, or to let Germany get bogged down in European affairs, and to get involved in a war against the Soviet Union... And not until all the belligerents have thoroughly exhausted each other will the non-aggressive powers come forward—of course "in the interests of peace" —with their own proposals, and dictate their terms to the powers that have frittered away their strength in making war on each other. A nice and cheap way of doing things!

Was there not a hint that if "they" could play at this game of the fresh-and-bright neutrals dictating their terms to the exhausted belligerents, then why should not "we" play it, too?

Britain and France, Stalin went on to say, had clearly encouraged Nazi Germany to attack the Soviet Union:

> They abandoned Austria, despite the obligations to protect her independence; they abandoned the Sudentenland, and threw Czecho-

slovakia to the wolves; in doing so, they broke every conceivable obligation; but after that, their press started its noisy campaign of lies about "the weakness of the Russian Army", the "breakdown of the Russian Air Force", the "disorders" in the Soviet Union. . . They kept on urging the Germans to go farther and farther east: "You just start a war against the Bolsheviks, and all will be well."

He then referred to "all the hullabaloo in the French, British and American press about a German invasion of Soviet Ukraine":

> They screamed, till they were hoarse, that since Germany was now in control of the so-called Carpathian Ukraine,* with about 700,000 people, the Germans would, not later than the spring of 1939, annex to it the Soviet Ukraine with a population of over thirty millions. It really looks as if the purpose of all this highly suspect screaming was to incense the Soviet Union against Germany, to poison the atmosphere, and provoke a conflict between us and Germany without any obvious reasons. There may, of course, be some lunatics in Germany who are thinking of marrying off the elephant (I mean Soviet Ukraine) to the gnat—the so-called Carpathian Ukraine. But let them have no doubt about it: if there are such lunatics, there are quite enough strait-jackets waiting for them here (*stormy applause*). . . It is significant that some politicians and newspapermen in Europe and the USA should now be expressing their great disappointment because the Germans, instead of moving farther east, have now turned to the west, and are demanding colonies. One would think that parts of Czechoslovakia were given to them as advance payment for starting a war against the Soviet Union; and now the Germans are refusing to refund the money and are telling them to go to hell. . . I can only say that this dangerous game started by the supporters of the non-intervention policy may end very badly for them.

In any case, Munich had brought no lasting peace. The world today was full of alarm and uncertainty; the post-war order had been blown sky-high; international law and treaties and agreements counted for very little. All disarmament plans had been buried. Everybody now was arming feverishly, not least the non-intervention states. "Nobody believes any longer in those unctuous speeches about the concessions made to the aggressors at Munich having started a new era of peace. Even the British and French signatories

* The eastern tip of Czechoslovakia, also known as Ruthenia.

of the Munich agreement don't believe a word of it. They are arming as much as the others are."

And Stalin added that, while doing her utmost to pursue a policy of peace, the Soviet Union could not look on impassively while 500 million people were already involved in war; and she had undertaken the task of greatly strengthening the military preparedness of the Red Army and the Red Navy.

Throughout, Stalin recalled, the Soviet Union had pursued a policy of peace. She had joined the League of Nations in 1934, hoping that, despite its weakness, the League could still act as a brake on aggression; in 1935 she had signed a mutual assistance pact with France, and another one with Czechoslovakia; a mutual assistance pact had also been signed in 1937 with Mongolia, and in 1938 a non-aggression pact with China. The Soviet Union wanted peace; she wanted peace and business relations with all countries, so long as these did not impinge on her interests; she stood for peaceful, close and good-neighbourly relations with all her immediate neighbours, so long as these did not try, directly or indirectly, to interfere with the integrity of her borders; she stood for the support of nations which had become the victims of aggression and were struggling for their independence; she did not fear the aggressors' threats, and would strike with double strength any warmongers who might try to violate Soviet territory. (*Long stormy applause.*)

The tasks of the Party in foreign policy were:

1) To pursue the policy of peace and of the consolidation of business relations with all countries;
2) To observe the greatest caution and not to allow our country to be drawn into conflicts by war *provocateurs*, who were in the habit of getting others to pull the chestnuts out of the fire for them;
3) To strengthen in every way the military might of the Red Army and Navy;
4) To strengthen the international bonds of friendship with the workers of all countries, workers in whose interest it was to maintain peace and friendship among peoples.

On the face of it, in view of what Stalin said of the complete breakdown of "international law" and international treaties, his speech suggested that, in this international jungle, the Soviet Union

would be wise to remain in splendid isolation; but in his precise
wording he evidently took some trouble not to slam the door in the
face of the French and British statesmen. The possibility of a late
deal with the West could perhaps still be read into the reference to
the Franco-Soviet mutual assistance pact. On the other hand he had
dwelt far more on the perfidiousness of the "non-aggressor" nations
than on that of the "aggressors", and he had almost gone so far as
to congratulate Germany on her wisdom in not having invaded the
Ukraine, as "the West" had allegedly urged her to do!

Not without significance were also Stalin's references to Russia's
"immediate neighbours". Had not some suspect negotiations been
going on between Germany and some of Russia's "immediate neighbours"? Had Nazi diplomacy not been active in the Baltic states?
Had not Beck raised the "question" of the Ukraine with Hitler at
Berchtesgaden on January 7, only to be told by the Führer that he
no longer regarded the Ukraine as topical.* And the Russians continued to suspect the Finns, who only a year before had celebrated
the twentieth anniversary of their liberation from "the Bolshevik
yoke" with the help of the Kaiser's army towards the end of the
First World War.

Such was the trend of Soviet policy on the eve of the Nazi march
into Prague. It was still a wait-and-see attitude; the menace of war
was already acute, but it was still not entirely clear what Hitler's
next move would be.

The Nazi entry into Prague on March 15 not only put a full stop
to Chamberlain's Munich illusions, but put the Soviet Union in a
position where a clear choice would have to be made before long.
It was already evident from Stalin's speech of March 10 that he was
anxious to keep out of it all—*unless* there was a possibility of stopping the aggressors through at least a partial restoration of
"collective security"—which could only mean the conclusion of an
anti-Hitler alliance by the "non-aggressive" powers.

*

* *Le Livre jaune français* (Paris, 1939), p. 72.

The German invasion of Czechoslovakia came to Russia as a shock —though not perhaps as a great surprise. When, on March 15, the blow fell, the Soviet reaction was fairly sharp. In reply to the official German notification that Bohemia and Moravia had been incorporated in the Reich as a "protectorate" and that the statute of Slovakia had been "modified" (it had been turned into a German satellite under Mgr Tiso), Litvinov sent the German Government a strongly-worded note. In it he recalled the Czechs' right to self-determination and denied the validity of President Hacha's surrender to Berlin. And Litvinov concluded: "The action of the German Government not only fails to lessen the dangers threatening world peace, but can, on the contrary, only intensify them, shake the political stability of Central Europe ... and strike another severe blow at the peoples' sense of security."

The alarm in Moscow was even greater than appeared on the surface. True, the papers were already full of stories from Prague about "German vandalism in Czechoslovakia" and about the "Gestapo terror" there—for instance, about a Karl Beneš, secretary of the Nieburg Communist Party organisation, having been beaten and tortured to death by the Gestapo (*Pravda*, April 1, 1939). But there was clearly nothing that the Soviet Union could have done about it at this stage. So attention suddenly shifted to London, Warsaw—and Lithuania, which had just had Memel "shamelessly extorted" from her by the Germans, as the Soviet press put it.

The Germans in Memel, the Hungarians in Ruthenia, the growing threats against Poland—all this was getting very near home.

Although the invasion of Czechoslovakia deeply shocked British public opinion, Chamberlain's own first reaction was mild, judging by his statement in the House of Commons on March 15. However, the outcry in the country compelled him to strike a different note in his Birmingham speech on March 17. This time he spoke of his "disappointment and indignation", and less than a fortnight later, on March 31, he announced the British Government's guarantee to Poland.

This extraordinary decision is perhaps best explained by a

particularly well-qualified observer, Robert Coulondre, who was French Ambassador in Berlin at the time: "Without any kind of transition, and with a rashness pointing to his genuine anger, Chamberlain turned a complete somersault. He went from one extreme to the other, and diplomacy, which is the daughter of wisdom and caution, does not like such extravagant behaviour. *Having been bamboozled by Hitler, Chamberlain was now going to be bamboozled by Colonel Beck,* and was going to ruin a game the outcome of which was of the most vital importance to the cause of peace."*

Immediately after the German invasion of Czechoslovakia the British Government had turned to the Soviet Union. On March 18 Halifax asked Maisky, the Soviet Ambassador, to call on him, and inquired what the Soviet attitude would be if Rumania became the object of an unprovoked aggression. The Soviet Government promptly replied by proposing a meeting at Bucharest of the six Powers most directly involved. The British Government rejected this and proposed, instead, on March 21, the publication of a joint Anglo-Franco-Soviet-Polish declaration saying that they would enter into immediate consultations about any joint action to be taken should the political independence of any European state be threatened. The Soviet Government, though disappointed by the rejection of its own proposal, agreed to such a declaration, provided Poland was one of the signatories. But on April 1 Chamberlain informed Maisky that he had dropped the idea.

On March 23, 1939, the Germans had occupied Memel. On that same day, Colonel Beck replied to the British proposal for a Four-Power Declaration, and argued against it. These multilateral negotiations would be very complicated and take time, and there was no time to lose; he therefore suggested the conclusion of a bilateral Polish-British agreement, without prejudice, of course, to any wider subsequent negotiations. What game was Beck playing? Certainly he was becoming distrustful of Hitler, and wished to strengthen his position by securing a British guarantee. At the same time he had no desire to enter into any sort of "defensive front" with the Russians, as this, he argued, might incense the Germans.

* R. Coulondre, op. cit., p. 263. (Emphasis added.)

In discussing the matter with Gafencu, the Rumanian Foreign Minister, he put forward the view that Hitler would not attack Poland, so long as the latter had not become involved with Russia; only a Polish-Russian alliance would produce a German invasion of Poland. "Despite the terrible threat hanging over his country, and despite the lesson of Czechoslovakia, Beck persisted in his more than dubious game of backing both horses."*

In the House of Commons on March 31 Chamberlain made his famous statement on Poland. A fortnight later he announced that the guarantee to Poland had been extended to Rumania and Greece. As Coulondre says: "The British Government was now crashing ahead so fast that it even rushed past the station at which it should have stopped. It was enough to look at the map of Europe to see what a serious diplomatic situation it had created. Rumania and Poland practically form a continuous front from the Black Sea to the Baltic, a front separating Germany from the USSR. Germany cannot attack Russia without going through Poland or Rumania, i.e. without bringing into play the Western guarantee, and without going to war against Britain and France. Thus, without having to commit himself, Stalin secured a Western guarantee in the East which he had sought in vain for ten years... It must now have been clear to Hitler that only by coming to an agreement with the USSR could he dodge that double front the day he decided to attack Poland."†

"Would it not have been much wiser"—Coulondre asks—"to stick to the Four-Power Declaration, as proposed on March 21, and, if Beck still refused to sign, to go right ahead with that Anglo-French-Soviet alliance which Churchill was demanding with prophetic foresight, and which the Russians were then prepared to sign?"

On April 1 the Soviet press prominently displayed Chamberlain's guarantee to Poland, but accompanied the story with an account of the House of Commons debate, in which Arthur Greenwood asked whether the Soviet Union had been brought into it, to which Chamberlain replied that discussions were in progress with numerous countries, including the Soviet Union. Three days later, in con-

* G. Gafencu, *The Last Days of Europe* (London, 1945), pp. 203–4.
† R. Coulondre, op. cit., pp. 263–4.

nection with Beck's visit to London, the Soviet press reported further House of Commons discussions. It reported Chamberlain as saying that the guarantee to Poland had marked a sharp change in British foreign policy. But already it focused all its attention on what was being said about the Soviet Union and the "trap" the Poles had laid:

Sir Archibald Sinclair said that the Soviet Union held the key to peace in Eastern Europe. British-Soviet cooperation was therefore of the utmost importance.

Mr Lloyd George asked why the British Government had not got Soviet support before entering into these colossal obligations. Britain should tell Poland that she could be helped only on certain conditions. In talking about the Soviet Union, Chamberlain, Lloyd George said, was merely trying to appease the Opposition. If Britain did not secure Soviet aid, her help to Poland would merely be a trap.

Mr Hugh Dalton hoped he would soon see some action about the Soviet Union, and not just vapid assurances.

The press reported that, according to a public opinion poll in Britain, eighty-four percent of the people now wanted close co-operation with the Soviet Union; but, it added, there was nothing to show that the Government was following suit. If the Labour and Liberal press were now saying that no resistance to German aggression could be effective without the Soviet Union, *The Times* and the *Daily Telegraph* were still beating about the bush, assuring Germany that no "encirclement" was contemplated, and trying to draw fine distinctions between Polish independence and Polish territorial integrity. "*The Times*", *Pravda* wrote on April 10, "is trying to suggest that this is a return to collective security; but it is not, if only because the Poles are still talking about 'holding the balance'."

All the same, something seemed at last to be stirring in Britain, and there was already much talk of conscription—which was, indeed, to be introduced at the end of April. But for a fortnight after the announcement of the guarantee to Poland, no new proposals came to Moscow from the West—or vice versa. It was not till April 15 that the British Foreign Office came forward with a proposal to the Russians that they give Poland, Rumania and other European states a unilateral guarantee against German aggression—in case these countries desired such help. It was for these countries to decide what kind of help would be convenient to them. This was unacceptable to Moscow.

More constructive, from the Soviet point of view, was a simultaneous French proposal for a joint Soviet-French declaration based on mutual assistance to each other, as well as to Rumania and Poland. The Soviet Government apparently sensed Daladier's dislike of the guarantee to Poland which Chamberlain had forced on him and which made him prefer the Russian alliance. So, "in order to coordinate the various British, French and Soviet proposals", the Soviet Government now came forward with the proposal for a straight Anglo-Franco-Soviet alliance, to be signed for a period of five or ten years. This alliance would provide that they undertake to render each other every help, including military help, in the event of an aggression in Europe on any of the three signatories, and also to render similar help to all East-European countries bordering on the Soviet Union between the Baltic and the Black Sea.

"This offer", Coulondre wrote, "was almost undreamed of at the time." He thought this was a tremendous step in the right direction, and attributed it to the fact that Litvinov, the "collective security man", with his obvious predeliction for the West, was still in charge of Soviet foreign policy. In actual fact such a proposal could not have been made simply on Litvinov's initiative. But the Chamberlain Government turned down the Soviet proposal which—Coulondre argued—could have still saved the day had it been seized with both hands.

Instead of accepting the Soviet proposal, the British Government started producing—in Coulondre's phrase—more and more sophisticated formulae, the purpose of which was to provide Soviet guarantees to countries that did not even want them. The British Government made it indeed clear, in a Note addressed to the French Government, that the various objections raised by Poland made any agreement with the Soviet Union very difficult.*

The "undreamed of offer" had been made by Russia—and had been rejected. A new approach was needed. It had now become necessary to give Soviet foreign policy not only a more flexible and opportunist character, but also to give it the maximum authority.

* R. Coulondre, op. cit., p. 263.

And Molotov's position in the Party was second only to Stalin's.
Just as in May 1941, with a German invasion threatening, Stalin was
to take over the Premiership, so in May 1939, with Europe on the
brink of war, Molotov took over the Foreign Commissariat. Litvinov
was temperamentally a "Westerner"—but he had received poor
thanks from the West. As a Jew, he had been fiercely abused by the
Germans for years. He was ill-suited for any new departures that
might now become necessary for Soviet foreign policy. In the eyes
of the Party he no longer carried sufficient authority, especially after
the rejection by London of the Soviet Plan of April 17.

There was no perceptible change in the tone of the Soviet press or in
official utterances after Molotov had become Foreign Commissar.
The press continued to report the great success in England and elsewhere of Russian anti-Nazi films like *Professor Mamlock* and
Alexander Nevsky; patriotic speeches continued to be made about
the might of the Red Army which would "smash any aggressor on
his own territory if he ever dared attack the Soviet Union"* and the
press continued to publish ominous little items like this one
in *Pravda* (May 16):

HITLER'S VISIT OF INSPECTION.
   Berlin, May 15 (TASS). Hitler today left for the Western frontier to
inspect the so-called Siegfried Line. He was accompanied by staff
officers and by Himmler, the head of the Gestapo.

* Thus, at the graduation ceremony of the Red Army academies on
May 7—a ceremony attended by Stalin, Molotov, Voroshilov,
Khrushchev, Bulganin, Zhdanov and others, Kalinin declared: "Our
people are convinced that, with an Army like ours, they can peacefully go on building and developing the Soviet state, a classless
socialist society and communism. The international situation
demands from you a state of constant preparedness. I hope you will
fully justify the confidence our people have placed in you." And
Colonel Rodimtsev, Hero of the Soviet Union (and a future hero of
Stalingrad), said at the same meeting: "We swear to carry out the
order of Comrade Voroshilov to smash any aggressor on his own
territory..."

Was this meant to suggest that Hitler might, indeed, turn on the West and that the Soviet Union and not the West had better hurry and join forces? At any rate, even a month after Molotov's appointment Nazi Germany was still treated as No. 1 Danger.

When the Supreme Soviet met at the end of May, A. G. Zverev, the Commissar for Finance, declared amid loud cheers that the expenditure on defence would be increased from twenty-three milliard roubles in 1938 to forty-one milliard roubles in 1939. "The stronger we are," he said, "the better will be the chances that peace will not be disturbed, and that the *Fascist aggressors will not dare attack our country.*" This could only mean Nazi Germany.

In its comments on this vast increase in military expenditure, *Pravda* (May 27) was full of the usual bluster:

> This figure of 40,885 million roubles means new guns, fast new planes, powerful new tanks... With such a mighty Red Army we can calmly look into the future, knowing that no provocation by our foreign enemies can catch us unawares. We can calmly go ahead with our third Five-Year-Plan... Provided with the most perfect equipment in the world, our Red Army will smash any enemy or any enemies, no matter where they come from.

This was clearly intended as a warning to *both* Japan and Germany.

One of the most important landmarks during that grim summer was Molotov's survey of the international situation before the Supreme Soviet on May 31.

He was highly critical of Britain and France, but the speech was, above all, *an attack on Germany.* After recalling the disasters that the Munich policy had already brought on Europe, Molotov said:

> The aggressive powers today are becoming more and more arrogant. On the other hand, the representatives of the democratic countries, having turned their backs on collective security, and having adopted a policy of non-resistance to aggression, are now trying to minimise the grave deterioration of the international situation.

Until very recently, Molotov continued, the responsible leaders of

France and Britain were happily contemplating the success of the
ill-fated Munich settlement.

But what was the result? Germany wasn't satisfied with getting the
Sudeten country, and simply proceeded to liquidate one of the Slav
countries, Czechoslovakia... This just shows what non-interference
produces... And, after that, the aggressor nations continued as before;
in April, Germany grabbed Memel from Lithuania, and Italy finished
off Albania. Things went from bad to worse: in April, too, the head of
the German State destroyed the Anglo-German naval agreement and
the Polish-German non-aggression pact... Such was Germany's answer
to the proposal of President Roosevelt, a proposal imbued with the
spirit of peace.

He then referred to the new political and military treaty between
Germany and Italy which, he said, was "aggressive by its very
nature".

In the past, these two countries pretended to be concerned with their
joint battle against communism. Hence all the fuss about the Anti-
Comintern Pact. Now the camouflage has been dropped... Both the
leaders and the press of the two countries openly talk about the new
treaty being directed against the main European democracies...

Although there were now some signs that the non-aggressive
countries were at last beginning to favour a front against aggression,
it still remained to be seen how serious this change of heart really
was. "It may well be that these countries may like to stop aggression
in some areas, but will not interfere with aggression in other areas."
And Molotov brought in that Stalin quote about the "chestnuts"
and about the need to beware of *provocateurs* who might try to drag
the Soviet Union into war.

He, clearly, continued to be very hostile to Germany, but was also
extremely distrustful of Britain and France; but even so, he said,
"There are some signs that the democratic countries have become
aware of the utter collapse of their non-intervention policy, and of
the need of creating a single front of the peaceful powers against
aggression. The British-Polish Pact *is* a new element in Europe, all
the more so as Germany has torn up *her* pact with Poland... And
there is also a tendency among the non-aggressive European powers
to seek the collaboration of the USSR in organising resistance to

aggression." That was why, he said, the Soviet Government had accepted the proposal of Britain and France to open negotiations for the purpose of strengthening the relations between these three countries, and for organising a peace front against any further development of aggression. "We entered into these negotiations with France and Britain in mid-April. These talks have not yet been concluded. But from the outset we realised that if there is really a desire to create an effective front of peace-loving countries against aggression, then the minimum conditions to be fulfilled are these:

1) There must be a purely defensive, but effective mutual assistance pact between Britain, France and the Soviet Union;
2) There must be guarantees by all three Powers to the countries bordering on the Soviet Union, and to other countries in Central and Eastern Europe;
3) There must be concrete agreements between the three about the immediate and effective aid to be rendered in the event of aggression against either of them or against the countries guaranteed by them."

Having elaborated at some length on the perplexities of pact-making for the protection of the many frontiers so precariously maintained between the Baltic and the Black Sea and between the Soviet Union and Nazi Germany, Molotov introduced another motif into his discourse which was like an echo of Stalin's speech of March 10.

Such are our talks with Britain and France. That does not mean that we intend to break off business relations with countries like Germany and Italy. At the beginning of 1938 Germany offered us a new credit of 200 million marks; but since no agreement followed, the question of this credit was dropped. However, at the end of 1938 the German Government again raised the question of economic talks, and of the 200 million marks credit. The Germans were ready to make certain concessions, and their Foreign Trade Ministry said that Herr Schnurre would come to Moscow. But instead it was decided that Ambassador Schulenburg would conduct the talks. Since there were some disagreements, the talks broke down. But now there are signs that the talks may be resumed. We also signed recently a profitable trade agreement with Italy...

In conclusion, Molotov said that relations with Poland had

"improved"; that relations with Turkey were "good", and that he
had recently warned the Japanese Ambassador that the Soviet
Union would defend both her own frontiers and those of the
Mongolian People's Republic against any Japanese-Manchurian
aggression.

> The Soviet Union is not what it was, say in 1921, though even some
> of our neighbours seem to have forgotten it. Nor is the Soviet Union
> what it was ten, or even five years ago; its strength is far greater. In
> spite of delays and hesitations, some democracies are becoming
> conscious of this simple truth; yet in any front of the peaceful powers
> resisting aggression the Soviet Union cannot but hold a place in the
> front rank.

What Molotov had said about trade talks with Germany did not,
on the face of it, amount to much; it might have been meant as a
mild warning to the West, where some of Chamberlain's close
associates still considered "trade talks" with Germany to be their
best hope of resuming an appeasement policy. Molotov was, of
course, aware of the long-standing tug-of-war going on in Britain,
below and above the surface, inside and outside the Tory Party,
between the advocates and the opponents of a pact with the Soviet
Union.

Until further notice the Soviet press maintained a fairly consistent
anti-Nazi line, playing the "Western" card. On June 9 Tass reported
from London Chamberlain's statement in the House of Commons
on the Franco-British-Soviet talks; there was, Chamberlain had said,
a common point of view about the main features of the intended
agreement, and to speed up the talks H.M. Government had decided
to send to Moscow a representative of the Foreign Office. This was
the beginning of the "Strang Mission". Special prominence was
given to influential utterances in Britain in favour of a pact with the
Soviet Union, notably to Churchill's article in the *Daily Telegraph*
on June 9. Churchill even went so far as to advocate a joint guarantee to the Baltic States and Finland, and declared that such a pact
was as much in the interests of the Soviet Union as it was in the
interests of France and Britain. But, said Churchill, there was no
time to lose.

At the same time, the Soviet papers continued to carry numerous stories about "German looting in Czechoslovakia" (Hubert Ripka in the *Spectator* quoted by *Pravda* on June 9), "Austria under the heel of the Nazi invaders" (*Pravda* June 16), "Executions in Spain" (*Pravda* June 15), and so on. Alongside with this went accounts about growing German pressure on Poland, and reports of some of the more violent speeches by Nazi leaders—such as Goebbels's attack on England in his Danzig speech at the end of June, with its "hands off Eastern Europe!" slogan. Altogether the growing violence over Danzig was being fully reported, and in a tone very far from friendly to the Germans. These, the Soviet press kept on suggesting, were out for trouble:

> Danzig is teeming with German military trucks that have come from Königsberg... Danzig is being invaded by hordes of "tourists" and other highly suspect elements... The German papers are continuing to carry screaming headlines about Poland's "aggressiveness". The *Völkischer Beobachter* is screaming that the Poles want to invade East Prussia, Pomerania, Silesia and other German territories.*

Although, whenever there was any vitally important business to discuss with Hitler, the British Government would send him Eden, Simon, Halifax—or Chamberlain in person, the British Prime Minister seemed to think that an experienced Foreign Office official, like Mr Strang, was more than good enough for Moscow. This choice had, indeed, been severely criticised by the Opposition press and Opposition speakers, who had argued that at least somebody of Halifax's or Eden's stature should be sent there. But, in Chamberlain's view Halifax had other things to do, while Eden was much too friendly to the Russians—he had already gone to Moscow in 1935— and Mr Strang would be better suited to what Chamberlain wanted to be no more than an exploratory mission—or merely a sop to the Opposition. He was determined to turn a deaf ear to all the warnings, coming from Churchill and others, that the time factor was of the utmost importance. It was indeed not surprising that the Strang appointment should have aroused little enthusiasm in Moscow.

* *Pravda*, July 2, 1939.

There is a remarkable passage in Maisky's reminiscences* about the visit he paid Halifax on June 12, the day of Strang's departure for Moscow:

> To get the three-power pact concluded with the utmost speed—for that was our basic object—and to discover our British partners' real intentions, the Soviet Government decided to invite Lord Halifax to Moscow... On June 12 I was instructed to call on Halifax in a personal capacity, and to urge him in a friendly but pressing way to go to Moscow without delay to complete the negotiations and to sign the pact.

After pointing out to Halifax the extreme urgency of the problem, Maisky said, "'If you can go to Moscow right away, Lord Halifax, I shall ask my Government to send you an official invitation.' A hard and mysterious look came over Halifax's face. He looked at the ceiling, then rubbed the bridge of his nose, and then solemnly declared: 'I shall bear it in mind.' I realised of course that he could not decide on this visit to Moscow without referring the matter to the Cabinet... After a week, there was still no reply."†

* I. Maisky, *Kto pomogal Hitlern?* (Who Helped Hitler?), Moscow, 1962. English translation, London, 1964.
† In conclusion, Maisky writes that he had an important postscript to make to this account of his meeting with Halifax on June 12. In the Documents of British Foreign Policy published later by the British Government, there was Halifax's own account of this meeting. According to this, Maisky had suggested that Halifax should go to Moscow "when things had calmed down", to which Halifax had replied that nothing would please him better, but that at the present moment it would be impossible for him to leave London.
Maisky then proceeds to demonstrate that, in Halifax's account of the same meeting, the Foreign Secretary had told "two untruths", both showing that, like Chamberlain, he was less than lukewarm about coming to a quick agreement with Moscow. This lack of enthusiasm, on both Halifax's and Chamberlain's part, is, of course, fully borne out by Churchill in what he said at the time and wrote later.
"It was decided to send a special envoy to Moscow. Mr Eden, who had made useful contacts with Stalin (in 1935) volunteered to go. This generous offer was declined by the Prime Minister. Instead, on June 12, Mr Strang, an able official, but without any standing outside the Foreign Office, was entrusted with this momentous mission.

Strang arrived in Moscow in the middle of June and had, together with the British Ambassador, Sir William Seeds, and the French Ambassador, M. Naggiar, a number of meetings with Mr Molotov. The first meeting on June 16, lasted an hour; another meeting on July 1 lasted an hour and a half; and still another, on July 8, two hours.

Let us remember that these discussions arose from the diplomatic exchanges that had gone on since April. After rejecting the "Litvinov Plan" on April 17, the British Government had asked the Soviet Union to enter into a number of unilateral commitments; in its Note of May 14—this was already after Molotov had taken over—the Soviet Government declared that the latest British proposals did not contain the principle of reciprocity, and put the Soviet Union in a position of inequality; the absence of these guarantees to the Soviet Union in case of aggression on the one hand, and the "unprotected position" of its North-Western frontiers, on the other, might well act as an incentive for the aggressors to attack Russia. It therefore proposed a more detailed version of the "Litvinov Plan" of April 17:

> An effective Anglo-Franco-Soviet mutual assistance pact, complete with (1) a three-power guarantee to the countries of Eastern and Central Europe exposed to aggression, these countries to include Latvia, Estonia and Finland, and with (2) a "concrete agreement" among the three powers as to the nature and the volume of the help they would render each other and to the guaranteed states. "Without such an agreement", the Note concluded, "the mutual assistance pacts may well remain suspended in mid-air, as we know from the experience of Czechoslovakia".*

This was another mistake. The sending of so subordinate a figure gave actual offence." (Churchill, op. cit., vol. I, p. 346.)

It should, of course, be remembered throughout that Maisky, a "Litvinov man" at heart, was more enthusiastic about the Tripartite Alliance as "the only way of stopping Hitler" than were either Stalin or Molotov.

* AVP SSR (Soviet Foreign Policy Archives) Anglo-Franco-Soviet talks, vol. III, f. 39, quoted in *Istoriya velikoi otechestvennoi voiny Sovietskogo Soyuza* (History of the Great Patriotic War of the Soviet Union), vol. I (Moscow, 1960). Referred to in future as IVOVSS.

The joint Anglo-French proposals of May 27, in reply to this
Note, were a marked improvement on earlier efforts; they provided
for direct Anglo-French aid to the Soviet Union in the event of a
"direct attack", but left the question of the Baltic States still un-
resolved. Molotov's new Note of June 2 now stressed the need for
"all-round, effective and immediate" mutual aid, and proposed to
cover Belgium, Greece, Turkey, Rumania, Poland, Latvia, Estonia
and Finland in the joint guarantees. It even provided that the mutual
assistance would apply in cases when one of the signatories had become involved in war by helping a neutral European country that
had applied for such help.* What Molotov was in fact suggesting
was a mutual assistance pact covering practically the whole of
Europe.

The talks were becoming increasingly complicated. The Russians
raised the question of "indirect aggression". This meant in the first
place, the use by Germany of the Baltic States as a base for aggression "with the connivance" of the governments of those countries.
The possibility of Russian preventive action here could, in the British
view, not be ruled out. The Russians also wanted to know if their
troops could have access to Polish territory in case of need. They
wanted a concrete agreement on the precise military contribution
the Soviet Union, Britain and France would make to the "common
effort".

Looking back on these crucial days Grigore Gafencu, the
Rumanian Foreign Minister, wrote: "The Western Powers were
seeking for a psychological effect (they did not hide this fact). They
wished to create a solidarity between the West and the East which
would prevent Hitler from starting his war. This plan was perfectly
justified . . . and any delay in its realisation seemed intolerable. The
Soviet view was equally tenable: Moscow did not want to engage
itself lightly. If despite agreement in principle, war broke out, the
greatest German effort might be made against the USSR."†

Anyway, the Strang-Molotov talks were leading nowhere, and,

* AVP SSR, vol. III, ff. 46–47.
† The trouble is that, as Stalin was to say to Churchill in 1942, he
(Stalin) knew perfectly well that such a "psychological effect" was
totally insufficient to restrain Hitler.

on July 23 Molotov finally proposed that France and Britain send a military mission to Moscow.

The manner and motions of this mission were to show before long how "intolerable" Mr Chamberlain thought "any delay". What he still wanted "without delay" was a "psychological effect"; on the other hand a military convention—to the Russians "the only real test of Western sincerity"—was precisely what he was not in a hurry to sign.

But were the Russians wholehearted about an alliance with Britain and France? On June 29 Zhdanov published in *Pravda* a sharply critical article on the Western Powers, almost suggesting that an alliance with the "Munichites" would be a doubtful asset. References to the Siegfried Line also appeared in the Soviet press from time to time, suggesting that France's striking power against Germany might be insufficient. And among the Soviet hierarchy there might well have been the lingering thought that, so soon after the Army Purges, the Red Army had better not take on a powerful enemy like Nazi Germany, *unless* some definite military convention could be reached with Britain and France. Short of this, it might (as Stalin had already suggested on March 10) be preferable to remain "neutral". But how?

Nor did it escape the Russians' notice that since Munich, and indeed to the very moment the war broke out, there were important people in power or near the levers of power in Britain and elsewhere who in their frantic efforts to appease Hitler, were prepared to go to almost any lengths.*

In all circumstances the Russians had to prepare themselves for an imminent Nazi thrust eastwards against Poland and the not unlikely event that such an offensive might encompass the Baltic States

---

* The list of appeasers—Mr Hudson, Sir Horace Wilson, Lord Kemsley, etc.—which emerges from the Dirksen archives, that is the papers of the German Ambassador in London until the outbreak of the war, captured by the Russians and published subsequently, *Dokumenty i materialy kanuna vtoroi mirovoi voiny. T.II Arkhiv Dirksena (1938–39)*, (Moscow, 1948), even allowing for a good deal of selective editing, certainly bears out what every experienced and sober observer of the political scene must have known or strongly suspected at the time.

and possibly Rumania, that is, a front extending from the Baltic to the Black Sea. Even if the German offensive stopped in the face of the Russian winter, the Russians must have feared a German invasion in the spring of 1940 with the West taking a ringside seat behind the Maginot Line, unless of course definite guarantees of co-ordinated military action were mutually provided.

On August 4, *Pravda* reported from London that Britain and France had agreed to send a military mission to Moscow. This report was accompanied by an account of the House of Commons debate, in the course of which Eden welcomed the decision. He thought that this would "resolve distrust", and hoped that these talks would soon lead to an agreement. He proposed, however, that, in addition to admirals and generals, the British Government should send "a representative political leader" to Moscow, "so that all the talks could be concluded within a week". There was no time to lose, Eden said, since Poland was now being threatened, as Czechoslovakia had been, and it was essential to create a peace front with the utmost speed, so as to discourage aggression. To these warnings Chamberlain turned a deaf ear.

But for several days after that very little more was said in the Soviet press about this military mission. For over a week a carefree holiday mood seems to have reigned in Moscow. On August 1, indeed, a monumental Agricultural Exhibition opened in the capital, with Molotov presiding over the opening ceremony. Stalin was represented by a colossal statue at the entrance of the Exhibition. Although, only a fortnight before, the Soviet press had reported a highly critical speech by Khrushchev on the state of stock-breeding in the Ukraine—a speech in which he castigated the half-heartedness of so many *kolkhozniki* who wholly lacked the proper collectivist spirit, and were, in fact, enemies of the collective sector of the *kolkhozes*—the opening of the Agricultural Exhibition gave rise to rapturous eulogies on the state of Soviet Agriculture.

> With this exhibition [*Pravda* wrote on August 1] we are celebrating a glorious victory of socialism. This is the tenth birthday of the *kolkhoz* system, and a report on its achievements. It was in the autumn of 1929

that the peasants started entering the *kolkhozes* by whole villages and districts. It was the year of the Great Change. The incantations of the Trotskyite and Bukharinite agents of Fascism about the inevitable clash between the workers and the peasants, and about the impossibility of building socialism in one country have been thrown into the dustbin of history. New machinery has taken the place of the individual peasant's plough, wooden harrow, sickle and scythe.

These raptures continued for several days, and 20,000 to 30,000 people a day visited the exhibition, with its ornate domes, Stalin-Gothic spires and its orgy of fountains, colossal statues of Lenin and Stalin, and with Vera Mukhina's giant silver statue of the worker with the hammer and the *kolkhoznitsa* with the sickle sweeping into a glorious future above the main entrance. The opulent and luscious exhibits in all the various palaces and pavilions were there to show that agriculture under the *kolkhoz* system had become a magnificently going concern, whereas, according to *Pravda*, the peasantry in Nazi Germany was "undergoing a process of continuous pauperisation".

Moscow was in a festive mood, and the blessings of peace seemed wonderful under the wise leadership of Comrade Stalin. No doubt, not all was well—least of all in a great number of *kolkhozes*—but conditions had certainly become easier in the last five years. The Exhibition teemed with lemonade and ice-cream stalls and eating places, and, in their light summer clothes, people looked cheerful, contented and even superficially prosperous. War seemed a long way away, whatever the papers said about "more Nazi provocations in Danzig".

At last, on August 12, *Pravda* announced the arrival in Moscow of the British and French Military Missions:

> The Missions, headed by Admiral Drax and General Doumenc, were met yesterday morning at the Leningrad Station by a number of Soviet personalities... Later in the day, Comrade V. M. Molotov received the leaders of the Missions. Present at the meeting were also Sir William Seeds, M. Naggiar, and the Deputy Foreign Commissar V. P. Potemkin... Later they were received by Defence Commissar

Voroshilov and the Chief of the General Staff of the Red Army, Army
Commander of the 1st rank, B. M. Shaposhnikov.

In the evening a banquet was given in honour of the British and
French Military Missions, and all the Soviet top brass were there—
Voroshilov, Shaposhnikov, Budienny, Timoshenko, heads of the
Kiev and Belorussian Military Districts and leaders of the Navy and
Air Force. "Friendly toasts were exchanged between Comrade Voro-
shilov and the heads of the British and French Military Missions."*

That was as much as the Soviet public were allowed to learn at
that stage about the Anglo-French visit. What did it really amount
to? The visit had been announced more than three weeks before; but
the British and French had obviously been in no great hurry to come,
having travelled by slow boat to Leningrad. Needless to say, nobody
had ever heard of Admiral Drax or General Doumenc. Why had
nobody of note come to Moscow—Halifax or Daladier?—not
Chamberlain, of course, for who would want to see *him*? All the
same, there was obviously "something in it" if all the top army and
navy and air-force leaders were attending the banquet... These were
the kind of confused impressions people had in Moscow at the time.
Certainly nothing had been done in London or Paris to fire the
Soviet public's imagination.

Present-day Soviet historians treat this Anglo-French Military
Mission with the utmost severity. "Here were generals and admirals
who had either reached the retiring age, or were holding only
secondary posts... The British Government's attitude to the Mission
was so frivolous that it had not even given them any powers. Only
towards the end of the talks, after a lot of insisting by the Soviet side,
did Drax produce some sort of credentials, but even these did not
allow him to sign any kind of agreement with the USSR. The credentials of the French general were no better. All they had been
empowered to do was to conduct negotiations with us." The *History*
recalls that after the Soviet Government had proposed that Britain
and France send military missions to Moscow, these people "had
taken eleven days to prepare for their departure, and had then taken

* *Pravda*, August 12, 1939.

six more days to travel by slow cargo-passenger boat to Leningrad, and thence to Moscow".*

The principle underlying the Soviet proposals was not only reciprocity, but also equality in the war effort to be put into this mutual assistance by the two sides. But even before Shaposhnikov outlined his proposals in detail, he had already been taken aback by the British reaction to his first mention of the "respective contributions":

> When B. M. Shaposhnikov said that the Soviet Union was ready to make available against the aggressor 120 infantry divisions, sixteen cavalry divisions, 5,000 medium and heavy guns, 9,000 to 10,000 tanks, and 5,000 to 5,500 bomber and fighter planes, General Heywood, a member of the British Mission, talked about five infantry and one mechanised divisions. This in itself was enough to suggest a frivolous British attitude to the talks with the Soviet Union.†

The *History* does not, however, mention the suggestions of the French, who had a numerically far larger army than the British.

The military convention the Russians proposed was to be based on three eventualities:

1) IF THE BLOC OF AGGRESSORS ATTACK FRANCE AND BRITAIN. In this case the Soviet Union will make available seventy per cent of the armed forces that France and Britain will direct against the "main aggressor", i.e. Germany. Thus, if they use ninety divisions, the Soviet Union will use sixty-three infantry divisions and six cavalry divisions, with the appropriate number of guns, tanks and planes—altogether about two million men.

In this case Poland must participate with all her armed forces, in view of her agreements with Britain and France. Poland must concentrate forty to forty-five divisions on her Western borders and against East Prussia. The British and French Governments must obtain Poland's undertaking to let the Soviet armed forces pass through the Vilno Bulge and, if possible, through Lithuania to the borders of East Prussia, and also, if necessary, through Galicia.

---

* IVOVSS, vol. I, p. 168. In Maisky's Memoirs Admiral Drax is made to look like someone straight out of P. G. Wodehouse.

† IVOVSS, vol. I, p. 169, quoting from AVP SSSR (Foreign Policy Archives), Anglo-French-Soviet Negotiations in 1939, v. III, f. 138.

2) IF THE AGGRESSION IS DIRECTED AGAINST POLAND
AND RUMANIA. In this case, Poland and Rumania must make
use of all their armed forces, and the Soviet Union will participate by
as much as 100 per cent of the forces employed against Germany by
Britain and France... In this case, an indispensable condition of the
Soviet Union's participation is that Britain and France should immediately declare war on the aggressor. Moreover, the Soviet Union can
take part in such a war only if the British and French Governments
come to a clear understanding with Poland and Rumania (and, if
possible, with Lithuania) about the free passage of the Soviet armed
forces through the Vilno Bulge, Galicia and Rumania.

3) IF THE AGGRESSOR ATTACKS THE SOVIET UNION BY
MAKING USE OF THE TERRITORIES OF FINLAND,
ESTONIA OR LATVIA. In this case France and Britain must not
only declare war on the aggressor (or the bloc of aggressors) "but must
also start active and immediate military operations against the main
aggressor", putting into operation seventy per cent of the forces
employed by the Soviet Union (the Soviet Union would put into
operation 136 divisions). "Since Poland is bound by her agreements
with Britain and France, she must intervene against Germany, and
must also, by agreement between herself on the one hand and Britain
and France on the other, give free passage to our troops through the
Vilno Bulge and Galicia... Should Rumania be drawn into the war,
a similar agreement should be made between Rumania, France and
Britain concerning the free passage of Soviet troops across Rumanian
territory."*

According to the Soviet version Admiral Drax thanked General
Shaposhnikov for outlining his plan, but it was not accepted by the
British and French, and there were no serious British or French
counter-proposals. Instead, both the French and the British made
the most of the "Polish obstacle". The British had, indeed, no
intention of bringing pressure to bear on the Polish Government.

The attitude of General Doumenc, head of the French Mission,
was rather different: "Twice he cabled the French War Ministry
saying he intended to send General Valin, a member of the Mission,
to Warsaw, in order to obtain the Polish Government's consent. But
the result was only a telegram from the French War Ministry to the

* IVOVSS, vol. I, pp. 169–70, quoting AVP SSSR (Soviet Foreign
Policy Archives).

French Military Attaché in Moscow proposing to postpone Valin's visit to Warsaw."*

All that the French and British found to propose, according to the Soviet *History*, was that the Soviet Union should declare war on Germany in the event of a German attack on Poland, but should take no military action before the German troops reached the Soviet borders. "All this shows that they were much less interested in helping Poland than in getting the Soviet Union involved in a war against Germany."†

Already in June 1939 the governments of Latvia and Estonia, frightened of both Germany and Russia, had, under German pressure, concluded "friendship pacts" with Germany. But Poland's position presented by far the most urgent problem since by August 15 the Germans were poised to invade her at any moment. Even in these conditions no progress was made in the Anglo-Franco-Soviet military talks in Moscow. On August 17, says the Soviet *History*, the talks were postponed until August 21, so that the British and French Missions could be given time to discover the real attitude of their respective governments to the passage of Soviet troops through Poland. The Admiral was still not in a hurry, whereas General Doumenc held that nothing was lost yet, but that there was no time to lose. He considered that, on that day, the Russians were still in dead earnest about the military convention. In his dispatch to Paris on August 17 he wired "There is a definite will on the part of the Russians not to stay outside as spectators, and a clear desire to commit themselves right up to the hilt. There is no doubt that the USSR wants a military pact; but she does not want from us a meaningless scrap of paper; Marshal Voroshilov assured me that all questions of mutual help, communications, etc., would be discussed without any difficulty, once what the Russians call 'the cardinal question'—the Russian access to Polish territory—has been satisfactorily solved."‡

That day, in desperation Doumenc even sent one of his aides,

* IVOVSS, vol. I, p. 170 quoting a French document originally captured by the Germans, and found in the German Foreign Office archives by the Russians. This episode is confirmed by Paul Reynaud in *La France a sauvé l'Europe* (Paris, 1947), vol. I, p. 580.
† Ibid., p. 170.   ‡ Paul Reynaud, op. cit., vol. I, p. 587.

Captain Beauffre, to Warsaw to see Marshal Rydz-Smigly, but to no avail; his reply was a repetition of his remark to the French Ambassador: "With the Germans we may lose our freedom, with the Russians we shall lose our soul."* Finally, on August 21 Admiral Drax said that he had received no further information from London, and proposed that the next meeting take place in three or four days.† At this point the Russians asked for a clear answer as to how the British and French visualised Soviet participation in mutual assistance in view of the Polish attitude; no reply was received.

In his conversation with the French Military Attaché on August 23—the day of Ribbentrop's arrival in Moscow—Voroshilov said: "We could not wait for the Germans to smash the Polish Army, after which they would have attacked us... Meantime, you would be stationed at your frontier, tying up perhaps ten German divisions. We needed a springboard from which to attack the Germans; without it, we could not help you."‡

It was with a touch of melancholy that Voroshilov said about the same time to General Doumenc, who had informed him of Daladier's latest telegram ordering him—without anything having been settled about Poland—to sign "the best possible military convention, with the Ambassador's consent, and subject to the French Government's subsequent approval": "We have wasted eleven days for nothing. We raised the question of military collaboration with France many years ago [an allusion to the abortive offer already made in 1935 by Soviet Ambassador Potemkin to M. Jean Fabry, then French Minister of War]. Last year, when Czechoslovakia was on the edge of the abyss, we waited for a signal from France; our Red Army was ready to strike. But the signal never came. Our government, and the whole of the Soviet people wanted to rush to the help of Czechoslovakia and to fulfil the obligations arising from the treaties. Now the British and French governments have dragged out these political and military talks far too long. Therefore other political

* Paul Reynaud, op. cit., vol. I, p. 587.
† IVOVSS, vol. I, p. 172, quoting AVP SSSR, Anglo-Franco-Soviet Negotiations, f. 204.
‡ IVOVSS, vol. I, p. 172, quoting Archives of Ministry of Defence of the USSR.

events are not to be ruled out. It was necessary to have a definite reply from Poland and Rumania about our troops' right of passage. If the Poles had given an affirmative answer, they would have asked to be represented at these talks."*

Although, in the Russian view, France was at least as much to blame for Munich as Britain, the breakdown of the Anglo-Franco-Soviet military talks in 1939 is attributed much more to Britain than to France. At the root of the trouble there was, among other things, that inept "guarantee" to Poland, which had only encouraged the Poles in their suicidal anti-Soviet policy—a guarantee the dangers of which the French Government had seen at once. In Russian eyes, the inconclusive talks with Admiral Drax demonstrated Chamberlain's continued resistance to a firm military alliance with the Soviet Union, as well as his determination not to overcome the Polish Government's objections to direct Russian aid. On the other hand, it seems obvious that Stalin and Molotov had been extremely distrustful of Britain and France throughout and had never been really enthusiastic about the alliance. Even if concluded, it might still have produced a "phoney war" in the west, and have helped Russia no more than the British "guarantee" helped Poland when it came to the test. Without the strongest military commitments by France, Britain and Poland, the alliance offered no attraction to them. Short of such commitments, a last-minute deal with Hitler was almost certainly at the back of Stalin's mind from April or May onwards.

* Paul Reynaud, op. cit., vol. I, p. 588.

Chapter II

THE SOVIET-GERMAN PACT

It is customary to look for turning points in history. Much has, of course, been read into Stalin's speech of March 10 with its phrase about the "chestnuts", suggesting a "curse on both your houses" and a desire to keep out of any military entanglements. Even more has been made of Hitler's speech of April 28, 1939, in which both the Polish-German non-aggression pact and the Anglo-German naval agreement were denounced, and in which the Führer refrained from his habitual attack on the Bolshevik menace. A shrewd observer like Robert Coulondre, the French Ambassador in Berlin, had at once considered this omission as very significant, and, in his dispatches to the Quai d'Orsay, had quoted authoritative German sources in support of his assessment. Gafencu also looked upon this Hitler speech of April 28 as a starting point: "Facing the failure of his Western policy, the Führer already contemplated an about-turn in his Eastern policy. Such a change ... would obviously find support among the German General Staff ... as well as in German economic circles."*

This was written in 1945 and since then there have been a variety of data to show that the matter was not as simple as that. We know, for instance, that it took Hitler a very long time to get used to the idea of a pact with Moscow, and that Ribbentrop, in particular, became enthusiastic about it some time before the Führer did. But none the less, it is probable that, already in April, after the British guarantee to Poland, he kept the possibility of an agreement with Moscow up his sleeve.

* G. Gafencu, op. cit., p. 175.

40

Although there is evidence to show that there were earlier contacts, the Soviet *History* now claims that it was the Germans who
made the first tentative approach to Russia on May 30, 1939, while
the Anglo-Franco-Soviet talks "were already in full swing".* On that
day Weizsäcker, the permanent head of the German Foreign Office,
told G. A. Astakhov, the Soviet chargé d'affaires in Berlin, that
"there was a possibility of improving Soviet-German relations". He
pointed out that, in renouncing the Carpathian Ukraine—which had
been handed over to Hungary in the partition of Czechoslovakia—
Germany had eliminated a *casus belli* with the Soviet Union. And
he went on to say: "If the Soviet Government wishes to discuss an
improvement in Soviet-German relations, then it should know that
such a possibility now exists. If, however, the Soviet Union wants to
persist, together with Britain and France, in its policy of encircling
Germany, then Germany is ready to meet the challenge."

The Soviet *History* reports that, at this stage, the Russians merely
replied that the future of Soviet-German relations depended primarily
on the Germans themselves, in itself a curious way of "rejecting"
their advances. And then, on August 3, according to the Soviet
History:

> Ribbentrop told G. A. Astakhov that there were no insoluble prob-
> lems between the USSR and Germany "in the whole area between the
> Baltic and the Black Sea. All questions could be solved if the Soviet
> Government accepted these premises." Ribbentrop made no secret of
> the fact that Germany had been conducting secret negotiations with
> Britain and France, but declared that "it would be easier for the
> Germans to talk to the Russians, despite all ideological differences,
> than with the British and the French". Having said that, Ribbentrop
> then resorted to threats. "If," he said, "you have other solutions in
> mind, if you think, for instance, that the best way of settling your
> problems with us is to invite an Anglo-French military mission to
> Moscow, then that's your business. For our own part, we don't mind
> all the screaming against us in the so-called West-European democ-
> racies. We are sufficiently strong to treat all this kind of thing with
> ridicule and contempt. There isn't a war which we couldn't win."†

* IVOVSS, vol. I, p. 174.

† IVOVSS, vol. I, p. 174, quoting Archives of the Ministry of Defence
of the USSR (Arkhiv MO SSSR).

Ribbentrop then proposed that Germany and the Soviet Union sign a secret protocol dividing into spheres of interest the whole area between the Black Sea and the Baltic. "Unwilling to enter into such an agreement with Germany, and still hoping for a successful conclusion of the military talks with Britain and France, the Soviet Government informed Berlin on August 7 that it considered the German proposal unsuitable, and rejected the idea of the secret protocol."*

In his dispatch of August 8, Astakhov expressed the view that the Germans would not observe seriously, or for any length of time, any obligations they might enter into under such an arrangement. "But I believe that, on a short-term basis, they would like to come to some kind of agreement with us along the lines suggested, and so to neutralise us. . . What would happen next would be determined not by any obligations entered into by the Germans, but by the new international situation that would be created."†

We need not here deal in detail with the familiar story of how the Nazi leaders, determined to strike at Poland, were growing more and more impatient at Moscow's reluctance to commit itself, and with the frantic "very urgent" telegrams that were being exchanged between Ribbentrop and the German Embassy in Moscow, or with how, in the end, in reply to Hitler's telegram, Stalin gave his assent to the pressing proposal that Ribbentrop arrive in Moscow "on August 22 or, at the very latest, on August 23". What is new is the way in which this whole episode is now handled by the Russians:

By the middle of August, the German leaders had become acutely worried. The German Embassy in Moscow was getting frantic wires asking what was happening about the Military Missions. Before these talks had started, Schulenburg [the German Ambassador] asked the Italian Ambassador, Rossi, to find out from Grzybowski, the Polish Ambassador, whether Poland would accept Soviet military aid. Schulenburg then promptly informed Berlin of the Polish Ambassador's reply: On no account would Poland allow Soviet troops to enter or even to cross Polish territory, or let the Russians use Polish air-

* Ibid., quoting Soviet Foreign Policy Archives (AVP SSSR).
† IVOVSS, vol. I, pp. 174–5, quoting Soviet Foreign Policy Archives (AVP SSSR).

fields. At the same time Schulenburg was instructed by Weizsäcker to tell the Soviet Government that if it preferred an alliance with England, Russia would be left face-to-face with Germany. By choosing instead an understanding with Germany, the Soviet Union would have her security guaranteed.*

Similar tempting promises were made to Astakhov, who reported:

> The Germans are obviously worried by our negotiations with the British and French military. They have become unsparing in their arguments and promises to avert an agreement. I consider that they are today ready to make the kind of declarations and gestures which would have been inconceivable six months ago.†

On August 15, Schulenburg told Molotov:

> At present they [the British and French] are again trying to push the Soviet Union into a war against Germany. This policy had very bad consequences for Russia in 1914. It is in the interests of both Germany and Russia to avoid a mutual massacre for the benefit of the Western democracies.‡

Schulenburg then proposed to Russia a non-aggression pact, complete with a protocol on the respective spheres of interest. Again the Soviet Government "declined",§ and Schulenburg, much discouraged, reported to Berlin that the Soviet Government took treaty obligations very seriously and expected the same attitude from its co-signatories.

By now the Anglo-Franco-Soviet military talks had, indeed, reached a deadlock, both on "numerical reciprocity" and, more immediately, on the Polish issue; and when, on August 20, Hitler sent his famous telegram to Stalin asking him to receive Ribbentrop "on Tuesday, August 22 or, at the latest, on Wednesday, August 23",

---

* IVOVSS, vol. I, p. 175, quoting DGFP, series D, vol. VII, p. 13.
† Ibid., quoting AVP SSSR (Soviet Foreign Policy Archives).
‡ IVOVSS, ibid., quoting Soviet Ministry of Defence Archives.
§ This does not tally with the German version, which says that Molotov first mentioned a non-aggression pact on August 15. The date is important. It was four days after the arrival of the Drax Mission about whose "seriousness" the Russians were now very doubtful. See W. R. Shirer, *The Rise and Fall of the Third Reich* (London, 1960), p. 521.

and saying that Ribbentrop would arrive with full powers for signing the non-aggression pact, "as well as the protocol", Stalin agreed.

It should, however, be remembered that, apart from the political soundings undertaken by the Germans in both Berlin and Moscow, there were also the trade negotiations which ran parallel with the political soundings, and had, of course, some bearing on them. Indeed, it was by announcing the Trade Agreement with Germany on August 21 that the Soviet Government prepared the ground for the much more spectacular and, to many, almost unbelievable announcement that was to come three days later. But the wording of the *Pravda* editorial of August 21 accompanying the announcement of the Trade Agreement was significant enough to anyone who could read between the lines—and, in this case, it did not even require outstanding political acumen to do so.

Shirer is probably quite right in saying that it was on August 19 that Stalin made his choice, unless it was on the 20th, after the receipt of Hitler's personal telegram.

> The best conclusion this writer can come to is that, as of August 14, when Voroshilov demanded "an unequivocal answer" on the question of allowing Soviet troops to meet the Germans in Poland, the Kremlin still had an open mind as to which side to join... At any rate, Stalin does not seem to have made his final decision until the afternoon of August 19.*

On the 19th, the Soviet press was, on the face of it, still violently anti-Nazi. It made it quite apparent that a German attack on Poland was now almost certainly a matter of days. Thus, *Pravda* of August 19 still published a TASS message from Warsaw under the heading: "GERMAN PROVOCATIONS IN DANZIG", and a TASS message from Berlin, under the heading: "ANTI-POLISH CAMPAIGN IN GERMANY":

> The *Völkischer Beobachter* today prominently displayed comments in the Italian press to the effect that the tension between Germany and Poland "can no longer be settled by a mere settlement of the Danzig

---

* Shirer, op. cit., p. 535.

question". All German papers are trying to present Poland as an "aggressor", and as the creator of "an intolerable situation". Britain and France are being attacked with special violence. In its editorial, the *Völkischer Beobachter* says: "The problem of Danzig and the Corridor are ripe for a German solution." The papers are openly threatening war. "Every day that's wasted," says the *Völkischer Beobachter*, "increases the danger of war."

By the 21st, the emphasis in the TASS reports from Berlin had slightly shifted, but only slightly; the main suggestion was still that a German attack on Poland was imminent; but now it was also suggested that Poland would be crushed within a very short time:

> *Berlin, August 20.* The threats against Poland today are even more violent. All the papers are screaming about the "Polish terror against Germans", and about "the crowding of Polish prisons by Germans". At the same time the German newspapers are writing about "the military weakness of Poland" and her incapacity to withstand a German blow.

It was not, however, this seemingly routine story which attracted the reader's attention that day, but the front-page editorial on the Soviet-German Trade and Credit Agreement. It started from afar, as it were:

> Even only a few years ago, Germany held first place in the Soviet Union's trade turnover. In 1931 Soviet-German trade amounted to 1,100 million marks. In view of the strained political relations, there was a marked decline in this trade. Until 1935, Germany was still first in the Soviet Union's foreign trade, but by 1938 she was down to fifth place, after Britain, the USA, Belgium and Holland. This loss of the Soviet market must have worried both German business circles and the German Government. That is why, since the beginning of last year, negotiations were conducted between the two countries, with certain intervals, on trade and credit questions with a view to enlarging Soviet-German trade. Despite difficulties that arose in these negotiations in view of the tense political atmosphere, there was a marked improvement in recent months. Thanks to the desire of both sides to improve commercial relations between the two countries, all matters of dispute have now been settled...

The editorial went on to say that a trade and credit agreement had been signed in Berlin on August 19 by Comrade Babarin, of the Soviet Trade Delegation, and Herr Schnurre. It was a satisfactory agreement: under it, Germany granted the USSR a credit of 200 million marks for purchases to be made in Germany during the next two years—mostly machine tools and other industrial equipment. The Soviet Union would supply, during the same period, "various commodities" for 180 million marks. The great advantage of the German credit was that it was in the nature of a financial loan, and the Soviet Union could pay German firms in cash. The annual interest rate on this loan was five percent, which was cheaper than the interest on previous loans. Also, the loan would not be repayable for seven and a half years.

This suggestion of peaceful German-Soviet trade relations for over seven years to come was sufficiently startling at a moment when the Germans were about to invade Poland. But the conclusion of the article was even more startling: "This agreement should greatly stimulate trade between the USSR and Germany, and *should become a turning point in the economic relations between the two countries.* The new trade and credit agreement between the USSR and Germany, though born in an atmosphere of strained political relations, is designed to clear this atmosphere. *It can become an important step towards a further improvement in not only the economic relations but also the political relations between the USSR and Germany.*"*

Clearly, the die was about to be cast. What also contributed to Stalin's decision to sign up with Germany was the situation in the Far East. In August 1939 the fierce battle of Halkin Gol was being fought against the Japanese, and the Russians were afraid of becoming involved in a two-front war—against Germany in Europe and against Japan in Asia. A pact with Germany would almost automatically end the war with Japan, Hitler's ally.

Ribbentrop's visit to Moscow and the signing of the Soviet-German Non-Aggression Pact of August 23 came almost as a complete surprise to the Russian public, and if nobody openly declared himself

* Emphasis added.

deeply shocked and scandalised, it was simply because it was "not done"—especially after the Purge years—to be openly shocked or scandalised by anything with which Comrade Stalin and Comrade Molotov were directly associated. It is, nevertheless, obvious that, at heart, millions of Russians were deeply perplexed by what had happened, after their country had been in the vanguard of the "anti-Fascist struggle" ever since the Nazis had come to power.* The mental alibis to which many Russians—whether workers or intellectuals—resorted, at least during the early stages of the Pact, were that Stalin and Molotov no doubt knew what they were doing; that they had, after all, kept the Soviet Union out of war (here was something corresponding roughly to the "cowardly relief and shame" reaction in the West at the time of Munich); and that the Pact, though distasteful, had been rendered inevitable by the attitude of France, Britain and Poland. Nor was it doubted that Stalin and Molotov must have had a great many reservations about the whole thing.

The reactions to the "deal" with Hitler were to undergo numerous changes during the twenty-two months the Pact was in force; but it seems clear that Stalin and Molotov were fully conscious of the mixed feelings with which the Pact was received in the country. Throughout the Pact period, the Soviet press, for example, maintained a marked aloofness *vis-à-vis* Nazi Germany. There were no favourable comments on any aspects of the Nazi régime at any time, and there was, strictly speaking, no reporting whatsoever on the German scene in the Soviet newspapers, beyond the reproduction of war communiqués and some official utterances by Hitler, especially when these concerned Soviet-German relations. Important news items, such as Stalin's toast during Ribbentrop's visit—"Since the

* This is also confirmed by the recollections of so competent an observer as Wolfgang Leonhard, whose account is based on first-hand experience at the time within the Comintern establishment: *Child of the Revolution* (London, 1957). At the same time, according to Jean Champenois, a leading French correspondent in Moscow, there was also widespread chuckling among many Russians about the punishment meted out to England and France "after all their dirty tricks".

German people love their Führer so much, let us drink the Führer's
health"—were carefully kept out of the Russian press.

During the week preceding Ribbentrop's visit, Aviation Day had
been celebrated on August 18, and half the front page of *Pravda* that
day was occupied by a drawing showing Stalin and Voroshilov sur-
veying a boundless airfield with thousands of planes on it. "Great and
touching is our airmen's love for Comrade Stalin", the editorial
wrote, while, on page 2, a famous airman commented rapturously
on "Comrade Stalin's profound knowledge in aviation matters",
and recalled some of the outstanding feats of Soviet aviation in
recent years and their heroes—Chkalov, Gromov, Grizodubova,
Raskova and Osipenko. The same paper reported, on its foreign
news page, "Jewish pogroms in Czechoslovakia" (TASS, Prague),
and "Persecution of Poles in Germany" (TASS, Warsaw).

On August 19, *Pravda* reported the Aviation Day meeting at
Tushino Airfield, attended by a million people: here also was a
picture of the Party and Army leaders present at the air display—
Stalin, Molotov, Voroshilov, Kaganovich, Zhdanov, Mikoyan,
Beria, Shvernik, Malenkov, Bulganin, Shcherbakov, Shkiriatov,
Budienny, Loktionov and Mikhailov. On August 20 the place of
honour was given to a "Letter from Prague", entitled: "The Czech
People are Not Defeated." And then, on August 21, there appeared,
as we have seen, the famous editorial on the Soviet-German Trade
and Credit Agreement, with its significant concluding paragraph,
foreshadowing a political *rapprochement* between the two countries.

But on the following two days—August 22 and 23—there was
still nothing of any importance, except the usual seemingly anti-
German news items like these: "Many Poles preparing to flee from
Danzig", or "Mass Arrests in Memel. Gestapo arresting not only
Poles, but also Lithuanians, Polish Press says."

On August 24 came the bombshell. Big front-page pictures in
Pravda showing Molotov, Stalin, Ribbentrop, Gaus, Deputy Secretary of State at the German Foreign Office and its legal adviser, and
an interpreter. The editorial on the Soviet-German Non-Aggression
Pact argued along the following lines:

The Pact was consistent with the Soviet Union's policy. "We stand for peace and the consolidation of business relations with all countries." Recalling Rapallo and the Soviet-German Neutrality Agreement of 1926, it said: "Yesterday's agreement follows in the footsteps of the 1926 agreement, except that it goes still further, since Art. 1 precludes any aggressive actions against the co-signatory either alone or with other Powers, while Art. 2 provides for neutrality in the event of an attack on either signatory by a third power." Art. 3 called for consultation on matters of common interest. Art. 4 was particularly important since it obliged the signatories not to take part in any grouping of Powers which might, directly, or indirectly, be aimed at the other signatory.

The editorial also highly commended Art. 5 providing for the peaceful and friendly settlement of any disputes and for the creation of commissions in the event of more serious conflicts, as well as Art. 6 which specified that the Pact was valid for ten years and was automatically renewable for five more years; here was a clear promise of a lasting peace. The last paragraph concerned ratification "as quickly as possible".

Below the picture of the Kremlin meeting there was this announcement:

> At 3.30 p.m. on August 23 a first conversation took place between ... V. M. Molotov and the Foreign Minister of Germany, Herr von Ribbentrop. The conversation took place in the presence of Comrade Stalin and the German Ambassador Count von der Schulenburg. It lasted about three hours. After an interval the conversation was resumed at 10 p.m. and ended with the signing of the Non-Aggression Agreement of which the text follows.

Another communiqué concerned the arrival in Moscow, at 1.30 p.m. on August 23, of "the Foreign Minister of Germany, Herr Joachim von Ribbentrop" and the persons accompanying him, among them Herr Gaus, Baron von Dörnberg, Herr P. Schmidt, Prof. G. Hoffmann, Herr K. Schnurre, etc. It also gave a long list of the personalities who had gone to the airfield to meet them, among them Deputy Foreign Commissar V. P. Potemkin; Deputy Commissar for Foreign Trade, M. S. Stepanov; Deputy Commissar of the Interior, V. N. Merkulov; the Chairman of the Moscow City Soviet, etc. Present were also members of the German Embassy, with

Ambassador von der Schulenburg at their head, as well as the Italian Ambassador and Military Attaché. On the following day *Pravda* briefly reported Ribbentrop's departure "at 1.25 p.m. on August 24". The same people who had come to meet him had also gone to see him off.

The editorial that day, however, dealt with nothing more exciting than the State purchases of vegetables.

For the next few days nothing more was said about the Soviet-German Pact and, surprisingly, there were no reports of any "spontaneous" and "enthusiastic" mass meetings anywhere in Russia approving it. The foreign press reactions, as reported in the Soviet Press, seemed remarkably inconclusive, except for the London *Star* which was reported to have blamed Chamberlain for what had happened. On August 29, *Pravda* quoted H. N. Brailsford, the veteran Labour journalist, as saying something similar. Equally inconclusive were the various news items printed—about military preparations in Poland, Britain, and so on.

Yet there was a great deal of uneasiness in the country; this may be gauged from the publication, on August 27, of an interview with Voroshilov in which he explained why the talks with Britain and France had broken down.

> The talks, he said, had stopped because of serious disagreements. The Soviet Military Mission took the view that since the Soviet Union had no common frontier with the aggressor (*sic*), she could help Great Britain, France and Poland only if her troops could cross Polish territory in order to make contact with the aggressor forces. The Poles said that they neither needed nor wanted Soviet help. Asked if there was any truth in the *Daily Herald* report that, in case of war, the Soviet Union would occupy parts of Poland and also help the Poles with planes, munitions, etc., Voroshilov said No, adding: "We did not break off the talks with Britain and France because we had signed a non-aggression pact with Germany; on the contrary, we signed this pact because, apart from anything else, the military talks with Britain and France had reached a complete deadlock."

The whole suggestion was that the Soviet Union was prepared to

go to war with Nazi Germany, but that she could not do so in view
of the attitude of Britain, France and especially Poland.

During the next few days the news continued to be highly confusing—more about Polish "defence measures", British "military
preparations", about an appeal by the Slovak Premier, Mgr Tiso,
asking Germany, on behalf of the Slovak population, to send troops
to Slovakia, about German ships leaving American ports, and so on.
On August 30 there were only short news items about "General
Mobilisation in Poland", and about Ambassador Nevile Henderson's
meeting with Hitler and Ribbentrop.

It was not till August 31—i.e. one day before the German invasion
of Poland—that Molotov made a statement on the Soviet-German
Pact before the Supreme Soviet. If, only four days before, Voroshilov
spoke of the breakdown of the talks with Britain and France more
in sorrow than in anger, Molotov started that day on his series of
anti-French and anti-British speeches, with lasting co-existence with
Nazi Germany as their keynote.

Since the 3rd Session of the Supreme Soviet, he said, the international situation had shown no turn for the better, either in Europe
or in the Far East. The talks with Britain and France had gone on
since April, i.e. for four months, and they had led to nothing. Poland
had made any agreement impossible, and, in her negative attitude,
Poland had been supported by Britain. He then ridiculed the British
and French military missions who had come to Moscow without any
powers or credentials; the whole thing "wasn't serious". Then came
his monumental defence of the Soviet-German Pact:

> We all know that since the Nazis came to power, relations between
> the Soviet Union and Germany have been strained. But we need not
> dwell on these differences; they are sufficiently familiar to you anyway,
> Comrades Deputies.
>
> But, as Comrade Stalin said on March 10, "we are in favour of
> business relations with all nations"; and it seems that, in Germany,
> they understood Comrade Stalin's statement correctly, and drew the
> right conclusions.
>
> August 23 must be regarded as a date of great historic importance.
> It is a turning point in the history of Europe, and not only Europe.
>
> Only recently the German Nazis conducted a foreign policy which
> was essentially hostile to the Soviet Union. Yes, until recently, in the

realm of foreign policy, the Soviet Union and Germany were enemies. The situation has now changed, and we have stopped being enemies. The political art in foreign affairs is ... to reduce the number of enemies of one's country, and to turn yesterday's enemies into good neighbours.

History has shown that enmity and war between Russia and Germany have never led to any good. These two countries suffered more from the last World War than any other.

Molotov obviously expected a new war in Europe to break out at any moment; but this did not seem to worry him unduly: "Even if a military collision cannot be avoided in Europe, the scale of such a war will be limited. Only the partisans of a general war in Europe can be dissatisfied with this."

The Soviet-German agreement has been violently attacked in the Anglo-French and American press, and especially in some "socialist" papers... Particularly violent in their denunciations of the agreement are some of the French and British socialist leaders... These people are determined that the Soviet Union should fight against Germany on the side of Britain and France. One may well wonder whether these warmongers haven't gone off their heads. [*Laughter.*]

Under the Soviet-German Agreement, the Soviet Union is not obliged to fight either on the British or the German side. The USSR is pursuing her own policy, which is determined by the interests of the peoples of the USSR, and by nobody else. [*Loud cheers.*]

If these gentlemen have such an irresistible desire to go to war, well then—let them go to war by themselves, without the Soviet Union. [*Laughter and cheers.*] We'll see what kind of warriors they will make. [*Loud laughter and cheers.*]

Molotov had set the tone of the "debate".

Soon afterwards Shcherbakov rose to speak: "Two great nations," he said, "have solemnly declared their good-neighbourly relations... And now the Western socialists are furious. For they would like the Soviet Union and Germany to attack one another."

What Molotov had said about the British and French, Shcherbakov continued, showed that, in their negotiations with the Soviet Union their attitude, especially that of the British, was insincere. There was no real desire to form a mutual assistance front. He then proposed that, in view of the "perfect clarity" of Molotov's statement, there should be no debate, that the policy of the Soviet government be approved and the Soviet-German agreement ratified.

Needless to say, neither Molotov nor Shcherbakov had any grounds for fearing a debate; but there is no reason to suppose that it would have been marked by any high degree of enthusiasm.

A few hours later the Germans invaded Poland. Nothing was said in Moscow at that stage of the role that the Soviet Union was going to play in the destruction of that country, except for a slightly mysterious TASS statement on August 30 denying that Soviet troops were being transferred to the Far East:

> On the contrary, TASS is authorised to state that, owing to the strained situation in the West, the garrisons on the Western frontier of the USSR are being reinforced.

Needless to say, Molotov's and Ribbentrop's Secret Protocol was not published. This, as we know, provided that "in the event of territorial and political transformations" the northern frontier of Lithuania would be the frontier of the Soviet-German "spheres of interest" in the Baltic States, and, roughly, the Narew-Vistula-San line the provisional demarcation line. The Soviet Union and Germany would subsequently decide whether to maintain an independent Polish state, and if so, within what frontiers.

Before long, as we shall see, the occupation by the Red Army of Eastern Poland was to be represented as "the liberation of Western Belorussia and the Western Ukraine" and as a means of saving these areas from the Nazis.

The present-day Soviet assessment of the Soviet-German Pact is that it was a measure that had been forced on Russia which simply had no alternative.* It is one of the very few points on which Khrushchev has never attacked or criticised Stalin, but has, on the contrary, fully justified his action.

* For example ex-Ambassador Maisky's criticism of British foreign policy in 1939 in his memoirs.

Chapter III

THE PARTITION OF POLAND

The coverage in the Soviet press of the German invasion of Poland was almost unbelievably thin. It looked as though there were a desire to make people think and talk about it as little as possible. An attempt was made to give the impression that this was a small local war, of no particular consequence to the Soviet Union, where life, thanks to the wisdom of Comrade Stalin, was going on normally and peacefully.

Much space was given in the press to a great popular fête at the Dynamo Stadium in Moscow on the eve of the German invasion of Poland, to another fête at Sokolniki a few days later, and to the International Youth Days which were celebrated in Moscow, Leningrad and Kiev at the end of the first week of the war (though the question which nations were represented at these Youth Days was left remarkably vague—and no wonder!).

In reporting the war itself, the Soviet press tried at first to sound as neutral and objective as possible. Both the German and the Polish communiqués were published; but controversial matters like the "Operation Himmler" at Gleiwitz—where Germans, dressed in Polish uniform, attacked a German wireless station—were carefully avoided.*

* In the Soviet post-war *History* of the war, on the other hand, the greatest prominence is given to this far-reaching Nazi provocation against Poland.

Miles

0   100   200

SWEDEN

Baltic Sea

ESTONIA

U

Riga

LATVIA

Annexed by
USSR
June·1940

Annexed by
GERMANY
April·1939

Memel

LITHUANIA

Vilno

Minsk

Königsberg

Lida

Danzig

EAST
PRUSSIA

Grodno

Baranovichi

Stettin

G
E
R
M
A
N
Y

Torun

Bialystok

Brest-
Litovsk

Pinsk

Oder

Poznan

WARSAW

BERLIN

Neisse

P O L A N D

Lodz

Oder

Lublin

Kovel

Lutsk

Rovno

PRAGUE

Cracow

Lwow

S
S
R

CZECHOSLOVAKIA

Ternopol

Stanislav

VIENNA

Danube

N

AUSTRIA

BUDAPEST

PARTITION OF
POLAND·1939

HUNGARY

Annexed by USSR

YUGO-
SLAVIA

Annexed by GERMANY

Hitler's Reichstag speech announcing the invasion of Poland was given under a three-column heading in *Pravda* on September 2. The speech was important since, in the course of it, Hitler said: "I can endorse every word that Foreign Commissar Molotov uttered in his Supreme Soviet speech," and proposed the ratification of the Soviet-German Pact. The news that Britain had declared war on Germany was given only a two-column heading.

Relations with Nazi Germany were what seemed to interest the Soviet Government most. On September 6, *Pravda* prominently reported that, in the presence of Ribbentrop, Hitler had received the new Soviet Ambassador, Comrade Shkvartsev and the Soviet Military Attaché, Comrade Purkayev. "After presenting his credentials, the Soviet Ambassador had a lengthy talk with Hitler."

Events in Britain and France were only very thinly reported, but, significantly perhaps, considerable interest was shown in the American attitude to the war in Europe.

But that "objectivity" in reporting the war in Poland did not last long. Ten days after the German invasion *Pravda* published its first "survey" of the Polish-German war which, it said, was marked by an extraordinarily rapid advance of the German troops; the absence of any proper fortifications in Western Poland and great German air superiority, as a result of which practically all Polish airfields, most of the Polish air force and most communication centres had been destroyed. The "survey" stressed the great superiority of the German land forces, with their large numbers of tanks and heavy guns, and also commented on the total lack of "any effective help" from Britain and France. Although, it concluded, a large part of the Polish Army had succeeded in crossing the Vistula, the Polish command was unlikely to continue strong resistance, since it had lost practically its entire military and economic base.

Better still was to come. Three days later, on September 14, a *Pravda* editorial argued that the Polish Army had *practically not fought at all.*

Why is this Polish Army not offering the Germans any resistance to speak of? It is because Poland is not a homogeneous country. Only sixty percent of the population are Poles, the rest are Ukrainians, Belorussians and Jews... The eleven million Ukrainians and Belorussians are living in a state of national oppression... The administration is Polish, and no other language is recognised. There are practically no non-Polish schools or other cultural establishments. The Polish Constitution does not give non-Poles the right to be taught in their own language. Instead, the Polish Government has been pursuing a policy of forced Polonisation...

The more heroic episodes of the Polish soldiers' resistance to superior German forces—whether at Hel or Westerplatte or in Warsaw—were not mentioned at all; instead, on September 14, *Pravda* reported that "after a tour of inspection of the Front, Hitler had arrived at Lodz at 3 p.m." Reports of German air attacks on railway trains and of "the flight of the Polish Government" were intended to convey the impression that by the middle of September Poland was in a complete state of chaos.

The full significance of the article on the Ukrainians and Belorussians soon became apparent. On September 17 Molotov made a broadcast in which he declared that two weeks of war had demonstrated the "internal incapacity" of the Polish State. All industrial centres had been lost; nor could Warsaw be considered any more the capital of the Polish State. No one knew where the Polish Government was. The situation in Poland therefore called for the greatest vigilance on the part of the Soviet Union. The Soviet Government had informed the Polish Ambassador, Mr Grzybowski, that the Red Army had been ordered to take under its protection the populations of Western Belorussia and the Western Ukraine.

Grzybowski had, indeed, been informed that day that although it had been neutral "up till now", the Soviet Government could no longer be neutral in the face of reigning chaos in Poland or the fact that "our blood-brothers, the Ukrainians and Belorussians, are being abandoned to their fate..."

And then came the *guerre fraîche et joyeuse*. In a few days the Red Army occupied vast stretches of country which had constituted the eastern half of Poland. The war communiqué of September 17 announced that the Red Army had crossed the Polish frontier all the way from Latvia to Rumania; that, in the north, Molodechno and Baranovichi had been occupied, and, in the south, Rovno and Dubno. Seven Polish fighters had been brought down, three Polish bombers had been forced to land, and their crews had been taken prisoner. By September 20 the Red Army had occupied Kovel, Lwow, Vilno and Grodno. Three Polish divisions had been disarmed, and 68,000 officers and men taken prisoner.

On September 19 a joint Soviet-German communiqué was published saying that the task of the Soviet and German troops was to "restore peace and order which had been disturbed by the disintegration [*raspad*] of the Polish State, and to help the population of Poland to reorganise the conditions of its political existence".

If, during the German invasion of Poland, the Soviet press was extremely reticent in its accounts of what was happening, and carefully refrained from any "straight" reporting, it now embarked on an orgy of rapturous articles and descriptive reports on the enthusiasm with which the Red Army was being welcomed by the people of the Western Ukraine and Western Belorussia—

Happy Days in the Liberated Villages (report from the Rovno area).
Jubilant Crowds Heartily Welcome N. S. Khrushchev.
Population to Red Army: "You have Saved our Lives!"

Such were some of the headlines. On September 20 *Pravda* reported "great animation in Lwow" and the great enthusiasm with which the people there had gone to see the film "Lenin in 1918".

Another report from the Rovno area read: "An old peasant, named Murash, went up to our soldiers. 'I am seventy,' he said, 'and I know that there is in Moscow a man who is the father of all the oppressed, a man who thinks of us and cares for us. And I know that his name is Joseph Stalin.'"

All the same, the Soviet hierarchy must have known that there was at least some slight uneasiness in the country over what was in effect a partition of Poland in the company of Hitler. Hence, for instance, the publication in *Pravda* on September 18 of a poem by Nikolai Aseyev called "Hold Your Heads Up"—

The landlords' (*panski*) flag has been trampled underfoot,
But you, Polish people, have not been humiliated. . .

You toilers of Poland, do not believe the tale
That we have stepped forward
Just to add to your sorrows.
If we have crossed the frontier,
It is not to make you afraid;
We do not want you to cringe to us;
Proudly you can hold up your heads.

In fact, the great majority of "real" Poles were to remain under German occupation, as most of the people in the areas taken over by the Russians were Ukrainians or Belorussians. As we now know, the NKVD soon got busy in the liberated territories of the Western Ukraine and Western Belorussia. The deportation to the east of "hostile" and "disloyal" Poles was to run into hundreds of thousands. They were to constitute a major political problem in 1941–2. The Polish soldiers captured by the Russians were demobilised before long, but most of the captured Polish officers were to remain in Russian captivity—with dire consequences, as we shall see.

The land reform in the liberated areas—a reform described in the Soviet press as early as September 27 as "the distribution of landlord estates"—began almost at once.

On September 27 *Pravda* published a map of Poland showing the provisional demarcation line between the Russian and German armed forces. This ran from the south-east corner of East Prussia down to Warsaw and then further south along the river San.

On the following day Ribbentrop came on his second visit to Moscow. On September 29 *Pravda* published a large front-page photograph showing Molotov signing the German-Soviet Agreement of Friendship and on the Frontier between the USSR and Germany; standing behind him were Ribbentrop, Stalin, Pavlov (the interpreter), and Gaus. The paper also spoke of the dinner given by Molotov in Ribbentrop's honour. Among those present were Forster, Gaus, Schnurre, and Kordt of the Ribbentrop party, Schulenburg and Tippelskirch of the German Embassy, as well as Stalin, Voroshilov, Kaganovich, Mikoyan, Beria, Bulganin and Voznesensky.

"Comrade Molotov and Herr von Ribbentrop exchanged speeches of welcome. The dinner took place in a friendly atmosphere."

That day the following Soviet-German Statement was published:

> Having signed today an agreement which finally settled the problems that had arisen from the disintegration of the Polish State, and having thus laid the solid foundations for a lasting peace in Eastern Europe, the Soviet and German Governments declare that the liquidation of the war between Germany on the one hand and Great Britain and France on the other would be in the interests of all nations.
>
> If, however, the endeavours of both governments remain fruitless, this will only show that Great Britain and France will bear the responsibility for continuing the war. If this war is to continue, the Governments of Germany and the Soviet Union will consult each other on the necessary measures to be taken.
>
> (Signed) *Molotov. Ribbentrop.*

Later, during the war, I had occasion to discuss with a number of Soviet intellectuals the effect this statement had in Russia at the time. It appeared that the "recovery" of Western Belorussia and the Western Ukraine had indeed caused much satisfaction, partly because it had pushed the Soviet frontier further west—and nobody had ever trusted Hitler. Secondly the one thing many people dreaded was that Britain and France might make peace with Germany. They knew that Russia had become thoroughly disreputable in French and British eyes over the "partition" of Poland, and feared that there might be a Western deal with Hitler at Russia's expense.

No sooner was the war in Poland over, than the Russians inflicted on Estonia, Latvia and Lithuania "mutual aid and trade agreements" under which the Soviet Union was given military, air and naval bases in all three countries. In that matter, too, the consummation of the secret protocol drawn up by Ribbentrop and Molotov, when the Soviet Nazi treaty was concluded, made steady progress. Vilno, however, which had been part of Poland, was handed back to Lithuania by the Russians after they had secured the required military hold on that small country, as they had on the two other Baltic States.

Meanwhile Molotov and Ribbentrop continued to go through all the usual motions of friendship. On September 29, before leaving Moscow, Ribbentrop declared in a statement to Tass:

> Again this visit to Moscow was too short, and I hope my next visit will last longer. All the same, we made good use of these two days.
> 1) German-Soviet friendship is now finally established;
> 2) Neither country will allow any interference from third parties in East-European affairs;
> 3) Both countries wish a restoration of peace, and they want Britain and France to stop their absolutely senseless and hopeless war against Germany;
> 4) If, however, in these countries, the warmongers gain the upper hand, then Germany and the USSR will know how to react to this.

He then referred to "the great programme of economic co-operation which had been agreed upon and which would be valuable to both countries", and, he concluded: "The talks took place in a particularly friendly and splendid atmosphere. I should like, above all, to stress the extraordinarily cordial reception given me by the Soviet Government and particularly by Herr Stalin and Herr Molotov."*

Looking back on this statement, a number of Russians later told me that it had created a "rather reassuring impression". Among many Russians there was the hope—or the illusion—that Ribbentrop perhaps belonged to that *Ostpolitik* faction in Germany who were decidedly against conflict with Russia. That was the impression that Stalin and Molotov also had; they were, moreover, convinced that Ambassador Count Schulenburg belonged to the old Bismarckian, no-war-with-Russia school of thought. In this they were right. The big question mark was Hitler himself.

On October 8, a week after the Ribbentrop visit to Moscow, Hitler made another peace offer to Britain and France, but it was rejected, again, one suspects, to the Russians' relief.

The Soviet Press during the weeks following the destruction of Poland makes pretty nauscating reading. Thus, *Pravda* of October 17

* *Pravda*, September 30, 1939.

published an article by David Zaslavsky, an old hack, ironically a Jew, whom Lenin had once described as "the most corrupt pen in Russia":

> In all seriousness, though scarcely able to suppress a smile, the French press has informed the world of a sensational piece of news. In Paris in such-and-such a street a new Polish Government has been formed, with General Sikorski at its head. The territory of this government consists, it appears, of six rooms, a bathroom and a w.c. Compared with this territory, Monaco is a boundless empire.
>
> In the Great Paris Synagogue, Sikorski addressed the Jewish bankers of Paris. The Synagogue was adorned with a flag with a white eagle, which the Chief Rabbi must have turned into kosher meat, since this is a bird that orthodox Jews do not, as a rule, use as food.
>
> In former Poland, the Jews used to be frightened to death of the Polish nobility and of pogroms, but the Jewish bankers in Paris had, obviously, nothing to fear from General Sikorski...

And more witticisms of the same kind; but not a word about the Nazis and Mr Zaslavsky's own fellow-Jews in "former" Poland. The cartoons in the press were becoming increasingly anti-British and anti-French. Thus Kukryniksy published one showing a "Capitalist" and a "Social-Democrat" locking a door marked "Democracy" and a "French Communist" peeping through the barred window. The Social-Democrat carried a shield marked "War for Democracy".

It was not till October 31 that Molotov made another speech before the Supreme Soviet—this was the famous speech in which he welcomed the disappearance of Poland, "that monster child of the Treaty of Versailles",* and declared that not Germany, but Britain and France were now the "aggressor" nations.

It was this speech which marked, as it were, the zenith of Soviet-German "friendship" and "solidarity"; first it dealt with Poland: "The rulers of Poland used to make a great fuss over the 'soundness' of their State and the 'might' of their Army. A short blow at

---

* A phrase for which, in retrospect, he was to be taken to task in vol. I of the official *History of the War*, published in 1960.

Poland from the German Army, followed by one from the Red
Army was enough to reduce to nothing this monster child of the
Treaty of Versailles."

He then dealt with the British and French guarantees to Poland,
and remarked "amidst general laughter" that "no one knew to this
day what kind of guarantees these were". He noted that the war in
the West had not yet developed.

"But the whole concept of 'aggression' has changed. Today we
cannot use the word in the same sense as three or four months ago.
*Now Germany stands for peace, while Britain and France are in
favour of continuing the war. As you see, the roles have been
reversed.*"*

He even improved on this performance by going on:

> Now Britain and France, no longer able to fight for a restoration of
> Poland, are posing as "fighters for democratic rights against Hitler-
> ism". The British Government now claims that its aim is, no more, or
> no less, if you please, "the destruction of Hitlerism". So it's an ideo-
> logical war, a kind of medieval religious war.
>
> One may like or dislike Hitlerism, but every sane person will under-
> stand that ideology cannot be destroyed by force. It is therefore not
> only nonsensical but also criminal to pursue a war "for the destruction
> of Hitlerism" under the bogus banner of a struggle for "democracy".
> And what kind of democracy is it, anyway, with the French Com-
> munist Party in jail?

It was only when dealing with the liberation of the Western
Ukraine and Western Belorussia that Molotov did drop something
like a hint that Germany, after all, still constituted a potential danger
to the Soviet Union: "Our relations with Germany have radically
improved. We are neutral. But we could not remain neutral in respect of Eastern Poland, *since this involved acute problems of our
country's security.** Moreover, the populations of Western Belorussia
and the Western Ukraine had been left to their fate, and this we
could not allow."

Since the incorporation of these territories in the Soviet Union,
Molotov said, the population of the country had grown by some
thirteen million people, over seven million Ukrainians, three million

* Emphasis added.

Belorussians, one million Poles and one million Jews. The war against Poland had cost the Soviet Union 734 dead and 1,862 wounded; and the Red Army had captured from the Poles 900 guns, 10,000 machine-guns, 300 planes, one million shells, etc.

He then spoke of the mutual assistance pacts with the Baltic States and, indeed, contended that these did not, in any way, constitute interference in their internal affairs.

This, however, did not end his diplomatic survey. Next on the list was Finland. Leningrad, Molotov said, was only twenty miles from the Finnish frontier, and could thus be shelled from Finnish territory. Lately there had been all kinds of absurd rumours. The Soviet Union was supposed to have demanded from Finland the transfer of Viborg and of the north side of Lake Ladoga. This was a lie.*

"Our demands are minimal. In our talks with Tanner and Paasi-kivi we proposed a mutual assistance pact on the lines of those signed with the other Baltic States. The Finns said they were neutral; so we did not insist. What we are asking for is only a small area of a few dozen kilometres north-west of Leningrad, in return for which we are willing to give them an area twice that size. We are also asking for a naval base at the western end of the Gulf of Finland. We have now a naval base at Baltiski in Estonia on the south side of the gulf; we want a similar base on the north side." Molotov argued that these demands were eminently reasonable, and regretted that the Finns were being difficult.†

He then briefly dealt with Japan, saying that between May and mid-September there had been heavy fighting in the Far East. Japan had wanted to annex a part of Mongolia; but if England's guarantee to Poland was a scrap of paper, the Soviet Union's guarantee to the Mongolian People's Republic was not. On September 15 peace had been restored between Japan and the Soviet Union.

In conclusion he remarked that the United States Government had lifted its embargo on arms to belligerent nations, and this, he said,

* Precisely the territory the Russians were eventually to annex.
† From the Finnish point of view these Russian demands did not look as trivial as Molotov tried to suggest, and events were soon to show that the Finns had good grounds for mistrusting Russia's intentions.

"aroused legitimate doubts". This complaint fitted, of course, the official line that not Germany, but Britain and France were now the "aggressors". This argument was illustrated a few days later by another Kukryniksy cartoon in *Pravda* showing British and French generals and capitalists in top hats queuing up for armaments in front of "Uncle Sam's Bargain Basement".

Molotov's speech of October 31, 1939 marks the end of the first phase of the Soviet-German "honeymoon". The recovery by the Soviet Union of Western Belorussia and the Western Ukraine—including some areas, such as Lwow, which had never been part of the old Russian Empire—suggested to many Russians that, from a national point of view, the *rapprochement* with Nazi Germany could have some distinct advantages. It is true that all these annexations were mixed up with "acute problems of our country's security" as Molotov had said, and this could primarily refer only to a potential danger from Nazi Germany. Nevertheless there was a widespread feeling in the country that "neutrality" paid; that as a result of the Soviet-German Pact the Soviet Union had become bigger and, as yet without too much bloodshed, more secure.

Following the partition of Poland, the western frontier of the Soviet Union had been moved several hundred miles further west; the Baltic States had been "neutralised" through the establishment of Soviet military bases there. There was, of course, that threat to Leningrad left which had now to be dealt with.

The "liberation" of Eastern Poland, with its 700 Russian dead, had been one of the cheapest wars ever fought and gave the pleasant illusion of the Red Army's invincibility. The Finnish war, with its enormous casualties (48,000 Russian dead alone) was to raise some highly awkward questions about the Red Army's overwhelming power and efficiency. Politically, the Finnish war could not, as we shall see, have been handled—at least in its initial stages—more ineptly than it was.

Chapter IV

FROM THE FINNISH WAR TO THE
GERMAN INVASION OF FRANCE

The Russians considered the Finnish frontier, running only twenty miles north-west of Leningrad, a potential threat to Russia's second largest city. The Russians, as Molotov said in his speech of October 31, were "only" asking that the frontier be pushed back "a few dozen kilometres", while a much larger area was to be given to Finland further north in return for this concession. Moreover, the Russians, anxious to control the Gulf of Finland and so to protect Leningrad and its sea route, had asked for a naval base, i.e. for the port of Hangö on the north side of the Gulf.*

The negotiations continued for two months, until at the end of November there was a frontier incident, real or imaginary. Despite Finnish denials the Russians claimed that the Finns had shelled the Soviet border killing several Russian soldiers. The Russians demanded that the Finnish Army withdraw twenty or twenty-five kilometres from the frontier. The Finnish Government denied that the incident had occurred and refused to comply. On November 29 Molotov sent a note to Irje Koskinen, the Finnish Minister in Moscow, in which he declared:

* In 1945, Paasikivi and Kekkonen, both future presidents of Finland, who had favoured accommodation with the Russians, told me that they had considered the Russian proposals moderate and understandable, and maintained that the war could have been avoided had their policy prevailed.

66

Having refused to withdraw their troops from the Soviet border by even twenty or twenty-five kilometres after the wicked shelling of Soviet troops by Finnish troops, the Government of Finland has shown that it continues to maintain a hostile attitude to the Soviet Union. Since it has violated the non-aggression pact . . . we now also consider ourselves free of the obligations arising from this pact.

On the same day Molotov made a radio announcement in which he said, in effect, that war had been declared on Finland since the two months' negotiations had only led to the shelling by the Finns of Soviet troops in the Leningrad area. He announced that the Soviet political and economic representatives in Finland had been recalled. At the same time Molotov also went out of his way to state that the Soviet Union "regarded Finland, no matter what its régime was, as an independent and sovereign State". This statement was all the more curious since, three days later, the Russians set up the "Finnish People's Government" of Terijoki under Otto Kuusinen.

"Spontaneous" mass demonstrations of anger were reported from all over the Soviet Union in *Pravda* of November 30, alongside the text of the Molotov broadcast. Here are a few headlines:

"Let us Strike Mercilessly at the Enemy!" (Mass meeting at the Bolshevik Plant in Leningrad).
Moscow: "We Shall Answer Fire with Fire!"
Kronstadt: "Our Patience is at an End!"
The People's Wrath: "Wipe the Finnish Adventurers off the Face of the Earth."
Kiev: "The Fate of Beck and Moscicki Awaits Them!"

On the following day, the Soviet press briefly reported "clashes between Soviet and Finnish troops".

More startling, however, was the "monitoring report, translated from the Finnish" of an alleged "Address by the Central Committee of the Finnish Communist Party to the Labouring People of Finland". And then on December 2, the Soviet press published this TASS report from Leningrad:

FORMATION OF A PEOPLE'S GOVERNMENT OF FINLAND
By agreement with the representatives of a number of Left-wing parties and with Finnish soldiers who had rebelled, a new government

of Finland—the People's Government of the Finnish Democratic
Republic—was formed at Terijoki today.*

The premier and foreign minister of this government was Otto
Kuusinen, one of the most active members of the Comintern for
many years past, and he had six ministers—somebody called Mauri
Rosenberg, the Minister of Finance, Axel Anttila, Minister of
Defence, Taure Lechin, Minister of the Interior and three others.
No one knew who exactly, with the exception of Kuusinen, these
people were. On the same day it was announced that diplomatic
relations had been established between the Soviet Union and the
Finnish Democratic Government.

The news of the formation of the new Finnish Government was
not only received "with jubilant enthusiasm by the people of Leningrad" but—already on the very day of its formation—"The *kolkhozniks* of Tataria 'heartily welcomed' the People's Government of
Finland".†

Kuusinen was going from strength to strength. On the following
day (December 3) *Pravda* published a front-page picture showing
Molotov signing the Mutual Assistance and Friendship Pact between
the USSR and the Finnish Democratic Republic. Standing behind
him were Zhdanov, Voroshilov, Stalin and Kuusinen. It was not
quite clear what had happened to the other members of the new
Finnish Government. The Pact provided that the "ratification
papers" would be "exchanged by the two governments at Helsinki".

The same issue of *Pravda* published a map showing the new
Soviet-Finnish frontier agreed upon between Molotov and Kuusinen:
apart from a lease by Russia of Hangö, only a small area of Finnish
territory north-west of Leningrad—less than half-way towards
Viborg‡—was to be ceded to the Soviet Union. In return, Finland
received large stretches of Karelia, including the whole Olonetz area,
east of Lake Ladoga.

It is more than doubtful whether these terms did indeed impress
the Finns by their show of "generosity". Be that as it may, the clause

* Terijoki is on the Gulf of Finland only a few miles across the
Finnish border. It used to be a favourite seaside resort with Petro-
graders before the Revolution.
† *Pravda*, December 2, 1939.   ‡ Viipuri in Finnish (see map).

Kakisalmi

Lake Ladoga

1940 Frontier

13th MARCH·1940

Viipuri

27th FEB·1940

12th DEC·1939
–11 FEB.·1940

Bjorko

Nykyrka

30th NOV·1939

Terijoki

Gulf of Finland

Kronstadt

LENINGRAD

N

SWEDEN

FINLAND

LENINGRAD

EST
LAT
LITH

POLAND

U S S R

Miles

0   10   20   30   40

SOVIET-FINNISH WAR
1939 – 1940

stipulating that the ratification papers were to be "exchanged" at
Helsinki between the Russians and Kuusinen was quite another
matter. It suggested that the "liberation" of Finland by the Red
Army, accompanied by the Terijoki Government, would only be a
matter of a few days, at most of weeks.

Both militarily and politically, Stalin's and Molotov's miscalculations could not have been worse. The "Terijoki Government"
was set up two or three days after Molotov had explicitly declared
his continued recognition of the Finnish Government at Helsinki,
and, except for the capture of Petsamo in the far north in the middle
of December, the Red Army's advance on either the Karelian
Isthmus or in Central Finland was extremely slow and arduous. The
"Mannerheim Line" was much stronger than the Russian command
had anticipated, and Finnish resistance was extremely tough. Indeed,
casualties were rapidly mounting. Anyone who lived in Leningrad
knew that the hospitals had difficulties in coping with the thousands
of wounded pouring in day after day. Meanwhile, the communiqués
were brief and unilluminating, except for showing that most of the
heavy fighting was taking place on the Karelian Isthmus. The dis-
concerted Soviet public soon guessed that the Finnish war was nothing like the walkover in Eastern Poland. Still, the myth of the
"Terijoki Government" had to be kept up for quite a while, as well
as the myth that the "White-Finnish Clique at Helsinki" was "unrepresentative" of the Finnish people.

Pravda even resorted to quoting from some article in a Rumanian
paper which was supposed to have said: "The present 'ruling circles'
of Finland consist chiefly of ex-Tsarist functionaries... Foreign
Minister Erkko recently recalled the happy times when Finland was
a Russian Grand-Duchy. General Mannerheim is particularly
attached to the good old Tsarist days, when he was a personal A.D.C.
to Nicholas II. It was Mannerheim who, in 1918, strangled Finland's
democratic freedoms with the help of foreign (*sic*) troops." *Pravda*
did not specify that the foreign troops in question were German
troops.

*

December 21, 1939 was Stalin's 60th birthday which, needless to say, was marked by an orgy of laudatory articles ("Stalin Continues the Work of Lenin" by Molotov, "Stalin and the Build-Up of the Red Army" by Voroshilov, "Stalin, the Great Engine-Driver of History", by Kaganovich, "Stalin is Lenin To-Day", by Mikoyan, etc.), poems and musical compositions, among them Prokofiev's, musically admirable, *Ode to Stalin*.

Two days later the press began to publish the birthday greetings Stalin had received from abroad. The place of honour was given to the telegram from Hitler, followed by that from Ribbentrop.

In his birthday greeting to Stalin on December 21, Hitler said:

> ... Please accept my most sincere congratulations. I send at the same time my very best wishes for your personal good health and for a happy future for the peoples of a friendly Soviet Union.
>
> *Adolf Hitler.*

Ribbentrop was even more gushing:

> Remembering the historic hours at the Kremlin which marked the beginning of a decisive change in the relations of our countries and which thus laid the foundations for long years of friendship between our two peoples, please accept my most cordial congratulations on your 60th birthday.
>
> *Joachim von Ribbentrop.*

Stalin sent Hitler a rather conventional telegram of thanks, but in his telegram to Ribbentrop he said: "The friendship between the peoples of the Soviet Union and Germany, cemented by blood, has every reason to be solid and lasting."

The impression persisted among the Soviet hierarchy that Ribbentrop was more wholehearted about the Soviet-German Pact than Hitler was. No doubt they would have preferred it the other way round.

Third on the list was the telegram from Kuusinen, followed by birthday greetings from Chiang Kai-Shek, Mgr Tiso, the President of Slovakia, Mr Sarajoglu of Turkey, and the particularly obsequious messages from the leaders of Estonia, Latvia and Lithuania. There were no birthday greetings from any Western leaders, who were

busy at the time expelling the Soviet Union from the League of
Nations.

Kuusinen wired: "In the name of the toiling people of Finland,
fighting hand-in-hand with the heroic Red Army for the liberation
of their country from the yoke of the White Guards, hirelings of
foreign imperialists, the People's Government of Finland sends its
warmest good wishes to you, Comrade Stalin, the great (*veliki*) friend
of the Finnish People."

A few days later Stalin replied: "To the Head of the People's
Government of Finland, Otto Kuusinen, Terijoki. Thank you for
your good wishes... I wish the Finnish people and the People's
Government of Finland a speedy and complete victory over the
oppressors of the Finnish people, the Mannerheim-Tanner gang."

Shortly before the Finnish war had begun, there was, at Munich,
an abortive attempt on Hitler's life. He had already left when the
explosion occurred, in which six persons were killed and sixty
wounded. Promptly Ambassador Shkvartsev called on Ribbentrop
to present him the condolences of the Soviet Government "in connection with the terrorist act in Munich, which had caused serious
loss of life". *Pravda* also reported that, according to Himmler, the
plot had originated abroad and that a reward of 800,000 marks
would be paid in any currency to anyone whose information would
lead to the discovery of the criminals. Hitler's Munich speech,
delivered before the explosion, was reported in *Pravda* under a
three-column heading.

During the Finnish war Soviet relations with Germany continued—
at least on the face of it—to be friendly, while the hostility to Britain
and France became much more strident than before. True, there
were, from time to time, some seemingly inexplicable deviations
from this obvious line; thus, at the end of November, *Pravda* surprisingly reproduced an article from the *Nineteenth Century*
(London) deeply sympathetic to Poland and describing the ruthless
bombing by the Germans of trains crowded with refugees. It was like
a confirmation of the numerous stories of German brutality in
Poland which Russian soldiers had brought back from there, and

which were widely current in Russia. *Pravda*'s inconsistency is but one of the minor mysteries in that very strange period in Russian history. Yet, on the surface, Soviet-German relations could not be better.

As the Finnish war progressed, the official Russian attitude to Britain and France became more and more hostile. Typical was *Pravda*'s New Year editorial on January 1, 1940: "Our country is the land of the greatest historical optimism. On the other hand, the capitalist world, as it enters 1940, is torn by agonising contradictions. Covering up their imperialist aims with hypocritical slogans about their 'battle for democracy', the British and French financial oligarchies, helped on by their faithful flunkeys from the Second International—Blum, Jouhaux, Citrine and Bevin—are kindling the flames of the new war."

The class war in Britain, France and the USA, said *Pravda*, was stronger than ever between the "overwhelming majority of the people" who did not want war, and a handful of capitalists who cared nothing for the people's blood and were only interested in their own profits: "All the honest sons and daughters of the British, French and American peoples have branded with contempt that gang—ranging from the Pope to the London stockbrokers—who have started all this screaming and yelling over the noble help given by the Red Army to the Finnish people struggling against their oppressors."

A few days later there were angry articles on "the shameful comedy of the 'expulsion' of the Soviet Union" from the League of Nations—a comedy staged by Britain and France. These were, moreover, now sending arms to Finland.

In themselves, the Anglo-French arms shipments to Finland did not matter very much; but it is quite obvious that the indignation the Russian attack on Finland had caused in Britain, France, America and Scandinavia, gave the Russian leaders food for anxious thought. They dreaded the possibility that Finland might become common ground for a reconciliation between Germany and the Western Powers, a reconciliation from which Russia would be made to suffer. This largely explains the eagerness with which they hastened to wind up the Finnish war and to make peace with the "Mannerheim gang" without waiting for the "Terijoki government" to make its triumphal entry into Helsinki. The idea of turning a "hostile" Finland into a "friendly" Finland with the help of this absurd device had miscarried completely and had merely silenced those Finnish elements—including men like Paasikivi—which had criticised their government for rejecting the original Russian proposals.

What then had been the progress of the actual military operations?

Neither at the time, nor later, did the Russians do much flag-waving over the Finnish war. It is now openly admitted that the first month of the war was an almost undiluted disaster. The most the Russians achieved in December was to advance, in the course of "very heavy fighting", between fifteen and forty miles; but, having reached the Mannerheim Line proper, with its network of powerful fortifications, they came to a halt. On the Karelian Isthmus, as well as in Central Finland, the Russians were handicapped by snow, in some places five or six feet deep. The few available roads were heavily defended by the Finns, and the Russians had practically no trained ski troops, in which the Finnish army abounded. To move heavy equipment on such terrain was as good as impossible. The Finns were heavily armed with automatic rifles and tommyguns, while the Russians were not. Temperatures—around minus 30°C. —were abnormally low. A large proportion of the Soviet troops "were simply unprepared for this kind of warfare; they had had no experience of moving on skis through lake and forest country, and had no experience at all of breaking through permanent lines of fortifications, or of storming pillboxes and other reinforced concrete structures".*

By the beginning of January, the offensive was stopped. Marshal Timoshenko was appointed Commander-in-Chief, and, for a whole month, the Russians planned and prepared for a break-through of the Mannerheim Line. Large reinforcements, especially of engineers, were to be mustered for the purpose. Massive support of tanks, planes and guns was provided for in an all-out offensive effort to overcome the Finnish fortifications. Moreover, three infantry divisions, reinforced by cavalry and tanks, were assigned the task of

* IVOVSS, vol. I, p. 266.

out-flanking the Mannerheim Line in the Viborg area across the ice of the Gulf of Finland.

The storming of the Mannerheim Line, preceded by a tremendous artillery barrage "from thousands of guns", did not begin till February 11. But the advance was still slow; although the Russians destroyed and captured many of the pillboxes, the Finns in the surviving pillboxes continued their desperate resistance, and casualties were very high on both sides. The steel and concrete fortifications of the Mannerheim Line, many of them connected by underground passages, with reinforced concrete walls three feet thick, were, indeed, in many cases almost invulnerable even to the heaviest pounding. It took nearly a week after a breakthrough along an eight-mile front before the Russians began to make any decisive progress. By February 21 most of the western part of the Mannerheim Line had been overrun, but the Russian losses had been so heavy that their forces had to be regrouped and further heavy reinforcements had to be brought up before the offensive could be resumed, what remained of the Mannerheim Line conquered and Viborg captured.

Full-scale operations were only re-started on February 28. As the Russians approached Viborg, they met with another major obstacle —the flooding of large areas by the Finns—but they finally reached the Viborg–Helsinki highway. By now the resistance of the Finnish Army had, in the main, been broken. On March 4, Mannerheim informed the Finnish Government that the Army could no longer resist successfully. The Soviet-Finnish Peace Treaty was signed in Moscow on March 12.*

* After the Finnish attempts to obtain German or American mediation had failed, tentative negotiations were started in January in Stockholm between the well-known Finnish playwright, Hella Wuolijoki—with Foreign Minister Tanner's consent—and Mme Kollontai, the Soviet Ambassador. A variety of negotiations continued throughout January and February, though the Finns still hoped to obtain substantial military aid—including troops—from Sweden, and also hoped that the Swedes would allow French and British troops to go to Finland via Sweden. On this point the Swedes, afraid of becoming involved in a major war, would not yield and, indeed, advised the Finns to make peace with the Russians on the best possible terms.

Almost throughout the "Winter War" there had been something
of a news blackout in Russia, even though people in Moscow, and
especially Leningrad, had a fair idea of what was going on. But very
little was said at first about the great offensive against the Mannerheim Line in February, and still less about the abortive advance into
Central Finland; and it was not till the first week of March, after
three months of inconclusive and mostly frustrating news, that the
Soviet press at last began to speak of "victories on the Mannerheim
Line". And then, suddenly, on March 12, it was announced that the
Peace Treaty between the USSR and Finland had been signed. The
signing was done by Molotov, Zhdanov and Vassilevsky on the
Russian side, and Ryti, Paasikivi and General Walden on the Finnish
side. The terms were harder than those originally proposed by the
Russians—let alone those originally "agreed to" by Kuusinen. Now
the whole Karelian Isthmus, including Viborg and numerous islands,
a part of Rybachi Peninsula on the Arctic, west of Murmansk, and
the country north of Lake Ladoga were annexed by the Soviet
Union; moreover, she received a thirty-year lease on Hangö for a
naval base. Nothing was said any more about the "Terijoki Government"; it might never have existed. All that it had achieved in effect
was to unify the Finnish people (many of whom had thought the
original Russian proposals quite reasonable), and to cause much
unnecessary resentment in Finland. Now this resentment was further
increased by the loss of Viborg.

Since, by March 5, the Red Army could easily have occupied
Helsinki and other parts of Finland, the Finns may be said to have
been let off lightly; nevertheless, without the loss of Viborg, it is just
conceivable that the Finns might have been less eager to attack the
Soviet Union in 1941. In itself, Viborg was of very little strategic
value, but its loss was keenly felt in Finland, where the many
thousands of "Viborg refugees" added greatly to anti-Russian feeling. During the War, many Russians agreed (on the quiet) that the
annexation of Viborg had been a serious mistake.

As distinct from Britain and France, Germany had, in the official
Russian view, remained commendably neutral during the Soviet-

Finnish war. Even so, the thought must have crossed the Russian leaders' minds that Germany might yet take advantage of Finnish grievances and longing for revenge. On the face of it, it is true, the Russians had attained their objective, which was to render Leningrad "invulnerable". This, as it turned out, short-lived advantage was outweighed by the fact that the performance of the Red Army in the Finnish War was far from good. There was a danger that the Germans might draw certain conclusions from this.

That the Soviet General Staff was not satisfied with the Red Army's record in Finland may be seen from the far-reaching measures that began to be taken soon afterwards to reorganise the Army. 1940 was to become, in General Zhukov's words, the "year of the great transformation" in the Red Army.

For all that relations with Germany had remained highly satisfactory on the surface throughout the duration of the Soviet-Finnish War. All the abuse in the Soviet press was reserved for the Western democracies which, it was now claimed, were more anxious than ever to "generalise the war" and to drag the neutrals into it. As early as January 17, *Pravda* began to speak about Anglo-French designs on the neutrality of the Scandinavian countries. Hitler's speeches continued to be politely reported, notably the one on January 30 in which he said that, thanks to the Soviet-German Pact, Germany had a "free rear" in the East: the state which Britain had guaranteed had disappeared from the face of the earth in eighteen days. *Pravda* also duly reported his threats to England and his announcement that "Germany would be victorious".

On February 11, with the Soviet-Finnish war still in full swing, a new Soviet-German economic agreement was signed. This, said *Pravda*, was a very good thing: "Present-day Germany is a highly-developed industrial power requiring many raw materials; and these the Soviet Union can largely supply. We also are a great industrial power; nevertheless, we can do with certain forms of imported industrial equipment... Our trade with Britain and France has dwindled, and the increase in our trade with Germany is only to be welcomed... The new economic agreement had been welcomed by

the *Völkischer Beobachter* and other German papers."* The volume
and exact nature of these exchanges was not stated. Three days later
Pravda reported another Hitler speech again boasting of the quick
victory over Poland and announcing that there was "more to come".
As *Pravda* put it: "'I am determined to pursue this battle to the
finish,' Hitler said with particular vigour."† There was a clear
suggestion here that an attack in the West was now in the offing.

Molotov waited till the end of March before making a statement to
the Supreme Soviet on the termination of the Finnish War and on
the international situation generally. This speech was, at least outwardly, the most violently anti-British and anti-French ever made.
He was no longer regretting the breakdown in the Anglo-French-
Soviet talks during the previous year; on the contrary, he now said
that "the Soviet Union had been determined not to become a tool in
the hands of the Anglo-French imperialists in their anti-German
struggle for world hegemony".

"The Anglo-French imperialists," he said, "wanted to turn the
war in Finland into a war against the Soviet Union. But they failed
in this, and the Soviet Union's relations with Germany continue to
be good." The Anglo-French hostility to the Soviet Union, he went
on, had been most violent in connection with the Finnish question,
and he then indignantly spoke of the police raid on the Soviet trade
delegation in Paris, and of the "virtual expulsion" from France of
the Soviet Ambassador, Jacob Suritz. The Soviet Government had
had to recall him.

After referring to the satisfactory economic relations with Germany, Molotov then complained of British and French interference
with Soviet-German trade: "They seize our ships in the Far East,
because they are alleged to 'help Germany'; yet Rumania sells half
her oil to Germany, and Rumania remains unmolested." He then
protested against the various "fabrications" concerning Russia's
alleged designs on India and other parts of the British Empire. "Our
policy is a policy of neutrality, and I know it isn't to the taste of the

* *Pravda*, February 17, 1940.
† *Pravda*, February 18, 1940.

Anglo-French imperialists, who want to inflict on us a policy of hostility and war against Germany."

Pointedly he remarked that Chamberlain, who had hoped that the Finnish War would develop into something different, was greatly distressed when he heard of the Finnish-Soviet peace settlement. He spoke of the 141 planes and the other equipment Britain had sent to Finland, and of the military help France and Sweden had given her.

He concluded somewhat morosely by saying that the war in Finland had cost the Soviet Union 48,745 dead and 158,000 wounded* —for a small "frontier rectification". Saying that the Finns were minimising their losses, Molotov then "estimated" that they had lost 60,000 dead and 250,000 wounded. These figures gave the Russians but little grounds for boasting, nor were they likely to foster Finnish-Soviet relations. Significantly he was very sparing in his praise of the generals who had conducted the campaign.

Altogether, as I was later told by many Russians, Molotov's report on the Finnish War had left them with an unpleasant and frustrating feeling. The only two things that could be said in favour of the war were that it had achieved its immediate objective (but at a terrible price, and in very unfortunate conditions)—and that it was now over. Here and there, questions were also asked about the "Terijoki Government", but it was soon made clear to the bright young people who asked them that they had better shut up.† *Pravda* briefly announced that, in view of the changed international situation, the Finnish "People's Government" had been dissolved. This was the end of that absurd experiment.

At one time, while the war was still on, *Pravda* had published a long list—covering two whole pages of the paper—of the officers and soldiers decorated for bravery; but there was remarkably little flag-waving over the conclusion of the Finnish War—much less, indeed, than over the "victory" won in Eastern Poland. Here at least much could be made of the, more or less genuine, enthusiasm with which the Ukrainians and Belorussians welcomed the Red Army; there was

* The Finns put the Russian losses much higher.
† Wolfgang Leonhard, op. cit., p. 86.

nothing like that in Karelia, where practically the entire population had been evacuated, or had fled, to Finland. Viborg, the only large city occupied by the Russians, had been abandoned by all its inhabitants. Above all there was the depressing effect of the heavy casualties suffered and of the suspicion that all was not perfect with the Red Army. Then, less than a month after the signing of the Soviet-Finnish Peace Treaty, Germany invaded Denmark and Norway. This gave rise to more anxiety.

During that short interval nothing of any consequence happened in Russia, with the exception of the meeting of the Supreme Soviet at the beginning of April which approved the 1940 budget. Already the effects of the Finnish War could be felt here. As *Pravda* wrote in its editorial of April 5: "The Supreme Soviet has approved the budget of the USSR for 1940. With great enthusiasm it voted a large increase in our defence expenditure. Our country must have an even more powerful Red Army and Navy if it is to discourage the warmongers. The fifty-seven milliard roubles to be spent on strengthening our defence will help the Red Army and Navy to solve any problems connected with the security of our State."

The tone of this editorial was remarkably free of the usual bluster, and was perhaps intended to convey that the Red Army would, in the future, give a better account of itself than it had done in the Finnish War.

Before the actual German attack on Denmark and Norway, the Soviet press tended to echo the German charges of "Anglo-French violations of Norwegian sovereignty". This was, indeed, the phrase used by *Pravda* on April 9. By the time the paper had been printed, the Germans were already busy occupying the two Scandinavian countries. During the days that followed, the Russian press continued, on the face of it, to follow the German line. Thus, on April 10, together with the news that German troops had occupied both Copenhagen and Oslo, the Soviet papers published under a three-column heading the "Memorandum of the German Government" which, they said, had been read over the radio by Goebbels. Two days later, TASS, in a message from Oslo, referred to Quisling as "the new head of the Norwegian Government". However, it did not deny the continued existence of the "other" Norwegian Government.

After that the German and British communiqués, as well as TASS reports from London were published with a certain air of neutrality and impartiality. In a variety of ways the fact was emphasised that the Soviet Union kept strictly neutral in the Scandinavian war. For example, on April 12, there was an angry official TASS denial of a *New York Times* story that most of the German troops that had occupied Narvik had travelled there by way of Leningrad and Murmansk.

Yet there seems little doubt that, in the eyes of the Soviet leaders, the war was spreading much too near home. Although at the time nothing was published about it in the Soviet press, much is made in the Soviet *History of the War* of the way in which direct Soviet diplomatic intervention saved Sweden from being occupied by the Germans: "After the Nazi invasion of Denmark and Norway, the Soviet Government informed Count Schulenburg, the German Ambassador in Moscow, that it was definitely interested in the preservation of Swedish neutrality."*

According to Soviet diplomatic documents quoted by the *History*, "both the Swedish Premier and the Swedish Foreign Minister, in addressing (Mme) A. M. Kollontai, the Soviet Ambassador, warmly thanked the Soviet Union for having restrained Germany and for having saved Swedish neutrality".

Meanwhile, the Soviet press went on with its rather routine and seemingly "neutral" coverage of the war in Norway, with occasional surveys stressing the general ineptitude of the Anglo-French operations. The last of these surveys appeared in *Pravda* on May 9, and concluded that the Germans had as good as won. On the following day the Germans struck out in the west.

Inside Russia the most important developments during the Norwegian war concerned the reorganisation of the Red Army. On May 8, 1940 an *ukase* of the Presidium of the Supreme Soviet

* IVOVSS, vol. I, p. 395.

announced the creation of new military titles*—Major-General, Lieutenant-General and Army General, in addition to the already existing title of Marshal of the Soviet Union. At that time four men held the rank of Marshal of the Soviet Union: Voroshilov, Timoshenko, Shaposhnikov and Kulik.† At the same time Voroshilov was appointed Deputy Premier and Chairman of the Defence Committee of the USSR; his previous post of Commissar of Defence went to Timoshenko. Corresponding titles were also created in the Soviet Navy. During the months that followed, the press was filled with army nominations and promotions, complete with pictures of all the new generals, which filled four pages of *Pravda* for days and days. Coinciding with the German invasion of France, this unprecedented publicity given to hundreds of Red Army generals was no doubt calculated to have a reassuring effect on the public.

* These replaced the clumsier and less "distinguished" titles, such as "Army Commander of the 1st Rank", the equivalent of "Army General".

† Shaposhnikov, a highly professional soldier whom the Soviets had inherited from the Tsarist Army, was to be Chief-of-Staff during a large part of the 1941–5 war; he retired, in the end, owing to ill-health. Kulik, on the other hand, was a political upstart who was to fade out soon after the beginning of the war. He was to be blamed for much of the unpreparedness of the Red Army in 1941, and, in particular, for having failed to equip it with up-to-date machine-guns and other automatic weapons, which at first placed the Russian infantryman at a terrible disadvantage against the German soldier.

Chapter V

RUSSIA AND THE FALL OF FRANCE-
BALTIC STATES AND BESSARABIA

During my war years in Russia I put these two questions to a great number of people: "What did you feel about the Soviet-German Pact?" and "At what point, while the Pact was in force, did you begin to have serious doubts about it?"

The answer to the first question was, almost invariably, something like this: "Everybody thought it nasty and unpleasant to have to pretend to make friends with Hitler; but, as things were in 1939, we had to gain time at any price, and there was no choice. We did not think that Stalin himself particularly liked the idea, but we had tremendous faith in his judgment; if he decided on the non-aggression pact with Hitler, he must have thought that there was no other way." The answer to the second question was invariably along these lines: "We started getting really nervous when we saw that Hitler had managed to smash the French Army within a month, or less. We had had considerable confidence in the French Army and had also heard a lot about the Maginot Line and—let's face it—we thought the war in France would last a long time, and that the Germans would be greatly weakened as a result. Selfish?—well, yes, we were, but who isn't? That we were frightened may be seen from the frantic haste with which, while the Germans were busy finishing off the French, we grabbed the Baltic States, Bessarabia and Northern Bukovina. And then came those draconian labour laws, the reorganisation of the Red Army, and all the rest of it. We never

83

expected for a moment that the Germans would attack and above
all invade us the way they did, but we felt that we had to prepare
for a very hard fight if Hitler were mad enough to turn our way."

And then there was a supplementary question which I liked to
ask. It was this: "Between the fall of France and the invasion of the
Soviet Union there was the war between Germany and England—
and what did you think of that?" Here the answers became much
more confused but, roughly, they boiled down to this: "We developed
a sudden contempt—yes, contempt—for the French. On England
our feelings were very divided. We had been conditioned to be anti-
British, what with Chamberlain, Finland and the rest. But gradually,
very gradually we began to admire the English—for standing up to
Hitler. There was a good deal in our papers about the bombing of
London, Coventry, and so on. We also began to feel sorry for the
English people, and—began to feel that, sooner or later, we might
have to face something similar. Our intellectuals felt particularly
strongly about it. The idea of a 'just war', a 'people's war' began
to cross some people's minds. But then, in May, there was Hess, and
we got fearfully suspicious of the English again."

Ever since September 1939, the official Soviet line had been that the
war between Britain, France and Germany was an "imperialist"
war; but, since the partition of Poland, the powers guilty of pursuing
this "imperialist" war were Britain and France, but not Germany.
They, and not Germany, were now the "aggressors". During the
Finnish War, Germany had been "neutral", while Britain and
France had demonstrated their deep hostility to the Soviet Union by
helping Finland with arms and volunteers, and by expelling Russia
from the League of Nations. The German occupation of Denmark
and Norway was at first widely attributed in the Soviet press to
Anglo-French "provocation", though soon afterwards the Russian
pleading with Germany not to occupy Sweden showed that they were
anxious to limit the damage in Scandinavia.

Soviet relations with Britain and France remained badly strained,
and the Soviet press angrily reported the persecution of the French
Communists—whom Moscow itself had put in a hopelessly awkward

and difficult position with its "imperialist war" slogans. The French working-class—and the Communists in particular—who in any other circumstances would have fought Nazi Germany whole-heartedly, were precisely the people who were being told by the Russians—and, more particularly by Dimitrov and the Comintern—that the war against Nazi Germany was an "imperialist" war and so, in consequence, not a "just" war. A different morale of the French Communists might not have made any great difference at the time of the German break-through into France in May 1940, and the French Army would probably have capitulated in any case; but, undoubtedly, Moscow helped in some degree to weaken French resistance, even though it was obviously in the Russians' interest to strengthen it and to keep Hitler pinned down in France as long as possible.

It was all very well for communist propaganda later to adopt the fashionable Ehrenburg line that France had been "betrayed" by her bourgeoisie, but the morale of the whole nation was low in May–June 1940, including that of the French working-class. The Soviet-German Pact and the subsequent Russian and Comintern propaganda about the "imperialist war" had placed the French Communists—whether leaders or rank-and-file—in a truly tragic dilemma. Many of them strongly suspected that they—and France—were being sacrificed by Moscow, to whom the survival of the Soviet Union, with the help of the Soviet-German Pact, was *the* Number One priority.*

Whether or not, as is now claimed by communists, certain French Communist leaders took a firm anti-German *lutte à outrance* line in the first week in June, the Soviet leaders were very careful at the time to avoid anything that might have caused Hitler the least offence. Nevertheless, there was a significant change in the tone of the Soviet press as the French tragedy developed. At first it was distinctly malevolent towards France and Britain. Thus in summing

* This tragic dilemma among the French Communists in the face of the Soviet-German Pact and the German invasion of France is examined in detail in the author's *France, 1940–1955* (London, 1956), pp. 179–202. This chapter was, significantly, omitted from the Russian translation published in Moscow in 1959.

up the results of the first five days of the military operations in the
West, *Pravda* wrote in its editorial of May 16:

> During these first five days, the German armies have achieved con-
> siderable successes. They have occupied the greater part of Holland,
> including Rotterdam. The Netherlands Government has already run
> off (*sbezhalo*) to England. It had been a long-standing ambition of the
> Anglo-French bloc to drag Holland and Belgium into its war against
> Germany... After the Germans had forestalled Britain and France in
> Scandinavia, these two countries moved heaven and earth to get
> Holland and Belgium into the war... So far, the Anglo-French bloc
> can boast of only one success: it has thrown two more small countries
> into the imperialist war; two more nations have now been condemned
> to suffering and hunger.
> No one will be deceived by the Anglo-French lamentations over the
> violations of international law. As soon as the war had spread to
> Norway, the British grabbed the Faröe and Lofoten islands—heaven
> only knows in virtue of what international law. We now see how great
> is the responsibility of the Anglo-French imperialists who, by rejecting
> Germany's peace offers, set off the Second Imperialist War in Europe.

There was no mention of the ruthless bombing of Rotterdam, and,
on the following day, in a review of the military situation describing
German successes, there were again the same phrases about the
Netherlands Government having "run off" to London, "leaving the
army and the country to their fate". On the same day *Pravda* published a particularly nauseating anti-British article by David
Zaslavsky.

But, during the following week, with the Germans crashing on
towards Dunkirk, the tone suddenly changed. The reports became
much more factual. Every important Churchill speech was quoted
at some length, as was also Reynaud's famous *patrie en danger*
speech to the Senate on May 21. Significantly, much space was given
to the question of American help to Britain and France. On June 5,
Churchill's post-Dunkirk speech—"we shall fight on the beaches...
we shall never surrender"—was published under a three-column
heading in *Pravda*. On the same day the paper announced that
Molotov had "raised no objection" to the British Government's
appointment of Sir Stafford Cripps as Ambassador to Moscow.

When the resistance of the French army finally collapsed by the middle of June, and Pétain asked the Germans for an armistice, the Russians seemed suddenly to become obsessed with one great fear: which was that Britain might make peace with Germany—for what would happen then? Most significant in this respect was the military survey in *Pravda* of June 20 by Major-General P. A. Ivanov: "Not only has the French Army been smashed, but France has now lost all her vital industrial centres. This is France's *débâcle*... Another of Britain's allies has been put out of action, and now Britain is left face to face with Germany and Italy. *Yet both sides have mighty economic resources, and therefore they may continue the war for a very long time yet, and it is much too early to try to foretell the outcome of this war.** It is highly symptomatic that the activity of the British air-force should have been switched from the battle in France to the bombing of economic targets in Germany." And there followed long and detailed accounts of British air-raids on Germany.† There was not the slightest suggestion any more that a peace settlement between Germany and Britain would be a good thing!

Stupefied by Hitler's overwhelming victory over France, Russia now dropped all further pretence of respect for the sovereignty of the Baltic States. Lithuania, Estonia and Latvia were occupied, draconian new labour legislation imposed on Soviet industry, Bessarabia and Northern Bukovina occupied—all this was being done within the last fortnight in June. Already on June 17, *Pravda* reported that there was "great rejoicing at Kaunas", as the Red Army entered Lithuania, adding significantly that "its Fascist dictator, Smetona" had "*fled to Germany*". During the following days, the Soviet press reported similar "jubilant demonstrations" from Tallinn and Riga. The governments of the Baltic States were accused of plotting against the Soviet Union and Latvia and Estonia, in particular, of having "grossly violated their mutual assistance pacts with the Soviet Union". This now demanded that "they set up governments which would respect their treaties with the Soviet Union and that they give free access to their territory to Soviet troops, which would guarantee that these treaties would be respected".‡

---

* Emphasis added.   † TASS, London, quoting Reuter.
‡ *Pravda*, June 17, 1940.

It was quick work. On June 18 it was already announced that Mr Paletskis "who had been put in a concentration camp by the [pro-Nazi] Smetona gang in 1939", had become Lithuanian Premier. Similar miraculous changes were to take place in the next few days in Latvia and Estonia. On the very day *Pravda* published the DNB report from Berlin of "Hitler's meeting with the French delegation in the Forest of Compiègne" it also described the "jubilant reception given to the Red Army by the Estonian people at Tallinn". Some time later Molotov was to explain the diplomatic background of the Russian invasion of the Baltic States as best he could; but every Russian clearly thought he understood why the Red Army had marched in—while Hitler wasn't looking.

The direct connection between the invasion of the Baltic States on the one hand, and the fall of France on the other, was so embarrassingly obvious that, on June 23, the Soviet Government found it necessary to publish this extraordinary statement—denying that it was "dissatisfied with the German successes in the West":

> In connection with the entry of Soviet troops into the Baltic States there are persistent rumours in the Western press about 100 or 150 Soviet divisions being concentrated on the German frontier. This is supposed to arise from the dissatisfaction felt in the Soviet Union over Germany's military successes in the West, and to point to a deterioration of Soviet-German relations.
>
> TASS is authorised to state that this is totally untrue. There are only eighteen to twenty Soviet divisions in the Baltic countries, and they are not concentrated on the German border, but are scattered throughout the Baltic countries.
>
> No "pressure" on Germany is intended and the military measures taken have only one aim: which is to safeguard the mutual aid between the Soviet Union and these countries.

As for Soviet-German relations, the TASS statement went out of its way to say that the occupation of the Baltic States—or Germany's victory in the West, for that matter—could not in any way affect them, though it was careful not to say whether, or not, the Baltic States had been occupied with German consent. "There is a deliberate attempt" (the TASS statement went on) "to cast a shadow on Soviet-German relations. In all this there is nothing but wishful thinking on the part of certain British, American, Swedish and Japanese gentlemen... They seem to be incapable of grasping the obvious fact that the good-neighbourly relations between the Soviet Union and Germany cannot be disturbed by rumours and cheap propaganda, since these relations are based not on temporary motives of an *ad hoc* (*konyunkturnyi*) character, but on the fundamental State interests of the USSR and Germany."

So far so good; but six days later it was announced that "the Soviet-Rumanian conflict over Bessarabia and Northern Bukovina" had been "satisfactorily settled". Whereupon the Soviet press proceeded to report the "jubilant" reception given by the population of these two areas to the Red Army.*

*

* According to the Russian post-war *History*, the Russians had become increasingly worried, especially since May 1940, by Rumania's "growing subservience" to Germany; both Tatarescu and King Carol, who had, for a time, tried to sit on the fence, were now beginning to lean heavily over to the German side. It was on June 26 that the Soviet Government presented what was in effect an ultimatum to the Rumanian Government demanding an "immediate solution" of the question concerning the return of Bessarabia to the Soviet Union. It also demanded the transfer to the Soviet Union of Northern Bukovina which was ethnically Ukrainian. An additional argument concerning Northern Bukovina was that "in November 1918 the People's Assembly (*veche*) of Bukovina had, reflecting the will of the people, decided in favour of joining Soviet Ukraine".

Davidescu, the Rumanian Ambassador in Moscow, declared, on the following day, his government's "readiness" to enter into negotiations with the Soviet Government; but the latter demanded a "clear and precise" answer. This came almost immediately, and on June 28 the Red Army began to move into the two areas.

On June 23 Germany had been informed of the Soviet demands on Rumania, "but had to declare that she was not interested in the question of Bessarabia". As the *History* says: "While the Battle of France was going on, it was particularly undesirable for the Germans to complicate their relations with the Soviet Union. Moreover, the Germans feared that, in the event of a Soviet-Rumanian conflict, Rumania might lose her oilwells, while Germany was extremely anxious that these should remain intact".

For hard-boiled "realism" the Russian conduct in this case was

During the few days separating the occupation of the Baltic States
and of Bessarabia-Bukovina, a number of other significant things
happened. On June 25 it was announced that diplomatic relations
had been established between the Soviet Union and Yugoslavia.
Milan Gabrilovic was appointed Ambassador to Moscow and
V. A. Plotnikov Ambassador to Belgrade.

But that was not all. On the following day came a real bombshell
of another kind—the *ukase* of the Presidium of the Supreme Soviet
placing Soviet industry virtually on a war footing. The eight-hour
working-day was now introduced, and the full six-day working-
week; more important still, workers and employees were now
tied to their particular enterprise or office, and there could no
longer be any migration of labour. The *ukase* also provided for
the most rigid disciplinary measures against absenteeism and similar
offences.

Needless to say, countless "spontaneous" meetings of workers
were reported from all over the country, all approving the *ukase*, the
purpose of which, according to all the speakers at these meetings,
was to increase the military might of the Soviet Union. The fall of
France was having its immediate repercussions inside Russia.

Speaking at a plenary session of the Soviet Trade Union
Federation on June 25, N. M. Shvernik said: "We are living in a
capitalist encirclement and the war is raging over great areas. It is
our good fortune not to be in the war, but we must be prepared for
all emergencies. We must do all we can to be many times stronger
than we are; we must in every way and at any moment be ready to
face every possible ordeal."

After the fall of France, it was only too clear to everybody that
there was only one country from which these "ordeals" could now
come. It was certainly not England, and not even Japan. And
Shvernik went on: "Comrades, as Comrade Stalin has taught us, the
most dangerous thing in the world is to be caught unawares. To be
caught unawares means falling a victim to the unexpected. Today

hard to beat. The *History* adds that, "with the best will in the world",
Britain was unable at the time to "interfere in Soviet-Rumanian
relations", since she was wholly tied up by the war in the West.
(IVOVSS, I, p. 281). Rumania joined the Axis in November 1940.

the international situation demands from us that we strengthen the defence of our country and the might of our armed forces day after day."

During that historic week, the coverage of events in the West showed a slight, if only very slight, pro-British bias. Churchill's speeches saying Britain would fight till final victory, were duly reported, and, as early as June 21, there was a first mention in the Russian press of de Gaulle and his refusal to surrender to the Germans. On the other hand, Pétain was reported as calling for the termination of the war between Germany and Britain; and the Soviet press also published the Franco-German armistice terms, and the report of the German High Command on the French campaign: 27,000 Germans killed, 18,000 missing, 111,000 wounded. Prisoners taken: 1,900,000, including five army commanders.

The fact that German losses were only about half of what had been the Russian losses in the "little" Finnish War cannot have passed unobserved. The secret hope that Germany would have found herself greatly weakened by her war in the West had been dashed to the ground. Now, for the first time, the Russians heard names bandied about which, before long, were to acquire so ominous a ring: Rundstedt, Kleist, Guderian.

For all that, the pretence that relations with Germany were good had still to be kept up. Alongside reports of the "election campaigns" in the Baltic States, the Soviet Press published extracts from a German White Paper disclosing "Anglo-French intrigues against the Soviet Union" at the time of the Finnish War, their plans to bomb Baku, and similar matters. And then came Molotov's Supreme Soviet speech of August 1, 1940 in which he commented in his own peculiar way on all the spectacular and tragic events of the last few months. In a devious and subtly ambiguous manner he intimated that he was not displeased and perhaps relieved—as he most certainly was—that Britain had not given up the struggle.

Germany has achieved a great success against the [Western] Allies. But she has not solved her fundamental problem, which is to stop the war on conditions desirable to her. On July 19 the *Reichskanzler* offered peace negotiations to Great Britain, but the British Government rejected his offer, interpreting it as a demand for capitulation. It replied that it would go on till final victory. The British Government has even broken off diplomatic relations with France. All this means that Great Britain does not wish to give up her colonies and wants to go on fighting for world domination, even though this will be much more difficult for her since the defeat of France and since Italy's entry into the war.

Having delivered this side-kick at "British imperialism", Molotov then proceeded: "The end of the war is not in sight. We are likely to be faced with a new stage of the war—a struggle between Germany and Italy, on the one hand, and Britain, *supported by the United States*, on the other." The reference to the United States was clearly intended to suggest that Germany's chances of winning the war were not necessarily good.

It is highly significant that even when things looked blackest for Britain, the Russians took a reasonably optimistic view of her chances; thus, the chief ideological journal of the Communist Party, *Bolshevik* of July 15, 1940 concluded its survey by saying that Britain was "far from finished", while a similar line had already been taken by the well-known economist, Prof. E. Varga in *Mirovoye Khoziaistvo i Mirovaya Politika* (World Economy and World Politics) early in June, when the collapse of France was already imminent.

As for the future of Soviet-German relations, Molotov merely repeated, almost word for word, the TASS communiqué of June 23: "There has recently been in the British and pro-British press much speculation on the possibility of discord between the Soviet Union and Germany. Attempts have been made to frighten us with the growing might of Germany. But our relations are not based on temporary *ad hoc* considerations, but on the fundamental state interests of the two countries."

What he said about Britain was at any rate distinctly less ill-tempered than anything said or published for a long time: "There have been no substantial changes in our relations with England. After all the hostile acts she has committed against us, it was hard to expect any favourable developments in Anglo-Soviet relations, *even though the appointment of Cripps as British Ambassador to Moscow may point to a desire on the part of Great Britain to improve her relations with the Soviet Union.*"*

The incorporation in the Soviet Union of the Baltic States, Bessarabia and North Bukovina was presented by Molotov in a manner that was to be expected. It was, no doubt, pleasing to see the Soviet Union recover some of the territories which had once belonged to the old Tsarist Empire, and even to annex an area— Northern Bukovina, including the large city of Czernowitz—which had never been part of it. Northern Bukovina, Molotov said, was chiefly inhabited by Ukrainians and Moldavians—and these, as well as the inhabitants of Bessarabia, had now become Soviet citizens "with great joy". There was now every reason to believe that relations with Rumania would become normal again. As for the Baltic States, Molotov explained their incorporation in the Soviet Union in the following terms:

> The mutual assistance pacts we had with Lithuania, Latvia and Estonia did not produce the desired results. The bourgeois cliques in these countries were hostile to the Soviet Union, and the anti-Soviet "Baltic Entente" between Latvia and Estonia was latterly extended to Lithuania.
> Therefore, especially in view of the international situation, we demanded a change in the government personnel of Lithuania, Latvia and Estonia, and the introduction into these countries of additional Red Army formations. In July free parliamentary elections took place in all three countries, and we can now note with satisfaction that the peoples of Lithuania, Latvia and Estonia in a friendly *élan* elected representatives who have since unanimously declared themselves in favour of the introduction of the Soviet system in all three countries, and for their incorporation in the USSR. Ninety-five per cent of all these people had previously formed part of the USSR (*sic*).

Molotov reckoned that, since September 1939, the population of the Soviet Union had increased by about twenty-three million people, all of which meant "an important increase in our might and territory".

Relations with Turkey and Iran, he went on, were now "fairly

* Emphasis added.

normal", despite the revelations in the German White Paper on the sinister role the two countries had played in the Anglo-French plotting against the Soviet Union. Relations with Japan—since the licking she had received at Halkin Gol—were now also "fairly normal", and a Manchukuo-Mongolian commission would shortly deal with the frontier problem between the two countries. And then: "I shall not dwell on our relations with the USA if only because there is nothing good to report. [*Laughter.*] We understand that some Americans don't like our successes in the Baltic countries." He also referred to the gold belonging to the Baltic States which the USA had "grabbed", even though the Soviet Union had bought this gold from them.

He ended with the suggestion that the war would continue for a long time; and that "the entire Soviet people" must remain in a state of "mobilised preparedness" in view of the danger of a military attack on them. "We must not be caught unawares by any 'accident' or any of the tricks of our foreign enemies."

Paletskis, Kirchenstein and Lauristin respectively representing Lithuania, Latvia and Estonia, spoke at this Supreme Soviet meeting, and on August 2 new laws were adopted on the "Formation of the Moldavian SSR", on the "Inclusion of Northern Bukovina and the Khotinsk, Akkerman and Ismail districts of Bessarabia in the Ukrainian SSR", and on the "Admission of the Lithuanian, Latvian and Estonian SSR's into the USSR". These laws were passed at the request of the parliaments of the three countries, and in virtue of Arts. 34 and 35 of the Soviet Constitution. The Presidium of the Supreme Soviet was instructed to fix the date for elections in the three countries. On August 10 *Pravda* published a "Poem on Stalin" by Salome Neris, a Lithuanian poetess.

Meantime, in the three Baltic States a purge was being carried out amongst "Fascist" and other unreliable elements, with Vyshinsky, Dekanozov and Zhdanov supervising these operations; estimates vary as to the number of persons deported from the Baltic Republics between July 1940 and the outbreak of the Soviet-German war, but it is not improbable that they ran into tens of thousands.

Although the Baltic States, like the rest of Europe, had been affected by the war in the West, consumer goods were still plentiful in cities like Tallinn and Riga, and even long afterwards, all the elaborate and ingenious pretexts Russians used to think up in 1940 for going on more or less official "missions" to these newly-recovered territories in order to replenish their wardrobes and buy other nice things continued to be a standing joke.

The elections in the three Baltic Soviet Republics followed the usual Soviet pattern, but Russians who visited these countries in the autumn of 1940 had no great illusions about their peoples' unanimous love for the Soviet Union. There were strong pro-Soviet currents among the Latvian working class, but that was about all. When the Germans overran the Baltic States in June–July 1941, they met with very little opposition from the population; certain elements continued to be violently anti-Soviet, as is admitted in much of the Russian post-war writing on that stage of the war. The Estonians, although most of them disliked the Germans, had strong affinities with Finland, and Finland was at war with Russia. . .

Chapter VI

RUSSIA AND THE BATTLE OF BRITAIN: A PSYCHOLOGICAL TURNING-POINT?

In post-war Soviet histories of the war, there is a marked tendency to minimise the importance of Britain's resistance to Germany between the fall of France and the summer of 1941; one Soviet author went so far as to say that the Battle of Britain was something of a myth; there had really been no such thing. There had been important air battles over Britain, but it had never come to a real clash between the "bulk" of the German and British forces. One explanation currently offered in recent histories is that Hitler's fear of the Red Army stopped him from making an all-out attempt to invade England.

Although this assertion may have some substance, one might as well recall that, on August 23, 1940, i.e. just as the Battle of Britain was about to start in real earnest, *Pravda* as good as egged Hitler on to attack England. In its editorial that day, celebrating the first anniversary of the Soviet-German Pact, it wrote:

> The signing of the Pact put an end to the enmity between Germany and the USSR, an enmity which had been artificially worked up by the warmongers... After the disintegration of the Polish State, Germany proposed to Britain and France a termination of the war— a proposal which was supported by the Soviet Government. But they would not listen, and the war continued, bringing hardships and sufferings to all the nations whom the organisers of the war had dragged into the bloodbath... We are neutral, and this Pact has made things

easier for us; it has also been of great advantage to Germany, *since she can be completely confident of peace on her Eastern borders.**

After referring to the Economic Agreement of February 11, 1940, the article concluded that Soviet-German relations had "honourably stood the test of time", which was all the more valuable with a great war raging elsewhere.

The most notable news items in the Soviet press during the last week of August and the beginning of September were a brief announcement on August 24 of Trotsky's death;† another Timoshenko speech on the reorganisation of the Red Army; a TASS denial of a Japanese report that Stalin had, at the end of August, discussed with Ambassador Schulenburg an agreement between the USSR, Germany, Italy and Japan on the abolition of the Anti-Comintern Pact: "TASS is authorised to state that this is a pure invention. During the last six or seven months Comrade Stalin has had no meeting with Schulenburg." On September 5, there was a report on the destroyers that the United States had given to Britain.

From September 9 on, following the first great German air-raid on London on the night of September 7, more and more space was devoted to the Battle of Britain—though it was never called that. There was at first scarcely any first-hand reporting of news from "our own correspondent", but the coverage, consisting chiefly of official German and British communiqués, extracts from DNB and Reuter reports, and quotations from the British and American press, etc., ran into two or three columns every day, and was reasonably well-balanced. Thus, on September 16 TASS reported from London: "According to Reuter, it was officially stated that the Germans lost today 185 planes, and the British 25." On October 1, there was a similar report from London saying that, during September, the Germans had lost 1,102 planes and at least 2,755 airmen, against a

* Emphasis added.
† This read as follows: "London, August 22 (TASS). London radio reports that Trotsky has died in hospital in Mexico City of a fractured skull, the result of an attempt on his life by one of the persons in his immediate entourage."

loss of 319 British planes. "168 British airmen baled out over British territory."

Despite the dryness of this reporting, the news from England undoubtedly stirred the imagination of the Russian public. Several Russians later told me that the most common reaction at the time had been: "Well, at last these German bastards are getting it in the neck from somebody." There was something else that made an even greater psychological impact. London was the first great city the bombing of which was being reported in the Soviet press in some detail. There had been practically nothing about the bombing of Polish cities, and the devastating German air-raid on Rotterdam had scarcely been mentioned at all. But now the papers were full of stories about "gigantic fires", casualties, evacuees, shelter difficulties, and the like, and the Russian reader began to see it all in terms of a human drama. Significantly, after reporting for several days that most of the German bombing was done in the East End, in the London docks, "in the poorer areas of the city", it was also reported some days later that "bombs had been dropped on Buckingham Palace".

And then about a month after the beginning of the bombing of London, there was the first major first-hand report in the Soviet press from the TASS correspondent in London. In *Pravda* on October 5, there appeared an account of "A Visit by the TASS Correspondent to one of the Field Batteries of Anti-Aircraft Guns in the London area". "The present system of anti-aircraft defences in England", it said, "is much more impressive than anything the Luftwaffe has yet encountered." After describing the battery's night operations, the TASS correspondent* went on:

> In the morning I was able to get more closely acquainted with the twenty soldiers manning the battery. Mostly these were young workers of twenty-three or twenty-four—miners, transport workers, printers, mechanics, besides a smaller number of employees and unskilled

---

* The TASS correspondent was Andrew Rothstein. Significant is not the fact that a British subject and a communist should have written so sympathetically of the British people, but that the Soviet press should have published every word of his story. Such things do not happen by accident in Russia.

labourers. Nine of the soldiers were trade union members, among them two miners. The food rations they got were satisfactory. The battery had been there only a few weeks. The cook (a corporal) who was a miner, coming from the same village as Jack Horner, the communist chairman of the South Wales miners' federation, showed me the menu. For breakfast they had tea, porridge, bacon (or sausage) and egg; for lunch, meat and two vegetables, and a sweet; at 5 p.m. they had tea, bread and butter (or marge), jam and biscuits; at 7 p.m. supper including another meat course. They were getting 12 oz of bread a day, 12 oz of meat, ½ lb of vegetables, 2 oz of fresh fruit, and a weekly ration of 3½ oz of butter.

The TASS correspondent added that there were "dozens of such batteries" in the London area, and commented on the comradely atmosphere amongst all these men: "The behaviour of the sergeants is entirely different from what it used to be during the 1914–18 war." This article caused a real stir in Russia. It was something quite new. There had never been any "human interest" stories in the Soviet press about the Germans and their "menus", let alone about Frenchmen and Norwegians. There was also a clear suggestion that this was a "people's war" in which the "proletariat" were playing as active a part as any, including Jack Horner's fellow villagers who could reasonably be supposed to be communists.

For a time, at any rate, a subtle kind of fellow-feeling for the British people was thus created in Russia. The intellectuals felt it, of course, most acutely. Anna Akhmatova wrote a poem on the bombing of London, which was not, however, to be published until 1943:

> Time, with its bony hand,
> Is now writing Shakespeare's twenty-fourth drama.
> No, let us sooner read Hamlet and Caesar and Lear
> Above the leaden river.
> No, let us rather accompany darling Juliet
> With singing and torches to her grave.
> No, let us sooner look into Macbeth's window,
> And tremble, together with the hired murderers.
> But not this, not this, not this.
> This one we cannot bear to read.*

* Anna Akhmatova, *Izbrannoye* (A Selection) (Tashkent, 1943), p. 12.

And Nikolai Tikhonov, full of foreboding, wrote another poem which was finally published in 1956:

> Through the night, through sheets of rain, and the wind
>   cutting his cheeks,
> Learning his lesson as he goes along,
> The man of London winds his way to the shelter,
> Dragging his rug along the watery pavement.
> There's the cold steel key in his pocket,
> A key to rooms now turned to prickly rubble.
> We still are learning lessons at our school desk,
> But at night we dream of the coming exam.*

Especially among the intellectuals, there had, all along, been a distaste for the Soviet-German Pact, and a growing feeling that what was now happening to England would, sooner or later, happen to Russia too: "At night we dream of the coming exam"....

On October 25 *Pravda* contained three news items, each significant in its own way: "Hitler meets Franco", which suggested that Russia was certainly in very strange company; "The Evacuation of Children from Berlin", which suggested that England was hitting back hard; and another TASS message from London saying that there had been great improvements lately in the organisation of air-raid shelters. And, two days later: "Roosevelt warns Pétain against collaboration with Germany and against declaring war on England." After that came the news of the Italian attack on Greece —suggesting that the war was now spreading to the Balkans, a point about which Russia had always been very sensitive.†

* *Literaturnaya Moskva* (Moscow, 1956), p. 499.

† Another curious news item during that week was the arrival in Moscow of Matias Rakosi, the Hungarian communist leader. It was stated that he had been in jail for fifteen years, and had now been released as a result of the recent Soviet-Hungarian negotiations.

Chapter VII

DISPLAY OF RUSSIAN MILITARY MIGHT—
MOLOTOV'S TRAGI-COMIC VISIT TO BERLIN

And then came November 1940. The Soviet Government clearly felt that the people needed reassuring. The November 7 celebrations of the 23rd anniversary of the Bolshevik Revolution were marked by a spectacular display of the Soviet Union's military might; this was not only meant to restore the Soviet public's confidence, but also to impress Germany. At the Bolshoi Theatre, on the eve of Revolution Day, there was the usual meeting at which Kalinin, the venerable President of the Soviet Union, spoke, saying that "of all the large States, the USSR is, in fact, the only one not to be involved in war, and is scrupulously observing its neutrality". To this *Pravda* added: "What we see in the capitalist world is a process of savage destruction of what generations of human beings had created. People, cities, industries, culture are being ruthlessly destroyed."*

In his Order of the Day, on November 7, the Commissar of Defence, Marshal Timoshenko declared: "The Red Army is prepared, at the first summons of the Party and the Government, to strike a crushing blow at anyone who may dare to violate the sacred frontiers of our socialist state."

As *Pravda* described it on November 9, the November 7 military display was a very big affair:

The military parade in the capital of our country was truly dazzling. Troops of every kind demonstrated before Comrade Stalin and the

* *Pravda*, November 9, 1940.

leaders of the Party and the Government their preparedness for the defence of the sacred frontiers of the Soviet Union. The parade demonstrated the real might of the Soviet Army. The squares of cities shook with the thunder of mighty engines, and the rhythmic march of the battalions. Our combat planes flew over our cities in impeccable formation. There were many of them everywhere: in Moscow, Riga, Lwow, Orel, Tallinn, Czernowitz, Voronezh, Kiev, Odessa, Archangel, Murmansk, Sebastopol, Tbilisi, Novosibirsk, Irkutsk, Erevan, Viborg, Krasnoyarsk, Baku, Alma Ata, Vladivostok and other cities. Altogether, over 5,000 combat planes of different types and classes took part in these air parades and, but for the bad weather in some places, there would have been 8,000. Our proud Stalin Hawks* flew these remarkable planes, the work of our glorious Soviet constructors.

It then spoke lyrically of the "growing army of Stakhanovites" who had also taken part in the parade, and of the thousands of children—those "Soviet children who have a happy, cloudless today and a secure tomorrow".

There was, of course, no suggestion that a high proportion of the 5,000 planes that had taken part in these air parades near the German, Finnish and Japanese borders, and elsewhere, were wholly obsolete. No doubt the general public knew no better, but the German military and air attachés at the Red Square parade may well have drawn more professional conclusions.

In Leningrad, where there appears to have been no air display owing to bad weather, the parade was directed by the commander of the Leningrad Military District, Hero of the Soviet Union, Lt.-Gen. Kirponos, who was to come to a tragic end in the Kiev encirclement, barely ten months later.

Looking back on this strange period, one has the curious feeling that, in his own way, Molotov was made to play in Russia the part of Laval; like Laval, he was *le vidangeur*, who had to do all the dirty work, while Pétain—and Stalin—tried to keep their hands relatively clean, and refrained, as far as possible, from any direct dealings with the Germans. It was significant that, in the TASS denial published

* "Stalin Hawks" was the affectionate term for Soviet airmen.

at the end of August,* a point should have been made of the fact
that Stalin had not seen the German Ambassador "during the last
six or seven months".

Molotov, on the other hand, was extremely busy and active.
Although he did not go to Laval's extreme of saying "*je souhaite la
victoire allemande*", it was his job to present to the Soviet people
the Soviet-German Pact at all its stages in the most favourable light
possible.

This does not mean that Molotov crawled and grovelled to the
Germans; on the contrary, he had, throughout, been thoroughly
hard-headed and businesslike in his dealings with them and was one
of the few men not to appear impressed, still less overawed, by
Hitler, when he at last met him face-to-face in Berlin on November 12, 1940.

This is borne out by the story of the events leading up to Molotov's
visit to Berlin in November 1940 and his handling of the matter. In
June, without asking the Germans' permission, the Russians had
occupied the Baltic States, Bessarabia and Northern Bukovina. The
Germans then became particularly alarmed by the Russians'
proximity to the Rumanian oilfields, a source of oil supremely
important to Germany. This started a process which, within a few
months, was to end in the complete German subjugation of
Rumania, and the virtual occupation of Bulgaria, to be followed by
the German invasion of Yugoslavia and Greece. The German
penetration of Rumania had begun, in a more or less camouflaged
form, soon after the Russian occupation of two of Rumania's
northern provinces and had coincided with Hitler's "Vienna
Award", under which a large part of Transylvania had been handed
over to Hungary. What was left of Rumania—now a plain Fascist
dictatorship under Antonescu†—was "guaranteed" by Germany
and Italy.

The Russians took the beginning of this German penetration of
the Balkans very badly, and charged the German Government with

* See p. 97.
† King Carol abdicated and went to Switzerland with Madame
Lúpescu, leaving the throne to his young son Michael.

violating Article III of the Soviet-German Pact which called for consultation. The Germans retorted that they had not been consulted about either the Baltic States or Bessarabia-Bukovina. A further complication arose from reports that German troops had been seen in Finland, ostensibly in transit to Northern Norway, and that Germany was selling large quantities of armaments to Finland. Worse still, at the end of September the Germans informed Molotov that a military alliance was about to be signed by Germany, Italy and Japan, an alliance which, the Germans claimed, was directed against the United States. Molotov reacted sharply to this piece of news, demanding full information on the treaty, and also pressed the Germans for more details on their activities in Rumania and Finland. A few days later the Germans informed Molotov that they were sending a "military mission" to Rumania, which produced from him the rejoinder: "How many troops does that represent?"

Relations were becoming severely strained between Berlin and Moscow, and on October 13, Ribbentrop sent a long, wordy and perhaps deliberately vague letter to Stalin, prophesying the early collapse of England and proposing that Molotov come to Berlin, "where the Führer could explain personally his views regarding the future moulding of relations between our two countries". He significantly added in an underlined passage that "it appears to be the mission of the Four Powers (the Soviet Union, Germany, Italy and Japan) to adopt a long-range policy . . . through the delimitation of their interests on a world scale".

It was obviously necessary for the Russians to try to find out what the Germans were up to next, and the invitation to Berlin was accepted. But there is nothing to show that they were genuinely interested in sharing the British lion's skin—anyway the lion was still alive—or in joining in any German-Italian-Japanese alliance against the United States. What they were worried about, above all, were the Balkans and Finland.

As we know from the German documents published since the war, Ribbentrop, during his first Berlin meeting with Molotov, harped above all on the imminent collapse of the British Empire, and suggested that, in the share-out of this Empire, the Russians might be interested in extending their "sphere of influence" to the south, particularly towards the Persian Gulf. Molotov was not impressed, any more than he was by Hitler's harangue, in the afternoon, about a "common drive towards an access to the ocean", implying that the Russians might perhaps be interested in India. Instead, Molotov fired question upon question at Hitler. "No foreign visitor," Schmidt, Hitler's interpreter later recalled, "had ever spoken to him in this way in my presence." Molotov wanted precise answers to his questions about the New Order in Europe and Asia, and, above all, about German machinations in Finland, Rumania, Bulgaria and Turkey—areas in which the Russians were directly interested. On the pretext that there might soon be a British air-raid, Hitler, completely taken aback by Molotov's manner, broke off the discussion until the next day.

When they met again on the 13th, Molotov once more showed no interest in the share-out of the British Empire, but argued, instead, that the German-Italian guarantee to Rumania was directed against the Soviet Union, and, since the Germans were unwilling to "revoke" it, Russia would be willing to give a similar guarantee to Bulgaria, a suggestion which Hitler took very badly. Bulgaria, the Führer said, had not asked for such a guarantee and, in any case, he would have to consult Mussolini on the subject. Again, thoroughly displeased with his troublesome and impertinent visitor, Hitler broke off the talk on the same pretext as on the previous night. He did not attend the gala banquet Molotov gave that night at the Soviet Embassy. This banquet—at which "friendly" toasts were exchanged by Molotov and Ribbentrop—was interrupted by an air-raid warning, soon to be followed by the drone of planes, and the guests scattered to shelters, Ribbentrop rushing Molotov to the near-by shelter of the German Foreign Office. While they were there, Ribbentrop pulled out of his pocket the draft of an agreement which, in effect, transformed the Three-Power Pact into a Four-Power Pact; under this, Germany, Italy and Japan recognised the present frontiers of the Soviet Union; while, according to the secret protocols defining each country's "territorial aspirations", the Soviet Union was to expand "in the direction of the Indian Ocean".

Again, the infuriating Molotov was not interested; and kept on
returning instead to questions like Finland, Rumania and Hungary,
and German plans for Bulgaria, Yugoslavia, Greece and Turkey;
he also continued to insist on the preservation of Swedish neutrality.

Ribbentrop, more and more exasperated, declared that Molotov
had not answered *the* fundamental question; which was whether the
Soviet Union would "co-operate in the great liquidation of the
British Empire". Finally, Molotov could not resist it: "If you are so
sure that Britain is finished, then why are we in this shelter?"*

The visit ended inconclusively, and a fortnight passed before
Stalin himself took up the ball and unlike Molotov in Berlin showed
some interest in joining the Three-Power Pact as a fourth member.
He might well have thought that he could not obtain any satisfaction
from Hitler by any other means.

His main proposals were that the Germans clear out of Finland;
that Russia sign a mutual assistance pact with Bulgaria, that she
establish a military and naval base within range of the Turkish
straits; and that Iran be recognised as a Russian sphere of interest.
Stalin must have known that there was but a small chance that Hitler
would accept these demands. Even at this late hour, Stalin still
made it clear that he was not interested in India or any other part of
the British Empire. His primary concern was that Hitler should leave
the Balkans and Finland strictly alone. No reply to these proposals
was ever received from Berlin.

How was the Molotov visit presented to the Soviet people? The
Soviet press certainly made a brave effort to show its readers that
the Soviet-German Pact was still a good thing, and that relations
with the Germans were still correct, if not cordial. And yet, the
Soviet newspaper reader, well-trained to read between the lines, must
have guessed that things had not gone too well, as he read the following items:

COMRADE V. M. MOLOTOV'S VISIT TO BERLIN, Berlin,
November 12 (TASS):

* Stalin was to tell Churchill about this parting shot in August 1942.
Churchill, *The Second World War*, vol. III, p. 586.

Comrade Molotov was given a festive (*torzhestvennaya*)* reception in Berlin. . . . Long before the arrival of his train at the Anhalter Bahnhof, there had assembled on the station platform the representatives of various German government organs, the representatives of the German High Command, the Diplomatic Corps of Berlin, members of the Soviet Embassy and Trade Delegation and foreign and German journalists.

The platform was decorated with flowers and evergreens, and the main entrance of the station with the State flags of Germany and the USSR. All the adjoining streets were crowded with people long before the arrival of the train.

Comrade Molotov was met by Foreign Minister von Ribbentrop; Commander of the OKW, General Field-Marshal Keitel; the head of the Labour Front, Dr Ley; the head of the German Police, Herr Himmler; the head of the German Government Press Office, Dr Dietrich, State Secretary Weizsäcker, Herr Steeg, the Burgomaster of Berlin, and many others.

Herr von Ribbentrop then accompanied Comrade Molotov to his Bellevue residence. The German press unanimously considers the arrival of Comrade Molotov as a fact of first-rate political importance.†

And then:

In the afternoon of November 12 a conversation took place in the new Chancellery between the Reichskanzler of Germany, Herr Hitler and Comrade Molotov, in the presence of Ribbentrop and the Deputy Foreign Commissar, V. G. Dekanozov. The conversation lasted more than two hours.†

On the following day, according to *Pravda*, Molotov had further conversations in Berlin, and left in the morning of November 14. The following communiqué was published:

In the course of his visit to Berlin on November 12–13, Foreign Commissar V. M. Molotov had a conversation with the Reichskanzler, Herr Adolf Hitler and Foreign Minister Herr von Ribbentrop. The exchange of views took place in an atmosphere of mutual trust and established mutual comprehension on all the important questions concerning the USSR and Germany. V. M. Molotov also had a conversation with Reichsmarschall Goering and another with Herr Hitler's deputy at the head of the National-Socialist Party, Herr Rudolf Hess.

* The Russian adjective is somewhere half-way between "festive" and "solemn". It might be translated as "V.I.P."
† *Pravda*, November 13, 1940.

On November 13, V. M. Molotov had a final conversation with Herr von Ribbentrop.*

Then there was another story on the "festive atmosphere" in which Molotov was seen off from the Anhalter Bahnhof. After 10 a.m. Ribbentrop had collected Molotov at the Bellevue Palace to accompany him to the station. Again the station was decorated with flags, flowers and evergreens, and Molotov and Ribbentrop reviewed a guard of honour.

> Apart from Ribbentrop, Molotov and his party were seen off by Reichsminister Dr Lemmers, Himmler, Ley, Dietrich, Weizsäcker; Himmler's deputy, Daluege; General Thomas representing Keitel [etc.]. Comrade Molotov was also seen off by members of the Soviet Embassy and Trade Delegation in Berlin, to whom he warmly said good-bye. Having thanked Herr von Ribbentrop for the reception he had been given, Comrade Molotov then took leave of the representatives of the German government who had come to see him off.*

Nothing was revealed at the time about the real nature of the Molotov-Hitler-Ribbentrop talks and although, in the final communiqué, there was that phrase about the "mutual trust", Russian readers had an uneasy feeling that something was not quite right. There was a little too much about the flowers and evergreens at the Anhalter Bahnhof, but no mention of any "friendly atmosphere" in the first report on the Hitler-Molotov meeting, even though it had lasted "more than two hours".

Could something be read into the fact that Keitel had merely sent his deputy to see Molotov off? And into the fact that Molotov had said good-bye "warmly" to the members of the Russian Embassy, but not to the Germans?† Needless to say, there was nothing in the Soviet papers about the British air-raid on Berlin, which had forced Ribbentrop and his guest into a shelter, where Molotov had made one or two caustic remarks. But these were to be quoted in Moscow *sub rosa* before long.

* *Pravda*, November 15.
† Perhaps the "warmth" was deliberately omitted in the account of Molotov's leave-taking, since the Germans present included such particularly unsavoury characters as Himmler and Daluege. Curious, too, was the omission of any mention of Molotov's second meeting with Hitler.

On November 18 the Soviet press printed photographs of Molotov and Hitler in the new Chancellery; Molotov had a completely non-committal expression, and Hitler one of those strained and oily semi-smiles, into which anything could be read. Molotov looked much the same in the photograph with Ribbentrop; but the latter at least tried to look a little more cheerful. It was exactly a month after the publication of these photographs that Hitler finally decided on Plan Barbarossa, i.e. the invasion of the Soviet Union.

Molotov's most unusual manner of talking to Hitler had certainly something to do with it. Although Hitler had considered an attack on Russia as early as the summer of 1940, his final decision was not taken until after his infuriating meetings with Molotov.

Chapter VIII

"1941—IT WILL BE A HAPPY YEAR"

On the face of it, nothing seemed to have changed in Russia as a result of Molotov's November visit to Berlin. And yet, all kinds of strange news items began to appear in the press: for instance, a TASS denial, on November 16, of an American report that Japan had offered the Soviet Union the whole or part of India in exchange for Eastern Siberia—a curious coincidence, to say the least, so soon after Hitler's mention of India to Molotov. Then, for two days (November 16–17), *Pravda* ran, for no apparent reason, two whole pages by André Maurois on "Why France Lost the War", which for all their crypto-Vichyism, were scarcely pro-German. On the next day there was a story about 400,000 Frenchmen being thrown by the Germans out of Lorraine, and there were numerous reports of "Famine in Paris". There were further suggestions of the Soviet Union not being really sympathetic to the Axis Powers; thus, on November 18, TASS denied a German story that Hungary had joined the German-Italian-Japan axis "with the approval and encouragement of the Soviet Union". Then, as later, there were frequent accounts of German air-raids on England (Coventry, Manchester, etc.) and of the air blockade of Britain, shipping losses, and so on.

One of the peculiarities of the Soviet-German Pact was that it provided for no "cultural" contacts between the two countries, and one of the few manifestations of a heightened Russian interest in German *Kultur* was Eisenstein's production, on November 22,

1940, of the *Walküre* at the Bolshoi Theatre. A peculiarity of this Eisenstein production was his original and unconventional treatment of the Wagner opera—with pantomime effects introduced, for instance, in Act I to illustrate Siegmund's narrative. Members of the German Embassy who attended the *première* referred to the "deliberate Jewish tricks" with which Eisenstein had desecrated the Master's work. But, on the other hand, Sieglinde was sung by Mme Spiller, who, according to Moscow gossip, was Molotov's lady-friend —perhaps a subtle compliment to the Germans.

Nothing much happened in December. There were the usual celebrations of Constitution Day, and there were many self-congratulatory articles saying that, in 1938, the Soviet Union had a population of 170 million, in 1939 one of 183 million, and in 1940, one of 193 million, since the Baltic Republics had joined the USSR and Bessarabia and Northern Bukovina had been freed from "the yoke of the Rumanian boyars".

The elections in the new Karelo-Finnish Republic, and in the Western Ukraine and Belorussia later in December proved a "dazzling victory of the Stalin Bloc of Communist and Non-Party Candidates". The press also reported that at a Supreme Soviet election meeting at Czernowitz, the candidate, General G. K. Zhukov, Commander of the Special Kiev Military District, had declared to his voters: "Under the wise leadership of Comrade Stalin, our country has become the mightiest country in the world"—a statement strangely contrasting with the much more cautious words General Zhukov was to use only a few months later.

The press continued to deal in some detail with the situation in Britain, with Churchill's statement that the danger of an invasion was not over, with British victories in the Western Desert and with Italian defeats in Albania. There was also a report of some particularly powerful new American bombers; altogether, much interest continued to be shown in American aid to Britain. Occasionally, there were also some more explicitly anti-Nazi items like this in *Pravda* of December 19: "Hungary: All Jews (except 3,500) Deprived of Voting Rights."

New Year 1941 was celebrated in Russia with the usual exuberance and in the customary holiday atmosphere, complete with the giant New Year parties for children, and celebrations in millions of homes. The editorials in the press tried to sound highly reassuring. On December 31, 1940 *Pravda* wrote: "We can look back on 1940 with a feeling of deep satisfaction... As Comrade Kalinin said on November 6, our economic progress resulted in an eleven per cent increase of production... Much was done in 1940 by the Party and the Government to increase the military might of the USSR and the defensive strength and military preparedness of the people. There have been great improvements in the training and education of the Army and Navy personnel, and important work is being done in the military education of the civilian population, and of our young people in particular... In all fields our successes have been stupendous."

And after recalling once again the incorporation of new territories in the Soviet Union, the editorial concluded: "1941 will be the fourth year of the third Stalinist Five-Year Plan. And as we enter 1941, which will be a year of an even more tremendous development of our socialist economy, the Soviet people are looking into their future cheerfully and full of confidence."

Ironically, during the next few days, the Soviet press spoke more and more frequently of the possibility of a German invasion of England, largely on the strength of speculation in the British press. Was there here a touch of wishful thinking? Even in February and March this motif was frequently to be found in the Russian papers.

Since the Molotov visit to Berlin and, even more so, since the middle of January, the Russians had, indeed, more and more cause for uneasiness, but they continued for as long as possible to hope that Germany was still not interested in the East. On January 7 a photograph—obviously old, and dating from September 1940—was published in *Pravda* showing a crowd of English children in a trench watching an Anglo-German dogfight in the sky. Would Hitler get bogged down in the West?

However, appearances had to be kept up. On January 11, *Pravda* announced "Another Victory of Soviet Foreign Policy": the signing of the Soviet-German Agreement on the State Frontier between the two countries, a frontier running from the Igorka river to the Baltic, mostly through "former Poland". There was a picture of Molotov and Schulenburg signing the agreement. The publication of the agreement was accompanied by a communiqué on reciprocal property claims in Lithuania, Latvia and Estonia and on the repatriation of Germans from these countries; as well as on a new Mikoyan-Schnurre economic agreement. All was well, *Pravda* suggested:

> The present agreement, based on the Soviet-German agreement of February 11, 1940, covers the period from February 11, 1941 to August 1, 1942 and marks the next stage in the economic programme approved by the Soviet and German Governments. It provides for a much larger volume of trade than that provided for during the previous period. The USSR will send industrial raw materials, oil products and foodstuffs, particularly grain... Germany will send us industrial equipment. This new economic agreement of January 10, 1941 marks a great step forward.

The exact volume and nature of this trade was kept dark at the time, and even today it remains one of the more obscure aspects of the last war. There are conflicting views as to the contribution these Russian supplies made to Germany's war economy. Certain German studies have tended to exaggerate their importance, while the Russians have tried, on the contrary, to minimise them. More recently Professor Friedensburg of the West German *Deutsches Institut für Wirtschaftsforschung* published a detailed study on the subject. According to him, Germany received from the Soviet Union between January 1, 1940 and June 22, 1941 roughly the following deliveries: 1·5 million tons of grain, 100,000 tons of cotton, 2 million tons of petroleum products, 1·5 million tons of timber, 140,000 tons of manganese and 26,000 tons of chromium.

The last two items were of course of great importance to Germany's war industry at the time when the British blockade had deprived it of many of its customary sources of supply. According to Friedensburg, Russia had not supplied them before the Soviet-German Pact had come into force. He also claims that the Russians had resold to Germany copper bought from the United States. On the other hand, the Russians seem to have received fairly little in return. According to the same author, German statistics for that period show a balance of 239 million Reichsmarks in the Russians' favour, while the Russian statistics for 1940 showed a balance of 380 million roubles also in their favour, a sum which the Hitler régime had never paid and which the author asserts the Russians themselves refrained from claiming after the war, suggesting that they found it more convenient to forget about it.

During May and June 1941 when Stalin dreaded more than ever a German attack, important raw materials such as copper and rubber were being rushed to Germany by express trains from the East and the Far East to keep Hitler happy in an effort of "appeasement" that was as frantic as it was futile. A few weeks later this copper, after processing, was used to kill thousands of Russians.

So, on the surface, all seemed well on January 10 when the new economic agreement was signed with Germany—an agreement which covered the period up to August 1, 1942—by which time the Germans were well on their way to Stalingrad and the Caucasus.

But only three days later a new kind of rot started. *Pravda* published the following ominous statement: "The foreign press has suggested that we had approved the entry of German troops into Bulgaria. If there are German troops in Bulgaria, they are there without our consent. We were never consulted." It had now become clear that the Germans had taken no notice of Molotov's plea that the "Eastern Balkans" were a Soviet sphere of interest. Yet, if the Russians were annoyed they still showed it only by small petulant pinpricks. Thus, for no obvious immediate reason, they attacked Knut Hamsun, calling him a "rotting corpse" who did not share his fellow-Norwegians' hearty dislike for German rule. "And to think that this corpse—rotting alive—used to be a highly popular author in our country!"*

Hitler's speech of January 30 was duly reported. He said that the outcome of the war had already been settled in 1940; that an all-out U-boat war against England would start in the spring, and that the

* *Pravda*, January 25, 1941.

Americans were "wasting their time". But what struck the Russians most was that there was no mention of the Soviet Union. Moreover, there was that ominous little phrase at the end: "I have calculated every conceivable possibility." Stalin knew that, by now, his December "proposals" had been ignored by Hitler.

Moscow's nervousness produced strange results. On January 30 there was an *ukase* of the Presidium of the Supreme Soviet appointing Beria, head of the NKVD, "General Commissar of State Security"; a few days later the People's Commissariat of the Interior (NKVD) was turned into two different commissariats—Interior (NKVD) under L. P. Beria and Security (NKB) under V. N. Merkulov.

The phrase "mobilisational preparedness" kept recurring over and over again in propaganda and the press; the *ukase* of the previous June on labour discipline was being more and more rigidly enforced, "slackers" and absentees in industry being subjected to ruthless punishment; great attention was being given to the training of young people for industry in a network of establishments like railway and FZO (factory) schools with their 600,000 pupils. These young people were intended to become an important labour reserve in the great national emergency.

In the middle of February, at the 18th All-Union Conference of the Party, long, detailed and rather critical reports were produced by Malenkov on the "Successes and Shortcomings of Industry and Railways", by N. Voznesensky on the "General Progress of the Economy of the USSR in 1941", and so on.

The usual glorification of the "invincible" Red Army, referred to as recently as December 1940 by Zhukov as "the mightiest army in the world", gave way to a more sober and critical assessment. On Red Army Day, February 23, 1941, the same General Zhukov clearly suggested in an article in *Pravda* that the Army was undergoing a process of transformation, which had not yet been completed, and that things were still far from perfect. 1941, he wrote, would be the year of the "great change" (*perelom*) in the Red Army, the year of "the reconstruction of the whole system of the soldiers' training and education". He congratulated himself on the changes that had already been made since the Finnish War, and pointed out that in August 1940 the officer's "single command" had been restored, which meant that the officer was no longer under the thumb of the commissar; as a result the status, responsibility and authority of the officers had been greatly increased. This, Zhukov emphasised, was the "essential foundation" on which the other reforms would be built.

He stressed the importance of military "professionalism" and attributed the spectacular defeat of the French Army in 1940 largely to the French soldiers' low standard of training, and to their unfamiliarity with modern weapons. In the Red Army such "sloppiness" would not be tolerated: "An imperialist war is raging round us. In the reconstruction of our system of military training we have achieved some unquestionable successes. The training is taking place in near-combat conditions, and we have improved the tactical skill of our troops; but it would be a grave error to be smug and complacent about it; much still remains to be done."

The whole article, without sounding alarmist, nevertheless betrayed a certain feeling of uneasiness, though it is impossible to say whether a man like Zhukov anticipated a German invasion only four months later; the whole suggestion underlying his article was that the "great change" in the Red Army was a fairly long-term affair which was not likely to be completed until 1942.

In reality the international situation in February 1941 was already rapidly deteriorating from the Russian point of view. The big question was whether Hitler would move west or east.

On February 16, the Soviet press quoted *The Times*—with some relief, one may suspect—on the continued danger of a German invasion of England; on February 25 it reported another Hitler speech promising more victories over the British, but again, as on January 30, there was *no mention of the Soviet Union*. And then the trouble in the Balkans started in real earnest. On March 3, Andrei Vyshinsky, Deputy Foreign Commissar, informed the Bulgarian Government that he "disagreed" with its decision to let German troops enter Bulgaria "to protect peace in the Balkans". "On the contrary," Vyshinsky said, "we consider that this measure will merely extend the area of conflict to the Balkans, and the Soviet Government cannot, therefore, support the Bulgarian Government's policy." This was blunt enough; it was, in fact, the first open and official clash between Soviet and German interests.

There were now German troops in Hungary, Bulgaria and Rumania. But on March 27 there was a popular uprising in Belgrade against Yugoslavia becoming a German satellite with the connivance of its rulers. A group of officers, with General Simovic at their head, had organised the *coup*, which took place two days after Premier Cvetkovic and his Foreign Minister, with Prince Paul's blessing, had signed in Vienna an agreement joining the Tripartite Pact between Germany, Italy and Japan. The Simovic revolt aroused great popular enthusiasm amongst the Serbs and incensed Hitler.

Thinking no doubt that the Germans would still "reckon" with the Soviet Union, and obviously unaware of Hitler's decision to invade Yugoslavia, the Soviet Government hastened to conclude a Friendship and Non-Aggression Pact with the new Yugoslav Government. Significantly, it did not dare propose to Yugoslavia a Mutual Assistance Pact which would have committed Russia to immediate military action, should Germany attack. Stalin and Molotov were wrong if they thought that such qualified support would frighten off Hitler.

On April 5 the Friendship and Non-Aggression Pact was solemnly signed in Moscow in the presence of Foreign Minister Simic, Ambassador Gabrilovic and two of his assistants on the Yugoslav side and Molotov, Stalin and Vyshinsky on the Russian side. Less than twenty-four hours later the Germans invaded Yugoslavia and the Luftwaffe dropped thousands of bombs on defenceless Belgrade. On April 7, *Pravda* carried on its back page, and in unspectacular type, a TASS message from Berlin saying that Germany had declared war on Yugoslavia and Greece and that the German Army had started military operations against these two countries. The massive bombing of Belgrade—Hitler's revenge for the "unheard-of" affront he had suffered—was played down—even though, as time was to show, Yugoslavia's gallant revolt and tragic resistance providentially delayed the invasion of Russia by a few weeks.

There was no official Russian reaction to the German invasion of Yugoslavia. All the Soviet Foreign Commissariat dared to do in the next few days was to instruct Vyshinsky to inform the Hungarian

Ambassador that "the Soviet Union could not approve of Hungary's attack on Yugoslavia".

On April 11 the Soviet press reported Churchill's speech saying that, for several months past, the Germans had concentrated large armoured and other forces in Bulgaria, Hungary and Rumania. But it refrained from any comment and, for the next few weeks, it reported in a routine and "objective" kind of way the Germans' progress in Yugoslavia, Greece and Crete. There were no lamentations over the tragic fate of the Yugoslavs with whom a Friendship Pact had so recently been signed. A showdown with Hitler seemed inevitable; Stalin's and Molotov's one aim now was to put off the evil hour—at any price.

Chapter IX

THE LAST WEEKS OF PEACE

In Soviet novels and films produced both during and since the War, the news of the Invasion of June 22, 1941 is often represented as a complete surprise. "Life was so peaceful and happy, and we were preparing to go on holiday when suddenly, on that lovely Sunday..." Oddly enough, that is precisely what happened to a great many ordinary Soviet citizens, who had been conditioned for years into thinking that the Red Army was the finest army in the world, and that Hitler would never dare attack Russia. Others, more sophisticated, reacted the way the hero of Simonov's novel, *The Living and the Dead* did: "It seemed that everybody had been expecting the war for a long time and yet, at the last moment, it came like a bolt from the blue; it was apparently impossible to prepare oneself in advance for such an enormous misfortune." But the politically minded people in Russia must have known for some time that the danger of war was immense, and there can be no doubt that the invasion of Yugoslavia must have deeply shaken both Stalin and Molotov.

For some months past, the Kremlin had been receiving specific and grave warnings. As early as February, after his visit to Ankara, Sir Stafford Cripps had told the Soviet Foreign Commissariat that the Germans were preparing to invade the Balkans and that they were also planning an attack on the Soviet Union "in the near future". About the same time, similar information had been given by Sumner Welles to Konstantin Oumansky, the Soviet Ambassador in Washington. And then, in April, there was Churchill's famous message to Stalin.* In the post-war *History* these warnings are treated somewhat ungraciously—they were "not disinterested warnings", the suggestion being that the British and Americans were merely trying to drag the Russians into the war and turn them into "England's soldiers". Instead, the *History* claims that Soviet Intelligence in Poland, Czechoslovakia and even Germany had kept the government fully informed on what was going on.

Be that as it may, it seems certain that Molotov and Stalin were both fully aware of the danger of a German attack but still hoped that they could put off the evil hour—at least till the autumn, when the Germans would not attack; and then by 1942, Russia would be better prepared for war.

Russia's Friendship Pact with Yugoslavia had not deterred Hitler; it had turned out a lamentable fiasco. True, there had been a number of subtle little "anti-German" demonstrations before that—a few pinpricks in the press, as we have seen, and a few other little demonstrations, such as the award of a Stalin Prize in March 1941 to Eisenstein's ferociously anti-German film, *Alexander Nevsky*, as well as to some other strongly-nationalist and implicitly "anti-invader" works like Alexei Tolstoy's novel, *Peter I*, Shaporin's oratorio, *The Field of Kulikovo*, and Sergeiev-Tsensky's novel on the Siege of Sebastopol. Behind the scenes at the end of March, Manuilsky, Vice-President of the Comintern, had even declared that, in his opinion, "a war with Nazi Germany could now scarcely be avoided". The story got round Moscow. Better still, in March a number of Russian officers of Timoshenko's entourage had invited the British Military Attaché to a party. The conversation had been guarded and non-committal until the atmosphere had warmed up— no doubt helped by the vodka—and, in the end, some of the officers went so far as to drink to "the victory over our common enemy".

* See p. 276.

In the course of the evening they had made no secret of their deep concern about the general situation, especially in the Balkans.*

Officially, no doubt, both Stalin and Molotov had to go on pretending that they were not frightened. After the signing of the Soviet-Yugoslav Pact Gabrilovic, Yugoslav Ambassador in Moscow (as he later told me himself), asked Stalin: "What will happen if the Germans turn on you?" To which Stalin replied: "All right, let them come!"

On April 13—the day Belgrade fell—the Soviet-Japanese Non-Aggression Pact was signed. It was a doubtful insurance, but still an insurance that the Russians took in view of the growing German menace. Everybody in Moscow was startled by Stalin's extraordinary display of cordiality to Matsuoka, the Japanese Foreign Minister, who had come from Berlin to Moscow to sign the Pact. He took the unprecedented step of seeing Matsuoka off himself at the railway station. He embraced him and said: "We are Asiatics, too, and we've got to stick together!" To have secured Japanese neutrality in these conditions, and the promise by Japan not to attack Russia regardless of any commitments she had signed "with third parties" was, in Stalin's eyes, no mean achievement. As long as Japan stuck to her word, it meant the avoidance of a two-front war, if Germany attacked. On that station platform Stalin was in an unusually exuberant mood, even shaking the hands of railwaymen and travellers as he walked down the platform arm-in-arm with Matsuoka.

True, he also threw his arm round the neck of Colonel von Krebs, the German Military Attaché, who had also come to see Matsuoka off, saying "We are going to remain friends, won't we?" But what mattered most to Stalin that day was his pact with Japan. Stalin had no great illusions about the Germans. Significantly, at the end of April, he telephoned Ilya Ehrenburg saying that his anti-Nazi novel, *The Fall of Paris*, could now be published. (Ehrenburg concluded

---

* Having heard about this, I asked Cripps in Moscow in July 1941 whether it was true. "Yes, that is, roughly, what happened. It was certainly something of a pointer. It was all the more significant since I, as Ambassador, continued to be as good as boycotted by both Stalin and Molotov." The story was also later confirmed to me by Colonel E. R. Greer, the British Military Attaché, though he was uncertain about the exact date of the incident.

from this call that, in Stalin's view, war with Germany was now inevitable.)

On May Day, there was a particularly impressive military parade in Red Square, complete with motorised units, many new KV and T-34 tanks, and hundreds of planes. It was rumoured in Moscow that all these troops were on their way to Minsk, Leningrad and the Polish border. Ambassador Count Schulenburg noted on May 2 that the tension in Moscow was growing, and that the rumours of a Soviet-German war were becoming increasingly persistent. On that day Hitler made his speech on the Balkan campaign; as in his two previous speeches, there was again no mention of the Soviet Union.

On May 5 a reception was given in the Kremlin to hundreds of young officers, new graduates of the military academies. Stalin spoke at this meeting. Officially, nothing was disclosed beyond what *Pravda* was to write on the following day. The article was entitled: "We must be prepared to deal with any surprises." "In his speech, Comrade Stalin noted the profound changes that had taken place in the Red Army in the last few years, and emphasised that, on the strength of the experience of modern war, its organisation had undergone important changes, and it had been substantially re-equipped. Comrade Stalin welcomed the officers who had graduated from the military academies and wished them all success in their work. He spoke for forty minutes and was listened to with exceptionally great attention."

Obviously he had said much more than that in *forty minutes*.

After the outbreak of the war, I was given a fairly detailed account of this meeting, to which great importance was attached in Moscow at the time. I gathered that the main points that Stalin had then made were these:

1) The situation is extremely serious, and a German attack in the near future is not to be ruled out. Therefore, "be prepared to deal with any surprises".

2) The Red Army is not, however, sufficiently strong to smash the Germans easily; its equipment is still far from satisfactory; it is still suffering from a serious shortage of modern tanks, modern planes and much else. The training of large masses of soldiers is still far from having been completed. The frontier defences in the new territories are far from good.

3) The Soviet Government will try, by all the diplomatic means at its

disposal, to put off a German attack on the Soviet Union at least till the autumn, by which time it will be too late for the Germans to attack. It may, or may not, succeed.

4) If it succeeds, then, *almost inevitably*, the war with Nazi Germany will be fought in 1942—in much more favourable conditions, since the Red Army will have been better trained, and will have far more up-to-date equipment. Depending on the international situation, the Red Army will either wait for a German attack, or it may have to take the initiative, since the perpetuation of Nazi Germany as the dominant power in Europe is "not normal".

5) England is not finished, and the weight of the American war potential is likely to count more and more. There is a very good chance that, after the signing of the Non-Aggression Pact with Japan, that country will stay quiet as far as the Soviet Union is concerned.

Stalin reiterated that the period "from now till August" was the most dangerous of all.*

Immediately following this Stalin speech to the young officers, there was a succession of desperate Russian attempts to "appease" the Germans in order to at least postpone the invasion, if there was to be one. On May 6 an *ukase* of the Presidium of the Supreme Soviet appointed Stalin, until then "only" Secretary-General of the Party, President of the Council of People's Commissars, i.e. head of the Soviet Government. Molotov became Deputy-President, whilst remaining at the same time Foreign Commissar.

The general public, not unnaturally, saw a danger signal in this appointment of Stalin as head of the government; in more normal conditions this would not have happened. One of the men most impressed by this government change was Count Schulenburg who, in a series of dispatches to Berlin, argued that Stalin was the most determined opponent of any conflict with Germany. But his counsels of moderation fell on deaf ears in Berlin; Hitler had decided long ago to attack Russia, regardless of what Schulenburg, an

* I have compiled this from several Russian verbal sources; all of them agreed in the main, and particularly on one of the most important points: Stalin's conviction that the war would "almost inevitably" be fought in 1942, with the Russians possibly having to take the initiative.

exponent of the traditional Bismarckian *Ostpolitik*, thought or advised.

The next few weeks were marked by a kind of cold-footed opportunism on Stalin's part; to impress Hitler with his "friendliness" and "solidarity" he took such incongruous and gratuitous steps as closing down the embassies and legations of countries now occupied by the Germans, such as Belgium, Greece and Yugoslavia, which implied a sort of *de facto*, if not *de jure* recognition of their conquest by Germany.*

For good measure, the strictest instructions were reiterated to the military authorities in the frontier areas and elsewhere on no account to shoot down any of the numerous German reconnaissance planes flying over Soviet territory. In May 1941, the Soviet Government went so far as to give official recognition to the short-lived pro-German and anti-British government of Rashid Ali in Irak—a country with which the Soviet Union had not had any diplomatic relations before.

Also in May, only a few days after Stalin had become head of the government, the Russians were puzzled and alarmed by the startling news of Hess's arrival in Britain. The news was presented in a highly confusing manner. TASS reported from Berlin on May 12 that, according to the Germans, Hess had "gone insane"; but this was not borne out by TASS dispatches from London, and the suspicion immediately arose of an Anglo-German deal—needless to say, at Russia's expense.

However, the Soviet press said very little about Hess; he was an awkward subject at a time when top priority had to be given to the development of cordial relations with Nazi Germany. Everything was done to keep the Germans happy, and considerable quantities

* This measure was, of course, not extended to the French "Vichy" Embassy in Moscow which had existed since 1940. The Ambassador was the erstwhile left-wing politician Gaston Bergery, whose American wife, a former Schiaparelli model, would tell Russians how nice Paris was under the German occupation: "*Les Allemands sont tellement corrects.*"

of oil and other materials in short supply were rushed to Germany without pressing for the delivery of industrial equipment from Germany due to Russia under the Trade Agreement.

Whereas Schulenburg remained amicable in his talks with Molotov, the German Government's response to Stalin's friendly economic and diplomatic gestures was precisely nil. It seems, therefore, that it was in sheer desperation that—exactly a week before the Invasion—Stalin decided to publish that famous TASS communiqué of June 14, a document which was to figure prominently in all Soviet histories of the war written under Khrushchev as the most damning piece of evidence of Stalin's wishful thinking, shortsightedness and total lack of understanding of what was going on in Germany even at that late hour. This is the text of the famous TASS communiqué:

> Even before Cripps's arrival in London and especially after he had arrived there, there have been more and more rumours of an "early war" between the Soviet Union and Germany. It is also rumoured that Germany has presented both territorial and economic claims to the Soviet Union... All this is nothing but clumsy propaganda by forces hostile to the USSR and Germany and interested in an extension of the war.
>
> TASS is authorised to state: 1) Germany has not made any claims on the USSR, and is not offering it any new and closer understanding; there have been no such talks.
>
> 2) According to Soviet information, Germany is also unswervingly observing the conditions of the Soviet-German Non-Aggression Pact, just as the USSR is doing. Therefore, in the opinion of Soviet circles, the rumours of Germany's intention to tear up the Pact and to undertake an attack on the USSR are without any foundation. As for the transfer to the northern and eastern areas of Germany of troops during the past weeks, since the completion of their tasks in the Balkans, such troop movements are, one must suppose, prompted by motives which have no bearing on Soviet-German relations.
>
> 3) As is clear from her whole peace policy, the USSR intends to observe the conditions of the Soviet-German Pact, and any talk of the Soviet Union preparing for war is manifestly absurd.
>
> 4) The summer rallies now taking place among Red Army reservists and the coming manœuvres have no purpose other than the training of reservists and the checking of railway communications. As everyone

knows, such exercises take place every year. To represent them as something hostile to Germany is absurd, to say the least.*

The *History* is no doubt quite right in saying that it was much too late in the day to "test" Germany's intentions; but, on the other hand it seems deliberately to exaggerate the TASS communiqué's soporific effect on the Soviet people.

The Russians were sufficiently used to reading between the lines of government communications not to overlook the innuendo of the phrase: "These troop movements, *one must suppose*, are prompted by motives which have no bearing on Soviet-German relations." Far from being unduly reassured by this TASS communiqué, a very high proportion of the Russian people spent the next few days anxiously waiting for Berlin "reactions" to it. According to Gafencu, the Rumanian Minister in Moscow, thousands of people were glued to their wireless sets listening to news from Berlin. But they listened in vain. The German Government did not respond in any way to the TASS statement, and did not even publish it. When, on the night of June 21, Molotov asked Schulenburg to call on him, it was too late.

Schulenburg, apparently wholly uninformed of Hitler's plans, was unable to give any answer to Molotov's anxious questions as to "the reasons for Germany's dissatisfaction"; and not until he returned to the Embassy did he receive Ribbentrop's instructions to go to see Molotov and, "without entering into any discussions with him" to read out to him a cabled document which, framed in Hitler's most vituperative manner, was in fact a declaration of war.† Sick at heart,

---

* In the recent *History* Stalin is taken severely to task for this TASS communiqué: "Up to the last moment I. V. Stalin tried to prevent a German attack and tried to influence the German Government. In order to test Germany's intentions and to influence her government, Stalin caused TASS to publish this communiqué... It reflected Stalin's incorrect assessment of the political and military atmosphere. Published at a time when war was already on our threshold, the TASS statement misguided Soviet public opinion and weakened the vigilance of the Soviet people and of the Soviet Armed Forces." (IVOVSS, vol. I, p. 404.)

† As Shirer says, "It was a familiar declaration, strewn with all the shopworn lies and fabrications at which Hitler and Ribbentrop had

the Ambassador drove back to the Kremlin just as dawn was breaking, and read the document to Molotov. According to Schulenburg's account, the Foreign Commissar listened in silence, and then said bitterly: "This is war. Do you believe that we deserved that?"

become so expert. . . Perhaps . . . it somehow topped all the previous ones for sheer effrontery and deceit" (op. cit., p. 847).

PART TWO

From the Invasion
to the Battle of Moscow

Chapter I

SOVIET UNPREPAREDNESS IN JUNE 1941

In the early morning hours of June 22, 1941, Plan Barbarossa—on which Hitler and his generals had worked for the last six months—came into action. And the Russians were not prepared for the onslaught.

The three-pronged German invasion, aiming at Leningrad in the north, Moscow in the middle, and the Ukraine and the Caucasus in the south, with the ultimate object of occupying within a short time practically the whole of European Russia up to a line running from Archangel to Astrakhan, was to prove a failure. But the first weeks of the war and, indeed, the first three-and-a-half months were, to the Russians, an almost unmitigated disaster. The greater part of the Russian air force was wiped out in the first few days; the Russians lost thousands of tanks; hundreds of thousands, perhaps as many as a million Russian soldiers were taken prisoner in a series of spectacular encirclements during the first fortnight, and by the second week of July some German generals thought the war as good as won.

How was this possible? Stalin's interpretation of these initial disasters—which was to remain the official version for many years afterwards—was that the element of *surprise* had been overwhelmingly in the Germans' favour. No doubt, Stalin himself later admitted that "certain mistakes" had been made on the Russian side; but there was no mention of these "mistakes" at first, and the only explanation given in July was the "suddenness and perfidiousness" of the German attack.

This explanation did not entirely satisfy the Russian people at the time; they had been told so much for years about the tremendous might of the Red Army that the non-stop advance of the German steam-roller during the first three weeks of the war—to Smolensk, to the outskirts of Kiev and to only a short distance from Leningrad —came as a terrible shock. There was much questioning and heartsearching as to what had gone wrong. But, in the face of the fearful threat of the destruction of Russia, and despite much *sotto-voce* grumbling, this was not a time for recrimination, and, whatever had gone wrong, and whatever the mistakes that had been made, the only thing to do was to fight the invaders. The mystique of a great national war, of a life-and-death struggle took deep root in the Russians' consciousness within a very short time; and the "national war" motifs of Stalin's famous broadcast of July 3 made such a deep impression precisely because they expressed the thoughts which, in the tragic circumstances of the time, the Russian people—consciously or unconsciously—wanted to hear clearly stated. Here at last was a clear programme of action for a stunned and bewildered nation.

But the fact remains that at first Russia proved totally unprepared to meet the German onslaught, and that in October 1941 the Germans very nearly won the war.

While Stalin was alive, no serious attempt was made openly to analyse the numerous long-term, as well as immediate causes of the military disasters of 1941; and it was not, in fact, till after the 20th Congress of the CPSU (Communist Party of the Soviet Union) in 1956, and Khrushchev's sharp, and at times even exaggerated, criticisms of Stalin's "military genius" that Soviet military historians got down to the job of explaining what really happened.

The explanations given for the disasters of 1941 are numerous and touch on a very wide range of subjects. Among the principal long-term causes some were historical (e.g. the 1937 purges in the Red Army); some were psychological (the constant propaganda about the invincibility of the Red Army); some were professional (lack of any proper experience of war among the Red Army as compared with the Germans and, in many cases, a low standard of training); some, finally, were economic (the failure of the Soviet war industries, despite the breathing-space provided by the Soviet-German Pact, to turn the Red Army into a well-equipped modern army).

Whether, as seems likely, the Red Army would have been perfectly fit to fight the Germans in 1942, it was obviously not in a condition to do so in 1941.

One of the most important recent Russian publications, printed in 1960, is the first volume of the official *History of the War*. This explains with refreshing candour many of the things that went wrong in 1941. In particular, it deals in considerable detail with the bad psychological conditioning for the "next" war of both the Red Army and the Soviet people generally.

Thus, it draws particular attention to the wishful thinking pervading the famous *Draft Field Regulations* of 1939 which said:

> Any enemy attack on the Soviet Union will be met by a smashing blow from its armed forces;
>
> If any enemy inflicts war upon us, our Red Army will be the most fiercely-attacking army the world has ever known;
>
> We shall conduct the war offensively, and carry it into enemy territory;
>
> The activity of the Red Army will aim at the complete destruction of the enemy and the achievement of a decisive victory *at a small cost in blood*.

The present-day *History* strongly criticises this document, as well as other pieces of military doctrine current in the Red Army before 1941.

> Soviet strategic theory [it says] as propounded by the Draft Field Regulations of 1939 and other documents did not prove to be entirely realistic. For one thing, they denied the effectiveness of the *blitzkrieg* which tended to be dismissed as a lopsided bourgeois theory. Soviet military theory was largely based on the principle of ending any attack on the Soviet Union with the complete rout of the enemy on his own territory.

Thus, the whole emphasis of Soviet military theory was on the *offensive*, and the failure of both Poland and France to break the

German attack was, all too easily, attributed to a) the lack of organised resistance and b) the nefarious activities of "fifth columns" in the rear in the case of France, and to the lack of national homogeneity in the case of the Polish army.

> Soviet strategy (says the *History*) considered *defence* as an essential part of war, but stressed its subsidiary role in relation to offensive operations. In principle, our strategy considered a forced *retreat* as a possibility, but only on a limited and isolated part of the front, and as a temporary measure, connected with preparations for the offensive. *The question of large forces having to break out of a threatened encirclement was never seriously examined at all*... (Emphasis added.)

This makes, indeed, ironical reading in the light of what happened in 1941. There is another important point the *History* makes—namely, the "deadening" effect on Soviet military thought of the Stalin "personality cult":

> This "personality cult" led to dogmatism and scholasticism, which impaired the independent initiative of military research. It was necessary to wait for the instructions by a single man, and to look for the confirmation of theoretical propositions, not in life and practical experience, but in ready-made formulae and quotations... All this greatly reduced the scope of any free discussions of military theory.*

There were other shortcomings. The Red Army had had very little actual experience of war. Its only major experience dated back to the Civil War of 1918–20, and the conditions in which that war was fought had very little relevance to modern warfare. Experience was, indeed, soon to show that heroes of the Civil War like Budienny and Voroshilov were completely out of their depth in the war conditions of 1941. True, there had, since then, been the war in Spain, in which the Russians had participated in a small way, but, as the *History* says,

> The limited and peculiar nature of the war in Spain was wrongly interpreted. Thus, the conclusion was reached that the concept of large tank units—though we were the first to have applied them in practice—was erroneous. As a result our mechanised tank corps were dissolved, and did not begin to be reconstituted again until the very eve of the German invasion.†

* IVOVSS, vol. I, p. 439.   † Ibid.

There had also been, in 1938–9, the successful battles against the Japanese at Lake Hassan and Halkin Gol, but these again were different from the vast war of 1941. Certain bitter lessons, it is true, had been learned from the Winter War in Finland, but had not yet been sufficiently implemented. As for the German invasion of Poland and France, there was still an irresponsible tendency in the Red Army to imagine that "it couldn't happen here". At least not along a vast front.

This irresponsible optimism and wishful thinking were faithfully reflected in the "political-educational" work done in the Red Army in 1940–1. The *History* now readily admits that some appalling mistakes were made in this education, especially in all questions concerning Germany. Under the influence of the Soviet-Nazi Pact, anti-Nazi propaganda was toned down to an almost unbelievable extent. Nothing was done to suggest that the Germans were Russia's most likely enemies in the next war. Instead, the Molotov line continued to be plugged that it was in the "state interests" of both countries not to attack one another. Much of the propaganda both in the army and among the Soviet people generally was, in 1940 and even in 1941, full of the most infantile wishful thinking.

> On the eve of the War (says the *History*) great harm was done by suggesting that any enemy attacking the Soviet Union would be easily defeated. There were popular films such as *If War Comes Tomorrow* and the like which kept rubbing in the idea. . . Even some army papers followed a similar line. Many writers and propagandists put across the pernicious idea that any fascist or imperialist state that attacked us would collapse at the very first shots, since the workers would rebel against their government. They wholly underrated the extent to which, in fascist countries, the masses had been doped, how terror had largely silenced the rebels, and how soldiers, officers and their families had all acquired a vested interest in military loot.*

Nevertheless, even after the war had started, Molotov and Stalin still continued to distinguish between the "long-suffering" German people and the criminal Nazi clique!

Such, according to the *History*, were the main factors of the psychological unpreparedness of the Soviet people and of the Red

---

* IVOVSS, vol. I, pp. 434–5.

Army in 1941, on the eve of the German invasion. The picture, it must be said, is slightly exaggerated because, as will have been seen from our story of the Soviet-German Pact period, there was unquestionably in the country a growing uneasiness which, especially after the fall of Yugoslavia in April 1941, developed into real anxiety.

No less serious than this psychological unpreparedness for an all-out war against Nazi Germany was the military unpreparedness of the Red Army both as regards the actual training of the men and the quantity and especially the quality of their equipment.

A major question that arises in this connection is whether the Soviet Government really made full use of the twenty-two months' respite given it by the Soviet-German Pact. The argument put forward by present-day Soviet historians is that the Soviet Union had a very sound economic and industrial base in 1940–1, that "the importance of the defence measures taken during these twenty-two months cannot be overrated", but that the net result of it all was not as good as might have been expected. On the one hand it is true,

> Soviet economy had a material and technical base which would permit it to embark on the mass-production of all forms of modern armaments ... and meet the needs of both the Armed Forces and the population in case of war... The armaments industry, based on a heavy industry, was able, before the war, to supply the Army with all the necessary equipment, to set aside reserves, and fully supply new formations with equipment once the war had begun. With vast raw material resources, the Soviet Union was economically prepared to repel a fascist aggression.*

The Soviet Union had the largest engineering industry in Europe, and some 9,000 large new industrial enterprises had been set up under the three Five-Year Plans—1,500 under the first, 4,500 under the second, and 3,000 during the first three years of the third (that is, up to 1941). In 1940 she produced 18·3 million tons of steel, 31 million tons of oil and 166 million tons of coal—these production figures were, moreover, to be substantially increased in 1941. Military expenditure had represented only 12·7 per cent of the budget during the Second Five-Year Plan, but had, since the begin-

* IVOVSS, vol. I, p. 405.

ning of World War II, risen to 26·4 per cent, and, in 1941, "there was a further increase in connection with the technical re-equipment of the Army". Since September 1939, in particular, measures had been taken by the Party and the Government to increase in the next one-and-a-half to two years the productive capacity of certain armaments industries, and particularly of the aircraft industry, by at least 100 per cent.

But all this planning was one thing, and the actual results were quite another. These, as the *History* admits, were still extremely disappointing by the end of 1940; nor were they spectacular by any means by the middle of 1941, at the time of the German invasion.

> The new Soviet models—the Yak-1 and Mig-3 fighters and the Pe-2 bombers—began to be produced in 1940, but only in very small quantities. Thus only twenty Mig-3's, sixty-four Yak-1's and one or two Pe-2's were produced in 1940. The position improved somewhat in the first half of 1941, when 1,946 of the new fighter planes—the Mig-3's, Lagg-3's and Yak-1's—were produced, as well as 458 Pe-2 bombers and 249 Il-2 *stormoviks*.
>
> But these quantities were totally insufficient to increase substantially the proportion of modern planes in the army, and, by June 1941, the great majority of army planes consisted of obsolete models.*

The performance of the tank industry was no better. In June 1941 the Red Army had a very large number of tanks, but nearly all of these, too, were obsolete.

The new tanks, the KV and the T-34—which were later to prove more than a match for the German tanks—were not yet in production in 1939; in 1940 only 243 KV tanks and 115 T-34 tanks were produced; not till the first half of 1941 was there an impressive increase; during that period 393 KV's and 1,110 T-34's came off the assembly line.

Similarly, the production of guns, mortars and automatic weapons proceeded at "an intolerably slow pace". For this the Deputy Commissars for Defence, G. I. Kulik, L. Z. Mekhlis and A. E. Shchadenko are blamed; Kulik, in particular, is taken to task for having neglected the production of automatic rifles, the value of

* IVOVSS, vol. I, p. 415.

which he persisted in denying, and the lack of which was to put the Russian infantryman at a great disadvantage. The production of ammunition in 1941 was lagging behind even that of the guns. Although the first special anti-tank rifles were made in Russia in 1940–1, these had not yet been supplied to the Army by the beginning of the war.*

Another very serious weakness of the Red Army was the absence of a large-scale automobile industry in the Soviet Union; in June 1941 the Soviet Union had a total of only 800,000 motor vehicles, and a large proportion of guns had to be drawn either by horses or by wholly inadequate farm tractors.

On the other hand Russian artillery is estimated by Russian experts to have been better than German artillery; jet rockets, first used in the Finnish War, began to be produced on a large scale in 1940–1, and Kostikov's famous *katyusha* mortars were extremely popular with the Red Army almost from the very beginning. They first came into action at Smolensk about the middle of July.

Radar was still in its infancy in the Red Army, and even ordinary wireless communications between army units were not the general rule. "Even the minimum requirements were not fulfilled in this respect. As a result a lot of obsolete material was used. Many officers did not know how to handle wireless communications . . . and preferred the old-fashioned telephone."†

In a highly mobile war this often proved quite useless.

This is just one example in many of the widespread professional inferiority of the Russian soldier and officer as compared with their German opposite numbers in 1941, and it was, in fact, not till 1943 that, in the estimation of the Russian military leaders themselves, the Russian soldier and officer became professionally as competent as the German, if not more so.

Very few officers or soldiers in 1941 had had any direct experience of war, and many of them were novices who had only lately been trained as "replacements" for the thousands of officers who had been purged back in 1937 and 1938. Although the officer's "single command" had been re-introduced in August 1940 through the eclipse of military commissars, an uneasy relationship continued

* Ibid., p. 416.   † Ibid., p. 455.

to exist between many officers and those Party and Komsomol
cadres in the Army which were expected to go on "helping" the
officers; and, in July, the fully-fledged military commissars were re-
introduced again. Although (in July 1940) fifty-four per cent of
officers were Party members or Party candidates and twenty-two
per cent were Komsomols, there remained, among the officers, a
constant after-taste of the Tukhachevsky affair, and a feeling of
strain between them and certain Party bosses in the army with their
anti-officer complex. It was not till the autumn of 1942, as we shall
see, that the officer fully came into his own rights.

The training of specialised troops—notably tank crews and airmen—had also been seriously neglected. There are some quite
astounding admissions on this score in the official *History*. Not only
was there a shortage of modern tanks and planes in the frontier
areas on the day the Germans struck, but there was also a serious
shortage of properly trained airmen and tank crews:

> The new tanks did not begin to arrive in the frontier zones until
> April–May 1941, and, on June 22, in all the five Military Districts, there
> were no more than 508 KV's and 967 T-34's in all. True, there were
> considerable numbers of old tanks (BT-5's, BT-7's, T-26's, etc.) but
> by June 15, only twenty-seven per cent were in working order.

Worse still—

> The training of specialists for the new tanks required a considerable
> time. Since there was a shortage of tank crews, it was necessary to
> transfer to the tank units officers, sergeants and soldiers from other
> army formations—from infantry and cavalry units. But time was too
> short to let these learn their job properly. By the beginning of the war,
> many tank men had had only one-and-a-half to two hours' experience
> in actual tank driving. Even many officers in tank units were not fully
> qualified to command them... Similarly, our airmen had not become
> properly familiarised with the new planes.*

Thus, in the Baltic Military District those operating the new
planes had had, by June 22, only fifteen hours' flying experience,
and those in the Kiev Military District as little as four hours—
extraordinary figures when one considers that in the US air force, for
instance, 150 hours' flying experience are required before combat.

* IVOVSS, vol. I, pp. 475–6.

Such were some of the extraordinary shortcomings in the Red
Army on the day the Germans attacked. There were many others,
with which the *History* deals in some detail.

The frontier was an extremely long one—the Finnish frontier,
between the Arctic and the Gulf of Finland about 750 miles long,
and the "German" frontier, between a point just east of Memel on
the Baltic and the mouth of the Danube in Rumania, over 1,250
miles long.

No doubt the Soviet Government took a few belated precautions
in May 1941; but the troops that were moved nearer the frontier
"were neither fully mobilised nor at full strength, and they lacked
the necessary transport. The railways worked according to a peace-
time schedule, and the whole deployment of these troops was carried
out very slowly, since it was not thought that the war would start in
the immediate future."

> By June 22, most of the troops in the frontier areas were scattered
> over wide spaces. In the Special Baltic Military District they were
> scattered over a depth of 190 miles from the frontier; in the Western
> District over a depth of 60 to 190 miles, in the Kiev District over a
> depth of between 250 and 380 miles.

The General Staff of the USSR assumed that these troops would
be brought up to full strength during several days that would elapse
between mobilisation and the actual beginning of military operations.

> The whole defence of the State frontier was based on the assumption
> that a surprise attack by Germany was out of the question, and that a
> powerful German offensive would be preceded by a declaration of
> war, or by small-scale military operations, after which the Soviet
> troops could take up their defensive positions... No operational or
> tactical army groups had been formed to repel a surprise attack.*

The *History* goes on to quote a table showing that in the main
invasion areas the Germans had a clear four or five-to-one superiority
over the Russians; but, in addition to this numerical superiority, they
also enjoyed great qualitative superiority, many of the Soviet
soldiers in the frontier areas being fresh conscripts—youngsters
without any knowledge or experience.

* IVOVSS, vol. I, p. 474.

There was also, as already mentioned, an appalling shortage of modern tanks on the Russian side, and of properly trained tank crews. The equipment of the frontier troops, says the *History*, "was not to be completed until the end of 1941 or the beginning of 1942".

Even grimmer is the story of how the modern Russian planes in the western areas were destroyed, mostly on the very first day of the invasion.

The fast new planes required longer runways than had existed before; and it so happened that in the summer of 1941 a whole network of new airfields was being built in the frontier zones. This building of new airfields and the reconstruction of the old ones was in the hands of the NKVD. And here comes, in the *History*, the suggestion of perhaps deliberate sabotage on the part of Beria's organisation. Taking no notice of the warnings from the military, Beria proceeded to build and rebuild a large number of airfields in the frontier areas simultaneously.*

> As a result, our fighter aircraft were concentrated, on June 22, on a very limited number of airfields, which prevented their proper camouflage, manœuvrability and dispersal. Also, some of the new airfields ... had been built much too close to the frontier, which made them specially vulnerable in the event of a surprise attack. The absence of a proper network of airfields on June 22 and the overcrowding of a small number of the older airfields—the location of which was perfectly well known to the enemy—account for the very grave losses our air force suffered during the very first days of the war.†

Everything else at the frontier went wrong on that 22nd of June. The carrying capacity of the railways in the frontier areas—all acquired since 1939—was three or four times lower on the Russian side than on the German side. Also, the building of fortifications along the "new" borders was only at an initial stage in June 1941. A plan had been drawn up in the summer of 1940 for fortifying this border, but it was a plan stretching over several years. The fortifi-

* In reality, there appears to be no "objective" proof that Beria was a traitor or a German agent, but he has always been available when in recent years awkward facts have had to be explained. This footnote should not suggest that the author has ever had any kindly feelings for Beria.
† IVOVSS, vol. I, pp. 476–7.

cations on the "old" (1938) border had been dismantled, and, on the "new" frontier only a few hundred pillboxes and gun emplacements had been built by the time the war started. Anti-tank ditches and other anti-tank and anti-infantry obstacles had been built to the extent of less than twenty-five per cent of the plan. The Germans were, of course, very well informed about these fortifications, airfields, etc. The *History* mentions not only numerous German commando raids that had taken place since 1939, but also the more than 500 violations of Soviet airspace by the Luftwaffe, 152 of them since January 1941. To avoid any unpleasantness with Hitler, the frontier troops, according to the *History*, had been given strict orders not to shoot down any German reconnaissance planes over Soviet territory.*

A significant conclusion made by the *History* is that the Soviet General Staff had some perfectly sound plans for "making the frontier much less vulnerable by the end of 1941 or the beginning of 1942", but that, in view of the German menace in 1941, everything had been done "too slowly and too late". And there follows the assertion that neither the General Staff, nor the Commissariat of Defence would have shown such incompetence "if there had not been those wholly unjustified repressions against the leading officers and political cadres of the Army in the 1937–8 Purge".

This reference to Tukhachevsky and the other victims of the Purge is, of course, a monumental understatement when one considers that perhaps as many as 15,000 officers—probably about ten or fifteen per cent of the total, but with a higher proportion of purgees in the higher ranks—were either temporarily, or finally eliminated. Among those temporarily eliminated were such distinguished soldiers as the future Marshals Govorov and Rokossovsky.

The mess and muddle on the Russian side of the frontier was, of course, in striking contrast with what was going on on the German side. Here, since the middle of 1940, i.e. even before Plan Barbarossa had been finally adopted on December 18, the Germans had been thoroughly preparing their ground for a possible attack on the Soviet

* *The History* actually attributes this order not to Stalin or Molotov, but to "traitor Beria" who had the frontier guards under his jurisdiction.

Union. Roads, including *autobahnen*, railways and a large network of airfields had been built during the year preceding the invasion; during that period the Germans had built or modernised no fewer than 250 airfields and fifty landing strips in Poland for their deadly Heinkels, Dorniers and Messerschmitts.

In the words of a German chronicler, "millions of German soldiers broke into Russia in June 1941, without enthusiasm, but with a quiet confidence in victory".*

* Philippi and Heim, *Der Feldzug gegen Sowjetrussland* (The Campaign against Soviet Russia) (Stuttgart, 1962), p. 11.

Chapter II

THE INVASION

And now began for the Russian people *l'année terrible*—the most
terrible it had ever known. In a matter of a few days and weeks
death and destruction swept over vast parts of the country. In the
frontier zones, and, indeed, much further inland, the concentrated
German onslaught smashed, captured or wholly disorganised the
Red Army units facing it; the Soviet air force was as good as wiped
out in the western areas on the very first day of the German
invasion; within five days the German forces had already captured
Minsk, the capital of Belorussia, well within the Soviet Union's 1938
borders; nor did it take much longer for the German armies to
occupy all the areas incorporated by the Soviet Union since 1939—
Western Belorussia, the Western Ukraine, Lithuania, Latvia and
Estonia. In the north, the Finns smashed through to the old 1939
border just north-west of Leningrad. By July 8, the Germans were
already crowing that the war in Russia was "practically" won.

There is no doubt that Russia was dazed by these terrible initial
reverses, and yet, almost from the first day, it was clear that it was a
*national war.** A feeling of consternation swept the country, but it

* This was something that was understood by the best foreign
observers of Russia. Thus a few days before I left London for Russia
on July 2, 1941, I had a long talk with the late Sir Bernard Pares
who said: "I can already see it's going to be a tremendous national
war, a bigger and better 1812." Similarly, at the end of June,

144

was combined with an under-current of national defiance and the apprehension that it would be a long, hard and desperate struggle.

Everybody realised that millions of lives would be lost, and yet only very few people seem to have visualised the possibility of utter military defeat and a total conquest of Russia by the Germans. In this respect the contrast with France during the German invasion of 1940 is very striking.

This fundamental confidence was characteristic of the attitude of the Russian people and of the large majority of the Ukrainians and Belorussians; it did not exist in Lithuania, Latvia, Estonia, or in the Western Ukraine, where pro-Nazi and other anti-Soviet influences were strong. In these areas the German invasion was either welcomed or suffered with relative indifference.*

The hostility with which the Russians were surrounded in parts of the Western Ukraine only recently incorporated in the Soviet Union, is well illustrated in the memoirs of General Fedyuninsky, who tells of how, in May 1941, his car broke down in a village near Kovel:

> There gathered around us a crowd of about twenty people. No one was saying anything. Some, especially the better-dressed ones, smirked maliciously at us. No one offered to help. No doubt, there were among them some poor people, who sympathised with us, who had received land from the Soviet authorities, and who were later to fight bravely in the Red Army or in Partisan units. But now they were silent, frightened by rumours of an early arrival of the Nazis and by threats from the kulaks and the Bandera boys.†

*

G. Bernard Shaw wrote in a letter to *The Times* that, with Stalin now on our side, we were sure to win the war. On the other hand, British military experts at War Office or Ministry of Information briefings very clearly suggested that they did not think the war in Russia would last more than a few weeks or, at most, months.

* B. S. Telpukhovsky, *Velikaya otechestvennaya voina Sovietskogo Soyuza, 1941–5.* (The Great Patriotic War of the Soviet Union). (Moscow, 1959), p. 39.

† General I. I. Fedyuninsky, *Podnyatyie po trevoge* (Raised by the Alarm). (Ministry of Defence Publishing House, Moscow, 1961). Bandera was a "Ukrainian Nationalist" who later openly collaborated with the Nazis.

What were the first days of the war like in the frontier areas invaded by the Germans? The memoirs of some of the Russian soldiers published in the last few years, especially those of General Fedyuninsky and of General Boldin, give a striking picture of those events.*

In April 1941 Fedyuninsky (who was later to play a distinguished role in the war—especially in breaking the Leningrad blockade) was appointed commander of the 15th Infantry Corps of the Special Kiev Military District, with his headquarters in the West-Ukrainian town of Kovel, some thirty miles east of the border between the Soviet Union and German-occupied Poland, and on the main line to Kiev.

> At the time of my arrival in Kovel, the situation on our Western frontier was becoming more and more tense. From a great variety of sources, and from our army and frontier-guard reconnaissance, we knew that since February German troops had begun to concentrate along our borders... Violations of our air-space had been on the increase in recent months... At that time we did not yet know that Stalin, disregarding the reports of our intelligence and of the commanders of our frontier districts, had badly misjudged the international situation and particularly the timing of the Nazi aggression.

The general found that the troops in the frontier areas were still on a peace footing and that the reorganisation was proceeding very slowly. The new planes and tanks which were to replace the obsolete models were arriving only at a very slow pace. The older officers, including some who had served in the Tsarist army, took a serious view of the coming war, but among the younger soldiers and officers, there was a good deal of deplorable complacency.

> Many of them thought that our Army could win an easy victory and that the soldiers of any capitalist country, including Nazi Germany, would not fight actively against the Red Army. They also underrated the military experience and the enormous technical equipment of the German Army. When the showdown came, the might of the German Army came as a complete surprise to some of our officers.

* General Fedyuninsky, op. cit., General I. V. Boldin, *Stranitsy Zhizni* (Pages from my Life). (Ministry of Defence Publishing House, Moscow, 1961).

Although the famous TASS communiqué of June 14 dismissed the rumours of Germany's aggressive intentions as "completely groundless", Fedyuninsky reiterates that "it was completely contrary to what we were able to observe in the frontier areas", and he tells the story of how, on June 18, a German deserter came over to the Russians. While drunk, he had hit an officer, and was afraid of being court-martialled and shot; he also claimed that his father was a communist. This German soldier declared that the German Army was going to invade Russia at 4 a.m. on June 22.

Fedyuninsky promptly 'phoned the local army commander, Tank General Potapov, but was told that the whole thing must be "a provocation", and that "it was no use getting into a panic about such nonsense". Two days later Fedyuninsky was visited by General Rokossovsky, who did not share Potapov's complacency, and seemed extremely agitated. In the early hours of June 22, Fedyuninsky was called over the telephone by Potapov, who ordered that the troops be ready for any emergency, but added that ammunition had not yet been distributed.

I had the impression that at Army Headquarters, they were still not quite sure that the Nazis had started a war.

The 15th Infantry Corps was expected to hold a line about sixty miles wide.

We had to deploy our forces and occupy our defensive positions under constant shelling and air bombing. Communications were often broken and combat orders often reached the units with great delay... Nevertheless, our officers did not lose control, and we reached the defensive positions where the frontier guards had already, for several hours, been waging an unequal struggle. Even the wives of the frontier guards were in the firing line, carrying water and ammunition, and taking care of the wounded. Some of the women were firing at the advancing Nazis... But the ranks of the frontier guards were melting away. Everywhere barracks and houses, set on fire by enemy shells, were blazing. The frontier guards were fighting to the last man; they knew that, in that misty dawn of June 22, troops were speeding to their rescue.

Throughout that first day, Fedyuninsky's troops withstood the German onslaught, but the Germans threw in more and more new forces, and towards the evening, the Russians, having suffered very

heavy losses, began to withdraw. The situation was further complicated by German paratroop landings in the Russian rear, as well as
by numerous false reports of other paratroop landings spread by
"enemy agents". In Kovel the Bandera gangs, acting as a German
fifth column, were causing havoc—attacking Russian army cars,
blowing up bridges, and spreading these false reports. As large
German armoured forces were approaching Kovel from the north-
west, along the Brest-Kovel road, it was decided to evacuate Kovel.
Parts of the 15th Infantry Corps continued to fight, while already
encircled by the Germans. Even so, in three days' fighting, the main
forces of the Corps had been pushed back only some twelve to
twenty miles from the frontier. Nevertheless, Kovel had to be abandoned, and new defensive positions to be taken up further east. But
before evacuating Kovel, the wounded and the families of army
officers had to be evacuated.

> Most officers' wives, used to frequent journeys, took only the bare
> essentials with them. But some lost their heads, and would take to the
> railway station things like prams, mirrors and even flower-pots...
> Those in charge of the evacuation had quite a job to bring these people
> to their senses...

The retreat was typical of so many similar retreats in June 1941.
The Germans had complete control of the air, and losses from
strafing were heavy; moreover saboteurs did their best to harass the
Russian retreat by blowing up bridges.

> Railway junctions and lines of communication were being des-
> troyed by German planes and diversionist groups. There was a
> shortage of wireless sets at army headquarters, nor did many of us
> know how to use them... Orders and instructions were slow in
> arriving, and sometimes did not arrive at all... The liaison with
> neighbouring units was often completely absent, while nobody tried
> to establish it. Taking advantage of this, the enemy would often pene-
> trate into our rear, and attack the Soviet headquarters... Despite
> German air supremacy, our marching columns did not use any proper
> camouflage. Sometimes on narrow roads, bottlenecks were formed by
> troops, artillery, motor vehicles and field kitchens, and then the Nazi
> planes had the time of their life... Often our troops could not dig in,
> simply because they did not even have the simplest implements.
> Occasionally trenches had to be dug with helmets, since there were no
> spades...

Yet despite the terrible losses suffered by the Russians, morale remained reasonably high. "It would, of course," says Fedyuninsky, "be wrong to deny that there were cases of 'nerves' or cowardice, but they were rather unusual, and rapidly overcome by the steadfastness shown by the majority of the soldiers, whose morale was sustained by the Party."

How heavy the losses were could be judged from a regiment Fedyuninsky reviewed one day: "It was now no larger than a peacetime infantry battalion."

It is curious how, after telling this desperate story of the 15th Infantry Corps retreat, and the story of the two regiments who broke out of a German encirclement after eight days' heavy fighting, Fedyuninsky then dwells on the effect on the troops of Stalin's famous broadcast of July 3.

> It is hard to describe the enormous enthusiasm and patriotic uplift with which this appeal was met. We suddenly seemed to feel much stronger. When circumstances permitted, short meetings would be held by the army units. To platoons and companies political instructors would explain the position at the Front, and tell them how, in response to the Party's appeal, the whole Soviet people were rising like one man to fight the holy Fatherland war. They stressed that the war would be very hard, and that many ordeals, privations and sacrifices were yet ahead, but that the Nazis would never defeat our powerful and hard-working people.

But the retreat continued, and by July 8 Fedyuninsky's troops had withdrawn to the Korosten fortified line in the Ukraine, already well inside the "old" borders of the Soviet Union. On August 12, after a further retreat towards Kiev, Fedyuninsky was summoned to Moscow, and ordered by General Vassilevsky to fly immediately to Leningrad, where the situation was becoming even more serious than in the south.

More dramatic and tragic still than Fedyuninsky's story of the first days of the war is that of General Boldin who, in the winter of 1941, was to become famous as the commander responsible for the defence of Tula.

He heard of the imminence of a German invasion on the evening
of June 21, while attending, with other officers, the performance of a
Korneichuk comedy at the Army Officers' club at Minsk.

Suddenly Colonel Blokhin, head of the intelligence department of
our special Western Military District, appeared in our box and leaning
over the shoulder of our commander, Army General Pavlov, whispered
something in his ear. "It can't be true," Pavlov said...
Turning to me, he said: "Seems nonsense to me. Our reconnaissance
reports that things are looking very alarming at the frontier. The
German troops are supposed to be ready for action—and even to have
shelled some of our positions." Then he touched my hand, and pointed
at the stage, suggesting we had better go on watching the play...

The play no longer meant anything to Boldin; he began to brood
about the alarming news that had been coming in for the last few
days—for instance, the news from Grodno on June 20 that the
Germans had taken down the barbed-wire entanglements barring
the Avgustov-Seini main road, that the rumbling of countless engines
could be heard that day from across the border, and that several
reconnaissance planes, some of them carrying bombs, had violated
Russian air space.

On the 21st, there had been reports of heavy German troop concentrations at various points, complete with heavy and medium
tanks. He was puzzled by the Army commander's "Olympian
calm"...

This calm did not last long. In the early hours of the morning,
Boldin received an agitated 'phone call from Pavlov, asking him to
come to Headquarters immediately.

Ten minutes later he was there.

"What's happened?" I said.
"Can't quite make out," said Pavlov, "some kind of devilry going
on. General Kuznetsov 'phoned from Grodno a few minutes ago. Said
the Germans had crossed the border along a wide front and were
bombing Grodno, with its army headquarters. Telephone communications have been smashed, the army units have had to change over to
radio. Two wireless stations are already out of action, must have been
destroyed... There have also been calls from Golubev of the 10th

Army and Colonel Sandalov of the 4th. Most unpleasant news. The Germans are bombing everywhere."

Our conversation was interrupted by a call from Moscow: it was Marshal Timoshenko, the Commissar of Defence, who wanted Pavlov to report on the situation... Soon Kuznetsov 'phoned again to say that the Germans were continuing their air attacks. Along thirty miles all the telephone and telegraph lines were down. Liaison between many units had been broken... During the next half-hour more and more news came in. The bombing was growing in intensity. They were bombing Belostok and Grodno, Lida, Brest, Volkovysk, Slonim and other Belorussian towns. Here and there, there had been German paratroop landings. Many of our planes had been destroyed on the ground, and the Luftwaffe were now strafing troops and citizens. The Germans had already occupied dozens of localities, and were pushing inland...

Then came another 'phone call from Timoshenko, who said:

"Comrade Boldin, remember that no action is to be taken against the Germans without our knowledge. Will you please tell Pavlov that Comrade Stalin has forbidden to open artillery fire against the Germans."

"But how is that possible?" I yelled into the receiver. "Our troops are in full retreat. Whole towns are in flames, people are being killed all over the place..."

"No," said Timoshenko, "there is to be no air reconnaissance more than thirty-five miles beyond the frontier."

I argued that since the Nazis had knocked out practically all our front-line air force, this was impossible anyway, and insisted that we throw in the full weight of our infantry, artillery and armour, and especially our anti-aircraft guns. But Timoshenko still said No;—only reconnaissance of not more than thirty-five miles inside enemy territory...

It was not till some time later that Moscow ordered us to put into action the "Red Packet", i.e. the plan for covering the State frontier. But this order came too late... The Germans had already engaged in full-scale military operations, and had, in several places, penetrated deep into our territory.

A few hours later, with Timoshenko's permission, Boldin flew to Belostok. His plane was hit by twenty bullets from a Messerschmitt, but nevertheless managed to land on an airfield twenty miles east of the city. A few minutes later nine German planes appeared over the airfield and dropped their bombs, without any interference; there were no anti-aircraft guns on that airfield. Several cars and Boldin's plane were destroyed.

Every minute counted. We had to get to the 10th Army Headquarters. There were no cars at the airfield, so I took a small truck, and together with some officers and a number of soldiers—twelve people in all—we got into it. I took the seat next to the driver, and told him to drive to Belostok.

"It's dangerous, Comrade General," he said, "twenty minutes before you landed, there was a German paratroop landing; so the commander of the airfield told me."

An unpleasant bit of news, but it couldn't be helped. It was incredibly hot, and the air smelt of burning...

At last we reached the Belostok main road. Through the windscreen I could see fifteen German bombers approaching from the west. They were flying low, with provocative insolence, as though our sky belonged to them. On their fuselages I could clearly see the spiders of the Nazi swastika.

On the way, Boldin stopped a crowd of workers wandering in the opposite direction.

"Where are you going?" I asked.

"To Volkovysk," they said.

"Who are you?"

"We had been working on fortifications. But the place where we worked is now like a sea of flames," said an elderly man with an exhausted look on his face.

These people seemed to have lost their heads, not knowing where they were going and why.

Then we met a few cars, led by a Zis-101. The broad leaves of an aspidistra were protruding from one of the windows. It was the car of some local top official. Inside were two women and two children.

"Surely," I said, "at a time like this you might have more important things to transport than your aspidistra. You might have taken some old people or children." With their heads bent, the women were silent. The driver, too, turned away, feeling ashamed.

And then came the German strafing.

Three volleys of machine-gun fire hit our truck. The driver was killed. I managed to survive, as I jumped out just in time. But with the exception of my A.D.C. and a dispatch rider, all were killed...

Nearby, I noticed the same old Zis-101. I went up to it. The women, the children, the driver were all killed... Only the evergreen leaves of the aspidistra were still sticking out of the window.

Horror piled upon horror that day. Belostok was in a complete state of chaos, at the railway station a train packed with women and children evacuees was bombed, and hundreds were killed.

At last, towards evening, Boldin reached the Headquarters of the 10th Army which had moved out of Belostok to a little wood some distance outside the city. It consisted of two tents, with a table and a few chairs. General Golubev was there, with a number of staff officers. He had been unable to communicate with the Front (i.e. Army Group) Headquarters as the telephone lines had been destroyed, and radio communications were being constantly jammed by the enemy. Golubev told Boldin:

> "At daybreak three German army corps, supported by masses of tanks and bombers, attacked my 5th infantry corps on my left flank. During the first hours, all divisions suffered very heavy losses..."

His face and voice showed that he was deeply shaken. Having asked my permission to light a cigarette, he unfolded a map:

> "To prevent our being outflanked in the south, I deployed the 13th mechanised corps along the river Kuretz, but as you know, Ivan Vasilievich, there are very few tanks in our divisions. And what can you expect from those old T26 tanks—only good enough for firing at sparrows..."

From his further report it emerged that both the aircraft and the anti-aircraft guns of the army corps had been smashed, and that spies had apparently informed the Germans where the army's fuel dumps were, for during the very first hours of the invasion, these had all been destroyed by bombing.

Then General Nikitin, commander of the 6th cavalry corps, arrived and reported how his men, after successfully repelling the first German attacks, had been almost wholly exterminated by German aircraft. The remnants of the cavalry corps had been concentrated in a wood north-east of Belostok.

Looking up from the map, General Golubev said:

> "It's hard, very hard, Ivan Vasilievich. My men are fighting like heroes. But what can you do against a tank or a plane? Where there

is any chance of clinging to something we hold on; we fight back from any strong position, and the enemy cannot dislodge us. But there are few such positions, and the Nazis drive their wedges forward, they avoid frontal attacks, they get round us; they gain both time and space. The frontier guards, too, are fighting well, but few of them are left and we have no means of supporting them. And so the Nazis advance, insolently, marching upright, behaving like conquerors. And that's on the very first day of the war! What'll happen after that?"

At that very moment communications with Minsk were re-established, and General Pavlov proceeded to give Boldin peremptory orders about the counter-offensive the 10th Army was to carry out that night. Boldin objected, pointing out that the 10th Army had been as good as wiped out. For a moment Pavlov seemed to hesitate, and then said: "These are my orders. It's for you to carry them out."

What, Boldin reflected, was the meaning of these totally un-realistic orders? And he related that, long after the war, he discovered that men like Pavlov used to issue such orders, "merely for the record, to show Moscow that something was being done to stop the Germans".*

The rest of this tragic chapter in Boldin's book deals with the attempts, during the 23rd, to mount a counter-offensive with the remnants of the 10th Army, some other units and the armoured corps under General Hatskilevich, which was still in comparatively good shape. But all day long the troops and the army headquarters were being attacked by enemy aircraft. One general was killed, and although Hatskilevich's tank crews fought bravely, they were begin-ning to run out of fuel. Boldin, unable to contact the Front headquarters, sent two planes to Minsk, begging for fuel to be flown to the headquarters of the 10th Army. But both planes were shot down.

---

* Boldin does not mention the fact that Pavlov was, soon afterwards, to be shot for his incompetence—or as a scapegoat. Pavlov is also mentioned in Ehrenburg's memoirs as one of the Russian generals he met in 1937 in Spain. He also refers to Pavlov's tragic end in 1941.

It was in this desperate situation that Marshal Kulik* suddenly arrived from Moscow.

He listened to my explanations, then made a vague gesture, and mumbled: "Yes, I see..." It was quite obvious that, when leaving Moscow, he had no idea that the situation was as serious as this. Soon afterwards, the Marshal left our command post. When saying good-bye, he said he would see what he could do.

As I watched his car driving away, I wondered what he had come for... I had known him as a man of energy and will-power, but now his nerves seemed to have given way. General Nikitin seemed to think so, too. When the car had disappeared in a cloud of dust, he remarked: "A strange visit"...

A few minutes later Hatskilevich arrived. He was in a state of great agitation. "We are firing our last shells. Once we've done that, we shall have to destroy the tanks."

"Yes," I said, "I don't see what else we can do."

Within a few hours, General Hatskilevich died a hero's death on the field of battle.

Surrounded on all sides—like the other troops in the famous "Belostok Pocket"—without ammunition, the generals, officers and soldiers under Boldin split into small groups, and started moving east, hoping for the best... Boldin's small group of men, who picked up more and more soldiers in the woods in the course of their forty-five days' trek—in the end there were 2,000 of them—finally managed to cross the front near Smolensk and to join the main Russian forces.

There were countless other units who did not have Boldin's good luck, and who were either wiped out by the Germans, or forced to surrender. Boldin admits that, during the first few days of the trek, the morale among some of his own soldiers was low, especially as a result of German leaflets saying: "Moscow has surrendered. Any further resistance is useless. Surrender to victorious Germany now." Yet most of them were not desperate, but angry.

*

* Kulik was a "Stalinist" upstart who had risen to the top of the Army hierarchy since the 1937 Purge. Little more was to be heard of him after the beginning of the war.

The first-hand accounts of Generals Fedyuninsky and Boldin confirm that Stalin and the Army High Command still seemed, even at the twelfth hour, to have hoped to avoid the war. It was not until the night of the invasion that urgent directives were sent out to the army secretly to man the gun emplacements along the frontier; to disperse the aircraft concentrated on the frontier-zone airfields, and to get the troops and anti-aircraft defences into a state of military preparedness. No other measures were prescribed and even these orders came too late.

Thus General Purkayev recalls that when he started moving his troops to the frontier, the war had already begun several hours before. Another commander, Army-General Popov, recalls that when the Germans started their air raids on Brest-Litovsk it all came as a complete surprise. A regiment which was rushed to the frontier from Riga was intercepted by superior German forces advancing north and practically exterminated.

The official Soviet *History* admits that in many frontier areas the Germans broke all resistance within a short time. Many troops went into battle completely unprepared and the Germans had little difficulty in breaking through the frontier defences. The Soviet air force was almost wiped out over large areas. During the first days of the war German bombers raided sixty-six airfields, especially those where the most modern planes were concentrated. Before noon, on June 22, 1,200 planes were destroyed, 800 of them on the ground. The Central Sector suffered the heaviest casualties of all—528 planes were destroyed on the ground and 210 in the air.

There were practically no reserves in the frontier areas; telephone and telegraph communications were disrupted in the very first hours of the war; army units lost contact with each other; some front commanders lacked the necessary operational and strategic training, and the experience required for the command of large operational forces in war conditions. Throughout the day the Soviet General Staff was unable to gain a clear idea of what was happening.*

Issued at 7.15 a.m. on June 22, the first directive of the General Staff to the frontier troops reflects their ignorance of the true situation and, seen in retrospect, has the ring of bitter travesty:

* IVOVSS, vol. II, pp. 20 and 28–29.

1) Our troops are to attack enemy forces with all the strength and means at their disposal, and to annihilate them wherever they have violated the Soviet border.
2) Our reconnaissance and combat aircraft shall ascertain where enemy aircraft and land-forces are concentrated. By striking mighty blows our aircraft are to smash the main enemy troop concentrations and their aircraft on its airfields. These blows are to be struck anywhere within sixty to a hundred miles of German territory. Memel and Königsberg are to be heavily bombed. Until further notice, no air attacks are to be made on Finnish or Rumanian territory.

This order, given after the Soviet air force had already been practically eliminated, could, naturally, not be carried out. By the end of June 22, the left flank of the German Army Group Centre had already advanced far beyond Kaunas, where it had routed the Russian 11th Army, now in disorderly retreat from Kaunas to Vilno.

No doubt, here and there, the Russians were able to hang on, as for instance the garrison of the Citadel at Brest-Litovsk, which, although surrounded on all sides and constantly bombed and shelled, held out for over a month, till July 24. When the Germans finally captured the Citadel, most of its defenders were dead or severely wounded. The main German forces in the area, however, by-passed Brest-Litovsk and pushed thirty-five miles east on the very first day of the war.

The first official communiqué, published at 10 p.m. on June 22, was probably intended to prevent panic or bewilderment among the Soviet population:

> In the course of the day, regular German troops fought our frontier troops and achieved minor successes in a number of sectors. In the afternoon, with advance field forces of the Red Army arriving at the frontier, the attacks of the German groups have been repelled along most of the frontier with heavy losses to the enemy.

That the General Staff itself had no very clear idea of what was happening on the first day of the war is confirmed by the second directive given to the troops in the frontier area. The South-Western Army Group was to start, on the very next day, a major offensive, which would lead, by the end of June 24, to the capture of Lublin, some thirty miles beyond the Soviet border! The North-Western

Army Group was at the same time to capture Suvalki, and all three Army Groups were, moreover, ordered to surround any German forces that had penetrated into Soviet territory.

Absurd though the order was, a pathetic attempt was made to carry it out; in a number of places the Russians succeeded in concentrating what tanks they still had in the frontier areas; but, in the absence of air support they were wiped out by German bombers.

The German advance continued almost without a hitch. Large Russian forces were trapped in the Belostok pocket and eleven divisions in the Minsk area. By June 28 the Germans had already reached the city of Minsk, were pushing deep into the Baltic Republics and were approaching Pskov, on the straight line to Leningrad.

A few days later the remnants of sixteen Russian divisions were facing two powerful German tank formations along the Berezina, and under these conditions it was unthinkable to form a new 220 miles long defence line; some delaying actions were, however, fought with great gallantry by the Russians, notably east of Minsk, at Borisov, where they threw in a large number of tanks, though most of them obsolete. These delaying actions to some extent helped to gain time in which to bring up reserves and organise a defence in depth in what already came to be known as the "Smolensk-Moscow direction".

Some minor delaying actions were also fought, with suicidal bravery, against the German Army Group South. Held up in the Rovno area and unable to pursue their advance towards Kiev, the Germans turned north and got bogged down for some time in what were described as "battles of local importance". But by July 9, the Germans had broken through to Zhitomir, which was captured, and were threatening to break through to Kiev and to encircle the main Russian forces in the Northern Ukraine. But here again, at Berdichev, the Russians threw in some armour and there was heavy fighting around Berdichev for almost a week.

Chapter III

MOLOTOV AND STALIN SPEAK

It was not until several hours after the Germans had invaded the Soviet Union that an official announcement was made over the radio by Foreign Commissar Molotov. "Men and women, citizens of the Soviet Union," he began in a faltering, slightly stuttery voice. "The Soviet Government and its head, Comrade Stalin, have instructed me to make the following statement:

> At four o'clock this morning, without declaration of war, and without any claims being made on the Soviet Union, German troops attacked our country, attacked our frontier in many places, and bombed from the air Zhitomir, Kiev, Sebastopol, Kaunas and some other places. There are over 200 dead or wounded. Similar air and artillery attacks have also been made from Rumanian and Finnish territory.

The next sentence betrayed Molotov's extraordinary dismay and suggested that, in its dealings with the Germans, the Soviet Government would have been willing to consider almost any concessions to put off the evil hour:

> This unheard-of attack on our country is an unparalleled act of perfidy in the history of civilised nations. This attack has been made despite the fact that there was a non-aggression pact between the Soviet Union and Germany, a pact the terms of which were scrupulously observed by the Soviet Union. We have been attacked even though, throughout the period of the Pact, the German Government had been

unable to make the slightest complaint about the USSR not carrying out its obligations. Therefore the whole responsibility for this act of robbery must fall on the Nazi rulers.

Molotov then spoke of the visit he had received at 5.30 in the morning from the German Ambassador, who had informed him that Germany had decided to attack the Soviet Union because of Russian troop concentrations on the frontier.

He stated emphatically that no Soviet plane had ever been allowed to cross the border, and he branded as "lies and provocations" the announcement over the Rumanian radio that morning that the Russians had bombed Rumanian airfields, and Hitler's statement "trying after the event to concoct stories about the non-observance of the Soviet-German Pact by the Soviet Union". But now that the Germans had attacked the Soviet Union, the Soviet Government had ordered its troops to repel the attack and to throw the Germans out of Soviet territory.

> This war has not been inflicted upon us by the German people, or by the German workers, peasants and intellectuals, of whose sufferings we are fully aware, but by Germany's bloodthirsty rulers, who have already enslaved the French, the Czechs, the Poles, the Serbs, and the peoples of Norway, Denmark, Holland, Belgium, Greece and other countries.

Molotov did not doubt that the Soviet armed forces would do their duty and smash the aggressor. He recalled that Russia had been invaded before, that, in the great patriotic war of 1812, the whole Russian people had risen as one man to crush Napoleon. The same would happen to "arrogant Hitler".

> The Government of the Soviet Union is deeply convinced that the whole population of our country will do their duty, and will work hard and conscientiously. Our people must be more united than ever. The greatest discipline, organising ability and selflessness worthy of a Soviet patriot must be demanded of everybody to meet the needs of the Army, Navy and Air Force, and to secure victory.
>
> The Government calls upon you, men and women citizens of the Soviet Union, to rally even more closely round the glorious Bolshevik Party, around the Soviet Government and our great leader, Comrade Stalin. Our cause is good. The enemy will be smashed. Victory will be ours.

There were a few catch phrases that stuck—about this being another "patriotic war" after the model of 1812; as well as the last paragraph: "Our cause is good. The enemy will be smashed. Victory will be ours (*pobeda budet za nami*)." But the general tone of the broadcast, and especially the complaint that the Germans had "made no demands" on Russia, left an uneasy, almost humiliating, feeling. It took twelve incredibly long and anxious days before Stalin himself broadcast to the Russian people.

In the midst of the conflicting, reticent and, to all appearances, untrue military communiqués, the Russian people derived what cheer they could from Churchill's historic broadcast on the night of June 22, less than twenty-four hours after the German invasion.

These were the passages that made a particularly strong impression on the Russians. He admitted that: "No one has been a more consistent opponent of communism than I have in the last twenty-five years. I will unsay no word that I have spoken about it." But then he went on, as only he could do:

> I see the Russian soldiers standing on the threshold of their native land... I see them guarding their homes where their mothers and wives pray—ah, yes, for there are times when all pray—for the safety of their loved ones... I see the ten thousand villages of Russia where the means of existence is wrung so hardly from the soil, but where there are still primordial joys, where maidens laugh and children play. I see advancing on all this in hideous onslaught the Nazi war machine... I see the dull, drilled, docile, brutish masses of the Hun soldiery plodding on like a swarm of crawling locusts. I see the German bombers and fighters in the sky, still smarting from many a British whipping, delighted to find what they believe is an easier and safer prey...

And then—the assurance that there would never be a deal with Hitler, and the promise that Britain would support Russia, and finally, the conviction that: "He [Hitler] wishes to destroy the Russian power because he hopes that if he succeeds in this, he will be able to bring back the main strength of his Army and Air Force from the East and hurl it upon this Island..."

The comments I heard from Russians were almost all along these lines: "We had heard about Hess; we suspected that there might well be a deal between Britain and Germany. We remembered Munich and those Anglo-Franco-Soviet talks in the summer of 1939. We had felt deeply about the bombing of London, but had, all along, been taught to distrust England. One of our first thoughts, when Germany invaded us, was that it had perhaps been done by agreement with England. That England should be an Ally—yes, an Ally—was more than we had ever hoped for. . ."

At last Stalin spoke. It was an extraordinary performance, and not the least impressive thing about it were these opening words: "Comrades, citizens, brothers and sisters, fighters of our Army and Navy! I am speaking to you, my friends!" This was something new. Stalin had never spoken like this before. But the words fitted perfectly into the atmosphere of those days.

Stalin began by saying that the Nazi invasion was continuing, despite the heroic defence of the Red Army, and although "the best German divisions and air force units had already been smashed and had found their grave on the field of battle". Understating the territorial losses already suffered, Stalin then said that the Nazi troops had succeeded in capturing Lithuania, a large part of Latvia, the western part of Belorussia and parts of the western Ukraine. German planes had bombed Murmansk, Orsha, Mogilev, Smolensk, Kiev, Odessa and Sebastopol. "A serious threat hangs over our country."

Did this mean, Stalin asked, that the German-Fascist troops were invincible? Of course not! The armies of Napoleon and of William II also used to be considered invincible; yet they were smashed in the end. And the same would happen to Hitler's army. "Only on our territory has it, for the first time, met with serious resistance." That a "part of our territory" had, nevertheless, been occupied, was chiefly due to the fact that the war had begun in conditions favourable to the Germans and unfavourable to the Red Army:

At the time of the attack, the German troops, 170 divisions in all, had been fully mobilised and were in a state of military preparedness along the Soviet frontier, merely waiting for the signal to advance. The Soviet troops had not been fully mobilised, and had not been moved to the frontier. Important, too, was the fact that Fascist Germany unexpectedly and perfidiously violated the 1939 Non-Aggression Pact between herself and the USSR, wholly indifferent to the consideration that she would be branded as the aggressor by the whole world.

Stalin then proceeded to justify the Soviet-German Pact.

One might well ask: How was it possible for the Soviet Government to sign a non-aggression pact with such inhuman scoundrels as Hitler and Ribbentrop? Had not a serious mistake been made? Of course not! A non-aggression pact is a peace pact between two states, and that was the pact that Germany proposed to us in 1939. No peace-loving state could have rejected such a pact with another country, even if scoundrels like Hitler and Ribbentrop stood at its head. All the more so, as this Pact did not in any way violate the territorial integrity, independence or honour of our country."

Stalin went on to say that the Pact had given the Soviet Union time to prepare against a German attack should Nazi Germany decide to embark on one.

This war has been inflicted on us, and our country has entered into a life-and-death struggle against its most wicked and perfidious enemy, German Fascism. Our troops are fighting heroically against heavy odds, against an enemy heavily armed with tanks and aircraft... The main forces of the Red Army, armed with thousands of tanks and planes, are now entering the battle... Together with the Red Army, the whole of our people are rising to defend their country.

The enemy is cruel and merciless. He aims at grabbing our land, our wheat and oil. He wants to restore the power of the landowners, re-establish Tsarism, and destroy the national culture of the peoples of the Soviet Union ... and turn them into the slaves of German princes and barons.

There should be no room in our ranks for whimperers and cowards, for deserters and panic-mongers. Our people should be fearless in their struggle and should selflessly fight our patriotic war of liberation against the Fascist enslavers...

After a reference to Lenin, Stalin said:

We must immediately put our whole production on a war footing, and place everything at the service of the Front and the organisation of the enemy's rout... The Red Army and Navy and the whole Soviet people must fight for every inch of Soviet soil, fight to the last drop of blood for our towns and villages... We must organise every kind of help for the Red Army, make sure that its ranks are constantly re-newed, and that it is supplied with everything it needs. We must organise the rapid transport of troops and equipment, and help to the wounded.

... All enterprises must intensify their work and produce more and more military equipment of every kind... A merciless struggle must be undertaken against all deserters and panic-mongers... We must destroy spies, diversionists and enemy paratroopers... Military tribunals should immediately try anyone who, through panic or cowardice, is interfering with our defence, regardless of position or rank...

And then came the famous "scorched-earth" instructions:

Whenever units of the Red Army are forced to retreat, all railway rolling stock must be driven away. The enemy must not be left a single engine, or a single railway truck, and not a pound of bread nor a pint of oil. The *kolkhozniki* must drive away all their livestock, hand their grain reserves to the State organs for evacuation to the rear... All valuable property, whether grain, fuel or non-ferrous metals, which cannot be evacuated, must be destroyed.

Then followed the "partisan war" instructions:

In the occupied territories partisan units must be formed... There must be diversionist groups for fighting enemy units, for spreading the partisan war everywhere, for blowing up and destroying roads and bridges and telephone and telegraph wires; for setting fire to forests, enemy stores and road convoys. In the occupied areas intolerable conditions must be created for the enemy and his accomplices, who must be persecuted and destroyed at every step...

This war, Stalin continued, was not an ordinary war between two armies; it was a war of the entire Soviet people against the German-Fascist troops. The purpose of this all-people war was not only to destroy the threat hanging over the Soviet Union, but also to help all the nations of Europe groaning under the German yoke. In this war the Soviet people would have faithful allies in the peoples of Europe and America, including the German people enslaved by their ringleaders... the Soviet people's struggle for the freedom of their country would be merged with the struggle of the peoples of Europe and America for their independence and their democratic freedoms:

> In this connection the historic statement of Mr Churchill on Britain's help to the Soviet Union and the statement by the United States Government on its willingness to help our country can only meet with a feeling of gratitude in the hearts of our people, and are highly indicative.

And then came the conclusion:

> Comrades, our forces are immeasurably large. The insolent enemy must soon become aware of this. Together with the Red Army, many thousands of workers, *kolkhozniki* and intellectuals are going to the war. Millions more will rise. The workers of Moscow and Leningrad have already begun to form an *opolcheniye* (home guard) of many thousands in support of the Red Army. Such *opolcheniye* forces must be constituted in every town threatened with invasion...
>
> A State Defence Committee* has been formed to deal with the rapid mobilisation of all the country's resources; all the power and authority of the State are vested in it. This State Defence Committee has embarked upon its work, and it calls upon the whole people to rally round the Party of Lenin and Stalin, and round the Soviet Government for the selfless support of the Red Army and Navy, for the routing of the enemy, for our victory...
>
> All the strength of the people must be used to smash the enemy. Onward, to victory!

The effect of this speech, addressed to a nervous, and often frightened and bewildered people, was very important. Until then there had been something artificial in the adulation of Stalin; his name was associated not only with the stupendous effort of the Five-Year Plans, but also with the ruthless methods employed in the collectivisation campaign and, worse still, with the terror of the Purges.

The Soviet people now felt that they had a leader to look to. In

* The members of this Committee, presided over by Stalin, were Molotov (Deputy Chairman), Voroshilov, Malenkov and Beria, a fact not mentioned in the 1961 *History*, which merely states that Stalin was Chairman.

his relatively short broadcast Stalin not only created the hope, if not yet the certainty, of victory, but he laid down, in short significant sentences, the whole programme of wartime conduct for a whole nation. He also appealed to the national pride, to the patriotic instincts of the Russian people. It was a great pull-yourselves-together speech, a blood-sweat-and-tears speech, with Churchill's post-Dunkirk speech as its only parallel.

An admirable description of the effect of Stalin's speech is to be found in Konstantin Simonov's famous novel, *The Living and the Dead*; here the speech was listened to in a field hospital:

> Stalin spoke in a toneless, slow voice, with a strong Georgian accent. Once or twice, during his speech, you could hear a glass click as he drank water. His voice was low and soft, and might have seemed perfectly calm, but for his heavy, tired breathing, and that water he kept drinking during the speech...
>
> There was a discrepancy between that even voice and the tragic situation of which he spoke; and in this discrepancy there was strength. People were not surprised. It was what they were expecting from Stalin.
>
> They loved him in different ways, wholeheartedly, or with reservations; admiring him and yet fearing him; and some did not like him at all. But nobody doubted his courage and his iron will. And now was a time when these two qualities were needed more than anything else in the man who stood at the head of a country at war.
>
> Stalin did not describe the situation as tragic; such a word would have been hard to imagine as coming from him; but the things of which he spoke—*opolcheniye*, partisans, occupied territories, meant the end of illusions... The truth he told was a bitter truth, but at last it was uttered, and people felt that they stood more firmly on the ground...
>
> And the very fact that Stalin should have talked about the unhappy beginning of a vast and terrible war without changing his vocabulary, and that he should have spoken in his almost usual way about the great but not insuperable difficulties that would have to be overcome— this, too, suggested not weakness, but great strength.
>
> "My friends", Sintsov repeated over and over again. And suddenly he realised that in all the great and even gigantic work that Stalin had been doing, there had been a lack of just these words: "Brothers and sisters! My friends!"—and, even more so, the feelings that stood

behind these words. Was it only a tragedy like the war that could give birth to these words and these feelings? ... Above all, what was left in his heart after Stalin's speech was a tense expectation of a change for the better.

This passage is all the more remarkable as it was written in 1958, when the general attitude to Stalin had already become extremely critical; but Simonov was clearly unwilling to distort history on this cardinal point. Other works written in the late 1950's, without exception, admit the extreme importance of Stalin's broadcast of July 3—even though some do not even mention his name, but merely speak of a "government communication".

Chapter IV

SMOLENSK: THE FIRST CHECK
TO THE BLITZKRIEG

The State Defence Committee, the formation of which Stalin had announced in his July 3 speech, was charged not only with the military conduct of the war but also with "the rapid mobilisation of all the country's resources". Among the decisions it made in these crucial days were many of far-reaching importance. They concerned the whole field of economic wartime organisation, including industrial mobilisation and the evacuation of whole industries to the east as well as reorganisation within the armed forces.

Militarily, the State Defence Committee decided to decentralise the command system to some extent by dividing the enormous front into three main sectors, each with a Command of its own. Voroshilov was appointed to command the "North-Western Direction", including the Baltic and Northern Fleets; Timoshenko was appointed to the "Western Direction", and Budienny to the "South-Western Direction", including the Black Sea Fleet. As principal members of their War Councils (i.e. the senior Party leaders for the areas concerned) they were given Zhdanov, Bulganin and Khrushchev respectively.

On July 16 the military commissars were re-introduced. L. Z. Mekhlis, head of the Political Propaganda of the Red Army, had fanatically supported this measure.*

* Mekhlis had been notorious in the past as one of the "purgers" of the Army, and was held directly responsible for the liquidation of

One cannot help suspecting that the re-introduction of commissars was something of a panic measure due to the fear of a latent, if not open, conflict between the Army and the Party, and the doubt whether some of the officers (many of whom had highly unpleasant memories of the purges) would prove reliable. It is difficult to be sure how much hostility to the Party there was among the officers. In the higher ranks, many veterans of the Revolution such as Budienny and Voroshilov were probably more "Party" than "Army", and others, like Konev, were half-and-half. But several of the brilliant younger generals, such as Zhukov, Tolbukhin, Rokossovsky and Govorov, were probably more "Army" than "Party". The last two, for instance, had themselves been purged in 1937 and, though now fully rehabilitated, must still have had a good many reservations about the Party, however strong their patriotism.

In fact the military commissars were to prove a cause of friction and were to be abolished again in the autumn of 1942.

Similarly, it was decided at the end of June to mobilise members of the Party and Komsomol as "*politboitsy*", i.e. "political soldiers" to be incorporated in the Army. Each *obkom* or *kraikom* (i.e. provincial party committee) was to mobilise within three days between 500 and 5,000 Communists, and place them at the disposal of the Commissariat of Defence. In this way 95,000 *politboitsy* were mobilised, and of these 58,000 were sent into the Army in the field within the first three months of the war.

Another measure was the approval of the constitution of the *opolcheniye*, i.e. mainly workers' battalions, in cities like Moscow,

Blucher. He was something of a "politisation" fanatic, and had been on particularly bad terms with Timoshenko. A protégé of Voroshilov, he was unpopular with the "younger" generals, and finally, in 1942, after the disastrous Kerch operation in the Crimea, he was demoted. He was sharply disliked not only by men like Zhukov and Rokossovsky, who did not favour the re-introduction of the officer-and-commissar dual command in the Army in 1941, but also, on more personal grounds, by some top-ranking members of the Politburo, such as Shcherbakov. The eventual abolition of dual command should not be confused with the Political Departments in the Army, which continued as before. On Mekhlis, see John Erickson, *The Soviet High Command*, London, 1962.

Leningrad, Kiev, Odessa, Makeyevka, Gorlovka and other industrial centres. These "home guard" units were to be used extensively—and often very wastefully—to fill in gaps at the front, notably in the defence of Moscow, Leningrad and Odessa. The story of these poorly-trained and poorly-armed units is one of the most tragic in the whole war. Judging from the available figures, the eagerness to join the *opolcheniye* varied from place to place. It was highest in Leningrad, rather lower in Moscow, and much lower in Kiev.

Apart from the *opolcheniye*, a variety of other emergency formations were constituted in both towns and villages, such as anti-paratroop units, and orders were given for air-raid precautions:

> All Soviet citizens between the ages of 16 and 60 (men) and 18 and 50 (women) must compulsorily take part in civil-defence groups to be constituted by enterprises, offices and house committees. The training in anti-aircraft and anti-gas defence is to be carried out by the Osoaviakhim.*

Another important set of instructions issued at the end of June concerned the organisation of partisan warfare in the enemy rear; but while the principle of the thing was important, large-scale partisan war behind the German lines did not develop until considerably later.

While the State Defence Committee were making these plans and also laying the foundations for a thorough economic reorganisation of the country, the military situation continued to be disastrous. At the beginning of July there were large gaps in the front. The "first echelon" of the Red Army had suffered such appalling losses in the first weeks of the invasion that it scarcely still counted as an effective force. The hopes of holding a new defence line (referred to by the Western press as the "Stalin Line") running from Narva on the Gulf of Finland, through Pskov, Polotsk, and then along the Dnieper to

---

* The Osoaviakhim was the "Society for aiding defence and the aircraft and chemical industries"; it was a "voluntary society", set up long before the war, for giving some military experience to the population. Later, during the war, it was renamed DOSAAF (Voluntary society for aiding the army, air force and navy).

Kherson on the Black Sea, had been smashed. And though there were still reserves of men, the Red Army was suffering severe shortages of weapons of all kinds.

In these circumstances the Soviet command had to decide on priorities, and it decided that the first priority was to make every effort to hold up the enemy in the "Smolensk-Moscow direction".

Seen in perspective, the battle of Smolensk was to mark the beginning of a new phase in the campaign and, indeed, to introduce a decidedly different pattern into the struggle between Nazi Germany and Soviet Russia. In the Smolensk area, for the first time, Soviet resistance succeeded in bringing the German *blitzkrieg* advance to a halt, if only for a couple of months. Thus, at the very centre of gravity of the invaders' attack, on the direct road to Moscow, the freedom of manœuvre of the German High Command was seriously restricted and its all-important time schedule upset.

It was on July 16 that von Bock's advance guards reached the outskirts of Smolensk—and ran into resistance such as they had not met before. Hitherto they had encountered only limited nests of resistance and relatively small units making heroic and suicidal last-ditch stands. This time they were met with firm resistance on a coherent and relatively wide front.

The Russians were determined not to allow the enemy to advance much further. They threw in reserves along a wide front from Velikie Luki to Mozyr, and their counter-attacks were successful in checking the German advance. Though Smolensk itself fell, heavy fighting continued in the area, and for the rest of July and August the Germans failed to break through the Russian line, firmly stabilised about twenty to twenty-five miles east of Smolensk—the Yartsevo-Yelnya-Desna Line.

As usual, German and Russian histories disagree about which side had the numerical advantage in men and material in the Smolensk battle. General Guderian, for example, has referred to "the Russians' great numerical superiority in tanks". In view of the heavy Russian losses earlier, this is extremely improbable, though it must be remembered that, after such a deep and rapid advance into enemy territory, many of the German tanks may not have been operational any more. Wear and tear would have taken their toll, and the supply lines were by now so extended (in a country with inadequate roads) that spares and fuel may well not have been arriving at the front quickly enough, or in the quantities needed.

Such numerical comparisons are, in any case, often misleading—whether in the heat of the battle, or after the event—and it would be fruitless to discuss the rival claims in detail here. There were, however, three factors which favoured the Russians in the battle around Smolensk: Firstly, the morale of the Russian troops was now much higher than it had been; the thought that they were not fighting in distant Belorussia, but literally on the road to Moscow had an important psychological effect. Secondly, Soviet artillery, which was almost the only weapon the Red Army had with which to fight both tanks and aircraft, was considerably better than the German. Thirdly, very important militarily and even more so psychologically, there was the first appearance of the devastating *katyusha* mortars. As Marshal Yeremenko later wrote:

> We first tried out this superb weapon at Rudnya, north-west of Smolensk. In the afternoon of July 15, the earth shook with the unusual explosion of jet mines. Like red-tailed comets, the mines were hurled into the air. The frequent and dazzling explosions, the like of which had never been seen, struck the imagination. The effect of the simultaneous explosion of dozens of these mines was terrific. The Germans fled in panic, and even our own troops near the points of the explosions, who for reasons of secrecy had not been warned that this new weapon would be used, rushed back from the front line.*

The Russians had also thrown in a few modern planes, so that German air supremacy was no longer quite as complete as it had been during the first three weeks of the war.

But whatever the numerical superiority of either side, the essential fact remains that the Russians succeeded in slowing down, and then halting, the German *blitzkrieg* just east of Smolensk—and that this had several important consequences.

From the Russian point of view it was a desperate rearguard

* *Voyenno-istoricheskii zhurnal*, 1959, No. 1, p. 51 (Historico-military Journal), quoted by IVOVSS.

action—but one on a large enough scale, and long enough sustained, to give the Russian High Command a breathing-space. The "Smolensk Line" was the shield behind which the Soviet armies were able to regroup, and bring up reserves, for the defence of Moscow. But for this, Moscow might well have fallen, as Hitler had originally planned, before the winter set in.

From the German point of view the Russian stand in the Smolensk area was the first check to their plans, and the resulting delay faced them with a major strategic problem.

On August 4, when the heavy fighting around Smolensk had already gone on for about three weeks, Hitler held a conference at Novy Borissov, at the headquarters of Army Group Centre. According to Guderian, who attended it, Hitler designated the industrial area of Leningrad as his primary objective. He had not yet decided whether Moscow or the Ukraine would come next, but seemed to incline towards the latter target... He hoped to be in possession of Moscow and Kharkov by the time winter began. But no decisions were reached on this day.*

For the next twenty days heavy, but still inconclusive fighting continued in the Smolensk area, and when Hitler held another conference on August 23, Guderian's pleading in favour of a concentrated drive on Moscow was turned down. Hitler had finally made up his mind to attack the Ukraine and the Crimea, saying that the raw materials and the agriculture of the Ukraine were vitally important to the prosecution of the war. As for the Crimea, it was "a Soviet aircraft carrier for attacking the Rumanian oilfields", and must therefore be eliminated. "My generals," he said, "know nothing about the economic aspects of war." Whether or not Hitler still thought that, under this new plan, Moscow could fall before the winter, it was clear to Guderian that this was now most unlikely, and he took Hitler's decision very badly—or at least so he said after the war. He was later to refer to Hitler's decision to move two armies and one tank group to the south, instead of concentrating the attack on Moscow, as a "fatal error".

*

* Heinz Guderian, *Panzer Leader* (London, 1952), pp. 189–90.

Though the Russians dismiss as fantastic the German claim to have captured 348,000 prisoners, over 3,000 tanks and over 3,000 guns in the Smolensk fighting, Russian losses were undoubtedly heavy. They themselves admit the loss of 32,000 men "missing", 685 tanks and 1,176 guns.* Nevertheless the Smolensk battle was one of the turning points of the war. The Russians had halted the German *blitzkrieg*, and had forced Hitler to change his plans. Furthermore, it had an important effect on morale within the Red Army. Whereas, initially, many Russian soldiers had been, as it were, psychologically overwhelmed by the power of the German army, and particularly by the number of their tanks, by the end of July more and more Russian soldiers had learnt to use weapons such as grenades and "Molotov cocktails" against tanks, and (perhaps because of pep-talks by the Army's propaganda services) a healthy hatred of the Germans more and more took the place of sheer fear. An important aid to morale was a lavish distribution of medals and decorations, though not as lavish as it became later. About a thousand decorations were awarded after Smolensk and seven men were given the title "Hero of the Soviet Union".

*IVOVSS, vol. 2, p. 77.

Chapter V

CLOSE-UP ONE: MOSCOW AT THE
BEGINNING OF THE WAR

I arrived in Russia on July 3, 1941, that is, twelve days after the
beginning of the German invasion. Geographically, the journey
from London to Moscow was of a kind that was only conceivable in
wartime: travelling with the second batch of the British Military
Mission, I was flown to Inverness, then to the Shetlands, and from
there, by Catalina flying boat—all in one sixteen-hour hop—to
Archangel. The last few hours we flew over the vast uninhabited
tundra country of the Kola Peninsula. Then, after flying over the
White Sea and Archangel harbour, we came down on the waters of
the Dvina river, some miles south of Archangel. Here, on board a
sort of large house-boat, a sumptuous supper had been laid on by
the local military authorities, and this supper continued, right
through the "white" night till two or three in the morning. Among
the members of this second batch of the Military Mission—the first
batch, with General Mason MacFarlane at its head, had flown to
Moscow a few days before—were two Home Office officials in
colonel's uniform, one a fire-fighting expert, who was taking a stirrup
pump to Moscow, and the other a shelter expert.
    Our hosts were a colonel and two majors, both extremely amiable,
and, as the evening progressed, other officers joined the party. Several
referred to Stalin's broadcast that day, and thought it would be a
very long and hard war, but that Russia would win it in the end.
One of the majors assured me that Moscow's air defences were such

175

that it would probably never be bombed, and that the same was true
of Leningrad.

All of them were eagerly interested in Britain with which Russia
had, obviously, had very little contact for a long time. The curious
thing was that both the colonel and the two majors showed a very
special interest in Rudolf Hess and seemed, in fact, rather worried
about him. They had read Churchill's speech and said that the
Russian people had been very gratified by it, though they knew that
Churchill had been one of the chief "interventionists" in the Civil
War; even so, one of them asked, was I really absolutely sure that
Hess's proposals had been turned down? They were, obviously, not
quite sure yet of either Britain's or America's disposition.

Outside, it had been a "white" night throughout. The fir trees on
the steep sandy banks of the river were silhouetted against the brief
twilight. There were lots of mosquitoes about. After a couple of
hours' sleep we were taken in motor-boats some distance up the river
and then by car to an airfield. At 6 a.m. the sun was already high in
the sky. Blades of grass and wild flowers were swept by the wind as
we walked to the plane. It was a luxurious giant Douglas, and for
three or four hours we flew over what looked like one vast interminable forest. Then, at Rybinsk, we crossed the Volga and, after
flying over some more thickly populated country, we reached the
outskirts of Moscow.

On the face of it, Moscow looked perfectly normal. The streets
were crowded and the shops were still full of goods. There seemed
no food shortage of any kind; in Maroseika Street, I walked that first
day into a big food shop and was surprised by the enormous display
of sweets and *pastila* and *marmelad*; people were still buying food
freely, without any coupons. In their summer clothes the young
people of Moscow looked anything but shabby. Most of the girls
wore white blouses, and the men white, yellow or blue sports shirts,
or buttoned-up shirts with embroidered collars. Posters on the walls
were being eagerly read, and there were certainly plenty of posters:
a Russian tank crushing a giant crab with a Hitler moustache, a
Red soldier ramming his bayonet down the throat of a giant Hitler-
faced rat—*Razdavit' fascistskuyu gadinu*, it said: crush the Fascist
vermin; appeals to women—"Women, go and work on the collective

farms, replace the men now in the Army!" On numerous houses the front pages of that morning's *Pravda* or *Izvestia* with the full text of Stalin's speech were stuck up, and everywhere crowds of people were re-reading it.

All sorts of peculiar things were happening: I saw the last issue of *Bezbozhnik*, the "godless" paper; it was entirely devoted to indignant denunciations of the Nazi persecutions of the Protestant and Catholic Churches in Germany! Clearly, Stalin was working for the greatest unity among the Russian people, and anti-religious propaganda had completely vanished since the war had begun. However, the *Bezbozhnik*'s *volte-face* was a bit blatant, and, in fact, this was to be its last issue. It was closed down "owing to paper shortage". Instead, Emelian Yaroslavsky, the "anti-God" leader, was publishing pamphlets like *The Great Patriotic War*, in the best nationalist tradition, which they were now selling on bookstalls.

Partly perhaps as a result of Stalin's warning against spies and "diversionists" there was a real spy mania in Moscow. People seemed to see spies and paratroopers everywhere. The British army N.C.O.s who had travelled with me from Archangel had a most unpleasant experience on that very first day. From the airfield, they had gone to Moscow in a lorry, together with the Mission's luggage. At a street corner they had been stopped by the militia; puzzled by the unfamiliar British uniforms, a crowd had gathered round them and somebody had said "parachutists", whereupon the crowd had grown angry and vociferous. So the N.C.O.s had to be taken off to a police station, where they were finally rescued by an Embassy official.

Everyone was being asked for papers on all kinds of occasions, and it was absolutely essential to have these in order, especially after the midnight curfew, when a special pass was required. Speaking anything but Russian aroused immediate suspicion.

Auxiliary militia-women were particularly keen. I remember walking with Jean Champenois* along Gorki Street at sunset, when suddenly a militia-woman pounced on him shouting: "Why are you

* The Agence Havas correspondent in Moscow who joined the Free French in 1941.

smoking?" and ordered him to put out his cigarette at once; she thought he might be signalling to German aircraft!

All day long, soldiers were marching along the streets, usually singing. The *opolcheniye* movement was in full swing; during those first days of July tens of thousands of men, many of them elderly, volunteered, appearing at assembly points—such as the one opposite the house I lived in, in Khokhlovsky Lane—by the hundred, all carrying small bundles or suitcases. After being sorted out—and partly rejected—they were sent to training camps.

Apart from that, the mood in Moscow still seemed reasonably calm. People could still be seen laughing and joking in the streets though, significantly, very few talked openly about the war.

I found the Lenin Mausoleum closed, and was waved away, but without any explanation, by two bayoneted guards. On the surface, life seemed, in many ways, to go on as before. Fourteen theatres were open and invariably crowded, and restaurants and hotels continued to be packed.

For all that, Moscow was preparing for air raids. Already on July 9, special trucks began to run along the tram-lines, distributing heaps of sand. That week I wrote an article on the London blitz and on British air raid precautions, and this was promptly published in *Izvestia*, was much talked about, and even produced some polemics on the pros and cons of pouring buckets of water over incendiaries, which I had declared to be wrong. My story of the London blitz was widely discussed, all the more so as during the Soviet-German Pact the Russian press had not dwelt very much on Britain's experiences of bombing.

The prospect of German air raids led, by the second week of July, to a large-scale evacuation of children from Moscow. Many women were also urged to leave and to work on *kolkhozes*. Railway stations were crowded with people who had permits to leave Moscow. Many of the women I saw at the Kursk Station on the night of July 11, on their way to Gorki, were weeping; many thought they would not get back to Moscow for a long time, and perhaps, for all they knew, the Germans would come.

*

Anglo-Russian relations were rapidly improving. Sir Stafford Cripps, who had been cold-shouldered by the Russians right up to the beginning of the Nazi invasion, had two meetings with Stalin in the second week of July, and on July 12 the Anglo-Soviet Agreement was solemnly signed by Molotov and Cripps in Molotov's office at the Kremlin, in the presence of Stalin, Admiral Kuznetsov, General Shaposhnikov, General Mason MacFarlane, and Laurence Cadbury, head of the British Trade Mission. Stalin, through an interpreter, talked at some length to Mason MacFarlane, and chocolates and Soviet champagne were served.

At Lozovsky's* press conference on the following afternoon, the Russians were still showing surprise at the signing of the agreement providing for mutual aid and promising not to make a separate peace with Germany. Lozovsky himself seemed pleasantly surprised, and said it was the biggest blow for Hitler, since it smashed his plan for fighting East and West separately. Asked whether the USA could be considered a silent partner to this agreement, he said gallantly: "The USA is too great a country to be silent."

The press set-up in Moscow during those first weeks of the war was a very strange one. The only official sources of information were the Soviet press with their war communiqués and their war *reportages*, and these press conferences held three times a week by Lozovsky.

The *reportages* in the press dealt chiefly with isolated cases of Russian bravery and heroism, though, occasionally, especially in the army paper, *Red Star*, there were some useful analytical articles. The communiqués tended to be cagey and often gave only the vaguest indications of where the fighting was actually taking place, but people soon learned to read between the lines. Fighting in "the Minsk direction" or "the Smolensk direction" usually meant that these cities had already been lost, and a study of the communiqué vocabulary taught one to understand the degree of the Russian setbacks; thus "heavy defensive battles against superior enemy forces"

* A Deputy Foreign Commissar and the Deputy-Chief of Sovinform-bureau. His chief in the latter organisation was that extremely hard "Stalinist" party boss, member of the Politburo, A. S. Shcherbakov.

meant that the Russians were in full and disorderly retreat; this was the worst of all the communiqué phrases.

The general tendency of Lozovsky's press conferences was to suggest that all the Russian setbacks were temporary; that, whatever the loss of territory, the Germans were not going to win; that Moscow and Leningrad, in any case, would not be lost; that Russian losses were admittedly high, but that German losses were higher still —the most questionable of his arguments; that relations between Germany and her satellites were highly strained, also a questionable proposition in the summer and autumn of 1941. Occasionally he revealed important facts—such as the destruction by the Russians of the Dnieper Dam or the deportation to the east of the entire population of the Volga-German Autonomous Soviet Republic—a matter of about half-a-million people. Major disasters, such as the capture by the Germans of many hundreds of thousands of prisoners, and the stupendous losses in aircraft, were not mentioned at all. On the other hand, he tended, if anything, to exaggerate the number of German tanks and aircraft engaged on the Russian Front; thus, he spoke of 10,000 German tanks taking part in the fighting.

Lozovsky was an Old Bolshevik, with a smooth, cosmopolitan veneer, a first-vintage émigré, who had spent many years in Geneva and Paris, had known Lenin, spoke good French, and, with his *barbiche* and carefully cut clothes, looked rather like an old *boulevardier*, whom one could well imagine on the terrace of the Napolitain during *la belle époque*. After the Revolution, he had been active on the *Profintern*, the Red Trade Union International, a body of small consequence, and later became a member of the Foreign Affairs Commissariat. With his Old Bolshevik background, he must have had some anxious moments during the Purges; nor can he have been happy during the Soviet-German Pact. However, Lozovsky was a good survivor though, personally, he did not fit very well into the Stalin-Molotov *milieu*. In 1943 he became a leading member of the Jewish Anti-Fascist Committee, and this led, in the end, to his downfall; in 1949, along with other prominent members of this Committee, that perfectly harmless old man was shot.

In 1941 he was considered—wrongly perhaps—as one of the Foreign Commissariat's survivors of the Litvinov era, more sympathetic to the West than Molotov, though, on one notable occasion, he very clearly dissociated himself from Litvinov. It was a curious incident: just a couple of days before the signing of the Cripps-Molotov agreement, Litvinov—who had been under a cloud since May 1939—was to speak on Moscow radio; but when it came to the point, he spoke only on the foreign wave-lengths, and in English. On the following morning, the Soviet press gave a few scraps of his broadcast; leaving out his "Let bygones be bygones" and "we have all made mistakes", it concentrated, instead, on the passage in which he asserted that the Germans were the common enemy and that "there must be no *de facto* armistice in the West". When Lozovsky was asked what role Litvinov was going to play in future, he replied, very reluctantly, that "Mr Litvinov would presumably broadcast again."

The sources of information available to the Russian public were pretty watertight. At the very beginning of the war all private wireless sets had to be handed in to the militia; only foreign diplomats, journalists and certain Russian officials were allowed to keep theirs: everyone else had only loudspeakers giving the Moscow programme. It certainly would have been unfortunate if some of the German propaganda stories had got round, especially from those rusty old White-Russian colonels with their alcoholic voices—that's at least how they sounded—who bellowed about "Stalin and his *zhidy* (yids)" preparing to flee the country, about their "fat bank balances at Buenos Aires", about the "millions of prisoners" taken by the Germans, the "desperate plight of the Red Army", "the imminence of the fall of Moscow and Leningrad", about the Germans bringing "real socialism to Russia", and the like.

Not that the news was by any means good—even without these German commentaries. Already, by July 11, it was known that the Germans were getting near Smolensk, and that most of the Baltic republics had been overrun; by the 14th, it was announced that fighting was taking place "in the direction of Ostrov"—which suggested a rapid German advance towards Leningrad from the south; by the 22nd, it was learned that the Finns were fighting "in the direction of Petrozavodsk"; by July 28, that the Germans were advancing on Kiev. But the fact that, by the middle of July, the

Germans seemed to have got stuck at Smolensk created in Moscow a curious state of euphoria, a feeling that perhaps the worst was over—even though the news from both the Leningrad Front and the Ukraine continued to be distressingly bad.

The first air raid on Moscow took place on the night of July 21; what was most impressive was the tremendous anti-aircraft barrage, with shrapnel from the anti-aircraft shells clattering down on to the streets like a hailstorm; and dozens of searchlights lighting the sky; I had never seen or heard anything like it in London. Fire-watching was organised on a vast scale. Later I heard that many of the fire-watchers had been badly injured by incendiary bombs, sometimes through inexperience but usually through sheer Russian foolhardiness. Youngsters would at first just pick up the bombs with their bare hands!

It was soon learned that there were three circles of anti-aircraft defences round Moscow, and that, during the first raid, barely ten or fifteen German planes (out of 200) had broken through. Some high explosive bombs and some incendiaries could be heard dropping, but only very few. There were quite a number of broken windows the next morning, a few bomb-craters, including one in Red Square, a few fires, which were rapidly put out, but nothing very serious. On the night of July 22, there was a second blitz, which also caused only limited damage, except that over a hundred people were killed when one big shelter off Arbat Square received a direct hit. But, as on the first night, only a very small number of planes got through.

The air raids continued, off and on, through the last days of July and most of August. In the instructions issued at the end of July it was now said that sand must be used against incendiaries, rather than water—though, in reality, water continued to be used as well.

No shirking was allowed in fire-fighting. Three fellows guilty of neglect, and so held responsible for the destruction by fire of a large warehouse worth three million roubles, were shot.*

I wrote at the time:

* A. Werth, *Moscow '41* (London, 1942), p. 100.

I wonder if Moscow is taking the blitz as well as London? People look grim; and there are mighty few bomb jokes. Perhaps people here feel *individually* more helpless than they do in London. Ambulances are comparatively scarce, and perhaps too precious to risk in a big blitz, and they therefore do not collect the wounded during a raid, but only after the all-clear has gone. Until then the wounded have only the local first-aid to rely upon. The fire-watching rules are very drastic, and a dangerous amount of sleep is lost ... nor are most of the shelters adapted yet for sleeping.*

But, on the whole, Moscow, during those two first months of the war, presented a rather paradoxical sight. Official optimism was being, more or less, kept up by the Press. The halting of the Germans at Smolensk was made out to be of the utmost importance, even though the news from other sectors of the front was still looking highly ominous. But at least the German advance was not what it had been during the desperate first fortnight.

Conditions in Moscow were becoming more difficult. If, at the beginning of July, there was no real shortage of anything—food and cigarettes in particular were plentiful, and so were even nice-looking boxes of chocolates "made in Riga, Latvian SSR", now already in German hands—some hoarding went on in a smallish way all the time, and, by July 15, the food shortage became very noticeable, and the mountains of cigarette packets displayed at almost every street corner rapidly disappeared. On July 18 drastic food rationing was introduced, and the population split up into favoured, semi-favoured and unfavoured categories, the rations of the latter being already extremely meagre. True, the *kolkhoz* markets continued to function, but prices were rising rapidly. There were still some consumer goods in the shops, and at the end of August I even managed to buy a fur coat of sorts—made of white Siberian dogskin—in a shop in Stoleshnikov Lane, where there was still a fairly good assortment of reindeer *polushubki* (fur jackets) and the like. I paid 335 roubles (about £7) for my "dog-coat"—which was cheap. But

* Ibid., p. 111.

other shops, I found, were already quickly running out of shoes, galoshes and *valenki* (felt boots).

Restaurants were, however, continuing as before, and good meals were still served in the big hotels—the Metropole, Moskva, or in restaurants like the famous Aragvi in Gorki Street. The Cocktail Hall in Gorki Street was also crowded; the theatres—fourteen of them—and the cinemas were working normally and many of them were competing in producing topical and patriotic shows. The Bolshoi Theatre was closed, but its *filiale* in Pushkin Street was working, and there were the usual crowds of young people clamouring outside for spare tickets, in case anybody had one, and, inside the theatre, giving frantic ovations whenever the famous tenors Lemeshev or Kozlovsky sang. At the Malyi Theatre they were playing Korneichuk's *In the Ukrainian Steppes*; when one of the characters said:

> There is nothing more maddening than when you're interrupted just as you are completing the roof of your cottage. If only we have five more years! But if war comes, then we shall fight with a fierceness and anger the like of which the world has never seen!

it brought the house down.

Whenever in cinemas Stalin appeared on newsreels, there was frantic cheering—which, in the dark, people presumably wouldn't do unless they felt like it. There could be no doubt about Stalin's authority, especially since that July 3 broadcast. He was the *khoziain*, the boss, who it was hoped knew what he was doing. Even so, people felt that things had gone badly wrong, and many were greatly surprised that Russia should have been invaded at all.

Patriotic plays were being concocted, such as *The Confrontation* in Tairov's Kamerny Theatre, in which a German agent finally gives up in despair, finding all the Russian people completely united; or plays about Suvorov or Kutuzov, those victorious "Russian ancestors". The Ermitage Garden continued to be crowded on Sundays by a half-civilian, half-military public; here, in a crowded hall, Busia Goldstein played Tchaikovsky's *Violin Concerto*, while in one of the theatres they were playing "satirical sketches" ridiculing Hitler and Goebbels, and German soldiers and German generals and

German paratroopers, who were always outwitted by the patriotic Russian villagers. None of it, perhaps, terribly convincing in the circumstances. Nevertheless, people enjoyed it, and laughed.

Poets and composers were busy writing patriotic poems or patriotic war songs, and soldiers would be seen marching down the streets singing the pre-war *Little Blue Scarf*, or *Katyusha* or *V boi za rodinu, v boi za Stalina* (Into battle for the country, into battle for Stalin), or Alexandrov's brand-new and solemn *Sacred War*, which was to remain a kind of semi-official anthem throughout the war years:

But alongside all this, many theatres continued as before—the Moscow Art Theatre going on with *The Three Sisters*, and *Anna Karenina*, and *The School for Scandal*, and the usual Bolshoi Ballet season opening at the end of September with *Swan Lake*, with Lepeshinskaya dancing... This only a few days before the Germans' "final" offensive began...

The British and American Embassies were very active during those days. Cripps and Steinhardt had become familiar Moscow figures, and could often be seen on newsreels. At the end of July diplomatic relations were restored with the Polish Government in London, though this was soon to lead to the first complications. When, a day or two after the Maisky-Sikorski Agreement of July 30, I asked Lozovsky whether the release of Polish war prisoners had begun and whether steps had been taken to form a Polish Army in Russia, he became extremely cagey, saying that such steps *were* being taken, but with the Poles "scattered all over the Soviet Union", there were a lot of practical problems still to be settled; nor could he state how many Polish prisoners there were, since this would give away vital secrets to the enemy.*

Soon after that Sikorski referred in a broadcast to the destruction

* See also p. 293.

of Poland by Germany and Russia in 1939, and demanded that Poland be restored within her 1939 frontiers. *Izvestia* immediately protested:

> Sorry, but frontiers are not immutable, and the British Government realises this, and has not guaranteed any East-European frontiers. Mr Eden said so the other day. But with goodwill on both sides, Poland and the Soviet Union will settle this question, as they settled so many other questions. Moreover, Russia did not want to "destroy" Poland, but merely wanted to prevent the Germans from getting too near Minsk and Kiev.

Diplomatic relations were also resumed with the exiled governments of Yugoslavia, Belgium and Norway. An important Anglo-Soviet decision was to occupy Iran; a decision which was to produce some unintentionally amusing stories in *Pravda*, whose correspondent, describing the enthusiasm with which the Soviet troops were welcomed by the Persian population, quoted one old man as saying: "I welcome you in the name of Article 6 of the Treaty of 1921." This also gave rise to some bitter jokes like this one: "Thank God we've occupied Persia; when the Germans have occupied the whole of Russia, we'll have somewhere to run away to."

The highlight of diplomatic activity during that grim summer was Harry Hopkins's visit to be followed later by the Beaverbrook visit.* All this, especially the Hopkins visit, had a cheering effect on the Russians. The exact purpose of the Hopkins visit was, of course, not disclosed at the time, except that it was assumed that the Americans were going to "help". Needless to say, among ordinary Russians there was already much talk about the necessity of a Second Front; why couldn't the British land in France? Very little was, as yet, said about this officially, but Party propaganda had, clearly, spread the word that this was very important, if not absolutely decisive. A good deal was made, as a sop to Russian morale, of British air raids on Germany, though everybody seemed to feel that that wasn't enough. . . But of the active and, at times, cantankerous correspondence that was already going on between Churchill and Stalin, nothing was yet known to the Russian public.

* See pp. 280 ff.

Both Sir Stafford Cripps and General Mason MacFarlane, the head of the British Military Mission, were well-disposed to the Russians, even though MacFarlane occasionally spoke of "this blood-stained régime" and Cripps had had to suffer a good many humiliations at the time of the Soviet-German Pact. I used to see a great deal of both of them during that summer and early autumn. Both considered the situation at the Russian front serious, but never hopeless, and were, clearly, convinced that the Russians would not be crushed, even though there were times when things looked pretty desperate—at the very beginning, and then after the Germans had captured Kiev and forced the Dnieper, and then again when they closed in on Leningrad, and started their "final" offensive against Moscow. But throughout, both considered Russia as a lasting and decisive factor in the struggle against Nazi Germany. Both were greatly impressed by Stalin, by his knowledge of details, though Cripps told me, about the middle of August, that, at least on one occasion, he had found Stalin "badly rattled", adding, however, that he may have been play-acting, and simply trying to get Britain and America to do more than they were doing. Cripps was, above all, impressed by the fact that, with possibly one exception, Stalin in his negotiations with the British and the Americans always expressed himself in terms of a *long war*; his request for aluminium, in particular, was taken by Cripps as an indication of Stalin's thinking a long way ahead.*

Some of the younger British and American diplomats and journalists, however, tended to think that the Russians were heading for catastrophe. One American woman-journalist thought she would, "as a nootral", stay on to see from her Hotel National window the Germans march through Red Square. Some even gloated over the enthusiasm with which the Latvians and Estonians were said to be welcoming the Germans. But, in the main, there was among the journalists a feeling of goodwill and admiration for the Russians.

Apart from the "bourgeois" journalists—who were very few at the beginning of the war, but who received reinforcements as time went on—there were the so-called "Comintern" journalists—correspondents of communist papers. They had had a difficult time during

* See also p. 282.

the Soviet-German Pact, and now kept rather aloof. Nor were the communist leaders from foreign countries—Pieck, Thorez, Ulbricht, Gottwald, Anna Pauker, Dimitrov—to be seen at all in 1941. It was scarcely known even whether they were still in Moscow.

Apart from the very small number of official communist correspondents—at least three of these were Americans and two were Spaniards—there were some other people vaguely connected with the Comintern, with the foreign services of Moscow radio, or with *Moscow News*, among them the once-famous Borodin, who had been Soviet Russia's foremost emissary in China; many of these were survivors of all kinds of purges, and some had been only recently allowed to return from exile; they were, as it were, the flotsam and jetsam of a now bygone era. The Russians did not encourage them to mix with "respectable" allied, though bourgeois, correspondents. One of the best of these seemingly lost souls was John Gibbons, a convinced Glasgow communist, who had fought the Black-and-Tans in his early youth and had, since the closing down of the *Daily Worker* in 1939, been working on Moscow Radio. He was one of the few people I knew who lived in the famous Comintern hotel, the Lux, in Gorki Street. His wife, a cosy sentimental fat woman, continued to pine for her native Southampton. But John Gibbons, though he had lived through many sombre crises since 1936, remained a strangely happy and balanced man. True, during the next grim winter of 1941–2, he was to suffer deeply from having tea without sugar and only a piece of dry bread, while his boss on Moscow Radio, with a higher-category ration card, was in the same office eating ham and eggs. "It's part of the system," he would say, "and no doubt they are right, but it was bloody unpleasant to *smell* the ham and eggs. All the more so as the boss thought it was quite normal, and never offered me even a scrap of the ham."

Chapter VI

CLOSE-UP TWO: AUTUMN JOURNEY TO THE SMOLENSK FRONT

The Battle of Yelnya, south-east of Smolensk, which went on throughout the whole of August, was not a major battle of the Soviet-German war, and yet one has to live back into the fearful summer of 1941 to realise how vital it was for Russian morale. Throughout August and part of September it was built up by the Russian press and by Russian propaganda out of all proportion to its real or ultimate importance, and yet here was not only, as it were, the first victory of the Red Army over the Germans; here was also the first piece of territory—perhaps only 100 or 150 square miles—in the whole of Europe reconquered from Hitler's Wehrmacht. It is strange to think that in 1941 even *that* was considered a vast achievement.

After the capture of Smolensk, the Germans were held up along most of the Central Front; but they had managed to drive a wedge south-east of Smolensk, capturing the town of Yelnya and a number of villages.

According to Guderian, there was some dispute among the German generals whether to defend the Yelnya salient, or to evacuate it; in the end it was decided to evacuate it, though at heavy loss of life—which clearly suggests that the Russians actually drove the Germans out, after weeks of heavy fighting. The price paid in human lives by the Russians for this "prestige victory" had been very high, and when, later in October, the big German offensive had

189

started against Moscow, the Russians in what had been the Yelnya salient were doomed to encirclement.

Although, until then, foreign correspondents had not been allowed at the Front, the Yelnya victory was something that called for world-wide publicity, and seven or eight were taken in cars on a week's trip, beginning on September 15. What, in retrospect, was so striking about it was a certain tragic pathos of the whole scene. Tragic was the town of Viazma, exposed to constant air attack from near-by German airfields; more tragic still were the young airmen at the small fighter airfield near Viazma—who, with their seven or eight sorties a day over the German lines, were on a constant near-suicide job; tragic, too, was the completely devastated countryside of the "Yelnya salient", where every village and every town had been destroyed, and the few surviving civilians were now living in cellars or dugouts.

Viazma, where we arrived in the late afternoon, looked almost normal, in spite of a large number of soldiers and bombed houses. It was a harmless little town, with its few government buildings in the central square, and a few derelict churches, and a statue of Lenin, and the rest of the town a mass of quiet provincial streets, with wooden houses and little gardens in front of them, and rows of rough wooden fences. In the gardens grew large sunflowers and dahlias; and old women, with scarves round their heads, chatted in front of the garden gates. The place could not have changed much since the days of Gogol.

The interview we had on that first night at Viazma with General Sokolovsky, at that time General Konev's Chief of Staff, was in the circumstances reassuring. He spoke in a quiet, even voice, describing what the Russian army had done on this Central Sector during the past few weeks. He attached the greatest importance to the fact that the Russians had stopped the German advance beyond Smolensk; claimed that "several German armies" had been smashed up in the last month, and that, in the first days of September alone, they had suffered 20,000 casualties; several hundred German planes had been shot down in this sector over a number of weeks. The *blitzkrieg* as such, he said, was over, and the process of "grinding down" the German war machine had now started in real earnest, and the Russians had even succeeded in recapturing a considerable slice of territory in this sector. To check the Russian counter-offensive, the Germans had had to bring up reinforcements in the last few days.

He thought German communications were being seriously interfered with by the partisans in the enemy rear. He also thought that Russian artillery was greatly superior to German artillery, though he admitted that the Germans still had great air and tank superiority. Another important point he made was that the Russian troops all had *polushubki* (sheepskin jackets) and other adequate winter clothes and they could stand even fifty degrees of frost; the Germans could not stand up to it. It was significant that he should, already then, have attached the greatest importance to the part winter was soon going to play. As an afterthought he said that he could only speak of the Central Front, and could not speak with first-hand knowledge of Voroshilov in the north and Budienny in the south, where, indeed, the situation was then extremely serious.

Asked whether, in view of what he had said, a new German offensive against Moscow was now impossible, he said: "Of course not. They may always try a last desperate gamble, or even a few 'last desperate' gambles. *But I don't think,*" he added firmly, "*that they will get to Moscow.*"

At sunset we drove to a small fighter base outside Viazma. Here were the "Stalin Hawks"—the *Stalinskie sokoly*—in their own surroundings. The moment we arrived, we heard the drone of engines and, despite the growing darkness, a Russian fighter swooped down and landed gracefully on the airfield.

A crowd of airmen on the ground ran up to the new arrival. The newly-landed plane was a fighter, but had been fitted with a bomb bay... The young pilot was, by now, busily examining one of the wooden wings which had been pierced by an anti-aircraft shell. He had dropped his bombs on a German airfield near Smolensk, and there had been some heavy anti-aircraft fire. He had set fire to a hangar, and seemed very pleased with the result. He was about twenty, but had done a good deal of flying. When asked how much flying a day he did, he said: "From here to the German lines—oh, five, six, seven raids a day; only takes about an hour or so, there and back." There was another young, fair-haired airman whom I asked how he liked the dangerous life; "I love it. It may be dangerous, but every moment of it is exciting. It's the best life there is. It's well worth it." (Did he really mean it? I wondered.)

Later we were shown a rocket that was used by these planes against tanks. Even so, there was something pathetic about these slow obsolete planes being used as supposed fighter-bombers—with probably very little effect, but at a terribly high cost in Russian lives.

That week spent in the Smolensk country—the Smolenshchina— was, in a sense, a heartening but also a highly tragic experience. This was, historically, one of the oldest of Russian lands, not Estonian, Latvian or even Belorussian or Ukrainian; this was very nearly the heart of old Muscovy. The ancient city of Smolensk was already in German hands, and the front was running some twenty or twenty-five miles east of it. There were villages through which we travelled where the Germans had not yet been. There were hardly any young men left in these villages; only women and children and a few very old men, and many of the women were anxious and full of foreboding. Many of these villages in the frontal zone had been bombed and machine-gunned. Some villages and small towns, like Dukhovshchina, had been completely wiped out by German bomb- ing, and the fields of rye and flax around them had remained unharvested.

And then there were the soldiers. We visited many regimental headquarters, some of them only a mile or two from the front line, and with shells frequently falling around. For the last month these men had been advancing, though at heavy cost. Many of the officers, like Colonel Kirilov, who received us on a wooded hill overlooking the German lines on the other side of a narrow plain, were like some- thing out of Tolstoy—brave, a little gruff, taking war in their stride;

some of these men had retreated hundreds of miles, but now they were happy to have stopped and even driven back the Germans. Kirilov had adopted as a "son of the regiment" a pathetic little fourteen-year-old boy, whose father and mother had both been killed in the bombing of a near-by village.

One night we stayed at a field hospital consisting of several large dugouts; two of them were still crowded with men who had been too severely wounded to be transported—men who had lost both their eyes, or both legs; only a week before, there had been hundreds of wounded in these dugouts. All the nurses were pupils of the Tomsk medical school, all young and extraordinarily pretty, as Siberian women usually are. There was a staff of seven surgeons, six doctors and these forty-eight nurses, and, only a week before, they had had to handle as many as 300 wounded a day. The operating dugout was well-equipped, and there were X-ray and blood-transfusion outfits. As yet, the chief surgeon, a Moscow man, said, they had not been short of any medical supplies.

But perhaps the optimism among the soldiers was more on the surface. I had a talk one day with a captain, whose home town was Kharkov, and who had studied history and economics at Kharkov University. He had been engaged in some heavy fighting round Kiev during the previous month, until his regiment had been moved to this Smolensk sector. He was in a gloomy mood. "It's no use pretending that all is well," he said: "The flag-waving, the hurrah-patriotism of our press are all very well for propaganda purposes to keep up morale; but it can be overdone—as it sometimes is. We shall need a lot of help from abroad. I know the Ukraine; I know how immensely important it is for our whole national economy. Now we have lost Krivoi Rog and Dniepropetrovsk, and without the Krivoi Rog iron ore, Kharkov and Stalino, if we don't lose them too, will find it hard to work at anything like full capacity. Leningrad, with its skilled labour, is also more or less isolated. And we just don't know how much further the Germans are going to push—with their troops already at Poltava, we may well lose Kharkov. We've been hearing for weeks about the Economic Conference that's to meet in Moscow; they say Lord Beaverbrook is on his way; I wonder what good it'll do..."

He went on: "This is a very grim war. And you cannot imagine the hatred the Germans have stirred up among our people. We are easy-going, good-natured people, you know; but I assure you, they have turned our people into spiteful *mujiks. Zlyie mujiki*—that's what we've got in the Red Army now, men thirsting for revenge. We officers sometimes have a job in keeping our soldiers from killing German prisoners; I know they want to do it, especially when they see some of these arrogant, fanatical Nazi swine. I have never known such hatred before. And there's good reason for it. Think of those towns and villages over there," he said, pointing at the red sunset over Smolensk; "think of all the torture and degradation these people are made to suffer." There was a flicker of mad hatred in his eyes. "And I cannot help thinking of my wife and my own ten-year-old daughter in Kharkov." He was silent for a time, controlling himself, and hammering one knee with his fingers. "Of course," he said at last, "there are the partisans; they are at least a *personal* solution to thousands of people over there. There comes a moment when people can't bear it any longer. They go off into the woods, in the hope that they may murder a German some time. Often it's like suicide; often they know that, sooner or later, they are almost sure to be caught, and to be put through all the beastliness the Germans are capable of..."

He then talked about the partisans generally, thought they were important, though not as important as they might be. And sooner or later, if the Russians went on retreating, the partisans would lose touch with their sources of supply, and would soon be short of arms. "No doubt they can continue to carry on sabotage in a small way, and various forms of passive resistance, but they may no longer constitute a serious armed force. If only we had fully prepared the partisan movement, if only we had piled up thousands of arms dumps throughout Western Russia. Something was done, but not nearly enough; and in the south there are, unfortunately, no woods..."

It was during this visit to the Front that I first met Alexei Surkov, the Russian poet, who was there as a war correspondent. Later during the war we recalled those days. "Those were fearful days," he said. "Do you know that we wanted to show you people some of our tanks—well, I can now tell you, we didn't have a damned thing!"

The town of Dorogobuzh—famous before the war for its cheeses— on the banks of the Upper Dnieper, which we reached one night, after travelling for hours along terribly muddy, bumpy roads, had been bombed by the Germans, and now nothing was left of it but the shells of the stone and brick buildings and the chimney stacks of the wooden houses; of its 10,000 inhabitants, only about 100 people were still there. In July, in broad daylight, waves of German planes had dropped high explosives and incendiary bombs over the town for a whole hour. There were no troops there at the time; men, women, children had been killed—nobody knew how many.

After spending the night in an army tent outside the town—we saw the next morning some fifty people, mostly women and some pale-looking children, lining up for food outside an army canteen in one of the few only half-destroyed buildings of the town—we drove to Yelnya through what was now "reconquered territory". There had been heavy fighting there. The woods were shattered by shellfire; there were, here and there, large mass-graves, with crudely-painted wooden obelisks on top of them, in which hundreds of Russian soldiers had been buried. The village of Ushakovo, where some of the heaviest fighting had taken place for over a month, had been razed to the ground; and only from the bare patches along the road could one roughly imagine where the houses had stood. In Ustinovka, another village some distance away, most of the thatched roofs had been torn away by bomb blast; the people in the village had fled before the Germans came; but now there were faint signs of life again. An old peasant and two little boys had returned since the Russians had recaptured the village, and were working in the deserted fields, digging up potatoes—potatoes that had been sown long before the Germans had come. And there was nobody else in the village, except an old woman, a blind old woman who had gone insane. She was there when the village was shelled, and had gone mad. I saw her wandering barefooted about the village, carrying a few dirty rags, a rusty pail and a tattered sheepskin. One of the boys said that she slept in her shattered hut, and they gave her potatoes, and sometimes soldiers passing through the village would give her something, though she never asked for anything. She just stared with her blind white eyes and never uttered any articulate words, except the word "*Cherti*"—the devils.

We drove on to Yelnya, through more miles of uncut fields. Once we drove off the road into a wood, because there were three or four German planes overhead. In the wood there were Russian batteries and other signs of military activity. Yelnya had been wholly destroyed. On both sides of the road leading to the centre of the town, all the houses—mostly wooden houses—had been burned, and all that was left was piles of ashes and chimney-stacks, with fire-places some way down. It had been a town of about 15,000 inhabitants. The only building still intact was a large stone church. Most of the civilians who had been here during the German occupation had now gone. The town had been captured by the Germans almost by surprise, and very few civilians had had time to escape. Nearly all the able-bodied men and women had been formed into forced-labour battalions, and driven into the German rear. A few hundred elderly people and children had been allowed to stay on in the town. The night the Germans decided to pull out of Yelnya— for the Russians were closing in, threatening to encircle the town— the remaining people of Yelnya were ordered to assemble inside the church. They spent a night of terror. Through the high windows of the church black smoke was pouring in, and they could see the flames. For the Germans were now going round the houses, picking up what few valuables they could find, and then systematically setting fire to every house in the town. The Russians drove into the town through the burning wreckage, and were able to release the now homeless prisoners.

In the course of this one and only visit to the Front we had talked to three German airmen, the crew of a German bomber that had been shot down almost immediately after their raid on Viazma.* All three were arrogant, boasted of having bombed London, and were quite sure that Moscow would fall before the winter.

They argued that the war against Russia had been rendered inevitable by the war against England; it was part of the same war; and once Russia had been knocked out, England would be brought to her knees. "And what about America?" somebody asked. "America, that's a long way away: *Amerika, das ist sehr weit.*" They also said that it had taken *five* Russian fighters to bring down their Heinkel. . .

* They had just missed the house where we were staying, but had killed several people in the house across the street. The episode is described in *Moscow '41.*

Chapter VII

ADVANCE ON LENINGRAD

While the Red Army succeeded in stabilising the Front east of
Smolensk, events in the north and, before long, in the south, took a
turn for the worse. The unequalled tragedy of Leningrad will be
related in some detail later in this book, and the German advance on
Leningrad need be mentioned only briefly here. The German plan
was to make one rapid thrust through Pskov, Luga and Gatchina to
Leningrad, and to capture the city, while the Finns were expected
to strike from the north. A second enveloping movement was to be
carried out round Lake Ilmen, and then on to Petrozavodsk, east of
Lake Ladoga, where the German troops were to join with the Finns.

The Russian troops of the "North-West Direction", under Voroshilov, had been routed in the Baltic Republics, and the Wehrmacht
crashed through to Ostrov and the ancient Russian city of Pskov on
their way to Leningrad, some 200 miles to the north. They had
captured Ostrov on July 10 and Pskov two days later. Another
German force, after capturing Riga and occupying the whole of
Latvia, was rapidly advancing into Estonia, with the Russians
retreating in disorder to Tallinn, the capital of Estonia and one of
the most important Soviet naval bases on the Baltic. Of the original
thirty divisions of the North-Western Front only five were now fully
manned and fully armed, the rest were left with a ten to thirty per
cent complement of either men or equipment.* By July 10, the

* IVOVSS, vol. II, pp. 78–79.

position was as disastrous as during the worst stages of the Russian retreat through Belorussia. The Germans had a 2·4 to one superiority in men, four to one in guns and nearly six to one in mortars, not to speak about tanks and aircraft.* To slow down the German advance on Leningrad, not only were some regular reserve troops thrown in, especially along the River Luga, but also freshly improvised *opolcheniye* units, consisting of workers' battalions, student and even schoolboy battalions, so characteristic of that *levée en masse* spirit which was to prove stronger in Leningrad than in almost any other Soviet city. Moreover, several hundred thousand civilians had been mobilised, early in July, to dig three lines of trenches, anti-tank ditches, and other, admittedly rudimentary, defences on the approaches to Leningrad. The "outer" line of defence was along the River Luga.

As it is now openly admitted, no fortifications of any kind existed in that part of Russia; for even though the Soviet Government had been extremely concerned about the security of Leningrad, and had even embarked on its Winter War of 1939–40 to push the Finnish frontier back, "it had never even occurred to anybody before the war that Leningrad might be threatened from the south or south-west".†

The Germans pushed on relentlessly, and reached the Luga river long before the Russian defences were complete. Nevertheless, by July 10, a long stretch of the Luga Line had been manned by the so-called Luga operational group, consisting of four regular infantry divisions and three divisions of Leningrad *opolcheniye*. The German

* In this, as in most other cases, there is a discrepancy between the Russian and the German estimates of the German forces involved. According to Telpukhovsky, op. cit., the Germans had assembled for their thrust against Leningrad 700,000 men, 1,500 tanks and 1,200 planes. The Germans, without giving any figure for the number of men in *Heeresgruppe Nord*, claim that it had only 900 tanks and 350 planes in its drive on Leningrad. (See footnote by its German editors, A. Hillgruber and J. A. Jacobson on p. 56 of the German translation of Telpukhovsky's book, *Die Sowjetische Geschichte des Grossen Vaterländischen Krieges, 1941–5* (The Soviet History of the Great Patriotic War 1941–5), (Frankfurt, 1961).
† IVOVSS, vol. II, p. 210.

advance was, indeed, slowed down, but the Germans succeeded in establishing a number of bridgeheads on the north side of the Luga.

Meanwhile, other German forces were overrunning Estonia on the west side of Lake Peipus. Breaking through to Kunda on the Gulf of Finland east of Tallinn on August 7, the Germans cut off the Russian forces who had retreated to the Estonian capital. Even before that, other German forces had pushed north to Kingisepp along the east bank of Lake Peipus, and the threat to Leningrad had grown immensely. The Germans had forced the Narva river and were not only advancing on the former Russian capital from the Narva-Kingisepp area, where the Russians had already suffered terrible losses in heavy fighting, and from the Luga area, but were also advancing to the east of Leningrad, both north and south of Lake Ilmen, with the obvious purpose of isolating Leningrad from the east and joining with the Finns on the east side of Lake Ladoga.

In July, the Finns had already struck out in two directions—across the Karelian Isthmus up to the frontier, and to the east of Lake Ladoga, towards Petrozavodsk, on the banks of Lake Onega.

A particularly harrowing episode was the attempt of the Soviet troops marooned at Tallinn to escape by sea. For over a month they had tried to stop the Germans capturing Tallinn from the south. A large part of the Soviet Baltic Navy was still at Tallinn, and the greatest possible number of troops were to be evacuated by sea. It was a kind of Dunkirk, but without air cover, all available Russian aircraft being concentrated in and around Leningrad, where the situation was already highly critical, as the Germans had by this time practically cut off Leningrad from the east.

At Tallinn there were 20,000 Russian troops, and these, together with the Baltic Navy, had tied up substantial German forces within a radius of ten to twenty miles for over a month. 25,000 civilians were mobilised to strengthen the defences to the south of the city, though how enthusiastic these Estonians were may be questioned.

The Germans started their all-out attack on Tallinn on August 19, but the Russians, supported by the guns of the coastal defences and warships, were able to hold their ground for nearly a week. On

August 26, however, the Germans broke into the city, and the Russian Supreme Command ordered the evacuation of Tallinn, all the more so as Leningrad badly needed what troops and ships could still be rescued. After two more days of intensive street fighting, the convoy of troop transports and warships sailed from Tallinn harbour. The Germans claimed that "not a single ship" would be able to leave Tallinn; but, according to the Russians, "most" of the ships, including the flag-ship *Minsk*, got through, despite constant attacks from German aircraft and torpedo boats, and floating mines which the Germans had scattered throughout the Gulf of Finland. The biggest losses were suffered by the trawlers and destroyers trying to take the convoy through the German minefields. In the end, the "greater part" of the ships, carrying several thousand soldiers, landed in Kronstadt or Leningrad.

The Russian naval garrisons of Dagö and other islands off the Estonian coast, held out till the middle of October, when the 500 survivors of the defence of Dagö succeeded in sailing under cover of night to Hangö, the Russian naval base in Finland, which was then still in Russian hands.

It was, in fact, not until the Russian armies had retreated—or fled might be the right word—to the immediate vicinity of Leningrad after the collapse of the "Luga Line", that they began to contain the Germans with any success. Voroshilov had lost his head completely, and it was not until General Zhukov was rushed to Leningrad at the beginning of September and reorganised the troops on the spot that the defence of Leningrad began in real earnest... It was to become the greatest of all the great Russian stories of human endurance. Never yet had a city of the size of Leningrad been besieged for nearly two-and-a-half years.

Chapter VIII

ROUT IN THE UKRAINE
"Khrushchev versus Stalin"

Meantime, as we have seen, Hitler had decided to strike his main blow, not at Moscow, but at the Ukraine. Abandoning, for the time being, the drive on Moscow, he had transferred some troops to the north to speed up the capture of Leningrad, and even larger reinforcements were sent to the Ukraine, which, together with the Crimea, he planned to overrun within a few weeks.

Early in July, the Russians had had a few local successes in the Ukraine; thus they had checked a German breakthrough to Kiev some ten or twelve miles outside the city. But at the end of July and the beginning of August, the *blitzkrieg* had been resumed. On August 17 the Germans occupied Dniepropetrovsk, at the far end of the Dnieper bend, and forced the Dnieper, despite the Soviet Supreme Command's order to hold the Dnieper Line at all costs. Kherson, Nikolayev and the iron-ore centre of Krivoi Rog were captured.

In the south-west Odessa was cut off by the Rumanians from the Soviet "mainland". Meanwhile, north of Kiev, the Germans had started another offensive in the general direction of Konotop, Poltava and, ultimately, Kharkov. Thus, by the beginning of September, Kiev formed, in fact, the tip of a long and constantly narrowing salient, the Germans having advanced far to the east both north and south of the Ukrainian capital.

It is here that we come to one of the major controversies of the

202

war—a controversy involving not only Hitler and his generals, but also Stalin and Khrushchev. Khrushchev was a Member of the War Council attached to the staff of Marshal Budienny, the C.-in-C. of the "South-Western Direction".* Present-day histories are untiring in their praise of Khrushchev who, as a member of the Politburo and as Secretary of the Central Committee of the Ukrainian Communist Party, aroused everywhere, they say, the patriotic fervour of the people of the Ukraine, and of Kiev in particular—even though, lacking the great proletarian and revolutionary traditions of Moscow and Leningrad, the *levée en masse* seems to have been considerably less spectacular there than in the other two cities. Moreover, Kiev had a peculiar mentality. Only some twenty years before it had been occupied in quick succession by the German and Austrian armies, who had put up a puppet ruler, Hetman Skoropadsky, at the head of the Ukrainian "state", by Ukrainian nationalists under Petlura, by Reds, Whites and Reds again and, for a short time, in 1920, even by Pilsudski's Poles. Older people may have remembered that the German-Austrian occupation of 1918 had not been as terrible as all that.

As by September 9, the Germans were advancing on Nezhin† from the north, and other German armies had penetrated far into the Dnieper bend in the south, and as no Russian reserves were available to check these two German advances, Budienny and Khrushchev decided to pull out of the Kiev salient.

On September 11, they informed Stalin that his previous instructions to despatch two infantry divisions from Kiev to stop the German advance in the north could not be carried out; that the

* It should be explained, to avoid confusion, that the "South-Western Direction" was one of the three "Directions" into which the whole Front had been split in July. Several "Fronts" (i.e. Army Groups) came under the authority of each "Direction". One of the "Fronts" that came under the authority of the "South-West Direction" was the "South-West Front", the principal victim of the Kiev encirclement. By October 1941, the Front was no longer divided into "Directions", but only into "Fronts" (i.e. Army Groups). In September the commander of the "Direction" was Budienny, the commander of the "Front" was Kirponos.
† Seventy miles ENE of Kiev.

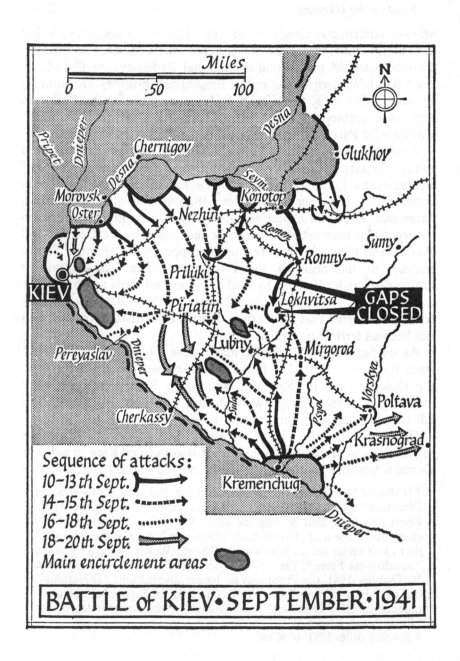

Miles

0   50   100

N

Pripet
Dnieper
Desna
Chernigov
Desna
Glukhov
Morovsk
Oster
Sevm
Konotop
Nezhin
Romen
Sumy
Romny
Priluki
Lokhvitsa
GAPS CLOSED
KIEV
Piriatin
Pereyaslav
Dnieper
Lubny
Mirgorod
Sula
Psyol
Vorskya
Poltava
Cherkassy
Krasnograd
Kremenchug
Dnieper

Sequence of attacks:
10–13 th Sept.
14–15 th Sept.
16–18 th Sept.
18–20 th Sept.
Main encirclement areas

BATTLE of KIEV · SEPTEMBER · 1941

Soviet armies in the Ukraine had been badly weakened by weeks of heavy fighting, and that, despite the Supreme Command's opinion to the contrary, they considered the time ripe for withdrawing to a new line in the east.

On that same day, in speaking to General Kirponos, commander of the South-Western Front, Stalin "emphatically rejected the proposal to abandon Kiev and to withdraw the troops from the Kiev salient to the River Psyol [in the Kursk-Poltava area]. He insisted that troops be taken from other sectors of the Front and thrown against the Germans advancing on Konotop [east of Nezhin]..." He also relieved Budienny of his command and replaced him by Timoshenko, who arrived in Kiev on September 13 to take up his new duties.

On that day, the bottleneck from which the four armies of the South-Western Front could have pulled out was only twenty miles wide—between Lokhvitsa and Lubny... Two days later, German tank formations closed this bottleneck.

Here we come to the climax of the Stalin-Khrushchev controversy, of which so much is made in the present-day *History*:

> On September 14 Major-General Tupilov, Chief of Staff of the South-West Front, considered it his duty to inform General Shaposhnikov, the Chief of Staff in Moscow, of the catastrophic situation... There were, he concluded, only a couple of days left. General Shaposhnikov called this report "panicky", asked the commanders of the South-West Front not to lose their heads and to carry out Comrade Stalin's orders of September 11.*

But on September 16, the Germans closed the bottleneck, and the four Soviet armies were surrounded... One of them, the 37th, was still holding the Kiev bridgehead on the west bank of the Dnieper. All these troops, says the *History*, had already suffered very heavy losses, "were disorganised and had lost most of their fighting capacity. All this could have been avoided if Budienny's and Khrushchev's advice had been followed in time."† After pointing out that the Supreme Command had a very erroneous idea of the whole situation, the *History* goes on:

* IVOVSS, vol. II, p. 108.   † Ibid., p. 108.

Since the Supreme Command still would not order a general retreat, the War Council of the South-Western Direction accepted N. S. Khrushchev's proposal to abandon Kiev and to lead the troops of the South-West Front out of the encirclement. Since the enemy had not yet consolidated his front along the Psyol, this seemed the only reasonable solution. On Budienny's and Khrushchev's behalf, this decision was transmitted verbally by General Bagramian to General Kirponos, who was then at Priluki, the headquarters of the South-West Front... Instead of immediately carrying out this order, Kirponos finally asked Moscow whether or not to carry out the instructions of the War Council of the South-Western Direction.*

It was not till 11.40 p.m. on September 17 that Shaposhnikov replied that the Supreme Command had authorised the abandonment of Kiev, but still said nothing about breaking across the river Psyol. Thus, two days were wasted in which substantial Russian forces could have broken out, but did not. What followed was an incoherent attempt to break out of the encirclement; it was all the more incoherent since communications between the various army headquarters were non-existent. Thus, separated from the other armies, the 37th Army continued its hopeless fight for Kiev during the next few days, and only then began—without any hope of success—to fight its way out.

Only some units succeeded in breaking out—for example one of 2,000 men with General Bagramian at their head. The General Staff of the South-West Front and members of its War Council, having been unable to find a single plane, followed Bagramian with 800 men, but were cut off by German tanks. Near Lokhvitsa, a battle raged for two days in the course of which General Kirponos was mortally wounded and M. A. Burmistrenko, a member of the War Council and Secretary of the Central Committee of the Ukrainian Communist Party, as well as the Chief of Staff of the Army Group, General Tupikov, were killed. Only very few members of the General Staff escaped. Tens of thousands of soldiers, officers and political personnel died in the unequal struggle, or were taken prisoner, many of them wounded.†

* IVOVSS, vol. II, p. 109.

† Ibid., p. 110. It is understood that Budienny, Timoshenko and Khrushchev escaped by air from Kiev.

The Germans claim that the Wehrmacht captured no fewer than 665,000 prisoners in the Kiev encirclement. According to the *History* there were 677,085 men on the South-Western Front at the beginning of the Kiev operation. But of these a total of 150,541 men had escaped encirclement. The troops that were encircled fought on through the greater part of September and suffered very heavy losses, while others succeeded in breaking out. Not more than one-third of the number of troops who had been originally surrounded were taken prisoner.* These Russian statistics would reduce the number of prisoners taken to about 175,000. One cannot help suspecting that the truth must lie somewhere half-way between the Russian and the German figures.

The question remains whether Stalin was not perhaps right, after all, to have clung to the Kiev salient for as long as he did. Paradoxically, the *History* suggests that this German victory in the Ukraine hopelessly upset Hitler's time-table.* This, indeed, coincides with the prevalent German view. In the opinion of some of the leading German generals, the time wasted on the Kiev operation very largely upset the plans of the German High Command to reach Moscow before the winter had set in. Thus Halder considered that the Battle of Kiev was the greatest strategic mistake in the Eastern campaign, an opinion shared by Guderian, who spoke of the Battle of Kiev as a great tactical victory, but doubted that great strategic advantages were to be derived from it.†

Guderian found some comfort, though not very much, in the thought that although "the planned assault on Leningrad had to be abandoned in favour of a tight investment" the prospects for occupying the Donets Basin and reaching the Don were now good. It is not quite clear, though, whether, at the time, he entirely agreed with the OKH's belief "that the enemy was no longer capable of creating a firm defensive front or offering serious resistance in the area of Army Group South".

In any case, however, the Germans had torn a 200-mile gap in the Russian front in the Ukraine, and, in the next two months, they occupied the whole Eastern Ukraine and nearly the whole Crimea,

* IVOVSS, vol. II, p. 111.
† Guderian, op. cit., pp. 225–6.

and were not thrown some distance back until after they had captured Rostov.

Although Odessa was to rank officially among the four "hero cities" (the others being Leningrad, Moscow and Stalingrad),* its defence against one German and eighteen Rumanian divisions between August 5 and October 16 by the Special Maritime Army under General Petrov was in reality something of a side-show in the general pattern of the war in 1941.

Reaching the Black Sea coast at the beginning of August, the enemy had cut off Odessa from the Russian "mainland", but this main Russian naval base in the western part of the Black Sea was able to maintain communications by sea with both the Crimea and the Caucasus. The Black Sea Navy and Marines played an important part in the defence of Odessa where extremely heavy fighting was raging at the end of August and losses in effectives reached as much as forty per cent overall, and in the case of the marines, as much as seventy to eighty per cent. In order to hold Odessa as long as possible, for this tied up considerable enemy forces, reinforcements were sent by sea, including a number of those invaluable *katyusha* mortars, whose mass production had only just begun.

It is remarkable, in view of the German air superiority, that the Russians should have been able to maintain, as they claim, regular sea communications from Odessa throughout the siege of the city. They even claim that they managed to evacuate by sea to the Caucasus 350,000 civilians, that is about half of the population, and some 200,000 tons of industrial equipment.

When practically the whole of the Crimea, with the exception of Sebastopol, had been overrun by the Germans, 80,000 soldiers and a considerable amount of military equipment were successfully transported by sea from Odessa to Sebastopol and the Caucasus—and

* It was long after the war that, on Khrushchev's initiative, Kiev was added to the "hero cities". In military quarters this decision was sharply criticised, one colonel, who had gone right through the whole war, telling me: "Hero city, my foot! It was one of our worst skedaddles."

this despite a large-scale attempt at sabotage by enemy agents who, at the height of the evacuation, set fire to numerous port installations.*

Odessa fell after two and a half months of extremely fierce fighting, and losses were heavy on both sides. The Russians were very surprised by the toughness of the Rumanian troops, since Rumania's military record, particularly in World War I, had not been exactly glorious. According to the Russians—always prone to exaggerate enemy losses—the Rumanians had lost 110,000 men at Odessa; but this is by no means a fantastic figure, since, according to the Rumanians, their army lost, between the outbreak of the war and October 10, 1941, as many as 70,000 dead and 100,000 wounded.†
Odessa and all the country between the Dniester and the Western Bug, were to be incorporated in Rumania under the name of Transniestria. There was, as we shall see, going to be a marked difference between the Rumanian and the German occupation régime.

Whether 175,000 prisoners were taken east of Kiev, or 400,000 or 600,000—all this Russian and German quibbling over figures is one thing; another is what all this represented in human terms.

A heavy silence hung over the whole question all through the war and, indeed, for many years after. Certainly, Molotov issued, from time to time, long Notes on the ill-treatment of Russian war-prisoners, or on atrocities committed by the Germans in the occupied areas of the Soviet Union. But these were clumsy documents, in which horrors were piled upon horrors to such an extent that those who read them, not only in the West, but even in Russia in 1941–3, only half-believed them—if that. Except for some atrocities the Germans had committed in the relatively small areas around Moscow that were liberated by the Russians in the winter of 1941–2, there was still very little first-hand information on the German occupation, or even on the German treatment of war-prisoners. Only after Stalingrad, when the Russians began to liberate enormous areas, did

* IVOVSS, vol. II, p. 118.
† Telpukhovsky, op. cit., German edition, p. 58.

the truth begin to emerge. And even then, not the whole truth. The full enormity of it did not begin to be measured until the liberation of Poland with its super-death-camps and the occupation of Germany when stock could at last be taken of what had happened to the Russians deported to Germany as slave labour, or captured as war prisoners, particularly in 1941–2.

For long after the war, very little was said about those who were taken prisoner in those early war days; a stigma was still attached to those unfortunate people.

The human tragedy of the Russian prisoners was not to be openly discussed in Russia until long after the war. By far the most graphic account of what it was like to have been trapped in the Kiev Encirclement was not to be written until twenty years after, and published in the form of a short story in *Novyi Mir* of January 1963. But though presented as fiction, it is the tale of one of its survivors, and has the ring of absolute authenticity.

In the thirty pages of *Through the Night*, Leonid Volynsky succeeds in telling the story of German captivity with the same concentrated intensity that Solzhenitsyn had given to his account of the Stalin labour camps.

The story begins on September 17, 1941 in a Ukrainian village, just as the German ring is about to close round the Russians.

> Many years afterwards, I read a book by von Tippelskirch, a German general, who wrote that the encirclement of our troops east of Kiev had tied down large German forces, and so ruined Hitler's game, since it delayed his offensive against Moscow.
>
> No doubt that's just how things happened... But we knew nothing about that. To hundreds of thousands of men trying during those nights to break out of the German ring ... groping their way through forests and marshes, and under a hailstorm of German bombs and shells ... all this was nothing but a vast and inexplicable tragedy.

On that night of the 17th, the narrator was wandering along a road; two or three thousand motor vehicles were burning; it was important not to let the Germans have them. That night, too, he saw a group of ten senior officers also walking towards Lokhvitsa (where there was believed to be a gap in the ring)—he recognised among them the Commander of the Front, General Kirponos.

Not until several years later did I learn that he shot himself that night—or it may have been the following night, having refused to fly off in a plane that had been sent for him with great difficulty... His remains have since been reburied in Kiev. With him also died a member of his war council, Burmistrenko, who had been the Second Secretary of the Central Committee of the Ukrainian CP before the war.*

On the following morning, the narrator and three other soldiers, seeing German tanks approaching, hid in an overgrown ravine. But the Germans noticed them, and proceeded to machine-gun the bottom of the ravine. One man was killed, but the three others surrendered. (The thought of suicide crossed the narrator's mind, but no more.) A German soldier, a decent and pleasant fellow at first sight, slapped their faces, and ordered them to empty their pockets. Closely followed by a tank, they had to run to a village called Kovali. By the end of the day, 10,000 prisoners were assembled there.

On the following morning, the "Commissars, Communists and Jews" were summoned to come forward, after the arrival of some fifteen SS-men in black uniforms and with skulls on their caps. Some three hundred came forward, were stripped to the waist and lined up in the yard. Then the interpreter, a young man, speaking with a strong Galician accent, shouted that some must still be hiding; and anyone who denounced a Communist, Commissar or Jew could take his clothes and other belongings. "And, among ten thousand men, you will always find a dozen or two such people; it may not be a high percentage, but there it is. Such people do exist, and always will." So, in the end, four hundred were shot, being taken away ten at a time, and ordered to dig their graves.

They all died silently, except one, who uttered heart-rending screams, as he crawled at the SS-men's feet: "Don't kill me! My mother is a Ukrainian." One of the SS-men kicked him in the face, and knocked his teeth out, and he was hauled off to the execution ground, his bare feet dragging through the dust.

The surviving war prisoners were marched first to one camp, and

* It is curious to note that, according to the official *History* Kirponos was "killed"; there is no mention of his suicide.

then to another, and the soldiers—"decent-looking, ordinary chaps, perhaps German working-men"—automatically shot any stragglers, or anyone falling down by the road-side. The rest of the story is one of such constant starvation, cold and humiliation that the prisoners rapidly lost all human semblance and human dignity. The narrator and two other men succeeded in escaping—but they were the lucky exceptions.

Chapter IX

THE EVACUATION OF INDUSTRY

The evacuation of industry threatened by the German invasion had been one of the Soviet Government's major concerns almost since the moment the war had begun. During the very first days of the war two important industrial centres were lost: Riga and Minsk; but there was nothing of outstanding industrial importance in Lithuania, the rest of Latvia, Belorussia, or the Western Ukraine. The great industrial areas of the European part of the Soviet Union threatened by the invasion, or, at any rate, by destruction from the air, were the whole of Central and Eastern Ukraine—including the Kharkov, Dniepropetrovsk, Krivoi Rog, Mariupol and Nikopol areas, and the Donbas—and secondly, the industrial areas of Moscow and Leningrad.

Whether or not the Soviet Government believed, in the early weeks of the war, that the Germans would reach Leningrad, Moscow, Kharkov, or the Donbas, it very rightly decided, there and then, to take no chances, and laid down as a firm principle the evacuation of all essential industries, and particularly the war industries, to the east. It knew from the start that this was a matter of life and death if the Germans were going to overrun large areas of European Russia.

This transplantation of industry in the second half of 1941 and the beginning of 1942 and its "rehousing" in the east, must rank among the most stupendous organisational and human achievements of the Soviet Union during the war.

A steep increase in war production and the reorganisation of the entire war industry on a new basis depended on the rapid transfer of heavy industry from the western and central areas of European Russia and the Ukraine to the distant rear, where it would not only be out of the German army's reach, but would also be beyond the range of German aircraft. As early as July 4, the State Defence Committee ordered the Chairman of the *Gosplan*, Voznesensky, to draw up a detailed plan for setting up in the east what was, in effect, "a second line of industrial defence". The aim was to organise a "coherent productive combination between the industries already existing in the east and those to be transplanted there".

The evacuation of industry to the Urals, the Volga country, Western Siberia and Central Asia, started at a very early stage of the war, not only from industrial centres immediately threatened by the Germans, but from other centres as well. Thus, as early as July 2, it was decided to move the armoured-plate mill from Mariupol in the Southern Ukraine, to Magnitogorsk, though Mariupol was still hundreds of miles away from the front. On the following day, the State Defence Committee, after approving the plans for the output of guns and small arms during the next few months, decided to transfer to the east twenty-six armament plants from Leningrad, Moscow and Tula. During the same week it was decided to send east part of the equipment, workers and technical staff from the diesel department of the Kirov Plant in Leningrad and the Tractor Plant in Kharkov. Another large plant for manufacturing tank engines was to be transferred from Kharkov to Cheliabinsk in the Urals.

At the same time, the conversion of certain industries was decided upon: thus, the Gorki automobile plant was to concentrate on the output of tank engines. These two decisions laid the foundations for a vast Volga-Urals combine for the mass-production of tanks. Similar steps were taken in respect of the aircraft industry.

With the German threat to the Eastern Ukraine growing, it was decided to evacuate without delay such vast enterprises as the Zaporozhie steel mills (Zaporozhstal). On August 7 orders were given to evacuate the enormous tube-rolling mill at Dniepropetrovsk. The first trains evacuating this plant left on August 9, and the ninth group of trains loaded with the plant's equipment, arrived at

Pervouralsk in the Urals on September 6. By December 24 it was in production again.

Many other large plants were also evacuated during August. The dismantling and loading of the equipment went on non-stop for twenty-four hours a day, often under enemy bombing. The size of the operation may be judged from the fact that in the case of Zaporozhstal alone, it required 8,000 railway trucks to evacuate the entire plant and its stocks. Most of the equipment, weighing some 50,000 tons, was put to work in the Magnitogorsk engineering combine.

On September 21, L. P. Korniets, of the Ukrainian Government, who supervised the evacuation, was able to report to the Government that "At Zaporozhie all plants have been evacuated. The evacuation took place in an organised manner, and with proper camouflage." He added that the raw materials were now being evacuated. In addition to the local workers, many hundreds of miners had been brought to Zaporozhie to help with the dismantling of the steel-mill equipment.

Rather less successful was the evacuation of some of the plants of the Donbas, which was overrun by the Germans more quickly than had been expected, and here the scorched-earth policy was extensively applied. Similarly, the Dnieper Dam was at least partly demolished by the retreating Russians. All the same, it had been possible to rescue a great deal: altogether, 283 major industrial enterprises had been evacuated from the Ukraine between June and October, besides 136 smaller factories.

More difficult, in the chaotic conditions of the first weeks of the invasion, had been the evacuation of the industrial plants of Belorussia, all the more so as the railways were under constant air bombardment; even so, some 100 enterprises (though not comparable in importance to those of the Ukraine) were evacuated, chiefly from the eastern parts of Belorussia (Gomel and Vitebsk).

The evacuation of Leningrad plants, and their workers, began in July after the Germans had reached the Luga river; but only ninety-two enterprises specialising in war production, and some workshops of the Kirov and Izhora plants were evacuated in time; the rest were trapped in Leningrad after the Germans had cut all the railway lines.

The large-scale industrial evacuation of Moscow was not started until October 10, with the Germans only a few miles away. But by the end of November 498 enterprises had been moved to the east, together with about 210,000 workers. No fewer than 71,000 railway wagons were required for this evacuation. During those grim winter months measures were also taken to evacuate from "threatened areas" like Kursk, Voronezh and the North-Caucasian provinces, as much as possible of the available food reserves, as well as the equipment of many light-industry factories.

This fantastic migration of industries and men to the east was not completed without considerable difficulties: there were gigantic bottlenecks at certain major railway junctions such as Cheliabinsk, and the evacuees suffered some terrible hardships on the way to the Urals, Siberia and Kazakhstan in the late autumn and at the height of winter.

Altogether, between July and November 1941 no fewer than 1,523 industrial enterprises, including 1,360 large war plants had been moved to the east—226 to the Volga area, 667 to the Urals, 244 to Western Siberia, 78 to Eastern Siberia, 308 to Kazakhstan and Central Asia. The "evacuation cargoes" amounted to a total of one and a half million railway wagon-loads.

This transplantation of industry to the east at the height of the German invasion in 1941 is, of course, an altogether unique achievement. But it would, at the same time be naive to assume that everything of any industrial importance was either evacuated in time, or destroyed on the strength of Stalin's "scorched-earth" instructions of July 3.

After the war, the Soviet Government officially claimed that, apart from destroying six million houses, leaving twenty-five million people homeless, slaughtering or carrying off seven million horses, seventeen million head of cattle, twenty million pigs, etc., the Germans and their allies had also "destroyed 31,850 industrial enterprises, employing some four million persons before the war, and had destroyed or carried away 239,000 electro-motors and 175,000 machine-tools".* Even allowing for the fact that, with an eye on

* Molotov's speech on Reparations on August 26, 1946, at the Paris Peace Conference for the Satellite countries, quoted in *Vneshnyaya*

reparations Molotov quoted some greatly inflated figures for the industrial equipment destroyed or looted by the Germans and their allies, his statement is, in fact, still an admission that a very important quantity of such equipment was left behind.

Everything tends to show that a very important part in this evacuation of industry and its "resettlement" in the east was played by Molotov, Beria, Malenkov and Kaganovich, but one would look in vain for any of these names in present-day accounts of this gigantic achievement which was ultimately to enable Russia to carry on the war. Instead, the names that are now given pride of place are Mikoyan and Kosygin, who remain among Mr Khrushchev's closest associates, and Voznesensky, who was shot, apparently in the course of the lurid "Leningrad Affair" in 1949.*

Especially when the Battle of Moscow was at its height, and after the Russian counter-offensive had begun, the Russian working-class worked with redoubled energy in resettling the evacuated war plants. Here was the combination of a great feat of organisation with an almost unparallelled example of mass devotion, for the men and women engaged in re-starting the evacuated armaments industry had to work at the height of winter, with worse than inadequate food and housing.

In October, many government departments, such as the People's Commissariats of Aircraft Production, Tank Production, Armaments, Iron and Steel, and Munitions were evacuated from Moscow to Kuibyshev. Voznesensky, the head of *Gosplan*, was instructed to send a weekly report to Moscow on the progress of the armaments industries. Similarly, a part of the *apparat* of the Central Committee of the CPSU had been evacuated to Kuibyshev and "was authorised to send recommendations and instructions to the regional party committees of the Volga, Urals, Siberian and Central-Asian provinces concerning the organisation of industries evacuated to these

---

Politika Sovietskogo Soyuza, 1946 (Soviet Foreign Policy 1946) (Moscow, 1947), pp. 296–7.
* See p. 359.

areas, and also concerning agricultural State purchases". Special
"evacuation bases" were established in industrial centres such as
Gorki, Kuibyshev, Cheliabinsk, Novosibirsk, Sverdlovsk, Magnitogorsk, Tashkent, etc.

Many evacuated factories were merged with local enterprises;
thus, a large tank plant from the Ukraine was integrated with a
number of local plants, to form a large combine which came to be
known as the "Stalin Urals Tank Works", while the Cheliabinsk
Tractor Plant, having merged with the evacuated Kharkov Diesel
Works and parts of the Leningrad Kirov Plant came to be popularly
known as "Tankograd".

Some of the "industrial giants" could not be transplanted as single
units, and had to be decentralised: thus part of the Moscow Ball-
Bearing Plant being re-settled in Saratov, another in Kuibyshev, and
still another in Tomsk. All this created a variety of new organisational problems.

During the war, I had the opportunity of talking to many workers,
both men and women, who had been evacuated to the Urals or
Siberia during the grim autumn or early winter months of 1941. The
story of how whole industries and millions of people had been moved
to the east, of how industries were set up in a minimum of time, in
appallingly difficult conditions, and of how these industries managed
to increase production to an enormous extent during 1942, was,
above all, a story of incredible human endurance. In most places,
living conditions were fearful, in many places food was very short,
too. People worked because they knew that it was absolutely necessary—they worked twelve, thirteen, sometimes fourteen or fifteen
hours a day; they "lived on their nerves"; they knew that never was
their work more urgently needed than now. Many died in the
process. All these people knew what losses were being suffered by
the soldiers, and they—in the "distant rear"—did not grumble
much; while the soldiers were suffering and risking so much, it was
not for the civilians to shirk even the most crippling, most heart-
breaking work. At the height of the Siberian winter, some people
had to walk to work—sometimes three, four, six miles; and then

work for twelve hours or more, and then walk back again, day after
day, month after month.

There was little or no exaggeration in the stories published in the
press—for instance the story of how, on an empty space outside
Sverdlovsk, two enormous buildings were erected in a fortnight for
a factory being brought from the Ukraine.

> Among the mountains and the pine forests there is spread out the
> beautiful capital of the Urals, Sverdlovsk. It has many fine buildings,
> but I want to tell you of the two most remarkable buildings in the area.
> Winter had already come when Sverdlovsk received Comrade Stalin's
> order to erect two buildings for the plant evacuated from the south.
> The trains packed with machinery and people were on the way. The
> war factory had to start production in its new home—and it had to do
> so in not more than a fortnight. Fourteen days, and not an hour more!
> It was then that the people of the Urals came to this spot with shovels,
> bars and pickaxes: students, typists, accountants, shop assistants,
> housewives, artists, teachers. The earth was like stone, frozen hard by
> our fierce Siberian frost. Axes and pickaxes could not break the stony
> soil. In the light of arc-lamps people hacked at the earth all night.
> They blew up the stones and the frozen earth, and they laid the
> foundations... Their feet and hands were swollen with frostbite, but
> they did not leave work. Over the charts and blueprints, laid out on
> packing cases, the blizzard was raging. Hundreds of trucks kept rolling
> up with building materials... On the twelfth day, into the new build-
> ings with their glass roofs, the machinery, covered with hoar-frost,
> began to arrive. Braziers were kept alight to unfreeze the machines...
> And two days later, the war factory began production.*

At the time, however, the press scarcely ever referred to the special
difficulties arising from war-time shortages. For example, a Government Instruction of September 11, 1941, laid down that steel and
reinforced concrete were to be used very sparingly, "and only in
cases when the use of other local materials, such as timber, was
technically wholly out of the question". So, especially in 1941, many
of the factory buildings were made of wood:

> These buildings were architecturally displeasing, and often altogether
> puny to look at; but... usually even large factory buildings were
> erected in a matter of fifteen to twenty days... People worked day and

* *Pravda*, September 18, 1942.

night—the scene of their work being lit by arc lamps or by electric bulbs suspended on trees... In one of the Volga cities the new buildings of the largest aircraft factory in the country were being built in this way... Even before the roof had been completed, the machine-tools were already functioning. Even when the thermometer went down to forty degrees below, people continued to work. On December 10, fourteen days after the arrival of the last train-loads of equipment, the first Mig fighter-plane was produced. By the end of the month, thirty Mig planes were turned out... Similarly, the last lot of workers of the Kharkov Tank Works left Kharkov on October 19; but already on December 8, in their new Urals surroundings, they were able to assemble their first twenty-five T-34 tanks, which were promptly sent to the front.*

Though a very high proportion of Soviet heavy industry, and especially war industry, was successfully moved to the east within four or five months, there was an inevitable drop in production in the meantime. There was, in fact, a gap of nearly a year—roughly from August 1941 to August 1942 when the Red Army was extremely short of equipment, and this shortage was very nearly disastrous between October 1941 and the following spring. It was, as we shall see, one of the principal reasons why the Battle of Moscow was only a partial, and not a complete victory. It also largely accounts for the Russians' grievous reverses of the following summer.

Even so, the increase in armament production immediately after the invasion was very considerable. In the whole of 1941 the aircraft industry produced a total of nearly 16,000 planes of all types, of which more than 10,000 were produced after the invasion, but mostly between July and October. The figures for the production of tanks and other weapons were equally striking, and the production of munitions of all kinds in the second half of 1941 was almost three times what it had been in the first. The tragedy of it was that, by October, all this progress came virtually to a standstill.

The difficulties facing the Soviet armaments industry in the east were enormous. Not all the workers of the evacuated plants could

* IVOVSS, vol. II, p. 151.

be transferred at the same time as the machinery; in many cases, for a variety of reasons, only forty or fifty per cent of the workers followed. There was also at first a very serious shortage of certain raw materials. High-grade steels for armour-plating, had, in the main, been produced in the Eastern Ukraine; this meant a fundamental reconversion of the various production processes in the east. This reconversion resulted in a temporary lowering of the output of the blast and open-hearth furnaces. There was an extreme shortage of molybdenum and manganese. A high proportion of the manganese had been produced in the Nikopol area, which was now under German occupation. New manganese mining areas had to be opened up in the Urals and Kazakhstan, where conditions of terrain and climate presented incredible difficulties. The Nikopol miners, who had brought to the east their mining equipment, started producing manganese ore, with the help of locally conscripted labour, in a remote part of Sverdlovsk province, where manganese mining had been only tentatively begun shortly before the war. The gradual organisation of the large-scale smelting of ferromanganese at the Kushvisk plant, in the Kuzbas and at Magnitogorsk was later described as "a stupendous industrial victory equal in importance to a major military victory". No more remarkable as a fact of human endurance was the development of molybdenum mines in the waterless steppe near Lake Balkhash in Central Asia.

When the Germans had overrun the Donbas, the Soviet Union lost over sixty per cent of her coal output, and the production of coal had to be stepped up in the Urals, the Kuzbas and Karaganda areas; in December 1941 it was decided to sink forty-four new mines within the next three months. Desperate efforts were also made to increase the output of aluminium, nickel, cobalt, zinc, oil, chemicals, etc., in the east.

The critical situation is best summarised in the second volume of the official *History*:

> In the late autumn of 1941 our country lived through its most difficult days, both militarily and economically. The front required more and more armaments and munitions, but owing to the evacuation of so many plants, the number of factories producing war equipment had sharply fallen... By the end of October, not a single plant in the south

was working. Of the blast furnaces in operation on June 1, only thirty-eight per cent were now working; of the open-hearth furnaces, only fifty-two per cent; of the electric-steel-smelting furnaces, thirty-eight per cent, of the rolling-mills, fifty-two per cent. Compared with June 1941, we were producing by the end of October 1941, thirty-three per cent of pig-iron, forty-two per cent of steel, forty-two per cent of rolled-iron. By December, the output of steel had dropped by two-thirds. We had lost all the coal mines of the Donbas and of the Moscow Basin; rolled non-ferrous metals were down to practically nothing, and the total industrial output had dropped since June by over fifty per cent.

It was the lowest point reached throughout the war.

The migration of the aircraft industry had a disastrous effect on the output of planes. This dropped in November to about thirty per cent of its September output; there was no means of replacing the heavy losses suffered by our air force in the battles of Moscow, Leningrad, etc. Only by concentrating all aircraft reserves on the most decisive sectors of the front could the Soviet air force carry on at all in the winter fighting of 1941–2.

Owing to evacuation, there was also a heavy drop in the output of tanks during the late autumn and winter months, and the same applied to the production of guns and munitions.

Nor was the conversion of peace production to war production easy: out of the thirty agricultural machinery plants earmarked for such conversion, only nine had the necessary equipment for doing so.

In the munitions industry there was a serious shortage of ferro-alloys, nickel, and non-ferrous metals. There were also desperate shortages of aluminium, copper and tin. The loss of the Donbas with its highly-developed chemical industries, and the evacuation of the chemical industries of Moscow and Leningrad, resulted in a sharp drop in the output of explosives. Out of the twenty-six chemical plants evacuated to the east only eight had reached their destination by the beginning of December, and only four of these had started production.

Between August and November 1941, 303 munitions plants were out of action; these used to produce every month many millions of shells, air bombs, shell-cases, detonating fuses, hand-grenades and some 25,000 tons of explosives.

There was a growing disproportion between the number of guns produced and the amount of ammunition available for each gun. In the second half of 1941 the front was chiefly using the ammunition reserves accumulated in peace-time. But after six months, these reserves were practically down to zero, while current production was fulfilling the army's needs only up to fifty or sixty per cent...

Apart from these heavy losses, Soviet industry also suffered from a serious shortage of manpower. The annual average of workers and employees in the national economy had dropped from 31·2 million in 1940 to 27·3 million in 1941; in November this figure had dropped to 19·8 million. Some had been left behind in the occupied areas; others were still on their way to the east. But on November 9, while the Germans were still prophesying the imminent fall of Moscow, the State Defence Committee laid down precise plans for the speeding up of production in the east, and, in particular, it stipulated that, in 1942, 22,000 planes and 22,000 to 25,000 heavy and medium tanks be produced.

Just as Russia was becoming industrially more and more dependent on the east, by the end of 1941 she had become almost equally dependent on the east for food.

The war had seriously lowered the efficiency of agriculture. Most of the men in the villages had been called up, including the tractor drivers who had been called up to drive tanks. Many of the horses, automobiles and tractors had been requisitioned for the Army. Practically all the agricultural work in Russia during the war was done by women and adolescents. In many *kolkhozes* the ploughing was reduced to the most elementary forms, while at harvest-time the population of the whole neighbourhood, including town-dwellers, was mobilised to help. Horses were used when they were still available, and when there were still tractors, they were usually fitted with gas generators, because of the oil shortage.

The territorial losses suffered in 1941 had an almost catastrophic effect on Russian food supplies. Before the war, the territory over-run by the Germans by November 1941 had produced thirty-eight per cent of the cereals, eighty-four per cent of the sugar, and contained thirty-eight per cent of the cattle and sixty per cent of the pigs. By January 1, 1942, the number of cows in the Soviet Union (not counting those in the occupied areas) had dropped from 27·8 million to 15 million and the number of pigs had dropped by over sixty per cent.

The Volga country, the Urals, Western Siberia and Kazakhstan

were to become the Soviet Union's "food base" for the greater part
of the war. The areas under cultivation were greatly extended, and
crops which had not been grown in these parts before, like sugar-beet
and sunflower, were introduced. With the loss of the Don and Kuban
country in the summer of 1942, the dependence on the "eastern food
base" was to become even greater.

Chapter X

BATTLE OF MOSCOW BEGINS—
THE OCTOBER 16 PANIC

In his statement to us at Viazma in the middle of September, General Sokolovsky had made three important points: first, that despite terrible setbacks the Red Army was gradually "grinding down" the Wehrmacht; secondly that it was very likely that the Germans would make one last desperate attempt, or even "several last desperate attempts" to capture Moscow, but they would fail in this; and, thirdly, that the Red Army was well-clothed for a winter campaign.

The impression that the Russians were rapidly learning all kinds of lessons, were dismissing as useless some of the pre-war theories, which were wholly inapplicable to prevailing conditions, and that professional soldiers of the highest order were taking over the command from the Army "politicians" and the "civil war legends" like Budienny and Voroshilov was to be confirmed in the next few weeks. Some brilliant soldiers had survived the Army Purges of 1937–8, notably Zhukov and Shaposhnikov, and had continued at their posts during the worst time of the German invasion; Zhukov had literally saved Leningrad in the nick of time by taking over from Voroshilov when all seemed lost. Apart from him and Shaposhnikov, Timoshenko—a first-class staff officer who had started his career in the Tsar's army—was almost the only one of the pre-war top brass to prove a man of ability and imagination.

The first months of the war had been a school of the greatest value to the officers of the Red Army, and it was above all those who had

225

distinguished themselves in the operations of June to October 1941 who were to form that brilliant *pléiade* of generals and marshals the like of whom had not been seen since Napoleon's *Grande Armée*. In the course of the summer and autumn important changes had been made in the organisation of the air force by General Novikov, and in the use of artillery by General Voronov; both Zhukov and Konev had played a leading role in holding up the Germans at Smolensk; Rokossovsky, Vatutin, Cherniakhovsky, Rotmistrov, Boldin, Malinovsky, Fedyuninsky, Govorov, Meretskov, Yeremenko, Belov, Lelushenko, Bagramian and numerous other men, who were to become famous during the Battle of Moscow or in other important battles in 1941, were men who had, as it were, won their spurs in the heavy fighting during the first months of the war. Distinction in the field now became Stalin's criterion in making top army appointments. It is, indeed, perfectly true that "the summer and autumn battles had brought on a military purge, as opposed to a political purge of the military. There was a growing restlessness with the incompetent and the inept. The great and signal strength of the Soviet High Command was that it was able to produce that minimum of high calibre commanders capable of steering the Red Army out of total disaster".*

Undoubtedly some of the commanders had only a purely nominal Party affiliation, and some of the new men, such as Rokossovsky, had actually been victims of the Army Purges of 1937–8, and so could not have had any tender feelings for Stalin.

The *Stavka*, the General Headquarters of the Soviet High Command was set up on June 23, and a few days later the State Defence Committee (GKO), consisting of Stalin, Molotov, Voroshilov, Malenkov and Beria; on July 10 the "*Stavka* of the High Command" became the "*Stavka* of the Supreme Command", with Stalin, Molotov, Voroshilov, Budienny, Shaposhnikov and General Zhukov, the Chief of Staff, as members. On July 19 Stalin became Defence Commissar and on August 7 Commander-in-Chief.

The Commissar system was greatly reinforced; the commissars, as "representatives of the Party and the government in the Red Army" were to watch over the officers' and soldiers' morale, and share with

* Erickson, op. cit., p. 624.

the commander full responsibility for the unit's conduct in battle. They were also to report to the Supreme Command any cases of "unworthiness" amongst either officers or political personnel. This was a hangover from the civil war, and, indeed, from the much more recent period when the officer corps was suspected of unreliability. In practice, in 1941, the commissars proved, in the great majority of cases, to be either men who almost fully supported the officers, or were, at most, a minor technical nuisance; but inspired by the same *lutte à outrance* spirit, and, faced daily by pressing military tasks, the old political and personal differences between officer and commissar were now usually less harsh than in the past. Even so, the dual command had its drawbacks, and, at the time of Stalingrad, the commissars' role was to be drastically modified.*

Whether or not there was any serious need for giving the officer a "Party whip", there was certainly even less need for the NKVD's "rear security units" to check panic through the use of machine-gunners ready to keep the Red Army from any unauthorised withdrawals. "What initial fears there might have been that the troops would not fight were soon dispelled by the stubborn and bitter defence which the Red Army put up against the Germans, fighting, as Halder observed, 'to the last man', and employing 'treacherous methods' in which the Russian did not cease firing until he was dead".† These "rear security units" were a revival of a practice inherited from the Civil War, and proved wholly unnecessary in 1941, the Army itself dealing rigorously with any cases of cowardice and panic.

The role of the NKVD in actual military operations remains rather obscure, though it is known that, apart from the Frontier Guards, who were under NKVD jurisdiction, and who were the first to meet the German onslaught, there were to be some very important occasions in which NKVD troops fought as battle units—for example at Voronezh in June–July 1942, where they helped to prevent a particularly dangerous German breakthrough. But there was a much grimmer side to the NKVD's connection with the Red Army; thus, not only Russian prisoners who had managed to escape from the Germans, but even whole Army units who—as so often happened

* See pp. 420 ff.   † Erickson, op. cit., p. 598.

in 1941—had broken out of German encirclement, were subjected
as suspects to the most harsh and petty interrogation by the O.O.
(*Osoby Otdel*—Special Department) run by the NKVD. In
Simonov's novel, *The Living and the Dead*, there is a particularly
sickening episode based on actual fact, in which a large number of
officers and soldiers break out of a German encirclement after many
weeks' fighting. They are promptly disarmed by the NKVD; but it
so happens that at that very moment the Germans have started their
offensive against Moscow, and as the disarmed men are being taken
to a NKVD sorting station, they are trapped by the Germans, and
simply massacred, unable to offer any resistance.

Apart from that, however, the NKVD interfered less than
before with the Red Army;* the border-line between the military
and the "political" elements in the Army was vanishing, and Stalin
himself presided over this development. Whatever he had done in
the past to weaken the army by his purges and his constant political
interference, he had learned his lesson from the summer and autumn
of 1941. Voroshilov and Budienny were pushed into the background
and the role of the NKVD bosses greatly reduced. The patriotic,
nationalist and "1812" line was wholeheartedly taken up by all
ranks of the army. All the military talent—discovered and tested in
the first battles of the war and, in some cases, before that in the Far
East—was assembled, all available reserves were thrown into battle,
including some crack divisions from Central Asia and the Far East,
a measure made possible by the Non-Aggression Pact concluded with
the Japanese in 1939.

Whatever bad memories and reservations the generals may have
had, Stalin had become the indispensable unifying factor in the
patrie-en-danger atmosphere of October–November 1941. There was
no alternative. The Germans were on the outskirts of Leningrad,
were pushing through the Donbas on their way to Rostov, and on
September 30 the "final" offensive against Moscow had started.

The Battle of Moscow falls, broadly, into three phases: the first
German offensive from September 30 to nearly the end of October;
the second German offensive from November 17 right up to Decem-

---

* This is not to say that the Army was left strictly to itself. Officers
were still subjected to NKVD surveillance.

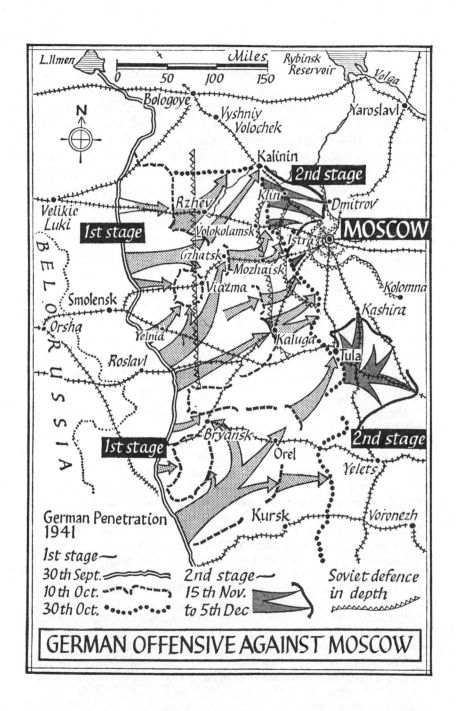

L.Ilmen   Miles   Rybinsk Reservoir
0   50   100   150   Volga

Bologoye
Vyshniy Volochek   Yaroslavl

N

Kalinin   2nd stage

Velikie Luki   Rzhev   Klin   Dmitrov
1st stage   Volokolamsk   Istra   MOSCOW
Gzhatsk
B   Mozhaisk   Kolomna
E   Smolensk   Viazma   Kashira
L   Orsha   Kaluga   Tula
O   Yelnia
R   Roslavl
U
S   1st stage   Bryansk   2nd stage
S   Orel   Yelets
I
A   Kursk   Voronezh

German Penetration 1941

1st stage —
30th Sept. ———   2nd stage —
10th Oct. –––––   15th Nov.   Soviet defence
30th Oct. •••••   to 5th Dec   in depth

GERMAN OFFENSIVE AGAINST MOSCOW

ber 5; and the Russian counter-offensive of December 6, which lasted till spring 1942.

On September 30 Guderian's panzer units on the southern flank of *Heeresgruppe Mitte* (Army Group Centre) thrust against Glukhov and Orel, which fell on October 2,* but were then held up by a tank group under Colonel Katyukov beyond Mtsensk, on the road to Tula. Other German forces launched full scale attacks from the south-west in the Bryansk area and from the west on the Smolensk-Moscow road. Large Soviet troop concentrations were encircled south of Bryansk and in the Viazma area due west of Moscow. The Germans had planned to contain Soviet troops surrounded in the Viazma area mainly by infantry, thus freeing their panzer and motorised divisions for a lightning advance on Moscow. But for more than a week, fighting a circular battle of extreme ferocity, the remnants of the 19th, 20th, 24th and 32nd Armies and the troops under General Boldin tied up most of the German 4th Army and of the 4th Tank Corps. This resistance enabled the Soviet Supreme Command to extricate and withdraw more of their front line troops from the encirclement to the Mozhaisk line and to bring up reserves from the rear.†

* The surprise was complete. The trams were still running at Orel when the German tanks broke in.

† IVOVSS, vol. II, p. 245. As usual in such matters, there are considerable discrepancies between German and Russian, and even between Russian accounts of the Viazma encirclement. The German claim, repeated by Tippelskirch, that "the Russians lost in the Viazma area sixty-seven infantry, six cavalry and seven tank divisions, totalling 663,000 prisoners, as well as 1,242 tanks and 5,412 guns", is dismissed by some Russians as "a piece of German day-dreaming, or a deliberate deception calculated to extract decorations and promotions from the Führer. In reality ten Soviet divisions (eight infantry, one motorised and one cavalry) were fighting against thirty or thirty-two German divisions. Moreover, these (encircled) Russian divisions, seriously weakened by earlier fighting, tied up thirty or thirty-two German divisions west of Viazma for a week (from October 6 to 13)." *Narodnoye opolcheniye Moskvy* (Moscow Home Guard), (Moscow, 1961), pp. 141–2.

The official *History*, while not accepting inflated German claims, suggests that a far greater number of troops were encircled at Viazma.

By October 6 German tank units had broken through the Rzhev-Viazma defence line and were advancing towards the Mozhaisk line of fortified positions some fifty miles west of Moscow, which had been improvised and prepared during the summer of 1941, and ran from Kalinin (north-west of Moscow on the Moscow-Leningrad Railway line), to Kaluga (south-west of Moscow and half-way between Tula and Viazma), Maloyaroslavets and Tula. The few troops manning these defences could halt the advance units of the *Heeresgruppe Mitte*, but not the bulk of the German forces.

While reinforcements from the Far East and Central Asia were on their way to the Moscow Front, the GKO Headquarters threw in what reserves they could muster. The infantry of Generals Artemiev and Lelushenko and the tanks of General Kurkin which fought here were, by October 9, placed under the direct orders of the Soviet Supreme Command. On the following day Zhukov was appointed C. in C. of the whole front.

But the Germans bypassed the Mozhaisk line from the south and captured Kaluga on October 12. Two days later, outflanking the Mozhaisk line in the north, they broke into Kalinin. After heavy fighting Mozhaisk itself was abandoned on October 18. Already on the 14th fierce battles were raging in the Volokolamsk sector, mid-way between Mozhaisk and Kalinin, some fifty miles north-west of Moscow.

The situation was extremely serious. There was no continuous front any more. The German air force was master of the sky. German tank units, penetrating deep into the rear, were forcing the Red Army units to retreat to new positions to avoid encirclement. Together with the army, thousands of Soviet civilians were moving east. People on foot, or in horse carts, cattle, cars, were moving east

It is also certain from numerous Russian break-out accounts that the number of Russian dead must have been enormous (cf. *Narodnoye opolcheniye Moskvy*, I. V. Boldin, op. cit., and others). It is perhaps significant that, while claiming 50,000 prisoners in the Briansk encirclement in October 1941, Guderian should, when referring to the Viazma encirclement, mention no figure at all for prisoners taken there. Maybe his figures disagreed with the official ones.

in a continuous stream along all the roads, making troop movements even more difficult.*

Despite stiff resistance everywhere, the Germans were closing in on Moscow from all directions. It was two days after the fall of Kalinin, and when the threat of a breakthrough from Volokolamsk to Istra and Moscow looked a near-certainty, that the "Moscow panic" reached its height. This was on October 16. To this day the story is current that, on that morning, two German tanks broke into Khimki, a northern suburb of Moscow, where they were promptly destroyed; that two such tanks ever existed, except in some frightened Muscovite's imagination, is not confirmed by any serious source.

What happened in Moscow on October 16? Many have spoken of the big skedaddle (*bolshoi drap*) that took place that day. Although, as we shall see, this is an over-generalisation, October 16 in Moscow was certainly not a tale of the "unanimous heroism of the people of Moscow" as recorded in the official *History*.

It took the Moscow population several days to realise how serious the new German offensive was. During the last days of September and, indeed, for the first few days of October, all attention was centred on the big German offensive in the Ukraine, the news of the breakthrough into the Crimea, and the Beaverbrook visit, which had begun on September 29. At his press conference on September 28 Lozovsky had tried to sound very reassuring, saying that the Germans were losing "many tens of thousands dead" outside Leningrad, but that no matter how many more they lost, they still wouldn't get into Leningrad; he also said that "communications continued to be maintained", and that, although there was rationing in the city, there was no food shortage. He also said that there was heavy fighting "for the Crimea", but denied that the Germans had as yet crossed the Perekop Isthmus. As for the German claim of having captured 500,000 or 600,000 prisoners in the Ukraine, after the loss of Kiev, he was much more cagey, saying that the battle was continuing, and that it was not in the Russian's interest to give out information prematurely. However, he added the somewhat sinister phrase: "The

* IVOVSS, vol. II, p. 244.

farther east the Germans push, the nearer will they get to the grave of Nazi Germany." He seemed to be prepared for the loss of Kharkov and the Donbas, though he did not say so.

It did not become clear until October 4 or 5 that an offensive against Moscow had started, and, even so, it was not clear how big it was. There was, needless to say, nothing in the Russian papers about Hitler's speech of October 2 announcing his "final" drive against Moscow.

However, Lozovsky referred to it in his press conference of October 7. He looked slightly flustered, but said that Hitler's speech only showed that the fellow was getting desperate.

"He knows he isn't going to win the war, but he has to keep the Germans more or less contented during the winter, and he must therefore achieve some major success, which would suggest that a certain *stage* of the war has closed. The second reason why it is essential for Hitler to do something big is the Anglo-American-Soviet agreement, which has caused a feeling of despondency in Germany. The Germans could, at a pinch, swallow a 'Bolshevik' agreement with Britain, but a 'Bolshevik' agreement with America was more than the Germans had ever expected." Lozovsky added that, anyway, the capture of this or that city would not affect the final outcome of the war. It was as if he was already preparing the press for the possible loss of Moscow. Yet he managed to end on a note of bravado: "If the Germans want to see a few hundred thousand more of their people killed, they'll succeed in that—if in nothing else."

The news on the night of the 7th was even worse, with the first official reference to "heavy fighting in the direction of Viazma".

On the 8th, while *Pravda* and *Izvestia* were careful not to sound too alarmed (*Pravda* actually started with a routine article on "The Work of Women in War-Time"), the army paper, *Red Star*, looked extremely disquieting. It said that "the very existence of the Soviet State was in danger", and that every man of the Red Army "must stand firm and fight to the last drop of blood". It described the new German offensive as a last desperate fling:

> Hitler has thrown into it everything he has got—even every old and obsolete tank, every midget tank the Germans have collected in Holland, France or Belgium has been thrown into this battle... The

Soviet soldiers must at any price destroy these tanks, old and new, large or small. All the riff-raff armour of ruined Europe is being thrown against the Soviet Union.

Pravda sounded the alarm on the 9th, warning the people of Moscow against "careless complacency" and calling on them to "mobilise all their forces to repel the enemy's offensive". On the following day it called for "vigilance" saying that, in addition to advancing on Moscow, "the enemy is also trying, through the wide network of its agents, spies and *agents-provocateurs*, to disorganise the rear and to create panic". On October 12, *Pravda* spoke of the "terrible danger" threatening the country.

Even without the help of enemy agents, there was enough in *Pravda* to spread the greatest alarm among the population of Moscow. Talk of evacuation had begun on the 8th, and foreign embassies as well as numerous Russian government offices and institutions were told to expect a decision on it very shortly. The atmosphere was becoming extremely tense. There was talk of Moscow as a "super-Madrid" among the braver, and feverish attempts to get away among the less brave.

By October 13, the situation in Moscow had become highly critical. Numerous German troops which had, for over a week, been held up by the "Viazma encirclement", had become available for the final attack on Moscow. The "Western" Front, under the general command of General Zhukov, assisted by General Konev, and with General Sokolovsky as Chief of Staff, consisted of four sectors: Volokolamsk under Rokossovsky; Mozhaisk under Govorov, Maloyaroslavets under Golubev and Kaluga under Zakharkin. There was absolutely no certainty that a German breakthrough could be prevented, and on October 12, the State Defence Committee had decided to call upon the people of Moscow to build a defence line some distance outside Moscow, another one right along the city border, and two supplementary city lines along the outer and inner rings of boulevards within Moscow itself.

On the morning of October 13, Shcherbakov, Secretary of the Central Committee and of the Moscow Party Committee of the

Communist Party, spoke at a meeting called by the Moscow Party Organisation: "Let us not shut our eyes. Moscow is in danger." He appealed to the workers of the city to send all possible reserves to the front and to the defence lines both inside and outside the city; and to increase greatly the output of arms and munitions.

The resolution passed by the Moscow Organisation called for "iron discipline, a merciless struggle against even the slightest manifestations of panic, against cowards, deserters and rumour-mongers". The resolution further decided that, within two or three days, each Moscow district should assemble a battalion of volunteers; these came to be known as Moscow's "Communist Battalions" and were, like some of the *opolcheniye* regiments, to play an important role in the defence of Moscow by filling in "gaps"—at a very heavy cost in lives. Within three days, 12,000 such volunteers were formed into platoons and battalions, most of them with little military training and no fighting experience.

It was on October 12 and 13 that it was decided to evacuate immediately to Kuibyshev and other cities in the east a large number of government offices, including many People's Commissariats, part of the Party organisations, and the entire diplomatic corps of Moscow. Moscow's most important armaments works were to be evacuated as well. Practically all "scientific and cultural institutions" such as the Academy of Sciences, the University and the theatres were to be moved.

But the State Defence Committee, the *Stavka* of the Supreme Command, and a skeleton administration were to stay on in Moscow until further notice. The principal newspapers such as *Pravda, Red Star, Izvestia, Komsomolskaya Pravda,* and *Trud,* continued to be published in the capital.

The news of these evacuations was followed by the official communiqué published on the morning of October 16. It said: "During the night of October 14–15 the position on the Western Front became worse. The German-Fascist troops hurled against our troops large quantities of tanks and motorised infantry, and in one sector broke through our defences."

*

In describing the great October crisis in Moscow it is important to distinguish between three factors. First, the Army, which fought on desperately against superior enemy forces, and yielded ground only very slowly, although owing to relatively poor manœuvrability, it was unable to prevent some spectacular German local successes, such as the capture of Kaluga in the south on the 12th, of Kalinin in the north on the 14th, or that breakthrough in what was rather vaguely described as "the Volokolamsk sector" to which the "panic communiqué", published on October 16, referred. Even long afterwards it was believed in Moscow that on the 15th the Germans had crashed through much further towards Moscow than is apparent today from any published record of the fighting. Only then, it was said, did Rokossovsky stop the rot by throwing in the last reserves, including scarcely-trained *opolchentsy*, and troops from Siberia as soon as they disembarked from the trains. There are countless stories of regular soldiers and even *opolchentsy* attacking German tanks with hand grenades and with "petrol bottles", and of other "last ditch" exploits. The morale of the fighting forces certainly did not crack. The fact that fresh troops from the Far East and Central Asia were being thrown in all the time, though only in limited numbers, had a salutary effect in keeping up the spirit of the troops who had already fought without respite for over a fortnight.

Secondly, there was the Moscow working-class; most of them were ready to put in long hours of overtime in factories producing armaments and ammunition; to build defences; to fight the Germans inside Moscow should they break through, or, if all failed, to "follow the Red Army to the east". However, there were different shades in the determination of the workers to "defend Moscow" at all costs. The very fact that not more than 12,000 should have volunteered for the "Communist brigades" at the height of the near-panic of October 13–16 seems indicative; was it because, to many, these improvised battalions seemed futile in this kind of war, or was it because, at the back of many workers' minds, there was the idea that Russia was still vast, and that it might be more advantageous to fight the decisive battle somewhere east.

Thirdly, there was a large mass of Muscovites, difficult to classify, who were more responsible than the others for "the great skedaddle"

of October 16. These included anybody from plain *obyvateli*, ready
to run away from danger, to small, medium and even high Party or
non-Party officials who felt that Moscow had become a job for the
Army, and that there was not much that civilians could do. Among
these people there was a genuine fear of finding themselves under
German occupation, and, with regular passes, or with passes of sorts
they had somehow wangled—or sometimes with no passes at all—
people fled to the east, just as in Paris people had fled to the south
in 1940 as the Germans approached the capital.

Later, many of these people were to be bitterly ashamed of having
fled, of having overrated the might of the Germans, of having not
had enough confidence in the Red Army. And yet, had not the
Government shown the way, as it were, by frantically speeding up on
all those evacuations from the 10th of October onwards?

Especially in 1942 the "big skedaddle" of October 16 continued
to be a nasty memory with many. There were some grim jokes on
the subject—especially in connection with the medal "For the
Defence of Moscow" that had been distributed lavishly among the
soldiers and civilians; there was the joke about the two kinds of
ribbons—some Moscow medals should be suspended on the regular
moiré ribbon, others on a *drap* ribbon—*drap* meaning both a thick
kind of cloth and skedaddle. There was also the joke of a famous
and very plump and well-equipped actress who had received a
Moscow Medal "for defending Moscow from Kuibyshev with her
breast".

I remember Surkov telling me that when he arrived in Moscow
from the front on the 16th, he phoned some fifteen or twenty of his
friends, and *all* had vanished.

In "fiction", more than in formal history, there are some valuable
descriptions of Moscow at the height of the crisis—for instance in
Simonov's *The Living and the Dead* already quoted. Here is a picture
of Moscow during that grim 16th of October and the following days
—with the railway station stampedes; with officials fleeing in their
cars without a permit; the *opolchentsy* and Communist battalion
men sullenly walking, rather than marching, down the streets,
dressed in a motley collection of clothes, smoking, but not singing;
with the "Hammer and Sickle" factory working day and night turn-

ing out thousands of anti-tank hedge-hogs, which are then driven to
the outer ring of boulevards; with its smell of burning papers; with
the rapid succession of air-raids and air-battles over Moscow, in
which Russian airmen often suicidally ram enemy planes; with the
demoralisation of the majority and the grim determination among
the minority to hang on to Moscow, and to fight, if necessary, inside
the city.

By the 16th, many factories had already been evacuated.

All the same, below all the froth of panic and despair there was
"another Moscow":

> Later, when all this belonged to the past, and somebody recalled
> that 16th of October with sorrow or bitterness, he [Simonov's hero]
> would say nothing. The memory of Moscow that day was unbearable
> to him—like the face of a person you love distorted by fear. And yet,
> not only outside Moscow, where the troops were fighting and dying
> that day, but inside Moscow itself, there were enough people who were
> doing all within their power not to surrender it. And that was why
> Moscow was not lost. And yet, at the Front that day the war seemed
> to have taken a fatal turn, and there were people in Moscow that same
> day who, in their despair, were ready to believe that the Germans
> would enter Moscow tomorrow. As always happens in tragic moments,
> the deep faith and inconspicuous work of those who carried on, was
> not yet known to all, and had not yet come to bear fruit, while the
> bewilderment, terror and despair of the others hit you between the
> eyes. This was inevitable. That day tens of thousands, getting away
> from the Germans, rolled like avalanches towards the railway stations
> and towards the eastern exits of Moscow; and yet, out of these tens of
> thousands, there were perhaps only a few thousand whom history
> could rightly condemn.*

Simonov wrote this account of Moscow on October 16, 1941 after
a lapse of nearly twenty years; but his story—which could not have
been published in Stalin's day—rings true in the light of what I had
heard of those grim days only a few months later, in 1942.

I also remember a very different kind of story—a story told me by a
leading woman-member of the Komsomol at the famous Trekhgorka

---

* Simonov, op. cit., p. 288.

Cotton Mill—a remarkable girl of about twenty-five, called Olga Sapozhnikova, who belonged to a long dynasty of Moscow cotton weavers. All her three brothers had been called up, and one was wounded and another "missing". She was a little plump and heavy, and had rough proletarian hands, with closely-clipped fingernails. And yet she had poise and character, and there was a solid kind of Russian beauty in that pale face, in her large, quiet grey eyes, firm jaw, finely shaped full mouth, and her white teeth showing when she smiled. Not a single nondescript feature about her; she belonged, even physically, to the proletarian aristocracy; her character, like her body, shaped by good tradition.*

The story she told me, on September 19, 1942, differed in one respect from present-day stories; she told me how even the bravest and most determined people in Moscow had felt uncertain of whether Moscow could be saved—or could be effectively defended had the Germans fought their way into the city.

"Those were dreadful days. It started about the 12th. I was ordered, like most of the girls at the factory, to join the Labour Front. We were taken some kilometres out of Moscow. There was a large crowd of us, and we were told to dig trenches. We were all very calm, but dazed, and couldn't take it in. On the very first day we were machine-gunned by a Fritz who swooped right down. Eleven of the girls were killed and four wounded." She said it very calmly, without affectation.

"We went on working all day and the next day; fortunately, no more Fritzes came. But I was very worried about father and mother [both of them old Trekhgorka textile workers], with nobody to look after them.

"I explained this to our commissar, and he let me go back to Moscow. They were strange, those nights in Moscow; you heard the guns firing so clearly. On the 16th, when the Germans had broken through, I went to the factory. My heart went cold when I saw that the factory had closed down. A lot of the directors had fled; but Dundukov was in charge; a very good man, who never lost his head. He handed out large quantities of food to us: I was given 125 pounds of flour, and seventeen pounds of butter and a lot of sugar, so that

* *The Year of Stalingrad*, pp. 252–4.

it should not fall into German hands. For me as a Komsomol—and a well-known Komsomol at that—it was not much use staying on in Moscow. The factory people suggested that I could evacuate father and mother to Cheliabinsk. But whatever was done about the old people, there was only one thing I could do, and that was to follow the Red Army. A lot of people had already left Moscow.

"I went and talked to mother. She wouldn't hear of Cheliabinsk. 'No,' she said, 'God will protect us here, and Moscow will not fall.' That night I went down to the cellar with mother; we took down a small kerosene lamp and buried all the sugar and flour and also father's Party card. We thought we'd live in the cellar if the Germans came; for we knew that they couldn't stay in Moscow for long. Perhaps I would have left with the Red Army, but it was hard to leave mother and father alone. That night mother cried, and said: 'The whole family has scattered; and are you going to leave me, too?' There was a feeling that night that the Germans might appear in the street at any moment; yes, it was possible, and Krasnaya Presnya was the part through which they would have come into Moscow. There were no trains any more by which we could leave, and what was father to do? He might have walked two or three kilometres, but no more...

"But they did not come that night. At the factory the next morning everything was mined; it was only a case of pressing a button, and the whole factory would have gone up in the air. And then came a phone message from Pronin, the Chairman of the Moscow Soviet, saying 'Absolutely nothing must be blown up.'

"And it was also on that day that the announcement was made that Stalin was in Moscow, and this made an enormous difference to morale; it now seemed certain that Moscow would not be lost. Even so, from the northern outskirts, people were being evacuated to the centre. There were continuous air-raid warnings and bombs fell. But on the 20th the factory was opened again; we all felt so much better and were quite cheerful again after that..."

It was, indeed, on October 17 that Shcherbakov announced on the radio that Stalin was in Moscow. At the same time he explained to the people of Moscow the "complexity" of the situation (in official Russian war-time terminology "complexity" always meant "gravity") as a result of the German offensive against the capital; he also explained why it had been necessary to take those numerous evacuation measures. He firmly denied the rumours about the imminent surrender of the city, rumours, he said, which had been spread by enemy agents. Moscow, he said, would be defended stubbornly, to the last drop of blood. "Every one of us, no matter what his work or his position, shall act like a soldier defending Moscow against the Fascist invaders."

Two days later, a state of siege was proclaimed in Moscow. This had partly been caused by the looting that had gone on, here and there, at the height of the panic; now all "breaches of law and order" were to be dealt with by emergency tribunals, and all spies, diversionists and *agents provocateurs* were to be shot on the spot. The maintenance of order inside Moscow was entrusted to the Commandant of the city and his NKVD troops. These, together with regular army units and newly-formed "Communist battalions" were to man the *gorodskiye rubezhy*, the defence lines just outside and inside Moscow. The state of siege had, by all accounts I was to hear later, a salutary, and, indeed, stimulating effect on morale.

By the end of October over two million people had been officially evacuated from Moscow; in addition, there were many others who had fled unofficially; many stories were current later, for instance about a very important person on Moscow Radio, who disappeared on October 16, and did not turn up again until three weeks later. Disciplinary action was taken in some cases against such "deserters", but there is no official record of the extent of these reprisals; it seems, however, that allowances were made for the general state of chaos in Moscow that day, and for the fact that people were genuinely frightened of falling under German occupation.

Many of those who had stayed on in Moscow later took some pride in not having lost their heads—or their faith in Moscow being saved,* and liked to recall the "heroic atmosphere" of half-empty Moscow in the second half of October and in November, with the

---

* Those who had fled retorted in some cases: "You didn't mind being occupied by the Germans—I did."

battle still raging not far away and, indeed, coming nearer and nearer in the second half of November. But it was now felt that the situation was well in hand and that a sudden German incursion into Moscow—which seemed so likely on that 16th of October—had become impossible.

Chapter XI

BATTLE OF MOSCOW II
STALIN'S HOLY RUSSIA SPEECH

In the first nineteen days of their offensive the Germans had advanced to less than fifty miles from Moscow at Noro-Fominsk and were even nearer the capital in the Volokolamsk area. But all the time the Russian resistance was stiffening and by October 18 counter-attacks slowed down the German advance. Losses were extremely heavy on both sides, there were signs of growing fatigue among the Germans, and between October 18 and the beginning of November they made very little progress.

German war memoirs stress the Wehrmacht's supply difficulties; but it is quite clear that the famous "Russian winter" was in no way decisive either in October or at the beginning of November. On the contrary, some of the Germans' difficulties arose from the fact that the roads had not yet frozen. To quote Guderian:

> On October 29 our leading tanks reached a point some two miles from Tula. An attempt to capture the city by a *coup de main* failed owing to the enemy's strong anti-tank and anti-aircraft defences; we lost many tanks and officers... The condition of the Orel-Tula road had meantime grown so bad that arrangements had to be made for the 3rd Panzer Division ... to be supplied by air... In view of the impossibility of launching a frontal attack on Tula, General Freiherr von Geyr suggested that in order to continue our advance we by-pass the town to the east... (He) was also of the opinion that *there was no possibility of using motorised troops until the frost set in.**

* Guderian, op. cit., p. 152. (Emphasis added.)

243

Guderian's argument that rain and mud interfered with the success of the first German offensive against Moscow seems futile, since it affected the Russians as much as the Germans; besides, Guderian himself admits that it was the defence put up by the Russians, and not the mud that stopped him from capturing Tula, this key position on the way to Moscow. Moreover, the Russians also sprang on him the unpleasant surprise of throwing in some of their T-34 tanks under Katyukov much to Guderian's disgust.*

On the night of November 6—that is, a week after the first German offensive against Moscow had virtually petered out, and ten days before the second offensive began—Moscow celebrated the 24th Anniversary of the Revolution. The Germans were still some forty miles from Moscow—in some places even nearer; and although the atmosphere in Moscow was that of a besieged city, with tens of thousands of wounded crowding the hospitals, and many thousands more arriving every day—the conviction that Moscow would not be lost had steadily grown in the past fortnight.

The usual Eve-of-Revolution Day meeting was held on that night of November 6 in the large ornate hall of the Mayakovsky tube station. The hall was crowded with hundreds of delegates of the Moscow City Soviet, and various Party and trade union organisations, and representatives of the Armed Forces. As many who attended that meeting later told me, the underground setting of the meeting was uncanny, depressing and humiliating.

Stalin's speech at the meeting was a strange mixture of black gloom and complete self-confidence. After recalling that the war had greatly curtailed, and in many cases wholly stopped, the peaceful building of socialism that had gone on for so many years, Stalin said:

> In four months of war, we have had 350,000 killed, 378,000 missing and 1,020,000 wounded. During the same period the enemy had lost over four and a half million in dead, wounded and prisoners. There can be no doubt that Germany, whose human reserves are running out, has been weakened much more than the Soviet Union, whose reserves are only now being fully deployed.

* Guderian, op. cit., p. 248.

It is extremely doubtful that anybody in Russia could have believed these figures; but it was perhaps essential to overstate the German losses in order to bring home his contention that the *blitzkrieg* had already failed. It had failed, Stalin said, for three reasons: the Germans, as could be seen from Hess's mission to England, had hoped that Britain and America would join them in their war against Russia or, at any rate, give Germany a free hand in the East; this had not come off: Britain, the USA and the Soviet Union were in the same camp. Secondly, the Germans had hoped that the Soviet régime would collapse and the USSR fall to pieces.

> Instead, the Soviet rear is today more solid than ever. It is probable that any other country, having lost as much territory as we have, would have collapsed.

Finally, the Germans had expected the Soviet armed forces to break down; after which they would, without further hindrance, push right on to the Urals. True, the German army was a more experienced army than the Soviet Army, but the Russians had the moral advantage of fighting a just war; moreover, the Germans were now fighting in enemy territory, far from their supply bases and with communications constantly threatened by the Partisans.*

> Our army, as against this, is fighting in its own surroundings, constantly supported by its rear, and supplied with manpower, ammunitions and food... The defence of Moscow and Leningrad show ... that in the fire of the Great Patriotic War new soldiers, officers, airmen, gunners, tank-crews, infantry men, sailors, are being forged—men who will tomorrow become the terror of the German army. (*Stormy applause.*)

For all that, said Stalin, there were also unfavourable factors, which could not be denied. One was the absence of a Second Front in Europe; whereas the Germans were fighting the Red Army with the help of numerous allies—Finns, Rumanians, Italians, Hungarians —there were no British or American armies on the European mainland to help Russia.

* This also was said more for effect. In 1941 partisan activity was still very weak and unorganised.

But there can be no doubt that the formation of a Second Front on the European mainland—and it unquestionably must come within a very short time (*stormy applause*)—will greatly facilitate the position of our army, and make things more difficult for the Germans.

The other unfavourable factor was the German superiority in tanks and aircraft. The Red Army had only a fraction of the tanks that the Germans had, even though the new Russian tanks were superior to those of the Germans. It was essential not only to produce far more tanks, but also far more anti-tank planes, guns, rifles, mortars and grenades, and to devise and make every kind of anti-tank obstacle.

After demonstrating that, far from being either "nationalists" or "socialists", the Nazis were imperialists of the worst kind, determined, in the first place to annihilate or enslave the Slav peoples, and after quoting some particularly revealing German "*Untermensch*" utterances, Stalin made his supremely significant appeal to the Russians' national pride—

And it is these people without honour or conscience, these people with the morality of animals, who have the effrontery to call for the extermination of the great Russian nation—the nation of Plekhanov and Lenin, of Belinsky and Chernyshevsky, of Pushkin and Tolstoy, of Gorki and Chekhov, of Glinka and Tchaikovsky, of Sechenov and Pavlov, of Suvorov and Kutuzov! The German invaders want a war of extermination against the peoples of the Soviet Union. Very well then! If they want a war of extermination they shall have it! (*Prolonged, stormy applause.*) Our task now ... will be to destroy every German, to the very last man, who had come to occupy our country. No mercy for the German invaders! Death to the German invaders!" (*Stormy applause.*)

There were not only moral reasons why these wild beasts would perish, Stalin went on. The "New Order" in Europe was not something that the Germans could rely on. Secondly—and here was still a faint echo of Stalin's previous distinction between the "Nazi clique" and the "German people"—the German rear itself was unreliable. The German people were tired of the war of conquest, which had brought them millions of casualties, hunger, impoverishment and epidemics.

Only the Hitlerite halfwits have failed to understand that not only the European rear, but the German rear is a volcano ready to blow up, and to bury the Hitlerite adventurers.

And thirdly, there was the coalition of the Big Three against the German-Fascist imperialists. This was a war of engines, and Britain, the USA and the USSR could produce three times as many engines as Germany.

He then referred to the recent Moscow Conference attended by Beaverbrook and Harriman,* to the decision to supply the USSR systematically with planes and tanks, to the earlier British decision to supply raw materials to Russia such as aluminium, tin, lead, nickel and rubber, and the latest American decision to grant the Soviet Union a one billion-dollar loan.

All this shows that the coalition between the three countries is a very real thing (*stormy applause*) which will go on growing in the common cause of liberation.

In concluding, Stalin said that the Soviet Union was waging a war of liberation, and that she had no territorial ambitions anywhere, in either Europe or Asia, including Iran. Nor did the Soviet Union intend to impose her will or her régime on the Slav or any other peoples waiting to be liberated from the Nazi yoke. There would be no Soviet interference in the internal affairs of these peoples. But to achieve this, the peoples of the Soviet Union must do their utmost to help the Red Army with armaments, munitions and food. And he ended on the usual note:

Long live our Red Army and our Red Navy!
Long live our glorious country!
Our cause is just. Victory will be ours!

Much more dramatic and inspiring was the setting in which Stalin delivered his speech to the troops on the following morning. In the distance Russian and German guns were booming, and Russian fighter planes were patrolling Moscow. And here, in the Red Square,

* See pp. 275 ff.

on that cold grey November morning, Stalin was addressing troops, many of whom had come from the Front, or were on the way to the Front.

Comrades! We are celebrating the 24th Anniversary of the October Revolution in very hard conditions... The enemy is at the gates of Moscow and Leningrad... Yet, despite temporary failures, our army and navy are heroically repelling the enemy attacks along the whole front.

Russia, Stalin went on, had survived worse ordeals than this; he recalled 1918, the first anniversary of the Revolution and, stretching some historical points, he said:

Three-quarters of our country was then in the hands of foreign interventionists... We had no allies, we had no Red Army—we were only beginning to create it—we had no food, no armaments, no equipment. Fourteen states were attacking our country then... And yet we organised the Red Army, and turned our country into a military camp. Lenin's great spirit inspired us in our struggle against the interventionists... Our position is far better than it was twenty-three years ago. We are richer in industry, food and raw materials than we were then. We now have allies, and the support of all the occupied nations of Europe. We have a wonderful army and a wonderful navy... We have no serious shortage of food, armaments or equipment... Lenin's spirit is inspiring us in our struggle as it did twenty-three years ago.

Can anyone doubt that we can and must defeat the German invaders? The enemy is not as strong as some frightened little intellectuals imagine...* Germany is, in reality, facing a catastrophe.

After reiterating that Germany had lost four and a half million men in the last four months, he went on:

There is no doubt that Germany cannot stand this strain much longer. In a few months, perhaps in half a year, maybe a year, Hitlerite Germany must burst under the weight of her own crimes.

Comrades, Red Army and Red Navy men, officers and political workers, men and women partisans! The whole world is looking upon you as the power capable of destroying the German robber hordes! The enslaved peoples of Europe are looking upon you as their

* In his memoirs, Ehrenburg, while welcoming the speech as a whole, described this phrase as particularly offensive and un-called for; in 1941 the intellectuals were no more, and no less worried than the rest of the Russian people. (*Novyi Mir*, January, 1963.)

liberators... Be worthy of this great mission! The war you are waging is a war of liberation, a just war. May you be inspired in this war by the heroic figures of our great ancestors, Alexander Nevsky, Dimitri Donskoi, Minin and Pozharsky, Alexander Suvorov, Michael Kutuzov! May you be blest by great Lenin's victorious banner! Death to the German invaders! Long live our glorious country, its freedom and independence! Under the banner of Lenin—onward to victory!

This invocation of the Great Ancestors—the great men of Russian civilisation—Pushkin, Tolstoy, Tchaikovsky, the great scientists and thinkers, and the great national heroes—Alexander Nevsky who routed the Teutonic Knights in 1242, Dimitri Donskoi who routed the Tartars in 1380 and Minin and Pozharsky who fought the Polish invaders in the seventeenth century, Suvorov and Kutuzov, who fought Napoleon—all this was meant to appeal to the people's specifically *Russian* national pride. With the Baltic States gone, with the Ukraine gone, it was in old Russia, one might almost say in old Muscovy, that the remaining power of resistance against the Germans was chiefly concentrated.

In wartime Russia, where every official utterance, and especially any word from Stalin was awaited with a desperate kind of hope, these two speeches, especially the one delivered in the dramatic setting of the Red Square, with the Germans still only a short distance outside Moscow, made a very deep impression on both the Army and the workers. The glorification of Russia—and not only Lenin's Russia— had a tremendous effect on the people in general, even though it made perhaps a few Marxist-Leninist purists squirm on the quiet. However, even these realised that it was this patriotic, nationalist propaganda which identified the Soviet Régime and Stalin with Russia, Holy Russia, that was the most likely to create the right kind of uplift.

In any case, it was not something entirely new. It was Stalin's nationalism which had, for years now, triumphed over Trotsky's internationalism; for years Stalin had already been built up in popular imagination as a state builder in the lineage of Alexander Nevsky (e.g. in the Eisenstein-Prokofiev film), of Ivan the Terrible and Peter the Great (e.g. in Alexei Tolstoy's novel).

Thus, in November 1941, all these reminders of the Tartar Invasion, of the Troubled Times, with their Polish invasion, and of 1812 did not fall on deaf ears. The Russian people felt the deep *insult* of the German invasion—it was something more deeply *insulting* than anything they had known before. In his 6th of November speech Stalin had not missed the chance of pointing out the difference between Napoleon and Hitler; Napoleon had come to a sorry end, but at least he had not brought to the invaded countries any *Untermensch* philosophy.

We shall deal more fully in a later chapter with the *mood* in Russia in 1941–2; here it is enough to say that in his two November speeches, Stalin had not only cleverly adapted himself to this mood, but he did everything to strengthen and encourage it.

It was, indeed, appropriate that such a mood should be encouraged, with the ancient Russian cities of Pskov, Novgorod and Tver (Kalinin) occupied by the Germans, with Leningrad virtually surrounded, and the Germans still battering against hastily improvised new Russian lines thirty or forty miles outside Moscow...

As a very orthodox Communist jokingly remarked to me some months later: "At that time it was absolutely essential to proclaim a 'nationalist NEP'."*

The importance of the two Stalin speeches is not underrated even in the "Khrushchevite" *History*:

> Stalin's two speeches had an enormous effect on the population in the occupied areas... Soviet airmen dropped behind the enemy lines newspapers with accounts of the November 6 meeting and of the Red Square Parade. These papers passed from hand to hand and were then kept as treasures. With tears of joy people learned that the Nazi stories about the fall of Moscow were nothing but stupid lies, and that Moscow was standing firmly like a rock. In hearing the voice of their beloved Party [euphemism for Stalin] they believed more firmly than ever in the might of the Soviet State, in the invincible will of the Soviet people to win, in the inevitable doom of the Nazi invaders...

* The New Economic Policy (NEP) introduced in 1921 had temporarily allowed some capitalist trading.

October and November 1941 were the grimmest months in the whole of the Soviet-German war, only to be equalled by October 1942, when the fate of Stalingrad hung in the balance.

By the end of September 1941, the greater part of the Ukraine had been lost, and the Germans were crashing ahead towards Kharkov, the Donbas and the Crimea. After the *débâcle* in the Battle of Kiev, in which the Russians—even according to their own admission—had lost in prisoners alone something in the neighbourhood of 175,000 men, the Germans, in the south, had a great superiority not only in men but in planes, tanks and guns.* Neither the *Stavka*'s order to organise a "stubborn defence" on the Perekop Isthmus in the Crimea, nor its order to build solid defences west of Kharkov or the Donbas could be carried out in time. The mobilization of many thousands of Donbas miners into the local *opolcheniye* and the efforts made by 150,000 miners to build new defence lines were of no avail. By September 29, the Germans broke into the Donbas which was then producing sixty per cent of the Soviet Union's coal, seventy-five per cent of its coking coal, thirty per cent of its pig-iron and twenty per cent of its steel. By October 17, Rundstedt's armies had overrun the whole Donbas and, after forcing the Mius river, entered Taganrog on the Sea of Azov; meantime, further north, Paulus's 6th Army was advancing on Kharkov, which was captured on October 24; the Russians had, during the previous days, been evacuating what industrial equipment they could. It was also then, with the Germans already at Taganrog, that Rostselmash, the vast agricultural-machinery plant at Rostov began to be evacuated to the east; this work continued almost till the last minute, often under German bombing.

On November 19, the Germans captured Rostov, after two days' bitter street fighting. But the High Command considered Rostov so important that even at the height of the Battle of Moscow, Timoshenko was given some reinforcements and ten days later, Rostov—"the gate to the Caucasus"—was recaptured by the Russians. It was the first major Russian victory, though the Germans were pushed only some thirty to forty miles to the west, where they entrenched

* Men, two to one; guns, three to one; planes, two to one. (IVOVSS, vol. II, p. 218.)

themselves along the Mius river. This victory was, according to the Russians (with some confirmation from the Germans) not only militarily but also politically important as it affected Turkey's policy towards Russia.*

In the meantime Manstein's 11th Army, supported by a Rumanian Army Corps, had broken into the Crimea, where the Russian forces retreated in disorder to Sebastopol. By mid-November the whole of the Crimea was in German (or Rumanian) hands, with the exception of Sebastopol, where three solid defence lines, ten miles in depth, had been organised. All enemy attempts to storm the naval base failed and under the command of Vice-Admiral Oktiabrsky and General Petrov the beleaguered fortress held out until July 1942. In underground workshops, more or less immune to the continuous bombing and shelling, Sebastopol made many of its own arms and ammunition. In November and December alone, it made 400 mine-throwers, 20,000 hand-grenades, and 32,000 anti-personnel mines, repaired numerous guns, machine-guns, and even tanks. At that time 52,000 men were defending Sebastopol, and for eight months they succeeded in tying up large German and Rumanian forces which, in the Russian view, would otherwise have been used to invade the Caucasus across the Kerch Straits.

Though thrown back from Rostov and held at Sebastopol, the Germans could still claim to have caused not only grievous military, but also immense economic damage to the Russians in the south.

The Russians' plight in the north was even more tragic. Except for a slender life-line across Lake Ladoga, the blockade of Leningrad had been complete by September 8, with the German capture of Schlüsselburg; on November 9, even the Ladoga gap was made almost unusable after the Germans had captured Tikhvin on the main railway line to the south-east of the lake. Leningrad seemed finally condemned to starvation, and it was not till December 9 that Tikhvin was recaptured, and the future began to look a little less desperate. It is rather remarkable that, at the very height of the

* The Russian attacks on Rostov in the south and Tikhvin in the north also helped to reduce the pressure on Moscow. Rostov was abandoned without Hitler's orders: hence the temporary disgrace of Rundstedt.

Battle of Moscow, the High Command should have been able to spare enough troops to recapture both Rostov and Tikhvin—even though these had obviously been looked upon as merely minimal objectives, which could not be followed up by either a recapture of the Donbas, or a major breach in the Leningrad blockade. For, at the time, Russia was not only short of trained soldiers, but also desperately short of arms. And, above all, it was clear that the Germans' Number-One target was still the capture of Moscow, despite the failure of their all-out October offensive.

Everything, by the beginning of November, tended to show that the Germans were preparing for another all-out attack, and were concentrating heavy forces not only west, but also north-west and south-west of Moscow. The failure of the first offensive had given the Soviet High Command just enough time to assemble large strategic reserves behind Moscow, and to strengthen their front line in all sectors.

The fact that Moscow was not captured in October had had an enormously salutary effect on the soldiers' morale. Some significance is today attached to the eagerness with which soldiers and officers were joining the Party and the Komsomol; within a month (October to November) the number of Party members in the three army groups outside Moscow rose from 33,000 to 51,000, and of Komsomol members from 59,000 to 78,000; it was at this stage in particular that the policy was adopted of admitting to the Party, with the minimum of formalities, almost any soldier who had distinguished himself in battle; the identification of Party and Country was at its height. Or rather, the Party adapted itself, as best it could, to the nationalist spirit of resistance.

After the failure of the first German onslaught on Moscow civilian morale improved also. The evacuation of Moscow had continued right through October and the first half of November; about half the population had gone, as well as a large part of the industry: thus, out of 75,000 metal-cutting lathes, only 21,000 remained in Moscow, whose industries were now concentrating chiefly on the manufacture of small arms, ammunition, and the repair of tanks and motor vehicles. The Moscow sky was dotted with barrage balloons, and there were anti-tank obstacles in most of the main streets, and a great many anti-aircraft batteries. These were far more numerous than before, and firewatching rules had become even stricter; thousands of Muscovites were engaged in fire-watching. The atmosphere was austere, military and heroic—very different from what it had been at the time of the panic exodus.

Although there was the general conviction that Moscow would not now be lost, the seriousness of the coming second offensive was not underrated. As was to be expected the Germans achieved considerable superiority in a number of places. Their first big blows fell on November 16 in the Kalinin-Volokolamsk sector of the front where they had three times more tanks and twice as many guns as the Russians. By November 22 they had broken into Klin north of Moscow and in the west to Istra, the point nearest to Moscow they were ever to reach in force. It was no doubt from Istra that German generals later remembered that they "could look at Moscow through a pair of good field-glasses". Istra is some fifteen miles west of Moscow.

There were many acts of heroism by Russian soldiers in the embittered fighting north of Volokolamsk, such as the many—if atrociously costly—feats by General Dovator's cossack cavalry (Dovator himself was to be killed during the Russian counter-offensive on December 19), or the suicidal resistance of Panfilov's anti-tank unit who were guarding the Volokolamsk highway at the Dubosekovo crossroads:

> On that day the Germans had hoped to break through to the Volokolamsk highway, and to advance on Moscow. After a massive air attack, German tommy-gunners tried to break into the Russian trenches, but were driven back by rifle and machine-gun fire. Then a second attack was launched by a fresh unit supported by twenty tanks... Using anti-tank rifles, hand-grenades, and petrol bottles the Panfilov men crippled fourteen of the tanks and the other six were driven back. Shortly afterwards the wounded survivors were again attacked by thirty more tanks. It was then that *politruk* (political instructor) Klochkov turned to the soldiers, saying "Russia is big, but

there is nowhere to retreat, because Moscow is behind us"... One by one the Soviet soldiers were being wounded and killed in a merciless fight which lasted four hours. The severely wounded *politruk* threw himself under an enemy tank with a bunch of hand-grenades and blew it up. The Germans, having lost eighteen tanks and dozens of men, failed to break through... *

There are various versions of the famous story of the "Twenty-eight Panfilov men"; what is curious about such stories of suicidal Russian resistance is that they are a little like a lottery or a lucky dip; numerous equally valiant deeds passed, if not unnoticed, at least unrecorded for posterity. But there were a few sample heroes, so to speak, who were to be built up in the popular imagination. The air force had its national hero in the famous Captain Gastello who, in the first week of the war, had crashed his burning plane into a column of German tanks; the infantry—its twenty-eight Panfilov men; the Partisans—and, by implication also the Komsomol and the Soviet people generally—were to have as their national heroine Zoya Kosmodemianskaya, the eighteen-year-old Moscow Komsomol girl, who had set fire to a German stable and was tortured and hanged by the Germans in the village of Petrishchevo near Moscow during the grim days of November 1941.† It so happened that the story of Zoya was discovered, together with her tortured and frozen body, with a rope round her neck, by Lidin, a *Pravda* reporter at the time of the Russian counter-offensive two weeks later... In reality, neither Gastello, nor the twenty-eight Panfilov men, nor Zoya were isolated cases of Russian bravery and self-sacrifice; there were very many others in the *levée en masse* atmosphere of November-December 1941.

On the southern flank of the Moscow front, the industrial city of Tula, joined to the capital by a narrow bottleneck, was in constant danger of being encircled. There was a particularly strong Party organisation in that old Russian centre of arms manufacture, and

* IVOVSS, vol. II, p. 261.
† Later in the war there was a similar "canonisation" of the "Young Guard" resistance group in the mining town of Krasnodon in the Donbas. A. Fadeyev later wrote a famous novel on them.

the workers' battalions took a very active part in the defence of their city, which was living in a sort of "1919" atmosphere, dramatically described by General Boldin, who was placed in charge of the defence of Tula on November 22. Guderian had failed already once to reach Tula, but had not abandoned his attempts to outflank and isolate it. On December 3 Tula was encircled, the Germans having cut both the railway and the highroad to Moscow. As Boldin tells the story:

> On December 3, sixteen enemy tanks, together with motorised infantry crossed the Tula-Moscow railway at Revyakino and occupied three villages... I was also told that, later in the day, the Hitlerites had cut in several places the Tula-Moscow highway, some ten miles north of Tula. "What shall we do now?" said Zhavoronkov (the local Party chief). "A strange question," I said, trying to sound cheerful. "We'll just go on defending Tula as before, and go on killing Fascists."
>
> Not for a moment did the roar of guns stop in and around Tula. I called up the command post of the 258th rifle division in the village of Popovkino, and asked for its commander, Colonel Siyazov. "Mikhail Alexandrovich," I had to bellow into the field telephone, "take immediate steps to clear the Germans off the Moscow highway!" Siyazov could hardly hear me. I had to spell out every word. Then I could faintly hear him say: "Comrade General, your order will be carried out. I am ordering the 999th regiment to attack."
>
> I asked Siyazov to inform me hourly. Not for a moment did I doubt that they would succeed. Then the phone rang from H.Q., and General Zhukov asked for me. I felt it would be an unpleasant conversation. And so it was. "Well, Comrade Boldin," Zhukov said, "this is the third time you've managed to get yourself encircled. Isn't it rather too much? I already told you to move your army headquarters and command post to Laptevo. But you were pig-headed, wouldn't carry out my order..." "Comrade Commander," I said, "if I and my army staff had left, Guderian would already be here. The position would be much worse than it is now."
>
> For a couple of minutes there was a loud crackle in the receiver, and finally I could hear Zhukov again. "What steps are you taking?" he said. I reported that the 999th rifle regiment of the 258th division had gone into action to clear the Moscow highway and that, moreover, an attack was being mounted against the Germans at Kashira. "What help do you need?" said Zhukov. "May I ask you to move the tanks of Getman's division southwards along the Moscow highway to meet

the 999th rifles?" "Very well, I shall," said Zhukov. "But you, too, do your stuff."

Siyazov went on phoning hour by hour. The 999th regiment had been fighting for seventeen hours when another phone call came. An overjoyed excited Siyazov reported: "Comrade Commander, Vedenin (the Regiment's commander) has just phoned to say that his men and the Getman tanks have joined up. Traffic may be resumed along the Tula-Moscow highway."*

At Tula, December 3 turned out to be the most critical day; at most other sectors of the front, however, the Germans had been virtually stopped about a week earlier, and already preparations were in full progress for the Russian counter-offensive which was to start on the 6th.

Towards the middle of their second offensive against Moscow, the Germans were beginning to suffer from the cold. A little over a week after Guderian had bitterly complained that he couldn't move his tanks because of the mud and was hoping for an early frost, which would make it easier to advance on Moscow, he started to complain equally bitterly about the frost for which he had longed. On November 6 he wrote:

> It is miserable for the troops and a great pity that the enemy should thus gain time while our plans are postponed until the winter is more and more advanced. It all makes me very sad... The unique chance of striking a single great blow is fading more and more. How things will turn out, God only knows.

And then he said that, on November 7, "we suffered our first severe cases of frostbite". By November 17 he sounded even more downcast:

> We are only nearing our final objective step by step in this icy cold and with all the troops suffering from this appalling supply situation. The difficulties of supplying us by railroad are constantly increasing... Without fuel, our trucks can't move... Yet our troops are fighting with wonderful endurance despite all these handicaps... I am thankful that our men are such good soldiers.

It was all most distressing. As he later wrote:

* Boldin, op. cit., pp. 184–5.

The 1941 harvest had been a rich one throughout the country, and there was no shortage of cattle. (But) as a result of our wretched rail communications only a small amount of food could be sent to Germany from the area of the Second Panzer Army.*

On November 17, we learned that Siberian troops had appeared... and that more were arriving by rail at Riazan and Kolomna. The 112th Infantry Division made contact with these new Siberian troops. Since enemy tanks were attacking simultaneously... the weakened troops could not manage this fresh enemy. Before judging their performance it should be borne in mind that each regiment had already lost some 500 men from frostbite, that, as a result of the cold, the machine-guns were no longer able to fire and that our 37-mm. anti-tank gun had proved ineffective against the Russian T-34 tanks. The result of all this was a panic... This was the first time that such a thing had occurred during the Russian campaign... The battle-worthiness of our infantry was at an end...

For all that, Guderian continued to attack Tula, and also records the fact that his troops did, at one moment, cut the Tula-Moscow highway as well as the Tula-Moscow railway; but it is clear from his story that something went wrong—though he does not say anything except that "the strength of the troops was exhausted, as was their supply of fuel."

All subsequent attacks on Tula failed, largely, according to Guderian, for the same reasons, and because on December 4 the thermometer had dropped to minus 31°C., and on the 5th to minus 68° (sic). This is a physical impossibility, and must be regarded, it seems, as a Freudian lapse, betraying Guderian's urge to blame everything on the weather!

The Russians, while denying that it was exceptionally cold in November, agree that it was very cold indeed in December; what they very rightly point out is that it is a stupid fallacy to imagine that Russian soldiers do not suffer, like anybody else, from extreme

---

* Guderian, op. cit., pp. 246–9. Here is also to be found the much more dubious story about the wonderfully good care the Germans were taking to supply the Russian civilians at Orel and elsewhere with food! As we shall later see, Orel suffered from an appalling famine in the winter of 1941–2 under Guderian's tender care. See p. 690.

cold! What they do say, however, is that the Soviet troops had far better winter clothing than the Germans:

> General Blumentritt bitterly admits that the German soldiers were destined to spend their first winter in Russia fighting heavily, and with nothing to wear but summer clothes, overcoats and blankets. At the same time, according to him, "most of the Russian effectives were well supplied with short fur jackets, padded jackets (*telogreiki*), felt boots (*valenki*) and fur hats with ear-flaps. They also had fur gloves, mittens and warm underwear." We can only agree with these lamentations of the beaten Nazi general. The facts he mentions merely show ... that the Soviet High Command proved more farsighted than the German High Command... For the first time in World War II the Nazi Army was passing through a severe crisis. The Nazi generals were deeply discouraged by the enormous losses their troops had suffered, and by their failure to end the war against the Soviet Union in 1941. All their hopes of warm, comfortable billets in Moscow had gone up in smoke...*

The almost astronomical figures of German losses quoted at the time for obvious propaganda purposes by both Stalin and the Sovinformbureau communiqués are not repeated in present-day Soviet histories of the War. In the course of the second German offensive against Moscow (November 16 to December 5), says the *History*, the German losses were: 55,000 dead, over 100,000 wounded and frostbitten, 777 tanks, 297 guns and mortars, 244 machine-guns, over 500 tommy-guns† which is a reasonable estimate, not greatly differing from the losses suggested, for instance, by Guderian.

The total German losses for the first five months of the war are now put not at Stalin's four and a half million, but at 750,000, not counting the losses of Germany's allies. This figure is even slightly lower than that given by the Germans themselves. As Hillgruber and Jacobsen say: "There is no doubt that German losses were very high during the first phase of the Russian campaign, especially during the Battle of Moscow... The total losses of the German army in the east were, up to December 10, 1941 (not counting the sick), 775,078 men (roughly, 24·22 per cent of the eastern armies which, on the average, totalled 3·2 million men). According to Halder's *Diary* the

* IVOVSS, vol. II, p. 268.   † Ibid., p. 265.

losses were as follows (in round figures) up to the second half of the second Moscow offensive:

Total up to 31 July	213,000 men
„ „ „ 3 August	242,000 „
„ „ „ 30 September	551,000 „
„ „ „ 6 November	686,000 „
„ „ „ 13 November	700,000 „
„ „ „ 23 November	734,000 „
„ „ „ 26 November	743,000 „

Of these nearly 200,000 were dead, including 8,000 officers.

As against this, the German authors glumly remark, 156,000 was the total of the German losses (of whom, some 30,000 dead) during the whole of the Western campaign in 1940!*

* B. S. Telpukhovsky, op. cit., German edition, footnote on p. 93.

Chapter XII

THE MOSCOW COUNTER-OFFENSIVE

In preparing for its winter counter-offensive, the Soviet High Command had a minimum and a maximum programme.* The minimum programme was to restore communications with blockaded Leningrad, to lift the threat hanging over Moscow, and to close the Germans' access to the Caucasus. The maximum programme was to break the Leningrad blockade, to encircle the Germans between Moscow and Smolensk and to recapture the Donbas and the Crimea. As things turned out, even the minimum programme was only partly carried out: Rostov, the "padlock of the Caucasus" had been liberated by the Russians at the end of November, and the Germans were pushed back to the Mius line, but apart from a local offensive in the Donbas, later in the winter, which recaptured a small salient including Barvenkovo and Lozovaya, the Russians got no further. In the Crimea, Sebastopol was holding out, but the Russian landing on December 26 on the Kerch Peninsula in the Eastern Crimea was to end in disaster in the following spring.† On the Leningrad front the recapture of Tikhvin on December 9 alleviated Leningrad's supply position considerably. But the land blockade as such continued. The Russian advance in the Moscow area was more spectacular, yet despite the liberation of large territories—one of the Russian thrusts, for instance, went nearly all the way to Velikie Luki, a matter of about 200 miles—the Germans succeeded

* As is implied in IVOVSS.   † See pp. 387-9.

L.Ilmen

Miles

0   50   100   150

Volga

LENINGRAD

Yaroslavl

Kholm

Kalinin

Klin

Dmitrov

Velikie
Luki

Solnechnogorsk

MOSCOW

Rzhev

Volokolamsk

B E L O R U S S I A

SPRING
1942

Gzhatsk

Mozhaisk

Kashira

Smolensk

Viazma

Kaluga

Orsha

Yelnia

Yasnaya
Polyana

Tula

Roslavl

Bryansk

Mtsensk

Orel

Yelets

Extreme limit of
German penetration

SPRING
1942

Kursk

Voronezh

Soviet offensive

Area liberated in
winter campaign,
1941–1942

N

MOSCOW · RUSSIAN COUNTER-OFFENSIVE

in holding the Rzhev-Gzhatsk-Viazma triangle of fortified hedgehog positions, less than a hundred miles west of Moscow.

It was Hitler who, against the advice of many of his generals—these advocated a major withdrawal—insisted on holding Rzhev, Viazma, Yukhnov, Kaluga, Orel and Briansk; and, with the exception of Kaluga, all these places were held. Many of the discouraged generals—among them Brauchitsch, Höppner and Guderian—were sacked, while von Bock fell "ill". In the north, von Leeb was also relieved of his command for reasons of "health" and was replaced by General Küchler, a more wholehearted Nazi. Hitler had been greatly disappointed by von Leeb's failure to capture Leningrad in August or September, just as he had been incensed by von Bock's failure to capture Moscow. Rundstedt also fell into temporary disfavour after the Russian recapture of Rostov.

The Russian counter-offensive was launched on December 5-6 along almost the whole 560 miles from Kalinin in the north to Yelets in the south, and during the very first days spectacular progress was made nearly everywhere. A characteristic of the fighting in winter conditions was the avoidance, as far as possible, of frontal attacks on the enemy's rearguard, and the formation of mobile pursuit units, calculated to cut the enemy's lines of retreat and create panic among them. Such pursuit units, comparable to the Cossacks of 1812, who mercilessly harassed the *Grande Armée*, were composed of tommy-gunners, ski troops, tanks and cavalry—notably the cavalry units under General Belov and General Dovator. But the results of these tactics often proved disappointing, and the cavalry units suffered particularly heavy casualties.

The behaviour of the Germans in this winter war varied from place to place; usually they still offered stubborn resistance, but were clearly obsessed by the fear of encirclement; thus, when by December 13 the Russians closed in on Kalinin and Klin and summoned the German garrisons to surrender, these rejected the ultimatum, but nevertheless hastened to pull out before it was too late—not without first, it is true, setting fire to as many buildings as possible. In other places, however, the German retreat often degenerated into a panic flight. West of Moscow and in the Tula area, miles and miles of roads were littered with abandoned guns, lorries and tanks, deeply embedded in the snow. The comic "Winter Fritz", wrapped up in women's shawls and feather boas stolen from the local population, and with icicles hanging from his red nose, made his first appearance in Russian folklore.

On December 13, Sovinformbureau published its famous communiqué announcing the failure of the German attempt to encircle Moscow, and describing the first results of the Russian counter-offensive. The newspapers published photographs of the outstanding Soviet generals who had won the battle of Moscow: Zhukov, Lelyushenko, Kuznetsov, Rokossovsky, Govorov, Boldin, Golikov, Belov and Vlasov, the future traitor!

By the middle of December the Red Army had advanced nearly everywhere between twenty and forty miles, and had liberated Kalinin, Klin, Istra, Yelets, and had completely relieved Tula; in the second half of December the offensive continued, the Russians recapturing Kaluga and Volokolamsk, where, in the main square, they found a gallows with eight bodies hanging from it—seven men and one woman. These were allegedly partisans whom the Germans had publicly hanged to terrorise the population.

If, on some sectors of the front the Germans were literally on the run, in others they continued to fight very stubbornly; thus, in Kaluga, one of the towns which Hitler had ordered to be held at all costs, the Germans were only driven out after several days of heavy street fighting.

True, the Germans were often handicapped by a shortage of adequate winter clothing; but the bitter cold and the deep snow did not make things easy for the Russians either. It should also be stressed that the Russians had no marked superiority, either in trained men or in equipment. According to the present-day Russian *History* the State Defence Committee and the *Stavka* had, on the eve of the Russian counter-offensive, failed, despite enormous efforts, to achieve the necessary superiority in the Moscow area, where the Germans had concentrated their most powerful army group. They still had a superiority of 1.1:1 in men, of 1.8:1 in artillery and of 1.4:1 in tanks, while Soviet troops, both in the Kalinin and the Moscow sectors, had been weakened by the defensive battle for the capital. The available strategic reserves which were thrown in, especially in the areas of the main thrusts, helped to overcome the enemy's superiority in manpower, but were not sufficient to tip the scales, the more so as the Germans still had more tanks and guns at their disposal.*

The Red Army was very severely handicapped by a shortage in motorised transport. There were only 8,000 trucks available on the Moscow sectors of the front, a totally inadequate number. Not even half of the required ammunition, food and other supplies could be delivered by motor transport, and many hundreds of horse-sleighs had to be used to make up for the shortage in trucks. Although the carrying capacity of the horse-sleighs was small, they had the advantage of getting through snow-drifts more easily than heavy lorries.

The shortage of the Red Army's motor transport in 1941–2 is very striking when one thinks of the hundreds of thousands of American trucks which were to increase so enormously the Red Army's mobility from 1943 on—but not before.

Numerous measures were taken, despite all these difficulties, to move the Army's supply bases nearer the Front; but if the great Russian counter-offensive in the winter of 1941–2 proved in the end to be only a partial success, it was due, as we shall see, to several factors; shortage of transport, especially as the lines of communications grew longer and longer; a growing shortage of arms and ammunition; and, finally, the exhausting nature of the winter war. Before spring came, the Red Army was terribly tired. Also, the High Command had made a number of errors.

In very heavy fighting during the whole of December, and the first half of January, the Red Army had driven the Germans a considerable distance away from Moscow; but the progress of the Russian offensive was very uneven; the northern flank had advanced furthest west—by some 200 miles, and the southern flank by nearly as much, but due west of Moscow itself, the Germans were clinging to their Rzhev-Gzhatsk-Viazma springboard. The *Stavka*'s directives of December 9 show that the Russian command was planning a vast

* IVOVSS, vol. II, p. 260.

encirclement of the German forces opposite Moscow, with one pincer striking north of them and the other south. Hitler, on the other hand, who after the purge among his generals had assumed the supreme command himself, ordered Army Group Mitte to defend fanatically the positions held west of Moscow, and to take no notice of the enemy breaking through on their flanks.

The Germans had suffered severe losses in the Battle of Moscow; they were fighting in unusual winter conditions, their morale was often low; nevertheless they continued to represent a formidable force.

By January 1, the Russians, drawing on their reserves, achieved equality in manpower and, on some sectors of the front, even a certain superiority in tanks and aircraft—tanks, 1.6:1, aircraft, 1.4:1 —but the Germans still had a 3:1 superiority in anti-tank weapons. In short, notwithstanding the Red Army's great successes in December and the first half of January, its superiority was, according to present-day Soviet historians, totally insufficient for the major offensive the Soviet Supreme Command had in mind.

It was very cold in January 1942,* and the heavy snowfall had made transport extremely difficult. Except for a relatively small number of ski troops, the Russian troops could, in fact, move only along the roads, and not without much difficulty at that. As the Russians advanced, the difficulties of using aircraft also increased, since there were no airfields ready for use in the newly liberated areas. Yet a further set of instructions dated January 7, 1942, confirms that the Soviet High Command was still determined to break up, encircle and destroy all the German forces between Moscow and Smolensk. But as the Russians advanced rapidly in the north, and only slowly in the centre, the line of the front had nearly doubled in length by the middle of January. On January 15, Hitler, though resigned to abandoning some territory, gave a further order to his troops to take up strong defensive positions east of Rzhev, Viazma, Gzhatsk and Yukhnovo. Rigorous disciplinary measures were introduced, and Halder, the Chief of Staff, issued a directive denouncing

---

* Temperatures averaged minus 20° to 25°C., (4° to 13° of frost Fahrenheit.)

panic and bewilderment and prophesying that the Russian offensive would soon peter out.

The Russian *History* now admits that the strengthening of German resistance by propaganda, disciplinary measures, and reinforcements from the west, was underrated by the Soviet High Command. Already on January 25, the Russians suffered their first major set-back in failing to take Gzhatsk by storm; in the south—west of Tula—the German resistance was stiffening as well, and on this sector of the front the Red Army came virtually to a standstill by the end of January.

But the Supreme Command still persisted with its plan for a big encirclement, and decided to drop a large number of paratroops in the enemy rear, to cut enemy communications and to serve as a link between the pincers which were expected to close round the Germans near Smolensk. Yet German resistance was increasing everywhere and all Russian attempts to break through to Viazma, the nodal point in the German defences, were doomed to failure.

In a number of places the Germans started counter-attacking. Renewed massive tank attacks, especially in the Viazma area, pro-duced more heroic deeds on the part of the Russians, similar to that of the Panfilov men at Volokolamsk in December. Inside a cartridge case embedded in a tree trunk a note was found after the war written by a dying soldier, Alexander Vinogradov, who, with twelve others, had been sent to stop German tanks from advancing along the Minsk highway—

> . . . And now there are only three of us left. . . We shall stand firm as long as there's any life left in us. . . Now I am alone, wounded in my arm and my head. The number of tanks has increased. There are twenty-three. I shall probably die. Somebody may find my note and remember me; I am a Russian, from Frunze. I have no parents. Good-bye, dear friends. Your Alexander Vinogradov. 22.2.42.

It is quite clear that the Russian High Command overrated both the Russian armies' driving force and the breakdown in the morale and organisation of the Wehrmacht after the setbacks they had suffered in December and the first part of January.

The plans to encircle and smash all the German forces between Moscow and Smolensk, as well as to recapture Orel and Briansk proved much too ambitious. With the Germans mostly dug in, and the Russians advancing, the conditions created by a particularly harsh winter ultimately affected the Russians more than it did the Germans. Not only were reserves in both men and equipment insufficient (industrial production of war material was, as explained before, at its lowest ebb), but what reserves were used were thrown in piecemeal. Thus, the *Stavka*'s order that Briansk be recaptured, and reinforcements be sent to that area, diverted the Red Army from its main aim, which was to smash the Germans in the Viazma area. The orders issued by the *Stavka* as late as March 20 that the Red Army should occupy a line close to Smolensk (Belyi-Dorogobuzh-Yelnya-Krasnoye, twenty-eight miles south-west of Smolensk), that it should join up with the Russians' units in the enemy rear, and that it should capture Gzhatsk by April 1 and Viazma about the same time, as well as Briansk, and capture Rzhev not later than April 5, turned out to be totally unrealistic.

The thaw that set in at the end of March reduced still further the Red Army's mobility; nor did the Red Army, by this time, have much air support, and its supply lines had practically broken down. By the end of March the Russian offensive came to a complete standstill. For many months after the offensive had stopped parachutists and other troops in the enemy rear under Cavalry General Belov, and the local partisans, continued to harass German communications,* but the net result of the January-March 1942 operations was bitterly disappointing after the enthusiasm caused by the Battle of Moscow proper.

Russian losses were much higher than those of the Germans; the troops were worn out, and the shortage of equipment and ammunition began to be keenly felt by the middle of February. True, large areas had been liberated—the whole of the Moscow province, most of the Kalinin province, the whole of the Tula, and most of the Kaluga province. But the large Rzhev-Gzhatsk-Viazma springboard, which was to continue to threaten Moscow, had remained in German

* According to the Russians the bulk of the men in the Suchevka pocket did not break out until the following June.

hands. Some deadly fighting was to go on for this in the summer of 1942, and it was not till the beginning of 1943 that the Germans were driven out of it. Many soldiers who had fought at various parts of the front later told me that perhaps the most heart-breaking months in their experience were February-March 1942. After the high hopes that had been raised by the Battle of Moscow, everything seemed to be going wrong again. The Germans had lost the Battle of Moscow, but they were clearly very far from finished.

Commenting on the results of the Russian winter offensive, the present-day Russian *History* makes the following important points:

> The moral effect even of the incomplete victory of the Red Army during the winter campaign of 1941–2 was enormous, and decisively strengthened the Soviet people's faith in ultimate victory;
> The effect on highly dubious neutrals like Turkey and Japan was little short of overwhelming;
> Thanks to the Russian winter offensive, it was now possible to stop the evacuation of central-Russian industry to the east, which meant that the output of armaments and munitions in the Moscow area in particular could be resumed and intensified; in some cases, plants were brought back from the east.

Nevertheless, the winter offensive did not achieve all the desired results:

> The offensive took place in exceptionally difficult conditions. The Red Army still lacked the experience of organising and conducting a large-scale offensive operation. The extreme cold, the deep snow, the very limited number of usable roads, severely limited manœuvrability. The delivery of supplies and the organisation of airfields met with enormous difficulties. *Nor could the country supply the Army with all it needed by way of equipment, armaments and munitions. All this had a bad effect on the tempo of the offensive, and on the performance of the troops, and often prevented the Red Army from making the best use of favourable conditions for the annihilation of large enemy group-ings.* This first attempt to mount a strategic counter-offensive and then a general offensive along the whole front was marked by some serious mistakes on the part of the Supreme Command, and of the command of separate army groups.*

> * IVOVSS, vol. II, p. 359. (Emphasis added.)

What were these mistakes and shortcomings?

1) The Supreme Command did not always make the best use of the reserves at its disposal. Often troops were thrown into battle without sufficient preliminary training. The recognition of this error was reflected in the new regulations issued by the State Defence Committee on March 16, 1942.

2) On the whole, the Red Army also lacked large mechanised and armoured units, which greatly reduced the troops' striking force and the speed of their advance; the Germans, on the contrary, used concentrated tank formations in their counter-attacks, even in the winter conditions of 1941-2.

What is more, having over-estimated the results of the December-January counter-offensive, the Supreme Command did not use its reserves rationally. In the course of the subsequent winter campaign, the *Stavka* scattered its reserves unnecessarily: nine new armies were thrown in: two were sent to the Volkhov Front, one to the North-West Front, one to the Kalinin Front, three to the Western (Moscow) Front, one each to the Briansk and South-West Front—

> When, at the final stage of the Battle of Moscow, conditions were thought favourable for encircling and routing of Army Group *Mitte*, the *Stavka* no longer had the necessary reserves, and the strategic operation, which had been successfully developing, remained uncompleted. If massed forces had been concentrated against Army Group *Mitte*—i.e. on the decisive "Western" Front—this Army Group would undoubtedly have been smashed.

3) The concentrated use of the air force at the initial stage of the Battle of Moscow could, for a number of reasons, not be kept up.

4) Partisan activity in the enemy rear was of great value to the Red Army, and had, according to Guderian's admission, a very depressing moral effect on the German troops. But many mistakes were also made in the conduct of partisan warfare;

> As it turned out, the constitution of large and vulnerable partisan formations proved a major error... The enemy did not have to deal with numerous and elusive small partisan bands over wide areas. Instead, he resorted to large military operations in the areas of partisan activity. This compelled the partisan units to adopt defensive tactics, which are not in the nature of partisan warfare, and their losses, therefore, were very heavy.

*

Stalin's Order of the Day on Red-Army Day on February 23, 1942
and on May-Day 1942 sounded, paradoxically, less optimistic than
his two speeches in November 1941 with the Germans right outside
Moscow. He no longer suggested that the war would be won "in six
months, perhaps in a year".

The hatred of the Germans had, if anything, grown since the Battle
of Moscow. In recapturing numerous towns and many hundreds of
villages, the Russian soldiers got their first first-hand experience of
the "New Order". Everywhere the Germans had destroyed whatever
they could; all but three houses had been burned down at Istra, for
instance, where they had also blown up the ancient New Jerusalem
Monastery. In several towns and villages, which the Red Army
entered, there were gallows with "partisans" hanging from them.
Later, in 1942, I explored some of the towns and villages that had
been occupied then destroyed by the Germans—it was always the
same grim story.

The Germans in towns and villages round Moscow; the Germans in
ancient Russian cities like Novgorod, Pskov and Smolensk; the
Germans in the suburbs of Leningrad; the Germans at Tolstoy's
Yasnaya Polyana; the Germans at Orel, at Lgov, at Shchigry, the
old Turgeniev country, the most Russian of all the Russian areas.
They were robbing, and looting and killing; when they were retreating they would burn down every house, and in the depth of winter
civilians were left without house and home. Nothing like this had
happened to Russia before—except under the Tartar invasions. The
anger and resentment against the Germans, mixed with a feeling of
infinite pity for the Russian people, for the Russian land, defiled by
the invader, produced an emotional reaction of national pride and
national injury which was extraordinarily well reflected in the literature and music of 1941 and the early part of 1942.

Some of the best poems, though unknown at the time—they were
not published until 1945—reflecting the bitter anxiety during the
first months of the invasion, were written by Boris Pasternak—

Do you remember that dryness in your throat
When rattling their naked power of evil
They were barging ahead and bellowing
And autumn was advancing in steps of calamity?

"Barging and bellowing" and "rattling their naked power of evil", as Pasternak put it, was not exactly the same thought—something like a "Martian Invasion"—conveyed by that horrible, inhuman little theme of Shostakovich's *Leningrad Symphony*? Today it may seem noisy, melodramatic, repetitive (the theme, is, indeed, repeated louder and louder and louder no fewer than eleven times); yet, as a documentary of 1941, as a reflection of the feeling that here was "naked evil" in all its stupendous, arrogant, inhumanly terrifying power over-running Russia there is almost nothing to equal it:

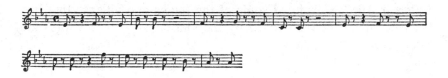

The lament for the Russian Land took on other forms, too. Konstantin Simonov's poems became immensely popular during that winter of 1941–2. For instance the agonising picture of the Russian retreat from the Smolensk province, with lines like these:

... And it seemed that outside every Russian village
Our grandfathers had risen from the dead,
And were shielding us with their outstretched arms,
And praying for us, their godless grandchildren...
Russia, our homeland, what is it? I ask you;
It's not Moscow houses, where we cheerfully lived,
It is rather these poor huts where our grandfathers laboured,
And the Russian graves with their simple crosses...

Here was a kind of nostalgia for the Russian *land*, even in its poorest and most archaic form.

Or the still more famous *Wait for me*, with its irrational, almost religious undertones:

Wait for me, and I'll return, only wait very hard.
Wait, when you are filled with sorrow as you watch the yellow rain;
Wait, when the winds sweep the snowdrifts,
Wait in the sweltering heat,
Wait when others have stopped waiting, forgetting their yesterdays.
Wait even when from afar, no letters come to you,
Wait even when others are tired of waiting. . .
Wait even when my mother and son think I am no more,
And when friends sit around the fire, drinking to my memory.
Wait, and do not hurry to drink to my memory, too;
Wait, for I'll return, defying every death.
And let those who did not wait say that I was lucky;
They will never understand that in the midst of death,
You, with your waiting, saved me.
Only you and I will know how I survived:
It's because you waited, as no one else did.

This literal translation naturally does not render the rhythm of the original; as a poem it is, in fact, very mediocre; but, nevertheless, from the autumn of 1941, when it was first published, right through 1942, it was the most popular poem in Russia, which millions of women recited to themselves like a prayer.

It is difficult at this distance, except for those who were in Russia at the time, to realise how important a poem like this was to literally millions of Russian women; no one could tell how many hundreds of thousands had died at the front since June 22, or had been taken prisoner or were otherwise missing.

Almost equally important were some other poets and writers. People were deeply moved for instance by *Zoya*, Margarita Aligher's poem on the partisan girl who was hanged outside Moscow—a poem later turned into a play. This represents the girl's hallucinations during the night between her torture by the Germans and her execution, Stalin appearing in the last scene to say that Moscow has been saved. Important, too, was Surkov's poetry, e.g. his prose poem, *A Soldier's Oath* written in 1941:

I am a Russian man, a soldier of the Red Army. My country has put a rifle in my hand, and has sent me to fight against the black hordes of Hitler that have broken into my country. Stalin has told me that the battle will be hard and bloody, but that victory will be mine.

I heard Stalin, and know it will be so. I am the 193 million of free Soviet men, and to all of them Hitler's yoke is more bitter than death...

Mine eyes have beheld thousands of dead bodies of women and children, lying along the railways and the highways. They were killed by the German vultures... The tears of women and children are boiling in my heart. Hitler the murderer and his hordes shall pay for these tears with their wolfish blood; for the avenger's hatred knows no mercy...

Of the greatest importance, too, as morale-builders, were Ehrenburg's articles in *Pravda* and *Red Star*—brilliant and eloquent diatribes against the Germans, which were very popular in the Army. They were, occasionally, criticised on the ground that he tended to ridicule the Germans, forgetting what a powerful, deadly enemy they were. His suggestion that *all* Germans were evil was, of course, at variance with the official ideological line (repeated once again in Stalin's order of the day of February 23), but "Ehrenburgism" was fully approved in the circumstances as the most effective form of hate propaganda. Nor was he alone in taking this propaganda line: there were also Sholokhov and Alexei Tolstoy, and many others. The "all Germans are evil" motif was to become even more outspoken in the fearful summer of 1942.

Chapter XIII

THE DIPLOMATIC SCENE OF
THE FIRST MONTHS OF THE INVASION

Diplomatically, the Soviet Union was in a very strange position at the time of the German invasion. The only two embassies in Moscow that seemed to count in the eyes of the Soviet authorities before that were the German and the Japanese Embassies, and, of all ambassadors, Count von der Schulenburg was the one the Russians cultivated most. The Japanese Ambassador was also being courted, especially since the Matsuoka visit a few months earlier.* As a gesture of appeasement towards Hitler, diplomatic relations had been broken off in May 1941 with Norway, Belgium, Yugoslavia and Greece; but Vichy France was represented by a full-fledged Ambassador, Gaston Bergery.

Apart from Sweden, Turkey, Iran, Afghanistan and Finland, very few neutral countries were represented; and if, with the American Embassy, under Laurence A. Steinhardt, relations were correct, but no more, the British Embassy, under Sir Stafford Cripps, was officially treated with deliberate coolness, almost bordering on rudeness. Cripps had the greatest difficulty in maintaining contact with the Soviet Foreign Commissariat, and, till the outbreak of the war in June 1941, he had not been privileged to meet Stalin, and had to content himself with occasionally seeing Vyshinsky, whose manner was far from forthcoming.

* See p. 121.

There is in Churchill's *Second World War** a very curious passage concerning the one and only message he sent Stalin on April 3, asking Russia, in effect, to intervene in the Balkans.

PRIME MINISTER TO SIR STAFFORD CRIPPS

Following from me to M. Stalin, *provided it can be personally delivered by you*:

I have sure information from a trusted agent that when the Germans thought they had got Yugoslavia in the net—i.e. after March 20—they began to move three out of the five Panzer divisions from Rumania to Southern Poland. The moment they heard of the Serbian revolution this movement was countermanded. Your Excellency will readily appreciate the significance of these facts.

Eden, in his dispatch to Cripps accompanying the Churchill message asked that Cripps should point out to Stalin (if he were to see him) that the Soviet Union now had an opportunity of joining forces with Britain in the Balkans by furnishing material help to Yugoslavia and Greece; this would delay a German attack on Russia.

Cripps meantime had sent a detailed letter along the same lines to Vyshinsky; and he therefore thought that Churchill's "fragmentary" message would do more harm than good.

I greatly fear that the delivery of the Prime Minister's message would not be merely ineffectual, but a serious tactical mistake. If, however, you are unable to share this view, I will of course endeavour to arrange urgently for an interview with Molotov.

"I was vexed at this," Churchill wrote, "and at the delay which had occurred."

After some acrimonious exchanges between Churchill and Cripps *via* Eden, Cripps finally wired more than a fortnight later (after Yugoslavia had already been invaded) that he had sent the text of Churchill's message to Vyshinsky; and on April 22 he wrote to Eden:

"Vyshinsky informed me in writing today that message had been conveyed to Stalin."

In the summer of 1941, in talking to me, Cripps alluded to this episode, when he said:

In London they had no idea what difficulties I was up against here. They did not want to realise that not only Stalin, but even Molotov

* Vol. 3, pp. 320–3.

avoided me like grim death; for several months before the war, Vyshinsky was my only contact, and a highly unsatisfactory one at that. Stalin, I can tell you, did not *want* to have anything to do with Churchill, so alarmed was he lest the Germans found out. And Molotov was no better. At the same time, they let it be understood that they didn't mind their military talking to our military.

Churchill later commented:

> I cannot form any final judgment upon whether my message, if delivered with all the promptness and ceremony prescribed, would have altered the course of events. Nevertheless I still regret that my instructions were not carried out effectively. If I had had any direct contact with Stalin I might perhaps have prevented him from having so much of his air force destroyed on the ground.

It was clear from what Cripps later said that the message could certainly not have been delivered "with all the promptness and ceremony prescribed" for the simple reason that Stalin would not even dream of having any such "ceremony". Finally, it is also clear that *this* particular message, suggesting that the Russians intervene in the Balkans, would have produced no results, since Stalin had firmly set his mind to continue in his policy of co-existence with Hitler. Moreover, it would have arrived too late to save Yugoslavia. But even if the Russians were frightened of being dragged into a Balkan war they might all the same have listened to Cripps when the latter persisted in warning them of the imminent German attack on the Soviet Union. At the same time Eden kept on warning Maisky who, as the latter later assured me, did not fail to pass these warnings on to Moscow. But it was no good.

Cripps had no reason to be satisfied with the Soviet leaders; nevertheless, when the invasion started, he did his utmost to restore normal relations between Britain and the Soviet Union. There is a suggestion in Churchill's *Second World War* that the Russians were at first wholly unresponsive to his famous broadcast of June 22—

> ... except that parts of it were printed in *Pravda* ... and that we were asked to receive a Russian military mission. The silence at the top was oppressive, and I thought it my duty to break the ice. I quite

understood that they might feel shy, considering all that had passed
since the outbreak of the war...*

Maybe they *were* shy; but, in reality, they were delighted and, as
I often heard it said at the time, "pleasantly surprised" by Churchill's
broadcast; with their peculiar mentality, they had thought an Anglo-
German deal not entirely out of the question, and they had been
confirmed in this suspicion ever since the Hess episode.

Although Stalin did not communicate with Churchill personally
until after the latter had written to him on July 7, he hastened to
establish close relations with Cripps. Barely a week after the
invasion, the first batch of the British Military Mission, with General
Mason MacFarlane at its head, flew to Moscow. At the same time
Cripps had been discussing with both Stalin and Molotov the terms
of a joint Anglo-Soviet Declaration, which was to be made public
on July 12. The idea of this joint declaration originated on the
Russian side, as is apparent from Churchill's message to Cripps of
July 10.

It is reasonable to suppose that if Stalin did not communicate with
Churchill immediately after the latter's broadcast of June 22, it was
because the Soviet Government was bewildered by what was happening. After all, it took Stalin fully eleven days after the invasion to
formulate anything in the nature of a policy statement even to his
own people. Also without necessarily feeling "shy", Stalin may well
have had a variety of long-standing inhibitions, doubts and reservations about British policy, and may have been anxious to secure
the Anglo-Soviet Declaration before proceeding any further. And
when, finally, on July 18, he did write to Churchill, it was to propose
the establishment of a Second Front—"in the west (northern
France) and in the north (the Arctic)".

> The best time to open this Front is now, seeing that Hitler's forces
> have been switched to the east... It would be easier still to open a
> Front in the north. This would call for action only by British naval and
> air forces, without landing troops or artillery. Soviet land, naval and air
> forces could take part in the operation. We would be glad if Great
> Britain could send thither, say, one light division or more of the

* Volume III, p. 340.

Norwegian volunteers, who could be moved to Northern Norway for insurgent operations against the Germans.

Churchill, in his reply of July 21, dismissed all this as totally unrealistic, including the Norwegian light division, which was simply "not in existence", but proposed a number of naval operations in the Arctic, and the establishment of a number of British fighter squadrons at Murmansk.

On July 26, Churchill wrote to Stalin again, saying that 200 Tomahawks would soon be sent to Russia; that two or three million pairs of ankle boots "should shortly be available in this country for shipment", and that, moreover, "large quantities of rubber, tin, wool and woollen clothes, jute, lead and shellac" would be provided.

All this was only a small beginning; but it should be remembered that in the summer of 1941 Britain was, in fact, Russia's only ally; the United States was not in the war yet. This would partly explain a certain petulance in Stalin's tone in his relations with Britain, and particularly with Churchill: this was the only country from which he could "demand" direct military co-operation; but since such direct military aid was clearly not forthcoming, the most important thing to do was to try to obtain from the West the maximum economic aid in the form of armaments and raw materials; and, in this respect, the United States was far more important than Britain.

The big question—and Stalin was fully aware of it—which bothered both Britain and the United States was whether Russian resistance to Germany could, or could not, last any length of time. As one could guess at the time, and as we know now, Churchill was by no means certain that Russia would "last" long.

The British military were almost unanimous in believing that Russia would be defeated in a short time: even at press conferences given during the first days of the war at the Ministry of Information in London, War Office spokesmen made no secret of it. Their tone became slightly different by the middle of July, largely, one suspects, as a result of the dispatches sent from Moscow by General Mason MacFarlane who, while referring occasionally to "this bloodstained régime", nevertheless did not underrate the fighting qualities of the

Red Army.* Mason MacFarlane, with whom I had numerous talks in Moscow, appeared convinced, even during the blackest moments, that the Russians were at any rate determined to fight a very long war, and that even the loss of Moscow—which was not to be ruled out early in October—would not mean the end.

Opinion at the American Embassy in Moscow was rather divided. The Military Attaché, Major Ivan Yeaton, was convinced that the Red Army would be smashed in a very short time; Ambassador Steinhardt took less gloomy a view; but the big clash between the two schools of thought was not to come until later, with the appointment as Lend-Lease representative in Moscow of Colonel Philip R. Faymonville. This appointment was made by President Roosevelt at Harry Hopkins's suggestion. Faymonville had accompanied Harriman to Moscow at the end of September, and he was convinced from the start that the Red Army's prospects were by no means as hopeless as Yeaton had been making out ever since the beginning of the invasion.

The fact that Faymonville should have been appointed to Moscow at Hopkins's suggestion was highly significant. It was Hopkins who unquestionably decided, during his visit to Moscow at the end of July that the Russians could, if not win the war, at any rate hold out for a very long time, and this was also the view held by Faymonville. And after the Battle of Moscow, Faymonville became finally convinced that the Russians would not lose the war.

Harry Hopkins's visit was of crucial importance to the whole future of American-Soviet and Anglo-Soviet relations. As Robert E. Sherwood wrote:

> The flight [from Archangel] to Moscow took four hours, and during it Hopkins began to be reassured as to the future of the Soviet Union. He looked down upon the hundreds of miles of solid forest, and he thought that Hitler with all the Panzer divisions of the Wehrmacht could never hope to break through country like this.

On arriving in Moscow

* See also p. 187.

Hopkins had a long talk with Steinhardt in which he said that the main purpose of his visit was to determine whether the situation was as disastrous as pictured in the War Department, and particularly as indicated in the cables from the Military Attaché, Major Ivan Yeaton.

The views of Ambassador Steinhardt, as described by Sherwood, tally with Steinhardt's attitude, as I was able to observe it in Moscow in the summer of 1941.

Steinhardt said [to Hopkins] that anyone who knew anything about Russian history would hardly jump to the conclusion that the Germans would achieve easy conquest. Russian soldiers might appear inept when engaged in offensive operations— they had done so in the Napoleonic wars and again in Finland. But when they were called upon to defend their homeland they were superb fighters, and there were certainly a great many of them. But, Steinhardt emphasised, it was supremely difficult for any outsider to get a clear picture of what was really going on ... because of the prevailing attitude of suspicion toward all foreigners and consequent secretiveness. Hopkins said that he was determined somehow or other to break through this wall of suspicion.*

Then came his account of Hopkins's first meeting with Stalin:

After Hopkins's introductory remarks to the effect that the President believed that the most important thing to be done in the world today was to defeat Hitler and Hitlerism, and that he therefore wished to aid the Soviet Union, Stalin spoke.
He welcomed Hopkins to the Soviet Union and then, describing Hitler and Germany, spoke of the necessity of there being a minimum moral standard between all nations. ... The present leaders of Germany knew no such moral standard and represented an anti-social force in the world today...
"Our views coincide," he concluded.
Then, turning to Hopkins's question what Russia would require that the USA could deliver immediately, and, second, what would be her requirements on the basis of a long war, Stalin listed in the first category anti-aircraft guns of medium calibre, together with ammunition— altogether 20,000 pieces of anti-aircraft artillery, large and small. Second, he asked for large-size machine-guns for the defence of his cities. Third, he said he needed a million rifles; "if the calibre was the

* *The White House Papers of Harry Hopkins*, by Robert E. Sherwood. Volume I, pp. 327–8 (London, 1949).

same as the one used in the Red Army, then he had plenty of ammunition."

In the second category, he mentioned first, high-octane aviation gasolene, second, aluminium for the construction of aeroplanes and, third, the other items already mentioned in the list already presented to our government in Washington.

And then came this striking remark from Stalin: "Give us anti-aircraft guns and the aluminium and we can fight for three or four years."

After a long meeting with Molotov, which was chiefly devoted to a somewhat inconclusive discussion about Japan, Molotov suggesting, in the course of it, that the United States give Japan "a warning" against attacking Russia, Hopkins had a second meeting with Stalin.

Since the outbreak of the war, Stalin said, the number of German divisions at the Russian front had been increased from 175 to 232, and he thought Germany could mobilise 300. Russia had only 180 divisions at the beginning, but had 240 now, and could mobilise 350.

> Stalin stated that he can mobilise that many by the time the spring offensive begins in May 1942... He is anxious to have as many of his divisions as possible in contact with the enemy, because the troops then learn that Germans can be killed and are not supermen... He wants to have as many seasoned troops as possible for the great campaign next spring.
>
> He made much of "insurgent troops" [i.e. partisans] fighting behind the enemy lines, and claimed that there had been no mass surrenders of troops on either side. He thought the Germans would soon have to go on the defensive themselves, but nevertheless, admitted that while the Russians had a large number of tanks and motorised divisions, none of them were a match for the German Panzer divisions. All the same, he believed that the large Russian tanks were better than any German tanks...
>
> The Red Army, he said, had now 4,000 large tanks, 8,000 medium tanks and 12,000 light tanks; the Germans had a total of 30,000 tanks.

His tank production now was only 1,000 per month, he said, and Russia would be short of steel.

> He urged that orders for this steel be placed at once. Later he said it would be much better if his tanks could be manufactured in the

United States. He also wished to purchase as many tanks as possible to be ready for the spring campaign. He said the all-important thing was the production of tanks during the winter—the tank losses were very great on both sides, but Germany could produce more tanks per month this winter than Russia. He would like to send a tank expert to the United States and would give the United States his tank designs.*

"He gave", Hopkins goes on, "a much more glowing account of Russia's aircraft position, and said that the German claims of Russian air losses were 'absurd'." Nevertheless, "he expressed considerable interest in training pilots in America, and left me the impression that there would soon be a shortage of pilots."

> Stalin repeatedly stated that he did not underrate the German Army. Their organisation was of the very best, and they had large reserves of food, men, supplies and fuel... The German Army is [therefore] capable of taking part in a winter campaign in Russia. He thought, however, that it would be difficult for the Germans to operate offensively much after September 1, when the heavy rains would begin. After October 1 the ground would be so bad that they would have to go on the defensive. He expressed great confidence that the line during the winter months would be in front of Moscow, Kiev and Leningrad, probably not more than 100 km. away from where it was now. He... thought the Germans were "tired", and had no stomach for an offensive... Though Germany could bring up forty divisions, making 275 divisions in all, these divisions probably could not get there before the hard weather set in.†

At this second meeting, Stalin again insisted that the Red Army's first need was anti-aircraft guns—"vast quantities of these to give protection to its lines of communications; secondly, aluminium for the construction of aeroplanes; thirdly, machine-guns and rifles."

As regards the ports of entry, he thought Archangel "difficult, but not impossible" since icebreakers could keep the port free all winter; Vladivostok he thought dangerous, as Japan could cut it off at any time, and the roads and railroads of Persia "inadequate".

> "He [Stalin] expressed repeatedly his confidence that the Russian lines would hold within 200 km. of their present position... and indicated that the front would be solidified not later than October 1."

---

* Sherwood, op cit., pp. 337–8.   † Ibid., p. 340.

It is clear from what Hopkins told Stalin that he was not entirely convinced that the Russians would survive the autumn:

"I was mindful of the importance that no (economic) conference be held in Moscow until we knew the outcome of the battle now in progress... This battle was still in the balance. Hence my suggestion that we hold this conference at as late a date as possible. Then we would know whether there was to be a front and approximately the location of the front during the coming winter months."

Nevertheless, basing himself on Stalin's belief that the front would be "solidified not later than October 1" Hopkins recommended to the US Government that such a conference (the future Stalin-Beaverbrook-Harriman conference) be held between October 1 and October 15.

In conclusion, Stalin said that he thought German morale pretty low, and that the Germans would be demoralised still further by an announcement that the United States was going to join in the war against Hitler.

Stalin [Hopkins continued] said it was inevitable that we [the USA] would finally come to grips with Hitler on some battlefield. The might of Germany was [still] so great that, even though Russia might defend herself, it would be very difficult for Britain and Russia combined to crush the German military machine... He believed the war would be bitter and perhaps long ... and he wanted me to tell the President that he would welcome American troops on any part of the Russian front under the complete command of the American Army... Finally, he asked me to tell the President that, while he was confident that the Russian Army could withstand the German Army, the problem of supply by the next spring would be a serious one and that he needed our help.

In a remarkable article on his meetings with Stalin, Hopkins later wrote:

... He welcomed me with a few swift Russian words. He shook my hand briefly, firmly, courteously. He smiled warmly. There was no waste of word, gesture or mannerism. It was like talking to a perfectly co-ordinated machine, an intelligent machine... The questions he asked were clear, concise, direct... His answers were ready, unequivocal, spoken as if the man had had them on his tongue for years... If he is always as I heard him, he never wastes a syllable. If

he wants to soften an abrupt answer...he does it with that quick
managed smile—a smile that can be cold but friendly, austere but
warm. He curries no favour with you. He seems to have no doubts.
He assures you that Russia will stand against the onslaught of the
German Army. He takes it for granted that you have no doubts,
either... He laughs often enough, but it's a short laugh, somewhat
sardonic perhaps. There is no small talk in him. His humour is keen,
penetrating.*

Although Hopkins had, obviously, come with instructions which
forbade him to assume that the Russians would *not* be beaten before
the winter had set in, Stalin not only enormously impressed him as a
person, but also convinced him that the Russians would hold the
Germans, and were preparing for a very long war. "A man," Sherwood wrote of the Hopkins-Stalin meetings, "who feared immediate
defeat would not have put aluminium so high on the list of priorities... The very nature of Stalin's requests proved that he was
viewing the war on a long-range basis."

And Sherwood added:

Hopkins later expressed extreme irritation with the military
observers in Moscow when they cabled darkly pessimistic reports that
could be based on nothing but mere guesswork coloured by prejudice.*

This Hopkins account of his meetings with Stalin is invaluable.
It is, in fact, the only detailed first-hand account there is of Stalin at
the height of the German invasion. Several points are worth noting.
Anxious to obtain American aid, Stalin painted a more favourable
picture than was warranted by the progress of the war at the end of
July 1941. He carefully avoided any suggestion of the Red Army's
acute shortage of tanks and aircraft. He knew that he could hardly
expect anything at once and therefore stressed himself the desirability of building up the Soviet air force and armour in readiness for
a spring campaign in 1942. He quite deliberately created the impression of planning for a long-term war. But he was not "currying
favours"; he took it for granted that it was in both Britain's and
America's interests to help Russia.

He went, of course, seriously wrong in assuming that the Germans

* Sherwood, op. cit., p. 345.

would not advance more than 125 miles, that the Russians would keep not only Moscow and Leningrad, but also Kiev, and that the front would become stabilised by the beginning of September, or the beginning of October at the latest. Was there not an element of bluff in his apparent optimism?

It was on the basis of Hopkins's reasonably optimistic forecast that the Stalin-Beaverbrook-Harriman conference was to meet on September 29, a day before the "final" German offensive began against Moscow.

The assurance given to Hopkins that Kiev would be held may well have accounted in part for Stalin's determination to hold on to the capital of the Ukraine; a decision which had, as we know, disastrous results.

One may well wonder, all the same, whether Stalin was not much more nervous about the general situation than would appear from Hopkins's account. The most striking suggestion that Stalin made to Hopkins was that he would "welcome American troops on any part of the Russian front under the complete command of the American Army". More alarmist still were to be some of Stalin's dispatches to Churchill after the greater part of the Ukraine had been overrun by the Germans. Thus, on September 3 he wrote:

> The position of the Soviet troops has considerably deteriorated in such vital areas as the Ukraine and Leningrad. The relative stabilisation of the front, achieved some three weeks ago, has been upset by the arrival of thirty to thirty-four German infantry divisions and enormous numbers of tanks and aircraft... The Germans are looking on the threat in the west as a bluff... They think they can well beat their enemies one at a time—first the Russians and then the British.
>
> The loss of Krivoi Rog, etc., (he went on) has resulted in a lessening of our defence capacity and *has confronted the Soviet Union with mortal danger*... The only way out of this more than unfavourable situation is to open a second front this year somewhere in the Balkans or in France... and simultaneously to supply the Soviet Union with 30,000 tons of aluminium by the beginning of October and a minimum *monthly* aid of 400 aeroplanes and 500 tanks (small or medium).

Without these two kinds of aid the Soviet Union will be either defeated or weakened to the extent that it will lose for a long time its ability to help its allies by active operations at the front against Hitlerism.*

And, ten days later, on September 13, Stalin again wrote to Churchill, saying that if the opening of a second front was not feasible at present, then—

it seems to me that Britain could safely land twenty-five to thirty divisions at Archangel or ship them to the southern areas of the USSR via Iran for military co-operation with the Soviet troops on Soviet soil in the same way it was done during the last war in France. That would be a great help.†

The suggestion that British troops should come to help Russia on Russian soil, as well as the warning that Russia might be defeated betrayed real anxiety on Stalin's part; nevertheless, he concluded his message to Churchill on a characteristic note of bravado. In reply to a British proposal that if, as a result of the situation at Leningrad, the Baltic Fleet were lost, the British should, after the war, make up for these Russian losses, Stalin remarked:

The Soviet Government... appreciates the British Government's readiness to compensate for part of the damage... There can be little doubt that, if necessary, the Soviet people will actually destroy the ships at Leningrad. But responsibility for the damage would be borne not by Britain but by Germany. I think, therefore, that Germany will have to make good the damage after the war.‡

The most direct example of Anglo-Soviet co-operation in 1941 was the joint occupation of Iran. After previous consultations with the British Government, the Soviet Government informed the Iranian

* Correspondence between the Chairman of the Council of Ministers of the USSR and the Presidents of the USA and the Prime Ministers of Great Britain during the Great Patriotic War of 1941–5, vol. I, p. 21 (Moscow, 1957), to be later referred to as *Stalin-Churchill Correspondence* or *Stalin-Roosevelt Correspondence*.
† Ibid., p. 24.
‡ Ibid., p. 25.

Government that it would "introduce Soviet troops into Iran in connexion with the widespread anti-Soviet activity of German agents in that country". The troops would be "introduced" in virtue of Article 6 of the Soviet-Iranian Agreement of 1921 which provided for such an occupation in the event of a third party threatening the independence of Iran and the security of the Soviet Union. The Soviet Note recalled that, since the German invasion of Russia, the Soviet Government had already sent three warnings to the Iranian Government but without any effect.

It was also on August 25 that the British Ambassador in Iran, Sir Reader Bullard, informed the Iranian Government of the entry of British troops into Iran. This joint occupation had the double purpose of preventing Germany from using Iran as a base of operations against both Russia and the Iranian oilfields, and of opening a supply route from the Persian Gulf to the Caspian Sea. Since the Allies, and, in particular, Churchill, considered both the other routes—via Vladivostok or via the Russian Arctic—highly precarious, this project was held to be of vital importance as an alternative. The joint operation went off remarkably smoothly; a new Iranian Government was set up, and before long, the pro-German Rezah Shah abdicated, to end his days in exile in Johannesburg, where he died in 1944.

> British and Russian forces met in amity, and Teheran was jointly occupied on September 17, the Shah having abdicated on the previous day in favour of his gifted twenty-two-year-old son. On September 20 the new Shah, under allied advice, restored the Constitutional Monarchy... Most of our forces withdrew from the country, leaving only detachments to guard the communications, and Teheran was evacuated by both British and Russian troops on October 18.*

*

* Churchill, op. cit., p. 432. Later, when Iran became the great route for supplies to Russia, numerous Russian, British and American troops were to be seen in Teheran once more. For a time after the evacuation of the Polish "Anders" army from Russia, the Poles were also very active at Teheran. The Russians, whom I was able to observe there at the end of 1943, made a point of being extremely "correct" in their behaviour, and drunkenness, not uncommon among the British and Americans, was strictly prohibited and

The Beaverbrook-Harriman Mission arrived in Moscow on September 28. Several meetings were held under the chairmanship of Molotov, and on two occasions Beaverbrook and Harriman had long conversations with Stalin. Beaverbrook was a strong "help-Russia" man, and the economic conference was a prelude to the granting of a first lend-lease loan of a billion dollars by the USA to the USSR. It was decided to ship a wide variety of arms, raw materials and machinery in considerable quantities to the Soviet Union, while in return certain Russian raw materials were to be delivered to the USA and Britain. The closing speeches of the conference by Beaverbrook, Harriman and Molotov were extremely cordial. Molotov stressed "the great political importance of the conference, which had foiled the Hitlerites' intention to destroy their enemies one by one, demonstrating to the world that a mighty front of freedom-loving peoples had been created, led by the Soviet Union, Great Britain and the USA." The final communiqué said that Britain and America were going to supply "practically everything that Russia had asked for".

As I noted in Moscow on October 4:

> The conference is over, and is being acclaimed on all sides as a huge success. Impressed by the remarkable speed with which the conference got through its work, people are perhaps apt to forget the limited scope of the talks and the limited possibilities of delivering the stuff to Russia... The Russian papers are making a big display of the success of the conference, of the "united anti-Hitler front" by three of the greatest industrial powers in the world, et cetera. People reading the papers in tram-cars appear to be pleased, though I don't think they are overwhelmed. They know that a fearfully hard winter is ahead of them...

And then:

---

severely punished. The Russians at that time did also engage in a good deal of propaganda in Persia, notably by opening a large hospital in Teheran. With the support of various public welfare schemes they encouraged a separatist movement in Persian Azerbaijan. In 1946, under American pressure, they had to abandon these political schemes and had to withdraw their troops.

Beaverbrook has been very much in the centre of things, and has pretty well eclipsed everybody, including Harriman ... and Cripps. This may be unfair, for Cripps and the Military Mission certainly did a lot to prepare the Conference... Even so, Beaverbrook's dynamics have unquestionably contributed to the success of the Conference; and his nightly talks with Stalin seem to have been decisive in smoothing away the rough edges... Beaverbrook has fully realised that the Russians are the only people in the world today who are seriously weakening Germany, and that it is in Britain's interest to do without certain things and to give them to Russia... He and Eden are said to be the most whole-hearted pro-Russians in the Cabinet now. At the little press conference yesterday he was bursting with exuberance. Slapping his knees he was saying that the Russians were pleased with Beaverbrook, and the Americans were pleased with Beaverbrook— "Now, aren't they, Averell?" to which Harriman replied: "Sure, you bet." ... Beaverbrook is praising Stalin up to the skies... I imagine he has been genuinely impressed by Stalin's practical mind, his organising ability, and his qualities as a national leader... At the Kremlin banquet last night, cold and sceptical Molotov made an unusually warm speech...*

The impression Beaverbrook gave of the Moscow visit not only to the correspondents on the spot, but also to Churchill in his dispatch of October 4—"the effect of this agreement has been an immense strengthening of the morale of Moscow"—and the comments made by the Russians seem wholly at variance with the account given after the war by Churchill:

Their reception was bleak and discussions not at all friendly. It might almost have been thought that the plight in which the Soviets

* Alexander Werth, *Moscow '41* (London, 1942), pp. 226–7. Beaverbrook's attitude to Russia had manifested itself much earlier as is borne out by the Harry Hopkins *Papers* on Churchill's famous "pro-Russian" broadcast of June 22: "He conferred that day principally with Beaverbrook and Sir Stafford Cripps... Although one would hardly have expected it of him, Beaverbrook was a vehement supporter of immoderate and unstinted aid to the Soviet Union and was subsequently an ardent, persistent and sometimes (to Churchill) embarrassing proponent of the Second Front. At the urging of these two men, as well as his own inclination, Churchill went on the air that Sunday with one of his most powerful speeches." (Sherwood, op. cit., p. 305.)

now found themselves was our fault. (They) gave no information of any kind. They did not even inform them of the basis on which Russian needs of our precious war materials had been estimated. The Mission was given no formal entertainment until almost the last night... It might almost have been that it was we who had come to ask favours.*

There is no doubt that at the time the Russians were extremely pleased with the political significance of the conference and the propaganda capital they could make of it and that they were anxiously looking forward to the long term prospect of American help on a large scale. On the other hand the British deliveries that were immediately available were, of course, a mere drop in the bucket.†

Even if "the reception was bleak"—although Beaverbrook then gave the very opposite impression—it is more than probable that the news from the front had something to do with it. While Beaverbrook and Harriman were still in Moscow, the great German offensive against Moscow had started, first in the Briansk and three days later in the Viazma sector. Whatever the future value of the Economic Conference was to be, the Battle of Moscow had to be won by the Russians alone with what was left of their operational equipment.

While Soviet diplomatic activity was chiefly concerned with the establishment of closer relations with Britain and the USA, the German invasion had created a number of additional diplomatic problems. Finland, Hungary, Rumania and Italy were now in a state of war with the Soviet Union, and Churchill was reluctant to declare war on Hungary, Rumania and especially on Finland; indeed, the

* Churchill, op. cit., p. 416.
† Churchill's message to Stalin of October 6, promised that the convoy, due to arrive at Archangel on October 12, would carry twenty heavy tanks and 193 fighter planes, the convoy due on October 29 140 heavy tanks, 100 fighter planes (Hurricanes), 200 Bren carriers, 200 anti-tank rifles and 50 two-pounder guns

problem of Finland was to lead to some considerable Anglo-Soviet friction.

Soviet relations with Vichy France were broken off, and, barely a week after the German invasion, Pétain authorised the formation of a French Anti-Bolshevik Legion; a number of Swedish volunteers also joined the Finnish Army, while a Blue Brigade was formed in Spain for operations in Russia, particularly at Leningrad. Turkey, Iran and Afghanistan hastened to assure Russia of their neutrality, though in the case of Iran these assurances were not accepted. Later in the year the Soviet Government demanded that Afghanistan expel numerous Axis agents from its territory—a demand with which the Afghan Government nominally complied, except that Signor Pietro Quaroni, the Italian Ambassador at Kabul, continued to remain at the centre of Axis activity in Afghanistan—until in 1943, after the fall of Mussolini, he was appointed Italian Minister to Moscow!

Much was made in Moscow of the German war on "Slavdom"; on August 10 and 11 the first All-Slav meeting was held. It called on all the Slav peoples to wage a holy war against Germany, and the appeal was signed by "representatives of the peoples of Russia, Belorussia, the Ukraine, Poland, Czechoslovakia, Yugoslavia and Bulgaria".

Already on July 18 a mutual-aid agreement had been signed in London between Maisky, representing the USSR and Jan Masaryk, representing the Czechoslovak Government in exile. The agreement provided for an exchange of ministers and the formation of Czecho-slovak military units under the command of a Czechoslovak officer approved by the Russians; these units would be under the supreme command of the USSR.

Dorothy Thompson relates that the only person in London she met in July 1941 who believed the Russians would not be crushed by the Germans was President Benes.* Russia's diplomatic relations with "independent" Slovakia had, of course, automatically lapsed, and were not mentioned.

The question of whether and on what terms diplomatic relations with Poland were to be restored presented a much trickier problem.

* Sherwood, op. cit., p. 320.

On the face of it, the Maisky-Sikorski agreement of July 30, 1941 was little different from the Soviet-Czechoslovak agreement twelve days before; in reality it touched on some extremely awkward matters.*

It must have been a little embarrassing for the Russians to agree to the first paragraph declaring all Soviet-German territorial agreements made in 1939 to be null and void; there was also the problem of Polish citizens in the Soviet Union, which had to be faced somehow. In order to resolve this awkward question a protocol was attached to the main agreement in which the Soviet Government granted an amnesty to "all Polish citizens now imprisoned in the Soviet Union, either as prisoners-of-war or for any other valid reasons".

Apart from that—as in the case of the Soviet-Czechoslovak Agreement—it provided for an exchange of Ambassadors and for mutual aid in the common war against Nazi Germany.

This agreement, which had been preceded by some acrimonious discussions on the future borders of Poland, was, in the event, to mark the beginning of another most unhappy phase in Polish-Russian relations. On the surface and for the moment, however, Soviet-Polish co-operation was developing normally and on August 14 a military agreement was signed in Moscow between the Soviet Supreme Command, represented by General Vassilevsky and by the Polish Supreme Command, represented by General Bogusz-Szyszko; within its terms General Sikorski appointed General Anders Commander-in-Chief of the Polish armed forces on Soviet territory, and it was announced that he "has begun to form the Polish Army". General Anders had been only just released from a Soviet jail.

On September 4, Mr Kot arrived in Moscow as the first Polish Ambassador, and in December General Sikorski came to Russia, and had some long—and highly awkward—conversations with Stalin. But this will be dealt with later.

Apart from Poland and Czechoslovakia, relations were also restored during the first months of the war with Yugoslavia, Norway, Belgium and Greece. There was also an important exchange of notes between Maisky and de Gaulle on September 27, 1941. The

* See also p. 186.

Soviet Government recognised de Gaulle as the leader of the Free French, proposed to de Gaulle all possible aid in his struggle against Germany, and expressed its determination to fight for the "complete restoration of the independence and greatness of France". De Gaulle replied in the same vein.

It is hardly surprising that the Japanese attack on Pearl Harbour should have come as a great relief to the Russians at a time when the Red Army had just launched their December counter-offensive on the Moscow sector of the front. It was, of course, possible that the flow of supplies from Britain and the United States would slow down as a result; but this consideration was outweighed by the immense fact that the USA had now entered the war and that the drive of the Japanese armed forces to the west and south had, at least for the time being, removed the threat of a Japanese attack on the Soviet Union.

On December 16 Roosevelt wired to Stalin proposing that the Russians take part in a conference at Chungking, along with Chinese, British, Dutch and US representatives. Stalin, in his reply, dodged the issue, though he added: "I wish you success in the struggle against the aggression in the Pacific."*

* *Stalin-Roosevelt Correspondence*, p. 18.

PART THREE

The Leningrad Story

Chapter I

THE DEAD OF LENINGRAD

There were many mass tragedies in the Second World War. There was Hiroshima, where 200,000 people were killed in a few seconds, and many thousands of others were maimed and crippled for life; there was Nagasaki, on which the second atom bomb was dropped. In Dresden 135,000 men, women and children were killed in two nights in February 1945. At Stalingrad on August 23, 1942, 40,000 people were killed. Earlier in the war, there had been the London Blitz and "small stuff" like Coventry, where some 700 people were killed in one night. There were the massacres in hundreds of "Partisan" villages in Belorussia; and there were the Nazi extermination camps where millions perished in gas chambers and in other horrible ways. The list is almost endless.

The tragedy of Leningrad, in which nearly a million people died, was, however, unlike any of the others. Here, in September 1941, nearly three million people were trapped by the Germans and condemned to starvation. And nearly one-third of them died—but not as German captives.*

* In the words of Harrison Salisbury, one of the best foreign observers of the Russian wartime scene: "This was the greatest and longest siege ever endured by a modern city, a time of trial, suffering and heroism that reached peaks of tragedy and bravery almost beyond our power to comprehend... Even in the Soviet Union the epic of

Leningrad—the old St Petersburg—had been the capital of the Russian Empire for over two centuries. With its Neva embankments, its bridges, its Winter Palace and Hermitage and dozens of other palaces, with its Admiralty and St Isaac's Cathedral, and its Bronze Horseman (the famous statue of Peter the Great), its Nevsky Prospect, its Summer Garden and its canals, with their hump-backed granite bridges, it was—and is—one of the most beautiful cities in the world.

For two centuries it had been not only Russia's capital, but its greatest cultural centre. No Russian city had so many literary associations as St Petersburg. Pushkin, Gogol, Dostoevsky, Innokenti Annensky, Blok and Anna Akhmatova, to mention only a few, would never have been what they were but for that haunting city— so dazzling in its grandeur, grace and harmony to Pushkin; so mysterious, so sinister, so surrealist, if one may say so, to Gogol and Dostoevsky; the Gogol of *The Nose*; the Dostoevsky of *The Idiot* and *Crime and Punishment*.

St Petersburg—Petrograd at the time—was also where the two Revolutions of 1917 had begun. In 1918, the Soviet Government moved Russia's capital to Moscow, and for three or four years afterwards, Petrograd was almost a dying city, hungrier than most. From 1919 to 1921 more than half its population had fled, and of those who had stayed behind, many thousands died of hunger. So hunger was not new to Leningrad. However, by 1924, its revival—above all, its industrial revival—began, and, by 1941, it was a flourishing industrial and cultural centre again and the greatest educational centre in the Soviet Union, with, proportionately, a larger student population than any other city.

Though no longer the capital of Russia, it had its own, slightly snobbish local patriotism, and tended to look down on Moscow as an upstart. It had, too, had its bad spells under the Soviet régime. Kirov had been assassinated here in December 1934, and that had

---

Leningrad has received only modest attention, compared with that devoted to Stalingrad and the Battle of Moscow. And in the west not one person in fifty who thrilled to the courage of the Londoners in the Battle of Britain is cognisant of that of the Leningraders." (*New York Times* Book Review, May 10, 1962.)

started the Great Purges of the late thirties. Leningrad had had its
share, perhaps more than its share, of the Stalin-Yezhov Purges.
Characteristically, a gifted writer and poet like Olga Bergholz, who
was to play so important a part as one of the principal "Leningrad-
can-take-it" speakers on the Leningrad radio during the famine winter of 1941–2, had spent several months in prison in 1937 on some
fantastic trumped-up charge. Other members of her family had also
suffered in the Purges. And yet, Olga Bergholz's book of reminiscences, *The Daytime Stars*, is one of the most moving books on the
fearful days of the Blockade. There is, for instance, an unforgettable
description of how, faint with hunger and with only a crust of bread
and one cigarette to last her a day—the other cigarette she kept for
her father—she wandered for ten miles through the snowdrifts and
across the ice of the Neva, almost stumbling over dead bodies, to see
her father, an elderly doctor, himself nearly dead of hunger, and
with patients around him dying. She is a typical Leningrad phenomenon—a woman who was ready to die for Leningrad, but who,
at heart, hated Stalin.

And so, in September 1941, three million people were trapped by
the Germans; never had a city of that size endured what Leningrad
was to endure during the winter of 1941–2.

Chapter II

THE ENEMY ADVANCES

In Leningrad the news on June 22, 1941 of the German invasion produced a wave of mass meetings, and in the next two weeks an immense number of Leningraders volunteered for the *opolcheniye* formations. At the great Kirov Works alone, 15,000 men and women applied for immediate military service. Not all these applications could be accepted, since it was essential that the Kirov Works should go on producing armaments. The original plan, therefore, to form fifteen workers' divisions had to be abandoned, and, on July 4, it was decided to limit the *opolcheniye* divisions to three, until further notice. By July 10, the first *opolcheniye* division was sent to the front, followed a few days later by the second and third. They had only a few days' training, which had taken place in the main squares of Leningrad. These three *opolcheniye* divisions were rushed to the so-called Luga defence line, which was 175 miles long and was only sparsely defended by three rifle divisions and the pupils of two military schools, who had also been rushed there from Leningrad. By July 14, the Germans had already succeeded in establishing a large bridgehead north of Luga, on the right bank of the Luga river; it was from there that they were to develop their subsequent offensive against Leningrad.

The situation was extremely grim, and it seems that Voroshilov, the C. in C. of the Northern Armies, and Zhdanov, head of the

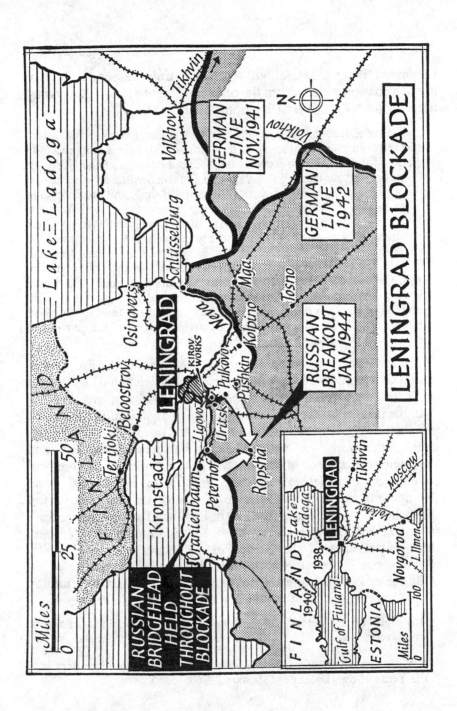

LENINGRAD BLOCKADE

GERMAN LINE NOV. 1941

GERMAN LINE 1942

RUSSIAN BREAKOUT JAN. 1944

RUSSIAN BRIDGEHEAD HELD THROUGHOUT BLOCKADE

Lake Ladoga

FINLAND

Miles
0   25   50

Tikhvin
Volkhov
Volkhov
N

Schlüsselburg

Osinovets

LENINGRAD
KIROV WORKS
Neva
Mga
Tosno
Kolpino
Pushkin
Pulkovo
Uritsk
Ligovo
Ropsha

Beloostrov
Terijoki

Kronstadt
Oranienbaum
Peterhof

FINLAND
Lake Ladoga
LENINGRAD
1938
1940
Tikhvin
MOSCOW
Volkhov
Novgorod
L. Ilmen
Gulf of Finland
ESTONIA
Miles
0   100

Leningrad Party organisation, were in a truly desperate state of
mind, as one may judge from the order read out to all the Red Army
units of the "North-West Direction" on July 14:

> Comrades Red-Army men, officers and political workers! A direct
> threat of an enemy invasion is now suspended over Leningrad, the
> cradle of the Proletarian Revolution. While the troops of the Northern
> Front are bravely fighting the Nazi and Finnish *Schützcorps* hordes all
> the way from the Barents Sea to Tallinn and Hangö, and are defending
> every inch of our beloved Soviet land, the troops of the North-Western
> Front, often failing to repel enemy attacks, and abandoning their
> positions without even entering into combat with the enemy, are only
> encouraging by their behaviour the increasingly arrogant Germans.
> Certain cowards and panic-stricken individuals not only abandon the
> Front without orders, but sow panic among the good and brave
> soldiers. In some cases both officers and political workers not only do
> nothing to stop the panic, and fail to organise their units for combat,
> but increase even more, by their shameful behaviour, the panic and
> disorganisation at the Front.

The order went on to say that anyone abandoning the Front without orders would be tried by a field tribunal which could order them
to be shot, "regardless of rank and previous achievements".*

In the middle of July the Leningrad Party organisation decided to
mobilise hundreds of thousands of men and women to build fortifications; the work was supervised by members of the city and
provincial committees of the Party, by secretaries of the regional
committees, etc. Several defence lines were built—one, from
the mouth of the Luga to Chudovo, Gatchina, Uritsk, Pulkovo and
then along the Neva; another, a line of Leningrad's "outer defences",
from Peterhof to Gatchina, Pulkovo, Kolpino and Koltushski; and
then several lines in the immediate neighbourhood of the city,
including one in the northern suburbs, facing the Finns.

By the end of July and the beginning of August nearly a million
people were engaged in the building of defences:

> People of the most different trades and professions—workers,
> employees, schoolchildren, housewives, scientists, teachers, artists,

---

* A. V. Karasev *Leningradtsy v gody blokady* (The Leningraders in
the Years of the Blockade) (Moscow, 1960), p. 65.

actors, students, etc.—worked with their picks and shovels. From morning till night they went on, often under enemy fire.*

Much of the digging done in these conditions, by people not used to this kind of work, was inevitably hasty and amateurish; many of the trenches dug were not deep enough, and the minefields and barbed-wire defences were often laid and built in a haphazard manner. Nevertheless, when one considers that the Germans had reached the Luga line, 125 miles south of Leningrad, within three weeks of the Invasion, and that it took them over six weeks after that to reach the outskirts of Leningrad, it is clear that this building of defence lines played an important role in saving Leningrad. Altogether, the people of Leningrad succeeded in digging 340 miles of anti-tank ditches, 15,875 miles of open trenches, and erecting 400 miles of barbed-wire defences, 190 miles of forest obstacles (felled trees, etc.), and 5,000 wooden or concrete firing points,† not counting the various defences built inside Leningrad itself.

But, except for one successful Russian counter-attack in the Soltsy area at the southern end of the "Luga Line", near Lake Ilmen, on July 14–18, the most the Russians could do was to hold the various defence lines between the Luga River and Leningrad as long as possible.

The state of mind of these hundreds of thousands of people who were digging trenches and building fortifications, day after day, can well be guessed; the spirit of self-sacrifice was there, sure enough, but mixed with a great deal of bitterness. General Fedyuninsky tells how, on one occasion, some miles outside Leningrad, he saw a large group of young and elderly women digging like mad: "You are digging well, girls," he remarked. "Yes," said an elderly woman, "we are digging well, but you fellows are fighting badly."‡ This was perhaps unfair; the soldiers were doing what they could; but there was everywhere a desperate shortage of both reserves and heavy equipment. Everywhere, except along part of the Luga Line, the Germans had great superiority. Thus, Major-General

* Ibid., p. 69.
† *Ognevyie tochki* (firing points) included not only proper pillboxes, but even the most rudimentary gun and machine-gun emplacements.
‡ Fedyuninsky, op. cit., p. 68.

Nikishov, Chief of Staff of the Northern (i.e. Finnish) Front, wrote
in August in a dispatch to Marshal Shaposhnikov:

> The difficulties in the present situation arise from the fact that
> neither divisional commanders, not army commanders nor the com-
> mander of the Army Group, have any reserves at all. Even the smallest
> enemy breakthrough has to be stopped up with improvised sub-units
> drawn from other parts of the Front.

Moreover, many of the *opolcheniye* troops had no experience at
all; the kind of hardships to which they were subjected may be
gauged from the example of the newly-formed 1st *opolcheniye*
division which, after a forced thirty-seven miles march, during which
they were constantly attacked by German aircraft, was promptly
thrown into battle against German motorised and panzer troops:

> This first battle which the men had ever fought proved a terrible
> ordeal both to them and their officers. Not only were they totally
> inexperienced, but they had no weapons with which to fight the enemy
> tanks, and when there were large-scale armoured attacks, they inevit-
> ably retreated.*

The strong Russian stand along a large part of the Luga Line since
the middle of July nevertheless forced the Germans to regroup their
forces and it was not till August 8 that the "final" offensive against
Leningrad began. The defenders of the Luga Line were outflanked
both in the west and in the east, and by August 21, they found
themselves at the tip of a salient, thirteen miles wide and nearly
130 miles deep, with the Germans crashing ahead towards the Gulf
of Finland south-west of Leningrad and towards Lake Ladoga
south-east of the city. For fear of being encircled, they had to pull
out—which they did in chaotic conditions. On August 21 the
Germans captured Chudovo, thus cutting the main Leningrad-
Moscow railway, and, by the 30th, after heavy fighting, they captured Mga, and cut Leningrad's last railway link with the rest of the
country. Having concentrated an enormous number of tanks and
planes both south-west and south-east of Leningrad, the Germans
now confidently expected to take the city by storm. Despite desperate
Russian resistance, the German forces broke through to the south

* Karasev, op. cit., p. 99.

bank of Lake Ladoga. They captured a large part of the left bank of the Neva, including Schlüsselburg, but failed to cross the river. Leningrad was now isolated from the rest of the country, except for highly precarious communications across Lake Ladoga. South and south-west of the city the position of the Russians was equally desperate, with the Germans having broken through to the Gulf of Finland only a few miles south-west of the city and attacking heavily in the Kolpino and Pulkovo areas some fifteen miles south of Leningrad. The Russians, however, maintained a large bridgehead at Oranienbaum, opposite Kronstadt, and to the west of the point at which the Germans had reached the Gulf. In the north, on September 4, the Finns occupied the former frontier station of Beloostrov, twenty miles north of Leningrad, but were thrown out on the following day.

As early as August 20, at the meeting of the Leningrad Party *aktiv*, Voroshilov and Zhdanov admitted the extreme seriousness of the situation. Zhdanov said that the whole population, and particularly the young, must be given a rudimentary training in shooting, grenade-throwing and street-fighting.

> Either the working-class of Leningrad will be turned into slaves, and the best among them exterminated, or we shall turn Leningrad into the Fascists' grave...*

On the following day the famous Appeal to the people of Leningrad, signed by Voroshilov, Zhdanov and Popkov, chairman of the Leningrad Soviet, was published:

> Let us, like one man [it concluded] rise to the defence of our city, of our homes and families, our freedom and honour. Let us do our sacred duty as Soviet patriots in our relentless struggle against a hated and ruthless enemy, let us be vigilant and merciless in dealing with cowards, panic-mongers and deserters, let us establish the strictest revolutionary discipline in our city. Armed with such iron discipline and Bolshevik organisation, let us meet the enemy and throw him back.

During those days there was no certainty at all that the Germans would not break into Leningrad. As Pavlov later wrote:

* D. N. Pavlov, *Leningrad v blokade* (Leningrad During the Blockade) (Moscow, 1961), pp. 14–15.

Everything had been prepared for destroying the enemy forces inside the city. Factories, bridges and public buildings were mined, and their wreckage would have fallen on the enemies' heads and stopped their tanks. The civilian population, not to mention the soldiers and sailors of the Baltic Fleet, were prepared for street fighting. The idea of fighting for every house was not an act of self-sacrifice, but aimed at destroying the enemy. Later, the experience of Stalingrad was to show that such warfare could succeed. . .*

This sounds rather like a piece of bravado; for the problem of feeding and supplying Leningrad, with its nearly three million population, would, in such conditions, have been infinitely more complicated than at Stalingrad. Nevertheless, it is certain, as I was told in Leningrad in 1943, that the possibility of gradually abandoning the southern (and main) part of the city, and of clinging on to the "Petrograd Side" and the Vassili Island on the right bank of the Neva was not entirely ruled out during those desperate days.

The shelling of Leningrad began on September 4, and on September 8, 9 and 10 the city was subjected to some particularly fierce air-raids. That of September 8 caused 178 fires, including that of the famous Badayev food stores—about the destruction of which such exaggerated stories were told, especially after the fearful famine had started. Firewatching was better organised on September 9, and all but a few incendiaries were rapidly put out. The anti-aircraft guns brought down five planes, but the slow Soviet *Chaika* fighters were almost helpless against the Messerschmidts; it was then that, in desperation, several Russian pilots rammed the German planes.

In these first major raids, the Germans also dropped many delayed-action bombs and land-mines, and, not being used to handling these, many volunteers (and there were volunteers for *everything* in Leningrad) lost their lives.

There are numerous stories of desperate fighting during those days at Pulkovo, Kolpino and Uritsk—the latter only two or three miles from the Kirov Works, in the south-west of Leningrad; but except for a footnote in the official *History* saying that Zhukov was in

* Pavlov, op. cit., p. 19.

command of the defence of Leningrad from September 11 till the middle of October, post-war accounts are silent about the changes that took place in the High Command. The dramatic story I heard from several people in Leningrad in 1943 was that about September 10, when there was practically complete chaos at the front, Voroshilov, believing that everything was lost, went into the front line, in the hope of getting killed by the Germans. But on September 11 Stalin dispatched Zhukov to Leningrad, and it was Zhukov who fully reorganised the defence of the city within three days; in a press interview I attended in Berlin in June 1945, Zhukov proudly referred to this fact, though without going into any details, and Vyshinsky said "Yes, it was Zhukov who saved Leningrad." It was, undoubtedly, during the short Zhukov reign—after which he was placed in charge of the defence of Moscow—that the front round Leningrad became stabilised.

Having failed to take Leningrad by storm, the German High Command (not unreasonably) supposed that the city would, before long, be starved into surrender. But Hitler, characteristically, ordered that no capitulation be accepted and that the city be "wiped off the face of the earth", as Leningrad would present a danger of epidemics and would, moreover, be mined, and so constitute a double threat to any soldiers entering it. This order (and, incidentally, the German failure to take Leningrad) was to be explained by Jodl at Nuremberg:

> Field-Marshal von Leeb, the Supreme Commander of Army Group North at Leningrad ... pointed out that it would be absolutely impossible for him to keep these millions of Leningrad people fed and supplied, if they were to fall into his hands, since the supply situation of the Army Group was catastrophic at the time. That was the first cause. But shortly before, Kiev had been abandoned by the Russian armies, and hardly had we occupied the city than one tremendous explosion after another occurred. The major part of the inner city was burned down, 50,000 people were made homeless. German soldiers ... suffered considerable losses, because large amounts of explosives went up into the air... The purpose of the order was exclusively that of

protecting German troops against such catastrophes; for entire staffs had been blown into the air in Kharkov and Kiev.*

An order from the Führer's headquarters, dated October 7, 1941 and signed by Jodl, reiterated the Führer's order not to accept capitulation "at either Leningrad or, later, Moscow". Refugees from Leningrad, says the order, must be driven back by fire if they approach the German lines, but any flight to the east by "isolated individuals", through small gaps in the blockade was to be welcomed, since this could only add to the chaos in eastern Russia. This order also said that Leningrad should be razed to the ground by air bombing and artillery fire.

The date of this document is significant: by the beginning of October, the Germans had given up hope of capturing Leningrad by storm. Leningrad, and most of the Leningrad isthmus continued to remain in Russian hands, and was tying down an army estimated by the Russians at 300,000 men. Although there was no guarantee that the Germans might not attempt another all-out attack on Leningrad, the desperate preparations made at the end of August and the beginning of September for defending every house and for destroying any German paratrooper landing in the large open squares of Leningrad lost their immediate urgency; nevertheless the building of firing points and pillboxes inside practically every house (especially corner buildings) continued right on to December; 10,000 soldiers and 75,000 civilians were engaged in this work.† 17,000 firing points were set up inside houses and over 4,000 pillboxes were built inside Leningrad, as well as fifteen miles of barricades. Mighty batteries of shore, naval and army artillery were being installed right round Leningrad, and the Baltic Fleet was invaluable. Even the gun from the cruiser *Aurora* which had given the signal for the storming of the Winter Palace in 1917, was now stationed on the Pulkovo heights, south of Leningrad. But, by a strange irony, though Leningrad was in grave danger, Moscow in October was in even greater danger, and, despite the blockade, 1,000 guns and considerable

---

* *Trial of German Major War Criminals*, vol. 15 (London 1947), pp. 306–7. (To be referred to in future as TGMWC.)
† Karasev, op. cit., p. 123.

quantities of ammunition and other equipment were flown from Leningrad to Moscow!* A grim thought, especially in view of the desperate shortage of ammunition on the Leningrad Front later in the winter, when the hunger blockade had enormously reduced the output of ammunition in Leningrad itself.

The immediate danger of a German occupation of Leningrad had been averted by the middle of September; but it was only too clear that, cut off from the "mainland", except for the Lake Ladoga route, the only real hope of keeping the city supplied with food, raw materials and fuel—as well as armaments and ammunition that could not be made on the spot—lay in the breach of the land blockade. In September the Russians made a desperate effort to drive the Germans out of the Mga-Siniavino salient, running to the southern shore of Lake Ladoga, and so to clear the Leningrad-Vologda railway line. But although the Russians succeeded in establishing a small bridgehead on the south bank of the Neva, west of Schlüsselburg, and even in holding it, right through the winter, at terrible cost in lives, the Germans had fortified the Mga-Siniavino area so strongly that no progress could be made, and the German defences here were not to be broken up until February 1943.†

* Karasev, op. cit., p. 133.
† The story of this futile attempt to capture the Mga salient, which ended with the last defenders of the Neva bridgehead being wiped out on April 29, 1942, was one of the most tragic episodes of Leningrad's attempt to loosen the German stranglehold.

Chapter III

THREE MILLION TRAPPED

So, by the beginning of September, Leningrad was completely isolated by land from the Russian "mainland", and nearly three million people had been trapped there. The only remaining communications were worse than precarious. In 1941 Russia was desperately short of planes, and, with the Germans enjoying complete air control in the Leningrad area, any Russian plane there was in grave danger of being shot down, even at night. Apart from that, Lake Ladoga, without any proper harbours, was the only route by which Leningrad could communicate with the "mainland".

How was it possible that so many people should have remained in Leningrad, even though the dire threat of a German occupation had hung over the city ever since the middle of July? And what hope was there of feeding this enormous population in case Leningrad was encircled?

It was clear, even during the war, that there had been some very serious miscalculations somewhere; but the factual material published in the last few years shows that this tragic situation was created by a whole series of specific mistakes. There had been lack of foresight on the part of the authorities who, primarily concerned with slowing down the German advance, had given almost no thought at all to the question of food supplies inside the city; also, for several crucial weeks, when the Germans seemed to have been stopped on the Luga Line, there had been an excess of optimistic propaganda; this was responsible for much wishful thinking among the people of Leningrad, who simply did not visualise the city being either occupied or blockaded.

This lack of foresight is illustrated by a number of striking facts. Thus, during the German *blitzkrieg* advance through the Baltic Republics and right into the Leningrad province in June and July, many thousands of tons of grain were evacuated by rail from areas about to be overrun by the Germans, but to the east, and not to Leningrad. At the same time, the evacuation of industrial plants from Leningrad continued to be delayed.

The very slow progress of the evacuation in July and August was due to wishful thinking: people did not believe that the Germans would come anywhere near the city. It is true that, owing to the danger of air-raids, children began to be evacuated in June and early July, but oddly enough to places like Gatchina and Luga, on the Germans' direct road to Leningrad. Soon afterwards they had to be hurriedly brought back to Leningrad, and some—but not all—were then evacuated to the east, where they remained in perfect safety until the end of the war.

Altogether the evacuation of Leningrad throughout July and August was very slow indeed. Only 40,000 people—mostly workers of plants earmarked for evacuation, and their families—left for the east, besides about 150,000 refugees from the Baltic Republics, Pskov, etc.

> Some local authorities regarded a refusal to be evacuated as a manifestation of patriotism, and actually encouraged such attitudes. One could often hear such officials say: "Our population is ready to dig trenches right in the front line, but it doesn't want to leave Leningrad." This was typical of Leningrad's mood, but it overlooked the fact that there were many people—children, old people and invalids, who were of no use to the defence of the city, and were merely a drain on the city's scant food reserves.*

Moreover, in July and August, most Leningraders did not know exactly where the Germans were, and since during those two months, the city was not being bombed, they adopted an optimistically complacent attitude.

* Pavlov, op. cit., pp. 58–59.

The situation called for strong administrative evacuation measures, but the authorities hesitated to apply them. As a result there were caught in the blockade 2,544,000 civilians (including 400,000 children) in Leningrad proper, and 343,000 people in the suburbs and other localities inside the ring of the blockade—a total of nearly three millions.*

To these "mouths to be fed" should, of course, be added the troops who were later to constitute the "Leningrad Front" proper. The mass-evacuation of civilians did not start until January 1942, across the Ice Road of Lake Ladoga. By this time, hundreds of thousands of civilians had already died of hunger.

The whole extent of the disaster of Leningrad cannot be fully understood without some knowledge of the food reserves available at the beginning of the blockade, of the rationing measures taken, and of the meagre supplies brought from outside against appalling difficulties.

On September 6, two days before the land blockade was finally complete, Popkov, head of the Leningrad Soviet, cabled to the State Defence Committee in Moscow, saying that there was very little food left in the city and urging that as much as possible be sent by rail immediately.†

But the railways had already been cut, and two days later, all other land communications as well. On September 12 it was established that, on the basis of the rationing system that had been introduced on July 18 in Moscow, Leningrad and other cities, the stocks available in Leningrad for both troops and civilians only amounted to:

Grain and flour	35	days' supply	
Cereals and macaroni	30	„	„
Meat, including live cattle	33	„	„
Fats	45	„	„
Sugar and confectionery	60	„	„

* Pavlov, op. cit., p. 60.
† On that day Popkov still hoped that Mga would be recaptured by the Russians. (Ibid., p. 60.)

In addition, the Army and the Baltic Navy had some small "emergency reserves" of food; but these did not amount to much.

Short of breaking through the blockade, and re-establishing rail communications with the "mainland", there was little hope of replenishing these meagre reserves. Lake Ladoga was very poorly equipped, and what little shipping it had was under constant German air attack. The food reserves in Leningrad were, moreover, constantly threatened with further destruction by air raids. Considerable quantities of grain, flour and sugar had already been destroyed, notably on September 8, largely because even some of the most elementary air-raid precautions had not been observed. There was still no centralised control, and the food in the city was held by numerous organisations; thus, for several days after the ring of the blockade had closed, it was still possible to eat in "commercial" restaurants, which were not subject to rationing, and which used up as much as twelve per cent of all the fats and ten per cent of all the meat consumed in the city. Certain tinned goods, such as tinned crab, could still be bought in shops without ration-cards for some time after September 8.

The explanation given now for all this carelessness is that both the civilian and the military authorities were so concerned with building defences and keeping the Germans out of Leningrad that they had "no time to give much thought to the problem of food.*
An example of the general confusion, both in Leningrad and elsewhere, quoted by the same author, is the order sent from Moscow to Leningrad, several days *after* the blockade had begun, to despatch several wagon-loads of sugar and confectionery from Leningrad to Vologda!

The first sign that the authorities were alarmed by the food situation in Leningrad was the decision, on September 2, to cut down rations to 22 oz. of bread a day for workers, 14 oz. for office workers and 11 oz. for children and dependants. On September 12, there was a second cut in rations—the bread ration now was just over 1 lb. for workers, 11 oz. for office-workers and children and 9 oz. for dependants.

* Pavlov, op. cit., p. 64.

There was also a reduction in the meat and cereals* rations, but, to make up for this, the sugar, confectionery and fats ration was increased as follows:

	Sugar and conf.	Fats
Workers	4½ lb. monthly	2 lb. 2 oz.
Employees	3 lb. 12½ oz. monthly	1 lb. 2 oz.
Dependants	3 lb. 5 oz. „	11 oz.
Children (to 12)	3 lb. 12½ oz. „	1 lb. 2 oz.

These sugar and confectionery rations of three to four pounds a month and of fats of one to two pounds a month, though by no means generous by ordinary standards, were wholly out of proportion with Leningrad's miserable food reserves; those in charge of Leningrad's defence still had the over-optimistic idea that the blockade would, somehow, be broken before long.

This did not happen, and to economise on "real" flour, the authorities soon had to embark on a feverish search for substitutes, which could be used as admixtures in the baking of bread. When, in September, several barges carrying grain were sunk by the Germans on Lake Ladoga, a large proportion of the grain was recovered by divers and though, normally, it would have been unfit for human consumption, this mouldy grain was to be used as an admixture. As from October 20, bread was composed of 63% rye flour, 4% flax-cake, 4% bran, 8% wholemeal, 4% soya flour, 12% malt flour, 5% mouldy flour; a few days later, with the malt flour reserves running out, new substitutes began to be used, such as cellulose, after it had been processed in a certain way, and cotton cake. "During that highly critical period, these substitutes represented a saving of twenty-five days' rations." True, the cellulose and mouldy flour gave the bread a mouldy and bitter taste, "but, in those days, taste was what people stopped worrying about".

Needless to say, oats which was intended as fodder for horses, was consumed by people, and horses—at least a small number of which it was essential for the Army to keep—were fed on tree leaves and the like. Other incredible substitutes for proper food were devised. In the port of Leningrad a stock of 2,000 tons of sheep guts was

* By cereals (*krupa*) are meant millet, rice, semolina, buckwheat, etc.

discovered; this was turned into a horrible jelly, the smell of which had to be neutralised through the admixture of cloves; at the height of the famine, this sheeps' gut jelly was often to be supplied to ration-card-holders instead of meat.

As distinct from all other cities in the Soviet Union during the war, where people could buy a few extras in the *kolkhoz* market, the population of Leningrad was absolutely and solely dependent on its ration cards.

There were, of course, some black sheep. In September and the first half of October there were numerous cases of fraud; many people managed to have two or more ration cards; often the cards of people who had died or left the city. There were also many cases of forged cards; since there was scarcely any lighting in the shops, the sales staff were often unable to distinguish between real and forged cards. Particularly atrocious were cases when ration cards were stolen. The loss of a card was often equal to a death sentence.

An employee of the printing works where ration cards were printed, was found in possession of 100 such cards; she was shot. It was also suspected that some forged cards had been dropped on Leningrad by German planes, to add to the confusion. In the middle of October a "re-registration" of all ration-cards holders was ordered; this showed that some 70,000 ration cards had, before that, been unnecessarily honoured. People had used the cards of the absent, the dead, or of some who were now in the Army.

At the height of the famine in December there was a "epidemic" of lost ration cards; in October 5,000 ration cards had been genuinely or fraudulently lost; in November the figure rose to 13,000, in December to 24,000. The usual story was that the card had been destroyed in an air-raid. It is perhaps surprising that not *more* people should have resorted to this subterfuge, since the difference between one and two ration cards in December often meant the difference between life and death. The authorities' refusal to replace these lost ration cards, except when such loss and destruction could be more or less satisfactorily proved, soon put an end to the "epidemic".

If, in September and October, most rations were still honoured, this was no longer true in November; the shortage of cereals, meat and fats was particularly serious, and card-holders had to accept

substitutes. Some of these, such as 6 oz. of egg-powder instead of
2 lb. of meat, were not "equivalents" by the widest stretch. Other
meat-substitutes were the horrible jelly from sheep's guts, or an evil-
smelling jelly made out of calves' skins, of which a stock had been
discovered in a warehouse. In November and especially December,
there were practically no fats (butter, oil or margarine) left, nor any'
kinds of substitutes.

During the first few months of the blockade the distribution of
food was rather chaotic; in theory, anyone could have his ration
coupon honoured anywhere; but this often produced queues of unequal length. In December, everybody had to register in a particular
shop; the distribution centres were thus able to send each shop
approximately its correct share—not that this meant that all ration
coupons could be honoured.

In November and December, the whole of Leningrad was living
on starvation rations; even many privileged ration holders (workers
and technical and engineering staffs)—representing 34·4% of the
population—died of hunger; still lower ration cards were held by
office workers (17·5%), dependants (29·5%) and children (18·5%).
This system has been severely criticised by Soviet authors—especially
in relation to children's ration cards: a child of eleven certainly
needed more food than a child of three, and it was particularly
unfair to put children on the even lower dependants card once they
had reached the age of twelve.

As we have seen, the first cut in rations was decided on September 2;
the second was on September 10, the third, on October 1, the fourth
on November 13, and the fifth, the all-time low, on November 20.
Already after the fourth cut, people began to die of hunger. Apart
from the food shortage, there was also a catastrophic fuel shortage
in Leningrad. Both oil and coal supplies were virtually exhausted
by the end of September. The only hope was to cut whatever timber
was still available in the blockaded territory.

On October 8, the City and Provincial Committees decided to cut
timber in the Pargolovo and Vsevolozhsk areas north of the city...

The wood-cutting teams consisted mostly of women and adolescents; they arrived in the woods without proper instruments or clothing, and there was no housing and no transport there. The whole plan was threatened with collapse. By October 24 only one per cent of the plan had been fulfilled... in one area, only 216 people were working, instead of 800 as originally planned... In the circumstances the Komsomols, mostly girls, were sent out to Pargolovo and Vsevolozhsk. Without warm clothes and shoes, and sometimes wearing only light shoes and overcoats, and suffering from hunger and cold, these girls of the Leningrad Komsomol nevertheless did wonders. Thus the girls of the Smolny area built, in forty degrees of frost [Centigrade], a narrow-gauge line from the forest to the nearest railway line. They built barracks, supplied them with rudimentary stoves, and so delivered substantial quantities of timber to Leningrad.*

This slightly eased the fuel situation in Leningrad, without, however, solving it. By the end of October, the city's electric-power supply was only a small fraction of what it had been. The use of electric light was prohibited everywhere, except at the General Staff, the Smolny,† Party offices, civil defence stations, and certain other offices; but ordinary houses, as well as most offices had to do without light throughout the long winter nights. Central heating was abandoned in flats, offices and houses, and in factories central heating was replaced by small wood stoves. Owing to the lack of electricity, most factories had to close down, or use the most primitive methods for making the machines turn at all—such as bicycle pedals. Tramcars were sharply reduced in number in October, and in November they stopped running altogether. No food, no light, no heat, and, on top of it all, German air-raids and constant shelling—such was the life of Leningrad in the winter of 1941–2.

* Karasev, op. cit., pp. 237–8.
† The headquarters of the Leningrad Defence Council under Zhdanov, and of the City Soviet and other central organisations. Originally a famous school for young gentlewomen, it had been the headquarters of Lenin and the Bolsheviks during the 1917 Revolution.

Chapter IV

THE LADOGA LIFELINE

With Leningrad firmly encircled by the Germans by the beginning of September, desperate remedies had to be devised for bringing supplies to the city. It could no longer be assumed that the blockade on land would be broken within a short time. Therefore, on September 9, the Leningrad War Council decided to build a harbour in the small bay of Osinovets, on the west bank of Lake Ladoga near the end of a suburban railway line, some thirty-five miles north-east of Leningrad. Through it some capital equipment could, it was reckoned, be evacuated from Leningrad, and food and other supplies brought in. The port was intended to handle twelve vessels a day by the end of September. The Ladoga naval flotilla, supplied with some anti-aircraft guns, was supposed to protect the new port.

Needless to say, with the Germans only some twenty-five miles south of Osinovets, their planes not only kept a constant watch on the new harbour, but also on the primitive little harbour of Novaya Ladoga on the south side of the lake through which the supplies went, as well as on any cargoes crossing the lake between the two points. Many tugs and barges were sunk during the first weeks of the "Ladoga Lifeline", including several with women and children evacuees from Leningrad.

*

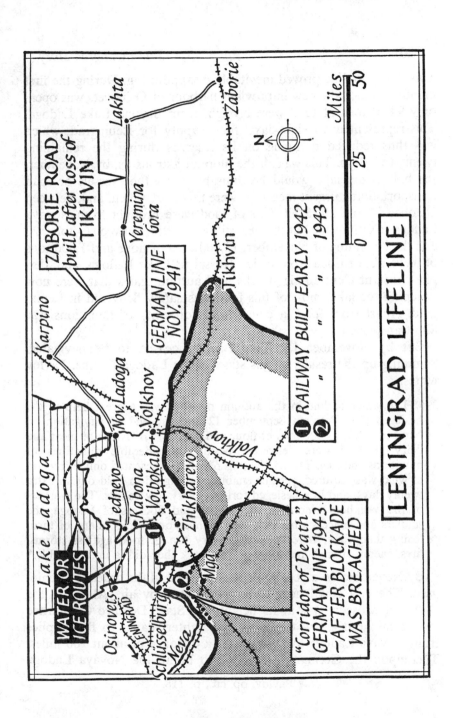

WATER OR
ICE ROUTES

Lake Ladoga

ZABORIE ROAD
built after loss of
TIKHVIN

Lakhta

Zaborie

Karpino

Yeremina
Gora

GERMAN LINE
NOV. 1941

Nov. Ladoga

Volkhov

Lednevo

Kabona
Voibokalo

Osinovets

LENINGRAD

Schlüsselburg

Zhikharevo

Mga

Volkhov

Neva

"Corridor of Death"
GERMAN LINE·1943
—AFTER BLOCKADE
WAS BREACHED

Tikhvin

N

Miles

0   25   50

❶ RAILWAY BUILT EARLY 1942
❷   "   "   "   1943

LENINGRAD LIFELINE

This flimsy lifeline proved inevitably disappointing. During the first month in which the new improvised harbour of Osinovets was open, only 9,800 tons of food were brought from beyond Lake Ladoga. This represented an eight-days' food supply for Leningrad, which was thus reduced to living on its reserves during the remaining twenty-two days. This was all the more disastrous as, by November, the half-frozen lake would be unusable for either vessels or road transport. Some urgent measures were therefore taken, and, between October 14 and 20, 5,000 tons of food were brought from Novaya Ladoga to Osinovets; but this was still very little. Between October 20 and the beginning of November, 12,000 tons of flour and 1,000 tons of meat were rushed from inside Russia to Lake Ladoga, and, despite constant German air attacks, and autumn gales that were now sweeping the lake, most of this food was safely delivered in Leningrad. Apart from food, a considerable quantity of munitions was also transported.

But by November 15, Lake Ladoga ceased to be navigable. Summing up the results of this stage of the Ladoga lifeline, Pavlov writes:

> The water lifeline in the autumn of 1941 was a great help to the besieged city. Between September 12 and the end of navigation on November 15, 24,000 tons of flour and cereals, 1,131 tons of meat and dairy produce were delivered, besides considerable quantities of munitions and fuel. The 25,000 tons of food represented only a fraction of what was required, yet this enabled Leningrad to hold out an extra twenty days, and in a besieged fortress every day counts. The workers of the Volkhov river fleet, the sailors and dockers of Ladoga, the soldiers and officers who took part in these operations, many of them losing their lives, were defending every ton of food against storms, fires, enemy aircraft and looting. The work they did is unforgettable.*

By November 16 a new phase was reached in the ordeal of Leningrad. The city could now be supplied only by air. Although the Battle of Moscow was at its height, the State Defence Committee gave Leningrad a few transport and fighter planes to fly supplies from Novaya Ladoga to Leningrad—a distance of about 100 miles. Thereupon the Germans proceeded to bomb the Novaya Ladoga

* Pavlov, op. cit., p. 118.

airfield, and two-thirds of the supplies had to be flown from airfields further inland. Moreover, the air convoys were constantly attacked by the Germans while flying over the lake, and a number of Russian planes were shot down. In view of the very limited cargo space, only pressed meat and other concentrated foodstuffs were delivered to Leningrad in this difficult and costly way. This small-scale "air-lift" could not, in the long run, solve the problem of feeding nearly three million people.

On top of it all, there now came some truly disastrous new military reverses. At the beginning of November, the Germans attempted to capture the whole southern bank of Lake Ladoga, including the railway junction of Volkhov; General Fedyuninsky's troops just managed to stop the Germans outside Volkhov; but, further east, the Germans succeeded in cutting the main Leningrad-Vologda railway line, and, on November 9, they captured Tikhvin. The loss of Tikhvin was critical. Small quantities of food could still, with great difficulty, be delivered by air. The problem of delivering larger quantities of food across Lake Ladoga, even when it was well frozen, became almost insoluble. The Volkhov and Novaya-Ladoga food bases had gone out of action when the Germans had cut the railway to the east of them. The new rail-head was now a small station called Zaborie, in wild forest country some 100 miles east of Volkhov and some sixty miles east of Tikhvin. Only a state of mind bordering on despair could have persuaded the Leningrad War Council to order the building of a "motor road" of nearly 200 miles, along old forest paths and through virgin forest, in a wide circle from Zaborie to Novaya Ladoga. Soldiers and peasants were mobilised to build this "road" at the height of winter; and it was actually completed on December 6. The whole area was almost uninhabited and:

> Along a large stretch, the road was so narrow that lorries meeting each other could not pass; moreover, the deep snow, the steep hills in a country wholly unfamiliar to the drivers led to constant breakdowns and stoppages. Fortunately, it so happened that three days after the road had been completed, the military situation sharply changed for

the better, with the Red Army's recapture of Tikhvin. It is obvious that the new road could not save Leningrad for any length of time. A convoy of trucks which left Zaborie for Novaya Ladoga took fourteen days to return to its base, and in three days, between Novaya-Ladoga and Yeremina Gora over 350 trucks had got stuck in the snow. These convoys had travelled at the rate of twenty miles a day...*

By driving the Germans out of Tikhvin and beyond the Volkhov river between December 9 and 15 General Meretskov's troops literally saved Leningrad.† The Germans, whose radio had screamed its head off about the imminent surrender of Leningrad the day Tikhvin fell, said very little about the loss of the Leningrad "padlock". Had Tikhvin remained in German hands, it is impossible to see how Leningrad could have been supplied, since the improvised 200-mile road was as good as useless. And, at that time, with the Russian counter-offensive at Moscow at its height, there could be no question of providing Leningrad with a sufficient number of transport and fighter planes for a super-airlift. Not only did General Meretskov's troops drive the Germans out of Tikhvin, but by the end of December the troops of the Volkhov Army Group had also driven the Germans a considerable distance away from Voibokalo, half-way between Volkhov and Mga (the latter still in German hands). By January 1, 1942, trains could travel all the way from Moscow and Vologda to Voibokalo, where the supplies were taken by lorry across the now frozen Lake Ladoga to Leningrad. But the organisation of the "Road of Life" across the ice of Lake Ladoga is a long and complicated story, and it would be wrong to suppose that, with the liberation of Tikhvin on December 9, Leningrad's supply troubles were over.

* Pavlov, op. cit., p. 155.
† Another great advantage of the recapture of Tikhvin was that it put an end to the threat of a German-Finnish "junction".

Chapter V

THE GREAT FAMINE

Already in November, people in Leningrad (in the first place, elderly men) began to die of hunger, euphemistically described as "alimentary distrophy". In November alone over 11,000 people died; the cut in rations on November 20—the fifth since the beginning of the Blockade—enormously increased the death-rate.

On paper, but only on paper, these all-time-low daily rations were as follows:

	Workers and Engin. and tech. staff	*Office Workers*	*Dependants*	*Children*
Bread	9 oz.	4½ oz.	4½ oz.	4½ oz.
Fats	⅔ oz.	⅓ oz.	¼ oz.	⅗ oz.
Meat	1¾ oz.	1 oz.	½ oz.	½ oz.
Cereals	1¾ oz.	1⅙ oz.	¾ oz.	1⅖ oz.
Sugar and conf.	1¾ oz.	1⅙ oz.	1 oz.	1⅗ oz.
Total	15 oz. or 1,087 calories	8⅙ oz. or 581 calories	7 oz. or 466 calories	8⅓ oz. or 684 calories

Even these incredible figures for calories, representing, especially for the last three categories, only a tiny fraction of the human body's requirements, are an "optimistic" exaggeration. Since the meat and fats rations were not honoured, or else were replaced by wholly inadequate substitutes (sheep-guts jelly, etc.), the calory content of the rations was even lower, except (it is claimed) in the case of children. In December 52,000 people died, as many as normally died in a year; while in January 1942, between 3,500 and 4,000 people died every day; in December and January 200,000 people died. Although, by January, the rations had been somewhat increased, the after-effects of the famine were to be felt for many months after; altogether, according to the official Russian figures quoted at the Nuremberg Trial, 632,000 people died in Leningrad as a direct result of the Blockade—a figure which is undoubtedly an under-estimate. In 1959 I was told by Shostakovich, who had been in Leningrad during the early stages of the blockade, that 900,000 people died, and even higher figures have been quoted.

Apart from hunger, people also suffered acutely from cold in their unheated houses. People would burn their furniture and books— but these did not last long.

> To fill their empty stomachs, to reduce the intense sufferings caused by hunger, people would look for incredible substitutes: they would try to catch crows or rooks, or any cat or dog that had still somehow survived; they would go through medicine chests in search of castor oil, hair oil, vaseline or glycerine; they would make soup or jelly out of carpenter's glue (scraped off wallpaper or broken-up furniture). But not all people in the enormous city had such supplementary sources of "food".
>
> Death would overtake people in all kinds of circumstances; while they were in the streets, they would fall down and never rise again; or in their houses where they would fall asleep and never awake; in factories, where they would collapse while doing a job of work. There was no transport, and the dead body would usually be put on a hand-sleigh drawn by two or three members of the dead man's family; often, wholly exhausted during the long trek to the cemetery, they would abandon the body half-way, leaving it to the authorities to deal with it.*

According to another witness:

> It was almost impossible to get a coffin. Hundreds of corpses would be abandoned in cemeteries or in their neighbourhood, usually merely wrapped in a sheet... The authorities would bury all these abandoned

* Pavlov, op. cit., pp. 136–7.

corpses in common graves; these were made by the civil defence teams with the use of explosives. People did not have the strength to dig ordinary graves in the frozen earth. . . On January 7, 1942 the Executive Committee of the Leningrad City Soviet noted that corpses were scattered all over the place, and were filling up morgues and cemetery areas; some were being buried any old way, without any regard for the elementary rules of hygiene.*

Later, in April, during the general clean-up of the city—which was absolutely essential to prevent epidemics, once spring had come—thousands of corpses were discovered in shelters, trenches and under the melting snow, where they had been lying for months. As the Secretary of the Leningrad Komsomol wrote at the time: "The job of disposing of these corpses was truly terrifying; we were afraid of the effect it might have on the minds of children and very young people. A dry matter-of-fact communiqué would have read something like this: 'The Komsomol organisations put in order all trenches and shelters.' In reality this work was beyond description."†

Hospitals were of very little help to the starving. Not only were the doctors and nurses half-dead with hunger themselves, but what the patients needed was not medicine, but food, and there was none.

In December and January the frost froze water mains and sewers, and the burst pipes all over the city added to the danger of epidemics. Water had to be brought in pails from the Neva or the numerous Leningrad canals. This water was, moreover, dirty and unsafe to drink, and in February, about one and a half million people were given anti-typhoid injections.

Between the middle of November and the end of December, 35,000 people were evacuated from Leningrad, mostly by air; on December 6 many people were allowed to leave the city across the ice of Lake Ladoga, but, up to January 22, this evacuation went on in an unorganised way: thousands simply proceeded across Lake Ladoga on foot, and many died before they even reached the south bank of the lake.

* Karasev, op. cit., p. 189.   † Ibid., p. 227.

It was not till January 22 that, with the help of a fleet of buses travelling along the new Ice Road, the evacuation across Lake Ladoga started in real earnest.

There is some conflicting evidence about the effect of the famine on people: on the whole, people just died with a feeling of resignation, while the survivors went on living in hopes: the recapture of Tikhvin and the slight increase in rations on December 25 had a heartening effect. Nevertheless, Karasev talks of numerous cases of "psychological trauma" produced by hunger and cold, German bombing and shelling, and the death of so many relatives and friends. There are no exact figures of the number of children who died of hunger; but the death-rate among these is believed to have been relatively low, if only because their parents would often sacrifice their own meagre rations.

Both local patriotism and an iron discipline, partly enforced by the authorities, account for the virtual absence of any disorders or hunger riots. That the measures taken against "anti-social" behaviour were extremely drastic may be judged from the statement by Kuznetsov, head of the Leningrad City Party Organisation, who said in April: "We used to shoot people for half-a-pound of bread stolen from the population." There were, inevitably, a few racketeers here and there; but, on the whole, the discipline was good. Pavlov tells the following significant incident:

> The driver of a truck was delivering loaves of bread to a bakery, when a shell hit the front of the truck and killed the driver... The loaves of bread were scattered over the pavement. Conditions were favourable for looting. Yet the people who gathered round the wrecked vehicle, raised the alarm, and guarded the bread till the arrival of another truck. All these people were hungry, and the temptation to grab a fresh loaf of bread well-nigh irresistible. And yet not a single loaf was stolen.*

Whether, on the other hand, as Pavlov implies, a man who started

* Op cit., p. 109.

screaming at people in a bread-queue urging them to loot the shop was an enemy agent or simply a man driven half-insane by hunger is difficult to say; many people were driven half-insane, as is suggested by Karasev and other writers.

Morale, even in the appalling conditions of the famine at its height, was kept up in all kinds of ways: there are many accounts of the theatrical shows that continued throughout the winter, given by actors almost fainting with hunger, and wearing (like the audience) whatever they could to keep themselves warm.

Much is also made of the role played by the Leningrad Komsomol organisations to help people in dire distress. The Komsomol organised *bytovyie otriady* ("everyday life teams") of several thousand young people:

> These teams consisted of a total of 1,000 young people; moreover, in each district, some 500 or 700 temporary helpers were frequently mobilised. Tired and worn out, these young people, mostly girls, would help the population to overcome their terrible difficulties. Visiting dirty and freezing houses, they would use their swollen hands, cracked with cold and hard work, to chop wood, or light the little *burzhuika* stoves, or bring pails of water from the Neva, or bring dinner from a canteen, or wash the floor or clothes, and the pathetic smile of a completely exhausted Leningrader would then express his gratitude for this hard and honourable work. In the Primorski district alone, the members of these Komsomol teams examined in February–March 1,810 flats, looked after 780 sick people and, altogether, helped 7,678 persons. . . The Komsomol teams were authorised to resettle people into more suitable houses, place homeless children in children's homes, and arrange about evacuations. . . Largely through the help of the Komsomol teams, over 30,000 orphans were settled in the eighty-five new children's homes set up between January and May 1942.*

Most of these children were the orphans of parents who had died in the famine.

If the civilian population of Leningrad had to suffer all the pangs of hunger, and many had to die, since there was no alternative so long as large scale evacuation was impossible, there could be no question

* Karasev, op. cit., p. 190.

of letting the soldiers starve; for everything ultimately depended on them. Even so, the soldiers' rations had to be cut, too. The Red Army rations established on September 20, 1941, amounted to 3,450 calories in the case of front-line troops and 2,659 calories in the case of "rear personnel", with two intermediary categories between them.

In the conditions of Leningrad such rations could not be maintained for long. Between the middle of November 1941 and February 1942, the ration of front-line troops was reduced to 2,593 calories, and that of "rear" troops to 1,605 calories; from November 20—that is, at the height of the hunger blockade—front-line soldiers were getting 1 lb. of bread and about 4 oz. of meat, besides small quantities of other food. This, at the height of winter, was far from satisfactory, though the knowledge of what was happening in Leningrad at the same time made the soldiers feel that they were highly privileged in comparison with the civilians. Whenever civilians visited the front, soldiers gladly shared their meagre rations with them. Moreover, most of the reserves of potatoes in Leningrad were handed over to the Army's field kitchens, and this created an illusion of "bulk"; also, the army bread was of slightly better quality than that given to civilians.

The soldiers, however, suffered severely from the Leningrad tobacco shortage, and all kinds of admixtures were devised—such as hops and dried maple leaves. Desperate remedies were resorted to in order to keep the troops well supplied with tobacco, which was found to be essential for morale. Very few soldiers, it was found, would agree to exchange their tobacco even for chocolate, which was among the "concentrated" foods brought to Leningrad by air.

Chapter VI

THE ICE ROAD

There were only two drastic remedies for the appalling famine from which Leningrad had suffered, especially since the end of October: one was the evacuation of as many people as possible; the other was the organisation of a reliable supply-line for food, fuel and raw materials. The organisation of an ice road across Lake Ladoga had been in the Leningrad authorities' minds ever since the blockade on land had closed round Leningrad on September 8; the lake was expected to freeze in November or early December. But everything depended on the intensity of the frost; to build a proper motor road across the ice, it was essential that the ice should be uniformly two metres thick. This thickness could be reached rapidly in only extremely cold weather of at least minus 15°C.

By November 17 the ice was only one metre thick, but by November 20—that day of the all-time-low ration cut in Leningrad —it reached a thickness of 1·8 metres; horse-drawn vehicles were sent across the ice, but the horses were so underfed that many of them collapsed and died. The drivers were instructed to cut up such horses, and deliver them to Leningrad as meat. At last, on November 22, the first motor transport ventured on to the lake; but the ice was still so thin that only small loads could be carried by the two-ton lorries, and even so, several of them fell through the ice. On the following day a system was adopted of attaching sleighs to the lorries, and putting most of the load on the sleighs, so as to spread out the pressure on the ice more evenly. Between November 23 and December 1 only 800 tons of flour were transported across the ice in these various ways, and, in the process, some forty lorries were lost, some of them falling through the ice, often together with their drivers. The results of this first attempt to use the Road of Life were negligible. It should be remembered that, at this time, Tikhvin was in German hands, and that most of the food transported during that week came from the meagre stores that had been accumulated on the south side of the lake before the fall of Tikhvin on November 9. New supplies—if any—were now expected to reach Lake Ladoga along the incredibly long improvised road from Zaborie, far to the east of Tikhvin. To maintain the starvation rations that had come into force in Leningrad on November 20, it was essential to bring to the city at least 1,000 tons of food a day, besides ammunition and petrol which were absolutely essential to the troops of the Leningrad Front. Even in the best possible conditions, not more than 600 tons a day could be expected from the Zaborie road. Thus, the liberation of Tikhvin on December 9 truly meant that Leningrad had been saved.*

Not that the recapture of Tikhvin solved all problems—far from it. Although Tikhvin, on the main Vologda-Leningrad line, had now become the main food base for Leningrad and became, as soon as it was recaptured, "like a gigantic ant-heap" (Pavlov), the task of transporting food and other supplies from Tikhvin to Leningrad was still an extremely arduous one. Since the Germans, in their retreat, had blown up all the railway bridges between Tikhvin and Volkhov, there was no alternative, for the time being, to transporting the supplies by road, namely from Tikhvin to a number of points on the lake, such as Kabona or Lednevo, a matter of over 100 miles of very bad winter roads. It was not till January 1 that the railway bridges between Tikhvin and Volkhov were rebuilt; by this time, the Germans had also been driven a long distance away from Volkhov and Voibokalo (roughly to their original "Mga salient" which they had captured in September), and it was Voibokalo, on the main

* Pavlov, op. cit., p. 156.

Leningrad-Vologda railway line, and just south of the Schüsselburg Bay, which became the main "food base". It was only some thirty-five miles from Osinovets, on the Leningrad side of the lake. What is more, during the following weeks, a branch line was built, in incredible winter conditions, from Voibokalo to Kabona, a matter of some twenty miles, so as to bring the trains right up to the lake, where the food was then put in lorries.

Although the food supplies in Leningrad were still worse than precarious at the end of December, the War Council decided to increase the bread ration slightly on December 25. This was not enough to reduce the death-rate, but it had an important effect on morale.

Altogether, between the beginning of the blockade on September 8 and January 1, some 45,000 tons of food were delivered to Leningrad in the following ways (in tons):

	By water	By air	By the ice road	Total
Grain and Flour	23,041	743	12,343	36,127
Cereals	1,056	—	1,482	2,538
Meat and meat products	730	1,829	1,100	3,659
Fats and cheese	276	1,729	138	2,143
Condensed milk	125	200	158	483
Egg powder, chocolate, etc.	—	681	44	725
Total:	25,228	5,182	15,265	45,675

Considering that there were about two and a half million people still in Leningrad, these quantities were, of course, extremely small, and, what is more, the quantities delivered by January 1 across the ice were worse than disappointing. It should, it is true, be added that, apart from food, a certain quantity of ammunition and petrol were also brought into Leningrad during this period.

Altogether, neither in December nor even in January, could the Ice Road be said to be working satisfactorily, and at the beginning of January Zhdanov expressed his extreme discontent at the way things were going. What complicated matters still further was the decrepit state of the small railway line (in the past a derelict suburban line, built long before the Revolution) between Osinovets and Leningrad. The railway even lacked water-towers, and engines had to be filled with water by hand, and trees had to be cut on the spot to supply them with damp and wholly inadequate fuel. The line which used to have one train a day, was now expected to carry six or seven large goods trains. The half-starved railwaymen were fighting against terrible odds.

There was also an acute shortage of packing material in Russia and a high proportion of the food taken to Leningrad was wasted as a result. It was not, in fact, until the end of January or rather, until February 10, 1942, when the branch-line from Voibokalo to Kabona was completed, and not until after a good deal of reorganisation had been done, that the Road of Life across Lake Ladoga began to work like clockwork. By this time several wide motor-roads had been built across the ice, and hundreds of lorries could now deliver food to Leningrad, and also evacuate many thousands of its inhabitants, many of them half-dead with hunger. The Germans did what they could to interfere both with the building of the railway line to Kabona and with the ice-roads themselves; these roads were both bombed and shelled, but Russian fighter planes protected them as far as possible, and traffic police were stationed along the roads. One of their duties was to lay little bridges across any holes or cracks in the ice made by German bombs or shells.

By January 24, 1942, food supplies had sufficiently improved to allow a second increase in Leningrad's rations; workers were now getting 14 oz. of bread, office workers 11 oz., dependants and children 9 oz., and front line troops 21 oz.; on February 11, the ration was increased for the third time.

On January 22 the State Defence Committee decided to evacuate half-a-million people from Leningrad; priority was given to women, children, old and sick people. In January 11,000 people were evacuated, in February 117,000, in March 221,000, in April 163,000; a total of 512,000. In May, after shipping on Lake Lagoda had been restored, the evacuation continued, and between May and November 1942, 449,000 more people were evacuated, making a total, in 1942, of nearly a million people. Moreover, the evacuation of industry, which had been so harshly interrupted in September 1941, was resumed: between January and April, several thousand machine tools, etc., were evacuated across the ice to the east. What is more, a petrol pipeline was laid, between April and June 1942, across the bottom of Lake Ladoga to supply Leningrad with fuel. The German attempts to wreck the pipeline by dropping depth-charges into the lake failed. Similarly, when the Volkhov power station resumed work in May 1942, an electric cable was laid across the bottom of Lake Ladoga, to supply Leningrad with electric power.

The Ladoga Life Line—ice in winter, water in summer, continued to function satisfactorily right up to January 1943 when the land blockade was broken and trains began, soon afterwards, to run through the narrow "Schlüsselburg Gap".

With the population enormously reduced, first by famine, and then by evacuation, feeding Leningrad no longer presented an insuperable problem. Indeed after March 1942, to make up for what the city had suffered, Leningrad rations were higher than in the rest of the country, and special canteens with extra-good food were set up, particularly for workers in poor health. Nevertheless, the winter famine had left a mark on very many people. During the summer months of 1942 a high proportion of workers were too ill to work— in one armaments plant mentioned by Karasev, thirty-five per cent of the workers were too ill to work in May, and thirty-one per cent in June. On May 23, 1942, the poet Vera Inber, whose husband worked in a Leningrad hospital, noted in her diary:

> Our hospital compound has been cleared of rubble, and has become almost unrecognisable—better even than before the war, I'm told. In place of heaps of rubbish there are now new vegetable plots. In the students' hostel they have opened a "reinforced nutrition" dining room; there are several in every district. Weak, pale, exhausted people (second degree distrophy) slowly wander about, almost surprised at the thought that they are still alive... Often they sit down for a rest, and expose their legs to the rays of the sun, which heals their scurvy ulcers... But among Leningraders there are also some who can no longer move or walk (third degree distrophy). They lie quietly in their frozen winter houses, into which even the spring seems unable to pene-

trate. Such houses are visited by young doctors, medical students and nurses; the worst cases are taken to hospital; we have put up 2,000 new beds in our hospital, including the maternity ward; so few children are born nowadays, one might say none are born at all!*

A very high death-rate persisted at least until April; and although, by June, people stopped dying of hunger or its after-effects, the strain of what they had lived through, as well as of the constant bombing and shelling of the city, continued to make itself felt. Karasev speaks of a widespread "psychic traumatisation", marked, in particular, by high blood-pressure; this condition was four or five times more frequent than before the war.

Nevertheless, with the population reduced to only 1,100,000 in April and to some 650,000 by November 1942, conditions of life became relatively more normal. 148 schools (out of some 500) were opened with 65,000 pupils, and the children were given three meals a day.

Although the front outside Leningrad seemed in 1942 to have been stabilised, the danger of another all-out German attempt to capture the city was ever-present, and there were several (more or less false) alarms. On the other hand, the attempts made by the Red Army to break the land blockade failed.

The news throughout the "black summer" of 1942 of the Germans crashing ahead into the Caucasus and towards Stalingrad, had a depressing effect. The fall of Sebastopol—which had so many points in common with Leningrad—seemed particularly ominous, and there was also a feeling that if Stalingrad fell, the fate of Leningrad, too, would be sealed.

The Russian counter-offensive at Stalingrad not only created a tremendous feeling of optimism in Leningrad, as it did in the rest of the country, but it also enormously improved the prospects of break-

* Vera Inber, *Pochti tri goda* (Nearly Three Years), (Leningrad, 1947), pp. 118–19.

ing the German blockade. This was now achieved as a result of a week's heavy fighting in January 1943, when the troops of the Leningrad Front under General Govorov and those of the Volkhov Front under General Meretskov, joined forces, and so hacked a ten-mile corridor through the German salient south of Lake Ladoga. Schüsselburg was recaptured and, in a very short time, a rail link was established with the "mainland" and a pontoon bridge built across the Neva; as a result, trains could travel from Moscow to Leningrad.*

But the memory of the terrible winter months of 1941–2 lingered on, and when I went to Leningrad in 1943, they were still the main subject of conversation.

* Vera Inber (op. cit., p. 194) wrote in March 1943, "only freight trains cross the pontoon bridge across the Neva at Schüsselburg. The railwaymen call this place 'the corridor of death'. It is under constant German shell fire."

Chapter VII

LENINGRAD CLOSE-UP

When I went to Leningrad in September 1943,* the German lines
were still two miles from the Kirov Works, on the southern outskirts
of the city. The total population had now been reduced to some
600,000, and the city, though as beautiful as ever, despite considerable damage caused by shells, bombs and fires, had a strange
half-deserted look. It was a front-line city, sure enough, and a high
proportion of its people were in uniform. There was practically no
more bombing, but the shelling was frequent, and often deadly. It
had caused great damage to houses, especially in the modern
southern parts of Leningrad, and many people would recall horrible
"incidents" when a shell had hit a queue at a tram-stop or a

* With the exception of Henry Shapiro of United Press who went
there a few weeks earlier, I was the only foreign correspondent
allowed to visit Leningrad during the blockade. To me, as a native of
Leningrad, who had lived there until the age of seventeen, this was a
particularly moving experience. After an absence of twenty-five
years, I visited all the familiar places, including the house where I
had spent my childhood and school years. Many houses in the street
had been destroyed by bombing and in the house where I had lived a
large number of people had died of hunger in 1941–2. I have described my visit fully in an earlier book (*Leningrad*, London, 1944),
but as it is out of print I make no excuse for reprinting from it, in
this chapter, a few accounts of visits and conversations which convey
something of the spirit of Leningrad during the blockade.

336

crowded tram-car: some of these had happened only a few days before.

Yet, in a strange way, life seemed almost to have returned to normal. Most of the city looked deserted and yet, in the late afternoon, when there was no shelling, there were large crowds of people walking about the "safe" side of the Nevsky Prospect (the shells normally landed on the other side*) and even little luxuries were sold here, unavailable at the time in Moscow, such as little bottles of Leningrad-made scent. And the "Writers' Bookshop" near the Anichkov Bridge in the Nevsky was doing a roaring trade in second-hand books. Millions of books had been burned as fuel in Leningrad during the famine winter; and yet many people had died before having had time to burn their books, and—a cruel thought—some wonderful bargains could now be got. Theatres and cinemas were open, though whenever the shelling started they were promptly evacuated. In the Marsovo Pole (the Champs de Mars) and in the Summer Garden—whose eighteenth-century marble statues of Greek gods and goddesses had been removed to safety—vegetables were being grown, and a few people were pottering around the cabbages and potatoes. There were also cabbage beds round the sandbagged Bronze Horseman.

Almost from the moment I arrived in Leningrad—after travelling there by plane via Tikhvin and then, at night, only a few yards above the waters of Lake Ladoga—I began to hear stories about the famine. For instance this conversation on the very first night with Anna Andreievna, the genteel old lady who looked after me at the Astoria:

> The Astoria looks like a hotel now, but you should have seen it during the famine! It was turned into a hospital—just hell. They used to bring here all sorts of people, mostly intellectuals, who were dying of hunger. Gave them vitamin tablets, tried to pep them up a bit. But a lot of them were too far gone, and died almost the moment they got here. I know what it is to be hungry. I was so weak I could hardly walk. Had to use a walking stick to support me. My home is only a mile away, in the Sadovaya... I'd have to stop and sit down every hundred yards... Took me sometimes over an hour to get home...

* See p. 361.

You don't know what it was like. You just stepped over corpses in
the street and on the stairs. You simply stopped taking any notice. It
was no use worrying. Terrible things used to happen. Some people
went quite insane with hunger. And the practice of hiding the dead
somewhere in the house and using their ration cards was very common
indeed. There were so many people dying all over the place, the
authorities couldn't keep track of all the deaths... You should have
seen me in February 1942. Oh, Lord, I looked funny! My weight had
dropped from seventy kilos to forty kilos in four months! Now I am
back to sixty-two—feeling quite plump...

On the following day I had a conversation at the Architects'
Institute, where they were already working on the future restoration
of the various historic buildings, such as the palaces of Pushkin
(Tsarskoye Selo) and Peterhof that had been wrecked by the
Germans:

We went on with this blueprint work right through the winter of
1941–2... It was a blessing for us architects. The best medicine that
could have been given us during the famine. The moral effect is great
when a hungry man knows he's got a useful job of work to do... But
there's no doubt about it: a worker stands up better to hardships than
an intellectual. A lot of our people stopped shaving—the first sign of a
man going to pieces... Most of these people pulled themselves together
when they were given work. But on the whole men collapsed more
easily than women, and at first the death-rate was highest among the
men. However, those who survived the worst period of the famine
finally survived. The women felt the after-effects more seriously than
the men. Many died in the spring, when the worst was already over.
The famine had peculiar physical effects on people. Women were so
run down that they stopped menstruating... So many people died that
we had to bury them without coffins. People had their feelings blunted,
and never seemed to weep at the burials... It was all done in complete
silence, without any display of emotion. When things began to improve,
the first signs were that women began to put rouge and lipstick on their
pale, skinny faces. Yes, we lived through hell right enough; but you
should have been here the day the blockade was broken—people in the
street wept for joy, and strangers fell round each others' necks. Now
life is almost normal. There is this shelling, of course, and people get
killed, but life has become valuable again.

Also, I remember this conversation, one day, with Major Lozak,
a staff officer who conducted me round the Leningrad Front:

In those days there *was* something in a man's face which told you that he would die within the next twenty-four hours... I have lived in Leningrad all my life, and I also have my parents here. They are old people, and during those famine months I had to give them half my soldier's ration, or they would certainly have died. As a staff officer I was naturally, and quite rightly, getting considerably less than the people at the front: 250 grams a day instead of 350. I shall always remember how I'd walk every day from my house near the Tauris Garden to my work in the centre of the city, a matter of two or three kilometres. I'd walk for a while, and then sit down for a rest. Many a time I saw a man suddenly collapse on the snow. There was nothing one could do. One just walked on... And, on the way back, I would see a vague human form covered with snow on the spot where, in the morning, I had seen a man fall down. One didn't worry; what was the good? People didn't wash for weeks; there were no bath houses and no fuel. But at least people were urged to shave. And during that winter I don't think I ever saw a person smile. It was frightful. And yet, there was a kind of inner discipline that made people carry on. A new code of manners was evolved by the hungry people. They carefully avoided talking about food. I remember spending a very hungry evening with an old boy from the Radio Committee. He nearly drove me crazy—he *would* talk all evening about Kant and Hegel. Yet we never lost heart. The Battle of Moscow gave us complete confidence that it would be all right in the end. But what a change all the same when February came and the Ice Road began to function properly! Those tremendous parcels that started arriving from all over the country—honey and butter, and ham and sausages! Still, our troubles are not at an end. This shelling can really be very upsetting. I was in the Nevsky once when a shell landed close by. And ten yards away from me was a man whose head was cut clean off by a shell splinter. It was horrible. I saw him make his last two steps already *with his head off*—and a bloody mess all round before he collapsed. I vomited right there and then, and was quite ill for the rest of the day—though I had already seen many terrible things before. I shall never forget the night when a children's hospital was hit by an oil bomb; many children were killed, and the whole house was blazing, and some perished in the flames. It's bad for one's nerves to see such things happen; our ambulance services have instructions to wash away blood on the pavement as quickly as possible after a shell has landed.

From that visit to Leningrad I brought back countless impressions of human suffering and human endurance. The front round

Leningrad had by this time become stabilised, and Leningrad, though still surrounded, was confidently watching the Germans in full retreat along most of the Russo-German front, and waiting for its own turn to be finally liberated. Although there was no longer any famine, life was still desperately hard for many people, not least the men and women of the Kirov Works, which were almost in the front line. Here, as well as in another important plant, I was not only shown what life was like then, but also told what it had been like during the famine. Here are two accounts. First a visit to an important factory making optical instruments:

Here most of the smaller wooden buildings had been used up for fuel during the previous two winters. It was a large factory building, the outer brick walls of which were marked by shell splinters. Comrade Semyonov, the director of the factory, with a strong hard face, and wearing a plain khaki tunic to which were pinned the Leningrad medal and the Order of Lenin, was a typical Soviet executive to look at and listen to—very precise and to the point. In his office was a collection of the various things the factory was now making— bayonets, detonators and large optical lenses, and on the wall were portraits of Stalin and Zhdanov... Altogether, I had noticed in Leningrad a certain aloofness towards Moscow, a feeling that although this was part of the whole show, it was also, in a sense, a separate show, one in which Leningrad had survived largely through its own stupendous efforts.

Semyonov said that this was the largest factory in the Soviet Union for optical instruments... "But during the first days of the war the bulk of our optical equipment was evacuated east, because this was considered one of the key factories for defence. One couldn't afford to take any risks with it. Early in 1942 we had a second evacuation, and those of the skilled workers who hadn't gone in the first evacuation were sent away—that is, those who were still alive."

"Already in the first weeks of the war, when most of our equipment and skilled men had been sent away, we started here on an entirely new basis—we started working exclusively for the Leningrad Front, and we had to make things for which we had the equipment— and there wasn't much of it. Our people had no experience in this kind of work. Even so, we started making things our soldiers needed most. But Leningrad has a great industrial tradition, a great industrial culture, and our hand-grenades and anti-tank-mine detonators turned out to be the best of any made. We made hundreds of thousands of these... Throughout the blockade we have also been repairing small arms, rifles and machine-guns; and now we are also working again on optical instruments—among them submarine periscopes. For our Baltic Fleet isn't idle, as you know..."

I asked Semyonov to tell me something about life at the factory during the hunger blockade. He was silent for a few seconds... "Frankly," he said, "I don't like to talk about it. It's a very bitter memory... By the time the blockade started half our people had been evacuated or had gone into the army, so we were left here with about 5,000. I must say it was difficult at first to get used to the bombing, and if anyone says it doesn't frighten him, don't you believe it! Yet, though it frightened people, it also aroused their frantic anger against the Germans. When they started bombing us in a big way in October 1941 our workers fought for the factory more than they did for their own houses. One night we had to deal with 300 incendiaries on the factory grounds alone. Our people were putting the fires out with a sort of concentrated rage and fury. They had realised by then that they were in the front line—that was all. No more shelters. Only small children were taken to shelters, and old grannies. And then, one day in December, in twenty degrees of frost, we had all our windows blown out by a bomb, and I thought to myself: 'No, we really can't go on. Not till the spring. We can't go on in this temperature, and without light, without water, and almost without food.' And yet, somehow—we didn't stop. A kind of instinct told us we mustn't—that it would be worse than suicide, and a little like treason. And sure enough, within thirty-six hours we were working again—working in altogether hellish conditions, with eight degrees of frost in the workshops, and fourteen degrees of frost in this office where you are sitting now. Oh, we had stoves of sorts, little stoves that warmed the air a couple of feet around them. But still our people worked. And, mind you, they were hungry, terribly hungry..."

Semyonov paused for a moment and there was a frown on his face. "Yes," he said, "to this day I cannot quite understand it. I don't quite understand how it was possible to have all that will-power, that strength of mind. Many of them, hardly able to walk with hunger, would drag themselves to the factory every day, eight, ten, even twelve kilometres. For there were no trams. We used all sorts of childish expedients to keep the work going. When there were no batteries, we used bicycle pedals to keep the lathes turning."

"Somehow, people knew when they were going to die. I remember one of our elder workers staggering into this office and saying to me: 'Comrade Chief, I have a request to make. I am one of your old workers, and you have always been a good friend to me, and I know you will not refuse. I am not going to bother you again. I know that today or tomorrow I shall die. My family are in a very poor way— very weak. They won't have the strength to manage a funeral. Will you be a friend and have a coffin made for me, and have it sent to my family, so that they don't have the extra worry of trying to get a coffin? You know how difficult it is to get one.' That happened during the blackest days of December or January. And such things happened day after day. How many workers came into this office saying: 'Chief, I shall be dead today or tomorrow.' We would send them to the factory hospital, but they always died. All that was possible and impossible to eat, people ate. They ate cattle-cake, and mineral oils—we used to boil them first—and carpenter's glue. People tried to sustain themselves on hot water and yeast. Out of the 5,000 people we had here, several hundred died. Many of them died right here... Many a man would drag himself to the factory, stagger in and die... Everywhere there were corpses. But some died at home, and died together with the rest of their family and, in the circumstances, it was difficult to find out anything definite... And since there was no transport, we weren't usually able to send people round to enquire. This went on till about February 15. After that, rations were increased and the death-rate dropped. Today it hurts me to talk about these things..."

One of the Leningrad memories that stands out most clearly in my mind is the afternoon I spent in September 1943 at the great Kirov Works, where work continued even then under almost constant shelling from the German lines barely two miles away. For here, even in 1943, one had a glimpse of Leningrad's darkest and grimmest days; to the Kirov workers these were not a memory of the past; they were continuing to live here through a peculiar kind of hell. Yet to these people, to be a Kirov worker, and to hold out to the end, had become like a title of nobility. The workers here were not soldiers; sixty-nine per cent were women and girls—mostly young girls. They knew that this was as bad as the front; in a way it was worse: you did not know the thrill of direct retaliation. The great revolutionary tradition of the Putilov, now the Kirov Works, had much to do with it.

The day before, in a children's rest home in Kamenny Island, I had talked to a girl called Tamara Turanova:

She was a little girl of fifteen, very pale, thin and delicate, obviously run down. On her little black frock was pinned the green-ribboned medal of Leningrad:

"Where did you get that?" I asked. A faint smile appeared on her pale little face. "I don't know what he was called," she said. "An uncle with spectacles came to the works one day and gave me this medal." "What works?" "Oh, the Kirov Works, of course," she said. "Does your father work there, too?" "No," she said, "father died in the hungry year, died on the 7th of January. I have worked at the Kirov Works since I was fourteen, so I suppose that's why they gave me this medal. We're not far away from the front." "Doesn't it frighten you to work there?" She screwed up her little face. "No, not really; one gets used to it. When a shell whistles, it means it's high up; it's only when it begins to sizzle that you know there's going to be trouble. Accidents do happen, of course, happen very often; sometimes things happen every day. Only last week we had an accident; a shell landed in my workshop and many were wounded, and two Stakhanovite girls were burned to death." She said it with terrible simplicity and almost with the suggestion that it wouldn't have been such a serious matter if two Stakhanovite girls hadn't lost their lives. "You wouldn't like to change over to another factory?" I asked. "No," she said, shaking her head. "I am a Kirov girl, and my father was a Putilov man, and really the worst is over now, so we may as well stick it to the end." And one could feel that she meant it, though it was only too clear what terrible nervous strain that frail little body of hers had suffered. "And your mother?" I asked. "She died before the war," said the girl. "But my big brother is in the army, on the Leningrad Front, and he writes to me often, very often, and three months ago he and several of his comrades came to visit us at the Kirov Works." Her little pale face brightened at the thought of it, and, looking out of the window of the rest home at the golden autumn trees, she said: "You know, it's good to be here for a little while."

The next day, after driving down the Peterhof Road through the heavily-battered southern outskirts of Leningrad, with the German lines running along the other side of the Uritsk inlet of the Gulf of Finland, I arrived at the Kirov Works, where I was received by Comrade Puzyrev, the director, a relatively young man with a strong, but careworn face...

"Well," he said, "you are certainly finding us working in unusual conditions. What we have here isn't what is normally meant by the Kirov Plant... Before the war we had over 30,000 workers; now we have only a small fraction of these ... and sixty-nine per cent of our workers are female. Hardly any women worked here before the war. We then made turbines, tanks, guns; we made tractors, and supplied the greater part of the equipment for building the Moscow-Volga canal. We built quantities of machinery for the Navy... Before this war started, we began to make tanks in a very big way, as well as tank and aircraft engines. Practically all this production of equipment proper has been moved to the east. Now we repair diesels and tanks, but our main output is ammunition, and some small arms..."

Puzyrev then spoke of the early days of the war at the Kirov works. It was a story of that *lutte à outrance* so typical of the people and workers of Leningrad. Like one man they reacted to the German invasion, but the highest pitch of self-sacrifice was reached as a result of the "Leningrad in danger" appeal made on August 21 by Voroshilov, Zhdanov and Popkov.

"The workers of the Kirov Plant," Puzyrev said, "were in reserved occupations, and hardly anybody was subject to mobilisation. Yet no sooner had the Germans invaded us than everybody without exception volunteered for the front. If we had wanted to, we could have sent 25,000 people; we let only 9,000 or 10,000 go.

Already in June 1941 they formed themselves into what was to become the famous Kirov Division. Although they had done some training before the war, they couldn't be considered fully-trained soldiers, but their drive, their guts were tremendous. They wore the uniform of the Red Army, but they were in fact part of the *opolcheniye*, except that they were rather better trained than other *opolcheniye* units. Several such workers' divisions were formed in Leningrad . . . and many tens of thousands of them went out from here to meet the Germans, to stop them at any price. They fought at Luga, and Novgorod and Pushkin, and finally at Uritsk, where, after one of the grimmest rearguard actions of this war, our men managed to stop the Germans, just in the nick of time. . . The fight put up by our Workers' Division and by the people of Leningrad who went out to stop them was absolutely decisive. . . It is no secret—a large proportion of the Workers' Divisions never came back. . ."

One felt that Puzyrev regretted at heart that such good industrial material should have had to be sacrificed on the battlefield; but, clearly, in 1941, when it was touch-and-go for both Moscow and Leningrad, such fine points had to be put aside; he was glad, all the same, that when the worst was over, many of the survivors had been taken out of the army and put back into industry.

He then spoke of the evacuation of the Kirov Plant. Before the German ring had closed, it had been possible to evacuate only one complete workshop—525 machine tools and 2,500 people. But nothing more could be sent east till the spring.

"However, our most highly skilled workers, who were badly needed in Siberia and the Urals, were evacuated by air, together with their families. They were flown to Tikhvin, but after the Germans had taken Tikhvin, we had to fly them to other airfields, and from there the people had to walk to the nearest railway station, walk through the snow, in the middle of a bitter winter, often dozens and dozens of kilometres. . . Already in the early part of the winter a lot of equipment from Kharkov, Kiev and other places, and also some from Moscow, had reached the Urals, and our skilled people were badly needed to handle the stuff and to organise production. Cheliabinsk, for example, had never made tanks before, and our people were needed for starting this large-scale production of tanks in the shortest possible time. . . We were then in the middle of that most critical transition period when industry in the west had ceased to function, and had not yet started up in the east. . . The people who left here in October were already working at full speed in their new place, 2,000 kilometres away, by December! . . . And in what conditions all this was done! Trains carrying the equipment were attacked from the air, and so were the transport planes taking the skilled Leningrad workers and their families from Leningrad. Fortunately the percentage of transport planes shot down was not high. But the flying had to be done mostly at night, in very difficult conditions. . ."

Puzyrev's story of the Kirov Plant during the worst months of the famine was much the same as the story told me by Semyonov, the director of the optical instruments plant:

"Those were terrible days," he said. "On December 15 everything came to a standstill. There was no fuel, no electric current, no food, no tram-cars, no water, nothing. Production in Leningrad practically ceased. We were to remain in this terrible condition till the 1st of April. It is true that food began to come in in February across the Ladoga Ice Road. But we needed another month before we could start any kind of regular output at the Kirov Works. But even during the worst hungry period we did what we could. . . We repaired guns, and our foundry was kept going, though only in a small way. It felt as if the mighty Kirov Works had been turned into a village smithy. People were terribly cold and terribly hungry. Many of our people died during those days, and it was chiefly our best people who died— highly skilled workers who had reached a certain age when the body can no longer resist such hardships. . .

"As I said before, there was no water and no electric current. All we had was a small pump which was connected with the sea down there; that was all the water supply we had. Throughout the winter —from December to March—the whole of Leningrad used snow for putting out incendiaries. . . The only very large fire was that of the Gostiny Dvor.* Here, at the Kirov Works, not a single workshop was destroyed by fire.

* The famous shopping arcade in the Nevsky Prospect.

"People were so faint with hunger that we had to organise hostels, so that they could live right here. We authorised others who lived at home to come only twice a week... At the end of November, we had to call a meeting to announce the reduction of the bread ration from 400 to 250 grams for workers, and to 125 grams for the others —and very little else. They took it calmly, though to many it was like a death sentence..."

And Puzyrev then said that the soldiers on the Leningrad Front asked that their own rations be reduced, so that so drastic a reduction in the rations of the Leningrad citizens could be avoided; but the High Command decided that the soldiers were receiving just a bare minimum for carrying on—which, at that time, was 350 grams of bread, and not much else.

"We tried to keep people going by making a sort of yeast soup, with a little soya added. It wasn't much better, really than drinking hot water, but it gave people the illusion of having 'eaten' something... A very large number of our people died. So many died, and transport was so difficult, that we decided to have our own graveyard right here... And yet, although people were dying of hunger, there was not a single serious incident... Frankly, I find it hard to this day to understand how people resisted the temptation of attacking bread vans or looting bakeries. But they didn't ... sometimes people came to me to say good-bye... They knew they were going to die almost at once. Later, in the summer of 1942, a lot of people who had survived the famine were sent east to supplement their comrades from Kiev, Kharkov and other places..."

By 1943, food was no longer a major problem in Leningrad; nevertheless, with the city under constant shellfire, and the German lines only two miles away, the Kirov Works continued to live through a hell that was only different in degree.

"How," I asked, "can you carry on at all when shellfire is heavy? Have you any casualties? And how do your people stand up to it?" "Well," he said, "there is, I suppose, a sort of Kirov Works patriotism. Except for one or two very sick people, I have never yet come across anybody who wanted to quit..."

He pulled out a drawer of his desk and brought out a pile of forty or fifty envelopes with postmarks. These were letters from Leningrad workers who had been evacuated, and who were begging to be allowed to return to Leningrad, alone or with their families.

"They know how difficult conditions here are," he said, "but they also know that they wouldn't be a food problem to us any longer. But we can't agree to their return. These skilled Kirov workers are doing a valuable job of work out there; here we haven't much equipment, and the place is run as a sort of emergency war factory. Not unlike Kolpino, some ten miles away from here, where munitions are turned out in underground foundries—right in the front line. . ."

"The way to keep the place going," he then said, "was by having it decentralised. We have divided up the work into small units, with only a corner of each workshop taken up with people and machinery; and this section, as far as possible is protected against blast and splinters. But misfortunes—or rather, a certain normal rate of casualties, will occur. This month—and it's been a relatively good month—we have had forty-three casualties—thirteen killed, twenty-three wounded and seven cases of shell-shock."

"You ask how they take it? Well, I don't know whether you've ever been for any length of time under shellfire. But if anybody tells you it's not frightening, don't you believe it. In our experience, a direct hit has a very bad effect for twenty-four or forty-eight hours. In a workshop that's had a direct hit, production slumps heavily during that time, or stops almost completely, especially if many people have been killed or injured. It's a horrible sight, all the blood, and makes even our hardened workers quite ill for a day or two. . . But after that, they go back to work, and try to make up for the time lost by what's called the 'accident'. But I realise all the same that working here is a perpetual strain, and when I see that a man or girl is going to pieces, I send him or her to a rest-home for a fortnight or a month. . ."

Later he took me round some of the workshops. It happened to be a quiet day, with almost no German shelling. The enormous plant was, I could now see, much more smashed up than the outside view from the street suggested. In a large space, with badly shattered buildings around, stood an enormous blockhouse. . . The concrete walls were twelve inches thick, and the roof was made of powerful steel girders. "Nothing but a direct hit from a large gun at close range can do anything to this," said Puzyrev. "It was built during the worst days when we thought the Germans might break through to Leningrad. They would have found the Kirov Works a tough proposition. The whole place is dotted with pillboxes like this one. . ."

Then we went into one of the foundries. One end of it was quite dark, but behind a strong brick partition the other half of it was lit up by flames inside the open furnaces, with their red-hot walls. Dark, eerie shadows of men, but again mostly of girls, were moving about in the red glow. The girls, with patched cotton stockings over their thin legs, were stooping under the weight of enormous clusters of red-hot steel they were clutching between a pair of tongs, and then you would see them—and as you saw it, you felt the desperate muscular concentration and will-power it involved—you would see them raise their slender, almost child-like arms and hurl these red-hot clusters under a giant steel hammer. Large red sparks of metal were flying and whizzing through the red semi-darkness, and the whole foundry shook with the deafening din and roar of machinery. We watched this scene for a while in silence; then Puzyrev said, almost apologetically, through the din: "This place isn't working quite right yet. We had a few shells in here the other day," and, pointing at a large hole in the floor now filled with sand and cement, "That's where one of them landed." "Any casualties?" "Yes, a few."

We walked through the foundry and watched more closely all that the girls were doing. As we were going out I caught a glimpse of a woman's face in the red glow of the flames. Her face was grimy. She looked an elderly woman, almost like an old gipsy hag. And from that grimy face shone two dark eyes. There was something tragic in those eyes—there was a great weariness in them, and a touch of animal terror. How old was she? Fifty, forty, or maybe only twenty-five? Had I just imagined that look of terror in her eyes? Was it that grimy face and the eerie shadows around leaping up and down that had given me that idea? I had seen some of the other girls' faces. They were normal enough. One, a young thing, even smiled. Normal —yes, except for a kind of inner concentration—as if they all had some bad memories they could not quite shake off. . .

*

Another striking memory is my visit to a secondary school in Tambov Street, in a modern and heavily shelled part of the city, three or four miles from the front. It was run by an elderly man, Tikhomirov, a "Teacher of Merit of the USSR", who had started as an elementary teacher back in 1907. This school was one of the few that had not closed down even at the height of the famine. On four occasions it had been heavily damaged by German shells; but the boys had cleared away the glass, bricked up the walls that had been smashed, and had put plywood in the windows. During the last shelling in May, a woman-teacher had been killed in the yard of the school.

The boys were typical Leningrad children; eighty-five per cent of the boys' fathers were still at the Leningrad Front, or had already been killed there, while many others had died in the Leningrad famine, and nearly all their mothers—if still alive—were working in Leningrad factories, or on transport, or on wood-cutting, or in civil defence. The boys all had a passionate hatred for the Germans, but were fully convinced by now that these *svolochi* (bastards) would be destroyed outside Leningrad before long. They had mixed feelings about Britain and America; they knew London had been bombed; that the RAF was "bombing the hell out of the Fritzes"; that the Americans were supplying the Red Army with a lot of lorries, and that they (the boys) were getting American chocolate to eat; but "there was still no Second Front".

The headmaster, Comrade Tikhomirov, told me how they had "stuck it, and stuck it fairly well. We had no wood, but the Leningrad Soviet gave us a small wooden house not far away for demolition, so we could use the timber for heating. The bombing and shelling was very severe in those days. We had about 120 pupils then—boys and girls—and we had to hold our classes in the shelter. Not for a day did the work stop. It was very cold. The little stoves heated the air properly only a yard around them, and in the rest of the shelter the temperature was below zero. There was no lighting, apart from a kerosene lamp. But we carried on, and the children were so serious and earnest that we got better results than in any other year. Surprising, but true. We had meals for them; the army helped us to feed them. Several of the teachers died, but I am proud to say that all the children in our care survived. Only it was pathetic to watch them during those famine months. Towards the end of 1941, they hardly looked like children any more. They were strangely silent... They would not walk about; they would just sit. But none of them died; and only some of those pupils who had stopped coming to school, and stayed at home, died, often together with the rest of the family..."

Tikhomirov then showed me an extraordinary document, which he called "our Famine Scrapbook", containing copies of many children's essays written during the famine, and much other material. It was bound in purple velvet, and the margins composed of rather conventional children's watercolours depicting soldiers, tanks, planes and the like; these surrounded little typewritten sheets—copies of typical essays written during the famine. One young girl wrote:

> Until June 22 everybody had work and a good life assured to him. That day we went on an excursion to the Kirov Islands. A fresh wind was blowing from the Gulf, bringing with it bits of the song some kids were singing not far away, "Great and glorious is my native land". And then the enemy began to come nearer and nearer our city. We went out to dig big trenches. It was difficult, because a lot of the kids were not used to such hard physical labour. The German General von Leeb was already licking his chops at the thought of the gala dinner he was going to get at the Astoria. Now we are sitting in the shelter round improvised stoves, with our coats and fur caps and gloves on. We have been knitting warm things for our soldiers, and have been taking round their letters to friends and relatives. We have also been collecting non-ferrous metal for salvage...

Valentina Solovyova, an older girl of sixteen, wrote:

> June 22! How much that date means to us now! But then it just seemed an ordinary summer day... Before long, the House Committee was swarming with women, girls and children, who had come to join the civil defence teams, the anti-fire and anti-gas squads... By September the city was encircled. Food supplies from outside had stopped. The last evacuee trains had departed. The people of Leningrad tightened their belts. The streets began to bristle with barricades and anti-tank hedgehogs. Dugouts and firing points—a whole network of them—were springing up around the city.
>
> As in 1919, so now, the great question arose: "Shall Leningrad

remain a Soviet city or not?" Leningrad was in danger. But its workers
had risen like one man for its defence. Tanks were thundering down
the streets. Everywhere men of the civil guard were joining up... A
cold and terrible winter was approaching. Together with their bombs,
enemy planes were dropping leaflets. They said they would raze Leningrad to the ground. They said we would all die of hunger. They
thought they would frighten us, but they filled us with renewed
strength... Leningrad did not let the enemy through its gates! The city
was starving, but it lived and worked, and kept on sending to the front
more of its sons and daughters. Though knocking at the knees with
hunger, our workers went to work in their factories, with the air-raid
sirens filling the air with their screams...

This from another essay on how the school-children dug trenches
while the Germans were approaching Leningrad:

In August we worked for twenty-five days digging trenches. We
were machine-gunned and some of us were killed, but we carried on,
though we weren't used to this work. And the Germans were stopped
by the trenches we had dug...

Another girl of sixteen, Luba Tereshchenkova, described how
work continued at the school even during the worst time of the
blockade:

In January and February terrible frost also joined in the blockade
and lent Hitler a hand. It was never less than thirty degrees of frost!
Our classes continued on the "Round the Stove" principle. But there
were no reserved seats, and if you wanted a seat near the stove or
under the stove pipe, you had to come early. The place facing the
stove door was reserved for the teacher. You sat down and were
suddenly seized by a wonderful feeling of well-being: the warmth
penetrated through your skin, right into your bones; it made you all
weak and languid; you just wanted to think of nothing, only to slumber
and drink in the warmth. It was agony to stand up and go to the
blackboard... At the blackboard it was so cold and dark, and your
hand, imprisoned in its heavy glove, went all numb and rigid and
refused to obey. The chalk kept falling out of your hand, and the lines
were all crooked... By the time we reached the third lesson there was
no more fuel left. The stove went cold and a horrid icy draught started
blowing down the pipe. It became terribly cold. It was then that
Vasya Pugin, with a puckish look on his face, could be seen slinking
out and bringing in a few logs from Anna Ivanovna's emergency
reserve; and a few minutes later, we could again hear the magic

crackling of wood inside the stove. . . During the break nobody would jump up because nobody had any desire to go into the icy corridors.

And this from another essay:

The winter came, fierce and merciless. The water pipes froze, and there was no electric light, and the tram-cars stopped running. To get to school in time, I had to get up very early every morning, for I live out in the suburbs. It was particularly difficult to get to school after a blizzard, when all roads and paths are covered with snowdrifts. But I firmly decided to complete my school year. . . One day, after standing in a bread queue for six hours (I had to miss school that day, for I had received no bread for two days) I caught a cold and fell ill. Never had I felt so miserable as during those days. Not for physical reasons, but because I needed the moral support of my school-mates, their encouraging jokes. . .*

None of the children who continued to go to school died, but several of the teachers did. The last section of the Famine Scrapbook, introduced by a title page with a decorative funeral urn painted in purple watercolour, was written by Tikhomirov, the headmaster. It was a series of obituary notes of the teachers who were either killed in the war or had died of hunger. The assistant headmaster was "killed in action". Another was "killed at Kingisepp", in that terrible battle of Kingisepp where the Germans broke through towards Leningrad from Estonia. The maths teacher "died of hunger"; so did the teacher of geography. Comrade Nemirov, the teacher of literature, "was among the victims of the blockade", and Akimov, the history teacher, died of malnutrition and exhaustion despite a long rest in a sanatorium to which he was taken in January. Of another teacher Tikhomirov wrote: "He worked conscientiously until he realised he could no longer walk. He asked me for a few days' leave in the hope that his strength would return to him. He stayed at home, preparing his lessons for the second term. He went on reading books. So he spent the day of January 8. On January 9 he quietly passed away." What a human story was behind these simple words!

*

* Curious that in all these ultra-patriotic essays there was not a single mention of Stalin.

I have described conditions in Leningrad as I found them in September 1943, when the city was still under frequent and often intense shell-fire. This shelling continued for the rest of the year, and it was not till January 1944 that the ordeal of Leningrad finally ended. During the previous weeks a large Russian armed force was transferred under cover of night to the "Oranienbaum bridgehead" on the south bank of the Gulf of Finland; and this force, under the command of General Fedyuninsky, struck out towards Ropsha, where it was to meet the troops of the Leningrad Front striking towards the south-west. During that first day of the Russian breakthrough no fewer than 500,000 shells were used to smash the German fortifications. About the same time, the Volkhov army group also came into motion, and, within a few days, the Germans were on the run, all the way to Pskov and Estonia. On January 27, 1944 the blockade officially ended.

All the famous historical palaces around Leningrad—Pavlovsk, Tsarskoie-Selo, Peterhof—were in ruins.

Chapter VIII

WHY LENINGRAD "TOOK IT"

Why *did* Leningrad "take it"? A glib, easy and, on the face of it, quite justified argument is that, with all road and rail communications cut, the people of Leningrad had no alternative to sticking it out, and had to be "heroic", whether they wanted to or not. Had they had time to get out, it is also argued, they would have been on the run, just as the people of Moscow were on the run on October 16, 1941. But that is not really the point. What is remarkable, once the city was surrounded, was not the fact that the people "took it", but *the way* they took it.

In his interesting study, *The Siege of Leningrad*, Mr Leon Goure suggests that a number of people in the city were in favour of surrendering it to the Germans and that, though not a majority, "the number of disaffected persons ... appears to have been far from negligible".* When I was in Leningrad I heard quite a few references to a German "fifth column" inside the city, and this is also mentioned in recent Soviet studies. But the evidence that more than a tiny minority wanted to surrender is very slender.

Mr Goure himself recognises that "patriotism, local pride, growing resentment of the Germans and reluctance to betray the soldiers" had much to do with the "maintaining of discipline". At the same time he places, in my view, undue emphasis on "an ingrained habit

* Leon Goure, *The Siege of Leningrad* (Stanford, 1962), p. 304.

355

of obedience to the authorities", "no prior experience of political freedom", the "Stalinist terror", and so on, and relies too much on the evidence of certain post-war refugees.*

There is much stronger evidence to show that the "Leningrad can take it" spirit was there from the very start. There was no one, except a few anti-communists, who even considered surrender to the Germans. At the height of the famine, a few people—who were not necessarily collaborators or enemy agents (as Soviet accounts assert), but merely people driven half-insane with hunger—did write to the authorities asking that Leningrad be declared an "open city"; but no-one in his right mind could have done so. During the German advance on the city, people soon learned what the enemy were like; how many young people had died through enemy bombing and machine-gunning while digging those trenches? And once the blockade was complete the air-raids began, together with the sadistic leaflets like that dropped on Leningrad on November 6, to "celebrate" Revolution Day: "Today we shall do the bombing, tomorrow you shall do the burying".

The question of declaring Leningrad an open city could never arise, as it did, for example, in Paris in 1940; this was a war of extermination, and the Germans never made a secret of it. Secondly, the local pride of Leningrad had a quality of its own—it was composed of a great love of the city itself, of its historical past, its extraordinary literary associations (this was particularly true of the *intelligentsia*) and also of a great proletarian and revolutionary tradition amongst its working-class; nothing could have so blended these two great loves for Leningrad into one thing as the threat of the annihilation of the city. Perhaps even quite consciously, there was also the old competition with Moscow: if Moscow were to fall in October 1941, Leningrad at least would hold out longer, come what may; and, once Moscow had been saved, it was a point of

* Ibid., pp. 304–6. Mr Harrison Salisbury, in *The New York Times* of May 10, 1962, takes the book to task on that score, recalling Hitler's directives to "erase St Petersburg from the face of the earth", adding that "we are not interested in preserving even a part of the population of this large city"—directives on the substance of which nobody in Leningrad could have had any serious doubts.

honour for Leningrad to do as well, and even better. Some of the most bitter anti-Stalinists like Olga Bergholz, were also the most fanatical Leningrad patriots. But sentiment, however praiseworthy, was not enough. No doubt, the army's record, right up to the moment when it retreated to the outskirts of Leningrad, had been disappointing; and the Leningrad authorities had, obviously, done a great deal of bungling too during those first two and a half months of the German invasion. The whole problem of evacuation, especially of children, had been grossly mishandled, and little or nothing had been done to lay in food reserves. But once the Germans had been stopped outside Leningrad, and once the decision had been taken to fight for every house and every street, the faults of the army and the civilian authorities were readily forgotten; for now it was a case of defending Leningrad at any price. It was only natural that very rigid discipline and organisation were necessary inside the besieged city; but this had little to do with "an ingrained habit of obedience to the authorities", or, still less, with "the Stalinist terror". Obviously, food had to be severely rationed; but to say that people in Leningrad worked and did not "rebel" (for what purpose?) in order to have a ration card—which, to many, did not even mean "the difference between life and death"—is to misunderstand the spirit of Leningrad completely. And there is little doubt that the Party organisation, after many initial blunders, played a very important role in keeping Leningrad going: first, by making rationing as fair as was humanly possible in incredibly difficult conditions; second, in organising civil defence inside the city on a vast scale; third, in mobilising people for cutting timber, peat, etc.; fourth, by organising the various "roads of life". And there is also no doubt that, in the midst of the most appalling hardships of the winter of 1941–2, organisations like the Komsomol showed the greatest self-sacrifice and endurance in helping people.

There can really be no comparison with London; the blitz was terrible enough, though it was not comparable to what German cities got a few years later. The bombing of London was really worse than the bombing or shelling of Leningrad, at least in terms of casualties. But only if one imagined that everybody in London was starving during the blitz winter, and ten or twenty thousand people were dying of hunger in London every day, would it be possible to put an equation mark between the two. In Leningrad the choice lay between dishonourably dying in German captivity or honourably dying (or, with luck, surviving) in one's own unconquered city. Any attempt to differentiate between Russian patriotism, or revolutionary ardour, or Soviet organisation, or to ask which of the three was the more important in saving Leningrad is also singularly futile: all three were blended in an extraordinarily "Leningrad" way.

Local "Leningrad" patriotism gave a special flavour to all three. In Leningrad in 1943 I could observe this on every occasion; to the people of Leningrad, their city, with all that it had done and endured, was something unique. They spoke with some contempt of the "Moscow skedaddle" of 1941 and many, among them that very remarkable man, P. S. Popkov, head of the Leningrad Soviet, felt that, after what it had done, Leningrad deserved some special distinction. One idea, very current at the time, was that Leningrad should become the capital of the RSFSR, i.e. of Russia proper, whereas Moscow would remain the capital of the USSR.

This Leningrad particularism was not at all to Stalin's liking. He must have known that there were much fewer pictures of him there than in any other city in the Soviet Union, and that Leningrad tended to look upon itself as being something rather distinct, both militarily and politically, from the "mainland". It was suspected in Moscow that Zhdanov (who had been a great chief in the days of the siege—quite regardless of all his previous "purge" activities and his subsequent vandalism in the cultural field) had become something of a Leningrad particularist himself, though he was not born there. There is little doubt that, especially after Zhdanov's death in 1948, Stalin decided to stamp out Leningrad's particularism. A remarkable museum, called *The Defence of Leningrad*, had been organised during and after the siege; this was a striking collection of documents and exhibits of every kind, illustrating the gigantic "mass effort" made by the Leningrad people, and their civilian and military leaders. This museum was closed in 1949. As Pavlov wrote in 1961:

This was totally unjustified, and most regrettable. Immensely valuable data were concentrated in this museum reflecting the heroic struggle of the besieged, the conditions in which Leningraders lived during the fearful time of the Blockade; the defence measures taken against the air-raids and artillery bombardments; the exhibits demonstrated the high degree of organisation in producing armaments and in building defences, in dealing with delayed-action bombs, and so on. The museum was a remarkable tribute to the inventiveness, stubbornness and courage of ordinary people. But this museum was organised in the days of the "personality cult" when the heroic deeds of so many Leningraders tended to be attributed to single personalities.

In 1957 (Pavlov goes on to say) a museum of the History of Leningrad was opened; but this, he says, "contains only a few rooms of exhibits relating to the war period; this 'museum', quite different from that assembled during the war, is utterly inadequate."

Not only was the museum of the Defence of Leningrad destroyed in 1949, but there was also the—still somewhat mysterious— "Leningrad Affair", in which Kuznetsov, Popkov and many other leaders of the defence of Leningrad lost their lives. Was the Leningrad Party organisation too "particularist", not sufficiently Stalinist? There have been no more than some vague references to it in Mr Khrushchev's speeches, with the suggestion that Malenkov played a particularly sinister role in this purge. It has also been suggested that both Stalin and Malenkov (who was an enemy of Zhdanov's) waited till Zhdanov was dead until they settled their scores with the Leningrad organisation, which had never been particularly loud in its praise of Stalin, least of all during the War and the Blockade.

Chapter IX

A NOTE ON FINLAND

One thing was very striking during the Leningrad Blockade; *the* enemy was Germany, and Finland was scarcely even mentioned. Yet the Finns were also at war with the Soviet Union, were taking part in the blockade of Leningrad, and their troops were within some twenty miles north and north-west of the city. Further east, they had penetrated deep into Soviet territory, and were holding a line along the Svir river, between Lake Ladoga and Lake Onega. The large Soviet city of Petrozavodsk, capital of the Karelo-Finnish SSR, was under Finnish occupation.

The position of the Finns in their war against the Soviet Union between 1941 and 1944 was, however, very unusual. They had many bonds with the Germans, but their war against Russia was still a "separate" war, and they were certainly less subservient to the Germans than were, for instance, the Hungarians and Rumanians. After the war they were to claim that they had not allowed German troops to operate against Leningrad from Finnish soil and that they had not taken part in the bombing or shelling of Leningrad.

There had, of course, been negotiations between Germany and Finland long before June 22, 1941 on joint operations against Russia. There is also no doubt that the Finns did, at one moment, push beyond the old frontier, since they captured the Russian frontier town of Beloostrov only twenty miles north-west of Leningrad; here, however, the Russians counter-attacked, and the Finns were thrown out on the very next day, after which this part of the front was stabilised.

The Germans were not satisfied with this, and on September 4, Jodl came specially to see Mannerheim and urged him to continue the Finnish offensive beyond the old border—i.e. against Leningrad. Mannerheim appears to have refused. At the trial of the pro-German Ryti after the war, the former head of the Finnish Government even argued that the Finns had really "saved" Leningrad:

> On August 24, 1941, I visited Marshal Mannerheim's headquarters. The Germans had been pressing us to advance on Leningrad, after crossing the old frontier. I said that the conquest of Leningrad was not our object, and that we should not take part in it. Mannerheim and War Minister Walden agreed with me, and rejected the German proposal. As a result, there arose the paradoxical situation in which the Germans were unable to advance on Leningrad from the north; in this way, the Finns defended Leningrad from the north.*

For all that, the Finns did take part in the encirclement of Leningrad; also, according to the German historian Walter Görlitz, the Finns *would* have attacked Leningrad had there been a final German onslaught on the city from the south; but this never took place.† They occupied considerable stretches of Soviet territory which had never belonged to them, notably east of Lake Ladoga. But although, as is evident from the Soviet armistice conditions presented to the Finns in 1944, there were some German troops stationed in Finland, there appears to be no evidence that they were ever used against Leningrad from Finnish territory. Whether Leningrad was ever shelled or bombed from Finnish territory is perhaps more doubtful; in 1943 I was shown one or two shell-holes on the *north* side of buildings in Leningrad, which suggested that some shells had been fired from Finnish territory. But even if these one or two shell-holes were genuine, there was certainly no regular shelling of Leningrad from the north. Notices in the streets of Leningrad declaring the southern "sheltered" side of the streets much safer than the north side, clearly

* See C. Leonard Lundin, *Finland in the Second World War* (New York, 1957).
† Walter Görlitz, *Paulus and Stalingrad* (London, 1963), p. 128.

implied that the shelling was all assumed to come from the south, i.e. from the Germans.

It is certain that any major offensive from the Finnish side during the most critical months of the Leningrad blockade, and heavy shelling from the north would have greatly added to Leningrad's troubles. That the Finns did not attack at that critical time was due to a number of factors: a certain distaste of many Finns at being allied to Hitler, who had ruthlessly invaded Denmark and Norway; the fact that Britain and, later, the United States, were allied with the Soviet Union; and a perhaps genuine reluctance on Mannerheim's part to take part in the conquest and destruction of Leningrad.

This does not mean that the Finnish *bourgeoisie* was not violently anti-Russian, as it had been ever since 1918, and even more since the Winter War of 1939-40. But grandiose ideas of a "Great Finland" stretching, according to some of the more absurd blueprints, as far as Moscow ("an old Finnish city, as its very name indicates") seem to have been limited to the lunatic fringe. Nevertheless, there were at least a small number of select Finnish troops which took part in the German operations against Russia proper, and, according to numerous testimonies I heard both during and after the war, particularly in the Smolensk and Tula areas, many of these Finnish soldiers behaved particularly brutally to the Russian civilian population—especially to girls and women—"worse even than the Germans".

As far as the military and political leadership of Leningrad were concerned, there seems, however, little doubt that they were conscious of a certain negative value of the role played by the Finns in the tragedy of Leningrad. When, after the Soviet-Finnish armistice, Zhdanov travelled to Helsinki, he had long and pointedly courteous conversations with Mannerheim and, as we know, the armistice terms finally agreed to, leaving nearly the whole of Finland unoccupied by Soviet troops, were much milder than might have been expected. With an eye on future relations with the Scandinavian countries, and no doubt remembering the fiasco of Kuusinen's "Terijoki Government" of 1939-40, the Russians made no attempt, either then or later, to turn Finland into a People's Democracy.

PART FOUR

The Black Summer of 1942

Chapter I

CLOSE-UP: MOSCOW IN JUNE 1942

I returned to England in November 1941, and did not go back to Russia again until May 1942—this time for the duration—sailing for twenty-eight days from Middlesbrough to Murmansk on the Liberty ship, the *Empire Baffin*, which formed part of the famous PQ-16 convoy. Soon after leaving Iceland, the convoy was subjected to six days' dive-bombing by the Germans, from their bases in Northern Norway. As we know from Churchill's letters to Stalin, the Admiralty expected half this convoy to be wiped out; but owing, apparently, to some faulty organisation on the Germans' part, only eight ships were sunk, out of a total of thirty-five. The Germans were to make up for it a month later with the next convoy, the PQ-17, threequarters of whose ships were destroyed.

In *The Year of Stalingrad* I described this extraordinary voyage of the PQ-16, the marvellous spirit shown by both the British and the Russian seamen who took part in it; the miserably poor protection given it by a couple of submarines and a few destroyers and corvettes—the two escorting cruisers having left it after the first German air-raid. About 160 men lost their lives in that convoy, and many others were wounded, and were, in the end, taken to the terribly crowded and under-equipped hospital at Murmansk.

At the end of May 1942 there were about 3,000 British "survivors" at Murmansk—many of them from the cruiser *Edinburgh*, which had been sunk shortly before. Despite frequent German air-raids, especially when a convoy landed there from the west,

365

Murmansk was still more or less intact at the time; and it was not until a month later that most of it was destroyed in a great fire-blitz. In the same book I described not only Murmansk in May 1942, but also my remarkable six-days' journey in a "hard"—i.e. third-class—carriage from Murmansk to Moscow during the first week of June. With the sun shining for nearly twenty-four hours in that part of Russia far beyond the Arctic Circle, summer had come in a rush within a few days, and the far north, with its millions of flowers, was extraordinarily beautiful. Of wonderful beauty too, in the midnight twilight, were Lake Imandra, in the mountainous country of Soviet Lapland through which we travelled a day after leaving Murmansk, and then the immense forests south of the White Sea and all along the Archangel-Vologda railway line, which we reached on the third day. Often the train would stop, and people would jump out to pick flowers and cranberries—which had been preserved by the snow through the winter.

The carriage was crowded with soldiers and civilians, and they presented a remarkable cross-section of Russian humanity. In *The Year of Stalingrad* I recorded dozens of conversations with soldiers, officers, railwaymen and all kinds of civilians, among them an eleven-year-old girl called Tamara, an evacuee from Leningrad, who had spent the winter in a small town on the White Sea and was now being taken by her mother to a *kolkhoz*, where her grandmother lived, in the more clement province of Riazan, south-east of Moscow.

All these people had something significant to say. Tamara had gone to school during her winter on the White Sea; she had with her several school books with pictures of Stalin and Voroshilov, as well as a game of snakes-and-ladders. She said she had had enough to eat at the school canteen, thought that "Hitler would have to be killed before things got better", but kept the carriage amused, all the same, by often singing in a shrill voice an optimistic ditty she had learned at school:

> Hitler sam sebé ne rad,
> Vziát' ne mózhet Leningrád,
> Vídit Névsky i sadý,
> I ni tudý, i ni sudý

Na Moskvú pustílsya vor,
Dáli tam yemú otpór,
Propádayut vse trudý,
I ni tudý, i ni sudý

(Hitler is cursing his luck, he can't take Leningrad; he can see the Nevsky and the gardens, but he's got stuck. Then the thief tried Moscow, but here, too, he got thrown back; all his efforts are in vain; he's stuck, he is stuck again).

Although enormous areas of Russia were still under German occupation, the fact that neither Moscow nor Leningrad had been lost gave people a certain amount of self-confidence; nevertheless, morale among them varied a great deal—partly depending on the amount of food they had had to eat. Civilians were badly underfed, and many suffered from scurvy; old women especially were tearful and pessimistic, and thought the Germans were terribly strong, and God only knew what might yet be in store for Russia during the coming summer. Railwaymen, though much better fed than most other civilians, were in a grim mood—all the more so as they had had an extremely hard winter on this Murmansk railway which had been continuously bombed by the Germans. Practically all the railway stations had been destroyed by bombing, and, off the line, there was also much wreckage of carriages and engines.

Morale among soldiers and officers was rather better: some of them spoke highly of the British Hurricanes that were operating at Murmansk; others talked about the "tremendous" casualties they had inflicted on the Germans and Finns on the Murmansk Front with their "miraculous" *katyusha* mortars. Many of the officers came from the Caucasus and the Ukraine; all spoke nostalgically of their homes and families there, but opinion seemed to be sharply divided between the optimists and pessimists: some thought the Germans might well overrun the rest of the Ukraine and the Caucasus, others that they hadn't a chance. All the same, they were far from under-rating the power of the Germans, and in their game of dominoes, they called the double-six "Hitler"—"because it's the most frightening of them all". The double-five was called "Goebbels".

In that part of Russia, Leningrad was an obsession with many of the people; they had seen thousands of Leningrad evacuees, many of them half-dead, and had heard the real and unvarnished truth about the dreadful famine winter there; many had friends and relatives in Leningrad, among them my friend Tamara, whose step-father was a Leningrad railwayman.

Civilians were extremely short of food, though the soldiers were well-supplied, and at railway stations it was only the soldiers who did a lot of trading with the peasants, bartering a small piece of soap or an ounce of tobacco for a dozen eggs or even half a chicken. The civilians had nothing to trade, and money was as good as useless; the peasants weren't interested. The civilians spoke with some bitterness of the "shameless profiteering" of which both the peasants and the soldiers were guilty.

The attitude to the Allies was extremely mixed. Many of these people had been travelling all the way from Murmansk, where they had seen ships bringing tanks and munitions and sacks of Canadian flour, but, on the whole, they tended to think that all this was small stuff. An old elementary school-teacher, suffering from scurvy, and now on his way to join his family in a fishing-village on the White Sea where he hoped to get more "wholesome food", talked to me a lot about England, saying that Churchill was, of course, an old enemy of the Soviet Union, and the Russians should, therefore be grateful that he at least wasn't on the side of the Germans; but he doubted whether there would be a Second Front for a very long time, at least so long as Churchill was in charge.

There was a moment of real excitement in the carriage when somebody brought in the news of a British 1,000-bomber raid on Cologne; suddenly England seemed to have become wonderfully popular. But the next day the mood was much less cheerful; it had been learned from somewhere that the Russians had just lost 5,000 men in the Battle of Kharkov, and that "70,000 were missing". This struck everybody as extremely disturbing and ominous, and the soldiers from the Ukraine and the Caucasus seemed particularly alarmed.

At last, on the fifth day, the train reached the great railway junction of Vologda. There were hundreds of evacuees at the station —mostly women and children—who had waited literally for days for their train, sleeping on railway platforms or in waiting-rooms, and with very little to eat, beyond the daily half-pound of bread which was distributed regularly—even though little else was.

Here I also saw several trains with hundreds of emaciated evacuees from Leningrad, and also a number of hospital trains, with hundreds of wounded from the Leningrad and Volkhov Fronts where there was heavy fighting again.

Having missed our connection at Vologda, we were stuck there for a whole day, and it was not till nearly a week after leaving Murmansk that I finally reached Moscow. During the last lap of the journey, the carriage was even more crowded than before; many soldiers had squeezed in at Vologda. I particularly remember one giant of a soldier, looking like Chaliapin in his youth, who devoured a pound of bread and six hard-boiled eggs all at one go. "You've got a pretty good appetite," I remarked. "I should say so," he replied. "I've got to make up for all last winter. *You'd* stuff yourself if you'd been there." He turned out to be one of the soldiers who had fought at Leningrad right through the winter.

One thing struck me at the time as very curious: throughout that week in the train from Murmansk to Moscow, nobody had mentioned the name of Stalin. Was his leadership being taken for granted, or were there some silent doubts about the great quality of his leadership? Was it not because the people of the north were more closely concerned with the Leningrad tragedy than with Moscow, and that it was in Moscow, which had been saved in the previous autumn "under Stalin's leadership", that his prestige was highest of all? Stalin was *in* Moscow. He belonged to Moscow, as it were, and had come to symbolise in popular imagination the capital's spirit of resistance.

In June 1942 Moscow was still very near the front line. The Germans were firmly entrenched at Rzhev, Viazma and Gzhatsk, rather less than eighty miles away. Nobody could be quite sure that the Germans would not attempt another all-out attack on the city. The last bombs had been dropped on Moscow in March, and although the anti-aircraft defences were said to be much better than in the summer of 1941, there was no certainty that air-raids would not begin again.

Moscow had a lean and hungry look. It had lived through a hard and, to many people, terrible winter. It was nothing compared with what Leningrad had suffered, but many individual stories were grim—stories of under-nourishment, of unheated houses, with temperatures just above or even below freezing point, with water-pipes burst, and lavatories out of action; and in these houses one slept smothered—if one had them—under two overcoats and three or more blankets. In June bread still sold in the open market at 150 roubles a kilo (thirty shillings a pound). There was almost no cabbage or other vegetables, and although the bread ration varied from 28 oz. to 14 oz. a day, the rations of other foodstuffs were often honoured in a most irregular way, or not at all.* What reserves of potatoes and vegetables there had been in the Moscow province had either been looted by the Germans or taken over by the Army. Sugar, fats, milk and tobacco were all very scarce. There was a peculiar form of profiteering which had developed in Moscow during the spring, when the owner of a cigarette would charge any willing passers-by two roubles† for a puff—and there were plenty of buyers.

People in the Moscow streets looked haggard and pale, and scurvy was fairly common. Consumer goods were almost unobtainable, except at fantastic prices, or for coupons, if and when these were honoured. In the big Mostorg department store strange odds and ends were being sold, such as barometers and curling-tongs, but

---

* In the case of "heavy" workers (railwaymen, for instance) the rations were as follows:

Bread	1½ lb. daily	Sugar	¾ oz. daily
Cereals	4 oz. „	Tobacco	½ oz. „
Meat	3½ oz. „	Tea	1 oz. a month
Fats	¾ oz. „	Fish	2½ oz. daily

Vegetables (cabbage or potatoes) ½ lb. to 1 lb. daily.
In most cases these rations were not fully honoured; in factories most of the food was handed over to the canteen. Rations for the three other categories were, of course, much lower.
† Nominally about a shilling.

nothing useful. In the shopping streets like the Kuznetsky Most, or Gorki Street, the shop windows were mostly sand-bagged and where they were not, they often displayed cruel cardboard hams, cheeses and sausages, all covered with dust.

There were other deplorable shortages. In dental clinics—with the exception of a few privileged ones—teeth were pulled without an anaesthetic. The chemists' shops were about as empty as the rest.

A large part of the Moscow province had been devastated; many villages had been burned down, and in towns like Kalinin, Klin or Volokolamsk life was slowly rising from the wreckage and rubble.

Moscow itself was very empty, with nearly half its population still away. Only half a dozen theatres were open in June, among them the *Filiale* of the Bolshoi, and tickets were easy to obtain. In the buffet, all they sold, for a few coppers, was—glasses of plain water. The Bolshoi itself had been hit by a ton bomb, and was out of action. There was a good deal of other bomb damage here and there, and the sky was dotted with barrage balloons.

The panic exodus of October 16 had remained a grim and, to many, a shameful memory. Hundreds of thousands who had left then had not yet returned. Many government offices were still in the east—at Kazan, Ulianovsk, Saratov, Kuibyshev and other places; the University and the Academy of Sciences had been moved east; many factories had also evacuated much of their equipment and many of their workers, and were working on skeleton staffs, if at all. On the other hand, those who had stayed on in Moscow during the two "danger months"—from October to December—now recalled with some pride of how they had stuck it through. Those had been heroic weeks, and there had been something great and inspiring in the very air of Moscow during that time, with barricades and anti-tank obstacles in the main streets, especially on the outskirts; the timid had gone, but the Kremlin had not budged. Stalin had remained in Moscow and, with him, the generals, and most of the Politburo. The Commissariat of Defence had not budged, nor had the Moscow Town Council, with Pronin at its head. Sure enough, there had been that panic on October 16, but the announcement on the following day that Stalin was in Moscow had had a great moral

effect on both the population, and on the soldiers fighting their
deadly battle on the outskirts of the capital.

But by February it was clear that the German rout had not been
complete. The Germans were still holding a mighty springboard at
Gzhatsk, Viazma and Rzhev, and this required a large concentration
of Russian troops to protect Moscow. Smolensk, which the Russians
had hoped to recapture, still remained far in the enemy rear. There
was a note of disappointment in Stalin's Red Army Day Order of
February 23.

And, in June 1942, there were many persistent rumours that
something had already seriously gone wrong at Kharkov, and that
the Germans were preparing for an all-out offensive in the south.

I had many opportunities, during the early summer months of 1942,
of seeing something of the devastation the Germans had caused
around Moscow. On the road to Klin, for instance, there was a great
deal of destruction, barely fifteen or twenty miles north-west of the
capital—bombed, burned and shelled houses, and a church with
half its dome blown away by a shell. This church was at Loshki,
twenty-eight miles from Moscow, and the town had been occupied
by the Germans in November 1941. At Istra, three houses had
survived out of 1,000, and, instead of 16,000 people there were now
only 300, most of them living in dugouts. At Klin over 1,000 houses
had been destroyed out of 12,000; this, according to later German
standards of destruction, could be called almost generous. It was
only because they had had to pull out in a hurry. Under their three
weeks' occupation, only 1,500 people had remained in the town,
out of 30,000; now 15,000 were back. Even if most of the town was
standing, the Germans had still done an enormous amount of looting; and the *kolkhozes* in the neighbourhood had suffered great
losses. Before the Germans came, 3,000 cows belonging to the
kolkhozes had been evacuated; but of the 4,500 cows belonging to
the peasants themselves, 3,000 had been driven away by the Germans. All this had seriously affected Moscow's food supplies. Soviet
propaganda at the time made much of the "destruction" and
"desecration" of Tchaikovsky's house at Klin, and of Tolstoy's

house at Yasnaya Polyana, near Tula, but the houses themselves were still standing, though much had been stolen from them or damaged. The Germans had, moreover, buried a lot of their dead right round Tolstoy's solitary grave in the park, and this, no doubt, was a form of "desecration". The Russians, after recapturing Yasnaya Polyana, threw all the German bodies out.

The large Tolstoy Centenary School, built near Yasnaya Polyana in 1928, had been burned down by the Germans, and here, as in so many other places they had committed various atrocities. I shall mention here just a couple of examples of what I saw and heard during those months.

Near the Tolstoy School, I went into one of the cottages of the village. Here I saw a young woman with a sad face. Her husband had been hanged right here, in the village. The Germans had suspected him of having punctured one of their tyres. They had hanged him along with another man, whom nobody in the village knew. On a bed, in the dark corner of the room, a child was sleeping. The woman told how she had gone away to another village to see her sister a few days before. And she then told the wild tormented story of her home-coming that day, when she had heard the news. Twice the Germans had stopped her on the way and had ordered her to peel potatoes. As she spoke, the child woke up, and as we sat there in the dark hut, her story was interrupted by the small girl's pranks and laughter.

Then the hanged man's mother arrived. She was a stronger character than the wife; she had seen it all happen, and she told her story firmly and coherently. She told how the Russian troops retreated, and then how the German tanks came into the village. And, soon after, there was a knock on the door of the hut, and a German with a torch said: "Six men will live here."

"They came and lived here," she said. "They were rough and coarse, but the Finns—for two of them were Finns and four were Germans—were even worse. The moment they took him away, one of the Finns, with a leer, told me they were going to hang him. I pushed him aside, trying to run after my son, but he knocked me down and pushed me into that small store-room and locked the door. Later a German came, and unlocked the door and said: 'Your Kolya's kaputt.' He and the other man remained hanging there for three days, and I could not go near them, but I could see them from this window swaying in the wind. Only three days later did the Commandant allow the bodies to be taken down. They were brought into this room, and laid down, right here. I untied their stiff creaking arms, and, as they began to thaw, I wiped the sweat and dirt off their poor faces. And so we buried them.''

Sitting there in the dark hut, with only a small oil lamp burning under the ikon (with Stalin's picture torn out of some magazine beside it), the old woman now wept softly. She said she had four other sons, all at the front, and said that one of them "wasn't writing any more". And in the dark corner of the hut the younger woman wept, and kissed and slapped, and then again kissed the hanged man's unruly laughing child.

I remember another journey later in the summer—this time to the Rzhev sector of the front, where there had been some very heavy fighting for weeks. Again we passed through Istra with its forest of chimney-stacks (that was all that was left of the town) and the ruins of the New Jerusalem monastery which the Germans had blown up; then we drove through Volokolamsk, where there was much less destruction, but where the Germans had hanged numerous "partisans". And then we stopped at Lotoshino. A number of people came up to our cars. There was a little man there, wearing a tattered cap and jacket, and with a bunch of spring onions under his arm. He had been here right through the German occupation. The first day the Germans came, he said, they hanged eight people in the main street, among them a hospital nurse and a teacher. The teacher's body was left hanging there for eight days. They had called for the people to attend the execution, but few went. The teacher was a Party member. The Germans had stayed in the town for three months, till January 2; a fortnight before, they had begun to burn down the town. The last houses weren't burned down till the eve of their departure. They appointed *starostas* (village mayors) from among the local inhabitants; later, when the Russians caught these *starostas*, they shot them.

As we stood there talking, a crowd of village kids gathered. They were mostly a bunch of ragamuffins in tattered clothes, and though many of them looked underfed, they were full of fun as they talked about the Germans. One or two even saw a humorous side to the teacher being strung up...

One boy, with a jolly laugh, told how he once set fire to a German store. "Then I ran away and hid on top of the stove, and was very scared; but one of the Germans came along and dragged me down, and kicked me in the arse, but nothing more happened. I suppose they forgave me. '*Kleiner Partisan*' they would call me, and give me another kick in the arse, and when winter came, they kept on screaming for fires and saying, '*Kalt, kalt, kalt!*' Or they'd keep on shouting '*Scheisse*' which means... I said I knew. "Actually," said the boy, "what saved us was the distillery. It kept them in good humour. They'd fill themselves up with vodka from the distillery storehouse, and then they'd sing German songs—don't know what the hell they sang; it sounded kind of mournful on winter nights—like dogs howling... And, of course, they fed their faces; they devoured everything—chicken and geese and pigs and ducks. They would chase the ducks and geese and beat them to death with sticks. And then they burned down the town. I avoided them the last days; they were in such a foul temper. And now," he went on, "people live here in dugouts (for all the houses have been burned down), or on the *kolkhoz* not far away. Tomorrow—on September 1—the school will open, but it's not our school, but another one, five kilometres away; our old school (he pointed at a patched-up building) was burned down, but has now been patched up as a hospital."

Three points emerge very clearly and indisputably from these (and many similar) accounts: firstly, that the public executions of communists and other "suspects"—usually branded "partisans"—were a common practice in towns and villages occupied by the Germans. Since these executions frequently took place "on the first day" of the occupation, they were apparently the work not of any special detachments under Himmler, but of members of the Army itself. It seems also true that the "communists" must have been picked as a result of denunciations either by willing collaborators, or by people frightened into doing so.* Secondly, that, already in 1941, the Germans were practising a scorched-earth policy, with incendiary teams burning down whole towns and villages before retreating—if they had the time to do so. Thirdly, that the Germans appointed Russian burgomasters in the towns and *starostas* in the villages—people picked from what they considered "reliable" elements, ex-bourgeois, or ex-kulaks. How many of these were willing collaborators, and how many had simply been bullied into accepting such jobs, and whether they deserved to be shot once the Russians returned (or even whether they actually *were* always shot) are questions on which very little light is thrown by either Russian or German authors. It is certain however, that many such Russian "collaborators" were playing a double game, and that some Soviet "underground" members were actually encouraged to join the German-appointed local-government agencies. As in all other Resistance movements, so in Russia, the Resistance had its "own" men and women "colonising" such German-appointed bodies, picking up information, and maintaining contact with partisans or other pro-Soviet elements.

* That executions were carried out by the Army is persistently denied by German generals, but, according to the Russian eyewitnesses I saw in 1942, it was "ordinary soldiers" who did the hanging. However, this is a much argued point, and it seems that the practice varied from place to place.

Chapter II

THE ANGLO-SOVIET ALLIANCE

The background to the Anglo-Soviet Alliance of May 1942 is too
well known to need detailed discussion here. In December 1941
Mr Eden had gone to Moscow, and Stalin and Molotov had asked
for a recognition of the Soviet frontiers as they stood at the time of
the German invasion. This meant a recognition of the new frontiers
with Finland and Rumania and the incorporation of the Baltic
States in the Soviet Union, as well as that of the territory which
Churchill still persisted in calling "Eastern Poland". But while
Churchill was prepared to give way on these questions, including
that of the Baltic States, he met with opposition from Washington,
where such an incorporation was regarded as being contrary to the
principles of the Atlantic Charter. The Soviet Government, no doubt
with some mental reservations, had subscribed to "the general
principles and aims" of the Atlantic Charter. Privately, the Russians
often said that if they had some "mental reservations", Churchill
had many more still. Ultimately, on May 23, during Molotov's visit
to London, Eden proposed to substitute for a territorial agreement
a general and public Treaty of Alliance for twenty years, omitting
all references to frontiers, and a treaty on this basis was signed on
May 26.

As for the question of the Second Front, this had first been raised
by Stalin in a letter to Churchill in the summer of 1941* and the

* See p. 278.

Russians had continued to press it on both the British and the Americans.

American proposals made in the spring of 1942, particularly General Marshall's proposal "that we should attempt to seize Brest and Cherbourg... during the early autumn of 1942" were not to Churchill's liking at all, even though he "did not reject the idea from the outset."*

Both in 1941 and during part of 1942 Churchill took the view that Russia was an "expendable" ally, and was at times highly pessimistic about her chances of survival. Thus, as we have seen, he took a much more dismal view of the Beaverbrook Mission to Moscow at the end of September 1941 than seemed warranted by Beaverbrook's own attitude. To Beaverbrook the Soviet Union was an ally of immense value, and he was anxious to back it at almost any price. Even after the Russians had repelled the first German onslaught on Moscow, Churchill thought that Russia's early defeat was not at all unlikely, and he felt with some bitterness—and perhaps a touch of malice—that they had "brought it upon themselves". In a letter to Sir Stafford Cripps, now evacuated to Kuibyshev, of October 28, 1941, he wrote:

> I fully sympathise with you in your difficult position, and also with Russia in her agony. They certainly have no right to reproach us. They brought their own fate upon themselves when... they let Hitler loose on Poland. They cut themselves off from an effective Second Front when they let the French Army be destroyed... If we had been invaded and destroyed in July or August 1940... they would have remained utterly indifferent.†

For one thing, Churchill was keenly aware that, at that stage, Britain would have to bear the brunt of any Second Front operation. So he preferred other ideas—a landing in French North Africa, or "Jupiter"—the liberation of Northern Norway, which would "represent direct aid to Russia", and he regarded 1943 as the earliest date for landings in France.

> In planning the gigantic enterprise of 1943 it was not possible for us to lay aside all other duties. Our first Imperial duty was to defend

* Churchill, op. cit., vol. 4, pp. 288–9.
† Churchill, op. cit., vol. 3, p. 420.

India... To allow the Germans and Japanese to join hands in India or the Middle East involved a measureless disaster to the allied cause. It ranked in my mind almost as the equal of the retirement of Soviet Russia behind the Urals, or even of their making a separate peace with Germany. At this date [spring 1942] I did not deem either of these contingencies likely, [but] our Indian Empire... might fall an easy prey... Hitler's subjugation of Soviet Russia would be a much longer and, to him, more costly task. Before it was accomplished the Anglo-American command of the air would have been established beyond challenge. Even if all else failed this would be finally decisive... *

Roosevelt was extremely sceptical about "any junction between Japanese and Germans" and was, like General Marshall, more favourable than Churchill to an attempt to open a Second Front in France in 1942.

That was certainly the impression that Molotov brought back from his visits to Washington and London in May-June 1942, and the present-day Soviet *History* makes the most of the fact that Roosevelt twice assured Molotov that the Second Front would be opened in 1942, and that General Marshall told him that the USA had every possibility of opening such a front. According to Hopkins, however, what Roosevelt had twice told Molotov was that he *expected* a Second Front to be opened in 1942. Hopkins also records that "Marshall felt that the sentence about the Second Front [which Molotov had drafted for the communiqué] was too strong, and urged that there be no reference to 1942", adding: "I called this particularly to the President's attention but he, nevertheless, wished to have it included".

The public statement issued on June 11 therefore included the sentence:

> "In the course of the conversations full understanding was reached with regard to the urgent task of creating a Second Front in Europe in 1942."

Now the fat was in the fire. Although Churchill discreetly omits to mention Roosevelt's responsibility for this statement, and felt forced to subscribe to it on Molotov's return from Washington to

* Churchill, op. cit., vol. 4, p. 288.

London, he insisted on handing to Molotov the now well-known
aide-memoire saying, *inter alia*:

> It is impossible to say in advance whether the situation will be such
> as to make this operation feasible when the time comes. We can there-
> fore give no promise in the matter, but, provided that it appears sound
> and sensible, we shall not hesitate to put our plans into effect.*

The plan in question, as we know, concerned "a landing on the
Continent in August or September 1942", and Molotov's great hope
was that "at least forty German divisions" would be drawn off from
the Russian front.

At the ceremony in London on May 26 at which the Anglo-Soviet
Treaty was signed very warm speeches were made by Molotov and
Eden, both of whom stressed the great importance of the alliance,
not only during the war, but also after the war. For all that, Churchill's attitude continued to be somewhat reserved. According to
both the Russians and Americans, relations between Molotov and
Roosevelt were much more friendly than between Molotov and
Churchill.† As Hopkins wrote to Winant after Molotov's visit was
over:

---

* Sherwood, op. cit., p. 582, and Churchill, op. cit., vol. 4, p. 305.
Churchill underlines the words "We can therefore give no promise in
the matter".

† Many anecdotes were told both then and later about Molotov's
week-end at Chequers. One diplomat told me it had all been "rather
like a Marx Brothers' film." Molotov's English was limited to three
words: "Yes", "no", and "second front". At dinner one night,
Molotov remarked on the extraordinary patriotic fervour of the
Russian people as displayed in this war—a fervour the depth of which
had even surprised the government. "The Old Adam coming out,
what?" Churchill growled. Molotov took some trouble to explain
that this was not only Russian patriotism, but also Soviet patriotism,
not quite the same thing. There was also this record of Molotov's
first impression of Churchill: "A very strong man—very strong."
Then, as an afterthought: "Unfortunately, he'll never make a good
communist." But the best stories about Molotov demanding his bedroom key, and the Russian search for bombs under his bed, the

Molotov's visit went extremely well. He and the President got along famously and I am sure that we at least bridged one more gap between ourselves and Russia. There is still a long way to go, but it must be done if there is ever to be any real peace in the world. We simply cannot organise the world between the British and ourselves without bringing in the Russians as equal partners. [As for the Second Front] I have a feeling that some of the British are holding back a bit, but all in all it is moving as well as could be expected.*

It was largely as a result of the Molotov visit to Washington that a new Lend-Lease agreement—or rather, a wider agreement on what was called the "principles of mutual aid against aggression"—was signed by Cordell Hull and Litvinov, the Soviet Ambassador, on June 11.

In Moscow it was decided to make immense political capital out of Molotov's visits to London and Washington. A special meeting of the Supreme Soviet at the Kremlin was called on June 18 to ratify the Anglo-Soviet Alliance. But for fully a week before that the Soviet press had built up the Molotov visits to the West as an event of the most far-reaching importance.

Molotov, flying in a fast British bomber high over Scandinavia, returned from London on June 13; but already on June 11 the Soviet press had published the full text of the Anglo-Soviet agreement, as well as the famous "Second Front" communiqué. On the 13th, it published the text of the Soviet-American agreement. The papers that day were, by Russian standards, spectacular. Over the front page of *Pravda* was splashed a photograph showing Eden and Molotov signing the alliance, with a pussy-face Maisky on one side and a cigar-chewing Churchill on the other. Here also were the text of the Soviet-American agreement, the text of warm bread-and-butter letters from Molotov to Churchill, Eden, Roosevelt and Cordell Hull; the text of Roosevelt's cable to Stalin thanking him for having sent

revolver on his bedside table, and the special way of making his bed, so that he could jump out in a hurry in case of anything, are told by Churchill himself. (Op. cit., vol. 4, p. 201.)

* Sherwood, op. cit., pp. 582–3.

Molotov to Washington on his "most satisfactory" visit, and Stalin's cable of thanks to Roosevelt, and so on. In his cables to both Churchill and Roosevelt, Molotov specifically referred to the "Second Front in 1942". Page two of *Pravda* prominently announced the decision of the Soviet Union and Canada to exchange diplomatic representatives. Such a display was enough to make any Soviet citizen extremely ally-conscious. In its editorial *Pravda* wrote that day:

> At countless meetings throughout the country the workers, *kolkhozniki*, intellectuals, soldiers, officers and political workers of the Red Army are expressing the greatest conviction that the strengthening of these bonds [between the Big Three] will hasten final victory... 1942 must become the year of the enemy's final rout. Our Soviet people have reacted with great satisfaction to the complete understanding concerning the urgent tasks for the creation of a Second Front in 1942.

During the days that followed the press kept up this optimistic Second Front barrage.

The splendours of the Supreme Soviet meeting—the first since the beginning of the war—contrasted strangely with Moscow's down-at-heel appearance. In the Kremlin, diplomats (many of whom had specially come from Kuibyshev) and members of the government were driving up in their limousines. Outside the main entrance of the palace I noticed a car flying a little Japanese flag. In the former Throne Room, completely rebuilt since the Revolution, Lenin stood in his floodlit niche above the rostrum. The Presidium of the Supreme Soviet sat on the left, and the members of the government on the right. On the platform behind the speaker sat members of the Politburo and other leading deputies. On the floor of the hall there was room for some 1,200 deputies of the two Houses sitting jointly— the Chamber of the Union and the Chamber of Nationalities. A large number of these had been flown from distant parts of the country, and there were many colourful oriental costumes and dresses in the front half of the floor. Many of the women wore bright scarves and sari-like dresses, and many men wore embroidered coloured caps, and many of the faces were Mongol, and others almost Indian-like. Among the members of both Houses were many soldiers in uniform, some wearing war decorations; but many seats were empty, partly owing to the difficulty of reaching Moscow at short notice, but chiefly because many deputies were at the front, while others had already been killed.

Then suddenly the whole building shook with applause as the State Defence Council, with Stalin inconspicuously among them, took their seats on the platform. For several minutes the deputies stood up and cheered, and shouted Stalin's name. Stalin and the others on the platform also rose, and Stalin himself clapped, in acknowledgment of the ovation he was receiving. Finally everybody sat down. Stalin was wearing a well-cut pale-khaki summer tunic—plain, without any decorations. His hair was much greyer and his build much smaller than I had imagined it to be, I had never seen Stalin before. There was a pleasant casualness in his manner as, in the course of the meeting, he talked informally to his neighbours, or as he turned round to exchange remarks with people behind him, or as he stood up with the rest and clapped somewhat lazily when, time after time, his name was being acclaimed by the Assembly.

Molotov was the first to speak, and for a long time he spoke about the principal episodes in the process of the *rapprochement* between Britain and the Soviet Union—the Cripps-Molotov agreement of July 12, 1941, the Hopkins, Beaverbrook and Eden visits; then he outlined the main points of the agreement now signed in London: the first part was, in the main, a repetition of the July 1941 agreement, now embodied in a regular treaty; the second part, on post-war co-operation was "in agreement with the main theses of the Atlantic Charter to which the Soviet Union had already subscribed in the past". He then quoted Stalin in confirmation of his further remark that the Soviet Union had no territorial ambitions anywhere, and said that, in terms of the Treaty, Britain and the Soviet Union would strive to "render impossible any future aggression by Germany, or any other State linked with her in her acts of aggression in Europe". (The Russians were at that time still very careful not to say anything that might conceivably offend Japan.) The Treaty, he said, was for twenty years, and subject to renewal, and he added:

I cannot but associate myself with the words of Mr Eden: "Never in the history of our two countries has our association been so close. Never have our obligations in respect of the future been more perfect." This is unquestionably a happy omen... The Treaty has met with the most favourable response in both Britain and the Soviet Union, while in the enemy camp it has caused confusion and angry hissing.

As the speech went on, one became aware of a feeling of impatience in the hall: What about the Second Front? At last Molotov came to that:

Naturally, serious attention was given to the problems of the Second Front, both in London and Washington. The results of these talks can be seen from the identical Anglo-Soviet and American-Soviet communiqués... This is of great importance to the peoples of the Soviet Union, because the establishment of a Second Front in Europe would create insuperable difficulties for the Hitlerite armies at our front. Let us hope that our common enemy will soon feel on his own back the results of the ever-growing military co-operation between the three Great Powers.

There was, according to next day's *Pravda*, "stormy, lengthy applause" at this point; in reality, I noticed that the applause might have been greater than it actually was: it seems obvious that the "let-us-hope" had had a somewhat damping effect—which was to be reflected in some of the later speeches.

Molotov then said that the results of his visit to Washington had been less definite than those of his visits to London, but he stressed that the Soviet-American agreement on present and future co-operation was only "preliminary", adding, however, that general problems of war and peace had been lengthily discussed by him and Mr Roosevelt, and that both the President of the United States and Mr Churchill had been very kind.

In conclusion, Molotov said:

Our strength is growing, our certainty of victory is stronger than it has ever been. Under the great banner of Lenin and Stalin we shall wage this struggle till complete victory, till the complete triumph of our cause and that of all freedom-loving nations.

Apart from discussing the British alliance, many of the other speakers took the opportunity to speak of their own constituencies.

Shcherbakov, representing Moscow, recalled the struggle for Moscow and said, amid a storm of truly emotional applause: "And now, Comrades Deputies, you can see your Capital intact!"

There was also a touch of emotion in the applause that greeted L. R. Korniets, a representative of the now almost completely occupied Ukraine. Korniets, with his heavy drooping "Ukrainian" moustache did not mince his words: "We hope," he said, "that from agreements and words, the great Western Powers will proceed to action."

Zhdanov, representing Leningrad, who received an ovation almost as great as that given to Stalin, said:

> The value of the Treaty is unquestionably enhanced by the fact that complete agreement was reached in London and Washington in respect of the urgent tasks for the creation of a Second Front in Europe in 1942...

He quoted a worker of the Kirov Plant (right in the front line) as saying:

> "It strengthens our conviction that Hitler and his bloody clique will be crushed in 1942. Let us work with double and treble energy in helping the Red Army to carry out its heroic mission."

Y. L. Paletskis, the Lithuanian representative, said he was convinced that there would not be "the slightest delay" in preparing the Second Front in Europe in 1942, as this was also in Britain's and America's interests; and the Latvian, Estonian, Georgian, Uzbek and other representatives spoke more or less on the same lines.

After three and a half hours of speeches, the Treaty was unanimously ratified. In *Pravda* on the following day Ehrenburg wrote a heartfelt couple of columns on "The Heart of England", in which he grew lyrical about London, its old stones, its soot and its "pastel skies". The raids on Cologne and the Ruhr were "only a beginning".

> Already the small children of France, looking across the misty sea, are whispering: "There's a ship over there." And the name of the ship is the Second Front.

The meeting of the Supreme Soviet was followed by a brief, one might say very brief, Anglo-Russian honeymoon. A few weeks later the sharp bickering over the Second Front began. It should be noted that at no time was the British *aide-memoire* mentioned on the Soviet side, or even hinted at—except perhaps for that "let us hope" in Molotov's speech.

There continued much suspicion on both sides*—right up to Stalin's speech on November 6, and the landing in North Africa a few days later. Much of the bad humour and, before long, anger on the Russian side was spontaneous, and largely caused by the pretty desperate outlook at the front; though, for a few weeks before the North Africa landing, some of the angry comments in the press may have partly been calculated to deceive the Germans.

* See pp. 473 ff.

Chapter III

THREE RUSSIAN DEFEATS:
KERCH, KHARKOV AND SEBASTOPOL

All the, admittedly superficial, rejoicing over the Anglo-Soviet
Alliance in fact coincided with one of the hardest periods of the war
in Russia; for in May the Russians had suffered disasters at Kerch
and Kharkov, and it was also obvious that the days of Sebastopol's
resistance were numbered.

After the Russians had been driven out of the Crimea in the autumn
of 1941, with the exception of Sebastopol which continued to be
held by a strong garrison, they undertook a combined operation
from the Caucasus in an endeavour to recapture the Kerch Peninsula, at the eastern extremity of the Crimea, and thus establish a
strong bridgehead from which eventually the whole Crimea could
be liberated and Sebastopol relieved. This was one of the largest
combined land-and-sea operations undertaken by the Russians
during the war. In the last week of December 1941, despite highly
unfavourable weather conditions and some heavy losses, they
succeeded in landing some 40,000 troops, occupying the whole
Kerch peninsula, and also (for a few days) the important city of
Feodosia on the Crimean "mainland".

It was at Kerch, incidentally, that the Russians received their first
evidence of large-scale German atrocities: soon after the German
occupation of Kerch in 1941, several thousand Jews had been

exterminated by one of Himmler's *Einsatzgruppen* and buried in huge trenches outside the town. Needless to say, Field-Marshal von Manstein, who was in command of the German 11th Army in the Crimea, later denied all knowledge of this.

The immediate result of the successful landing at Kerch was to reduce the German pressure on Sebastopol, and Manstein was later to admit that the Russian landing had created an immense danger to the German forces in the Crimea.*

But owing to shortage of trained men, or equipment, or both, or because of some very serious miscalculation on the part of the Russian High Command, the successful Kerch landing was not followed up except by a few abortive sorties, and on May 8 von Manstein launched an all-out offensive against the Russian forces in the Eastern Crimea. This opened with a concentrated air attack on the Russians, who suffered heavy casualties and were forced to retreat to a fortified line known as the Turkish Wall. But the German onslaught was much too strong:

> Our forces proved themselves incapable of holding the Turkish Wall, and retreated to Kerch. The local command had shown itself incapable of using the air force effectively, and our troops retreated under constant German air attacks... By the 14th the Germans broke into the southern and western outskirts of Kerch, and between the 15th and 20th our rearguard units fought desperately to enable our main forces to cross the Kerch Straits to the Taman Peninsula [on the Caucasus side of the five-mile-wide straits]. Even so, it proved impossible to carry out the evacuation in an organised manner. The enemy captured practically all our military equipment, which was then used against the defenders of Sebastopol.†

It was in these laconic words that the recent Soviet *History* described the first of the great disasters suffered by the Russians in the Crimea.

This disaster is attributed by the *History* to a faulty organisation of defence, the "shallow operational disposition of the troops" and the lack of essential reserves. Other reasons were "the thoughtlessness of the army headquarters, the absence of camouflage at the

* E. v. Manstein, *Verlorene Siege* (Lost Victories), Bonn, 1955, p. 246.
† IVOVSS, vol. 2, p. 405.

command posts, which had failed, moreover, to move from place to place, with the result that in their very first raids, the Luftwaffe smashed up these command posts, thus wrecking all communications. The different headquarters were, moreover, unaccustomed to the use of radio." Lt. Gen. Kozlov, the commander of the Kerch Army Group, and his top commissar, Mekhlis, as well as numerous other officers and commissars, were demoted, and Mekhlis, who was at that time both Vice-Commissar of Defence and one of the heads of the Political Administration of the Red Army was relieved of both these posts and demoted to the rank of corps commissar. Mekhlis and the officers of the Kerch group were accused of having "wasted hours arguing about the situation at fruitless sessions of the War Council", instead of acting. In particular, they had been too slow in withdrawing the troops to the Turkish Wall, and this had been fatal to the whole defensive operation.*

Although some publicity was given at the time to the disgrace of Mekhlis, one of the villains of the Army Purge in 1937–8, little, if anything, was said about the holocaust among the other officers responsible for the Kerch disaster. It seems obvious that the demotion of Mekhlis was at least partly intended as a political operation (he was deeply detested by the "younger" generals); but how far he (and the other officers) were used as scapegoats for a perhaps inevitable failure (for German air superiority at Kerch was overwhelming) is anybody's guess. What is certain, however, is that the Kerch disaster paved the way for an even greater disaster: that of Sebastopol. After the liquidation of the "Kerch front", von Manstein was free to concentrate all his forces in the Crimea against Sebastopol which had held out ever since October... Sebastopol was, however, a "noble", not a "shameful" disaster.

Like the Battle of Kiev in 1941, the so-called Battle of Kharkov in May 1942 was to become the subject of some of Khrushchev's angry posthumous recriminations against Stalin.

According to the present-day Soviet *History*, the Soviet Supreme Command had made numerous mistakes in its planning of the

* Ibid., p. 406.

spring operations. First, because of the concentration of enemy forces in that area, it had expected the main German blow to fall on Moscow:

> Instead of concentrating large forces on the south-western and southern front, and creating an insuperable defence in depth in these areas, the *Stavka* continued to strengthen the Briansk front, whose main forces were protecting the Tula-Moscow axis.

Secondly, the Soviet Supreme Command simply over-rated its own strength and under-rated that of the Germans:

> In planning large offensive operations in the summer of 1942 which would clear the invaders out of the Soviet Union, and so liberate millions of people from the German yoke, the Soviet Supreme Command over-rated the successes of our winter offensive, and had not taken sufficient notice of the fact that, after the defeats it had suffered, the German army had restored its battle-worthiness, and was still full of offensive possibilities.*

The Russian rout at Kharkov in May 1942 was more heavily concealed from the public than almost any other Russian defeat; perhaps the great *rapprochement* then in progress with Britain and the United States had much to do with it, or perhaps also the fact that Stalin himself—at least according to present-day accounts— had played a leading role in conceiving and, worse still, in persisting in, this disastrous operation.

In March 1942 the Supreme Command had considered a plan for a large offensive in the Ukraine which would carry the Red Army all the way to a line running, north-to-south, from Gomel to Kiev, and then, roughly along the right bank of the Dnieper, through Cherkassy, and on to Nikolaev on the Black Sea. Owing to shortage of reserves, this plan was abandoned in favour of a more modest offensive, the main object of which was the liberation of Kharkov. One Russian blow was to be struck from the north of Kharkov, the other from the south—from the so-called Barvenkovo salient which the Russians had recaptured during the winter.

It so happened that the Germans were planning an offensive in the same area, but the Russians got in their blow first when they

* IVOVSS, vol. 2, p. 404.

started their offensive towards Kharkov on May 12. The real trouble was that Russian superiority in the area was far from overwhelming and, worse still (as events were soon to show) the Germans had powerful mobile reserves in the neighbourhood, and the Russians had not. The Soviet historian, Telpukhovsky sums up this battle as follows:

> To smash our offensive, which had begun on May 12, a strong formation of German troops, supported by large numbers of tanks and aircraft, struck a powerful blow at our 9th Army in the Slaviansk and Barvenkovo areas on May 17. Our troops had to withdraw to the left bank of the Donets, thus exposing the flank of the Soviet shock troops advancing on Kharkov. By cutting the communications of our troops advancing on Kharkov, the Germans placed these in an extremely difficult position, and they were forced, with very heavy fighting, to withdraw to the east, suffering serious casualties in the process.*

The more recent *History* is much more explicit about this episode: it says that the advance on Kharkov was persisted in at the demand of Stalin, and despite the protests of Khrushchev, who saw that these troops were walking into a trap. Further, it tells how the Russian tank reserves were thrown in too late to save the situation. Finally, it admits that a large number of Russian troops were encircled, and that in the hard-fought attempts to break out "many brave men" died, including the deputy commander of the South-West Front, Lt. Gen. Kostenko, the commander of the 6th Army, Lt. Gen. Gorodnyansky, the commander of the 57th Army, Lt. Gen. Podlas and many other high-ranking officers. Although many of the troops broke out by escaping across the Donets, others continued to fight in the encirclement until May 30.

> The offensive against Kharkov which had begun so successfully, thus ended in the rout of three armies of the South-Western and Southern Front.†

The *History* also mentions the fact that, as a member of the War Council of the South-Western Front, Khrushchev urged Stalin to stop the advance on Kharkov and to concentrate the Russian forces

---

* Telpukhovsky, op. cit., p. 119.
† IVOVSS, vol. 2, p. 415.

on smashing the German counter-offensive. But Stalin insisted on the Russians continuing their advance on Kharkov—"which," says the *History*, "complicated the situation still further."*

Whether this is strictly true or not (and one must remember that the *History* was written after the XXth Congress, and goes out of its way to magnify Khrushchev's role in the war at Stalin's expense), it is interesting to note that this particular episode was dealt with at considerable length in Khrushchev's "Secret Report" at the XXth Congress in February 1956. The main points he made were these:

> When an exceptionally serious situation developed in the Kharkov area, we correctly decided to drop the operation whose objective was to encircle Kharkov... We informed Stalin that the situation demanded changes in the operational plans...
>
> Contrary to common sense, Stalin rejected our suggestion and ordered that the Kharkov operation be continued, although by this time many of our army units were themselves threatened with encirclement and extermination...
>
> I telephoned Vassilevsky (the Chief of Staff) and begged him to explain the situation to Comrade Stalin. Vassilevsky replied, however, that Comrade Stalin did not wish to hear any more about this operation... I then telephoned Stalin at his villa. Malenkov answered the phone. I said I wanted to speak to Stalin personally. Stalin informed me through Malenkov that I should speak with Malenkov... I asked again to speak to Stalin himself. But Stalin still said no, though he was only a few steps from the telephone. After "listening" in this manner to our plea, Stalin said: "Let everything remain as it is."
>
> And what was the result? The worst that could be expected. The Germans surrounded our armies and we lost hundreds of thousands of our soldiers.†

Whether in reality the Russians lost, as Khrushchev claimed, "hundreds of thousands of our soldiers", the Germans, at any rate, claimed 200,000 prisoners.

In any case, the facts about the "Battle of Kharkov" were kept

---

* IVOVSS, vol. 2, p. 414.

† *The Dethronement of Stalin: Full Text of the Khrushchev Speech* (*Manchester Guardian* reprint, 1956), p. 21. I have slightly abridged the text, and made a few corrections in the rather clumsy translation of this version of the "Secret Report".

extremely dark at the time, except for a strange communiqué at the end of May which put the Soviet losses at "5,000 killed and 70,000 missing", in its own way an admission that something had gone seriously wrong. It caused considerable consternation. There was even a clumsy attempt to represent the "Battle of Kharkov" as a Russian victory: early in June, the foreign press were specially taken to a German war prisoners' camp near Gorki; the 600 or 700 prisoners we were shown had, indeed, been captured during the *first* stage of the Kharkov Battle—i.e. during the Russian offensive of May 12–17. Most of them, while deploring their *Pech*, their "bad luck", were extremely cocky for all that; they claimed to be convinced that Germany would smash Russia in 1942, and they did not believe for a moment in any Second Front materialising in time.*

The third great defeat suffered by the Russians in the summer of 1942 was at Sebastopol; but, unlike Kerch and Kharkov, Sebastopol was one of the most glorious defeats of the Soviet-German war. In many ways, except for its tragic end, the nine-months' siege of Sebastopol had the same quality of human endurance and solidarity as the siege of Leningrad. Local patriotism, based on the historic memories of the *other* siege of Sebastopol in 1853–4, complete with "great ancestors" like Admirals Nakhimov and Kornilov, besides the peculiar revolutionary and patriotic traditions of the Black Sea Navy, had a decisively important effect on the morale of both soldiers and civilians. Important, too, were the very strong and efficient local party and Komsomol organisations. Towards the end, the last-ditch resistance was also encouraged by the simple and tragic fact that, with the exception of a very, very few top-ranking personnel, who got away dangerously by submarine, there was no alternative to imprisonment by the Germans but a fight to the last round.

* A visit to this camp, a former monastery, in which the Germans were fairly comfortably housed and better fed than most Russian civilians, and many conversations with the Germans there, are described in *The Year of Stalingrad*, pp. 87–89. Most striking was the Germans' *Herrenvolk* attitude to their Rumanian fellow-prisoners, of whom there were half a dozen in the camp.

As we have seen, the Germans had overrun the whole of the Crimea in October 1941—with the exception of Sebastopol. The siege of the great naval base began on October 30, and the first attempt by the German 11th Army under von Manstein to break through to Sebastopol, defended on land by a semi-circle of three more or less well-fortified lines, lasted from October 30 to November 21. A very important part in repelling this first great German onslaught was played by the guns of the Black Sea Navy, and by the naval marines fighting on land; these, like the men of the Baltic Fleet at Leningrad, were among the toughest Russian troops. The most famous case of suicidal resistance by the Russians during that first German attack was that of the five Black Sea sailors, with *politruk* (political instructor) Filchenkov at their head who, having run out of ammunition, threw themselves with their last remaining hand-grenades under the advancing German tanks, and so prevented a break-through to Sebastopol from the north-east. This heroic deed of the "five sailors of Sebastopol" was to become the subject of many songs and poems, among them a very beautiful song by Victor Belyi.

Although the Germans and Rumanians already had a great superiority in manpower, as well as vast superiority in aircraft and tanks, Sebastopol was protected on land by good natural defences, and the navy, with its powerful guns, was of considerable help. In November 1941 the Russians had over 50,000 combat troops in Sebastopol, including 21,000 marines. The Germans and Rumanians, according to Russian sources, had at least twice as many.

The first German attack, which continued for three weeks, barely dented the first of the three defence lines here and there, the only important German gain being the capture of the Balaclava Hills, east of Balaclava—which itself remained in Russian hands. Rather more successful was the second German-Rumanian attack between December 17 and 31, when the enemy pushed the Russians back to a line about five miles to the north of Sebastopol, and also made minor advances due east of the city; but this also came to a halt on December 31, partly as a result of the successful Russian landing on the Kerch peninsula, which as we have seen diverted many German troops from Sebastopol. The most famous Russian exploit during that second German offensive against Sebastopol was that of a handful of Black Sea sailors who, for three days, defended Firing Point No. 11 in a village called Kamyshly till they were all dead or dying. When the firing point was recaptured by the Russians, they found a note written by one of the men:

> Russia, my country, my native land! Dear Comrade Stalin! I, a Black Sea sailor, and a son of Lenin's Komsomol, fought as my heart told me to fight. I slew the beasts as long as my heart beat in my breast. Now I am dying, but I know we shall win. Sailors of the Black Sea Navy! Fight harder still, kill the mad Fascist dogs! I have been faithful to my soldier's oath.—Kalyuzhnyi.*

A remarkable story of how Sebastopol lived through the nine months of the siege was told after the war by B. A. Borisov who was Secretary of the Sebastopol Party committee and Chairman of the city's Defence Committee for the whole period. He tells of the Sebastopol airmen, such as Yakov Ivanov, who rammed enemy planes usually at the cost of their own lives; of the way in which practically the entire population of Sebastopol had to be moved into shelters, cellars and, especially, caves during the first two German offensives, so fierce and continuous was the bombing of the city; of the vast cave near the Northern Bay in which a giant workshop— ("Spetskombinat No. 1") was set up—where the people manufactured mortars, mines and hand-grenades, and another, ("Spetskombinat No. 2"), near Inkerman, where clothing and footwear were made on a large scale in underground cellars previously used for storing Crimean champagne. He tells of the underground schools that were organised for the children in Sebastopol itself, of the numerous reinforcements that came to Sebastopol by sea, first after the fall of Odessa, and later, from the Caucasus. Most pathetic of all perhaps was the extraordinary elation and optimism that swept Sebastopol in January and February, after the failure of the second German offensive against the city, and after the successful Russian landing at Kerch. It was then thought that if both Kerch and

* In all post-Stalin books, including the official *History*, mentioning this episode, the words "dear Comrade Stalin" are replaced by dots, or omitted altogether.

Sebastopol held, the whole Crimea would soon be liberated. People moved out of their shelters and caves back into their battered houses, and the young people made a special effort to repair as many houses as possible. Even tram-cars began to run along the streets of Sebastopol, though the Germans were only five miles to the north. On May Day, which was almost exactly six months after the siege had begun, there were numerous meetings and celebrations, despite several air-raids and German shelling.

But that day our troops were preparing to help our troops on the Kerch peninsula; for these were expected to start their offensive at any moment. Both at Sebastopol and at the front everybody was talking about the Crimea being liberated and the siege of Sebastopol lifted. Everybody was in an exalted holiday mood.*

Then came the tragic news of the loss of Kerch, and Sebastopol now had to prepare for the worst. A somewhat disorderly evacuation of children and old people was started. The sea communications with the mainland had already become highly precarious. Half the Komsomols in Sebastopol (among them many girls) volunteered for the Army, and the others remained in the city to work double shifts, in the Sebastopol armaments works. Once more people had to be moved from their houses back to shelters and caves.

And now the last ordeal began. About May 20 it was learned from reconnaissance, and from messages received from the partisans in the Crimean mountains, that vast numbers of German troops were converging on Sebastopol. On June 2 the Germans began to bomb Sebastopol with hundreds of planes, and every day hundreds of heavy shells would explode in the city. In six days the Germans dropped 50,000 high-explosive and incendiary bombs on Sebastopol, besides thousands of shells; the destruction was terrible, and the casualties very high. The Germans were using a giant · siege gun called Dora, which had originally been ·built to smash the heaviest fortifications of the Maginot Line.

Then, on June 7, the final German-Rumanian offensive against Sebastopol was launched. Because of great German air superiority,

* B. Borisov. *Sevastopoltsy ne sdayutsya* (Men of Sebastopol Do Not Surrender). (Simferopol, 1961), p. 130.

the Russian airfields around Sebastopol were now almost completely
out of action, and sea communications between Sebastopol and the
Caucasus had virtually been cut by the Luftwaffe. Such small
quantities of food, arms, raw materials and petrol as still reached
Sebastopol from the mainland were now usually brought by submarines or small craft. Submarines were also used for evacuating
the wounded. It is obvious that they could take very few and that
most of the wounded remained in the blazing inferno of Sebastopol.
The local "armaments industry" could no longer cope with the
urgent needs of the troops, and the constant bombing and shelling
made the distribution of food and water to the crowded caves and
other shelters almost impossible.

After three weeks' very heavy fighting, which then continued for
a couple of days in the streets of Sebastopol, the Germans occupied
what was left of the city. In the July heat, the stench from the countless unburied bodies was such that the last defenders fought wearing
their gasmasks. Meantime, an evacuation of sorts was attempted
from Cape Chersonese, some eight miles west of Sebastopol. Here,
at night, one plane was able to land, and take away a few of the
wounded; also a submarine picked up Admiral Oktiabrsky, General
Petrov, General Krylov and other top-ranking Army and Party
personnel.

In the course of his narrative Borisov draws some remarkable
portraits of the leading male and female members of the Sebastopol
Komsomol—all of them young people of infinite patriotism, endurance and devotion to duty—who were either killed in the fighting
round Sebastopol, or were killed or taken prisoner after the Germans
had entered the city. He dwells, in particular, on the tragic fate of
two leading Komsomol members, a man and a woman—Sasha
Bagrii and Nadya Krayevaya. Like so many others, they had waited
in vain at Cape Chersonese for either a plane or a ship; one plane
did land in the middle of the night, but could only take away a few
wounded and a few "seniors". When dawn came, the shelling of the
airfield was resumed, and no more planes could be expected. Nor
could any ships reach Chersonese. Noticing a large accumulation of
soldiers and civilians near Cape Chersonese, the Germans started
shelling them.

Bagrii and Nadya then joined one of the rearguard units... Taking rifles and cartridges from dead sailors, they tried with the others to break through to the Crimean hills to join the partisans. But in the shelling half the brave people were killed... A second attempt to break through was no more successful, and as the Germans started their final attack, the shots from the Russians became fewer and fewer... Most of the survivors now counter-attacked with nothing but their bayonets. Nadya was killed. The last that was heard of Sasha Bagrii was this: he was seen, scarcely able to move, in a column of prisoners. Then he was seen, half-dead and spitting blood first at Bakhchisarai and then at Simferopol. And here there were traitors who denounced him to the Germans. And the Germans did not forgive all that he had done for his country and for Sebastopol... *

I was to see Sebastopol in May 1944, after it had been recaptured by the Russians; I was then to hear many more harrowing stories of those last agonising days of Sebastopol in June and July 1942. All that was known in Moscow in July 1942 was that very few of the defenders of Sebastopol had got away. Twenty-six thousand Russian wounded were said to have fallen into German hands, besides an unspecified number of other soldiers. The Germans claimed to have captured 90,000.†

In Moscow one thing had been clear: after the German victory at Kerch in May, the fate of Sebastopol was sealed; the only question was how long it would hold out. It held out longer than could reasonably have been expected, and this heroic defence was contrasted, not without some sarcasm, especially by Ehrenburg, with the "gutless" surrender of Tobruk only a week earlier.

* Borisov, op. cit., p. 176.
† This figure is not necessarily exaggerated. According to the postwar Soviet *History*, there were 106,000 Russian troops, including 82,000 combat troops, at Sebastopol, when the final German onslaught began, as against 203,000 German and Rumanian troops, including 175,000 combat troops. The vast German-Rumanian superiority in equipment was greater still, except in guns—

	German-Rumanian	Soviet
Guns of all kinds	780	606
Tanks	450	38
Aircraft	600	109

The news of the imminent fall of Sebastopol had been broken as gently as possible to the Russian people; but the Russian reader had learned to read between the lines. Each communiqué adjective was, as it were, a code word which meant something quite definite. Thus, "fierce fighting" (*ozhestochennyie boi*), "stubborn fighting" (*upornyie boi*) and "heavy fighting" (*tyazhelyie boi*) meant three different things; "heavy fighting" meant that things were going very badly; this phrase was more and more frequently used in the communiqués on Sebastopol during the last fortnight the city held. On June 25 Sebastopol was "holding out against superior enemy forces"; on June 28, *Pravda* already spoke of the "immortal fame of Sebastopol"; on June 30, Ehrenburg wrote in *Red Star*—

> The Germans boasted: "We shall drink champagne on June 15 on the Grafsky Embankment"... Experts foretold: "It's a matter of three days, perhaps a week." We knew how many planes they had, and they knew how hard it was to defend a city with all its roads cut. But they forgot one thing: Sebastopol is not merely a city. It is the glory of Russia, the pride of the Soviet Union. We have seen the capitulation of towns, of celebrated fortresses, of States. But Sebastopol is not surrendering. Our soldiers do not play at war. They fight a life-and-death struggle. They do not say "I surrender" when they see two or three more enemy men on the chessboard.

This was clearly a crack at Tobruk. However, the end of Sebastopol was now clearly in sight. On July 1 the communiqué said:

> Hundreds of enemy planes are dropping bombs on our front lines and on the city. They are making more than 1,000 sorties a day. Every defender of Sebastopol is endeavouring to kill as many Germans as possible.

And, on July 3, the communiqué said that, after a siege of 250 days, the Soviet troops had abandoned Sebastopol on the order of the High Command.

Three days later Admiral Oktiabrsky who had escaped from Sebastopol by submarine with other top military leaders, published in *Pravda* a detailed account of the battle of Sebastopol, turning a military defeat into a great moral victory. He gave some unbelievably high figures of the German and Rumanian losses (300,000 killed and wounded) during the 250 days' siege, but avoided all reference to the number of Russians left behind, including the 26,000 wounded left in the ruined town or on the beaches—without a ship to take them away...

The men and women of Sebastopol had rendered a great service to the rest of the Russian forces by tying down von Manstein's 11th Army for so long and preventing it from operating on the "main" front.

Chapter IV

THE RENEWAL OF THE
GERMAN ADVANCE

Though Sebastopol did not finally fall until the beginning of July, its fate was already sealed at the time of the meeting of the Supreme Soviet on June 18 to ratify the Anglo-Soviet Alliance. There had, too, been the disasters at Kerch and Kharkov in May. And yet on June 21 the Army paper *Red Star* wrote:

> The German Army is still stubborn in defence. But it has been deprived of that offensive drive it had before... But though the enemy is still strong, one thing is clear. There cannot be a German offensive like last summer's. The question facing Germany now is not to conquer the Soviet Union, but to hang on, to last out somehow. Not that it will stick to defensive warfare throughout... But its offensive operations cannot go beyond the framework of limited objectives.

Equally surprising, in the light of the real situation, was the publication by Sovinformbureau on June 22 of *A Review of The First Year of the War* giving the following figures for casualties in support of the statement that the Red Army had shaken the German war machine so badly that the ground had been prepared for the smashing of the German Army in 1942:

		Germany	USSR
Killed, wounded and prisoners	about	10,000,000	4,500,000
Guns lost	over	30,500	22,000
Tanks lost	over	24,000	15,000
Planes lost	over	20,000	9,000

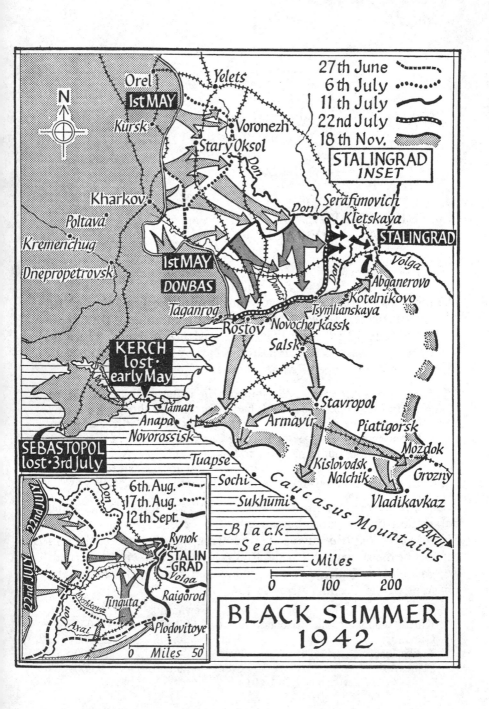

BLACK SUMMER 1942

These figures for German casualties were, to say the least, improbable and have not been reproduced in post-war Soviet histories. At the time even the most credulous readers took them with a large pinch of salt. Much more plausible are the figures given in General Halder's diary for German casualties (excluding the sick):

Up to 15.2.42— 946,000
„ „ 10.5.42—1,183,000
„ „ 20.5.42—1,215,000
„ „ 10.6.42—1,268,000
„ „ 30.6.42—1,332,000
„ „ 10.7.42—1,362,000
„ „ 20.7.42—1,391,000
„ „ 31.7.42—1,428,000
„ „ 10.8.42—1,472,000
„ „ 20.8.42—1,528,000
„ „ 31.8.42—1,589,000
„ „ 10.9.42—1,637,000

This means that, by the end of the winter campaign, the Germans had suffered nearly a million casualties; then, after a relative lull, between February and May (which had, however, still cost them some 200,000 casualties), the Germans had half-a-million casualties between the beginning of the May operations and the *beginning* of the Stalingrad Battle. So even the pre-Stalingrad phase of the 1942 campaign was very far from having been a walkover for the Germans.

The figure in the Russian *Report* of June 22 for Soviet casualties is less fantastic, and is if anything an under-estimate. And though the German losses in heavy equipment are grossly exaggerated, the Russian losses, curiously enough, may *also* have been exaggerated, considering the great shortage of planes and tanks from which the Russian armies had suffered almost from the outset, and the very slow rate at which these were being produced, especially between October 1941 and March 1942.

The stupendous losses of equipment given in the table may have been calculated to impress upon Soviet industry the gigantic size of reinforcements and replacements required from it, and upon the

Western Allies the wholly inadequate help they had been sending up till then.

> Naturally [the Sovinformbureau statement went on] on a front as long as this the German High Command can concentrate here and there a sufficient number of forces... in order to achieve certain successes. That is what happened, on the Kerch peninsula... But such local successes cannot decide the outcome of the war. The German Army of 1942 is not what it was a year ago. *The picked German troops have, in the main, been destroyed... The German army cannot carry out offensive operations on a scale similar to last year's.* [Emphasis added.]

But even if this optimistic propaganda was believed for a short while it was very soon to be disproved by events and as the German offensive progressed throughout the summer of 1942, the feeling that Russia—Holy Russia—was again in mortal danger grew from day to day. True, there was not the same feeling of bewilderment as in the early days of the invasion in 1941, and the German failure to seize either Moscow or Leningrad had created an undercurrent of hope—and perhaps even the conviction—that "something" good would happen again. Even so, whereas the communiqués in May and the greater part of June were vague but reasonably optimistic, those that followed were to spread almost undiluted gloom throughout the country.

Hitler's Directive No. 41, drawn up in the spring of 1942 outlined the main aims of the German summer campaign; but certain important changes were then made in the course of the campaign itself. Briefly, Hitler's plan boiled down to this: first, liquidation of the Russians in the Crimea (Kerch and Sebastopol); second, the capture of Voronezh, which would present the double advantage of constituting a serious German threat both to Central Russia south-east of Moscow (Tambov-Saratov area), as well as to Stalingrad; third, the encirclement and liquidation of the main Russian forces inside the Don bend, with one German pincer striking south-east from Voronezh, and the other north-east from Taganrog; fourth, after thus clearing the way to Stalingrad, either capture the city on the

Volga, or at any rate destroy it completely by bombing, and then turn due south towards the Caucasus, and capture the oil areas of Maikop, Grozny and Baku, and finally reach the southern frontier of the Soviet Union, which would probably bring Turkey into the war on the side of the Axis Powers. The plan also provided, among other things, for another attempt to capture Leningrad.

But once the campaign had started, a number of major and, as it proved, fatal, changes were made in this plan. First the Russians stopped the Germans at Voronezh and secondly, they did not allow themselves to be trapped—at least not in large numbers—inside the Don Bend. These, and a few other factors (such as the easy German capture of Rostov) made Hitler change his original plan. As Chuikov was to comment later:

> This logical and coherent plan was abandoned; and so, instead of doing his utmost in using the bulk of his forces to capture Stalingrad during the third phase of the campaign, and then proceed to capture the oil areas in the Caucasus, Hitler decided to carry out two operations *simultaneously*: capture Stalingrad *and* invade the Caucasus.*

The big German offensive which began over a wide front on June 28—i.e. a few days before the fall of Sebastopol, which was by now a foregone conclusion—assumed at first all the old characteristics of the *blitzkrieg*. Telpukhovsky's semi-official history of the war, published in 1959 briefly sums up the situation in June-July as follows:

> Our forced abandonment of the Crimea and our defeat at Kharkov substantially changed the situation along the whole southern part of the front in the Germans' favour. Once more the enemy was able to take the initiative... On June 10 the Germans started offensive operations in the Kharkov sector, and on June 28 they launched a major offensive in the Kursk-Voronezh sector... They broke through our defences south of Kursk and on July 8 came very close to Voronezh. However, the stubborn resistance and the counter-attacks

---

* V. I. Chuikov, *Nachalo puti* (The Beginning of the Road). (Moscow, 1959), p. 18.

of the Soviet troops of the newly-formed Voronezh Front stopped the German advance, and the Nazi high command therefore turned part of these troops towards the south, along the right bank of the Don— on the way to Stalingrad.

... The Soviet troops, retreating under the pressure of superior enemy forces, nevertheless resisted heroically, and thus gained valuable time, which was used for throwing in reserves and strengthening the defensive capacity of Stalingrad... But with 1,200 planes in this area of the front, the enemy had great superiority in aircraft, as well as in guns and tanks.*

Within a short time the parts of the Donbas still in Russian hands were overrun, the important industrial city of Voroshilovgrad (Lugansk) falling on July 19. More rapid still was the German advance further north into the Don country; and only at Voronezh, further north still, were the Germans stopped. Here the Russians succeeded in averting the danger of a German breakthrough to the Tambov-Saratov area—which would have meant that Moscow's main communications with the east would be cut before long. It is still not clear, despite much discussion by historians of both sides, whether such an advance on Tambov-Saratov ever entered the German plans; but the possibility was clearly envisaged on the Russian side, and very strong Russian forces were concentrated for that reason in the Voronezh area.

Communications with the east and south-east had already become highly precarious; the Caspian-Volga waterway, with its ships and tanker-fleet was one of the principal Russian supply-lines, the equivalent of ten railways. Practically all the Caucasus oil came along the Volga route. After the ice had melted in the spring of 1942 enormous quantities of Caucasian oil had been shipped to Moscow and central Russia—the equivalent of about a year's reserve; but with the beginning of the summer campaign German bombing of the Volga line made it more and more hazardous. Russia's alternative oil supplies from the east depended on the railways running through the Saratov-Tambov area, which was one reason for the Russian determination to stop the Germans at Voronezh at any price. The grave danger of a critical oil shortage was emphasised in

* Telpukhovsky, op. cit., pp. 119–20.

Moscow in July 1942, when the most drastic cuts were made in petrol rations, even for some of the most privileged categories of users.

Except for the very important German failure to break through at Voronezh,* the general outlook was very serious indeed. The breakthrough into the wide open spaces of the Don country was bad enough; but the real shock to the Russian people came with the announcement on July 28 that Novocherkassk and Rostov had been lost. This meant that the Germans were now going to invade the Kuban and the Caucasus. At the same time, they were already far inside the Don country, and were busy forcing the Don on the southern side of the bend at Tsymlianskaya, on the way to Stalingrad.

What happened at Rostov? Many dark hints were dropped at the time both in the press and in private conversations. The gist of it all was that certain Red Army units had panicked and fled, and that officers and generals had lost their heads under the fierceness of the German onslaught. This time the Germans had attacked Rostov from the north and north-east, and not from the west, as in 1941; east and north-east Rostov had no defences to speak of. It was made clear in the press that no orders had been given to abandon the city, and that here was a clear case of disobedience. Many were shot and demoted: generals, officers and ordinary soldiers. There is no doubt that a cry of "Pull yourselves together!" went through the country; and this cry was loudly echoed in the press. It talked more and more in the days that followed of the "iron discipline" that had been introduced, and the fall of Rostov was openly attributed to "cowards and panic-stricken creatures" who had failed in their duty to defend the city.

There are some rather puzzling aspects about the whole "Rostov

---

* In Moscow at the time some military observers, e.g. General Petit, the French military attaché, who had close contacts with Russian top brass, attached the utmost importance to this; had the Germans broken through at Voronezh, Moscow might have been encircled; by spreading south, the Germans were much less dangerous, and were less likely to achieve any quick and decisive results.

affair". Militarily, it is extremely doubtful whether, in the circumstances of July 1942, it could have been held for any length of time,
and it has even been suggested (perhaps with some hindsight) that
any attempt to make of Rostov another "Sebastopol" could only
have ended in encirclement which, in turn, would have entailed the
useless loss of many thousands of valuable troops. It seems clear
that, on the pretext that Rostov had been abandoned without orders,
the government was going to use the tremendous shock caused in the
country by the fall of the city for a vast psychological, as well as
organisational operation.* Anyone who was in Russia at the time
knows that the great anxiety that had been mounting throughout
July reached something very like panic the day the fall of Rostov
was announced. Looking back on this period there is no doubt that
the psychological operation undertaken as a result of the fall of
Rostov was highly salutary; throughout August, the mood in the
country continued to be grim, but no longer panicky, and by some
curious instinct, people were expecting a change for the better as
the Germans approached Stalingrad.

It was after the fall of Rostov that the Russian command called a
halt with Stalin's "not a step back" order, read to the troops on
July 30, and although this was very far from being literally carried
out—for the retreat continued rapidly in the Northern Caucasus and
(more slowly) in the Don country, on the way to Stalingrad, *something*, as we shall see, had changed in comparison with the earlier
part of the summer campaign.

More valuable contributions to our understanding of this period
than the official histories are the reminiscences by a number of
Russian generals who played an active part in the operations, such
as Marshal Yeremenko's and Marshal Chuikov's. No doubt, like
generals the world over, they have axes to grind about some of their
colleagues; but what emerges most clearly from their reminiscences
(and this was not altogether clear at the time) is not only that some
Russians generals were good, and others quite useless, but that the
morale and efficiency of some of the troops was high, while other
Russian troops retreating to Stalingrad were almost completely
demoralised.

* See pp. 414 ff.

An even more vivid picture of what was going on in the south is given in certain novels written after the war, such as Fadeyev's *Young Guard*, or in films like the much more recent *Ballad of a Soldier*—with all the roads teeming with refugees who were being attacked from the air; trains that were being wrecked by German bombers; troops in more or less disorderly retreat—scenes of horror reminiscent of the worst days of 1941 but with the difference that in 1942 there was practically nowhere further to retreat to. Or more precisely, the limits were Stalingrad and the Caucasus foothills. There was a frantic feeling in the country that if the Germans were not to be stopped there, then the war would be as good as lost.

The military situation at the end of July and the beginning of August was certainly looking serious for the Russians. There was very heavy fighting inside the Don Bend, and the Germans had already crossed the river at Tsymlianskaya. They were clearly on their way to Stalingrad. Meanwhile, the Russians were in full retreat in the Kuban. By August 3 the Germans, advancing from their Tsymlianskaya bridgehead, had reached Kotelnikovo, and they then continued their advance, more slowly, towards Stalingrad until August 18. The only redeeming feature was the Russian success in firmly holding the country north of the Don Bend as well as a number of bridgeheads within the bend itself, notably at Kletskaya. They also later captured a bridgehead at Serafimovich, which, as we shall see, was to play an important part in the Russian counter-offensive at Stalingrad in November.

In the Caucasus the German advance was much more rapid. By August 11 the fighting had spread in the west to the oil town of Maikop, and to Krasnodar and the Germans were penetrating the mountains on their way to the Black Sea coast. In their southern thrust, they had, by the 21st, occupied the famous watering places, Piatigorsk, Essentuki and Kislovodsk in the Caucasus foothills, and soon afterwards planted the Nazi flag on the top of Mount Elbrus. In their south-eastern drive they were crashing ahead towards the vital oil areas of Grozny and Baku.

Chapter V

PATRIE-EN-DANGER AND THE POST-ROSTOV REFORMS

It is often assumed that what was published in Russia during the war was "just propaganda", as indeed it often was, and that the real truth is told in the present post-Stalin histories, which it often is not.

To anyone who, like myself, was in Russia at the time, present-day Soviet histories depict the whole period in over-simple terms.

I noted in my Moscow diary, which I quote in *The Year of Stalingrad*, the extraordinarily emotional atmosphere that summer, for instance even at any routine Tchaikovsky concert—as though all Russian civilisation were now in deadly danger. I remember the countless tears produced on one of the worst days in July 1942 by the famous love theme in Tchaikovsky's *Romeo and Juliet* Overture. Irrational no doubt, but true!

Significant of the sense of deadly danger was also the poem called *Courage* that Anna Akhmatova wrote during that summer (though it was not to be published until a year later):

> We know what today lies in the scales
> And what is happening now.
> The hour of courage has struck on the clock
> And courage will not desert us.
> It is not frightening to fall dead under enemy bullets

410

It is not bitter to remain homeless.
But we shall preserve you, our Russian speech,
Our great Russian word.
We shall carry you to the end, free and pure,
  And give you to our grandchildren and save you from bondage,
For ever.

It was during that summer that Shostakovich's famous *Leningrad Symphony* was first performed in Moscow. The impact of the first movement depicting the German invasion—which was now continuing—was truly overwhelming.

These emotional undertones, with the frantic *patrie-en-danger* mood, and in particular the psychological shock deliberately provoked after the fall of Rostov (and the changes it paved the way for) are scarcely mentioned at all in the Soviet histories. Curiously, a better picture of the mood of the people can be gained from the literature and indeed from the propaganda articles in the press at the time.

So far two feelings had characterised the literature and propaganda of that summer of 1942. One was the same love of Russia that had been so typical of all the writing at the height of the Battle of Moscow—only it was now a love that had even greater warmth and greater tenderness. It was, too, specifically a love of Russia proper, to which—apart from the Caucasus—the German advances had by now reduced the European part of the U.S.S.R. The other was hate—hate, no longer mingled with ridicule, or scarcely so (except for the "Winter Fritz" who still loomed large at the Moscow Circus). It grew during those summer months till it reached a paroxysm of frenzy during the blackest days of August. "Kill the German" became like Russia's Ten Commandments all in one. Sholokhov's *The School of Hate*, the story of a Russian prisoner who had suffered hell at the hands of humorously-sadistic Germans, published in several papers on June 23 had a profound effect. Poignant and convincing, it set the tone of much of the hate propaganda during the weeks that followed.

Ehrenburg, too, was a very important factor in the great battle for Russian morale in the summer of 1942; every soldier in the Army read Ehrenburg; and partisans in the enemy rear are known to have readily swopped any spare tommy gun for a bundle of Ehrenburg clippings. One may like or dislike Ehrenburg as a writer, but during those tragic weeks he certainly showed a genius for putting into biting, inspiring prose the burning hatred Russia felt for the Germans; this man, with his cosmopolitan background and his French culture, had grasped by intuition what the ordinary Russian really felt. Ideologically, it was unorthodox, but tactically, in the circumstances, it was thought right to give him a free hand. Read later in book form, his articles no longer make the same impression; but one must imagine oneself in the position of a Russian in the summer of 1942 who was watching the map and seeing one town going after another, one province going after another; one must put oneself in the position of a Russian soldier retreating to Stalingrad or Nalchik, saying to himself: How much farther are we going to retreat? How much farther *can* we retreat? The Ehrenburg articles helped such a man to pull himelf together. It wasn't Ehrenburg only; but Ehrenburg certainly holds a central place in the battle for Red Army morale. His articles were printed chiefly in *Red Star*, the army paper, and reprinted in hundreds of Front sheets. Some of the writings of Alexei Tolstoy, Simonov, Surkov and many others, also had an important effect on morale.

Simonov's play, *The Russian People*, printed in full in *Pravda* in July and performed in hundreds of theatres throughout the country, was typical of the "all Russians are united" motif: here, in a seaside town, a sort of miniature Sebastopol, a handful of Russians, an old ex-Tsarist officer among them, fight the Germans till nearly all are killed; they are touchingly frail human creatures fighting against a terrible inhuman machine. The emotional appeal of the play was overwhelming in the conditions of 1942; I remember how, at the Filiale of the Moscow Art Theatre, there was complete silence for at least ten seconds after the curtain had fallen at the end of the third act; for the last words had been: "See how Russian people are going to their death". Many women in the audience were weeping. Needless to say, there was a happy ending; in the last act the town was recaptured by the Red Army. It could not have been otherwise in those days: for a *Journey's End* driven to the very end, would have been too depressing. The feeling of hate for the Germans, already very strong in *The Russian People* (significant that it should have been called *Russian*, rather than "Soviet People")* grew in intensity during the summer and culminated in Simonov's famous *Kill Him!* poem. Another writer of considerable importance as a morale-builder was Alexei Surkov, the "soldier's poet", as distinct from Simonov, more the "officer's poet", besides many others like Semyon Kirsanov, Dolmatovsky, etc. Surkov's poem *I Hate* was published in *Red Star* of August 12 and concluded with the lines:

> My heart is as hard as stone,
> My grievances and memories are countless,
> With these hands of mine
> I have lifted the corpses of little children . . .
>
> I hate them deeply
> For those hours of sleepless gloom.
> I hate them because in one year
> My temples have grown white.
>
> My house has been defiled by the Prussians,
> Their drunken laughter dims my reason.
> And with these hands of mine
> I want to strangle every one of them.

And here was Ehrenburg at the height of the Russian retreat in the Northern Caucasus, and with the Germans breaking through to Stalingrad:

---

* It was later, but only later, when the danger was over, that Simonov was rather sharply criticised in retrospect for having made his characters look such "amateur partisans", guided no doubt by the finest patriotic motives, but still lacking all the organisational precision of the Communist Party. Their resistance was marked, as it were, by *partisanshchina* in the bad sense, i.e. a spontaneous act of self-sacrifice, without proper organisation behind it. This criticism was very similar to that which, in 1948, condemned Fadeyev's famous novel, *The Young Guard*, published two years before. Here also the young heroes of a Resistance group in the mining town of Krasnodon were charged, in retrospect, with *partisanshchina*. Worse still, Fadeyev, the official criticism said, had failed to point out that "in reality" all the Resistance Movement in the occupied territories had been directed by the Party, i.e. more or less directly from Moscow and by its representatives in German-occupied areas. Fadeyev was made to rewrite the novel.

... One can bear anything: the plague, and hunger and death. But one cannot bear the Germans. One cannot bear these fish-eyed oafs contemptuously snorting at everything Russian ... We cannot live as long as these grey-green slugs are alive. Today there are no books; today there are no stars in the sky; today there is only one thought: Kill the Germans. Kill them all and dig them into the earth. Then we can go to sleep. Then we can think again of life, and books, and girls, and happiness. ... Let us not rely on rivers and mountains. We can only rely on ourselves. Thermopylae did no stop them. Nor did the Sea of Crete. Men stopped them, not in the mountains, but in the suburban allotments of Moscow. We shall kill them all. But we must do it quickly; or they will desecrate the whole of Russia and torture to death millions more people.*

And on another day he wrote:

We are remembering everything. Now we know. The Germans are not human. Now the word "German" has become the most terrible swear-word. Let us not speak. Let us not be indignant. Let us kill. If you do not kill the German, the German will kill you. He will carry away your family, and torture them in his damned Germany... If you have killed one German, kill another. There is nothing jollier than German corpses.

These two propaganda themes were to continue, both before and after the fall of Rostov. But after its fall, a new note was also sounded—partly in support of the organisational changes being introduced into the Red Army. Self-pity and hatred of the Germans were no longer enough. Partly no doubt to explain to an acutely anxious country the disasters that had befallen the Red Army since May, the new line now taken was that the Army itself was largely to blame for what was happening—and *not* the Government—or Stalin.

In retrospect the violent criticisms of the Red Army that were made at this time seem unfair. They ignored the fact that in the summer of 1942 the Russians were still seriously short of heavy equipment, and that along most of the front in the south the Germans had a great superiority in tanks and, especially, in aircraft.

After the fall of Rostov there was a ruthless tightening up of discipline in the army—ruthless to the point of summary executions, all down the scale, for disobeying orders or displaying cowardice. Then

* *Red Star*, August 13, 1942.

too there was a propaganda drive in which the soldier's and the officer's personal honour and loyalty to his regiment were constantly invoked. One over-enthusiastic propagandist pointed out that even when a regiment received orders to retreat, it was still a blot on the regiment's reputation. More important still, it was impressed upon the soldiers that the country was disgruntled and disappointed in its own army. Political commissars were called upon to circulate among the troops plaintive and contemptuous letters received from soldiers' relatives.

Finally the post-Rostov changes marked the beginning of a rise in the status of officers in the Red Army. There was for instance the creation of new military decorations *for officers only*: the Orders of Suvorov, Kutuzov and Alexander Nevsky—significantly named after the "Great Ancestors".* This was part of the drive, which was to take on spectacular proportions soon afterwards, to create something like a new officer caste which would be thoroughly competent and, at the same time, smart and decorative. The "old warhorse", slovenly in his attire and easygoing in his soldiering, was more and more discredited in the post-Rostov propaganda drive. Before long, the dual command of officer-and-commissar was to be scrapped once again in favour of the officer's "sole command".

It was not until the height of the Stalingrad battle that epaulettes and a lot of gold braid were added to officers' uniforms—epaulettes like those which angry soldiers had torn off their officers' shoulders back in 1917. Out of the fire and smoke of Stalingrad the gold-braided officers emerged; in this gold braid the fires of Stalingrad were reflected, as it were. It was that which made those gold-braided epaulettes so popular and acceptable.† Their introduction was like a collective reward to the whole officer class of the Soviet Union. The

---

* There had already been an Alexander Nevsky Order under Nicholas II who had conferred it in 1912 on Poincaré, then French Prime Minister. Suvorov was Catherine II's most famous general, and Kutuzov was the victor of Napoleon in 1812.

† Much of this gold braid was imported from England, and the Russian request for vast quantities of it at first struck the British (as an Embassy official told me at the time) as "absurdly frivolous". They did not grasp the full significance of these exports until later.

gold braid also emphasized the *professionalism* of the Red Army. It was no longer a revolutionary army of *sans-culottes*; the time was drawing close when the Red Army would have its word to say as the greatest national army in Europe; it was only right that its officers should be as smartly dressed as the British and American officers— not to mention the German officers. It was psychologically very sound that the gold braid should have made its appearance during Stalingrad, and not before; fine uniforms would have looked all wrong in retreat. Nevertheless, the process of smartening up the Soviet officer, both inwardly and outwardly, was begun in the "psychological operation" that followed the Rostov disaster.

Since the Russian people had no sources of information except the Soviet radio and the press, the news and propaganda that these produced were, of course, of the utmost importance. Everybody, especially during those anxious days, waited frantically for the nightly communiqué, and most people had learned to read between the lines, and to decipher the adjectives. Propaganda articles were read with enormous interest by tens of millions of people. Ehrenburg, Sholokhov and Alexei Tolstoy (probably in this order) were immensely popular, as we have seen. So were some of the war correspondents' articles which, without necessarily telling all the truth, were known to tell at least some of the truth. Russia is probably also the only country where poetry is read by millions of people, and during the war, poets like Simonov and Surkov were read by everybody.

It is therefore interesting to see how the press handled the grim situation both before and after Rostov.

During the first week of July, the emphasis was on the heroic struggle of the men and women of Sebastopol which had just ended. Then, with the German offensive developing all over the south, the emphasis was, more and more, on "Holy Russia" and on hatred of the enemy. "Hatred of the Enemy" was the title of the *Pravda* editorial of July 11. The tone was still appealing, rather than threatening, as it was to become after Rostov:

> Our country is living through serious days. The Nazi dogs are
> frantically trying to break through to the vital centres of our country...

The wide steppes of the Don are spreading before their greedy eyes. Dear comrades at the Front! Your country believes in you. It knows that the same blood flows in your veins as in those of the heroes of Sebastopol... May holy hatred become our chief, our only feeling. This hatred combines a burning love of your country, anxiety for your family and children, and an unshakable will for victory... We have every chance to win. The enemy is in a hurry; he wants to achieve results which would forestall the Second Front. But he will not escape this danger. The stubbornness of the Soviet people has destroyed more than one enemy plan before now...

Here was a warning not to expect too much from the Allies, and to depend on Russia's own will to save herself.

A higher pitch of emotional patriotism, combined with the hatred motif, was reached by Simonov's poem, "Kill Him!" published in *Pravda* the day Voroshilovgrad fell—

If your home is dear to you where your Russian mother nursed you;
If your mother is dear to you, and you cannot bear the thought of the
    German slapping her wrinkled face;
If you do not want the German to tear down and trample on your
    father's picture, with the Crosses he earned in the last war;
If you do not want your old teacher to be hanged outside the old
    school-house;
If you do not want her, whom for so long you did not dare even kiss,
    to be stretched out naked on the floor, so that amid hatred, cries
    and tears, three German curs should take what belongs to your
    manly love;
If you don't want to give away all that which you call your Country,
Then kill a German, kill a German every time you see one...

And so on, and so on.

The young Communists' paper, *Komsomolskaya Pravda* tended rather more than *Pravda* to invoke the memory of Lenin, as well as memories of the Civil War. On the whole, it went in for "pep talks" rather than lamentations of the Ehrenburg variety. On July 24, foreshadowing, as it were, the more determined tone of the post-Rostov period, it recalled the heroic battles of the Civil War "under the banners of Stalin and Kirov, Voroshilov and Ordjonikidze"—

Yes, we remember how Stalin saved the south in incomparably more difficult conditions than the present ones. "We had no line of retreat left," Voroshilov later related, "but comrade Stalin did not worry about that. His one thought was to smash the enemy, to win at any price. . ." So it was at Tsaritsyn in the autumn of 1918. So it will be again now. Our army is convinced of it. Our entire people are convinced of it. . . So let us close our ranks, young friends, more vigorously, and smash the hated invaders. . . *

The first press reactions to the fall of Rostov were still fairly mild, and the *Pravda* editorial of July 28 tended to blame the absence of the Second Front for what had happened, enumerating the nine infantry and two armoured divisions that had arrived "from France and Holland" in the last few weeks. But something clearly happened on July 29 at the highest Government and Party level; for, on July 30, (the day of Stalin's "Not a step back" order) *Pravda* set a new tone altogether:

> Iron discipline and a steady nerve are the conditions of our victory. "Soviet soldiers! Not a step back!"—Such is the call of your country. . . Our Soviet country is large and rich, but there is nothing worse than to imagine that you can, without making a maximum effort, yield even an inch of ground, or abandon this or that town without fighting to the last drop of blood. The enemy is not as strong as some terrified panic-mongers imagine.

What followed was even stronger meat:

> Every soldier must be ready to die the death of a hero rather than neglect his duty to his country.

Four times in the editorial the phrase "iron discipline" was used.

> During the Civil War Lenin used to say: "He who does not help the Red Army wholeheartedly, and does not observe its order and iron discipline is a traitor". . . And at the 8th Congress of the Party, Stalin said: "Either we shall have a strictly disciplined army, or we shall perish." Today the officer's order is an iron law.

Red Star that day was even more explicit. It gave the same quotation from Lenin with this addition from the same speech: "He who does not observe order and discipline is a traitor, *and must be mercilessly destroyed.*"

* It is curious that the paper should have then prophesied that the Germans would be stopped at Stalingrad (the former Tsaritsyn).

Now is not the time when a coward or traitor can rely on mercy. Every officer and political worker can, with the powers given him by the State, see to it that the very idea of retreating without orders becomes impossible... Not a step back: such is the country's order, the order of our leader and general, Comrade Stalin.

The "power" given to the officer and commissar mentioned here was nothing less than the right to shoot or to order the summary execution of traitors or cowards.

On August 1 *Red Star* added a macabre (and so far unpublicised) detail to the familiar story of the 28 Panfilov men who had died in the battle of Moscow, fighting against German tanks to the last man:

They dealt with one contemptible coward. Without any preliminary discussion all the Panfilov men fired at the traitor; that sacred volley symbolized their determination not to retreat another step, and to fight to the bitter end.

It also recalled Shchors, the Civil War hero, one of whose rules was: "A soldier who has left the battlefield without officer's orders is shot like a traitor."

There is good reason to believe that, on the strength of these new "iron discipline" rules about "traitors" and "cowards", certain commissars in the Red Army went too far during the week that followed. Nothing else would explain the extraordinary editorial of *Red Star* on August 9, which said that one must, after all, discriminate between incorrigible cowards and men who had momentarily lost their nerve:

The War Commissar (says the Statute of the Presidium of the Supreme Soviet) is the representative of the Party and the Government in the Red Army and, together with the officer, he bears full responsibility for the performance of military tasks and ... for the determination to fight to the last drop of blood... If you see that you have before you an obvious enemy or defeatist, a coward or panic-monger ... then it is no use wasting any propaganda or persuasion on him. You must deal with a traitor with an iron hand. But sometimes you come across people who need your temporary support; after that they will firmly take themselves in hand...

This was, clearly, a warning to trigger-happy commissars ready to kill off all "cowards".

The second part of the same editorial already foreshadowed the coming abolition of the commissars in their present rôle:

It is a great mistake to imagine, as some comrades do, that in battle the political commissar must act in precisely the same way as the officer, on the ground that, in the midst of a battle, there is no time to argue; that the only thing to do is to give orders, and to punish if these orders are not obeyed. Naturally, every soldier bears the gravest responsibility for the non-fulfilment of his superior's orders on the battlefield. *But the commissar's task is, first and foremost, to eliminate the possibility of such things happening. And his chief weapon is political agitation, the Bolshevik persuasion of men.* [Emphasis added.]

Thus this truly historical article in the Red Army's paper not only sounded the alarm over the excessively ruthless and perhaps irresponsible application of the new "iron discipline" rules, but also brought to the surface the chronic conflict that had been brewing for a long time between the officer and the commissar. In applying the new rules, the commissars (generally harder and more rigid people than the officers) had apparently gone to extremes which the officers in many cases resented. *Red Star* clearly suggested now that the meting out of punishment was not the commissar's primary job, and that in fact, it wasn't his job at all, but the officer's; the commissar's primary job was "agitation and Bolshevik persuasion". This was a very clear indication that the two functions would soon be sharply divided. After this *Red Star* protest against the indiscriminate shooting of "cowards" the ferocious articles in the press stopped almost completely.

Another theme that kept on recurring in Soviet propaganda was "Don't ever surrender. Captivity in Germany is worse than death." *Pravda* of August 13, quoted with appropriate comments, numerous letters from Germany, including one from a German woman called Gertrude Renn, and dated February 2, 1941:

It is very cold, nearly as cold as in Russia. A lot of potatoes this winter got frozen. These are given to the Russians who devour them raw. At Fallingbostell 200 or 300 Russians die every week, from hunger or cold. After all, they don't deserve anything else.

Whether genuine or not, this letter certainly sounds perfectly plausible in the light of what one learned then or later about Russian war-prisoners in Germany. For all that, especially in 1942, a black mark was almost automatically placed against the name of any Russian soldier who had fallen into German hands, while Russians who escaped from German captivity (or even broke out of a German encirclement) were, as a rule, treated as "suspects". Some were cleared; others put in "punitive battalions", others still, as we know from certain recent publications, were sent to Russian "labour" camps.

I recall a grim conversation I had with a Russian colonel shortly before the fall of Sebastopol, where many thousands of Russians were to fall into German hands.

What was it, the Colonel said, that made Sebastopol so different from Tobruk or Singapore? "Isn't it because of the Russian's more intense hatred of the enemy, and because of the British temptation to surrender when all hope of holding out is lost? Is not the good treatment of British war prisoners by the Germans part of a definite policy—aiming at stopping the British from fighting to the last man?"

"Do you then suggest," I said, "that if the Germans treated Russian war prisoners better, Sebastopol would have fallen long ago?" "No," he said rather angrily, "because such calculations don't enter the head of a Russian soldier, still less a Soviet sailor. These people loathe the guts of every German. Besides, they know that by fighting this hopeless battle of Sebastopol till the very end, they are tying up very large German and Rumanian forces, and are so helping the rest of the Front. Here is heroism—but heroism plus definite orders."

I then brought up the question of the International Red Cross, the Geneva Convention, and so on. Would it not be better if Russian war prisoners were given some International Red Cross protection, for instance, as Molotov had indeed suggested? The colonel said to this: "I am not so sure about that. The damned Germans are going to trick the International Red Cross, anyway, at least as far as our prisoners are concerned. We treat the German war prisoners reasonably well* because, in the long run, it's a policy that will pay—not

* This was, of course, much too sweeping a statement.

that we like doing it. These swine are better fed than millions of our civilians—and that's a galling thought. But would a convention with the Germans on war prisoners be a good thing? Our troops have gone through hell, and will go through many more hells before we are finished with this war. And in such a hell—I am ready to admit it—the thought that a comfortable bed and breakfast—the kind of thing British prisoners get—may be secured by the simple gesture of surrendering to the Germans might be bad for morale. Not every man in our army has the makings of a hero. So let him die, rather than surrender... Listen, this is a terrible war, more terrible than anything you've ever seen. It's an agonising thought that our prisoners are starved to death in German camps. But, politically, the Germans are making a colossal blunder. If the Germans treated our prisoners well, it would soon be known. It's a horrible thing to say; but by ill-treating and starving our prisoners to death, the Germans are *helping* us."

The interesting thing is that the Germans used very much the same kind of reasoning; German propaganda aimed at impressing upon every soldier that falling into Russian hands was equal to suicide: either he would be immediately shot, or die a slow agonising death "in Siberia". This was, roughly, the story of every German prisoner whom I was to see later in the Don country, at Stalingrad and in numerous battles after Stalingrad, when the fear of encirclement became a kind of obsession with the German army, and even led to some unexpected withdrawals. Also, rather than surrender, many SS-men committed suicide.

It will be convenient here to look a little beyond the pre-Stalingrad phase of the war, and deal with the next stages in the process which began immediately after the fall of Rostov. These next steps may be said to fall under three headings: the "inner" smartening-up of the officer corps through the promotion of many young officers who had shown a high degree of technical competence during the war, and the demotion or shelving of the "old war-horses", a process which had already had its precedent in 1941 with the removal from key positions in the Army of men like Voroshilov and Budienny. This shelving of the "old war horses" served to divert popular annoyance about the military defeats from the Party (including Stalin) to "certain" Army leaders. Secondly, there was the "outer" smartening-up of the Soviet officer through the introduction of smarter uniforms, complete with epaulettes and gold braid. Thirdly, the process begun soon after Rostov of drawing a clear line between the officer's and the commissar's respective roles (see the *Red Star* editorial of August 9 quoted above) was brought to its logical conclusion on October 9, when the officer's "sole command" was at last restored.

The contrast between the old and new types of officer was vividly brought out in Korneichuk's play *The Front* which is worth examining, if only because of the enormous publicity given to it.*

The main theme of the play was the conflict between Army-General Gorlov, Commander of a Front (i.e. army group) and his subordinate, Major-General Ognev, in command of one of the armies. Gorlov is an amiable man, brave, with a fine Civil War record, but wholly unsuitable for modern warfare.

He pokes more or less good-natured fun at the "specialists", and proudly claims: "I have never gone through any of your academies or universities; I am not one of your theorist chaps. I'm an old war-horse." Personal bravery, to him, is the secret of military success. "We'll smash any enemy," he says, "not with wireless operators, but with heroism and valour." He is surrounded by toadying nonentities who flatter him; they are men with none of Gorlov's fundamental honesty. Among them are his intelligence chief, the editor of the Front newspaper, a war correspondent, and his liaison officer. All of them are drawn in a highly satirical vein.

The central figure in the opposite camp is Ognev, a young general with a mastery of modern warfare. He is supported by Gorlov's brother, director of a large aircraft factory, and worshipped by Gorlov's own son. The atmosphere in Gorlov's headquarters is thoroughly easy-going, with frequent supper parties, toasts and smug speeches. Ognev is disgusted by all this, and Gorlov's brother, who has come on a tour of inspection from Moscow (where he had discussed aircraft production with Stalin himself) is taken aback by all

* Korneichuk told me soon afterwards that the "general idea" of the play had been given to him by Stalin himself.

this and then reports to Moscow on the very unsatisfactory job his brother is doing. The central episode is one where the two schools of thought clash in a military operation which Gorlov completely bungles; then the situation is saved, at heavy cost, by Ognev's much clearer vision of the Germans' intentions and by his far better organisation.

In the very first scene the following typical conversation occurs:

General Gorlov (to Udivitelny, the Intelligence Chief): How many German tanks are there at Kolokol station?
Udivitelny: Fifty, comrade commander.
Gorlov: Not more?
Udivitelny: Maybe they've brought up a few more in the last five days, but I shouldn't think so.
Gorlov: But Ognev says they've got three hundred.
Udivitelny: But how's that possible, comrade commander? I don't imagine they've got more than five hundred along the whole Front.
Gorlov (to Ognev): There you are!
Ognev: Why then are they bringing up petrol at such a rate to Kolokol?
Udivitelny: I couldn't say. I suppose they are preparing for the next offensive. They've got stores there, anyway.
Ognev: Who is in command of the Germans here?
Udivitelny: I really don't know. Before, they had that—what d'you call him; difficult sort of name; can't remember; Major-General von something-or-other. He was replaced. Who the present Von is I couldn't say.
Ognev: What fire power have they got?
Udivitelny: Well, the usual four divisions—with a seventy per cent complement; couldn't tell you exactly.
Ognev: Have they got any ski regiments?
Udivitelny: I don't suppose so. Maybe a few small groups. Why, the Germans weren't preparing for winter.
Ognev (yelling): God damn you! What the hell do I care what *you* think? What I want to know is what the Germans have actually got. Answer me: do you know, or don't you know?
Kolos (commander of the cavalry group): Volodya, please. . .
Gorlov: Why yell like this; this isn't a bazaar.
Ognev: You ask him why he is lying like a carpet-vendor at a bazaar. What the hell does he mean by "maybe" and "I suppose so", "That's possible", and "I don't imagine so". How can you issue orders if that's all your Intelligence produces? What data have you?

With the snow-storm raging for five days, what kind of data could you have got from your air reconnaissance? What else do you know? Nothing. And in these five days the Germans might have done any damned thing.

Here was the official condemnation by the Party of Russia's peculiar brand of Blimps; these, in September 1942, were produced as an answer to the bewildered questions why the Germans were again, for the second year in succession, overrunning vast areas of Russian territory.

In the last act, after a hard victory has been won, and disaster averted by Ognev, despite Gorlov's original orders, Gorlov is dismissed from his post. He is bewildered, but begins to understand, and accepts his removal with good grace. In the course of the action, his son, one of Ognev's most devoted admirers, is killed. Gorlov is not treated viciously in the play, and whoever has seen *The Front* at the Moscow Art Theatre will remember the pathetic, almost Chekhovian figure Gorlov cuts in the last act when played by the great Moskvin.

But the play is intended to convey an optimistic message. In the end, not only Gorlov, but his whole *entourage* disappear; and they are replaced by other men like Ognev, who have been brought to the surface by the war itself, and who, in addition to their "academic" training, have also learned a great deal from direct military experience. Ognev is very much the *new* type of the Soviet officer and, in a sense, the publication of the play in September 1942 constitutes an important link between the immediate "post-Rostov" reforms and their logical sequel, the heightening of the officer's role in the Red Army, his "glamourisation" through the introduction of new uniforms, and above all, the abolition of the commissars and the restoration of "sole command".

That many "Ognevs" had been exiled and even shot in the 1937-8 Purge is, needless to say, not even alluded to in Korneichuk's play. Rokossovsky, for one, was well aware of it; and that may be why he (and many other officers) did not care for the play. They felt, moreover, that it produced some awkward discussions among the troops themselves, and caused some disrespectful questions to be asked. Paradoxically, the play was, on the one hand, a Party-versus-Army

demonstration, but, on the other, an exaltation of the professional
soldier at the expense of the old civil war hack with his more "revolutionary" tradition.

The full restoration of the officer's "single command" was contained in the *ukase* of the Presidium of the Supreme Soviet of
October 9, which abolished the Institute of the Political Commissars
in the Red Army. The *ukase*, alluding to the friction that often used
to arise inside an army unit between the officer and the commissar,
especially during the hard weeks of the retreat, explained that there
was now no further need for political commissars in the old sense;
they had originally been introduced during the Civil War to keep
an eye on the officers, many of whom had belonged to the old
Tsarist Army and "who did not believe in the strength of the Soviet
regime and were even alien to it."

Without as much as alluding to the reduced rôle of the commissars under Tukhachevsky, and the "politisation" of the Army
after the purges, the abolition of "dual command" in 1940, at Timoshenko's insistence, and its reintroduction once more at the beginning
of the German invasion in 1941, the *ukase* merely said that, since the
Civil War, a large number of officers had been trained under Soviet
conditions, and that, during the present war, "an enormous number
of new and experienced officers have emerged; they have acquired
the greatest experience, have proved their devotion to their country,
and have grown in stature both militarily and politically."

> On the other hand the commissars and political workers have greatly
> increased their military knowledge; some of them have already been
> given commanding posts ... while others may be employed as officers
> right away, or after a certain period of military training... In the cir-
> cumstances, there is no longer any reason for having political
> commissars in the Red Army. What is more, the perpetuation of the
> Institute of Political Commissars may act as an obstacle in achieving
> the best results in the command of the troops; this, in itself, would put
> the commissars in a false and awkward position. The time has therefore
> come for establishing complete Single Command, and for placing upon
> the officer the sole responsibility for military decisions...

Thus dual control was abolished; the commissar was turned into the officer's "deputy in the political field"; he was also an officer, but usually of junior rank and was, above all, in charge of political education, propaganda, welfare, etc. The important thing was that he could no longer interfere with the officer's decisions, least of all with his operational decisions.

Another great practical advantage of this reform, after the terrible losses suffered since June 1941, was the great increase, within a short time, in officer *cadres* drawn from the ranks of ex-commissars, most of whom had had first-hand experience of the war.

The *ukase* replaced the "institute" of political commissars and political instructors (the opposite numbers of the n.c.o.'s) by an "institute" of "deputy-commanders in the political field in army units, staffs, sub-units, military schools, and in the central ... offices of the People's Commissariat for Defence. . ."

The *Red Star* editorial of October 11 pointed out that numerous commissars had had a gallant war record; there had been many cases when an officer was killed or wounded, and the commissar took over his duties. Many such commissars had already been given officers' posts. The article emphasised that the latest *ukase* was, in effect, the last phase of a process that had gone on for a long time. Distorting history pretty mercilessly by omitting all that had happened in the late 1930's and also since the war, it set out to show that the latest reform, was in effect, merely an application of the army reform Frunze had advocated back in the early 'twenties. Tukhachevsky, that opponent of "dual command" was, of course, not mentioned.

Having extolled the merits of "single command", *Red Star* nevertheless went on to say that the new reform did not mean any lowering in the standard of political education and Bolshevik agitation in the army.

> The officers' deputies in the political field must continue this propaganda ... They must go on forging men of iron, capable of the greatest fearlessness, of the greatest spirit of self-sacrifice in this battle against the hated Hitlerites.

In conclusion it said that the Red Army would very shortly be endowed with 200 new regimental commanders and 600 new battalion commanders drawn from the ranks of the ex-commissars.

All this was, in a sense, a clear victory of the "Army" over the "Party".

Together with this reform came the introduction of the new uniforms. A little later, in 1943, in addition to new uniforms, a whole code of manners was introduced for officers; above a certain rank, for instance, they could not travel by public transport, and were not allowed to "carry paper parcels". Altogether a number of points from the etiquette of the old Tsarist Army were revived.

Chapter VI

STALIN ROPES IN THE CHURCH

The establishment of correct and even seemingly cordial relations between Church and State had been one of the imperatives of Soviet Government policy ever since the beginning of the war. Even before the war, especially since the publication of the "Stalin" Constitution of 1936 which guaranteed freedom of religious beliefs, the cruder forms of anti-religious propaganda had been largely abandoned. As we have seen, one of the most comic episodes in this process had been the decease, a fortnight after the German invasion, of Emelian Yaroslavsky's famous "anti-God" weekly, *Bezbozhnik*.*

The aim of the Soviet Government was to create absolute national unity; and, with a very high proportion of soldiers in the Army coming from peasant families, among whom religious traditions were still strong, it was important to do nothing that would offend their religious "prejudices". With government propaganda becoming more and more patriotic and nationalist, complete with invocations of the great national heroes of the past, including a saint of the Orthodox Church—St. Alexander Nevsky—it was impossible to treat the Church as a hostile element in what soon came to be known as "the Great Patriotic War". It was, indeed, essential to secure the utmost co-operation from the Church, and to induce the clergy to do patriotic propaganda among the faithful, and support the Soviet regime, rather than look for salvation to the Germans who, despite

* See p. 177.

all the monstrosities of their occupation policy, still gave some encouragement to the Orthodox Church which they regarded (not unreasonably) as an element with serious grievances against the Soviet system. To the Soviet Government the Church was, in effect, a potential Fifth Column, which it was imperative to win over.

Some of the Orthodox clergy in the occupied areas certainly collaborated with the Germans, or pretended to—particularly during the earlier stages of the war—while some members of the Ukrainian church hierarchy were wholly subservient to Berlin to the end. In 1941 and 1942 there were many instances of the Germans posing as liberators of the Christian faith in the occupied areas. General Guderian mentions, for example, the town of Glukhov, near Briansk, where "the population asked our permission to use their church as a place of worship once again. We willingly handed it over to them."* In their radio propaganda the Germans made much of this "revival" of religion in the areas they had occupied, and the fact that some priests were said to have joined the partisans was insufficient to cancel out these German claims entirely. Moscow was particularly sensitive, in 1942, to hostile propaganda, especially in the United States, on the ground that there was no "freedom of religion" in Russia.

A curious landmark in the story of the Russian church during the war was the publication by the Moscow Patriarchate, in August 1942, of a sumptuously-bound and admirably printed and illustrated volume called *The Truth about Religion in Russia*. Its flyleaf claimed that 50,000 copies had been printed. The Central Committee itself had not produced such a typographical masterpiece for years; there was obviously a great deal behind this publication. It was certainly intended partly for foreign consumption.

Much of the book had been written (or purported to have been written) by Father Sergius, Metropolitan of Moscow and Kolomna, and *locum tenens* of the Patriarchal Throne since the death of the Patriarch Tikhon in 1925. Although Tikhon's anti-Soviet attitude was well known, Sergius nevertheless recalled that, according to Tikhon, the "Soviet order means the rule of the people ... and is, therefore, firm and unshakable". Sergius further recalled (a rather

* Guderian, op cit., p. 228.

piquant touch) that Tikhon had "explicitly condemned" the schism
in the Orthodox Church, brought about by the Karlovite* sect, who
for years had waged war against the Metropolitan Evlogi of Paris,
the head of the "true" Russian church in Western Europe. The
Karlovites were *émigré* extremists who later identified themselves
with the teachings of Hitler. The Orthodox Church, as represented
by Sergius, was the old Russian Church, but deprived of the financial
and other earthly privileges it had enjoyed under the Tsars. In the
old days the Tsar himself had been head of the Church; but the
separation of Church and State was, in Sergius's opinion, all to the
good.

This attack on the "Karlovites" was in fact a disguised attack on
Father Vvedensky's "Living Church" which had created a schism,
not among the émigrés, but in Russia itself. This Living Church had
been encouraged by Lunacharsky and other members of the Soviet
government in the early years of the Revolution. This attack on
"schisms" in 1942 clearly showed that the Soviet Government was
willing to throw Vvedensky and his "Living Church" overboard; it
had, indeed, been a failure; people went to a Vvedensky church only
when there was no "real" church in the neighbourhood. The "Living
Church" was, indeed, to be disbanded in 1943. It went, as it were,
into voluntary liquidation, with Vvedensky recanting, and its priests
and bishops submitting to the authority of Sergius, who was elected
Patriarch in 1943.

The disappearance of the Vvedensky Church was in the logic of
things: it was important to the Soviet Government that there should
be only *one* Russian Church.

In *The Truth about Religion in Russia* Sergius wrote that the loss
by the Church and the monasteries of land and other property did
not denote persecution, but "a return to Apostolic times when priests
pursued their profession. . . more in accordance with the teachings
of Christ." The separation of Church and State had had a purifying
effect on the Church; now only true believers went to church, and
nominal Christians had dropped out. No doubt he regretted that

---

* Named after Karlovac in Yugoslavia, a centre of violently anti-
Moscow religious activity among the White-Russian émigrés. See W.
Kolarz, *Religion in the Soviet Union*, p. 41 (London 1961).

communists should "adhere to the anti-religious standpoint". It was certain, however, that anti-religious propaganda had been in decline for several years past, and had disappeared completely since the beginning of the war.

Since the beginning of the war, Sergius went on, the attitude of the Church had been clearer than ever. It rejected absolutely Hitler's "crusade" for its liberation. Although no priests were attached to the Red Army, the Church constantly prayed for this Army, and also said innumerable prayers for individual soldiers at their families' request. In their sermons Russian churchmen now constantly referred to the Nazis as the successors of "the foul hounds"—the Teutonic Knights, whom St Alexander Nevsky, the patron saint of Leningrad, had routed in 1242 on the ice of Lake Peipus.

Sergius went on to say that he had recently addressed an Epistle to the Orthodox faithful in occupied territories, telling them that they must never forget that they were Russians and that they must do nothing, wittingly or unwittingly, while under the German yoke, which would be a betrayal of their homeland.

He also said that the Church had proved its patriotic fervour not only in words, but also in deeds; it was helping the Red Army not only with prayers, but also with gifts and collections. Thus the Holy Trinity Church at Gorki had recently collected a million roubles for the Defence Fund.

The book also devoted much space to the "chaos" in the Orthodox Church abroad. Those who saw eye to eye with the Russian Church, it said, were dismissed or persecuted by the Germans: this was true of Gabriel, Patriarch of Serbia, of Chrysanthos, Metropolitan of Athens, and Stefan, the Bulgarian Metropolitan, "who because of his great sympathy for the patriotism of the Russian Orthodox Church," had fallen into disfavour with the Germans and was "frequently attacked in the pro-Nazi press."

> Great sympathy for the patriotism of the Russian Church has also been shown by the Near-Eastern Patriarchs of Alexandria, Antioch and Jerusalem, as well as by Benjamin Fedchikov, Metropolitan of the Aleutians and North America [who represented the Moscow Patriarchate under that picturesque title in the United States]. He has worked steadily in favour of American aid to Russia, despite the Theophilites,

an Orthodox sect, who have been engaged in anti-Soviet propaganda, and have been urging President Roosevelt to send an ultimatum to the Soviet Government demanding guarantees of "religious freedom" in Russia after the war.

The book further contained a sharp attack on certain "church quislings", notably in the Ukraine, who, after accepting the authority of the Moscow Patriarchate, were now serving Hitler in fostering Ukrainian "nationalism". In an Epistle addressed to the Ukrainian faithful, Sergius stated that Bishop Sikorsky had presented himself to the German authorities as the "Archbishop of Luck and Kovel and Head of the Ukrainian Orthodox Church." This imposter "had promised his faithful co-operation to the Germans, whom he had addressed as the liberators of the Ukrainian People'".

The true Orthodox Church in the Ukraine, said Sergius, was the Church which was "sharing all the hardships and sorrows of the Russian people."

The second part of the book told of the German destruction of numerous valuable churches (notably the New Jerusalem Monastery at Istra and the Novgorod churches), and of the fearful atrocities committed by the enemy in occupied areas. Conscious of the sufferings inflicted by the Germans on the Russian people, the book said, the priests had nearly everywhere [*sic*] refused to fraternise with the German "liberators".

For all that, in 1942, the Church was still very down-at-heel, and it was not till later that steps were taken to restore church buildings— buildings of "historic value"—and that the Patriarch and the newly formed Synod were given decent quarters in Moscow. These measures, and others of a financial nature were taken after the establishment of a special Department for Church Affairs at the Council of People's Commissars, with a Mr Karpov at its head—a comrade who had been a police official in charge of church matters and who was now sometimes jokingly referred to in Moscow as "Narkombog" or "Narkomop", i.e. People's Commissar for God, or People's Commissar for Opium (for the people).

But in the summer of 1942, churches in Moscow—and even

"Moscow Cathedral", which had never been more than a very large and ugly and relatively modern suburban church—were still a dismal and depressing sight. The cathedral remained one of the few Moscow centres of organized, professional and completely unashamed begging, even though the rouble notes and twenty-kopek pieces they were given can hardly have been of any value to the wretched tattered old women. The congregation consisted chiefly of elderly people, though there were also some young women—many of them with children. They kept passing on to the altar slips of paper with the names of those they wished included in the prayers. Then there were collections "for the poor" and "for the restoration of the church"—which it certainly badly needed. Only very few soldiers could be seen among the congregation. The priests' robes were on the shabby side, though the robes and crown of the Metropolitan Nicholas looked impressive enough; but there seemed a shortage of both incense and candles, and the singing was poor and uninspired. The whole scene was drab and miserable.

By 1943 there was already a great improvement. The church attendance, especially on Easter night, was extraordinarily high; whole streets adjoining the twenty-five or thirty churches in Moscow were crowded with people who could find no room inside. A Party member told me: "The Party and the Komsomol have been much impressed by the number of people who went to church this Easter—much more even than usual." One explanation was that people knew that the Church was no longer frowned upon by the authorities. Significantly, there were many more soldiers in the churches in 1943 than there had been in previous years.

The establishment of more "correct" relations with the Church in 1942–3 was part of both a short-term and a long-term policy. It was certainly part of that drive for "complete national unity", which the grim situation of 1942 demanded. The Church derived considerable benefits from it and, in return, became increasingly vocal in its loyalty to the regime, even to the point of saying special prayers for Stalin, and treating him as an "anointed of the Lord", though no doubt in only a figurative way.

Internationally the "reconciliation" with the Church served a great variety of purposes: it made a good impression on the Allies, particularly the United States; it made the Moscow Patriarchate play the role of a sort of Greek-Orthodox Vatican, intolerant of any suspect "sects". Leaders of the Russian Orthodox Church were also encouraged to fraternise for instance with leaders of the Anglican Church, and were prominent in such organisations as the All-Slav Committee, and were even used to add the weight of their authority to more dubious bodies such as the Committee of Inquiry into the Katyn Murders* After the war the Metropolitan Nicholas, in his golden robes also added lustre to international Peace Congresses where he spoke alongside other leading Soviet personalities like Korneichuk and Ehrenburg.

Looking beyond 1942, we may briefly summarise the story of State-Church relations during and just after the War. As Walter Kolarz was to write later in his excellent *Religion in the Soviet Union*,

> The ideological content of Soviet communism in 1941 or 1943 was infinitely more patriotic than it was in the twenties or early thirties. All sorts of nationalist contraband had infiltrated into the official communist ideology ... The Church found Stalin's revised communism attractive to its traditional way of thinking.†

Kolarz also recalls how in 1941–3 the church leaders assisted the war effort not only in words but also in deeds. When a tank column christened "Dimitri Donskoi"‡ paid for out of funds collected by the Church was handed over to the Army, the Metropolitan Nicholas spoke of Russia's "sacred hatred of the fascist robbers" and referred to Stalin as "our common Father, Joseph Vissarionovich".

In September 1943 a sort of "concordat" was concluded between the Church and the State, after Stalin had himself received all the

* See p. 661.
† Kolarz, op. cit., p. 49.
‡ The valiant Russian Prince who routed the Tartars on the Field of Kulikovo in 1380. An oratorio in his honour by Yuri Shaporin had been given a Stalin Prize in 1941 just before the war.

three Metropolitans (Sergius, Alexis and Nicholas), at the Kremlin. As a result of this meeting the Church was allowed to elect its Patriarch and to re-establish a proper ecclesiastical government, the Holy Synod. The Russian Orthodox Church was allowed to resume publication of the *Journal of the Moscow Patriarchate* which had been suspended in 1936, and to open a limited number of theological seminaries and academies. The Church was also recognised as a "juridical person" entitled to own property.

The official recognition of the Patriarchal Church as the sole legal representative of the Orthodox Christians became fully operative in October 1943 with the appointment of the "Council for the affairs of the Russian Orthodox Church" under the above mentioned Karpov, which was to act as the go-between between the Patriarchate and the Soviet Government. It issued licences for the opening and restoration of churches; and another of its duties was to look after the material interests and even personal comfort of the Patriarch and his closer collaborators.

The Patriarchate became, as it were, part of the Soviet Establishment. It not only made a great show of the Church's loyalty to the regime, and of a special devotion to Stalin personally, but it also became a political instrument of considerable international importance.

Sergius, the first war-time Patriarch, died in May 1944, and was succeeded by Alexis, the Metropolitan of Leningrad and Novgorod. By the time Alexis was elected, the Russians had practically won the war; but this did not mean that the Church had outlived its usefulness from Stalin's point of view.

> Church support was still needed to enhance the respectability of the Soviet Government ... and was particularly essential in the fight against centrifugal forces in the borderlands. ... Outside the new Soviet borders there was even more for the Church to do as an ally of the Soviet State. The Red Army was now operating in countries with an Orthodox population—Rumania, Bulgaria and Serbia—and the Russian Orthodox Church could assist in promoting ... friendship among the Orthodox peoples of the Balkans.*

The unspectacular election of Sergius as Patriarch in 1943 by a

* Kolarz, op. cit., p. 56.

handful of metropolitans and bishops contrasted strikingly with the sumptuous election of Alexis in February 1945 attended by 204 ecclesiastical dignitaries and laymen. Among the guests were the Patriarchs of Antioch and Alexandria and the representatives of other Balkan and Near-East Patriarchs. Metropolitan Benjamin of North America was also present, and alluded approvingly to the old messianic traditions of the Russian Orthodox Church by saying that Moscow might yet become "The Third Rome".

Stalin was all in favour of Moscow's becoming a sort of "Vatican" of the Orthodox Church, and Alexis was given every encouragement to extend his foreign contacts and to claim for himself and his Church a leading position in the religious world. On April 10, 1945 Stalin had another meeting with the Patriarch Alexis and the Metropolitan Nicholas, and gave the Patriarch every encouragement for his forthcoming journey to the Near and Middle East—a journey which lasted four weeks. A special plane, piloted by a Hero of the Soviet Union, was placed at the Patriarch's disposal. The political implications of all these contacts were obvious enough; and, as already said, the Church hierarchy, and in particular the Metropolitan Nicholas were to lend special respectability to a variety of committees of inquiry, as well as to the Peace Movement in its various international manifestations, such as the famous congress of the Partisans of Peace at the Salle Pleyel in Paris in 1949.

There was much talk in Moscow, especially towards the end of the war, about Stalin, the ex-seminarist, having a soft spot for the Church, which was thought to be somehow associated in his mind with the Muscovite State and with his "forerunners", the Moscow Tsars.

The international purpose served by the Church was also only too obvious. It did its best to establish a friendly contact with certain other Churches; a great fuss was made over the visit to Moscow of the Archbishop of York whose only complaint was that the bearded old gentlemen would insist on kissing him on every possible occasion; he thought this "constant diving into their whiskers" was being a bit overdone. Sir Archibald Clark Kerr (later Lord Inverchapel), the British Ambassador told me, at the end of 1944, about a meeting he had with Stalin, at which the Marshal assured him that "in his own way, he also believed in God." "I dare say," Clark Kerr commented, "he had his tongue in his cheek when he said so; but it is surely interesting that he should have thought it politic to make such a remark to me!"

The *modus vivendi* established between the Church and the State during the war was of considerable mutual benefit, though no doubt it made many diehard communists squirm at times; it was all very "un-Leninist". Stalin's apparent wish that the Russian Orthodox Church should become a sort of "Vatican" for all Orthodox Christians throughout the world, met with a considerable measure of success, though not complete success. The resistance to the whole concept developed after the war, together wth the intensification of cold-war currents.

It is true that, even at the height of the Stalin-Patriarch honeymoon, both the Party and the Komsomol continued to discourage religious practices among their members, and no chaplains were ever attached to the Red Army. But active anti-religious propaganda in Russia was not to be resumed on a large scale until after Stalin's death.

The Russian Orthodox Church was traditionally anti-Catholic; nevertheless with the establishment of a Polish Army in Russia in 1943 and the subsequent liberation of Poland by the Red Army, Stalin was very anxious, at one stage, to normalise relations with the Catholic Church as well. In this he was much less successful. And, on one famous occasion, he even had a big practical joke played on him by an obscure American parish priest.*

* See p. 844 ff.

PART FIVE

Stalingrad

Chapter 1

STALINGRAD: THE CHUIKOV STORY

Broadly speaking, the Battle of Stalingrad may be divided into the following stages:

(1) July 17 to August 4, when the main fighting was still inside the Don Bend. Here the Russians attempted, on the strength of the "not-a-step-back" slogan at least to slow down the German advance. On the north side of the Bend, the Russians fought stubbornly in order to preserve at least a few bridgeheads. It was also hoped that, by slowing down the German advance, time would be gained for strengthening the "defences" of Stalingrad, which were being built by thousands of people in a feverish hurry but, as time was to show, without much effect.* Nevertheless, authorities such as General Yeremenko claim that the fighting outside the Don Bend was very valuable in slowing down the German advance, and in preventing them from either trapping large numbers of Russian troops inside the bend, or capturing Stalingrad at one fell swoop.

(2) August 5 to August 18. Having previously forced the south side of the Don at Tsymlianskaya, large portions of the German 6th Army, supported by General Hoth's panzer army, were now trying to outflank the Russians by striking towards Stalingrad via

* Yeremenko admits that only a quarter of these defences had been completed by August, and badly at that. (Yeremenko, op. cit., p. 76.) Moreover, these rudimentary defences were neither properly manned nor armed.

441

Kotelnikovo, Abganerovo and Plodovitoye, south-east of the city. By August 14 nearly the whole of the country inside the Don Bend (except for a few Russian-held bridgeheads in the north) had been overrun by the Germans. Besides attacking Stalingrad from the south, the Germans were also advancing on the city from the west and the north-west.

(3) August 19 to September 3. The fighting in the country between Don and Volga now reached its height. Although, south-east of the city, the enemy was held for some days along the Axai and then the Myshkova rivers, the Germans broke through to the Volga north of Stalingrad, forming there a five-mile-wide salient. This happened on August 23, a day which was also marked by a 600-bomber raid on Stalingrad. Despite the seemingly chaotic conditions created in the city by this super-air-raid, in which 40,000 were killed, neither the military nor the civilian authorities quite lost their heads; to avoid encirclement and also to stop the Germans from striking south from their Volga salient north of Stalingrad, the Russians hastened to retreat to the city. The German Rynok-Yerzovka salient north of Stalingrad was "stabilised".

(4) Between September 4 and 13 the fighting was concentrated on the "outskirts" of Stalingrad, but with the Germans breaking through to the Volga south of Stalingrad as well, the Russian 62nd Army found itself isolated from the rest of the Russian forces. On September 12 General Chuikov was appointed commander of the 62nd Army.

(5) The period from September 13 to November 18 was marked by the historic battle inside Stalingrad. By the middle of October, the Russians were holding only three small bridgeheads; but still the Germans were unable to dislodge them, despite a "final" offensive in the first half of November. The bulk of the Russian artillery was on the other side of the Volga and so relatively invulnerable, despite great German air superiority.

Then came the Russian counter-offensive:

(1) November 19 to December 11, during which period the Russians succeeded in finally encircling the Germans and Rumanians at Stalingrad.

(2) December 12 to January 1, which was chiefly marked by the

Hoth-Manstein attempt to break through to the encircled Stalingrad
troops, by its failure, a further widening of the Russian ring round
Stalingrad and the complete rout of the Italians on the Don.

(3) January 10 to February 2, 1943 marked by the final liquidation
of the German and Rumanian forces inside the Stalingrad "cauldron".

In considering the defensive stage of the Stalingrad battle, the
most important piece of evidence available, both on the military
aspects and on Russian morale, is the remarkable book *The Beginning of the Road* by General (now Marshal) Chuikov, who was the
Commander of the 62nd Army throughout the Stalingrad siege. Published in 1959, it is the best account of this complicated battle. It is
also one of the most candid books published by any Russian
General.*

Chuikov, who until the beginning of 1942 had been Soviet Military
Attaché at Chungking, was sent to the Stalingrad front at the beginning of July, when the Germans were advancing across the Don
country. In his account of the retreat to Stalingrad he gives a very
frank picture of the uneven morale of both troops and officers, including senior officers.

> Thus at the railway station of Frolovo [west of Stalingrad] I ran into
> the headquarters of the 21st Army. The H.Q. was on wheels. Every-
> thing, including Army Commander Gordov's sleeping outfit, was on the
> move—in cars and lorries. I did not like such excessive mobility. One
> could feel a lack of stability, and a lack of determination. They looked
> as though they were trying to get away from their pursuers—every-
> body, including the Army Commander.

A few days later, travelling west towards the Don, he also saw
evidence of very low morale:

> I saw how these people were moving along the waterless Stalingrad
> steppe from west to east, eating up their last reserves of food, and over-
> come by the stifling heat. When I asked them: "Where are you going?
> Who are you looking for?" they gave senseless answers: they all

* An English version of the expurgated 1961 edition was published
in London in 1963.

seemed to be looking for somebody on the other side of the Volga, or
in the Saratov region. . . In the steppe, I met the staffs of two divisions
who claimed to be looking for the H.Q. of the 9th Army. These staffs
consisted of a few officers sitting in three or fours cars, loaded to the
brim with petrol tins. In reply to my questions: "Where are the Germans? Where are our units? Where are you going?" they didn't know
what to say. It was, clearly, not going to be easy to restore the morale
of these people and the fighting spirit of the troops in retreat. . .

Some of the generals were no better. General Gordov, who had
been commander of the 21st Army, was appointed commander of the
64th Army, with Chuikov as his Deputy.

On the night of July 19 we met at the H.Q. of the 64th Army. . . I
had never met him before. He was a general with greying hair and
with tired grey eyes which seemed to see nothing, and whose cold
expression seemed to say: "Don't tell me about the situation, I know
all about it. There's nothing I can do about it, since such is my
fate."

Being in a defeatist mood, Gordov ordered that only part of his
Army should hold positions inside the Don Bend, and that the reserves be left on the east side of the Don. Chuikov was critical of this
decision, but adds that "General Gordov was not a man who tolerated any contradiction from his inferiors."

Nevertheless, only a few days later, Gordov was summoned to
Moscow and was appointed to the even higher post of commander
of the Stalingrad Front (i.e. Army Group). Meantime, Chuikov was
left as acting commander of the 64th Army. On July 25 the troops
under his command made contact with the Germans at Nizhne-
Chirskaya, in the south-east corner of the Don Bend. After describing a ferocious two-day battle, in the course of which many German
tanks were destroyed, and the Germans also suffered heavy casualties from the Russian *katyusha* mortars, Chuikov then relates how
the Germans nevertheless succeeded in breaking through the Russian
lines inside the Don Bend.

We had no tanks left, but I sent along several battalions of marines
to fill in the gap. . . It seemed that we would manage, in the end, to
close the breach. But here, unfortunately, a panic started. It did not
start in the front line, but in the rear. It started among the medical

personnel, in the artillery park and our transport units, all of them on the right bank of the river. They had heard from somewhere that the German tanks were within a couple of miles. In those days such a piece of news was sufficient to drive all these people in disorder to the river crossing. Through channels unknown to me this panic spread to the front line troops.

To stop this mass of people and vehicles from rushing towards the Don, I sent several members of my staff and my artillery chief, Major-General Brout, to the crossing. It was all too late and in vain. Enemy aircraft spotted this large concentration of people and cars at the river crossing, and proceeded to bomb it. In the course of this bombing General Brout... and several other officers of the Army H.Q. were killed.

By nightfall the Germans had destroyed the bridge, but one infantry division and some other small units were still inside the Don Bend. What happened next was only too typical of the lack of co-ordination at the top on the Russian side. In Chuikov's absence, the Chief of Staff of the 64th Army gave orders to these troops to retire beyond the Don. Arriving back at headquarters, Chuikov was appalled by this news, and promptly countermanded the order which might have led to another stampede and panic, particularly in the absence of any crossing in that area. The troops successfully dug in inside the Don Bend, and so filled the breach at the end of three days' heavy fighting.

Generals the world over have axes to grind, and Chuikov is no exception. Throughout this narrative he contrasts good troops with bad troops, good leadership with bad leadership. Thus, when he learned, at the height of the fighting inside the Don Bend, that General Kolpakchi had been relieved of his command of the 62nd Army, and had been replaced by Lieutenant-General Lopatin, he was far from pleased:

A cavalry man in the past, General Lopatin had lately been in charge of an army which, during the fighting on the Don, had become so scattered across the steppes that it was extremely difficult to assemble it again.

Plump and fair and outwardly very calm, Lopatin treated me to an excellent lunch at his command post, but informed me that, in the absence of munitions, the 62nd Army could not carry out the orders of the Army Group's chief of staff... I at once felt he lacked self-confidence, and doubted whether he could hold the right flank on the Don, since his troops were half-encircled.*

Under constant air attack, Chuikov spent the rest of the day circling about the Don steppes, looking for Lopatin's "lost divisions." Meanwhile, General Shumilov had been appointed commander of the 64th Army, and Chuikov was ordered to report to Gordov at Stalingrad.

At Stalingrad on August 1, I found Gordov (so downcast only a few days before) in a gay, almost jocular mood. In talking to air-force General Khrukin, he sounded entirely self-confident, as though the Nazis were on the point of being wiped out at any moment. "The Germans," he said, "have got bogged down in our defences, and with one blow we can destroy the whole lot." Remembering my vain search in the steppe for the lost divisions, which had just vanished, I came to the conclusion that the Commander of the Stalingrad Front simply did not know what was going on. He was full of wishful thinking, and did not even know that, having broken across the Don at Tsymlianskaya and pushing, as they were, towards Kotelnikovo, the Germans were preparing to strike a mighty new blow, this time at Stalingrad itself. He would scarcely listen to my explanations, and cut me short by saying: "I know about the general situation as well as you do."

Full of foreboding, Chuikov returned to the front; but was no longer able to cross the Don; practically all the country inside the Bend had now been overrun by the Germans.

As an example of the chaotic lack of liaison between Russian units fighting inside the Bend, Chuikov tells how, while the 33rd Guards Division of the 62nd Army held up the Germans along a narrow sector of the front for several days, destroying or putting out of action no fewer than fifty German tanks and fighting almost literally to the last man, the troops on either side of them were doing nothing, "simply waiting for something to happen"; before long, they were attacked by strong German forces which broke through their lines.

* Yeremenko in his book (*Stalingrad*) defends Lopatin by saying that, since he was commander of the 62nd Army in July–August, he deserves a little share of its fame. To Chuikov he was a person to be got rid of as quickly as possible.

The heroic stand of the 33rd Guards Division, had thus been almost in vain.

Yet as late as July 26 General Lopatin was sending optimistic reports to headquarters about important German forces being on the point of being encircled. "It was like the story of the man," Chuikov commented, "who said he had caught a bear. 'Well, bring him along.' 'I can't, the bear won't let me.' "

By the time the 62nd Army had retreated beyond the Don, it had been decimated, and needed strong reinforcement.

On returning to the Front on August 2, Chuikov found that the situation had badly deteriorated. Large German forces, outflanking the main Russian forces, had forced the Don at Tsymlianskaya, and after capturing Kotelnikovo, were advancing north towards Stalingrad in a wide semi-circle through Plodovitoye and Tinguta in the Kalmuk steppes. In many places, the Russians were being smashed by heavy air and tank concentrations. Thus, two days later Chuikov learned that a troop train unloading fresh Siberian troops at Kotelnikovo station had been attacked by German aircraft and tanks and the losses had been so appalling that the colonel in command of these troops now retreating in disorder towards Stalingrad, was found in a state of complete nervous collapse.

> I remember his pale face and his trembling voice. He was in a bad state... "Comrade General," he said, "I am a Soviet officer, and I cannot survive the death of a large part of my division. It is hard for me to assemble the survivors, who are completely demoralised. I cannot therefore continue to command the division."
>
> I could not leave this without doing something about it... A few hours later when Colonel Voskoboinikov came to himself, I called in to see him, the chief of staff and the head of the division's political department. I ordered all three to establish contact with the troops scattered between Zhutovo and Abganerovo, and to take up firm defensive positions on the north side of the Axai river.

Despite heavy losses among the Russian troops, Chuikov succeeded in organising a defence line on the Axai river, and, on August 6, launched some successful counter-attacks against the Germans and Rumanians.

As a result of this battle of August 6, the enemy suffered heavy losses. We captured eight guns and many small arms. I found that the scattered troops I had assembled during the retreat, had not lost their fighting spirit, and fought well. They boldly went into attack, and did not panic when the enemy counter-attacked. That was the main thing.

Farther east, at Abganerovo and Tundutovo, where other units of the 64th Army were now concentrated, the Germans had also failed to break through. On that day, Chuikov was also glad to learn that Gordov had been replaced by Yeremenko as commander of the Stalingrad Front—though later he was not to remain on the best of terms with him.

The German advance on Stalingrad from the south and south-west was being slowed down; but other difficulties were still in store. A large ammunition dump south of Stalingrad had been destroyed by the German bombers, and the troops were, before long, to experience a serious shortage of ammunition. Even so, Chuikov, assisted by Ludnikov and other future heroes of the defence of Stalingrad, held the Axai line for over a week; but with the Germans outflanking all these troops from the east, they were ordered to withdraw north to the next natural defence line, the Myshkova river, some forty miles south of Stalingrad. During this fighting in the country between Don and Volga, virtually on the outskirts of Stalingrad, despite all the setbacks suffered inside the Don Bend, the Russians began to fight as seldom before. Chuikov gives many examples of suicidal resistance when Russian soldiers, with grenades tied round them, would throw themselves under enemy tanks. Many of the fresh troops that had only recently been incorporated in the 62nd and 64th Army were "acquiring new experience every day, and were rapidly turning into mature and hardened troops". The German plan—to break through to the Volga and at the same time to encircle both the 62nd and 64th Army—failed. These two armies were to bear the brunt of the Stalingrad fighting, the former inside Stalingrad, the latter south of it.

Hitler had ordered that Stalingrad be taken on August 25. On the tragic day of August 23 the Germans broke through to the Volga north of Stalingrad, on a five-mile front; on the same day, 600 planes attacked the city, killing some 40,000 civilians.

> The enormous city, stretching for thirty miles along the Volga, was enveloped in flames. Everything around was burning and collapsing. Sorrow and death entered into thousands of Stalingrad homes.

Many thousands of civilians fled across the Volga; but Chuikov stresses the determination shown by both the army and the civilian authorities to save Stalingrad at any price. North of the city, the Germans failed to widen their five-mile salient, while, in the south, the 64th Army was still preventing them, at that stage, from breaking through to the Volga.

But, during the days that followed, the German pressure grew worse and worse.

> The troops of the 62nd and 64th armies were retreating towards their final positions, inside Stalingrad. The roads were crowded with refugees. Peasants from collective and state farms were migrating, with their families and their livestock, many also taking their agricultural implements with them, and converging on the Volga ferries.

Chuikov, returning from a visit to the east side of the Volga a few days later, describes the scene at one of the ferries:

> From time to time a German shell would burst in the river, but this indiscriminate shelling was not dangerous... From a distance we could see that the pier was crowded with people. As we drew closer many wounded were being carried out of trenches, bomb-craters and shelters. There were also many people with bundles and suitcases who had been hiding from German bombs and shells. When they saw the ferry arriving they rushed to the pier, with the one desire of getting away to the other side of the river, away from their wrecked houses, away from a city that had become a hell. Their eyes were grim and there were trickles of tears running through the dust and soot on their grimy faces. The children, suffering from thirst and hunger, were not crying, but simply whining, and stretching out their little arms to the water of the Volga.

During the last week of August and the first ten days of September, the Germans were advancing on Stalingrad from all directions, despite stiff Russian resistance; they had great superiority in weapons, above all in aircraft. By September 10 they broke through to the Volga south of Stalingrad, near Kuporosnoye, cutting the 62nd Army from the 64th. As a result the 62nd Army was isolated within an irregular German "horse-shoe" of which the northern tip reached the Volga at Rynok and the southern tip at Kuporosnoye, about twenty miles downstream. At the time, the German air force did as many as 3,000 sorties a day; the Russians barely did more than 300. Nor did the Russians have any tanks to speak of.

> The enemy had complete air superiority. This had a particularly depressing effect on our troops; and we were feverishly trying to think up some solution... A part of our anti-aircraft defences had been completely smashed, and most of the rest were moved to the left bank of the Volga. Here the guns could fire at German planes hovering over the river and over a narrow stretch of the right bank; this, however, did not prevent German planes from being suspended over the city and the river from dawn to dusk...

By September 10, morale among the troops was still very low.

> The heavy casualties, the constant retreat, the shortage of food and munitions, the difficulty of receiving reinforcements ... —all this had a very bad effect on morale. Many longed to get across the Volga, to escape the hell of Stalingrad... On September 14 I met the former commander of the 62nd Army [Lopatin]; I was struck by his mood of despair, by his feeling that it was impossible and pointless to fight for Stalingrad... As politely as possible, I suggested he report to the War Council [on the other side of the Volga]—in other words leave Stalingrad altogether. This depressed mood of the former commander of the army was contagious... Three of my aides, the men in charge of tanks, artillery and the engineering troops, all claiming to be ill, hastened to go beyond the Volga... All this was beginning to affect the ordinary troops...

Chuikov, aided by Divisional Commissar Gurov, General Krylov, and others proceeded to give a number of pep-talks to the troops; about the same time, the War Council of the Stalingrad Front issued its famous order: "The enemy must be smashed at Stalingrad." This had an electrifying effect on all the officers, soldiers and political personnel of the 62nd Army.

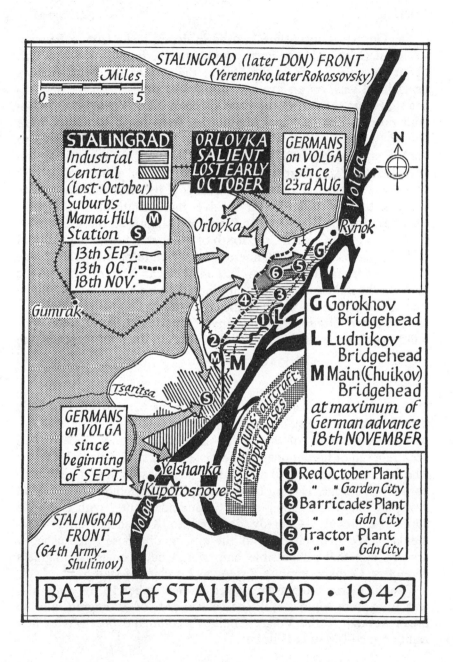

Miles
0 5

STALINGRAD
Industrial
Central
(lost·October)
Suburbs
Mamai Hill   **M**
Station   **S**

13th SEPT.
13th OCT.
18th NOV.

ORLOVKA SALIENT LOST EARLY OCTOBER

GERMANS on VOLGA since 23rd AUG.

STALINGRAD (later DON) FRONT
(Yeremenko, later Rokossovsky)

N

Orlovka

Rynok

Gumrak

Tsaritsa

GERMANS on VOLGA since beginning of SEPT.

Yelshanka

Kuporosnoye

STALINGRAD FRONT
(64th Army–Shulimov)

Russian guns; aircraft; supply bases

G Gorokhov Bridgehead
L Ludnikov Bridgehead
M Main (Chuikov) Bridgehead
at maximum of German advance
18th NOVEMBER

❶ Red October Plant
❷ " " Garden City
❸ Barricades Plant
❹ " Gdn City
❺ Tractor Plant
❻ " " Gdn City

BATTLE of STALINGRAD · 1942

The German "horse-shoe" varied in depth; apart from a Russian salient at Orlovka in the north, the western extremity of which was about eleven miles from the Volga, the rest of the 62nd Army's bridgehead was, on an average, about five miles deep on September 13, before the first of the great German offensives against Stalingrad proper. The principal landmarks, from north to south, were Rynok (to the north of which the Germans had crashed through to the Volga on August 23), Spartakovka Garden City, then the Stalingrad Tractor Plant Garden City, with the Tractor plant itself nearer the Volga; then, the Barricades Garden City, and the Barricades Plant, to the east of it, also on the river bank; south of that, also on the river, was the Red October Plant, and slightly to the south-west, the Red October Garden City, south of which was the famous Mamai Hill, the highest point in Stalingrad, for which ferocious fighting was to go on for months. Mamai Hill marked, as it were, the border between the industrial north of Stalingrad and the business, administrative and residential south of the city, with its two railway stations, its Red Army House, its Univermag (department store), and other buildings that were to become famous during the later stages of the battle.

It was on September 12, two days after the 62nd Army had been isolated from the rest of the Soviet troops that Chuikov was appointed commander of the 62nd Army. The gloomy Lopatin had been relieved of his command, and his chief of staff, General Krylov, who had had a fine record at Odessa and Sebastopol, had been temporarily in charge. Having been appointed commander of the 62nd Army by the War Council of the Stalingrad Front, "with Comrade Stalin's approval", Chuikov declared to Khrushchev and Yeremenko: "We shall either hold the city or die there." Khrushchev assured him that all possible help would be given to Stalingrad's defenders. Chuikov kept on Krylov as his chief of staff.

The big German offensive started on September 13. Its main aim was to capture Mamai Hill, the central part of Stalingrad, and so break through to the Volga. Chuikov's command post was at first right on top of Mamai Hill, but:

The constant bombing and shelling of the hill continuously smashed our communications, which made it impossible to direct the troops... So we moved to the Tsaritsa ravine, leaving only an observation post on top of the hill... During that whole day of the 13th, none of us, either officer or soldier, had had anything to eat. Our lunch was being cooked in a small house on the side of the hill, but an enemy bomb destroyed both the kitchen and our lunch. Our cook tried to cook our dinner in a field kitchen, but this was also smashed by a direct hit. Our cook wasn't going to waste any more food on us, so we stayed hungry all day. Glinka, our cook, and Tasya, our waitress, were delighted when we transferred them to the new command post.

This was a large, roomy and well-protected dugout, near the Volga, and between the two railway stations, which had earlier been the H.Q. of the Stalingrad Front.

Chuikov describes how, after their initial successes on the 13th, the Germans, now full of confidence, proceeded to occupy the central part of Stalingrad.

Our counter-attacks before daybreak were not unsuccessful at first; but once the sun had risen German planes, in groups of fifty or sixty, proceeded to bomb our counter-attacking forces non-stop... Our counter-attack failed. By noon, the enemy brought into action numerous tanks and motorised infantry... The main blow was aimed at the Central Station. This was an attack of exceptional strength. Despite enormous losses, the Germans were now crashing ahead. Whole columns of tanks and motorised infantry were breaking into the centre of the city. The Nazis were now apparently convinced that the fate of Stalingrad was sealed, and they hurried towards the Volga... Our soldiers—snipers, anti-tank gunners, artillery-men, lying in wait in houses, cellars and firing-points, could watch the drunken Nazis jumping off the trucks, playing mouth organs, bellowing and dancing on the pavements.

Hundreds of them were killed, but more and more German troops were flooding the centre of Stalingrad. The fighting was now within 800 yards of the 62nd Army's command post. That night, Chuikov threw in his small reserve of nineteen tanks, to stop the Germans from breaking through to the Volga and to the Army H.Q.

It was during the critical night of September 14–15 that the famous Rodimtsev Division, 10,000 strong, began to arrive across the Volga.

Except for anti-tanks guns, the bulk of the division's artillery was to stay on the left bank. Two infantry regiments of the Rodimtsev division were ordered to "clear the centre of Stalingrad" of the Germans, and another was ordered to occupy Mamai Hill and dig in there. Throughout the 15th, the fighting was extremely heavy; the Central Railway Station changed hands several times, and, by the end of the day "it was hard to decide who was in possession of Mamai Hill". However, on the morning of the 16th, Mamai Hill was recaptured by the Russians, and the fighting for the Hill was to continue almost uninterruptedly until the end of January.

It was at the height of this fighting that the troops of the Stalingrad Front attempted to break through the German "Rynok" salient from the north. Chuikov tells with some irony how this offensive, conducted by Yeremenko and his deputy, the same old Gordov, came to nothing. For a few hours on September 18 the Stalingrad sky was clear of German aircraft; they had gone to deal with the attempted Yeremenko breakthrough; soon afterwards they were back over Stalingrad.

During that day the fighting was chiefly on Mamai Hill and around the Central Station. The top of Mamai Hill was again recaptured "by the remnants of Sologub's division" and Colonel Yelin's regiment, which had advanced between 100 and 150 yards that day. On the other hand, the Central Station was lost to the Germans that night, after five days' bloody, often hand-to-hand fighting.

> By this time [Chuikov relates] we had nothing left with which to counter-attack. General Rodimtsev's 13th Division had been bled white. It had entered the fray from the moment it crossed the Volga, and had borne the brunt of the heaviest German blows... They had had to abandon several blocks of houses inside central Stalingrad, but this could not be described as a withdrawal or a retreat. There was nobody left to retreat. Rodimtsev's guardsmen stood firm to the last extremity, and only the heavily-wounded crawled away... From what these wounded told us, it transpired that the Nazis, having captured the station, continued to suffer heavy losses. Our soldiers, having been cut off from the main forces of the division, had entrenched themselves in various buildings around the station, or under railway carriages— usually in groups of two or three men—and from there they continued to harass the Germans night and day...

There is no doubt, as Chuikov himself admits, that it was the men of the Rodimtsev Division who saved Stalingrad during the second half of September. But he pays this tribute a little reluctantly: the reason being that, for months afterwards, the Rodimtsev Division continued to receive incomparably more publicity in the Soviet press (and, consequently, throughout the world) than any other. In reality, it had suffered such appalling losses that, after the end of September, it played only a minor part in the Stalingrad fighting and occupied a relatively quiet sector.

Supplies for the 62nd Army inside Stalingrad had all to come from across the Volga; and the river, which is over a mile wide at Stalingrad, was under constant bombing during the day, and artillery and mortar fire during the night.

Units which had succeeded in crossing the Volga during the night, had to be put in position at once, before dawn, and all supplies had to be immediately distributed among the troops, since they would otherwise have been destroyed by bombing... We had neither horses nor cars ... everything that was brought across the Volga had to be carried to the firing line by the soldiers themselves—those very soldiers who, during the day, had to repel fierce enemy attacks and who at night, without sleep or respite, had to carry ammunitions, food and engineering equipment to the front lines. This was terribly exhausting, and inevitably lowered their fighting capacity; and yet, that is how it went on in Stalingrad, day after day, and week after week, as long as the Battle of Stalingrad continued.

Another absolutely vital factor of the Stalingrad fighting (but one to which Chuikov refers as little as possible) was that practically all the artillery, *katyusha* mortars, etc.—were on the other side of the Volga, and these represented a formidable force. Victor Nekrasov, the future novelist, who spent virtually the whole of the Stalingrad battle as a lieutenant of the Batyuk Division, in the Mamai Hill sector, told me:

Especially towards the end of October, when we had nothing but a few small bridgeheads left on the right bank of the river, the number of troops there was extremely small. Perhaps 20,000 in all.* But, on the other hand, the other side of the Volga was a real ant-heap. It was there that all the supply services, the artillery, air-force, etc. were concentrated. And it was *they* who made it hell for the Germans.

Exactly the same point is made by Konstantin Simonov in his new novel, *Men Are Not Born Soldiers*, an important corrective to the Chuikov story:

> *We could certainly not have held Stalingrad had we not been supported by artillery and* katyushas *on the other bank all the time.* I can hardly describe the soldiers' love for them... And as time went on, there were more and more and more of them, and we could feel it. It was hard to imagine at the time that there was *such* a concentration of guns firing their shells at the Germans, morning, noon and night, over our heads!†

Even so, to the Russians on the bridgeheads, Stalingrad continued to be a peculiar kind of hell. Thus, of the reinforcements that came from across the river Nekrasov told me:

> There were times when these reinforcements were really pathetic. They'd bring across the river—with great difficulty—say, twenty new soldiers: either old chaps of fifty or fifty-five, or youngsters of eighteen or nineteen. They would stand there on the shore, shivering with cold and fear. They'd be given warm clothing and then taken to the front line. By the time these newcomers reached this line, five or ten out of twenty had already been killed by German shells; for with those German flares over the Volga and our front lines, there was never complete darkness. But the peculiar thing about these chaps was that those among them who reached the front line very quickly became wonderfully hardened soldiers. Real *frontoviks*.

In his account Chuikov refers to several "critical" days at Stalingrad, between September 12, when he took over the command of the 62nd Army and the middle of November, when the last German offensive failed. In fact, every day was "critical", except that some

* A leading Soviet military expert, General Talensky, in speaking to me about Stalingrad in 1945, put the figure rather higher: about 40,000. There was, he said, physically no possibility of having more people on the bridgeheads.
† Znamia, No. 11, 1963, p. 7.

days were even more so than others. Thus, September 21 and 22—
i.e. a week after the Rodimtsev Division had joined in the fighting—
were specially "critical". It was then that the Germans occupied a
large part of the "business quarter" of Stalingrad and split the 62nd
Army in two by breaking through to the Central Pier on the Volga.

One of the grimmest stories of Russian endurance that Chuikov
tells is that of the 1st battalion of Colonel Yelin's regiment; this
battalion had, for days, been fighting for the railway station; when
the Germans captured this, the Russian survivors entrenched themselves in a stone building in the neighbourhood, and finally only six
survivors, all more or less seriously wounded, made their way to the
Volga, and even so not until they had completely run out of ammunition. Here they improvised a raft of sorts, and drifted downstream,
and were finally picked up by a Russian anti-aircraft crew and sent
to hospital. They had eaten nothing for three days. The dead and the
heavily wounded had been left behind in their last stronghold inside
central Stalingrad, now in the hands of the Germans.

The loss of the Central Pier required a reorganisation of the communication lines across the Volga. The Volga river flotilla continued
to function, despite heavy losses, both north and south of the Central
Pier; moreover, a foot-bridge, resting on empty iron barrels, was
built across the river, farther to the north.*

To strengthen the rapidly dwindling Rodimtsev division, a number of other famous divisions† were transported to Stalingrad at the
end of September—Batyuk's (largely composed of Siberians) and
Gorishnyi's. Rodimtsev was reinforced by 2,000 new men. Both sides
had suffered staggering losses in the fighting in central Stalingrad.
But, according to Chuikov, the Germans' breakthrough to the Volga
at the Central Pier was only a "partial success", since their attempt
to outflank the Russians to the north of them along the river failed

* The official map (in IVOVSS, vol. 2, p. 440) shows that south of
the Central Pier the Russians still held a small bridgehead in central
Stalingrad, barely half a mile wide and a few hundred yards deep, on
September 26; it was later abandoned, but it is not clear exactly when.
† The term "division" is in the case of Stalingrad misleading, since
many of these "divisions" were only 2,000 or 3,000 strong and often
even smaller.

completely. Here the Germans came up against the stubborn resistance of the Rodimtsev, Batyuk and Gorishnyi divisions, the Batra-
kov Brigade, and other troops. In this attempt, the Germans lost
"dozens of tanks and thousands of men".

By September 24 the Germans had occupied most of central Stalingrad, and now aimed their main blows at the industrial area in the
north. Chuikov quotes with much satisfaction a German observer,
General Hans Dörr, who described the war in north Stalingrad as
follows:

> These battles were in the nature of a positional or "fortress" war.
> The time for big operations was over... We now had to fight on the
> Volga heights cut by ravines; this industrial area of Stalingrad, built on
> extremely uneven ground, and composed of buildings built of stone,
> iron and concrete, presented new difficulties. As a measure of
> length, a metre now replaced a kilometre. Fierce actions had to be
> fought for every house, workshop, water-tower, raised railway track,
> wall or cellar, and even for every heap of rubble. There was nothing,
> even in World War I, to equal the enormous expenditure of ammu-
> nition. The no-man's land between us and the Russians was reduced to
> an absolute minimum, and, despite the intensive activity of our
> bombers and our artillery, there was no means of widening this "close
> combat" gap. The Russians were better than the Germans at camou-
> flage, and more experienced in barricade fighting for separate houses;
> their defence lines were very strong... The catastrophe that later fol-
> lowed has eclipsed these weeks of "siege". But it is the story of heroic
> deeds by small units, storm groups and many nameless German
> soldiers..."

If the Germans had reason to congratulate themselves on the
heroism of their soldiers, the Russians had even more reason to
do so, especially as German superiority in tanks and aircraft continued to be very great. By and large, the Germans, supported
by aircraft and tanks, attacked during the day. For the Russians, as
Chuikov says, "the night was their element". The effectiveness of the
German tanks and aircraft was, however, limited by two factors:
observing that the Germans were not good at precision bombing,
Chuikov had devised a tactic of "close combat", whereby the no-

man's land never exceeded "the distance of a hand-grenade throw": this kept the Russian front lines more or less immune from air attack; as for the tanks, these found it more and more difficult to operate as the mountains of rubble accumulated in the streets of Stalingrad. Highly favourable to the Russians, too, was the powerful fire of the guns and *katyusha* mortars from the other side of the river; these caused havoc among any German troop concentrations, and in the German positions, which were usually more exposed, and less well camouflaged than the Russians'.

On September 27, the Germans began their first big offensive against the industrial area of Stalingrad. "Hundreds of dive-bombers" attacked the Russians, and the Germans, though suffering heavy losses, crossed the Russian minefields and advanced between 2,000 and 3,000 yards. Gorishnyi's troops lost the top of Mamai Hill and what was left of them entrenched themselves on its north-east slope. "One more such day," Chuikov commented, "and we would have been thrown into the Volga."

Chuikov sent an S O S to the War Council* asking for reinforcements, especially in the air. Two infantry regiments, under General Smekhotvorov crossed the Volga that night and were promptly sent to reinforce the troops in the Red October Garden City. The remnants of Gorishnyi's and Batyuk's troops counter-attacked on Mamai Hill. On the morning of September 28 the Germans resumed the attack, their planes concentrating not only on the Russian troops, but also on the Volga shipping. Of the six cargo ships on the Volga, five were put out of action that day. Some oil tanks in the neighbourhood of Chuikov's command-post were set on fire by German bombing.

> The staff at my command post were choking with the heat and smoke. The fire of the flaming oil tanks was crawling down to our dugouts. Every dive-bomber attack was killing people and putting our wireless sets out of action. Even Glinka, our cook, who had set up his field kitchen in a bomb crater, was wounded.

And yet, the German attacks lacked the coherence and self-assurance of the previous day.

> Supported by tanks, entire battalions would hurl themselves into the attacks, and this enabled us to concentrate our artillery fire on them. . .

* To Mr. Khrushchev personally, according to his 1959 book.

I then appealed for help to General Khrukin, commander of our air force, and he threw in all he had. It was during this big Russian air-raid that Batyuk's and Gorishnyi's troops again attacked Mamai Hill; they made an appreciable advance, though they failed to seize the summit, which remained a no-man's land, and continued to be shelled by both sides. That day, the Germans lost 1,500 men in dead alone, and some fifty tanks. On Mamai Hill alone, there were 500 German corpses.

Chuikov admits, of course, that the Russian losses were very heavy too.

Our tank units had 626 casualties (dead and wounded), Batyuk lost 300 men and the Gorishnyi Division, though continuing to fight, was bled white. Many hundreds of Russian wounded were now on the river bank, waiting to be evacuated; with the shipping losses that day this was no easy task. The delivery of ammunitions had also become extremely difficult. And, meantime, reconnaissance reported that the Germans were preparing to launch another major attack against the Red October plant. The real battle for industrial Stalingrad was only beginning.

On September 29, the Germans proceeded to "liquidate" the eleven-mile-deep and three-mile-wide "Orlovka" salient to the northwest of the industrial area of Stalingrad. Here again we find in Chuikov's book some angry polemics against the command of the Stalingrad Front (now called the Don Front)* beyond the German

* The changes in name, and in command, of the "fronts" to the north and south of Stalingrad have led to a lot of confusion. In early August Yeremenko was in command of the army groups both north (the "Stalingrad Front") and south of the city, with Golikov as his deputy in the south (the "South East Front")—and also of the troops inside the city. Then on September 28 (i.e. before the Orlovka battle), according to both Yeremenko and the official history 'IVOVSS, vol. 2, p. 444) the army group to the north, previously the Stalingrad Front, was renamed the "Don Front", ånd placed under General Rokossovsky, and that to the south was now called the "Stalingrad Front" and was under Yeremenko "as before". Chuikov's troops in the city came under command of the "new" Stalingrad front and were therefore still under Yeremenko. So when Chuikov criticises the "Stalingrad Front" for not helping in the Orlovka battle from the north, he must really mean what had then become the Don Front. He is therefore in fact criticising Rokossovsky and not, as would appear, Yeremenko.

"Rynok" salient to the north of Stalingrad. Twice before Yeremenko (and his deputy, Gordov, Chuikov's *bête noire*) had failed to break through the German salient and come to the rescue of the 62nd Army.

Chuikov argues that the existence of the Orlovka bulge gave the troops in the north a wonderful opportunity to cut through the German "Rynok" salient, which was only five miles wide; but once again, when the German attack on the Orlovka salient was serious, the opportunity to help the 62nd Army was missed.

The small number of troops under Andrusenko, Smekhotvorov and Sologub defending the Orlovka bulge, had already suffered very heavy losses in the first two days of the German attack. Some, under Andrusenko, were then encircled, and fought on for nearly another week. Then, having run out of ammunition, 120 men broke out of the encirclement on the night of October 8; the remaining 380 were left behind, dead or severely wounded.

> A few days before, the command of the Stalingrad [Don] Front asked me what measures I was taking to hold the Orlovka bulge... What could I reply? The best answer would have been that the Stalingrad [Don] Front should strike out from the north at the rear of the German divisions attacking Orlovka. But no one was planning such a blow. For my own part, I had no reserves. With the Germans threatening to strike a powerful blow at the Stalingrad Tractor Plant and the Barricades Plant, I could not afford to help those in the Orlovka bulge.

Marshal Yeremenko, in his book, *Stalingrad*, published in 1961, i.e. two years after Chuikov's book, treats the liquidation of the Orlovka bulge as an inevitable war casualty, and makes no attempt to answer Chuikov's very serious charges of apathy and inactivity on the part of the commanders of the army-group to the north. It may well be that, with an eye on the coming Russian counter-offensive, the commanders of the "Stalingrad" or "Don" Front preferred to remain inactive, trusting that Chuikov would somehow succeed in holding his Stalingrad bridgeheads. If so, it was a dangerous gamble, since on October 14, as we shall see, and again in November, the 62nd Army was very nearly wiped out.

*

For the Russians, October was the cruellest month in Stalingrad. On October 1, Major-General Guriev's 39th Guards Division arrived in Stalingrad, where it was to defend the Red October Plant for many critical days. (Some of its survivors were later to fight all the way to Berlin). On the same day, another famous division crossed the Volga —that of Colonel Gurtiev. These men, many of them Siberians, were to bear the brunt of some of the heaviest fighting in the northern part of Stalingrad during October.*

> Equally tough new troops were the guardsmen under General Zholudev. These were really guardsmen. All of them were young and tall, and healthy, many of them in paratroop uniform, with knives and daggers tucked into their belts. They went in for bayonet charges, and would throw a dead Nazi over their shoulder like a sack of straw. For house-to-house fighting, there was no one quite like them. They would attack in small groups, and, breaking into houses and cellars, they would use their knives and daggers. Even when encircled, they went on fighting, and would die crying: "For country and Stalin! But we shall never surrender."†

For Chuikov himself, October started particularly badly. His H.Q. near the Barricades Plant again happened to be close to some oil tanks; these were set aflame by German bombers, and the burning oil poured across the H.Q.'s dugouts towards the Volga, and enveloped them in a sea of flame.

> At first we almost lost our heads. What were we to do? Then my chief of staff, General Krylov, gave the order: "Sit tight. Stay in the un-damaged dugouts and keep up radio communications with the troops!" Then he said to me in a whisper: "Do you think we can hold out?" "Yes," I said. "At a pinch, we've got our revolvers." "All right," he said. We understood each other perfectly.
> I must admit that when I first looked out of the dugout, I was dazzled by the flames and overwhelmed. But Krylov's order brought me to my senses... Though encircled by flames, we continued to work, and to direct the troops.

* Gurtiev himself was to be killed at Orel in the summer of 1943.
† In the second (1961) edition of Chuikov's book the mention of Stalin is deleted—both here and practically everywhere else.

The fire went on for several days, and we had no other H.Q. in reserve. All our troops, including our engineers, were fighting the Germans. So we had to carry on as best we could—in the surviving dug-outs, in holes and trenches, often under enemy fire. We did not sleep for several days and nights.

In these conditions, Chuikov was exasperated by the frequent phone calls from General Zakharov, Yeremenko's chief of staff, ostensibly asking for all kinds of details (which, in the circumstances, Chuikov was unable to supply) but, in fact, anxious to make sure that Chuikov's H.Q. still existed.

It was neither funny nor easy to spell out code words over the wireless with bombs and shells landing all round us. These unnecessary talks often resulted in the radio operators being killed, with the microphones in their hands.

Here, as elsewhere in the book, the *frontovik*'s contempt for the staff officer living in relatively normal surroundings on the "safe" side of the Volga comes out strongly.

Worse still, after the flames had abated three days later, the Germans began to shell and bomb the Army H.Q. Numbers of men at the H.Q. were killed or wounded. With great difficulty, the H.Q. was moved at night some 500 yards farther north, to the H.Q. of General Sarayev's division, which had been practically wiped out, and was now being reconstituted on the other side of the Volga.

During all that first week of October, there had been heavy fighting in the industrial area of Stalingrad. By October 7, the Germans captured part of the Tractor Plant Garden City. Often the Russians had some good luck, though. A *katyusha* hit at 6 p.m. that day wiped out a whole battalion of advancing German troops. Smekhotvorov's troops were, meantime, fighting a stiff battle in the Red October Garden City. One building there changed hands five times during the day.

By October 8 it was clear that the Germans were preparing for an all-out offensive. Hitler had promised his vassals to capture Stalingrad within the next few days. The German soldiers would shout from their trenches: "*Russ, skoro bul-bul u Volga.*" ("You'll soon be blowing bubbles in the Volga.") The German planes were showering leaflets on the city... These showed us surrounded on all sides by tanks and guns, and also mockingly reminded us of the "Stalingrad Front's" failure to break through to us from the north.

For four days—between the 9th and the 13th of October—there was a relative lull, and then, on October 14, all hell broke loose. Before this "final" German offensive, the depth of the main bridge-head held by the 62nd Army—i.e. the distance between the Volga and the front line was about two miles. If, Chuikov argues, the Germans had organised their attack properly, they could have broken through in one and a half or two hours. But the precautions taken by the Russians and the incredible stubbornness of their troops prevented catastrophe. Nevertheless, it was touch-and-go.

Here is Chuikov's description of this "unforgettable" day:

The 14th of October marked the beginning of a battle unequalled in its cruelty and ferocity throughout the whole of the Stalingrad fighting. Three infantry and two panzer divisions were hurled against us along a five-km. front... There were three thousand German air sorties that day. They bombed and stormed our troops without a moment's respite. The German guns and mortars showered on us shells and bombs from morning till night. It was a sunny day, but owing to the smoke and soot, visibility was reduced to 100 yards. Our dugouts were shaking and crumbling up like a house of cards... The main blow was delivered against Gorishnyi's, Zholudev's and Gurtiev's troops, and the 84th tank brigade—all in the general direction of the Stalingrad Tractor Plant and the Barricades Plant. By 11.30 a.m. 180 German tanks broke through Zholudev's positions to the stadium of the Tractor Plant... By 4 p.m. Sologub's, Zholudev's and Gurtiev's troops... were encircled but still fighting.

The reports from the various units were becoming more and more confusing... The command and observation posts of regiments and divisions were being smashed by shells and bombs. At my Army's command post thirty people were killed. The guards scarcely had time to dig the officers out of the smashed dugouts of the Army H.Q. The troops had to be directed by radio; transmitters had been set up on the other side of the Volga, and we communicated with them, and they then passed on our orders to the fighting units on this side of the river.

... By midnight it was clear that the invaders had surrounded the Stalingrad Tractor Plant, and that fighting was going on in the workshops. We reckoned that the Germans had lost forty tanks during the day, and around the Tractor Plant there were 3,000 German dead. We also suffered very heavy losses that day. During the night 3,500 wounded soldiers and officers were taken across the Volga; this was a record figure.

The Germans had managed to advance two kilometres (over a mile and a quarter) during the day; they had captured the Tractor Plant and had, indeed, cut the Russian forces in two. To the north of the Tractor Plant there was now only a small area in Russian hands: the small number of troops there were under the command of Colonel Gorokhov.

On the 15th the Germans continued to attack strongly; again thousands of bombs were showered on the Russians, and the German tommy-gunners were trying to break through to Chuikov's Army H.Q.

But von Paulus [says Chuikov] was short of that one battalion which might have captured the Army headquarters, only 300 yards away. And yet we decided not to move, and to fight on.

Nevertheless, Chuikov does not hesitate to describe the situation as "desperate"; owing to constant German air attacks, radio was working intermittently, not only on the right bank of the river, but also on the left bank, where an emergency command post had been set up. This was particularly serious since most of the Russian artillery was on the left bank, and communications were, for a time, as good as paralysed.

The Russian losses were mounting up at a disastrous rate. In two days' fighting Zholudev's and Gorishnyi's troops had lost seventy-five per cent of their effective. On the night of October 15–16 a regiment under Colonel Ludnikov crossed the Volga and entered the fray to the north of the Barricades Plant. But, as Chuikov says, this regiment, and the miserable remnants of the Gorishnyi and Zholudev divisions would have been helpless against overwhelming German strength but for the Russian artillery on the other side of the river, the guns of the Volga flotilla and the *stormovik* planes which, with heavy losses, were breaking through the clouds of German planes and attacking the advancing German troops. On the night of October 17–18 two more regiments of the Ludnikov division crossed the

Volga. That was also the night on which Chuikov was to receive a
visit from General Yeremenko.

I went to meet him at the pier. Shells were exploding all over the
place, and the Germans were shelling the Volga with their six-barrel
mortars. Hundreds of wounded soldiers were crawling to the pier.
Often we had to step over dead bodies.

The meeting with Yeremenko was not a very happy one. Chuikov
clamoured, above all, for ammunition, and when, on the following
day, he heard what was to be sent, he was furious. Instead of a
month's supply, he was now promised a day's supply. He protested
strongly, and the figure was "slightly revised".* Altogether, Chuikov

* Yeremenko gives a rather more dramatic account of his visit
(*Stalingrad*, pp. 233–4).

"In talking on October 15 on the phone to Chuikov, I felt that the
Army Commander's spirit had somewhat deteriorated. So I decided,
without delay, to visit the 62nd Army. The situation that had developed there was, indeed, alarming. Mamai Hill and (the adjoining)
height 107·5 . . . were in enemy hands, and the Germans were domi-
nating the city and keeping our river crossings under intensive fire,
and so paralysing them . . . (Chuikov) rather strongly protested
against my visit, since it meant crossing the Volga under intensive
shelling, and then walking five miles along the shore under rifle,
machine-gun and mortar fire. . . However, we were used to that kind
of thing; we had experienced such fire hundreds of times; in August
and September the H.Q. of the War Council of the Front, being
situated in the centre of Stalingrad, had been under constant bombing and shelling."
He then describes how he sailed for ten km. up the river, despite
constant shelling, and landed near the Red October Plant. Owing to
the constant German flares it was light all the time. Although all
along the embankment mountains of wreckage were piled up and the
whole area was riddled with shell-holes and bomb-craters, there was
an "extraordinary animation" along this embankment: reinforcements and supplies were arriving all the time in a continuous stream,
and the wounded were being evacuated—and all under constant
shell-fire. Before Yeremenko had reached Chuikov's H.Q. near the
Barricades Plant, "a number of the comrades accompanying me had
been killed or wounded by bomb or shell splinters". Yeremenko also
tells how, while at Chuikov's H.Q., he talked to the commanders of

does not seem to have cared for visitors: he vetoed a visit to Stalingrad by Manuilsky on behalf of the Central Committee. He declared that the Stalingrad troops did not need any pep talks from Manuilsky and it would only annoy Comrade Stalin if Manuilsky got killed—which was quite possible in the circumstances.

With the Germans increasingly active on the bank of the Volga near the Tractor Plant, Chuikov found it necessary to move his headquarters farther south, to a ravine near Mamai Hill. These dugouts were to remain the Army H.Q. till the end of the Stalingrad Battle. This H.Q., inside the Volga cliffs was just over 1,000 yards from Mamai Hill—for that was now the maximum depth of the main Stalingrad bridgehead still in Russian hands.

On October 19 and 20 the Germans continued their attacks, chiefly in the Barricades and Red October areas, but they already seemed to lack their former punch. Judging from the prisoners' statements, morale among the German troops, especially the newcomers, was low. The Russians were, however, also very short of troops, and Chuikov had to scrape the bottom of the barrel by drawing on all kinds of people in the Army's rear services—shoemakers, tailors, and men in charge of horses, stores, etc.

> These poorly trained or wholly untrained people became "specialists" in street fighting, as soon as they stepped on to the ground of Stalingrad. "It was pretty terrifying," they would say, "to cross over to Stalingrad, but once we got there we felt better. We knew that, beyond the Volga there was nothing, and that if we were to remain alive, we had to destroy the invaders."

---

some of the famous Stalingrad divisions. Particularly pathetic was his talk with Colonel Zholudev, who had lost practically all his men in the last German offensive. "Over a thousand German planes attacked us, and then we were attacked by 150 German tanks, followed by waves of infantry. And yet nobody abandoned his post." Zholudev spoke to Yeremenko with tears in his eyes...

It appears from his account that while the War Council of the Front was now stationed on the other side of the Volga, some ten km. south of the main fighting, it had been in central Stalingrad during August and part of September. This is apparently also where Khrushchev (and Malenkov?) were stationed at the time.

In his story, Yeremenko does not mention any disagreement with Chuikov.

It should be added that, by this time, the "prestige value" of having fought at Stalingrad was enormous.

Summing up the results of the fierce ten-days' fighting between October 14 and 23, Chuikov says:

> Both the Germans' strength and our strength were on the wane. In these last ten days, the Germans had once again cut our army in two, and had inflicted on us very serious losses. They had captured the Tractor Plant, but had failed to destroy either the northern group [under Gorokhov] or the Army's main forces south of it. Yet the Germans still had reserves, as we knew from our reconnaissance... But our forces had been decimated; the 37th, 208th and 193rd divisions were little more than numbers. All they represented was a few hundred rifles.

The Germans renewed their attacks in the Barricades and Red October sectors, and between the two factories they were now within 400 yards of the Volga. The last Russian Volga crossing was then in range of machine-gun fire. Stone walls had to be erected across the ravines to stop these machine-gun bullets—no easy task in the circumstances.

On October 27, parts of a new division under General Sokolov began to arrive at Stalingrad; but the crossing of the Volga met with great difficulties. Meantime, the Germans had struck another violent blow at the Red October Plant, and captured the north-west part of the factory's territory. It was here that one of the most famous and deadly battles was to be fought for weeks afterwards.

Pending the arrival of reinforcements, Chuikov was reduced to all kinds of "psychological" expedients.

> One day we had the good luck of discovering on the battlefield three half-wrecked tanks, including one flame-throwing tank. We quickly had them repaired, and Colonel Wainrub, my tank commander, decided to throw in these tanks along Samarkand Street, where the Germans had nearly broken through to the Volga... The attack started early in the morning, on October 28, before daybreak. The attack was supported by artillery and *katyusha* fire. We failed to capture a large area, but the effect was very impressive all the same. The flame-throwing tank destroyed three enemy tanks, and the other two killed off the Germans in two trenches, which were promptly taken over by our men... The Nazi

radio started screaming about "Russian tanks", as though trying to justify Paulus's failure to finish us off.*

After two more days of heavy German attacks against Ludnikov's, Gurtiev's and Batyuk's men, there came a lull.

By October 30 we began to feel that we were winning the battle. It was clear that Paulus was no longer able to repeat his October 14 offensive which brought us to the brink of catastrophe.

But it was not over yet. The bridgeheads held by the Russians were only a few hundred yards deep in some places, and during the first ten days of November, the Russians made many attacks, mostly at night, in a vain attempt to enlarge them, if only slightly.

On November 11, the Germans launched their last major attack on the defenders of Stalingrad. Advancing along a three-mile front, five German divisions, supported by tanks and aircraft, tried to crash through to the Volga at one fell swoop. But the Russians were so well entrenched that the Germans made only little progress. The fighting went on, in Chuikov's words, "for every brick and stone, for every yard of the Stalingrad earth".

At Mamai Hill Batyuk's troops fought desperately against advancing enemy forces. Factory chimneys were crashing down under the blow of shells and bombs. The heaviest blows were struck at Ludnikov's and Gorishnyi's men. By noon, out of the 250 soldiers of the 118th Guards regiment, only six men were left. The colonel of the regiment was severely wounded. Throwing in reserves, the Germans then broke through to the Volga along a 500-yard stretch; thus, for the third time, the 62nd Army was cut in two, and Ludnikov's division was cut off from the rest. But nowhere else did the Germans make any appreciable progress. Heavy fighting continued, as before, at the Red October and Barricades, and round Mamai Hill. . .

The 62nd Army had received some reinforcements during the previous days; in particular a large number of sailors of the Pacific

* This story of the three tanks is reminiscent of another piece of Russian "bluff" at Stalingrad, as described in one of Nekrasov's stories—that of a soldier who, with one machine-gun, pretended to have a whole trenchful of soldiers with him—a story which, he assured me, was based on fact.

Fleet had been drafted into Gorishnyi's division. These Siberians were tough fighters.

The German attacks continued on the following day, without much effect, and, by the middle of November 12 the offensive had petered out. Nevertheless, the Germans had gained a little ground and had reduced the area in Russian hands still further. In some places, the distance between the German lines and the Volga, now covered with ice-floes, was barely 100 yards wide. Also, the Ludnikov division was now isolated from the rest of the 62nd Army on a small bridgehead south of the Barricades, now in German hands. Most of the Red October Plant had also been captured by the Germans. During the days that followed, the Russian attempt to break through the 500 yard German salient on the Volga dividing them from Ludnikov's men, failed. These had to be supplied by small PO-2 reconnaissance planes at night, and it was not until several days later that a few small "armoured" cutters*) of the Volga Flotilla reached the Ludnikov bridgehead through the ice-floes and evacuated 150 wounded men.

But Ludnikov's men had to fight on for more than another month before breaking out of their virtual encirclement.

It was only a week after the Germans' last all-out attempt to dislodge the Russians from the remaining Stalingrad bridgeheads that the great counter-offensive started, the Russian troops of the Don and North-West Fronts striking out from the north, and those of the Stalingrad Front from the south, and the two closing the ring at Kalach, at the eastern end of the Don Bend only four days later.

The news of the counter-offensive†—which had been expected for some time—was received with immense joy and relief by the men of the 62nd Army. Stalin's forecast of November 7 that "there would soon be a holiday in our street" was coming true.

For all that, the position of the 62nd Army at Stalingrad continued to be a highly uncomfortable one. In the north, there was the small bridgehead held by Gorokhov's men. Then, near the Barricades, there was another small bridgehead of half a square mile held by

---

* According to Yeremenko, any bullet could have pierced this "armour".

† See pp. 493 ff.

Colonel Ludnikov's men. The main bridgehead, about five miles long, was, in Chuikov's words, "a narrow strip of ruins".

The left flank of the main bridgehead, held by Rodimtsev's men, was a strip of land only a few hundred yards wide. The maximum depth of the bridgehead, east of Mamai Hill, was only a little over a mile. Chuikov's H.Q. was inside the Volga cliffs, east of Mamai Hill; he also had an observation post between the two, on the railway embankment. All the Russian positions were under German shell-fire, and most of them were even exposed to machine-gun fire. With the Germans holding part of the Mamai heights, they were able to subject the Russian Volga crossings to precision shelling. So Chuikov's two immediate targets were to join up with Ludnikov's men and to recapture the Mamai heights, which would in effect double the depth of the bridgehead there.

By November 20 the Volga, covered with ice-floes, was no longer navigable, and, with the great counter-offensive having begun, the 62nd Army could no longer expect any reinforcements in either men or equipment, anyway. Only small quantities of food and ammunition could be flown over by PO-2 reconnaissance planes. It was not till December 16 that the Volga froze, and individual soldiers could now bring ammunition over the ice in small sleighs.

The problem of dislodging the Germans from their Barricades salient on the Volga was no easy one. They had entrenched themselves in the ruins of factory buildings, and two days of heavy shelling from the other side of the Volga did not make them give up. It took several days of often hand-to-hand fighting, with Ludnikov's men attacking from the north, and Gorishnyi's men from the south, before the salient was eliminated, with heavy casualties on both sides. The junction was not made till December 23.

On December 25 Guriev's men stormed the parts of the Red October Plant in German hands; here it also came to hand-to-hand fighting for every room and workshop. The Germans had turned the main office of the Red October Plant into a powerful firing-point; and their resistance ended only when the whole building was smashed by artillery fire at close range. This kind of house-to-house fighting was to continue almost to the end. As Chuikov says:

The streets and squares of Stalingrad continued to be deserted.

Neither we nor the Germans could act openly. Whoever stuck his head out or ran across the street was inevitably shot by a sniper or tommy-gunner.

Chuikov says that, even after they knew they were encircled, the German troops continued to fight well, and remained confident that Manstein's tank army would break through to relieve them.

Up to the end of December they continued to live in hopes and put up a desperate resistance, often literally to the last cartridge. We practically took no prisoners, since the Nazis just wouldn't surrender. Not till after Manstein's failure to break through did morale among the German troops begin to decline very noticeably.

The growing shortage of both food and ammunition began to tell. Nevertheless, in numerous places in Stalingrad, even after January 10, when the final liquidation of the "cauldron" had begun, the stiff resistance of the Germans continued, notably in the Mamai Hill area, which they were determined to hold to the last. Here they continued to resist and even to counter-attack up to January 25, i.e. a week before the final surrender of the German Stalingrad forces.

Chapter II

THE "STALINGRAD" MONTHS IN MOSCOW—
The Churchill Visit and After.

Unlike the early months of the Invasion, when the communiqués
were cagey in the extreme, the war communiqués in the summer
and autumn of 1942 were, on the whole, remarkably candid. The
loss of this or that town was sometimes only admitted after a few
days' delay and the communiqués often used euphemisms such as
"the approaches of Stalingrad" when in reality the fighting was
already inside the city; but the general picture was almost perfectly
clear throughout. From the beginning of August (after the post-
Rostov reforms) to August 25—which started, as it were, a new
phase in the fighting—the communiqués were almost calculatedly
cruel in their candour. As early as August 8, the communiqué spoke
of fighting "north of Kotelnikovo", which meant that the Germans
had crossed the Don in strength and were now advancing on Stalingrad from the south. More depressing still were the parts of the
communiqués dealing with the German lightning advance into the
Kuban and the Caucasus. In quick succession the losses of Krasnodar, the capital of the Kuban, of the oil city, Maikop, of
Mineralnyie Vody, Piatigorsk, Essentuki and Kislovodsk, the
famous watering-places in the foothills of the Caucasus were
announced. It was also admitted that the Germans were breaking
through the mountains on their way to Novorossisk and the Black
Sea Coast, and that, in the Eastern Caucasus, they were pushing on

towards the oil city of Grozny and the Caspian, with Baku as their target.

No doubt, there were stories of outstanding heroic deeds performed by individual units, and on August 19, Sovinformbureau published some more than improbable figures of German losses. On the same day, the *Red Star* found some solace in the thought that the Germans were attacking on a much smaller front than in 1941, and with less "sureness of touch" than even in July 1942; more and more, the German offensive was working "in fits and starts", and the Russian resistance in the Don Bend had already upset Hitler's time-table.

The swift German advances into the Kuban and the Caucasus had a very depressing effect in Moscow, though some experts were saying that the real test would come once the Germans had reached the mountains. Nevertheless, the loss of the Kuban country, one of the richest agricultural areas of Russia, was keenly felt. Even more was the thought that millions more Russians would now be under German occupation. But as the Germans approached Stalingrad, there was a curious feeling from the start that here it would come to a real showdown. The very name *Stalingrad*, with all the legends woven round it since the Civil War, suggested that the place had a sort of symbolic (therefore political) significance, and that Stalin's own prestige was directly involved. It is hard to say by what subtle propaganda this idea was put across, but the germs of the "Stalingrad legend" were there even before the battle had started.*

Yet it would be absurd to say that the possibility of the loss of Stalingrad was excluded; on the contrary, between the end of August and, roughly, the last week of October, everybody was extremely conscious that the situation at Stalingrad was highly critical.

It was while the military situation in Russia looked particularly desperate that Churchill arrived in Moscow on August 12. The

---

* I find that in my Diary I wrote as early as July 13: "Black as things are, I somehow feel that Stalingrad is going to provide something very big. Stalin's own prestige is involved." (Quoted in *The Year of Stalingrad*, p. 140).

Russians were in full retreat in the North Caucasus, and the Germans were approaching Stalingrad, and about to break through to the Volga north of the city.

Since the brief Anglo-Soviet honeymoon, which had culminated in the meeting of the Supreme Soviet of June 18, relations had been rapidly deteriorating. The correspondence between Churchill and Stalin, especially in July and the beginning of August, points to growing exasperation on both sides. The three main points were the Second Front, the sending of convoys to Northern Russia and the Poles.

Churchill had become increasingly doubtful about the possibility of running convoys to Murmansk and Archangel. As early as May 20 he wrote that the PQ 16 convoy of thirty-five ships had left for Russia, but that "unless the weather is again favourable enough to hamper German air operations, we should expect the greater part of the ships and the war materials they carry to be lost." He proposed therefore that the Russians try to bomb German air bases in Northern Norway. Stalin replied that the Russians would give the convoy what air cover they could, but did not answer Churchill's suggestion about the bombing of Norwegian airfields; the Russians, obviously had no bombers available for the purpose.

As it happened, twenty-seven out of the thirty-five ships of the PQ 16 (the one on which I sailed) got through to Murmansk; but the next convoy, the PQ 17 ended in disaster. Churchill wrote Stalin a long letter on July 18. He recalled that Britain had started running small convoys to Russia as early as August 1941, and that these were not interfered with until December. The problem had become much more difficult after that. In February 1942 the Germans had moved "a considerable force of U-boats and a large number of aircraft" to Northern Norway; nevertheless, the convoys "got through with varying, but not prohibitive losses". Not satisfied with these results, the Germans then sent their surface forces to the north.

> Before the May convoy (PQ 16) was sent off, the Admiralty warned us that the losses would be very severe if, as was expected the Germans used their surface forces to the east of Bear Island. We decided to sail the convoy. The attack by surface forces did not materialise, and the convoy got through with a loss of one-sixth, chiefly from air attack.

But in the case of the PQ 17 convoy the Germans at last used their forces in the manner we had always feared... At the moment only four ships have arrived at Archangel, but six others are in Novaya Zemlya harbours. These may, however, be attacked from the air separately.

In short, Churchill announced his decision to discontinue the Arctic convoys until further notice:

> We do not think it right to risk our Home Fleet eastward of Bear Island... If one or two of our most powerful types were to be lost or even seriously damaged while the Tirpitz and her consorts... remained in action, the whole command of the Atlantic would be lost.

Food supplies by which Britain lived would be affected; and her whole war effort would be crippled.

> Above all, the great convoys of American troops across the ocean, rising presently to as many as 80,000 a month, would be prevented... and a really strong Second Front in 1943 rendered impossible.

Churchill had decided to cancel the PQ 18 convoy, but proposed to send "some of the ships" to the Persian Gulf instead. The same letter also mentioned the "three divisions of Poles" who were anxious to get out of Russia, together with their women and children. Stalin had agreed to their departure, but now Churchill was anxious:

> I hope this project of yours, which we greatly value, will not fall to the ground on account of the Poles wanting to bring with the troops a considerable number of women and children. The feeding of these dependants will be a considerable burden to us. But we think it well worth while bearing that burden for the sake of forming this Polish army which will be used faithfully for our common advantage.

These Poles were to move to Iran and Palestine, and Churchill was obviously in a hurry to get them all out of Russia.

On July 23 Stalin sent a furious reply to this message:

> I gather, first, that the British Government refuses to go on supplying the Soviet Union with war materials by the northern route, and secondly, ... is putting off the (Second Front) operation till 1943... Deliveries via Persian ports can in no way make up for the loss... In view of the situation on the Soviet-German Front, I state most emphatically that the Soviet Government cannot tolerate the Second Front in Europe being postponed till 1943.

Stalin also violently criticised the Admiralty for mishandling the PQ 17 convoy, its dread of losing any warships, and its virtual decision to abandon the supply ships to their fate:

> Of course, I do not think that steady deliveries to northern Soviet ports are possible without risk or loss. But then no major task can be carried out in wartime without risk or losses... The Soviet Union is suffering far greater losses, and I never imagined that the British Government would deny us delivery of war materials precisely now, when the Soviet Union is badly in need of them.

Churchill was, clearly, thoroughly nettled by this obvious charge of gutlessness and bad faith, and in his very next message offered to meet Stalin at Astrakhan or in the Caucasus. He said that another effort would be made to run a convoy to Archangel in September.

Stalin replied on July 31 inviting Churchill to Moscow. "The members of the Government, the General Staff and myself cannot be away at this moment of bitter fighting against the Germans."

Churchill promptly accepted to go to Moscow.

Churchill's story of that famous visit to Moscow is too well-known to need recalling here in any detail. But a few points should be mentioned. The visit was, obviously, distasteful to him. The task of telling Stalin that there would be no Second Front in 1942 "was like carrying a large lump of ice to the North Pole." The conversations ranged from extreme unpleasantness to a superficial mateyness; but there is little doubt that there was much about Stalin that impressed Churchill.

> I met for the first time the great Revolutionary Chief and profound Russian statesman and warrior with whom for the next three years I was to be in intimate, rigorous, but always exciting, and at times even genial association.

During his first meeting he gave him all the good reasons for not opening a Second Front in Europe in 1942, but then told him of operation "Torch" (the landing in North Africa). Stalin "became intensely interested", and finally said: "May God prosper this undertaking." Stalin had quickly grasped the strategic advantages of "Torch":

He recounted four main reasons for it: it would hit Rommel in the back . . . it would overawe Spain; it would produce fighting between Germans and Frenchmen in France; it would expose Italy to the whole brunt of war.

I was deeply impressed with this remarkable statement. It showed the Russian dictator's swift and complete mastery of a problem hitherto novel to him.

According to Churchill this first meeting went off remarkably well, but the next meeting was much less pleasant, and Churchill thought that, in the interval, Stalin had been influenced by the Council of Commissars, "who had not taken the news I had brought as well as he did." In an *aide-mémoire* Stalin handed Churchill during this second meeting he violently protested against the British decision not to have a Second Front in Europe in 1942. Further Notes were exchanged, to no great purpose.

In retrospect, the most interesting part of Churchill's story is Stalin's assessment of the military situation in Russia: he said a) that, with twenty-five divisions defending the Caucasus, the Germans would not cross the mountain range, and would not break through either to Baku or to Batum and, in two months, snow would make the mountains impassable, and b) that he had other solid reasons for his confidence, *including a counter-offensive on a great scale.*

My own feeling (Churchill wrote to Attlee and Roosevelt) is that it is an even chance they will hold, but CIGS will not go as far as this.*)

There was also some inconclusive talk of a joint Soviet-British operation in Northern Norway.

Churchill records no talks with Stalin on the subject of the Poles; all he says is that, on his last night in Moscow, he had a meeting with General Anders. Of this he gives no details.

On his last night (before seeing Anders) Churchill had gone to Stalin's private flat in the Kremlin to have dinner.

Molotov was also summoned. Stalin introduced me to his daughter, a nice girl, who kissed him shyly, but was not allowed to dine. . . The greatest goodwill prevailed, and for the first time we got on to easy and friendly terms. I feel I have established a personal relationship which will be helpful. . .

* Churchill, *The Second World War*, vol. IV, pp. 425–8.

He would rather have lorries than tanks, of which he is making 2,000 a month. Also, he wants aluminium. On the whole, I am encouraged by my visit to Moscow... Now they know the worst and, having made their protest, they are entirely friendly, and this in spite of the fact that this is their most anxious and agonising time. Moreover, Stalin is entirely convinced of the great advantages of "Torch"... *)

Such is the gist of Churchill's story of his visit to Moscow in August 1942. The attitude to the Churchill visit, and to the Western Allies generally, on the part of the Moscow population is a rather different story. Not only had the "Second Front communiqué" of June 11 been played up to a fantastic degree by the Soviet press, but it was also linked in the public mind with Stalin's somewhat ill-considered May-Day Order about "driving the Fascist invaders out of the Soviet Union in 1942." It was assumed that Stalin would have never issued such an order without being as good as certain that there would be a Second Front in the West.

Not only was the Russian population suffering very serious hardships (the winter had been terrible, and the spring and summer were not much better), but, when the military situation began to look truly catastrophic in July and August, the question of a Second Front in the immediate future became to many Russians almost a matter of life and death. It should also be remembered that nearly every Russian one met had a father or brother, or son—or several brothers or sons—in the army, or else dead, wounded or missing. In the villages there were hardly any men left at all except youngsters or very old people.

Even at the height of the "honeymoon" there had been distrust of the Americans and especially of the British. The ratification of the Anglo-Soviet Alliance had been marked by a display of a lot of Soviet flags on public buildings, but no British flags. As we have seen, invidious comparisons were made between the desperate resistance at Sebastopol and the "gutless" surrender at Tobruk. I remember an educated-looking old woman in a tramcar saying:

* Ibid., pp. 450–1.

"You can't possibly trust the British. Young people are not educated enough to know; but I know all about Dis-ra-eli" (she uttered the four-syllable name with a snarl); others were very distrustful of Churchill, whose attitude to Russia was often contrasted with that of Roosevelt, who was assumed to be much friendlier. During June, July and August, I visited a variety of schools and talked to many young people. They were friendly; but there was only one thing they really wanted to know, and that was whether there was going to be a Second Front, and if so, when.

There was little propaganda to popularise the British and American Allies. In June there were a few posters—one of three darts of lightning, with the Soviet, the American and the British flags striking down a toad-like Hitler, green with fear. Except for some newsreels of the Molotov visit to the USA and England, nothing much was made of the alliance in either cinemas or theatres; and the only "pro-Allied" show I remember was a variety show at the Moscow Ermitage—which ended, somewhat fatuously, with an exotic-looking young woman playing *Tipperary* on an accordion, and singing in a mixture of broken English and Russian, after which the whole company burst into what was meant to be a sort of Anglo-Soviet-American dance, in the setting of a great display of allied flags. The audience showed very little enthusiasm. This was at the beginning of July; the show was stopped soon after, and the three darts-of-lightning posters also disappeared, as well as the displays of the "Victory in 1942" slogan.

One of the minor accompaniments of the Anglo-Soviet Alliance and the American-Soviet Agreement was the formation in June of an Anglo-American Press Association; besides being a gesture of special goodwill on the part of the Russians who had authorised this purely Anglo-American association to be set up, it gave them an opportunity to concentrate their propaganda efforts on the British and American press.

As time went on, the exasperation about the lack of a Second Front grew. Stories went round Moscow of German leaflets showered on the Russians, saying "Where are the English?"* or "The

* These were almost exactly like those dropped on French troops in 1939 and 1940.

Rumanians and Hungarians are better allies to us than the English are to you."

In this atmosphere, the news of Churchill's visit was received with rather mixed feelings. The first guess made by people like Ehrenburg was, roughly, the correct one: that Churchill had come to "plead with Stalin and to withdraw the Second Front communiqué". Apart from that the Russians were completely silent; and the two other sources of information, or rather, sources of hints, seemed unable to agree. The British Embassy kept hinting that Stalin and Churchill were "getting on like a house on fire" and, on the last day, Sir Archibald Clark-Kerr described the meeting as "an epoch-making event"—which was going to create a lot of confusion soon afterwards. Mr. Harriman and the Americans, on the other hand, kept on suggesting that the meetings had not gone well at all, and that if the Russians were to expect any immediate results from these bad-tempered meetings, they were going to be disappointed. It was also learned that the British had asked for air bases in the Caucasus, a proposal the Russians had rejected. However, even the Americans admitted that the atmosphere had improved somewhat towards the end, and was "almost jovial" at the Kremlin banquet. It was said that Churchill had complimented Stalin on the "splendid Russian soldiers" to which Stalin had replied "Don't exaggerate. They aren't all that hot. In fact they are pretty bad still. But they are learning and improving every day; and they'll be all right before long."

The Russian public saw nothing of Churchill; he did not go to any theatre show; there was no embassy reception of any kind, and he even decided not to see the British and American press, who were seen instead by the Ambassador who then uttered that ill-considered phrase about the "epoch-making event".

However, the newsreel men were kept busy, and on his arrival at the airfield, Churchill's V-sign was interpreted by some Russians who saw it on the screen as meaning "Second Front". (In a cinema I heard a young girl, when the band played "God Save the King", asking her girl friend what the tune was, and receiving the reply: "Don't you know? That's the 'Internationale' in English.")

The communiqué published at the end of the Churchill visit and the editorials in the Russian press spoke of the close bonds between

Britain and the Soviet Union, but were not very illuminating, and did not suggest any immediate results. Significantly, the Army paper, *Red Star*, did not publish an editorial of its own, but merely reprinted the *Pravda* editorial. Also, on the day of Churchill's departure, when, in his final statement, he said that he had "spoken his mind" to Stalin, *Pravda* printed an angry Yefimov cartoon ridiculing the German cardboard defences on the Channel—a theory Dieppe was, unfortunately, going to disprove a few days later. Not that the Russians thought that Dieppe had proved anything, except perhaps a desire on the part of the British to show that the Second Front was "impossible".

The Russians also disliked Churchill's "hobnobbing" with General Anders during his Moscow visit, even though he appears to have had only one short meeting with him. It was (probably correctly) assumed that the stories Churchill was told about the "imminent" defeat of the Red Army (whether he believed them or not) emanated in the first place from Anders, who, as the Russians knew only too well, was in a great hurry to pull the greatest possible number of Poles out of Russia. The story widely current in Moscow that Churchill had encouraged the Poles to leave the "sinking ship" added to Russian annoyance.

These stories did not appear in the press, but it should be remembered that the Party went in for a good deal of verbal propaganda, and kept up a fairly heavy barrage in this way against both the "saboteurs of the Second Front" and, more particularly, against the Poles. In ideological terms, there were many "class enemies", and Churchill and certainly the Anders' Poles were amongst them. The fact that these Poles had some highly understandable grievances against the Russians was, of course, overlooked.

On August 23 Stalingrad was bombed by 600 planes and to the north of the city the Germans broke through to the Volga; this was not announced at the time. For the next week the communiqués rather vaguely (but ominously) spoke of "intensive" fighting northeast and north-west of Stalingrad, with occasional mentions of some local success. During the first fortnight of September, the whole tone of the press was distinctly nervous in its comments on Stalingrad; and it was not till September 20 (five days after the arrival of the Rodimtsev division) that it began to speak of "heroic Stalingrad".

During the greater part of September, the press blew hot and cold: while admitting that the situation at Stalingrad was very serious, it gave some general reasons for being reasonably confident. Thus, much was made of the enormous progress made by the war industries, of the supplies that were now reaching the army, and of the growing discouragement among the Germans. In particular, much as he may have disliked doing it, Ehrenburg frequently quoted desperate letters to German soldiers at the Russian front about the terror and horror of "British thousand-bomber raids". There was no Second Front, but the RAF was, all the same, having its uses.

Two things began to characterise the Soviet press coverage of Stalingrad during the last ten days of September: the detailed description of the peculiar nature of the fighting there (above all, the house-to-house fighting) and the birth of the Stalingrad Legend. Thus, on September 22, *Red Star* published an extremely detailed article on the technique of house-to-house (and even floor-to-floor and room-to-room) fighting.*

As for the Legend, the press was no longer as reticent as it had been during the first half of September. "Heroic Stalingrad" and the "heroic defenders of Stalingrad" now became daily phrases in the press. Simonov, Grossman, Krieger, and many other Soviet writers and journalists depicted the pathos, the grim and heroic atmosphere of the Stalingrad Battle. It was not until later that anyone questioned whether these articles were first-hand. After the war, General Chuikov, in particular, debunked some of this reporting. But this was not always fair. Many Soviet reporters and, especially, photographers and cinema operators lost their lives at Stalingrad and in other battles.

Early in September the Russian press had applied the word "Verdun" to Stalingrad, and this word was seized on by the world press. But by the end of September, the Soviet press dismissed the parallel as absurd. Thus Yerusalimsky wrote in *Red Star* of September 27 that Stalingrad "by far exceeded Verdun", and pointed out

* See *The Year of Stalingrad*, pp. 218–9.

that "Verdun was a first-class fortress; Stalingrad is not. Also, the Russian offensive in the east in 1916 diverted great German forces from Verdun; ... now the opposite is true."

October 1942 was, as Stalin was to say a year later, the month in which the Soviet Union was in even greater danger than she had been at the time of the Battle of Moscow. The Battle of Stalingrad was going badly and on October 14 the city was very nearly lost. There was also an acute deterioration in Anglo-Soviet relations. Wild accusations were hurled at Britain for playing a double game—which were not unrelated with the extremely critical position at Stalingrad about the middle of the month.

The intensification of the Anti-British campaign (which had somewhat abated at the time of the Churchill visit and the Dieppe fiasco) had started some time before—to be precise, at the time of Wendell Willkie's visit to Moscow about September 20. Willkie had come as President Roosevelt's personal representative, and was made a great fuss of. His whole attitude to Russia contrasted, in Russian eyes, very favourably with Churchill's. Photographs of him in the company of Stalin and Molotov appeared in every paper, and the most was made of his public utterances. He was shown a number of war factories and was taken on a trip to the Rzhev sector of the front west of Moscow, where the Russians were fighting a particularly fierce and heartbreaking "diversionist" action against the Germans, and suffering heavy losses with very little to show for it.

Several times Willkie clearly suggested that Roosevelt was all in favour of the Second Front that year, but he had met with opposition from the British generals, and from Churchill himself.

I particularly remember the morning of September 26, just after his return from the Rzhev sector of the front, when he invited me to breakfast at the Soviet Guest House in Ostrovsky Lane. He was wearing a smart blue silk dressing gown with white spots, and was the picture of health and vigour. He looked like a man who would live to be ninety. How great his personal charm was everybody knows. The Russians were doing him proud; there was caviare for breakfast, and even grapes, the first I had seen that year.

"It's a very tricky problem I'm up against," he said. "How is one to explain to the American public that the Russians are in a very grave situation but that their morale is first-rate for all that?... I know the country is full of the most appalling personal tragedies but, at the same time, if I were to repeat all the wild talk I heard at dinner yesterday from Simonov, Ehrenburg and Voitekhov, with all their abuse of the Allies, I think it would make a very bad impression in the States...

There followed this striking illustration of the grave doubts that existed in Washington in the summer of 1942 about Russia's power of survival.

"After all", said Willkie, "things are not as desperate as one thought they might be by now. Egypt is okay; the Russians are holding out, and even Stalingrad is still in their hands. I don't mind telling you that when I was leaving Washington five weeks ago, the President told me: '... I just want to warn you. I know you've got guts, but you may get to Cairo just as Cairo is falling, and you may get to Russia at the time of a Russian collapse'."

I suggested to Willkie that the President was not perhaps being as competently informed from Moscow as he might be (I had in mind the pessimists at the US Embassy, particularly General Michela and Colonel Park), to which Willkie nodded. Speaking of the Second Front, he thought it was taking a terrible risk to postpone it till 1943; for what if Russian offensive capacity was meantime reduced to nothing? (This, incidentally, showed that if the Russians told Churchill something about their planned counter-offensive, they hadn't told Willkie anything about it—why spoil his Second Front fervour?).

The same day he made a statement to the Anglo-American press in which he spoke with real emotion of the great Russian spirit of self-sacrifice he had observed everywhere; and then he uttered the famous phrase which was going to cause a lot of trouble:

Personally I am now convinced that we can help them by establishing a real Second Front in Europe with Great Britain at the earliest possible moment our military leaders will approve. And perhaps some of them will need some public prodding.

The Russians took him at his word, and stick-in-the-mud British

Blimps (modelled on Low) began to appear in Russian cartoons. Churchill was furious, since Willkie's statement had, in his view, undone much of the good of his own visit a month before, when he thought he had convinced the Russians that the Second Front in the near future was impossible. And although Stalin knew about "Torch" (which Willkie perhaps did not) the Russian press embarked on a savage anti-British campaign during October, when the situation at Stalingrad looked particularly desperate.

On October 6, barely a week after the Willkie statement, Yefimov published in *Pravda* a vicious cartoon of a number of bald-headed and walrus-moustached Blimps sitting round a table and facing two dashing young soldiers in American uniform. These two were labelled "General Guts" and "General Decision", while the Blimps were called "General What-if-they-lick-us", "General What's-the-hurry", "General Why-take-risks", and so on. On the same day Stalin answered the three-point questionnaire sent him by Henry Cassidy, the A.P. correspondent. In his answer he said that the Second Front "occupied a place of first-rate importance in the current situation"; that "the aid of the Allies to the Soviet Union has so far been little effective", and that it was essential that the Allies "fulfil their obligations fully and on time"; and, finally, in reply to Cassidy's question: "What remains of the Soviet capacity for resistance?" Stalin said:

> I think that the Soviet capacity of resisting the German brigands is in strength not less, if not greater, than the capacity of Fascist Germany, or of any other aggressive power, to secure for itself world domination.

Molotov added fuel to the flames by resorting to a curious trick. For nine months there had been lying in his folders a Note on war-crimes from the Czech Government and the French National Committee and endorsed by Governments of other Nazi-occupied countries. He now replied to this Note and, in the last paragraph he said:

> The Soviet Government considers it essential that any of the leaders of Nazi Germany who happens to be in the hands of States fighting against Hitler Germany be tried without delay by a special People's court, with all the rigour of the criminal law.

This Note was published on October 15 (one of the grimmest days in the Stalingrad fighting). Its meaning was rubbed in four days later when *Pravda* published a violent editorial on Rudolf Hess:

> So it now appears that Rudolf Hess arrived in England dressed as a German airman; therefore, he is not being treated as one of the chief war criminals, but is, instead, being treated as a mere "war prisoner". So it was enough for this notorious war criminal to dress up ... in order to evade his responsibility for his countless crimes, and thus *to turn England into a sanctuary for gangsters.*

Not to treat Hess as a war criminal, *Pravda* went on, was to treat him as "the representative of another State, as Hitler's envoy."

And then came the story of "Hess's wife":

> It is not accidental that Hess's wife should have appealed to certain British representatives to be allowed to join her husband. It would seem from this that Frau Hess does not consider him a prisoner-of-war. It is time we found out whether Hess is a criminal ... *or the pleni-potentiary representative of the Nazi Government in England, with all the privileges of immunity.*

Maybe the story of Hess's wife was a pure invention; or maybe it had been planted on the Russians by some diplomatic tipster. The purpose of this violent anti-British campaign is still not clear, and there are several possible explanations: the most pleasant is that Stalin knew about "Torch", and was trying to mislead the Germans —to make them think that there was nothing to worry about in the west. Certainly, the German press had an orgy of hee-hawing over the Anglo-Soviet quarrel over Hess. But there are also other possible explanations: things at Stalingrad were going badly, and a scapegoat was necessary, and, in any case, many Soviet leaders had a bee in their bonnet about "Lady Astor", the "Cliveden Set" and other alleged British supporters of a deal with Hitler at Russia's expense. Although these were mentioned occasionally, the Hess article was the most vicious anti-British attack throughout the war, and it certainly stirred up a great deal of anti-British feeling in Russia. The day the article appeared, I remember seeing a Polish officer standing in a queue outside one of the Gastronome shops in Moscow; people started shouting at him, "Instead of queuing up for delicacies, you English had better do a little fighting." When he explained that he was a Pole, they left him alone.

The only comic relief was provided by the British Ministry of Information paper published in Moscow, the *Britansky Soyuznik*. A day or two after the *Pravda* editorial on Hess, amongst a lot of notes on culture in England was a photo of "Madame Hess" giving a lunch-time piano recital at the London Royal Exchange. It was, actually, Dame Myra Hess, but how were the Russians to know that this was not Hess's wife playing to London bankers and stockbrokers?

The British reaction to the "sanctuary for gangsters" editorial were so sharp that the Russians decided not to persist in their campaign, though the bad humour persisted. At a public lecture given by Professor Yudin, one of the Party's great ideologists, on October 28, he argued that the reasons for the absence of the Second Front were *entirely political*: that unfortunately there were very strong Munichite influences inside the British Government. He almost suggested that the purpose of the Hess article had been to stir up British public opinion, so that it should insist that the "Munichites" be thrown out of the British Government. Asked why the British Government was incapable of breaking this resistance, he said: "I am not suggesting that Churchill cannot break it, but—". He shrugged his shoulders.

At the same time, however, Yudin was very optimistic about the outlook at the front; thanks to the resistance of Stalingrad, the Germans had already lost their summer campaign, and he was confident that neither the Japs nor the Turks would budge now. He already declared that Stalingrad would prove the great turning-point in this war.

He even alluded to some peace-feelers the Germans had put out *via* Japan, but said that it no longer depended on Germany when the war would end; whether or not there was going to be a Second Front, the Soviet Union would fight on till the final defeat of Germany.

At the end of October the whole tone of the Russian press became, indeed, much more optimistic. The communiqués and the press reports in the middle of the month had dwelt on the extreme seriousness of the situation; but by the end of October the worst seemed to be over. On October 28 Alexandrov wrote in *Pravda*:

> The defence of Stalingrad has held up the Germans for three months. This means that at Stalingrad they lost the most precious time they had this year for offensive operations.

In other words, the terrible danger that the country had felt in July and August had already been averted. Not that Stalingrad itself was necessarily out of danger yet, and nearly the whole of the Northern Caucasus was in German hands. Although they had been held up at Mozdok on the way to Baku and had not advanced much beyond Novorossisk on the Black Sea, the Germans suddenly scored a major success on November 2 by breaking through to Nalchik on the way to Vladikavkaz, the northern terminus of the Georgian Military Highway—the gate into Transcaucasia.

Even so, the whole atmosphere in Moscow on the eve of the 25th anniversary of the October Revolution was distinctly optimistic. Something had clearly changed since the grim months of July and August. The biggest front-page publicity was given, on November 6, to the "Oath of the Defenders of Stalingrad" addressed to Stalin:

> ... The enemy's aim was to cut our Volga waterway and then, by turning south to the Caspian, to cut off our country from its main oil supplies... If the enemy succeeds, he can then turn all his strength against Moscow and Leningrad...

Even at that stage, Stalingrad still said "if he succeeds", and not "if he had succeeded". Apart from this reservation, the tone was confident throughout. After enumerating all that the defenders of Stalingrad had achieved and the losses the Germans had suffered there, they recalled Stalin's role in the defence of Tsaritsyn (the old name of Stalingrad) during the Civil War, and they declared themselves firmly convinced that, "fighting as we are under your direct guidance ... we shall strike another smashing blow at the enemy and drive him away from Stalingrad."

The Oath to "dear Joseph Vissarionovich" did not go so far as to say that Stalingrad *would* be held; but the way in which they associated the city with the name and prestige of Stalin made failure extremely unlikely.

In sending you this letter from the trenches, we swear to you, dear Joseph Vissarionovich, that to the last drop of blood, to the last breath, to the last heart-beat, we shall defend Stalingrad... We swear that we shall not disgrace the glory of Russian arms and shall fight to the end. Under your leadership our fathers won the Battle of Tsaritsyn. Under your leadership we shall win the great Battle of Stalingrad.

The whole tone of the Oath was so confident that there was now, if anything, a tendency to underrate the dangers Stalingrad was still facing; nevertheless, people still felt instinctively that the worst was over, and this instinct proved right. The letters people were getting from soldiers in Stalingrad greatly contributed to the optimism. These were not official missives like the "Oath", each word of which had no doubt been carefully vetted by the political big-shots on the spot, but private letters; and in these it was clear that, despite the fearful mental and bodily strain, Russian soldiers were becoming immensely proud of *being* in Stalingrad. To the Germans, on the other hand, the idea of being sent to Stalingrad was becoming increasingly terrifying.

Not only had the Soviet press been conducting an anti-British campaign in October, but the Churchill-Stalin correspondence during this period was far from cordial. Stalin acknowledged the arrival of the PQ 18 convoy at Archangel rather curtly; he also dismissed Churchill's estimate of German aircraft production as inaccurate; and in reply to Churchill's long letter of October 9 pressing him to accept an Anglo-American air force in the Caucasus (but also informing him that the Arctic convoys would have to be cut down) Stalin merely said: "Your message of October 9 received. Thank you. J. Stalin."

However, with the situation in the Caucasus deteriorating (Nalchik had been captured by the Germans on November 2) Stalin, in his letter of November 8 showed renewed interest in the offer of twenty Anglo-American squadrons for the Caucasus.

In view of all the unpleasantness, especially in October, between the Soviet and British Governments (Churchill was particularly furious about the Hess outburst) Stalin's November 6 broadcast came as a pleasant surprise to the Western Allies. No doubt he knew by this time that Operation "Torch" had already started and that Rommel was in retreat in the Western Desert. He repeatedly stressed the importance of the Anglo-American-Soviet alliance, though he sounded ironical about the British in Libya, where they were fighting "only four—yes, four—German and eleven Italian divisions." He also said that, if only there were a Second Front, the Germans would by now have been driven back to Pskov, Minsk and Odessa. He spoke with satisfaction of the great improvement in the Russian fighting, and of the enormous progress made by the Soviet industries in the east. He also argued that the Germans had failed in their main objective which was not the occupation of the Caucasus (this was only their "secondary" objective) but the encirclement of Moscow from the east, after the fall of Stalingrad.

His Order of the Day on November 7 followed much the same line; without alluding either to "Torch" or to the coming Russian offensive, it used, however, a phrase which enormously cheered—and intrigued—the Russians: "There will be a holiday in our street, too," meaning "it will soon be our turn to rejoice".

The news of the North African landing two days later created a big impression in Moscow. Without understanding the enormous organisational complexity of the landing, people had the pleasant feeling that things in the west were at last on the move—not that this was quite the same as the "Second Front" they had hoped for. Later, in Stalingrad, I was told that the news of the North-African landing was flashed to all the army units and had a very good effect. In his second letter to Cassidy, dated November 13, Stalin expressed great satisfaction over the successful progress of the North-African campaign. "It opens the prospect of the disintegration of the Italo-German coalition in the nearest future", he wrote, adding that the operation clearly showed that the Anglo-American leaders "were capable of organising a serious war campaign" and that, in the Western Desert "the enemy troops had been smashed with great mastery." He predicted that Italy would soon drop out of the war. Although it was too early to say to what extent the North-African campaign would relieve the pressure on the Soviet Union, he thought the effect would be "appreciable".

Stalin also said that the campaign "created the prerequisites for establishing a Second Front in Europe, nearer to Germany's vital centres", and would "shake France out of her lethargy".

Although many Russians were scandalised by the American deal with Darlan, we now know that Stalin himself took a completely cynical or "realistic" view of the whole thing—which is scarcely surprising when one looks back on 1939. In his letter to Churchill of November 27 he wrote:

> As for Darlan, I think the Americans have made skilful use of him to facilitate the occupation of North and West Africa. Military diplomacy should know how to use for the war aims not only the Darlans, but even the devil and his grandmother.

Altogether, after the North-African landing, there was a very marked improvement in inter-allied relations. As Clark-Kerr, the British Ambassador remarked to me a few days later: "The Kremlin is now sending out warm rays."

Chapter III

RUSSIANS ENCIRCLE THE GERMANS AT STALINGRAD

There was only a lapse of thirteen days between the "Oath by the Defenders of Stalingrad" and the beginning of the great Russian counter-offensive which ended in the Stalingrad victory two and a half months later. But in the course of these thirteen days the Germans launched one more desperate offensive against Chuikov's 62nd Army whose position had been rendered even more difficult than before by the icefloes on the Volga. These had practically stopped all communications across the river, and had made it almost impossible even to evacuate the wounded. And yet, once this last German offensive was smashed, the morale of the defenders of Stalingrad was higher than ever, all the more so as they had an inkling that something very important was about to happen.

Later, Stalingrad soldiers told me with what frantic joy, hope and excitement they heard the sound of distant but intensive gun-fire on November 19, between 6 and 7 a.m., that most silent hour of the day in Stalingrad. They knew what that gun-fire meant. It meant that they would not have to go on defending Stalingrad through the winter. Through the darkness, with scarcely a glimmer of light—for it was a dim, damp, foggy dawn—they listened, as they put their heads out of their dugouts.

Neither on November 19, when the Don Army Group under Rokossovsky and the South-West Army Group under Vatutin struck out southward towards Kalach, nor on the 20th, when the Stalingrad

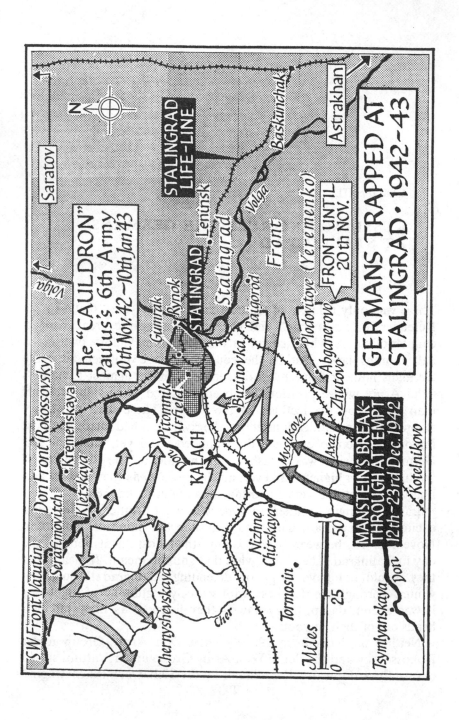

GERMANS TRAPPED AT STALINGRAD · 1942~43

Astrakhan

STALINGRAD LIFE-LINE

Saratov

The "CAULDRON"
Paulus's 6th Army
30th Nov.'42–10th Jan.'43

Baskunchak

Volga

Leninsk

STALINGRAD

Stalingrad

Front

Volga

Plodovitoye (Yeremenko)

FRONT UNTIL
20th NOV.

Gumrak

Rynok

Raigorod

Abganerovo

Zhutovo

Don Front (Rokossovsky)

Kremenskaya

Buzinovka

Pitomnik Airfield

Don

KALACH

Myshkova

Aksai

Kotelnikovo

MANSTEIN'S BREAK-
THROUGH ATTEMPT
12th–23rd Dec. 1942

Kletskaya

Serafimovitch

S.W. Front (Vatutin)

Cherryshevskaya

Nizhne
Chirskaya

Tormosin

Cher

Miles

0   25   50

Tsymlyanskaya

Don

Army Group under Yeremenko struck north-west from the area
south of Stalingrad to meet them was anything officially announced.
Nor was there anything in the communiqué of November 21. With
unconscious irony, *Pravda* devoted its editorial that day to "The
Session of the Academy of Sciences at Sverdlovsk."

It was not till the night of November 22 that a special communiqué announced the tremendous news that Russian troops had
struck out "a few days ago" from both north-west and south of
Stalingrad, that they had captured Kalach and had cut the two railway lines supplying the Germans in Stalingrad, at Krivomuzginskaya
and at Abganerovo. It was not yet explicitly stated that the ring
around the Germans in Stalingrad had been closed, but the communiqué spoke of very heavy losses inflicted on the enemy, of 14,000
enemy dead, 13,000 prisoners, et cetera.

The excitement in Moscow was tremendous, and on everybody's
lips there was this one word: "*nachalos!*"—"it's started". Some
instinct suggested to everybody that something very big could be
expected from this offensive.*

The main points about this second and decisive phase of the Stalingrad battle are:

1) The three Russian "Fronts" together had 1,050,000 men
against an almost equal number of enemy troops; about 900 tanks
against 700†; 13,000 guns against 10,000; and 1,100 planes against
1,200.

On the other hand, in the "main blow" sectors, Russian
superiority was overwhelming which, according to the *History*, had

---

* It is interesting to note that, a few days later, Colonel Exham, the
British military attaché, reckoned that this offensive "would take
the Russians all the way to Kharkov" before the end of the winter,
whereas General Michela and Colonel Park of the US Embassy were
saying that it was "darned smart of the Germans to get themselves encircled at Stalingrad, and to tie up enormous Russian forces in this
way—which would cause the Russians no end of embarrassments."

† IVOVSS, vol. 3, p. 26. Elsewhere the *History* claims that the
Russians had 1,200 tanks, most of them modern, whereas at Moscow
they had only scraped together 750, mainly obsolete.

never before been achieved in this war: a three-fold superiority in men and a four-fold superiority in equipment, especially in artillery and mortars.

Practically all this equipment had been made by Soviet industry during the summer and early autumn months, and only a small number of Western tanks, lorries and jeeps were used. Up to February 1943, 72,000 Western lorries had been delivered to Russia, but only a very small proportion of these were available by the time the Russian Stalingrad offensive began.

2) Morale among the troops was extremely good.

3) The plan for the counter-offensive had been worked out "collectively" since August, chiefly by Stalin, Zhukov* and Vassilevsky, in consultation with the commanders of the local Army Groups—Vatutin, Rokossovsky and Yeremenko. In October and November Vassilevsky and Zhukov visited the areas of the coming operations.

4) The preparations for the offensive were an enormous feat of organisation and had been conducted with the greatest secrecy; thus, for several weeks before the offensive all mail was stopped between the soldiers of the three Army Groups and their families. Although they bombed the railways leading to the area north of the Don, the Germans never got a clear idea of how much equipment and how many troops were being brought (mainly at night) to the area north of the Don and to the two main Russian bridgeheads inside the Don Bend; and the Germans never thought that the Russian counter-offensive (if any) could assume such vast proportions. More difficult still was the task of transporting vast numbers of troops and enormous quantities of equipment to the Stalingrad Front, in the south. The heavily-bombed railway line east of the Volga had to be used, and pontoons and ferries had to be organised across the Volga, almost right under the Germans' noses. Unlike the country north of

* Zhukov, in order to make the "final arrangement", visited Vatutin's H.Q. on November 5 and that of Yeremenko on November 10. (IVOVSS, vol. 3, p. 26). But the idea that he was probably the real brain behind the operation is minimised in recent histories.

the Don, where there were some forests, camouflage in the barren steppes south of Stalingrad was particularly difficult.

Even so, the Germans still had no idea of the weight of the coming Russian onslaught.

5) The German command, and Hitler in particular, were so obsessed with the prestige problem of capturing Stalingrad that they did not give sufficient attention to consolidating the two flanks of what can conveniently be called the Stalingrad salient. Strictly speaking, it was not a salient: there was a clear "front" on its north side, but in the south there was a sort of vast no-man's-land running through the Kalmuk steppes all the way to the northern Caucasus, with a few thin lines held here and there, mostly by Rumanian troops. In the north, too, some of the sectors of the front were held by Rumanians. The Rumanian troops had fought well round Odessa and in the Crimea, but at the beginning of winter in the Don steppes their morale was low. Here they were clearly not fighting Rumania's battle, but Hitler's, and their relations with the Germans were far from satisfactory at any level. Further west on the Don, there were Italian troops, whose morale was also far from good. The Russians were fully aware of this, and rightly regarded the sectors held by Rumanians and Italians as the weakest.

The offensive started along a wide front to the north of the salient at 6.30 a.m. on November 19 with an artillery and *katyusha* barrage; and Russian infantry and tanks began their advance two hours later. Owing to bad weather, little aircraft was used. In three days Vatutin's troops advanced some seventy-five miles, routing in the process the Rumanian 3rd Army and a number of German units that were hastily sent to the rescue of their allies. Despite strong resistance from the Germans and also some Rumanian units, Vatutin's troops of the South-West Front reached Kalach on the 22nd, meeting there Yeremenko's forces which had broken through from the south, with rather less resistance from the enemy.

In the fighting, four Rumanian divisions were encircled, and soon afterwards surrendered, with General Lascar at their head. The same fate befell another encircled Rumanian group commanded by General Stenescu. The routing of the Rumanian 3rd Army, as a result of which the Russians took some 30,000 prisoners, had a far-reaching political effect on Hitler's relations with his allies. For one thing, after that Rumanian troops were placed under much stricter and more direct German supervision.

Yeremenko's Stalingrad Army Group, starting their attack one day later, advanced even more rapidly towards Kalach which it reached within less than three days, thus forestalling the North-Western Army Group and taking 7,000 Rumanian prisoners. The right flank of Army Group Don, under General Rokossovsky had also struck out to the south on November 19, one of its prongs breaking through to General Gorokhov's bridgehead on the Volga north of Stalingrad.

Within four and a half days the encirclement of the Germans in Stalingrad was completed. The "ring" was neither very thick—it varied from twenty to forty miles—nor very solid, and the obvious next task was to strengthen and widen it. During the last days of November the Germans made an attempt to break through the "ring" from the west, but they failed despite a few initial successes. What the Russians feared most was that Paulus's 6th Army and units of the 4th Panzer Army inside Stalingrad would attempt to break out and abandon Stalingrad; but there was no sign of this happening and, paradoxically, during the Russian breakthrough on the Don many Germans fled to Stalingrad "for safety".

Some interesting details on the scene of this great battle were given me by Henry Shapiro, the United Press Correspondent in Moscow, who was allowed to visit it a few days after the "ring" had closed. He went by train to a point some hundred miles north-west of Stalingrad, and travelled from there by car to Serafimovich, on that bridgehead on the Don which the Russians had captured in heavy fighting in October, and whence Vatutin hurled his troops towards Kalach on November 19.

> The railway line nearer the front had been heavily bombed by the Germans; all stations were destroyed, and the military commandants and railway personnel operated the railway traffic from dugouts and ruined buildings. All along the railway towards the front there was a

tremendous continuous flow of armaments: *katyushas*, guns, tanks, ammunition—and men. The traffic continued day and night, and it was the same on the roads. It was particularly intense at night. There was very little British or American equipment to be seen, except an occasional jeep or tank; about ninety-nine per cent of the stuff was Russian-made. A fairly high proportion of the food was, however, American—especially lard, sugar and spam.

By the time I got to Serafimovich, the Russians were not only consolidating the "ring" round Stalingrad, but were now making a "second ring"; it was clear from the map that the Germans at Stalingrad were completely trapped, and couldn't get out... I found among both soldiers and officers *a feeling of self-confidence, the like of which I had never seen in the Red Army before. In the Battle of Moscow there was nothing like it.* (Emphasis added.)

Well behind the fighting-line there were now thousands of Rumanians wandering about the steppes, cursing the Germans and desperately looking for Russian feeding-points, and anxious to be formally taken over as war prisoners. Some individual stragglers would throw themselves on the mercy of the local peasants, who treated them charitably, if only because they were not Germans. The Russians thought they were "just poor peasants like ourselves".

Except for small groups of Iron-Guard men who, here and there, put up a stiff fight, the Rumanian soldiers were sick and tired of the war; the prisoners I saw all said roughly the same thing—that this was Hitler's war, and that the Rumanians had nothing to do on the Don.

The closer I moved to Stalingrad, the more numerous were the German prisoners... The steppe was a fantastic sight; it was full of dead horses, while some horses were only half-dead, standing on three frozen legs, and shaking the remaining broken one. It was pathetic. 10,000 horses had been killed during the Russian breakthrough. The whole steppe was strewn with these dead horses and wrecked gun-carriages and tanks and guns—Germans, French, Czech, even British (no doubt captured at Dunkirk)..., and no end of corpses, Rumanian and German. The Russian bodies were the first to be buried. Civilians were coming back to the villages, most of them wrecked... Kalach was a shambles: only one house was standing...

General Chistiakov, whose H.Q. I finally located in a village south of Kalach—the village was under sporadic shell-fire—said that, only a few days before, the Germans could still fairly easily have broken out of Stalingrad, but Hitler had forbidden it. Now they had missed their chance. He was certain that Stalingrad would be taken by the end of December.*

German transport planes, Chistiakov said, were being shot down by the dozen, and the Germans inside the Stalingrad pocket were already short of food, and were eating up the horses.

The German prisoners I saw were mostly young fellows, and very miserable. I did not see any officers. In thirty degrees of frost they wore ordinary coats, and had blankets tied round their necks. They had hardly any winter clothing at all. The Russians, on the other hand, were very well-equipped—with *valenki*, sheepskin coats, warm gloves, et cetera. Morally, the Germans seemed completely stunned, unable to understand what the devil had happened.

On my return journey I saw General Vatutin in a dilapidated school-house at Serafimovich for a few minutes at four in the morning... He was terribly tired; he had not had a proper sleep for at least a fortnight, and kept rubbing his eyes and dozing off. For all that, he looked very tough and determined, and was highly optimistic. He showed me a map on which the new Russian sweep into the western part of the Don country was clearly marked.

My impression was that while the capture of Serafimovich in October had cost the Russians heavy casualties, their losses in this well-planned breakthrough were incomparably smaller than those of the Rumanians and Germans.

At this time, the Germans and their allies were still occupying vast territories of south-east Russia. The whole of the Kuban country and parts of the Northern Caucasus were in their hands; they were still at Mozdok on the road to Grozny, and at Novorossisk on the Black Sea. On November 2 they had captured Nalchik and had nearly captured Vladikavkaz, at the northern end of the Georgian Military Highway, though here the Russians scored a major success on November 19 by throwing in a strong force and hurling the Germans back to the outskirts of Nalchik. At Mozdok, the Germans had failed to make any appreciable advance since the end of August. For months now Mozdok, like Stalingrad, had continued to figure in

* The Manstein offensive helped to upset this Russian time-table; if Stalingrad had fallen in December, the Russians might, indeed, have reached the Dnieper during their winter campaign, and might not have lost Kharkov, as they did in March 1943.

the communiqués. By aiming to drive the Germans out of the whole Don country west of Stalingrad, right up to Rostov and the sea of Azov (to begin with), the Russians rightly reckoned that if they succeeded in this they would almost automatically force the Germans to pull out of the Caucasus and the Kuban.

The even more ambitious Russian "Plan Saturn", adopted by the Supreme Command on December 3, a fortnight after the counter-offensive had started was, first, to liquidate the German forces trapped at Stalingrad and then capture the country inside the Don Bend, including Rostov, and to cut off the German forces in the Caucasus. According to the *History** Stalin telephoned Vassilevsky, the Chief of Staff, then in the Stalingrad area, on November 27 demanding top priority for the liquidation of the German Stalingrad forces, leaving the rest of "Plan Saturn" to the troops of Vatutin's South-West Front.

> In the first days of December the troops of the Don and Stalingrad Fronts began their offensive against the enemy forces trapped in Stalingrad. But no substantial results were achieved. That was why the Soviet Command decided to strengthen the Soviet forces in this area very considerably, and to make more thorough preparations for the operation. New units from the *Stavka* Reserve were being thrown in, including the 2nd Guards Army under the command of Lieut-Gen. Malinovsky.†

The Germans had made a first attempt to break through to Stalingrad from the west at the end of November, but had failed. After that the Germans reorganised their forces by forming a newly-named Army Group called "Don", the purpose of which was a) to stop the Russian advance into the Don country and b) to break the ring round Stalingrad. This Army Group included all the German and allied troops between the Middle Don and the Astrakhan steppes, and its two big striking forces were to be concentrated at Tormasin inside the Don Bend and at Kotelnikovo, south of the Don Bend and some ninety miles south-west of the Stalingrad pocket. Field-Marshal von Manstein, the "victor of the Crimea", whose prestige was high in the German army, was placed in charge of these operations.

* IVOVSS, vol. 3, p. 43.   † Ibid., p. 43.

But the formation of the great striking force, especially at Tormasin, met with considerable delays due to enormous transport difficulties. According to the Russians, these were largely due to constant partisan attacks on the railways, so that reinforcements could only be brought to the Don country from the west in all kinds of roundabout ways. As time was short, Manstein decided to attack with the Kotelnikovo striking force only. Later he explained:

> It was closer to Stalingrad, and it did not have to force the Don on its way there. There was a good hope that the enemy would not expect a big offensive in this sector... Facing the Kotelnikovo group there were, indeed, at first, only five Russian divisions, as against fifteen facing the Tormasin group.*

On December 12 Manstein's Kotelnikovo forces, including several hundred tanks,† struck out on a narrow front towards Stalingrad along the railway from the Caucasus. In three days it advanced thirty miles, despite strong Russian resistance. On December 15 the Germans succeeded in forcing the Axai river, but to the north of it the Russians had taken up defensive positions, and were receiving considerable reinforcements. The German advance was slowed down; but by December 19, with hundreds of bombers supporting them, they reached the Myshkova river, the last natural barrier between them and Stalingrad. They forced this river, too, and then, in von Manstein's words, the Germans "could already see the glow in the Stalingrad sky." That glow was all that von Manstein was to see of Stalingrad. Postponing the "Operation Saturn" plans to "liquidate the Stalingrad bag", the Russian High Command gave first priority to smashing Manstein's Army Group advancing from Kotelnikovo, and also his forces in the Tormasin area.

To deal with the former, Russian reinforcements were rushed to the Myshkova river, barely twenty-five miles from the Stalingrad "bag", in particularly difficult conditions. Malinovsky's 2nd Guards Army had to travel over 125 miles from beyond the Volga to reach its destination; it was a forced march of twenty-five to thirty miles a day through the snow-covered steppe and in a howling blizzard. By the time Malinovsky's men reached the Myshkova river, which the

* von Manstein, op. cit., p. 353.
† The Germans say about 250, the Russians 600.

Germans had already forced in several places, they were very short of petrol, and replenishments were delayed by the weather and the state of the roads. The Russians had to fight for several days with infantry and artillery alone, and it was not till December 24 that their tanks were able to enter the fray. But the Germans were held, and then on the 24th the Russians struck out with both tanks and aircraft, and hurled them back to the Axai River where they were determined to make a stand; but now the Russian forces were striking heavier and heavier blows, and the Germans were driven back to Kotelnikovo. This they abandoned on December 29, and the remnants of Manstein's troops hastily retreated to Zimovniki and thence beyond the river Manych on the way to the Northern Caucasus. This river was fully sixty miles south-west of Kotelnikovo, where the Manstein offensive had started on December 12.

In this attempt to break through to Stalingrad the Germans had lost (according to Russian claims) 16,000 dead alone, and a high proportion of their tanks, guns and vehicles. A few days after it was all over I was to see the scene of this extraordinary German retreat, all the way from the Myshkova river to Zimovniki.

A question that puzzled the Russians at the time, and for a long time afterwards, was why Paulus, with the rescue force only some twenty-five miles from the Stalingrad cauldron, did not attempt to break out to meet it, or at least make its advance to Stalingrad easier by a counter-attack which would at least have drawn off some of the Russian forces.

Since the war, a great deal has been written on this highly controversial operation—by von Manstein himself, by Walter Goerlitz, by Philippi and Heim and others. First of all, it still remains something of a puzzle what von Manstein (or "Gruppe Hoth", as the Germans usually call it) hoped to achieve, short of getting the whole of the German forces at Stalingrad to break out; for it is very hard to see how Gruppe Hoth could have hoped to hold a narrow corridor to Stalingrad for any length of time, without the Russians cutting it. It seems clear that von Manstein undertook this operation with the "mental reservation" that, having broken through to Stalingrad, or got sufficiently near it, he could either persuade Hitler to give Paulus the order to pull his forces out of the Stalingrad cauldron, or confront Hitler with a *fait accompli* based on the *force majeure* argument that there was no other way.

There were four days, between December 19 and 23, while Gruppe Hoth was holding the bridgeheads, north of the Myshkova river, when Paulus could have attempted a breakout with some chance of success. Manstein had two different operations in mind: first, Operation *Wintergewitter* which aimed at establishing a link between Gruppe Hoth and Paulus's forces, largely for the purpose of rushing supplies by land to Stalingrad, since the airlift to Stalingrad had as good as broken down; and, secondly, Operation *Donnerschlag*, meaning the breakout from the cauldron of the whole Stalingrad force. Paulus argued that he needed several days for preparing either operation; the troops were in very poor physical condition, and needed food and other supplies ("at least ten day's rations for 270,000 men"), and there was also a desperate shortage of petrol; also 8,000 wounded would first have to be evacuated. In the last analysis, it seems apparent that, whether there was a good chance or not for the Stalingrad forces to break out, *both Paulus and von Manstein dithered during those four crucial days of December 19 to 23, since no permission had been received from Hitler to abandon Stalingrad.* Neither, it seems, was prepared to act without Hitler's express permission, since such a major act of disobedience to the Führer would set up a dangerous "revolutionary" precedent which might have a disastrous effect on the discipline of the Wehrmacht generally. Moreover, Hitler, they thought, might countermand any order that he had not himself given.

What also made Paulus hesitate (unlike at least one of his generals, von Seydlitz, who favoured a breakout) were the extravagant promises showered on him by Hitler: Goering had "guaranteed" that the troops at Stalingrad could be adequately supplied by air, and so could easily hold out till the spring of 1943, by which time the whole of the Don country would presumably be reconquered by the Germans. After the failure of Manstein's attempt to break through to Stalingrad, Paulus (and Manstein, for that matter) consoled themselves with the thought that, despite the failure of the airlift, the German forces in the Stalingrad cauldron were still serving a useful purpose in tying down large Russian forces, while Manstein was now able to devote himself to an even more vital task than saving the 6th Army—namely, to keep the Rostov-Taman Gap open, and so enable the much larger German forces in the Caucasus and Kuban to pull out with the minimum of loss.

According to Walter Goerlitz, Paulus had, for many years, been a Hitler enthusiast, and therefore meekly accepted Hitler's order to cling to Stalingrad whatever the sacrifice. It was not till after the attempt on Hitler's life of July 20, 1944 that he was prevailed upon to join hundreds of other German officers and generals in their appeal to the German army and people to overthrow Hitler. Goerlitz thus tends to demolish the legend, partly built up by the Russians, that "von Paulus" (as they invariably called him) was a rather noble anti-Nazi figure. It is true that he later settled in Eastern Germany and advocated, right up to the time of his death in 1957, the closest co-operation between Germany and the Soviet Union. (Which does not prevent him from having been one of Hitler's most wholehearted planners of both the war in Poland and the invasion of Russia in 1941).

Recently, there have been some German writers to take the view that all the controversy of what Manstein and Paulus should have done between December 19 and 23 evades the main issue, which was simply that the Manstein offensive had been badly planned and that Paulus could not have broken out. As Philippi and Heim say:

> There is really nothing to show that in those late December days a break-out of those down-at-heel troops was still possible, even when one considers that the prospect of breaking through to freedom would encourage them to perform superhuman deeds of valour. When, on December 21, the OAK6 (i.e. the command of the 6th Army) des-cribed the proposed breakout as a *Katastrophenlösung* ... it was right in the sense that this could only amount to a gesture of despair by a large mass of people in very poor physical condition trying to fight their way to the Myshkova, across fifty km. of snowbound steppes and against a perfectly fresh, intact and heavily-armed enemy. The conditions for *Donnerschlag* and *Wintergewitter* were equally un-favourable.*

* Philippi and Heim, op. cit., p. 195.

Whether this is correct or not will no doubt remain a matter of controversy among military historians; judging from the Germans I saw in Stalingrad over six weeks later, they must still have been in reasonably good condition around December 20; they had by then been encircled for less than a month, and were not yet anywhere near real starvation. They also said that they were still "full of fight" at the thought of von Manstein about to break through to Stalingrad. Even in January, those still in reasonably good condition fought with the greatest stubbornness during the Russian liquidation of the cauldron.

While the 2nd Guards Army under Malinovsky was about to hurl back the Germans from the Myshkova River, the Vatutin-Golikov advance into the Don country from the north was successfully continuing.

Advancing rapidly both into the Middle Don and further west, this time with considerable air support (4,000 sorties in the first few days of the offensive), they routed the remnants of the Rumanian 3rd Army, the Italian 8th Army and dislocated that German "Tormasin" striking force which was planning to attempt a break-through to Stalingrad—to coincide with the "Kotelnikovo" thrust. An area of some 15,000 square miles was liberated. To quote the *History*,*

> A smashing defeat was inflicted on the Italian 8th Army and on the left flank of Army Group "Don". Five Italian divisions were smashed ... and one brigade of Blackshirts. In the autumn of 1942 this army had about 250,000 men and now lost about one half of its effectives. Heavy losses were also inflicted on operational group "Hollidt", belonging to the left flank of Manstein's Army Group "Don". Five of its infantry divisions and one tank division were smashed... †

* IVOVSS, vol. 3, p. 50.
† After quoting an Italian eyewitness account (Giusto Tolloy, *Con l'armata italiana in Russia*, Torino, 1947) on the encirclement of large Italian forces south of Boguchar and the panic caused among the Italian officers and soldiers, the *History* protests against certain Italian allegations that many thousands of Italian war prisoners

After the failure of the Hoth-Manstein group to break through to Stalingrad, and its retreat to Kotelnikovo and beyond, Malinovsky's troops pursued them beyond the Manych River, and were planning to break through to Rostov from the south-east. But there is no doubt that the Russian offensive, which had achieved such spectacular results since November 19, and right through the rest of November and December in the Don country, was now, by the beginning of the New Year, to meet with much stiffer German resistance. It was essential for the Germans to keep the "Rostov Gap" open as long as possible, for this remained the main escape route for the German forces which were now—at the beginning of January—hastily beginning to pull out of the Caucasus and the Kuban. Thanks to Stalingrad, Hitler's attempt to conquer the Caucasus had been a complete failure.

---

failed to return after the war. It argues that many of those whom the Italians counted as war prisoners had, in fact, found their death in battle "and found their grave in the steppes of the Don." It quotes Khrushchev's speech at Tirana (Albania) in 1959 saying that war was "like a fire—easy to jump in, but not so easy to jump out. Well, the Italians just got burned in the War." It adds, however, that a large number of Italians who had survived the Don Battle were murdered by the Germans, particularly at Lwow in 1943, after they had refused—this was after the fall of Mussolini—to swear allegiance to Hitler.

There is, in reality, another explanation for the failure of many of the Italians in Russia to return to Italy after the war; and there was a great deal of talk about this in Moscow towards the end of the war: although the leaflets dropped on Italian troops urging them to surrender to the Russians promised that they would be sent to a "warm climate", many thousands of Italian war prisoners were actually sent to camps in northern and central Russia, where large numbers died of pneumonia, tuberculosis, et cetera.

Chapter IV

STALINGRAD CLOSE-UPS

Close-Up I: The Stalingrad Lifeline.

By January 1, 1943, the Germans inside the Stalingrad Pocket—an oval measuring about forty-four miles from west to east and fourteen miles from north to south—had been isolated from the outer world, except for some transport planes, for over six weeks. By December 24 all hope of being rescued by von Manstein's "Gruppe Hoth" had vanished.

It was during the first fortnight of January that, with a small group of other correspondents, I was able to travel along that fantastic railway east of the Volga which had been for months the only lifeline for the Russian troops defending Stalingrad. It was along this line, too, that troops, equipment and supplies had been taken in October and November to the area south of Stalingrad, whence Yeremenko had struck out on November 20.

Leaving Moscow on the morning of Monday, January 3, 1943, we travelled in an old-fashioned, pre-revolution sleeping car attached to the Moscow-Saratov express. The candlesticks were still inscribed "Compagnie Internationale de Wagon-Lits", and the washstand had beside it a brass plate saying, first in pre-revolutionary Russian spelling, and then in French: "*Sous le lavabo se trouve un vase*". Not that, in travelling in such relative luxury we were getting anything unheard of in the Soviet Union even in 1942–3; there were other people in the sleeping car—higher officials, "intellectuals" on some special mission, officers from the rank of colonel up, et cetera.

508

There was, of course, no dining car, and we had to do with "dry" rations, supplemented by the tea provided by the amiable old *provodnik*'s samovar. The other carriages of the train were, however, "hard" third-class carriages, packed mostly with soldiers, and, with all the windows shut, extremely hot, stuffy and smelly with that characteristically Russian blend of smells, leather boots, black bread, cabbage fumes and *makhorka* tobacco.

It was foggy and thawing the day we left Moscow, and icicles were dripping outside the carriage window. We passed Kashira, with its burned-out houses, remnants of the German advance on Moscow a year before—grim days which now seemed very far away. Since the Stalingrad encirclement one now felt that nothing like that could ever happen again. . .

The next morning we reached Tambov and in the afternoon, Kirsanov. The station platform was crowded. Just outside it was a big open-air *kolkhoz* market. It worked mostly on a barter basis. Butter cost here a third of the Moscow price, but most of the eggs and butter were bought with tobacco or soap... There were crowds of young soldiers on the platform, some carrying whole bundles of brand-new rifles. Many were about eighteen, and seemed to be leaving home for the first time; on the platform were also crowds of elderly and old women, many of them crying, and a few making the sign of the Cross as they kissed the boys good-bye. The boys pretended to be quite unperturbed, and argued vigorously with the woman guard in the next carriage who claimed vociferously that it was full up. They squeezed in all the same. . .

At Saratov the next morning it was sunny and very cold, minus 25°C. and with deep snow. Saratov, with its handsome wide avenues, looked unusually prosperous. Numerous leading educational establishments had been evacuated here from Moscow,

Leningrad and other places, and the city had been nicknamed
"Professaratov". . . Theatres (including an opera house) and several
cinemas were going strong. We had a large meal at the Railwaymen's
Club. . .

That night our carriage was joined on to a goods train. It had grown
dark by now, and there was just enough light to see an immense
number of trains of every kind at and around Saratov Station, and
to realise its importance as a railway junction. . . We crossed the
great bridge across the Volga, and then travelled through what the
maps called "Autonomous German Volga ASSR", and it seemed
clear now why the Soviet Government did not wish to take any
chances with the Volga Germans. They were deported, a whole half-
million of them—to Kazakhstan in August 1941. There had already
been some cases of railway sabotage in the "Autonomous German
Volga Republic" (with "Engels" as its capital!) at the very beginning of the war, and also stories of German airmen brought down
over the area, being given shelter by the local Germans.

On Wednesday morning, Moscow seemed very far away. All night
the train had travelled at good speed, and we were now in the endless waterless steppes of the Trans-Volga country. There was very
little snow, and through it rose tufts of untidy brown grass. We had
just passed several wrecked railway-carriages, and beside the siding
lay another railway wagon, its wheels in the air. It had already gone
rusty. At the small station I talked to a group of railwaymen. Among
them was an elderly man from Tomsk, a dour Siberian with a long
greyish moustache and a wrinkled face. "Stalingrad," he said, "yes,
it's over there—not very far away, about a hundred kilometres from
here. Oh yes, in October we were right in the thick of it. Can't tell
you how many times we were bombed—but it was a hell of a lot of
times. See that?" he said, pointing at the overturned wagon. "I drove
that train. *They* were lucky that day. Three direct hits on my train.
Just went up in the air. Only the engine and the front carriage rolled
on, all the rest was torn away and wrecked." I looked down the

line: there was the wreckage of many more wagons and also of several lorries and armoured cars which must have been part of the train's cargo. "Were many killed?" "Thirty-five," said the Tomsk man. "Thirty-five railwaymen and three soldiers. Their graves are over there," he said pointing to the east, a little way off the line. And it was strange how, in saying it, this tough Siberian said not *mogily,* but the affectionate diminutive *mogilki,* little graves.

A young railwayman joined in. He was fair and blue-eyed, and spoke with a soft southern accent. "I've been working on this line right through the Stalingrad business," he said. "We railwaymen are really the same as soldiers. All the supplies to Stalingrad came along this line, so you can imagine the attention the Fritzes paid it. All around here has been bombed to blazes, except one small hut." Not far away from the railway line were more craters and piles of twisted metal, but also large numbers of new rails, stacked up. "We've got these spare rails all down the line," he said. "And the railway was never put out of action, except occasionally for a couple of hours. When you think of the amount of traffic along this line these last five months, they didn't really hit many trains." "That's true," said the Tomsk man, "but they gave us a lot of trouble dropping the bombs just beside the railway, and wrecking all the telephone and telegraph wires." The young railwayman smiled. "Well, it's a great comfort to know it wasn't in vain. The Fritzes are running like rabbits now. Yes, there were some fearful moments, but down here we never thought they'd get away with it. We used to see a lot of people straight from Stalingrad, and *they* never lost hope. . ." He was from Bessarabia. "I got away by the skin of my teeth when the Rumanians surrounded our village. Followed the Red Army across the Pruth. I know I'll soon be back in Bessarabia, drinking good Bessarabia wine. It's a better country than this, I can tell you," he said, looking at the desolate steppe.

Another railwayman joined in, and also thought he would soon be "back home at Kupiansk, in the Ukraine, near Kharkov". He was our engine-driver; his face was grimy with coal-dust, but his white teeth and pink gums were bright and moist as he smiled, and he had laughing Ukrainian eyes. I knew the name of Kupiansk only too well; it was the important railway junction which was among the first places the Germans had seized at the beginning of their summer offensive. . .

He talked about the chaos of the evacuation from the Ukraine in June 1942. "I was lucky," he said. "We received the order to evacuate the rolling stock. There was no time to look for my family, who were in a village nearby. At all the stations there were mobs of people hoping—often against hope—to be evacuated to the east. And then, would you believe it, at the third railway stop, right there on the station platform, were my wife and my little daughter. I shoved them quickly into one of the goods trucks, and so we all got away. Incredible luck, don't you think?" His wife and child were at Saratov now.

At length the train moved. For a long time we travelled through the steppe, without any sign of human life, except occasional haystacks. Then we passed some low L-shaped mud-huts, the same colour as the earth. These were Kirghiz huts. There was a pale-blue sky over this ocean of perfectly flat steppe—it was like the first shots of Pudovkin's *Storm over Asia*. In fact, this *was* Asia; according to the map, the railway twice crossed through stretches of country which belonged administratively to Kazakhstan. How clearly one realised now why the men fighting at Stalingrad felt that beyond Stalingrad "there was nothing". Thousands had travelled to Stalingrad along this line.

Another station with L-shaped mud-huts, with two large shaggy camels outside one of them, the same colour as the huts and the earth, also some horses, and an old Kirghiz woman, a perfect Asiatic with a long padded coat and a white cloth round her head, below the fur cap with earflaps. Her face was wrinkled, dark-brown, with narrow eyes. Here also were several soldiers, most of them Mongols. A young Russian soldier, with weather-beaten face and red eyes, came up, asked for newspaper to roll some cigarettes and said he had heard that Tsymlianskaya on the Don and Nalchik in the Caucasus had been liberated from the Germans. He had just come from Stalingrad, along the railway from Leninsk. He had been in Stalingrad for two months. "Now the Fritzes are trapped like rats," he said. "But the *svolochi* are still cocky, shouting '*Russ, sdavais!*' (Russian, surrender!). But things are going fine. They still have those transport planes to drop them food during the night; but when they try to get there during the day, we shoot every damned one of them down." Except for the redness of his eyes, due to chronic lack of sleep, he seemed none the worse for his two months at Stalingrad— though these last two months had, of course, been nothing like the terrible months of September and October... A train coming the other way passed us; it had anti-aircraft guns on board, many wrecked Russian planes, and also a long string of oil tanks, coming from where—Baku perhaps? For this was the only remaining line linking northern Russia with the Caucasus.

Leninsk, near the end of the branch line running from Baskunchak, was as far as we could go by rail. It was some thirty miles from Stalingrad on the other side of the Volga, was the principal supply base for Stalingrad itself, and also for the Stalingrad Front... Practically all the troops and equipment for the "southern pincer" had come through here. It was also to Leninsk that the wounded from Stalingrad were normally evacuated. It had very strong anti-aircraft defences, and was relatively undamaged. It still had the appearance of an old-time district town. The wide main street was composed of shabby little brick houses, while in the side-streets there was nothing but wooden cottages, many with very beautiful wood carvings around the windows. The old-time atmosphere of this provincial backwater contrasted strangely with the modern slogans painted on every wall: "Men of the Red Army, remember at Stalingrad your responsibility to your country!" "Drive the German rats from the walls of Stalingrad!" "Glory to the men of Stalingrad!" and so on. In the small public park was a statue of Lenin, and on the airfield just outside the town were numerous "aero-sleighs", with Red Cross markings, for the transport of the wounded.

We had a meal at the officers' mess, and met two surgeons from Leninsk Hospital. One of them, a small and dapper man, had gone through the whole of the Stalingrad battle at this transit hospital. "One of the worst features of this war," he said, "is that the proportion of the severely wounded is much higher than it was in any other war. It used to be eighty per cent light cases, and twenty per cent severe cases; now the severe cases are around forty per cent. Head injuries are much more frequent than in the last war, owing to mortar shells and bombs. It's the same on the German side; we know it from German army doctors we have taken prisoner." He said that most of the German and Rumanian prisoners suffered from frostbite. They were simply unprepared for this winter weather, and really seemed to imagine they were going to take Stalingrad in September and end the war! The Rumanians have those high fur hats, which look very decorative but don't protect the lower half of the face, or even the lower half of the ears. And instead of felt *valenki* the Germans now have some ridiculous ersatz *valenki* made of straw, and with wooden soles; the things are so clumsy that they can't even walk in them."

The atmosphere in the officers' mess was jovial, and there was little talk of all that this corner of Russia had gone through in the last months. A few toasts were drunk to "our gallant Allies"—not without a little touch of irony.

One of the girls who was serving us had a bandage tied round her cheek. I asked if she had been wounded. Next to me sat a pompous stout major. "Ah, yes," he said, "she was wounded. Our people are wonderful; when they are lightly wounded, they just go on with their work, wouldn't dream of stopping." "Nonsense," said the older surgeon, "she's just got a gumboil."

My heart warmed to the major; here was Gogol's immortal blowhard Nozdrev back again, and in the Red Army at that, and thirty miles from Stalingrad!

We had to wait for our bus in a room beside an empty hospital ward, with two young nurses as our hostesses. The hospital was empty now, though the beds were all made, ready to receive any sudden arrivals. But for several days now there had been no wounded from Stalingrad; the Germans in the "bag" were perhaps running out of ammunition one of the girls suggested.

The girls were called Valya and Nadya. Valya was lively, red-cheeked and flirtatious in a coy way. She was twenty-one and married, with her husband in the Army. She was in uniform, and when the war broke out had been studying biochemistry at the university. The other girl had one of those full but pale Russian faces with large grey eyes, with perfect large white teeth and lips that were full without being sensuous.

From time to time they would put on a well-worn record on their portable gramophone—bits from *Werther* or *Manon* of all things. When the gramophone played, they were silent.

Nadya wore a red woollen jumper which stressed the paleness of her beautiful face. "I am not a nurse," she said, "I am a medical statistician, attached to this hospital base." "*Some* statistics you must have had to do here through the autumn," I remarked. "Yes," she said, "*some* statistics." Her home was in Stalingrad, and her address was 24 Frunze Street. It seemed odd that anyone should have an *address* at Stalingrad! "You should go to Stalingrad after the war," she said, with a faint smile. "Not that you will find my house there any more. It was destroyed like the rest of the city. And what a pity! We had those lovely boulevards, and so many fine new buildings, and public parks, and the new Volga Embankment; and, on Sundays, there were lots of young people everywhere, and lots of trees and flowers, and all those steamer and sailing-boats and motor-boats on the Volga. It was a gay town. I was in my last year at school when the war started, and I joined up as a medical worker, after a short training."

A copy of Simonov's poems was lying on the table. I asked Valya if she liked Simonov. "Yes, very much; we all do." "What, *Wait for me*?" "Yes, that, and much else." "Dear Simonov," said Valya sentimentally. Nadya said: "We'll have a glorious life after the war. Stalingrad will be very beautiful again. We shall again go for holidays to the Caucasus, as we did before the war."

It was confirmed that day that the Germans had begun to pull out of the Caucasus; Nadya's daydreaming wasn't so fantastic, after all.

We set out that afternoon from Leninsk to Raigorod across the delta-land of the Volga, between the narrow Akhtuba river and the Volga proper; flat wooded country with several roads running to the Volga crossings opposite Stalingrad or south of it. There was a

lot of traffic that afternoon, mostly army lorries, and an occasional
peasant sleigh; and once we passed a sleigh drawn by a camel. Most
of the life here seemed concentrated in the fishing villages on the
Volga itself. Most striking along these roads through the delta-land
were not only the numerous boards with Stalingrad slogans on them,
but also notices like "Trench" and "Warming Station". These were
part of the organisation of the "lifeline"; the warming stations were
dugouts, with a heated stove, off the road, where soldiers could stop
to get warm; while the trenches were refuges during German air
attacks. Many dead horses were lying about, most of them half-
decayed, but now frozen. Our driver was a youngish man, who had
been in Odessa during the siege, and had been evacuated by sea at
the last moment; it was a fearful business, he said, as the ships were
attacked by dive-bombers all the time, and many were sunk.

"I know these roads only too well," he said. "They used to be
constantly attacked from the air. It was along these roads that we
carried men and supplies to Stalingrad. Machine-gunning was the
Fritzes' favourite sport; they killed lots of people and horses; but,
especially after August, we had fighters in the air, and hundreds of
lorries got through daily. My worst experience was on August 23,
during the big raid on Stalingrad. You can't imagine what it was
like. The whole city was burning like a giant bonfire. There was the
awful crash of masonry. I'd drive along a street between burning
houses, and dozens of planes were in the air; and suddenly a large
house would collapse just in front of you, and with all the dust you
could hardly see where you were going; and there were a lot of dead
people lying around. But I got away, and my lorry didn't have as
much as a scratch. Right over the pontoon bridge, with stuff dropping into the water all round. The bridge didn't last long, I can tell
you. . ." And, after that, day after day, he went on taking munitions
to Stalingrad—"this side of the river, of course"—and evacuating
the wounded. "It was a difficult time," he summed up in a typical
understatement. "But it's going to be all right now."

We were not allowed to go to Stalingrad as yet, but by now we
were only a few miles away and at nightfall that evening we could
see in the west a glow in the sky, and hear a gun firing every minute
or so. It was relatively quiet at Stalingrad that night; but it was the

eve of Rokossovsky's ultimatum to Paulus, and two days later the final liquidation of the German 6th Army was going to begin.

At last we reached the Volga crossing some fifteen miles south of Stalingrad. A few faint lights were flickering in the dark. The thud of sporadic gunfire had grown much fainter. We drove smoothly over a wide pontoon bridge, lying flat on the ice. In the sky, on the right, was still that dim glow, that faint halo over Stalingrad. "It used to look different," the driver remarked, "when the whole town was burning for weeks. At Leninsk the whole sky used to be lit up at night." The bridge must have been nearly a mile long, though, in the dark, it was hard to say exactly. The bank on the other side was much steeper, and then we drove through a darkened village and then, through ten or fifteen miles of steppe, on to Raigorod.

We were billetted in a large hut requisitioned by the Army, and were given a meal—borshch and some wonderfully cooked mutton —by a plump Ukrainian girl from Kharkov and an elderly man with a hooked purple nose and a little toothbrush moustache; he was a Jew who had been a miner in the Donbas. He was talkative, but very gloomy, since his family had been left behind. As he plaintively pleaded for the Second Front, one felt he was pleading for his wife and children.

After supper we received a visit from Major-General Popov, our first contact with the command of the Stalingrad Front. He had a typical Volga-Russian face, with high cheek-bones, lively dark eyes and a brisk business-like manner. He was one of the men who had organised the transport across the Volga of a large part of Yeremenko's army which had struck out from here towards Kalach on November 20. "These bridges played a great part in our offensive, though not at the very beginning; for, before the river froze, most of the stuff had to be taken across in boats. In fact, our most difficult problem was to supply Stalingrad itself. It couldn't be done from here; it had to be done direct from the opposite bank; for two weeks, before the Volga was properly icebound, hundreds of soldiers would crawl on their bellies across the thin layer of ice, dragging behind them little sleighs with a couple of ammunition boxes—as much as the ice was likely to hold. The Germans continued to shell the river. All the same, most of them got across. Now the ice on the Volga is thick enough to be used for lorries and horse vehicles, though not strong enough for tanks; but we've got plenty of bridges now."

General Popov said it took three to five days to lay a pontoon bridge. In spite of all their bombing raids and reconnaissance flights the Germans had no idea until it was too late what a large number of troops had been brought over. Most of the work was done at night, and during the day the troops were scattered in small groups over large areas. The Russians, he said, now had some American Dodges and jeeps, but not many; they also used many "trophy" trucks made in practically every country in Europe; the French Renault trucks were particularly numerous. He hoped the production of these had been greatly reduced since the great RAF raids on the Paris works. . .

Close-Up II: The Scene of the Manstein Rout.—A Cossack Town Under the Germans.—Meeting General Malinovsky.

The next day—January 7, 1943, we travelled in a blizzard across the completely flat and uninhabited Kalmuk steppes. Though it snowed heavily, it was not very cold—between minus 5° and minus 10° centigrade. We were no longer in cars, but in a dilapidated old bus, used until recently as an ambulance for taking the wounded to Leninsk. In the middle stood a small metal stove—a *burzhuika*—which was being conscientiously stoked with small bits of wood by Gavrila, an elderly north-Russian *muzhik* with a kindly rough-hewn face and a stubbly chin. He looked like a good-natured bear. Occasionally the *burzhuika* smoked ferociously and the smoke mingled with the fumes of the exhaust pipe seeping into the bus through the half-broken back door. This strange-looking dismantled ambulance was typical, in a way, of the shortage of proper motor transport from which the Red Army was still suffering.

Gavrila had two sons in the army and had no news of one of them almost since the beginning of the war. During the whole Stalingrad battle he had been a stretcher-bearer attached to this ambulance. "It was no fun for the wounded," he said, "to travel in this bone-rattler. But our men can stand a lot. It's true that before being sent off on their journey they always got a shot of morphine. . ."

It was about a hundred miles from Raigorod to Abganerovo on the Stalingrad-Caucasus railway, and another sixty from there to Kotelnikovo.

Not very far west of Raigorod was a string of lakes in the Kalmuk steppes which had been the first line of defences protecting the right flank of the Germans' Stalingrad salient. From a distance, through the heavily falling snow, one could see a patch of the black water of one of the salt lakes, and a little farther along we stopped to look at an enormous dump of wrecked German tanks and armoured cars. All this wreckage had been collected over a fairly large area around the lakes—where the Russians had crashed through the lines held by the Rumanians. Thousands of Rumanians had surrendered here on November 20 and 21. There was no sign of them now except for a few tin hats, half-filled with snow. They had a large "C" in front and the Royal crown of Rumania; "C" stood for Carol, even though Carol was no longer king.

As we drove through the steppes the snow was coming down so heavily that our conducting officer, Colonel Tarantsev, wondered whether we'd make it. However, by the afternoon the weather cleared and the steppe was dazzling-white in the sun as we approached the Stalingrad railway. At one point we crossed the Axai River; here also Rumanian helmets were lying about, half-buried in the snow, and a lot of wrecked vehicles, but no German helmets. It had been further west that the Germans had crossed the Axai in their last push, and it was not until we reached Abganerovo and Zhutovo on the Stalingrad-Caucasus railway line that we first saw the traces of the Manstein offensive of only a few days before. Abganerovo had been completely wrecked by bombing during the German summer offensive, but there was a lot of rolling-stock on the railway. Zhutovo was some ten miles down the line, which ran parallel to the road. A number of goods trains steamed past; the Russians had already put the line back to the broad Russian gauge.

Zhutovo looked a pleasant enough village, with gardens and orchards and small Russian cottages. A crowd of youngsters gathered round us, and also two young women with babies in their arms. The women told the usual story of how they had hidden in cellars during the last German occupation. "Thank God," one of them said, "our people came back soon, and the Germans hadn't even time to burn down our houses." There were two little boys there, aged about ten. One wore an enormous high sheepskin hat which came right down over his ears; the other wore a pair of army boots, about six sizes too large for him. "Where did you get all this?" I asked. "Got my hat off a dead Rumanian," Number One said proudly. "And these boots?" "Oh, that's off the dead Fritz, over there in the orchard. Would you like to see him?" I followed the two boys along a narrow path. Here, among the apple-trees, lay the dead German. His face was covered with snow, but his feet, purple and glossy like those of a wax figure, were bare. He had no overcoat, only an ordinary tunic with an eagle and swastika. "Why don't they take him away?" I asked. "The soldiers will take him away some time, I suppose," said the owner of the boots; "they've got other Fritzes to collect round here. He's no bother in the cold weather."

Was the little fellow callous? I don't know... The Germans had brought war so deeply into his life, had made him live so intimately in the company of death, that one could hardly blame him. Corpses had become part of his daily routine, and to him there were only good corpses and bad corpses. A few days later I heard of a village on the Don where the kids used a frozen German as a sleigh for sliding down a hill... I don't know if this story was true.

Kotelnikovo, which was to be our base for about a week, was a large town of some 25,000 people, and it had been occupied by the Germans and Rumanians between August 2 and December 29, when von Manstein's troops were driven out after their abortive attempt to break through to Stalingrad, and I soon heard what it had been like under the German occupation. Kotelnikovo had been in the operational zone throughout the occupation, and the German Army seemed to have been in full authority there; moreover, it was considered Cossack country, and the Germans refrained here from large-scale savagery. Edgar Snow and I were billeted in a small wooden cottage belonging to an elementary teacher, who was living there with her very decrepit old mother and her only child, a fifteen-year-old boy called Gai. Her husband was a railwayman, but had not been heard of since last June.

Kotelnikovo was not a story of great German atrocities. It was simply a story of German contempt and of Russian bitterness and humiliation, as told by the forty-year-old Russian school-teacher and her fifteen-year-old son. Just that—nothing more. But quite enough.

It was a sprawling town, with an administrative and shopping centre, and an important railway depot; the rest of the town consisted of many long streets of wooden cottages and gardens; all round was the flat steppe of the trans-Don country. Our house had two small rooms—the kitchen and the bedroom. Between the two was a large Russian stove, and it was very warm. Elena Nikolaevna was exuberant, plump, with fat arms and two golden front teeth that glittered in the light of her one and only kerosene lamp. After presenting us to *babushka*, a tiny shrivelled creature who sat huddled in a corner of the kitchen, near the blacked-out window, she took the kerosene lamp and showed us into the bedroom, leaving *babushka* in the dark. "Babushka will be all right," she said, "she is used to peeling potatoes in the dark." In the bedroom were two large beds, a table and a book-case. "What a life we've had these last five months!" she exclaimed. "First we had some Rumanians here, and then the Germans—a tank crew of five men. Rough, hard people; but then, I suppose, they looked upon us as enemies. Don't know what they would have been like in peace-time. . ."

A plane was zooming overhead. "That's a German plane; I know it by the sound. Makes me a bit nervous when they fly about at night. It's these transport planes that still try to take food to the Germans encircled at Stalingrad." Suddenly we heard a stick of bombs go off with a whine and somewhere, a long distance away, there was the sound of two not very loud explosions.

At the end of July the Secretary of the *Raikom* told Elena Nikolaevna that she and her family would be evacuated; but the Germans bombed the railway station to blazes, and occupied the town on August 2, before anything could be done. So all the teachers were left behind. One of them went to see the German commandant to ask when the schools would open, but was told "not yet". So the teachers were left without any jobs. The population were summoned to a meeting to elect a *starosta*, or mayor, but the first two were invalidated by the Germans, and in the end they virtually appointed a railwayman called Paleyev to be *starosta*. He seemed a good man; but later he must have sold himself to the Germans. There were also some railwaymen who formed the local police; they would bully the local people, make them carry bricks, and dig, and build fortifications for the Germans.

"But how did you live?"

"One can hardly call it living. We were very short of food—nine ounces of flour a day per person, and nothing else. I used to do some work for the Rumanian officer when he lived here; but all he would give me for a whole day's washing was half a loaf. It was a shame. But then, I suppose, the Rumanians didn't have much. Some of the soldiers, far from giving us anything, asked for food; I'd give them a slice of bread, it was better that way; they would have taken it anyway. The Germans are a proud people, very different from the Rumanians. Occasionally they'd give me something—a tin of fish or a few cigarettes. All the time they were here they gave me two tins of fish; it wasn't much, was it? I used to wash and scrub for them all day, and they'd send me out for water to the well. It was a slave's life. And Gai, my boy and *babushka* and I had to live in the little kitchen, all huddled together, and the five Germans lived here, in this room; some sleeping on the bed, and the others on the floor. They had a lot of drink and food, and thought at first they were staying here indefinitely. In the morning they'd shout '*Matka, Wasser zum waschen!*' They used to call everybody *Matka*, damned cheek! In the middle of December one of the man said: '*Russ nicht zurück*, we've chased them fifty miles away'. It's quite true, the firing could no longer be heard. But on December 28 one of the men said: '*Russ kommt zurück*'. You see, one wants to live, especially when you've got a young boy to look after, so I expressed no joy. Four of them went away without a word, only the fifth one said: '*Auf wiedersehen, Matka*'. They were very gloomy. They weren't so bad, those five Germans, but they thought we were just their slaves. In other houses they behaved much worse, and the Rumanians were terrible—wouldn't leave the women alone. There was a lot of rape in the town. I didn't hear of anybody being shot; but thirty, or maybe fifty people were taken away by the Germans. Or perhaps they followed them voluntarily, people like the *polizei*. They were going to mobilise all the young people for work in Germany, and they sent out leaflets, but I don't think they had time to do anything much. . ."

And then she described how, on the last night, the Germans set fire to all the public buildings in Kotelnikovo; but they hadn't time to burn down the whole town; there was much firing going on, and, in the middle of the night¹ he streets were empty: the Germans had gone and the Russians had not yet come in.

So this was the room where the German tank crew had lived. The house was intact; partly no doubt because it was hardly worth looting. Here was a book-case with school-texts of physics and chemistry and Russian literature, and a lot of family photographs on the wall; and the Germans had left behind—how odd to find it here, in the wilds of the trans-Don steppes!—a map and index of the Paris Metro, and a copy of the *Wittgensteiner Zeitung* of December 4 with an editorial: "*50.Geburtstag Francos: der Erretter Spaniens*".

The next morning we met Gai, Elena Nikolaevna's fifteen-year-old son. He was fairly tall, but extraordinarily thin. He had a bright, intelligent, slightly monkey-like face, and spoke beautiful Russian in a clear, silvery voice. "Is that what the Germans have reduced you to?" I said. "No, I was always rather thin; but it was, of course, upsetting to live under the Germans; they got on one's nerves; and also, we didn't have enough food. But when I went with mother last year to Stalingrad to see a well-known specialist, he said I was quite all-right, just a little anaemic. . . I am sorry I wasn't here last night, but when the Germans were here I never went out at night, and very seldom even during the day—one just didn't feel like it. Now I go out to see my comrades—the ones I used to go to school with." "Yes, it's a blessing," said Elena Nikolaevna, "Gai will now be able to go to school again. He is the cleverest boy in his form—full marks in every subject. He has read all the classics, but his chief interest is science, and he wants to go into the Navy. . ."

I was to have many other talks with Gai after that. He would talk about anything—about himself, and his future career, and the

Germans, and the films he had seen. "I like American films," he said. "Here in Kotelnikovo *Song of Love* and *The Great Waltz* and Chaplin's *City Lights* were a great success. Before the war we had a very good time, you know. I was a Pioneer myself, and would be in the Komsomol by now, but for the German occupation. All our young people were preparing to be engineers, or doctors, or scientists. I want to enter the Naval Academy. If the Germans had stayed, the girls would have been expected to wash floors and the boys to look after the cattle. They didn't regard us as human beings at all. . . That's just how it was under the Germans." "Did they kick you about?" "No, they simply took no notice of me. Sometimes they'd ask: 'What form are you in?' or 'Where's your father?' I'd say he was in the Red Army. They would look cross, but say nothing." "Did they ever say what sort of government they were going to set up here?" "Yes, they would say: 'Everybody will work for himself; no more *kolkhozes* and no more communism. We aren't going to stay here; we have only come to liberate you from the Jews and the Bolsheviks'. They put up pictures of Hitler on the walls; they were called 'Hitler the Liberator'. He hardly looked human. Completely beastly face. Like a savage from the Malayan jungle. Terrifying. They opened the church; first they had a Rumanian priest, later a Russian. I once went when the Rumanian was still there. Inside were crowds of Rumanian soldiers. At one point they'd all go down plunk on their knees. Then they would carry round a dish, and the Rumanians would put money on it—roubles, or marks or lei. . . It didn't make much difference. All money was pretty useless. The mark was worth ten roubles, but the marks they had here were occupation marks, without a water-mark, and were as good as useless. . . The Germans had a passion for destroying things. They tore up all the vegetables in our allotment. And they burned down the public library the last night they were here, and they wouldn't even leave my little library alone," said Gai, pointing at the bookcase. "They tore up the Russian magazines, and tore out of the books all the Stalin and Lenin pictures. So silly, don't you think? It was those tank men. Queer chaps. You should have seen them at Christmas. They went all sloppy. They had got a lot of parcels from Germany. They lit a tiny paper Christmas tree, and unwrapped enormous cakes, and opened tins, and winebottles, and got drunk, and sang sentimental songs about something or other." "Where were you at that time?" "Just where we always were, next door in the kitchen." "Did they not offer you any wine or cake?" "Of course not; wouldn't even occur to them. They didn't look upon us as *people*." "Weren't you hungry?" "Of course I was, but I would have hated to take part in their festivities." He produced a lighter from his pocket. "They left it here by mistake. I found it under one of the beds. We have no matches, so it's a useful gadget to have. But I don't like having anything from those people... Yes, I lost a lot of weight. The bombs got on my nerves, I suppose, and also the feeling that I was no longer a human being. They never stopped rubbing that in. They had no respect for anybody—they'd just undress in front of women; we were just a lot of slaves. And there was also no food; no *kolkhoz* market, and it's very bad for your system if you get no fats," he concluded with a scientific air.

Elena Nikolaevna would talk a lot about herself and about *babushka*, her mother. She was the last survivor of a Cossack family, ruined during the Civil War. Her father had been a small farmer in a Cossack *stanitsa* on the Don; but he hadn't much of a business head, and the farm had gone to pot during the Civil War, so he sold his farm to a *kulak* for ten sacks of flour. They moved to Novocherkassk, but in the typhus epidemic both her father and her brother died. "I was only eighteen then, and I entered the Komsomol, and got a small scholarship for the Novocherkassk music school, where I was taught singing"; but she couldn't make much of a living with that, and it was not enough to support her mother as well, so when her future husband, a railwayman, asked her to marry him, she agreed.

"He's a good man, my husband, though he hadn't much education. But he is in the right Bolshevik traditions; his father also had been a railwayman for forty years, and had received an inscribed gold watch from Kaganovich himself." Later, after settling down in Kotelnikovo in her husband's little house, she took a correspondence course in elementary teaching. It was during the days when thousands of schools were opening throughout the Soviet Union, and Elena Nikolaevna was as good as anybody for this simple job. This coquette of thirty-eight or so no doubt dreamed of all she might have been but for the Civil War. "I used to look pretty good and *kulturno*," she said, "when I was younger, with my hair waved and with a nice summer frock." And she described how she had her two perfectly good front teeth crowned in gold, because it was "fashionable" at the time.

And *babushka* sat in the corner, and would say how awful it was with those Germans in the house, and "I would cry and cry, thinking I would soon die, and how awful it was to leave my dear ones in all this misery... But now that our own dear people are back I think I'll live to a hundred," she said as her little face screwed up into a toothless smile... And she'd go on, talking almost to herself: "I used to know English and American gentlemen. My husband used to be an *izvoshchik*, had a fine phaeton on springs; he used to drive English and American gentlemen across the Don; they were engineers. That was a long time ago, still under the Tsar..."

And Elena Nikolaevna's husband, the railwayman? They had last heard of him in June 1942. He was at Voronezh then. Now that the postal service had been restored at Kotelnikovo, they might hear from him soon. They might—or they might not...

"You can say what you like," Elena Nikolaevna said one day (not that anybody had said anything), "but our Soviet régime is a good régime. Even *babushka*, to whom it was all very strange at first, has now become very fond of it. And look at this little house of ours. Five roubles rent a month is all I pay; you wouldn't get a house so cheap in any other country." Here was, indeed, a strangely mixed family: the grandmother still thinking of the good old days under the Tsar, the mother with her Cossack background and her *petit bourgeois* instincts; the father a real Soviet proletarian; and the boy who could only see a happy future for himself under the Soviet system with its stress on education—to all these people the Germans were unspeakably odious.

This was not quite general in a town like Kotelnikovo; I saw a large Cossack family on whom a number of Germans had also been billeted; they had been allowed to keep a cow and dozens of chickens, and a sort of *modus vivendi* had been established between themselves and the Germans, "who were very fond of eggs and milk".

One of the members of this family worked on a near-by *kolkhoz,* and contributed what she could to the "good living" of both her family in Kotelnikovo and of their German guests. The *kolkhozes* in the area had not been disbanded, though the Germans kept promising that they would be under the New Order.

The German capture of Kotelnikovo on August 2 had been so sudden that only about one-third of the population could be evacuated—and in terrible conditions at that. Many had been bombed on the railway or machine-gunned on the roads, and much of the cattle that was being evacuated to the Astrakhan steppes had also been killed in air-raids before it reached its destination. According to Comrade Terekhov, chairman of the local executive committee who had taken up his duties again the day after the town was liberated, four people were shot by the Germans for harbouring a Soviet officer; and some 300—mostly young people—had been taken away to Germany as slave labour; many more would have been taken, and the whole town would have been destroyed if the Germans had had time to do so. Some, he said, had collaborated voluntarily with the Germans, and had left with them; others, including several railwaymen, had been forcibly drafted into the *polizei*, and, though they had to go through "certain motions", they had remained loyal to the Soviets. Certain cases of "excessive mateyness" with the Germans were going to be looked into. . .

Outside Kotelnikovo the Russians had captured an enormous ammunition dump, two Fokke-Wulf 189's, completely intact, and a number of other German aircraft. The Russian air force sergeant to whom I talked said he didn't care for the idea of using German planes: "It's a tricky business. Our anti-aircraft gunners are too sharp for that. At Stalingrad we got five Me.109's in perfect condition, and we thought we'd use them. All five were shot down by our own guns the very first day. Damned if I'd go up in a German plane. Signalling is all very well, but the chap on the ground thinks the Fritz is cheating, and he just won't miss a chance of having a crack at a Messerschmidt. . ." He said these planes here had got stuck for lack of water. It often happened on these improvised airfields in the steppe.

There was still a good deal of air activity; from increasingly distant airfields—their closest base was now at Salsk, 125 miles from Kotelnikovo and 220 miles from Stalingrad—the Germans were still trying to send their transport planes to Paulus's trapped army. They were being shot down by the dozen, and very few were now getting through. Goering's promise to Hitler to carry 500 tons of supplies a day to Stalingrad had proved a complete myth. The many captured German airmen we saw during those days were obviously disheartened by the "near-suicide" job they had to do, and doubted whether Stalingrad could hold out, though several argued that, in the spring, there would be a new German offensive, and that Stalingrad would be taken. Rostov would "certainly" not be abandoned. The captured infantry-men—many of whom had wandered about the steppe for a week trying to catch up with the rapidly retreating Germans and were very hungry—were even more demoralised. The fanatical Nazis, especially among the Goering boys, still thought a defeat of Germany quite impossible, but thought the war might end in a draw: Stalingrad was already having *that* effect on them.

The nearest we got to the front was at Zimovniki some sixty miles down the Stalingrad-Caucasus line. The Germans had cleared out of the town only two days before, and were now fighting a stiff rearguard action some five miles south of it. There was intense air activity. As we approached Zimovniki across miles and miles of completely flat snow-covered steppe (we passed another enormous ammunition dump the Germans had abandoned in a hurry) Russian fighters zoomed overhead every minute; dogfights were going on not far away, and the fighters were also pursuing the retreating Germans. But they were now retreating more slowly: the remnants of their two tank divisions which had tried to break through to Stalingrad had been reinforced by the SS Viking Division, brought up from the Caucasus. Gunfire could be heard very clearly, and once a shell landed a short distance away, a cloud of yellow smoke rising from it. Now and then there came from the south a loud booming noise; that was the famous Russian *katyusha* mortar in action. The pleasant little town had been badly damaged by shelling, and a grain elevator was still burning; the local inhabitants told much the same story as in other liberated towns; during the four days' fighting at Zimovniki they had hidden in cellars, with very little food, and only snow to suck, instead of water.

The street signs were still in Rumanian or German, and on the pedestal of the Lenin statue there was only half a leg still standing. The big clubhouse had been used as a barracks by the Germans. The whole floor was covered with bundles of straw on which they had slept. The rostrum was still decorated with fir-branches and the tables and the heaps of straw were littered with what looked like the remains of a Christmas party—dozens of empty wine and brandy bottles, mostly French, empty tins and German cigarette and biscuit cartons. Here also lay a pile of magazines, one of them showing German soldiers basking in deck-chairs on a verandah overlooking the Black Sea—was this Anapa?—and carrying a touristy article on *"Der herrliche Kaukasus und die Schwarzseeküste"*. So they had already been making themselves at home in the Caucasus. The magazine was only three weeks old; now they were beating it from the Caucasus as fast as their legs would carry them...

Much grimmer was the sight in the little park behind the club-house. Russian soldiers were digging a common grave for the Russians who had been killed at Zimovniki only two or three days before. There, in the park, seventy or eighty Russian corpses were placed in rows, in horrible frozen attitudes, some sitting up, some with their arms wide apart, some with their heads blown off; also, some elderly bearded men, and young boys of eighteen or nineteen with open eyes... How many common graves like this were being dug every day along the 2,000 mile front?...

Marshal Malinovsky, Mr Khrushchev's Minister of Defence, now very heavy, stout and seemingly humourless, and well over sixty, was a very different man in 1943. He was then a dapper young Lieutenant-General of forty-four, a very fine specimen of military manhood, admirably groomed in his smart uniform, tall, handsome with long dark hair brushed back, and with a round sunburned face, which did not show the slightest sign of fatigue after several weeks of continuous campaigning. He looked much less than forty-four. He was then still in command of that 2nd Guards Army which had played a leading part in smashing Manstein's Kotelnikovo offensive. Before long he was going to succeed Yeremenko as commander of the Stalingrad Front (to be renamed the "Southern Front") and was going to recapture Rostov in February 1943.

He received us on January 11 at his H.Q. in the large school-house in a big village on the Don. After telling us of his experiences as a soldier of the Russian Expeditionary Force in France in World War I,* Malinovsky outlined the first stage of the Stalingrad battle, which ended with the encirclement of the German forces and the Russian westward drive into the Don country. The second stage was to have begun on December 16, but the Russians were fore-stalled by von Manstein's thrust towards Stalingrad on the 12th.

* At *that* time he told the story as mildly and as "tactfully" as possible. As a member of the Expeditionary Corps of 20,000 men he had, together with the others, sailed from Vladivostok to Marseilles via Singapore and the Suez Canal; he had fought at Laon and Arras; he had seen British and Anzac troops in action, as well as French *poilus*, Malgaches and Senegalese. At Amiens the Russians had fought side-by-side with the British. With a significant little smile Malinovsky said: "I liked those English and Scottish troops; they are slow, but they are reliable. I liked the way they shaved every morning and went into action smoking their pipes." Later, the Revolution broke out in Russia and "there was some trouble with the Russian troops in France." They did not feel any longer like "fighting for France"; they were put in a camp at Courtine; here there was more trouble, and the French shot three or four hundred of them. However, the bulk of the Russians were sent home in the end, except for some who had stayed in France, usually because of some French woman. When he returned to Russia, he joined the Reds in the Civil War. Later, the story of the massacre of the Russians at Courtine was to be told in Russian books (and, indeed, by Malinovsky himself) in much stronger terms.

He said that this striking force was composed of three infantry and three tank divisions, one brought from the Caucasus and another from France. They had about 600 tanks* and were well supported from the air.

After describing the Russian rearguard action between December 12 and 16, the "defensive battles" fought for the next week on the Axai and the Myshkova rivers, the Russian counter-offensive which had hurled the Germans beyond Zimovniki, and the other offensive which had smashed the German "Tormasin Group" in the Middle Don, Malinovsky made a number of significant points:

> For the first time the Germans are showing signs of great bewilderment. Trying to fill in gaps, they are throwing their troops about from one place to another—which shows that they are short of reserves. Many of their troops are retreating west in a disorderly way, and abandoning enormous masses of equipment. Such troops are an easy target for our aircraft. Most of the satellite troops have been knocked out altogether.
>
> The German officers we have captured are extremely disappointed in their high command and in the Führer himself. They have none of the self-assurance they had last summer.
>
> We have considerable difficulties arising from our long lines of communication, but we are overcoming them fairly successfully. And the Red Army has certainly changed and evolved. There were some truly revolutionary changes in the Red Army organisation in the summer of 1942.†
>
> Secondly, there is far more drive and punch in our troops than there used to be; our winter offensive of 1942–3 is on a much larger scale than that of the winter of 1941–2. Our men have far greater experience, and an intense hatred of the Germans. And they can now face situations which they could not face a year ago—for example an onslaught by 150 enemy tanks. Well-armed with anti-tank weapons, our troops successfully faced such attacks in this last Manstein offensive.

On the Stalingrad encirclement he said:

> Stalingrad is an Armed Prisoners' Camp, and its position is hopeless. The liquidation of the "cauldron" has begun, and the enormous losses the Germans will have suffered in Stalingrad will have a decisive

* According to the Germans about 250.
† This was a clear allusion to those "post-Rostov" reforms described in an earlier chapter.

effect on the war. Their attempts to supply Stalingrad from the air now that it is outside the reach of their fighters have been a complete failure.

He thought the Germans were still strong in the air, for all that, and also still had a very great number of tanks. The Waffen-SS were ferocious fighters; but the quality of the other German troops varied greatly.

He was cautious in his forecast for 1943: he was pretty sure that Rostov would be liberated, but would not commit himself to more "for the present". He thought limited German counter-offensives still possible, but none of any decisive importance. But he stressed that the Russians were still going to have a very hard time, that their sacrifices were "unprecedented in history", and he appealed for a much greater effort in the west. North Africa, he suggested, was only a small beginning, with little direct effect on German pressure in the east. He said that no allied equipment had yet been used on this front, except some American lorries.

Malinovsky treated us to a generous lunch (with "trophy" French brandy and German cigars to conclude), and talked wittily and informally, again recalling some of his experiences in France in World War I. His toast was uttered with great warmth and friendliness:

> Victory (he said) is the sweetest moment in the life of every soldier, and I am sparing no effort to achieve it. We Soviet people realise the technical difficulties of a Second Front in Europe; we are, for the present, fighting without it, but we firmly believe it will come very soon. Show your people how pure and clear our aims and motives are. We want freedom—and let us not quibble over certain differences in our conception of freedom; these are a secondary matter—and we want victory so that there may be no war again.

That evening, after seeing some more German airmen who had just been brought down—we travelled through a blizzard back to our Kotelnikovo "base".

There were many heavy snowfalls throughout the first half of January, but the weather was relatively mild—usually between minus 5° and minus 10° centigrade. It was not till towards the end of the

Stalingrad mopping-up, i.e. the second half of January and the early days of February that the frost became truly ferocious: minus 30° and minus 40° centigrade. I was, indeed, going to find this out for myself; for a fortnight later I was to return to the Stalingrad area. And this time to Stalingrad itself.

Chapter V

STALINGRAD: THE AGONY

On January 1, Sovinformbureau published a very long special communiqué on the results of the first six weeks of the Russian offensive in the Stalingrad and Don areas. Not only, it said, had twenty-two enemy divisions been surrounded, but thirty-six had been smashed in the six weeks' fighting. We need not quote here the figures of the enemy tanks, planes, guns, et cetera, captured or destroyed; they were obviously exaggerated—for instance 3,250 tanks and 1,800 aircraft.*

What was interesting, in the light of subsequent attempts to minimise Zhukov's role in the planning and execution of the Battle of Stalingrad, was the concluding statement:

> These operations took place under the command of Colonel-General Vatutin, Commander of the South-West Front; Colonel-General Yeremenko, Commander of the Stalingrad Front; Lieut.-General

* In an interview on the twentieth anniversary of the Battle of Stalingrad, published in *Pravda* on February 10, 1963, Marshal Malinovsky gave the following figures for German losses including all that was finally captured or destroyed in the Stalingrad "bag" during that battle, i.e. up to February 2: 2,000 tanks, 2,000 planes, over 10,000 guns and mortars and 70,000 motor vehicles. Except for the last, these figures are less than the Sovinformbureau statement claimed on January 1, 1943—a statement which did not cover what was to be captured later in the "cauldron".

Rokossovsky, Commander of the Don Front; Lieut.-General Golikov, Commander of the Voronezh Front, and under the general leadership of Army General Zhukov, Colonel-General Vassilevsky and Colonel-General of Artillery Voronov.

There now remained the job of liquidating the German Stalingrad Cauldron. The trapped Germans had nothing more to hope for. Not that the troops in the Stalingrad trap were yet fully aware of the whole ghastly truth. The officers kept telling them not to be unduly disturbed by the rapidly diminishing food rations; the Führer would see to it that everything turned out all right, despite von Manstein's failure to break through. And in any case, they were told, their presence in Stalingrad was a great embarrassment to the Russians and, in the general scheme of things, a great service to the Führer and the Fatherland.

Paulus's forces had been encircled since November 23 and their supplies were running down. Goering's promises to fly 500 tons of food, fuel and ammunition a day to Stalingrad had proved a mirage. Before long the Luftwaffe was only bringing in 100 tons a day and, towards the end of December, even less. The number of planes lost was growing daily. By the middle of December the troops began to eat what was left of the Rumanian cavalry division's horses.

The Germans' growing shortage of ammunition made an enormous difference to the troops of the Russian 62nd Army still holding the Stalingrad bridgeheads. It was now almost safe to carry large dishes of hot food to the front-line troops in broad daylight, barely forty yards away from the German lines. It was equally safe—according to Stalingrad standards of safety—for whole convoys of horse-sleighs to cross the Volga during the day.

At the end of December Grossman wrote in *Red Star*:

> Those Germans who, in September, broke into houses and danced to the loud music of mouth-organs, and who drove about at night with their headlights full on and who, in broad daylight, would bring up their shells in lorries—these Germans are now hiding among the stone ruins... Now there is no sun for them. They are rationed to twenty-five or thirty rounds a day, and they are to fire only when attacked. Their food ration is four ounces of bread and a little horse-flesh.

There, like savages grown over with wool, they sit in their stone caves, gnawing at a horse's bone... Fearful days and nights have come to them. Here, in the dark cold ruins of the city they have destroyed they will meet with vengeance; they will meet it under the cruel stars of the Russian winter night.

Such was the outlook inside Stalingrad itself; it was no better in the open steppes, nearer the centre of the "ring", at Gumrak, or that airfield of Pitomnik which so few of the Junker 52's were now succeeding in reaching. The Germans in the west had been driven far away—into the Salsk steppes and beyond the Donets, and the Germans at Stalingrad were hopelessly isolated.

During the first week of January the troops of the Don Front under Rokossovsky and Voronov were preparing, in the steppes between the Don and the Volga, for the final onslaught. Knowing, however, that the Germans still had much equipment inside the ring, and in order to avoid "unnecessary bloodshed", General Voronov, "representative of the general headquarters of the Supreme Command of the Red Army", and General Rokossovsky, commander of the Don Front, sent an ultimatum to Colonel-General Paulus, on January 8.

The German 6th Army, formations of the 4th Panzer Army and units sent to them as reinforcements have been completely surrounded since November 23... The German troops rushed to your assistance have been routed, and their remnants are now retreating towards Rostov... The German air transport force which kept you supplied with starvation rations of food, ammunition and fuel, is frequently compelled to shift its bases and to fly long distances to reach you... It is suffering tremendous losses in planes and crews and its help is becoming ineffective...

Your troops are suffering from hunger, disease and cold. The severe Russian winter is only beginning... You have no chance of breaking through the ring surrounding you. Your position is hopeless and further resistance is useless.

Voronov and Rokossovsky therefore offered a termination of hostilities and a capitulation on the usual terms:

Arms, equipment and munitions to be turned over to the Russians in an organised manner and in good condition;

Life and safety guaranteed to all soldiers and officers who cease
hostilities; and upon the termination of the war their return to
Germany or to any country the prisoners of war may choose.

All prisoners may retain their uniforms, insignia, decorations and
personal belongings and, in the case of high officers, their side-arms.
All prisoners will be provided with normal food, and all in need of
medical treatment will be given it.

The ultimatum finally stated where Paulus's representative,
travelling in a passenger car flying a white flag, was to appear at
10 a.m. on the following morning, January 9. The ultimatum ended
with the warning that if it was rejected, "the Red Army and Air
Force will be compelled to wipe out the surrounded German
troops" and that "you will be responsible for their annihilation".

The ultimatum was rejected. But not quite off-hand. The German
generals must have taken time to consult Hitler and to think it over.
Afterwards, Russian officers at Stalingrad told me that, after the
presentation of the ultimatum there was a short uncanny truce, when
no guns were fired on either side. Not only the official Russian
envoys but also some other Russians (including a staff officer I
knew) ventured right across the no-man's-land and actually talked
to some Germans urging them to lay down their arms. But Hitler
would not hear of any capitulation, and von Manstein, too, now
thought it in his own interests to sacrifice the German and Rumanian
troops in the Stalingrad "Bag", and failed to inform Paulus of
the real situation, thus leaving him to grope in the dark.*

At 8 a.m. on January 10, the Russian attack was begun with a
barrage from 7,000 guns and mortars along the southern and western
side of the pocket, the density of the barrage reaching in some places
170 guns or mortars per kilometre. Russian planes were meantime
bombing the German positions farther inland. After an hour,
Russian tanks and infantry were thrown in. Despite some desperate
resistance from the Germans, who had strongly fortified the whole

---

* H. M. Waasen. *Was geschah in Stalingrad? Wo sind die Schuldigen?* (What happened at Stalingrad? Where are the guilty men?).
(Salzburg, 1950), p. 69.

area, the Russians advanced in some places during the first day between three and five miles.

As a Russian writer wrote:

> The enemy suffered enormous casualties from our barrage. Our infantry swiftly advanced through the enemy front lines. At every step there were blackened German bodies, wrecked enemy guns and mortars, shattered dugouts and pillboxes. The country, white the day before, was now grey with soot and smoke and dotted with thousands of black shell-holes... And yet the Germans, frightened by "Russian atrocity" stories, continued to resist like hounded wolves.*

It took three days of heavy fighting to snip off the western extremity of the pocket—some 250 square miles. During the following days the advance was much more rapid; the Russians captured the whole middle part of the pocket, including Pitomnik, with the Germans' largest airfield.

On January 17, the Russian command sent Paulus another capitulation offer, and although at least two German generals—von Seydlitz and Schlömmer—were in favour of accepting it, Paulus still had no authority to do so. By this time the Russians had recaptured nearly half the cauldron; but German resistance was still stiff; the western part of the cauldron was studded with hundreds of pillboxes and other firing points; Sovinformbureau's interim report of January 17 spoke of 1,260 pillboxes and fortified dugouts, 75 fortified observation posts and 317 gun or mortar batteries that had been captured or destroyed during the first week's fighting; it also gave a long list of equipment captured or destroyed, including 400 planes, 600 tanks and 16,000 trucks, most of which had, however, been out of action through lack of petrol. The Germans killed during that first week were put at 25,000, but, significantly, the number of prisoners taken—less than 7,000—was still very low, and even many of these appear to have been Rumanians.

On January 22 the Russians started on their final onslaught. The Germans were now retreating in disorder to Stalingrad, and by the 24th, the Russians had reached that line of Stalingrad's "outer defences" which they had themselves held till September 13. "The

* Zamiatin, *Stalingradskaya Bitva* (The Battle of Stalingrad) (Moscow, 1946), p. 56.

German troops, suffering incredible hardships," a Russian military
expert, Colonel Zamiatin, wrote, "now began to realise more fully
the complete hopelessness of their position, and began to surrender
in groups." At the same time, some of the sick and wounded in the
area the Germans were abandoning, were being killed off rather than
being left to the Russians.

But Hitler and Manstein were still insisting that the Germans in
the Stalingrad pocket continue their resistance. Paulus was promoted
to the rank of Field-Marshal, even though he continued to inform
Manstein of the hopelessness of resisting any longer. According to
some German accounts the demoralisation among both soldiers and
officers was now rapidly growing, and there were ugly scrambles at
Gumrak, the last German airfield, where officers paid large bribes to
airmen for a seat on the last departing planes.*

On January 26 the Russian troops both from the north and the
west broke into Stalingrad itself, and at last, at Mamai Hill, joined
with units of Chuikov's 62nd Army which, throughout December
and January, had continued to harass the Germans, especially in
the Mamai Hill, Barricades and Red October areas.†

Although the Germans and especially the Rumanians (including
General Dimitriu) were now surrendering in much larger numbers—
the Rumanians appear, for one thing, to have been deprived even of
their starvation rations since January 20—some heavy fighting still
continued in the streets of Stalingrad for the next five days, and it
was not till January 31 that Field-Marshal Paulus surrendered at his
H.Q. in the basement of the Univermag department store.

Later, when I got to Stalingrad, I heard the story from the man

* Heinz Schröter. *Stalingrad*... quoted by IVOVSS, vol. 3, p. 60.
† During the big Russian counter-offensive in November, troops of
the Don Front broke through to Colonel Gorokhov's little bridgehead north of Stalingrad, in the Rynok area; but had failed to reach
Chuikov's main bridgehead. As a result, for two more months, the
bulk of the 62nd Army was still isolated from the rest of the Russian
forces. Although, during these two months, the Germans were unable to attack the 62nd Army in force, Chuikov speaks with some
bitterness in his book of the "others'" failure to break through to
Stalingrad from the north in November, when the conditions for
doing so had greatly improved.

who had captured Paulus: a youngster with a turned-up nose, fair hair and a laughing face, Lieutenant Fyodor Mikhailovich Yelchenko, whom one could not imagine being called anything but "Fedya". He was bubbling over with exuberance as he told his story—the lieutenant who had captured the Field-Marshal.

On January 31—the day after the tenth anniversary of the Hitler régime, a day on which the Führer had failed to speak—the Russians were closing in on central Stalingrad from all directions. The Germans were frozen, starving, but still fighting. First, after a heavy artillery and mortar barrage, the whole square in front of the Univermag was captured by the Russians, who then began to surround the building. From time to time, flame-throwers also came into action. Yelchenko said that, in the course of the day, he had learned from three captured German officers that Paulus was in the Univermag building. "We then began to shell the building (my unit was occupying the other side of the street, just opposite the side entrance of the Univermag), and as the shells began to hit it, a representative of Major-General Raske popped out of the door and waved at me. It was taking a big risk, but I crossed the street and went up to him. The German officer then called for an interpreter, and he said to me: 'Our big chief wants to talk to your big chief'. So I said to him: 'Look here, our big chief has other things to do. He isn't available. You'll just have to deal with me.' All this was going on while, from the other side of the square, they were still sending shells into the building. I called for some of my men, and they joined me—twelve men and two other officers. They were all armed, of course, and the German officer said: 'No, our chief asks that only one or two of you come in.' So I said: 'Nuts to that. I am not going by myself.' However, in the end, we agreed on three. So the three of us went into the basement. It is empty now, but you should have seen it then. It was packed with soldiers—hundreds of them. Worse than any tramcar. They were dirty and hungry and they stank. And did they looked scared! They all fled down here to get away from the mortar fire outside."

Yelchenko and the two other men were ushered into the presence of Major-General Raske and Lieut.-General Schmidt, Paulus's chief of staff. Raske said that they were going to negotiate the surrender on Paulus's behalf, since Paulus "no longer answered for anything since yesterday". It was all a bit mysterious, Yelchenko said; he couldn't quite figure out who was in charge. Had Paulus passed his authority on to Raske, or was he simply avoiding a personal surrender, or had there been some disagreement between Paulus and the others? Probably not, for Raske and Schmidt kept going into Paulus's room, apparently consulting him on the coming capitulation. Perhaps Paulus was merely unwilling to negotiate with the little Russian lieutenant direct. However, Yelchenko was, in the end, shown into Paulus's room. "He was lying on his iron bed," said Yelchenko, "wearing his uniform. He looked unshaved, and you wouldn't say he felt jolly. 'Well, that finishes it,' I remarked to him. He gave me a sort of miserable look and nodded. And then, in the other room—the corridor, mind you, was still packed with soldiers— Raske said: 'There's one request I have to make. You must have him taken away in a decent car, under proper guard, so the Red Army soldiers don't kill him, as though he were some vagabond.'" Yelchenko laughed. "I said 'Okay'". Paulus had a car duly sent for him, and was taken to General Rokossovsky's place. What happened after that I don't know. But for two days afterwards we were gathering in prisoners all over the place. And the other fellows, on the north side, also surrendered three days later. But even in this part of Stalingrad there was still some fighting for a few hours after Paulus had been caught; however, when they learned what had happened, they began to surrender without any further trouble."*

* It is amusing to note that there should be no mention in the official *History* of Lieutenant Yelchenko, or of his unconventional and presumably "undignified" story of how the German C. in C. at Stalingrad surrendered. Instead, it merely says that the Univermag was surrounded, and that while the firing was continuing, Paulus's A.D.C. "came out of the basement and expressed his willingness to negotiate. Soon afterwards representatives of the Soviet Command arrived on the spot and presented an ultimatum which was accepted by the German command. After all formalities had been completed, Field-Marshal Paulus, his Chief of Staff Lieut.-General Schmidt, and his A.D.C. Colonel Adam, together with a group of staff officers, were delivered to the H.Q. of the 64th Army." (IVOVSS, vol. 3, p. 61.)

Fifteen other generals surrendered at the same time, and the mass-surrender of the German troops now began. A last pocket, in the northern part of Stalingrad was, however, still holding out. Russian planes showered leaflets on this last group; to these were attached real photographs of Paulus being questioned by a Russian general; perhaps there were no facilities for manufacturing a block in a hurry; or perhaps a "real photograph" seemed more convincing. In the end, the Russians had to use heavy artillery before this last group of Germans finally surrendered on February 2. Among these were eight more generals, including some of the more fanatical Nazis, such as Lieut.-General von Arnim, a cousin of the other von Arnim of North-African fame. Over 40,000 German soldiers and officers now surrendered.

According to the official Russian announcement made on February 2, 330,000 men had been encircled in November; but between November 23 and January 10, when the liquidation of the Stalingrad Pocket began, 140,000 men had died in the fighting, or from hunger and disease. By January 10, according to Colonel von Kulowski, the General Quartermaster of the 6th Army, there were 195,000 men to be supplied, including police and Todt personnel.* Twenty-four generals, including a Field-Marshal, had been captured, besides 2,500 other officers; the final number of prisoners was now put at 91,000, which meant that about 100,000 men had been killed or died between January 10 and February 2, and over 200,000 since the November encirclement. The booty enumerated in this final report on the entire operation since January 10 mentioned 750 planes, 1,550 tanks, 480 armoured cars, 8,000 guns and mortars, 61,000 trucks, 235 munitions dumps, and vast quantities of other equipment.

In their final report to Stalin, Lieut.-General Rokossovsky and his chief of staff, Lieut.-General Malinin wrote:

It seems a little odd that Paulus should have been taken to the H.Q. of General Shumilov, commander of the 64th Army, whose role in the defence of a relatively quiet southern sector of the Stalingrad Front has been unspectacular, and not to General Chuikov, the No. 1 hero of the defence of the city.

* The Todt Organisation, often using foreign labour, was concerned with the building of roads, fortifications, etc.

Carrying out your order, the troops of the Don Front at 4 p.m. on February 2, 1943, completed the rout and destruction of the encircled group of enemy forces in Stalingrad. Twenty-two divisions have been destroyed or taken prisoner... The military operations in the city and area of Stalingrad have ceased.

Russia was not noisily exultant, but happy; truly happy for the first time since the war had begun. Now everybody knew that victory would come. There was a feeling of deep, but not vociferous national pride; it was clear at last that all the sufferings and hardships and loss of life had not been in vain. And it was a thousand times right that the Germans should now proclaim their three days of National Mourning, a humiliation the Nazi Government and the German people had so amply deserved.

No one doubted that this was *the* turning-point in World War II.

On the next day the Russian papers published the first photographs of the surrender: long black serpents of German war prisoners winding their way across the ice of the Volga; Paulus, with a very strained look, seated at a table in a small room and being questioned by Generals Rokossovsky and Voronov, and a young man, Major Diatlenko, interpreting; and a picture of a number of captured generals standing on a snowy field; standing to one side and frowning, and almost turning his back on the Germans stood General Dimitriu, wearing a tall sheepskin hat.

He had obviously a grudge; for had not the Germans deprived the Rumanians of even their starvation ration twelve days before?

The papers also printed histories of the 6th Army which, under von Reichenau, had invaded Belgium and had entered Paris, and had then taken part in the invasion of Yugoslavia and Greece. In 1942 it had broken through from Kharkov to Stalingrad. Hitler was particularly proud of this army, and of its enormous striking power. There were also biographies of Paulus, who had fought in World War I, and, more recently, in Poland and France.

The Germans had started the rumour that Paulus had committed suicide.

Two days later I was to see him and the other Stalingrad generals in the flesh.

Chapter VI

CLOSE-UP: STALINGRAD AT THE
TIME OF THE CAPITULATION

Our two planes landed in the early afternoon of February 3 in the
middle of a vast snow-covered steppe. It was sunny and very cold,
with a fierce wind blowing from the east. There was a village at the
edge of the airfield and a few administrative buildings. Tufts of
white smoke were rising from the chimneys. There was no bomb
damage. We were somewhere north-west of Stalingrad.*

The night before I had listened to the German radio: they were
playing lugubrious Wagnerian music—the Siegfried funeral march
over and over again, and *Ich hatt' ein' Kamaraden. Götterdäm-
merung*—a nice word which must have given Hitler the creeps. *Ich
hatt' ein' Kamaraden...* Yes, and not just one, but 330,000 of
them.

At the air force canteen, where we had to wait for a long time,
there were three Soviet correspondents in army uniform—Olender
of *Red Star*, Rosovsky of *Izvestia*, and another man whose name I
forget. They had been to Stalingrad off and on. Olender talked about
Gumrak, just west of Stalingrad, where he had witnessed the biggest
slaughter of Germans ever. "The place is just littered with thousands
of them; we got them well encircled, and our *katyushas* let fly. God,
what a massacre! And there are thousands and thousands of lorries
and cars, most of them dumped in the ravines; they had neither the

* This was the largest party of foreign correspondents—about
twenty—taken anywhere since the beginning of the war. Only six or
seven were taken on the Kotelnikovo trip described in Chapter IV.

544

time nor the means to destroy them, and thousands of guns. Sixty or seventy per cent of the lorries and guns can be repaired and used again. . . And we actually captured a food dump—four or five days before the end! How they must have kicked themselves for having lost *that*!"

"They are uncanny and terrifying," one of the others said, "some of those surviving villages in the pocket; for some of them did survive. A few peasants are still there; fortunately, most of the others had been driven beyond the Don long before the encirclement. Even in that tiny area there was a brand of partisans. Well, not exactly partisans, but desperate people who were hiding, waiting for our troops to come up. There was a half-demented old man who, taking advantage of the general bewilderment among the Germans—that was an hour before we arrived—hid in a hole in the ground and managed to shoot twelve Fritzes. He had a score to settle with them. Somebody said they had raped his daughters, or something, but I never found out exactly."

Then a gruff captain with a drooping moustache, who had just come in, joined in the conversation. He talked about the tremendous amount of equipment the Germans had abandoned at Pitomnik and its airfield, where the fighting had been very stiff; the Germans had an enormous concentration of pillboxes which, in the end, had had to be smashed by a powerful barrage of guns and *katyushas*. "The place is now littered with thousands of dead frozen Fritzes. Our guns also smashed nearly all the planes on Pitomnik airfield; several Ju 52's among them. . . Before the war, Pitomnik was a wonderful fruit tree nursery; the finest apple, pear and cherry trees were grown there; now everything is destroyed."

"Close-by," he went on, "we found an open air camp for Russian prisoners. Yes—open-air, with barbed-wire round it. It was dreadful. There were originally 1,400 men there, whom the Germans forced to work on fortifications. Only 102 survived. You might say the Germans had nothing to eat themselves; but the starvation of the prisoners began long before the encirclement. Unfortunately, finding a few half-dead people lying there among the many frozen corpses, our men started, there and then, to feed them on bread and sausage, and several died as a result. . . ."

A couple of young soldiers then joined us. One was an Ukrainian who talked of his parents and wife who were in Kiev; he had had no news from them. "But the way things are going," he said, "we may soon be there." And he grinned. "Yesterday," he said, "I went down to the Volga hoping to catch some fish through a hole in the ice. And there I saw thousands of German prisoners being taken across the river. God, they looked a mess; dirty; long shaggy beards some of them had; all of them were unshaven, a lot of them had ulcers and boils, and their clothes were terrible. Three of them just collapsed and died of cold, there and then."

"We try to feed them and give them what clothes we can spare," one of the Russian correspondents said with a look of distaste, "but many of them are far-gone, and there just isn't any hospital accommodation for them at Stalingrad; so they have to be marched to a sorting-out camp first." "I shouldn't worry about them too much," said the Ukrainian. "Think what they've done to our people. And how do I know they haven't killed or starved to death *my* wife, or *my* father and mother. . ."

Outside, there was an astonishingly perfect tricolour landscape— a bright red sunset that was almost too like those crudely-coloured picture postcards one used to get in France before the war; to the east, a spotless blue sky and all around, as far as the horizon, the boundless white steppe. Apart from a few sentries there was nobody to be seen; the two planes had departed, and there were no other aircraft. The wind had dropped, and all was strangely still on this cold winter evening. "How far is it to Stalingrad?" I asked one of the soldiers. "About fifty miles," he said.

We spent the night in a large village a few miles away. This was a part of the country that had never been occupied by the Germans, and the village people—especially the women—were "getting a bit tired of having our soldiers about for months and months—for they never stop asking for things". Next morning we were driven for about an hour through the snow-covered steppes (it was now minus

20° centigrade) to another village; we were never told its name. The reason for such secrecy was obvious: for here we were going to see the German generals. What if German paratroops suddenly landed here, in a desperate attempt to rescue them (which was unlikely), or if they tried to bomb them out of existence, now that they were of no further use to the Reich and might even prove a liability?

It was a village of rather flimsy wooden cottages with a few trees and with no local inhabitants by the look of it; everywhere there were soldiers, but no civilians. The generals were living in four cottages—five or six in each. We could not enter their room, and had to speak with them—if they were willing to talk—through the door from the passage. Some were in the background, sitting or standing, with their backs more or less turned on us. It was rather like being in the zoo, where some animals showed interest in the public, and the others sulked. Some of those in the background turned to the door from time to time and glared. The first thing that hit you in the eye were their orders, medals, crosses—some of them almost like mantelpiece ornaments—pinned to their uniforms. Some were wearing monocles—looking like caricatures of Erich von Stroheim—almost too good to be true. But they varied a lot. Some tried to make the best of it. General von Seydlitz—who was, before long, to play an important part in the "Free Germany" set-up—tried to see the funny side of it all; so did General Dubois who grinned and said, as if asking us not to be frightened, that he was an Austrian; and General von Schlömmer, who also grinned and said: "Come on, come on; now what do you want to know?" and familiarly patted one of our conducting officers on the shoulder, and, pointing to his new epaulettes, said: "*Was?—neu?*" with a comic look of surprise, and an almost approving nod, as much as to say: "Well, I suppose you *are* a real army by now".

The most unpleasant of them was General von Arnim. He was enormously tall, with a long twisted nose, and a look of fury in his long horse-like face with its popping eyes. He had a stupendous display of crosses and medals. When somebody asked why the Germans had allowed themselves to be trapped at Stalingrad, he snarled: "The question is badly put. You should have asked how we held out so long against such overwhelming numerical superiority!"

One of the sulking ones in the background then said something about hunger and cold. When somebody suggested that the Russian Army was perhaps better than the German Army and certainly better led, von Arnim snorted and went almost purple with rage. I then asked how he was being treated. Again he snorted. "The officers," he said reluctantly, "are correct. But the Russian soldiers— *das sind Diebe, das sind Halunken. So eine Schweinerei!*" He fumed. "Impudent thieves! They stole all my things. *Eine Schweinerei!*" *Vier Koffer!* Four suitcases, and they stole them all. The soldiers, I mean," he added as a concession. "Not the Russian officers. *Die Offiziere sind ganz korrekt.*" These people had looted the whole of Europe; but what was that compared with his four suitcases? When a Chinese correspondent asked about Japan, he said stiffly, with another devastating glare: "We immensely admire our gallant Japanese allies for their brilliant victories over the English and the Americans, and wish them many more victories." Then he was asked what all those crosses and mantelpiece ornaments were, and he rattled them off one after another—the golden frame with the black spider of a swastika was, he said, the *Deutsche Kreuz in Gold,* and the Führer himself had designed it. "One would have thought that you'd have a slight grudge against the Führer," somebody suggested. He glared and merely said: "The Führer is a very great man, and if you have any doubts, you will soon have occasion to put them aside." The man was one of the few German generals who was to keep completely aloof, during the rest of the war, from the Free German Committee.

One thing was astonishing about these generals. They had been captured only a couple of days before—and yet they looked healthy and not at all undernourished. Clearly, throughout the agony of Stalingrad, when their soldiers were dying of hunger, they had continued to have more or less regular meals. There could be no other explanation for their normal, or almost normal, weight and appearance.

The only man who looked in a poor shape was Paulus himself. We weren't allowed to speak to him*; he was only shown to us so that we could testify that he was alive and had not committed

* I later learned that he had firmly refused to make any statement.

suicide. He stepped out of a large cottage—it was more like a villa—gave us one look, then stared at the horizon, and stood on the steps for a minute or two, in a rather awkward silence, with two other officers, one of whom was General Schmidt, his chief of staff. Paulus looked pale and sick, and had a nervous twitch in his left cheek. He had a more natural dignity than the others, and wore only one or two decorations. The cameras clicked and a Russian officer politely dismissed him, and he went back into the cottage. The others followed and the door closed behind him. It was over.

In the village the soldiers were joking about some of the German generals. "They're damn lucky," one of them said, "living in decent houses, and getting three big meals a day. And some of them have still got plenty of cheek. I must tell you a funny story. It's a fact. They have a girl barber—a Russian Army girl—to go and shave them every morning. One of them got fresh with her the very first day, and pinched her bottom. She resented it and slapped his face. He's now so scared of having his throat cut that he won't shave any more, and is growing a beard!"

We were driven to another village where we were received by General Malinin, General Rokossovsky's chief of staff. Malinin had a strong, typically North-Russian face; he was a native of Yaroslavl, and was now forty-three. He had fought in the Civil War, and had attended the Military Academy for two years in 1931–3; he fought in Finland, and had been with Rokossovsky during the Battle of Moscow. Later, he was to become Zhukov's chief of staff and, in that capacity, took part in the capture of Berlin.

For the last two or three days "Cannae" had suddenly become a catchword with the Red Army; the papers were full of it and Stalingrad was being described as an ideal "Cannae" operation, the most perfect since Hannibal's. Malinin also talked about it; it seemed almost as odd to hear this former Yaroslavl peasant lad talk of Cannae, here in the middle of the Don steppes, as if he had suddenly started reciting the Aeneid... He then paid a tribute to Stalin, under

whose direction this operation had been carried out and then spoke
with obvious feeling of the ordinary Russian soldiers:

> The network of roads and railways (he said), was very weak; and
> yet there was never a shortage of food, munitions or petrol. Every
> soldier, every driver, every railwayman understood the tremendous
> aim before us. The railwaymen ran more trains than seems humanly
> conceivable. The lorry-drivers who, normally, should not work more
> than ten hours a day in winter, often went on working on our transport
> columns for twenty-four hours on end.

He was certain that the Germans could have broken out of Stalingrad at the early stages of the encirclement, if Hitler had allowed it.

Asked about allied equipment and supplies, Malinin said that
there were "a certain amount of American food", a few Dodge
lorries, and a few Churchill tanks—they were good, but there were
only very few of them.

As we now know from German sources, one of the immediate
consequences of the encirclement of the German forces at Stalingrad
in November was an extreme shortage of winter clothing there. In
November, seventy-six railway wagons of winter clothing had got
stuck at Yasinovataya railway station, seventeen at Kharkov, forty-
one at Kiev, and nineteen at Lwow. The German High Command,
not wanting to give the Stalingrad troops the idea that they would
not win the battle before winter, had been in no hurry to send them
winter clothing. The combination of cold and very low rations—
towards the end, these were reduced to two ounces of bread a day
and scraps of horse-flesh (with the generals receiving, in theory, five
ounces of bread)—enormously increased the death-rate among the
Germans especially in January. Not that the cold was uniformly
intense. It was very cold (minus 20° to minus 25° centigrade) in the
second half of December; it was much milder during the first half
of January (usually between 5° and 10° below), but became extremely cold after that, the temperature falling at times to minus 25°,
30° and 40°. And even 45°.

On the night of February 4 I learned what 44° of frost means in
practice, and what it must have meant to the Germans at Stalingrad

—and to the Russians for that matter; for it would be a great mistake to imagine that a Russian—no matter how well clad—*likes* 44° of frost. . .

We set out at 3 p.m. on our fifty mile trek from General Malinin's headquarters to Stalingrad. Our Army driver said we would make it in four to five hours; it took us nearer thirteen.

There were half-a-dozen of us in a wretched van, without any seats or benches, sitting or half-lying on bags or pieces of luggage. Every hour it became colder and colder. To add to our misery the back door of the van had no glass in it; it was almost as cold as driving in an open car.

It was a pity not to travel through this battle area during the day, but it couldn't be helped. Even so, I remember that night as one of my strangest experiences during the whole war. For one thing, I had never known such cold in all my life.

In the morning it had been only minus 20°, and then it was minus 30°, then minus 35°, then minus 40° and finally minus 44°. One has to experience 44° of frost to know what it means. Your breath catches. If you breathe on your glove, a thin film of ice immediately forms on it. We couldn't eat anything, because all our food—bread, sausage and eggs—had turned into stone. Even wearing *valenki* and two pairs of woollen socks, you had to move your toes all the time to keep the circulation going. Without *valenki* frostbite would have been certain, and the Germans had no *valenki*. To keep your hands in good condition, you had to clap them half the time or play imaginary scales. Once I took out a pencil to write down a few words: the first word was all right, the second was written by a drunk, the last two were the scrawl of a paralytic; quickly I blew on my purple fingers and put them back in the fur-lined glove.

And as you sit there in the van all huddled up and feeling fairly comfortable, you cannot bear to move, except your fingers and toes, and give your nose an occasional rub; a kind of mental and physical inertia comes over you; you feel almost doped. And yet you have to be on the alert all the time. For instance, I suddenly found the frost nibbling at my knees: it had got the right idea of attacking the tiny area between the end of my additional underwear and the beginning of the *valenki!* . . . Your only real ally, apart from clothes, on such occasions is the vodka bottle. And, bless it, it didn't freeze, and even a frequent small sip made a big difference. One could see what it must be like to fight in such conditions. For the last stage of the Battle of Stalingrad had been fought in weather only a little milder than it was on that February night.

The nearer we got to Stalingrad, the more bewildering was the traffic on the snow-bound road. This area, in which the battle had raged only so very recently, was now hundreds of miles from the front, and all the forces in Stalingrad were now being moved—towards Rostov and the Donets. About midnight we got stuck in a traffic jam. And what a spectacle that road presented—if one could still call it a road! For what was the original road and what was part of the adjoining steppe that had been taken in by this traffic—most of it moving west, but also some moving east—was not easy to determine. Between the two streams of traffic, there was now an irregular wall of snow that had been thrown up there by wheels and hoofs. Weird-looking figures were regulating the traffic—soldiers in long white camouflage cloaks and pointed white hoods; horses, horses and still more horses, blowing steam and with ice round their nostrils, were wading through the deep snow, pulling guns and gun-carriages and large covered wagons; and hundreds of lorries with their headlights full on. To the side of the road an enormous bonfire was burning, filling the air with clouds of black smoke that ate into your eyes; and shadow-like figures danced round the bonfire warming themselves; then others would light a plank at the bonfire, and start a little bonfire of their own, till the whole edge of the road was a series of small bonfires. Fire! How happy it made people on a night like this! Soldiers jumped off their lorries to get a few seconds of warmth, and have the dirty black smoke blow in their faces; then they would run after their lorry and jump on again.

Such was the endless procession coming out of Stalingrad: lorries, and horse sleighs and guns, and covered wagons, and even camels pulling sleighs—several of them stepping sedately through the deep snow as though it were sand. Every conceivable means of transport was being used. Thousands of soldiers were marching, or rather walking in large irregular crowds, to the west, through this cold deadly night. But they were cheerful and strangely happy, and they kept shouting about Stalingrad and the job they had done. Westward, westward! How many, one wondered, would reach the end of the road? But they knew that the *direction* was the right one; perhaps few were yet thinking of Berlin, but many must have been thinking of their homes in the Ukraine. In their *valenki*, and padded jackets, and fur caps with the earflaps hanging down, carrying tommy-guns, with watering eyes, and hoarfrost on their lips, they were going west. How much better it felt than going east! Yet from the west others were coming—these were merely a trickle. But they also had their story to tell—these peasants in horse-sleighs and horse-carts, and these citizens of Stalingrad walking or driving home through the night—driving home into the ruins. And around all this bustle of trucks, and horse-sleighs, and covered wagons, and camels, and soldiers shouting, and soldiers swearing, and soldiers laughing and dancing joyfully round the bonfires filling the air with acrid smoke, lay the silent snow-covered steppe; and, as the headlights shone on the steppe, and you looked, you saw dead horses in the snow, and dead men, and the shattered engines of war. We were now in the "pocket". And, ahead of us, the searchlights were spanning the sky —the sky of Stalingrad.

It was not till 4 a.m. that we reached Stalingrad. It was terribly cold, and the night was pitch-black, except for a few dim lights here and there. Dazed with cold, we stepped out of our van. Somebody shouted a few yards away; somebody else waved a lantern. "Two here," the man with the lantern said, "two more farther along." He lit up a hole in the ground. "Go down there, and get warm." The hole was little wider than a man's body. Sliding on the slippery boards, and clutching at the ice-covered sides of the tunnel, we slithered down into the dugout, a drop of twenty or twenty-five feet. Warmth! How cosy the miserable hole looked, and how sweet the fumes of the *makhorka* smelled! There were four men down there— two of them sleeping on bunks, the other two crouching by the small iron stove. Both of these were young fellows—one almost a boy, with a little fair down on his chin. The other one, Nikolai, was a tougher soldier, though scarcely more than twenty-three. The other two yawned and fell asleep again. We were offered two of the bunks, covered with thick brown army blankets; but the dugout, lit by a kerosene lamp made of a shellcase, with its top flattened to catch the wick, was crowded, and we sat up most of the time. Nikolai treated us to hot tea out of old cans and, once we had thawed, we vaguely began to take things in. These men belonged to one of the guards regiments that had just completed the liquidation of the German 6th Army, and were now having a few quiet days before being sent on to the front. "When it gets light," said Nikolai, "you'll be able to see the Barricades and the Tractor Plant over there; it looks as if they were standing, but they're gone. There's nothing left of Stalingrad; not a thing. If I had any say in the matter, I'd rebuild Stalingrad somewhere else; it would save a lot of trouble. And I'd leave this place as a museum."

"It's funny," said the younger boy, "to think how quiet it is now. Only three days ago there was still fighting going on. This is a lousy dugout; it's one our people built. The German dugouts are much better. In these last weeks, they hated coming into the open; they can't stand the cold... Filthy, dirty; you wouldn't believe in what filth they lived there. Scared of the cold, and scared of our snipers, and of *katyusha*, of course." The lad shook his head and gave a boyish giggle. "Funny blokes, really. Coming to conquer Stalingrad, wearing patent-leather shoes. Thought it would be a joy-ride. Just go and have a look at them at Pitomnik. Parasites!" he concluded with that favourite Red Army man's word, a word coined back in '41.

"*Katyusha*", said Nikolai, "has done a wonderful job. We got an enormous crowd of them encircled at Gumrak, and they wouldn't surrender. So we got fifty or sixty *katyushas* round them, and let fly... My God, you should have seen the result! Or else we gunners would go up to their pillboxes and smash them up at thirty yards. It was really the guns that did the main job in this liquidation; we had complete superiority in artillery. But they can be tough, for all that. No, they don't like surrendering, not they! On the last day we got to a house where there were fifty officers; they kept firing and firing. It was only when four of our tanks came right up to the house that they put up their arms. Ah, well," he said, sipping hot tea out of the can, "just one more Stalingrad, and they'll be finished!"

"They were in a bad way all right," said the third man, who now woke up—a dark Armenian with a hooked nose, dark beady eyes and a funny accent. "Down at Karpovka, the Germans were eating cats. They were hungry and very cold, and many died of the cold. The local people somehow managed to survive: they had hidden chunks of frozen horse-flesh; and had to manage on that. It was better than cats, anyway. An old woman who lived in a dugout there said the Germans took her dog away and ate it. Yet the German Commandant kept a cow, and he wouldn't allow it to be slaughtered; it made the Fritzes very angry. In the end he had to give way, though. There was also an old priest there, and back in August the Germans opened a church for him. He used to pray for the victory of the Christ-beloved Hosts—which might have meant anything. Some of the people thought it was a great joke."

The soldiers laughed. "Never mind," said Nikolai. "It may now soon be over. I am a factory worker and when we recapture Kharkov, I hope I get my old job back. All very well sitting in trenches and dugouts. But I've been at it since 1940. It's been a long road to Stalingrad, seeing I started this war at Lwow. I was stationed there before the war. Queer lot, the Poles. Before the war, we had to deport the more unreliable elements—all sorts of people. They kept saying: 'We don't want to be either German or Soviet'. That's understandable. But then why, I ask you, when the Germans were coming in at one end of the city, and we were leaving from the other end, did the Poles—youngsters mostly, boys and even girls of fifteen—keep firing at us from every window? Of course, there are different kinds of Poles; some were very friendly and hospitable; it's a question of *class*, I suppose. . ."

It was odd to hear again about this old, old Russo-Polish enmity, even here, in a dugout in the ruins of Stalingrad. . .

In the end, we snatched a couple of hours' sleep, and about 8 a.m. crawled up the slippery tunnel. Here was Stalingrad.

*

It wasn't quite what I had expected. For a moment, I was dazzled by the sun shining on the snow. We were in one of those Garden Cities which the Russians had lost in September. Most of the cottages and trees had been completely smashed. To the right, in the distance, there were large imposing-looking blocks of five or six-storey buildings; they were, in reality, the shells of the buildings of central Stalingrad. On the left, a couple of miles away, there rose a large number of enormously high factory chimneys; one had the impression that there was, over there, a live industrial town; but under the chimneys there was nothing but the ruins of the Tractor Plant. Chimneys are hard to hit, and these were standing, seemingly untouched. It was still very cold, though a little less so than during the night.

At length we drove off, down towards the Volga, through the wreckage of the Garden City and past some smashed warehouses and railway buildings. The wind from across the Volga had swept much of the country bare, and the earth was deadly-frozen with patches of snow here and there, and a pale-blue sky above. A few frozen dead Germans were still lying by the roadside. We crossed the railway-line. Here were railway carriages and engines piled on top of each other, in an inextricable tangle of metal. High cylindrical oil tanks standing alongside the battered railway-line were crumpled up like discarded old cartons and riddled with shell-holes, and some had fallen down completely. On the other side of the road was a honeycomb of trenches and dugouts and shell-holes and bomb-craters; and then, beyond the railway, the road made a sharp hairpin bend, and before us was the white icebound Volga, with the misty bare trees of the delta-land on the other side, and, beyond it, the white steppes stretching far into Asia.

The Volga! Here was the scene of one of the grimmest episodes of the war: the Stalingrad lifeline. The remnants of it were still there: those barges and steamers, most of them smashed, frozen into the ice. Now a thin trickle of traffic was calmly driving across the ice: cars and horse-sleighs, and some soldiers on foot. The Volga was frozen over, but not entirely—not even after the fierce frost of the past fortnight. There were still a few shining blue patches of water, from which women were carrying pails. We drove down from the cliffs to the Volga beach, crowded with hundreds of German "trophy" cars and lorries, and were now on Russian soil that the enemy had never taken.

That night we saw General Chuikov, a tough, thick-set type of Red Army officer, but with a good deal of *bonhomie*, a sense of humour and a loud laugh. He had a golden smile: all his teeth were crowned in gold, and they glittered in the light of the electric lamps. For there *was* electric light in this large dugout built into the cliff facing the Volga, which had been his headquarters during the latter stages of the battle. With him was General Krylov, his chief of staff, who had also survived the siege of Sebastopol.

Chuikov gave us his whole evening and talked solidly for at least an hour and a half describing the whole progress of the Battle of Stalingrad. Since then he has published a full account of the battle, from which I have quoted in an earlier chapter; so I shall mention here only a few specially characteristic points of his story, as told immediately after the German capitulation. The story he told us then was, in essence, the same as that in the book, though then he did not allow himself various indiscretions, particularly about his fellow-generals and about the very uneven morale in the Red Army during the earlier stages of the 1942 campaign, which do appear in the book. There was, however, one small but significant detail. When asked whether Stalin had visited the city during the siege, as rumour had it, Chuikov then replied: "No. But Khrushchev and Malenkov were both here, practically all the time between September 12 and December 20. Stalin, meantime, was working on the gigantic offensive operation of which you can now see the first results.*

He spoke of the important role played by the 62nd Army in slowing down the German advance through the Don country in July and August, then of the great German onslaught on Stalingrad on September 14, and of various stages of the battle.

* Malenkov's presence is not mentioned either in the official history or any other recently published accounts. Though not yet a Politburo member, he was, as member of the GKO, even more important.

Then he came to the story of the 14th of October:

It was the bloodiest and most ferocious day in the whole battle.
Along a front of four to five kilometres, they threw in five brand-new
infantry divisions and two tank divisions, supported by masses of
infantry and planes... That morning you could not hear the separate
shots or explosions; the whole thing merged into one continuous
deafening roar... In a dugout the vibration was such that a tumbler
would fly into a thousand pieces. That day sixty-one men in my headquarters were killed. After four or five hours of this stunning barrage,
the Germans advanced one and a half kilometres, and finally broke
through at the Tractor Plant. Our men did not retreat a step here, and
if the Germans still advanced, it was over the dead bodies of our men.
But the German losses were so great that they could not keep up the
power of their blow, and were not able to widen their salient along the
Volga.

He paid tributes to several of the Stalingrad divisions—to
Zholudev's which had defended the Tractor Plant almost to the last
man, to Ludnikov's, to Rodimtsev's, and many others, adding rather
pointedly that although Rodimtsev's division had played an enormous part in "saving" Stalingrad in September, "there was no
division which had not also "saved" Stalingrad at one time or
another.*

Chuikov also said that after the great counter-offensive had
started to the north and south, things inside Stalingrad became much
easier; all the same, the 62nd Army had been ordered to "activise"
its front with constant attacks on the Germans now encircled in the
Stalingrad "pocket". Chuikov spoke of his men with a note of
fatherly affection. He was also popular with the soldiers; many
Stalingrad soldiers later told me that they admired him immensely

* Then, as later, Chuikov felt that Rodimstev had been given a
disproportionately large share in the press accounts of the Battle of
Stalingrad—at the expense of others whose military record was at
least as remarkable. In his book he explains how this happened:
at the height of the fighting in October and November, Soviet correspondents were not allowed to enter the most dangerous areas in
Stalingrad, and had to stay in the more quiet southern part of the
city, then held by the remnants of the Rodimtsev Division. They had
plenty of time to talk to Rodimtsev—and to write him up.

for his extraordinary personal bravery, and for his self-control—
"There isn't another man in a thousand who wouldn't have lost his
head on that 14th of October."

I was not to see Chuikov again until June 1945; by then he was
one of the conquerors of Berlin. The prosperous abandoned Nazi
villas with their rose and jasmine bushes and the motor boats on the
Wannsee seemed a million miles away from the dead frozen winter
soil of that night at Stalingrad, from that icebound Volga, into which
the wreckage of barges and steamers was frozen.

"It's been a long and a hard way," said Chuikov that day in
Berlin. "But mind you," he added, flashing his gold teeth, "speaking
of those barges and steamers, it wasn't as bad as you think. It was a
devil of a job getting the stuff to Stalingrad, but we got ninety per
cent across for all that!"

The morning after our evening with Chuikov I climbed up to the
little war memorial they were putting up on top of the cliff. A
Russian soldier and two German prisoners were working on it. One
had a growth of black beard, the other of reddish beard. A little
Bashkir soldier with a strong humorous Mongol face and deep
laughing slanting eyes came up to me and started telling me in
broken Russian how he had fought at the Red October Plant during
the worst of the Stalingrad Battle. Then he said, pointing at the two
Fritzes digging the frozen earth round the memorial: "Can you talk
their language?" "Yes." "Then come and talk to them." "*Na, wie
geht's?*" Cheerfully, with a look of surprise, but emphatically the
dark German said: "*Ganz gut!*" "So you haven't been murdered by
the Russians after all?" "No," he said, cheerfully again. I translated
to the Bashkir. "To think what they've done. During the evacuation
they sank a steamer on the Volga, with three thousand women and
kids. Nearly all killed or drowned," he said, "and now they're wearing our *valenki.*" True enough, both of them were wearing *valenki.*
One was wearing a dirty German grey-green overcoat, but below it
were all sorts of bits of clothing, and the other wore a padded Russian army jacket, and they both had fur caps of sorts. "Yes," said
Black Stubble, "the Russians gave us these *valenki. Die sind prima!*"

They were both from Berlin; I asked if they still thought Hitler the greatest man in the world. They protested vigorously; Red Stubble said he had once been a Young Communist, and Black Stubble said he had been a Social Democrat. "*Ach*, all the misery that Hitler has brought to the world and to Germany," Red Stubble said sententiously. "Stalingrad—yes, but in Germany it's just as bad: Cologne and Düsseldorf and parts of Berlin, and it's going from bad to worse." They were both on the skinny side, but looked reasonably fit, and said they were getting plenty of food now, and were surprised at being so well treated. The Russian sergeant who was in charge of the two Germans had been listening to our conversation with a touch of tolerant amusement. Now he called them back to get on with the job. "How are they?" I said to him. "They're all right, *nichevo. Ludi kak ludi.* (Like any other people)".

In and around the Red October Plant fighting had gone on for weeks. Trenches ran through the factory yards and through the workshops themselves; and now at the bottom of the trenches there still lay frozen green Germans and frozen grey Russians and frozen fragments of human shapes; and there were helmets, Russian and German, lying among the brick debris, and now half-filled with snow. There was barbed wire here, and half-uncovered mines, and shell cases, and tortuous tangles of twisted steel girders. How anyone could have survived here was hard to imagine; and somebody pointed to a wall, with some names written on it, where one of the units had died to the last man. But now everything was silent and dead in this fossilised hell, as though a raving lunatic had suddenly died of heart failure.

It was still 30° below zero. That afternoon we also went up the deadly slopes of Mamai Hill along a narrow path about 100 yards long. Already on the summit the Russians had erected a rough wooden obelisk painted bright-blue, with a red star on top. Among the fractured stumps of fruit-trees lay more helmets, and shell-cases, and shell splinters and other metal junk. There were patches of snow on the ploughed-up frozen ground, but no dead except for a solitary large head, completely blackened with time, and its white teeth grinning; had he been a Russian or a German? A major said that the Russians had been buried, but that 1,500 Germans were still stacked up on the other side of the hill. How many thousands of shells had pierced this ground where only six months before the water-melons were ripening? A Russian tank was standing there, half-way up the hill, facing the summit, and burned-out.

I remember, we then drove into central Stalingrad, along a long, long avenue with shattered trees on either side, running parallel to the Volga. We passed tramcars—many of them, all blasted, smashed and burned out; had they been standing here since the great bombing of August 23? . . . One could see it now: Stalingrad was one of the modern cities of Russia; its entire centre, like its factories, had been built in the last ten or twelve years. Here were large blocks of flats, all burned out, of course, and public buildings in the main square, with the wrecked railway station at one end. This, too, had changed hands several times in deadly fighting in September. . . In the centre of the square there was a frozen fountain with the half-shattered statues of children still dancing round it.

We got out here. There was an enormous heap of litter piled up in one corner of the square—letters, and maps and books, and snapshots of German children, and of German middle-aged women with smirking self-contented faces standing on what looked like a bridge over the Rhine, and a green Catholic prayer book called *Spiritual Armour for Soldiers*, and a letter from a child called Rudi writing that "now that you have taken *die grosse Festung Sewastopol* the war will soon be ended against *die verfluchten Bolschewiken, die Erzfeinde Deutschlands.*"

We walked down the main avenue running south, between enormous blocks of burned-out houses, towards the other square. In the middle of the pavement lay a dead German. He must have been running when a shell hit him. His legs still seemed to be running, though one was now cut off above the ankle by a shell, and, with the splintered white bone sticking out of the frozen red flesh,

it looked like something harmlessly familiar from a butcher's
window. His face was a bloody frozen mess, and beside it was a
frozen pool of blood.

In the other big square some houses had been wrecked, but two
were standing there, squat and solid, though burned-out: the Red
Army House and the Univermag Department Store.

After visiting the scene of Paulus's surrender and talking to
Lieutenant Yelchenko who had captured the Field-Marshal,* we
went out into the street again. Everything around was strangely
silent. The dead German with his leg blown off was still lying some
distance away. We crossed the square and went into the yard of the
large burned-out building of the Red Army House; and here one
realised particularly clearly what the last days of Stalingrad had
been to so many of the Germans. In the porch lay the skeleton of a
horse, with only a few scraps of meat still clinging to its ribs. Then
we came into the yard. Here lay more horses' skeletons and, to the
right, there was an enormous horrible cesspool—fortunately frozen
solid. And then, suddenly, at the far end of the yard I caught sight
of a human figure. He had been crouching over another cesspool,
and now, noticing us, he was hastily pulling up his pants, and then
he slunk away into the door of a basement. But as he passed, I
caught a glimpse of the wretch's face—with its mixture of suffering
and idiot-like incomprehension. For a moment, I wished the whole
of Germany were there to see it. The man was perhaps already dying.
In that basement into which he slunk there were still two hundred
Germans—dying of hunger and frostbite. "We haven't had time to
deal with them yet," one of the Russians said. "They'll be taken
away tomorrow, I suppose." And, at the far end of the yard, beside
the other cesspool, behind a low stone wall, the yellow corpses of
skinny Germans were piled up—men who had died in that basement—about a dozen wax-like dummies. We did not go into the
basement itself—what was the good? There was nothing we could
do for them.

This scene of filth and suffering in that yard of the Red Army
* See page 540 ff.

House was my last glimpse of Stalingrad. I remembered the long anxious days of the summer of 1942, and the nights of the London blitz, and the photographs of Hitler, smirking as he stood on the steps of the Madeleine in Paris, and the weary days of '38 and '39 when a jittery Europe would tune in to Berlin and hear Hitler's yells accompanied by the cannibal roar of the German mob. And there seemed a rough but divine justice in those frozen cesspools with their diarrhoea, and those horses' bones, and those starved yellow corpses in the yard of the Red Army House at Stalingrad.

Chapter VII

"CAUCASUS ROUND TRIP"

"*Kaukasus—hin und zurück*"—Caucasus round trip: that's what German soldiers used to say with a touch of irony and some bitterness when it was all over. The German invasion of the Caucasus had lasted six months; in August 1942 they overran vast territories there as quickly as they were to evacuate them again in January–February 1943.

Their hurried evacuation of the Caucasus was, of course, a direct result of the encirclement of the Germans at Stalingrad and the subsequent recapture of the Don country by the Russians. If the Russians had succeeded in January 1943 in closing the "Rostov bottleneck" and, better still, in also occupying the Taman Peninsula, that Germany escape route to the Crimea across the Kerch Straits, all the German forces in the Caucasus would have been trapped.

In the last five months of 1942, with attention focused on Stalingrad, the Soviet press gave relatively little space to the fighting in the Caucasus, and, for many years afterwards, very little was written about the Caucasus campaign. Coming on top of the loss of Rostov at the end of July 1942, its first phase was one of the Russians' bitterest and most humiliating memories. Despite Stalin's "Not a step back" order flashed to every unit of the Red Army at the end of July, the Russians were on the run, throughout August, in the Kuban and the Northern Caucasus as they had not been since some of the worst days of 1941. The communiqués during August were

564

unspeakably depressing: it was clear that the Kuban country—the richest remaining agricultural area this side of the Urals—was being abandoned "under the pressure of superior enemy forces". By August 20 an enormous territory had been overrun by von Kleist's Heeresgruppe A; the whole of the Kuban country was now in German hands, and the Germans were penetrating into the Caucasus proper and driving on, in the west, to the Black Sea coast, after capturing Krasnodar, the capital of the Kuban, and Maikop, the third most important oil centre in the Caucasus. In the east, they were on their way to the two great oil centres, Grozny and Baku.

When the Russians had failed to stop the Germans on the Don at the beginning of August, the German advance through the Kuban had assumed all the characteristics of the *blitzkrieg*. The Germans had overwhelming superiority in tanks and aircraft, and only here and there, particularly along the rivers, did the Russians fight a rearguard action of sorts, but without much effect. According to Russian accounts, the roads were crowded with thousands of refugees, trying to escape, with their cattle, to the mountains; others stormed trains at every railway station; but, in reality, the German advance was so rapid that probably not very many civilians actually got away.* For the same reason it was practically impossible to evacuate any of the industries and the most the Russians could do in Maikop was to blow up the derricks and other installations and destroy what oil reserves were still there; the German oil engineers

---

* According to General Tyulenev, many thousands got away all the same, but in the worst possible conditions. "Even the smallest railway stations were cluttered with thousands of refugees. Despite intensive German bombing, and though having exhausted their meagre food supplies, all these people were trying to get away from the German avalanche." There was, he further relates, such an influx of refugees—weeping women and children—into the Caspian ports like Makhach-Kala and Baku, where they were desperately hoping to be taken across the Caspian, that a serious danger of epidemics arose; the local Party organisations made a frantic effort to house a large number of these refugees in local *kolkhozes* and to ship the rest to Krasnvodsk, on the other side of the Caspian, and beyond. (I. V. Tyulenev, *Cherez Tri Voiny* (Through Three Wars) (Moscow, 1960), p. 176.)

who arrived soon afterwards found that it would take a very long
time before Maikop could produce any oil again.

To the Russians, the abandonment of the Kuban and the northern
fringes of the Caucasus proper were, sentimentally, a particularly
painful and shameful memory; and yet, almost all German writers
on the Caucasus campaign are agreed that the Russians did the only
sensible thing they could do in the circumstances, which was not to
allow themselves to be trapped by the highly mobile advancing
German forces, and to escape to the relative safety of the mountains.

As it turned out, the German plan for the conquest of the
Caucasus was over-ambitious. It was one of Hitler's less happy
brainwaves. His original plan, as we have seen, had been to capture
Stalingrad first, with far larger forces than were ultimately sent there,
and then to overrun the Caucasus, chiefly from the Caspian side, to
begin with, with Grozny and Baku as No. 1 target. After the easy
capture of Rostov, Hitler imagined that the Russians were so weak
that he could divide his forces in two, one to capture Stalingrad and
the other to conquer the Caucasus. He had long had his eye on the
Caucasian oil and thought that, by cutting the Volga supply route
and also capturing the three Caucasian oil cities, he could knock out
Russia economically in a very short time. The capture of Baku was
scheduled for the middle or end of August.

There is no doubt that the Germans again underrated the Russian
capacity of resistance; in the Caucasus, as elsewhere, they tried to do
too many things all at once: a) in the east, break through to Grozny
and then, along the Caspian, to Baku; b) in the middle, break
through to Vladikavkaz (Orjonikidze) and cross the great Caucasus
mountain range along the Georgian Military Highway into Transcaucasia and, perhaps simultaneously, along the parallel Ossetin
Military Highway, as well as further west across the mountain passes
of Klukhor, Marukh and Sancharo—a straight cut to the Black Sea
coast between Sochi and Sukhumi, whence the Germans could then
overrun Transcaucasia from the west and reach the Turkish border;
c) in the west, to break through to the Black Sea at Novorossisk and,
farther south—which was much more important—at Tuapse,
whence they could follow the Black Sea coast all the way to Batumi.

General Tyulenev, the Commander of the Transcaucasian Front, has since then written that if, instead of trying to do too many things all at once, the Germans had concentrated the bulk of their forces in the east, they might have broken through to Grozny and even to Baku. Instead, Tyulenev argues, they were determined to grab the Black Sea coast as well, partly in order to eliminate the Russian Black Sea Navy, which would have had to scuttle itself, and partly in order to get Turkey into the war on the German side. Tyulenev actually refers to certain units in the German armies invading the Caucasus which were held in reserve for "operations in the Middle East and for joining up with Rommel's forces in Egypt!" It is scarcely surprising that Churchill was extremely worried about the German advance into the Caucasus and offered Stalin a large Anglo-American air force which would "defend the Caucasus". And, as we have seen, Stalin did not reject the proposal off-hand.

The Russian command obviously felt that the danger of a German breakthrough to Grozny and Baku was very real. Throughout August and September 90,000 civilians were mobilised for day-and-night work on fortifications, gun emplacements, anti-tank ditches, et cetera, at Grozny, Makhach-Kala and the "Debrent Gate" on the Caspian, as well as at Baku itself, round which ten defence lines were built. In fact, however, the Germans were stopped at Mozdok, about sixty-five miles west of Grozny, and were prevented, during weeks and months of intense fighting, from enlarging the bridgehead they had seized on the south side of the Terek river, and so driving on to Grozny. It came as a complete surprise to the Germans that the Russians had, in addition to the armies that had escaped them, sufficient reserves in the Caucasus to stop them at Mozdok—a place-name which, like Stalingrad, first appeared in the communiqué on August 25, and continued to figure in subsequent communiqués right up to January.

The Russian troops at Mozdok belonged to the so-called Northern Group of General Tyulenev's "Transcaucasian Front". The troops that had retreated from north to south belonged to two "Fronts", the "Southern Front" under the luckless Marshal Budienny, and the "North-Caucasian Front" under General Malinovsky. Malinovsky was to play a very active part in the subsequent Caucasus fighting, but Budienny appears again to have soon faded out of the picture, since the troops of the "Southern Front" were merged on August 11 with Malinovsky's armies or with the "Black Sea Group" under General Petrov (of Sebastopol fame) which formed part of the "Transcaucasian Front". This "Black Sea Group" held the coast and the adjoining mountains between Novorossisk and Sochi.

Not only did the Russians have considerable reserves in the Caucasus, which stopped the Germans at the most crucial points—after everything, or nearly everything, that was strategically expendable had been expended—but, from September right on to the end of the campaign, they succeeded in bringing very substantial reinforcements to the Caucasus, despite enormous transport difficulties. Men and a great deal of heavy equipment (guns, tanks, et cetera) came across the Caspian from Krasnovodsk to Baku, and thence by train or road; the Russian troops in the west were supplied, broadly, the same way. Mortars, small arms, ammunition and much else came from more or less improvised factories and workshops in Transcaucasia. Transcaucasia also provided the Russian armies of the Caucasus front with much of their food. Both men and supplies were also brought by sea from Batumi to Tuapse.

No doubt the German advance had been spectacular throughout August, and in September the Germans scored a further success in the north-west by capturing the whole Taman Peninsula, as well as the naval base of Novorossisk. Not that they could use the port effectively, since the opposite side of the bay was still held by the Russians, who kept it under shell-fire. But the Germans' desperate attempts to break through to Tuapse, farther south, which was the real key to the Black Sea coast all the way to the Turkish border, failed completely. This failure is attributed by General Tyulenev to several factors; the extreme toughness of the Russian troops and sailors, the natural obstacles on the way to Tuapse (mountains and forests), but above all, perhaps, the stupendous amount of plain spade-work done by both soldiers and civilians in building gun emplacements, digging anti-trench ditches, and in some cases, felling century-old trees over threatened roads. This work was done not only on the road to Tuapse, but along mountain passes, on the road to Baku, and all along the Georgian and Ossetin Military Highways crossing the main mountain range.

> Within a few weeks the entire Caucasian theatre of war became a network of defences. People worked till they nearly collapsed, with bloody rags round their blistered hands. Sometimes they had little or nothing to eat for days, but they still went on with the work even at night, and despite enemy air-raids... By the beginning of autumn about 100,000 defence works were built, including 70,000 pillboxes and other firing-points. Over 500 miles of anti-tank ditches were dug, 200 miles of anti-infantry obstacles were built, as well as 1,000 miles of trenches. 9,150,000 working days were expended on this work.*

Tyulenev pays a special tribute to General Babin, head of the engineering troops of the Transcaucasian Front who succeeded in "sealing up the Caucasus against the enemy's infantry and tanks". He succeeded in this despite the extremely difficult conditions arising from the shortage of implements and explosives.†

Thus the Germans failed to break through both to Grozny in the east and to Tuapse in the west. In the "middle", they tried to cross the Caucasus range along three famous mountain passes, but although, from the top of these 9,000-foot high mountains they could see the Black Sea in the distance, they were held up there, too. Tyulenev describes some particularly ferocious fighting high up in the mountains throughout September, and the enormous difficulties of bringing up supplies to the troops there with little U2 planes or with mules and donkeys. A still more difficult problem was evacuating the wounded. The blizzards that began to sweep the mountains at the beginning of October forced the Germans to abandon their attempt to break through to the Black Sea across the high mountain passes.

At the beginning of November the Germans made one final bid to break through to both Grozny and Tbilisi by another route, and to

* Tyulenev, op. cit., p. 188.
† When in 1946 I travelled along the Georgian Military Highway, in an army truck from Vladikavkaz to Tbilisi, I was indeed amazed at the number of pillboxes that had been dug into the mountainside, back in 1942.

outflank the Russian forces at Mozdok from the south. On November 2 they captured Nalchik, the capital of Kabarda, and pushed on to Vladikavkaz (Orjonikidze), the capital of Northern Ossetia at the northern end of the Georgian Military Highway, and also on the way to Grozny from the south-west. But the Russians had time to regroup, and only a few miles to the west of Vladikavkaz they delivered a smashing blow at the advancing German armoured columns, and finally hurled them back to Nalchik. Three well-manned defence lines had been built outside Vladikavkaz, and Russian tanks and artillery, operating from here, inflicted a heavy defeat on the Germans. The Russians put the German losses during the five days' fighting at 140 tanks, 2,500 motor vehicles and much other equipment, and the German casualties at 5,000 dead.

In any case, the Germans undertook no further offensives after that and went over to the defensive at both Mozdok and Nalchik. They were hoping to resume their conquest of the Caucasus with renewed strength in the spring—if all went well at Stalingrad.

As we have seen, it did not. By the beginning of January, the troops of the "Stalingrad Front", shortly to be renamed "Southern Front" and to be placed under the command of Malinovsky, instead of Yeremenko, were advancing beyond Kotelnikovo towards Salsk and Tikhoretsk, with the ultimate object of capturing Rostov and of closing the "Rostov Gap" to the German forces in the Caucasus. General Petrov's task was to strike east from the Black Sea coast towards Krasnodar and Tikhoretsk, and join up there with the troops of the "Southern Front", thus not only closing the Rostov Gap but also cutting off the German forces in the Caucasus from the Taman Peninsula, their escape route to the Crimea. For a large number of reasons this Russian plan failed. The Germans, rapidly transferred strong armoured forces from the Caucasus to the Zimovniki-Salsk-Tikhoretsk area to slow down the Russian advance on both Rostov and Tikhoretsk. After their heavy fighting since the beginning of Manstein's Kotelnikovo offensive, the Russian troops of the "Southern Front" were short of tanks and other equipment, and the new tanks they were asking for were slow in arriving.

MID·NOV.1942

End of December 1942
Beginning of Feb. 1943 ·····
End of February "
March — 1943
German counter-offensive

KURSK SALIENT

Orel

Kursk

Voronezh

MID·NOV.1942

N

Kharkov

Don

Stalingrad

Volga

Zaporozhie

Stalino

Donets

Don

Kotelnikovo

Taganrog

Rostov

Zimovniki

Manych

Kerch

Taman

Krasnodar

Novorossisk

Mineral Vody

Piatigorsk

Black Sea

Nalchik

Miles

0   100   200

MID·NOV.1942

Vladikavkaz

RUSSIAN WINTER OFFENSIVE · 1942-43

With the Stalingrad railway junction still inside the "Stalingrad Bag", there was no railway link with central Russia, and the road communications were slow and very long (about 220 miles from the nearest railhead). As for General Petrov's "Black Sea Group", it was also faced with supply difficulties; the gales on the Black Sea had rendered its chief supply lines precarious and, moreover, heavy rains and floods seriously slowed down its progress towards Krasnodar. This was not liberated by the Russians until February 12, i.e. over a month after the offensive had begun.

There is much disagreement between German and Russian commentators on the German withdrawal from the Caucasus; according to the Germans, it was a "planned" withdrawal; according to the Russians it was a "disorderly retreat". In particular, the Russians make much of the complete demoralisation among the Rumanian and Slovak troops which took part in the German conquest of the Caucasus, and point to the large quantities of equipment the Germans abandoned in a hurry at certain railway junctions like Mineralnyie Vody, where the Russians captured 1,500 wagon loads of equipment. But there is, in fact, little to show that, in their pursuit of the retreating Germans, the Russian troops of the "Northern Group" of the "Transcaucasian Front" (among them those who had fought for months at Mozdok) succeeded in either capturing or destroying many. Most of the German troops in the Caucasus got away, either through the Rostov Gap, or to the Taman Peninsula. According to German commentators, it was Hitler's pet idea to hold this peninsula with the strongest possible forces as a springboard for a future reconquest of the Caucasus. This is today considered as a cardinal mistake on Hitler's part; instead of staying idle in the Taman Peninsula, these 400,000 troops could have made all the difference to the German's chances in the subsequent fighting on the Don and the Eastern Ukraine.*

The German withdrawal from the Caucasus was rapid, but still not rapid enough to prevent the application of "scorched earth" methods

* Cf. Philippi and Heim, op. cit., p. 203.

on a very considerable scale. In their retreat, the Germans destroyed or half-destroyed a very large number of towns and villages. Earlier on during their occupation of the Kuban they had confiscated or "bought" from the population large quantities of food and livestock.

In invading the Caucasus, the Germans had laid great store on the "disaffection" towards Moscow on the part of the various Caucasian nationalities, and indeed the Russians themselves were far from certain about the loyalty of these people, and some even had doubts about the Cossacks of the Kuban—that "Vendée" of the Russian Civil War where, moreover, the Soviets had had some particularly serious trouble at the time of the Collectivisation drive.

I remember a significant conversation on the subject with Konstantin Oumansky on July 24, i.e. on one of the blackest days of the Black Summer of 1942.

I must say I am a little worried about the Caucasus. Even when a Russian or an Ukrainian is not particularly pro-Soviet, he still remains patriotic; he will fight for a United Russia, or the Soviet Union, or whatever you like to call it. But the Tartars in the Crimea are, to a large extent, disloyal. They were economically privileged by the wealthy tourist traffic before the Revolution, and now they have not been so well-off. But they never liked us. It is well-known that during the Crimean War they gladly "collaborated", as we'd now say, with the English and the French. And, above all, there are religious factors which the Germans have not failed to exploit. Nor do I trust the mountain peoples of the Caucasus. Like the Crimean Tartars, they are Moslems, and they still remember the Russian conquest of the Caucasus which ended not so very long ago—in 1863. The only fully pro-Soviet and pro-Russian nation in the Caucasus are—for obvious historical reasons—the Armenians. The Georgians are not so hot.

"What, even with Stalin a Georgian?"

Yes, because a lot of Georgians—well, you know yourself what kind of people they are. Southerners, like Italians, a lazy, wine-drinking, pleasure-loving bunch. No doubt we have several excellent Georgian generals in the Red Army, and some fine Georgian soldiers, but they are not altogether typical of the Georgians as a whole...

"And the Cossacks?"

They have their grievances against us. But they are Russian, so they'll be all right. Maybe a few will rat on us, but certainly not many.

The Soviet authorities were, indeed, rather worried about the Caucasus and, particularly, about the Moslem nationalities there. This uneasiness extended, to some extent, also to certain Moslem nations of Central Asia, particularly the Uzbeks, though not to the Kazakhs who had much weaker historical and religious traditions of their own than the Uzbeks, and had proved the most "assimilable" of the Central Asian peoples, and had provided some of the toughest soldiers to the Red Army. Altogether, the Kazakh's military record throughout the war was to prove outstandingly good, and in Stalingrad itself some of the finest soldiers were Central Asians—Bashkirs, Kirghizes and, above all, Kazakhs. The Tartars— i.e. the Volga Tartars, not the Crimean Tartars—also had an excellent record.*

Since the rapid loss, during the first weeks of the invasion in 1941, of non-Russian areas like the Baltic Republics, the war had been fought on Russian and Ukrainian territory whose populations could (except in the Western Ukraine) be considered wholly, or almost wholly, loyal. But with the Germans breaking into the Caucasus and approaching the borders of Asia, the Soviet authorities were faced with a number of new problems. Their experience of the Crimean Tartars had been an unhappy one, and the question arose how the Caucasus would behave. There also seemed, at this stage, some need to preach loyalty to the Uzbeks, among whom Moslem traditions were still strong. The propaganda among the Uzbeks took on some

* During the first year of the war, military decorations were distributed much less lavishly than later. Up to October 5, 1942, 185,000 persons had been decorated. By nationalities, the list was headed by Russians (128,000), followed by Ukrainians (33,000), Belorussians (5,400), Jews (5,100), Tartars (2,900), Mordvinians (1,100), Kazakhs (1,000), Georgians and Armenians (900 each), Latvians, Uzbeks, Bashkirs, Karelians (400 each), Ossetins, Azerbaijanis, Chuvashs (300 each). There followed a dust of various small or tiny nationalities of Siberia, the Caucasus and Central Asia, besides 14 Gypsies, 7 Assyrians, 230 Poles, 98 Greeks, 37 Bulgars, 10 Czechs and 9 Spaniards. (Table from E. Yaroslavsky's *Twenty-five Years of the Soviet Régime*, Moscow, 1942.)

extravagant forms; thus, on October 31, 1942, the whole second page of *Pravda* was printed in Uzbek, with a Russian translation opposite. This missive "From the Uzbek People to the Uzbek Soldiers" and signed by leading personalities in Uzbekistan "on behalf of over two million Uzbeks", was an extraordinary piece of florid oriental prose:

> Beloved sons of the people, children of our heart!... Remember, your ancestors preferred to gnaw through the chains with their teeth, rather than live as slaves... Remember, Hitler is not only the sworn enemy of all the European nations and, above all, the Slav nations, but he is also the sworn enemy of the peoples of the east. Behold the fate of the Moslem peoples of the Crimea and the Caucasus; their peaceful villages are being burned and looted by the Germans. Quickly destroy the enemy, or these beasts will slay your grey-haired grandfathers, and your fathers and mothers, and violate your wives and brides, and crush your innocent babes underfoot, and destroy your canals, and turn flourishing Uzbekistan into a sun-scorched desert...

It went on and on for four columns, recalling all the national heroes of the Uzbek people who had valiantly fought against the Mongol conquerors, and the great writers and poets of the Uzbek people, who had lived in the ancient cities of Samarkand and Ferghana and Bokhara, all of which Hitler now intended to destroy. But the main point of this "missive" was that Hitler was the deadly enemy of the Moslem peoples as could be seen from the atrocities he was committing against the Moslems in the Crimea and the Caucasus.

Had some German propaganda, one could only wonder, reached Uzbekistan to show that the Germans were favouring the Moslems in both the Crimea and the Caucasus?

Needless to say, this kind of Soviet propaganda among the peoples of the Caucasus had started even earlier, immediately after the German invasion of the Kuban. All over the Caucasus "anti-Fascist" meetings were being organised. Great publicity was given to the enthusiasm with which all the Caucasian peoples had supported these meetings; particular prominence was given in the Soviet press to a vast "anti-Fascist" rally at Vladikavkaz at the end of July. There was a curiously appealing, not to say cringing, note in the flattery that was now addressed to the peoples of the Caucasus. Thus, on September 1, *Pravda* published this appeal in enormous letters:

> Mountain peoples of the Northern Caucasus, Cossacks of the quiet Don, swift Kuban and stormy Terek; peoples of Kalmukia and Stavropol! Rise for the life-and-death struggle against the German invaders! May the plains of the Northern Caucasus and the Caucasus foothills become the grave of the Hitlerite robbers!

On September 3, in an article entitled "The Peoples of the Caucasus and the Stalin Constitution", *Pravda* wrote:

> In the old days, that jewel among the nations—the Caucasus—shone but dimly. Now it glitters in the constellation of Soviet cultures.

On September 6, in connection with another "anti-Fascist" rally, this time in Transcaucasia, it wrote:

> Peoples of Transcaucasia! To the Germans you are merely "natives". The German monster wants to cut the Caucasus armies from the rest of the Red Army, and to cut off the Caucasian nations from the rest of the Soviet family of nations.

There was a clear suggestion in all this that the Soviet authorities were nervous about German policy in the Caucasus, not only vis-à-vis the Moslems, but also the Georgians, Armenians, Azerbaijanis— and even the Cossacks.

This anxiety, as it turned out, was largely unjustified, all the more so as the Germans stayed only a short time in both the Kuban and the Northern Caucasus, and their policy was, to say the least, a confused and contradictory one. Nevertheless the anxiety was not entirely groundless.

We need not deal here with the various grandiose German "schemes" for the Caucasus, whether Rosenberg's or the others, all of which were to remain mere paper theories. All the same, some rather incoherent attempts were made to exploit the Cossacks' "anti-revolutionary past". Savagely anti-Bolshevik Cossack generals of the Civil War days like General Krasnov and General Shkuro were brought to the Kuban, and were expected to help in converting the Cossacks to "collaboration". Whereas Rosenberg had expressed the view that the Cossacks were essentially Russians, and should, therefore, be treated more harshly than the Ukrainians (whom, unlike Erich Koch, the Reichskommissar for the Ukraine, he chose not to regard as *Untermenschen*), the German Army adopted the policy that the Cossacks were potential 'friends", who should be exempted from the *Untermensch* status. Cossacks were, as far as possible, to be drafted into the German Army. As we have seen, for instance in Kotelnikovo, which was considered a Cossack or semi-Cossack town, the Germans refrained from committing any major atrocities, though they did, in fact, nothing to endear themselves to the population—which they treated with much disdain. As regards "reforms", like abolishing the *kolkhozes*, they did not go beyond vague promises.

It was, roughly, the same in the Kuban country, except that here certain German officers established an experimental "Cossack District" with a population of about 160,000. All kinds of promises were made, including that of an early dissolution of the *kolkhozes*. Although Rosenberg's Ministry, as well as the SS objected to the experiment at first, the Army pursued it until the day in January 1943 when the Germans had to pull out of the Kuban.

> A local police force was recruited. By January 1943 the District's borders were to be expanded, and a Cossack Army commander was to be appointed... Far-reaching reforms were contemplated in agriculture, though, in practice, little was achieved. Other plans called for the recruitment of 25,000 Cossack volunteers to fight with the German Army, but again there was no time to implement them.*

The purpose of this "realistic" Army policy, was, as Alexander Dallin says, to secure as much cannon-fodder for the German Army as possible. He also argues that the experiment was intended to show that once "the Soviet population was given a chance to work out its own problems ... it was generally inclined to work more whole-heartedly with the Germans." He also notes that:

> When Kleist's army withdrew from the Kuban considerable numbers of Cossack refugees joined in the exodus, and by late 1943 more than 20,000 Cossacks—or rather men claiming to be Cossacks—were fighting in various German-sponsored formations.

* Alexander Dallin, *German Rule in Russia* (London, 1957), p. 300.

Even so, it is fairly clear from Mr Dallin's account that the great majority of the Cossack population on the Don, Kuban and Terek did not collaborate, and that many, indeed, offered passive and often active resistance to the Germans. Cossack partisan units were operating in many areas, and some took an active part in the liberation of Krasnodar in February. And even if the Germans succeeded in collecting 20,000 Cossacks—or pseudo-Cossacks—in a vast area of a few million people, the "achievement" can only be regarded as a relative failure. The very fact that many of these "Cossacks" only "claimed to be Cossacks" suggests that the number of real Cossacks of the Don, Kuban and Terek who joined the Germans was not large.

Over 100,000 Cossacks had been in the Red Army since the beginning of the war and some, like the famous Dovator Corps, which had harassed the Germans for weeks in the Battle of Moscow, had acquired almost legendary fame. Many thousands—among them most of the Dovator Corps—had died fighting the Germans. No doubt many Cossacks had mental reservations about the Soviet régime, but in the patriotic atmosphere of 1942 it would have been absurd of the Germans to expect much co-operation from the Cossacks, with their nationalist Russian traditions.

To expect a sinister émigré adventurer like General Krasnov, head of the "Central Cossack Office" in Berlin to win over the Cossacks and—in the words of another Cossack adventurer in German pay, Vasili Glazkov—"to recognise the Führer Adolf Hitler as the supreme dictator of the Cossack Nation" was naive, to say the least.

The few "Cossack" bands the Germans did scrape together for the German army were later to become notorious, especially in the Ukraine, for their acts of banditry. Which, in itself, was not, of course, entirely alien to certain Cossack traditions either.

The German courting of the Moslems in the Caucasus was part of Hitler's lunatic schemes for bringing Turkey into the war and for advancing from the Caucasus into the Middle East; Moslem fighting units were to be formed in the Caucasus and these were to take part in bringing the whole Middle East into the German orbit. On the other hand, Hitler appears to have treated with great scepticism Rosenberg's ideas about a "Berlin-Tbilisi Axis". In December 1942 he said:

> I don't know about the Georgians. They do not belong to the Turkic peoples. *I consider only the Moslems to be reliable...* I consider the formation of these battalions of purely Caucasian peoples as very risky, but I see no danger in the establishment of purely Moslem units... In spite of the declarations of Rosenberg and the military, I don't trust the Armenians either.*

The question whether the Georgians, Armenians and Azerbaijanis would have co-operated with the Germans never came to the test; all we know is that several divisions composed of these nationalities were formed in the autumn of 1942 to fight on the *Russian* side, though there were, of course, a number of émigrés—mostly Georgians—who had come to the Caucasus with the German Army and were waiting for the entry of the German troops into Baku, Tbilisi and Erevan.

But the Germans did make contact with some of the Moslem nationalities in the Northern Caucasus, as well as with the more-or-less Buddhist Kalmuks to the east of the Kuban. Their capital of Elista in the sparsely inhabited Kalmuk steppes was occupied by the Germans for about five months, and émigrés like the notorious Prince Tundutov were busy knocking together Kalmuk military units of sorts for the German Army. Towards the predominantly Moslem mountaineers of the Northern Caucasus—the Chechens, Ingushi, Karachai and Balkarians—the German Army adopted a "liberal" policy. Promises were made for the abolition of the *kolkhozes*; mosques and churches were to be reopened; requisitioned goods were to be paid for; and the confidence of the people was to be won by "model conduct", especially in respect of women. In the Karachai region a "Karachai National Committee" was set up. The same happened in the Kabardin-Balkar area, though the Moslem Balkars were more outspokenly pro-German than the mostly non-Moslem Kabardinians. Although the Germans did not penetrate far into the Chechen-Ingush ASSR (south of Grozny), these two peoples appear to have made no secret of their sympathy for the

* Quoted by Dallin, op. cit., p. 251.

Germans. They were to suffer for it later, like the peoples who had actually collaborated.

The high point of German-Karachai collaboration was the celebration of Bairam, the Moslem holiday, in Kislovodsk on October 11... High German officials were presented with precious gifts by the local committee. The Germans... pledged the early dissolution of the collective farms and announced the formation of a Karachai volunteer squadron of horsemen to fight with the German Army.

Similarly, on December 18:

The Kurman ceremonies were held at Nalchik, the seat of the local administration of the Kabardino-Balkar area. Again gifts were exchanged, with the local officials giving the Germans magnificent steeds and receiving in return Korans and captured weapons. Bräutigam (of the Rosenberg Ministry) made a public address about the lasting bonds of German friendship with the peoples of the Caucasus.*

Exactly a fortnight after this moving ceremony, the Germans abandoned Nalchik and were on the run.

The Germans apparently amassed only a very small number of soldiers from amongst their Moslem friends in the Caucasus, and the most active collaborators naturally followed the German Army in its retreat to the north. The grandiose scheme for the conquest of the Middle East with the help of the Caucasus mountaineers was off.

The Moslem nationalities whose representatives had fraternised with the Germans were to suffer for it. The "liquidation" of the Moslem areas was decreed by the Supreme Soviet on February 11, 1944. When I visited Kislovodsk, Nalchik, Vladikavkaz and other towns in the Northern Caucasus in 1946, people were still talking of the "liquidation" of the Chechens, Ingushi, Karachais and Balkars. In a few days the NKVD had herded everyone of these nationalities into railway carriages and packed them off "to the east". As a frightened and embittered Kabardinian told me at Nalchik: "It was a terrible business seeing them all—men, women and children— being sent off like this; but you *can* say it was a tremendously efficient piece of organisation—yes, terrifyingly efficient." "And

* Dallin, op. cit., pp. 246-7.

what about the Kabardinians?" I asked. "Well," he said, "we got away with a few bumps and bruises. Some of our people also did a few foolish things. One Kabardinian prince, who lived high up in the mountains, could think of nothing better than to send a superb white charger to Hitler personally."

In his "secret" report at the XXth Congress, Khrushchev was to refer to these mass deportations in the following terms:

> At the end of 1943... a decision was taken to deport all the Karachai... The same lot befell, in December 1943, the population of the Autonomous Kalmuk Republic. In March 1944 all the Chechen and Ingushi people were deported and their Autonomous Republic liquidated. In April 1944 all Balkars were deported to faraway places and the Kabardino-Balkar Republic was renamed Kabardinian Republic. The Ukrainians avoided this fate only because there were too many of them... Otherwise he (Stalin) would have deported them also.
>
> Not only no Marxist-Leninist but also no man of common sense can grasp how one can make whole nations responsible, including women, children, old people, Communists and Komsomols, and expose them to misery and suffering for the hostile acts of individual persons or groups of persons.*

These five nationalities—or what was left of them—were, indeed, allowed to return to their homes after Stalin's death. Khrushchev's indignation would perhaps have been more convincing if he had extended it to the fate of two other nationalities, the Crimean Tartars and the Volga Germans; for these were not allowed to return to their homes, either then or later.†

* *The Dethronement of Stalin* (*Manchester Guardian* reprint, 1956), p. 23.
† Perhaps there is something in the argument that the German boasts, in 1943, of having left a "fifth column" behind in the Caucasus in the shape of Germany's Moslem friends convinced the Kremlin that something drastic should be done about the "disloyal" nationalities. A particularly boastful article about Germany's "allies" in the Caucasus appeared in Goebbels's paper *Das Reich* of February 21, 1943 (cf. Dallin, op. cit., p. 251.)

PART SIX

1943: Year of Hard Victories— the Polish Tangle

Chapter I

AFTER STALINGRAD.—THE BIRTH OF "STALIN'S MILITARY GENIUS"

With the victory of Stalingrad the Soviet Union had won her Battle of Survival, and now the war entered an entirely new phase. Anxiety over the ultimate outcome of the war vanished almost completely; and there were even moments of excessive optimism and over-confidence, such as those after the Russian liberation of Kharkov in February. Less than a month later, Kharkov was again to be lost.

This setback acted as a reminder that, despite Stalingrad, the Germans were still far from finished, and that there was perhaps some justification, after all, for Churchill's forecast, made at the time of the Stalingrad victory, that the war might last till 1945—a forecast which greatly annoyed the Russians at the time. Nevertheless, nobody in Russia doubted any longer that ultimate victory was now a foregone conclusion; the only question was: "How long will it take?" And this was inevitably linked with the other question of what Britain and the United States were going to do.

There were moments of optimism, after Stalingrad, when soldiers would say that the Red Army could smash the Germans single-handed, and that Russia would therefore not need to "share the fruits of victory" with anybody. This line was to be discouraged by Stalin himself, who, on one occasion in 1943, bluntly declared that Russia could not win the war by herself.

In 1943, the official Russian attitude to Britain and America was

585

much better than it had been in 1942, when nervousness over the
ultimate outcome of the Battle of Stalingrad tended to produce outbursts of bad temper like the whole Hess affair. In 1943, victory—
though still distant—was already in sight, and it was important to
start making plans with Britain and America for a peace settlement.
Discussions which were, in the end, to lead to the Teheran Conference, had already begun. The Allied victories in North Africa were
being given considerable publicity in the Soviet press. Although this
was "not the Second Front yet", it was very far from negligible,
especially as it was certainly drawing away from the Russian front
at least part of the Luftwaffe, as was also the bombing of Germany.
But there were still to be many ups and downs in the Russian
appreciation of the Western war effort; the landing on "the island of
Sicily" was deliberately to be played down, though, later in the year,
maximum publicity was to be given to the fall of Mussolini.

Another factor which greatly contributed to a more friendly
attitude to the Allies was the very considerable increase, in the
course of 1943, of lend-lease supplies. If there was still very little
allied equipment in the Red Army at the time of Stalingrad, this was
no longer true. Not only were there many Western bomber and
fighter planes in the Russian air force, but everywhere in the Red
Army there were now hundreds of Dodges and Studebakers and
jeeps, and a considerable proportion of army rations was American
food. It gave rise to some wisecracks: thus, spam was invariably
referred to as "Second Front", and egg-powder used to be called
"Roosevelt's eggs" (*yaitsa* being the Russian word both for "eggs"
and "testicles"). But they were pleased to have it, all the same.

After Stalingrad, too, Soviet foreign policy became much more
active than it had been. In 1942, except for the "Second Front" and
"Hess" campaigns, the Soviet Government had avoided any major
unpleasantness with the world at large. There were occasional
criticisms of Turkey and Sweden, but these never assumed the
proportions of a "campaign"; the handling of Japan, then at war
with Britain and the United States, was exceedingly tactful and
cautious, as at least up to October the possibility of a Japanese stab-
in-the-back could not be entirely ruled out. Much more remarkable
was the great reticence, throughout 1942, in respect of the Polish

Government in London, and almost no publicity was given to the departure from Russia of the Anders Army.*

But, soon after Stalingrad, attitudes to foreign governments began to be more selective. Apart from Japan, to which the Russians remained formal but polite, a sharp line began to be drawn between good and bad governments. The Polish Government in London soon became the blackest sheep of all, and the campaign against it began in real earnest in February 1943, and soon led to the breaking off (or rather, "suspension") of diplomatic relations. This was followed by the formation of a Polish Army on Russian soil independent of the London Government. That this trouble with the Poles was going to create considerable complications with Britain and America could, of course, be foreseen; but the Russians tried—not unsuccessfully—to "localise" the quarrel, at least for a time. At Teheran, indeed, the Polish Problem was going to be as good as shelved.

On the other hand, the real friends of Russia were proclaimed to be the Czechs, the Yugoslavs and—the French. All three were represented by fighting units on the Russian Front, and the French Normandie Squadron was given particularly wide publicity. The Czech and Yugoslav token forces fitted well into the general pattern of the "All-Slav solidarity" propaganda; as for the French squadron, which fought gallantly throughout 1943, and was to suffer very heavy casualties, it symbolised, as it were, the solidarity between the Soviet Union and all the nations of occupied Europe—not only the Slav nations.

After Stalingrad the Russian attitude to Germany's satellites also changed sharply. The rout of the Rumanians and Italians in the Don country between November and January, and the terrible losses inflicted on the Hungarians at Kastornoye a little later, had struck a fearful blow at Hitler's Grand Coalition. Although, in 1941, Lozovsky at his press conferences, as well as the Russian press, used to ridicule Hitler's attempts to "make these people fight for him", it was well known that, numerically, at any rate, they represented a considerable contribution to Germany's armed strength, and there were times when both the Hungarians and the Rumanians had fought very well indeed. At Odessa, at Sebastopol, and in the

* See Part VI, Chapter 6.

Caucasus, the Rumanian troops had been of considerable help to the Germans.

Now, in a military sense, Hitler's Grand Coalition had as good as ceased to exist. There were still some hardened Hungarian troops, and the Finns; but the latter were a rather special case, since they were fighting their "own", "independent" war. In any case, as Mathias Rakosi, the Hungarian Communist leader, wrote in *Pravda* in February 1943, two-thirds of the Hungarian forces in the Soviet Union had been wiped out; there was a political crisis in Hungary; and the Government was already trying to "get out of the war". The Russians began to pay more and more attention to signs of rebellion against the Germans in the satellite countries.

In short, after Stalingrad the stage was set for a big Russian international game. Significantly, it was in 1943, only a few months after Stalingrad, that the Comintern, dormant for at least two years, was called upon to dissolve itself. This was an essential preliminary to the international policies on which Stalin and Molotov were now embarking.

The Stalingrad victory brought about a number of other changes. Whereas in 1941 and 1942 the whole emphasis in Soviet propaganda was on *Russia*, on the great *Russian* national heritage that was in danger, and so forth, after Stalingrad, the word *Soviet* came into its own again. More and more was made of the fact that a victory like Stalingrad was not just a question of "*Russian* guts"; these "guts" would have been quite helpless—as the 1914–18 war had shown— but for the stupendous *Soviet* organisation behind them. And who was the real backbone of this organisation but *the Party*?

Another development after Stalingrad was the systematic build-up of Stalin as a military genius. After Stalingrad, *but not before.*

We may here usefully look back a little. Russia, in terms of personal security and *habeas corpus*, had never been a comfortable place to live in, either under Lenin or under Stalin. The ruthless collectivization drive had brought about fearful hardships, but by 1936—the year of the "Stalin Constitution"—*zhit' stalo legche, zhit' stalo veselei*: life had become "easier and more cheerful". Stalin was taking the credit for it, and the vast propaganda machine of the Party had by now embarked on the "personality cult" in earnest. And there *was* a Five-Year Plan mystique in the country. Then came the Purges: in the Party, in the Army, among the intelligentsia. There were hundreds of thousands, perhaps millions, who were directly affected ("many thousands" of officers in the Red Army alone, Khrushchev said), and millions more who had lost relatives and friends in the Purges. "Thirty-seven"—the height of the Purges—became a fearful memory. And yet Stalin's personal prestige had been surprisingly little affected. There was a kind of obsession with "capitalist encirclement" and, above all, with Nazi Germany, and it seems that countless people believed, or half-believed that there could be no smoke without fire, and that there must have been "some" reason for the great public purge trials of Kamenev, Zinoviev, Rykov, Piatakov, Bukharin, Radek and the rest. In many minds, Trotsky had been built up into a diabolical figure with countless accomplices inside Russia. There were also many—including many of those arrested—who were genuinely convinced that much injustice was being done without Stalin's knowledge, and that it was the fault first of Yagoda and then of Yezhov. When the Purges more or less came to an end, and Yezhov vanished in 1939, to be replaced by Beria, the story was put about by Party propagandists, that Stalin himself had stopped the Purges.*

The glorification of Stalin—helped by better economic conditions, a sense of great industrial achievement and the feeling that Russia had become "invincible"—reached quite fantastic proportions in 1939. For Stalin's 60th birthday, Prokofiev wrote an exquisite piece of music, called *Ode to Stalin*, with incredible words like these:

> Never have our fertile fields such a harvest shown,
> Never have our villagers such contentment known.
> Never life has been so fair, spirits been so high,
> Never to the present day grew so green the rye.

* In reality the purges continued, though on a smaller scale, even in 1939. Kosarev, for example, head of the Komsomol for several years, was shot on Stalin's instructions, in March 1939, for having more or less openly protested about the earlier purges. This was revealed in *Pravda* in December 1963.

O'er the earth the rising sun sheds a warmer light,
Since it looked on Stalin's face it has grown more bright.
I am singing to my baby sleeping in my arm,
Grow like flowers in the meadow free from all alarm.
On your lips the name of Stalin will protect from harm.
You will learn the source of sunshine bathing all our land.
You will copy Stalin's portrait with your tiny hand.*

No doubt Prokofiev wrote the music to this with his tongue in his cheek, making the rapturous *kolkhozniks* sing some of their words in a C-major scale going up and down and up and down again; but he wrote it all the same.

Propaganda had also drummed into the people that the Soviet-German Pact had been an act of wisdom—or at any rate the least of all evils, and, for a time, there was undoubtedly some satisfaction at the thought that, with the occupation of Western Poland, the Baltic States and Bessarabia, Russia had virtually regained her old frontiers. At the same time, there was unquestionably a growing feeling of anxiety, especially after the rapid collapse of France and, even more, after the German invasion of Yugoslavia and Greece. Yet there was still the widespread feeling that Stalin—the boss, the *khoziain*—knew what he was doing.

Then came the Invasion which seemed at first like an apocalyptic kind of disaster. Millions wondered how "Great", "Wise" Stalin had allowed all this to happen. Had there not been some fearful miscalculations somewhere? It is said that Stalin lost his head at first, and even uttered in a moment of despair that—perhaps genuine—phrase about "the whole work of Lenin being destroyed." But if he felt desperate, he certainly did not show it—except once in a letter to Churchill in August 1941. His broadcast of July 3, for all its alarming undertones, had a reassuring effect on the country. The

* S. Prokofiev. *Zdravitsa* (*Ode to Stalin*). *For Chorus and Orchestra.* State Music Publishers, Moscow (1946 reprints of both orchestral score and piano score). It is not stated who was responsible for the English translation of the "folk texts", described as being of Russian, Ukrainian, Kurdish, Belorussian, Mariisk and Mordva origin. The rest of the libretto is at least as adulatory of Stalin as this short quotation.

general feeling among the people seems to have been that, for better or for worse, Stalin was *with them*, that he, like the country, had been let down, and that he was now asking for the country's confidence. And, since there was nowhere else to turn to, the people "accepted" Stalin's leadership.

In the first few months of the war—right up to the Moscow Victory—the references to Stalin in the press became much fewer and the pictures of him were now few and far between. But after the Moscow victory his prestige was again largely restored—though there were still a great many mental reservations about him, above all in Leningrad. Two points undoubtedly counted in his favour: first, that he had not lost his nerve on October 16, and had not fled from Moscow; and the idea that "Stalin had stayed with us" had a very important psychological effect on both the Moscow population and on the Army. Secondly, there was that Red Square parade on November 7 at which his Russian nationalist speech made a tremendous impression.* To the Army, Stalin became, more than before, something of a father-figure. And the soldiers *did* go into battle crying "*za rodinu, za Stalina*". Victor Nekrasov, the novelist, who did *not* like Stalin—for he had lost many of his friends in the Purges —told me in 1963 that he, too, had led his men into battle with that cry. Stalin, as he put it, had bungled things terribly at the beginning of the war; and yet, later, people instinctively felt that here was a man with nerves of steel, who, when things looked blackest of all, had pulled himself together and had not lost his head.

After the Battle of Moscow Stalin's stock went up and the poets began to sing his praises again. But by that time Stalin was willing to share the credit for the victory of Moscow with others, particularly with generals like Zhukov and Rokossovsky.

Then came the Black Summer of 1942. In a sense, Stalin's position was even more difficult then than it had been in 1941. His great argument in 1941 had been that a powerful army launching a surprise attack on a country, however strong, had an immense initial advantage. But now, in 1942, this argument no longer held good, except that Russia was still suffering economically from the "surprise attack". So when the black days came—first with Kerch,

* See pp. 247–9.

Kharkov and Sebastopol, and then with the German advance on
Stalingrad and the breakthrough to the Caucasus—explanations
were needed. As we have seen, scapegoats were found: first, the
Allies who had not started the Second Front, and secondly, the Army
itself. What was happening was not the fault of the Party, still less
of Stalin, but was due to lack of discipline in the Army, bad leadership, and so on.

There may well be very good reasons to suppose that the post-
Rostov army reforms, which began to work wonders, were in reality
much more the work of Zhukov and Vassilevsky than of Stalin, and
that things had come to such a pass that he had to agree to them
whether he liked them or not. But the credit for them was given to
Stalin. This, with his "not a step back" order, was built up into the
idea that all would be well now that Stalin had taken things in hand.

In view of Khrushchev's allegations in his "Secret Report" to the
XXth Congress that Stalin was a military ignoramus, and of the
comments of foreign observers that though he was polite to
foreigners he was extremely rude to Russians of whatever rank, it is
interesting to have Marshal Yeremenko's account of a Defence
Committee meeting in the first week of August 1942, just before
Stalingrad. Yeremenko had been in hospital, recovering from a leg
wound, when he was summoned to the Kremlin:

> Leaving my stick in the hall, I carefully but briskly entered the study
> of the Commander-in-Chief and Head of the State Defence Com-
> mittee... Standing at his desk, Joseph Vissarionovich had just finished
> a telephone conversation. Several other members of the Defence
> Committee were in the room.
> ... J. V. Stalin came up to me, shook hands, and closely looking at
> me said: "So you consider you are fit again?" "Yes, I have fully
> recovered," I replied.
> One of those present then said: "Looks as if his wound was still
> bothering him; he's limping badly." "Please don't worry," I said, "I
> am quite all right."
> "That's fine," said Stalin, "Let's consider that Comrade Yeremenko
> has fully recovered, and let's get down to business. We need you very
> badly."

... The Defence Committee was working on the measures to be taken for straightening things out in the Stalingrad area. The problem under discussion was the appointment of the commander to a new Front.

Summing up the discussions, J. V. Stalin turned to me:

"The situation at Stalingrad calls for urgent measures... The Defence Committee has decided to divide the Stalingrad Front into two distinct fronts, and to appoint you commander of one of them."

Yeremenko accepted the post, and Stalin then told him to go to the General Staff and study there all the necessary operational and organisational details, and to return in the evening with Vassilevsky, the Chief of Staff. The final decisions would be taken then.

Saying good-bye, Stalin then said: "Will you work out a schedule, so as to be able to leave for Stalingrad the day after tomorrow."

Yeremenko then relates how he spent the day at the General Staff and what he learned there about the very threatening outlook in the Stalingrad area.

In the evening I returned to the Commander-in-Chief. Here were also the Chief of Staff, General Vassilevsky, Major-General Ivanov, also of the General Staff, and General Golikov... After the usual welcome, J. V. Stalin ordered Comrade Vassilevsky to report on the draft decision about the new re-arrangement of the army groups.

While Comrades Vassilevsky and Ivanov were spreading out the maps, J. V. Stalin came up to me and feeling the two gold wound stripes on my tunic, remarked: "It was quite right to introduce these wound stripes. People should know those who have been shedding their blood fighting for the country..."

After Vassilevsky's clear and laconic report, there was a long discussion, in the course of which Yeremenko argued against the splitting of the Stalingrad Front in two, since the border between two fronts always tended to be vulnerable.

Having said my piece, I stopped, waiting for observations, if any. Rather to my surprise, and apparently to that of the others, Stalin reacted rather nervously to my suggestion. This nervousness may well have been caused by the telephone conversations he had just had, in our presence, with a number of fronts... We could feel that he was being given bad news, and that they were all asking for help. The situation was, indeed, very tense. Our troops were continuing to retreat. At that moment I could not help thinking of the great responsibility for the future of our country, of the fearful burden that had been placed on the shoulders of Joseph Vissarionovich, who was both head of the Government and Commander-in-Chief.

After a few minutes, Stalin said to Vasilevsky, with a touch of irritation:

"Let us stick to our decision. Cut the Stalingrad Front in two, with the river Tsaritsa . . . as the border-line."

There followed a discussion on how the new fronts were to be named; and when Yeremenko again asked for permission to speak, Stalin smiled, and now said very calmly: "Go ahead." Yeremenko then asked that he be appointed to the command of the South-East Front, i.e. to the right flank of the two army groups at Stalingrad, since it was from this area that the main blow could be struck at the Germans.

I added that my "soldier's heart" was more attuned to offensive than even to the most responsible defensive operations.

All those present carefully listened to me. Having stalked up and down the room, Stalin then said: "Your proposal deserves serious attention; but it's a matter for the future. Our present job is to stop the Germans."

Filling his pipe, he paused. I took advantage of this and said: "I mean the future, and I agree that now we must stop the Germans at any price."

"You understand the position correctly," said Stalin. "That is why we decided to send you to the South-East Front, where they are advancing from Kotelnikovo to Stalingrad. The new front must be built up quickly and along new lines. You have the necessary experience; you did it with the Briansk Front. So go off, or rather fly off, to Stalingrad tomorrow. . ." In concluding, Stalin stressed, as he turned to me, that it was essential to reinforce discipline among the troops, and to take the most drastic measures.

At 3 a.m. all questions were settled, and Stalin wished me military success. . . We all left filled with thoughts of our immense responsibility. . . .*

Although later, in 1963, Yeremenko joined in the fashionable game of criticising Stalin as a war leader, and made much of his

* A. I. Yeremenko. *Stalingrad* (Moscow, 1959), pp. 33–39.

"erroneous" decision to split the "Stalingrad Front" in two (a decision which, as we have seen, was to be reversed a few weeks later), several important points emerge from Yeremenko's 1959 description of his meeting with Stalin. First, that the Defence Committee was doing important *team* work, and that the "erroneous" decision about the Stalingrad Front may have been taken by others, and only endorsed by Stalin; second, that he had a good grasp of military affairs (an impression borne out by Churchill, Hopkins, Deane and many others); thirdly, that he and his team were in direct communication with the entire Front and had to take vitally important decisions every day; finally, that, despite moments of "nervousness" and "irritation", understandable in the highly critical atmosphere of August 1942, Stalin could be a good listener when his generals had anything to say. Nor does the Yeremenko story suggest that in the grim days of 1942 Stalin was either arrogant or overbearing; on the contrary, he could be both friendly and considerate. His closest associates in 1942 were, as we know, Zhukov and Vassilevsky, and it was they, in fact, who planned the Stalingrad counter-offensive—with Stalin's blessing.

This was made perfectly clear in the official announcements on the Stalingrad operations; and it was not till February 1943 that new phrases like "Stalinist strategy", the "Stalinist military school of thought" and even "the military genius of Stalin" first made their appearance in the Soviet press, and not least in the *Red Star*. What the military artisans of the victory of Stalingrad—men like Zhukov, Vassilevsky, Voronov and Rokossovsky—thought of this in private is anybody's guess. But these very first phrases in the Soviet press, soon after Stalingrad, about "Stalin's military genius" started a new process which was to lead to some curious and, in the end, some highly pernicious results.

The destruction of the German 6th Army at Stalingrad was part of a vast military plan, the "ideal" aim of which was to carry the Red Army along a wide front all the way to the Dnieper before the spring. Long before the Germans had capitulated at Stalingrad, the Russians were moving westwards in a number of places. But German resistance in the Don country and east of Rostov had stiffened very considerably since the beginning of January, and the plan for closing the "Rostov Gap" had failed. The Russians did not capture Rostov until the middle of February; and by this time the German forces in the Caucasus had either entrenched themselves on the Taman Peninsula, or had slipped through the Rostov Gap.*

Much more successful for the Russians—at least until the German counter-offensive began—were their operations in the Upper Don and East-Ukrainian areas. On January 26, Voronezh (now a heap of ruins) was liberated by troops of General Golikov's Voronezh Front, and the first half of February was marked by a quick succession of Russian victories. After their liberation of Voronezh, they inflicted a major rout on the Hungarian 2nd Army at Kastornoye, west of Voronezh—where, according to the Russians, over 100,000 Hungarians were killed or taken prisoner; German commentators do not deny that the Hungarians were virtually eliminated from the Eastern Front by the Kastornoye rout. Although in the south (i.e. north of the Sea of Azov) the Germans firmly held the Mius Line defending the southern part of the Donbas, the Russians were now on the move along a wide front in the north, between Voronezh and Boguchar, overrunning the Kursk province and penetrating into the North-Eastern Ukraine and the northern Donbas from the east and north-east. Valuiki, Lisychansk, Izyum and the great engineering centre of Kramatorsk (though now reduced to another heap of ruins) were recaptured during the first week of February, and, a few days later, Volchansk, Chuguyev and Lozovaya. On the 16th, after heavy fighting, Golikov's troops entered Kharkov, the fourth-largest city in the Soviet Union. Meantime, farther south, Vatutin's troops of the South-West Front liberated the great industrial centre of Voroshilovgrad, while Novocherkassk and Rostov were liberated by the troops of the Southern Front under Malinovsky.

After the capture of Kharkov, Golikov's and Vatutin's troops continued their advance, and, with the capture of Pavlograd on the 17th, the Russians were almost in sight of the Dnieper Line, barely

* See pp. 570 ff.

twenty miles to the west. It was at this stage that the Germans began preparing their counter-offensive, their "revenge for Stalingrad". In March, caught on the hop, the Russians were, indeed, going to lose some of the territory gained in the winter offensive, including Kharkov.

Between Stalingrad and the first indications of the coming German counter-offensive the mood in Russia was exuberant, and it was during this period that phrases like "Stalin's military genius" began to be used in the press. The prospect of recapturing the whole of the Donbas and reaching the Dnieper Line before the spring was alluring, and the capture of Kursk and Kharkov seemed to exceed even the rosiest hopes. The Soviet press was full of articles on the importance of recapturing the Donbas—which meant coal and steel. The tone of the press became even more exuberant after the liberation of Kharkov; *Red Star* wrote on February 16:

> The capture of Kharkov is ... another triumph of that Stalinist strategy which has already achieved so much during the past winter. Frantically the enemy clung on to Kharkov... The Germans tried to hold us on the Donets river ... but all the fortified lines were broken, one after another... Finally, the battle continued inside Kharkov itself, but here also those divisions with arrogant names like Grossdeutschland, Reich and Adolf Hitler were smashed... And now it is we, and not the Germans, who are going to plan the future course of the war.

Two days later, the same paper exalted the skill of the Red Army: not only had it liberated immense territories, but in doing so it had been constantly encircling and destroying the enemy; thus, the Italians had been encircled and routed at Millerovo and the Hungarians at Kastornoye, not to mention the Germans at Stalingrad. And again it referred to Cannae, "where Hannibal, with his 50,000 Carthaginians had routed 70,000 Romans." "Cannae" had become part of the Red Army's strategy. *Red Star* went on to say that all that had happened in the last months had finally shown that "the vaunted superiority of German military thought" had proved a myth, even though it was a myth that had even survived the 1914–18 war. Now "Stalinist strategy" was triumphant. It is significant that it was soon after the capture of Kharkov that Stalin assumed the rank and title of Marshal of the Soviet Union.

During these exuberant weeks of February 1943 more credit began to be given to the Communist Party than ever before. Here were the first signs of a renewal of the old tensions between "Party" and "Army", although, right to the end of the war the two continued to be identified with each other, rather than contrasted. The Party was, as it were, now living in the reflected glory of the Army, or was it *vice versa*, since the official propaganda now went out of its way to point out that all that was best in the Army was "Party"?

Thus, at the height of the rejoicing over Kharkov, *Red Star* wrote on February 19: ·

> The Party has thrown its best sons into the fray. How many times in moments of crisis, both at Moscow in 1941 and at Stalingrad in 1942, did the courage and toughness of Communists save the situation! The Party organisation is the real backbone of the Army. All the magnificent achievements of our Army are due to the fact that the Red Army's military doctrine is based on the well-tested principles of the wisest doctrine in the world—that of Marx, Engels, Lenin and Stalin.

In short, "innate Russian virtues" were indispensable, but they were merely the raw material with which the régime was forging victory. More and more, as the war approached a victorious conclusion, did the concept of "Soviet patriotism" take the place of "Russian patriotism" of the dark days of 1941–2. And Stalin was increasingly built up into the symbol of this Soviet patriotism.

It is, however, significant that Stalin never quite forgot the fearful days of 1941 and 1942, when he had to depend almost exclusively on specifically *Russian* nationalism to save the situation; and, at the end of the war, he singled out the *Russian* people as those whose determination to win the war and defend the Soviet State had been greatest of all.

Chapter II

THE GERMANS AND THE UKRAINE

Now that the Red Army had begun to drive the Germans out of the Soviet Union and, in particular, out of the Ukraine, we must look at German policy in the occupied areas—if it can be called a policy. For, in reality, this policy was a story of almost unrelieved bestiality, occasionally mixed up with the more farcical aspects of Nazi ideology.

Thus, as early as 16 July, 1941, Hitler had already decided that the Crimea was to become a purely German colony, from which all "foreigners" were to be deported or evacuated. It was to become the "German Gibraltar" in the Black Sea. To Robert Ley, Chief of the German Labour Front and the Strength Through Joy movement, it was to become a gigantic spa, a favourite playground for German youth. Later, Hitler also played with the idea of settling the South-Tyrolean problem with Mussolini by resettling in the Crimea the German-speaking inhabitants of the Italian part of the Tyrol.

After the fall of Sebastopol in July 1942, Manstein, "the Hero of the Crimea", was to be presented with one of the former Imperial palaces on the Crimean "Riviera". One of Rosenberg's more lunatic discoveries was that the Crimea was, "geo-politically", part of the Germanic heritage, since it was in the Crimea that the last Goths had survived as late as the 16th century. In December 1941 he had proposed to Hitler that the Crimea be renamed "Gotenland":

I told him that I had also worried about the renaming of the cities.

599

I thought of renaming Simferopol Gotenberg, and Sebastopol Theo-
dorichhafen. . . *

In reality, whatever Hitler's post-war plans were, it was awkward,
while the war was still on, to proceed with a total evacuation of all
"foreigners" (i.e. non-Germans) from the Crimea, especially as the
Crimean Tartars were not only gladly collaborating with the Germans, but were actually supplying the Wehrmacht with a certain
number of soldiers.

But the Crimea was still a minor sideshow, compared with the
Ukraine. This was an immense territory with nearly forty million
inhabitants before the war, a proverbial "bread-basket", and a
source of coal, iron ore and steel.

It would be idle to deal here in detail with all the conflicting
policies that existed amongst the Nazi hierarchy in respect of the
Ukraine. Rosenberg clearly tried to distinguish at first between the
"evil" Great-Russians and the Ukrainians who could be used as a
bulwark against the Russians. Early in 1941 Rosenberg argued, in
his usual insane way, that Kiev had been the centre of the
Varangian State, which accounted for the strongly Nordic and
superior racial features of the Ukrainian people.

Then, in May, he drafted instructions for the future German rule
in the Ukraine. Retreating slightly from his goal of immediate state-
hood, he now envisaged two stages: during the war, the Ukraine was
to provide the Reich with goods and raw materials; after that "a free
Ukrainian state in closest alliance with the German Reich" would
assure German influence in the east:

> To attain these goals, one problem . . . must be attacked as rapidly
> as possible: Ukrainian writers, scholars and politicians must be put to
> work to revive an Ukrainian historical consciousness, so as to over-
> come what Bolshevik-Jewish pressure has destroyed in Ukrainian
> *Volkstum* in these years.

A new "great University" in Kiev, technical academies, extensive
German lecture tours, the elimination of the Russian language and
the intensive propagation of German language and culture were
integral parts of this programme. He spoke in terms of extending the

* Dallin, op. cit., pp. 254–5.

future "Ukrainian State" all the way from Lwow to Saratov on the Volga.*

This seemingly "liberal" Rosenberg Plan, as well as all its subsequent variants, met with no favour from Hitler, Goering, Himmler or, for that matter, Erich Koch, Reichskommissar for the Ukraine, who pointedly set up his headquarters in the provincial town of Rovno, and not in Kiev, which was not to be given even the semblance of a "capital". The various émigrés, who had been hanging round Rosenberg for years, such as the senile Skoropadsky, who had been the German-appointed Hetman of the Ukraine back in 1918, were not taken seriously by any of the top Nazis—except by Rosenberg himself. Even Bandera, the ferociously anti-Polish and anti-Jewish Ukrainian "nationalist" leader in the Western Ukraine, was arrested by the Germans at the beginning of the war, and sent to Berlin, where he was interned till 1944 when the hard-pressed Germans decided that he might still have his uses. Meantime Galicia (i.e. the Western Ukraine) was simply incorporated in the German-ruled Government-General of Poland. Melnik, another Ukrainian nationalist leader, was no luckier than Bandera.

To Hitler, to Goering, to Himmler and to Erich Koch the Ukrainians were *Untermenschen*, just like the Russians. Goering is quoted as having said: "The best thing would be to kill all men in the Ukraine . . . and then to send in the SS stallions.†

He also cheerfully envisaged the possibility in 1941 of twenty or thirty million people dying of hunger in Russia during the following year. Koch, a representative of the most extreme *Untermensch* school of thought, was appointed overlord of the Ukraine at Goering's insistence.

For a short time after the German occupation of the Ukraine a small number of Ukrainian "nationalists" still tried to make their voice heard, especially in parts of the Ukraine, such as Kharkov, still nominally under the jurisdiction of the Army and not of Koch. But they received no serious encouragement from anybody.

The Ukraine was, to the Germans, first and foremost a source of food; secondly, of coal, iron and other minerals; and thirdly, of slave labour.

* Dallin, op. cit., pp. 108–9.   † Dallin, op. cit., p. 123.

Yet, the agricultural deliveries from the Ukraine turned out much smaller than the Germans had budgeted for, while the German attempts to revive the Donbas, Krivoi Rog and other industrial areas, was to prove a complete failure; the Germans actually had to send coal to the Ukraine from Germany! Both in agriculture and industry they met with great passive resistance; moreover, agriculture was short of machinery, and the Germans had to export certain quantities of such machinery to the Ukraine; the industrial plants had largely been evacuated to the east, and in those coal and iron ore mines which had not been put out of action by the retreating Russians, there was both a shortage of skilled labour (many of the miners having been evacuated) and various kinds of passive resistance from the miners who were still there.

According to German statistics, non-agricultural deliveries from the east (i.e. from *all* the occupied Soviet territories, and not just the Ukraine) totalled 725 m. marks' worth; these were offset by an export of 535 m. marks' worth of equipment and coal to the east, thus leaving a net profit of 190 m. marks! To this should be added various local deliveries to the German Army, estimated at 500 m. marks; but even so, the total balance remains unimpressive. According to Dallin's calculations, based on the available German statistics, and even including the east's agricultural deliveries, "the contributions of the occupied east to the Reich . . . amounted to only one-seventh of what the Reich obtained during the war from France!"*

Even if the greater part of what the Germans got out of the occupied Soviet territories came from the Ukraine, that enormous and wealthy country cannot have supplied to the Reich more than one-tenth of what the Germans had pumped out of France. The desire for even plain economic collaboration was lacking.

For two things characterised the German occupation of the Ukraine: the massacre of the Jews, and the deportation of millions of young Ukrainians to Germany as slave labour.

Even assuming that industrial production in the Donbas, Krivoi Rog and Zaporozhie could be made to work (and the "proletariat", or what was left of it was even more anti-German than the rest of the Ukrainian population) any such possibility was made even more

* Dallin, op. cit., p. 407.

remote by Sauckel's policy of draining all industry in the east of its manpower and deporting it to Germany.

The deportation of slave labour from the Ukraine began in a big way as early as February 1942.

We shall have to return to the topic of German occupation policy and methods in Soviet territories, and in the Ukraine in particular. But here is a sample of what they looked like in purely human terms. It is an account of my visit to the great city of Kharkov after its first—and only brief—liberation by the Russians in February 1943, at the height of the post-Stalingrad offensive.

Chapter III

KHARKOV UNDER THE GERMANS

There was some argument before the war whether Kharkov was the third-largest or only the fourth-largest city in the Soviet Union; according to some figures, it had just a few thousand more inhabitants than Kiev. But be that as it may, Kharkov was, in February 1943, the first city with a population of nearly a million to be liberated from the Germans, and this, in itself, was extraordinarily interesting. How had such a city lived under the Germans for a year and a half?

Before the war, it had been a great industrial city, but practically all its heavy industry had been evacuated in the autumn of 1941; ethnically, it was predominantly Ukrainian, but nearly a third of the population were Russians.

When I went there in February 1943 the Russian liberation of Kharkov was still highly precarious; the Red Army's communication lines were long and very bad, and the danger of a German counter-offensive could not be ruled out. The high spirits among the Russian soldiers noticeably declined even during the three days I was there.

The German occupation of Kharkov (which was in the Military Zone, and not under the authority of Erich Koch) was marked by the following features:

Acute hunger among civilians, especially during the first winter of the occupation;

Terror, especially against suspected Soviet sympathisers;

Extermination of the Jews;

The toleration of a Black Market, in which the German soldiers played a very active part;

No encouragement given by the German authorities to any Ukrainian nationalist movements, but, at the same time, a readiness to sow discord between Ukrainians and Russians;

The stamping out of Russian and Ukrainian cultural life, and the abolition of all education, except some elementary schools;

A certain encouragement to the artisans and to shopkeepers, but only the most half-hearted attempt, by German Big Business, to revive Kharkov as a great industrial centre;

A readiness on the part of some of the Ukrainian *petite bourgeoisie* (artisan and shopkeeper types) to adapt themselves as best they could to a difficult situation, and, above all, to survive;

Acute resentment against the Germans because of the deportation of so many of the younger people as slave labour to Germany;

The existence of a Soviet underground, and a widespread anti-German feeling in the city, above all among children and adolescents deprived of their education;

What "local government" there was—the Ukrainian Burgomaster and his town council—was completely under the thumb of the German military authorities. The Burgomaster, Alexander Semënenko, who followed the Germans when they left, and then returned with them in March 1943, was later, in 1944, to play a minor part in Berlin in the various attempts to set up an Ukrainian National Committee.

That evening, a few days after the Russians had entered Kharkov, the front was still only a very short distance away; and for half-an-hour before landing our plane had been flying under fighter escort.

It was thawing. The large blocks of houses near the airfield had all been burned out. A wrecked Heinkel was lying on the airfield; but here also were half-a-dozen Russian fighter planes—not wrecked, but very much alive. Two of them had just escorted us here. But the airfield was in a mess; all hangars gone, and all the other buildings gone. A young air force sergeant, shaking his head, remarked:

"We're in a real jam here. With this thaw, communications have gone to hell, and we even have to fly the petrol here... Before leaving, they wrecked everything at this airfield. They also caused great damage to Kharkov with their air-raid the day after they were thrown out..."

It was a long way from the airfield to Kharkov. Most of the larger buildings on the way had been burned out, though the small cottages with their vegetable gardens were standing. We stopped at one of these cottages which had been turned into an air force officers' mess. Our host was a handsome air force colonel with a fair beard, Neomtevich by name, who had distinguished himself in many battles, and had started fighting back in 1941, in Belorussia.

"What a wollop we got from the Germans then!" he remarked. "They were really expecting us to give up the ghost; and, I can tell you: it *was* a job keeping the show going. Now we are doing well, but not nearly as well as we should like to. It's all very well talking about 'Kiev next month'. No; we've got to regroup. Our communications are absurdly long, and very bad indeed. Our nearest railway that's functioning is over sixty-five miles away. The Germans have certainly buggered up the railway; and you should see what they've done to Kharkov railway station—a mountain of wreckage which will take weeks to clear..."

He was not at all optimistic about the immediate prospects of the Russian offensive; he thought it had come near the end of its tether, and after three months' continuous fighting the Russian soldiers were physically exhausted. "As it is," he said, "we are living mostly on 'trophy' food; with so few roads, our supplies have gone to pot. Not that this selection is bad," he added, pointing at the table and pouring me out a glass of reasonably good *mousseux*. The wine was French or Hungarian, the sardines Portuguese; there were chocolates from Vienna and pickled lemons, probably from Italy. "At Valuiki," he said, "we captured an enormous food dump. My men and I just stacked a couple of tons into planes, and brought it here."

"The Ukrainian Government," he said, "arrived in Kharkov yesterday. They intend to set up the Ukrainian capital here, till Kiev is liberated." Then he made a face. "Don't know that it's a good idea," he added. "Maybe they're in too great a hurry..."

After sampling some of this produce of Hitler's New Order, we drove on. Kharkov seemed endless; we drove for miles through suburban and town areas before we reached the centre of the city, marked by the high tower of an onion-domed church, and, further to the left, high up on the hill, by an agglomeration of fourteen- or sixteen-storey skyscrapers built during a brief constructivist period in the late '20's. These were the skyscrapers of Dzerzhinsky Square. But, as we were to discover the next day, most of them had been burned out by the Germans before they left, and only two—which had housed some of the central industrial administration of the Ukraine—were still intact, except that the Germans had mined them before leaving.

We were put up in a small well-built house in the residential and almost undamaged part of Sumskaya Street, the main street of Kharkov. The house was guarded by half-a-dozen tough soldiers with pistols and tommyguns. Kharkov was still considered far from safe as there might be many German spies and agents around. These soldiers belonged to General Zaitsev's division, which had been the first to break into Kharkov, and were very pleased with themselves.

The house, like most houses in Kharkov, had neither electricity nor water. We had to live by candle-light, and water was brought from somewhere in pails.

There had been 900,000 people in Kharkov before the war, but when the war spread to the Ukraine, and the refugees started pouring in from the west, this figure swelled to 1,200,000 or 1,300,000. Later, in October 1941, with the Germans approaching, the evacuation of Kharkov began in real earnest. Most of the larger plants were more or less successfully evacuated, among them the great Tractor Plant, with nearly all its workers. By the time the Germans came, some 700,000 people were left in the city. Now there were only 350,000. What had happened to the rest?

According to the Russian authorities, the disappearance of half the population of October 1941 is accounted for as follows: it has been established that 120,000 people, mostly young people, had been deported as slaves to Germany; some 70,000 or 80,000 had died of hunger, cold and privation, especially during the terrible winter of 1941–2; some 30,000 had been killed by the Germans, among them some 16,000 Jews (men, women and children) who had remained behind in Kharkov; the rest had fled to the villages. Various checks I made in the next few days suggested that the figure for deaths from hunger, et cetera, was slightly, but not greatly, exaggerated; so too was that for non-Jews shot, but the figure for the Jews was correct. On the other hand, the figure for slave-labour deportations was, if anything, an under-estimate.

The next day the lime-trees and poplars in Sumskaya Street were white with hoar-frost. Poplars! This was the Ukraine, the south, two-thirds of the way from Moscow to the sea. Everywhere there were still German notice-boards: *Parken Verboten*, and this *verboten* and that *verboten*. The street signs were in German, too, and on one house was the ominous notice-board "*Arbeitsbehörde Charkow*". This was where they mobilised people to be sent to Germany.

In Dzerzhinsky Square, with its enormous burned-out or mined skyscrapers, there were large crowds of people; most of them were shabby, undernourished, haggard, and with a look of great nervous strain. Only the crowds of young boys looked normal; and they were lively and talkative. But, looking at the adults, one could readily believe that many thousands had died of undernourishment—even here, in this rich part of the Ukraine.

These people in the streets of Kharkov were enormously talkative; one felt that all of them wanted to tell some story. I remember, for instance, a misshapen, very sick-looking little man. He said he was arrested soon after the Germans came; they kept him locked up at the International Hotel (now burned out) in this very square, and they kept him there, almost without food, for a fortnight. Then he was released. But it had been a harrowing experience; because every night he could hear people being taken away to be shot; many of them were communists who had been denounced to the Germans. He had been an optician before the war; in the end, he got a job

from the Germans in the big Kharkov electrical plant, which a big
German concern had taken over; but since the Russians had
evacuated all the machinery, the Germans had had to bring their
own, and never employed more than 2,500 workers there, as against
25,000 before the war. Once a day there was a hot meal, and the
bread ration was 11 ounces. "The pay," he said, "was supposed to
be one rouble seventy kopeks an hour, but at the end of a fortnight
I went to collect my wages, and the German clerk handed me
seventy-five roubles. When I objected, the German said: 'There were
taxes to deduct, and you can take it or leave it; and another word
from you, and you'll get your face knocked in.' Finally I couldn't
stand it any longer, and the Germans let me go, because I was a
sick man." Later he made a meagre living by selling spectacles in
the market.

It was clear that thousands of people had managed to keep body
and soul together by selling and buying in the black market; people
with jobs, people without jobs—all had to do it. "If you had money,"
one woman said, "you could buy anything you wanted from the
German soldiers. They had wrist-watches by the dozen. They'd take
them off people in the street, and then sell them in the market."
"And not only wrist-watches," another woman joined in, "In broad
daylight my daughter was stopped by a German soldier; he had
taken a fancy to her shoes, and ordered her to take them off. He sold
them in the market, or sent them home." "Your daughter was
lucky," said the little man, "or else she must be very ugly. They
would often compel girls to follow them." Many of those standing
around shouted that that was true, and, worse still, many girls were
forced into army brothels; they'd just go and pick up the good-
looking ones in a queue at the *Arbeitsamt*. And, of course, there was
now a lot of v.d. in the city. . .

Then people talked about the hangings. Public hangings. It was
that which seemed to have left the deepest impression of all. At the
corner of Sumskaya and Dzerzhinsky Square there was a large
burned-out building which had been the Gestapo headquarters. Now
several women told excitedly how in November 1941 the population
was summoned to the square to hear a German announcement; and
when a crowd had gathered, several people inside the Gestapo

building were thrown over the balconies, with ropes tied round their necks, and the other end tied to the balcony rail. That day many people were hanged in many parts of Kharkov. There were quite a lot of traitors, who had denounced these Reds to the Germans. . .

Two or three other women talked about how the children had become undisciplined and demoralised. The schools had been closed, and little boys had to beg in the street, or else they'd have little handcarts and carry the German soldiers' kit, and luggage, and black-market packages, and earn a few roubles that way. "Half the people," one pale-faced woman said, "expected their small children to work for themselves. . . Small children, hungry, having to fend for themselves; have you heard anything like it? Under Stalin children get the best of everything, but not under these German swine. And now a lot of them will be good-for-nothings, thieves and little hooligans. But then how could you help it, with bread costing 150 roubles a kilo in the black market?"

I then got into conversation with a man called Cherepakhin, a working-class type who claimed to have been in the Communist underground during the occupation, and told many harrowing stories about the Gestapo. "It may be un-Marxist to say so," he said, "but the Germans *are* a bad lot—practically every one of them. If there are exceptions, I haven't come across any." But he had met some Italians in Kharkov, and they were really quite different from the Germans. They hated the Germans, and he was sure the Italians would soon get out of the war. "A lot of these Italians were really decent chaps," he said. "I managed to get a set of guitar strings for one of them, and he asked me, on the quiet, to the house where he and a number of other Italians were living; and there they would curse Hitler, and play the guitar and sing. They had little to eat, but they gave me some nice wine from a straw-covered bottle. Good chaps. But they were miserable, and they hadn't even any proper shoes, and suffered from the cold. I also talked to a lot of Hungarians; and although a lot of them are thieves and black-marketeers, most of them were good fellows at heart, and hated the Germans."

"There was no love lost between the Germans and their allies," Cherepakhin said. "Only Germans were admitted into the principal restaurants in Kharkov—not their so-called Allies."

He then told me how the Germans discriminated between the Russians and the Ukrainians; many Ukrainians served in the local police—many of them were more or less forced into it. Somehow, the Germans preferred Ukrainians to Russians, though, in reality, most of the Ukrainians hated them as much as the Russians did; even the Ukrainian nationalists, who thought they'd have a wonderful time under the Germans, were soon going to be disappointed.

I happened to talk to one of them in the street that day. He was an elderly man with a small red nose, and round face, and wore a shabby coat and frayed grey flannel trousers, and shoes that were split on the sides. He said he had taken a job on the town council, but had found it didn't pay. The Germans paid him only 400 roubles a month, and he had a wife and child to keep, and he couldn't live on that. So he took to black-marketing, too. He would travel beyond Poltava, and bring bags of flour to Kharkov. As we passed a new picture of Stalin and another of Voroshilov stuck up on a bombed wall, he gave a faint shrug. "The Germans certainly made a mess of things," he said. "They promised us a New Europe, but then everything went wrong." Maybe, he said, the Germans would come back, but that would no longer do any good to anybody. They'd missed their chance. Even this little collaborator had received mighty little satisfaction from the Germans... He had wanted one of his brothers in France and another in Yugoslavia to "come home" to Kharkov, but now it was useless.

Of course, there were people, especially of the artisan and shopkeeper class who, without being "unpatriotic", had tried to adapt themselves as best they could to the German occupation.

One such citizen was the lady barber who used to come in the mornings to shave us and the Red Army officers living in the same house. With her came her "assistant", a pretty boy of fifteen with blue eyes and long eyelashes. He was much more anti-German than she was. He told the familiar story of how the Germans used to hang people from balconies; and one day he saw—this was early in the Occupation—how they marched fifteen Red Navy sailors through the streets. Hitler had said, the boy declared, that Bolshevik sailors were not to be shot, but drowned. They were manacled, and as they were being led along, there were crowds of people on either side of the street, weeping. The sailors sang the song of the Black Sea Fleet, *Raskinulos' more shiroko*. And still weeping, people joined in the song. "The Germans," the boy said, "took them handcuffed to the river, and there they drowned them. I didn't see it myself, but others told me. . ."

"The kids in Kharkov," the boy went on, "used to sing a song, and the Germans got furious whenever they heard it—

> Doloi tserkov, doloi khram,
> Doloi Hitlera trista gram,
> Davai kluby i kino
> Davai stalinskoye kilo.*

He also told me how they took 16,000 Jews, kids and grand-mothers and all, to the brick-works outside the town and there after a fortnight in a camp, they killed the lot; they also sent thousands and thousands of people to Germany—pushed them into railway carriages like a lot of cattle.

The buxom young lady barber, with rouge, lipstick, manicure and perm, and now wearing a red beret and a white overall, admitted that she had lived better than most people under the Occupation. She had worked in a barber's shop near the main railway station, paying fifty per cent of the takings to her Ukrainian boss. It was a small place, but very busy. The boss was a good man; she didn't know what he was doing now. The barber's shop had been destroyed the week before, along with the railway station and all the surrounding buildings. She was as talkative as barbers are. "Germans or no Germans," she said, "one's got to live. With a ration of 11 ounces of bread, you just couldn't do it. I've got a child of four, and my husband has been away for over three years. And the prices in the market were just awful—130 or 150 roubles a kilo of bread. You should have seen how happy people were last May, when they thought the Red Army was returning. But it didn't, and I had to go on with my job in the barber's shop. A lot of the Germans, I must

> * To hell with the church,
> To hell with the cathedral,
> To hell with Hitler's 300 grammes;
> Let's have workers' clubs and cinemas,
> And Stalin's kilogram (of bread).

say, were quite nice people. There was a major who, for a long time, used to come in for a shave every day, and once or twice I cut him slightly, and I'd say: '*Ach, entschuldigen sie bitte, Herr Major!*' and he'd laugh and say: '*Ach, das tut nichts.*' And the German officers certainly tipped very well. The face-cream, the eau de Cologne and the powder we'd buy from German soldiers in the black market. . . Of course, awful things used to happen. All those hangings; made one ill for days. . . And it was awful about the Jews, too. They'd drive them in an endless procession through the streets, many of them pushing wheelbarrows or prams with babies inside, and they'd all weep and wail. I could understand their wanting to send the Jews away somewhere—but to kill them all in this awful way, that was going a bit far, don't you think?" Then she said: "Yes, the Germans can be very cruel people. But some were nice. And some of the officers were quite crazy about our women; positively sentimental. . . But then our women are so much more attractive than German women. And these German women were certainly bitches. They behaved as if the place belonged to them. There were hundreds of them here. The best flats were commandeered for German families, and they and some Ukrainians would open shops and restaurants. . . If any Russian had a decent flat, he was sure to be thrown out. . ."

I also heard something of the tragi-comedy of the Ukrainian nationalists. When the Germans first came to Kharkov, a bunch of Ukrainian nationalists started a newspaper called *Nova Ukraina*. On the face of it, there wasn't a single known person among the contributors; they wrote under pseudonyms. The principal writer signed "Petro Sagaidashny"—the name of an old Ukrainian hero. He was head of a self-appointed Ukrainian Propaganda Department, and, for a short time, the Germans patronised these people. But two months later, several of the ringleaders were shot by the Germans themselves. To the survivors the Germans made it quite clear that *they* were the bosses. This was rubbed in in a thousand different ways: for example, all sign-posts and street-names were written in German first and only then (and not always) in Ukrainian. Although an Ukrainian operetta was performed at the theatre the programmes were printed in German only.

A professor of the Kharkov Technical Institute, Kramarenko, who became burgomaster of one of the Kharkov districts, at first conducted a strong pro-German campaign; he made speeches in favour of developing a "Ukrainian national consciousness". Then, when he and his friends realised that the Germans were not interested in Ukrainian independence or autonomy, they rebelled; Kramarenko was dismissed from his post and shot soon afterwards.

Lubchenko and other Ukrainian intellectuals who ran the *Nova Ukraina* paper also soon realised that they were kidding themselves; it was the last straw when, in March 1942, the Germans ordered them to remove from the front page of the paper the Hetman's Trident, a token of Ukrainian autonomy or independence. For even if Rosenberg's *Ostministerium* was sympathetic to such Ukrainian ambitions, it had very little influence either with the military authorities in the Eastern Ukraine, or with Erich Koch in the Western and Central Ukraine; since the beginning of 1942, when the Ukraine began to be treated first and foremost as a reservoir of slave labour, there could no longer be any doubt about dominant German attitude to the Ukraine.

The fact that, in some of the surviving elementary schools pictures were displayed not only of Hitler but also of "Hetman" Petlura, who had been assassinated by a Jew in Paris in 1928, could be considered no more than a piece of primitive anti-semitic propaganda. It did not imply any promise of Ukrainian autonomy or independence.

To the German Army, the Ukraine was colonial territory in which the position of Ukrainian adolescents, who eked out a meagre living by carrying the Germans' luggage, was rather like that of young Arabs in Algiers in the heyday of French colonialism. The very young, who had benefited most from the Soviet régime, were among the most fanatical anti-Germans, and there was also no getting away from the fact that millions of Ukrainians were on the "other" side— fighting in the Red Army, or working in the Soviet war industries.

But to the German soldiery Kharkov was something of a metropolis, and here many of them were having a good time. The theatres were patronised chiefly by Germans and the programmes were arranged accordingly. They had Viennese operettas, grand opera (*Aïda* and *Don Quixote*) and, frequently, a *Grosses Wagner Konzert*. Most of the performers were German or Austrian. There were many restaurants, cafés and brothels; and whole German families had come here to open businesses. Some local inhabitants also managed to get licences for small shops and booths, and a number of Armenians had opened restaurants and night-clubs in various parts of the city. The occupation, clearly, had its profiteers—and they were not all Germans.

It was part of the German policy in the Ukraine to wipe out the intellectuals. The Ukrainian nationalists were treated badly enough; but even worse was the fate of those whom the Germans thought pro-Soviet. I saw several professors and teachers of Kharkov University and of some of the thirty-five technical and other colleges that had existed here under the Soviets. These men had survived the occupation; but many of their colleagues had died. Some had been shot, either because they were Jews or were Party members, or suspected of being Party members; some had committed suicide. Others had died of starvation, especially in the winter of 1941–2. Several university buildings were destroyed by the Germans before they left; but even while they were here, they had looted the libraries and the laboratories. The teachers who had survived had lived from hand to mouth, making home-made matches or soap, and selling them in the black market. Except for a few small laboratories, all higher education had been closed down; so had all the 137 secondary schools of Kharkov; only twenty-three elementary schools had been allowed to open under the Germans. Hospitals had either been taken over by the German army, or had come almost completely to a standstill owing to lack of food and medical supplies. One story—hard to verify—was that there was one flourishing school, in which the Germans trained adolescents as spies—not only Ukrainians, but even some Jewish children, who were to act as *agents provocateurs*.

There was no constructive planning to speak of. Everything in the Ukraine was being more or less destroyed and dissolved, with nothing to take its place. Local administration was run by Germans, or Ukrainian adventurers, or a few White émigrés, usually with no understanding or experience. The Ukraine was nothing but a source of food, raw materials and slave labour, and the raw materials and food were not produced in the quantities the Germans had hoped for. The Soviet scorched earth policy in the industrial areas had created immense difficulties for the Germans from the outset; labour willing to work for them was short, and, in the Donbas in 1943 they were reduced to turning tens of thousands of Soviet war prisoners into improvised miners.

Nor was the return of the Russians an occasion for unanimous rejoicing in Kharkov. I saw two large letter-boxes marked U.N.K.V.D.—the Ukrainian Security Police—into which people were invited to drop denunciations and other relevant information. Here was scope for some ugly vendettas. And at the former Gestapo prison, now burned out, I could see civilian prisoners being escorted into the basement for questioning by the NKVD. Scared relatives were hanging about the prison, some of them with parcels of food.

The atmosphere in Kharkov was becoming more and more depressing during those three days. There was no further mention of the Ukrainian Government being there. Had they already left? For there were more and more rumours of a great German counter-offensive having started—and this was soon to be officially confirmed. The railway to Kharkov had not been restored and an early thaw had set in, which made the Russian soldiers shake their heads. Kharkov was as good as cut off from the Russian rear.

True, the Russians were re-opening schools and hospitals in a small way, and tearing down German street signs; but, with every hour, the feeling of uneasiness grew.

*

It was a harrowing experience to go to the main market on my third afternoon. Most of the trading was over. But at one stall they were still selling little glasses of millet or sunflower seed, and, at another, battered tubes of German toothpaste or tins of shoe-polish, and primitive lighters made of aluminium scrap, and selling at sixty roubles apiece. All the same there were still large crowds in the market, dismally eyeing this junk. Among them were many soldiers. The women behind the stalls looked shabby, worried, under-fed.

Then I noticed two weird ghost-like figures in terrible rags. I remember one of them particularly: he had a long face that was nothing but bone and a dirty-white skin, and long red stubble grew from his chin; his eyes were blue and enormous and in them was a look of helpless suffering; his lips were parched and cracked, and his breath smelled of death. The rags he was wearing were the remains of a discarded Italian uniform. He was a Smolensk peasant, and had been captured by the Germans at Millerovo in the summer of 1942. He and the other man had come from a war prisoners' camp in a place called Sobachi Pitomnik, or Dog Farm. For months they had lived there on starvation rations, and most of their pals had died. Now when the Russians had come, they had been let out, but had to go back to the camp every night. Nobody was taking care of them, and they had wandered about Kharkov, looking for food. No one in the market had given them anything, and the military were treating them with suspicion.

This widespread callousness was another product of the German occupation, plus the NKVD. For to the Russian authorities, they had surrendered to the Germans, and could not be treated as deserving cases before closer investigation. One Russian soldier remarked: "Don't you get het up about them. For all we know, they may have been left here by the Germans as spies or diversionists." "They don't look like it, do they?" "Maybe not," he replied, "But one can't be too careful these days. The NKVD had better find out who they are. And anyway," he added, "there are plenty of other things to worry about. . ."

These Russian war prisoners could still have been saved by their own people; but they weren't. No doubt, conditions in Kharkov that afternoon were exceptional, but still the harrowing episode made one think of the whole ghastly tragedy of Russian war prisoners.

The soldiers in our house that night were no longer as cheerful as they had been. The Germans, they said, were attacking strongly at Kramatorsk and elsewhere west of Kharkov, and large numbers of wounded had started pouring into the town. These wounded were saying that the SS Panzer divisions were attacking in great strength.

We left Kharkov the next day, with a feeling of foreboding. The Germans returned, not at once but over a fortnight later, on March 15. One of the first things the SS did was to butcher 200 wounded in a hospital, and set fire to the building.

This recapture of Kharkov was their "revenge for Stalingrad"; but it was only a relatively small revenge. The early thaw, which had caught the Russians on the hop, and had forced the Soviet High Command to abandon Kharkov, was now beginning to work in the Russians' favour. The ice on the Donets had become so thin that the German tanks could no longer cross it, and the Russians had by now dug in along the Donets line. Here the front became more or less stabilised till July.

Chapter IV

THE ECONOMIC EFFORT OF 1942-3—
THE RED ARMY'S NEW LOOK—
LEND-LEASE

The Red Army of 1943 was very unlike the Red Army of 1941 or even 1942. We have already described the post-Rostov reforms to smarten up the officer corps, to increase its authority through the abolition of dual command, and to heighten the discipline among the troops. In 1942, there had been many heroic episodes in the Red Army, but also many cases of demoralisation and even panic; Ehrenburg in his *Memoirs* recalls a colonel, in the summer of 1942, saying bitterly to him: "There has never been such a skedaddle yet."*

After Stalingrad, the overall morale of the Red Army was incomparably better than it had been either in 1941 or in 1942; there were many desperately difficult moments still, and some serious setbacks, such as the loss of Kharkov in March 1943; but the ultimate defeat of the Germans was no longer in doubt. Secondly, the *quality* of the troops was far better than it had been in 1941 and 1942; as Stalin said to Churchill in August 1942: "They are not so hot yet, but they are learning, and they'll make a first-class army before long." It was, indeed, during 1942 that the type of the hardened soldier, the *frontovik*, gradually developed.

* *Novyi Mir*, January 1963, p. 87.

But this general improvement in the quality of the Red Army was not only due to psychological causes. In 1941 and 1942 the Russian troops had had the deeply depressing feeling of having to fight against a *stronger* enemy; heroism, guts, self-sacrifice were all very well, but what could they do against an enemy whose infantry, with its variety of automatic weapons, had far greater fire-power than themselves, and who had far more tanks and planes?

Today it is admitted that Soviet armaments production did not reach a satisfactory level until the autumn of 1942. The evacuation of hundreds of plants from west to east in the autumn and winter of 1941 had resulted in an almost catastrophic drop in arms production, which largely accounted for the disappointing results of the Russian Moscow counter-offensive in the winter of 1941–2 and for the disasters of the summer of 1942.

After the loss of the Krivoi Rog iron ore, the Donbas coal, and the Ukrainian electric power-stations, there was a serious shortage in the east (where most of the armaments industry was now concentrated) of both power and metals. The total fuel resources were only half of what they had been before the war. The engineering works of Siberia and the Urals could not work at full capacity, and, during most of 1942 the output of tanks, planes, guns and ammunition was well below the Red Army's requirements. Draconian measures had to be taken to increase output. New coal-mines had to be speedily sunk; new power-plants had to be built; the People's Commissariat for Coal had some 200,000 more or less "improvised" new miners placed at its disposal, and a special food reserve had to be constituted to keep them going. Tens of thousands of new miners were sent from various parts of the country to the Karaganda coal area in Kazakhstan—nearly all of them women and very young people, who had to be trained in the shortest possible time. The morale of the Russian women, conscious of working for their husbands or sons or brothers in the Army was particularly admirable. Though less spectacular than the Battle of Stalingrad, the stupendous mass-effort made by the women of Russia during the war, whether in industry or agriculture, had nothing to equal it.

Despite these efforts, the shortage of coal, metals and electric power was still serious even in 1943. Though coal production in the east increased substantially in 1943* the total produced was still nowhere near the 166 million tons produced in 1941.

In 1943 oil resources were very low, too; Maikop had been put out of action by the retreating Russians; Grozny, with its refineries, had suffered severely from German bombing; and during the temporary breakdown of communications, in the Stalingrad period, many of the Baku wells had to be temporarily closed down. Instead, a special effort was made to develop the "Second Baku" in the east at top speed.

The coal shortage had to be met (particularly for transport and urban needs) by the substitution of peat and timber; in Moscow, thousands of students, office and factory workers were made to spend their summer holidays in improvised timber camps.

New industrial "giants" had to be speedily built—thus an enormous new power station was built in 1942 at Cheliabinsk to supply dozens of armaments works over a large area, and a gigantic new blast furnace (the famous "No. 6") was completed during the year at the Magnitogorsk Metallurgical Combine. Altogether, although the Soviet engineering industry had lost half its potential through the German occupation of the Ukraine and other areas, it had, in the main, overcome its difficulties by 1943.†

All this had a decisive effect on Soviet arms production. A tremendous effort was put into creating an air force superior to the Luftwaffe; gone were the grim days of 1941 when most of the Russian planes were suicidally obsolete. The principal planes that began to be produced in quantity in 1942 were the Il-2 stormovik (low-flying attack plane), and the Pe-2 operational dive-bomber; and the La-5 fighter, which was better than the Messerschmidt 109, but

---

* In 1943, the principal coal areas in the east produced the following amounts: Karaganda, 9·7 m. tons (an increase by 2½ m. tons over 1942); Kuzbas, 25 m. tons (4 m. tons more than in 1942); Urals, 21 m. tons (5 m. more than in 1942 and 9 m. more than in 1940). Finally, the "Moscow coal basin", with its very inferior coal, produced in 1943 14 m. tons. After the liberation of the Donbas its badly-wrecked mines were producing only 35,000 tons a day at the end of 1943—i.e. at the rate of 11 million tons a year.

† IVOVSS, vol. III, p. 161.

not as good as the Messerschmidt 109F or 109G. In 1943 the La-5-FN, which proved better than any German fighter, including the Fokke-Wulf 190, went into mass-production, and, in May, so did the Yak-9, with a 37 mm. gun, which was superior to German fighters with their 20 mm. guns. The Tu-2 dive-bomber went into mass-production in September, and the Il-2 stormovik was steadily improved and was developed by the end of the year into a two-seater plane, with increased fire power. The average monthly production of planes rose from 2,100 in 1942 to 2,900 in 1943, of which 2,500 were combat planes. Altogether, in 1943, 35,000 planes were produced, thirty-seven per cent more than in 1942, and including eighty-six per cent of combat planes. The proportion of stormoviks and fighters was particularly high. At the height of the summer battles of 1943 more than 1,000 Il-2's were produced every month—over one-third of the total of aircraft produced.

A little grudgingly the present-day *History* adds that there were also some Western planes in the Red Army; but the Hurricanes and Tomahawks were obsolete, and much inferior to both Russian and German fighters; the Airocobras and Kittyhawks which began to be used on the Russian front in the autumn of 1943, were excellent, "but there weren't enough of them."*

The output of tanks had also been seriously slowed down by the evacuation of industry to the east; nevertheless, great progress was made in tank construction throughout 1942. Two-thirds of all Soviet tanks were made by three "giant plants" in the east—the Ural-mashzavod, the Kirov Plant at Cheliabinsk, and Plant No. 183. Some spectacular improvements were made in 1942 for speeding up the production of tanks; thus the turrets of the T-34 medium tank were stamped instead of being cast. The T-34 was, altogether the best medium tank of World War II—as many German experts were to agree—and it continued, throughout 1943, to undergo various further improvements. In September 1943, to meet the challenge of the new German Tiger tank, the Russians began mass-producing the heavy JS ("Stalin") tank, with armour one-and-a-half times thicker than that of the Tiger, and described in the Soviet *History* as "the best heavy tank in the world."

* IVOVSS, vol. III, p. 216.

The average monthly output of Soviet tanks in 1943 was over 2,000, which was a little less than in 1942; but in 1943 the production of light tanks was almost discontinued, whereas, at the beginning of 1942, these still accounted for half the total. Altogether, in 1943, 16,000 heavy and medium tanks were made; 4,000 mobile guns and 3,500 light tanks. This total was eight-and-a-half times more than in 1940 and nearly four times more than in 1941.

A substantial number of tanks was received from Britain and the USA in 1942 and 1943, but Soviet historians are even more critical about them than about the British planes. Fifty-five per cent of the tanks received in 1942 were light tanks; in 1943 the proportion of light tanks was even higher—seventy per cent. The quantities received were described as "mediocre", and the quality left much to be desired.*

The output of guns and mortars was also greatly increased by 1943, that of guns of different calibres amounting that year to no less than 130,000; altogether, as D. F. Ustinov, the Minister of Armaments wrote in 1943: "A great density of fire for every kilometre of front is now the usual thing." From the beginning of 1943, there was also a vast improvement in the fire power of the infantry: in 1943 the number of submachine-guns was three times, and of light and heavy machine-guns two-and-a-half times, that of 1942. The vast superiority in fire-power of the German infantry of 1941 was now a thing of the past. One can well imagine the difference this made to Russian morale. The German *avtomatchik* was no longer, as he was in 1941, an object of terror or despair; practically every Russian soldier was now an *avtomatchik* himself.

*

* IVOVSS, vol. III, p. 214. The *History* adds that Allied authorities, e.g. Liddell Hart, now readily admit that "the tanks the Russians used were almost entirely home-made." Some of the tanks the Russians had received in 1941–2, particularly the Matildas, had proved to be particularly bad, and "as inflammable as a box of matches", as a disgruntled colonel told me at the Rzhev front in the summer of 1942.

Food production presented another major problem. Many of the Soviet peasants may have remained fundamentally hostile to the *kolkhoz* system; but there is no doubt that, by and large, they were as deeply affected as the working-class by the *patrie-en-danger* mystique of 1941–2. Almost all able-bodied men from the villages were drafted into the Army in the course of the war, and very many tractors and horses were requisitioned by the Army. Yet the remaining village population, consisting almost entirely of women, adolescents and old people, worked heroically, often in the most appalling conditions, to produce food. Cows were often used as draught animals, and some cases are even known of women drawing ploughs themselves. Even more than in the factories was there a deep consciousness of working "for" the sons and husbands and brothers who had gone to fight the Germans.

The scale of the food problem can be seen from the fact that, in 1942, only fifty-eight per cent of the pre-war area under cultivation was in Soviet hands; the rest had been occupied by the Germans. With the recovery of the Northern Caucasus and other areas, the proportion was sixty-three per cent in 1943; but the number of cattle was sixty-two per cent of the low pre-war total; that of horses, thirty-seven per cent; that of pigs, twenty per cent. The production of artificial fertilisers was down to very little, and there was often no petrol for the remaining tractors. It is one of the wonders of Russian character plus Russian organisation that a still worse food shortage should have been avoided. Although food supplies continued to be very poor in the cities, especially for "dependents" with their miserable rations, the fact remains that the Army was reasonably well fed, especially from 1943 onwards, and so too were most of the skilled industrial workers.

It is quite obvious that lend-lease supplies played an important part in improving the Army's diet, especially from the beginning of 1943. Of very great importance to the Red Army, too, were the growing numbers of Studebakers, Dodges and Willys jeeps—commonly known in the Red Army as *villises*—which so greatly increased its mobility. They were still not in great evidence at the time of Stalingrad, but, as I know from my own experience, they became an integral part of the Russian military landscape after about March 1943. These lorries and jeeps certainly contributed to the "new look" and to the tremendous and constantly-growing fighting power of the Red Army after Stalingrad.

This question of American, British and Canadian help to the Soviet Union had both political and psychological aspects.

In 1942, Allied aid was certainly not taken very seriously; in 1941–2, American shipments still amounted to only 1·2 m. tons and British shipments to 532,000 tons. Some of the heavy equipment sent that year (Hurricanes, Matilda tanks, etc.) was unsatisfactory. In 1943 British shipments remained stable but American shipments were enormously stepped up, rising to 4·1 m. tons (and over 6 m. tons if one includes the first four months of 1944). This included over 2 m. tons of food. Besides this, the U.S.A. sent the Soviet Union between 22 June 1941 and 30 April 1944:

6,430 planes	17,000 motor-cycles
3,734 tanks	991 m. cartridges
10 minesweepers	22 m. shells
12 gunboats	88,000 tons of gunpowder
82 smaller craft	130,000 tons of TNT
210,000 automobiles	1·2 m. km. of telephone wire
3,000 anti-aircraft guns	245,000 field telephones
1,111 oerlikons	5½ m. pairs of army boots
23 m. yards of army cloth	
2 m. tyres	
476,000 tons of high octane petrol	Other industrial equipment:
99,000 tons of aluminium	$257 m. worth (including
and duraluminium	oil refinery equipment,
184,000 tons of copper and	electrical equipment,
copper products	excavators,
42,000 tons of zinc	cranes,
6,500 tons of nickel	locomotives, et cetera)
1·2 m. tons of steel and	
steel products	
20,000 machine-tools	

Between June 22, 1941, and April 30, 1944, Britain dispatched 1,150,000 tons, of which 1,041,000 tons arrived. This included:

5,800 planes	33,000 tons of copper

4,292 tanks

12 minesweepers

103,000 tons of rubber

35,000 tons of aluminium

29,000 tons of tin

48,000 tons of lead

93,000 tons of jute

besides relatively small quantities of other raw materials, explosives, shells and other army equipment, as well as over 6,000 machine tools and £14 m. worth of other industrial equipment. The total value of Canadian deliveries for the same period was about 355 m. dollars, and included 1,188 tanks, 842 armoured cars, nearly a million shells, 36,000 tons of aluminium and 208,000 tons of wheat and flour, besides a number of smaller items.*

By the end of the war the figures were higher still. According to General Deane, over fifteen million tons were shipped to Russia between October 1941 and the end of the war. In his view the most important items were:

1) 427,000 trucks, 13,000 "combat vehicles", over 2,000 Ordnance vehicles and 35,000 motor-cycles;
2) Petroleum products (2,670,000 tons);
3) Food (4,478,000 tons), including flour. "Assuming that the Red Army had an average strength of 12 m. men, this meant a half pound of fairly concentrated food for each per day";
4) Railways equipment.

Altogether, he says, including a vast number of other items (medical supplies, clothing, boots, et cetera), "our supplies and services amounted to about eleven billion dollars. They may not have won the war, but they must have been comforting to the Russians."†

These figures are, in their own way, highly impressive; for instance those showing that a high proportion of the boots and clothing-material of the Red Army was American-made, and that America and Britain also delivered important quantities of strategic raw materials, aviation petrol, and much else. The planes and tanks, though of uneven value, were not to be sneezed at either. But they still constituted a relatively small proportion of all the planes and

* Commissariat for Foreign Trade Statement published in *Pravda* in June, 1944, a few days after the Normandy Landing.

† John R. Deane. *The Strange Alliance* (London 1947), pp. 93–95.

tanks used by the Red Army. According to Stalin's election speech in 1946, the Soviet Union produced about 100,000 tanks, 120,000 planes, 360,000 guns, over 1·2 m. machine-guns, 6 m. tommyguns, 9 m. rifles, 300,000 mortars, some 700 m. shells, some 20 billion cartridges, etc., during the last three years of the war.

Assuming that Stalin's figures are correct, they would suggest that the Allied heavy equipment (tanks and planes) amounted to between ten and fifteen per cent of the total. N. Voznesensky, the head of the Gosplan, argues in his book, *The War Economy of the Soviet Union*, published in 1948, that the Allied deliveries in 1941, 1942 and 1943 amounted to only four per cent of the Soviet Union's total production. This purely quantitative statement was misleading, since 1941 could not be considered a "lend-lease" year at all, and 1944, a peak year in allied deliveries, was omitted altogether.

From my personal observation I can say that, from 1943 on, the Red Army unquestionably appreciated the help from the West— whether in the form of Airocobras, Kittyhawks, Dodges, jeeps, spam, army boots, or medicines. The motor vehicles were particularly admired and valued. And the fact remains that the Allied raw materials enormously helped the Soviet war industries. But this still does not dispose of the profound emotional problem created by the simple fact that the Russians were losing millions of men, while the British and Americans were losing much fewer people.*

It was partly because of this feeling in the country that the Soviet Government liked to say as little as possible about Western deliveries; nor did it probably particularly like to advertise its dependence on the capitalist West for certain forms of equipment. This attitude was, understandably, resented in the West, and the first major incident over Russian "ingratitude" occurred in March 1943 when the US Ambassador, Admiral Standley, complained at a press conference of the "ungracious" Soviet attitude to both private Aid-to-Russia donations and American help generally.

The Russians were extremely annoyed by this protest; nevertheless, a few days later, the press published a very full account of a

* An important exception were the Russian airmen who warmly appreciated the Allied bombings of Germany, and the fact that many German fighter planes were immobilised in Germany.

statement by Stettinius showing just how much had been sent to the Soviet Union since the beginning of the war. For one thing, as Standley had pointed out, it was essential to appease Congress, where much was being made of these charges of Russian ingratitude.*

But this sudden generous acknowledgement of Western aid in the Soviet press in March 1943, though provoked by the Standley incident, had a long-term purpose as well. In a sense, Stalin was already on his way to Teheran with a Big-Three peace at the back of his mind. Apart from the extremely unpleasant "special" problem of Poland which was on the point of blowing up, the Soviet Government was much more "pro-Western" throughout 1943 than it had ever been. Paradoxically, it was in its official utterances *more* pro-Western during that year than were the Soviet people as a whole.

* In my Diary entry for March 9, 1943, I find the following: "The Russian censorship, after five hours' high-power telephoning, passed the text of the Standley statement. The people at the press department looked furious. Kozhemiako, the chief censor, was white with rage as he put his name to the cable. His mother had died of starvation in Leningrad... Another Russian remarked tonight: "We've lost millions of people, and they want us to crawl on our knees because they send us spam. And has the 'warmhearted' Congress ever done anything that wasn't in its interests? Don't tell me that Lend-Lease is *charity*!"

Chapter V

BEFORE THE SPRING LULL OF 1943—
STALIN'S WARNING—THE GERMANS'
"DESERT POLICY"

The great Russian drive in the winter campaign of 1942–3 from
Stalingrad to Kharkov and beyond, and the Germans' forced withdrawal from the Caucasus were not the only major Russian successes
during that period. After all the losses the Germans and their allies
had suffered in the south, they were visibly more and more short of
trained manpower. This largely accounts for their decision, in
March 1943, to abandon the Gzhatsk-Viazma-Rzhev springboard,
that "dagger pointing at Moscow", to which they had clung so
desperately ever since their first setbacks in Russia in the winter of
1941–2. It will be remembered that although the Russians had
driven the Germans back from Moscow along a wide front, they
had failed to dislodge them from their Gzhatsk-Viazma-Rzhev
springboard barely 100 miles from the capital.

Throughout the Black Summer of 1942 this remained a potential
threat to Moscow; but the Russians' main concern was less an
attack on the capital than a German attempt to hold the "springboard" with the minimum number of men, and to transfer the rest
to the south—to Stalingrad and the Caucasus. So, throughout the
summer and autumn of 1942 the Russians did their utmost to tie up
as many German troops as possible west of Moscow by constantly
attacking and harassing them. Those battles outside Rzhev were
among the most heartbreaking the Russians ever had to fight. They
were attacking very strong German positions; Russian losses were

629

much higher than the Germans, and so bitter was the fighting that very few prisoners were taken.

I visited the Rzhev sector during the rainy autumn of 1942 after the Russians had recaptured a few villages at fearful cost, but had each time been repelled from the outskirts of Rzhev. I was struck by the intense bitterness with which the officers and men spoke of their thankless task.

The roads that autumn were like rivers of mud, and countless ambulances had to travel over a "carpet" of felled tree-trunks covering the road, an agonising bone-rattling and wound-tearing experience for the wounded.

That autumn I saw something of the German "desert" policy in a few of the villages recaptured by the Red Army. Thus, in the village of Pogoreloye Gorodishche, a large part of the population had died of hunger; many had been shot; others had been deported as slave labour, and the village had been almost completely destroyed.

Now, in March 1943, fearing to be outflanked by the Russians from the south (and, eventually, of being trapped in that great "twixt-Moscow-and-Smolensk" encirclement which the Russians had failed to carry through in February 1942) the Germans simply pulled out of the "Moscow springboard", though with some heavy rearguard actions, notably at Viazma, and destroying as much as time would permit them.

The official Soviet report, published on April 7, 1943, on the effects of the "desert policy" the Germans had systematically carried out in the newly-liberated areas west of Moscow was a harrowing catalogue of mass shootings, murders and hangings, rape, the killing or starving to death of Russian war prisoners, and the deportation of thousands as slave labour to Germany. Kharkov was almost mild in comparison. The report noted that most of the shootings of civilians had been done by the German army, not by the Gestapo or the SD. The towns were almost totally obliterated—as I could indeed see for myself soon afterwards. At Viazma, out of 5,500 buildings, only fifty-one small houses had survived; at Gzhatsk, 300 out of 1,600; in the ancient city of Rzhev, 495 out of 5,443. All the famous churches had been destroyed. The population was being deliberately starved. 15,000 people had been deported from these three towns alone. The rural areas were not much better off: in the Sychevka area, 137 villages out of 248 had been burned down by the Germans. The list of war criminals appended to the Report was headed by Col.-Gen. Model, commander of the German 9th Army and other army leaders who had "personally ordered all this". The report noted that the destruction was "not accidental, but part of a deliberate extermination policy," which was being carried out even more thoroughly in these purely-Russian areas than elsewhere.

It is scarcely surprising that, as the Red Army moved farther and farther west, it became increasingly angry at the sight of all this bestiality and destruction.

The Russians scored two other important military successes at the beginning of 1943: they captured the strategically important Demiansk salient north of Smolensk and, more spectacular, after several days' extremely heavy fighting—with the troops of the Leningrad Front striking east and those of the Volkhov Front striking west across the German Lake Ladoga salient—the Russians cut a seven-mile-wide gap in the Leningrad land blockade. It was through this gap, which included the town of Schlüsselburg, that a railway line was built within a few weeks, and so linked Leningrad with the "Mainland". The trains had to travel through a corridor constantly exposed to German shell-fire, and the journey called for the greatest bravery on the part of the railwaymen. But though frequently shelled, this railway through what came to be known as "the corridor of death" carried on, and the thought of no longer being entirely cut off by land from the "mainland" had a very heartening effect on the 600,000 people still living in Leningrad. The city was, nevertheless, to remain under German shell-fire for another year.*

*

* See Part III.

All this was satisfactory. Nevertheless, the violent German counter-offensive which started at the end of February and led to the Russian loss of Kharkov, Belgorod and a large part of the northern Donbas was a disappointing conclusion to the glorious "Winter of Stalingrad".

In his Red Army Day order of February 23 Stalin spoke in glowing terms of the winter offensive, saying that "the mass expulsion of the enemy from the Soviet Union had begun." But he warned the army and the country against excessive optimism—no doubt fore-seeing some major setbacks.

The figures he gave for total enemy losses were, as usual, improbably high. In three months, he said, the Germans and their allies had lost 7,000 tanks, 4,000 planes and 17,000 guns; 700,000 enemy soldiers had been killed and 300,000 taken prisoner. Since the beginning of the war, the enemy casualties had amounted to nine million men, among them four million killed. In the Soviet Union things were going much better, both in the army and in industry, whose output of armaments had "enormously increased".

If, Stalin said, the German army was more experienced at first than the Red Army, the opposite was now true. The Red Army had now become a *cadres* army, and the quality and skill of the Soviet soldier had greatly increased. The German losses, on the other hand, were compelling the German High Command to draw low-quality soldiers into the army. Also, Russian officers and generals were now superior to their German opposite numbers. The Germans' tactics were banal and when the situation no longer corresponded to one outlined in his Field Regulations, the German officer lost his head. Yet this did not mean that the German Army was finished:

> The German Army has suffered a defeat, but it has not yet been smashed. It is now going through a crisis, but it does not follow that it cannot pull itself together... The real struggle is only beginning... It would be stupid to imagine that the Germans will abandon even one kilometre of our country without a fight.

Stalin's statement was remarkable in two respects: it was a warning to the Red Army that very heavy fighting was still in store; and, as events were to prove before long, the Germans were already on the point of launching their counter-offensive. Russian reconnaissance must have shown by February 23 that it was coming.

Secondly, of all Stalin's war-time statements, this one was by far the least pro-Ally. Without mentioning North Africa—where the Allies' progress was admittedly slow at the time—Stalin said that the Soviet Union was "bearing the whole brunt of the war." The compliments he had paid the Allies in November 1942 on their North Africa landing were not followed up. What they were doing was small stuff compared with Stalingrad and the rest.

What nettled the British and Americans even more was that, after paying a warm tribute to Soviet industry, Stalin should have made no mention at all of Lend-Lease and other Western supplies which were now beginning to arrive in very substantial quantities, partly along the newly-reorganised Persian route. It was this Stalin Order of February 23 which was really at the root of the "Standley incident" described in the last chapter.

A strange dual phenomenon was to characterise Soviet foreign policy during the rest of 1943: an almost constantly growing cordiality towards the United States and Britain (all, as it were, in preparation for Teheran at the end of the year) but, at the same time, an extremely "anti-Western" stand on the Polish issue. It already looked as though Stalin, while anxious to cultivate the best possible relations with the Western Allies, had made up his mind that Poland was an issue which the Soviet Union was going to settle her own way. It was the biggest test-case of all; and one, as de Gaulle was to observe during his visit to Moscow at the end of 1944, which was "the principal object of his (Stalin's) passion, and the centre of his policy".*

From the end of March until early July there was a relative lull on the Soviet-German Front—in fact the longest lull from then until the end of the war. But both sides were preparing feverishly for the summer campaign which was to begin on July 5 with the stupendous

* C. de Gaulle, *Salvation, 1944-6* (New York, 1956), p. 74.

Battle of Kursk, the last major battle that most (though not all) Germans were still confidently expecting to win—thanks largely to their new Panther and Tiger tanks and Ferdinand mobile guns. Yet within five days the Germans had lost the battle, and the Russians then were able to fight their way to the Dnieper and beyond.

But this long three-months' lull was marked by political events of far-reaching importance, among them a further *rapprochement* with Britain and the United States, characterised by such "gestures of goodwill" as the dissolution of the Comintern and, on the other hand, the breach with the Polish Government in London and the laying of the foundations for an entirely new Polish régime.

Chapter VI

THE TECHNIQUE OF BUILDING A NEW POLAND

The Breach with the London Poles

Poland occupies the central place in the diplomatic battle between Russia and her Western Allies—a battle which began long before the war was over. Despite all official attempts to play it down or to localise it, it was the problem which had, since the early part of 1943 (and even before) tended to poison East-West relations.

Throughout the Soviet Union's Battle of Survival of 1941-2, from the invasion to the Stalingrad victory, the Soviet Government had been on its best behaviour—at least most of the time—in its relations with the outside world. There had been a strident outcry, largely for home consumption, for a Second Front during the agonising summer of 1942, but apart from that and the snarling about Hess, the Soviet Union was, in the main, being thoroughly conciliatory in her relations with the West.

The only allied and "friendly" country with whose government relations were continuously strained was Poland. This was, indeed, a very special case. The trouble inevitably went back to the fact that Germany and Russia had "partitioned" Poland in 1939, and that several hundred thousand Poles had been taken prisoner or deported by the Russians; there were Poles scattered all over the Soviet Union; and among these Poles there were numerous war prisoners, including some twelve to fifteen thousand officers and N.C.O.'s.

According to the Polish Government, the officers had been in three

635

large camps—at Kozelsk, Starobelsk and Ostashkov until the spring of 1940; but by the end of 1941, despite pressing inquiries, no trace could be found of any of them, except for some 400 who had been transferred from one of these camps in the spring of 1940 to the camp of Griazovetz, near Vologda.

The fate of these missing officers was to become a major bone of contention between the Russians and the "London" Poles. It was also to provide the basis for one of the master-strokes of Goebbels's propaganda machine—the story of the mass-graves in Katyn forest, near Smolensk, which we shall discuss later in this chapter.

Under the terms of the Sikorski-Maisky Agreement of July 30, 1941, concluded in London, diplomatic relations between the two Governments were restored, and a Polish Army was to be organised in Russia "under the orders of a chief appointed by the Polish Government, but approved by the Soviet Government". It would be under the Supreme Soviet Command, but this would include a Polish representative.

The Agreement further said that, after the restoration of diplomatic relations, the USSR would "grant an amnesty to all Polish citizens imprisoned in Soviet territory whether as war prisoners or for any other reason." The very word "amnesty" in this context was, of course, more than distasteful to the Polish Government, but conditions were too serious for quibbling.

General Sikorski went to Moscow in December, 1941—with the Germans still only a few miles from the Soviet capital—and confirmed the Polish promise to set up a Polish Army on Soviet territory, which would fight the Germans beside the Soviet Army. Even with Russia in a highly precarious military position, Stalin would not agree during the meeting with Sikorski to the restoration of Poland within her pre-September 1939 frontiers, and the Polish territorial claims continued to be a chronic subject of dispute between the Russian and Polish "allies". But a more serious and immediate problem was the Polish Army in the Soviet Union.

*

This army began to be formed in 1941 by General Anders, who had himself been a prisoner of the Russians, and was understandably anti-Russian at heart.

Later, after the breach with the London Poles, Vyshinsky made a savage indictment against Anders and the Polish government in London. He began by recalling that the Polish-Soviet agreements of 1941 provided for:

> A Polish Army to be formed on Soviet soil, the number being fixed at 30,000 men. General Anders himself had proposed that "when a division was ready for action, it should be immediately sent to the front."
>
> The supplies given to the Polish Army were the same as those given to Soviet Army units in process of formation. Moreover the Soviet Government had granted the Polish Government an interest-free loan of sixty-five million roubles, which, on January 1, 1942, was increased to 300 millions, plus a free gift of equipment to Polish officers, amounting to fifteen millions.
>
> Vyshinsky said that, by October 25, 1941, the Polish Army already counted 41,561 men, including 2,630 officers. In December Sikorski proposed that this figure be increased to 96,000 men, representing six divisions.

Despite great difficulties, there were already divisions with 73,415 men in the Polish Army in December 1941.

But at this point, according to Vyshinsky, it began to be increasingly clear that the Poles were double-crossing the Russians; that they had no intention of letting their men be killed at the Russian front, and were making one excuse after another for not letting them fight.

> Some of the troops (Vyshinsky claimed) were to be ready for action by October 1, 1941; but they were not. While the Soviet Government did not wish to hurry the Poles, it began, after five months had elapsed since the beginning of the Army's formation, to ask questions, in virtue of the Agreement of August 14, 1941. This had said that the Polish Army units would be sent to the front as soon as they were fully ready for action. As a rule, they would not go into action in less than one division, and would be used in accordance with the Soviet Command's operational plans.
>
> Later, however, Anders declared that he considered the use of single divisions undesirable, even though (Vyshinsky added) single brigades were used at other fronts.

Then Anders promised that the whole Polish Army would be ready for action on June 1, 1942; however, before long, the Polish Government finally refused to send any Polish troops to the Soviet front.

It is perhaps scarcely surprising that the Polish Army under Anders had no desire to fight on the Russian front after all that had happened since 1939. They had some very grim memories of the N.K.V.D. camps and also grave misgivings about the fate of the missing Polish officers, a crucial point Vyshinsky dodged.

In Ehrenburg's *Memoirs*—though he also dodges this question—there is this striking passage on the early stages of Polish-Russian "friendship":

> At the beginning of December (1941) I happened to attend near Saratov a parade of General Anders's army, composed of Polish ex-war-prisoners. General Sikorski arrived, accompanied by Vyshinsky. I don't know why Vyshinsky, of all people, should have been chosen for this ceremony. Perhaps because he was of Polish descent? I could not help remembering him in the rôle of Public Prosecutor in the Purge trials... He clicked glasses with Sikorski and there was a sugary smile on his face. Among the Poles there were many gloomy men, deeply embittered by what they had lived through; many of them could not restrain themselves and openly admitted that they hated us. I felt that these men could not let bygones be bygones. Sikorski and Vyshinsky referred to each other as "allies", but behind these pleasant words one could feel deep animosity.*

The "Anders' Poles" had certainly had a more than raw deal in Russia since 1939—though it was perhaps tactless and ungracious of them to complain so frequently after the outbreak of the Soviet-German war of their miserable living and food conditions: after all, the Russian people as a whole were also suffering terrible hardships during that winter.

Nor is it surprising that the Russians were not especially anxious to have on Russian soil a "reactionary" Polish army, commanded by virulently anti-Russian officers—particularly if it was being of no help in fighting the Germans—and that Stalin agreed to Churchill's proposal that the Anders' Poles should leave Russia via Iran. Many

* *Novyi Mir*, 1963, No. 1, p. 73.

Russians regarded their departure as a good riddance; but it so happened that the Anders' army left Russia on the eve of the Battle of Stalingrad. To the Russian people this looked like rats leaving a ship they thought was sinking. All this was very unfair; but it was all part of that tragic conflict which went back to 1939.

In any case, the Poles held rather a special place in the Russians' scheme of things; many Russian soldiers had taken part in the Polish campaign of 1939, and they had been struck by the almost general hostility of the Poles; similarly, there were Russian soldiers who, when abandoning cities like Lwow in 1941, claimed to have been fired on by Poles while the Germans were entering the city from the other end.

It is perhaps significant that on General Gundorov's "All Slav Committee" which was particularly active in 1942, and was marked by a special Russian affection for Yugoslavs, Czechs and pro-Soviet Bulgarians, the Poles played very little part. This was a curious movement with sentimental "Pan-Slav" and even Orthodox Church undertones.

In short, the Russians had many mental reservations in respect of the Poles—and no doubt a very bad conscience as a result of the 1939 deportations. And among the top-ranking Russians there was great uneasiness about the "missing officers" about whom the London Government never ceased asking questions.

But in any case Stalin had some definite ideas about the future of Poland. He was not going to subscribe to the "Riga frontiers" of 1921. Nor was he going to tolerate a Poland run by anti-Russian elements. Of one thing he was profoundly convinced—and that was the deep-seated hostility existing between Poles and Russians. Even in later years, long after the war, he continued to be highly sceptical about any assurances that the Poles and Russians were "getting on splendidly"—he used to say that it would, perhaps, take two generations or more to overcome the innate prejudices existing on both sides.

Stalin's Polish policy had been planned in advance, though it is doubtful whether he could have anticipated Goebbels's Katyn bombshell. But this bombshell, in fact, only precipitated the process Stalin had planned. The all-out campaign against the Sikorski Government's territorial claims had started almost immediately after Stalingrad, and *before* the Katyn blow-up. It was indeed, after Stalingrad (and not before) that the diplomatic activity of the Russians became very intensive, complete with the production of (as yet secret) blue-prints for the future of Eastern Europe.

The trouble over Poland, which had been simmering for a long time, began to boil over in February, 1943.

The Russian post-Stalingrad winter offensive was still at its height and the Red Army was continuing its advance west of Kharkov. The Ukrainian Government arrived in Kharkov (only to leave again a few days later, it is true), and in the official Ukrainian Government newspaper *Radyanska Ukraina* (Soviet Ukraine) printed in Kharkov on February 19, there appeared an article by Alexander Korneichuk, the well-known Ukrainian playwright—who had written *The Front* in 1942—and in this article, reprinted on the following day in *Pravda*, the Soviet-Ukrainian point of view was clearly stated.* For, apart from being a problem concerning the Soviet Union as a whole, Poland was also treated then, as later, as a problem specifically affecting the Ukrainian S.S.R.

Shortly afterwards, Korneichuk was, somewhat symbolically, appointed Soviet Vice-Commissar for Foreign Affairs "in charge of Slav countries". He did not hold the job for very long though, partly perhaps because diplomacy was not quite in his line and partly perhaps because the foreign press tended to make the most of the fact that he was married to Wanda Wassilewska, a Polish Communist writer who had been a Soviet citizen since 1939, and was even a member of the Supreme Soviet.

Ever since the renewal of diplomatic relations between Poland and the Soviet Union in the summer of 1941 the frontiers had been a bone of contention between the two Governments. Sikorski himself, though willing, at heart, to take a realistic view of the situation, had never officially abandoned Poland's claims to the 1939 frontiers. He

* See p. 642.

was always considering his own diehards; though the indications are that he was prepared, eventually, to compromise, and his "minimum" was the preservation by Poland of Lwow. Later it was argued that, if only Sikorski had remained alive, relations between the Soviet Government and the Polish Government in London would not have deteriorated as much as they did; but this is doubtful. Sikorski was still alive when the Soviet Government "suspended" diplomatic relations; Sikorski was still alive when the Union of Polish Patriots—that first nucleus of a pro-Soviet Government in Poland—was set up and the decision was taken to form the new Polish Army in Russia.

There are, however, indications that the Russians did not hold Sikorski personally responsible for the "Katyn Scandal", but some of the diehards in and around his Government, especially their *bête noire* General Sosnkowski, the Chief of Staff; and it is also true that at no moment after the suspension of relations with the Polish Government in April 1943 did the Russian press attack Sikorski personally. But, looking back on it now, it is doubtful whether Sikorski would have been able to play a part much greater than that to be played later by Mikolajczyk.

The main lines of Russia's Polish policy may be said to have been laid down in the early part of 1943. The Katyn scandal only precipitated an inevitable breach.

The eastern frontier was to be, roughly, the Curzon line, and Poland was to expand westwards instead, though no exact borderline was yet mentioned.

The Polish Government was to be a "friendly Government".

A lasting settlement of Poland's frontiers was to be achieved, and although the Russians at first refrained from indicating officially what Poland's frontiers in the west would be, a new Polish paper published in Moscow, *Wolna Polska* (Free Poland) openly raised the question in March 1943. Somebody called Andrzej Marek wrote that Poland should be given the essential parts of Silesia and, naturally, the mouth of the Vistula, "with wide access to the sea". The coastline from Danzig to Memel, he said, should be Polish and

East Prussia should "cease to be an everlasting springboard for German aggression against the Poles, Russians, and the Baltic peoples. It should be Poland's bridge to the sea, and not the barrier between her and the sea". These still relatively modest claims were to be greatly exceeded later by the Oder-Neisse frontier.

The Poles, in short, were expected to sink their past differences with the Russians and Ukrainians, to become "good Slavs", and stop thinking about *cordons sanitaires* and other Pilsudskian heresies.

As already said, Korneichuk opened the debate on February 19:

> It would seem (he wrote), that in the hard times through which the Polish people are living all layers of Polish society would be united by the same national feeling, and by the same sacred thought; to drive out the Germans... But no, there are large groups of Poles in London who are doing their best to shatter the united front of Hitler's enemies. A Polish newspaper, printed on good English newsprint, recently dismissed the outcry for the Second Front as "cheap demagogy". And at a recent meeting in Edinburgh Professor W. Wielhorski said: "Every Pole must consider it his duty to fight for the inviolability of our eastern areas."
>
> The Polish *szlachta* [landed gentry] have learned nothing. They have never recognised the Ukrainian people...

Korneichuk then gave a long list of the benefits that the Western Ukraine had derived during its incorporation in the Soviet Union, between 1939 and 1941—the creation of schools and hospitals, land reform, struggle against illiteracy, unemployment and prostitution.

On March 2 a *Tass* communiqué declared that this Polish attempt to deny the Ukrainians and the Belorussians their rights was "contrary to the Atlantic Charter... Even Lord Curzon, hostile though he was to the Soviet Union, understood that Poland could not claim Ukrainian and Belorussian territories."

Then it sounded the motif that the Polish Government in London was *not representative of the Polish people.*

It was all well orchestrated.

Wolna Polska made its first appearance a few days later. It declared itself to be the organ of the Union of Polish Patriots, and aimed at "uniting all Polish patriots living in the USSR, regardless of their past, their views and their convictions, in the joint task of waging an uncomprising struggle against the German invaders. . ." The aim, the paper said, was to "regain for Poland every inch of Polish ground, but not to claim an inch of other people's land."

Other articles were published by Wands Wasselewska, Wiktor Grosz and others, calling for friendship with the Soviet Union and denouncing both the London Government and various Polish "quislings".

Many wondered at first who these people of the Union of Polish Patriots were. Only one, its President, Wanda Wassilewska, was well known. But she was in a somewhat ambiguous position, being, at the time, a member of the Supreme Soviet of the USSR, and moreover, the third wife of Korneichuk, the newly appointed Vice-Commissar for Foreign Affairs. Then there was Colonel Berling, one of the very few officers who had refused to follow Anders's Army to Iran. There were some other Poles—Borejsza, the editor of *Wolna Polska*, and Victor Grosz, Jedrichowski, and Modzelewski—mostly young and unknown people whom the collapse of Poland had, in one way or another, brought to the Soviet Union. Many of them were Jews. Who were the public to whom the Union of Polish Patriots in the USSR were appealing?

In March, this still seemed very vague. There were hundreds of thousands of Poles and Polish Jews scattered over large parts of the Soviet Union—mostly people who had been deported by the Russians in 1939–40 from Western Ukraine and Belorussia, including some ex-war-prisoners who had not had time to be incorporated in the Anders Army. There were others who had come voluntarily, to escape from the Germans in 1941, but how many of these could be called real Poles—rather than Ukrainians, Belorussians or Jews— was in some doubt; and, altogether, it seemed doubtful whether many of these people were "Polish Patriots" in the Moscow sense. Even a well-known Russian said to me, when he heard of the decision to form a Polish division on Russian soil, that he did not quite see how it could be done, for it was not much use putting nothing but Ukrainians or Jews into the "Polish Division", and as for

real Poles, the only ones who would be willing to enter such a division would be Polish Communists; and these were a *rara avis.*

Yet neither the Union of Polish Patriots, nor, still less, the Polish
Division (later followed by three more divisions formed on Soviet
soil) turned out to be a joke, as not only the enemies of the whole
scheme, but also many friendly sceptics seemed to expect at the
time. It was not until the Kosciuszko Division made its appearance
in July 1943 that most of the sceptics recognised that the Russians
had, somehow, pulled it off. As for the Union of Polish Patriots,
nondescript though it may outwardly have been, it had created the
ideological basis for that New Poland, of which the Kosciuszko
Division was to be the first important manifestation.

It was certainly not accidental that throughout April all the loyal
friends of the Soviet Union should have been built up in the Soviet
press. It was as if their activities were being compared with the
"reprehensible and shortsighted" conduct of the London Poles.
Thus, great publicity was given to the Czechoslovak unit that fought
its first great action—a very costly but successful action—on the
Soviet front. Great prominence was also given to the resistance
movements in France, Belgium, and Norway, and more particularly
to the French Normandie Squadron already fighting on the Russian
front on de Gaulle's initiative.

The Czechoslovak unit fighting on the Russian front won the
greatest fame of all during those days. It was not a large unit—
2,000 or 3,000 men under the command of Colonel Svoboda, who
was later to become Minister of War in the Czechoslovak Government in Prague. In March it went into action and on April 2, the
Russian communiqué told the story of its first great engagement.
Two things were, politically, of the greatest importance; first, that,
unlike the Anders Army, the Czechoslovak unit was fighting on the
Soviet front; secondly, that it was doing so with the blessing of the
Czechoslovak Commander-in-Chief, President Benes, and of the
Czechoslovak Government in London. The unit was, of course,
under the operational command of the Russians.

On April 8, Alexander Fadeyev wrote a glowing account of the

Czechs' heroism and, two days later, warm congratulations were sent to Colonel Svoboda by President Benes, by the Minister of Defence (also in London), and by the Czechoslovak Communist deputies who were then in Moscow, Gottwald, Kopecky and others. Captain Jaros who was in command of one of the companies during the heavy fighting in the Kharkov area, and had been fatally wounded, was posthumously awarded the title of Hero of the Soviet Union. Svoboda received the Order of Lenin, and eighty-two other men of the Czechoslovak unit were decorated by the Russians.

Such relations with the Czechs contrasted strangely with the first-class row with the London Poles which was on the point of reaching its climax.

From the beginning the Polish Government's principal worry had been the fate of the Polish officers who had been in the Soviet Union since the debacle in 1939. Where were they? In their many conversations with Stalin, Molotov and Vyshinsky during the winter of 1941–2, General Sikorski, General Anders (who had himself been in Russian prisons for many months), Ambassador Kot, and other Polish representatives kept on raising this question. The Russians (according to the Poles)` never gave a definite answer, saying that these prisoners would eventually turn up or that they had perhaps escaped to Poland, or Rumania, or Manchuria or, finally (a very belated afterthought of Stalin's) that some of them might have been trapped by the Germans during the invasion of the Soviet Union.

The announcement by Goebbels's propaganda machine in the middle of April, 1943, that the Germans had found several mass graves in the Katyn Forest near Smolensk containing the bodies of thousands of Polish officers, was therefore well timed to exacerbate further the strained relations between Moscow and the London Poles.

The Germans had set up a much publicised Committee of Inquiry which had "proved" that these Polish officers had been shot by the Russians in 1940.

The news was sprung on a startled Russian public in an official communiqué on April 16:

> "Goebbels's gang of liars have, in the last two or three days been spreading revolting and slanderous fabrications about the alleged mass

shootings by Soviet organs of authority in the Smolensk area, in the spring of 1940. The German statement leaves no doubt about the tragic fate of the former Polish war prisoners who, in 1941, were in areas west of Smolensk, engaged on building, and who, together with many Soviet people, inhabitants of the Smolensk Province, fell into the hands of the German hangmen, after the withdrawal of Soviet troops from Smolensk... In this clumsy fabrication about numerous graves which the Germans are supposed to have discovered near Smolensk, Goebbels's liars mention the village of Gnezdovaya; but they deliberately omit to mention the fact that it was precisely here, near Gnezdovaya, that archaeological excavations were in progress on the so-called Gnezdovsky Tumulus... With this faking of facts, and these stories of Soviet atrocities in the spring of 1940, the Germans... are trying to shift on to the Russians the blame for their own monstrous crime...

"These professional German murderers, who have butchered hundreds of thousands of Polish citizens in Poland, will deceive no one with such lies and slander..."

All this was a little mystifying; for it seemed to suggest that, although the Poles had no doubt been murdered, the Germans had invented the story about the mass graves at Smolensk. It was not at all clear what the Gnezdovsky Tumulus had to do with it all.

The position became a little clearer a few days later; or, at least, one thing now became perfectly clear—and that was that Goebbels had engineered a first-class diplomatic row.

On the 19th, the *Pravda* editorial indignantly wrote:

Goebbels's fabrication has been taken up not only by his German scribes, but, to everybody's amazement, by the ministerial circles of General Sikorski... The Polish Ministry of Information knows perfectly well the purpose of this German provocation, for it says itself: "We are used to the lies of German propaganda, and can understand the purpose of its latest revelations." Yet, in spite of this, the Ministry of Information can think of nothing better than to appeal to the International Red Cross with the request to "investigate" something that never existed, or, rather, had been fabricated by the hangmen of Berlin, who are now trying to attribute their crime to the Soviet organs [i.e., the NKVD]. They have been caught by this German bait. It is not surprising that Hitler should also have appealed to the International Red Cross. Yet this is not the first case of its kind: already in Lwow in 1941 they staged "The victims of Bolshevik Terror".

Hundreds of witnesses then showed up the German liars. [The article then referred to Sovinformbureau's statement on the subject of August 8, 1941.]

Feeling the indignation of the whole of progressive humanity over their massacres of peaceful citizens, and particularly of Jews, the Germans are now trying to rouse the anger of gullible people against the Jews: for this reason they invented a whole collection of mythical "Jewish Commissars" who, they say, took part in the murder of the 10,000 Polish officers. For such experienced fakers it was not difficult to invent a few names of people who never existed—Lev Rybak, Avraam Borisovich, Paul Brodninsky, Chaim Finberg. No such persons ever existed either in the "Smolensk Section of the OGPU", or in any other department of the NKVD. In the light of these facts, the request made by the Polish Ministry of National Defence to the International Red Cross can be regarded only as a demonstration of their desire to give direct aid to Hitler's forgers and *provocateurs*.

And then, two days later, a Tass statement said that this *Pravda* editorial "fully reflects the attitude of Soviet leading circles".

The statement made by the Sikorski Government on April 18 makes matters worse, since it identifies itself with the provocative statement of the Polish Ministry of Defence... The fact that the anti-Soviet campaign started simultaneously in the German and the Polish press, and is being conducted on the same plane—this amazing fact allows one to suppose that this campaign is being conducted as a result of an agreement between the German occupants in Poland and the pro-Hitlerite elements of the ministerial circles of Mr Sikorski. The Polish Government's statement shows that the pro-Hitlerite elements have great influence in the Polish Government and that they are taking new steps to worsen relations between Poland and the USSR.

The Soviet case was not at all well presented. Detailed facts and figures were missing. Something of the secretiveness that had surrounded the whole affair of the "missing Polish officers" was still maintained. To the Russians, the allegations were "beneath contempt". They would say what there was to say once the Red Army got to Smolensk. Now there was only one thing to do: draw the political conclusions.

On the evening of April 27 it was announced that the Soviet Government had suspended diplomatic relations with the Polish

Government. The announcement was contained in a letter from Molotov to Romer, the Polish Ambassador in the USSR.

The word used was "*prervat*" (suspend), not "*porvat*" (break off), and those who believed that the breach was only temporary, at first attached some importance to this fine point of Russian grammar.

The Polish Ambassador himself suggested at first that the quarrel might be patched up, and that he "would soon be back in Moscow". He was clearly upset at what had happened, but made a point of being very "correct" about the Russians at the press conference he gave to the British and American correspondents the night the "suspension" was announced. He said he had refused to accept the Russian Note, because the motives were "unacceptable". He argued that an article in the official Polish paper in London, the *Dziennik Polski* had, on April 15, rejected the German proposal to appeal to the International Red Cross; but he did not know when and how exactly this appeal had finally been made, and on whose authority. Instead, speaking studiously more in sorrow than in anger, he made a few general complaints about the Russians. According to the lists of the Polish Embassy, he said, there had been 400,000 Poles in the Soviet Union. Since then 95,000 soldiers and 40,000 civilians had gone to the Middle East. The Polish soldiers had been demobilised in 1939, but the officers and N.C.O.'s were kept in camps. The Polish Government had asked the Russians in vain to give them lists of these officers and N.C.O.'s; and, unlike Kozielsk, *the camps of Starobelsk and Ustashkovo had not been occupied by the Germans*. If the Polish officers and N.C.O.'s had been transferred to Smolensk, the Polish Government had not heard of it until now. It was apparent that if the Russians had left the Poles behind to fall into German hands, the Russians did not wish to admit it, and were, therefore, humming and hawing. It was most unfortunate, and had played into the hands of German propaganda. "*Je ne crois pas au crime russe—* I don't believe in a Russian crime", he said, "only why could they not be franker with us?" He said the three camps in question had been closed between April and June 1940, and it had been believed that the officers had been scattered through the Soviet Union in small groups. The news that they had been left behind near Smolensk was something quite new.

In these camps (he said), there had been 12,500 officers and N.C.O.'s and when the Polish Army began to be formed, it was found that only a handful of officers were available.

He then talked about the 570 children's homes, schools, canteens, old people's homes, and other Polish institutions which had been set up in the Soviet Union, and had mostly been run on lend-lease stuff by 420 *personnes de confiance* appointed by the Polish Embassy at Kuibyshev, but had latterly been taken over by the Russians. After that, all these centres had lost contact with the Embassy. He had heard of Madame Wassilewska but did not know what she was doing or was proposing to do.

And then, on January 16, the Soviet Government went back on its former decision to allow certain categories of people from Eastern Poland to rank as Polish citizens. I (Romer) had been discussing this question with the Russians for some time, and it is most disappointing to me that these negotiations should now have had to be suspended.

He ended, however, on a note of confidence, saying he thought the quarrel would yet be patched up.

I have quoted Romer's statement because, a few days later, Vyshinsky was to answer him, though *not* on the crucial point of the "missing officers." Romer's suggestion that it would "blow over" was not justified. The Russians, having in effect broken off relations with the London Government, were now going to get tough.

Romer was not to forestall Vyshinsky. From the Russian point of view he was no longer Ambassador, and, therefore, had no business to give interviews. None of his statements was passed by the censorship, *not even the statement that he did not believe the Russians had committed the Katyn crime!*

On the very next day, while *Pravda* was fuming against the "Polish Imperialists" and "German agents", Wanda Wassilewska came out with an article in *Izvestia* which was a landmark in the history of Polish-Russian relations. After making the usual charges against the London Government of preventing active resistance to the Germans

* After recapturing the Katyn area the Russians tried to prove that the Polish officers had been shot by the Germans. See pp. 661 ff.

in Poland, and of haggling, instead, over Poland's eastern frontiers, she said that this Government had "done everything to silence progressive Poles abroad" and to "undermine the Poles' confidence in their natural ally, the Soviet Union."

"Yet every honest Pole knows that such an alliance is a matter of life and death to his country, especially now when Europe's and Poland's fate is being settled on this front."

And then she came to her main point: she said that *another Polish Army might shortly be constituted on Soviet soil*, which would fight side by side with the Red Army, as the Czechoslovak troops and the French airmen were already doing. *This Polish Army would not be under the jurisdiction of the Polish Government in London.*

What this meant was that a new Polish Army, drawn from Polish citizens in the Soviet Union, and former Polish citizens (though Wassilewska did not mention this point) would shortly be formed on Soviet soil. It now seemed likely that the point about Polish nationality which the Russians had, for a short time, stretched in favour of the Anders Army, might now be stretched again for the benefit of the new Polish Army, and, indeed, stretched much farther.

The question as to who would replace the London Government from the point of view of authority was left vague; but, for the present, the new Polish Army would, in fact, owe its allegiance to the Soviet Government pending the formation of a *real* Polish Government. Many sceptics wrongly thought that what was contemplated was merely a "token force", or even only a "gesture".

From now on, Soviet policy had two objectives—to denounce and debunk the Polish Government in London as "unrepresentative", and to proclaim its intention of supporting those wishing to build a "free, strong, and democratic Poland". On May 6, Stalin answered the questions of Ralph Parker, the *Times* correspondent, as follows:

Q. Does the Government of the USSR desire to see a strong independent Poland after the defeat of Nazi Germany?
A. Unquestionably.

Q. What, in your view, should be the basis for relations between Poland and the USSR after the war?

A. Sound good-neighbourly relations and mutual respect, or, if the Polish people desire it, a basis of mutual aid against the Germans, the principal enemies of both the Soviet Union and Poland.

On the same day, Vyshinsky called a press conference and produced his long indictment against the London Government. He spoke in a particularly harsh and snarling manner, reminiscent of his manner as Public Prosecutor in the notorious purge trials of 1936–8.

He began by giving his account, quoted above,* of the formation of the Anders army, and then went on to deal with the charges that it had been undernourished.

He argued that, owing to the Pacific War and other causes, there was a food shortage in Russia in 1942. Non-combat troops could, clearly, not be as well fed as combat troops. As the Polish Command persisted in not wishing them to fight, they had to be regarded as such. Finally, on April 1, it was decided that the rations would be cut down to 44,000, and that those over and above that figure could leave the Soviet Union.

In March 1942, 31,488 soldiers and 12,455 members of their families were evacuated. But while refusing to fight, said Vyshinsky, *the Polish Government desired to go on mobilising new units*; however, in reply to the Polish Note of June 10, 1942, on the subject, the Russians refused to allow any further mobilisations. *It was then that the question of total evacuation was raised, and in August* 1942 *a further* 44,000 *soldiers and* 20,000 *to* 25,000 *dependents left the country.*

Thus, already in 1942, 75,491 soldiers and 37,756 members of their families left the Soviet Union.

All the assertions, he said, that the Soviet authorities prevented Polish citizens in the Soviet Union (who were "not numerous") or members of Polish soldiers' families, from leaving the country, were a lie.

Here, of course, was a sticky point. There were believed to be some 300,000 or 400,000 Polish citizens, including Jews, still in the Soviet Union. But (a) had they expressed the wish to leave for Iran, rather

* See p. 637.

than wait for Poland to "open" and, (b) even if they did, and there was no means of transport, could it be said that they had been "prevented" from leaving? Further, very many of those whom the Polish Government considered Polish citizens, were no longer Polish citizens in the eyes of the Russians. At least, not as far as joining the Anders Army was concerned—though points were, in fact going later to be stretched in the case of the Kosciuszko and other Russian-formed divisions.

Vyshinsky partly explained the problem when he said that, in the early stages of Polish-Soviet relations in 1941, it was agreed by the Russians that Polish nationality could be regained by the *Poles* of Western Ukraine and Belorussia—this with a view to their joining the Anders Army.

The Polish Government did not, however, consider itself satisfied, and pressed for the cancellation of Soviet nationality for other inhabitants of Western Ukraine and Belorussia.

Far from satisfying this claim, the Russians decided, once the Anders Army had left, that there was no longer any purpose in making an exception for the Poles, and all former Polish subjects in Western Ukraine and Belorussia, *again* became Soviet citizens, in terms of the original Soviet *ukase* of November 29, 1939. This decision was taken on January 16, 1943.

This was the subject that had been Ambassador Romer's chief concern when diplomatic relations between Poland and the Soviet Union were broken off.

The second part of Vyshinsky's statement dealt with the large network of Polish welfare organisations, to which Romer had referred in the statement quoted above:

After referring to the twenty "agencies" the Polish Embassy had set up in the Soviet Union, ostensibly for the purpose of dealing with these welfare organisations, and quoting numerous cases of more than "incorrect" Polish behaviour, Vyshinsky said that the Polish Embassy people, including Ambassador Kot, instead of busying themselves with the welfare of their fellow-citizens were, in reality, engaged in espionage. Many, he said, were arrested, some expelled from the Soviet Union, and others sentenced to a number of years' imprisonment. (It all savoured a bit of 1937!)

Soon afterwards it was learned that the Union of Polish Patriots had largely been put in charge of these schools, hospitals, et cetera.

Decision to form Polish Army in the Soviet Union

On May 9, it was officially announced that the Council of People's Commissars had agreed to the request of the Union of Polish Patriots in the USSR concerning the formation on Soviet soil of the Tadeusz Kosciuszko Division which would fight against the German invaders, alongside the Red Army. The statement added: "The formation of this division has already begun."

That same day, there was a great All-Slav meeting in Moscow. Greetings were sent to Stalin, Churchill, Roosevelt and Benes. Representatives from all the Slav countries were there, among them Colonel Svoboda, the Commander of the Czechoslovak unit which had distinguished itself so well on the Russian front at the end of March; the Metropolitan Nicholas was there in his robes and tiara; a girl who had escaped from Dachau also spoke, and the introductory speech was made by Fadeyev, President of the Writers' Union, who said:

> The Russian people are totally opposed to the thoroughly reactionary idea of Pan-Slavism, which Russian Tsarism tried to use in its imperialist ambitions. The Russian people are united with the other Slav peoples in their struggle against the common foe on a basis of equality and of profound respect for their freedom, and their national honour and dignity.

But the real *clou* of the meeting was the presence of Wanda Wassilewska and Colonel Berling. Wassilewska, tall, dark, more highly strung than ever, exclaimed:

> From here, from the Eastern Front we shall break through to Poland, a great strong and just Poland. Polish brethren! Listen to the shots fired on the Eastern Front!... And shame on those who are urging you to follow a policy of disastrous inactivity!

Colonel Berling, an ugly, burly man with cropped hair, and looking older than his age, said:

> The road to our homeland lies across the battlefield, and we, Poles in the Soviet Union, are now taking this road.

In the next two months there were to be many more discussions around the Polish problem; violent editorials about the London Poles, meetings by the Union of Polish Patriots, etc. *Wolna Polska* published more revelations about the high officers of the Anders Army and about Anders himself who, according to Zygmunt Berling, now Commander of the Kosciuszko Division, had said that he was glad the Polish Army was being trained on the Middle Volga, because, with the collapse of the Red Army, the Poles could get away to Iran along the Caspian, and then "they could do what they liked". Berling also said: "What an opportunity Anders missed when he could have thrown one Polish Division into the Battle of Moscow, and failed to do so!" He also referred to General Okulicki, Anders's chief of staff (and later, in 1945, the chief defendant in the Moscow trial of the Polish Right-wing Underground) who

> was sabotaging the supply base on the Caspian through which British arms and food were to come to the Anders Army from Iran... The Polish warehouses at Teheran were bursting with stuff in 1942—stuff that the British had been sending—and food was going rotten. But the Anders Command would not allow a single British rifle, tank or case of food to be sent to Russia, and the supply base was to be used for one thing only—the evacuation of the Polish troops from Russia.

But all this recrimination was becoming ancient history (not, however, ancient history of no consequence), and what was of immediate interest now was the development of Russian Policy towards the "other" Poland, and, in the first place, the progress of the new Polish Division. I was to see the Kosciuszko Division on July 15, and it was something of a revelation.

The camp of the Polish Division was in a beautiful pine forest, on the steep banks of the Oka river, about two-thirds of the way from

Moscow to Riazan. In the surrounding villages, in that heart of hearts of Great-Russia, it was odd to see soldiers in Polish uniform wearing square *confederatka* caps, talking to the local inhabitants. No Polish soldiers had ever been anywhere near these parts since 1612, in the days of Ivan Susanin! However, these were in khaki, and not in the dazzling costumes they wore in 1612, if one is to believe the costume designers of the Bolshoi Theatre!

It was a large camp, with well-built wooden barracks and everywhere there were Polish inscriptions, slogans and symbols. The whole forest was teeming with white Polish eagles. We arrived there on the night of the 14th, and the 15th was Grünwald Day, when the Kosciuszko Division was to take the oath on the large parade ground. Grünwald was a battle in the Middle Ages which the combined forces of Slavdom—Poles, Russians and also Lithuanians —had fought against the Teutonic Knights, and by which they had delayed the Germanic expansion to the east. To the Poles it was what the Battle of the Ice, fought on Lake Peipus by Alexander Nevsky in 1242, was to the Russians. It was also a great symbol of Slav unity.

On that night of the 14th, there were many guests seated round the supper table in a large army hut: some Russian generals, Commandant Mirlès, representing the French airmen in France, Czech officers—in short, representatives of all the nations fighting on the Soviet-German Front. For reasons of etiquette, or rather for fear of being snubbed, the Poles had not invited any official British or American representatives. A Russian general called Zhukov— only a namesake of the Marshal's, and, according to the London Poles, an NKVD general—was the principal Russian attached to the Polish division, and had played a leading part in its training, organisation and equipment.

Many Poles who were later to become familiar figures I saw there for the first time. Major Grosz—later General Grosz who was to become one of the chief political advisers of the Polish General Staff; Captain Modzelewski, a seemingly modest and quiet little man, who was later to become Polish Ambassador to Moscow and then Foreign Minister; Captain Borojsza, who was later to become "dictator" of the Polish Press.

And there was a priest there, Father Kupsz, who was said to have been a Polish partisan, and who had recently smuggled himself into Russia. Father Kupsz was a young man with mousey hair and very cagey.

The proceedings on the night of the 14th were presided over by Wanda Wassilewska, and by Colonel Berling.

The next day started with an open-air mass. This was totally unlike the Red Army. An open-air Catholic altar had been erected in an open space in the forest, and Father Kupsz officiated. The altar was decorated with three large panels, one with a symbolic picture of the Christian Faith protected by a Polish soldier, the middle panel showed a Polish eagle, and, below it, a crown of thorns surrounding the figures 1939, 1940, 1941, 1942 and 1943, and with enough room left for one, or, at most, two more dates; the third panel represented a scene of the Nazi terror in Poland. The altar was decorated with flowers and fir-branches and an orchestra of two violins and several brass instruments took the place of the organ. Hundreds of soldiers were kneeling down as they prayed, and later many of them, and scores of auxiliary service girls in khaki, received the holy sacrament. All this in the middle of the pine-forest made a memorable picture.

The most important event of the day was the long march-past of the Kosciuszko Division, preceded by their taking the oath, and the presentation to the Division of its banner with the white Polish eagle on a red-and-white background, inscribed "For Country and Honour" on one side, and a portrait of Kosciuszko on the other. Everywhere, there was a great display of Polish national symbols, and no suggestion that this was in any way a Russian show—except that the Polish spokesmen continuously emphasised their gratitude to the Soviet Union and the Red Army. In the oath, which, phrase after phrase, thousands of Polish soldiers repeated in chorus, standing there on the parade ground, they swore not only that they would fight to the last drop of blood to liberate Poland from the Germans, but they also swore fidelity to their Russian allies "who had put the weapons of war into their hands". And then the march-past began.

It went on for nearly two hours. On the grandstand decorated with Polish, Russian, British, American, Czech and French flags, stood Wanda Wassilewska, Berling and other Polish and Russian officers, and Allied representatives. The men were mostly between twenty-five and thirty-five and were in good trim; the officers wore spruce khaki uniforms and square caps with the Polish eagle; the soldiers wore dark khaki summer tunics as they marched past, the band playing military marches. The formation of the division had started in April, but the intensive training had not begun till early June. They were not a fully trained division yet, but what had been done was described by French and other Allied representatives as very remarkable. No secret was made of the fact that the division had been trained almost exclusively by Russian officers. But the most notable feature was the equipment. Eighty per cent of the equipment was automatic or semi-automatic; several of the companies also had long "stove-pipe" anti-tank rifles; there were several machine-gun units and artillery units, a number of mortar units, and finally some thirty T 34 tanks. All the equipment, except for a few American trucks and jeeps, was Russian.

This equipment was particularly interesting to see, as it was the equivalent of that of a regular Russian Guards infantry division, and the wealth of anti-tank weapons made one realise why, in the previous ten days' fighting, the Germans had failed so completely in their Kursk offensive. A Polish officer remarked (and this was later confirmed by General Zhukov) that the fire power of this division was seven times greater than that of a regular division of the Polish Army in 1939. It was stated that by October the Kosciuszko Division would be ready for action. This was to prove correct, and the Division fought with distinction and heavy casualties in its very first engagements.

What of the human material?

No precise figure could be obtained, but the great majority of the nearly 15,000 officers and men appeared to be Poles—but Poles from parts of Poland taken over by the Russians in 1939. What Russian I did hear spoken in the division—and nearly everybody was speaking Polish—was spoken with a Polish accent. A considerable number of the officers—in fact nearly all of them—had served in the Red Army; and many of them were decorated. One had the Stalingrad medal. But he was unmistakably a Pole, a native of Lwow, who had been mobilised into the Red Army at the beginning of the war. The problem of "nationality" was now solved in a curious and "non-committal" way: the principle on which people were drafted into the Polish division was whether they "felt" Polish. Anyone from the Western Ukraine or Belorussia who "felt" Polish could enter the division. In fact, I talked to a few soldiers who, while calling themselves Poles, said that "in a way" they were sorry to have moved from the Red Army into this Polish division. Very few of the officers and men had served in the Anders Army but there were many who had been "about to join" it when it left for Iran. The soldiers were told that those whose nationality was in doubt could later opt for Polish or Soviet citizenship. This applied to both Poles and persons holding Soviet passports now. There were said to be six per cent of Jews, two per cent of Ukrainians and three per cent of Belorussians in the division. Many of the men were ex-Polish war-prisoners who had come from strange and remote places in the Soviet Union, to which many had been deported as long ago as 1939. Others were deported civilians. In the course of the day I saw a crowd of these. They looked ragged, verminous and demoralised; they had lived in shocking conditions for a long time, and had also had a very hard and long journey from Siberia or Central Asia.

One officer remarked, as I was talking to them: "A lot of our soldiers looked just like that when they first arrived—and now look how spick and span they are." It was true enough, and while no one could deny that many of the Poles in the east had had a very raw deal, this division at last provided a solution for them, and most of them apparently welcomed it. It did mean, if nothing else, that unless killed *en route*, they would be among the first to re-enter Poland; and now, after the tremendous Russian victory at Kursk, the prospect was no longer a remote one.

Among those ragged verminous new arrivals, there was, however, one man in a half-demented hysterical state. He was a dark little man who shrieked a wild incoherent story in very good French— a story of how he had worked before the war on *Le Peuple*, the Socialist paper in Brussels, of how he then fled from Vilna to Sweden with a "temporary" British passport just before the Red Army arrived, of how he then got to Brussels again in 1940. And then the Germans came, and he was put in a concentration camp, but later he was released and went to Lithuania, and here he fell into Russian hands, and then, he cried hysterically, "*depuis trois ans je ne suis plus parmi les vivants!*" He did not seem to relish his "resurrection" by means of the Kosciuszko Division, nor the clarification of his national status.

More refreshing was a group of Polish youngsters who had been mending roads for the German Army near Kalinin, but had joined a Russian partisan unit and had finally got across the German lines.

As regards the trained soldiers, the impression one had was that although they were a very mixed lot, the patriotic propaganda was having the desired effect. They were well-disciplined, well-fed, well-clothed and the idea of being "the first Poles to enter Poland" had its attractions. There was a strong element of flattery in the propaganda and many of these people who had been at a loose end were made to feel important now. Many of them were, in fact, Poles whom Anders would have mobilised (and taken away to Iran), if he had been given time to do so.

A press conference was given by Berling and Wassilewska. Berling said he was born near Cracow in 1896 and had served in Pilsudski's Polish Legion in the last war. (Nobody was tactless enough to ask against whom they had fought then.) He was on the general staff of the Anders Army but disagreed with Anders's political line. He said that the principal criterion in selecting and mobilising people into the Kosciuszko Division was the man's own conscience; if he considered himself a Pole, he was accepted. Other points he made were:

> It is not certain whether we shall accept Poles who served in the German Army. We may take those who deliberately came over to the Red Army; but shall be much more careful with those simply taken prisoner.
>
> We have 600 women doing mostly auxiliary work in our division, also nurses...
>
> No political work is done in the division. But care is taken of cultural activities and a big effort is being made to stamp out illiteracy.

Most of the people have been in the Soviet Union since 1941, or earlier (*sic*); many left their homes as civilian refugees (*sic*). Some have their families in the Soviet Union, and the Union of Polish Patriots is taking care of them.

Father Kupsz has been here only a short time, but judging from the number who attended mass this morning, a high proportion of our soldiers feel the need for religious services.

Wanda Wassilewska, in a somewhat pugnacious mood said that the division clearly showed that all foreign suggestions that it would be merely a token force were utter nonsense. She said she was born in Cracow in 1905, had graduated at the University of Cracow, was a member of the National Committee of the Polish Socialist Party until the collapse of Poland. She had been a journalist, and, since 1934, an author. She came to the Soviet Union in September, 1939. (She did not mention the fact that she was a member of the Supreme Soviet.)

The Union of Polish Patriots (she said) was established in April, 1943. The Union had directly appealed to Marshal Stalin for assistance; and had offered to provide the people who would do the Union's work. The Union of Polish Patriots had three objects: (1) stimulate the formation of Polish armed forces in the Soviet Union; (2) satisfy the cultural needs of the Poles in the Soviet Union; and (3) build a network of Polish schools and take care of the children.

There was no full record of all the Poles in the Soviet Union. The areas over which they were scattered were so enormous that it had not been possible to get in touch with everybody.

The Polish organisations—schools, hospitals, et cetera, run by the Polish Embassy at Kuibyshev were quite unsatisfactory; the Union of Polish Patriots had taken the whole thing over. By September 1, there would be enough schools for all Polish children in the Soviet Union.

It was difficult to say whether any *rapprochement* with the Polish Government in London was possible.

The Union of Polish Patriots merely dealt with Poles in the USSR; it had no pretension of being an *ersatz* Polish Government.

But it strongly felt that the future Government of Poland must come from the people, not from the émigrés. Poland must be democratic, not feudal.

Sikorski [who shortly before had been killed in a plane crash] was a good, honest man, but he was too weak, and he was unable to resist the pressure of the reactionaries.

The Union of Polish Patriots was not conducting any propaganda inside Poland, but, the very existence of a Kosciuszko Division here would certainly make the strongest impression on the Polish people—especially once it started, together with the Red Army, driving the Germans out of Poland.

Clearly, the whole thing was of far-reaching political importance, and this is not altered by the fact that both Wassilewska and Berling were—for different reasons—to disappear as leaders of the movement before very long. Other, and stronger, people were to take their places.

Katyn

In September, 1943, the Russian Army recaptured Smolensk from the Germans, and soon people in Moscow were asking when light would at last begin to be thrown on the Katyn murders. But for a long time nothing happened, and it was not till January, 1944, that the Russians published their findings, and also invited the Western press in Moscow to visit the mass graves.

On January 15 a large group of Western correspondents, accompanied by Kathie Harriman, the daughter of Averell Harriman, the United States Ambassador, went on their gruesome journey to look at the hundreds of bodies in Polish uniforms which had been dug up at Katyn Forest by the Russian authorities. It was said that some 10,000 had been buried there, but actually only a few hundred "samples" had been unearthed* and were filling even the cold winter air with an unforgettable stench. The Russian Committee of Inquiry, which had been set up, and was presiding over the proceedings, consisted of forensic medicine men, such as Academician Burdenko, and a number of "personalities" whose very presence was to give the whole inquiry an air of great respectability and authority; among them were the Metropolitan Nicholas of Moscow, the famous writer Alexei Tolstoy, Mr Potemkin, the Minister of Education, and others. What qualifications these "personalities" had

---

* The London Poles alleged that only 4,000 were buried at Katyn and that there were two other "Katyns" inside Russia which had not been discovered.

for judging the "freshness" or "antiquity" of unearthed corpses was not quite clear. Yet the whole argument turned precisely on this very point: had the Poles been buried by the Russians in the spring of 1940, or by the Germans in the late summer or autumn of 1941? Professor Burdenko, wearing a green frontier guard cap, was busy dissecting corpses, and, waving a bit of greenish stinking liver at the tip of his scalpel would say "Look how lovely and fresh it looks."

Hundreds of pages have been written about the findings of the Committee of Inquiry set up in April, 1943, by the Germans and of the Russian Committee of Inquiry of January, 1944. Both cases have been very fully summarised in a number of books, particularly in General Anders's *Katyn*. Anders's conclusion, of course, is that, however many millions of people the Germans had murdered elsewhere, there was not the slightest doubt that in this case the Russians were guilty.

While this is more than probable, if not *absolutely* certain, it must be said that the Russians conducted their publicity round the case (including the visit of the Western press to Katyn) with the utmost clumsiness and crudeness. The press was allowed to attend only one of the meetings of the Russian Committee of Inquiry, which questioned several witnesses. Among them were a Professor Bazilevsky, an astronomer, a doddery little man whom the Germans were said to have persuaded or compelled to become the assistant burgomaster of Smolensk; he declared that his chief, a quisling who had since fled with the Germans, had told him that the Polish officers were to be liquidated; a notebook said to belong to this ex-burgomaster was produced with this significant, if somewhat cryptic, entry: "Are people in Smolensk talking about the shooting of the Poles?"

Among other witnesses was a girl who had been a servant at the former NKVD villa* taken over by the Gestapo, where the German killers lived. She related how lorries used to drive into the forest and how, soon afterwards, with her employers absent from the villa, she could hear shots being fired some distance away.

There was also a railwayman who explained how it was impossible to evacuate the Poles from the camps near Smolensk in July

* Why *was* there such a villa near Katyn Forest? One might well have wondered.

1941 during the German advance. The railways were in a state of grave disorganisation, with the Red Army in full retreat.

Another witness declared that on the roads leading to Katyn Forest he had met large lorries covered with tarpaulins from which came a terrible stench of corpses—the inference being that not all the killing had been done at Katyn, and that many bodies had been brought by the Germans from elsewhere—indeed old, 1940 corpses, which would help to confirm *their* story about these Poles having been killed in 1940. One very scared peasant admitted that he had been bullied by the Germans into testifying as they wanted him to, during *their* inquiry into the Katyn murders. All this was very thin.

One strange peculiarity of the one and only session of the Committee of Inquiry which the foreign press was allowed to attend was that it was not permitted to put any questions to the witnesses. The whole precedure had a distinctly prefabricated appearance.

Altogether, the Russian starting-point in this whole inquiry was that the very suggestion that the Russians might have murdered the Poles had to be ruled out right away; the whole idea was insulting and outrageous, and there was, therefore, no need to dwell on any facts which might have led to the Russians' "acquittal". It was essential to *accuse* the Germans; to *acquit* the Russians was wholly irrelevant.

The circumstances of the captivity and the exact number and whereabouts of the Polish officers and N.C.O.'s, in fact, continued to be treated as a "State secret" which concerned the Russian authorities only. No outsider was ever shown the three camps "near Smolensk" at which the Poles were supposed to have been trapped by the Germans.

It must be said that the Russians did not do much to destroy the "London-Polish" arguments for disbelieving the Russian version. For one thing, they did not even trouble to deal with the circumstantial evidence which, on the face of it, was favourable to them.

First, whatever the Germans said to the contrary, the technique of these mass murders was German, rather than Russian; in countless other places exactly the same technique had been used by the Gestapo in their mass murders. The record of the NKVD, on the other hand, rather suggested that people in their care did frequently die in large numbers—but through neglect, overwork, bad food and exposure to cold, rather than in any kind of mass murders. Secondly, why kill them in 1940 when Russia was at peace, and there could be no urgency for exterminating even these "class enemies"?

Then there was the question of the bullets; the Poles had been murdered with *German* bullets, a fact which—judging from his *Diary*—had greatly perturbed Goebbels. Anders quotes a witness as suggesting that these "Geco" bullets had been sold in large numbers by Germany to the Baltic States, and that the Russians had helped themselves to them there. But this argument is not perfect: the Russians were supposed to have murdered the Poles in March, 1940, and they did not fully occupy the Baltic States until three months later.

We now know the London-Polish story about the proposed Russo-German exchange of these officers for 30,000 Ukrainians held by the Germans, the subsequent refusal of the Germans to "accept" them, and the "mistake" made by the NKVD in misinterpreting Stalin's alleged order to "liquidate" the camps. But this story still needs a lot of clarification.

A not wholly convincing pro-Russian argument was that Katyn Forest used to be the favourite excursion place for the people of Smolensk, which had not been surrounded by barbed wire until after the Germans had come in July 1941. It was very hard to say whether this was true or not. The Russian argument was that there had been no barbed wire round Katyn Forest before the German invasion, and that, in the circumstances, it was ridiculous to suggest that people would have been allowed to picnic on fresh mass-graves!

Finally, the Germans had been in Smolensk since July 1941; was it conceivable that they would not have heard about the shooting of the Poles until two years later? But all this, too, was very thin.

On the other hand, was it not possible that the Germans had murdered the Poles in 1941—with a view to "planting" them on the Russians two years later? Since there might well have been serious doubts about the exact "age" of the corpses, this was just conceivable, except for the extreme obscurity surrounding the three camps "near Smolensk" at which the Poles were supposed to have been kept after being transferred there from the three original camps.

Then, there was another version which was put forward by some members of the British Embassy in Moscow at the time—and that is that the Russians did not murder the Poles in 1940, "which made no sense", but in 1941, during their stampede, when they lost their heads and decided that it was impossible to evacuate the Poles, but also most undesirable to leave this "bunch of Fascists" in German hands.

If this had happened, that would explain why the Russians were so infernally cagey whenever Sikorski or Anders kept asking about the missing officers. But it would still not explain why not a single message had been received in Poland from any of them—except the lucky 400 near Vologda—after the three original camps had been disbanded.

The *material* evidence produced by the Russians that the Poles had been murdered in 1941 and not in 1940 was very slender, one must say. Correspondents who looked at it were not impressed: newspapers and letters dated *both* 1940 and 1941 (all of them in very small numbers) were, together with other undated objects, such as tobacco pouches, medals and a fifty-dollar bill, displayed in show cases.

Sceptics inevitably wondered whether those few 1941 newspapers or one or two unmailed postcards could not have been slipped into the dead men's pockets at some time between September 1943 and January 1944. In 1943 the Germans had certainly put on show many thousands of "1940" objects supposedly found on dead Poles.

The Russians, in presenting their case to the outside world, had certainly taken no notice at all of what would, in Western terms, be regarded as *evidence*. The idea that foreign experts should have been invited to take part in the inquiry was dismissed by the Russians as "insulting". The answer to such a suggestion would have been: "Are you suggesting that Professor Burdenko or Alexei Tolstoy, or the Metropolitan Nicholas could tell a lie?" True, even a benevolent foreigner might say: "Well, if he thinks it in the interests of his country that he should tell a lie, wouldn't Tolstoy or the Metropolitan do it?" But then such an argument would also have been dismissed by the Russians as "hostile". Also, there was the perennial element of distrust: even if the Russians were one hundred per cent sure of their case, what certainty was there that a foreign expert might not prove either ignorant or malevolent, in expressing the view that the corpses, for all their "freshness" were three-and-a-half and not two-and-a-half years old.* There was always a risk of "Western bad faith".

The Western correspondents who had been allowed to visit Katyn in such peculiar circumstances were put in an extremely difficult— indeed impossible—position; they could do little more than say what they had been shown; and even any implied criticism of the Russian handling of the whole case, however mild, was deleted by the Soviet censorship. Also, to suggest that the Russian case was as bad as Goebbels's case, or even worse, was something one couldn't do in wartime; it was imperative not to play into the German's hands. Might it not also have been *this* consideration which prompted Miss Harriman to state in January 1944 that she was "satisfied" that the Russian version was correct?

Looking back on it now, with all the evidence accumulated by the "London Poles", which broadly tallies with the German version, one can only wish the Russians would open up their secret archives on the whole Katyn case. They must know far more than could be revealed in the days when Beria was head of the NKVD. It was surely also Beria who was Culprit No. 1 in either case—whether the Poles were murdered in 1940 or whether they were left behind in 1941, for the Germans to murder. But it would, even now, no doubt be too much to expect Moscow to make a clean breast of it merely for the sake of historical truth. Katyn, to the Russians, as well as to the Poles, is still so explosive a word that there is a kind of tacit agreement to say nothing about it. To the Russians it has, one feels, remained an embarrassing subject, whatever their true beliefs as to what really happened.

* The "freshness" of the corpses is attributed by Anders to the fact that the Russians made a bad mistake in burying them in sandy soil, in which they tended to become "mummified". In damp soil nothing but unidentifiable skeletons would have been found by the Germans.

All the same, the Russians might help to clear up the mystery in their own favour if only they would produce documentary evidence to show that the murdered Poles had really been in "Camps No. 1 ON, No. 2 ON, and No. 3 ON, 25 to 45 km. west of Smolensk" in the summer of 1941. There must be *something* about it in the archives of the NKVD—if the Poles really were in these camps at that time. *But were they?* In Poland, to this day, very, very few—if any—believe in the NKVD's innocence.

And it is, of course, well known that at the Nuremberg Trial, where the same old Bazilevsky repeated the same old story,* the Tribunal found the evidence on Katyn much too thin to take account of it in the final indictment of the Germans.

For years Katyn Forest was going to cast a shadow on Russo-Polish relations. It almost seemed as if there was a kind of curse on the relations between the two Slav peoples. For even if, despite Katyn, the Red Army, entering Poland, together with the Moscow-made Polish Army, was at first welcomed by the Polish population, more bitter feeling was, before long, to be created by what came to be known in London as "the monstrous crime against Warsaw". But in reality, as we shall see, the two cases are not identical, or even comparable.

* TMGWC, vol. 17, pp. 355–62.

Chapter VII

THE DISSOLUTION OF THE COMINTERN
AND OTHER CURIOUS EVENTS IN THE
SPRING OF 1943

Living and working conditions were still very hard for most of the
civilian population in 1943. In essential industries people worked
overtime—eleven, twelve hours. The labour shortage was such that,
for simpler operations, children were employed in some plants for
periods ranging from four to six hours a day.* Rations, especially
for dependents and non-working children, were miserably poor;
everything in the *kolkhoz* markets was scarce and very expensive.
In the cities, there was a black market of sorts, with sugar, for
instance, fetching as much as 3,000 roubles a kilo. (About £30 per
lb.)

In 1943, a "deep war", in Ehrenburg's phrase, had set in; peace
had become a distant memory and victory was still a long way ahead,
in a dim future. There was still no "real" second front, and though
between March and June there was an extraordinary display of
official cordiality towards the Western allies, this contrasted
strangely with the much more morose attitude towards them on the
part of the general public. The feeling that the Allies were not pulling their weight, despite North Africa and the bombing of Germany,
was very widespread. It is usually assumed that "the good Russian
people" are much more pro-Western than their government; at this

* Ehrenburg, *Ludi, Gody, Zhizn* (People, Years, a Lifetime), *Novyi
Mir*, No. 3, 1963.

time the opposite was the case. The official cordiality was no doubt tactical, rather than genuine.

First of all, soon after the uncomplimentary Stalin Order of February 23, the Soviet authorities, swallowing their pride, hastened to react to the Standley incident in a manner most agreeable to Roosevelt. Then there was the breach with the London Poles— which was likely to generate strong anti-Soviet sentiment in Britain and the United States, and it was essential, therefore, for the Russians to try to "localise" the Polish problem, and not allow it to affect Soviet-Anglo-American relations unduly. Hence perhaps the record warmth *vis-a-vis* Britain and America in May and June 1943.

Although the loss of Kharkov was keenly felt, the winter campaign had still, on balance, been a magnificent success. Whether, as the Russians said, the Germans and their allies had lost 800,000 men, or only the 470,000 which the Germans admitted, the replacement of even this lower figure in time for the summer offensive was well-nigh impossible, all the more so since the Satellites had not the capacity, and still less the desire, to waste more of their men on "Hitler's war" which was now more than unlikely to be won. In spite of this, the Russians awaited the summer campaign with a touch of nervousness, for the memories of the terrible last two summers—1941 and 1942—were still fresh.

On the eve of this decisive military showdown of July 1943 rumours became more frequent than at any other time in the war of separate peace offers by the Germans to both Russia and the West. In his May Day Order Stalin actually referred to these peace-feelers; and it is reasonable to suppose that the great display of official Russian cordiality towards the West was at least partly determined by nervousness at the possibility of a deal between Germany and the Western Powers. Similar suspicions existed on the other side too; for we know that Allied soldiers in the Mediterranean area were told that the war there would have to be pursued with the greatest possible vigour "in case the Russians packed up". Some suspicion was also aroused in the West by the curious and unexpected Russian move of setting up a "Free German Committee",* with the Wilhelmian black-white-red as its colours, which were still believed to be cherished by a great part of the officer corps.

Unlike his Red Army Day Order of February 23, Stalin's May Day Order of 1943 was full of friendly words for the Western Allies. After describing the great winter campaign in Russia, and after referring to the German counter-offensive at Kharkov which had been carried out thanks to the thirty divisions brought from the west (the only barbed "second front" reference in the whole statement) but which had, nevertheless, failed to become a "German Stalingrad", Stalin then spoke in glowing terms of "our victorious Allies in Tripolitania, Libya and Tunisia", and of "the valiant Anglo-American airmen" who were "delivering smashing blows on both Germany and Italy, thus foreshadowing the establishment of a second front in Europe".

The Germans and their allies, he said, were in an increasingly bad mess, and there was more and more talk in the foreign press of German peace-feelers aimed at splitting the Anglo-American-Soviet alliance. The German imperialists, Stalin said, were treacherous people, and liked to judge others by their own standards. Nobody would fall for that kind of bait, and peace would be attained only through the complete rout of Hitler's armies, and *the unconditional surrender* of Nazi Germany.

> But though catastrophe was staring Germany and Italy in the face, this still did not mean that the war was as good as won. Some very hard battles were still facing the Soviet Union and the Western allies, but the time was approaching when, *together with the armies of its allies, the Red Army would break the back of the Fascist Beast.*

During the days that followed, the Soviet press was more pro-Ally than ever before. On May 9, Stalin warmly congratulated Roosevelt and Churchill on "the great victory in North Africa", and all over the country coloured posters were displayed of three equal-sized bolts of lightning, bearing the British, American and Russian colours, breaking the Beast's back. It was a mangy, hyena-like beast with a Hitler head.

* See pp. 733 ff.

The end of the Tunisian campaign had raised high hopes—perhaps excessively high hopes—in Russia.

In any case, the space allotted in *Pravda* to the Allies was unusually large. The following long articles (*podvals*, the equivalent of the *Times* "turnover") appeared in *Pravda* in May and June:

	May	June
Germany	1	2
Germany's satellites	1	2
Britain and USA	4	6
Occupied Slav countries	7	2
France and Belgium	1	2
Neutrals	1	–

The articles on the Allies concerned the blows against Italy, the submarine war, the British Navy, the RAF and American war industries. Moreover, the principal Western statesmen were generously reported—

	Columns			Columns
May 21, Churchill	5	June 2, Sumner Welles	1½
„ 22, Eden	1	„ 8, Churchill	4
„ 26, Stettinius	2	„ 8, Eden	1
„ 28, Roosevelt	3	„ 22, Cripps	1

What impressed Soviet military commentators most was that, in Tunisia, the English and Americans had won their first major land battle. This was represented as the prelude to much bigger land operations in Europe. The air forces were preparing the way for them.

On May 22—largely as a gesture to impress Britain and America—the dissolution of the Comintern was announced. This took the form of a Resolution by the Presidium of the Executive Committee of the Communist International. It declared the whole organisation to be "out of date", and that it was even "becoming an obstacle in the way of the further strengthening of the national working parties." It then explained that the war had demonstrated a very important fact:

> Whereas in the Axis countries it is important for the working class to strive to overthrow the government, in the United Nations countries it is, on the contrary, the duty of the working class to support the governments' war effort.

This strange document concluded: "The Executive Committee calls upon its supporters to concentrate on the smashing of German fascism and its vassals."

It was signed by the following members of the Presidium: Gott-wald, Dimitrov, Zhdanov, Kolarov, Koplenig, Kuusinen, Manuilsky, Marty, Pieck, Thorez, Florin, Ercoli (i.e. Togliatti), and also the following representatives of the Sections: Biano (Italy), D. Ibarruri (Spain), Lechtinen (Finland), Anna Pauker (Rumania), M. Rakosi (Hungary).

A few days later, in a statement to Harold King of Reuters, Stalin declared the dissolution to be "right and timely".

> It showed up the Nazi lie that "Moscow" intended to interfere with the lives of other states, or to "bolshevise" them... It also facilitated the work of all patriots for uniting all the progressive forces, regardless of party allegiance and political beliefs... It was particularly timely just when the Fascist beast was exerting his last reserves of strength that the freedom-loving nations should organise a common onslaught on him, and so save all nations from the Fascist yoke...

It was well-known that both Churchill and Roosevelt had pressed for this step. Stalin had always replied that the Comintern was moribund, and did not matter. What he did not say, however, was that this "moribund"—and now dead—body comprised many future leaders of the "new democracy" in Europe—Thorez, Togliatti, Gottwald, Kopecky, Dimitrov, Pauker, Rakosi, et cetera. They led at the time a very retiring existence either at Ufa or in Moscow, where most of them lived in the grubby Hotel Lux in Gorki Street, only very occasionally wrote in the Soviet press, and were seldom seen in public, except at the very end of the war. But they were kept in reserve. Even so, many wondered whether Stalin had not a genuine grudge against the Comintern leaders. Had not Dimitrov overdone his "imperialist war" stuff in 1939-40. And *who* had thought up the "Kuusinen government"?

In my Diary notes during the few weeks before the Battle of Kursk I find a record of a number of conversations with Russians on the dissolution of the Comintern. One said that "it must have been a very hard decision for Stalin to take; after all, he had sworn on Lenin's tomb never to abandon the cause of the world revolution. But just like his 'socialism in one country' this decision was another sign of Stalin's greatness that he could adapt himself to changed conditions". Another Russian described it jokingly as "our NEP in foreign policy"; and still another said that "Stalin had been a bit fed-up with the Comintern for some time, especially for their screaming about the 'imperialist war' in 1939–40". This had caused no end of damage in a country like France, and had also grossly misled the Soviet Government on a number of occasions.

Then there was the rather spectacular visit on May 30 of ex-Ambassador Joseph Davies, of *Mission to Moscow* fame, who had done his utmost to explain the Purge Trials in a manner most favourable to the Soviet Government. On arriving in Moscow, he got the Russians to paint "Mission to Moscow" in white paint on the fuselage of his plane. He went to see, as he called them, "his old friends" Mikoyan, Vyshinsky and Judge Ulrich. The film of his *Mission to Moscow* was full of absurdities—Vyshinsky with a great black beard, Mrs Molotov speaking pidgin Russian, and so on. They showed it at the Kremlin the night he was there, and the big Russian bosses laughed themselves nearly sick, but agreed that the film was friendly, and useful in debunking the Red bogey idea, still, according to Davies, very strong in the USA. The British Embassy were pretty mad with Davies about the monocled silly-ass who was supposed to represent Lord Chilston, the British Ambassador, scared to death of OGPU microphones, and so on. The US Embassy and the American press were uniformly hostile to Davies, partly because of his peculiar showmanship, and partly because of his excessive display of pro-Soviet sentiment, not to say sentimentality. Davies, for his part, was very pleased with the dissolution of the Comintern and remarked that when he was Ambassador in Moscow, he used to say to Litvinov that the Comintern—the stick with which everybody beat the Soviet Union—was the real source of all the trouble.

*

Sandwiched between the Dissolution of the Comintern and Stalin's statement on it were the celebrations of the first anniversary of the Anglo-Soviet Alliance which took the form of enthusiastic articles in the press, messages from Kalinin to George VI, and so on. On June 9, the anniversary of the Soviet-American Agreement, the papers were full of compliments to the USA, complete with expressions of gratitude for lend-lease shipments. Said *Pravda*: "The Soviet people not only know about them, but they highly value the support coming from the great Republic beyond the ocean." The most important thing now, *Pravda* said, was not to give Hitler any respite.

This constant boost of the Allies in May and June, and the great ideological concessions the Russians were making to the West were not, of course, without reference to the military situation. A period of extremely hard fighting was imminent, and the Russians were hoping that a tremendous new effort (now that North Africa was a closed chapter) would be made by the Allies in the near future.

In its "Second Anniversary of the War" statement on June 22, 1943, Sovinformbureau went so far as to say that "*without a second front victory over Germany is impossible.*" The main theme of the statement was that thanks to the Red Army, which was tying up 200 German and thirty satellite divisions, the Western Allies had been given enough time to prepare themselves for an all-out attack on the Axis on the continent of Europe.*

Was the Sovinformbureau statement merely another tactical move to butter up the allies, or was it a sign of genuine nervousness on the eve of the great summer battles?

For June 1943 was certainly an anxious month. Everybody felt that the storm might break at any moment. Many were surprised

* This statement said that, in two years, Germany and her allies had lost 6·4 m. men in killed and prisoners, 56,000 guns, 42,000 tanks, 43,000 planes. The Soviet Union had lost 4·2 million men in killed and missing (i.e. including prisoners), 30,000 guns, 30,000 tanks, 23,000 planes. It then dealt with the Partisan movement which it credited with having killed 300,000 Germans, wrecked 3,000 trains and over 3,000 bridges, destroyed "hundreds of tanks", et cetera, all of which is highly improbable, since the Partisan movement did not assume major proportions until the second half of 1943.

that the Germans had not attacked yet. There was intense air activity on both sides. On several nights the Germans raided Gorki, causing much damage to its industrial areas, especially to a large tank-assembly plant. There were also raids on Kursk, Saratov, Yaroslavl, Astrakhan, et cetera, and the Germans also dropped mines on the Lower Volga. The Russians raided Orel and other places. Altogether, it was clear that the Kursk-Orel area would be the main battleground; and when the German offensive began, it completely lacked all elements of surprise. Even their famous new weapons, the Tiger and Panther tanks were no secret. A number of them had been captured near Leningrad, and two were even included in the Trophies Exhibition in Moscow during June. They had undergone all the necessary Russian experiments for knocking them out.

On June 11 I recorded a conversation with a Russian correspondent who had just been to Kursk. He said the Russian equipment there was truly stupendous; he had never seen anything like it. What was also going to make a big difference this summer was the enormous number of American trucks; these were going to increase Russian mobility to a fantastic degree. The Russian soldiers were finding them excellent.

On the same day I also wrote:

> Molotov today gave a lunch to celebrate the anniversary of the Soviet-American agreement. He was extremely friendly, and kept talking about not only wartime, but also post-war co-operation between the Big Three. All the toasts dealt indeed with this tripartite association continuing after the war. Clark Kerr said he was glad the Anglo-Soviet alliance had turned out such a sturdy child; it had looked a bit bandy-legged at first. Admiral Standley dwelt on Lend-Lease deliveries, which had been a bit slow at first, but were very satisfactory now, with a lot of stuff all over the place, with Oerlikons on Russian ice-breakers and British guns on the Red October battleship. . . The Russians are thinking (or talking) more and more in terms of a Big-Three peace after the war. . .

During the second half of June there had been two air-raid warnings in Moscow. In fact, on June 9, some stuff had been dropped on the outskirts, though not on Moscow itself. The planes were on their way to Gorki. Even so, instructions were given to the civil defence people in Moscow to be on the alert.

On June 19 Ehrenburg published a rather alarmist article about future air-raids on Moscow: "Don't forget that they are still at Orel; forget that they are no longer at Viazma. They will not take Moscow, but they hate Moscow, the symbol of their failures; and they will try to cripple and disfigure it."

In June I saw a great deal of the airmen of the French Normandie Squadron, a mixed bunch ranging from Paris communist workers talking with a delightful *faubourg* accent to the ginger-haired Vicomte de La Poype. The Russians were astonished that a *vicomte* should want to fight on the side of the Bolsheviks. But the most impressive amongst this marvellous group of fellows was the commander of the Squadron, Commandant Tulasne, small, handsome, with something of the finesse of Alfred de Vigny's officers.

The squadron was formed in Syria in 1942. For political reasons, de Gaulle had decided to send this small French force to Russia. They had been here since the end of 1942, had already been in action, and, by June, the squadron had shot down fifteen German planes, for the loss of three. Now, in June 1943, they were preparing for those big battles in which so many of them were going to lose their lives. They got on well with the Russian mechanics at the air-base, and also had plenty of fun with the girls in the near-by village. They flew Yak-1's, which they said they liked.

Tulasne, whom I met at lunch on June 17 at General Petit's (the French Military Attaché), said that things were still very quiet in the Briansk sector (where the French had their base), but that "it" might start at any moment. The Russians were busy raiding German communications with 200 bombers and 200 fighters at a time; they were using Russian bombers during the day, and American bombers at night; the Germans had hardly any night fighters here, so busy were they over Germany.

The French, he said, were eating the same food as the Russians, and had got to like *kasha* and cabbage soup; but they seldom got fresh meat, and usually American spam or galantine, which was a bore. The more recent French arrivals were finding living conditions rather primitive, but were quite happy otherwise. The village girls were "very friendly".

The story of the Normandie Squadron was to become one of the proudest French exploits during World War II, and one of the most tragic. In the battles of the Kursk-Orel area in the summer of 1943 about *two-thirds* of the first batch of the Normandie Squadron were killed, among them Lefevre and Tulasne. Later, others came to take their place, and their last battles were to be fought in East Prussia where, supplied with the best Russian fighters, the Yak-3, they wrought terrible havoc on the now tottering Luftwaffe, once bringing down nearly 100 in three days. The *vicomte* was born under a lucky star, and, together with three others, was awarded the title of Hero of the Soviet Union, and ultimately safely returned to France. But Tulasne was the man whom the veterans of the Normandie Squadron remembered best.

The fearful losses in the Normandie Squadron give one some idea of the losses suffered by the Russian air force generally.

Partly because of the growing Great-Russian nationalism, and partly perhaps to impress the Western Allies (who had been so pleased with the dissolution of the Comintern) Stalin decided in June 1943 in favour of a new National Anthem to replace the *International*. At the end of the month, members of the Central Committee listened to some of the first attempts, but were not satisfied; it was not till the beginning of 1944 that the Party anthem (with new "nationalist" words) was adopted as the national anthem, and the *International* became the party anthem!

These manifestations of friendliness to the Allies—all with an eye on a Big-Three peace—were partly offset by an innovation of a different order. To show, as it were, that Marxist consciousness was still alive, and that there was no "ideological NEP", there appeared in June, ostensibly under the auspices of *Trud* and the Soviet trade unions,

a new journal called *War and the Working Class*. This declared in
its very first issue that its main object was to show up crypto-Fascist
elements abroad, who were unfavourable to the Soviet concept of a
Big-Three Peace. "It would be ridiculous to deny," it said, "that
certain difficulties exist in the relations between the different members of the anti-Hitler coalition," and it went hammer-and-tongs for
the American isolationists, for the English "Cliveden Set" and other
"Munichites". These "semi-allies of Hitler" tended nowadays to do
their dirty work through the medium of "certain Polish circles who
had learned nothing". It then spoke favourably of a "Directorate of
the principal powers" which would "render account" to the wider
international organisation of all the nations. The Russian conception
of a United Nations Organisation "directed" by the Great Powers—
or rather, by the Big Three—was beginning to take shape.

What with air-raids on Gorki and air-raid warnings in Moscow,
there was a distinct feeling of nervousness in Moscow during June
and the beginning of July. The feeling that more loss of life was in
store was nicely reflected in this genuine story a Russian told me
about the charwoman in his office. On hearing somebody say that
the Second Front was absolutely necessary, she exclaimed: "God
forbid! As if one Front wasn't enough!" She had two sons in the
Army.

On July 6 it was officially announced that the German offensive
had started in a very big way just where it had been expected—in
the Kursk salient, between Belgorod and the Orel Bulge.

Chapter VIII

KURSK: HITLER LOSES HIS LAST CHANCE OF TURNING THE TIDE

Already in February, after Stalingrad, Hitler had declared that it was essential for the German Army "to make up in summer what had been lost in winter." This was not easy since the Germans and their allies had lost well over half a million men, perhaps as many as 700,000. Despite the "total mobilisation" introduced in Germany, only about half the losses could be replaced by the beginning of the summer fighting, according to German sources. Hitler's prestige had suffered severely from Stalingrad, and the recapture of Kharkov had not made up for it. The rout of the Germans in North Africa and the prospect of an early invasion of Italy, with unpredictable (or perhaps all-too-predictable) political consequences, had added to Hitler's discomfiture. The war in Russia could scarcely be won any longer, but what Hitler badly needed was a spectacular victory—something similar to the Russian victory at Stalingrad. The "Kursk salient" between Orel in the north and Belgorod in the south (a salient which the Russians had captured in the previous winter) seemed the most obvious place for inflicting a sensational defeat on the Russians.

The Russians looked upon the Kursk salient as their springboard for the reconquest of the Orel and Briansk country to the north-west, and of the Ukraine to the south-west, and there were enormous Russian troop concentrations in it. Ever since March the Russians had been fortifying the salient with thousands of miles of trenches, thousands of gun emplacements, et cetera, and the defence in depth along the north, west and south sides of the salient extended as much as sixty-five miles.

In the spring of 1943, according to German sources, Hitler was determined for both political and economic reasons to hold a front running from the Gulf of Finland down to the Sea of Azov, and to inflict a resounding defeat on the Russians with his "Operation Citadel" in the Kursk salient. To trap vast numbers of Russians there would greatly change the whole strategic position in the Germans' favour, and might even make a new offensive against Moscow possible.

As the Germans now tell the story:

> The Kursk salient seemed particularly favourable for such an attack. A simultaneous German offensive from north and south would trap powerful Russian forces. It was also to be hoped that the operational reserves the enemy would throw into the fray could be smashed. Moreover, the liquidation of this salient would greatly shorten the front... True, there were some who argued even then that the enemy would expect the German attack precisely in *this* area and ... that there was therefore the danger of losing more German forces than destroying Russian forces... But Hitler would not be convinced, and thought Operation Citadel would succeed, provided it was undertaken *soon.**

But the operation was delayed owing to unfavourable terrain conditions and also to the slowness with which the German divisions were being replenished. In the circumstances General Model, commanding the German troops north of the salient declared that the operation could not succeed without strong reinforcements by heavy modern tanks, superior to anything the Russians had. The attack was therefore postponed once again till the middle of June, and meantime numerous new Tiger and Panther tanks and Ferdinand mobile guns were rushed from armaments works in Germany straight to the front. But there were further hesitations and delays caused, among other things, by Hitler's fear that Italy was on the point of dropping out of the war. When he had satisfied himself that Mussolini was not giving up, Hitler decided to stick to his original plan.

* Philippi and Heim, op. cit., pp. 209–10.

The Kursk victory, he declared, would fire the imagination of the world.

Meanwhile the Russians under Zhukov and Vasilevsky had not wasted their time, and nothing suited them better than that the Germans should attack them where they were strongest of all. The extent of the Russian concentration of armaments in the main battle area may be judged from the fact that, in less than three months, some 500,000 railway wagons loaded with every kind of equipment had been brought from inside Russia to the Kursk salient.

The Germans had accumulated 2,000 tanks round the salient (according to the Russians, over 3,000), more than half of them in the southern sector commanded by General Hoth, and nearly 2,000 planes.

To quote Philippi and Heim:

> With such heavy German concentrations, Hitler looked forward to the battle with great confidence. He was sure that the northern and southern striking force would break through and close the ring east of Kursk. But, contrary to expectations, it took only a very short time to realise that the offensive was a failure, even though our troops exerted themselves to the utmost. Our attacking forces, though penetrating into the deep Russian defences, were suffering very severe losses, and on July 7 the Russians threw in increasingly heavy tank forces. The German 4th Panzer Army had to fight particularly heavy tank battles, in which the most it could hope to do was not to be driven back. Serious doubts grew as to the success of Operation Citadel. Hitler nevertheless ordered on July 10 the offensive to continue. That was the day on which the Western Allies landed in Sicily, and he needed his "Kursk victory" more than ever.
>
> In reality, after the initial tactical successes, the Battle of Kursk had long before come to a standstill, and on July 12 the Russian command suddenly struck out towards Orel, in the rear of the German 9th Army [at the north side of the Kursk salient]... On July 13 Hitler reluctantly ordered Operation Citadel to be discontinued. This decision was further prompted by the Italians' failure to defend Sicily, and the possibility of having to send German reinforcements to Italy.*

* Ibid., p. 212.

In four days the Germans succeeded in no more than denting the Kursk salient—by some ten miles along a front of about twelve miles in the north, and by some thirty miles along a thirty mile front in the south. About 100 miles still separated the two German forces when the battle came to a standstill.*

Nearly the entire German panzer force had been used up to an irreplaceable extent, and the initiative was finally lost by the Germans and taken over by the Red Army. Despite very heavy losses they had also suffered in the Battle of Kursk, the Russian command was now still able to launch its summer offensive along a very broad front, with superior forces.

There was tremendous tension in Moscow when it was first learned that the German offensive had begun. The news was contained in an article, redolent of nationalism, in *Red Star*:

> Our fathers and our forebears made every sacrifice to save their Russia, their homeland. Our people will never forget Minin and Pozharsky, Suvorov and Kutuzov, and the Russian Partisans of 1812. We are proud to think that the blood of our glorious ancestors is flowing in our veins, and we shall be worthy of them. . .

What was being fought in the very heart of Russia, in Turgeniev country, was a modern kind of Battle of Kulikovo† on the outcome of which so much depended.

On the very first day of the battle two things were clear: that Germany had thrown tremendous forces into the battle and that they were suffering losses on an unprecedented scale, and were not getting much in return. The communiqué of the first day's fighting read:

> Since this morning our troops have been fighting stubborn battles against the large advancing forces of enemy infantry and tanks in the Orel, Kursk and Belgorod sectors. The enemy forces are supported by large numbers of aircraft. All the attacks were repelled with heavy losses to the enemy, and only in some places did small German units

* See map p. 686.
† In which Prince Dimitri Donskoi routed the Tartars in 1380.

succeed in penetrating slightly into our defence lines. Preliminary reports show that our troops . . . have crippled or destroyed 586 enemy tanks. . . 203 enemy planes have been shot down. The fighting is continuing.

It was the 586 tanks which captured the country's imagination; there had never been anything like it in one day. The feeling it produced was like that in London at the height of the Battle of Britain when it was announced that 280 German planes had been shot down in one day.

On July 6 the communiqué again spoke of a slight Russian withdrawal, and the number of tanks was now 433, and of planes, 111. On the 7th, it was 520 tanks and again 111 planes. On the 8th, the Russians were already counter-attacking, and the German losses for the day were put at 304 tanks and 161 planes.

By the 9th, the four days of anxiety came to an end; not that the anxiety was ever acute after those first 586 tanks. "The Tigers are Burning" was the title of a report from the front, and there appeared statements by bewildered German prisoners on "the carnage among the German troops, the like of which they had never seen".

"Our medical staff were unable to cope with all the wounded. One medical orderly told me that the dressing station was like a slaughterhouse to look at", a German corporal in the Belgorod area was quoted as saying.

On July 15 the Russian communiqué announced that the Russian counter-offensive against Orel had begun, and that, in three days since the break-through in several parts of the Orel salient, the Soviet troops had advanced between fifteen and thirty miles.

On the 24th there was a Stalin Order to Generals Rokossovsky, Vatutin and Popov announcing the "final liquidation of the German summer offensive" and the recapture of all the territory the Germans had gained since July 5. It recalled that in the Orel-Kursk and the Belgorod areas the Germans had concentrated a total of thirty-seven divisions—seventeen tank, two motorised and eighteen infantry— but they had not taken the Russians by surprise and had failed completely in their design to cut through to Kursk. The legend that in summer the Germans always advanced had been dispelled once and for all. The German losses were put at 70,000 killed, 2,900 tanks,

195 mobile guns, 844 field guns, 1,392 planes and over 5,000 motor vehicles.

What was being emphasised in all front reports was the extraordinary sureness of touch the Russians had shown in this battle. No doubt some of these figures were exaggerated, but even if the Germans lost 2,000 and not 3,000 tanks (and after the war they admitted that their tank forces at Kursk had been virtually frittered away), it was good enough. But it was easy to imagine that if 70,000 Germans were killed in the Kursk fighting, the Russian losses must have been very high, too. Examples of extraordinary courage and endurance by the Russians were reported—for instance of soldiers staying put in their trenches while the heavy German tanks were sweeping across them, and then firing at them from behind.

Altogether, it was reckoned that some 6,000 tanks and 4,000 planes were involved in the Battle of Kursk on the two sides. It was a concentrated carnage within a small area more terrible than had yet been seen. When, a few weeks later, I travelled through the fair Ukrainian countryside from Volchansk to Valuiki and then to Belgorod and Kharkov, I could see how the area to the north of Belgorod (where the Germans had penetrated some thirty miles into the Kursk salient) had been turned into a hideous desert, in which even every tree and bush had been smashed by shell-fire. Hundreds of burned-out tanks and wrecked planes were still littering the battlefield, and even several miles away from it the air was filled with the stench of thousands of only half-buried Russian and German corpses.

But for those who survived these were great days in Russia. What might be called the era of the Victory Salutes opened on August 5, 1943, following the special Stalin announcement that Orel and Belgorod had been liberated.

The deep voice of Levitan, Moscow Radio's star announcer, now uttered for the first time phrases which were to become like sweet and familiar music during the next two years:

Order by the Supreme Commander-in-Chief to Col.-Gen. Popov,

Col.-Gen. Sokolovsky, Army General Rokossovsky, Army General Vatutin, Col.-Gen. Konev...

Today, August 5, the troops of the Briansk Front, in co-operation with the troops of the Western and Central Fronts captured, as a result of bitter fighting, the city of Orel.

Today also the troops of the Steppe and Voronezh Fronts broke the enemy's resistance and captured the town of Belgorod.

After naming the units which were the first to break into these two cities, and saying that they would now be named "Orel regiments" and "Belgorod regiments", there came, for the first time, an announcement like this:

> Tonight at twenty-four o'clock, on August 5, the capital of our country, Moscow, will salute the valiant troops that liberated Orel and Belgorod with twelve artillery salvoes from 120 guns. I express my thanks to all the troops that took part in the offensive... Eternal glory to the heroes who fell in the struggle for the freedom of our country. Death to the German invaders.
> The Supreme Commander-in-Chief,
> Marshal of the Soviet Union,
> STALIN.

With only some slight variations in the wording this was to become the consecrated text which Russia was to hear over the radio more than three hundred times before the final victory over Germany and Japan.

Yes, the era of the Victory Salutes had begun.

On the next day, August 6, the communiqué said that the troops that had captured Orel were pursuing the enemy to the west and had captured Kromy and seventy other localities, while, in the south, a large-scale offensive was successfully developing towards Kharkov.

There was nothing fortuitous or arbitrary in the Russian decision to celebrate the victory of Kursk with those first victory salvoes and fireworks. The Russian command knew that by winning the Battle of Kursk Russia had, in effect, won the war.

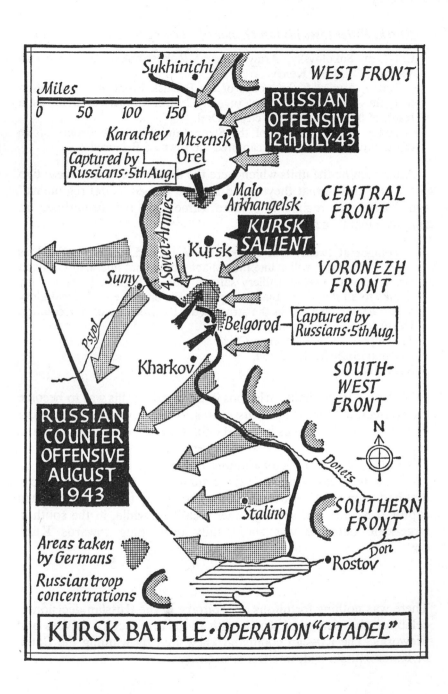

Miles

0   50   100   150

Sukhinichi

WEST FRONT

RUSSIAN
OFFENSIVE
12th JULY·43

Karachev   Mtsensk
Orel

Captured by
Russians·5th Aug.

CENTRAL
FRONT

Malo
Arkhangelsk

KURSK
SALIENT

Kursk

4 Soviet Armies

VORONEZH
FRONT

Sumy

Belgorod — Captured by
Russians·5th Aug.

Psiol

Kharkov

SOUTH-
WEST
FRONT

RUSSIAN
COUNTER
OFFENSIVE
AUGUST
1943

N

Donets

Stalino

SOUTHERN
FRONT

Don

Rostov

Areas taken
by Germans

Russian troop
concentrations

KURSK BATTLE · OPERATION "CITADEL"

This is also the view taken by post-war German historians. Thus, in the opinion of Walter Goerlitz, Stalingrad was the politico-psychological turning-point of the whole war in the east, but the German defeat at Kursk and Belgorod was its military turning-point.*

* Walter Goerlitz. *Paulus and Stalingrad*, p. 288. (London, p. 288).

Chapter IX

OREL: CLOSE-UP OF A PURELY RUSSIAN CITY UNDER THE GERMANS

The recapture of the ancient Russian city of Orel and the complete liquidation of the Orel Salient which, for two years, had constituted a threat to Moscow, were a direct sequel of the German rout at Kursk.

Orel was, in 1943, among the first of the larger purely Russian cities to be liberated; it was, moreover, one where (as distinct from the Don country and the Kuban) the Germans had been for nearly two years—since October 1941.

In the second week of August I was able to travel by car from Moscow to Tula, and then to Orel. The following account, based on notes written at the time, describes what the edge of the Orel Salient looked like, and what I found inside the Salient, particularly at Orel itself.

The thistles were as tall as a man; the thistles and the weeds formed a thick jungle, making a belt some two miles wide, and stretching west and east, and then south, nearly all the way round the Orel Salient. In this jungle, through which the dusty road from Tula now ran, there was death at every footstep. "*Minen*" in German, "*Miny*" in Russian, old and new notice-boards were saying; and, in the distance, up on the hill, under the hard blue summer sky, were

688

distorted shapes of ruined churches and fragments of houses, and chimney-stacks. These miles of weeds and thistles had been a no-man's-land for nearly two years. Those ruins on the hill were the ruins of Mtsensk; two old women and four cats were the only living creatures the Russians had found there when the Germans pulled out on July 20. Before departing they had blown up or set fire to everything—churches and houses and peasant cottages and all. In the middle of last century Leskov's—and Shostakovich's—"Lady Macbeth" had lived in this town; it was strange to think that this drama of blood and passion should have taken place in a town now smelling of blood shed for such different reasons.

We drove through the jungle up to Mtsensk. No, *one* small brick house had somehow survived. "Feeding Point", a notice outside said. "Here you can receive your dry ration, breakfast, lunch and dinner." And, beside it, was another notice: "The enemy has destroyed and looted this town, and driven away its inhabitants; they are crying for revenge."

Achtung, Minen. Achtung, Minen... "They're the devil," said the colonel who met us at Mtsensk. "Along only 100 yards just off this road we dug up 650. There was very tough fighting round here. German *Jaeger*—tough troops, very good troops, can't deny them that. But the mines are bad, very bad. Every damned day something happens. Yesterday a colonel came down this road on horseback; the horse kicked an anti-personnel mine—and there you are: horse and colonel both phut." He talked of new delayed-action mines found in German dugouts. Contraptions in which the acid eats through the metal; some take two months to blow up. And there were also booby-traps, plenty of them. These mines and booby-traps had become one of the Germans' most important weapons in 1943. and were the Russian soldiers' greatest worry and chief topic of conversation.* Mines had caused terrible casualties to the Russians in the Orel fighting, and were going to cause many more at Kharkov and elsewhere. As we talked to the colonel, a horse-cart drove past and in it were two moaning soldiers, with blood streaming from their heads; they had just been blown up on a mine...

* Many mines—both Russian and German—made in 1943, were cased in wood and so were particularly hard to detect.

In the last few days, only about 200 people had come back to Mtsensk, out of its original population of 20,000. These two hundred had been hiding somewhere in the countryside.

Along the road to Orel, with fields and beautiful woods on either side, there were no villages anywhere, and only notice-boards among the rubble giving the name the village had had. The German "desert zone" had now spread all the way from Rzhev and Viazma to Orel.

Orel, not so long ago a pleasant provincial backwater, still full of Turgeniev memories and associations, was badly shattered. More than half the town was destroyed, and some of the ruins were still smoking. The bridges over the Oka had been blown up, but a temporary wooden bridge had already been built, and army lorries were driving west, and ambulances were coming in from Karachev—thirty miles further west—where there was heavy fighting.

How had Orel lived through nearly two years of German occupation? Of 114,000 people now only 30,000 were there. Many had been murdered; many had been hanged in the public square—that very square where there were now new graves of the first Russian tank crew that had broken into Orel, and also of General Gurtiev, of Stalingrad fame, who was killed here the morning the Russians fought their way into the city. Altogether, 12,000 people were said to have been murdered, and about twice as many deported to Germany. But there were also many thousands who had joined the partisans in the forests round Orel and Briansk—for this (especially the Briansk area) was active partisan country.

The Germans had appointed a Russian burgomaster, who had now fled with them; and they had brought to the Orel countryside some former Russian landowners or landowners' sons—White Guardists they called them. But whether they got their former estates back was not quite clear. In most places, the *kolkhozes* had not been dissolved. A little private enterprise was encouraged—but goods were so short that it never came to anything. True, I found in a pile of junk in a street a broken bottle, and on it a label saying first in Russian and then in German: "Fruchtwasser-Fabrik, NOS-DRUNOW UND Co., Orel, Moskauer Str. 6." It would have been interesting to talk to Nosdrunow, the Mr Schweppes of German Orel; but he was not to be found.

The winter of 1941–2 had been the hardest of all. People had died by the hundred of starvation. Later, they began to receive 7 ounces of bread a day if they worked for the Germans in one way or another. And then there was all the horror of the Russian war prisoners' camp; and here I first learned at first hand of the German policy towards Russian war prisoners, as it changed after Stalingrad. Until then, they were allowed to die like flies; after that they were being blackmailed or flattered into joining the Vlasov Army.

Stiff, pop-eyed, blue-eyed General Sobennikov, now chief of the Garrison of Orel, had taken part in the great July offensive and now talked about it. By July 15, after three days' heavy fighting, the Russians had broken through the main lines of the German defences round the Orel salient. There had never been, he said, such a heavy concentration of Russian guns as against these defences; in many places the fire-power was ten times heavier than at Verdun. The German minefields were so thick and widespread that as many mines as possible had to be blown up by the super-barrage, in order to reduce Russian casualties in the subsequent break-through. By July 20, the Germans tried to stop the Russian advance by throwing in hundreds of planes; and it was a job for the Russian anti-aircraft guns and fighters to deal with them. In the countless air-battles there were very heavy casualties on both sides. Many French airmen were killed, too, during those days.

How important it was for the Germans to hold Orel, he said, could be seen from the order of General von Schmidt (since replaced by General Model) saying that Orel must be held to the bitter end.

"And it certainly was," said the General. "The German troops were tough; nearly all held out and only very few surrendered. None of the prisoners we took were older than thirty—picked troops, healthy, good troops; when Comrade Ehrenburg now talks about the German army being composed of gouty old men suffering from piles, he is talking through his hat. Yes, good troops, though morally damaged, all the same. Kursk and the rest has had a demoralising effect on them. Prisoners also told us that the fall of Mussolini had made a deep impression on the German soldiers—though some continued to believe their officers' stories that Mussolini was a very sick man."

Then he told the complicated story of how Orel has been almost completely surrounded by August 3, and how, finally, in the early hours of August 5, the Russians broke into Orel.

Our broadcasting armoured car, playing the *International* and *The Holy War* and *The Little Blue Scarf*, was among the first to break into the city; it had a tremendous effect on the population, who poured into the streets, even though the fighting was still going on. The Germans were still using mobile guns and tanks against us, and their tommy-gunners in the attics also bothered us a great deal. General Gurtiev was killed by one of them. Delayed action mines were still exploding, and in the midst of all this din, the loud-speaker was bellowing its patriotic songs. It was not till the next day that the tommygunners were all wiped out, though a few may still be in hiding. And there may still be hundreds of delayed-action mines at Orel, though we've already picked up 80,000 in the area. That's why no troops are stationed in Orel yet...

Yes, I drove into Orel on the morning of the 5th. You can imagine the dawn, and the houses around still blazing, and our guns and tanks driving into town, covered with flowers, and the loud-speaker bellowing *The Holy War*, and old women and children running among the soldiers, and pressing flowers into their hands and kissing them. There was still some firing going on. But I remember how an old woman stood at the corner of Pushkin Street, and she was making the sign of the Cross, and tears were rolling down her wrinkled face. And another elderly woman, well-educated judging by her speech, ran towards me and gave me flowers, and threw her arms round my neck, and talked, and talked and talked; through the din I couldn't hear what she was saying, except that it was about her son who was in the Red Army.

Now there's heavy fighting going on at Karachev. We have some British and American tanks there, but not many. The German air force is again very active, making a thousand sorties a day. What they are fighting is much more than a rearguard action, now that we are pushing on to the Dnieper.

*

Orel had been liberated only five days before, but already the Soviet authorities were fully established here. Most public buildings had been destroyed, but in a small house in a side street, Comrade M. P. Romashov, Partisan chief of the area, and Hero of the Soviet Union, was installed as president of the Provincial Executive Committee. He had many stories to tell of partisan warfare, of battles with punitive expeditions, and of partisan raids on columns of civilians who were being driven west. The partisans would kill the German escort, and the civilians would then scatter through the forests.

A check-up was going on among civilians at Orel, and party members especially had to account for their behaviour during the twenty months of occupation. Orel had been captured on October 2, 1941 by Guderian's tanks with such suddenness that many people had been trapped. On Romashov's desk I saw a note, written in an illiterate hand by a woman who said that she—a member of the Communist Party—and her two children had been trapped here on October 2, and that, to keep herself and her children alive, she had had to take a job as a cleaner at a German office.

They looked, from a distance, like soft greenish-brown rag dolls lying over the parapet of a trench from which they had been exhumed. Two Russian officials were sorting out skulls, some with bullet-holes at the back, others without. From the trench came a pungent mouldy stench. The rag dolls were bodies dug from trenches outside the large brick building of Orel Prison. Two hundred had been exhumed, but, judging from the length and depth of the trenches, there were at least 5,000 more. Some of these "samples" were women, but most were men; half of them were Russian war prisoners who had died of starvation or various diseases; the rest were soldiers and civilians who had been shot through the back of the skull. Many of them had been killed at 10 a.m. on Tuesdays or at 10 a.m. on Fridays; methodically, the Gestapo firing squads would visit the prison twice a week. Besides these, many others had been murdered at Orel; some had been publicly hanged as "partisans" in the main square.

*

One day at Orel I went to a charming old-time house, with classical pillars and an overgrown garden, which had once belonged to a relative of Turgeniev's. Turgeniev himself had often lived here, and this was obviously, in his mind, the scene of *The Nest of Gentlefolk.* The place could have scarcely changed since the 1840's, when the good and saintly Liza decided, in this very house, to retire to a convent since happiness in this world had been denied her.

The house had been the Turgeniev Museum, and I talked to the old man who was still in charge. He had been in the Gestapo prison for three months, and had heard the volleys on those Tuesday and Friday mornings. Both his assistants at the Museum had been shot as "communist suspects".

The old man—whose name was Fomin—spoke of the fearful famine in Orel. For a long time no food at all, not even the tiny ration of bread, had been given to the people. As you went along the streets in the winter of 1941-2, you would stumble over people who had collapsed and died. That winter, with great difficulty, he and his wife had bartered what possessions they had for some potatoes and beetroot. What later helped people to survive was their vegetable gardens.

Ten thousand books of the Turgeniev Library, he said, had been taken away by the Germans and many other exhibits—Turgeniev's own shotgun, for instance—had simply been looted. However, he said, thank God, the house had survived. Turgeniev's country house, at Spas Lutovino, between Orel and Mtsensk, had been burned down.

One night at the *gorsoviet* (town soviet), with a starry sky outside and a red glow of burning villages in the west, Karachev way, I met a strangely assorted pair—a local doctor and a local priest.

Dr Protopopov who, with his little beard and pince-nez, looked like something out of Chekhov, told how in spite of everything, the Germans allowed him to attend to the sick and wounded Russian war prisoners. It was a nightmarish story of starvation and neglect, which only he and a few devoted assistants had tried to remedy in a small way, by collecting food from the local population—even though they had less than nothing to spare—and by smuggling it into the hospital. Some of the severely ill prisoners, were moved by the Germans in horse-sleighs, at the height of winter, to another hospital, many miles away. The Russian staff had protested in vain, and had wrapped as many of the men as possible in blankets. But nearly half of them died during the journey. That other "hospital", from what he had heard, was little better than a death-camp, anyway.

The priest was a grubby old man of seventy-two, very deaf, with a white beard and a silver chain and cross, who said that if many Russians worked for the Germans, it was only because they would have died of hunger otherwise. He was allowed to visit the Russian war prisoners; they were being starved; on some days, twenty or thirty or forty would die. But after Stalingrad the Germans had begun to feed them a little better; and then started urging them to join the Russian Liberation Army.

He said that, up to a point, the Germans had encouraged the churches: it was part of their anti-communist policy. But in reality it was the churches which had unofficially organised Russian "mutual aid circles" to help the poorest people and also to do what they could for the war prisoners. Father Ivan said that "in view of the circumstances", he had ceased to be a village priest in 1929, and when the Germans came he thought he could help the Russian cause by serving in a church again. "Around me," he said, "there gathered a nucleus of believers, and we were given a church. I must say that, under the Germans, the churches flourished in Orel; and they became—that's what the Germans didn't expect—active centres of Russian national consciousness." But the man who supervised the churches for the German command was not, as one would have expected, a bishop, but a civilian functionary called Konstantinov, a "white" Russian; the churches were thus deprived of all autonomy, and even the rubber stamp of each church was locked up in Konstantinov's desk—a fact Father Ivan thought particularly outrageous. His immediate senior was Father Kutepov, who had a much larger church; and Father Kutepov told him never to mention the Metropolitan Sergius of Moscow, and to pray for Metropolitan Serafim, who was in Berlin and was approved by the Germans.

"I didn't like that," said Father Ivan, "and I avoided mentioning either. Yes, the churches were crowded—and there were five of them at Orel. Sometimes German soldiers—five or ten at a time—would come to our service, and they behaved very well, I must say." Then the old man told the strange story of how on Easter Night in 1942 and again in 1943 a few hundred war prisoners were allowed to come to church.

"When our people were told that the war prisoners would attend service, there was great rejoicing, and they swarmed to the church bringing the prisoners gifts... It was so wonderful to see our poor war prisoners come to church on Holy Easter Night. They were very sad, but there was great happiness shining in their eyes as they saw all the love and affection the people of Orel were showing them."

The doctor, who had been listening to the old priest, was becoming more and more irritated. "If they were all that happy," he said, "how was it that thousands of them died of starvation? Wasn't it a case of allowing a few prisoners, specially picked ones, to go to your Easter service? Just for effect. And your dates are all wrong. I can swear to it that no prisoners were allowed to go to church in 1942. It was only afterwards, after Stalingrad that the Germans started on all those tricks to get the surviving war prisoners to join the Vlasov Army."

The priest had, of course, been taken in by the Germans, especially by the fact that they were opening churches that had been closed for fifteen years or more. But what was the purpose of this German church policy amongst people whom they were determined to starve out anyway? Was it not a case of trying to create as much mental confusion as possible among the Russians? The curious thing was that the churches did become centres of "Russianism", despite the clear anti-Soviet stand taken—at least at first—by some of the priests, and despite the Germans' expectation that the churches would be centres of anti-Soviet propaganda.*

* Some Nazi officials had serious suspicions from the start about the churches exercising an undesirable "nationalist" influence on the *Untermenschen*. On the other hand, certain German generals, e.g. Guderian, later spoke selfrighteously of the satisfaction they had in

Some other strange characters had been active in Orel during the two years of the German occupation. The schools (except a small number of elementary schools and a school for juvenile spies—like the one I had already heard of in Kharkov) were closed. The bitterness among adolescents, who had been pampered under the Soviets, was particularly acute. The teachers—even of the schools that had been closed—were ordered to attend the lectures of an individual who spoke Russian with a queer accent, and called himself Oktan. His lectures were called a "course in pedagogical re-education". Oktan also edited a Russian-language paper in Orel called *Rech*, in which the gist of his "lectures" was published. Its subjects were "The Russian is uncreative by nature and is destined to obey orders"; "The revision of the Russian historical past"; "What an Aryan must be like". In the paper he preached a "total revaluation of cultural values"; Tolstoy was declared to be a worthless writer; Russian music was deprecated, and Wagner declared the greatest musical genius of all time. Needless to say, not all teachers were "invited" to Oktan's lectures; many had been arrested, while others had fled.

The general impression was that in the victorious days of 1941–2, the Germans had a number of nondescript Russian adventurers and hangers-on who were preparing to play some still undefined part in the Germanisation of a purely-Russian area like Orel.

There were also other lunatic happenings. There were some people of German descent who had lived at Orel for generations. They were sent to Lodz to have blood-tests taken to see if they were real Aryans.

Another memorable impression of Orel was the condition of the railways. I had never seen such thorough destruction before. In the Stalingrad area, only six months before, the destruction was still primitive, and could be easily repaired. But here, in the Orel area,

---

allowing the Russians in occupied towns to open their churches. Guderian is, however, careful not to say a word about the death from starvation that thousands of war prisoners and also thousands of civilians suffered in towns like Orel which, in 1941–2, were under the direct jurisdiction of his (Guderian's) own troops.

the Germans had used a special engine which, as it went along, destroyed both rails and sleepers. To use any railways in these newly-liberated territories, the Russians had to rebuild them practically from scratch.

On September 1 I also went to Kharkov, which the Russians had recaptured in their sweep towards the Dnieper. This was a hideous experience; for, as we travelled at night in a number of jeeps from Valuiki to Kharkov, one of them struck a mine and three of our travelling-companions were killed—Kozhemiako and Vasev of the Foreign Office press department, and a young captain, Volkov, whom I had already met at Stalingrad. Only the army driver, though slightly injured and almost insane with shock, survived. Kozhemiako had had both legs blown off and died within an hour without regaining consciousness.* At dawn, after the other two bodies had been found—one of them had been hurled fifteen yards off the road—we continued our grim journey. It was then that we crossed the fearfully devastated country north of Belgorod where some of the fiercest fighting in the Battle of Kursk had taken place in July. "Not a live spot", as the Russians say, was to be seen for miles around, and the air was filled with the stench of half-buried corpses.

Belgorod had suffered less from shelling than one would have expected, and there were many people around. The rich farm country between Belgorod and Kharkov was, however, cultivated only to the extent of about forty per cent—which was different from the Western Ukraine. But in 1943 this area was already very near the front line, and the Germans didn't bother.

Kharkov had suffered some additional damage since I was last there in February, but, apart from the massacre of 200 or 300 Russian wounded in a hospital by SS-men when they recaptured

---

* Vasev was a well-meaning but dull little man, but Kozhemiako, an exceptionally handsome young Leningrad man, had, despite a basic hardness of the "Stalinite" official, a charming manner and a great sense of humour. He spoke perfect English, though he had never been abroad. Had he lived he would almost certainly have rapidly climbed to the top of the diplomatic ladder.

Kharkov in March, the Germans had behaved with greater restraint than during the first occupation. They were nervous, and what shootings were done were done in secret—no more public executions. But people were still rounded up in the street and sent to Germany. From May onwards, the German manner had softened considerably, and the Ukrainian papers published on May 2 an official Order on the better treatment of Russian war prisoners; here too, it was part of the policy of getting them to join the Vlasov Army.*

During the April-to-June lull the Ukrainian papers under German control spoke high-mindedly of "Two Great Nations Preparing". Some German soldiers were beginning to speak with regret of Germans and Russians bleeding each other white for the ultimate benefit of the British and Americans. However, during the first three days of the Battle of Kursk, the German-run papers sounded triumphant; but their tone soon changed.

* There is an account of Vlasov himself in the Memoirs of Ilya Ehrenburg (*Novyi Mir*, January 1963) who met him in the spring of 1942, shortly before he was taken prisoner by the Germans. Vlasov was a man of boundless personal ambition and one of Stalin's favourite generals. He was rapidly rising to the top of the Red Army hierarchy, when the Germans captured him. His dazzling military career in Russia was at an end and Ehrenburg believes that Vlasov was sufficiently ambitious and cynical to see a great future for himself only in the event of a German victory. The Germans formed an Army, which he commanded, of "volunteers" from among the Soviet soldiers they had captured. It is certain that a high proportion of these were virtually conscripted by the "join or starve technique". After the war, Vlasov was captured by the Americans, handed over to the Russians and hanged. Many Vlasovites remained in Western Europe, but those who were handed over to the Russians or caught by them were in most cases sent to camps and not amnestied until after Stalin's death. A number of special studies of the "Vlasovites" have been written in the USA, notably *Soviet Opposition to Stalin* by George Fischer (Harvard U.P., 1952) and several chapters in *German Rule in Russia* by Alexander Dallin (London, 1957).

Chapter X

A SHORT CHAPTER ON A VAST SUBJECT: GERMAN CRIMES IN THE SOVIET UNION

Orel was the scene of numerous German crimes, and the wooded Orel and Briansk areas were notorious for their Partisan activity. It therefore seems timely and appropriate at this point to deal briefly with these two aspects of the war in Russia: (a) German crimes and (b) the Partisans.

In a book on the Soviet-German war of 1941–5 the crimes and atrocities that the Germans committed in the vast areas they occupied between 1941 and 1944 should, on the face of it, hold a very important place. But if one dealt with them in great detail the book would be in danger of assuming altogether impossible proportions. The subject is, indeed, vast. At the Nuremberg Trial, in particular, selected crimes and atrocities were discussed rather repetitively, but by no means exhaustively; and even these "selected" crimes committed by the Germans in the Soviet Union occupy a large proportion of the twenty-two volumes of the trial record. There can be no question of trying to summarise here the findings of the Nuremberg Trial even briefly—let alone all the other trials of war criminals. If the main aspects of German misdeeds are enumerated here, it is, above all, as background to the numerous examples cited in the course of the narrative of German behaviour in Russia—and in

700

Poland, for that matter. Insofar as these crimes can be classified at all, we find that, at Nuremberg, they fell roughly into the following categories:

(1) There was the general *Untermensch* "philosophy" which underlay the German attitude to the Russians, a "philosophy" illustrated by Field-Marshal von Reichenau's instructions for the Army's conduct in 1941 on Russian territory, or by Himmler's famous Poznan speech in which he said, "I am not interested in the slightest if 10,000 Russian females die of exhaustion digging an anti-tank ditch for us, provided the ditch is dug". Or else, there are the "realistic" utterances by Hitler, Goering and others to the effect that for all Germany cares, thirty million Russians may die of starvation in a very short time, and that it is not the business of the Germans to feed either the civilian population or the war prisoners. Millions of war prisoners and probably millions of civilians died as a result of this policy, especially in the first two years of the war. Although some Nazis like Rosenberg drew a distinction between the Russians—who were the arch-enemy—and the Ukrainians and other nationalities—who were to become some sort of protégés of the Reich—men like Erich Koch, the Reich Commissioner for the Ukraine, had no use whatsoever for any such fine distinctions, and his administration of the Ukraine was dictated by the usual Nazi *Untermensch* approach.

(2) There were special orders, such as the "Commissar Order" under which commissars (or, in practice, any recognisable communist, Jew or other suspect, for that matter) were not to be treated as war prisoners, but simply shot. Several generals tried after the war to explain that this order was largely "theoretical", since it was not applied by the German Army. This is a gross overstatement, or a quibble, since the "commissars" were, as a rule, taken over by Himmler's SD before the other prisoners were sent to camps under Army jurisdiction. Another order, called "Kugel" (i.e. Bullet), which was rigorously applied to the Russians, provided for the shooting of any war prisoners who had attempted to escape, or were suspected of any kind of clandestine activity in camps.

(3) There was the deportation to Germany of nearly three million Russians, Belorussians and especially Ukrainians as slave labour.

The treatment of these was much worse than that of the forced labour from most other countries.

(4) There were the indiscriminate shooting of hostages and "suspects" in occupied territories, people who might in any way be connected with the partisan movement or the Soviet underground; particularly in Russia and Belorussia numerous villages were not only burned down, but their inhabitants, including women and children, simply exterminated. As has often been observed, there was, in the Soviet Union, not *one* Oradour, or *one* Lidice, but hundreds. In every Soviet town and city there were Gestapo headquarters, where various atrocities and tortures took place, and everywhere there were crowded prisons; before the Germans left the prisoners were usually indiscriminately murdered.

(5) There was the specific German practice of exterminating the entire Jewish population; these massacres were chiefly the work of special *Einsatzkommandos* under Himmler's authority, and practically all the generals claimed after the war "never to have heard" of these massacres, though they often took place under their very noses. The massacres of Jews were carried out on a vast scale; thus, at Babyi Yar, near Kiev, about 100,000 Jews—men, women and children—were massacred, not to mention countless other cities, all the way from Krasnodar in the south, with its gas wagon which killed 7,000 people, or Kerch in the Crimea (where the Russians first discovered hundreds of bodies of both Jews and war prisoners) to Tallinn, in Estonia, in the north. To take the example of Tallinn, which I saw myself: there, in a place nearby called Klooga, I saw the charred remains of some 2,000 Jews, brought from Vilno and other places, who had been shot and then burned on great bonfires they themselves had been ordered to build and light. With the Red Army approaching, a small number of Jews had escaped this SD massacre, and were there to tell the full story. I particularly remember the story told by one of the survivors: a "kindly" SD man, trying to comfort a weeping child, said to it: *"Aber Kleiner, weine doch nicht; bald kommt der Tod."**

* "My little one, don't cry like this; death will soon come". A very full and poignant account of this harrowing Klooga affair was given by John Hersey in *Life* Magazine in October 1944.

And this is without mentioning the vast extermination camps like Auschwitz, Maidanek and many other where Jews (including many Russian Jews) were gassed, shot and otherwise killed by the million.*

(6) Next to the Jews in Europe, six millions of whom perished at the hands of the Germans (and it took rather more than a handful of "bad" Germans to carry out all this "work"), the biggest single German crime was undoubtedly the extermination by hunger, exposure and in other ways of perhaps as many as three million Russian war prisoners. Many were shot, many died in concentration camps during the later stages of the war (especially at Mauthausen), some were even used for vivisectionist and other "scientific" experiments. The evidence is so vast and overwhelming that one can only pick at some of it at random.

Thus, at the beginning of 1942, Rosenberg, writing to Keitel, thought it scandalous that out of the 3,600,000 Russian prisoners, only a few hundred thousand were still fit for work, so appalling were the conditions in which they had been kept. Goering about the same time complained to Ciano of the cannibalism among Russian war prisoners, adding, as a great joke, that it was now going a bit far: they had even eaten a German sentry! Hitler's policy during the pre-Stalingrad period was, clearly, to demonstrate the *Untermensch* nature of the Russians, precisely by reducing them to cannibalism.

We have echoes of this contempt for the "subhuman" Russian war prisoners even in recent German writing, e.g. in that odious little novel, *The Road to Stalingrad* by Benno Zieser†:

> The Ruskies were completely debilitated. They could hardly keep on their feet, let alone perform the physical effort required of them... Among them were mere kids, as well as bearded old men who could have been their grandfathers. Without exception, they all begged for a

* According to the unspeakable Ohlendorf, one of the *Einsatzkommando* leaders in Russia, giving evidence at Nuremberg, gas wagons had largely to be discontinued, since they caused "spiritual shock" to the killers—not because they were full of corpses, but because the corpses were mixed up with a lot of excrement, produced by the victims in their death agony. This particular commando had murdered 90,000 people in a little over a year.

† Ballantyne Books, New York, 1957, pp. 29–32.

scrap of food or a cigarette. They whined and grovelled before us... These were human beings in whom there was no longer a trace of anything human...

And then—

> When we [threw them a dead dog] there followed a spectacle that could make a man puke. Yelling like mad, the Russians would fall on the animal and tear it to pieces with their bare hands... The intestines they'd stuff in their pockets—a sort of iron ration.

And so on. Almost too nauseating to quote. And we know from countless other pieces of evidence that this is precisely the kind of thing that happened to hundreds of thousands, indeed millions, of Russian war prisoners, especially before Stalingrad.

Thus, a Hungarian tank officer wrote soon after the war:

> We were stationed at Rovno. I woke up one morning and heard thousands of dogs howling in the distance... I called my orderly and said: "Sandor, what is all this moaning and howling?" "Not far from here," he said, "there's a huge mass of Russian prisoners in the open air. There must be 80,000 of them. They're moaning because they are starving."
>
> I went to have a look. Behind wire there were tens of thousands of Russian prisoners. Many were on the point of expiring. Few could stand on their feet. Their faces were dried up and their eyes sunk deep in their sockets. Hundreds were dying every day, and those who had any strength left dumped them in a vast pit.*

Apart from the deliberate starving of Russian war prisoners, there were also the massacres. Some significant evidence on this score was produced at Nuremberg, for instance by Erich Lahousen, of Admiral Canaris's *Abwehr*. He spoke, in particular, of two specially charming characters with whom he had conferred at the beginning of the war in Russia. One was General Reinecke, known as *"der kleine Keitel"*; he was Chief of the General Army Office belonging to the OKW; the other was Obergruppenführer "Gestapo" Müller, a division chief of the Central Board of Reich Security (RSHA). The latter was "responsible for the measures regarding the treatment of Russian war prisoners," i.e. executions.†

* Dr Sulyok. *Deux nuits sans jour* (Two Nights Without Day), p. 88 (Zurich, 1948).   † TGMWC, vol. I, pp. 278 ff.

Lahousen: The purpose of the conference was to examine the orders received on the treatment of these prisoners... The substance of these orders dealt with two groups of measures. First was the killing of Russian commissars. Second was the killing of those elements who, according to the special segregation by the SD, could be identified as Bolshevists or as active representatives of the Bolshevist attitude to life... General Reinecke explained that the war between Germany and Russia was unlike any other war. The Red Army soldier ... was not a soldier in the ordinary sense, but an ideological enemy. An enemy to the death of National-Socialism, and he had to be treated accordingly.

Lahousen then said that Reinecke, a good Nazi, was not satisfied with the "ice age" mentality of some of the officer corps. On behalf of Canaris he (Lahousen) protested against these executions, and particularly against their taking place publicly. They had a terrible and devastating effect on the morale and discipline of the German troops. Moreover, this kind of thing could only increase the Russians' resistance to the utmost.

Müller rejected my arguments. The sole concession he made was that the executions ... should not take place in the sight of the troops, but in a secret place... The SD *Einsatzkommandos* were in charge of singling out persons in camps and in p.o.w. assembly centres, and of carrying out the executions... The sorting out was done in the most arbitrary way: Jewish or Jewish-looking or other racially-inferior types were picked for execution, or else they were picked according to their "intelligence".

Reinecke held that the Russians were different from others, and should be treated differently from Western p.o.w.'s. The camp guards should have whips, and should have the right to resort to firearms if necessary.

Lahousen then said:

The greater number of prisoners remained in the theatre of operations, without proper care... Many of them died on the bare ground. Epidemics broke out and cannibalism manifested itself.

In the circumstances, he said, Hitler ordered that no Russian war prisoners were to be brought to Germany.

Asked to what extent the Wehrmacht was responsible for the ill-treatment of Russian war prisoners, Lahousen said:

The Wehrmacht was involved in all matters which referred to the war prisoners, except the executions, which were carried out by the commandos of the SD and the RSHA. The victims were selected before the rest were taken to Army camps.

Except that some generals at Nuremberg tried to argue that it was difficult unexpectedly to have to feed so many p.o.w.'s, there is nothing to show that the Army did anything to oppose the policy of extermination of the Russian war prisoners, at least during the first twelve or eighteen months of the war.

More than that: some of these "gentlemanly" German generals were consciously starving the Russian war prisoners. At the Nuremberg Trial, apart from the famous Reichenau order issued at the beginning of the Russian campaign, there was also an order from Field-Marshal von Manstein, containing the following:

> The Jewish-Bolshevist system must be exterminated... The German soldier comes as the bearer of a racial concept. [He] must appreciate the necessity for the harsh punishment of Jewry... The food situation at home makes it essential that the troops should be fed off the land, and that the largest possible stocks should be placed at the disposal of the homeland. *In enemy cities, a large part of the population will have to go hungry. Nothing, out of a misguided sense of humanity, may be given to prisoners-of-war or to the population,* unless they are in the service of the German Wehrmacht.*

It is these kind of gentlemanly orders, not from Himmler, or Hitler, but also *from the generals* which are responsible for the starving to death of probably over two million war prisoners during the first year of the war.

Although, in the end, Manstein had to admit at Nuremberg that he had signed the order, he began by saying that it had "escaped his memory entirely".† No doubt much else had escaped his—and his fellow-generals'—memory "entirely", including the Army's frequent and very close co-operation with the *Einsatzkommandos* and other professional killers.

It was not till well into 1942 that the surviving Russian war prisoners began to be looked upon as a source of slave labour. Thus,

---

* TGMWC, vol. 21, p. 72. Emphasis added.   † Ibid., p. 73.

Field-Marshal Milch thought it "very amusing" that 30,000 Russians should have to man the German anti-aircraft guns against British and American planes.

It was towards the end of 1942, also, that the Germans started a form of blackmail against the surviving Russian war-prisoners: either go into the Vlasov Army* or starve.

But there were many who would not serve Vlasov; and many of these, including high-ranking Soviet officers, were to be found towards the end of the war at Dachau and Mauthausen, alive or dead—mostly dead. It was also Russian prisoners who, more than any other nationality, were given the privilege of *Aktion Kugel*.

> This was one of the numerous methods of dealing with "undesirables". A "K" (i.e. Kugel) prisoner was taken at Mauthausen to the "bathroom". This bathroom in the cellars of the prison building near the crematorium was specially designed for both shooting and gassing. The shooting took place by means of a measuring apparatus, the prisoners being backed towards a metrical measure with an automatic contraption releasing a bullet in the neck as soon as the moving plank determining his height touched the top of his head. If the transport consisted of too many *Kugel* prisoners, no time was wasted on measurements and they were exterminated by gas laid on in the "bathroom" instead of water.†

Russian prisoners were also used for freezing experiments and a variety of other entertainments devised by Himmler and some of the "scientists" of the Third Reich.

The whole story of the Russian war-prisoners—second only, in the number of people involved, to that of the Jews—is so horrible that it is almost difficult to believe. The Russians themselves have never quoted any clear figures on the number of Soviet soldiers captured by the Germans; but when one considers that the total loss in human life has been put at twenty millions, the loss of some three or four million men who died in German captivity does not sound improbable. The following table compiled by Alexander Dallin on the strength of an OKW document for May 1944 is probably quite correct:

* See p. 698.
† TGMWC, vol. 3, p. 207.

	In OKH custody in occupied Sov. territory	In OKW custody in Germany and Poland	Total
Total number of captured			5,160,000
Of these, transferred from OKH to OKW area		3,110,000	
Remaining under OKH control	2,050,000		
Recorded deaths in p.o.w. camps and compounds	845,000	1,136,000	1,981,000
Released to worker's or military status	535,000	283,000	818,000
Escapes		67,000	
Exterminations		473,000	
Not accounted for	495,000		1,308,000
Death and disappearance in transit		273,000	
Surviving as p.o.w.'s	175,000	878,000	1,053,000

This would mean that, except for the 800,000 "released" and the one million still alive, practically all the rest must be dead, i.e. over three millions.

On the strength of other German sources, Dallin puts the figure by the end of the war even higher. The total of Soviet war prisoners is put at 5,754,000, of whom 3,335,000 were captured in 1941, 1,653,000 in 1942, 565,000 in 1943, 147,000 in 1944 and 34,000 in 1945. These last four, and especially last three figures seem rather less probable. Where, in 1943, would the Germans have captured over half-a-million prisoners, not to mention the figures for 1944, let alone 1945?

*

What added to the tragedy of the Russian war prisoners was also that those who had joined the Vlasov army—mostly simply to save themselves from a slow death by starvation—were to be broken in mind and spirit even while the war was still in progress. Many became merely cynics and bandits, and when they returned to Russia, they were treated as criminals or near-criminals. But even the homecoming of those who had never joined Vlasov was far from always being an occasion for rejoicing. As Ilya Ehrenburg wrote in his *Memoirs*—

> In March 1945 my daughter Irina went to Odessa on behalf of the *Red Star*. British, French, Belgian war prisoners liberated by the Red Army were being repatriated from there. There she also saw a troop transport arriving from Marseilles with our own war prisoners on board, among them some who had escaped from German camps and some who had fought together with the French maquis. Irina told me that they were met like criminals, that they were isolated, that there was much talk of their being sent to camps. . ."*

But that is a different story. Here we are concerned with German crimes in the Soviet Union. In addition to the innumerable German crimes against persons, there were also the German crimes against Soviet private and public property: the Germans had laid waste vast areas; in three years they had destroyed hundreds of towns and thousands of villages. If some villages and some cities like Kharkov, Odessa or Kiev were only partially, but not completely destroyed, it was only because their retreating armies had not had enough time to complete the work of destruction. In other cities, like Rostov, Voronezh or Sebastopol (as well as Warsaw)—to mention only a few of those I have seen myself—the destruction was very nearly 100 per cent.

* *Novyi Mir*, 1963, No. 3, p. 138.

Chapter XI

THE PARTISANS IN THE
SOVIET-GERMAN WAR

In the summer of 1942 they used to sell in Moscow a pocket-size book of 430 pages called *The Partisan's Guide*. 50,000 copies, it said, had been printed. It purported to deal with all the problems besetting a Partisan's life. Here were precise instructions, often with explanatory drawings, on the chief "tactical rules of partisan warfare"; on the use of firearms captured from the enemy; on the destruction of enemy tanks and planes; on the best ways of wrecking enemy troop-trains and motor transport, of killing enemy motorcyclists by stretching a wire across a road; on reconnaissance work; on camping and camouflage. An interesting, and, in a way, highly pathetic chapter was on "emergencies"—for instance on the kind of moss and bark that can be eaten when there is nothing else to eat. There was also advice on first-aid, hand-to-hand fighting, and on "how to live in the snow".

The appendix consisted of a Russian-German phrase book: "*Halt! Waffen hinlegen!*" "*Ergieb dich!*" "*Raus aus dem Wagen!*" "*Bei Fluchtversuch wird geschossen!*"

And then: "*Sie lügen!*" "*Wo befinden sich deutsche Truppen?*" "*Wo noch?*" "*Wo sind Minen gelegt?*"*

* "Halt! Lay down your arms!" "Surrender!" "Get out of the car!" "Anyone who tries to escape will be shot." "You are lying." "Where are the German troops?" "Where else?" "Where are the mines laid?"

710

The superficial impression the book made on the uninitiated reader was that the Russian Partisan was a sort of glorified boy-scout, and that although it must be difficult to "live in the snow" and not very satisfactory to eat moss and bark in emergencies, the Partisan's life was a wonderful life all the same.

Partisan (i.e. guerrilla) warfare in German-occupied territory held an important place in both government propaganda and actual military planning almost from the beginning of the war in 1941. Stalin, in his famous broadcast of July 3, 1941, called for a vast partisan movement in the enemy rear, and on July 18 the Central Committee of the CPSU issued a decree (*postanovleniye*) on "The Organisation of the Struggle in the Enemy Rear" which explained that it was essential "to create intolerable conditions for the invaders, to disorganise their communications, transport", etc., and calling on "Soviet clandestine organisations" in occupied territories to exert their utmost energies to that end. In popular propaganda much was made of historic precedents—the peasant bands in 1812 who harassed Napoleon's *Grande Armée*, and the numerous Soviet guerrilla bands who played so important a role in the Civil War—in Siberia, the Ukraine, and so on. A certain romantic halo was made to surround the partisan leader and his men, and in the grim summer and autumn of 1941 press, radio, theatre and cinema tried (rather feebly) to cheer up Soviet citizens with stories of more or less unbelievable partisan exploits in Belorussia and other occupied territories. In December 1941, at the height of the Battle of Moscow, Zoya Kosmodemianskaya, who became a *partizanka* behind the enemy lines and was publicly hanged by the Germans in the village of Petrishchevo near Moscow, was built up into a national heroine and a symbol. But Zoya, like many others, had been sent behind the enemy lines for some immediate "diversionist" purpose, and so was not typical of the proverbial partisan who, under German occupation, spontaneously rose *on the spot* against the oppressors of his country.

Historically, the Russian partisan movement of 1941–4 is one of the most complicated and least thoroughly explored aspects of the Soviet-German war. To a large extent it is not only unexplored, but will remain, like the resistance movements in Yugoslavia, France and other countries, also largely *unexplorable* for the simple reason that all the participants of many partisan operations died, and there is nobody left to tell the story.

Much misinterpretation also arose from the over-glamourisation and over-magnification of the partisan movement by Soviet propaganda during the early stages of the war. This exaggerated interpretation has its German counterpart: according to the current German version, partly supported by certain Americans, there was no partisan movement in the Soviet Union at first, since both in Belorussia and the Ukraine the population was thoroughly well-disposed towards the Germans, and it was only afterwards, because of German "mistakes", that an anti-German partisan movement developed at all.

This is, of course, also a gross over-simplification. The truth is that in the grim months of 1941, following the invasion, everything in the vast newly-occupied territories was in a state of flux and chaos, and very little, if anything, had been done to organise a partisan movement in these parts of the country *in advance*. In Soviet jargon, no "material base" had been laid for it—no secret arms dumps, food stores, medical stores, etc., which would have constituted such a base.

There were, especially in Belorussia, a considerable number of Russian officers and soldiers who had been originally encircled by the Germans, and were then hiding in the woods, still hoping to find their way to the Russian Front, living as far as possible on the help of the local peasantry, and finally forming themselves into partisan bands.

The woods were also a place of escape for certain party and Soviet officials in Belorussian cities, for whom it was difficult to conceal their identity, for railwaymen and others who, having been caught by the Germans doing sabotage (or being suspected of such sabotage) had little alternative to "joining the partisans". But, for a long time, all this was sporadic and unorganised, and the Soviet authorities in Moscow, though liking to talk about the partisans and the role they were playing in the enemy rear, had much more immediate problems on their hands between the time of the Invasion and the Battle of Moscow.

In 1941, the partisans could wait. They required a considerable economic and organisational effort on the part of Moscow if they were to become effective at all.

And although, in 1942, the partisan movement in the Ukraine, in the Leningrad province, in Belorussia, as well as in certain Russian areas like Smolensk and Briansk, began to be taken much more seriously than before, there is still little doubt that in the Black Summer of 1942 the partisans were again a long way down the Soviet party and military authorities' list of priorities.

This is not to say that there was not a partisan movement of some importance in 1942, but it had not yet become the broad mass movement into which it was to develop in 1943. The contrast was, indeed, amazing, as many partisans have since written, between 1941, when they had nothing except some rifles and a few hand grenades, and 1943, when they had mortars and even some artillery. The lack of arms, much more than any goodwill towards the Germans, explains why there was no major partisan movement in 1941.

Present-day Soviet historians distinguish between the more-or-less sporadic and still largely unorganised partisan movement in 1941–2 and the (mostly) highly-organised partisan movement of 1943.

Thus, in his well-known history of the war, B. S. Telpukhovsky makes no big claims for the partisans in 1941:

> Already at the end of July 1941 there were 200 partisan detachments or groups in the Leningrad province. In September 1941 there were fifty-four such partisan detachments in the Orel province and thirty-two in the Kursk province.

But he does not specify how large these "groups" and "detachments" were; they often consisted of only a few dozen men, or even fewer. He then says: "During the first period of the war the partisans chiefly destroyed small enemy garrisons, regimental headquarters, motorised columns, etc.", which suggests that their main activity was in the nature of smash-and-grab raids.

True, during the Battle of Moscow, and often as a result of substantial units having been *sent* behind the enemy lines, partisan activity reached bigger proportions; thus, with 10,000 partisans operating in the enemy rear in the Moscow, Tula and Kalinin provinces, the attacks on German trains and motorised columns assumed a certain immediate importance.

There were then some partisan leaders, such as M. Gurianov, whose men killed about 600 Germans, but who himself was captured and hanged by the Germans and posthumously awarded the title of Hero of the Soviet Union. Another partisan leader, Solntsev, was publicly hanged at Ruza, in the Moscow province, on December 21, 1941.

Altogether, in the winter of 1941–2, the 10,000 partisans taking part (in their own way) in the Battle of Moscow, are credited with having destroyed 18,000 Germans.

It was not till May 30, 1942 that, on the initiative of the Central Committee, the *Stavka* created in Moscow a "Central Staff of the Partisan Movement" and, later in the year, similar special "Central Staffs" for the partisans of the Ukraine and Belorussia. The partisan movement certainly grew in 1942, though it had not yet become the mass movement it was to be in 1943. The slowness of the development was at least partly attributable to the shortage of arms. The personnel and supplies that Moscow could send the partisans by air in 1942 were still very limited, and many partisan units had to be left entirely, or almost entirely, to their own devices, like raiding German arms dumps and depending on the more or less voluntary help of the peasantry.

Telpukhovsky readily admits that German policy in the occupied areas enormously stimulated the partisan movement, notably in suitable "partisan country" like many parts of Belorussia or the Orel-Briansk forest zone. The régime of terror in the cities, the mass deportation of young people to Germany, which began as early as March 1942, deeply affected the civilian population.

Obvious parallels for this can be found elsewhere; thus, in France, the biggest factor that swelled the ranks of the *maquis* was the introduction of forced labour in Germany. In Russia, the *Untermensch* treatment meted out to the population acted as an additional incentive to fight the Germans by joining the partisans. But, as in France, the number of effective partisans was inevitably limited for a time by the shortage of arms.

It would be idle to speculate about what motives were the most important in persuading people to take the desperately dangerous step of joining the partisans—pure disinterested patriotism? injured national pride? a desire to get away from the Germans and their oppression and deportations? an attachment to the Soviet régime and to Stalin, now identified more than ever with the idea of "Russia"? All these motives mattered, but their order of importance obviously varied from place to place. Much is made in present-day Soviet histories of the leading role played in *all* partisan activity by the *Party*—all the way from the Central Committee in Moscow to the clandestine party *obkoms* and *raikoms* (provincial and district committees) still operating in the German-occupied areas and to party members who were commanders of the various partisan units.

At the same time, there is a tendency to minimise the role played in the partisan movement, especially in Belorussia, by the officers who, though encircled by the Germans in 1941, had evaded capture and went on fighting as partisans instead.

We shall later deal with some specific cases of partisan activity in 1941, 1942 and 1943; but Telpukhovsky claims that as early as the summer of 1942 the partisans tied up "enormous numbers" of German troops and police (either German, allied, or mercenary); that in the Briansk area alone 30,000 Hungarian troops were used for fighting the partisans and that in the summer and autumn of 1942, the partisans in various parts of the Soviet Union had wrecked as many as 3,000 German trains. This sounds like an exaggeration.

In September 1942, when things looked blackest in the south and south-east, Stalin issued a special order to the partisans saying, that, with German rail and road communications now longer and more vulnerable than ever, it was immensely important to start blowing up railways, bridges and trains; it is probable, therefore, that these big wrecking activities began towards the end of 1942, rather than in the summer.

1942 saw the development of "partisan regions"—*partizanskie kraya*—where there were no Germans and where the partisans had, in most cases, re-introduced the Soviet régime. Such "partisan regions" were to be found in the northern (wooded) parts of the Ukraine, in large parts of Belorussia, in the Briansk forests, in the Orel province where 18,000 partisans (belonging to fifty-four detachments) controlled an area comprising 490 villages; in the Leningrad province and south of it, such as the famous "partisan region" round Porkhov. Substantial areas in the Smolensk province were also controlled by 22,000 partisans belonging to seventy-two detachments. In the winter of 1942–3, according to Telpukhovsky, the "partisan regions" accounted for as much as seventy-three per cent of the whole area of Belorussia (a proportion reduced to sixty per cent by the official *History*.)

Officially, the "partisan regions" were the "supply bases" for the partisan troops, and, by the middle of 1942, runways began to be built in these and were soon used by planes bringing supplies from the "mainland" and evacuating wounded partisans and other persons. Supplies were also amassed locally; thus, on January 1, 1943, in the Baturinsk district in the Smolensk province there were supply dumps amounting to 207 tons of rye, 700 tons of potatoes and 1,000 head of cattle.

There is no doubt that by the autumn and winter of 1942 the partisans played an important part in wrecking the long lines of German communication to the Stalingrad area; we know, for instance, that the Manstein offensive of December 12 had been delayed by the slowness—caused by partisan action—with which military supplies were reaching the Don country.

Nevertheless, the partisans did not become an enormous mass movement until *after* Stalingrad. There was now an additional incentive to joining the partisans: the near certainty of fighting on the winning side and of not dying in vain. This was a motive which some partisans of older standing were later to treat with some bitterness. There was also the simple fact that in 1943 most of the partisan units were well-supplied by Moscow; they now had mortars and even heavy guns, including special anti-tank guns for destroying locomotives, more adequate food supplies and, very important, medical supplies. One of the horrors of the early days of the partisan movement was the almost total lack of medical supplies, which condemned many of the even lightly-wounded to death.

According to Telpukhovsky, "the partisan movement began to expand enormously after the Red Army had begun its Stalingrad counter-offensive". In this connexion he quotes the following significant figures for the largest partisan area, Belorussia:

February 1943,   65,000 armed partisans
June 1943,   100,000 ,,   ,,
October 1943,   245,000 ,,   ,,
December 1943 360,000 ,,   ,,

In the Ukraine, by the end of 1943, there were 220,000 armed partisans, and "many tens of thousands" in the parts of the RSFSR (i.e. Russia proper) still in German hands. Often, he says, whole families, or even entire villages would join the partisans, if only to evade ruthless German punitive expeditions.

On July 14, 1943, the Soviet Supreme Command ordered the partisans to start an all-out Rail War. Preparations for this had obviously already been made, for on July 20–21 great co-ordinated blows were struck at the railways in the Briansk, Orel and Gomel areas, to coincide with the Russian offensive against Orel and Briansk following the Kursk victory. During that night alone 5,800 rails were blown up. Altogether, between July 21 and September 27, the Orel and Briansk partisans blew up over 17,000 rails.

In Belorussia the partisans did even better. Between January and May, even before the official Rail War had begun, they had derailed 634 trains. On August 3, the partisans started another great wrecking operation on the Belorussian railways, two-thirds of which were put out of action, sometimes for weeks on end. Thus, the Molodechno-Minsk railway was blocked for ten days. Altogether, between August and November, 1943, in Belorussia:

200,000 rails were blown up;
1,014 trains were wrecked or derailed;
814 locomotives were wrecked or damaged;
72 railway bridges were destroyed or damaged.

The Germans became increasingly alarmed by these developments. On November 7, 1943, Jodl admitted that in July, August, and September that year there had been 1,560, 2,121 and 2,000 railway-line explosions (*Streckensprengungen*) respectively; and these, he said, had had a great effect on military operations and the withdrawal of troops (*Räumungstransporte*).

Telpukhovsky's semi-official History claims that in three years (1941–4) the partisans in Belorussia killed 500,000 Germans, including forty-seven generals and Hitler's High-Commissioner Wilhelm Kube (who, as we know from German sources—though the Russians for some reason don't mention this—had a partisan time-bomb put under his bed by his lovely Belorussian girl-friend).

In the Ukraine, according to the same writer, the partisans killed 460,000 Germans, wrecked or damaged 5,000 locomotives, 50,000 railway wagons, 15,000 automobiles, etc. Some of these figures, especially the total of nearly one million Germans killed by the Belorussian and Ukrainian partisans, sound distinctly exaggerated.

According to Telpukhovsky and other official and semi-official Soviet histories, "all the main work of the partisans" was directed by the Party. In the parts of Belorussia still occupied by the Germans in early 1944, there were 1,113 primary party organisations in partisan detachments and brigades, 184 clandestine territorial party organisations, including nine *obkoms* (provincial committees), and 147 town and district committees (*gorkoms* and *raikoms*). The membership of all these had risen during the war from 8,000 to 25,000. The number of party members among the Ukrainian partisans in 1943 was 14,000, and there were 26,000 komsomols—i.e. only about fifteen percent of the total number of partisans; the proportion of party and komsomol members among the Belorussian partisans was even lower, if anything. Among the Belorussian partisans, we are also told, there were 1,500 Poles, 107 Yugoslavs, 238 Czechs and Slovaks, and some Rumanians and Italians, and even "many Germans".

The official Soviet thesis is that, especially since the autumn of 1942, there was the strictest co-ordination between Moscow and the Army Command on the one hand, and the partisans on the other. The latter wrecked trains, blew up railways, killed German garrisons, etc., as part of a general plan, the main lines of which were laid down by Moscow.

Up to a point, this is true. The military effectiveness of the partisans grew enormously once they began to receive supplies, officers, etc., from the "mainland". But this version of the partisan story, making the partisans out to be a sort of Second Red Army fighting in the enemy rear, grossly over-simplifies the human aspects of the Partisan Drama. For it was drama. The partisans were not like an army that was methodically supplied with food, medical care and arms, and which had an enemy in front of it, and nowhere else.

There are two recent books, one on the Kaluga and Briansk partisans, *Narodnyie mstiteli*—"The People's Avengers"—by V. Glukhov (Kaluga, 1960), and another, much bigger book published by the Belorussian Academy of Sciences at Minsk in 1961, called *Iz Istorii partizanskogo dvizheniya v Belorussii, 1941–4* ("From the History of the Partisan Movement in Belorussia"), the latter consisting of forty-five "memoirs" written by leading participants of the partisan war in Belorussia.*

Both books are very badly written and put together; they are hideously repetitive, and some of the exploits described are almost worthy of the Baron von Münchhausen; and yet, the very repetiveness of the themes, and a variety of small details explain more fully than the much smoother official histories the constant nervous strain, the helpless suffering and the frequent horrors of partisan warfare. One of the main obsessions of the partisans was something scarcely known to the regular Red Army: the constant look-out for traitors and the physical and psychological *need* to kill them—such as *starostas*, burgomasters and policemen appointed by the Germans. There are several accounts in Glukhov's book of the hanging of traitors and of raids on the police stations of the German-recruited *Polizei*.

* There are, of course, countless other books on the partisans, starting with Vershigora's famous *People with a Clear Conscience* on the Ukrainian partisans, published in 1948, and Ivan Kozlov's book on the partisans and the communist underground in the Crimea (*V Krymskom Podpoliye*, 1950), but many of them are more romanticised than these two recent books.

Another constant worry was the attitude of the peasantry who kept them, more or less willingly, supplied with food and who, in doing so, were exposing themselves and their families to the most savage reprisals by the Germans—regular troops, SS, SD, etc.—or their underlings—Vlasovites, Cossacks, German-hired police, and so on. For if, as already said, there was one Oradour in France and one Lidice in Czechoslovakia, there were hundreds in the Soviet Union.

Living conditions among the partisans were nearly always terrible, at least until the beginning of 1943, when they began to receive considerable supplies from the "mainland". More terrifying even than the shortage of arms and food was the lack of medical supplies. There is a reference to this in the reminiscences of F. G. Markov, commander of the Vileya Partisan Unit, who was one of the first partisan leaders in Belorussia. He began to fight as a partisan in August, 1941.

> I should like to make a brief but affectionate mention of those humble and modest doctors who, in incredibly difficult conditions, *without any instruments or medical supplies or even bandages*, still managed to save the lives of hundreds of partisans. I particularly want to mention Dr Podsedlovsky, Dr Moisei Gordon and his wife, Noema Borisovna Gordon, Dr G. D. Mogilevchik, Dr I. V. Vollokh and others.*

This quotation is also interesting in another respect: most of the partisan doctors mentioned appear to be Jews, which is in striking contrast with the virtual lack of any reference to Jews taking part in the partisan war—despite the very large Jewish population in Belorussian towns like Minsk, Gomel, Pinsk, Vitebsk, etc.† Did most of the Jews not even try to escape their fate, or did the partisans not want them? Or were they—apart from these few doctors—already wholly isolated—or dead—by the time the partisan movement got into its stride?

The first partisan units were formed in the occupied parts of the

---

* *Iz istorii partiz. dvizh. v. Belorussii*, p. 282.
† One of the few references to Jewish partisans is to be found in Ehrenburg's Memoirs. He met in Lithuania, in 1944, a partisan band of 500 young Jews (men and women) who had escaped from the Vilno ghetto. (*Novyi Mir*, No. 3, 1963).

RSFSR and in Belorussia in 1941 in a variety of ways. Thus, one of the first partisan units formed at Polotniany Zavod near Kaluga lasted from October 11, 1941, to January 19, 1942. It was first composed of an anti-paratroop "destroyer" battalion; then it was joined by escaped Russian war prisoners; during the three months of the Battle of Moscow, it attacked German road columns. Finally, betrayed to the Germans by a traitor, it was more or less exterminated.

No doubt some of the partisan stories in the Glukhov book read rather too much like Cowboys-and-Red-Indians stuff. It was all very well for the partisans to attack a German headquarters and break up their Christmas party with a few hand grenades; but it was often the villagers who suffered most from such escapades:

> On January 17, 1942, in the village of Vesniny, there was a rough engagement between partisans and Germans. The Germans lost a few dozen men, killed or wounded. But they then started encircling the village. The partisans, having run out of ammunition, pulled out. The Germans then took their revenge. In two days 200 people, mostly women and children, were shot.*

Similarly, other villages suspected of partisan sympathies were dealt with with special savagery. At Rasseta 372 people were killed; at Dolina, 469, again mostly women and children.†

The deportation of villagers and the shooting of villagers by the Germans, ostensibly for "partisan sympathies" is an ever-recurring theme. In the Kaluga province alone, 20,000 civilians were shot, according to this book. Near Briansk, in the Ludinovo and Dyatkovo districts the Germans (and Hungarians) killed, up to November 1942, 2,000 civilians and burned down 500 houses. 5,000 civilians were deported as slave labour. Owing to this "scorched earth" policy, the Briansk partisans had a particularly hard winter in 1942–3. But with supplies coming from the "mainland" in the spring of 1943, things began to look up for them, and, in the following summer, the Briansk partisans were preparing for their all-out Rail War. As the Red Army was approaching Orel, they also issued "last warnings" to "traitors" (there are facsimiles of the leaflets in Glukhov's book)—

* Glukhov, op. cit., p. 38.   † Ibid., p. 87.

the *starostas*, burgomasters, Russian policemen and "legionaries" (apparently Vlasovites), giving them a last chance to turn their weapons against the Germans by joining the partisans. Some, but not very many, did. (Many, not unnaturally, suspected a trap.)

More harrowing even than the numerous "Oradours" and "Lidices" in the Kaluga-Orel-Briansk provinces, described in Glukhov's book, are those destroyed in the Osveia and Rossony districts in northern Belorussia in March 1943. This was partisan country; and although the German punitive expedition failed to trap the partisans, they occupied for a time the Osveia district. When, after forty days' fighting, the partisans returned to their base, they found that the Germans had burned down 158 villages. All able-bodied men had been deported as slaves and all the women, children and old people murdered.

> When the partisans returned, there were corpses everywhere. Only those who had followed the partisans had survived. Many thousands had been murdered.*

The troops of the punitive expeditions were usually composed of German regulars, or SD and SS troops, sometimes with an admixture of Cossacks, German-appointed policemen, and even Slovaks. Some of these, as well as some Cossacks, went over to the partisans in a few cases.

The atrocities committed against both captured partisans and allegedly pro-partisan peasants and their families must rank among the worst atrocities committed by the Germans and their stooges, and that is saying something.

Few of these Partisan stories are well-written, and the themes are nearly always the same. And yet the general picture that emerges is harrowing enough. It is not only one of great bravery and enterprise —for it takes a brave man to join the partisans—but also one of a world in which human life is terribly cheap. There are many boasts of "hundreds" of Germans being killed even in some relatively small partisan engagement, and of dozens of trains being wrecked; there

* *Iz istorii partiz. dvizh. v Belorussii*, p. 46.

are lamentations over the extermination of thousands of women and children in the "partisan areas" by *Einsatzkommandos* and other punitive troops; there are fewer references to the losses suffered by the partisans; but these must have been extremely heavy, especially at the beginning, when small improvised groups were either wiped out by the Germans, or died of cold and hunger and illnesses and wounds in the forest camps. These early units had mostly been improvised by Russian soldiers left behind the enemy lines, and by local communists.

A glimpse into the German methods of dealing with partisans and "partisan regions" is also provided by a number of German documents. Thus, at the Nuremberg Trial a report was read from the (German) General Commission for Belorussia, dated June 5, 1943, on the results of an anti-partisan operation called "Cottbus". The figures given were: enemy dead, 4,500; dead suspected of belonging to bands, 5,000; German dead, 59.

> These figures (the report went on) indicate again a heavy destruction of the population... If only 492 rifles are taken from 4,500 enemy dead, this shows that among them were numerous peasants from the country. The Dirlewanger Battalion especially has the reputation for destroying many human lives. Among the 5,000 people suspected of belonging to bands, there are numerous women and children. By order of the chief of the anti-partisan units, SS Obergruppenführer von dem Bach-Zelewski, units of the Armed Forces have also participated in the operation.*

Von dem Bach, a Himmler nominee in charge of the anti-partisan operations in the Soviet Union, who was later to distinguish himself as No. 1 killer in the German repression of the Warsaw rising in 1944, giving evidence at Nuremberg, explained that the anti-partisan operations were mainly carried out by regular Wehrmacht formations, and that the high military leaders had ordered the greatest severity in dealing with partisans.

Col. Telford Taylor (U.S. Prosecution): Did these measures result in the killing of an unnecessarily large number of civilians?
Von dem Bach: Yes...

* TGMWC, vol. 3, p. 174.

Taylor: Was an order issued by the highest authorities that the German soldiers who had committed offences against the civilian population were not to be punished in a military court?
Von dem Bach: Yes, there was such an order... The Dirlewanger Brigade consisted for the greater part of previously convicted criminals, among them murderers and burglars. These were introduced into the anti-partisan units partly as a result of Himmler's directives which said that among the purposes of the Russian campaign was the reduction of the Slav population by thirty millions.*

Hence the destruction of hundreds of villages and the massacre of thousands of civilians, including women and children, in the "partisan regions". Among the "enemy killed", as the above report shows, there were thousands of unarmed peasants in this one operation only. And there were very many more. And most of this "anti-partisan activity", as Bach-Zelewski stressed was "mainly undertaken by Wehrmach formations", the "principal task of the *Einsatzgruppen* of the SD" being "the annihilation of the Jews, Gypsies and political commissars."†

In a Hitler order, dated December 16, 1942, and signed by Keitel, there is also the following:

If the repression of bandits in the east, as well as in the Balkans, is not pursued by the most brutal means, the forces at our disposal will, before long, be insufficient to exterminate this plague. The troops, therefore, have the right and the duty to use any means, even against women and children, provided they are conducive to success. Scruples of any sort are a crime against the German people and against the German soldiers... No German participating in action against bandits and their associates is to be held responsible for acts of violence either from a disciplinary or a judicial point of view.‡

This directive was issued at the time of the Stalingrad encirclement and as the partisan movement was getting into its stride.

German savagery did not stop the development of the partisan movement which went from strength to strength in 1943 and 1944. So numerous did the partisans become that the Germans even made some feeble belated attempts at winning them over with "anti-communist" propaganda.

* TGMWC, vol. 4, pp. 26 ff.   † Ibid., p. 26.
‡ TMGWC, vol. 7, p. 59.

With the Red Army approaching, the partisans sometimes occupied entire towns a day or two in advance, thus preparing the way for the regular Russian forces. When these arrived the partisans were almost automatically drafted into the Red Army. It was fairly easy · in the case of those young people who had joined the partisans at the later and "safer" stage; the old guerilla fighters, with a mentality of their own, sometimes with an anarchist and even a "bandit" streak, inherited from the old Russian *partizanshchina* tradition, did not always find themselves at home in the regular army. It was not altogether unlike the problem de Gaulle had in France in drafting the Home Resistance (the *Francs-Tireurs-Partisans* and other FFI formations) into the regular army. The big difference was that the FFI had no great respect for the regular French army, largely composed of ex-Vichyites; the Russian, Belorussian and Ukrainian partisans—even though they may have felt some bitterness at having been neglected by Moscow for so long—were proud, all the same, in 1943 and 1944, to join the Red Army, with its Stalingrad record behind it. Once in the Red Army, they were frequently used for reconnaissance and other peculiarly "partisan" jobs.

Before being drafted into the Red Army, the partisans all had to undergo a medical test; not surprisingly, some twenty percent of them—many suffering from tuberculosis—were unfit for military service after all the physical and mental strain they had gone through in the last one, two, or even three years.

These are just a few of the elements of a human drama forming part of the even vaster drama of the Soviet people between 1941 and 1945. The romantic figure of the partisan, as he had existed and had been built up in popular imagination, during the civil war was something of an anachronism in the context of World War II. "Joining the partisans" could, in 1941, be a "personal solution" to many people with their backs to the wall; but as an effective fighting force, with a direct bearing on the progress of the war, the partisan movement did not become truly effective until late 1942, or rather, the spring of 1943.

The partisans were active in a great number of places—all the way from the Leningrad province to the Crimea; but the most important partisan activity inevitably took place in the geographically most suitable areas—the Russian forest country (Leningrad, Porkhov, Briansk), Belorussia, and some northern sections of the Ukraine.*

In addition to these "rural" partisans, with their traditional forest camps, there were the "urban" partisans who are, however, often hard to distinguish from the Soviet "underground" proper which, in varying degrees, existed in all towns under the occupation. The risks taken by these people were, in a way, even greater than those taken by the partisans proper.

The most famous case of urban resistance was that of the Young Guard in the mining town of Krasnodon in the Donbas; but this act of collective patriotism and martyrdom was by no means unique, any more than was that of Zoya who was hanged by the Germans in a village outside Moscow, in December 1941, and became, like the Krasnodon Heroes, a national symbol. The build-up of national heroes and martyrs was very much of a lottery; many fought and died, and never became famous.

At the height of the partisan movement, in 1943–4, there were at least half-a-million armed partisans in the Soviet Union. How many partisans and how many persons "associated" with them lost their lives in combat, or as a result of the German punitive expeditions is very hard to say; but in Belorussia alone about a million persons are estimated to have been killed in the course of the partisan war.†

* The partisans certainly succeeded in 1942, and especially 1943, in creating among the Germans a feeling of acute insecurity, particularly on roads and railways. Fernand de Brinon, the French quisling who was taken on a visit to Russia in 1943, describes the dread of partisans he observed among the German soldiers and officials who took him on his tour. (*Memoires*, Paris, 1948, pp. 141 ff.)

† For further details see John A. Armstrong (ed.) *Soviet Partisans in World War II*. (Univ. of Wisconsin Press, Madison, 1964.)

Chapter XII

PARADOXES OF SOVIET FOREIGN POLICY
IN 1943—THE FALL OF MUSSOLINI
—THE "FREE GERMAN COMMITTEE"

On October 1943 the foreign ministers of the Big Three—Molotov,
Cordell Hull and Eden—met in Moscow; this meeting was, among
other things, intended to prepare the ground for the "Summit" at
Teheran a month later. But during a great part of 1943, before clear
decisions had been taken to hold these two conferences, the Soviet
attitude to the Western Allies remained puzzling and full of apparent
contradictions. This attitude was partly, at any rate, determined by
what was happening at the time on the Russian Front. At the time
of Stalingrad, Stalin had been full of praise for the Anglo-American
landing in North Africa; in February, with the Germans about to
start their Kharkov counter-offensive, he began complaining again
of the absence of a Second Front. Then, in March, partly in response
to Admiral Standley's complaint about Russian ingratitude, the
Soviet press started playing up Western aid, and the breach with the
London Poles was followed, as we have seen, by rapturous accounts
of the Allied achievements in North Africa. Soon afterwards came
the dissolution of the Comintern, a gesture intended to impress
Western opinion.

One cannot, however, escape the impression that this great
cordiality shown to the Allies had something to do with the situation
on the Eastern Front: on the eve of the Nazi offensive at Kursk, the
Soviet public were very anxious, and, for once, it was apparently
thought expedient to magnify, rather than minimise, the Western
war effort.

But, as we know from the Stalin-Churchill correspondence during that period, relations were in reality far from cordial. Churchill tried to cheer Stalin with stories of 400-bomber raids on Essen (March 13); but, while not denying the value of such raids, Stalin was not satisfied. On March 15 he complained of major operations in North Africa again being postponed, and said that "Husky", the planned landing in Sicily, "can't possibly replace the second front in France."

> The Soviet troops [he wrote] fought strenuously all winter. Hitler is taking all measures to rehabilitate and reinforce his army for the spring and summer. A great blow from the west is essential. There is grave danger in delaying the Second Front in France.

Churchill went on sending him messages about "1,050 tons of bombs we've flung on Berlin" (March 28).

Stalin thanked him for the information and then graciously added (or was he being heavily ironical?):

> Last night with my colleagues I saw *Desert Victory*. It splendidly shows how Britain is fighting, and skilfully exposes those scoundrels— we have them in our country too—who allege that Britain is not fighting but merely looks on. *Desert Victory* will be shown to all our armies at the front.

But a few days later he blew up, after Churchill had told him that there would, for the present, be no more Arctic convoys, with the Tirpitz, Scharnhorst and Lützow around. "I consider the step as catastrophic," Stalin wrote on April 2. "The Pacific and the Southern [Iran] routes can't make up for it."

Again Churchill wrote (April 6) of 348 aircraft over Essen; Stalin welcomed the intensified bombing of Germany: "It evokes the most lively echo in the hearts of many millions in our country." On April 10, Churchill reported that 502 aircraft had attacked Frankfort, and promised to send films of bombed Germany "which might please your soldiers who had been in many Russian towns in ruins"; he also assured Stalin that the 375 Hurricanes and 285 Airocobras and Kittyhawks which were to have been delivered by the Arctic route, were being sent as quickly as possible through the Mediterranean.

This strange blend of pleasantness and unpleasantness was followed by the Russian breach with the London Poles, with Churchill frantically pleading with Stalin not to make the breach final. Sikorski was a good man, he argued, and anyone replacing him would be worse. He also declared that, according to Goebbels, the Russians were now setting up a new Polish Government—a story that Stalin hastened to deny as "a fabrication" (May 4).

On June 10, with the German offensive in the offing, Stalin grew furious with Churchill again. Writing to Roosevelt that day, he declared: "Now in May 1943 you and Churchill have decided to postpone the Anglo-American invasion of Western Europe till the spring of 1944. Now again we've got to go on fighting almost single-handed," and, on the 24th, in his letter to Churchill, he became really violent:

> The Soviet Government could not have imagined that the British and US Governments would revise the decision to invade Western Europe which they had adopted earlier this year... We were not consulted. *The preservation of our confidence in the Allies is being subjected to a severe stress.*

On June 27 Churchill angrily replied that Stalin's reproaches left him "unmoved", recalled that England had to fight Germany single-handed till June 1941, and that, anyway "you may not even be heavily attacked by the Germans this summer. That would vindicate decisively what you once called the 'military correctness' of our Mediterranean strategy."

Only a week later, the Germans struck out at Kursk.

Stalin's anger and recrimination may partly be due to the nervousness he felt about the outcome of the battle; once this had been won, he no longer worried too much about the Second Front. His line now was that it would come when it came; that Russia, though losing a terrible number of men, should be thankful for whatever the West contributed—lend-lease, or the fall of Mussolini—and that she should meantime make preparation for a big Tripartite Conference. In view of the delays in the Second Front, Stalin was more determined than ever not to give way on a question like Poland. At the

same time he felt that, on the German question, he might take certain
purely unilateral precautions.

It was while the successful Russian offensive, following the rout of
the Germans at Kursk, was in full swing that Mussolini fell from
power.

Until then, the Russian press had treated the Italian campaign
with a deliberate show of disdain. The invasion of Sicily was being
pointedly and invariably referred to as "operations in the *island* of
Sicily". But the fall of Mussolini, on the other hand, suddenly convinced the Russians that the Italian campaign, "miserable" though
it was in purely military terms, could be extremely important politically. The effect on Germany and on her satellites of Mussolini's fall
was not something that could be ignored.

On July 27 *Red Star* commented on Mussolini's fall in the following pungent piece containing some phrases directly borrowed from
Churchill (like "the jackal"), handsomely putting the importance of
Mussolini's fall side-by-side with the victorious Russian summer
campaign:

> ... this jackal, in June 1940, stabbed bleeding France in the back. ..
> Italy was hopeless even in her fight against little Greece. The fighting
> in Africa did not bring Mussolini any laurels either... The British
> offensive smashed the Italo-German army... The military situation of
> Fascist Italy became altogether hopeless when, like a fool, Mussolini
> threw himself into the adventure of conquering Russia, by Hitler's
> side... The best Italian divisions were sent there: Celere, Sforzesca,
> Giulia, and others; but they found their graves in the Don and
> Voronezh steppes. In Russia they lost 100,000 men in killed and
> prisoners. Then came Tunis...
> And now ... the British and Americans have, in a short time, over-
> run the greater part of Sicily. The jackal had boundless greed, but his
> teeth were rotten... And now he has been forced to abandon his post
> of Dictator... These twenty-one years of Mussolini's dictatorship are
> the gloomiest period in the whole of Italy's history... Mussolini sold
> Italy to Hitler.

And the article already foreshadowed a lenient Russian attitude
to the Italian people.

The Germans, these sworn and time-honoured enemies of the Italian people, became masters of Italy through the services of their flunkey, Mussolini. Mussolini, the traitor to Italy's interests, will as such go down to his grave... The liquidation of the German offensive in the east in the summer of 1943 was a mighty blow at Hitler. The collapse of his ally, Mussolini, is another mighty blow.

Not that that was quite enough. The theme of much of the comment about that time was that, splendid though the political achievements of the Allies were in Italy, there was a growing danger of the Germans now trying to drag out the war; therefore it was necessary to strike at Germany herself; i.e. land in France.

It is doubtful, however, whether the Russians had any serious illusions left on the possibility of such a landing in 1943.

Two developments of the summer of 1943, after the victory of Kursk, concerned Russian policy *vis-à-vis* Germany. First, with the liberation of large areas of the Soviet Union, some terrible German atrocities had come to light; and these called for a definite policy of ruthless punishment; on the other hand, pending an agreed Anglo-American-Soviet policy on Germany, it was felt that certain political precautions were called for, now that Hitler's last hope of defeating the Russians had been smashed at Kursk.

So only a few days after this victory, there were these two seemingly contradictory manifestations of the Soviet attitude to Germany. One was the Krasnodar trial, where a handful of Russian traitors were sentenced to death for collaborating with the Gestapo in exterminating 7,000 Jewish and other Soviet citizens, chiefly by means of the *dushegubka*, the word for "soulkiller", which was applied to the gas wagon which the Gestapo had used to exterminate its victims—men, women and children. It was the first public trial in Russia in which Gestapo horrors were revealed to the world with a mass of details which at that time were still completely new. In the light of later discoveries—such as Maidanek and Auschwitz—the Krasnodar revelations were small stuff; but they were almost the first concrete example of their kind, and made a deep impression on soldiers and civilians alike. The trial was fully reported for days at the beginning of the Russian Orel offensive. As "hate propaganda" it was first-rate, but all these details of how screaming children were pushed into the gas wagon were so horrifying that not only did the press abroad tend to play down the Krasnodar trial, but even in Russia some sceptics wondered whether the whole thing hadn't been somewhat touched up for propaganda purposes—little knowing that Krasnodar, with "only" 7,000 victims, was merely a minor episode in the Gestapo's and the SD's activities throughout Europe.

And then another startling development took place. On the very day after the Krasnodar verdict the Russian press came out with a spectacular display of the fact that a Free German Committee, composed of anti-Nazi war prisoners and a few German émigrés in Russia, had been formed. In Russia it at first caused some mental confusion; for it was certainly a curious development coming, as it did, on top of the Krasnodar trial, at that time the high-water mark of anti-German "bestiality" propaganda. Abroad, it aroused acute suspicion in many quarters. It was whispered that the Russians were preparing for a separate peace with Germany, perhaps even with Hitler... Molotov assured the British Ambassador that the whole thing was nothing but propaganda intended to create confusion in the minds of the German army and people, and so lower their resistance, which "Vansittartite" and "Ehrenburg" propaganda was obviously not doing; but the fact that the decision to form this Free German Committee had been taken unilaterally, without any consultation with the Allies, left, at least for some time, many doubts in the minds of "ill-disposed" people abroad. There can, indeed, be little doubt that, at least until Teheran at the end of 1943, there was some fear, not least on the British-American side, of a "dirty deal". It is perhaps characteristic that during the fighting in Italy, where, especially during the autumn and winter, there were many hard and heart-breaking moments, with little prospect of any early progress, the British troops at Monte Cassino and Monte Camino should (as we know) have been repeatedly told: "We've got to stick it, because if we have no foothold in Europe at all (and there won't be anything in France till next year) the Russians, tired of losing so many men, may pack up."

On the very day of the opening of the Krasnodar trial, the Russian press published with great prominence a written statement by a German officer, *Oberleutnant* of tanks Frankenfeld who said that, till the end, he had fought with distinction, but that he considered Germany's persistence in continuing the war as senseless and suicidal.

> ... On July 8 it became clear to us that the offensive had failed and that the whole year's campaign was lost. Now, much as it hurts me, I am absolutely convinced of the inevitable defeat of Germany: the only questions are: how soon?—in two or six months?—and where?—in the east or in the west?
>
> What was I to do? Die in the next days or months, without doing the German people any good? ... and knowing that the continuation of the war would lead only to the senseless use of gas and even more fearful casualties? The future of the German people is wholly in the hands of the victors.

Taking a long view of it, he decided to "hasten Germany's defeat".

But this was only a small prelude to what was to come five days later when, under enormous headlines, the formation of the Free German Committee was announced. The announcement took a peculiar form: the reproduction, in the Russian press, of the first number of *Freies Deutschland*, "Free Germany", organ of the National Committee. This paper explained that on July 12 and 13 (that is at the very time the Russian Orel offensive had begun) a conference had taken place in Moscow among German officers and soldiers, together with various anti-Nazi Reichstag deputies and writers who had been in Moscow since before the war.

The delegates, the Soviet press said, came from all the German war-prisoners' camps in the Soviet Union, men of different social classes and of different political and religious views. The Committee was elected unanimously. The President was Erich Weinert, well-known German communist writer, and the vice-presidents, Major

Carl Hetz, and Lieutenant Graf von Einsiedel. (The latter explained, at the time of his capture, that he was a grandson of Bismarck's and said he regretted that Hitler had ignored Bismarck's golden rule not to attack Russia and the West at the same time.)

The Committee said that Germany was now in deadly danger, and in fact used many of the arguments that were to be used a year later by those who attempted to assassinate Hitler in July 1944.

> Hitler is dragging Germany down the abyss... Look what is happening at the fronts; in the last seven months Germany's defeats are unparalleled in history: Stalingrad, the Don, the Caucasus, Libya, Tunis. Hitler, who is responsible for all this still stands at the head of our State and our Army... British and American troops are on the threshold of Europe.
>
> Look what is happening at home: through the allied bombings, Germany has already become a theatre of war... Facts are inexorable: the war is lost. But the attempt to drag out the war at a fearful price can only lead to the catastrophe of the nation. *But Germany must not die.*
>
> If the German people continue inertly to follow Hitler, then he can be overthrown only by the armies of the Coalition. But that would mean the end of our national independence and the partition of our country.
>
> If the German people have the courage to free Germany of Hitler... then Germany will have won the right to decide her own fate, and other nations will respect her... But no one will make peace with Hitler; therefore the formation of a genuine National Government is an urgent task... Such a government can be formed only by men who have risen against Hitler and are resolved to render harmless the enemies of the people—Hitler, his patrons and companions.
>
> Such a Government will recall the troops to the German frontier. Only under such a government can Germany, as a sovereign state, discuss the conditions of peace.
>
> The forces in the Army, true to their Fatherland, must play a decisive part in this. Our aim is a Free Germany, i.e. a strong democratic power totally unlike the impotent Weimar Republic...

The programme included the abrogation of anti-minority and racial laws, the restoration of trade unions, freedom of trade (i.e. no "bolshevisation"), the liberation of the victims of Nazi terror; the just and merciless trial of war criminals and war culprits.

German soldiers and officers (it concluded), you have the weapons in your hands. German people! organise resistance units inside the country! For People and Fatherland! For immediate Peace! For the Salvation of the German People! For a Free Independent Germany!

The document was signed by Major Karl Hetz, Major Heinrich Homann, Major Stesslein, several captains and lieutenants, dozens of NCO's and privates; Anton Ackermann, a Chemnitz trade union official; Martha Arendsee, Reichstag Deputy; Johannes Becher, writer, Willi Bredel, writer, Wilhelm Florin, Wilhelm Pieck, Walter Ulbricht, all Reichstag deputies; Gustav Sobottka, trade union leader of Ruhr miners; and two more writers, Erich Weinert and Friedrich Wolf. (Weinert had just written a book of anti-Nazi poems, called *Dank für Stalingrad,* which was published in Moscow; much of it was emotional German verse, with the then, in Russian eyes, somewhat unfashionable theme: "My beloved German people, how low have you fallen!")

Naturally, all this was not, strictly speaking, committing the Soviet Government in any way. It was the Free German Committee, without any authority, and not the Soviet Government that was promising the Germans "sovereignty" if an anti-Nazi "National Government" were set up. Obviously, the Soviet Government could make no such promises to Germany without consultation with the Allies.

Nevertheless it was, both internally and internationally, a curious step to take, and during the period that followed, some odd reactions to it could be observed both in Russia and abroad.

The truth is that the Free German Committee had by this time become an important basis for Russian propaganda in Germany, and especially among the German army. Speakers from the Free German Committee talked daily and nightly to Germany from Moscow radio. Hundreds of thousands of copies of *Freies Deutschland* were printed weekly and showered over the German lines. It was a large, extremely well printed and well produced paper, with a mass of good reading matter: but in this paper the Soviet Union's benevolence to the German people seemed to be so great that every possible precaution was taken to keep copies of *Freies Deutschland* out of the hands of foreigners, especially of foreign diplomats and correspondents in Russia. For, without the full acceptance by such readers of the view that this was propaganda, and nothing but propaganda, calculated to undermine German morale, it might have given rise to all sorts of undesirable comments, especially in the American press hostile to Russia. Nor were Russians allowed to read it, except for that first number. The thing was intended for Germany, and for Germany only.

Whether, in setting up this Free German Committee and in printing this "Free German" paper (whose Wilhelmian black-white-and-red border particularly scandalised so many "Comintern" Germans in Russia), the Soviet Government was also thinking in terms of "just in case" will perhaps never be definitely established. But it is certainly quite conceivable that there was an element of "insurance" in all this—for, supposing there *was* a palace revolution in Germany, and the Generals took over from Hitler, and attempted to negotiate a general peace, or a separate peace with the West, the Free German Committee and its later by-product, the *Bund Deutscher Offiziere*, with several of the Stalingrad generals among them, who were now calling for the overthrow of Hitler, might have become a useful diplomatic weapon in the hands of the Russians. All kinds of possibilities can, indeed, be envisaged if the plot against Hitler in July 1944 had succeeded; and if that had happened, the Free German Committee might have been of some value to the Soviet government. Also, one never could tell—it might come in useful even after the complete defeat of Germany; for there was not sufficient reason to suppose that complete unanimity would reign forever among the occupying powers. Also, from the standpoint of German internal propaganda, it was important to be able to impress upon the German people, if necessary, that the Russians were *the first* to have set up a Free German Committee, and that Stalin's benevolence was of more lasting consequence than all Ehrenburg's bloodcurdling threats. As it happened, the Free German Committee proved to be of only small practical importance; but in July 1943 there were still all kinds of possibilities in the future, and perhaps the Russians thought they had better be prepared for them. It should also be remembered that this was *before Teheran*: and suspicions of a possible double-cross by the "other fellow" existed—though only faintly—on both sides.

Perhaps the Russians also thought that the German defeat at Kursk might have greater immediate repercussions inside Germany than it actually had.

If the Free German Committee was not to play any political part whatsoever, it was because the Nazis kept control of Germany and the German people till the very end. Later, after Germany's surrender, some of the old German communists, who had been in Russia since before the war, were sent to Germany to do some "organisational" work; the soldiers on the Free German Committee, and on the *Bund Deutscher Offiziere* were not going to play any appreciable part in this sequel.* It was indeed, obvious from the start that at least a great part of the Free German Committee—which actually included among its rank-and-file members some SS men!—was never intended to be anything but a tool of Russian propaganda. Barring, of course, an "accident" to Hitler.†

* It is notable, all the same, that Field-Marshal Paulus, General Korfes (also of Stalingrad), and some others settled in East Germany and adopted a pro-Russian line.
† In *Child of the Revolution*, Wolfgang Leonhard, who was one of the contributors to the Free German paper in 1943–4, describes the consternation some aspects of the "Free German" move caused among the German communists then in the Soviet Union, especially the Wilhelmian black-white-red colours which, more than the "Weimar" colours, were expected to appeal to German soldiers and officers.

Chapter XIII

STALIN'S LITTLE NATIONALIST ORGY
AFTER KURSK

With the great victory of Kursk in July 1943 and the subsequent
rapid advance of the Red Army along a vast front towards the
Dnieper and beyond, the conviction grew in the country that the war
had been as good as won, though final victory was still very far
ahead, and would still cost another million lives or more.

Leningrad was still under German shellfire, but Moscow, with its
frequent victory salvoes and fireworks, was now completely out of
danger; symbolically, in August 1943, the whole diplomatic corps
was allowed to return to Moscow from Kuibyshev—Japs, Bulgarians and all.

On August 22, a programme of urgent reconstruction measures
was published. The purpose of this programme was, as far as
possible, to put the liberated areas on their feet again, so that they
should not be a lasting burden to the rest of the country. It provided,
among other things, for the supply of seeds for autumn sowing, for
the return of the cattle and tractors that had been evacuated before
the retreat, for the emergency reconstruction of railways, railway
buildings and for the building of rudimentary dwellings for railwaymen.

From now on, to the end of the war, there was a curious clash of
two conflicting tendencies, both of them characteristic of the personality of Stalin. The Marshal combined in a strange way an urge to
return to a semblance of "Leninist purity" with a streak of the most

738

jingoist Great-Russian nationalism. In his *Memoirs* Ilya Ehrenburg
says that it was in 1943, after Stalingrad and especially after Kursk,
that this Great-Russian jingoism manifested itself with particular
vigour, and made a writer like Lydia Seifullina squirm. "I always
considered myself a Russian; but since my father was a Tartar, I
shall damn well call myself a Tartar from now on. I don't like this
Russian ultra-nationalism," she said.

The Russian ultra-nationalism took on peculiar forms in 1943
and made some foreign observers go so far as to talk about a "return
to Tsarism". And not only foreign observers, but some startled
Russians too. A typical 1943 film was Eisenstein's *Ivan the Terrible*,
specially made on Stalin's orders, and depicting the cruel but wise
State-Builder of Muscovy as the obvious forerunner of Stalin. The
most striking example of the new measures was the decision to set
up nine "Suvorov Schools" in the liberated areas—i.e. Cadet schools
closely modelled on the pre-Revolution Cadet Corps. The "cult of
the uniform", which had begun at the time of Stalingrad, was now
in full swing. More than that: the Suvorov Schools (nine of 500
pupils each) were clearly intended to create something of an "officer
caste".

There was certainly something "Tsarist" about these Suvorov
Schools. In a statement to *Red Star* on August 25, 1943, Lieut.-Gen.
Morozov, head of the Military Education Establishments, said:

> The Suvorov Military Schools are established, as is indicated by the
> instructions of the Council of People's Commissars and of the Central
> Committee of the Party, after the manner of the old Cadet Schools.
> This means that the pupils will receive here not only a complete
> secondary education but also an elementary knowledge of military
> problems. Having completed his education in a Suvorov School, such
> a boy will become a worthy Soviet officer. The whole system of this
> education is based on the idea that the *military consciousness should
> penetrate into the pupils' flesh and blood at an early age.* At the end
> of his studies, the young Soviet officer must be a model of patriotism,
> culture, and a high standard of military knowledge... The curriculum
> will be more extensive than in an ordinary secondary school. Already
> at eight he will start learning a foreign language. On many routine
> details *we are consulting old officers who received their education in
> the old Cadet schools...* The boys will be chosen from among the sons

of soldiers and partisans, and also from among children whose parents were killed by the Germans... The uniforms are modelled on Red Army uniforms, with epaulettes and other markings; so that *from childhood the boys should develop a feeling of love and respect for the uniform... We have already received many applications, for an officer considers it an honour that his son should carry on his military traditions.* (Emphasis added.)

For some weeks afterwards the press, particularly the military press, went on publishing articles by old generals, notably by Lieut.-Gen. Shilovsky, giving an attractive account of their days in the old Cadet School under the old régime.

A year later, when I visited the Suvorov School at Kalinin, I found that, among the subjects the budding little officers were taught were English, fine manners and old-time ballroom dances (the waltz, the mazurka, the pas-de-quatre, etc.). On the walls, there were large pictures of Suvorov, but also equally large ones of Stalin and of numerous Red Army generals.

All this went together with the revival of the Church in Russia, already described. September 1943 saw the crowning of the Patriarch of Moscow, and the visit of the Archbishop of York.

No doubt all this was partly intended for foreign consumption; it was useful to put Churchill and Roosevelt in a good mood, and to get the *New York Times* to talk about a "return to Tsarism" and even perhaps to capitalism. But it was more than that: the dissolution of the Comintern, the establishment of the Suvorov Schools, General Krivitzky's articles, in October 1943, on "the glorious traditions of General Brusilov",* the election of the Patriarch, and the orgy of gold braid and new uniforms—uniforms for diplomats, uniforms for railwaymen ("and why not," Ehrenburg later said, "for poets, with one, two or three lyres on their epaulettes?")—all this was strangely significant of the Stalinist Great-Russian ultra-nationalism of 1943—a year that contrasted so strikingly with the *année terrible* only two years before, or even with one year before.

*

* The most successful Russian general of World War I.

Not that the "Socialist" side of things was being entirely neglected: alongside with the Suvorov Schools for a new officer caste a large network of Trade Schools for metal workers and others was to be set up in nine of the liberated areas; and there was nothing "Tsarist" about these; and, in 1944, as we shall see, there was a return, in some respects, to "Leninist Purity" and a drive for greater "Soviet-consciousness"; but this was, somehow, less striking than the manifestations of Great-Russian ultra-nationalism of 1943.

It all had a certain bearing on Stalin's relations with Britain and America. It seems significant, for instance, that in the November 7, 1943, slogans the very mention of *capitalism* should have been avoided.

The first of the slogans said: "Hail the 26th Anniversary of the Great October Socialist Revolution which overthrew the power of the *Imperialists* in our country, and proclaimed peace among all the nations of the world!"

And the other slogans were "Long live the victory of the Anglo-Soviet-American Coalition!" "Long live the valiant Anglo-American troops in Italy!" "Greetings to the valiant British and American airmen striking at the vital centres of Germany!", etc., etc.; and this was when the British Ambassador, Sir Archibald Clark Kerr, told me that Stalin had assured him that "in a way, he, too, believed in God."

How deep this regard for the Allies was in Party and Komsomol circles may, however, be questioned. On October 27, at a meeting celebrating the 25th anniversary of the Komsomol—that was the time of the Foreign Ministers' Conference in Moscow, and the "November slogans" had already been published—N. A. Mikhailov, Secretary of the Central Committee of the Komsomol, paid tributes to Lenin, Stalin, the Army, and the Party, but did not mention the Allies at all.

There was below the surface something of a conflict at that time between "Holy Russia" and the "Soviet Union". Sometimes compromises were reached between the two. Thus, on the question of the new State Anthem a curious compromise was reached at the end of 1943. No new Anthem by Shostakovich or Prokofiev was approved; but the new nationalist and Stalinist words were pinned to the *old* Party anthem, which became the State Anthem of the Soviet Union, while the *Internationale* became officially the anthem of the Party! There had been tremendous competition in the writing of the new anthem, and on January 5, 1944, it was announced that over 200 also-rans—172 poets and seventy-six composers—had been paid "consolation prizes" of between 4,000 and 8,000 roubles each!

Meantime—i.e. between July and November 1943—the Red Army was making a spectacular advance in the Ukraine and elsewhere.

Kharkov was captured by General Konev (Steppe Front), with the aid of General Vatutin (Voronezh Front) and General Malinovsky (South-West Front) on August 23.

The next great victory was General Tolbukhin's in the far south when, after breaking through from the Voroshilovgrad area to the Sea of Azov, his troops captured Taganrog, which the Germans had held ever since the autumn of 1941. 5,000 German prisoners were taken.

On August 31, Rokossovsky (Central Front) captured Glukhov and penetrated deep into the northern Ukraine.

Farther south, the Donbas was being rapidly overrun, the Germans fearing encirclement and pulling out, after wrecking factories and coalmines.

On September 8, a Stalin Order covering the whole front page of every newspaper, and addressed to Tolbukhin and Malinovsky, declared that in six days' skilful and rapid operations, the whole of the Donbas had now been liberated.

On September 10, with the aid of a naval landing west of the city, Tolbukhin and Malinovsky captured Mariupol on the Sea of Azov.

In the far south the last two German strongholds in the Caucasus were being mopped up. After five days' heavy fighting the troops of General Petrov and the naval units under Vice-Admiral Vladimirsky captured Novorossisk on September 16—or rather the ruins of that important naval base. The Taman peninsula was cleared by October 7, most of the Germans escaping to the Crimea across the straits of Kerch.

On the 21st, Rokossovsky took the ancient city of Chernigov, already reduced to ruins by German mass bombings in the summer of '41; and, on the 23rd, Konev took Poltava (also almost completely destroyed by the retreating Germans); on the 29th, breaking through to the Dnieper, Konev took Kremenchug.

On the 25th, Sokolovsky (Western Front) took Smolensk.

By the end of the month, as was officially stated, the Red Army was advancing on Kiev, in the Ukraine, and on Vitebsk, Gomel and Mogilev in Belorussia.

If September was marked by a spectacular amount of territory liberated, October was marked by something even more important— the forcing of the Dnieper. The German hope of "holding the Dnieper line" was smashed.

The great optimism after the forcing of the Dnieper may be gauged from a poem by Surkov printed on October 8:

> ... Avenging Russia is advancing;
> Ukraine and Belorussia, wait and hope;
> The Germans have not long left to torment you,
> The evil days of your bondage are numbered,
> From the high banks of the Dnieper
> We see the waters of the Pruth and the Niemen.

Russo-Ukrainian Unity was the subject of many articles, and was symbolised in the establishment of a new high decoration, the Order of Bogdan Khmelnitsky.*

No doubt, in earlier Soviet interpretations, the celebrated 17th century Hetman was not quite as great a man as he was now made

---

* For some reason, the Khmelnitsky order was not widely awarded, and never became popular in the army; it seemed an unnecessary rival to the Suvorov, Kutuzov and Nevsky orders which had the prestige of Stalingrad attached to them. Moreover, it caused some embarrassment when a number of Russian officers of Jewish race refused the Khmelnitsky order on the ground that the glorious Hetman had been guilty of a considerable number of pogroms. (Similarly several Poles refused the Suvorov Order, Suvorov having been one of the worst oppressors of the Polish people.)

out to be; in fact, he was described in the 1931 edition of the Soviet Encyclopaedia as a double-crosser of the worst sort, and indeed something of an agent of the Polish *szlachta*; but now a different view was taken:

> A Knight of the Order of Bogdan Khmelnitsky—that is a proud title, (wrote *Red Star*). The life of Bogdan Khmelnitsky is an example of the decisive struggle for the brotherly union of the Ukrainian people and its elder brother, the Russian people. Khmelnitsky clearly realised that the free and prosperous development of the Ukraine was possible only in the closest union with Russia. The Soviet people who finally completed the union of all Ukrainian lands into one mighty state,* under the Red Banner of the Soviets, particularly value Bogdan Khmelnitsky's immortal deed.

On October 14, Malinovsky captured Zaporozhie, and, on the 23rd, Tolbukhin captured Melitopol. The Crimea was now about to be cut off from the mainland. The actual penetration of the Russians into the Crimea did not, however, succeed, and had to be postponed till the spring of '44. A particularly brilliant stroke was Malinovsky's surprise attack on Dniepropetrovsk, on the lower Dnieper, which was captured on October 25. The German "Dnieper Line" was cracking from top to bottom.

* Meaning the incorporation of parts of the Western Ukraine formerly ruled by Austria-Hungary and, after World War I, by Poland, Rumania and Czechoslovakia.

Chapter XIV

THE SPIRIT OF TEHERAN

It is unnecessary to go once again over the ground of the Foreign
Ministers' Conference in Moscow in October 1943, or of the Teheran
Conference a month later, both of which have been described in
some detail by Churchill, in the Hopkins Papers, in General John
Deane's *Strange Alliance*, and elsewhere. What we are chiefly concerned with here are the Soviet reactions to these two momentous
events, which are, of course, major landmarks in Soviet-Western
relations during the war.

It may seem surprising that the war in Russia had gone on for
over two years, and that it was not till the end of 1943 that these
first two full-dress meetings among the Big Three leaders should
have taken place. In 1941, it is true, Hopkins, Beaverbrook, Harriman and Eden had all visited Moscow; in May 1942 Molotov had
travelled to Washington and London, and Churchill had come to
Moscow on his dismal visit in August 1942, in the course of which
he had not found Stalin or the other Soviet leaders in a particularly
happy or receptive mood. Stalingrad was, just then, on the eve
of its grimmest ordeal, and the Germans were well inside the
Caucasus.

In October 1943, the Russians were winning one victory after
another, day after day. If, before Kursk—which in July 1943 had
started an uninterrupted succession of Russian victories—the

Russians were worried and on edge, and were clamouring for vigorous action in the west, which would draw some forty or fifty German divisions from the Soviet Front—in October 1943, the Soviet Government, and indeed Soviet opinion, were taking things much more calmly. The Russians were losing thousands of men every day, but the Second Front was no longer, to them, a matter of life or death. It now began to be taken for granted that the war would be won anyway—and that the Western Allies were quite prepared to fight the war to a victorious finish, but with a maximum loss of life to the Russians, and a minimum loss of life to themselves. This was now accepted with a kind of bitter resignation.

Even so, the Allies had their uses; they were supplying substantial quantities of lend-lease equipment to Russia; and, as Stalin said to Eden in October 1943, he did not ignore the fact that the *threat* of a Second Front in Northern France had, in the summer of 1943, pinned down some twenty-five German divisions in the west, beside the ten or twelve German divisions that were tied up in Italy. For the time being Stalin was reasonably satisfied; though he had not stopped worrying about "Overlord"—the cross-Channel landing in Northern France—again perhaps being unduly delayed. It was the common belief in Moscow (a belief fed by American indiscretions) that Churchill was still anxious to extend operations in the Mediterranean, but was continuing to surround "Overlord" with all kinds of conditions and reservations.

This was the Number One question which, in the Russian view, needed clearing up at the Foreign Ministers' Conference that met in Moscow on October 19, 1943.

There had, as already said, been very few top-level Government contacts between the Russians and the Anglo-Americans, and the Moscow Conference was the first Big-Three meeting of its kind. It came at a good moment, after three months of uninterrupted Russian victories.

That this Conference took place in Moscow, and not elsewhere, was because Stalin, too busy with his own war, would not go abroad, and would not even let Molotov go—for instance, to Casablanca. It was not merely a technical matter; Stalin's line was that the Soviet Union was bearing the brunt of this war, and that it was for the "others" to travel to Moscow. Even if Cordell Hull was an old man and a sick man, it couldn't be helped. For the Summit Meeting with Roosevelt and Churchill, Stalin was willing to stretch a point and go to Teheran, close to the Soviet border, but he would not go to Habanniya or Basra, let alone Cairo. It was not only that Stalin as Commander-in-Chief could not absent himself for more than a few days; nor was it primarily a question of security; it was above all, a question of prestige: "We aren't going hat-in-hand to the West; let the West come to us." It made in the Soviet Union just the kind of impression Stalin meant it to make.

As long as the Western Allies were not doing any very serious fighting anyway, and had made it amply clear that no "real" Second Front was to be expected in the near future, and since the Red Army still seemed to have a very long way ahead of it, there was, to the Russians, no urgent need for a Big-Three Conference.

But by October 1943 the situation had changed. There was room for joint military planning; within a few months, the Red Army might well be across the Soviet borders, and the defeat of Germany was becoming, more and more, a tangible reality. The big question now was *how long* the war was to last. Since the month before Kursk, when the Russians officially stated that the Soviet Union could not win the war single-handed, there had been a certain departure from this position.

The statement was still true, but no longer in such absolute terms.

Paradoxically, one opinion expressed to me in a moment of indiscretion at the time of the Moscow Conference by Alexander Korneichuk, who was then one of the Foreign Vice-Commissars, was: "Things are going so well on our front that it might even be better *not* to have the Second Front till next spring. If there were a Second Front right now, the Germans might allow Germany to be occupied by the Anglo-Americans. It would make us look pretty silly. Better to go on bombing them for another winter; and also let their army freeze another winter in Russia; then get the Red Army *right up* to Germany, and *then* start the Second Front." Quite obviously a man like Korneichuk was anxious that the Russians should occupy Poland *before* the collapse of Germany or a *de facto* surrender to the West.

The Moscow Conference went on for no less than twelve days, and was marked by an extraordinary round of sumptuous lunches, ballet shows, embassy receptions and a super-banquet at the Kremlin described in lurid detail by General Deane, the head of the newly-appointed US Military Mission to the Soviet Union. There had never been anything like it in wartime Moscow, now deep in the Russian rear.

Eden had several meetings with Stalin and found him, on the whole, in good humour, though still ironical about the Western war effort—apart from the bombing of Germany, which pleased him greatly. "Hit the *svolochi* hard, the harder the better!" he said, thumping the table with his fist. His chief concern was the date of "Overlord"—and in this he was glad to receive full support from the Americans. The Americans, for their part, were anxious to obtain a promise of Russian participation in the war against Japan. Both questions were discussed at the Moscow Conference, though no clear decisions were to be taken until Teheran.

Stalin, for his part, was satisfied with the Americans' support of "Overlord". As General Deane wrote a little later, at the time of Teheran: "[Most of] the Americans at the Conference met Stalin for the first time. They were all considerably and favourably impressed by him, perhaps because he advocated the American point of view in our difference with the British. Regardless of this, one could not help but recognise qualities of greatness in the man..." To which, on a technical plane, he added:

> Stalin is a master of detail... and has an amazing knowledge of such matters as characteristics of weapons, the structural features of aircraft, and Soviet methods in even minor tactics.*

In a sense, the Moscow Conference was a rehearsal for Teheran; but it also achieved some "positive" results of its own—the setting up of a European Advisory Commission, a Commission for Italy

* John R. Deane, *The Strange Alliance* (London, 1947), pp. 47 and 152.

(which would include British, American, French, Greek and Yugoslav representatives, while Vyshinsky was going to represent the Soviet Union); there had been "sincere and exhaustive discussions" on the measures to be taken to hasten the end of the war against Germany and her satellites, and on the setting up of "close military co-operation between the three Powers in future"; it was also agreed that the "closest co-operation" must continue between the three Powers after the war. A Four-Power Declaration (the work chiefly of Cordell Hull) was signed on the unconditional capitulation of the Allies' "respective" enemies; in addition to the Big Three, the Chinese Ambassador in Moscow also signed this document on his country's behalf. (The Russians were no longer much scared of provoking the Japanese and were anxious to please Hull who had set great store on this Declaration, which gave China a Great-Power status.) Another of the statements foreshadowed the constitution of a United Nations Organisation. The Conference also published a statement on Austria, in effect warning the Austrians not to co-operate with Germany to the bitter end, and urging them to contribute to their own liberation—a principle of which much was later to be made in Rumania, Bulgaria, etc. Finally the Conference published a Roosevelt-Churchill-Stalin declaration on war criminals. They established the principle that these criminals would be returned for trial to the country where the alleged crimes had been committed.

Eden and Cordell Hull were optimistic both during and after the Conference. During an interval at the Bolshoi (they were playing the inevitable *Swan Lake*) I remember Eden telling me: "This is a good conference—better late than never. But the question of travelling to Moscow is infernally complicated. Here we've got to set up the right kind of machinery—we want it, and the Russians want it, too. If the machine is functioning, we'll find it much easier to deal with a problem like Poland. What we are striving for is to get the machinery set up, and to set as many things as possible down on paper."

He got this "machinery" in the form of the European Advisory Commission, but it was quite clear that both at the Moscow Conference and, later, at Teheran, Poland was among the problems that were inevitably shelved. At the Moscow Conference there was much talk of getting both Turkey and Sweden into the war, but this led to nothing. On direct Soviet-Western military co-operation the Russians were still reserved, and did not respond very favourably at first to the American proposal for shuttle bombing, with the setting-up of US air bases in Soviet territory. Nothing was going to be decided about this until February 1944.

Cordell Hull, though very tired at the end of the Conference, received the Press at the US Embassy and sounded very pleased:

> When I started out over here, (he said) most people thought that nothing would come of this meeting, *since Russia was liable to go the isolationist way.** Yet we exchanged at length our views, and were tremendously gratified to find that the Soviet statesmen were more and more disposed towards the view that isolationism was bad... Now the spirit of co-operation has been born, and we can begin to build. Now, indeed, was the time to get together. The foundations have been laid. Some problems are delicate and complicated, but with the spirit of harmony existing between us, nothing can bring estrangement."

He then hinted that the three heads of governments would meet shortly, and sounded particularly pleased with the Four-Power Declaration which included China. There was, however, still a Herculean task ahead of the Allies—problems like the future of Poland and Germany had not yet been settled, but consultation on both questions were in progress.

He also said that AMGOT (Allied Military Government in Occupied Territories) would gradually disappear and that the EAC would have an ever-growing number of problems to deal with. And then:

> Stalin is a remarkable person showing at once unusual ability and judgment and a grasp of practical problems. He is one of the leaders who, together with Roosevelt and Churchill, has a responsibility which no other man may have in the next 500 years... There is no hard feeling among the Russians about the Second Front, as far as I know... I do not know of two nations with fewer antagonistic interests and more common interests than the USA and Russia...

* It is amusing to think that, just as Hull dreaded Russian isolationism so, by 1945, the Russians dreaded American isolationism—one reason, by the way, why they insisted on UN having its headquarters in the USA.

Eden also was very pleased with the Conference:

> When we first arrived here, we thought the prospects were very bleak, and that all the Russians would do would be to scream for the Second Front. I should be surprised if they started screaming now, for they now know it *is* coming. Instead, this Conference was very big stuff, the beginning of a new form of co-operation between us. The teamwork was admirable. Today I discussed military problems with Molotov for two hours. Poland? Yes, it will be discussed through diplomatic channels. . .

On October 30, as President of the Anglo-American Press Association I presided at the lunch we gave to Eden and Cordell Hull (represented by Harriman) at the Hotel National. We did not think Molotov and the other top Russians would come, but much to our surprise the Protocol Department rang up and hinted that invitations would be welcomed. Here was real cordiality! True, Molotov did not come, but Vyshinsky and Litvinov did. In my speech of welcome I referred, among other things, to Eden's and Litvinov's gallant stand at Geneva and at Nyon, and made a crack or two at Chamberlain— without naming him—which went down very well. Eden sat to my right, and the terrible Vyshinsky (now with a sugary smile) to my left, and the whole atmosphere was very matey indeed. Quoting Churchill's remark, earlier in the year, about the "autumn leaves", Vyshinsky said: "Well, it is customary for the autumn leaves to fall in autumn, but if they fall in spring—well, I suppose that's okay, as long as they *do* fall." (He was now clearly resigned to the Second Front in 1944). Litvinov said the League of Nations had unfortunately turned out to be a Tower of Babel, not a solid Pyramid; the nations of the world must do better next time.

Harriman was in a slightly truculent mood and pointedly talked about the war in the Pacific, saying that if it hadn't been so successful there wouldn't be much prospect of America helping with the Second Front in Europe.

At the extravagant Kremlin Banquet that crowned the Conference, Stalin seemed in an exuberant mood. Despite all the earlier unpleasantness over the Northern convoys, he now paid a tribute to the British Navy and the Merchant Fleet: "We don't talk much about them, but we *do* know what they do." The new head of the British

Military Mission, General Giffard Martel rapturously congratulated Stalin on the forcing of the Dnieper only shortly before: "No other Army in the world could have performed such a feat!" The short era of mutual compliments and congratulations had set in.

The two chief American military representatives in the Soviet Union, the anti-Soviet General Michela, and General Faymonville who was notorious for the optimistic analyses of the military situation in Russia he had been sending Roosevelt ever since 1941, often to the disgust of the State Department—were both withdrawn and replaced by a regular Military Mission with General John R. Deane at its head. The Russians were soon to find him a very tough negotiator, who was particularly sticky in organising lend-lease deliveries, always first asking the Russians for full explanations as to whether they *really* needed the stuff for military purposes, or merely for post-war reconstruction.

The Soviet press was very pleased with the Foreign Ministers' Conference. The Revolution-Day Festivities on November 6 and 7, which were marked by tremendous fireworks in honour of the liberation of Kiev by Vatutin's troops, took place in an exuberantly cheerful atmosphere.

Stalin's speech reviewing the events of 1943—"the year of the great turning-point"—in which he paid the warmest tributes both to the Red Army and to the Russian war effort, was also particularly cordial in its comments on the Anglo-American Allies.

> Taking together the blows struck at the Germans and their allies in North Africa and Southern Italy, the intensive bombing of Germany ... and the regular supplies of armaments and raw materials that we are receiving from our Allies, we must say that all this has greatly helped us in our summer campaign... The fighting in Southern Europe is not the Second Front, but, all the same, it is something like the Second Front... Naturally, only a real Second Front—which is now not so far away—will greatly speed up victory over Nazi Germany, consolidate still further the comradeship-in-arms of the Allied States.

He was particularly pleased with Italy dropping out of the war, thought that Germany's other satellites, knowing that "only bumps and bruises were now in store for them," were frantically looking for ways and means of getting out of Hitler's clutches. He suggested that, in 1944, Germany would lose all her allies. She was now clearly "facing catastrophe".

On the night of the 7th Molotov gave his biggest war-time party. The whole diplomatic corps were now back in Moscow, and it was an extremely sumptuous and exceedingly drunken affair. Molotov was going round the guests, proposing innumerable toasts, and, towards the end of the evening, had to be supported on both sides in his further progress through the crowded rooms of the Spiridonovka. He was jovial and looked like a man who was relaxing—certainly for the first time in more than two years. But he carried his liquor much better than others. The first to leave were the Japanese diplomats who had been received with marked coolness; but not very long after, they were followed by a procession of Excellencies who were simply carried out, feet first. The British Ambassador had fallen flat on his face on to a table covered with bottles and wine-glasses, and had even slightly cut himself. There was also something of a row between Molotov and the Swedish Minister, whom Molotov upbraided for the peculiar "neutrality" Sweden had been pursuing. The said Minister was soon afterwards recalled by his Government. The whole party sparkled with jewels, furs, gold braid, and celebrities. The gold braid on the new Russian pearl-grey diplomatic uniforms rivalled that of the generals and marshals. Shostakovich was there in full evening dress—looking like a college boy who had put it on for the first time—and there were dozens of other stars of the literary, musical, artistic, scientific and theatrical firmaments. The party had something of that wild and irresponsible extravagance which one usually associates with pre-Revolution Moscow. There never was to be another party quite like it in subsequent years. But Molotov must have enjoyed it. There was something splendidly Muscovite in this entertainment of watching Ambassadors in all their regalia falling flat on their faces and being carried out by

Russian underlings whose chuckles kept breaking through their expression of deep concern.

We need not recount here the familiar story of the Teheran Conference, except to say that the Russians were satisfied with it—as far as it went. A firm decision had at last been taken to launch "Overlord" in May, an operation that would be supported by a great Russian offensive. Also increased help was to be given to Tito's Partisans.

Some of the remaining "military" decisions—e.g. concerning the eventual entry of Turkey into the war on the side of the Big Three— were to remain a dead letter.

The Partition of Germany was discussed, but no definite decisions were taken; an agreement of sorts was reached on the approximate future frontiers of Poland, though the question of the Neisse frontier was left unsettled and the question of the Polish Government was shelved.

Churchill had pleaded in favour of a lenient Russian treatment of Finland, and had received some half-assurances from Stalin on that score. In the end, Finland was to be let off fairly lightly by the Russians, less because of any half-promises made to Churchill, than in virtue of Russia's own peculiar "Scandinavian" policy, with Swedish neutrality as its centre.

Stalin promised to take part in the war against Japan after the capitulation of Germany, but on terms still to be settled.

None of this was publicly disclosed at the time; what was announced in the final communiqué was that:

> We have concerted our plans for the destruction of German forces. We have reached complete agreement as to the scope and timing of the operations which will be undertaken from the east, west and south. Our offensive will be merciless and cumulative.

The Russians were going to get their *real* Second Front at last. It was on this note—which caused immense satisfaction in Russia— that the victorious but very hard year of 1943 ended for her. A year that had carried the Red Army all the way from Stalingrad and the

Caucasus to Kiev and beyond. Over two-thirds of the German-occupied territory had been liberated. But it was still a long way to Berlin.

Perhaps Stalin was not bluffing when he said at Teheran that the Red Army was growing war-weary, and that it needed something to encourage it. The Teheran communiqué did it.

It came as a shock to many when, less than two months after Teheran, *Pravda* published its famous "Cairo Rumour" story about secret separate peace negotiations going on between Britain and Germany "somewhere in the Iberian Peninsula". Was this calculated to discourage that excessive post-Teheran euphoria that had developed in Russia, or was it a reflection of Stalin's irritation with Churchill who had been much more "difficult" at Teheran than Roosevelt had been? Significantly, the Americans did not figure in the "Cairo Rumour" story; Roosevelt was treated throughout as a very loyal friend and ally of the Soviet Union.

This is not altered by the fact that Roosevelt failed to give any serious thought to the tentative Russian suggestions—both in 1943 and in 1944—for large-scale economic co-operation between Russia and America after the war, complete with a seven-billion-dollar loan for Russian reconstruction. Such "co-operation" was known to be favoured by certain important American business interests, but frowned upon by others, among whom, it was believed, was Ambassador Averell Harriman.

PART SEVEN

1944: Russia Enters Eastern Europe

Chapter I

SOME CHARACTERISTICS OF 1944

1943 was, in the Russian phrase, the *perelom* year—the year of the great turning point. Since Stalingrad and especially since Kursk the Red Army had been sweeping west almost without a break. Two-thirds of the vast territory occupied by the Germans in 1941–2 had been liberated by the end of 1943, and although the Germans still held most of the Western Ukraine and of Belorussia and the whole Baltic area, and were still shelling Leningrad, the Russians were preparing for the final expulsion of the Germans from the Soviet Union in 1944. What is more, the Red Army, on its way to Germany, was going to find itself in non-Russian territory all the way from the Balkans to Poland, and this was going to create a number of new political, diplomatic and psychological problems. Since Stalingrad and especially since the fall of Mussolini, Germany's satellites (Finland, Rumania, Bulgaria, Hungary, Slovakia) were looking for ways and means of getting out of "Hitler's war" with the minimum damage to themselves. Already very early in 1944 the first peace-feelers were put out by Finland, Hungary and Rumania. The Teheran Conference had finally convinced these countries that the fighting alliance of the Russians and Anglo-Americans was a much more solid enterprise than German propaganda had tried to make out. The more conservative elements in these countries were hoping to soften the rigours of a Russian occupation by an active partici-pation of Britain and the United States in any kind of peace settlement. Thus, Admiral Horthy, in his first peace-feeler, was ready to break with Hitler provided Hungary was jointly occupied by Soviet and Anglo-American troops.

Poland continued to be the central problem in East-West relations, and was to lead to many new complications in the course of 1944; not that it was, in essence, a problem very different from say, Rumania, Bulgaria or even Czechoslovakia; but it turned out to be *the* test-case on which a seemingly uncompromising stand was taken by both the Russians and the Western Powers. In the case of Czechoslovakia, for instance, there was some friction and unpleasantness between Benes and the London Government-in-exile on the one hand, and Gottwald, Kopecky and the other "Moscow Czechs" on the other,* but it did not come to an open conflict until long after the war. The Russians maintained reasonably correct relations with the Czechoslovak "London Government", and never attempted to set up a rival pro-Communist Czechoslovak Government either in Moscow or in the liberated part of Czechoslovakia. Whether the Russians had any long-term plans for the future or not, they seemed willing to try out the Czechoslovak experiment of an East-West Co-existence Shopwindow.

On the face of it, President Benes's visit to Moscow in December 1943, almost immediately after Teheran, and the signing of a Soviet-Czechoslovak Pact of Friendship, Mutual Assistance and Post-War Co-operation, were a great success, even though the atmosphere surrounding the visit was not free from all kinds of mental reservations —not least in the relations between Benes and Zdenek Fierlinger, the Czechoslovak Ambassador, who was working hand-in-glove with Gottwald and Kopecky, and was to be one of the villains of the Prague *coup* of 1948. But much was made of the blessing given by Benes to the Czechoslovak Army units fighting on the Soviet Front, and to their Commander, Colonel Svoboda. On December 18 Stalin had a meeting with Benes, in the presence of Molotov and Fierlinger, and some surprise was caused by the absence of any phrase like "cordial atmosphere" in the official statement that such a meeting had taken place. It was known that, with Stalin's blessing, the Czech

---

* Gottwald, for example, criticised the Czechoslovak Government in London (in some articles in *Pravda* and elsewhere) for not encouraging a more vigorous resistance to the Germans inside Czechoslovakia.

Communists had been accusing Benes for some time of not encouraging a more active Resistance movement in Czechoslovakia; I gathered from Benes—whom I saw a few days later—that Stalin had raised this question, too. Unlike the Poles, the Czechs in London were a "good" London Government, but they were a *London* Government for all that; and Stalin's tentative suggestion that they move to Moscow met with no response from Benes.

Nevertheless, Benes's farewell speech on December 23 was marked by extreme cordiality, except that the Russians were not perhaps altogether pleased with his reference to the new Soviet-Czechoslovak Pact as *one of* the most important pillars on which the future policy of Czechoslovakia would be built.

Looking back on 1943, Russia had every reason to be in an optimistic mood, though, to individual Russians, the war, with its fearful casualties, continued to be a very grim reality. More and more young men were being drafted daily into the Red Army, and it was only too common to meet elderly men and women who had already lost several or all of their sons in the war. According to official figures published after the war, there were about seven million men in the Army at the beginning of 1944, and since at least five million men had, by then, been lost in two-and-a-half years' fighting, (not to mention the wounded), it is easy to imagine how deeply the war had affected practically every family in the country.*

Work in the war industries, largely run by women, adolescents and elderly men, was desperately hard, with overtime, compulsory subscriptions to State loans, various "competitions", practically no holidays and often very little food. Eighty to ninety percent of the mostly meagre rations were handed over to the factory canteens. The *podsobnyie khoziaistva* (auxiliary farms), usually no more than vegetable plots, attached to each factory, produced some extra

* The exact number of troops in the Red Army, Navy and Air Force are not easy to ascertain; General Deane, head of the US military mission in Moscow since 1943 thought there were "on the average" twelve million men, but these, of course, also included non-combat troops.

vegetables, but food supplies were still far from good. To the ordinary worker, the *kolkhoz* markets were of little help because of the still exorbitant prices.

Doctors, surgeons and teachers were all hideously overworked. There were not nearly enough surgeons to deal adequately with all the wounded during major military operations, and many lives were lost as a result.

The conditions in some—though not all—of the secondary schools of Moscow in 1944 may be illustrated by the comments made to me by an eleven-year-old boy about that time. There were thirty-five pupils in his form, and one fearfully overworked woman-teacher for *all* subjects: history, geography, arithmetic, natural science and Russian. All the food the children got at school was a slice of bread with some "nasty bitter jam—American stuff made of oranges"; some of the kids threw this *drisnya* (diarrhoea) out of the window. Among the boys, this youngster told me, there was a good deal of lawlessness, "hooliganism" and thieving; in a short time three pen-holders, a cap and a pair of gloves had been stolen from him. Most of their fathers were in the Army (or dead), and most of their mothers were working endlessly long hours in a factory. Among these youngsters there were clear signs of escapism: they no longer sang the usual patriotic songs, but an "escapist" song from a recent film about Kostya, a swaggering beau in the docks of Odessa, or, worse still, a "hooligan" (i.e. obscene) version of the same song. The war was, clearly having a bad effect on secondary education, and may well account for the extensive wave of juvenile crime that was to mark the immediate post-war years in Russia.

There was a serious shortage of teaching staff in 1944, and both the elementary and secondary schools suffered most from it. Also, in Moscow—now deep in the rear—the very young were less conscious of the immediate war tension as life was returning to "normal", except for the shortage of everything. On the other hand, vocational and trade schools, whose purpose was to create large industrial labour reserves, were given priority; similarly, top priority was given to the training of more and more new soldiers.

*

The spirit of the Russian working class was still good, despite unquestionable signs of physical fatigue. It was better still in the Army. Not only was there a feeling of great elation among the soldiers, as every day brought new victories, but there was a great national pride, a sense of achievement, and a well-cultivated desire for more and more distinctions, medals and decorations. These medals and decorations ran into many millions, and acted as a great incentive to every soldier. There were already "Stalingrad medals" and "Leningrad medals" and "Sebastopol medals" and "Moscow medals" and the end of the war was to see new medals "for the capture of Bucharest", "for the liberation of Warsaw"—as well as Belgrade, Budapest, Vienna, Prague and Berlin medals, besides a whole range of new decorations.

In the Army both Stalin and the generals were popular. I remember the tragic, but typical case of a nineteen-year-old boy I knew, Mitya Khludov. He belonged to a well-known Moscow merchant family, whose survivors had inevitably had a difficult time during the early years of the Revolution. He was in an artillery unit during the Battle of Belorussia in the summer of 1944. He wrote me a letter, in which he said: "I am proud to tell you that my battery has done wonders in knocking the hell out of the Fritzes. Also, for our last engagement, I have been proposed for the Patriotic War Order, and, better still, I have been accepted into the Party. Yes, I know, my father and my mother were *burzhuis*, but what the hell! I am a Russian, a hundred percent Russian, and I am proud of it, and our people have made this victory possible, after all the terror and humiliation of 1941; and I am ready to give my life for my country and for Stalin; I am proud to be in the Party, to be one of Stalin's victorious soldiers. If I'm lucky enough I'll be in Berlin yet. We'll get there—and we deserve to get there—before our Western Allies do. If you see Ehrenburg, give him my regards. Tell him we all have been reading his stuff... Tell him we really hate the Germans after seeing so many horrors they have committed here in Belorussia. Not to mention all the destruction they've caused. They've pretty well turned this country into a desert."

Ten days later Mitya's sister had another letter from him, this time from a hospital. He had been wounded, but said he was feeling better and would soon be back with his battery. He gave no details of his injury. But a few days later he died. We learned later that he had died in one of those terribly overcrowded field hospitals in which it was physically impossible to give the wounded all the individual attention and care that they needed.

Mitya's enthusiastic feeling of being "one of Stalin's soldiers" was not the only reaction. But this nationalist mood with its eagerness for medals and distinctions, and its hatred of the Nazis who had "humiliated" Russia, was probably the most widespread of all, and was shared by most of the peasant lads in the Army. Such moods were, of course, encouraged by the *politotdels*, the Army's propaganda services. Others were conscious of belonging to a lost and condemned generation which was destined to be sacrificed—a mood reflected in that pathetic little literary masterpiece by Emmanuel Kazakevich, *The Star*, the story of a reconnaissance raid, written towards the end of the war. The consciousness of living close to death runs through most of the Soviet writing during the war— whether in Surkov's poetry, or Siminov's poetry and plays, or Grossman's and Kazakevich's stories and novels. In the poems of Simeon Gudzenko, a remarkable poet (discovered during the war by Ehrenburg) there was a slightly different *frontovik* mentality; war to such men is a desperate, but still fearfully exciting gamble, and, after the war, such men felt a nostalgia for it. He, like so many others, also hoped it would be a better and freer Russia after the war.

1944 was to be known as the year of the Ten Victories.

1. In January the Leningrad Blockade was finally broken. After a tremendous artillery barrage from the Oranienbaum Bridgehead, the Russians broke through the powerful German ring of concrete and armoured pillboxes and minefields and joined with other Russian forces striking from the east; losses were very heavy on both sides, but within a week the Germans were on the run, and did not stop until they reached Pskov and the borders of Estonia. There was immense rejoicing among the 600,000 people who were still living in Leningrad after the fearful thirty-months' siege. In retreating, the Germans had destroyed many historic buildings, among them the palaces of Pushkin (Tsarskoie Selo) and Pavlovsk, south of Leningrad.

2. In February and March the troops of the 2nd Ukrainian Front under Konev (assisted by those of the 1st Ukrainian Front under Vatutin) first encircled several German divisions in the Korsun Salient on the Dnieper, and then, in their famous "Mud Offensive", crashed right through into Rumania, after forcing the Bug, the Dniester and the Pruth. They were then held up for a few months outside Jassy in Northern Rumania.

3. In April Odessa was liberated, and in May the Crimea was completely cleared.

4. In June Finland was knocked out by the Russian breakthrough to Viborg (Viipuri) across the Karelian Isthmus. Then, having reached the 1940 Finnish border, the Red Army stopped of its own accord, without pursuing its advance on Helsinki.

5. No less spectacular than Konev's offensive across the Ukraine into Rumania in March was the liberation of Belorussia, after the Russians had broken through the powerful German Bobruisk-Mogilev-Vitebsk line. Nearly thirty German divisions were trapped, chiefly around Minsk, and the Russians advanced almost as far as Warsaw, where the Armija Krajowa* insurrection had by then begun. In the course of this offensive the Red Army liberated a large part of Eastern Poland (including the new provisional capital of Lublin), nearly the whole of Lithuania, and, after forcing the Niemen, reached the frontiers of East Prussia.

6. In July, in a parallel offensive, the Red Army liberated the Western Ukraine, including Lwow, forced the Vistula and, after an abortive attempt to break through to Cracow, established the important bridgehead of Sandomierz on the west bank of the Vistula, south of Warsaw. But after its failure to take Warsaw, the Red Army did not pursue its task of breaking through to Germany at any price. Here, in Poland, the concentration of German forces was, indeed, heavier than anywhere else.

7. Instead, in August, the Red Army struck out in the south—in Moldavia and Rumania—and, after trapping fifteen or sixteen German divisions as well as several Rumanian divisions in the Jassy-Kishenev "pockets", swept into Rumania, precipitated

* The Armija Krajowa (or A.K.) was the Polish underground resistance movement directed from London.

Rumania's surrender, overran Bulgaria, reached the borders of Hungary, and established contact with the Yugoslavs.

8. In September Estonia and most of Latvia were freed of the Germans. Thirty German divisions remained, however, in Kurland peninsula, and remained there, as a "nuisance" force, till the capitulation of Germany in May 1945.

9. In October, the Red Army broke into Hungary and Eastern Czechoslovakia, joined up with the Yugoslavs and took part in the liberation of Belgrade. In Hungary the fighting was exceptionally fierce, and the fight for Budapest at the end of the year lasted several months. The city was not captured until the following February.

10. In October also, the Red Army attacked in the extreme north, threw the Germans out of Petsamo, in the Finnish salient running to the Arctic, and broke into Northern Norway.

The victories of 1944 were spectacular, but very few of them were easy victories. The Germans fought with extreme stubbornness in Poland (especially in August, when the Russians were stopped outside Warsaw), at Ternopol in the Western Ukraine (which, with its three weeks' intensive street fighting, was reminiscent of Stalingrad); and, later, in Hungary and Slovakia. German resistance was also particularly fierce in all areas on the direct road to Germany, notably in the areas adjoining East Prussia and, later, in East Prussia itself.

The Germans were, at last, obviously outnumbered. The Allies had been advancing in the west since June, and by September Germany had lost all her allies, except for a few Hungarian divisions.

Yet the German tendency to resist the Russians at *any* price, and to resist the Western Allies less strongly, became more and more pronounced as the war was moving to its close. The Vistula line opposite Warsaw; Budapest; East Prussia; and, later, the Oder Line, were defended more desperately by the Germans than any line or position in the west. Apart from the sweep across the southern Ukraine in March, and the sweep across Rumania in August (both following an encirclement of large German forces), and the minor operation in northern Norway, none of the Russian offensives in

1944 were in the nature of a walkover, and the nearer the Russians got to Germany, the more desperate became German resistance.

If, in 1941 and even in 1942, the German soldier seemed to so many Russians a soulless, but formidably efficient robot, the Russian attitude to the Germans changed very perceptibly during 1943 and 1944—but in two different directions. There were still some formidable German soldiers, particularly the Waffen-SS, ready to fight to the last round, and even known to commit suicide rather than surrender. But the ordinary German war prisoner was no longer the arrogant individual he used to be in 1941 and 1942. Now more and more German prisoners tended to whine, and tried to look pathetic, and spoke of "Hitler kaputt"; the 1941 and 1942 desire to beat up and even kill German prisoners had now largely disappeared; after a short time the Russian soldiers' anger cooled down, and they would even give newly-captured Germans food, saying: "go on, stuff yourselves, you bastards."

But there was another side to the "German problem". Nearly every liberated town and village in Russia, Belorussia or in the Ukraine had something terrible to tell.

In Belorussia, hundreds of villages in alleged "Partisan country" had been burned down, and their inhabitants either murdered or deported. Everywhere large cities had been systematically destroyed; in the Ukraine, where there was relatively little scope for partisan warfare, the Germans had deported a very high proportion of the young people; everywhere, in the towns, the Gestapo had been active, and people had been shot or hanged. The *Einsatzkommandos* and other troops had been busy exterminating partisans or alleged "accomplices" of partisans—often whole villages, including women and children. In hundreds of towns there had been the systematic massacre of Jews. In Kiev, for example, tens of thousands of Jews had been exterminated in a gully outside the city called Babyi Yar. Every Ukrainian and Belorussian city had its own horror story. As the Red Army advanced to the west, it heard these daily stories of terror, and humiliations and deportation; it saw the destroyed cities; it saw the mass-graves of Russian war prisoners, murdered or starved to death;

it saw Babyi Yar with its countless corpses, among them the corpses
of small children; and, in the Russian soldiers' mind, the real truth on
Nazi Germany, with its Hitler and Himmler and its *Untermensch*
philosophy and its unspeakable sadism became hideously tangible.
All that Alexei Tolstoy and Sholokhov and Ehrenburg had written
about the Germans was mild compared with what the Russian
soldier was to hear with his own ears and see with his own eyes and
smell with his own nose. For wherever the Germans had passed,
there was a stench of decaying corpses. But Babyi Yar was small
amateur stuff compared with Majdanek, the extermination camp
near Lublin where one and a half million people had been put to
death in a couple of years, and which the Russians captured almost
intact in August 1944.* It was with the whiff of Majdanek in their
nostrils that thousands of Russian soldiers were to fight their way
into East Prussia... There was the "ordinary Fritz" of 1944, and
there were the thousands of Himmler's professional murderers; but
was there a clear dividing line between the two? For had not
"ordinary Fritzes", too, taken part in the extermination of "partisan
villages"? And did not the "ordinary Fritz", in any case, approve of
what his SS and Gestapo colleagues were doing? Or didn't he
approve? Here was both a psychological and political problem which
was to give the Soviet government and the Red Army command a
good deal of trouble, especially in 1944 and 1945.

The Teheran communiqué had created in Russia a feeling of
euphoria: but for a number of reasons this did not entirely suit Stalin
and the Party. Stalin had apparently been irritated by Churchill's
half-hearted attitude to "Overlord", and also by his repeated
grumbling about "the Polish Problem", on which Stalin held strong
views. So in January 1944 *Pravda* launched, as already said, its
"Cairo Rumour" about separate peace talks "between two leading
British personalities and Ribbentrop in a coastal town of the Iberian
Peninsula"—a story which was later implicitly repudiated by Stalin
himself in the Red Army Order of February 23. This story was
followed by a particularly savage attack by Zaslavsky in *Pravda* on

* See pp. 889 ff.

Wendell Willkie (of all people) who had raised some questions—in a very mild form—about what the Russians were going to do about Poland, the Baltic States, the Balkans and Finland.

Willkie, said Zaslavsky, was using the phraseology of the "enemy camp"; and then he went off the deep end:

> It is high time it was understood that the question of the Baltic States is an internal Soviet matter which is none of Mr Willkie's business. Anyone interested in such questions should take the trouble to become acquainted with the Soviet Constitution and with that democratic plebiscite which took place in these Republics; and let him also remember that we know how to defend our Constitution.
>
> As for Finland and Poland, not to mention the Balkan countries, the Soviet Union will manage to thrash things out with them, without any assistance from Mr Willkie.

Zaslavsky indeed thought it "most peculiar" and highly suspect that Willkie should dare suggest that a "crisis" among the United Nations might be approaching over this question of Russia's small neighbours.

Appearing in *Pravda* a month after Teheran, this strident cry of "Hands off Eastern Europe", with its suggestion of a definite Russian "sphere of influence" was much more indicative of coming disagreements than Willkie's article to which Zaslavsky had so violently objected.

All kinds of little pinpricks continued in the Soviet Press, particularly against the British; thus, in March, *Pravda* publicised a story of German war prisoners—now re-taken by the Russians—who had allegedly been exchanged for British war prisoners in North Africa on the understanding that they would not fight the *British* again, but were, however, free to go and fight the Russians.

Above all, there continued to be a chronic irritation over the Polish Problem. The Russian offer to amend the Curzon Line in Poland's favour by giving her Bialystok and a large area around it failed to meet with any favourable response from the Polish London Government. This was also held responsible for alleged anti-Russian activities by the Armija Krajowa in Poland who wrote in their clandestine press that there was "nothing to choose between Hitler and Stalin", and who (the Russians alleged) even

directly collaborated with the Germans by denouncing to them certain Belorussian underground leaders as Communists. It was also
reported in the Russian press that General Anders had arrested fifty
Polish officers in Teheran for wanting to join the Polish Army in the
Soviet Union. Then, in January 1944, the Russians were greatly
annoyed by the reservations and innuendos in the British and
American press concerning the Soviet methods of conducting the
investigation into the whole lurid business of the Katyn murders.

However, with the Second Front in Normandy approaching, the
Russian attitude to the West grew considerably more cordial, though
the Polish Problem still continued to poison East-West relations,
which became particularly strained at the time of the Warsaw rising
in August. But, by October, the atmosphere again changed for the
better, and Anglo-Soviet relations never seemed as overwhelmingly
good as during the Churchill-Eden visit to Moscow that month. Even
the most sceptical became convinced that, by that time, both Stalin
and Churchill thought it expedient to remain on the best of terms,
at least so long as the war with Germany was still going on. It was,
indeed, not till some weeks after Yalta in February 1945 and very
near the end of the war in Europe that the Polish Problem became
acute again, only to go from bad to worse once the war was over.

In 1944, with the end of the war in sight, a great deal of stock-taking
began to be done by Stalin and the Party. The reconstruction and
population problems in Russia required some long-term decisions;
also, the ideological "deviations" and the Russian-nationalist departures from "Leninist purity" during the war—and, indeed, for some
time before the war—required some serious adjustments. Finally, the
very fact that millions of Russian soldiers were now fighting in
"bourgeois" countries in Eastern and Central Europe raised a number of altogether new psychological problems. One of these was to
be created by the Russian soldiers' first contact with the department
stores of Bucharest.

Chapter II

CLOSE-UP I: UKRAINIAN MICROCOSM

A "Little Stalingrad" on the Dnieper

Nikopol with its manganese, Krivoi Rog with its iron ore, and the whole of Right-Bank Ukraine (i.e. the Ukraine west of the Dnieper) —that great colonial domain of Erich Koch and that future (if not present) No. 1 granary of the greedy *Herrenvolk*—it was not easy for Hitler to say goodbye to all these. Without them, *Grüne Mappe*** and the rest of his superman blueprints were only fit for the wastepaper basket.

At the end of 1943 the Russians had already eaten some distance into Right-Bank Ukraine. At the end of September and the beginning of October they had performed one of their most astonishing feats in the war: under cover of night, many thousands of men had forced the mighty barrier of the Dnieper at many points. They had done it *s'khodu*, that is, "on the march". No sooner had they reached the Dnieper than thousands rowed or paddled across in small craft, on improvised rafts, on a few barrels strung together, or even by clinging on to planks or garden benches. The Germans, who had boasted of their impregnable *Ostwall* on the right bank of the Dnieper, were taken completely by surprise. Their allegedly powerful fortifications along the whole length of the Dnieper had, in fact, not been built, and what fortifications there were had certainly not been manned in time. If any serious resistance came from the Germans

---

* Göring's June 1941 "Directives for the Control of Economy in the Occupied Eastern Territories".

anywhere, it was dealt with by the Russian artillery on the east bank of the river. In one place as many as sixty tanks, with all openings puttied up, actually advanced under water and forded the river. Enough Russians crossed the river to form a number of bridgeheads on the other side: Vatutin's troops established several in the neighbourhood of Kiev, and, further south, Konev's set up no fewer than eighteen; and though, in the next few days, seven were lost with very heavy casualties, the remaining eleven merged into one. As soon as the big bridgeheads had been firmly established, the Russians laid pontoons across the river, and German air attacks on these were usually successfully repelled thanks to the powerful concentration of Russian fighters. The Russians also used two brigades of paratroopers to set up the bridgeheads. At the Kremlin banquet during the Foreign Ministers' Conference in Moscow in October 1943, General Giffard Martel, head of the British Military Mission, said that no army in the world could have performed the feat of crossing the Dnieper as the Red Army had done.

On the face of it, it looked like a reckless improvisation, but in reality the whole operation—barrels, garden benches and all—had been carefully planned in advance, and high decorations had been promised to those who particularly distinguished themselves in forcing the Dnieper: over 2,000 were, indeed, decorated afterwards. The Germans' "Maginot Line" on the Dnieper proved very largely a piece of bluff, and once the pontoons and ferries were completed, vast quantities of heavy Russian equipment were taken across the river, and, on November 6 the Russians liberated Kiev, the capital of the Ukraine. Despite various ups and downs (such as Vatutin's temporary loss of Zhitomir, west of Kiev, later in November) the 1st and 2nd Ukrainian Fronts had, by January, captured substantial territories on the right bank of the Dnieper, Vatutin's 1st Ukrainian Front* having advanced along a wide front some 125 miles west of the river, and Konev's 2nd Ukrainian Front some ninety miles. Still farther south there were Malinovsky's 3rd Ukrainian Front and Tolbukhin's 4th Ukrainian Front. These four Fronts were to liberate nearly the whole of Right-Bank Ukraine between January and the beginning of May 1944.

* The former Voronezh Front.

Obviously over-rating their own strength, and under-rating the drive and skill of the Red Army, the Germans were still determined —or at least Hitler was—as late as January 1944 to clear the Russians out of the whole of Right-Bank Ukraine—to begin with. With that end in view, they clung like grim death to their Korsun-Shevchenkovo salient on the Dnieper, about fifty miles south of Kiev, and stretching some thirty miles along the west bank of the river. North of this relatively narrow salient were Vatutin's troops;* south of it Konev's troops of the 2nd Ukrainian Front (formerly "Steppe Front"). Hitler's plan was to attack the Russians from this salient both north and south of it, and so to recover the whole of Right-Bank Ukraine for Germany—a plan as unrealistic as so many other Hitler plans during the later stages of the war.

The Russian command thought differently. Here, it seemed to them, was a golden opportunity of inflicting a "second Stalingrad" on the Germans—though admittedly, on a smaller scale.†

The similarities between the two operations were, indeed, striking enough. It was a case of encircling the German forces by the Russian northern (Vatutin) and southern (Konev) pincers joining somewhere west of the "bag", and of preventing the Germans outside it from breaking through to their encircled comrades. In this case, the rôle of Manstein was played by the German 8th Army under General Hube; the most important difference between the Stalingrad and the Korsun situation was that the Germans trapped at Korsun *did* try to break out, with the result that the Russians had to fight on "two fronts", as it were, on either side of the circle they had made round the "Korsun" Germans.

On February 3rd the great news was announced that, after three days' heavy fighting the troops of the 1st and 2nd Ukrainian Fronts, one striking south-east from Belaya Tserkov, the other, striking

* On March 1, 1944, General Vatutin was fatally wounded by a band of Ukrainian nationalists and Marshal Zhukov took over the command of the 1st Ukrainian Front on the following day.

† See insert map, p. 829.

north-west from Kirovograd, had effected their junction near Zvenigorodka, and had thus cut off the large German "Korsun" salient. The German divisions had been encircled, and the sixteen-day battle to liquidate them began. On February 9, Gorodishche, inside the Korsun "bag", was captured; on the 14th, Korsun itself was taken, and although that day the German forces, trying to break through the ring from outside, made some slight advance, on the 15th their further attempts to break through were already "successfully repelled". On the 18th, the Germans were wiped out in the whole Korsun "ring". The Russians claimed 55,000 German dead and 18,000 prisoners, 500 tanks, over 300 planes and much else.

It was in February and the beginning of March that all the four Ukrainian Fronts came into violent motion. After liquidating the Germans in the Korsun Salient, Konev's 2nd Ukrainian Front swept all the way into northern Rumania within a few weeks; north of it, General Zhukov's 1st Ukrainian Front, meeting with much stiffer resistance (it was getting nearer Germany than any other) still advanced along a wide front as far as the Carpathians and almost as far as Lwow, capturing Rovno, Erich Koch's Ukrainian "capital" in the process. To the south of the 2nd Ukrainian Front, Malinovsky's 3rd Ukrainian Front pushed on, in a spectacular sweep, to Kherson, Nikolaev and Odessa, which they captured at the beginning of April; and Tolbukhin's 4th Ukrainian Front, after finally dislodging the Germans in February from the Nikopol bridgehead on the left bank of the Dnieper, undertook its spectacular reconquest of the Crimea.

While Zhukov was crashing ahead in the northern Ukraine and Malinovsky along the Black Sea coast, on March 5 Konev launched his great offensive against the German 8th Army under General Hube—the "Manstein" who had failed to rescue the Germans trapped at Korsun. After a week's heavy fighting in incredibly difficult conditions (an early thaw had set in) Konev captured the town of Uman, Hube's principal base; after which the troops of the 2nd Ukrainian Front drove on to the Bug and beyond, not to stop until they had invaded Rumania the last week in March. They had covered a distance of over 250 miles in less than a month.

It was soon after the liquidation of the Korsun "bag" and on the day after Konev's capture of Uman that I had the good fortune of being the only Western foreign correspondent authorised to visit the 2nd Ukrainian Front, where I spent one of the most illuminating weeks of all my war years in the Soviet Union. My principal companion was Major Kampov, an officer of General* Konev's staff, who was to remain a life-long friend, and who was to become famous after the war as the novelist "Boris Polevoi".

On March 12 I was flown in an army plane from Moscow across the Dnieper and over Cherkassy to a place called Rotmistrovka which had been, until February, in the northern part of the Korsun salient. On the following day I was to fly in a tiny U-2 plane to Uman, which had just been recaptured by Konev's troops.

It was at Rotmistrovka that I first met Major Kampov. He looked pale and physically—though not mentally—tired; his uniform was grubby, and the mud was splashed right up his army boots. For three years he had been at it; in the grim autumn of 1941 he had broken out of an encirclement in the Kalinin Province after losing most of his men; he had taken part under Konev in the heartbreaking Rzhev offensive in 1942; but now he had eight months of continuous victories behind him. He was slim, dark, and had grey laughing eyes with a quietly humorous expression. Maxim Gorki, in his youth, must have looked a little like him (except that one of his eyes was half closed as a result of shell-shock).

"You couldn't have come at a better moment," he said, "do you know what happened today? Our troops have already crossed the Bug." This was great news. The Bug, on the way to Odessa and Rumania, was said to be one of the most heavily fortified German lines. (In practice, as I later learned, it was nothing of the kind, since

* He was to be promoted to the rank of Marshal later in 1944.

before reaching the Bug the Germans had lost all their heavy equipment).

The "Mud Offensive" was in full swing. It was one of the most extraordinary things that had happened; it was contrary to all rules of warfare. Barely three weeks after the liquidation of the German troops trapped at Korsun, Konev had struck out at a time when the Germans had least expected it. So deep and impassable was the Ukrainian mud.

During that week in the Ukraine I was to hear—and, indeed see— a great deal of the "Little Stalingrad" of Korsun. Since then I have read both Russian and German accounts of the operation, and whereas, by and large, the Russian and German versions of what happened at Stalingrad coincide, there are some major differences in the two versions on Korsun.

According to the official Russian *History*, the German troops still in the bag after a fortnight's heavy fighting, and after the failure of the Germans to break through from outside, made a final bid to break out of the encirclement on the night of February 16–17. Despite a violent blizzard, they were heavily attacked, first by artillery and mortar fire and by "light bomber planes", and then by machine-gun fire, and Russian tanks and cavalry.

> Only a small group of enemy tanks and armoured cars, carrying the generals and senior officers, succeeded, thanks to the blizzard, in breaking out of the encirclement in the Lisyanka area, leaving their troops to their fate. Before that, they had succeeded in evacuating 2,000 to 3,000 officers and soldiers by air. The whole operation ended in the liquidation of ten enemy divisions and one brigade. 55,000 Nazi officers and soldiers were killed or wounded, and 18,000 taken prisoner. The enemy also lost all his equipment, all of which had a highly demoralising effect on other units of the German Army in the Ukraine.*

German writers, on the other hand, have tried to minimise the disaster. According to Manstein† only six divisions and one brigade were encircled, totalling 54,000 men—a figure which the Russians

* IVOVSS, vol. IV, p. 68.
† Op. cit., p. 585. There is also a detailed account of this battle in Mellenthin's *Panzer Battles*.

challenge on the strength of German army documents captured at the time. Other German historians, such as Philippi and Heim, while (as usual) putting the whole blame on Hitler for trying to hang on to the "utterly useless" Korsun salient at all, claim that when the 50,000 encircled troops still left there attempted their desperate breakthrough on February 17, 30,000 got out, and some 20,000 "were lost", besides the entire equipment of all the divisions that had been encircled.*

What is certain is that the breakthrough of February 17—unsuccessful according to the Russians, partly successful according to the Germans—was very costly for the Germans.

In view of the conflicting post-war versions, it may be interesting to quote Major Kampov's very dramatic eye-witness account given me at the time.

After describing how the Vatutin and Konev troops had formed their ring round the salient on February 3, Kampov said:

"Having broken through with our tanks and guns and mobile infantry, we now had to face *both ways* in the 'ring'—and, for a time, this was very hard. We were shelled from both sides, and we had to attack unceasingly to widen our 'ring'—which, at first, was often only some two miles wide. Of course, we suffered very heavy losses. Even so, after six days, we had managed to widen the ring to nearly twenty miles at its narrowest point.

"At the beginning of the encirclement the area of the 'bag' was almost 240 square miles, and for a long time we had to fight not only the troops inside, but also those outside—and these amounted to no fewer than eight Panzer divisions.† They were under the command

---

* The big margin between the German admission of a loss of 20,000 men and the Russian claim of 80,000 German dead, wounded or prisoners, is perhaps due to the Germans referring only to the "final" breakthrough attempt without taking account of the extremely heavy fighting that had gone on for a fortnight for the liquidation of the "bag". When the casualties the Germans suffered during this period are added to the 20,000 men lost on February 17, the Russian figure of 80,000 becomes much less improbable.

† Seven, according to Philippi and Heim.

of General Hube. Inside the ring there were ten divisions, including a tank division, plus the Belgian SS Wallonia Brigade. Degrelle, the Belgian top Nazi, was among them but, along with several German generals, he escaped by plane. Pity; it would have been interesting to 'interview' him. The Belgian SS were all underworld thugs and adventurers of the worst kind.

"We had very strong forces in our 'ring' and Hube's troops did not make much progress. As for the 'bag', our policy was to slice it into bits, and deal with each bit separately. In this way we wiped out village after village in which the Germans had entrenched themselves —it was bloody murder. I'm afraid some of our own villagers perished, too, in the process: that's one of the cruellest aspects of this kind of war.

"Anyway, four or five days before the end, the Germans had only an area of about six miles by seven and a half, with Korsun and Shanderovka as its main points. By this time the whole German 'bag' was under shell-fire, but they still held out, because they were hoping for the miracle to happen—the miracle of Hube's breakthrough from outside. But all these German high hopes rapidly began to fade out. And then Korsun fell, and a tiny area round Shanderovka was all that was left.

"I remember that last fateful night of the 17th of February. A terrible blizzard was blowing. Konev himself was travelling in a tank through the shell-battered 'corridor'. I rode on horseback from one point in the corridor to another, with a dispatch from the General; it was so dark that I could not see the horse's ears. I mention this darkness and this blizzard because they are an important factor in what happened. . .

"It was during that night, or the evening before, that the encircled Germans, having abandoned all hope of ever being rescued by Hube, decided to make a last desperate effort to break out.

"Shanderovka is a large Ukrainian village of about 500 houses, and here Stemmermann's troops—he was the last general left in the 'bag', the others having fled—decided to spend their last night and to have a good night's rest. Konev learned about those plans, and he was determined to prevent them at any price from having a rest, and effecting an organised escape—or any kind of escape—the next morning. 'I know this is a hell of a night, with this blizzard blowing, but we must get night bombers to deal with the situation,' he said. He was told that, in weather like this, it was practically impossible to do anything with bombers, especially with so small a target as Shanderovka. But Konev said: 'This is important, and I cannot accept these objections as final. I do not want to give any orders to the airmen, but get hold of a Komsomol air unit, and say I want volunteers for the job'. We got a unit composed mostly of Komsomols; all without exception volunteered. And this is how it was done. The U-2 played an immensely important part in this. Visibility was so bad that nothing but a slow low-flying plane like the U-2 could have achieved anything at first. The U-2s located Shanderovka in spite of the blizzard and the darkness. Not for a moment did the Germans expect them. They flew down the whole length of Shanderovka and dropped incendiaries. Many fires were started. The target was now clearly visible. Very soon afterwards—it was just after 2 a.m.—the bombers came over and the place was bombed and blasted for the next hour. Our artillery, which was only three miles away now, also concentrated its fire on Shanderovka. What made it particularly pleasant for us was our knowledge that the Germans had chased every inhabitant out of Shanderovka into the steppe. They had wanted the place all to themselves for their sound night's rest. All the bombing and shelling compelled the Germans to abandon their warm huts, and to clear out.

"All that evening the Germans had been in a kind of hysterical condition. The few remaining cows in the village were slaughtered and eaten with a sort of cannibal frenzy. When a barrel of pickled cabbage was discovered in one hut, it led to wild scrambles. Altogether they had been very short of food ever since the encirclement; with the German army in constant retreat, they didn't have large stores anywhere near the front line. So these troops at Korsun had been living mostly by looting the local population; they had done so even before the encirclement.

"They had also had a lot to drink that night, but the fires started by the U-2s, and then the bombing and the shelling sobered them up. Driven out of their warm huts they had to abandon Shanderovka. They flocked into the ravines near the village, and then took the

desperate decision to break through early in the morning. They had
almost no tanks left—they had all been lost and abandoned during
the previous days' fighting, and what few tanks they still had now
had no petrol. In the last few days the area where they were concentrated was so small that transport planes could no longer bring them
anything. Even before, few of the transport planes reached them,
and sometimes the cargoes of food and petrol and munitions were
dropped on our lines.

"So that morning they formed themselves into two marching
columns of about 14,000 each, and they marched in this way to
Lysianka where the two ravines met. Lysianka was beyond our
front-line, inside the 'corridor'. The German divisions on the other
side were trying to batter their way eastward, but now the 'corridor'
was so wide that they hadn't much chance.

"They were a strange sight, these two German columns that tried
to break out of the encirclement. Each of them was like an enormous
mob. The spearhead and the flanks were formed by the SS men of
the Wallonia Brigade and the Viking Division in their pearl-grey
uniforms. They were in a relatively good state of physique. Then,
inside the triangle marched the rabble of the ordinary German
infantry, very much more down-at-heel. Right in the middle of this,
a small select nucleus was formed by the officers. These also looked
relatively well fed. So they moved westward along two parallel
ravines. They had started out soon after 4 a.m., while it was still
completely dark. We knew the direction from which they were
coming. We had prepared five lines—two lines of infantry, then a
line of artillery, and then two more lines where the tanks and cavalry
lay in wait. . . . We let them pass through the first three lines without
firing a shot. The Germans, believing that they had dodged us and
had now broken through all our defences, burst into frantic jubilant
screaming, firing their pistols and tommy-guns into the air as they
marched on. They had now emerged from the ravines and reached
open country.

"Then it happened. It was about six o'clock in the morning. Our
tanks and our cavalry suddenly appeared and rushed straight into
the thick of the two columns. What happened then is hard to describe. The Germans ran in all directions. And for the next four hours

our tanks raced up and down the plain crushing them by the hundred. Our cavalry,* competing with the tanks, chased them through the ravines where it was hard for tanks to pursue them. Most of the time the tanks were not using their guns lest they hit their own cavalry. Hundreds and hundreds of cavalry were hacking at them with their sabres, and massacred the Fritzes as no one had ever been massacred by cavalry before. There was no time to take prisoners. It was a kind of carnage that nothing could stop till it was all over. In a small area over 20,000 Germans were killed. I had been in Stalingrad; but never had I seen such concentrated slaughter as in the fields and ravines of that small bit of country. By 9 a.m. it was all over. 8,000 prisoners surrendered that day and during the next few days. Nearly all of them had run a long distance away from the main scene of the slaughter; they had been hiding in woods and ravines.

"Three days later at Djurzhantsy we found the body of General Stemmermann. Soon afterwards General Konev had a good laugh when the German radio announced, with all sorts of details, how Hitler had personally handed him a high decoration. For General Stemmermann was dead, right enough. I saw his body as it lay there. Our people had laid him out on a rough wooden table in a barn. There he lay, complete with his orders and medals. He was a little old man, with grey hair; he must have been a *Corpsstudent*† in his young days, judging from the big sabre scar on one cheek. For a moment we wondered whether it wasn't all a fake; perhaps an ordinary soldier had been dressed up in a general's uniform. But all Stemmermann's papers were found on the body. They might have

---

* This appears to be one of the few operations so late in the war in which cavalry played any substantial role. Certain cavalry units, such as the famous Cossack Corps under General Dovator (who was killed on December 19, 1941) had played a part in the Battle of Moscow and in the subsequent Russian counter-offensive, but their losses had been extremely heavy at the time. While propaganda greatly exaggerated the military importance of the Dovator Corps, General Malinovsky, whom I saw on the Don at the time of Stalingrad, referred to cavalry as "very beautiful and picturesque, but pretty ineffective in this kind of war—what can a horse do against a German tommy-gun?"

† Member of a German students' duelling association.

faked all the obvious papers, but they could scarcely have had the idea of forging a Black Forest gun licence, complete with the man's picture, and issued in 1939. . . We buried him decently. We can afford to bury a general decently. The rest were dumped in holes in the ground; if we started making individual graves—we don't do that even for our own people—we would have needed an army of grave-diggers at Korsun. . . And there was no time to waste. The general is very particular about corpses—they must be cleared away in two days in summer, in three days in winter. . . But dead generals aren't all that frequent, so we could give him a proper burial. Anyway, he was the only general there with any guts. All the rest of them had beat it by plane.

"Had he committed suicide?" I asked.

"No, a shell splinter got him in the back—but many of the SS-men did commit suicide, though hardly any of the others.

"Altogether, the Germans lost over 70,000 of their best troops in their attempt to hold the Korsun salient, 55,000 dead and 18,000 prisoners."

"What had they done with their wounded? Is it true that they killed them off?"

"Yes. And that no doubt contributed to the hysteria that marked their last night at Shanderovka. The order to kill the wounded was strictly carried out. They not only shot hundreds of them—shot them as they usually shoot Russians and Jews, through the back of the head, but in many cases they set fire to the ambulance vans, with the dead inside. One of the oddest sights were the charred skeletons in those burned-out vans with wide bracelets of plaster-of-Paris round their arms or legs. For plaster-of-Paris doesn't burn. . .

"The Korsun debacle prepared the ground for our present spring offensive. It was psychologically immensely important. To some extent the Germans had forgotten Stalingrad; at any rate, the effect of Stalingrad had partly worn off. It was important to remind them. It's going to heighten enormously their fear of encirclement in future."

I find it hard to say whether Kampov's figures are any more correct than post-war Russian or German figures; and whether it is true, as appears from his account, that no Germans broke out at all;

probably some did—particularly the generals. Or perhaps they left by air a few days before. But, unlike the dull "technical" tone of most of the post-war military literature, Kampov's account—even allowing for a little romancing, especially about the cavalry—seems to give a striking and truthful picture of both the hysterical and desperate mood of the hardened Nazi troops as they found themselves trapped, and of a real ruthlessness—"no time to take prisoners"—among the Russian troops at the end of a fortnight's extremely costly fighting against both sides of the "ring".

Konev's Blitzkrieg through the Mud

The Ukrainian mud in spring has to be seen to be believed. The whole country is swamped, and the roads are like rivers of mud, often two feet deep, with deep holes to add to the difficulty of driving any kind of vehicle, except a Russian T-34 tank. Most of the German tanks could not cope with it.

General Hube's 8th Army, having failed to break through to the Korsun bag, and having suffered very heavy losses in the process, decided, in spite of it all, to hold its part of the line running from Kirovograd in the south to Vinnitsa in the north, namely the line south of the Korsun "bag", now in Russian hands, and some forty miles north of the town of Uman. The Germans assumed that while the *Schlammperiode*—the deep-mud period—continued, there was nothing to fear, and, mobilising thousands of Ukrainian civilians, they were busy fortifying their new line north of Uman.

It was on March 5, with the mud and "roadlessness" at their worst, that Konev started his fantastic "Blitzkrieg through the Mud". It started with a gigantic artillery barrage against the German lines; within six days, the Germans were driven forty miles back, and chased out of Uman. The mud was such that they abandoned hundreds of tanks and trucks and guns, and fled—mostly on foot— to Uman and beyond. At one railway station the Russians captured a newly-arrived train with 240 brand-new tanks. Usually, however, the Germans burned or blew up both lorries and tanks.

Although Russian tanks were able to advance through the mud, the artillery lagged behind; and it was very often a case of Russian infantry, sometimes supported by tanks, but sometimes not, pursuing German infantry. Konev's Mud Offensive was "against all the rules", and the Germans had certainly not expected it. The Russian infantry and tanks rapidly advancing to the Bug and beyond—and, before long, towards Rumania—were being supplied with food, munitions and petrol by a large number of Russian planes. These also did some strafing of German troops, and would have done more but for the weather. The only vehicles, apart from T-34 tanks, that advanced fairly successfully through the mud were the Studebaker trucks, for which the Russian soldiers were full of praise.

Very striking, as I was to discover in the next few days, was the high morale of the Russians and the poor morale of the Germans, who had been unnerved by the Korsun disaster, by the suddenness of Konev's March 5 offensive and by the loss of practically all their heavy equipment.

With the permission of General Konev, the Major and I flew in two tiny U-2 planes from Rotmistrovka to Uman the next day. Flying in a U-2 is what, in childhood, one imagined flying to be like. Stuffy, closed passenger planes are nothing like it. Sitting in the open seat behind the pilot I somehow felt that I was really flying for the first time. At no more than sixty miles an hour we flew over the house-tops of Rotmistrovka; children in gardens and people on the roads waved, and we waved back. We flew mostly at twenty or thirty yards above the ground. At first the cold wind hurt my eyes, but when the pilot passed me a pair of goggles it was perfect. Like a bird, the plane dived down valleys and ravines, then darted up over hills and woods, and circled over towns and villages which were of special interest. The snow had disappeared, and there was spring in the air. The earth was dark-brown and almost black, and the trees were still bare, but one already imagined the harvest rising from the rich wet earth. We circled all over the "Korsun salient". Some villages were intact, but very few people were to be seen, and hardly any cattle. But other villages, especially Shanderovka, where the Germans had spent their last night, were nothing but a heap of rubble, though many cherry and apple trees were still standing among the ruins. From Shanderovka, through the hilly country to the west, there ran two roads, like two glossy brown ribbons, along which, on that February 17, the Germans had gone to their death.

Then we circled over a plain: hundreds of German helmets still lay about, but all bodies had been buried; and soon the grass would grow over the many thousand Germans who had been slaughtered here.

Next came several lines of trenches—these had been German trenches till March 5. Having crossed these shattered German lines, we flew for many miles over roads that presented the strangest spectacle. They were cluttered up with thousands of burned-out lorries, and hundreds of tanks and guns which the Germans had abandoned in their panicky retreat through the mud. And this strange, static procession of burned-out vehicles stretched all the way to Uman.

After about two hours in the U-2 we landed on Uman airfield. Here were several wrecked German planes, and, at the far end of the field, the enormous steel skeleton of a burned-out German transport plane, a Junkers 323.

The Major talked about his boss, General Konev. "Konev", he said, "is an old soldier. He fought in Siberia during the Civil War. There he organised partisan bands, then brigades, finally divisions; he was political commissar of one of the partisan divisions and commanded an armoured train which fought against the Japs. Later, armed with a rifle, he took part in the storming of Kronstadt during the Rebellion there in '21. Both in Siberia, and in Kronstadt, he had Fadeyev, the writer, with him; they have remained old friends ever since.

"They call him 'the general who never retreated'. That is, of course, untrue; we all retreated in '41, but Konev less than most, and he was one of the first to counter-attack—at Yelnia in August '41, and it was also he who advanced further than anyone else in the winter counter-offensive of '41–42.

"You've never met him? He is 48, almost bald and grey-haired. He is broad-shouldered, and can be very stern. But usually there is a gay twinkle in his eyes. Usually he wears glasses and is a great reader. He carries a library with him; he likes to read Livy, and also our classics, whom he loves to quote in conversation—something from Gogol, or Pushkin, or *War and Peace*. He lives in a simple peasant hut, and when he travels along the front he wears a cloak so as not to embarrass the soldiers by his presence. He is very austere in his habits; doesn't drink, and objects to others getting drunk. He is very exacting both to himself and others. Of his peace-time hobbies the one he misses most is partridge shooting; he is a great shot. What else can I say about him? He has a smattering of English and can read it fairly easily. He admires Stalin both as a leader and as a writer, and is a strong Party man. I have seen him reading a Stalin Order, and have heard him say: 'That's really first-class. That's the way to write. Everything fits. There is *thought* behind every word.'" A typical 1944 comment on Konev—and Stalin!

In the next few days I was told by the military authorities at Uman that the total losses the Germans had suffered in the week since Konev's March 5 offensive were: over 600 tanks (250 of them in good condition), 12,000 lorries (most of them destroyed), 650 guns and fifty ammunition and supply stores. In a week the Germans had lost about 20,000 dead, but only 25,000 prisoners; they were still desperately avoiding being taken prisoner. The Russian losses also had been heavy during the breakthrough attempt, but very light since then, with the Germans on the run.

I also remember a very revealing talk I had with an air force colonel during that week at Uman—revealing, because his attitude to the Western Allies—now in March 1944—was so much warmer than what one had found in the Red Army before. He talked of the way the air force was supplying the army, as it was advancing "towards Rumania" (the words "Rumania" and "Mamalyga"* were on every soldier's tongue in that part of the world), with food, ammunition and petrol; and then he said:

"The German air force is much weaker now than it used to be. Very occasionally they send fifty bombers over, but usually they don't use more than twenty. There's no doubt that all this bombing of Germany has made a lot of difference to the German equipment, both in the air and on land. Our soldiers realise the importance of the Allied bombings; the British and Americans, they call them '*nashi*'—that is '*our*' people... A lot of the German fighters now have to operate in the west and we can do a lot of strafing of German troops, sometimes even without much air opposition." And he added: "Those Kittyhawks and Airocobras are damned good—not like last year's Tomahawks and Hurricanes—which were pretty useless. But here we mostly use Soviet planes, especially low-flying *stormoviks* which scare the pants off the Germans..."

The Turbulent Town of Uman—Dostoevskian Bishop and other odd characters

In a way, the small town of Uman was a microcosm of the whole Ukraine. Its population had dropped from 43,000 to 17,000. To live here for a week was to see something of nearly every aspect of Ukrainian life under the German occupation—except heavy industry of which there was none for many miles around. Uman was the centre of a large rural area, one of the richest in the Ukraine, noted for its wheat, sugar-beet, maize, fruit and vegetables. Like many other towns in the Ukraine, its population before the war had been about one-quarter Jewish; now you did not see a single Jewish face in the streets. Half the Jews had escaped to the east in 1941, but the 5,000 who had stayed—children and all—were herded one night into a big warehouse: all the windows and doors were boarded up and hermetically sealed, and all of them died of suffocation within a couple

* Mamalyga is maize porridge, the staple diet among poorer Rumanians; these were condescendingly referred to as *mamalyzhniki*, i.e. mamalyga-eaters.

of days. The Ukrainians in the town did not talk much about it: they seemed to look upon it as rather a routine matter under the Germans. There were now partisans in the town, and there had been a Soviet underground during the occupation. There had also been various kinds of collaborators, and Ukrainian nationalists, and, strangely, the Red Army was still often referred to as "the Bolsheviks" or "the Reds", as though they were something extraneous to this turbulent part of the Ukraine, with its old Petlura and Makhno traditions.* But the biggest obsession was deportation. Nearly 10,000 young people from Uman had been deported as slave labour. Only few had escaped by joining the partisans, not strong in this part of the Ukraine.

The day we arrived Uman presented a fantastic sight. One large building in the centre of the town was still smouldering. The streets were crammed with burned-out German vehicles, and were littered with thousands of papers, trodden into the mud: office records, private documents and letters, photographs, and also whole bundles of well-printed coloured leaflets in Ukrainian exalting the "German-Ukrainian Alliance". One said "Down with Bolshevism" and showed a manly hand in a green sleeve tearing down a red flag with the hammer-and-sickle; another showed a German soldier shaking hands with another person in an unrecognisable pearl-grey uniform. "Our alliance will give happiness to all the nations of Europe"; still another called "Oath to the Fatherland" showed a crowd of gallant horsemen raising their arms to heaven and swearing: "None will lay down his arms while our Ukraine is enslaved by the Bolsheviks".† Among all this rubble, in a vacant space between two houses, lay a

* Petlura, head of an ephemeral Ukrainian nationalist "Government" in 1918, and Makhno, head of a peasant anarchist movement during the Civil War, were both notorious for their banditry and anti-Semitic pogroms. Petlura was assassinated by a Jew in Paris in 1928.
† These leaflets were apparently part of one of the half-baked attempts to set up an anti-Russian and pro-Nazi "Ukrainian Army" along Vlasov lines. These attempts came to little, and it was not till the end of 1944, when Bandera, Melnik and other Ukrainian "nation-

dead German soldier—a young lad, of not more than eighteen, with the face of a sleeping child. But his belly had been crushed—probably by some vehicle in the mad stampede which had accompanied the Germans' panicky flight from Uman.

A standing joke was one of a German general driving out of Uman on a rickety old farm tractor with a camel-like movement, one of the few vehicles able to cope with the deep mud.

There were very few people in the streets of Uman that day; they still seemed frightened to come out after all the firing during the previous days, and there were no militia in the streets, but, instead, weird figures on foot or on horseback—men with high fur caps, with red ribbons attached. Many were wearing German army overcoats. These were partisans from the neighbourhood. I talked to some of them. One, a young fellow in a blood-stained German overcoat, told a long story of how he had been arrested and tortured by the SD; how he had then escaped to the partisans, how the Germans had then murdered his wife, who had stayed at Uman. He said this with an uncanny calm. "There were lots of traitors in this town," he said; "and the worst was the chief hangman of the SD, a bastard called Voropayev; but now the NKVD have got him under lock and key. We'll see that *he* gets hanged all right."

Another of the partisans was a fat man, clean-shaven with a greasy cap on the back of his head: he might well have come straight out of a pub in Leeds or Manchester. He had worked at the railway depot at Uman as the chief liaison man with the partisans—"We are helping the Soviet authorities," he said, "to catch all the spies and traitors".

*

alists" were liberated by the Germans, that they encouraged something of an anti-Soviet guerrilla war in the Western Ukraine, which was to last till 1947. There had, of course, been isolated anti-Soviet guerrilla bands before that, some independent of the Germans. It was one such band that assassinated General Vatutin near Kiev in March 1944. At the end of the war, a number of SS officers took part in this Ukrainian guerrilla war against the Soviets. Bandera was released by the Germans in September 1944 and Melnik a month later. (See Dallin, op. cit., p. 624.)

Major Kampov and I stayed at an improvised Russian officers' hostel, and saw a wonderful variety of people at Uman during that week. The house had been inhabited by German officers until a few days before, and a good search had been made for mines and booby-traps; one had been found inside the tinny old piano; if anyone had struck one of the keys, it would have popped off.

The next day there were not only many soldiers, but also rather more civilians than before in the streets of Uman, with its small, nondescript, mostly ex-Jewish houses in the centre, and its more pleasant Ukrainian thatched cottages with gardens on the outskirts. I mixed with a large crowd of civilians who had come to the main square for the military funeral of a Russian tank-crew. Almost the sole subject of conversation was deportation to Germany. Practically all the young people in the town had been deported. The technique of deportation varied from time to time; in some places, the Germans had started by offering tempting labour contracts; once a few dozen people had fallen for the offer, the rest were mobilised compulsorily. But there were ways of dodging deportation—if one was lucky and wealthy enough to be able to bribe a German doctor or a German official. There was much corruption among the Germans. Self-mutilation was also fairly commonly practised to avoid deportation.

I also heard stories of Russian Cossacks serving under the Germans. They were a bad lot. A few days before the Germans evacuated Uman, some of these Cossacks—so the story went—were let loose, and looted part of the town, and raped several girls; they were said to have been wearing Red Army uniforms and the Germans said they were a Russian advance unit. One theory was that the Germans wanted the population to be terrorised at the thought of the Russians' coming, and to flee to the west.

The Gestapo and SD had been very active in Uman. The Jews had all been murdered; but the Gestapo had also been active among non-Jewish civilians; later, I went to see the field outside the prison, and here were the fresh bodies of some seventy or eighty civilians whom the Germans had shot before leaving Uman. Among them were a lot of ordinary peasants and peasant women, suspected of, and imprisoned for, "partisan" activity; among the dead bodies I also saw a little girl of six, still with a cheap little ring on her finger. She must have been shot so that she wouldn't tell. I also saw the Gestapo H.Q. with hideous instruments—such as a hard-wood truncheon with which prisoners' hands were smashed during interrogation.

We spent one evening at the Town Soviet. What a strange assembly of people were round the supper table! Mayor—i.e. Chairman of the City Soviet—Zakharov, a small palefaced man, with dark hair brushed back, had been one of the chief partisan leaders of the Ukraine. He had been wounded three times; here also was the former Bishop of Taganrog; and a doctor, a typical old-time intellectual, with a little beard and glasses, looking rather like Chekhov; and an elderly woman teacher, and a stout clean-shaven man in a semi-military tunic, who looked a typical Party man, but who declared himself to be a banker. "A banker!" I said, "how do you mean?" Yes, he was a banker all right; he was the head of the Moldavian branch of the Soviet State Bank; and now that the Red Army was beyond the Bug and would soon be in Bessarabia, he was expecting soon to take up his former duties again.

The Mayor was not an Ukrainian, but a Russian. He had been appointed Mayor by the military—"subject to the population's subsequent approval." It made me wonder whether the Army did not prefer to see real Russians in responsible administrative jobs in large Ukrainian towns, immediately they recaptured them, rather than Ukrainians—who might be more tolerant of the frailties of Ukrainian human nature. Was it a coincidence that in Uman, and before that in Kharkov, and after that, in Odessa, the Mayor should have been a Russian? Yet, in the purely Russian town of Voronezh, the Mayor was an Ukrainian.

In the Ukraine, with only small forests, the Mayor said, the partisans could operate only in small groups; the largest of the five groups he had organised were two of 200 to 300 men each, operating in the Vinnitsa forests. They had their wireless receiving sets, and they multigraphed leaflets with Soviet war news for distribution in the towns and villages. They were short of arms, and as a general rule they accepted no one without arms; volunteers were told to join the Ukrainian police force, obtain as many arms and as much ammunition as possible, and then come back. The Vinnitsa partisans had had many bloody battles with both German punitive expeditions and Cossacks, and, compared with Belorussia and other more wooded parts of the country, their casualties were very heavy. Working round Uman was particularly difficult, because there were hardly any forests around here. Nevertheless, the five units had succeeded in derailing forty-three trains with military equipment in 1943 alone, and had other daring exploits to their credit.

Being wounded in July 1941, Zakharov said, he had been unable to follow the Red Army, and had been taken prisoner by the Germans. But he escaped and came to Uman, which was already under German occupation; he had arrived in October 1941, and, since then, he had been "working for the good of his country." In 1942 he was arrested by the Gestapo and savagely beaten and injured in the spine; "so I know how the Gestapo question people". He was later released, and disappeared for a while, appearing afterwards at Vinnitsa, complete with a beard and priestly robes. For long intervals he would vanish to the woods where the partisans knew him as "Uncle Mitya".

"It was a hard and grim life", he said, "they were merciless and so were we. And we shall be merciless with the traitors now." He spoke in a soft, rather tired voice. "It's no use crying in wartime," he remarked. "Though there were not many of us, we still managed to worry the Germans a lot; in the smaller towns and the villages round Vinnitsa, we would put up notices at night saying: 'You are the bosses from 7 a.m. to 7 p.m.; we are the bosses from 7 p.m. to 7 a.m., and you are forbidden to come out of your houses.' And, by heaven, they usually obeyed the order; and when they didn't they were often sorry..."

As for life in the town of Uman during the occupation it was, on a small scale, much what I had already seen in Kharkov—the virtual abolition of schools, and a great deterioration in the health services; the number of clinics was cut down by three-quarters. Most of the small workshops had disappeared with the killing of the Jews. The one important industry of the town, the large sugar refinery, had been destroyed by the Germans. It was urgent to restore it. In one respect though, it was very different from Kharkov; in this rich agricultural area, there was always sufficient food to keep people more or less alive.

I asked Zakharov about the agricultural policy and administration.*
On the whole, the Germans considered this part of the Ukraine very much their granary, and they had done all they could to keep agriculture going. They had not split up the farms; or rather, for propaganda purposes, they had, in some parts, distributed the land among the peasants on one collective farm in a hundred, with the implication that this would also be done on the other farms sooner or later. They had made various other promises, but no one trusted them, and meantime they stuck to the *kolkhoz* organisation as being the easiest to handle. The cultivation in the main had not been as thorough as before the war, because there weren't enough tractors, even with those the Germans had imported; the peasants often had to plough the fields with horses and even cows; but two things had assured a good sowing of winter wheat: the rubber truncheon of the German officials, and much more so, the solid belief that the Russians, and not the Germans, would reap the harvest in 1944. . . Revolting conditions existed in many villages. The *starosta* was appointed by the Germans—he might have been a good man, or a bad man, or simply a weak man; but above him there was always an SS chief. "There's one village I know," said Zakharov, "and it's not the only one of its kind—where the SS man would order the *starosta* to supply him with girls every night, including young girls of thirteen or fourteen."
"Here at Uman we had three *Gebietskommissars* in succession:

* The best and most detailed account we have on the German agri-cultural policy in the Ukraine will be found in Alexander Dallin's *German Rule in Russia*. This shows that the underlying policy was exploitation pure and simple, and that the attempt to depart from the *kolkhoz* system and make other concessions to the peasants so that they should produce more were either very half-hearted or were sabotaged by *Untermensch* maniacs like Erich Koch, the German overlord of the Ukraine. What with future plans for colonising the Ukraine with Germans, the Ukrainian peasants' distrust of the Germans was complete.

the *Gebietskommissar* was the Chief for the civilian population. He was assisted by a number of SS officers. Then there was the Military *Kommandatur*; then there was the agricultural chief for the area, the *Landwirtschaftsführer*, a brute called Botke, who on his day off would go to the prison to watch, and take part in, the examination and torture of prisoners; he was a real sadist. The Burgomaster of Uman was a *Volksdeutscher** called Gensch, and he had an Ukrainian assistant called Kwiatkiwski. The police were composed of the Gestapo, the S.D., and an auxiliary Ukrainian police force. Into this they simply mobilised people; some of the Ukrainian police immediately escaped and joined the partisans, with the firearms they had received, or had managed to take. The Ukrainian policemen who have stayed behind—though the Germans tried to get most of them away, whether they wanted to or not—will be individually examined. Some of them undoubtedly worked for their country, though in German service; but those who were traitors shall be treated accordingly".

"There seems to have been a lot of contradictory orders as regards Right Bank Ukraine," the Mayor said. "I know of three orders: the first was 'don't destroy'—it came from Hitler himself at a time when the Germans were still confident they would recover all the ground lost on the Right Bank; then there was a second order, from one of the generals of the 8th Army, which said 'destroy'; and since then, there has been a third one, again saying 'Don't'. I don't know who is responsible for this one. So they may still have a few illusions left; but they can't last long now! In the towns, however, they have always tried to destroy at least the main buildings; you'll have seen something of that here in Uman; they were in a devil of a hurry here, so most of the damage is limited to the big buildings on the outskirts, especially near the airfield. And, of course, there's also the power-station which nearly everywhere is among the first things to go. . . ."

By far the most colourful of the Mayor's guests that night was the priest, the Archierei, i.e. the Bishop of Taganrog, a bishop of the

* German-speaking and of German descent, though not of German nationality.

"black" or monastic clergy. He was a handsome man, with a whimsical look in his eyes, rosy cheeks and a blond, silky beard. He was certainly a bit of a rogue.

He drank vodka like a Hero of the Soviet Union on leave, but carried it remarkably well, except that his humour grew more whimsical and crazy as the evening went on. Heaven knows what he really thought at the back of his mind as he sat there, the guest of honour at the Bolshevik Mayor's supper table. He must have chuckled to himself at the thought of it; in fact, his whole conversation was like one unceasing chuckle. "Ah," he said, "the morning the Red Army walked into Uman, and some of the dear boys came into my house, and embraced me and asked me for a drink, I brought out a bottle of vodka, and, believe it or not, I drank to Joseph Vissarionovich Stalin! Drank to him for the first time in my wicked life! That's what the Germans did to me!" he chuckled gaily. "They made me face death three times; I spent sixty-six days in jail because I wouldn't knuckle under them; not I! But they're terrible people, and if you don't wish to perish, you have to keep your wits about you. Now look at this," he said, pointing at his enormous diamond cross, "do you think they would have let me keep this if they had seen it? Not they—not the thieves and robbers that they are. Why, it's worth, I am told, well over a hundred thousand roubles. I received it five years ago from the Patriarch Sergei himself. I hid it in a nice cosy safe place as soon as the Germans came: I wasn't going to take any chances with this precious cross Sergei had given me as a token of his esteem."

"I had a lot of trouble with the Germans, I can tell you," he said, "I really suffered for my country. How I adore the Red Army!" he cried, and, bending over the shoulder of the major sitting beside him, he kissed the epaulette with a loud voluptuous smack. "You don't mind, Comrade Major, do you? Let me kiss it again!" (Gosh, I thought to myself, the old buffoon, Father Karamazov come to life again!) I also thought for a moment the Major would resent this piece of buffoonery, but he took it like a man, and merely laughed. "Oh, I know", the High Priest went on, "the Germans pretended they were great Christians; they opened five churches in this town of Uman—but what for? For German propaganda, for un-Christian, heathen propaganda. And when they saw that it had no effect, they turned against the church. The men of the *Kommandatur* would break into the church during Divine Service, and they carried rubber truncheons. They were afraid of our Russian nationalism. What quarrels, what arguments we had with them! They expected us to recognise the Metropolitan Serafim of Berlin—a Nazi, I tell you. But they said he was the real head of the Russian Church and declared that that holy man the Patriarch Sergei was—I hardly can repeat it—an impostor, who had been appointed by Stalin. 'No', I said, 'he has not been appointed by Stalin, but by the Metropolitans...' 'Oh', they said, 'they're just a small group of impostors, a bunch of Kremlin stooges...' I said, 'No, the Patriarch of Moscow is the only Head I can recognise'. But these arguments really started later. At first, I must say that, to my eternal shame, I thought I could take advantage of the Germans' arrival, and open a few churches at Taganrog—for at that time I was still at Taganrog. They sounded encouraging at first—no use denying it. Only, my troubles soon started. I was told that I was expected to make a speech to the faithful, denouncing the Moscow Patriarch and accepting the authority of their Berlin Metropolitan. They even said I should say prayers for a German victory. I failed to do either, and was, of course, duly reported, and ordered to go to Rostov, where I was hauled over the coals by a big German chief, who said: 'Look here, Your Eminence, if you think the German Army needs your prayers, you are quite wrong. But don't make any mistake about it; we give good marks to those who do pray for us, and bad marks to those who do not. And, he added, 'the bad marks can be very bad indeed'. What a nasty, horrid man he was!"

For a long time there was no serious trouble, but then, suddenly, he was ordered to leave Taganrog for Kakhovka, in the Ukraine, where the Germans again brought pressure to bear on him, this time in real earnest. They wanted him as "an Ukrainian Bishop" to make a public denunciation of the Patriarch Sergei, and to write a long article which the papers throughout the Ukraine would publish. Again he chuckled into his blond silky beard. "I wrote them an article—it made their hair stand on end! So they simply locked me up—they locked me up in a dark cell without a window; and they starved me, and often left me for a whole day without water. I stayed in that cell for sixty-six days and nights... And as I sat there in the dark, hungry and thirsty, I kept saying to myself: 'I am doing the right thing. How can I not recognise the Patriarch who gave me my diamond cross? How can I not recognise Stalin? He gave me my passport.' And I said to myself: 'No, I shall not work for the enemies of my people, even if it costs me my life'."

It was not quite clear how and why he was let out in the end; but it seems that he was deprived of his large church, and given only a small church at Uman. He had one more argument with the Germans, though, and quite recently. "One day the *Gebietskommissar* called for me, and said: 'Now what do you make of this? The Archbishop of York has visited Moscow.' (The German papers were, indeed, full of it.) 'What do you make of the Anglo-Saxons and the Bolsheviks conquering Europe?' I said I did not make anything of it. I tried to sound as simple as I could, and I said: 'Whatever happens, it will be the will of God'. The *Gebietskommissar* got very angry and said: 'I am not asking for any emotional utterances from you ... I want you to think in a rational spirit.' I said he could not expect me to be too rational; I was a Priest, and therefore whatever God the Father and His Son, Jesus Christ, decided, was good enough for me.' And I quoted to him the Lord's Prayer—'Thy will be done.' He didn't like it, and told me to go to hell." And, with a chuckle, he added: "Fancy telling a Bishop to go to Hell!"

I asked what he was going to do now. "Now", he cried, "now I shall be happy... Happy and frightened..." "Why frightened?" "Ooh! I am frightened, frightened of the Patriarch", he squealed, becoming more and more Dostoyevskian in his buffoonery. "Ooh! He is such a great man. Such a powerful mind. Do you know that his skull is sixty-three centimetres in circumference? A great brain. After all", he explained in a dramatic whisper, "I did work with the Germans; oh, only a teeny-weeny bit, but I worked with them all the same... It's true, I refused to pray for a Hitler victory; nor did I write the article that they demanded from me denouncing the Moscow Patriarch... But still I am frightened. Sergei—he is *such* a disciplinarian! But I am not frightened of Joseph Vissarionovich, who knows I am loyal. He, in his infinite wisdom knows that I am not like the Bishop of Vinnitsa. He escaped to Germany by plane; they even took some cattle away by plane. They took sheep and bishops away by air!" He giggled, and repeated "Sheep and Bishops!" And, turning to the Mayor, he said: "I know you'll agree with me that Joseph Vissarionovich will not be angry with me... But Sergei, oh I am frightened of that great, grand old man! But perhaps his great heart will soften when he learns that I had to live in hiding the last three weeks the Germans were here. And I also want to write a little book which will be a devastating answer to the foul and libellous book that was written by a *Volksdeutscher* called Albrecht, about our Orthodox Church, and I want to print on the cover a large black serpent with a swastika on its tail... But I shall atone for my sins. I shall serve my country, great Mother Russia, and her great Soviet Government, and pray for them as long as I live... And so, for the second time in my sinful life, let me drink with you all to our great leader Stalin!"

We drank to Stalin. Our host and the others listened to all this with tolerant amusement. The Archierei was a typical case, an average case. He was no hero, but he had not "collaborated" whole-heartedly; that, at least, was fairly clear. Everybody understood that, in the past, he could have had but little love for the Soviet régime, and one had to make allowances for this. He had, for a short time, taken advantage of the Germans' apparent desire to encourage the revival of the Orthodox Church, but had soon realised that they were only out for their own ends.

The roads continued to be rivers of mud, but one morning the Major wangled a Studebaker in which we drove to the Bug, west of Uman. Though the Red Army was well beyond the Bug, on its way to Rumania, there were many people on the road: soldiers who were wading through the mud towards the Bug, and they were jovial and in high spirits; and new labour battalions of peasants who were being sent to repair the railway, and who were not looking too pleased to be dragged away from their farms; and, lastly, new army recruits, who were going to Uman to report for service in the Red Army—now that, with the liberation of this part of the Ukraine, they had become available. Some of these looked singularly unenthusiastic; "however," said the Major, "they'll soon get used to the idea when they see so many of their fellow-Ukrainians, with high decorations, in the Red Army." There was no doubt, he said, that the German occupation had demoralised many people in this part of the country, and while they hated the Germans, they had also lost much of their "soviet-consciousness" and had become parochial in their outlook.

We stopped in one or two villages; they had not suffered much from the war; nor had more than two Germans ever been stationed there; nevertheless the German officials regularly came on a weekly inspection, and slackness and absenteeism were severely dealt with; a German surveyor with a whip travelled around the fields in a *brichka* and threw his weight about. In case of any trouble the police were called for. Suspected slackers were beaten up. Proportionately, there were much fewer deportations to Germany from these villages than from the towns; the food deliveries were rigorously exacted, and the peasants said that in fact the whole output of the *kolkhoz* was taken by the Germans, and they themselves had to live on whatever their "individual" plots yielded; however, in summer, most of the perishable fruit and vegetables were left to them, too, as the Germans did not have enough transport to take them away. The Germans had made vague promises of splitting up the land among the peasants after the war, but there were few illusions on that score.

This part of the Ukraine had been treated as an important source of food for Germany. Even so, the area under cultivation was only eighty percent of pre-war; but even this was better than the country round Kharkov, where I had been in the previous summer, and where only forty percent of the land had been cultivated. About two months before the Germans left, they started taking much of the livestock to Germany. This, of course, created much anti-German feeling. Even so, and even despite the deportations, many peasants were aloof and seemed indifferent to what was happening; it was clear that the Soviets—or "the Reds", as the peasants here called them—would have a job to develop a proper "soviet-consciousness" among these people. As Kampov said: "They lived reasonably well under the occupation; for the sly Ukrainian peasant is the greatest virtuoso in the world at hiding food. He always hid it from us; you can imagine how much better still he hid it from the Germans! And now that the Germans have disappointed them, they hope that maybe *we* shall scrap the *kolkhozes*. But we won't. . ."

Ukrainian Deportees

Nearly four million *Ostarbeiter* from the Soviet Union—most of them from the Ukraine—were deported as slave labour to Germany; and, in the Ukraine, this was No. 1 grievance against the Germans. Not only the deportations themselves but, even more so perhaps, the way in which they were carried out.

In Uman, I had long talks with two local girls, Valya and Galina, who had managed to return from deportation. Valya, a dark little girl of twenty, must have been pretty only two years before, but now was broken, and looked like a frightened little animal. To get away from Germany she had put her hand under a flax-cutting machine and had all four fingers cut off.

"On February 12, 1942, at two in the morning, the Ukrainian police came, followed by some German gendarmes in green uniform, and I was taken away under escort to School No. 4. From there, together with a lot of other girls, we were taken at 5 a.m. to the railway station, and packed into goods wagons—seventy of us. . .

"After a very long journey we got to some town, where we were put in a camp, all the women were made to strip and were sent to be deloused. Then, before reaching Munich, we were taken to a village called Logow. There we lived in a camp, until a manufacturer arrived, and he took us all to a flax-combing factory. We lived there in a barracks attached to the factory—it was really a sort of camp too. A little farther away, lived some French and Belgian war prisoners; and in another part of the camp were some Polish and Jewish girls. I stayed in this place seven and a half months. We got up at five in the morning, and, without food, we went on working till two in the afternoon. Then we would get two spoonfuls of boiled turnip and a slice of bread, which included sawdust and other substitutes. After that another shift came on, and it worked until eleven or twelve o'clock. For an evening meal we received three or four small baked potatoes and a cup of ersatz coffee; that was all the food we ever got.

"The Germans in the factory were very brutal. I was once beaten by a German woman. It was when I told her that the machine was out of order. She slapped my face and punched me, as if it was my fault. Another time when the machine went wrong, the foreman also hit me, saying I was a *'verdammte Bolshevik'*. He hit and hit me again, and I cried.

"There was so much flax-dust in the place, they had to keep the electric light on all day. It was a terribly depressing place. We received no money at all. I was so sick of all this, of the dust, and the bad food, and the beatings, and my clothes that were all going to pieces, because they would not give us any work clothes, and all the insults, and all the *'verdammte Bolshevik'* and that cold, contemptuous air with which the Germans talked to us and looked at us, as though we weren't real people, that my nerves began to go to pieces. There was some wild garlic growing outside, and we used to pick it, and rub our gums with it, because we were all developing scurvy, and our teeth were beginning to fall out; but the Director once arrived and said it was *verboten* to chew garlic because he could not stand the stink. At the railway station one day—we were made to unload coal once a week—there was another row over the garlic; one of the foremen, seeing me chewing garlic, kicked me in the shins, and hit me over the face; but the other girls began to scream at him; so he stopped. I was so sick at heart, I wanted to throw myself under the train that day; but I remembered my parents, and I felt sorry for them. I sometimes thought I might get one of the Belgians or Frenchmen to make me pregnant, because sometimes they sent pregnant girls home. But the very thought of it revolted me; was I an animal to have a child from a stranger? I was a virgin, and what would my parents say if I came home to them in that condition?

"I did not throw myself under a train; and yet, as the days went on, I grew more and more desperate. I knew that if I did not do something, I should die a slow death. And then, one morning, without premeditation, I did it. It just occurred to me in a flash. I was working on a machine, with a great knife going up and down and cutting the flax threads. And, almost without thinking, I suddenly put my hand under the knife. I did not lose consciousness; I was still quite tough then; I only shut my eyes, and then, when it happened, I was frightened to look. Then I called for the German woman working next to me; and she screamed and ran for the foreman; he was a fat fair-haired man, about thirty-eight and very deaf, and she took some time to explain what had happened. He came rushing along, and I was taken off to the infirmary, where they made me a tourniquet and bandaged me up. The foreman was very worried; some kind of commission was expected that day to come and inspect the place, and he thought he might get into trouble. Some Frenchmen and Belgians then led me to our barracks; I was nearly unconscious by the time we got there. The Director had still not been informed. The foreman went to him to report; and the Director ordered that an ambulance be sent for which would take me to the hospital in Munich, about ten miles away. It was almost a pleasure to be in the hospital. My hand hurt me; but I was put in a clean bed, with white bed-linen. They did not give me much food, but what I got was nice and tasty. I stayed there about a month; then the Director asked that I be sent back to the factory. He urged me to stay on; said that he would appoint me one of the managers of the camp; I don't know exactly what he was up to, I think he wanted to avoid paying my fare to the Ukraine. For four months he kept me there.

Finally, I was sent home by the Munich *Arbeitsamt* (Labour Office). It was by pure accident that this happened. One day when I was going to Munich for a dressing, I talked to a German woman who advised me to go to the *Arbeitsamt*. She was a kind woman, and even paid my fare, and told me exactly where to go. There, at the *Arbeitsamt*, they gave me a paper, and the police took me off to the station the next day and put me in a goods carriage along with several other Ukrainians. At the factory, the night before I left, the Director seemed much annoyed, but said nothing. I was given a pailful of boiled turnips, and a loaf of bread, and the people in the camp gave me their day's ration, and a few odds and ends they had saved up. But during many days, on that long journey, I had nothing to eat.

Now that I think of it, I realise that for two months they had not paid me anything; and later they paid me seventy pfennigs a week. And when we said to the foreman who was paying out the money: 'Why so little?' he would shout *'Ruhig'*. ('Be quiet!'). . . God, how they tormented us", Valya said, almost with a shudder. "It was so bitterly insulting, the way these people behaved to us. They looked at us with such contempt. Why? I ask you, Why? Was that the kind of life I was preparing for? I was growng up happily, in our Ukraine. Why should my life have been broken like this?" And then, as an afterthought: "There was another girl in the factory, and she decided to follow my example. But the Germans guessed this time that it had been done deliberately; and she was not allowed to go home. So she lost her hand for nothing."

Galina Ivanovna's experience was very similar to Valya's—yet she was, temperamentally, an entirely different woman, and, in a way, more typically Ukrainian with her sarcastic humour, and her singular contempt for the Germans "who did not know what good food was until they got to the Ukraine."

She was small and perky and fair, with the perfect comedian's face, with lively blue eyes and a little turned-up nose. She laughed a great deal, but it was not a kindly laugh; she was a mimic and satirist. She wore a pale-blue dress and a cocky little hat with a feather. She was about thirty, and physically slightly faded, which was not surprising after all she had gone through. She had been an actress before the war in the First Kolkhoz Theatre in Kiev, where she played small parts in Ukrainian peasant comedies. She quoted a few bits from her parts, but never got very far with them. . . "Oh dear, I've just forgotten everything", she said, "It seems such ages ago since I was an actress in Kiev. . . An actress", she repeated with a bitter little laugh. "Being a *putzfrau* (charwoman) is now more in my line of business. My husband used to be one of the stage managers at the theatre. Now he's somewhere in the Red Army. I haven't heard from him for years. . . He's from Uman."

Galina Ivanovna had been in Germany, and her story is the story of millions of Europeans—with variations. "The real trouble", she began, "started here in Uman when a German called Graf Spretti* arrived here in February '42 to recruit labour. The Germans announced a big meeting at the Cinema. A lot of us went there, just to see what it was all about. So Spretti said: 'I want you people of Uman to go voluntarily to Germany to help the German army.' And he promised us the moon. But we had a fair idea of how much such promises were worth, so we said: 'But what if we don't want to go?' Then Graf Spretti gave us a dirty look and said: 'In that case you will be politely requested to go all the same.' That was on February 10 and two days later they started rounding up people in a house-to-house search—the police, armed with rifles, would go from one house to the other and collect the younger people. We were taken to a big school, and at five o'clock in the morning we were taken to the railway station; we were put in railway carriages, and these were locked up. Some of the people had some food with them, and it was shared. We were told that we'd be fed at Lwow, but when we got there, we were given nothing at all, not even water.

"We stopped there at the railway station for a whole night, and then we went on to Przemysl. At Przemysl the Germans unlocked the carriages, and started examining our luggage."

"What kind of carriages were they?" I asked.

"What kind?" she said, almost surprised at my question. "Just ordinary goods carriages; we all sat or lay on the floor; there were no benches. There were about sixty or seventy people to a carriage. Anyway, as I was saying, they came to examine our luggage at Przemysl. 'What do you want all this luggage for?' the Germans said. 'There's any amount of stuff you can buy in Germany—fancy taking all these filthy clothes to Germany.' So they took away nearly all the clothes we had, and all the heavier luggage, and left us with just small bundles..."

The whole journey, which lasted a month, was a nightmare. In a camp near Przemysl, where they were kept for a fortnight, they were

* He is mentioned in the Nuremberg Trial as one of Sauckel's recruiting officers.

given hardly any food. Several of the girls fell ill, and a few died. Then, in Western Germany, they were taken to another camp; here at least there were some British and French prisoners who would throw them some food over the fence.

"The friendliness of the English and French", Galina said, "cheered us up a little bit. They would throw us bits of chocolate and some kind of wafers—very nice they were, with sweet little seeds inside them. We always thought the English, French and Russians were all very different people, but it turned out that we are all much the same. Only the Germans are different.

"And then, women and factory managers, and all sorts of people arrived one day at the camp. We were lined up in the snow—four rows of us—and these people kept walking up and down and inspecting us. So two hundred of us were picked by one of the factory managers, and we were taken by train to a barracks, with barred windows—the place was inside the factory grounds in a small town near Ulm. We were received there by a bunch of gendarmes, who said: '*Aha, Kommunisten*'. This place was much worse than the other camp. Before going to work we stayed in the barracks for three days, with only raw turnips and raw potatoes to eat, and one only nibbled at it, it was no use trying to eat a lot of the stuff... But at least there were bunks of sort to sleep on—hard and filthy, but still bunks...

"Later, they began to heat the stove, so we were at least able to cook what little food there was. On the fourth day we were taken to work. It used to be a hat factory; now they made helmet linings, or rather the sort of caps worn under the helmet. They made them of rabbit skins. We were given no gloves and our shoes also were falling to pieces. Our hands got into a terrible condition with handling those rabbit skins and treating them in some kind of acid." Galina Ivanovna showed her hands; they were small and well-shaped, but they looked scarred and the flesh round the nails seemed to have been eaten away. "Yes," she went on, "I lived in that factory barracks for eight months and twenty days; and to give you an idea of the condition in which we girls were, I'll say something which may seem indelicate—but I hope you'll understand. 180 girls were working there, and most of them didn't have what girls have every month;

the barracks were thirty yards away from the factory, and we never got outside the factory grounds, except on our 'day off'. We were under constant guard.

"We worked ten or twelve hours a day, and on our 'day off' we were always taken to the goods station to unload railway trucks. We were made to wear an 'Ost' badge—a blue badge with white lettering—but were never allowed to go into town. They actually charged us fifty pfennigs for the badge. For seven days' work we received one mark twenty pfennigs, and for fifty pfennigs we bought Sprudel—soda water—there was nothing else we could buy. I remembered now how Graf Spretti had told us that we'd wear silk stockings, and have 100 marks a week. At first when we arrived, we were promised new clothes and blankets; all we got was one blanket each, and once a fortnight they'd give us a tiny bit of soap with which to wash ourselves and wash our clothes. In our part of the barracks there were 180 girls, but in the other parts of the building there were 200 more women, all Ukrainians, or from Kursk, and 200 lads, from fifteen to twenty-three. What they gave us to eat was blue cabbage, turnips and sometimes some spinach, and 100 grammes per day of margarine to cook the stuff in—100 grammes for 100 people, that is, one gramme per day. Really nourishing, what! In other buildings there were Czechs and Poles and Greeks, and Belgians, and Frenchmen. We weren't allowed to speak to them—but we did all the same.

"The Poles and the French were better off than we were. They received twenty-five to thirty-five marks a week. The Poles had to wear a badge with a yellow 'P', the Belgians and the French were not expected to wear any badge. No difference was made between Ukrainians and Russians—both were treated the same. The Belgians and the Czechs, the Frenchmen and the Italians were all very decent to us, and gave us things. The Poles were more aloof. The Italians spoke longingly of macaroni.

"We used to meet the other girls in the lavatory, and there we'd talk—talk in bad German. One day one of the Italian girls said to me: 'You are even unluckier than we are. They say you are being treated like this because you are Communists. But, believe me, we are far more Communist than you are. Come on, let's sing the

International. And there, in the ladies' lavatory, the two of us softly sang the *International*, each to her own words.

"We once even threatened a hunger strike when the food had become altogether impossible, and we were developing scurvy so that our hands and arms swelled and our eyebrows started falling out, and the hair on our heads got all brittle. . .

"During air raids we were all driven into a big basement covered over with cement, and the door was locked from outside. The Germans went to their own shelter. When the air-raid warning started, the *chefs*, as they were called, came rushing in, brandishing whips, and drove us into the cellar. I lived through seven or eight big raids. One big bomb fell near the cathedral of Ulm, and wrecked the Rathaus, and demolished a small factory where they made some kind of metal tubing; 120 of our Ukrainians who were working there, were killed. . ."

"But what were the Germans like with whom you had to work?" I asked.

Galina Ivanovna merely screwed up her face. "There was one fat German in our factory. He once came into our barracks, and said: 'Ah, Ukrainian girls,' and said he liked Ukrainian songs, and would we sing to him. So we said: 'Alright, only we don't get much to eat, and will you give us something if we sing.' So he said yes. So we sang, in the dark miserable barracks, and as we sang the tears trickled down our faces. When we had finished, he said: 'That was very nice.' And he pulled out a five mark note and asked for three marks change." Galina laughed angrily. "As if he didn't know we had nothing. Still, he insisted, so we scraped together what pfennigs we had, and it came to two marks thirty. He seemed annoyed it wasn't more, but took the change and went away. "And then," she went on, "there was a foreman who worked in our workshop. He had a tiny bit of ground near our barracks, where he grew vegetables. He was a fat man with a shaved head and a concertina neck. What a fuss he made of his plot! He managed to grow a sunflower, and in case the sparrows picked at it, he put a pair of old pants over it; honest to God, he did. So I said to him one day: 'In our country we grow sunflowers by the mile, how many pairs of old pants do you think we'd need if we used your agricultural methods? There wouldn't be enough pants in the whole of Germany...' He looked kind of sheepish."

"Bah", said Galina, "these Germans—they're really unlike all other people. Now the French—they're quite different. We used to see them on Sundays at the goods station. We used to talk to them. And some of our girls went further than talking. The point is that if a Ukrainian girl gets pregnant, she is sent home. There was a dark shed behind one of the large piles of coal, and there some of our girls would go in the evening and make love with the French. God knows, they were so hungry and worn-out, they didn't really want to make love, but they hoped they might get pregnant. And the French were friendly—real comrades. There was one Frenchman I knew, who managed to escape from the factory. The night before he escaped, he said to me: 'There's a little corner near the stove in the workshop, and I'll leave you a note—try to pick it up tomorrow morning.' I went and looked for the note, and I found it, and with it were three bars of chocolate. The note said: 'This is all I've got. Good luck to you. I have run away. I hope they don't catch me.' They didn't catch him, though they sent the police all over the place. None of us said we knew anything. There was this strange solidarity among all of us non-Germans; a real fellow-feeling, a common hatred of the Fritz... And that feeling that we were not alone kept us going for a time, in spite of everything... But my health was becoming so bad that I felt that if I stayed on much longer, I should fall ill and die. And I did not want to die. There was an Austrian there called Hans, who worked in our workshop. He showed me a pamphlet about Thaelmann and said: 'Although Thaelmann is a German, he is a good man.' I said I doubted whether any German could be a good man. He gave me a queer look and for a moment I wondered if he wasn't a provocateur. Then I said: 'Oh God, what do I care, anyway? I want to go away, back home, and if I don't, I'll just *vergift* myself, poison myself...' Then Hans said: 'You won't betray me, will you? Here are six cigarettes'—and he slipped them into my hand—'Boil them, and let the infusion wait for an hour, and then drink it. It will give you a bad heart, and they may send you home. But don't give me away.' I did as he told me, but I was in such poor health that my stomach couldn't take it, and I was sick. I told him what had happened and he gave me six more cigarettes, telling me to try again. This time it was successful. It gave me terrible palpitations, and I was in a state of complete physical collapse. There were moments when I thought I'd die. I was taken to hospital. They x-rayed me three times, and decided my heart was so bad I would either soon die or be a cripple for life, so they gave me a certificate allowing me to go back to the Ukraine. But before that happened, I stayed in hospital for two months and five days. They patched up my hands, which were in a terrible state, and I had many visitors—there was a Greek girl who came to see me, and two Serbian girls; these were among the best. Altogether the Serbians and the Czechs were the best people of all; the French also were good, for instance Henri, who escaped and left me those three bars of chocolate; he was a real Communist. On the whole, all the foreigners in Germany were terribly decent people, and we had with them a common language as we never had with any Germans... Well, that's not perhaps quite true; there were two decent Germans I knew during all those months. One was a girl called Frieda. She knew much more about what was happening in the world than I did. I knew nothing—except from her. It was she who would tell me about the war in Russia—where the Red Army was. She got very excited at the time the Germans were stopped at Stalingrad. My feeling was that she was a double agent. She pretended to work for the Nazis, but she was also an agent of the Popular Front. She often talked to me, and warned me, and told me to warn the other girls that any Ukrainian girl who was intimate with a Frenchman or any other foreigner was liable to be shot. Frieda was a damn good girl. There was also another girl called Amalia—I didn't know her so well. But I later learned that both Frieda and Amalia had been shot by the Gestapo. But, in general the Germans are a wicked and crazy people."

Finally Galina returned to Uman, after another harrowing two months' journey. She was a physical wreck by then, and spent three months in bed at the house of some people who had befriended her. After that she took a job as a *putzfrau*—a cleaner—at a hotel occupied by German officers. But her troubles were not yet over.

She was now faced with a complicated family situation—strangely reminiscent of the turbulent years of the civil war in the Ukraine, when so many families were divided against themselves. Her brother Kiril had been a machine-gunner in the Red Army; he was taken prisoner by the Germans but escaped, and later turned up as a civilian in his native village where he set up shop again as a watchmaker. He had a wife who, before the war, was an active member of the Komsomol. "Three months ago she was arrested and taken away, and rumour had it she was shot", Galina said. "The strange thing was that the *starosta* had denounced her to the Germans, and when they came, they knew exactly where to find her; for she had been hiding in a cellar for the last month. And from what I have heard from my brother Kiril and also from my mother, there's little doubt that the *starosta* had learned from my other brother, Fedor, where Kiril's wife was in hiding. For Fedor, though my brother, is a thoroughly bad lot. He was a member of the Ukrainian *polizai*, and he must have told the *starosta*. This bad brother is probably still in hiding in our village; and, if it hasn't been done already, I shall denounce him myself to the Red Commandant. . ."

(6) *The Wail of the German stomach*

The German prisoners I saw near Uman were a very mixed bunch. All of them were bitterly disappointed at having been caught, when most of the Germans had got away beyond the Bug. The Austrians were already claiming to be "quite different from the Germans", though one I saw had obviously been brought up in the best Nazi tradition. Then there was one German optimist, a deserter, who had a Ukrainian girl friend who had hidden him during the German withdrawal from Uman. He was now hopefully wondering whether the Russians wouldn't allow him to settle here in the Ukraine, which he thought a lovely country, and he was also most devoted to his *Freundin*. Such things do happen even in the best of regiments. But depressed and bewildered though they were by their defeats in the Ukraine, and, of course, personally upset at being taken prisoner by the Russians, with only the remotest prospect of seeing Germany again soon, there was still much fighting spirit left in many of the

German soldiers I saw. They were hoping for something—they did not quite know what. Those from the Rhineland were more precise than the others. The allied bombing had made them angry, rather than downhearted. I remember a sergeant, Willi Jerschagen, from Remscheid on the Rhine. The town had been bombed to blazes, and yet his wife and parents were still living there among the ruins. His wife had a job in a steel mill, and had no intention of going away to any other part of Germany. "It'll be the same everywhere, so I might as well stay here," she had written recently.

And the great hope of this woman, and of Willi himself, and of other people of Western Germany was—*Vergeltung*. The Führer had promised this revenge on England; but they were growing impatient, and the people in Western Germany were now saying: "What about these weapons?" The V-1's over London were, indeed, not to start until a little later.

As the Germans were being pushed out of the Ukraine the songs the Wehrmacht sang began to have a mournful note. These ditties were very similar, though every regiment seemed to have its own variant. They went like this:—

> Nema kurka, nema yaika,
> Dosvidania khozyaika; or
>
> Nema pivo, nema vino,
> Dosvidania Ukraina; or
>
> Nema kurka, nema brot,
> Dosvidania Belgorod; or
>
> Nema kurka, nema soup,
> Dosvidania Kremenchug,

which, in this mixture of German, pidgin Russian and pidgin Ukrainian, means—"No more chicken, no more eggs, good-bye, land-lady; No more beer and no more wine, good-bye, Ukraine; No more chicken, no more bread, good-bye, Belgorod; No more chicken, no more soup, good-bye Kremcnchug". And many more on the same lines. And, more generally, the bitter disappointment and disillusionment was expressed in these lines, known to every German soldier:

"Es ist alles vorueber, es ist alles vorbei,
Drei Jahre in Russland und nix ponimai",—

"It is all over, it is all gone; three years in Russia, and can't understand anything".

Chapter III

CLOSE-UP II: ODESSA, CAPITAL OF RUMANIAN TRANSNIESTRIA

April and May 1944 saw the final expulsion of the Germans from the southern parts of the Ukraine. The troops of Konev's 2nd Ukrainian Front swept all the way into northern Rumania, and it was not till they had reached a line some twelve miles east of Jassy that the front became temporarily stabilised. On April 2 Molotov, announcing the invasion of Rumania, hastened to declare that the Soviet Union did not aim at altering the "social order" (i.e. capitalism) in that country. The troops of Malinovsky's 3rd Ukrainian Front had meantime advanced along the Black Sea coast, liberating Kherson, Nikolaev and Odessa, and, on April 11, the beginning of the Russian invasion of the Crimea, Hitler's last stronghold on the Black Sea, was announced. Within a month, the Crimea was cleared.

The great peculiarity of Odessa, "the Russian Marseilles" was that, except for the last few weeks when the Germans took over, it had not been under German rule. As a reward for Rumania's participation in the war against the Soviet Union, Hitler had given her a large and rich territory in the southern Ukraine stretching all the way from Bessarabia to the Bug; this included the great Black Sea port of Odessa, and the whole area was incorporated into "greater Rumania" as a new province under the name of Transniestria (i.e. the land beyond the Dniester).

Malinovsky liberated Odessa on April 10, and the Germans, fearing encirclement, had left in a frantic hurry, some by sea, under almost constant Russian bombing and shell-fire, others by the last remaining road between Odessa and the Dniester estuary, where a ferry took them across to the parts of Bessarabia and Rumania which the Russians had not yet occupied. By the time Odessa fell, this road was littered with hundreds of wrecked and abandoned German vehicles. Though in a desperate hurry to get out of Odessa, the Germans had had time to turn the harbour, most of the factories and many other large buildings, into smouldering heaps of wreckage.

I drove to Odessa on a beautiful spring day in mid-April from a point just north of Nikolaev, on the east side of the Bug. The Bug had been the frontier between German-occupied and Rumanian-annexed Ukraine, and civilians were not allowed to travel between the two except by very special permission. But since February 1944 the Germans no longer took any notice of the fiction of "Transniestria" being part of Rumania.

They had tried to drive away the cattle; but as they could not get the cows across the Bug, they shot them, and the green banks of the river were littered with dozens of brown carcasses of dead cows which were beginning to stink.

It was typical steppe country between the Bug and Odessa, and sometimes there was no village in sight for miles as one drove between the immense green carpets of winter wheat which had been duly sown in the autumn, and which the Russians were now going to harvest.

Here and there, there were fallow patches, but not many. But one of the strangest sights on this road were some completely deserted villages; they did not look like Russian or Ukrainian villages. Their houses were painted in bright colours, and they had spired churches —Lutheran churches, or maybe Catholic churches, for by the roadside there were also one or two Catholic shrines. These were German villages—villages of German colonists who had lived here for 150 years, and had latterly acted as quislings everywhere, filling administrative and police jobs placed at their disposal by the Germans on the eastern side of the Bug. Those who had stayed in this "Greater

Rumania", had acted as an arrogant German minority, and had no doubt already been preparing unpleasant surprises for the Rumanian "majority". But the rapid advance of the Red Army had obliged them to abandon their homes. Later, in Odessa, I was to see a paper called *Der Deutsche in Transniestrien*, in which the province was in fact treated as part of the German heritage, and the Rumanians were not mentioned once! Nevertheless, until only a few weeks before, Hitler still felt obliged to keep up the myth of Greater Rumania, and the pretence that Transniestria was a Rumanian province and Odessa a Rumanian city.

We approached Odessa at dusk, and as we drove towards the Black Sea, the country became hillier, and here and there were signs of fighting. All along the road we had passed many dead horses, and here, on these wind-swept hills above the Black Sea there were many more, and some bomb craters, and, here and there, some dead men. At one point we passed an enormous war memorial the Rumanians had erected to commemorate their Odessa victory of 1941. It was here, through these hills, that the Russian ring of defences round Odessa then ran.

And then we came to Odessa, and in the streets there was a sharp smell of burning.

Odessa was completely dark. All the power stations had been blown up by the Germans who had full control of the city in the last fortnight and, worse still, there was no water—except for very limited quantities drawn from Artesian wells inside the city. The normal supply of water came from the Dniester, thirty or forty miles away, and the mains had been blown up. Now, as during the two months' siege in the grim autumn of 1941, Odessa was relying on its own wells. At the Hotel Bristol, where we stayed, the washing ration was one bottle per day.

This Bristol Hotel, a great big absurd-looking building with ornate caryatids going three storeys up, was in Pushkin Street, and all its windows were broken. It had two hall porters, an old man with a black beard, a former Odessa docker or *bendyuzhnik*, with a gruff voice and loud ugly laugh, and his assistant, a little old man with a grey *barbiche* and a leer. The two of them would stand on the pavement outside, and, watching the Odessa girls in their light dresses walk past in groups of four or five, they would make lewd remarks, and the little man with the grey *barbiche* and the leer would then tell remarkable anecdotes, for instance about two girls who were living in the same house as himself, and of how the one specialised in Rumanian, and the other in German officers, and how they would compare notes.

No inhibitions here. This was Odessa with its perpetual whiff of the underworld, which recalled the glories of Isaac Babel's Benya Krik, the king of the Odessa gangsters, and which even a hundred years of Soviet rule may never quite eradicate.

It wasn't quite the Odessa one had known in the past. For one thing, it was an Odessa without Jews, and they had been an essential part of the Black Sea port—they and the Armenians and Greeks and other Mediterranean or quasi-Mediterranean fauna.

But there was still the Odessite who, whether he was Ukrainian, or Russian, or Moldavian, was Odessite first and foremost, speaking a jargon of his own, with his own idiom and his own accent. Obviously, many of them took like a duck to water to the seemingly easy-going life of Antonescu's Odessa, with its restaurants and black market, its brothels and gambling dens, lotto clubs and cabarets, and its semblance of European culture, complete with opera, ballet and symphony concerts.

There were the Siguranza, the Rumanian secret police, and the Bolshevik underground—literally underground in the Odessa catacombs—and the Jews, many thousands of whom had been murdered by the Rumanians; but the occupation (or rather, annexation) régime was different in many other ways from the German occupation régime I had seen in cities like Voronezh, Orel or Kharkov.

While the Axis's prospects of winning the war seemed good, the Rumanians were planning to turn Odessa into a sort of brighter and better Bucharest. Not only were there the restaurants, and shops and gambling dens, and the solemn appearance of Antonescu in the former Imperial Box at the Opera, but there was a serious attempt to convince the people that they were, and were going to remain, part of Greater Rumania. Unlike the Germans in occupied cities, the Rumanians did not close down either the University or the schools; school-children had to learn Rumanian, and university students were warned that if they did not learn Rumanian within a year, they would be expelled—though after Stalingrad the Rumanians were no longer insistent on this point. They continued to distribute a Rumanian geography book, translated into Russian, which demonstrated that practically the whole of southern Russia was, "geopolitically", part of Rumania and was largely inhabited by descendents of the ancient Dacians. Those who could prove any Moldavian blood were promised various privileges: to have a Jewish grandmother was dangerous, but to have a Moldavian grandparent was like a title of nobility.

There was one aspect of Odessa which was not to be found in any of the German-occupied cities. *Odessa was full of young people.* It was a happy fluke: the Rumanians had regarded "Transniestria" as part of their country, and its inhabitants as future Rumanian citizens. No doubt, after Stalingrad, they were no longer so sure about keeping Odessa, but the fiction still had to be kept up. Therefore, the great majority of young people in Odessa were not deported to Germany, or anywhere else. Nor had they been called up into the Rumanian Army, since they were totally unreliable from the Rumanian point of view. Only during the last few weeks, when the Germans had taken over, were some unlucky Odessites deported to Germany; but most had dodged deportation, thanks, partly, to the Soviet underground.

During those first days of the liberation, there were still plenty of signs of the Rumanian occupation régime that had lasted for two-and-a-half years.

All down Pushkin Street (spelled *Pušchin* on the white-and-blue Rumanian street plates that were now being taken down) and the other famous acacia-lined Odessa streets, named after the city's 18th century French founders (Richelieu, De Ribas, Langeron) there were still advertisements of lotto clubs and cabarets, and shop-signs with *Bodega* written on them (the *Bodegas* were now closed) and remnants of a proclamation printed in Rumanian, German and Russian (but *not* Ukrainian): "We Ion Antonescu, Marshal of Rumania, Professor L. Alexeanu, Civil Governor of Transniestria", etc., etc. A large building had a notice up: "*Guvernamantul Trans-nistriei*", and the bus signs—not that there were any buses now—said that the first bus from the *Aeroport* to *La Gara* (Station) left at 7.15 a.m. The musical programmes referred to the "*Teatrul de Opera & Balet, Odesa*"—which, incidentally, showed that it was not true that the city had been re-named Antonescu, and had merely lost one *s*. There had been many other entertainments in Odessa, even the Symphony Orchestra of the Luftwaffe had given a concert—though this was on March 27, during the German régime—and they played Schubert's Unfinished, and Beethoven's Violin Concerto, and Tschaikovsky's Fifth. There were also several dressmakers' *ateliers*, and many other small shops, whose proprietors had now vanished. Free Trade—of sorts—seemed to have been in full swing in Odessa while the Rumanians were there. The Rumanians were speculators, and half the people of Odessa, and more perhaps, were speculators, too. Was not speculation and trade in the Odessite's blood? Rumanian generals used to bring whole trunkloads of ladies' under-wear and stockings from Bucharest, and get their orderlies to sell them in the market. Even now there were quite a few things to buy in the market—German pencils, Hungarian cigarettes, German cigarettes (called "Krim", and made in the Crimea), and even bottles of scent—and some stockings, though these were becoming scarce now, and could only be bought under the counter. Now the militia was keeping an eye on all this trading, and the Odessites in the market looked somewhat subdued. The noisiest person was a blind man, accompanied by an old woman who rattled her money-box in people's faces; and the blind man was singing in a whining penetrating voice:

> Znayut vse moyu kvartiru,
> Tam zhivu sredi mogil,
> Rvalis tam snaryady zlyie,
> Zhizn svoyu tam polozhil.

> ("Everybody knows my dwelling;
> There I live among the graves,
> Where the wicked shells were bursting,
> There I lost my youthful life.")

They were selling jam at twenty roubles a pot and bread at ten roubles a kilo (which was very cheap); there was plenty of milk, and they were also selling German bottles of apple-juice. The silk stocking under the counter were now fetching 300 roubles.* And the saleswomen were still talking of marks when they meant roubles. The wrapping paper used was German newspapers.

Later, all these "New Order" luxuries were to disappear, and prices went up.

Although the port with its docks and grain elevators was a heap of smouldering ruins, the famous marine promenade overlooking the port and the sea was crowded as usual with young people. Many of them were sitting on benches or on the steps of the Great Staircase (of Eisenstein's *Potemkin* fame). I remember, in particular, two youngsters—one fair, the other with the beginnings of a black moustache, who were commenting, in their Odessa jargon, on the terrible destruction the Germans had caused to the port and other parts of the city—particularly to the factories at Moldovanka and Peresyp. They also recalled how, during the last fortnight of the German occupation, they and their friends had hidden in cellars and in the catacombs—for it was no good going out into the street, not even before the 3 p.m. curfew, because the Germans might nab you, and deport you to Germany, or simply kill you. They used elaborately abusive language about the Germans, and said the Rumanians were exceedingly fed-up when the Germans took everything over in February. "I wonder," black moustache said, "what the Reds are going to do about sea bathing." (In Odessa, too, many talked about "The Reds"). During the previous summer, he said, the Rumanians had allowed only one beach to be used, and on hot days as many as 20,000 people would queue up. Now that the damned Germans had mined all the beaches, there mightn't be any bathing at all this year. On the whole, they were pleased that the "Reds" had come, because it was really *terrifying* under the Germans. The Rumanians at least left "most people" in peace, though others, especially the Jews, had had great trouble with the Siguranza. But, on the whole, the

---

* Nominally £6, but the value of Russian currency (except for rationed goods) had depreciated so much during the war that the figure is meaningless.

Rumanians didn't interfere too much with people. *Mozhno bylo zhit*—"one could live", and there was plenty of food in the market, and the Rumanian soldiers always had a variety of things to sell. "What happened to the Jews?" I asked. "Oh," said the fair-haired boy, "they say they bumped off an awful lot, but I didn't see it. Some were allowed to escape—with a little money you could buy *anything* from the Rumanians, even a passport in the name of Richelieu. We had a family of Jews living in our cellar; and we took them food once a week. The Rumanian cops knew about them, but didn't bother. They said that if so many Jews were bumped off, it was because the Germans had demanded it. 'No dead Jews, no Odessa', they said. Anyway, that's what the Rumanians told us."

Professor Alexeanu, the civil governor of the Transniestria, had taken up his residence in the beautiful Vorontzov Palace on the Marine Promenade; in Soviet times it had been turned into the Pioneers' Palace. Now it was going to be turned into the Pioneers' Palace once again. Alexeanu, people in Odessa said, had been rather easy-going, except that he gave the Siguranza an entirely free hand. When he was removed in February 1944, it was because of the terrible amount of embezzlement of which he was said to be guilty. He did not spend his money on civic welfare, but rather, on a nice pair of legs. True, he pretended to be interested in the welfare of schools and the university, and it wasn't until the Germans came in February 1944 that the university laboratories and everything else were looted. Alexeanu, as somebody said, "was tall, long-faced, with brown hair, the kind of man women like". His *chef de cabinet* was one Cherkavsky, a White Russian, but the bulk of Alexeanu's staff came from Bucharest.

Alexeanu was succeeded as civil governor by General Potopianu, who had besieged Odessa back in 1941. He was a bit less easy-going than Alexeanu, but anyway he hadn't much say any longer. For from February the Germans were, unofficially, in control of everything and, from April 1, officially.

Towards the end of the occupation, the Germans scrapped the very name of Transniestria, and took over the railways and every-

thing else (much to Antonescu's indignation). They were greatly
worried about two things—that some of the Rumanian generals in
Odessa, or elsewhere, might "do a Badoglio" on them; and about
the spread of communism and defeatism among the Rumanian
soldiers.

Before the Germans had taken over, Transniestria had thirteen
districts, each under its own prefect; in Odessa itself there was a
mayor, Herman Pintia, formerly mayor of Kishenev. The police was
Rumanian, on the lines of the Soviet militia; but there was, moreover, the Siguranza.

Pintia was deposed by the Germans who appointed in his place a
Russian quisling called Petushkov. He was the last mayor of Odessa.
He arrived on March 24 and left again on April 9. He had been
Mayor of Stalino under the Germans; he was an engineer, a fat
podgy little man of forty-six; a German major did all his work.

Under the Rumanians, thirty churches were open in Odessa,
among them a few Lutheran and Roman Catholic churches. The
Orthodox clergy at Odessa were ordered by the Rumanians to sever
all connection with the Moscow Patriarchy, and to accept the
authority of the Metropolitan Nikodim of Odessa, a man who saw
eye to eye with the new masters. The Rumanians sent a church
mission of twelve priests to Odessa, headed by one Scriban, a
theology professor from Bucharest. These priests took over some of
the best houses in Odessa, including those of the Metropolitan and
other Bishops; they also took over all the best parishes. Father Vasili,
the Priest of the Uspensky Cathedral, told me that, as a result, the
Russian priests were put "in a highly unfavourable position, and
many were reduced to finding themselves new parishes in the
countryside." Father Vasili declared that the Rumanian priests in
Odessa went in for highly riotous living, and the worst offender of
all was Scriban himself. Scriban had made a racket of his job: he
would authorise Russian priests to take this or that parish, and the
better the parish, the higher his rake-off.

Finally, he was sent back to Bucharest, because his behaviour was
becoming too scandalously notorious, and instead there came the
Metropolitan Vissarion of Bessarabia and Czernowitz. He made a
solemn and triumphal entry into Odessa, with Rumanian cavalry

escorting his carriage, but soon afterwards great rows started between him, representing the Church, and Governor Alexeanu, representing the temporal power. The final result was that the Metropolitan Vissarion, who had entered Odessa like a Tsar, left for the railway station in a droshki, with one suitcase.

There was little or no *Herrenvolk* stuff about the Rumanians, and for that matter, not much love lost between Rumanians and the Germans, except perhaps at the very top level. Conquerors and conquered found common ground in business and in the black market. But neither Ukrainians, Russians nor Rumanians could, after all, take Transniestria very seriously. For one year (up to Stalingrad) it seemed possible that the Rumanians had come to stay: but not after that. Many "free-enterprise" enthusiasts among the Odessites must then have gone much more cautiously about their co-operation with the new masters. These were, moreover, becoming visibly dejected since the rout of the Rumanian troops on the Don, and were increasingly frightened of the Germans throwing them out of Transniestria altogether. It was known that even Antonescu was now resenting Hitler's growing demands for more and more Rumanian cannon fodder.

What had the Siguranza done in Odessa? The Russians said that they were as bad as the Gestapo: that they had not only shot 40,000 Jews* in a place called Strelbishche Field, but had also, especially during the early part of the occupation, shot about 10,000 others, many of them communists or suspected communists, or hostages taken after the shooting of Rumanian officers in the streets, cases of bomb-throwing, etc. The only redeeming feature of the Siguranza, according to the Russians, was that they were extremely corrupt, and many Jews who could afford it could buy "Aryan"

---

* There were over 150,000 Jews in Odessa in 1941, but about two-thirds had been evacuated by sea with most of the army and many of the other civilians. When, in June 1944, I went to Botoşani, in the part of Rumania occupied by the Russians, I found there a large Jewish population which had *not* been exterminated by the Rumanians, despite German demands. There was some disagreement in the Rumanian Government on this issue (see Reitlinger. *The Final Solution*. London 1953, p. 404.)

papers, or, at any rate, be allowed to escape to the countryside. There is evidence to show that the Rumanians, while themselves ready to kill Jews, resisted German "interference" in Odessa.

There is some doubt, too, about the real importance of the Soviet "underground" operating from the inextricable labyrinth of the Odessa catacombs, with their dozens of miles of subterranean passages, some of them as much as 100 feet underground. Many romantic stories (notably by V. Katayev) were written towards the end of the war about the "only urban partisans in the world", and about some of their communist chiefs, such as S. F. Lazarev, I. G. Ilyukhin and L. F. Borgel,* who functioned throughout the Rumanian occupation and spread perpetual terror among the invaders. It seems that, in reality, the Soviet underground in Odessa used the catacombs (which had many secret entrances *inside* houses) only in cases of great emergency and that, although some food and arms dumps were hidden there, very few people (if any) actually *lived* in the catacombs for any length of time. Some Jews were said to have lived there right through the occupation, but the extreme damp of the catacombs makes this highly doubtful.

What is certain, however, is that *after the end of 1943* (but not before), and particularly during the last (German) month of the occupation the catacombs became much more important. Thanks to the Soviet underground organisations, they became a refuge for young people in danger of deportation, and for a number of Alsatian, Polish, and especially Slovak deserters from the German Army. Some of the partisan chiefs I saw in Odessa soon after the liberation (and pretty thuggish *bendyuzhnik* types they were), claimed that there was a well-armed army of 10,000 men in the catacombs (who bought most of their arms in the black market from Rumanian or German soldiers) complete with a "catacomb hospital" with "twelve surgeons and 200 nurses", and not only a "catacomb bakery" but even a "catacomb sausage factory"; but this is not certain by any means, and must be taken with serious reservations. Except during the last weeks of the occupation, when Odessa was under the Germans, the usual incentives (such as the danger of deportation) for a big partisan movement were simply not

* V. Katayev, *Katakomby* (The Catacombs), (Moscow, 1945).

there; and even later a great number of people who went into the
catacombs were passive rather than active partisans. All I saw in
the catacombs were several machine-gun nests covering the essential passages; emergency food stores, artesian wells and arms dumps.
A few thousand people may well have stayed in the catacombs
during the last few critical weeks; but the claims made to me by the
partisan chiefs that the Odessa underground had killed "hundreds
of Germans", that it had prevented them from destroying the whole
of Odessa (it had not stopped them from destroying the harbour and
practically all the factories) had a certain *histoire marseillaise*
quality. It is perhaps significant that serious Soviet post-war studies
of the war say very little of the "catacomb partisans", and certainly
do not describe them as a major underground army which (as the
partisan chiefs claimed on April 14, 1944) "could have occupied
Odessa and thrown out the Germans if the Red Army had not
arrived in time". Such boasts were wholly unsubstantiated.

I saw many war prisoners that week at Odessa, among them, the
Slovaks and the Alsatians who had joined the partisans. They were
in fine fighting spirit, especially the Slovaks, and also some Poles,
and they were typical of the Occupied Europe during those days—
typical of its rapidly rising hopes. The Rumanian war prisoners were
all down-at-heel, both physically and morally, and one of them, when
asked what he had done during the war, jovially declared that he had
been a deserter for three years. Another was a cheery Bucharest
taxi-driver, who said he hoped King Carol and Madame Lupescu—
a very good woman, he said—would come back, because in their
days life was gay and there was a lot of business for taxi-drivers.
And the question they were all asking—hopefully—was "Has
Bucharest been taken yet?"
      The Germans, however, sulked, and few would commit themselves
to saying Hitler had lost the war. They seemed, in fact, rather proud
to think that nearly all the Germans had managed to get out of
Odessa before it was too late.
      The centre of Odessa had in the main survived, though most of the
factories in the suburbs had been destroyed. But life—a new Soviet

life—was already beginning to take shape here and there. At the Vorontzov Palace—now again the Pioneers' Palace—whose glass dome had been shattered by a Russian shell that was aimed at the port—children were invited to register again.

The matron of the Pioneers' Palace was indignant. "Such barbarism," she said. Alexeanu had lived here in grand style with his mistress, and, not unnaturally, he had "restored" the Palace, according to his own taste, and had given the Empire drawing room with the chandeliers new cream-coloured walls. "And the cream-coloured paint," she said, "is smeared over the mural of the pre-revolutionary squalor in which the children of Russia had then lived; and, similarly, on the opposite wall Alexeanu has destroyed forever the beautiful mural painting of Comrade Stalin clapping his hands as the happy Soviet children dance round him."

I was to see Odessa again, nearly a year later, in March 1945. By then it had become the port of embarkation for thousands of British, American, French and other prisoners of war, who had been liberated by the Red Army in Poland, Silesia, Pomerania and East Prussia. They were living in barracks, school buildings, and in villas near the Arcadia Beach. Sailors, British and American mostly, were dancing and drinking hard among the dusty palm trees of the lounge of the Hotel de Londres, now de-mined (it was roped off during my first visit). Food was scarce—even at the Hotel de Londres—and Odessa had a hungry look, much leaner than in 1944. There were still no buses or trams, and the market looked poverty stricken. Banditry was rife. Shady characters were slinking about the streets at dark, and robberies and murders were a nightly occurrence. Were *they* using the catacombs now—to dodge the Russian police? The port, it is true, was working, and pale, yellow-skinned German prisoners were clearing away the rubble. Much of the wreckage had indeed been cleared, though only a small part of the port was usable, with one American and one British transport moored to the quay, and the breakwater was still smashed in two places. Hundreds of British or French or American P.o.Ws. would march joyfully through the wrecked dockland of Odessa to the ship that was awaiting them;

they would jeer at the Germans, and the Germans would make philosophical remarks to each other about the changing fortunes of war, or merely glare disconsolately.

I wondered then why Odessa was scarcely being restored at all, and why food and living conditions generally were harder than they were in so many other liberated cities. Was not Odessa, I wondered, being indirectly punished for that relatively easy time it had had in the Transniestria days, and for the eagerness with which so many of its citizens had entered into the spirit of night-clubs, bodegas and black-marketing? Not out of real disloyalty, but rather out of an innate and frivolous liking for petty business.

For several years after the war there was a feeling that Odessa was in poor odour in Moscow and was low on the list of priorities for reconstruction.

Chapter IV

CLOSE-UP III:
HITLER'S CRIMEAN CATASTROPHE

Post-war German historians hold Hitler exclusively responsible for the "senseless disaster" that the German Army suffered in the Crimea in April–May 1944, complete with their abortive "Dunkirk" at Sebastopol, perhaps the most spectacular defeat of all inflicted on the Germans since Stalingrad.

Hitler's determination to cling on to the Crimea, even though the whole Ukrainian mainland to the north of it was now in Russian hands, had been dictated by his usual political and economic considerations, besides the sentimental rubbish about the Crimea having been "the last stronghold of the Goths" and still being potentially a wonderful playground for *Kraft durch Freude*. It was even said that Hitler intended to retire to the Tsar's palace of Livadia in his old age.

With Turkey beginning to lean heavily the other way since Teheran, it was essential to impress upon her that Germany was still powerful on the Black Sea; secondly, obsessed by economic considerations, Hitler was determined not to allow the Russians to use the Crimea as a springboard for massive air attacks on the Rumanian oil fields—Germany's most important source of oil. Ironically, it was exactly two days before the Russians undertook their attack on the Crimea that the Americans, operating from southern Italy, dropped their first big bombs on Ploesti—which Hitler thought he could make invulnerable against air attacks by hanging on to the

827

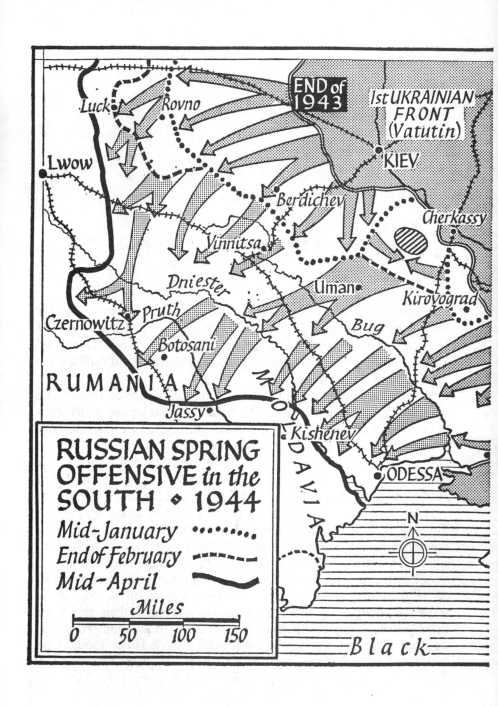

Luck
Rovno
Lwow
Czernowitz
Pruth
Dniester
Botosani
RUMANIA
Jassy
Berdichev
Vinnitsa
Uman
Bug
Kisheney
Kirovograd
Cherkassy
KIEV
1st UKRAINIAN FRONT (Vatutin)
END of 1943
ODESSA
MOLDAVIA
Black

RUSSIAN SPRING
OFFENSIVE in the
SOUTH ◆ 1944
Mid-January ....
End of February ----
Mid-April ~~~~

Miles
0   50   100   150

N

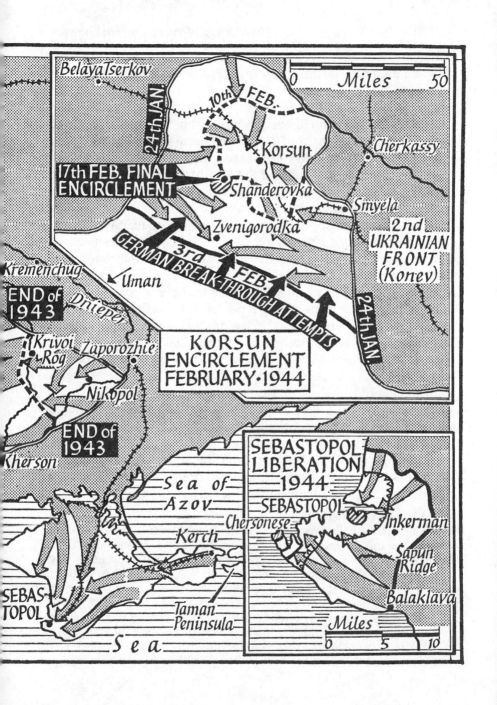

Belàya Tserkov

24th JAN.

10th FEB.

0 ——— Miles ——— 50

Korsun

Cherkassy

17th FEB. FINAL
ENCIRCLEMENT

Shanderovka

Smyela

2nd
UKRAINIAN
FRONT
(Konev)

Zvenigorodka

Kremenchug

Uman

GERMAN BREAK-THROUGH ATTEMPTS

3rd
FEB.

24th JAN.

END of
1943

Dniepei

Krivoi
Rog

Zaporozhie

KORSUN
ENCIRCLEMENT
FEBRUARY · 1944

Nikopol

END of
1943

Kherson

Sea of
Azov

SEBASTOPOL
LIBERATION
1944

SEBASTOPOL

Chersonese

Inkerman

Kerch

Sapun
Ridge

Balaklava

SEBAS-
TOPOL

Taman
Peninsula

Miles

0   5   10

Sea

Crimea!* Anyway, by May 1944, the Russians were already at Odessa, not much farther away from Ploesti than Sebastopol.

The Russians recaptured the Crimea within a month. The attack began in the north on April 11. In the course of the previous winter the troops of Tolbukhin's 4th Ukrainian Front had established a bridgehead on the south side of the Sivash, the narrow inlet between the Crimea and the mainland. It had been one of the boldest operations of its kind. After a heavy barrage against the relatively slender Rumanian positions on the south side of the Sivash, a considerable number of Russian troops got across by various means and established a bridgehead on the south side. After that hundreds of soldiers spent hours waist-deep or shoulder-deep in the icy and very salt water of the Sivash—the salt eating into every pore and causing almost unbearable pain—laying a pontoon across the inlet. Although the Russians suffered heavy losses in this double operation, the bridgehead was firmly established and fortified.†

And so, on April 11, after a heavy artillery barrage, thousands of Russian troops and hundreds of tanks poured from the bridgehead into the interior of the Crimea.

Simultaneously other Russian forces attacked the German defences on the Perekop Isthmus, but this was more in the nature of a diversion and, with the troops from the Sivash bridgehead threatening to cut off Perekop from the south, the Germans and Rumanians hastily abandoned the elaborate twenty-mile-deep defences they had been built on the Isthmus.‡

* Philippi and Heim, op. cit., p. 243.

† Curiously, at the time there was no announcement in the Russian press of this bridgehead, and later in newspaper articles and films (like *The Third Blow*) the establishment of the bridgehead was represented as the first part of Tolbukhin's April offensive. Perhaps it was feared that the bridgehead might yet be lost, so it was better to say nothing meantime.

‡ It had been the well-guarded "gate" of the Crimean Tartars up to the 18th century, and the main fortified position of Wrangel's "Whites" in 1920. In 1941 the Isthmus was poorly fortified and manned and the Germans broke through with relative ease.

Within two days Tolbukhin's troops overran the whole northern part of the Crimea, and captured Simferopol, its capital. Meantime Yeremenko's special Black Sea Army, advancing from east-Crimean bridgeheads (also established during the winter) struck out west along the southern coast of the Crimea, capturing Kerch, Feodosia, Gurzuf, Yalta and Alupka, and continuing to pursue the Germans retreating to Sebastopol.

Hitler's decision to hold the Crimea was one of his most insane inspirations. According to present-day Russian sources, the Russians succeeded in achieving overwhelming supcriority there. Whereas there were 195,000 German and Rumanian troops in the Crimea, the Russians had 470,000 and a similar superiority in tanks, guns and aircraft.* The Russians also had great naval superiority on the Black Sea.

About half of the German 17th Army holding the Crimea consisted of Rumanians; and Antonescu had argued months before with Hitler in favour of evacuating these Rumanian troops; the attempt to hold the peninsula struck him as totally unrealistic. But Hitler would not hear of it. Many of the Rumanian troops, realising no doubt that Sebastopol—to which all the German troops were now rapidly converging—would be a death-trap, and that they would, in any case, be the last to be evacuated, hastened to surrender to the Russians in the northern Crimea, at Simferopol, and along the coast.

By April 18, the bulk of the German forces had rapidly retreated to Sebastopol which Hitler now declared to be "Festung Sewastopol". This would have to be held indefinitely by some 50,000 men; the others could be evacuated; the Russians had held Sebastopol for 250 days in 1941–2, and had created a "Scbastopol Legend"; the Germans must now do at least as well.† On April 18 the front ran in a semi-circle east of Sebastopol, and was twenty-five miles in length.

In their hurried retreat to Sebastopol, the German troops nevertheless caused considerable destruction. They destroyed the whole sea-front at Yalta, but had no time to destroy the rest of the town

* IVOVSS, vol. 4, p. 89.

† According to German sources Hitler thought it essential to hold Sebastopol at least until he had repelled the expected Normandy landing six or eight weeks later.

(including the Chekhov Museum, where the writer had lived) or the former palaces at Alupka, one of which had been presented to Manstein "the conqueror of the Crimea" by "the grateful German nation" back in 1942. It was in these palaces that the Yalta Conference was to meet less than a year later.

It was later argued on the Russian side that if only the Red Army had begun to storm Sebastopol immediately after April 18, and had not waited till May 5, very few of the German troops could have got away at all; but the storming of Sebastopol required a high concentration of troops, guns and tanks, a thorough organisation of airfields, etc., and this needed some time. According to Tolbukhin, no successful all-out attack was possible without about a fortnight's preparation.

It will remain one of the puzzles of the war why, in 1941–2, despite overwhelming German and Rumanian superiority in tanks and aircraft, and a substantial superiority in men, Sebastopol succeeded in holding out for 250 days and why, in 1944, the Russians captured it within four days. German authors now explain it simply by the great Russian superiority in effectives, aircraft and all other equipment. But did not the Germans and Rumanians enjoy much the same kind of superiority in 1941–2? Was there not something lacking in German morale by April 1944—at least in a remote place like the Crimea? For, as we know, the Germans could still put up suicidal resistance once on German soil.

A moot question is how many Germans were actually evacuated from the Crimea between April 18 and May 13. According to a Russian general I saw at Sebastopol at the time, only 30,000 got away; according to German war prisoners taken, at least twice as many. Post-war German accounts say that 150,000 got away, but that "at least 60,000 Germans" were "lost" in the Crimea; as well as enormous masses of equipment, while sixty ships were sunk. The

Russians put the enemy losses in the Crimea much higher—50,000 (nearly all Germans) killed and 61,000 taken prisoner (30,000 of them at Chersonese)—a total loss of 111,000; but these (especially the prisoners) obviously included a great number of Rumanians. German authors today are surprised that the Russian Black Sea fleet allowed so many ships to get away; the Russian answer to this is that the sea between Sebastopol and Rumania was heavily mined, but that many German ships, with 40,000 men on board, were sunk all the same, mostly by aircraft between May 3 and 13.

Anyway, whether the Germans lost (as they now admit) at least 60,000 men or (as the Russians claim) nearer 100,000 men, the whole Crimean operation, and Hitler's futile attempt to stage a German version of the "Heroic Defence of Sebastopol" is now admitted to have been one of the Führer's prime blunders. German histories today say that the German commander of the 17th Army, Colonel-General Jaenicke, was made a scapegoat by the Führer. In fact he informed Hitler that he could not hold Sebastopol and was relieved of his command on May 3, and was replaced by General Allmedinger. Whether, at heart, the latter had any more hope than Jaenicke is hard to say; but he was apparently a more wholehearted Nazi. The big Russian onslaught began two days after his appointment.

In his farewell message, which the Russians captured at the time, Jaenicke wrote:

> "The Führer has ordered me to take up new functions. This means a bitter good-bye to my Army. With deep emotion I shall remember your exemplary courage. The Führer has entrusted you with a task of world-historical importance. At Sebastopol stands the 17th Army, and at Sebastopol the Soviets will bleed to death."

There had been some heavy fighting on the outer defences of Sebastopol since April 18, particularly in the valley of Inkerman; but it was not till May 5 that the Russians attacked Sebastopol in strength from the north, in order to draw there as many German troops as possible. Having achieved that, the Russians launched, on May 7, an all-out attack on Sapun Ridge, a hill 150 feet high, with several lines of German trenches, which was "the key to Sebastopol". The artillery and *katyusha* barrage, supported by aircraft, lasted several hours, and then the ridge was stormed by infantry. There were heavy losses on both sides, but once Sapun Ridge was taken, the road to Sebastopol was clear. Two days later, on May 9, Hitler resigned himself to abandoning the Crimea and ordered evacuation. But it was already too late and the 50,000 German troops left around Sebastopol were now doomed.

The successful if costly Russian capture of Sapun Ridge was accompanied by attacks on other parts of the "impregnable" Sebastopol defences, and by the 9th, the Russians began to pour into Sebastopol from all directions. Several thousand Germans were killed or captured in Sebastopol itself, while the rest—about 30,000 —abandoned the city and retreated across the moors to the Chersonese Peninsula. Here there were three isthmi, one less than two miles wide, and the others less than a mile wide, and across the first isthmus the Germans had laid minefields and had built an "earth wall" with fortifications of sorts consisting of barbed-wire fences and a series of dugouts and machine-gun nests—nothing very solid, but hard to approach because of the minefield.

The distance between the first line of defence and the tip of the Chersonese Promontory, with the ruins of its white lighthouse, was about three miles. The fortifications across the other two isthmi were much more rudimentary. It was in this small area of about three miles by about one and a half that the Germans were going to make their last stand, still in the desperate hope that ships would come to take them away.

And so, on the 9th, after abandoning Sebastopol, 30,000 Germans retreated across the bleak moors outside Sebastopol to the Chersonese Promontory—the very place to which the last Russian defenders of Sebastopol had retreated in July 1942, only to be exterminated or taken prisoner.

German prisoners later said that the morale was low among the troops, but that the officers kept on assuring them that ships would come. The Führer had promised it... For three days and nights the Chersonese was that "unspeakable inferno" to which German authors now refer. True, on the night of May 9–10 and on the following night two small ships did come and perhaps 1,000 men were taken aboard. This greatly encouraged the remaining troops.

The Germans still had one small fighter airfield on Chersonese; but since it was now under constant Russian shell-fire, it could not serve much purpose.

The Russians were not, however, going to allow any more Germans to be evacuated by sea; on the night of May 11–12, several more ships approached Chersonese, but two were sunk by Russian shell-fire and the rest turned tail. That was the night on which the Russians decided to finish off the 30,000 Germans. By this time the sight of the ships that had come and gone without landing had seriously demoralised the German troops. They had already been heavily bombed and shelled for two days and nights; and on the night of May 11–12 the *katyusha* mortars ("the Black Death" the Germans used to call them) came into action. What followed was a massacre. The Germans fled in panic beyond the second and then the third line of their defences, and when, in the early morning hours, Russian tanks drove in, they began to surrender in large numbers, among them their commander, General Böhme and several other staff officers who had been sheltering in the cellar of the only farm building on the promontory.

Thousands of wounded had been taken to the tip of the promontory, and here were also some 750 SS-men who refused to surrender, and went on firing. A few dozen survivors tried in the end to get away by sea in small boats or rafts. Some of these got away, but often only to be machine-gunned by Russian aircraft. These desperate men were hoping to get to Rumania, Turkey, or maybe to be picked up by some German or Rumanian vessel.

My trip to the Crimea on May 14–18 was perhaps the strangest Crimean holiday anyone had ever had.

On the morning of the 14th I flew from Moscow to Simferopol. The plane circled over the Sivash, where the Russian offensive had started a month before, and then over the Perekop Isthmus, where the Germans had built their defences in depth. It was just as well the Russians had by-passed Perekop.

With its poplars, the country round Simferopol looked like the Touraine. All the apple, peach, cherry and apricot trees were in blossom. Simferopol, small and nondescript, except for a few small mosques, had suffered some bomb-damage, but not much. More characteristic of the Crimea were the Tartar villages, with their mosques and the peculiar Tartar cottages with flat roofs and open verandahs. We drove through several such villages on our way to the mountains and the south coast, and the Tartars looked on, morose and scared.

Then we came to the south coast of the Crimea. At Alushta many houses had been burned out, and the beach was mined and roped off by barbed-wire fences; yet the scenery was of a picture-postcard beauty—a land of vineyards and cypresses, where the fruit-trees and the lilac were now in bloom and houses were bright with the flaming red of the bougainvilia, the lavender clusters of glycinium and the gardens golden with the yellow bushes of laburnum. Farther west, on the pale blue sea, lay the giant shape of Ayu Dag, the rock which, according to local legend, was the devil who had been turned into a granite bear trying in vain to drain the Black Sea by drinking it dry. To the right, there rose into the sky the high lilac outline of Ai-Petri, its peaks wrapped in cloud.

At Yalta, the "Nice" of the Crimea, the whole sea front had been burned down by the Germans, but there was little destruction between Yalta and the spot where the road turns inland. We passed the imperial palaces at Alupka, and several sanatoria, now crowded with Russian wounded, and many of them, though bandaged or on crutches, waved cheerfully as we drove past. (The Germans had also made great use of the Crimea as a gigantic military hospital ever since they had come here in the autumn of 1941).

Nothing was more striking than the contrast between this drive along the picture-postcard coast and the country round Sebastopol. There was nothing here but bleak, windswept moors, and a few houses, now all destroyed. The Valley of Inkerman was like the Valley of Death. It is separated from Sebastopol by Sapun Ridge, and this also looked one of the most melancholy spots on earth, now pockmarked with shell-holes, like all the country around. God knows how many men died here on May 7. In the plains around Sapun Ridge and along the road that runs to Sebastopol through the Valley of Inkerman, the air was filled with the stench of death. It came from the hundreds of horses still lying there, inflated and decaying by the roadside, and from the thousands of dead, many of whom had not been buried deep enough, or even not yet buried at all.

Here, more than anywhere else, one felt that one was driving over layers and layers of human bones—of those who died in the Crimean War, and in the fighting in 1920, and in 1941–2 during the deadly 250-day siege of Sebastopol, and now again. . .

From a distance Sebastopol, with the long and narrow bay beyond, looked like a live city, but it also was dead. Even in the suburbs, at the far end of the valley of Inkerman, there was hardly a house standing. The railway station was a mountain of rubble and twisted metal; on the last day the Germans were at Sebastopol they ran an enormous goods train off the line into a ravine, where it lay smashed, its wheels in the air. Destruction, destruction everywhere.

Sebastopol itself, bright and lively before the war, was now melancholy beyond words. The harbour was littered with the wreckage of ships the Russians had sunk during the last days of the German evacuation.

It was hard to imagine how people could have lived and fought here during that summer of 1942, in the midst of the stench of hundreds of unburied corpses. And then it all lit up in a flash: on the remnants of the old Navy monument on the sea front, I noticed an inscription scratched with a knife or a nail, and written no doubt during the last days of the agony of July 1942:

> You are not the same as before, when people smiled at your beauty. Now everyone curses this spot, because it has caused so much sorrow. Among your ruins, in your lanes and streets, thousands and thousands of people lie, and no one is there to cover their rotting bones.

It was strange to wander along the deserted streets of Sebastopol, so full of historic memories of the Crimean War with that Mikhailovsky

Fort—still, more or less, undamaged across the bay—where young Tolstoy had taken part in the siege of 1854–5, and so full of the more agonising memories of 1942.

In one of the few bigger buildings (patched up by the Germans since 1942) I saw the Mayor of Sebastopol, Comrade Yefremov; he had been mayor during the siege of 1941–2. Now, he said, the streets were deserted because the people living in the outskirts had not yet lost the habit of looking upon this as *verboten* territory. The soldiers also had gone, except for some Black Sea sailors manning the anti-aircraft guns. For the last two years, these men had been day-dreaming of the day when they would stand again on guard at Sebastopol. . . The famous Naval Museum had, in the main, survived the siege, but all its exhibits had been taken away to Germany by the Organisation Rosenberg "with the Wehrmacht's permission", as a notice inside said. It was written in German, Rumanian, Tartar and Russian, Russian coming last.

30,000 civilians had survived the 1941–2 siege of Sebastopol, but some 20,000 were deported by the Germans or shot as suspected soldiers in disguise; and 10,000 had been allowed to stay in Sebastopol, or rather in its northern suburbs. Yefremov also alluded to the Crimean Tartars, who had played a particularly cruel game in hunting down disguised Russian soldiers. Altogether, the Tartars' record was as bad as could be. They had formed a police force under German control and had been highly active in the Gestapo. . .

Chersonese was gruesome. All the area in front of the Earth Wall and beyond was ploughed up by thousands of shells and scorched by the fire of the *katyusha* mortars.

Hundreds of German vehicles were still there, or were being carted away by Russian soldiers. The ground was littered with thousands of German helmets, rifles, bayonets, and other arms and ammunition. Some of this stuff was now being piled up by Russian soldiers assisted by meek German war prisoners who looked almost happy to be alive. There were also numerous German guns around, and a few heavy tanks—but only few, for the Germans had either lost or evacuated the rest of them long before.

Over the ground were also scattered thousands of pieces of paper
—photographs, snapshots, passports, maps, private letters—and
even a volume of Nietzsche carried to the end by some Nazi superman. Nearly all the dead had been buried, but around the shattered
lighthouse dead Germans and rafts were bobbing in the water, as it
beat against the tip of the Chersonese Promontory—bodies of men
who had tried to escape on the rafts. They were some of those 750
SS-men who had made a last stand around the lighthouse, and would
not surrender. And here, among these dead bodies, on the water-
edge, was another weird shape: something that looked like a skeleton
with only a few rags still clinging to it: and one of the rags still had
white-and-blue stripes: the *telniashka* (singlet) of a Black Sea sailor.
Was he one of those who, nearly two years before, had fought here
to the last—just like these Germans—on this very Chersonese
Promontory, and had been left here on this desolate spot, to rot
away unburied?

Around the lighthouse, the blue sea was calm, and perhaps, not
very far away some rafts were still drifting over the sea, with
desperate men clinging to them, drifting over waters where only
three years before, the pleasure steamers still cruised between
Odessa, Sebastopol and Novorossisk. Of the three, only Odessa still
looked like a city. Novorossisk, like Sebastopol, was also a heap of
ruins.

My last night in the Crimea, I spent in the midst of the rich juicy
green steppe. It had rained heavily during the previous evening and
throughout the night. I was billeted in the clean little Tartar cottage;
there was an old man there, and an old woman, and their son, a boy
of fifteen or sixteen. They had, behind the house, a large vegetable
garden, all their own; the vegetables were coming up luxuriantly,
and beyond the vegetable plot were immense fields of green wheat.
But the Tartar family were morose and frightened, scarcely said a
word, and the woman claimed to be very ill. The land had been
intensely cultivated. The Germans, still hoping until April to hold
the Crimea, had encouraged the Tartars to sow and plant wherever
possible, and the Tartars had worked hard.

I remember the look of fear that came over the old man when a Soviet officer knocked on the door in order, as it turned out, merely to billet me on him.

The 500,000 Crimean Tartars were, before long, to be deported *en masse*—women, children and all—to "the east" for having collaborated with the Germans. The Crimea was eventually turned over to the Ukrainian SSR, and nothing more was said of the Tartars, even though Mr Khrushchev was to be very indignant about the "racialist" and "un-Leninist" mass deportation of *other* entire nationalities. But the Crimean Tartars (or the Volga Germans, for that matter) were not mentioned, and they were never allowed to return.

Chapter V

THE LULL BEFORE D-DAY—
STALIN'S FLIRTATION WITH THE
CATHOLIC CHURCH—"SLAV UNITY"

By the middle of May 1944 the Soviet-German Front came to a
relative standstill. Except for the enormous "Belorussian Bulge" in
the middle, where the Germans were still nearly 250 miles inside
Soviet territory, the Soviet-German Front ran in an almost straight
line from the Gulf of Finland, near the former Estonian border,
down to Northern Rumania and Bessarabia. To the north, the Baltic
Republics were still in German hands; so was most of Belorussia;
but most of the Ukraine had been liberated, with the front now running a short distance to the east of Lwow. It was expected that,
within the next few months, not only would the whole of Soviet
territory be cleared of Germans, but that the Red Army would
penetrate deep into eastern and central Europe—Poland, Czechoslovakia, Rumania and Hungary, and possibly Germany. Finland
was not yet out of the war, the tentative armistice talks in Moscow
with Enckel and Paasikivi having broken down. Vyshinsky announced this breakdown on April 22, indicating that the Red Army
would have to make the Finns see reason before long. Since Finland
had not suffered 'a military defeat, there was still much opposition
to accepting the stiff armistice terms, complete with a demand for
$600 million in reparations.

*

Soviet policy in relation to the countries of eastern Europe called
for some clarification; and almost the moment Soviet troops had
entered Rumanian territory, Molotov convened a press conference
on April 2 and officially announced that the Soviet Union did not
aim at acquiring any Rumanian territory or at making any changes
"in the existing social order in Rumania." The entry of Soviet troops
into Rumania was exclusively dictated by military necessity and the
continued resistance of enemy troops in that country. So there was
to be no forced "bolshevisation" or even "socialisation" of
Rumania, no abolition of private enterprise, perhaps even no
abolition of the monarchy. All this, in principle, was a matter for
the Rumanians themselves to decide. It was no use, at this stage,
either alarming the Rumanians, or upsetting the Western Allies with
the prospect of revolutionary changes in the countries of eastern
Europe. Already, various Rumanians were in contact with the
British and the Americans, with a view to getting out of the war, and
it was no good frightening them off. The question of the Rumanian
Government, as distinct from the "social order" could be tackled
once the Red Army was well inside Rumania—unless, in the interval, "the people" (as Stalin said) were to change the government
themselves; for the present, the Russians occupied only a small area
in north-east Rumania. "No claims on Rumanian territory" did not,
of course, relate to Bessarabia or Northern Bukovina, both of which
had been incorporated in the Soviet Union in 1940.

The Second Front decided upon at Teheran was now known to be
due in a matter of weeks. The feeling widely expressed among
ordinary Russian soldiers and civilians was that it would be "too
easy", now that the Red Army had already pulled most of the chestnuts out of the fire, and that if the British and Americans were going
to land in France now, it would be less out of any feeling of comradeship for the Russians than out of pure self-interest and even
self-protection, since they feared that the Russians might now well
smash Germany "single-handed".

These views were soon discouraged by Stalin, whose May-Day
1944 Order was particularly cordial to the Western Allies. After

recalling that the Red Army had advanced in a little over a year from the Volga to the Sereth, he said:

> We owe this success in a large measure to our great Allies, the United States and Great Britain, who are holding the front in Italy and are diverting from us a large part of the German troops, and who are also supplying us with highly valuable raw materials and armaments, are systematically bombing military objectives in Germany and are so undermining her military power.

In paying a tribute to the Soviet rear, Stalin said:

> In the past year hundreds of new factories and mines have come into operation, dozens of electric power stations, and many railway lines and bridges. Millions more Soviet people have entered industry.

Then, after a tribute to Russia's women, intelligentsia, and collective farms, Stalin said:

> The satellites must now see clearly that Germany has lost the war. *But their Governments cannot be relied upon to break with Germany, and the sooner the people take over and make peace, the better.*

The Red Army, he said, had reached the Soviet frontier along 250 miles, and more than three-quarters of occupied Soviet territory had now been liberated. But to drive the Germans out of the Soviet Union was not sufficient. The wounded German beast must be finished off in his lair.

This phrase (though usually amended to "Fascist beast") was to become No. 1 slogan during the next twelve months.

And as if to discourage any ideas that the Red Army had already done the job, and that the Second Front was no longer all that important, he added:

> The liberation of Europe, and the smashing of Germany on her own soil can be done only on the basis of joint efforts from the Soviet Union, Great Britain and the United States as they strike from the east and the west... There is no doubt that only such a combined blow can smash Hitler Germany.

This was, politically, an important statement.

*

There was much display of cordiality towards the Allies during May: at a ceremony of the British Embassy on May 10 the G.C.B.E. was conferred on the Soviet Chief of Staff, Marshal Vassilevsky, and hundreds of other decorations were awarded. Molotov and Clark Kerr exchanged speeches.

On May 26, the second anniversary of the Anglo-Soviet Alliance was marked by warm editorials in the principal papers.

On May 25 and 27 Churchill's and Eden's speeches were reported at great length, and the Molotov-Eden exchange of anniversary messages was particularly cordial. Eden was clearly alluding to the coming events when he spoke in his message of the "mighty onslaught" in which "our two peoples, hand-in-hand with our American and other allies", would win the war. Such a victory, he said, would strengthen the bonds of friendship and understanding on which the Anglo-Soviet alliance was based.

The suspension of diplomatic mail from Britain created a very happy impression in Russia. It was clearly an indication of what was coming—and coming soon. Alexei Tolstoy jokingly remarked to me one day: "If we Bolsheviks had done anything so outrageous, nobody would have been surprised; but if the correct English do such a thing, then they surely must have good reasons for doing so."

The Second Front—the Normandy Landing—came a few days later.

With the Russians preparing for their summer offensive which was expected to take the Red Army into Poland, this country, more than any other, continued to be in the centre of the Soviet Government's preoccupations. In April and May there were a number of curious developments: the visits to Moscow of Father Orlemanski, of Dr Oscar Lange, and of the leaders of the "Democratic Polish Underground."

The visit of Father Orlemanski, a parish priest from Springfield, Mass., was probably the most curious episode in the whole diplomatic history of the Soviet Union. People rubbed their eyes when they looked at the front page of *Pravda* of April 28 showing Stalin and Molotov smiling benignly in the company of the Rev. Stanislaw

Orlemanski "who has come here to study the problems of the Poles and the Polish Army in the Soviet Union".

Stalin and Molotov were obviously anxious, through their contacts with Orlemanski, to kill three birds with one stone: to make a good impression on the Catholics in the United States; to appease and, if possible, win over the powerful Catholic clergy in Poland— who were, for the most part pro-London—as well as the numerous priests in Lithuania and Belorussia; and, possibly to lay the foundations for a rapprochement with the Vatican.

After about a week there, Orlemanski came out with a statement on the Moscow radio:

> Dear fellow countrymen (he said), I left home on April 17. I came through the United States, Canada, and Alaska, and across Siberia to Moscow. I travelled very comfortably. I had never flown before, and now I flew all the way from Chicago to Moscow! I am an American of Polish origin, and I am a Roman Catholic priest. Moreover, we are four brothers, all priests in the United States.

After this pleasant introduction, Father Orlemanski, the parish priest from Springfield, Mass., said that as soon as he had heard of the formation of the Kosciuszko Division on Soviet soil, he decided to help, and in November 1943, formed the Kosciuszko League at Detroit. This, he said, was a great success. He continued: "Having achieved all this, I felt that I must inform myself more completely on the plans and aims of the Polish emigrants in the USSR." He said he had come with Cordell Hull's personal okay.

> First of all I went to Zagorsk where there are Polish children. At the school there I attended the lessons in Polish history. May I, as a neutral observer and practical American, say that the present conditions could not be better. We Poles must be grateful to the Soviet Government for their kindness, and we must try to preserve these institutions. I was told that there are such institutions in the whole of Russia.

All this sounded somewhat naïve. Then he described his visit to the Polish Army: Here he felt "quite at home". While he was there, 8,000 new soldiers from Ternopol and from other liberated parts had joined. "I told the soldiers that I considered the arms in their hands as the key to a free Poland."

Finally came his statement on his first two-hour meeting with Stalin and Molotov:

> I cannot repeat all that was said. But I must say that Stalin is a¹ friend of the Poles. He wants to see a strong, powerful, independent and democratic Poland which would effectively defend her frontiers. Stalin does not intend to interfere in internal Polish affairs. He wants Poland to be friendly and to co-operate harmoniously with the Soviet Republics. . .
> We are Slavs. Allied, Poland and the Soviet Union will be the mightiest power in the east. It will be of the greatest benefit to both. It will guarantee peace for hundreds of years. Long live the United States of America. Long live the Soviet Union. Long live a free, strong, independent and democratic Poland!

All this was reported verbatim, and in all seriousness, in the Soviet press, as was also his statement on the following day:

> I want to make the historic statement (*sic*) that the future will prove that Stalin is a friend of the Roman Catholic Church. Our religion will be the religion of our ancestors, and Marshal Stalin will not tolerate any violation of this.

He went on to say that there were five chaplains in the new Polish Army and that the Bishop of newly-liberated Luck (in the Western Ukraine) had promised to send several more priests into the army.

> I had another meeting with Stalin and Molotov (he continued), and the result has exceeded all my expectations. Marshal Stalin and Mr Molotov are two great men: I am most grateful to both these gentlemen for the democratic reception that was given me during my stay in Moscow.

Perhaps the Soviet press had its tongue in its cheek when it used the English word "gentleman" in quoting Orlemanski's broadcast.

But less than a fortnight later Orlemanski was back in the States—and in the soup. For it turned out that Orlemanski represented nobody, and was either a well-meaning simpleton or else a practical joker, in which case his visit to Stalin was the biggest hoax ever played on the Kremlin. In any case, Father Orlemanski's immediate superior, Bishop O'Leary, reprimanded and repudiated the Kremlin visitor on his return to the USA, and Orlemanski had to "repent" before being reinstated. After that Stalin came to the conclusion, either that he had been fooled, or else that Cardinal Spellman and the rest of the hierarchy but not Orlemanski, were the people who really mattered among the Catholics in the USA. The official repudiation of a Catholic priest who had consorted with the Devil naturally had the very opposite effect on the Polish and Lithuanian clergy to what Stalin and Molotov had hoped for when they devoted so much of their time to their unusual visitor from the USA. This was no joking matter: for the attitude of the Polish clergy mattered greatly in a question like the recruitment of Poles into the "Moscow-made" Polish Army. As we shall see, this Army, by the end of 1944, when part of Poland had already been liberated, consisted of about 300,000 men. With the active co-operation of the Church and the Armija Krajowa it might have been much larger.

Father Braun, the unofficial representative of the Vatican in the Soviet Union (and *he* was not going to do anything to help the Kremlin) thought the Orlemanski visit the biggest joke for years. Father Braun, of Alsatian origin, but American nationality, was the priest of the only Catholic church in Moscow. It happened to be next door to the NKVD headquarters and was jokingly referred to as Notre-Dame de Lubianka. Father Braun had had a good deal of trouble with the Soviet authorities during the eight or nine years he had been in Russia; in return he was an unfailing source of information to many foreigners, who had come to Russia with an open mind. During the earlier part of the war he had lived in two rooms at the French Embassy, till he was more or less turned out by the rather pro-Soviet and anti-clerical French Minister, M. Roger Garreau. The US Embassy took him under its wing after that.

Professor Oscar Lange of Chicago University, who was to become a prominent personality in post-war Poland, came to Moscow soon after Father Orlemanski, and was also photographed in the company of Stalin and Molotov, and made numerous speeches, in which, more intelligently than Orlemanski, he advocated close bonds between Russian and the New Poland. The Russians publicised the eminent Professor's preference for the "Moscow" Poles in order to make the maximum impression in the USA.

*

Throughout May, Poland continued to be front-page news. With obvious relish the Soviet press reported on May 19 that General Zeligowski, a popular Polish veteran then in London, had more or less rebelled against the London Government by saying that the alliance of the Slavs was the only salvation for Poland, and that, by refusing to adopt this slogan, the London Government was playing into the hands of the Germans. The Russians gladly forgave Zeligowski the *coup de force* with which he had snatched Vilno away from Lithuania in 1920, and even the contemptuous remarks he now made about the Lithuanians, whom he described as a nondescript alien body in the Slav world. In London many Poles tried to explain Zeligowski's change of heart by simply saying the poor old boy had gone gaga.

But the biggest surprise was still in store.

On May 24 the Union of Polish Patriots issued a statement saying:

> A few days ago delegates of the People's Council of Poland (*Krajowa Rada Narodowa*) arrived in Moscow... This Council was established in Warsaw on January 1, 1944, by the democratic parties and groups struggling against the German occupants. The following are represented in the K.R.N.: The Opposition groups of the *Stronnictwo Ludowo* (Peasant Party), the P.P.S. (Socialist Party), P.P.R. (Workers'—in fact, Communist—Party), the Committee of National Initiative non-party democrats, the underground trade-union movement, the Youth Struggle Movement (*Walki Mlodych*), groups of writers and other intellectual workers, artisan and co-operative groups, representatives of the underground military organisations—the National Guard, the National Militia, the Peasant Battalions, local military formations of the *Armija Krajowa*, etc.

These were alleged "dissidents" of that A.K. which was under the orders of the London Government. The statement went on:

> It has become necessary to form a centre of struggle and co-ordination... The emigré Government is not fighting the Germans; instead, it is calling for inactivity. Its people sometimes even murder resistance leaders... In 1943 hopes were rising in Poland, but, at the same time, the German terror was growing in intensity... The National

Council, at its very first meeting, took the highly important decision to unify all the partisan groupings, armed units, etc., struggling with the occupants, and to merge them into a single People's Army (*Armija Ludowa*)... The National Guard, the National Militia, a large part of the Peasant Battalions, etc., have entered this. The Polish people have responded with enthusiasm. In a few months a network of local—rural, urban, and provincial—organisations was set up by the National Council. The struggle against the occupants has been greatly intensified.

The statement concluded by saying that the Delegates of the National Council of Poland came to Moscow, firstly to become acquainted with the work of the Union of Polish Patriots in the USSR, and with the state of the first Polish Army; and secondly in order to establish contact with the Allied Governments, including the Government of the Soviet Union.

It was also announced that, on May 22, Stalin had received the Polish delegates, with Mr "Morawski" at their head, that the conversation lasted for over two hours, and that Molotov and Wanda Wassilewska were present.

That was the first news the world was to hear of the "Left Underground" in Poland, and of a National Council of Poland that had allegedly been in existence there for over five months. It was also the first mention of the name of Morawski, later known at Osóbka-Morawski. The London Poles lost no time in debunking the delegates in Moscow as a bunch of communist stooges or adventurers with no following whatsoever, the National Council as a pretentious fake, etc., etc.

Indeed, Morawski and the other delegates whose names (or even pseudonyms) were not disclosed at the time (though many knew that they included Bierut, Andrzei Witos, and some others who were to become prominent before long), stayed for some time in the Soviet Union, and some did not go home until the Red Army had marched into Poland in the following July. On June 8 Morawski gave an interview to *Tass* in which he said that nearly 100,000 Polish troops were now on Soviet soil; among their leaders were General Berling,

Alexander Zawadski (recently promoted to the rank of general by the Russians), and that great Gargantuan character, General Karol Sweszczewski, famous in the Spanish Civil War under the *nom de guerre* of General Walter.* Already acting like something of a Provisional Government, the delegates of the National Council conferred on General Berling, on the Council's behalf, the Grunwald Cross 1st class.

Among other things the delegates had come to Moscow to ask for arms. They received some satisfaction from the Russians but none from the British and the Americans who continued to supply the Armija Krajowa. But the political significance of the arrival in Moscow of this "delegation" was much greater than its military significance. They were, in fact, a nucleus of that "Lublin Committee", which was, before long, going to be the *de facto* government of Poland. In the course of his interview with *Tass*, Morawski expressed his gratitude to the Red Army and his affection for Stalin.

Nor were the Yugoslavs being neglected in this bid for Slav Unity.

In April a regular military mission from Tito arrived in Moscow, and on May 20 it was announced that Stalin had had a long meeting the day before with Generals Terzic and Djilas, "representing the National Liberation Army of Yugoslavia". Terzic, it was explained, was "the head of the Yugoslav Military Mission in the USSR". Whether this was recognised by the Royal Yugoslav Government no longer mattered; the Soviet Union had already given *de facto* recognition to Tito. Simic, the Yugoslav Ambassador had declared himself a Titoite some time before, and when two members of the Yugoslav Embassy, returning to Moscow, were met by the Embassy car flying the Tito flag with the red star, they ordered the chauffeur to take it down. This he refused to do, and told the two diplomats they could walk into Moscow for all he cared. It is not recorded how they reached town, but they refused to accept the Embassy's *fait accompli*, and stayed for some days at the Hotel National, whereupon they were recalled by the Royal Government.

* In 1947, as Deputy Minister of Defence, he was assassinated by Ukrainian terrorists near the Ukrainian border.

On the same day as the announcement of Stalin's meeting with the Yugoslav generals, an interview, given by Tito to the A.P. was prominently published in the Soviet press. Tito explained that 50,000 square miles and five million people were under his jurisdiction; he asked for UNRRA help, and for the recognition of the National Liberation Committee as the Government of Yugoslavia. A few days later Lieut.-Gen. Milovan Djilas published a long article in the Russian press on the four years of the war of liberation in Yugoslavia. In the course of it he violently denounced Mihailovic. He also commented on Stalin's shrewdness and clarity of vision, and his hatred of empty phrases:

> He takes a problem and you can just see him polishing it and sharpening it. He did not ask us a single irrelevant question, and he answered our questions remarkably quickly and to the point. He has an excellent knowledge of Yugoslavia and her personalities, and he interprets these men with remarkable correctness and shrewdness.*

Poland, Czechoslovakia, Yugoslavia—the future was taking shape.

* In retrospect Djilas was to paint a very different picture of Stalin in his *Conversations with Stalin*, published in 1962.

Chapter VI

THE RUSSIANS AND THE NORMANDY LANDING

Officially, relations continued to be excellent between the Soviet Union and the Western Allies at the time of the Normandy Landing. Only a few days before, the American shuttle-bombing bases in the Ukraine had come into operation. Flying Fortresses started coming in from Italy after dropping their bombs on Debrecen, Ploesti and other Hungarian and Rumanian targets; and then flying back to Italy and dropping more bombs on the way.

It was strange to see there, at Poltava and Mirgorod, in the heart of the Gogol country, those hundreds of G.I.'s eating vast quantities of American canned food—spam, and baked beans and apple-sauce —drinking gallons of good coffee, making passes at the giggly Ukrainian canteen waitresses, and commenting flatteringly on the Ukrainian landscape, which was "just like back home in Indiana or Kentucky". Many of them, it is true, had serious doubts about the usefulness of these shuttle-bombing bases, and thought them more in the nature of a political demonstration of "Soviet-American solidarity", or as a precedent which might come in useful in the Far East if and when. . .

Judging from General John R. Deane's account,* the Russians had never been very keen on the whole idea and had been difficult and obstructive for months before the bases actually came into operation in early June 1944.

* *The Strange Alliance.*

Soon afterwards, in a surprise night raid on the principal (Poltava) base the Germans destroyed forty-nine out of the seventy Flying Fortresses on the ground.* My own impression at the time was that the Russians were extremely embarrassed at having failed to protect the base effectively with either fighters or anti-aircraft guns but that they were, on the whole, relieved when, before very long, these American bases were scrapped altogether, despite the enormous effort and money that had been sunk into them. The very idea of American air bases on Soviet soil somewhat went against their grain; nor did they care for the idea of the Ukrainians in a war-devastated part like the Poltava Province (Poltava itself had been completely destroyed) being able to observe at close quarters the "high living" of the American G.I.'s, with their P-X, and their enormous meals.

The shuttle-bombing bases came into operation only a few days before the Normandy Landing. I happened to be at the Poltava base when the news broke, and immediately flew back to Moscow, arriving there in the afternoon of June 6.

The first wave of excitement over the Second Front had subsided, but people were happy.

The newly-opened "commercial" restaurants were packed that night with people celebrating—not only British and Americans, but many Russians, too. (A party of Jap diplomats and journalists also came to one, and behaved and danced provocatively and ostentatiously and were nearly beaten-up by some Americans.)

The news of the Normandy landing had missed the morning papers, but Moscow radio had been giving news of it in successive bulletins. On the night of the 6th General Deane and General Burrows, heads of the American and British military missions, spoke on Moscow radio, the latter in Russian (of sorts). On the 5th, there had been enthusiastic articles in the Russian press on the capture of

* Two Americans and thirty Russians were killed in this raid, mostly by anti-personnel mines with which the Germans had peppered the airfield before dropping their heavy bombs.

Rome, and now, on the 7th, the great news of the Normandy landing was splashed over four columns, with a large picture of Eisenhower. But there was no comment yet. The Russians wanted to be absolutely sure that the landing was a success. A curious feature of this Russian reporting on the Second Front was that, although facilities had been given to Russian correspondents to be on the spot, no news from any Russian correspondent was published.

The articles were mostly by military and naval experts, and dealt with the technicalities of the landing operations, the part played by the allied air-forces, etc., and for some days rosy forecasts were avoided. Almost the only non-technical article was written by Ehrenburg, and, in the circumstances, it was particularly inept. It was a sloppy, emotional piece on France, which would have been all right, if only there had been something on the same lines about Britain and America; but, as it was, it lacked all sense of proportion. It was all about the French people, the French Resistance, French paratroops that had landed in Normandy, the tradition of Verdun, the Unknown Soldier who had now risen from his tomb to fight *le Boche*, etc. Those really responsible for the operation he swept aside in a polite sentence: "We admire the valour of our Allies—the British, Canadians, Americans." And then he immediately proceeded to wallow in his Francophilia.

Was this a purely personal reaction of Ehrenburg's, the old habitué of the Rotonde? Perhaps, and yet in a film produced some time later on the liberation of France, the British and Americans were also made to play a sort of incidental role—or something that could be taken for granted—while the men who played the most prominent part in saving France were—the French, assisted by the Red Army, the heroes of Stalingrad, etc.

Rather more legitimate were the frequent suggestions in the Soviet press that the Russians had, in fact, enormously facilitated the task of the Allies, and had already done the greater part of the work in smashing the Germans. Patrick Lacey, of the BBC, was quoted with pleasure as saying that "but for the Russians, D-Day would have been impossible." A Kukryniksy cartoon, on June 11, showed Hitler as a rat, with its head already caught in the Russian trap and the British-American sword *then* descending upon its hind quarters.

A week passed before Stalin indicated the official line. This was wholly unlike Ehrenburg's.

In a statement to *Pravda*, Stalin said:

After seven days' fighting in Northern France one may say without hesitation that the forcing of the Channel along a wide front and the mass-landings of the Allies in Northern France have completely succeeded. This is unquestionably a brilliant success for our Allies. One must admit that the history of wars does not know of an undertaking comparable to it for breadth of conception, grandeur of scale, and mastery of execution.

Invincible Napoleon shamefully failed in his plan to force the Channel and to conquer the British Isles. Hitler the hysteric, who, for two years, boasted that he would force the Channel did not even venture to carry out his threat. Only the British and American troops succeeded with flying colours in carrying out the gigantic plan of forcing the Channel and of landing in force on the other side. History will record this action as an achievement of the highest order.

After this statement the press became very warm to the Allies and, on the initiative of the People's Commissariat for Foreign Trade, only a few days after the opening of the Second Front, the Soviet press published for the first time (and not merely in the form of a statement by Roosevelt or Stettinius) a long list of arms and other deliveries received since the beginning of the war from Britain, the United States and Canada.*

Not long after D-Day all Russian attention was again focussed on the Soviet-German Front. In a way, this was natural, for now the Red Army was making an all-out bid to put all Germany's satellites out of action, and to break into Germany itself. Only four days after D-Day the Russians, under Marshal Govorov, struck out at Finland and, after eleven days of heavy fighting on the Karelian Isthmus, Viipuri was captured. On June 23 began the great offensive in Belorussia, that was to carry the Red Army far into Poland. And no sooner had the front become more or less stabilised there in

* This list of deliveries from the three countries up to April 30, 1944, is given on pp. 625–6.

August than the Russians struck out at Rumania, Bulgaria and Hungary—and, in Russian eyes, the war in the west again became relatively small stuff.

At first the Allies, held up at Caen and Saint-Lo, had made little progress—which produced some critical notes in the Russian press; then it became "extraordinarily easy"; and when Paris was liberated, it was the French Resistance who received most of the credit in the Russian press (even though only a few days before, *à propos* of Warsaw, an official Soviet statement ridiculed the suggestion that, in conditions of modern warfare, any city could be liberated by forces inside it). Indeed, it was not long after the Russian summer offensive had begun in Belorussia that *Pravda* wrote on July 16:

> The Red Army's offensive has not only made an enormous gap in the eastern wall of Hitler's European fortress, but has also shattered the arguments of Nazi propaganda. The myth that Germany's main front is now in the west has burst like a soap bubble. . . German commentators are now speaking with terror of the battle in the east which, they say, has taken on apocalyptic proportions.

Naturally, the suggestions put forward by some military commentators in Britain that the Germans were deliberately pulling out of Belorussia as a result of the Normandy landing, were strongly resented by the Russians. As the Russian commentator was to say, "this nonsensical talk did not stop until we had paraded 57,000 newly-captured German prisoners, complete with dozens of generals, through the streets of Moscow." That was on July 17, after the enormous German routs at Vitebsk, Bobruisk, and Minsk.

Even when the campaign in France was developing highly favourably, the Soviet press still published little more than the official communiqués from the Western Front, and few despatches from the Russian correspondents attached to SHAEF appeared in print. It was not until the end of 1947 that one of them, A. Kraminov, wrote a long retrospective account of the Second Front, and if the sentiments and ideas he expressed then were the same as they had been in 1944, it would scarcely have been good inter-allied manners to publish his cables while the war was still in full swing. He treated the institution of SHAEF war correspondents as a gigantic publicity machine for armies and even for individual generals (Montgomery, in his view, was the worst publicity-monger of all); of Montgomery's military gifts he spoke with some disdain, gave the British army no credit for holding the Allies' left flank at Caen, and wrote with typical Russian anger of both the conception of strategic bombing and of the "barbarous and futile" use made of the air force in Normandy where cities like Caen were wrecked and thousands of civilians killed for no valid military reason. It is true that he spoke with admiration of both Patton and Bradley, but treated Eisenhower as a "good chairman", and no more.

In 1944, however, it was not yet the fashion to speak in rude terms of the Second Front. Though terribly belated, it was still regarded as a real help and as a guarantee that the war would end soon. It made the imminent collapse of Germany more tangible than ever; and the Russians were not altogether surprised at the attempt made on July 20 to assassinate Hitler.

The failure of the attempt was received in Russia with undisguised relief. Although the Russians had, in a way, prepared for such an eventuality with their Free German Committee, the setting up of a "respectable" (i.e. pro-Western) German Government, with the British and Americans now firmly established on the Continent, might have created a situation which would almost certainly have turned out detrimental to Russia. There was nothing the Red Army wanted more at this stage than to "finish off the fascist beast in his lair".

This did not prevent them from letting, or even encouraging, Field-Marshal Paulus (who had kept silent until then) publish a statement calling on the German people to "change the State leadership". The wide use made of this statement in leaflets showered over the enemy lines was intended to demoralise the German soldiers, even though the results of similar attempts in the past had been disappointing, especially if measured by the number of Germans voluntarily surrendering to the Red Army.

Chapter VII

GERMAN ROUT IN BELORUSSIA:
"WORSE THAN STALINGRAD"

The great Russian summer offensive started a little over a fortnight
after D-Day in the West, and, somewhat symbolically, on June 23,
the day after the third anniversary of the German invasion of the
Soviet Union. The rôles had now been completely reversed. In the
last two years, despite extremely heavy losses in both men and
equipment, the Russians had gone on building up a tremendously
effective, competent and powerfully equipped army, while Germany's reserves in manpower were now in constant decline.*

* Some very interesting percentage figures are published in Vol. V
of the Soviet *History*, showing that between Stalingrad and the end of
the war the Russians increased *only slightly the number of soldiers
in their Army*, but *increased enormously the quantity of equipment.*
(IVOVSS, Vol. V, p. 467).

The following table illustrates this point admirably:

Date	Effectives	Guns and Mortars	Tanks	Aircraft
Nov. 19, 1942	100	100	100	100
Jan. 1, 1944	111	180	133	200
Jan. 1, 1945	112	217	250	343

The increase in the number of trucks must have been greater still.

858

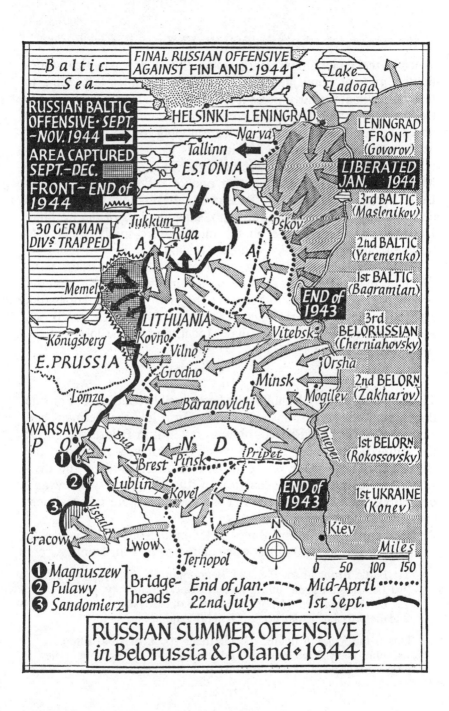

FINAL RUSSIAN OFFENSIVE AGAINST FINLAND · 1944

RUSSIAN BALTIC OFFENSIVE · SEPT. –NOV. 1944

AREA CAPTURED SEPT.–DEC.

FRONT– END of 1944

30 GERMAN DIV? TRAPPED

LENINGRAD FRONT (Govorov)

LIBERATED JAN. 1944

3rd BALTIC (Maslenikov)

2nd BALTIC (Yeremenko)

1st BALTIC (Bagramian)

3rd BELORUSSIAN (Cherniahovsky)

2nd BELORN. (Zakharov)

1st BELORN. (Rokossovsky)

1st UKRAINE (Konev)

END of 1943

Baltic Sea

Lake Ladoga

HELSINKI — LENINGRAD

Narva

Tallinn
ESTONIA

Pskov

Tukkum

Riga

L A T V I A

Memel

Königsberg

E. PRUSSIA

LITHUANIA

Kovno

Vilno

Vitebsk

Orsha

Minsk

Mogilev

Dnieper

Grodno

Lomza

Baranovichi

WARSAW

P O L A N D

Bug

Brest

Pinsk

Pripet

Lublin

Kovel

Vistula

Cracow

Lwow

Terhopol

Kiev

N

Miles

0   50   100   150

❶ *Magnuszew*
❷ *Pulawy*
❸ *Sandomierz*
} Bridge-heads

End of Jan. ·----·   *Mid-April* ·········
22nd July ·—·—·   *1st Sept.*

RUSSIAN SUMMER OFFENSIVE
in Belorussia & Poland · 1944

Whereas the Soviet Union now had her British and American allies fighting a major campaign in France, and tying down (according to Russian estimates) thirty percent of Germany's combat troops, the troops of all Hitler's remaining allies were becoming more and more unreliable and their governments were hoping to get out of the war at the first convenient opportunity. It is ironical that one of the reasons why Hitler was determined to cling on to the Vitebsk-Mogilev-Bobruisk Line at the east end of the great "Belorussian Bulge" penetrating deep into Russia was that its loss would have a demoralising effect on the Finns who, since the loss of the Karelian Isthmus and Viipuri earlier in the month, were sorely tempted to resume their armistice talks with the Russians.

Field-Marshal von Busch, the commander of Army-Group *Mitte* which occupied Belorussia, had been pleading with Hitler to pull out of Belorussia, or at least to "shorten the line". All that Hitler did, after five days of inevitable German defeats, was to sack von Busch and replace him by Field-Marshal Model, one of the losers of the Battle of Kursk.

The Russian offensive began in the best possible conditions. For one thing, until the very last days of the May-June lull, the Germans had expected the next big Russian blow to fall, not in Belorussia, but in the southern part of the front, between the Pripet Marshes and the Black Sea. The Russian concentration of no fewer than 166 divisions* in Belorussia had been done with the utmost secrecy and discretion, and when the blow fell the Germans were taken almost completely by surprise.

The campaign, starting along a 450-mile front (which was to extend later to over 600 miles) was conducted by four fronts:

1st Baltic Front under General Bagramian,
3rd Belorussian Front under General Cherniakhovsky,
1st Belorussian Front under General Rokossovsky,
2nd Belorussian Front under General Zakharov.

* This is the Russian figure; the Germans speak of "140 rifle divisions, plus forty-three panzer and mechanised formations (*Verbände*)" (Philippi and Heim, op. cit., p. 247).

The first two were under the general command of Marshal Vassilevsky and the last two under that of Marshal Zhukov.

The Russians made no secret of the fact that this was, in a sense, their revenge for 1941 and that it was they who now had enormous superiority over the Germans, with 166 divisions (including reserves) in Belorussia, 31,000 guns and mortars, 5,200 tanks and self-propelled guns, and at least 6,000 planes. Their superiority over the Germans was: 2 to 1 in men; 2·9 to 1 in guns and mortars; 4·3 to 1 in tanks; and 4·5 to 1 in planes.*

This looked, indeed, like 1941 the other way round! In the breakthrough areas, the density of artillery was often as much as 320 guns per mile. For several weeks enormous reserves of ammunition, petrol and food had been accumulated behind the Russian lines; 100 trainloads had been arriving daily for the four Fronts, besides large quantities brought by lorries (chiefly American). A large fleet of motor ambulances was in readiness, as well as hospital accommodation of 294,000 beds for the wounded.†

A fleet of 12,000 lorries was in readiness to transport 25,000 tons of ammunition, petrol, etc., to the advancing troops in a single journey. It was—with the possible exception of Kursk—the most thoroughly prepared of all the Russian operations, with everything worked out down to its finest detail, and nothing left to improvisation, as had been the case in the past, even at Stalingrad, chiefly because of serious shortages in equipment and motor transport.

One characteristic of the Belorussian campaign was the very important part played by the partisan formations behind the German lines. Despite some particularly savage German punitive expeditions against the Belorussian partisans in January-February 1944, and again in April, with massacres of entire villages (for example, the village of Baiki in the Brest province where 130 houses had been

---

* IVOVSS, vol. IV, p. 164. German sources put the Russian superiority even higher.
† Ibid., p. 166.

burned down and 957 people massacred on January 22, 1944), the
partisans of Belorussia still constituted an appreciable armed force
of 143,000 men on the eve of the offensive. There was close co-
ordination between the Red Army Command and the partisans who
succeeded between June 20 and 23, in putting practically all the
Belorussian railways out of action—precisely what the Red Army
needed to paralyse the movement of German supplies and
troops.

From the very start, the Russian offensive was tremendously successful. Between June 23 and 28 the four Russian Fronts broke through
the German lines in six places, and encircled large German forces at
Vitebsk and Bobruisk. Tens of thousands of Germans were killed
and some 20,000 taken prisoner in these two encirclements alone.
After the Germans' loss of the Vitebsk-Orsha-Mogilev-Bobruisk
line, Hitler sent a frantic order to hold the Berezina line. But in this
the Germans failed completely. Striking out from north-east and
south-east, the Russians entered Minsk, the capital of Belorussia,
on July 3, and in the process encircled large German forces in a
vast "bag" east of Minsk—a total of about 100,000 men, the
majority of whom surrendered. Some 40,000 were killed or wounded,
but 57,000 Germans, with several generals and dozens of officers at
their head were marched in July 17 through the streets of Moscow.
The purpose of this unusual procedure was to disprove both the
German claims of a "planned withdrawal from Belorussia", and
suggestions in the British and American press that if the Russian
campaign in Belorussia was a "walkover", it was because large
numbers of German troops had been moved to fight the Western
Allies in France.
    That parade of 57,000 Germans through Moscow was a memor-
able sight. Particularly striking was the attitude of the Russian
crowds lining the streets. Youngsters booed and whistled, and even
threw things at the Germans, only to be immediately restrained by
the adults; men looked on grimly and in silence; but many women,
especially elderly women, were full of commiseration (some even
had tears in their eyes) as they looked at these bedraggled "Fritzes".

I remember one old woman murmuring, "just like our poor boys ...
tozhe pognali na voinu (also driven into the war)".

The Russian soldiers fighting in Belorussia did not, on the whole,
feel quite so charitable towards the Germans. Everywhere the retreating Germans had tried to destroy as much as they possibly could.
At Zhlobin, the Russians saw a trench with 2,500 corpses of newly-
murdered civilians, and it is estimated that well over a million people
had been murdered in Belorussia during the German occupation—
among them the entire Jewish population and many hundreds of
thousands of partisans and their "accomplices", including women
and children.

Most of Belorussia, and the country east of it between Smolensk
and Viazma, had been turned into a "desert zone". In the spring of
1944, anticipating a probable withdrawal from Belorussia, the Germans had ordered that the winter crops be ploughed under, and had
tried to prevent spring sowing. They even devised special rollers to
destroy the crops. Practically all the cities were in ruins. It is true
that with nearly sixty percent of the rural areas more or less under
partisan control (and even jurisdiction, complete with Soviet
administrative and party organs) these orders could not be put into
effect in many places. General Tippelskirch, Commander of the 4th
German Army which took part in the Belorussia retreat, later
referred to "a vast wooded and marshy area from the Dnieper nearly
all the way to Minsk which was controlled by large partisan formations, and was never in three years, either cleaned up, still less
occupied by German troops."[*]

Nevertheless, the Germans succeeded in turning most of Belorussia into a "desert zone". In the villages (according to Russian
figures) over a million houses were destroyed; and when I travelled
through Belorussia, shortly after the German rout, there was extremely little livestock to be seen.

Here (as distinct from the Ukraine) a large number of young
people had evaded deportation by joining the partisans; but even so,

[*] K. Tippelskirch. *Istoriya vtoroi mirovoi voiny.* [Russ. ed.] p. 445.

380,000 had been deported from Belorussia to Germany. The destruction in the cities was appalling: nearly all factories and public buildings had been destroyed, and at Minsk the majority of all other houses had been burned down, too. If the large Government House and some other public buildings and nineteen out of 332 industrial enterprises had survived, it was only because they had been rapidly de-mined as soon as the Russian troops had entered the city. In Minsk alone 4,000 delayed-action bombs, mines and boobytraps had to be unprimed. The Red Army was full of admiration for those engineers "who never made more than one mistake."

The "bagging" of 100,000 Germans east of Minsk meant that the Red Army had torn a 250-mile gap in the German front, and that the road was now almost clear into Poland and Lithuania.

On July 4, even before the final liquidation of the Minsk "bag", the Soviet Supreme Command set new targets for the four fronts fighting in Belorussia: they were to advance, within a very short time into eastern Latvia, Lithuania, and on to Vilno, Kaunas, Grodno and Brest-Litovsk, and to force the Niemen in several places, with a subsequent advance to the East Prussian border and (farther south) into Poland.

The Red Army continued to advance at great speed, covering between ten and fifteen miles a day; on July 8 Baranovichi was taken; on July 13 Vilno fell to the troops of Cherniakhovsky, on July 18, Rokossovsky's troops crossed into Poland, and on July 23, captured Lublin—an event of far-reaching political consequences. On July 28 they captured Brest-Litovsk, and the whole of Belorussia was cleared of the Germans.

According to the Germans themselves, the Russian offensive in Belorussia was the gravest defeat ever inflicted on the Wehrmacht on the Eastern Front. Between twenty-five and twenty-eight German divisions were destroyed, a loss of at least 350,000 men. In the words of the *Official Journal of the OKW* the rout of Army Group *Mitte* (in Belorussia) was "a greater catastrophe than Stalingrad."* This figure of twenty-five divisions or 350,000 men lost occurs in other

* *Kriegstagebuch des OKW*, IV–I, pp. 13–14.

German post-war accounts. Thus, Guderian speaks of the "destruction of Army Groupe *Mitte*" and of "the total loss of some twenty-five divisions." The events, he says, were "so shattering" that "Hitler moved his headquarters in mid-July from Obersalzberg to East Prussia."*

The routing of Army Group *Mitte* in Belorussia had created highly favourable conditions for other Russian army groups to come into action. On July 13 the 1st Ukrainian Front under Konev started its Lwow-Sandomierz operation; in the north, the 3rd Baltic Front liberated Pskov on July 18 and broke into southern Estonia; the 2nd Baltic Front broke into southern Latvia, while the 1st Baltic Front under Bagramian, after capturing Yelgava (Mitau) broke through on July 31 to the Gulf of Riga at Tukkum, thus cutting off the whole of the German Army Group *Nord* in Estonia and Latvia from the rest of the German forces. However, three weeks later, the Germans succeeded in hacking out a twenty-mile corridor south of the Gulf of Riga and thus partly restoring land communication between Army Group *Nord* and western Lithuania and East Prussia.

Although, in Belorussia and eastern Lithuania the Russians had scored one of the greatest victories of the war—and one from which the Germans could never recover—their further progress from about July 25 to the end of August was much slower for a number of obvious reasons: long-drawn-out communications, fatigue among the troops, and the throwing in of heavy German reserves against the Russian attempt to advance both beyond the Niemen into East Prussia, and along the Narew and upper and middle Vistula into central Poland. By the end of August, when most of the operations between Yelgava in Latvia, and Jozefow, a hundred miles south of Warsaw, came to a standstill by order of the Soviet Supreme Command, the front ran about half-way across Lithuania, then a short distance from the eastern border of East Prussia, and then, roughly, along the Narew and Vistula into central Poland.

*

* Guderian, op. cit., p. 336. Philippi and Heim speak of twenty-eight divisions and 350,000 men.

By this time Poland had become the scene of the most dramatic military and political events. On July 23, the left flank of Rokossovsky's 1st Belorussian Front, including the 1st Polish Army, had already liberated the ancient Polish city of Lublin. On July 31, the blunted spearhead of the right flank of the same 1st Belorussian Front reached "the outskirts of Praga" across the Vistula opposite Warsaw; on August 1, the Warsaw Uprising of the *Armija Krajowa* under General Bór-Komarowski began.

Chapter VIII

WHAT HAPPENED AT WARSAW?

It was shortly before the beginning of the Warsaw tragedy that events of far-reaching political importance took place in the Russian- -liberated parts of Poland.

As we have seen, Lublin was liberated by the Russians on July 23, and two days later the Soviet Foreign Office published a statement on the attitude of the Soviet Union to Poland; simultaneously a Manifesto was published, dated July 22 and signed at Chelm (a frontier town inside Poland), announcing the formation of the Polish National Liberation Committee, before long to be known as the "Lublin Committee".

The Russian statement said that the Red Army, together with the Polish Army fighting on the Soviet Front, had begun the liberation of Polish territory. The Soviet troops, it continued, had only one object: to smash the enemy and to help the Polish people re-establish an independent, strong, and democratic Poland. Since Poland was a sovereign state, the Soviet Government had decided not to establish any administration of its own on Polish soil, but had decided to make an agreement with the Polish Committee of National Liberation concerning the relations between the Soviet High Command and the Polish administration. The statement added that the Soviet Government did not wish to acquire any part of Polish territory or to bring about any changes in the social order of Poland, and that the presence of the Red Army in Poland was simply necessitated by military requirements.

The *Rada Narodowa* (the "underground parliament"), in a document dated "Warsaw (*sic*), July 21", issued a decree, which was published in Chelm on the following day, in the first issue of the "official" paper, *Rzeczpospolita*, ordering the formation of the Polish Committee of National Liberation.

The principal members of the Committee were:
President and Chief of the Foreign Affairs Department: E. B. Osóbka-Morawski.
Deputy-President and Head of the Department for Agriculture and Agrarian Reform: Andrzei Witos.
Deputy President: Wanda Wassilewska.
Head of National Defence Department: Col.-Gen. M. Rola-Zymierski.
His Deputy: Lt.-Gen. Berling.

There were fifteen other appointments, among them that of S. Radkiewicz, the notorious head of security, and five whose names were not disclosed, since they were still in German-occupied territory.

The Committee's "Manifesto" stated that it had been nominated by the *Krajowa Rada Narodowa*, "a body comprising representatives of the Peasant Party and other democratic elements inside Poland", and "recognised by Poles abroad—in the first place by the Union of Polish Patriots in the USSR and by the Polish Army formed in the Soviet Union." It denounced the London emigré government as a "usurper" government that had adopted the "fascist" constitution of 1935. The National Committee, on the other hand, recognised the "democratic" constitution of 1921 until the Constituent Assembly met and decided otherwise.

The Manifesto emphasised the new era of Slav unity; it said that the frontiers between Poland and the Soviet Union would be settled on an "ethnical" basis and by mutual agreement, and that, in the west, Poland would regain her old territories in Silesia, along the Oder, and in Pomerania. East Prussia would also be included in Poland. The 400 years of fruitless enmity between the Slav peoples were now at an end, and the Polish and Soviet flags would wave in the wind side by side as the victorious troops marched into Berlin. . .

The Manifesto then enumerated the various items of the reconstruction programme, and stressed the need for a general land reform. On nationalisation it was cautious; it said that the Polish State would take over large enterprises now run by the German State and German capitalists, and, "as economic relations were being regulated, property would be returned to its owners." All this was still exceedingly vague.

The Manifesto said that comradeship-in-arms would strengthen Poland's friendship with Great Britain and the USA, and that Poland would strive to maintain her traditional bonds of friendship and alliance with France.

The personnel of the National Committee was a rather mixed bunch; Dr Drobner—head of the Department for Labour and Health—for instance, was a right-wing Socialist; Witos was (like Mikolajczyk) a veteran leader of the Popular Peasant Party (he was soon to be eliminated); but the key positions were obviously held by men of the PPR (the Communist Party)—to which Bierut, the President of the *Krajowa Rada Narodowa*, at that time also belonged. Osóbka-Morawski was made President of the Committee—not perhaps because he was an outstanding personality, but because he was one of the few Socialists available. This was freely admitted (much later, it is true) by many of the PPR men.

On July 23 a number of decrees were issued by the *Rada Narodowa*—one establishing a High Command of the Polish Army, another placing the Union of Polish Patriots under the authority of the National Committee, and so on.

We now come to one of the most controversial episodes of the war in the East—the tragedy of the Warsaw Rising of August-September 1944. The "London-Polish" version of what happened is too familiar to need recalling in detail. Bór-Komarowski, the leader of the uprising, has told his story of "Russian treachery"; so has Stanislas Mikolajczyk in his *Rape of Poland*,* Mikolajczyk's book in particular, keeps on referring to General Rokossovsky's head-quarters as "only a few miles" outside Warsaw, and to the Red

* See his Chapter VI called "Betrayal".

Army as being "in the suburbs of Warsaw from which it wouldn't budge." The fact that Warsaw and the Red Army were separated by a wide river, the Vistula, is only very incidentally referred to. His implication is that the Vistula was no serious obstacle and that, if they had wanted to, the Russians could easily have captured Warsaw, and so saved the city from destruction, and also saved many of the 300,000 Poles who were to perish in the two-months' fighting-cum-massacre inside the city. If the Russians did not capture Warsaw, it was not, according to Mikolajczyk, because they could not do it, but for purely political reasons: it did not suit them to have the Polish capital "liberated" by a popular rising, directed by Bór-Komarowski and other "agents" of the London Government. Both Bór-Komarowski and Mikolajczyk make the most of the following facts: (1) a Moscow broadcast at the end of July specifically calling on the people of Warsaw to rise against the Germans; (2) the Russian refusal to allow planes from the west that had dropped supplies on Warsaw to land on Russian airfields, and (3) the lack of proper Russian support for the gallant attempt of the Polish troops under General Berling to force the Vistula in the immediate neighbourhood of Warsaw, and the disciplinary action taken against Berling for failing to hold the bridgehead, or rather, for making the attempt at all.

The Churchill-Stalin correspondence during the period of the Warsaw rising is marked by a tone of increasing exasperation on the part of Churchill about the Russians' unco-operative attitude, and by growing anger on the part of Stalin against the Warsaw "adventurers" who had dragged the people of Warsaw into a senseless rebellion without co-ordinating their actions with the Red Army Command.

On August 4 (i.e. three days after the beginning of the rebellion) Churchill wired to Stalin:

> At the urgent request of the Polish underground we are dropping, subject to the weather, about sixty tons (on Warsaw)... They also say they appeal for Russian aid which seems very near. They are being attacked by one and a half German divisions.

On August 5 Stalin replied:

> I think the information given you by the Poles is greatly exaggerated and unreliable... The Polish émigrés claim that they have all but captured Vilno with Home Army units... This has nothing to do with the facts. The Home Army consists of a few detachments misnamed divisions. They have neither guns, aircraft nor tanks. I cannot imagine detachments like these taking Warsaw, which the Germans are defending with four armoured divisions, including the Hermann Goering Division.

On August 8 Stalin reported to Churchill on the meetings that had taken place in Moscow between Mikolajczyk and the "Lublin Poles", but suggested that the meeting had, so far, been fruitless. Nevertheless, on August 10, Churchill thanked Stalin for bringing the two sides together, and also said that Polish airmen from the west had dropped more supplies on Warsaw. "I am so glad to learn you are sending supplies yourself. Anything you feel able to do will be warmly appreciated by your British friends and allies."

But it was not long before Churchill began to suspect foul play on the part of the Russians. He telegraphed to Eden (then in Italy) on the 14th:

> "It certainly is very curious that at the moment the Underground Army has revolted the Russian Armies should have halted their offensive against Warsaw and withdrawn some distance. For them to send machine-guns and ammunition [to Warsaw] would involve only a flight of 100 miles."*

Two days later, according to Churchill, Vyshinsky informed the American Ambassador that the Soviet Government could not object to English and American aircraft dropping arms in the region of Warsaw, but they did object to their landing on Soviet territory, "since the Soviet Government do not wish to associate themselves either directly or indirectly with the adventure of Warsaw."

On August 16, Stalin sent—though in a milder form—a message to the same effect to Churchill.

There was great agitation in London and Washington, and on August 20 Churchill and Roosevelt sent a joint message to Stalin beginning: "We are thinking of world opinion if anti-Nazis in

* Churchill, op. cit., vol. VI, p. 117.

Warsaw are in effect abandoned", and pleading for Big-Three co-operation in the matter.
Stalin replied on August 22:

> Sooner or later the truth about the handful of power-seeking criminals who launched the Warsaw adventure will be out. They... have exposed practically unarmed people to German guns, armour and aircraft... Every day is used, not by the Poles for freeing Warsaw, but by the Hitlerites who are cruelly exterminating the civil population.
> From the military point of view the situation which keeps German attention riveted to Warsaw, is highly unfavourable both to the Red Army and to the Poles. Nevertheless, the Soviet troops, who of late have had to face renewed German counter-attacks, are doing all they can to repulse the Hitlerite sallies and to go over to a new large-scale offensive near Warsaw. I can assure you that the Red Army will spare no effort to crush the Germans at Warsaw and liberate it for the Poles. This will be the best, really effective, help to the anti-Nazi Poles."

Churchill went on speaking in terms of the Russians' "strange and sinister behaviour". He attributed the Russians' unwillingness to let Western planes land behind the Russian lines to the blackest villainy. "They did not mean to let the spirit of Poland arise again in Warsaw. Their plans were based on the Lublin Committee."*

But then, he says, "On September 10, after six weeks of Polish torment, the Kremlin appeared to change their tactics."

> That afternoon shells from the Soviet artillery began to fall upon the eastern suburbs of Warsaw, and Soviet planes appeared again over the city. Polish communist forces, under Soviet orders, fought their way into the fringe of the capital. From September 14 onward the Soviet air force dropped supplies, but few of the parachutes opened and many of the containers were smashed and useless.

And then:

> The following day the Russians occupied the Praga suburb, *but went no further*. They wished to have the non-Communist Poles destroyed to the full, but also to keep alive the idea that they were going to their rescue.†

On October 2, a little over a fortnight later, Bór-Komarowski capitulated to the Germans.

---

* Ibid., p. 24.   † Ibid., p. 127 (emphasis added).

According to the Russian official *History*, in order to understand the situation one has to go back to the directives given by the Soviet Supreme Command to the various fronts on July 28. These directives included the following:

> The 3rd Belorussian Front was ordered to capture Kaunas by August 1 or 2, and then push on to the East Prussian border;
> The 2nd Belorussian Front was also ordered to advance, farther south, via Lomza, towards the East Prussian border;
> The 1st Belorussian Front was ordered, after capturing Brest and Siedlce, to occupy Praga (opposite Warsaw) between August 5 and 8, and to establish a number of bridgeheads south of Warsaw on the western bank of the Vistula.

The right flank of the 1st Belorussian Front indeed clashed with the Germans on July 31 "on the close approaches to Praga, the suburb of Warsaw on the right bank of the Vistula". Meantime, the left flank of the 1st Belorussian Front forced the Vistula south of Warsaw and captured the small bridgeheads of Magnuszew and Pulawa. The capture of these bridgeheads was followed by frantic German attacks on them; though the Russians were not to be dislodged, they were not strong enough to enlarge them.

Something obviously went seriously wrong with the Russian military plans at the end of July and beginning of August. Under the dateline "Outside Warsaw, August 1" (the day the Warsaw Rising began), Makarenko wrote in *Pravda* of August 2:

> On to Warsaw! In an offensive there is a moment when the military operation reaches its culminating point and, having acquired its necessary pressure and impetus, goes ahead without any doubt as to what will happen next. At such a time when the full strength of the offensive comes into motion, it starts advancing in great strides, and then no power can stop its victorious forward march.

Whatever exactly this verbiage was supposed to mean, every reader must have interpreted it as signifying that the Red Army would be inside Warsaw within a few days. On August 3, the Soviet papers published a map showing the front running a few miles from the Vistula, just east of Praga, though on a very narrow salient. The talk in Moscow was that Rokossovsky was going to capture Warsaw on August 9 or 10. And then something went wrong: apparently that *coup de main*, of which Guderian was to speak, had not come off. The news from Warsaw grew more tragic every day. Then, for nearly a fortnight there was a news blackout in Russia as far as the Warsaw sector was concerned, and it was not till August 16 that an ominous communiqué was published saying that "east of Praga our troops have been repelling the enemy's large-scale attacks, and have abandoned Ossow." Ossow was only a short distance from Praga, and there was no real indication how far the Russians had been pushed back.

After denouncing the decision taken by the AK command, with the blessing of the Polish Government in London, to start the Warsaw uprising on August 1 as an anti-Soviet "political operation", and after describing the wholly inadequate quantities of arms available inside Warsaw, the Soviet *History* goes on to say:

> The very first day proved highly unfavourable to the insurgents... They failed to capture the strategic points in the city, the railway stations or the Vistula bridges... As a result, the Germans were able to bring up heavy reinforcements. The commanders of some of the AK detachments, discouraged by all this, dissolved them or took them out of Warsaw. Yet, despite these unfavourable conditions, the struggle continued, and greatly grew in vigour when the population of Warsaw joined in... Rank and file members of the AK, unaware of the political schemes of their leaders, fought bravely against the Nazis... However, the forces were too unequal... In the second half of August the situation became truly tragic, with the Germans carrying out Hitler's orders to wipe Warsaw off the face of the earth.*

The explanation now given is that although "in principle" (as could be seen from Stalin's letter to Churchill of August 16), the Soviet Government did not wish to be associated with the Warsaw Rising (on which it had not even been consulted), it nevertheless "did all it could" because many thousands of Warsaw patriots had joined in the struggle.

* IVOVSS, vol. IV, p. 243.

In reply to the Western charge that the "Soviet Command had deliberately stopped its troops at the gates of Warsaw and so condemned the insurgents to death", the *History** says:

> People who say this have never taken the trouble to study the possibilities of the Red Army at the time of the Warsaw Rising. Here are the real facts:
>
> In the second half of July the troops of the 1st Belorussian [Rokossovsky] and of the 2nd Ukrainian [Konev] Front entered Polish territory and began to advance towards the Vistula... At the end of July, even before the beginning of the Warsaw Rising, the tempo of the offensive had greatly slowed down. The German High Command had by this time thrown very strong reserves against the main sectors of our advance. German resistance was strong and stubborn. It should also be considered that our rifle divisions and tank corps had suffered heavy losses in previous battles; that the artillery and the supply bases were lagging behind, and that the troops were short of both petrol and munitions.
>
> Infantry and tanks were not receiving nearly enough artillery support. During the delays in re-basing our air force on new airfields, this was much less active than before. At the beginning of the Belorussian Campaign, we had complete control of the air. At the beginning of August our superiority was temporarily lost. In the 1st Belorussian sector between August 1 and 13 our planes carried out 3,170 sorties and the enemy planes 3,316.
>
> Consequently, after a long forty-day offensive, with enemy resistance much stronger than it was, our troops could not maintain the high tempo of our advance, and give immediate help to the Warsaw rising. This was quite obvious to the German command. Thus General Tippelskirch writes: "*The Warsaw Rising started on August 1, at a time when the strength of the Russian blow had exhausted itself.*" The task was rendered all the more difficult as we were faced with the problem of forcing the Vistula.

And then:

> On August 1, troops of the left flank of the 1st Belorussian Front approached Warsaw from the south-east. In approaching Praga, the 2nd Tank Army met with fierce enemy resistance; the approaches to Praga had been heavily fortified... It was also here that *the Germans*

* IVOVSS, vol. IV, pp. 244 ff (emphasis added).

concentrated a heavy striking force of one infantry and four Panzer divisions, which struck out at the beginning of August and drove the 2nd Tank Army away from Praga, before the bulk of our troops had had time to approach this Warsaw suburb.

The very difficult position in which the 2nd Tank Army found itself at Praga may be measured by its losses.

In its battles fought on Polish territory—at Lublin, Deblin, Pulawa and the approaches of Warsaw—it had lost about 500 tanks and mobile guns. Under the weight of the German offensive it had to retreat from Praga, take up the defensive and repel the German attacks...

There followed weeks of confused fighting both north and south of Warsaw on the eastern bank of the Vistula and also on the three bridgeheads the Russians had captured on the western bank—at Magnuszew, Pulawa and Sandomierz—all a considerable distance from Warsaw. Everywhere the Germans were now throwing in heavy forces.

It is not clear from this *how far* away from Praga the Russians were thrown back, but they were certainly a considerable distance to the east of Praga by the middle of August, when Churchill was desperate to get Western planes to land behind the Russian lines.

Here I can supplement the *History* with what General Rokossovsky, commander of the 1st Belorussian Front, told me at Lublin on August 26, 1944.

My informal and off-the-record conversation with Rokossovsky (after a great ceremony in the main square for the unveiling of a cenotaph to those who had fallen in the Battle of Lublin) was a brief but significant one. Here is what he said:

"I can't go into any details. But I'll tell you just this. After several weeks' heavy fighting in Belorussia and eastern Poland we finally reached the outskirts of Praga about the 1st of August. The Germans, at this point, threw in four armoured divisions, and we were driven back."

"How far back?"

"I can't tell you exactly, but let's say nearly 100 kilometres (sixty-five miles)."

"Are you still retreating?"

"No—we are now advancing—but slowly."

"Did you think on August 1 (as was suggested by the *Pravda* correspondent that day) that you could take Warsaw within a very few days?"

"If the Germans had not thrown in all that armour, we could have taken Warsaw, though not in a frontal attack; but it was never more than a 50–50 chance. A German counter-attack at Praga was not to be excluded, though we now know that before these armoured divisions arrived, the Germans inside Warsaw were in a panic, and were packing up in a great hurry."

"Wasn't the Warsaw Rising justified in the circumstances?"

"No, it was a bad mistake. The insurgents started it off their own bat, without consulting us."

"There was that broadcast from Moscow calling on them to rise."

"That was routine stuff. [sic.] There were similar calls to rise from *Swit* radio [the AK radio], and also from the Polish service of the BBC—so I'm told, though I didn't hear it myself. Let's be serious. An armed insurrection in a place like Warsaw could only have succeeded if it had been carefully co-ordinated with the Red Army. The question of timing was of the utmost importance. The Warsaw insurgents are badly armed, and the rising would have made sense only if we were already on the point of *entering Warsaw*. That point *had not been reached at any stage,* and I'll admit that some Soviet correspondents were much too optimistic on the 1st of August. We were pushed back. We couldn't have got Warsaw before the middle of August, even in the best of circumstances. But circumstances were not good, but bad. Such things do happen in war. It happened at Kharkov in March 1943 and at Zhitomir last winter."

"What prospect is there of your getting back to Praga within the next few weeks?"

"I can't go into that. All I can say is that we shall try to capture both Praga and Warsaw, but it won't be easy."

"But you have bridgeheads south of Warsaw."

"Yes, but the Germans are doing their damnedest to reduce them. We're having much difficulty in holding them, and we are losing a lot of men. Mind you, we have fought non-stop for over two months now. We've liberated the whole of Belorussia and nearly one fourth of Poland; but, even the Red Army gets tired after a while. Our casualties have been very heavy."

"Can't you help the Warsaw insurgents from the air?"

"We are trying; though, to tell you the truth, it isn't much good. They are holding only isolated spots in Warsaw, and most of the stuff will fall into German hands."

"Why can't you let British and American planes land behind the Russian lines, after dropping their supplies on Warsaw? There's been an awful stink in England and America about your refusal. . ."

"The military situation east of the Vistula is much more complicated than you realise. And we just don't want any British and American planes mucking around here just at the moment.* I think in a couple of weeks, we'll be able to supply Warsaw ourselves from low-flying planes if the insurgents hold any recognisable area in the city. But this high altitude dropping of supplies on Warsaw by Western planes serves practically no purpose at all."

"Isn't all this massacre and destruction in Warsaw having a terribly depressing effect on the Polish people here?"

"Of course, it has. But a fearful mistake was made by the AK leadership. *We* (the Red Army) are responsible for the conduct of the war in Poland, *we* are the force that will liberate the whole of Poland within the next few months, and Bór-Komarowski and the people around him have butted in *kak ryzhy v tsirke*—like the clown in the circus who pops up at the wrong moment and only gets rolled up in the carpet. . . If it were only a piece of clowning it wouldn't matter, but the political stunt is going to cost Poland hundreds of thousands of lives. It is an appalling tragedy, and they are now trying to put the blame on us. It makes me pretty sick when I think of the many thousands of men we have already lost in our fight for the liberation of Poland. And do you think," he concluded, "that we would not have taken Warsaw if we had been able to do it? The whole idea that we are in any sense afraid of the AK is too idiotically absurd."

*

* This may or may not be the true explanation, but it tallies with the usual Russian cageyness at times of reverses.

There were two strange and, in some ways, pathetic figures at a press conference given by General Rola-Zymierski, the "Minister" of Defence of the Lublin Committee, later that day: two AK officers, Colonel Rawicz and Colonel Tarnawa, who said they had left Warsaw on July 29 on the initiative of "a strong minority" of AK officers inside Warsaw to establish contact with Mikolajczyk (who was then in Moscow), in a last-minute endeavour to persuade the London Government to use all its influence to call off the rising that was being prepared for August 1—for, on July 25, they had already received orders from General Bór-Komarowski to prepare and stand by. They claimed that it was clear that the insurgents could not possibly hold Warsaw unless they struck out at the very last moment, with the Russians practically inside the city. Unfortunately, it had taken the two colonels nearly a fortnight to reach Lublin, and it was then too late.

Colonel Rawicz, a smart, dapper little man in a new uniform, but with a look of grief and bewilderment in his eyes, said that headquarters had given the order for a rising as soon as the Russians were twenty miles away from Warsaw; he and many other officers felt it would be folly to do it until the Russians had reached the Vistula bridges.

"We did not think," he said, "that the Russians could enter Warsaw before August 15. But the man-in-the-street (and you know how brave and romantic our Warsaw people are) was convinced the Russians would be there by August 2; and with tremendous enthusiasm they joined in. . ."

Rawicz was in a state of great emotion as he spoke about Warsaw and its destruction and there were tears in his eyes as he mentioned his wife and daughter, who were "still there", in that burning inferno. He reckoned that 200,000 people had already been slaughtered.

It was all tragic, and a little mystifying. Had these two men really acted in good faith (I felt that they had) in their attempt to avert the disaster? Were they, as London was later to call them, deserters from the AK cause?

*

According to the *History*:

> At the beginning of September, with the Germans having now
> turned their main attention to our bridgeheads on the west side of the
> Vistula, we were able to concentrate sufficiently large forces which ...
> finally captured Praga on September 14. Thus, there was a consider-
> able improvement in the Warsaw sector of the front, and there was
> now a good prospect of giving direct support to the Warsaw Rising.
> This was the task with which the 1st Polish Army [under General
> Berling] was entrusted. On September 15 it entered Praga, and began
> to prepare the forcing of the Vistula and the establishment of bridge-
> heads in Warsaw itself.

After describing this operation, carried out with the help of
amphibious vehicles, and supported by Russian artillery and aircraft, the *History* then goes on to say that between September 16
and 19, six battalions crossed the Vistula, that the Polish soldiers
and officers fought heroically, but that they were helpless against
the very heavy fortifications from which the Germans were able to
prevent any extension of the bridgehead. Moreover, the insurgents
failed to co-ordinate their actions with the Polish forces on the
bridgehead. On September 21 German tanks and infantry attacked
in strength, splitting up the bridgehead and inflicting very heavy
casualties on the Poles. On September 23 the Poles had to evacuate
the bridgeheads and return to the east bank of the Vistula, suffering
very heavy losses.

Such is the present Russian version of the abortive "Berling
operation" undertaken (according to the "London" Poles) on
Berling's own initiative and without Russian support. After its
failure, Berling was recalled to Moscow "for further training".

Quoting Soviet Ministry of Defence archives, the *History* then
gives a long and impressive list of arms, food and other material
dropped on Warsaw by the Soviet air force between September 14
and October 1, the eve of Bór-Komarowski's capitulation. There
were altogether over 2,000 Soviet sorties over Warsaw.

The *History* also dwells on the very heavy Russian casualties in
the fighting in Poland during that period. Thus, between August 1
and September 15 the 1st Belorussian Front lost 166,000 men (killed

and wounded) and the 2nd Ukrainian Front (in August only) 122,000 men.

Finally, when the position in Warsaw had become completely hopeless, says the *History*, the Red Army command proposed to the Warsaw insurgents, to fight their way across the Vistula under Russian artillery and aircraft protection; but only a small number of Warsaw fighters took advantage of this offer.

In conclusion, the *History* quotes Gomulka's merciless indictment of the AK leadership in Warsaw who "committed a fearful crime against the Polish people by launching the insurrection without previous co-ordination with the Red Army command."

Such is the present-day Russian—and Gomulka—version of the Warsaw tragedy. It evades the awkward questions of the Moscow radio appeals at the end of July to the people of Warsaw to "rise" (though it criticises the *Swit* broadcasts)* and the Russians' refusal to let supply planes from the West land on Soviet airfields.

But the really crucial question is whether the Russians *could* have forced the Vistula at Warsaw in either August or September; and on this the Russian evidence to the contrary seems impressive, reinforced as it is by the opinion of General Guderian who wrote:

> It may be assumed that the Soviet Union had no interest in seeing these (pro-London) elements strengthened by a successful uprising and by the capture of their capital... But be that as it may, an attempt by the Russians... to cross the Vistula at Deblin on July 25 failed, with the loss of thirty tanks... We Germans had the impression that *it was our defence which halted the enemy rather than a Russian desire to sabotage the Warsaw uprising.*

And then:

> On August 2 the 1st Polish Army... attacked across the Vistula with three divisions in the Pulawa-Deblin sector. It suffered heavy casualties, but secured a bridgehead... At Magnuszew a second bridgehead was established. The forces that crossed here were *ordered to advance along the road running parallel to the Vistula to Warsaw, but they were stopped at the Pilica.*

* The *Swit* broadcasts were those of the "pro-London" Poles.

Guderian clearly believes that there was a serious Russian attempt to capture Warsaw in the first week of August. He then goes on:

> The German 9th Army had the impression, on August 8, *that the Russian attempt to seize Warsaw by a* coup de main *had been defeated by our defence, despite the Polish uprising, and that the latter had, from the enemy's point of view, been begun too soon.**

This is an important piece of evidence, which tallies, to an extraordinary degree, both with what was said in Moscow at the very beginning of August when the capture of Warsaw by the Red Army was expected "at any moment", and with what was being said in Lublin at the end of August, at the height of the Warsaw tragedy.

The only conclusion this author, at any rate, has been able to reach is that in August and September 1944 the available Red Army forces in Poland were genuinely not able to capture Warsaw which Hitler was determined to hold. For Warsaw was on the Russians' shortest road to the heart of Germany.

It might, of course, be argued that if the Russians had wanted to capture Warsaw *at any price*, that is, by transferring whole armies to the Vistula from other fronts at short notice (not an easy task), they might conceivably have captured it. But this would have upset their other military plans like steadily advancing on East Prussia, routing the Germans in Rumania, joining with the Yugoslavs and breaking into Bulgaria and Hungary.

There is no question but that the Warsaw rising was a last desperate attempt to free Poland's capital from the retreating Nazis and at the same time to prevent the Lublin administration from gaining a foothold and establishing itself in Warsaw once the victorious Soviet army had entered the city.

Once more in Poland's history this valiant struggle for independence was defeated by the overriding, although conflicting, great-Power interests of other states. Still, with Moscow determined, ever since the beginning of the war and especially since April 1943, to control the future destinies of Poland, Bór-Komarowski would have been eliminated one way or another by the

---

* Guderian, op. cit., pp. 358–9. (emphasis added.)

Russians, as they managed a few years later to rid themselves of Mikolajczyk.

The story of the end of the Warsaw tragedy, and of German bestiality under the leadership of the notorious SS Obergruppen-führer von dem Bach-Zelewsky, assisted by equally notorious murder gangs like the Kaminsky Brigade, is well known, as is also Hitler's maniacal order of October 11 to "raze Warsaw to the ground".

300,000 Poles lost their lives in Warsaw. When the Russians finally entered Warsaw in January 1945, more than nine-tenths of the city had been almost as completely destroyed as had been the Warsaw Ghetto in 1943.

Chapter IX

CLOSE-UP: LUBLIN—
THE MAIDANEK MURDER CAMP

It was a beautiful sunny day as we flew at the end of August 1944 from Moscow to Lublin over those hundreds of miles of Belorussian fields, marshes and forests that had been recaptured by the Red Army in the great battles of June and July. Belorussia looked more wretched and ruined than any part of the Soviet Union, apart from that terrible "desert" that stretched all the way from Viazma and Gzhatsk to Smolensk. There were scarcely any cattle to be seen outside the villages, most of which had suffered partial or complete destruction. This was mostly partisan country and, flying over Belorussia one realised once more how dangerous and precarious their life had been. Contrary to what is often believed, there are no immense forests in Belorussia stretching over hundreds of miles; there are mostly only patches of forest seldom more than five or ten miles wide. Even many of these patches were yellow—set on fire by the Germans, to smoke the Partisans out. A ferocious life-and-death struggle had gone on here for two years or more; one could tell that even from the air.

Then we flew over Minsk, and it all seemed a shambles, except for the enormous grey Government Building. Minsk had also had its torture-chambers at the Gestapo headquarters, and its mass graves of slaughtered Jews. It was hard to grasp that, only three years before, it had been a prosperous industrial city.

We flew on to Lublin, into Poland. The rural scene here looked very different. Outwardly at least, the country looked almost un-

884

scathed by war. The Polish villages looked intact, with their white-washed houses and their well-kept and prosperous-looking Catholic churches. The front was not very far away from here, and we were flying low; children waved as we roared past; and in the fields there were many more cattle than in any part of the Soviet Union where the Germans had been; and most of the land was cultivated. We landed a good distance outside Lublin, and the villages through which we then drove along a terribly dusty road looked much the same as from the air—all fairly normal-looking, with a large number of cattle about, and the landscape dotted with haystacks. . .

I was to stay several days in Lublin. The streets were crowded, which they seldom were in any newly-liberated Russian town; there was also great activity in the market place. Everywhere there were many Russian and Polish soldiers. Before leaving, the Germans had shot 100 Polish prisoners in the old Castle; but apart from a few burned-out buildings, the city was more or less intact, complete with the Castle, the Radziwill Palace and the numerous churches.

Yet this first impression of normality was a little deceptive. The German occupation—which had now lasted five years—had left a deep mark on the people of Lublin, and the arrival of the Russians here had not set their minds at rest; far from it. And, for over two years now, Lublin had, as it were, lived in the shadow of Maidanek, the great extermination camp only two miles away. When the wind blew from the east it brought with it the stench of burning human flesh from the crematoria chimneys.

At dinner on the night of our arrival with some of the local worthies and some of the "Lublin Poles"—among them Colonel Wiktor Grosz whom I had already met in Moscow*—I sat next to

---

* A few months before, Grosz, as one of the leading lights of the Union of Polish Patriots, had tried to go to London to present to the British Government the "Moscow Poles'" point of view, but had been refused a visa. Grosz was a brilliant writer, and spoke excellent English. He was to become one of the chief foreign policy advisers of the "Lublin Committee" and was later to play a leading rôle at the Polish foreign ministry in Warsaw until his premature death only a few years later.

Professor Bielkowski, who had, before the war, been Assistant
Rector of Lublin University; he was one of the few Polish intellectuals who had survived the German occupation. Lublin
University, he said, was closed by the Germans, and the Library
looted; but he was given a wretched job in the Archives where he
was expected to dig up books and documents to show that this part
of Poland was *urdeutscher Boden* (ancestral German territory).
"The whole thing was a mockery," he said, but would not go into
any details on how the "research work" was conducted, or on what
results it had produced. He had obviously collaborated in a small
way to save his life. And he was ready to admit that he was one of
the few Polish intellectuals to have escaped.

"The Germans' policy," he said, "was to exterminate the Polish
intelligentsia; and now that they are going to be thrown out of
Poland before long, they want to make sure that our power of
national recuperation is reduced to zero, if possible. In the last few
days I have learned that the Germans have murdered dozens more
of our professors—in addition to the thousands and thousands of
our intellectuals who have already perished in their concentration
camps." He gave a long list of names. "They wanted Poland to be
an inert mass of peasants and labourers, without leadership and
without any kind of national prestige."

"And the clergy?" I asked.

"Yes, I'll grant you, the Church has done its best to maintain a
sense of national cohesion and consciousness in Poland; but there
are going to be complications now: most of the priests are pro-AK
and anti-Russian."

"How are things here in Lublin?"

"You'll no doubt see Maidanek tomorrow; that's one aspect of
Lublin. For the rest—well, things are taking shape, but slowly. There
is a lot of worry and uncertainty. People are obsessed with the idea
of Warsaw burning and its people being butchered by the Germans."

"What's the feeling among the Polish people about the Russians?"

"Quite good," he said, "yes, quite good. Of course, I may be
more pro-Russian than most Poles. I studied in St Petersburg; I like
Russian people, and admire their great civilisation. But it's no use
denying it: there's a terribly old tradition of mutual distrust between

Poles and Russians. Now, for the first time, I think, a real attempt is being made by the Russians to come to a lasting understanding with the Poles. But we Poles have been kicked around so much that the idea of a Russo-Polish bloc takes time to sink in. And now there are plenty of poisonous stories going around about Warsaw. Quite unjustified, I think. I have talked to many Russian officers; they are very fed-up at having so far failed to take Warsaw... And there are other things, too. Our people want Vilno and Lwow to be included in Poland. I know we can't have Vilno, which has been promised to the Lithuanians, but the Russians are being sticky even about Lwow..."*

He then talked about Maidanek, where over one-and-a-half million people had been murdered in the last two years—many Poles amongst them, and people of all kinds of nationalities, but, above all, Jews.

"What," I asked, "has been the attitude of the Polish people to the massacre of the millions of Jews?"

"This is a very tricky subject; let's face it," said the Professor. "Owing to a number of historical processes, such as the Tsarist government's Jewish policy of confining most of the Jews in the Russian Empire to Poland, we have had far too many Jews here. Our retail trade was entirely in Jewish hands. They also played an unduly large part in other walks of life. There's no doubt that the Polish people wanted the number of Jews in Poland reduced. They wanted part of them to emigrate to America, to Palestine, or perhaps to Madagascar; there was such a scheme before the war. But that was one thing," he added a little glibly. "What the Germans did is quite another thing; and this, I can tell you, genuinely revolted every one of our people..."

During the next few days I spent several hours in the streets of Lublin talking to all kinds of people. Despite some bomb damage here and there, the city had preserved some of its old-time charm. On Sunday, all the churches—and there were said to be more

* Incorporated into the Soviet Union at the partition in 1940 and kept by her after the war.

churches per square mile in Lublin than in any other Polish city—
were crowded. Among the faithful, kneeling and praying, there were
many Polish soldiers. People were rather better dressed than in
Russia, though many looked distinctly worn out and undernourished,
and under great nervous strain. The shops were almost empty,
though there was a good deal of food in the market place. But the
food was dear, and there was much animosity against the peasants
who were described as "a lot of bloodsuckers"; there were also many
stories of how the peasants "crawled" to the Germans; a German
soldier only had to appear in a Polish village, and the peasants were
so scared they'd bring out roast chickens, and butter and eggs and
sour cream... On the other hand, the Russian soldiers had been
given strict orders to pay for everything and the peasants were not
keen at all to give anything away for roubles.* People—many of
them very humble-looking working people, talked freely about the
German occupation; many had lost friends and relatives at
Maidanek; many more had had members of their families deported
as slave labour to Germany; they also talked about that terrible first
winter of 1939–40, when there was a regular trade in children: whole
trainloads of children—whose parents had been killed or arrested—
children from Poznan and other places taken over by the Germans
would arrive in Lublin, and a child—often starved and half-dead—
could be bought for thirty zloty from German soldiers. They talked
of people who were publicly hanged in the main square of Lublin
and of the torture chambers of the Lublin Gestapo. "Anyone," said
an elderly woman looking like a schoolmistress, "could be taken
there: if a German thought, as he passed you in the street, that you
had given him a dirty look, that was enough. To kill a human being
—it was as easy as stepping on a worm and squashing it." During
the German occupation, most people in Lublin had gone hungry,
and the peasants had not been helpful; and now there was no certainty that things were going to be much better. Still, to many it had
been a pleasant surprise to see real Polish soldiers in Polish uniforms
arrive here from Russia; the Germans had always denied that there

* This polite Russian behaviour was to change in time; but at first
the Russians behaved in a very disciplined and "correct" way to the
Polish peasants.

was a Polish Army in Russia. On the other hand, there were—
especially among the better-dressed people—grave misgivings about
the Russians, and strong AK sympathies; and there was also much
talk of 2,000 AK men having been arrested by the Russians in the
Lublin area alone. Many questions were, of course, also asked about
the Polish troops in Italy and France, and, on many Poles, the
arrival of British and American correspondents in Lublin made a
particularly strong impression: dozens of people, with a suggestive
look in their eyes, would give us flowers. One young man, I remember, took me aside and drew my attention to a large inscription
painted on a wall; it said "MONTE CASSINO". "Monte Cassino,"
he said, "that's a Polish victory won on the *other* side, and we are
particularly proud of it... It was *our* people who painted the
inscription." "*Your* people?" I said, "You mean the *Armija
Krajowa?*" He nodded. "The war seems to be going well," he said,
"but you realise there are many *buts*, many, many *buts*... There's
Warsaw, and we don't trust these Lublin Committee people... Well,
you know what I mean... And 2,000 arrests." He was a pink-
cheeked young man of about twenty-three with carefully-plastered
hair which, however, strangely contrasted with his shabby clothes;
he had worked as an accountant under the Germans, but was also
active in the Polish "London" underground. Now, he said, he was
going to be mobilised into the Polish Army. "Seems reasonable
enough, I suppose," he said, "to be mobilised to fight the Germans,
though I can't say I am particularly delighted to fight under Russian
orders..."

Since the end of the war, there have been numerous accounts of
various German Extermination Camps—Buchenwald, Auschwitz,
Belsen and others—but the story of Maidanek has not perhaps been
fully told to Western readers; moreover, Maidanek holds a very
special place in the Soviet-German war.

As they advanced, the Russians had been learning more and more
of German atrocities and the enormous number of killings. But,
somehow, all this killing was spread over relatively wide areas, and
though it added up to far, far more than Maidanek, it did not have

the vast monumental, "industrial" quality of that unbelievable Death Factory two miles from Lublin.

"Unbelievable" it was: when I sent the BBC a detailed report on Maidanek in August 1944, they refused to use it; they thought it was a Russian propaganda stunt, and it was not till the discovery in the west of Buchenwald, Dachau and Belsen that they were convinced that Maidanek and Auschwitz were also genuine...

The Russians discovered Maidanek on July 23, the very day they entered Lublin. About a week later Simonov described it all in *Pravda*; but most of the Western press ignored his account. But in Russia the effect was devastating. Everybody had heard of Babyi Yar and thousands of other German atrocities; but this was something even more staggering. It brought into sharper focus than anything else had done the real nature, scope and consequences of the Nazi régime in action. For here was a vast industrial undertaking in which thousands of "ordinary" Germans had made it a full-time job to murder millions of other people in a sort of mass orgy of professional sadism, or, worse still, with the business-like conviction that *this was a job like any other*. The effect of Maidanek was to be enormous, not least in the Red Army. Thousands of Russian soldiers were made to visit it.

My first reaction to Maidanek was a feeling of surprise. I had imagined something horrible and sinister beyond words. It was nothing like that. It looked singularly harmless from outside. "Is *that* it?" was my first reaction when we stopped at what looked like a large workers' settlement. Behind us was the many towered skyline of Lublin. There was much dust on the road, and the grass was a dull, greenish-grey colour. The camp was separated from the road by a couple of barbed-wire fences, but these did not look particularly sinister, and might have been put up outside any military or semi-military establishment. The place was large; like a whole town of barracks painted a pleasant soft green. There were many people around—soldiers and civilians. A Polish sentry opened the barbed-wire gate to let our cars enter the central avenue, with large green barracks on either side. And then we stopped outside a large barrack marked *Bad und Desinfektion II*. "This," somebody said, "is where large numbers of those arriving at the camp were brought in."

The inside of this barrack was made of concrete, and water taps came out of the wall, and around the room there were benches where the clothes were put down and *afterwards* collected. So this was the place into which they were driven. Or perhaps they were politely invited to "Step this way, please?" Did any of them suspect, while washing themselves after a long journey, what would happen a few minutes later? Anyway, after the washing was over, they were asked to go into the next room; at this point even the most unsuspecting must have begun to wonder. For the "next room" was a series of large square concrete structures, each about one-quarter of the size of the bath-house, and, unlike it, had no windows. The naked people (men one time, women another time, children the next) were driven or forced from the bath-house into these dark concrete boxes—about five yards square—and then, with 200 or 250 people packed into each box—and it was completely dark there, except for a small skylight in the ceiling and the spyhole in the door—the process of gassing began. First some hot air was pumped in from the ceiling and then the pretty pale-blue crystals of Cyclon were showered down on the people, and in the hot wet air they rapidly evaporated. In anything from two to ten minutes everybody was dead. . . There were six concrete boxes—gas-chambers—side by side. "Nearly two thousand people could be disposed of here simultaneously," one of the guides said.

But what thoughts passed through these people's minds during those first few minutes while the crystals were falling; could anyone still believe that this humiliating process of being packed into a box and standing there naked, rubbing backs with other naked people, had anything to do with disinfection?

At first it was all very hard to take in, without an effort of the imagination. There were a number of very dull-looking concrete structures which, if their doors had been wider, might anywhere else have been mistaken for a row of nice little garages. But the doors— the doors! They were heavy steel doors, and each had a heavy steel bolt. And in the middle of the door was a spyhole, a circle, three inches in diameter composed of about a hundred small holes. Could

the people in their death agony see the SS-man's eye as he watched
them? Anyway, the SS-man had nothing to fear: his eye was well-
protected by the steel netting over the spyhole. And, like the proud
maker of reliable safes, the maker of the door had put his name
round the spyhole: "Auert, Berlin". Then a touch of blue on the
floor caught my eye. It was very faint, but still legible. In blue chalk
someone had scribbled the word *"vergast"* and had drawn crudely
above it a skull and crossbones. I had never seen this word before,
but it obviously meant "gassed"—and not merely "gassed" but,
with that eloquent little prefix *ver,* "gassed out". That's this job
finished, and now for the next lot. The blue chalk came into motion
when there was nothing but a heap of naked corpses inside. But
what cries, what curses, what prayers perhaps, had been uttered
inside that gas chamber only a few minutes before? Yet the concrete
walls were thick, and Herr Auert had done a wonderful job, so
probably no one could hear anything from outside. And even if they
did, the people in the camp knew what it was all about.

It was here, outside *Bad und Desinfektion II,* in the side-lane
leading into the central avenue, that the corpses were loaded into
lorries, covered with tarpaulins, and carted to the crematorium at
the other end of the camp, about half-a-mile away. Between the two
there were dozens of barracks, painted the same soft green. Some
had notice-boards outside, others had not. Thus, there was an *Effek-
ten Kammer* and a *Frauen-Bekleidungskammer;* here the victims'
luggage and the women's clothes were sorted out, before they were
sent to the central Lublin warehouse, and then on to Germany.

At the other end of the camp, there were enormous mounds of white
ashes; but as you looked closer, you found that they were not perfect
ashes: for they had among them masses of small human bones: collar
bones, finger bones, and bits of skull, and even a small femur, which
can only have been that of a child. And, beyond these mounds there
was a sloping plain, on which there grew acres and acres of cabbages. They were large luxuriant cabbages, covered with a layer of
white dust. As I heard somebody explaining: "Layer of manure,
then layer of ashes, that's the way it was done... These cabbages

are all grown on human ashes... The SS-men used to cart most of the ashes to their model farm, some distance away. A well-run farm; the SS-men liked to eat these overgrown cabbages, and the prisoners ate these cabbages, too, although they knew that they would almost certainly be turned into cabbages themselves before long..."

Next we came to the crematorium. It was a great big structure of six enormous furnaces and above them rose a large factory chimney. The wooden structure that used to cover the crematorium, as well as the adjoining wooden house, where *Obersturmbannführer* Mussfeld, the "Director of the Crematorium" used to live, had been burned down. Mussfeld had lived there among the stench of burned and burning bodies, and took a personal interest in the proceedings. But the furnaces stood there, large, enormous. There were still piles of coke on the one side; on the other side were the furnace doors where the corpses went in... The place stank, not violently, but it stank of decomposition. I looked down. My shoes were white with human dust, and the concrete floor around the ovens was strewn with parts of charred human skeletons. Here was a whole chest with its ribs, here a piece of skull, here a lower jaw with a molar on either side, and nothing but sockets in between. Where had the false teeth gone? To the side of the furnaces was a large high concrete slab, shaped like an operating table. Here a specialist—a medical man perhaps?—examined every corpse before it went into the oven, and extracted any gold fillings, which were then sent to Dr Walter Funk at the Reichsbank...

Somebody was explaining the details of the whole mechanism; the furnaces were made of fibreproof brick, and the temperature had always to be maintained at 1,700° centigrade; and there was an engineer called Tellener who was an expert in charge of maintaining the right temperature. But the corroded condition of some of the doors showed that the temperature had been increased above normal to make the corpses burn more quickly. The normal capacity of the whole installation was 2,000 corpses a day, but sometimes there were more corpses than that to deal with, and there were some special days, like the great Jew-extermination day of November 3, 1943, when 20,000 people—men, women and children—were killed; it was impossible to gas them all that day; so most of them had been shot and buried in a wood some distance away. On other occasions many corpses were burned outside the crematorium on enormous funeral pyres soaked in petrol; these pyres would smoulder for weeks and fill the air with a stench. . .

Standing in front of the great crematorium, with human remains scattered on the ground, one began to listen to all these details with a kind of dull indifference. The "industrial report" was becoming unreal in its enormity. . .

Besides the charred remains of Mussfeld's house, there lay piles of large black cans, like enormous cocktail shakers, marked "Buchenwald". They were urns and had been brought from that other concentration camp. People from Lublin who had lost a relative at Maidanek, somebody said, would pay substantial sums to the SS-men for the victim's remains. It was another loathsome SS racket. Needless to say, the ashes with which the cocktail shakers were filled were nobody's ashes in particular.

Some distance away from the crematorium, a trench twenty or thirty yards long had been re-opened and, looking down through the fearful stench, I could see hundreds of naked corpses, many with bullet-holes at the back of their skulls. Most of them were men with shaved heads; it was said that these had been Russian war prisoners.

I had seen enough, and hastened to join Colonel Grosz, who was waiting beside the car on the road. The stench was still pursuing me; it now seemed to permeate everything—the dusty grass beside the barbed wire fence, and the red poppies that were naïvely growing in the midst of all this.

Grosz and I waited there for the rest of the party to join us. A Polish youngster with tattered clothes and a torn cap, and barefooted, came up and talked to us. He was about eleven, but talked of the camp with a curious nonchalance, with that *nil admirari* that had become his outlook on life after living for two or three years in the immediate proximity of the Death Camp. . . This boy had seen everything, at the ages of nine, and ten and eleven.

"A lot of people in Lublin," he said, "lost somebody here. In our village people were very worried, because we knew what was going on in the camp, and the Germans threatened to destroy the village and kill everybody in case we talked too much. Don't know why they should have bothered," the boy said with a shrug, "everybody in Lublin knew anyway." And he recounted a few things he had seen; he had seen ten prisoners being beaten to death; he had seen files of prisoners carrying stones, and had seen those who collapsed being killed with pickaxes by the SS-men. He had heard an old man screaming while he was being chewed up by police dogs... And, looking across the fields of cabbages growing on human ashes, he said, almost with a touch of admiration: "Everything is growing well here—cabbages, and turnips and cauliflowers... It's all land belonging to our village, and now that the SS are gone, we'll get the land back."

There was much coming and going on the road—hundreds of men and women were going into and out of the camp; Russian soldiers were being taken in large parties to be shown the pits and the gas chambers and the crematoria; and Polish soldiers of the 4th Division and new Polish recruits. It was policy to make them see it all, and to impress upon them—in case they were not yet sufficiently impressed—what kind of enemy they were fighting. A few days before a crowd of German prisoners had been taken through the camp. Around stood crowds of Polish women and children, and they screamed at the Germans, and there was a half-insane old Jew who bellowed frantically in a husky voice: "*Kindermörder, Kindermörder!*"* and the Germans went through the camp, at first at an ordinary pace, and then faster and faster, till they ran in a frantic panicky stampede, and they were green with terror, and their hands shook and their teeth chattered...

I shall describe only briefly some of the other aspects of that vast industrial enterprise that the Murder Camp represented. There were those trenches in Krempecki Forest, a few miles away, where they murdered 10,000 Jews on that 3rd of November. Here speed was even more important than business. They shot them, without taking off their clothes, even without taking the women's handbags and the children's toys away. Amongst the stinking corpses, I saw a small child with a teddy-bear... But this was unusual; the great principle

* Child-murderers.

of the Murder Camp was that nothing should be wasted. There was, for instance, that enormous barn-like structure which had contained 850,000 pairs of boots and shoes—among them tiny baby shoes; now, by the end of August, half the shoes had gone: hundreds of people from Lublin had come and taken whole bagfuls of shoes.

"How disgusting," somebody remarked.

Colonel Grosz shrugged his shoulders. "What do you expect? After having had the Germans here for years, people stopped being squeamish. They had lived for years buying and selling and speculating; they are short of shoes, so they say to themselves: 'These are perfectly good shoes; someone will get them eventually; why not grab them while the going's good?'"

And then—perhaps the most horrifying thing of all—there was the enormous building called the "Chopin Lager", the Chopin Warehouse, because, by a curious irony, it happened to be in a street called after the composer. Outside, there was still a notice, with the swastika on top, announcing a German public meeting:

> *Kundgebung.*
> *Donnerstag, 20, Juli 1944.*
> *Reichsredner P.G. Geyer.*
> *Im Hause der Nazional-Sozialisten, Lublin.**

One wondered what kind of cheerful news the *Partei-Genosse* had to tell the Maidanek murderers a couple of days before the Russians entered Lublin, and while most of the Germans must have been busy packing up. It was also the day of the bomb that had failed to kill Hitler. . .

The Chopin Warehouse was like a vast, five-storey department store, part of the grandiose Maidanek Murder Factory. Here the possessions of hundreds of thousands of murdered people were sorted and classified and packed for export to Germany. In one big room there were thousands of trunks and suitcases, some still with carefully written-out labels; there was a room marked *Herrenschuhe* and another marked *Damenschuhe*; here were thousands of pairs of

---

* Meeting, Thursday, July 20, 1944. Speaker from the Reich, Party Comrade Geyer, in the House of National Socialism, Lublin.

shoes, all of much better quality than those seen in the big dump near the camp. Then there was a long corridor with thousands of women's dresses, and another with thousands of overcoats. Another room had large wooden shelves all along it, through the centre and along the walls; it was like being in a Woolworth store: here were piled up hundreds of safety razors, and shaving brushes, and thousands of pen-knives and pencils. In the next room were piled up children's toys: teddy-bears, and celluloid dolls and tin automobiles by the hundred, and simple jigsaw puzzles, and an American-made Mickey Mouse... And so on, and so on. In a junk-heap I even found the manuscript of a Violin Sonata, Op. 15 by somebody called Ernst J. Weil of Prague. What hideous story was behind this?

On the ground floor there had been the Accounts Department. Letters were strewn all over the place; mostly letters from various SS and Nazi organisations to the "Chopin Lager, Lublin", asking to be sent this and that. Many of the letters were orders from the Lublin SS and Police Chief: on November 3, 1942 a carefully-typed letter instructed the Chopin Lager to supply the Hitler Youth Camp, Company 934, with a long list of articles including blankets, table linen, crockery, bed-linen, towels, kitchen utensils, etc. The letter specified that all this was wanted for 4,000 children evacuated from the Reich. There was another list of articles for 2,000 German children who required "sports shirts, training suits, coats, aprons, gym shoes, skiing boots, plus-fours, warm underwear, warm gloves, woollen scarves". The department store was euphemistically called "Altsachenverwertungsstelle, Lublin" (Lublin Disposal Centre for Second-hand Goods). There was also a letter from a German woman living in Lublin asking for a pram and a complete layette for her newborn child. Another document showed that in the first few months of 1944 alone eighteen railway wagons of goods from the Lublin warehouse had been sent to Germany.

The joint Russo-Polish Tribunal investigating the Maidanek crimes sat in the building of the Court of Appeal at Lublin. It included many leading Polish personalities—the President of the District

Court, Czepanski; Professor Bielkowski (whom I had already met); a round stout prelate, Father Kruszinski, Dr Emil Sommerstein, the leading Jewish member of the Lublin Committee, and a former Sejm deputy, and Mr Witos, the Commissioner for Agriculture. That these people were not Russian stooges could be seen from the eagerness with which one of the members insisted on telling the foreign press that the Russians had arrested 2,000 AK men in the Lublin District. In an introductory speech, the Polish president of the tribunal gave the history of Maidanek camp, a lurid catalogue of all the various ways in which people were tortured and killed. There were SS-men who specialised in the "stomach-kick" or the "testicle-kick" as a form of murder; other prisoners were drowned in pools, or tied to posts and allowed to die of exhaustion; there had been eighteen cases of cannibalism in the camp even before it had officially become, on November 3, 1943, an extermination camp. He spoke of the chief of Maidanek. *Obersturmbannführer* Weiss, and his assistant, a notorious sadist, Anton Thumann, and Mussfeld, the chief of the crematorium, and many others.

Himmler himself had twice visited Maidanek and had been pleased with it. It was estimated that 1,500,000 people had been put to death here. The big fry had, of course, fled, but six of the small fry—two Poles and four Germans—had been caught, and, after a trial, they were all hanged a few weeks later.

The four Germans—three of them SS-men—were professional killers; but it seemed a little hard on the two young Poles, both of whom had originally been arrested by the Germans and had then "sold themselves" to them, in the hope of surviving.*

The press and radio in the West were still sceptical. Typical was the BBC's refusal to use my story, as was also this comment of the *New York Herald Tribune* at the time:

> Maybe we should wait for further corroboration of the horror story that comes from Lublin. Even on top of all we have been taught of the maniacal Nazi ruthlessness, this example sounds inconceivable. . .

* The interrogation of these men is described in my article, "First Contact with Poland", published in the *Russian Review, No. 1.* (Penguin Books. 1945).

The picture presented by American correspondents requires no comment except that, if authentic [*sic*] the régime capable of such crimes deserves annihilation.

I saw a great deal during those days of the members of the "Lublin Committee"—Obsóbka-Morawski, its chairman, General Rola-Zymierski, and several others. The New Poland was still in its infancy, and less than one-quarter of Poland's territory had yet been liberated. No industrial centres, except Bialystok, mostly in ruins, had yet been recaptured, and it was still too early to do any large-scale planning. For the present, the Committee was obsessed with some immediate problems, such as rationing in the towns, the creation of regular government jobs in Poland, so as to get people away from the hand-to-mouth existence they had led under the Germans, and the mobilisation of conscripts into the Polish Army, despite the resistance coming from the AK men. Osóbka-Morawski had seen Mikolajczyk in Moscow earlier in the month, and what seemed to worry him most at the time was the support the London Polish government was still getting from Britain and the USA.

There could be no question of an amalgamation between the London Government and the Lublin Committee. "We are willing to accept Mikolajczyk, and Grabski, and Popiel and one more, and *that is all*," Osóbka-Morawski said. He added that the Lublin Committee could accept only the 1921 constitution, but London stuck to the "fascist" constitution of 1935. Unlike the Americans, Clark Kerr, the British Ambassador in Moscow, had told him that he fully approved of the 1921 constitution—but it was just a bit awkward what to do with President Raczkiewicz.

"I was going to tell him where he could put him," Osóbka-Morawski said, and suddenly grinned like a schoolboy. "Anyway," he concluded, "the sooner we resume conversations with Mikolajczyk, the better for him; for time is working for us. We are anxious to come to a settlement, and that's why we offered him the premiership. But he had better accept soon, or the offer may not be repeated." (Which is precisely what happened.)

Chapter X

RUMANIA, FINLAND AND BULGARIA
PACK UP

Apart from Poland, the Red Army had a lot of other fish to fry. In that summer and autumn of 1944 Hitler's satellites were collapsing one after the other, and it was important to speed up the process. Below the surface, there was rivalry between the Soviet Union and the British and Americans in the Balkans, and Moscow thought it essential to occupy Rumania, Bulgaria and Hungary as quickly as possible.*

Events in Rumania followed upon one another with fantastic speed during that month of August 1944. Since the late spring the Russians had held a line running (west to east) from the Carpathian foothills across Moldavia and Bessarabia just north of Jassy and Kishenev, and then along the Dniester to the Black Sea some thirty miles south of Odessa. The Moldavian sector was held by the troops of the 2nd Ukrainian Front under Malinovsky, the Bessarabian sector by those of the 3rd Ukrainian Front under Tolbukhin, which also held an important bridgehead on the right bank of the Dniester just south of Tiraspol. Facing them, east to west, were the Rumanian 4th Army, the German 8th Army, the German 6th Army and the Rumanian 3rd Army, the whole, under the command of General

* Some (perhaps over-suspicious) Russians attributed Churchill's wish to get the Red Army to capture Warsaw at any price to a desire to slow down its progress in south-east Europe.

Friessner, forming Army Group *Süd-Ukraine* consisting of some fifty divisions, half of them Rumanian.

On August 20 both the Ukrainian fronts struck out with forces estimated by the Germans at "ninety infantry divisions and forty-one tank and three cavalry formations".*

As the same writers say:

> The avalanche had now been set in motion and nothing could stop it on its way to the Rumanian interior. It was all the easier for the enemy since half the divisions of Army Group *Süd-Ukraine* were Rumanian, and the Russians deliberately struck their first blows at them. But it was not till August 22 that the full extent of the catastrophe could be measured... With its sixteen divisions the German 6th Army was trapped in the Kishinev area and the Rumanian 3rd Army along the Black Sea coast. In the general confusion no one did anything to blow up the bridges across the Pruth and the Danube and, for the Russians the road was now clear to Bucharest and the Dobrudja.

This roughly corresponds to Russian accounts of the same operation which, within a few days, was to knock Rumania straight out of "Hitler's war". As General Talensky told me in 1945:

"The Germans holding the line north of Jassy were worried, for this was our road to the Rumanian oil and to the Balkans. They concentrated here practically all that was left of the Rumanian Army, which now formed part of the German Army Group *Süd-Ukraine*. The Germans had strongly fortified their lines though, in fact, they were pretty sure that the Central Front was engaging all our attention, and that there was little to fear for the present.†

"So our attack of August 20 came like a bolt from the blue... By August 23 fifteen German divisions were trapped. Unlike the Rumanians, who either offered no resistance or even (in a number of cases) turned against their 'allies', the Germans resisted fiercely at first; some 60,000 were killed, but, in the end, we bagged 106,000 prisoners, among them two corps commanders, twelve divisional

* Philippi and Heim, op. cit., p. 259.
† This is corroborated by German evidence showing that, in July, a number of strong German formations were moved from Rumania to other parts of the front. See Philippi and Heim, op. cit., p. 260.

commanders and thirteen other generals. Two corps commanders and five divisional commanders were found dead. We also captured or destroyed 338 planes, 830 tanks and mobile guns, 5,500 guns and 33,000 trucks... It was a classically-done job."

Nearly the whole of the German 6th Army was destroyed; but most of the German 8th Army hastily retreated west to the Carpathians.

Jassy had been captured on the 22nd and Kishenev on the 24th; during the following week the Russians overran the whole of eastern Rumania, and on the 30th Malinovsky's troops triumphantly entered Bucharest and the oil capital of Ploesti. Little more than a week later Tolbukhin was overrunning Bulgaria.

Meantime the political unrest that had been growing in Rumania for months past came to a head. Antonescu, whose last hope rested in the German and Rumanian forces holding the Jassy-Dniester Line, had had an inconclusive last meeting with Hitler on August 5, and although he urged Hitler to send several panzer formations to Rumania, the Führer still did not think the situation in Rumania desperate, and still imagined that Antonescu had the Rumanian Army behind him. The total lack of enthusiasm for fighting the Russians shown on August 20 by the Rumanian troops came as a shock to Hitler, and this was to be followed by an even greater shock three days later when King Michael appointed General Sanatescu head of the Government and had both Ion Antonescu and Michael Antonescu interned at the Palace.

On August 25, the Soviet Foreign Office published a statement recalling its earlier statement of April 2 that the Soviet Union did not intend to change "the social order in Rumania" and saying that the Rumanian Army could keep its arms if it were ready to fight the Germans and Hungarians. The Rumanian troops must help to liquidate the Germans; this was the only way in which military operations in Rumania could rapidly end and the essential conditions be created for an armistice between Rumania and the Allies.

Two days later it published another Note saying that the Armistice terms which had been rejected by Antonescu, had now been accepted by King Michael and General Sanatescu. It further said that Bucharest was now being firmly defended by the Sanatescu Government against the Germans, and that the German Military Mission, with General Hansen at its head, had been interned. The King's Declaration announcing a change of government and a change of policy had caused great rejoicing in Bucharest. The Germans, however, were wreaking vengeance on the city by bombing and shelling it. In the Carpathians and in Transylvania Rumanian troops were now known to be fighting the Germans. In Transylvania the Germans were planning to set up a puppet government under Horea Sima.

The Note then said that Mr S. Vinogradov, the Soviet Ambassador in Ankara,* had been informed by the Rumanian Minister there that the new Rumanian Coalition Government was composed of the four principal parties led by Maniu, Bratianu, Petrescu and Patrasceanu, the last-named a Communist.

The Rumanian communication to Vinogradov also said that the government was willing to accept the armistice terms, which provided, among other things, for a complete breach with Germany, for the Rumanian army now fighting against Germany, for the restoration of the Soviet-Rumanian border of 1940, and for compensation to the Soviet Union. The Soviet Government, on its side, subscribed to the cancellation of Hitler's "Vienna Award" handing over to Hungary a large part of Transylvania.

For a week after the change of government in Rumania, the Rumanian troops held Bucharest as best they could, though it does not seem that there were any large German forces around after the Jassy-Kishenev debâcle. But there was much nuisance shelling and nuisance bombing of the Rumanian capital, and the people feared a German counter-offensive and an attempt to recapture Bucharest. It was therefore with some relief that most of Bucharest welcomed the Red Army on August 30. The Soviet press reported that the Red Army aroused feelings of "wonder and surprise" in Bucharest: the

* Later for many years Ambassador in Paris.

Rumanians were amazed at the quantity of heavy Russian equipment and could hardly believe at first that most of it was Soviet-made. "The courtesy is overwhelming," one Soviet reporter wrote. "No sooner does one of our comrades produce a cigarette than dozens of hands holding burning lighters are stretched out to light it for him". The communists were displaying posters everywhere welcoming "*Maresalul Stalin, genialul comandat al armatei rosii*". "And everybody is down on Antonescu", the Soviet press also reported. The Dictator was still locked up in the Royal Palace.

In all these Soviet reports there was a note of condescension, sometimes a note of contempt for all this "hearty cringing"; they made a distinction, however, between the "sincere joy of the ordinary Rumanian people" and the half-hearted relief felt by the "bourgeois loafers" in whom Bucharest abounded (and who would no doubt have preferred to see American and British troops).

For the first time the Russian troops were seeing a "real" Western capital, with shops, theatres, cafés and all the paraphernalia of the bourgeois way of life. This in itself, as we shall see, was going to raise something of a psychological and almost ideological problem inside Russia.

At that stage the Soviet Government raised no objections to the composition of the new Rumanian Government and was in a hurry to conclude an armistice with Rumania; however, before long, it began to bring strong pressure to bear on the "double-crossing elements" in the Rumanian "democratic bloc". Under Russian pressure Sanatescu was later replaced by General Radescu and, finally, by the much more pliable Petru Groza. The very cordial Russian attitude to the young King, who at first was given a high Soviet decoration, also changed before very long, and later the terrible Mr Vyshinsky was sent down to Bucharest to bully the life out of him.

But that came later. Early in September the Rumanian Armistice Delegation arrived in Moscow. It was received in style—almost like representatives of a new Allied Power—and lived in luxury at the Government Guest House in Ostrovsky Lane.

Although the delegation was headed by Prince Stirbea who, earlier in the year, had established contact with the British in Cairo, most of the talking was done by the communist leader, the new Minister of Justice, Mr Patrasceanu, a man of drive and ability and great personal charm.*

With him was his pretty young wife. Mme Patrasceanu was a product of French culture in Rumania; elegant, petite, vivacious, she evoked visions of the rue de la Paix. She would come to tea and cocktail parties given by British and American correspondents and would bring a whiff of Guerlain into the dingy rooms of the Hotel Metropole. With a playful grimace she would chatter about the "frightful" week in Bucharest before the Russians came, and when the Germans were dropping bombs on the city *all* the time. She said that King Michael was *un très joli garçon* and *most* intelligent; and she related how difficult life had been for her under the Fascist régime. "Of course, even our Rumanian Fascists aren't quite like the Germans; my husband was in a concentration camp, but I can't really say he was ill-treated; I could visit him and take him food parcels."

At his press conferences, Mr Patrasceanu graphically described the *coup d'état* of August 23, and the way in which Antonescu was trapped by "our King"; he also stressed the heroic deeds of the Rumanian troops during the days when Bucharest was being bombed and shelled by the Germans, and concluded that the Rumanians were a peace-loving and democratically-minded people who at heart had always hated the Germans.

Of the difficulties that were likely to arise inside the new coalition he said nothing. In the background, at one of his press conferences, sat a Mr Popp, the Minister of Agriculture, but he had little to say about land reform, and preferred to let Patrasceanu do the talking.†

That month Armistice Delegations were simply queueing up in

* He was later to be shot as a "Titoite".
† Privately, Mr Popp remarked to me that the Germans would have found it difficult to drag the Rumanians into the war against Russia, if the Russians hadn't recklessly grabbed Bessarabia and Bukovina from them in 1940.

Moscow. No sooner had the Rumanians gone than the Finns were ready to be received. The Rumanian Armistice was signed on the 12th, and the Finnish on the 19th; and then came the Bulgarians.

In June, after their capture of Viipuri (Viborg), the Russians had stopped at the 1940 Finnish frontier, and did not go beyond it. They were giving the Finns time to reflect. But the Finns refused to be rushed.

It was not till the beginning of the Russian invasion of Estonia, that they became thoroughly alarmed. For what if the Russians were to land troops from Estonia in the most vital parts of Finland, just across the Gulf of Finland? In the first week of August President Ryti, the person most responsible for the recent last-ditch agreement with Germany—an agreement under which the Finns would not conduct separate peace negotiations without Germany's approval— very suddenly resigned, and the Finnish Parliament, ignoring the usual procedure in these matters, passed a law handing over the President's powers to Field-Marshal Mannerheim. Keitel, who rushed to Helsinki on August 17, was informed by Mannerheim that the Ryti-Ribbentrop agreement was "off".

On August 25 the Finnish Minister in Stockholm handed a Note to the Soviet Ambassador, Mme Kollontai, asking that an Armistice Delegation be received in Moscow. The Soviet Government agreed, provided Finland publicly announced its breach with Germany and demanded that all German troops be withdrawn from Finland by September 15. If the Germans refused, the Finns would disarm them and hand them over to the Allies as war prisoners. The Soviet Note added that it was sent in agreement with Britain, and with no objections from the United States.

Despite some hedging by the Finns on the question of "disarming" the Germans, a cease-fire was agreed to, to take place on September 4 along the Finnish frontier of 1940.

The Finnish Armistice Delegation, headed by K. Enckel, arrived in Moscow on September 14 and the Armistice was signed on the 19th. The chief Soviet negotiator was Zhdanov, who soon afterwards became head of the Allied Control Commission in Helsinki. The

300 million dollars-worth of reparations in kind—the hardest of the
armistice terms—were spread out over six years, later to be extended
to eight years; the 1940 frontier was restored; the Russians renounced their claim on Hangö but, instead, leased the territory of
Porkkala Udd, only a few miles from Helsinki, as a military base,*
and the Petsamo area, with its nickel mines and its outlet to the
Arctic, "voluntarily" surrendered to Finland in 1920, was now
returned to the Soviet Union. The loss of Karelia and Petsamo
implied the repatriation to Finland of some 400,000 people who did
not want to stay under Soviet rule and the loss of substantial timber
and hydroelectric resources. The agreement not to occupy Finland
with Russian troops was a gesture of goodwill to the Finns themselves and a gesture of reassurance to the Scandinavian countries
generally.

When Zhdanov, who had stood at the head of the defence of
Leningrad, went to Helsinki, he conferred politely for two hours
with "fascist Beast" Mannerheim, the object of so many vicious
Russian cartoons; and in October Stalin sent a friendly message to
the Finnish-Soviet Friendship Society in Helsinki, whose president
was none other than that conservative but ultra-realist new Premier,
Paasikivi himself.

In the end, the Finns did not do much to "disarm" the Germans,
and there does not appear to have been any actual fighting between
Finns and Germans. What in fact happened was that the Germans
withdrew from most of northern Finland of their own free will, after
burning down all the towns and villages (to be later rebuilt with
UNRRA help). What fighting there was was done by Russian troops
under Marshal Meretskov who broke through the strong German
lines west of Murmansk, and then captured Petsamo and Kirkenes,†
the latter inside Norway. Everything in northern Norway was
burned down by the Germans who then withdrew by sea. The rest
of Norway remained under their occupation till May 1945. But the
fact that even a small part of Norway was liberated by the Red

---

* The Russians renounced this some years after the war.
† The German air base whose main purpose had been to smash the
convoys from England to Murmansk and Archangel.

Army continued to be of some sentimental value in Soviet-Norwegian relations for some years after the war.

The story of Bulgaria can be told very briefly. Although Britain and the United States were at war with Bulgaria, the Soviet Union was not, and there was a Bulgarian Minister in Moscow (or Kuibyshev) throughout the war. The Germans had used Bulgaria as a source of raw materials and as a military and naval base, but the Russians, making allowances for the widespread pro-Russian sentiment in Bulgaria and the weakness of its government, had shown considerable tolerance to that country for a long time, even despite serious provocations—for instance when the Germans freely used Bulgarian ports during their evacuation of the Crimea. But by August 1944, the situation had changed. When the Red Army overran Rumania, several armed German ships escaped from there to Bulgarian ports, and were not interned. These ports were also alleged to harbour German submarines.

On August 26, Draganov, the Bulgarian Foreign Minister, made a "neutrality" declaration and promised that any German soldiers in Bulgaria would be disarmed if they refused to withdraw from the country.

The Russians did not think this good enough and declared war on Bulgaria on September 5. Three days later Tolbukhin's troops invaded Bulgaria. They met with no resistance, and were received with enthusiasm. On the following day as a result of an anti-German insurrection in Sofia, Kimon Georgiev's "Fatherland Front" Government was formed and declared war on Germany. The bloodless Two Days' War was over. Messages of brotherly affection were sent by the Bulgarian Government to Tito, and a Bulgarian Army was getting ready to fight the Germans. The "revolutionary enthusiasm" in Bulgaria was much deeper and more general than in Rumania.

Before many weeks had passed, the Russian press noted with satisfaction that all over Bulgaria People's Courts had been set up to try war criminals, and that the Bulgarian Army was being purged of all its "Fascist elements".

The Armistice between the Allies and Bulgaria was signed in Moscow on October 28.* Bulgaria, like Rumania, had entered the Soviet "sphere of influence".

The link-up between the Red Army and Tito's Yugoslavs took place at the end of September. On the 29th a TASS communiqué announced that, in order to be able to attack the Germans and Hungarians in Hungary from the south, the Russians had asked permission from the Yugoslav Committee of National Liberation to enter Yugoslav territory. On October 4 it was announced that the Russian and Yugoslav armies had joined forces in an unspecified town in the Danube valley.

On October 20, Tolbukhin's troops and Tito's Yugoslavs entered Belgrade together amidst great popular rejoicing.

On the same day Malinovsky's troops took Debrecen in eastern Hungary, but the Russian advance in Hungary, though rapid at first, was then slowed down by very stiff German and Hungarian resistance, especially as the Russians approached Budapest in November.

The Germans had, by then, foiled Horthy's attempt to "do a King Michael on them", and Hitler and Salasi, the Hungarian Fascist leader, decided at their meeting early in December, to hold Budapest "at any price". Although, officially, the Germans expressed their confidence in being able to hold Budapest, it was known that many of its industries were now being evacuated to Austria.

It took some time to set up at least the nucleus of a "democratic régime" in Russian-occupied Hungary. It was not till December 20 that it was announced that a Hungarian Provisional National Assembly had been formed at Debrecen, "the citadel of Hungarian Freedom—that Debrecen where Kossuth raised the flag of independence in 1849".

On the following day the Soviet press announced:

> At the beginning of December, under the chairmanship of Dr Vasary, the mayor of Debrecen, a group was formed of representatives

* One of the Bulgarian signatories was N. Petkov, the Agrarian leader, who was to be tried and shot soon after the war as a Western "agent".

of the different Hungarian parties. In the liberated territory the election of delegates to the Provisional National Assembly took place between December 13 and 20. 230 delegates were elected, representing the democratic parties, the town and village councils and the trade and peasant unions... The Assembly opened with the playing of the Hungarian National Anthem. The meeting was held in the Reformation College where, in 1849, Kossuth proclaimed the independence of Hungary...

An Address to the Hungarian People was adopted which said:

It is time to make peace. Salasi is an usurper... We call upon the Hungarian people to rally to the banners of Kossuth and Rakoszi and to follow in the footsteps of the Honweds [volunteer militia] of 1848. We want a democratic Hungary. We guarantee the inviolability of private property as the basis of our social and economic order. We want Land Reform... Turn your arms against the German oppressors and help the Red Army... for the good of a Free and Democratic Hungary!

Two days later a Provisional Hungarian Government was formed; no Communist leaders were included in it—it would have been premature when a large part of Hungary, including Budapest, was still in German hands. The premier was General Miklos; the other ministers included a peasant leader, Ferenc Erdei, Janos Göngös, Count Gesa Teleki, and General Janos Veres, the Minister of Defence, a Horthy man, who had been Hungarian chief of staff since April 1944, was then arrested by the Germans, but managed to escape.

This assortment of back-the-winner Hungarian gentlemen were not to stay long at the head of affairs. "Kossuth" was a convenient symbol, but did not mean much. Nor did Rakoszy. It was the other Rakosi who was waiting for the signal to enter the stage.

It was also in the eventful autumn of 1944 that in "independent" Slovakia a great rising took place against the Germans by Slovak partisans, supported by Red Army units and by part of the Slovak Army. In the end, the rising was crushed by strong German forces that were rushed to Slovakia, though some partisans escaped to the mountains. Although, at the time, there was a virtual news blackout about the whole tragic business, there was later to be much recrimination, on the part of the Russians, both against the "dubious" and "half-hearted" rôle played in the rising by the Slovak Army and by the Czechoslovak Government in London which had not given the insurrection sufficient encouragement.* Both the Slovak Insurgents and the Soviet troops, fighting in incredibly difficult conditions in the Carpathians, suffered very heavy casualties.

Significantly (and the London Government was largely to be blamed for this) only about a thousand men from Bohemia and Moravia came to join in the Slovak rising, the average unromantic Czechs preferring not to stick their necks out.

The facts available on the Slovak rising are numerous, but highly confusing, and the Russian presentation of the rôle played by the non-communist elements in Slovakia has been far from generous.

There was also much recrimination in the opposite direction, and in Slovakia, to this day, there continues to be some ill-feeling against the Red Army amongst many non-communists, whose stories about having been "let down" are not unlike those still current amongst pro-Western elements in Poland.

* The Slovak Communist Party, allegedly riddled with "bourgeois nationalists", was also to be blamed for its half-heartedness and for its failure to carry out the instructions of the Central Committee of the Czechoslovak C.P. (IVOVSS, vol. IV, p. 318).

Chapter XI

CHURCHILL'S SECOND MOSCOW VISIT

In October 1944 the Red Army was overrunning Estonia and Latvia in the north; farther south, General Cherniakhovsky's troops first set foot on German soil at the eastern tip of East Prussia; but what interested—and worried—Churchill above all were first, the Polish Problem and second, the Russian penetration of the Balkans and Central Europe—by which he meant, in the first place, Hungary.

He was ready to write off Rumania and Bulgaria as part of the Russian sphere, but was not prepared to do so in the case of Yugoslavia, Hungary and, above all, Greece. The Kings of Greece and Yugoslavia were looking to Britain for protection against communism and although the Russians were losing thousands of men every day in the heavy fighting in Hungary, he felt that Hungary, like Yugoslavia, should at least be the object of an East-West compromise.

As we know from Churchill's own account* the whole question of the Balkans, including Hungary, was "settled" in a few minutes between him and Stalin. During their very first meeting on October 9, he scribbled on a half-sheet of paper his proposal for Russian or British "predominance"—Rumania: Russia 90%, the others, 10%; Greece: Britain (in accord with USA) 90%, Russia, 10%; Bulgaria: Russia, 75%, the others, 25%; Yugoslavia and Hungary: 50–50%.

* Churchill, op. cit., vol. VI, p. 198.

I pushed this across to Stalin... Then he took his blue pencil and
made a large tick upon it, and passed it back to us... At length I said:
"Might it not be thought rather cynical if it seemed we had disposed
of these issues... in such an offhand manner? Let us burn the paper."
"No, you keep it," said Stalin.

As Churchill himself says, even in retrospect, relations between
him and Stalin were never better than they were during that October
visit to Moscow. Shortly before that, he had gone out of his way to
flatter the Russians by saying that they had "torn the guts" out of
Hitler's war machine. The British Ambassador, Sir Archibald Clark-
Kerr was eager to make the Churchill-Eden visit to Moscow an
overwhelming success and something of a personal triumph for himself.* Since the British statesmen were the guests of the Soviet
Government, Clark-Kerr (at Churchill's suggestion, it is true)
organised a banquet and, for the first time in his life, Stalin dined
at the British Embassy. The Ambassador also exercised all his diplomatic skill and charm on the two sets of Poles. He tried to be
particularly nice to Bierut and Osóbka-Morawski who had been
offended by the treatment given them by Churchill and Eden, who
looked upon them as a pair of Russian "quislings" who had gone so
far as to declare that the "Polish people" did not want Lwow. Clark-
Kerr also hoped that he had persuaded Mikolajczyk during this
Churchill-Eden visit to return to Moscow after a flying visit to
London, and to go to Poland immediately to form the new government there. When Mikolajczyk failed to return, Clark-Kerr felt he
had been badly let down.

Outwardly, an unprecedented atmosphere of cordiality surrounded the Anglo-Soviet talks; for several minutes a thunderous
ovation at the Bolshoi Theatre greeted Churchill and Stalin as they
both appeared in the State Box.

On October 18, at the end of his Moscow visit, Churchill received
the press in the large Ambassador's study; outside the large windows
were the bare trees and an autumn twilight, and in the study hung

---

* He was very conscious of his historic rôle as wartime Ambassador
to Russia. Asked, before leaving Moscow for Washington in 1945,
what had impressed him most in Russia, he said unhesitatingly,
"Stalin." Stalin had gone out of his way to be pleasant to him.

the large oil paintings of Queen Victoria, King Edward VII in his regalia, Queen Alexandra, King George V and Queen Mary. Wearing a lounge suit with a blue bow tie, Churchill looked in good form. He began by jokingly referring to his days as a war correspondent in South Africa and to "the bitter irritation of having my dispatches censored: and I sympathise when a good story is spoilt by the blue pencil—or it may be the red pencil here."

When I last came to Moscow (he said), Stalingrad was still under siege, and the enemy was sixty or seventy miles from this city, and he was even nearer Cairo. That was in August 1942... Since then the tide has turned, and we have had victories and wonderful advances over vast expanses... Coming back here, I find a great sense of hope and confidence that the end of the trials will be reached... Some very hard fighting will yet have to be done. The enemy is resisting with discipline and desperation, and it is best to take a sober view of the speed with which the conclusion will be reached on the Western Front. But there is good news everyday, and it is difficult not to be oversanguine.

After referring to the "circle of fire and steel" closing in on Germany and the hunger, cold and shortages with which Germany was now faced, Churchill said:

It is a great change from the days when England and her Empire were left alone to face the mighty power of Germany... As for our work here, I shall only say this: after Quebec and the long discussions I had with my great friend President Roosevelt, I thought it right to see my other friend—as I think I may truly call him—Marshal Stalin.

The smooth working of interallied relations, he said, was greatly assisted by these conferences. In the course of these Moscow talks, "we were most deeply involved in the anxious questions concerning Poland, and I am quite sure I am entitled to say that very definite results have been gained and differences have been sensibly narrowed. The Polish question stands in a better position than it did and I have good hope we shall reach full agreement eventually among all the parties concerned. Undoubtedly, we must not allow Poland to become a sore place in our affairs. We British went to war for Poland, and our sympathy for Poland is great, and Britain has a special interest in her fortunes, now that Poland is about to be liberated by the great manly efforts of our Allies." He made no reference whatsoever to the Warsaw tragedy which had come to its gruesome end only a fortnight before.

Churchill then referred to the "surprising events" that had been occurring in the Balkans, and said that each of the Balkan problems was difficult to handle by correspondence, which was another good reason for coming to Moscow. Eden here had had "a hard time". But very sensible results had been achieved in co-ordinating the policies of the two governments in these regions. Then he spoke of the atmosphere of "friendship and comradeship" that had marked these Moscow talks:

> We both have our armies in the field and I am glad the Russians no longer have the heavy feeling that they bear the whole brunt. . . Unity is essential if peace is to be secure. Let us cast our eyes forward beyond the battle-line to the day when Germany has surrendered unconditionally, beaten to the ground, and awaiting the decisions of the outraged nations who saved themselves from the pit of destruction that Hitler had digged for them.

He ended with a Churchillian tirade on Anglo-Russian-American friendship:

> This friendship, in war as in peace, can save the world, and perhaps it is the only thing that can save the peace for our children and grandchildren. In my opinion, it is a goal easily attainable. Very good, very good are the results in the field, very good the work behind the lines, and hopes are high for the permanent results of victory.

He also referred to "the great regard, and respect, and great confidence" he felt for "the great chief of the Russian State".

The Russians present at the conference were very pleased with the statement; they saw in Churchill a strong supporter of a Big-Three policy.

No doubt there were difficulties—no real progress was made during the long talks with Mikolajczyk, Romer and Grabski on the one hand, and the Lublin Poles on the other; nor did the agreement on the Balkans amount to very much, except that the Russians seemed ready to abandon Greece—but some useful talks had taken

place on the possible partition of Germany, and, above all, Churchill
had secured some fairly precise assurances from Stalin about the
Russians joining in the war against Japan within three months after
the defeat of Germany. At Roosevelt's request the discussion of the
disagreements that had arisen at Dumbarton Oaks over UNO was
postponed till the next Big-Three meeting.

So the results of the Moscow talks were rather a mixed bag.
Nevertheless, there was a general impression that Churchill and
Stalin were now on excellent terms, and that Churchill was now
genuinely starry-eyed about "the great chief of the Russian State",
partly perhaps under the influence of Clark-Kerr.

The extreme cordiality in the Churchill-Stalin relations is reflected
in the correspondence they exchanged during and just after the
Moscow visit. These letters are reproduced in the volume published
in Moscow in 1957, though they are not quoted by Churchill himself.

Thus, his letter of October 17, in which he asked Stalin to see
Mikolajczyk—"in whose desire to reach an understanding with you
and with the National Committee I am more than ever convinced"
—concludes with the words:

My daughter Sarah will be delighted with the charming token from
Miss Stalin and will guard it among her most valued possessions.
I remain, with sincere respect and goodwill,
Your friend and war comrade,
Winston S. Churchill.

On October 19, Stalin wrote:

Dear Mr Churchill,
On the occasion of your departure from Moscow please accept from
me two modest gifts as souvenirs. The vase, "Man in a Boat" is for
Mrs Churchill and the vase "With Bow against Bear" for yourself.
Once again I wish you good health and good cheer.
J. Stalin.

In reply Churchill wrote:

My dear Marshal Stalin,
I have just received the two beautiful vases... We shall treasure
them amongst our most cherished possessions... The visit has been
from beginning to end a real pleasure to me... most particularly

because of our very pleasant talks together. My hopes for the future alliance of our peoples never stood so high. I hope you may long be spared to repair the ravages of war and lead All The Russias out of the years of storm into glorious sunshine.

Your friend and war-time comrade,

Winston S. Churchill.

After a further message of overwhelming cordiality sent during his and Eden's return journey, Churchill sent Stalin from London an almost gushing message of thanks for the "Russian products" (obviously caviare) that had been added to the English party's luggage:

> It is only since my arrival in London that I have realised the great generosity of your gifts of Russian products for myself and members of my mission. Please accept the warmest thanks of all who have been the grateful recipients of this new example of Russian hospitality.*

At all the Moscow parties, Churchill had, indeed, shown a gargantuan liking for caviare.

Throughout the visit, Stalin had gone out of his way to show Churchill and Eden the greatest friendliness; he had even gone to see them off to the airfield. There had been nothing like it since the Matsuoka visit in 1941. The communiqué recorded "considerable progress" in the talks on Poland, "greatly reduced differences" and "dispelled misunderstandings"; agreement on Bulgaria, and agreement on a joint policy on Yugoslavia—the Yugoslavs would, of course, be "free to choose their own system", but meantime there would be a fusion of the National Liberation Committee and the Royal Yugoslav Government.

* Stalin-Churchill correspondence, pp. 263–6.

Chapter XII

STALIN'S HORSE-TRADING WITH
DE GAULLE

There is a long story behind de Gaulle's visit to Moscow in December 1944. During the Soviet-German Pact the Soviet Union had established diplomatic relations with the Vichy Government, though the Vichy Ambassador, M. Gaston Bergery and his American wife, Bettina, the ex-Schiaparelli mannequin, did not arrive in Moscow until April 25, 1941, i.e. after the German invasion of Yugoslavia. When he presented his credentials to Kalinin in the presence of Molotov, and urged Russia to "take part in the organisation of the New Order in Europe", his speech was met with stony silence from the Russians. On the following day, Mr Bogomolov, the Soviet Ambassador to Vichy France, who happened to be in Moscow at the time, called on Bergery and explained to him, in "ideological terms", why the Soviet Union did not think it possible to accept Germany's hegemony in Europe.*

Diplomatic relations with Vichy were, of course, broken off the moment the Germans invaded the Soviet Union. The first direct contacts between the Free French and the Russians were made as early as the beginning of August 1941 on de Gaulle's initiative when M. Jouve, de Gaulle's unofficial representative in Turkey, called on Mr S. Vinogradov, the Soviet Ambassador there and informed him

* G. Gafencu. *Préliminaires de la guerre à l'Est*. (Paris, 1944), pp. 234–5. Bogomolov was to become Ambassador to the various "allied" (i.e. exiled) governments in London.

918

that de Gaulle, whom he had just seen at Beirut, would like to send two or three Free French representatives to Moscow. Without insisting on recognition—official or unofficial—of the Free French by the Soviet Government, de Gaulle was anxious to establish direct relations with the Russians, instead of dealing with them, as hitherto, through the British. According to the Soviet account of the meeting, Jouve pointed out that, in General de Gaulle's view, the Soviet Union and France were both continental Powers which had problems and aims different from those of the Anglo-Saxon states. And Jouve added:

> General de Gaulle talked a lot about the Soviet Union. Her entry into the war, he said, represented for us a great chance on which we had not counted before. He also said that while it was impossible to say when exactly victory would be won, he was absolutely certain that, in the end, the Germans would be smashed.*

During the same week MM. Cassin and Dejean called on Mr Maisky, the Soviet Ambassador in London proposing to him the establishment of "some kind of official relations" between the Soviet Union and the Free French. They suggested that these relations be modelled on those existing between the Free French and the British Government. On September 26, 1941, Maisky informed de Gaulle that the Soviet Union recognised him as the leader of all the Free French who had rallied to him, "regardless of where they were". It also promised the Free French all possible aid in the common struggle against Germany and her allies.†

De Gaulle was anxious, almost from the outset, to give tangible form to the military co-operation between the Free French and the Soviet Union, and wanted to send to Russia a French division then stationed in Syria. But this apparently met with opposition from the British and, in April 1942, Dejean proposed that the French send to Russia thirty airmen instead, and thirty ground staff—to begin with.

Thus the foundations were laid for that French Normandie Squadron which arrived in Russia later in the year. No doubt they

---

* *Sovietsko-Frantsuzskie otnosheniya . . . 1941–1945.* (Moscow 1959), pp. 43–44.
† Ibid., p. 47.

were little more than a token force, but they represented an important political factor and a symbolic link between Russia and the French Resistance. The French airmen fought gallantly on the Russian Front, suffered very heavy casualties, and Russian military decorations were lavishly conferred on them. Great publicity was given to this French unit.

In March 1942 a small diplomatic mission, headed by M. Roger Garreau, and with General E. Petit as the Military Attaché, arrived in Moscow. Garreau was (at least at that stage) a strong supporter of de Gaulle and, in his conversations with the Russians, never made any secret of the disagreements between de Gaulle on the one hand and the British and Americans on the other.*

Garreau (like de Gaulle) attached the greatest importance to the support given by Russia to the Free French, and on March 23, 1943, went so far as to tell Molotov that "but for the Soviet Government's support, Fighting France would not have survived the great November (1942) crisis when various attempts were made in North Africa to set up quite a different government."†

In June 1943 the question arose of recognising the French Committee of National Liberation in Algiers, and on the 23rd, the British Ambassador, in a letter to Stalin, said that he had learned "with alarm" of the Soviet intention of recognising this Committee.‡ Under British and American pressure, this recognition was delayed, but when it was finally granted in August 1943, the Soviet "formula" of recognition was much shorter and more straightforward than that of the British and American Governments, with its numerous con-

---

* In this he was closely following de Gaulle's example in London. In talking to Soviet diplomats the General frequently complained about the British Government: thus, on November 26, 1941, in reply to Ambassador Bogomolov's remark that he regularly read his (de Gaulle's) paper, *France*, de Gaulle angrily snapped back: "That isn't my paper, that's the paper of the British Ministry of Information." On another occasion, on September 26, 1942, he told Bogomolov that the British were trying to build up Herriot as his rival, adding "with great irritation" that the British were trying all the time to overthrow him by making use of all sorts of other people. (Ibid., pp. 50 and 96).
† Ibid., p. 118.   ‡ Ibid., p. 167.

ditions and reservations. When, finally, in August 1944, the de Gaulle Government established itself in Paris, the Russians pressed Britain and the United States for an early recognition as the French Provisional Government. So, on the whole, de Gaulle had every reason to be satisfied with the backing the Soviet Government had given him ever since 1941.

His decision to go to Moscow to see Stalin at the end of 1944 had been largely determined by a good deal of irritation and annoyance caused him by the British and Americans, by their "domineering" position in France, and by his desire to show that he had an independent policy and was nobody's satellite. The Russians, for their part, were interested in France in so far as this was a country in which the communists had played a leading part in the Resistance and were making their influence felt inside the French Government.

And yet, in the conditions prevailing at the end of 1944, the most important question for the Russians was to finish the war against Germany as quickly as possible, and Stalin expected the French communists to subordinate their own political interests to this end— as we know, for instance, from the instructions Stalin obviously gave Maurice Thorez soon afterwards to approve the dissolution of the Patriotic Militias (the para-military communist organisations of the Resistance), and to co-operate with de Gaulle.* During de Gaulle's visit to Moscow Stalin made a point of urging the General half-jokingly "not to shoot Thorez—at least not for the present"—since the communist leader was going to behave as a good patriotic Frenchman. Thorez, who had been in Moscow throughout the war, had returned to France in November 1944—where he had just been amnestied for his "desertion" from the French Army in 1939, and was later (in 1945) also going to be appointed one of the Ministers of State in de Gaulle's government.

De Gaulle's visit to Moscow was, above all, a move to break away from an excessive dependence on Britain and the USA. In those pre-atomic days de Gaulle continued to think of France and Russia— as he had already done in 1941—as the two great future military

* See the author's *France 1940–1955* (London, 1956), pp. 244–5.

Powers on the Continent of Europe which could keep Germany down, and whose points of view and interests were different from those of the "Anglo-Saxons". It was precisely on this point that, in 1944, Stalin was unable to see eye-to-eye with de Gaulle—for the simple reason that, in purely military and economic terms, France was totally insignificant compared with Britain and America. So, much to de Gaulle's disappointment, Stalin refused to take France seriously at that stage as a military ally. Instead, Stalin tried to use de Gaulle as a means of breaking Western unity over the Polish question. De Gaulle, for his part, tried to force the hands of Britain and America by getting Stalin to accept the annexation of the Rhineland by France. In the end, de Gaulle refused to recognise the Lublin Committee, and Stalin refused to recognise the Rhine frontier, and de Gaulle finally "triumphed" by taking back to Paris a Franco-Soviet Treaty of Alliance, on the lines of the Anglo-Soviet Pact of 1942. But this was by no means everything that either de Gaulle or Stalin had originally hoped to achieve.

There was something slightly comic about the whole de Gaulle-Bidault visit that December. The Russians treated the French with a good deal of condescension, and the French, at the time, felt this very keenly, though there is not the slightest suggestion of that in de Gaulle's *Memoirs*.

Travelling via Baku and Stalingrad, de Gaulle, Bidault, General Juin and a handful of diplomats arrived in Moscow on December 2. First de Gaulle dropped a brick at Stalingrad where there was a reception in his honour at which he presented the city with a memorial tablet from the people of France. In his speech he referred to Stalingrad as "a symbol of our common victories over the enemy", a description of the defence of Stalingrad which the Russians did not much relish, especially coming from a Frenchman.

At the Kursk Station in Moscow two days later, the French party were met by Molotov and a guard of honour. The Diplomatic Corps were also there in force, and a large crowd had gathered outside the station, attracted by the numerous official cars. Emerging from the station, de Gaulle looked at this big crowd in the square: and the crowd looked back, not quite sure who he was, and nobody even murmured "Vive de Gaulle!" or anything. So he drove off, wondering what a queer country this was.* In 1944, de Gaulle was a very great man in France, and it shocked him not to be treated as such anywhere else.

The minutes of the three Stalin-de Gaulle meetings on December 2, 6 and 8, as published by the Soviet Foreign Ministry in 1959, as well as the minutes of the Molotov-Bidault talks† are of the greatest interest, since in substance and especially in their overtones they differ considerably from de Gaulle's rather glib account of what happened. The minutes are also one of the few first-hand accounts we have of how Stalin conducted negotiations during the war.

During de Gaulle's first meeting with Stalin the General started by saying that the real trouble with France was that she did not have any alliance with Russia, and, also, that her eastern frontier was very vulnerable.

Yes, said Stalin, the fact that Russia and France were not together had been a great misfortune for Russia, too. He then asked de Gaulle whether French industry was being restored.

> *De Gaulle*: Yes, but very, very slowly. There are terrible transport difficulties and a coal shortage. In order to equip her army, France has to appeal for arms from the Americans and, for the present these won't give her any. It will take France two years to restore her industry.

Stalin expressed some surprise at this, and said that Russia was not finding the restoration of industry such an insuperable problem. The south of France had been liberated without difficulty, and there had not been much fighting in Paris, so what was the trouble?

De Gaulle said that most of the French rolling stock had been destroyed and that much of what was left was being used by the British and Americans.

* In his *Memoirs*, de Gaulle writes: "A considerable crowd had gathered, from which rose a hum of sympathetic voices." Op. cit., p. 68; I was there, and was totally unaware of any kind of "hum".
† *Sovietsko-Frantsuzskie otnosheniya, 1941–45.* (Moscow, 1959).

Rather with the suggestion that it was these who were doing most of the fighting in France, Stalin then asked how France stood for officer *cadres*.

De Gaulle replied that in 1940 the Germans had captured nearly the whole French Army and most of the officers. Only a small number were left in North Africa, and these were now fighting in France. Some had betrayed their country by collaborating with Vichy. So a lot of new officers now had to be trained.

Stalin: The reason why I asked about this is that everywhere— whether in Poland, Hungary, Rumania or Yugoslavia—the Germans always try to round up officers and pack them off to Germany. But how do you stand for airmen?

De Gaulle: We have very few airmen, and even those we have need complete re-training, as they are unfamiliar with modern planes.

Stalin: Now the French airmen of the Normandie Squadron are doing very well on the Russian Front; so if you are so hard up for airmen, we could perhaps send them back to France?

De Gaulle: No, no, this is quite unnecessary. They are contributing nobly to the common cause while in Russia.

Stalin: I suppose you have very few training schools for airmen?

De Gaulle: Yes, very few, and very few planes.

Having got over this phase of the talk, in which he had to act the poor relation (there is no mention of these remarks in his *Memoirs*), de Gaulle tried to get down to more serious business. It would be a good thing for both France and Russia, he said, if the Rhineland could be joined to France. Maybe the Ruhr would have to be given an international régime, but not the Rhineland proper.

Stalin asked how Britain and America looked upon this, to which de Gaulle replied that these had already let France down in 1918 by insisting on a temporary arrangement, which just didn't work. As a result, France was again invaded. Perhaps Britain and America had learned their lesson, but he couldn't be sure.

Stalin: As far as I know, the British are considering a different solution: an international control of Rhineland-Westphalia. What you are proposing is something quite different. We must find out what Britain and America think about it.

De Gaulle: I hope the matter may be examined by the European Advisory Commission.

Stalin: Yes.

De Gaulle then went on with his sharp criticism of Britain and America. They were neither geographically nor historically on the Rhine, and the French and Russians had had to pay a heavy price for this. Even though they were fighting there now, they would not be on the Rhine forever, while France and Russia would always remain where they were. The full-scale intervention of Britain and America always took place in peculiar conditions—much too late; as a result, France was nearly destroyed in 1940.

Stalin was not convinced. The strength of Russia and France alone were insufficient to keep Germany in order. The experience of the two world wars had demonstrated this. Frontiers in themselves were not of decisive importance; what mattered was a good and well-commanded army. It was no use relying on the Maginot Line, or Hitler's *Ostwall*. And when de Gaulle still persisted, Stalin said:

> Please understand me. We simply cannot settle this question of France's eastern frontier without having talked about it to the British and the Americans. This and many other problems must be decided jointly.

Obviously not at all satisfied with this, de Gaulle tried to approach the question from a different angle by bringing up Germany's eastern frontier.

> *De Gaulle*: If I understand the question correctly, the German frontier should run along the Oder and then along the Neisse, that is, west of the Oder.
>
> *Stalin*: Yes, I think the old Polish territories—Silesia, East Prussia, Pomerania—should be returned to Poland, while the Sudeten country should be given back to Czechoslovakia.

But he did not rise to the bait.

Throughout the de Gaulle-Bidault visit, Stalin was, significantly, in regular communication with Churchill. The day after his first meeting with de Gaulle he cabled to Churchill saying that he had informed de Gaulle that the question of Germany's western frontier could not be settled independently of Britain and the United States. As regards the Franco-Soviet Pact, he had told de Gaulle that the matter would require a many-sided examination. Churchill, in reply, indicated his preference for a Tripartite Pact.

It was during the Molotov-Bidault meeting of December 5 that the Russians bluntly raised the question of the recognition of the Lublin Committee by France.

Molotov: Why shouldn't France and the Polish Committee exchange official representatives? After all, both Britain and the USSR entertain relations with both the Yugoslav Liberation Committee and the Royal Yugoslav Government. By establishing official relations with Lublin, France would not need to break with the Polish émigré government.

Molotov then said that he liked the French draft of the Soviet-French Pact, but the Soviet Government considered that the signing of this Pact should go together with the establishment of official French relations with the Lublin Committee.

Bidault, obviously taken aback, said he was surprised that the Franco-Soviet Pact should have this *condition préalable* attached to it; for their own part, the French also had some questions they would like urgently settled: for instance, that of the Rhine frontier.

Molotov dodged the issue, without telling Bidault that Stalin had already cabled to Churchill about it. Instead, he stressed that the Soviet Union was still bearing the brunt of the war and that, in signing a Pact with France, she would like a definite decision to be taken about Poland; this would be of the greatest importance to the implementation of the Pact.

During the second Stalin-de Gaulle meeting on December 6, Poland was the main topic. De Gaulle referred to the old cultural and religious bonds uniting France and Poland, and (without mentioning the anti-Soviet *cordon sanitaire*) said that France had tried, in 1918, to turn Poland into a great anti-German force. Unfortunately, men like Beck had tried to make an agreement with Germany, and were both anti-Russian and anti-Czech. He [de Gaulle] was all in favour of both the Curzon Line and the Oder-Neisse Line.

He had no objection to an Anglo-Franco-Soviet bloc; but he would like a straight Franco-Soviet Pact to begin with.

Stalin (still busy consulting Churchill) said he thought the matter could be settled in the next few days. He would like, instead, to return to the question of Poland. He hoped France would adopt, *vis à vis* Poland, a more realistic attitude than that shown by Britain and the United States. The British Government had, unfortunately, got itself tied into knots with both the Polish Government in London and Mihailovic, who was now "hiding somewhere in Cairo". The London Poles were playing at musical chairs, while the Lublin Poles were carrying out a land reform, similar to what France had done in the 18th century. He went on to demonstrate that the London Government were becoming more and more discredited in Poland and talked at some length of the "folly" of the Warsaw rising, saying that the Red Army could not have taken Warsaw in time, with its guns and shells lagging 200 miles behind.

De Gaulle was not convinced about the London Government being "discredited" in Poland, and said it would become more apparent what the Polish people really felt once the whole country had been liberated.

On December 7, Stalin cabled Churchill saying that he and his colleagues had approved Churchill's idea of a Tripartite Anglo-Franco-Soviet Pact, and had submitted it to the French, but had not yet received a reply.

That same day Bidault told Molotov that it was not satisfactory for France to simply "join" in the old Anglo-Soviet Pact; it might give rise to the idea that France figured in such a Pact as a kind of junior partner. Molotov brushed this argument aside, and returned to the question of French recognition of the Lublin Poles. This was an aspect of the Franco-Russian talks on which Stalin was *not* keeping Churchill informed—though the British Embassy in Moscow knew, of course, more or less what was going on.

During his third meeting with Stalin on December 8 de Gaulle again announced that Germany was France's Number One Problem and that "so long as the German people existed, there would always be a menace." And again he started on the Rhine frontier. It was essential for France and Russia to join forces. Britain, which was "always late", could rank only as a "second-stage" ally, and the United States as a "third-stage" ally. Neither could be depended upon in the great moment of danger, and under a Tripartite Pact all immediate action would inevitably be slowed down by the British.

Stalin agreed that a straight Franco-Soviet Pact would make France more independent in relation to "other countries", but since it would be difficult for Russia and France alone to win the war, he still preferred a Tripartite Pact.

De Gaulle then said that the Tripartite Pact was "un-French"; it would, in present circumstances, stress France's inferiority *vis-à-vis* England; it would be easier for France to deal direct with Russia; France was uncertain about Britain's future attitude to Germany, and, moreover, she was expecting all kinds of difficulties with the British both in the Middle East and the Far East.

Stalin remarked that the Tripartite Pact was Churchill's idea, and that he [Stalin] and his colleagues had agreed to the British proposal. True, Churchill had not vetoed the Franco-Soviet Pact, but, all the same, he preferred the Tripartite Pact.

> If we shelve this (Stalin continued), Churchill will be offended. However, since the French are so anxious to have a straight Franco-Soviet Pact, let me suggest this: if the French want us to render them a service, then let them render us one. Poland is an element in our security. Let the French accept in Paris a representative of the Polish Committee of National Liberation, and we shall sign the Franco-Soviet Pact. Churchill will be offended, but it can't be helped.

"You have probably offended Churchill before," de Gaulle said.

"I have sometimes offended Churchill," Stalin replied, "and Churchill has sometimes offended me. Some day our correspondence will be published, and you will see what kind of messages we have sometimes exchanged."

There seems, at this point, to have been an embarrassed silence and then Stalin suddenly asked de Gaulle when he intended to return to France. De Gaulle said he was hoping to leave in two days.

After a somewhat irrelevant digression on the aircraft factory the French guests had visited, de Gaulle remarked that he much regretted that there could be no Franco-Soviet Pact, and it would now be necessary to start discussing a Tripartite Pact. He appreciated Stalin's policy on Poland, but it was not at all clear what the Lublin Committee represented.

The meeting broke up in a chilly atmosphere.

Later that day Bidault called on Molotov and said there had perhaps been some "misunderstanding" about the Lublin Committee. Anyway, de Gaulle intended to see the member of this Committee on the following day. Molotov said he hoped this meeting would make a great difference, and meantime he and Bidault could work on the draft of *the Franco-Soviet Pact.*

De Gaulle was no more impressed by Bierut, Osóbka-Morawski and Rola-Zymierski than Eden and Churchill had been, and agreed, in the end, before leaving Moscow, to no more than sending an "unofficial" French representative to Lublin, and "quite independently" of the Franco-Soviet Pact.

Such was the horse-trading that went on for over a week between Stalin and de Gaulle—each, in his own way, trying to pull a fast one on Britain and the United States.

The atmosphere surrounding this French visit to Moscow was not devoid of comedy. One day, de Gaulle and Bidault were taken for a ride on the Metro, where nobody took any notice of them and where they were pushed about and had their feet trodden on mercilessly. Bidault seemed particularly outraged when he told me about it. In their negotiations, he said, the Russians were pretty rough: "*Ça manque d'élégance, ça manque de courtoisie. C'est un régime brutal, inhumain*". As for the people in the Metro: "*Ces gens sont muets. Ont-ils des sentiments?*"* One assured him that they had, though not necessarily for official French visitors, of whom they knew little or nothing. And the people on top, Bidault fumed, were mean and

* "There's a lack of graciousness, a lack of courtesy. A brutal, inhuman régime. . . " "Are these people mute? Have they any feelings at all?"

*accrocheurs.** He twisted his wrist about in the air. He also thought
their whole ideology completely cockeyed—an incredible medley of
Hegel, Marx and Stalin—what kind of political philosophy was that?
He thought that in a completely ruined Europe, there would be a
wave of something more extreme than communism, as understood
here; and "they must be terrified of Trotskyism!"

Something wasn't quite clicking. As a Russian colonel whom I met
at the great reception given at the French Embassy said: "You know,
we can't really take the French terribly seriously. Toulon and Kronstadt and *l'alliance Franco-Russe* with Marseillaise and God Save
the Tsar don't mean a damned thing to the present generation of
Russians!"

All the same, that Embassy reception was really something. There
was an enormous tricolour flag outside, floodlit in the blizzard, and
the Embassy teemed with dozens of celebrities—Ulanova and
Lepeshinskaya and Ehrenburg and Prokofiev amongst them. The
gallant French airmen of the Normandie Squadron, who had been
decorated by de Gaulle that morning, were also there. With surprising graciousness, de Gaulle was doing the round of the guests. When
he came to me I mentioned his visit to Stalingrad. *"Ah, Stalingrad!"*
he said, *"c'est tout de même un peuple formidable, un très grand
peuple." "Ah, oui, les Russes. . ." "Mais non,"* said de Gaulle with
a touch of impatience. *"Je ne parle pas des Russes, je parle des
Allemands. Tout de même, avoir poussé jusque là!"*†

In later years, when de Gaulle started on his "Paris-Bonn Axis"
and publicly embraced Adenauer, I often remembered that remark.
Was he, in 1944, still full of professional admiration for an Army
that had smashed the French Army in five weeks? Or was this
astonishing remark a reaction to the condescension with which Stalin
had spoken to him, only a few days before, of the French Army,

---

* Sticky.

† "Ah, Stalingrad! All the same, they are a pretty tremendous people,
a very great people." "Ah yes, the Russians. . ." "No, I'm not talking about the Russians; I mean the Germans. Fancy having pushed
all *that* far!"

most of which had been taken prisoner by the Germans in 1940? Or did de Gaulle perhaps want to remind the Russians that they, too, had been on the run, and that thanks to their geography, they had been able to run much farther even than the French had run in 1940?

At the Kremlin banquet on the last night Stalin behaved with a mixture of truculence, bonhomie and buffoonery ("*il avait l'air de se foutre un peu de nous,*" one of the French guests later remarked), and it was not till after de Gaulle had made an angry and spectacular exit that the Russians finally decided to sign the Franco-Soviet Pact without the Polish "counterpart", except for a very minor face-saver. The Russians only signed the Pact in these conditions because they thought it might still come in useful at some later date, and would also help the French Communists. But, throughout the de Gaulle visit, they made no secret of their low opinion of France's contribution to the allied war effort, and the idea of basing the future security of Europe and of the Soviet Union in the first place on a Franco-Russian alliance struck them as unrealistic.

Stalin did not raise a finger to get de Gaulle invited to Yalta two months later. In December 1944 what mattered to Stalin were Britain and the USA, with their armies and air forces and economic resources.

It is more than improbable that Stalin would have agreed to the Rhine frontier independently of them even if de Gaulle had agreed to recognise the Lublin Committee. The only deal that Stalin had proposed was the signing of the Franco-Soviet Pact (even at the risk of annoying Churchill) in exchange for a French recognition of Lublin.

But to de Gaulle this Pact was still important as part of that "independent" French policy—the "Between-East-and-West" policy —that he and Bidault tried (unsuccessfully) to pursue for two years after the war.

Chapter XIII

ALTERNATIVE POLICIES AND IDEOLOGIES
TOWARDS THE END OF THE WAR

The last three months of 1944 were marked by a variety of Russian
military campaigns in preparation for the final onslaught on Nazi
Germany between January and May 1945. In the north the Red
Army overran the Baltic Republics, where they met with a somewhat
mixed reception from the population. There were Estonian, Latvian
and Lithuanian formations in the Red Army, and much was also
made in the Soviet press of a Communist-inspired partisan movement
in both Latvia and Lithuania; but while, in the larger cities like
Tallinn and Riga, the working-class welcomed the Red Army with
apparent enthusiasm, the peasantry were lukewarm. The middle-
class, and the many government officials who had more or less
collaborated with the Germans, had either followed them in their
retreat, or were now lying low. All three countries had their own
Nazis and their own Gestapo men. When I went to Tallinn in
October 1944, I saw furtive and anxious looks on a good many
faces, especially among the better-dressed people. The NKVD were
becoming very active, and thousands of Balts were to be deported
in the next few years.*

By the end of October all the three Republics were liberated, with
the exception of the Courland peninsula (where thirty German
divisions were to remain trapped till the end of the war). By that

* In Solzhenitsyn's famous *One Day in the Life of Ivan Denisovich,*
several seemingly quite harmless Balts figure among the convicts.

932

time over 300 square miles of German territory in East Prussia had also been conquered by the Russians. The great exodus of the German population from East Prussia had begun, many fleeing to Königsberg, others further west.

The fighting for these small areas of German territory had been extremely heavy. The Russians were also meeting with very strong German resistance in Slovakia and Hungary, where the Red Army's progress was very much slower than it had been in Rumania. Budapest was not to fall till February 13, 1945.

In Poland the front had become more or less stabilised in September, but it was generally expected that the final blow at Nazi Germany would be struck from here.

Fighting, however, continued on the Sandomierz bridgehead, south of Warsaw which the Germans were attacking with great determination. Among the Red Army soldiers there was now a feeling of impatience—and distrust. In November 1944 I was shown a letter from a soldier who was fighting "somewhere in Poland"— apparently at Sandomierz:

> As before, I am on my way to Berlin. True, we may not get there in time, but Berlin is precisely the place that we *must* reach. We have suffered enough, and we deserve the right to enter Berlin. Our "military rank" entitles us to it, while the Allies are not entitled to it. They probably wouldn't understand, but Fritz understands it only too well. Hence the frantic resistance with which we are meeting. They keep shelling us morning, noon and night, and must have brought pretty well everything they had in the west. They obviously prefer to be licked by the Allies, and not by us. If that happened, it would really *hurt* us. I trust, however, you will soon hear some good news from us. Our fellows' fury and thirst for revenge after all we have seen are more intense than ever. Even in the days of our retreat it was nothing like it...

But the question of who would reach Berlin first—and this had already become a real obsession with many Russian soldiers—was now thought to be no longer a military, but a diplomatic question, which would *have* to be settled in the Russians' favour.*

* At any rate, all Russians were convinced that there was such a diplomatic agreement, and the soldiers had no doubt whatsoever that the Allies *could* have taken Berlin had they wanted to, but that the

It is probably true to say that the Red Army as a whole was prepared to lose many thousands of men in the Battle of Berlin, rather than see the British and Americans get there first with a minimum loss of life. It was, obviously, also politically important, from the Russian standpoint, to record in every German mind the fact that Berlin had not been voluntarily surrendered to the Western Allies, but had been conquered by the Russians in bloody battle.

A very large number of new questions arose during the latter half of 1944, now that the war was moving to its close—questions concerning foreign policy, internal policy, as well as a variety of cultural and ideological problems. A paradoxical aspect of Russia at that time was that the gigantic human losses it had suffered and the immense devastation wrought by the retreating German armies, as well as great hardships and shortages in both town and country, were combined with a nation-wide feeling of pride and an immense sense of achievement.

The Soviet Union was faced with the vast problem of economic reconstruction and the at least equally serious population problem. Today it is estimated that, by the end of the war, the Soviet Union

---

Allied governments decided against it for political reasons—namely, so as not to antagonise the Russians unduly. As we know, Eisenhower, fearing that German resistance might continue for a very long time in the mountainous "Southern Redoubt", gave priority over Berlin to the occupation of southern Germany and western Austria, despite angry protests from Churchill who thought it politically of the utmost importance for the Western Powers to occupy Berlin before the Russians got there. It has, nevertheless, been suggested that there was a Stalin-Roosevelt agreement behind Eisenhower's choice. But, as Stettinius says: "I know of no evidence to support the charge that President Roosevelt agreed at Yalta that American troops should not capture Berlin ahead of the Red Army." (*Roosevelt and the Russians: The Yalta Conference*, London 1950, p. 264). The fact remains that had the Western Powers occupied Berlin before the Russians, it would have created violent anti-American feeling in Russia, especially in the Army. Roosevelt was no doubt aware of it. By the time Truman took over, the final Russian offensive against Berlin was on the point of starting.

had lost, in one way or another, about twenty million people, among them at least seven million soldiers. Although no exact figures are available, it would seem that these seven million include some three million soldiers who died in German captivity. Further, several million civilians died under the German occupation, including about two million Jews who were massacred, besides the victims of the German anti-partisan punitive expeditions; about a million people died in Leningrad alone, while the sharp lowering of living and food conditions throughout Russia, the shortage of medical supplies, etc., must account for a few million more deaths. Several hundred thousand also died in the various evacuations in 1941 and 1942, in the strafing of refugees and the bombings of cities. Thus in Stalingrad alone some 60,000 civilians were killed.

One of the characteristic developments of 1944 was the new Family Code embodied in the Supreme Soviet Decree of July 8, 1944. The two main purposes of the reform were to discourage "loose living" after the war, and to increase the birth-rate. The decree established the Order of "Mother-Heroine" for mothers of ten or more live children, the Order (three classes) of "Motherly Glory" for mothers of nine, eight or seven live children, and the "Motherhood Medal" (two classes) for mothers of six or five live children. A progressive scale of monetary grants was laid down. Thus, at the birth of a third child the mother received 400 roubles, at the birth of the fourth, 1,300 roubles, and so on, till 5,000 roubles for the tenth, eleventh, etc., child. Especially after the monetary reform of 1947 it became positively good business to produce children *ad infinitum*. The system was, in substance, not unlike the French *allocations familiales* established after the Liberation.

The same decree made divorce very much more difficult, troublesome, and costly than it had been. The most controversial part of the decree concerned "lone" (i.e. unmarried) mothers. Alimony was abolished, though not retroactively. Monetary grants were allowed to unmarried mothers, and they could also, if they wished, hand their child, or children, over to a State institution, with the option of claiming them back at any time. This measure was dictated partly by wartime conditions which, especially in the war zones and the newly-liberated areas, made it both difficult and embarrassing to enquire too closely into a child's parentage. Secondly, in view of the larger number of women than men in Russia towards the end of the war, this decree was, in fact, intended to encourage the production of "illegitimate" children by relieving unmarried mothers of all, or most of the financial responsibility for them. The rather crude demographic principle underlying it was "illegitimate children, rather than none at all". In later years, this part of the 1944 decree was to be severely criticised, since, with the encouragement it gave the professional seducer, it went counter to the "cult of the family" and that high standard of morals the rest of the decree was striving to bring about, notably by making the registration of marriage compulsory before the father could incur any legal and financial responsibilities for the children. *De facto* marriages, without registration, were no longer legally valid, and the children remained officially "fatherless", even if the father was a model family man. The decree of August 8, 1944, besides providing various financial benefits relating to pregnancy and confinement, also imposed a heavy tax on bachelors over twenty-five and a smaller tax on couples with fewer than three children. The law of 1936 prohibiting abortion remained in force, and was not to be changed until many years after the war.

As important as the population problem after the war was that of the economic restoration of the country. Hundreds of cities and towns and thousands of villages had been wholly or partially destroyed by the Germans, much livestock and agricultural machinery had been taken, and the great question that began to be discussed at top level as early as 1943 was how this economic restoration was to be financed. There were, in principle, three possible sources: the Soviet Union's own admittedly depleted resources; a large foreign loan—inevitably from the United States; and, finally, substantial German reparations in kind, and similar reparations, on a smaller scale, from Germany's allies. (The ideal would have been a combination of all three). The armistice terms accepted by Finland and Rumania in 1944 were the first examples of such limited reparations agreements. Finland, for example, agreed to pay 300 million dollars over a period of six years, later extended to eight years. At Yalta, Stalin was to propose that Germany pay Russia ten billion dollars in kind, a figure to which Churchill, in particular, strongly objected.

A further source of "reconstruction expenses", as the post-war years were to show, were the various trade agreements and other financial arrangements made between Russia and the countries of Eastern Europe.*

But this was still in the future, and the problem that preoccupied Stalin and the other Russian leaders, from 1943 on, was an American loan of seven billion dollars or more. American visitors to Russia, representing important business interests, such as Donald M. Nelson and Eric Johnston, favourable to a programme of large-scale American exports to Russia after the war, and seeing this as a precaution against a possible post-war slump in the USA, were taken very seriously by the Russians, especially at the height of the Big-Three harmony, roughly between the middle of 1943 and the Yalta Conference in February 1945. At the same time, the Russians felt certain ideological and political inhibitions about such a loan, since they feared that excessive financial dependence on the United States might well go counter to their own security considerations. Put perhaps a little crudely, there was a conflict between *reconstruction* and *security*. Speedy and relatively easy reconstruction meant a certain dependence on the United States, but it also inevitably meant a greatly-reduced degree of Soviet control over eastern Europe and parts of central Europe, which represented, in the Russian military conception of 1944–5, an indispensable security precaution against a new German aggression or against any kind of aggression from the West. Loose talk in the United States about a "war with Russia in fifteen years' time" had already begun in 1944, and was to become more and more widespread once the first American atom bomb had been dropped.

In the end, the American loan of seven billion dollars came to nothing. But it seems certain that the Russian leadership was to some extent divided on the question and that, inside the Party itself, there were roughly three tendencies, often in conflict inside the

* The Yugoslavs were the first to rebel against such agreements which were highly advantageous to Russia, but unfavourable to them.

minds of the same people. There were, to quote William Appleman
Williams's definition,* the "softies", the "conservatives" and the
"doctrinaire revolutionaries".

Since many Soviet leaders combined all three tendencies in varying degrees, it is impossible to say how large each "school of
thought" was. The pattern also varied greatly from year to year.
There were certainly far more "softies" in 1944 than there were to
be in 1947 or 1948.

Perhaps the most diehard "softy" was Litvinov, who remained
one even as late as 1947. I had a conversation with him at the reception given by Molotov on Red-Army Day in February 1947
which threw some light on what had happened. Taking me aside,
he suddenly started pouring his heart out. He said he was extremely
unhappy about the way the Cold War was getting worse and worse
every day. By the end of the war, he said, Russia had had the choice
of two policies: one was to "cash in on the goodwill she had accumulated during the war in Britain and the United States." But *they*
(meaning Stalin and Molotov) had, unfortunately, chosen the other
policy. Not believing that "goodwill" could constitute the *lasting*
basis for any kind of policy, they had decided that "security" was
what mattered most of all, and they had therefore grabbed all they
could while the going was good—meaning the whole of eastern
Europe and parts of central Europe. At this point, Vyshinsky walked
past, and gave us both an exceedingly dirty look. Litvinov was never
to appear at any public reception again. Ivy Litvinov's reckless
indiscretions at the same party—remarks made for anybody to hear
—added to Molotov's great displeasure.

In the end, for a variety of reasons, it was the "conservative"
policy that prevailed, i.e. the policy lying half-way between the
"softy" policy and the "world revolution" policy. The "conservative" policy finally adopted by Stalin was a rejection of the "world
revolution" idea, at least in any foreseeable future (his advice that
the Communist "patriotic militia" be disbanded in France after the
liberation is a case in point); at the same time, the security of the
Soviet Union, as he saw it, required a strict Russian control of

* *The Tragedy of American Diplomacy* (New York, 1962), pp.
222–3.

eastern Europe, a control that became increasingly strict as the cold war developed. The most important landmark in this process was the "stalinisation" of Czechoslovakia in February 1948.

The "softy" attitude was not perhaps widespread among the Party hierarchy in 1943–4, but it certainly was among the general public, and most of all, perhaps, among the Russian intellectuals. Their great belief was that, after the war, Russia would be able to "relax".

In Moscow, in particular, there were some extraordinary signs of relaxation by the middle of 1944, with a kind of foretaste of easier living conditions, of post-war prosperity and of a growing frivolity in public taste.

Although the "commercial restaurants" and "commercial shops" which opened in April 1944 had nothing to do with that ideological "softness" against which the Party journals were to protest before long, they undoubtedly contributed to the easy-going mood among the more privileged sections of the Moscow population, and even among wider sections. Foreigners in Moscow, and especially the English, with their ideas on war-time austerity, were scandalised by anything so "undemocratic" as these shops and restaurants where people with a lot of money could buy any luxuries they liked. In such restaurants, a good meal, including drinks, cost about 300 roubles or, at the "diplomatic" rate, about £6 per head. These shops and restaurants represented a sort of legal black market.

After a ruinous party for four at the Moskva Restaurant on May-Day, 1944 (there was a jazz band playing, and the meal, with two bottles of wine, cost nearly £30) I asked Boris Voitekhov, the writer, a diehard party-man, about the "party line" on these commercial restaurants.

"This country," he said, "is in a tragic plight after three years of war. Look at our women, for instance. When I see how they work—how they run our agriculture, and look after their children, though tired and dirty and hungry, how they drive steamships and fly aeroplanes—it brings a lump to my throat. It affects me more even than the Red Army, with its fearful casualties. There are people in our country who are literally dying of hunger. At first sight, the commercial restaurants are a scandal. But they are not. And I'll tell you why. It is sentimental democracy to say you mustn't allow an officer on leave to have a night out at the Moskva. What he eats and drinks is a drop in the ocean and won't help the poor and the starving. It is also a good thing when a factory director from the provinces, who has been reporting on his work to the Kremlin, can go somewhere for a decent meal. It keeps him in good humour, makes him think kindly of Moscow, and has a good effect on his work. And even if there are twenty or thirty crooks and racketeers out of every hundred people in the restaurant, it doesn't matter. Crooks don't last long in our country."

People were, in fact, glad to have commercial restaurants and commercial shops to go to. Especially the shops. These gave even the poorly-paid a chance to have an *occasional* treat, such as buying some chocolates or cream cakes, even at an absurd price, and so, for once, getting something different from the same dreary old rations. The restaurants were mostly frequented by highly-paid industrial executives, writers, artists and scientists and, above all, by officers on leave who were only too glad to "blow" a whole month's unspent salary on a night out.

These commercial shops and restaurants were also part of a long-term policy for regulating prices in the *kolkhoz* markets, and their introduction was, in fact, to be a first step towards the abolition of rationing two years after the war, after a further series of price adjustments and the monetary reform.

But whether commercial restaurants and shops were an economically sound proposition or not in the long run, by the middle of 1944 they certainly created a somewhat frivolous illusion of "back to normal" and post-war prosperity. And that at a time when a very, very hard war was still being fought.

There were other signs of frivolity and escapism. The famous *chansonnier* and *diseur* Alexander Vertinsky, after spending more than twenty years as an idol of the Russian émigrés in Paris, New York and, finally, Shanghai, turned up in Moscow. His recitals of "decadent" songs drew immense crowds, including hundreds of soldiers and officers. Although he was never reviewed or advertised in the press, posters announcing Vertinsky recitals were stuck up all over Moscow, and the story went that he was the protégé of high-up NKVD officials who loved him after years of confiscating thousands of his gramophone records which travellers had tried to smuggle into Russia! Another theory was that he had been a Soviet spy while posing as an émigré. The fact remains that his songs, with their quaint exoticism, were thoroughly escapist and wildly popular in the Moscow of 1944.

Both songs and films were tending to become escapist. The most popular song hits in 1944 were two songs by Nikita Boguslavsky from a film called *The Two Pals*—*The Dark Night* and *Kostya, the Odessa Mariner* already referred to; both were later to be denounced as examples either of escapism, or of "tavern melancholy"— *kabatskaya melankholiya*.

The Russian people in 1944 liked to think that life would soon be easier, and that Russia could "relax" after the war. The "lasting alliance" with Britain and the USA had much to do with it. In the middle of 1944 Konstantin Simonov, with his genius for scenting the mood in the country, produced a play called *So It Will Be*, in which officers home on leave were seen preparing to settle down to a pleasant, easy life in a nice Moscow flat, where even that proverbial bully, the *upravdom*, the manager of the block of flats, was a personification of kindness and efficiency. "The wounds of war, however deep, will soon heal," one of the officers said. And another, after something of a *crise de conscience*, decided that his wife and child, who had been missing for years in German-occupied territory, must be considered as finally lost, and that he might as well start life again with a professor's sweet young daughter. It was the very anti-thesis of the *Wait for Me* mood of Simonov's 1941-2 poetry. In 1944 the cinemas were showing American films, among them a particularly inane Deanna Durbin film, for which thousands queued for hours.

Some Party members were full of easygoing ideas. One very tough Party member remarked to me in 1944: "We also have our softies in the Party—people who think of the future of Anglo-Soviet and American-Soviet relations in terms of the *Britansky Soyuznik**

* The British Ministry of Information weekly which sold about 50,000 copies in those days.

942 *1944: Russia Enters Eastern Europe*

with its sickly rubbish about '400 Years of Anglo-Russian Friendship'. It is high time they read some Lenin."

Even some notoriously tough party members were not quite immune against this relaxed atmosphere. Thus, in the summer of 1944, with the Second Front in full swing, the writer Vsevolod Vyshnevsky remarked at a VOKS* party (maybe he would not have made the same remarks anywhere else):

> When the war is over, life in Russia will become very pleasant. A great literature will be produced as a result of our war experiences. There will be much coming and going, with a lot of contacts with the West. Everybody will be allowed to read anything he likes. There will be exchanges of students, and foreign travel will be made easy.

It was even widely suggested that light reading would be encouraged. Thus, there was a scheme for starting a library of thrillers and detective stories in Russian—mostly translated from English— under the general editorship of Sergei Eisenstein, that great lover of Western thrillers.

The first serious warning against these "Western" and "bourgeois" tendencies came from a certain Solodovnikov, writing in the official Party magazine *Bolshevik*, in October 1944:

> Recently views have been expressed in various quarters to the effect that, after the war, art and literature will follow the "easy road", and will, in the first place, be calculated to entertain. The supporters of this view talk of the development of light comedy and other thoughtless forms of entertainment, and object to big and serious subjects being included in art and literature. Such views receive support from part of our audiences. Such tendencies must be fought. They are reactionary, and in flat contradiction with the Lenin-Stalin view that art is a powerful weapon of agitation and education among the masses.

He not only fumed against "frivolous" art, but also against "refined" art which was calculated only for "the bloated upper ten thousand".

On the whole, however, he spoke highly of Soviet literary and artistic production during the war—and was particularly enthusiastic

* Society for Cultural Relations with Foreign Countries.

about the music produced by Shostakovich, Prokofiev, Miaskovsky, Khachaturian and Shebalin.*

He also warned Russian artists against aping "Western, especially German"† models and deplored the wartime tendency to wax enthusiastic over ikons and religious music, merely on the ground that they formed part of the Russian "national heritage", a marked departure from the 1941–2 line.

The rapid succession of events in 1944 raised a number of other new problems in the eyes of the Party. Deep below the surface, there was a fundamental rivalry between the Party and the Army. During the first three years of the war, the Party was usually only too glad to identify itself with the Army. But with the end of the war in sight, it decided that it was time to regain something of its former identity. During the first two years of the war, the emphasis in nearly all official propaganda had been on "Holy Russia", and it now seemed important to revive a greater Soviet-consciousness. The Party also had to take account of the fact that many people in the occupied areas had been demoralised by Nazi propaganda and by the re-introduction of private enterprise (only small-scale, but still private enterprise), that the Red Army was now fighting in "bourgeois" countries, which created a number of new psychological problems.

For the first two or three years of the war (whatever was said later to the contrary) there had been a tendency for the Party to get lost in the crowd. Especially in the Army, the Party had become diluted by the easy admission of new members, whose numbers had grown between 1941 and 1944 from about two to six million.

In 1944 there came a change. *Pravda* of June 24, 1944 still placed the Communist's *practical wartime value* above all other qualities.

* All these were to be fiercely denounced as "formalists" in 1948. (see the author's *Musical Uproar in Moscow*, London, 1949).
† This was a polite way of avoiding any mention of Britain and the USA.

Personal qualities are, at the present time, tested, above all, by the party candidate's contribution to the struggle with the enemy. Every candidate or member of the Party must be in the front rank of those carrying out the required military, economic or political tasks. The Communist at the front must be brave and spontaneously willing to do the most dangerous jobs. That is why the Communist's authority is so high in the Red Army, and why hundreds of thousands of soldiers, before going into battle, now apply for membership.

But, by September 1944, bravery was no longer enough. As *Red Star* wrote on September 27:

The ideological training of members is now more necessary than ever. The Party organisations in the Army have done much in this respect—but not enough. The Army's Party Organisations largely consist of young party members and are being replenished by more young men *who have been tested as brave soldiers but who, politically, are insufficiently experienced.* More attention must be given to the ideological upbringing of candidates and members.

Secondly ... the front now runs *through territory outside our borders. To find his way about in these new conditions, a Communist needs a sound ideological equipment more than ever* (emphasis added).

As the war was moving to its close the admission of new Party members was tightened up. "What we need now is not quantity but quality," *Red Star* wrote on November 1, thus completely abandoning its earlier position. It now recalled that the rules of admission to the Party had been relaxed early in the war,* and now argued that far too many people, including soldiers who had never been in any battle at all, had been admitted to the Party. The Party's representatives within the Army had often "misused the authority given them" and had admitted far too many people into the Party. Now, "the chief object of the Army's party organisations must be the ideological-political education of communists and their absorption into Party work." The same line was taken by *Bolshevik* in October 1944 which declared: "In the complex international

* It recalled the two decrees of August and December 1941, the latter issued at the height of the Battle of Moscow. Under this any officer or soldier "who has distinguished himself in battle" could be admitted to the Party after a three months' candidate stage.

situation facing the Soviet Union, the Party member needs a compass, and there is no better one than Marxist-Leninism." It recommended the intensive study of the Stalinist *Short History of the Communist Party*.

The same *Bolshevik* article then referred to two recent Central Committee decrees which concerned newly liberated areas. It was remarkably outspoken in commenting on the Central Committee's Decree on Belorussia:

> Ideological and political education is of exceptional importance in the newly-liberated areas... The enemy has spread the poison of racialist theories in these areas, inciting Ukrainians against Russians, Belorussians against Lithuanians, Estonians against Russians, etc... The Nazi invaders have also inflamed private-property instincts among these peoples. They liquidated the *kolkhozes*, distributed the land among German colonists, destroyed the intelligentsia, encouraged trading and profiteering, and played off workers and peasants against each other...

In short, political education in these newly-liberated areas must be intensified. And *Bolshevik* also emphasised a number of awkward facts seldom, if ever, mentioned in the daily press at the time:

> White emigrants, Ukrainian nationalists, Bandera, Bulba and Melnikov bands are being extensively used by the Germans in the Ukraine... These contemptible flunkeys of Hitler placed their nationalist slogans at the service of German imperialism, and also actively participated in the massacres* organised by the Germans. The Party organisations must intensify their work, especially in the rural areas of the Ukraine. They must remember that until this German-Ukrainian nationalism is completely weeded out, the restoration of the Ukrainian economy and national culture is impossible.

But what worried the Party above all, perhaps, was the widespread hope, both in the liberated territories, *and inside the Army*, with its millions of peasant conscripts, that the *kolkhoz* system would be "changed".

*

* The massacres obviously refer to the massacres of Jews, though these are, as usual, not specifically mentioned.

If the Germans, despite the general beastliness of their occupation régime, had succeeded, on the Russians' own admission, in creating anti-Soviet moods in both Belorussia and the Ukraine, particularly among private-enterprise enthusiasts, there was, obviously, also a parallel danger of Russian soldiers becoming infected by their contact with the bourgeois way of life in countries like Rumania, Poland, Hungary and Czechoslovakia.

The problem was not, of course, entirely new. In 1939 the Red Army had occupied eastern Poland and, in 1940, the Baltic States. There had then been a rush by Soviet citizens, on one pretext or another, to Lwow and Tallinn and Riga to buy up trunkfuls of clothes, and shoes and handbags while stocks lasted. But that had been relatively small stuff. Now hundreds of thousands, or millions of Russian soldiers were seeing countries where housing conditions were often better than in Russia, where farms were more prosperous-looking, and where there was still something to be bought in the shops. Rumania in 1944 was not overflowing with consumer goods, but there was much more to be found in the Bucharest department stores than in the completely bare shops in the Soviet Union. About that time I remember Konstantin Simonov wearing in Moscow a wonderfully loud tweed suit acquired in Bucharest. And, until further notice, Rumania was going to remain a "bourgeois country"; Moscow had assured the Western allies that no changes in Rumania's "social structure" were contemplated. There was all the more reason to debunk the Western way of life, as seen in Rumania, and to warn Russians against being taken in by the "tinsel" of Bucharest.

Typical of this campaign was a series of articles by Leonid Sobolev in *Pravda* in September 1944:

> Fantastic Transniestria has again become the Soviet province of Odessa. The unfortunate Rumanian people have had to pay millions (*sic*) of lives for that spectacle... Our Soviet people were united, and that is why we have won. Here in Rumania it is different: on the one hand there are the Rumanian people, on the other, the political adventurers... What patriots there were in Rumania were lost in a bewildered, befuddled crowd... Rumanian intellectuals tell me that in 1939 all resistance to Hitler would have been useless... One would

think that one man's resistance to one tank would also be useless—yet such things happened at Sebastopol.

After a satirical and contemptuous description of Bucharest, with "its tinsel, vulgarity and commercialism", its "sickening cringing to the Red Army", and its "well-dressed people sitting at café tables", and "traders and speculators, sitting on the high seats of horse-carriages, and looking like old posters of *burzhuis*", Sobolev then said that "this tinsel of Bucharest" was not typical of Rumania. At Constanza there were 80,000 people, but not a single theatre, no concert hall, no local newspaper and only two secondary and two elementary schools.

> "We shall pass through many foreign countries yet. Soldiers! your eyes will often be dazzled; but do not be deceived by these outward signs of their so-called civilisation! Remember, real culture is that which you carry with you... When the war is over, foreign nations will resume their own lives, but there will always remain in their hearts the memory of your great human culture, of the soul of the Soviet people—of that people who shed their blood so that millions might be free and happy."

He then went on to say that the Rumanian countryside was poor, and that all the loot went to Bucharest:

> Quietly, with an ironical smile, our soldiers march along these sumptuous streets... The Rumanians had expected "Russian beasts" to enter the city. They were expecting murder and robbery and rape. Nothing like that happened... A few bandits in Russian uniform who were caught turned out to be Rumanian deserters...

Soviet comments on the Slav countries—Bulgaria, Yugoslavia, Czechoslovakia—were somewhat different, even though these, too, had their "well-dressed people sitting at café tables"—especially Czechoslovakia. For one thing, there was more good feeling for the Russians there than there was in Rumania, let alone Hungary.

Also, whatever official writers said, the Russian soldiers were far from always being gallant knights in shining armour. If, in the southern and central-European Slav countries, their conduct was reasonably good (though far from perfect—the Yugoslavs had a great deal to say later on that score), it was worse in Rumania and worse still in Hungary and Austria. Nor was it by any means exemplary in Poland. Sometimes this conduct varied from army to army. Malinovsky's troops had a worse reputation than others, and the Kazakhs and other Asiatics sometimes emulated their forebears, the warriors of Genghis Khan, especially in Germany, where anything from wrist-watches to young boys attracted their covetous attention.

It is not denied by the Russians themselves that some Russian troops ran wild, especially in Germany; but here there were, of course, some weighty extenuating circumstances.

PART EIGHT

Victory—And the Seeds
of the Cold War

Chapter I

INTO GERMANY

The final Russian offensive against Germany, which was not to stop until her capitulation nearly four months later, began on January 12. On the following day the Russians published this communiqué:

> The troops of the 1st Ukrainian Front under Marshal Konev (Chief of Staff, General Sokolovsky) took the offensive on January 12 in the area west of Sandomierz and, despite bad weather, which made air support impossible, broke through the enemy's strong defences along a twenty-five mile front. Our artillery barrage was decisive. In two days the troops advanced twenty-five miles and the width of the breakthrough is now forty miles. 350 localities have been occupied.

The statement that the Russian offensive was started "without air support" had a diplomatic story behind it.

In 1948 the Russian Foreign Ministry published the letters exchanged between Churchill and Stalin before and during this January offensive.

After the Germans had launched their Ardennes Offensive, which had placed the Anglo-American troops in a "difficult position" (the Russian publication said), and Britain was threatened with "a second Dunkirk", Churchill sent the following message to Stalin on January 6, 1945:

> The battle in the west is very heavy and, at any time, large decisions may be called for from the Supreme Command. You know yourself . . . how very anxious the position is when a very broad front has to be defended after temporary loss of the initiative. It is General Eisenhower's great desire and need to know in outline what you plan to do. . . [Can we] count on a major Russian offensive on the Vistula front, or elsewhere, during January? . . . I regard the matter as urgent.

951

On the next day Stalin replied that it was "very important to make use of our superiority in artillery and aircraft", for which clear weather was essential—and the weather prospects were bad—but "in view of the position of our allies on the Western Front, Headquarters of the [Soviet] Supreme Command has decided to complete the preparations at a forced pace and, disregarding the weather, to launch wide-scale offensive operations against the Germans all along the Central Front not later than the second half of January."

On January 9, Churchill replied with overwhelming gratitude:

> "I am most grateful to you for your thrilling message. I have sent it over to General Eisenhower for his eyes only. May all good fortune rest upon your noble venture. The news you give me will be a great encouragement to General Eisenhower because ... German reinforcements will have to be split."

The Russian offensive was duly launched on the 12th—even earlier than Stalin had promised: five days later, Churchill cabled to Stalin thanking him "from the bottom of his heart" and congratulating him on "the immense assault you have launched upon the Eastern Front."

Later, in February, in an Order of the Day, Stalin claimed that the Russian offensive had undoubtedly saved the situation in the West: "The first consequence of our winter offensive was to thwart the German winter offensive in the West, which aimed at the seizure of Belgium and Alsace, and enable the armies of our allies, in their turn, to launch an offensive against the Germans."

Churchill, while quoting some of this correspondence, gives it rather less dramatic significance. He describes it, nevertheless, as "a good example of the speed at which business could be done at the summit of the alliance." Also, "it was a fine deed of the Russians and their chief to hasten this vast offensive, no doubt at heavy cost in life. Eisenhower was very pleased indeed."*

*

* Churchill, op. cit., vol. VI, p. 244. On the other hand, Chester Wilmot, in describing the military events in the West in December 1944-January 1945 in *The Struggle for Europe* greatly minimises the effect of the Russian offensive on the situation on the Western Front.

On January 14, two days after Konev's thrust from the Sandomierz bridgehead, the 1st Belorussian Front under Marshal Zhukov (Chief of Staff, General Malinin) struck out from their two bridgeheads south of Warsaw, and from another one to the north. After surrounding Warsaw, the two groups entered the Polish capital (or rather, its ruins) on the 17th. Units of the Polish Army took part in this operation.

The timing of the Russian offensive on the middle Vistula appears to have come as a surprise to the German High Command. True, an eventual Russian thrust in the "Warsaw-Berlin direction" was to be expected, and the Germans had built seven defence lines between the Vistula and the Oder. But in January they expected that, before attacking here, the Russians would try to destroy the thirty German divisions trapped in Courland and also strike their heaviest blow in Hungary. The concentration of German forces along the middle Vistula was therefore not as great as it might have been. The enormous superiority the Russians achieved in this "sector of the main blow" may be gauged from the following figures quoted by the *Soviet History*:

> The 1st Belorussian and 1st Ukrainian Fronts had 163 divisions, 32,143 guns and mortars, 6,460 tanks and mobile guns and 4,772 aircraft. The total effectives were 2,200,000 men. Thus we had in the Warsaw-Berlin direction [at the beginning of the offensive] 5·5 times more men than the enemy, 7·8 times more guns, 5·7 times more tanks, and 17·6 times more planes.*

Further north, the troops of Rokossovsky's 2nd Belorussian Front also struck out.

By the 18th the whole picture was clear: Konev was overrunning southern Poland on his way to Silesia; Zhukov, central Poland towards the heart of Germany; Rokossovsky, northern Poland on the way to Danzig. Meantime in the south, General Petrov (4th Ukrainian Front) was advancing in the Carpathians and, in the

---

* IVOVSS, vol. V, p. 57. This great superiority was, of course, far from being maintained throughout the subsequent fighting; with the Germans throwing in reserves, there was to be some extremely bitter fighting in many areas for the next four months, e.g. on the Oder, at Königsberg, etc.

LIBERATION of POLAND and
INVASION of GERMANY • 1945

north, Cherniakhovsky (3rd Belorussian Front) was breaking deep
into East Prussia.

A few dates and place names should suffice to illustrate the success
of this offensive:

January 18   Rokossovsky captured the fortress of Modlin.
             Konev captured Piotrkow.
January 19   Konev captured Cracow, almost intact.
  „   20   Cherniakhovsky captured Tilsitt in East Prussia.
  „   21   Cherniakhovsky captured Gumbinnen, and Rokos-
             sovsky Tannenberg, also in East Prussia.
  „   23   Zhukov captured Bygdoszcz (Bromberg) and Konev
             broke into Silesia and reached the Oder along a forty-
             mile front.
January 24–6 Zhukov captured Kalisz, "on the way to Breslau".
             Rokossovsky broke through to the Bay of Danzig,
             thus almost isolating the German forces in East
             Prussia; Konev broke into the Polish Dombrowski
             coal basin.
January 29   Zhukov crossed the 1938 frontier into Germany,
             south-west of Poznan. Poznan, and its large German
             garrison, was encircled and, two days later, Zhukov
             penetrated into the province of Brandenburg, on his
             way to Frankfurt-on-the-Oder.

That was the setting in which Hitler was "celebrating" the 12th
anniversary of his accession to power—with the Russians inside the
province of Brandenburg! One last obstacle, the Oder, and then—
finis.

There was panic in Berlin. Hundreds of thousands of refugees
were fleeing along all roads to Berlin and beyond, in twenty-five or
thirty degrees of frost. Many died by the roadside, and thousands
were suffering from frostbite when they reached Berlin. If they were
not, as a rule, strafed from the air, it was because among this torrent
of refugees, with their lorries, horse-carts, hand-carts, babies and
animals, there were also many non-Germans—war prisoners and
slaves of all nationalities, who were being forcibly evacuated—away
from the front, away from the Russians. Hospitals in Berlin were
packed, the military barracks were almost empty, and the life of the
capital was made an endless misery by massive air-raids from the
West, the most devastating of which precisely coincided with this

influx of refugees from the East. The most fearful were the thousand-bomber night raids at the beginning of February, which set miles and miles of the city ablaze.

Before abandoning Tannenberg, the Germans blew up the immense Tannenberg war memorial and took to Berlin the remains of Hindenburg and his wife. "We shall put it up again when East Prussia is liberated", the radio announcer said dismally. But Dittmar, the "radio general", was saying: "The position on the Eastern Front is incredibly grave", and they were interrupting the programmes with announcements of *Terrorbomber*, here, there and everywhere.

On January 30 Hitler himself spoke, lugubriously, like a voice from the grave. It was the last time his people were going to hear him speak. "By sparing my life on July 20, the Almighty has shown that He wishes me to continue as your Führer." No word of comfort, still less of apology came from him. Only: "German workers, work! German soldiers, fight! German women, be as fanatical as ever! No nation can do more." He then started prophesying how Europe, with Germany as her spearhead (*an der Spitze*), would yet defeat the hordes that England had called up from the steppes of central Asia.

Meanwhile, thousands of refugees were chasing along the *Autobahnen* and other roads to Berlin, where nobody wanted them. Berliners, aided by the police and the SS, were driving them farther away—where to? 150,000 of those who had not fled to Berlin, fled to "impregnable" Königsberg, only to be trapped there, until the German garrison hacked a path through the Russian lines and they could flee to Danzig along the icy wastes of the lagoon and the strip of snow-covered dunes. But, before very long, Danzig itself was going to be cut off by the Russians.

The Russian offensive across Poland and deep into Germany was spectacular. The Germans retreated to the Oder, but leaving behind various garrisons for delaying actions. The largest delaying force was that progressively isolated in an ever-shrinking area of East Prussia; but there were also garrisons at Poznan, Torun and, later, at Schneidemühl and Breslau. A handful were still resisting desper-

TOWARDS
VICTORY
APRIL-MAY
1945

3rd BELORᴺ
(Vassilevsky)

2nd BELORᴺ
(Rokossovsky)

1st BELO-
RUSSIAN
(Zhukov)

BRITISH
(Montgomery)

Hamburg

Swinemünde
Waren
Stettin

BERLIN
Küstrin
Wittenberg
Frankfurt
Cottbus
Oder

TORGAU

JUNCTION
MADE BY
RUSSIANS &
AMERICANS
26th MAY

Leipzig
Dresden
Elbe

1st UKRAINE
(Konev)
Görlitz
Breslau
20th APRIL
Neisse

Miles
0   50   100   150

N

Karlsbad
PRAGUE
C Z E C H O S L O V A K I A

4th UKRAINE
(Yeremenko)
20th APRIL

Nuremberg
Pilsen

Regensburg
Danube
Passau
Krems

2nd UKRAINE
(Malinovsky)

AMERICANS
Munich

VIENNA

BUDAPEST

3rd UKRAINE
(Tolbukhin)

A U S T R I A
H U N G A R Y

Danube

Klagenfurt

ITALY

BRITISH
(Alexander)
Trieste

JUGO-

SLAVIA

20th APRIL

Last German
movements

ately in the castle of the Teutonic Knights at Marienburg. In their retreat through Poland the Germans destroyed what they could— railway bridges above all—but they had no time to destroy Lodz or Cracow, or the great sources of wealth that Silesia represented to the new Polish State.

In many of the conquered towns of Germany there was a babel of tongues—French war-prisoners who had worked on the land ("It was we Frenchmen who ran the agriculture of East Prussia in the last two years," some of them later claimed); British prisoners, many of them survivors of Dunkirk and almost old residents; American newcomers—G.I.'s captured at Bastognes a few weeks before, who had gone into Germany from one end, and were now coming out at the other; Dutch workers, Belgian workers, French workers, Polish slaves, Russian slaves, Italians—not much better than slaves either —it was rather crazy, jolly and chaotic.

Later, in March, I was to see many British, American, French and other ex-war prisoners who were being sent home by sea via Odessa. The first days of their liberation had been pretty rough-and-tumble, and each had some tragic, or comic, story to tell. A kind of real international solidarity had developed among them, and if things sometimes went wrong, as they were bound to do, it couldn't be helped. The Russian armies had plenty of other things to worry about but, by and large, the repatriation through Odessa was done as well as could be expected in exceptionally difficult circumstances.*

*

* Some had even arrived in Odessa with their "wives", mostly Ukrainian girls who had been deported to Germany. I saw six English lads with Ukrainian "wives"—they all claimed to have gone through some sort of religious marriage ceremony in Germany—and all six couples lived happily together in Odessa in a schoolroom. There was a seventh couple—a London lad with a German girl from East Prussia, a plucky young thing who, he claimed, had saved both his life and that of a Russian officer, who had thereupon given them his blessing. Unfortunately, the Ukrainian girls—rather raw village specimens they were—were not allowed to go to England with their Tommy husbands, and the poor plucky German girl was informed by the British repatriation authorities that her "husband" already had a wife in London.

Despite the spectacular Russian advance through January and February, and great superiority in both men and every kind of equipment, the Germans were not cracking up yet. Ehrenburg's daily outbursts of gloating, mostly on the subject of "see-how-they-run", did not strictly correspond to the facts. I remember a Russian major saying to me: "In some places their resistance reminds me of Sebastopol; those German soldiers can be quite heroic at times." And a professional soldier wrote in *Red Star* in February:

> How fierce the battles are in the Poznan area may be judged from this episode: in one of the suburbs of Poznan some five hundred German soldiers and officers were cut off from the rest. Having entrenched themselves in a number of stone buildings, they continued to resist our advancing troops till they were nearly all destroyed. Only the last fifty Germans, who realised the uselessness of further resistance, surrendered.

The Germans were certainly not easily surrendering to the Russians; their chief hope, except when trapped or left behind for delaying actions, was to get beyond the Oder. By the end of January the German losses since the beginning of the offensive were put by the Russians at 552 planes, 2,995 tanks, 15,000 guns and mortars, 26,000 machine guns, 34,000 motor vehicles, 295,000 dead—but only 86,000 prisoners; and even this figure may have been an exaggeration. Throughout February, the Russian advance went on relentlessly. Every night the German radio played light music—what else were they to do? And then a male voice would say dismally that here was the report from the Führer's headquarters: "After heroic resistance, Elbing has fallen... The enemy has broken into Posen and Schneidemühl... The Bolsheviks are suffering enormous losses. They lost 7,500 tanks in the last month. But the V-bombing of London continues..." Then there would be atrocity stories about such-and-such little girls and somebody's 87-year-old grandmother having been raped. Next, another military march and again: *Terrorbomber, Terrorbomber* over such-and-such cities. Finally the same old baritone would then sing his little song: "*Geht zu Bett und geht zu Ruh, geht dem neuen Morgen zu*",* or the Fräulein would wind

* "Go to bed and go to sleep, until the morning comes".

up reassuringly, and yet rather conscious, one felt, of the silliness of the remark: "Good night, and sleep really well."

The Russian press published many lurid accounts of Berlin, especially after the immense fire raid of February 4. But so far the big land offensive in the West had not yet started, and the Russians tried to push on as fast as they could.

On February 1 Rokossovsky took Torun by storm, after a six-days' siege.

On February 6, Konev forced the Oder along a wide front in Silesia and isolated Breslau.

By February 9, Königsberg was almost entirely encircled, and a German prisoner was reported as saying:

> There is not much enthusiasm amongst the troops who have been ordered to defend Königsberg to the last. All are tired, and the soldiers are silently watching the panic among the civilians; it has a depressing effect on soldiers and officers alike. The city is full of gloomy rumours. All the schools, theatres and railway stations are packed with wounded. The civilians have been told that they must get out of Königsberg as best they can.

On February 10 Rokossovsky took Elbing, and on the 14th Zhukov took Schneidemühl, after several days' street-fighting. On February 23, after a month's siege, Zhukov took Poznan and its citadel, the last German stronghold there. General Chuikov, of Stalingrad fame, and a specialist in street-fighting took a leading part in the fighting there. 23,000 prisoners were taken. That was the day on which the Allies launched their offensive in the west.

A few days before, one of Russia's most brilliant young soldiers, General Cherniakhovsky was fatally wounded outside Königsberg. Marshal Vassilevsky took over the command of the 3rd Belorussian Front.

During March, the war in the East became somewhat less spectacular than in January and February. Everywhere the Germans were resisting fiercely. Vassilevsky was battering at Königsberg which, reduced to a heap of rubble, was not going to fall until April 9.

Zhukov's and Rokossovsky's troops were closing in on Danzig from different directions. By the middle of March Danzig was completely isolated, except by sea; on March 28 Gdynia was taken, with its harbour wrecked, but its modern Polish-built town—called "Gothenhafen" during the German rule—more or less intact. Not so Danzig, which fell on March 30, after several days' fierce street-fighting. The beautiful medieval city had been reduced by then to a smoking ruin, but the Polish flag was solemnly hoisted on what was henceforth to be known as Gdansk. Ten thousand German prisoners were taken, but many more than that were dead. Many civilians in and around Danzig committed suicide, so great was the fear of falling into Russian hands. I was later to see a German Army leaflet printed during the last days of the defence of Danzig; it was full of last-ditch resistance slogans and stories of Russian atrocities, and it promised a mighty German counter-offensive. Significantly, there was no mention of Hitler in it.

It was, more or less, the same at Königsberg. When it fell, 84,000 prisoners were claimed there, and 42,000 German dead, though the Russians also had lost many thousands of men. A few thousand half-demented civilians were still living among the ruins, among them many Russian war prisoners and deportees. Except for some minor mopping-up operations still to be done, East Prussia had vanished from the map by the middle of April. The country was to become partly Russian, partly Polish. Most of the Russian troops in East Prussia could now be moved to the Oder where, with the bridgeheads the Russians already held on its west bank, the stage was now set for the final onslaught on Berlin. Meanwhile, after the fall of Danzig, Rokossovsky was pushing along the Baltic towards Stettin.

For a time, during that first half of April, attention shifted to the south. Even before the fall of Budapest in February, the "Democratic Government" of Hungary at Debrecen asked for an Armistice, and this was signed in Moscow on January 20 by Göngös, Weres and Balogh on behalf of Hungary and by Voroshilov on behalf of the three Allied Powers. As *Red Star* wrote on the following day:

> Hungary was Hitler's last satellite in Europe, and the most stubborn of all. Not until the Red Army had occupied a large part of Hungary

did the Horthy Government feel obliged to break with Germany...
But the Germans organised a *coup d'état* in Budapest and Salasi, a
ruffian with a criminal past, and head of the Crossed Arrows,* became
head of the new puppet government... His aim was simply to defend
Austria's frontiers with the help of Hungarian "volunteers". But even
Hitler, in his New Year message, had to admit that the partnership
was coming to an end.

The Hungarian Democratic Government at Debrecen decided then
to declare war on Germany and sued for an Armistice... The terms
are generous, especially when one considers that Hungary was Hitler's
first and last satellite, and that the Hungarian troops behaved abomin-
ably at Voronezh, on the Don, at Orel, Chernigov and Kiev... The
300 million dollars' reparations (200 to the Soviet Union, 100 to
Yugoslavia and Czechoslovakia) spread over six years, are generous...
Territorially, Hungary returns to her 1937 frontiers, and Hitler's
Vienna Award of 1940 is thus cancelled... Hungary must now take
part in the war against Germany... Meantime, the Soviet troops are
completing the liberation of Budapest.

Budapest fell at last on February 13. 110,000 prisoners were
taken, among them Col.-Gen. Pfeffer-Wildenbruch. Eleven panzer
divisions—which might have served a better purpose elsewhere—
were now thrown into Hungary, since Hitler was eager to save
Vienna at any price. After the fall of Budapest the Germans
launched a strong counter-offensive and the Russians even lost some
ground. It was not till the end of March that both Tolbukhin and
Malinovsky could say that the German counter-offensive had spent
itself. On March 29 the Russians crossed into Austria; on April 4,
Malinovsky captured Bratislava, the capital of Slovakia and, on the
13th, after a week's heavy fighting inside the city, Malinovsky and
Tolbukhin occupied Vienna.

A novel feature of the Vienna fighting was the announcement by
Tolbukhin that rank-and-file Nazis had nothing to fear. All kinds of
other surprising phrases began to appear in the Soviet press at the
time: "The Viennese are helping the Red Army, and they fully
understand that the Soviet Union is not fighting against Austrians."

* A Hungarian Nazi organisation.

"The Austrians' hatred for Prussianised Germany has deep historic roots..." And, after the fall—or "liberation" as it was called—of Vienna, the Soviet press was full of pleasant little stories of how the Russian soldiers went on pilgrimages to the grave of their favourite composer, Johann Strauss "who had written the music for the film *The Great Waltz*". Wreaths were also laid on the grave of Beethoven.

Meantime Yeremenko had taken the place of Petrov as commander of the 4th Ukrainian Front, and the sweep through Czechoslovakia also gained in momentum. On April 26, Malinovsky entered Brno, the capital of Moravia. However, in the end, neither he nor Yeremenko was destined to liberate Prague. On the very last day of the war, it was Konev's tanks which made a spectacular breakthrough to the city from Saxony in the north, just as street fighting in Prague was becoming serious and the danger of the city's destruction was growing from hour to hour. The part played in the Prague fighting by the Vlasov troops, who deserted their German masters and went over to the Czech Resistance movement makes one of the strangest stories of this phase of the war; but, for a long time, neither the Russians nor the Czechs liked it mentioned.

By the middle of April, with the Russians deep inside Austria and Czechoslovakia and the Western Allies sweeping across Western and Southern Germany, and Zhukov, Konev and Rokossovsky holding the Oder Line, the time was ripe for the final attack on Berlin.

A short digression is called for, however, on the tricky subject of Russian policy towards Germany when the Red Army began to occupy German territory. After all that the Germans had done—and horrors like the destruction of Warsaw and the extermination camps at Maidanek and Auschwitz were still fresh in every soldier's memory—there was no sympathy at all for the German people. No doubt, there was much respect for the German soldier, but that was different. Having fought the Germans for nearly four years on Russian soil, and having seen thousands of Russian towns and villages in ruins, the Russian troops could not resist their thirst for revenge when they finally broke into Germany.

Ever since Russian troops had been on German soil, some rough things had been going on. In the first flush of the invasion of Germany, Russian soldiers burned down numerous houses, and sometimes whole towns—merely because they were German! (I was to see this later, for instance in a large East Prussian town like Allenstein. The Poles who had taken over the city—now re-christened Olsztyn—were furious at all the repairing and rebuilding they had to do in a town which had originally fallen almost intact into Russian hands). There was also a great deal of looting, robbery and rape. The rape no doubt included many genuine atrocities; but as a Russian major later told me, many German women somehow assumed that "it was now the Russians' turn", and that it was no good resisting. "The approach," he said, "was usually very simple. Any of our chaps simply had to say: '*Frau, komm,*' and she knew what was expected of her... Let's face it. For nearly four years, the Red Army had been sex-starved. It was all right for officers, especially staff officers, so many of whom had a 'field-wife' handy—a secretary, or typist, or a nurse, or a canteen waitress; but the ordinary Vanka had very few opportunities in that line. In our own liberated towns, some of our fellows were lucky, but most of them weren't. The question of more-or-less 'raping' any Russian woman just didn't arise. In Poland a few regrettable things happened from time to time, but, on the whole, a fairly strict discipline was maintained as regards 'rape'. The most common offence in Poland was '*dai chasy*'—'give me your wrist-watch.' There was an awful lot of petty thieving and robbery. Our fellows were just crazy about wrist-watches—there's no getting away from it. But the looting and raping in a big way did not start until our soldiers got to Germany. Our fellows were so sex-starved that they often raped old women of sixty, or seventy or even eighty—much to these grandmothers' surprise, if not downright delight. But I admit it was a nasty business, and the record of the Kazakhs and other Asiatic troops was particularly bad."

The posters put up in Germany, during the first weeks of the invasion, such as: "Red Army Soldier: You are now on German soil;

the hour of revenge has struck!" did not make things any easier. Moreover, the press propaganda of Ehrenburg and others continued to be very ferocious indeed.

Here are some samples from Ehrenburg's articles during the invasion of Germany:

> Germany is a witch... We are in Germany. German towns are burning, I am happy...
>
> The Germans have no souls... An English statesman said that the Germans were our brethren. No! it is blasphemy to include the child-murderers among the family of nations...
>
> Not only divisions and armies are advancing on Berlin. All the trenches, graves and ravines filled with the corpses of the innocents are advancing on Berlin, all the cabbages of Maidanek and all the trees of Vitebsk on which the Germans hanged so many unhappy people. The boots and shoes and the babies' slippers of those murdered and gassed at Maidanek are marching on Berlin. The dead are knocking on the doors of the Joachimsthaler Strasse, of the Kaiserallee, of Unter den Linden and all the other cursed streets of that cursed city...
>
> We shall put up gallows in Berlin... An icy wind is sweeping along the streets of Berlin. But it is not the icy wind, it is terror that is driving the Germans and their females to the west... 800 years ago the Poles and Lithuanians used to say: "We shall torment them in heaven as they tormented us on earth"... Now our patrols stand outside the castles of the Teutonic Knights at Allenstein, Osterode, Marienburg...
>
> We shall forget nothing. As we advance through Pomerania, we have before our eyes the devastated, blood-drenched countryside of Belorussia...
>
> Some say the Germans from the Rhine are different from the Germans on the Oder. I don't know that we should worry about such fine points. A German is a German everywhere. The Germans have been punished, but not enough. They are still in Berlin. The Führer is still standing, and not hanging. The Fritzes are still running, but not lying dead. Who can stop us now? General Model? The Oder? The Volkssturm? No, it's too late. Germany, you can now whirl round in circles, and burn, and howl in your deathly agony; the hour of revenge has struck!...

And, after visiting East Prussia, Ehrenburg wrote: "The Niezschean supermen are whining. They are a cross between a jackal and a sheep. They have no dignity. . . . A Scottish army chaplain, a liberated prisoner-of-war, said to me: 'I know how the Germans treated their Russian prisoners in 1941 and 1942. I can only bow to your generosity now.'"

It did not take very long for both the Party and the Command of the Red Army to realise that all this was going too far. The troops were getting out of hand, and, moreover, it was clear that, before long, the Russians would be faced with a variety of political and administrative problems in Germany which could simply not to be handled on the "anti-Marxist" basis that "all Germans are evil." The alarm, not so much over "atrocities" as over the totally unnecessary destruction caused by the Red Army in the occupied parts of Germany, was first reflected in the *Red Star* editorial of February 9, 1945:

> "An eye for an eye, a tooth for a tooth" is an old saying. But it must not be taken literally. If the Germans marauded, and publicly raped our women, it does not mean that we must do the same. This has never been and never shall be. Our soldiers will not allow anything like that to happen—not because of pity for the enemy, but out of a sense of their own personal dignity. . . They understand that every breach of military discipline only weakens the victorious Red Army. . . Our revenge is not blind. Our anger is not irrational. In an access of blind rage one is apt to destroy a factory in conquered enemy territory —a factory that would be of value to us. Such an attitude can only play into the enemy's hands.

Here was a clear admission that factories—and much else—were being burned down by Russian troops—simply because they were "German property".

On April 14, Ehrenburg's hate propaganda was stopped by a strong attack on him in *Pravda* by G. F. Alexandrov, the principal ideologist of the Central Committee. According to Ehrenburg's post-war *Memoirs* this attack was launched on direct instructions from Stalin. Alexandrov's article, "Comrade Ehrenburg is Oversimplifying" took him up on two points: first of all, it was both un-Marxist and inexpedient to treat *all* Germans as sub-human;

"Hitlers come and go, but the German people go on forever", Stalin himself had said in a recent speech; and Russia would have to live with the German people. To suggest that every German democrat or Communist was necessarily a Nazi in disguise was absolutely wrong. The article clearly suggested that there were now certain Germans with whom it would be necessary for the Russian authorities to co-operate. Secondly, Alexandrov objected to Ehrenburg's *Red Star* article two days before, called "That's Enough!" in which he had raged against the ease with which the Allies were advancing in the west and the desperate resistance the Germans were continuing to offer the Russians in the east. Ehrenburg had said that this was so because, having murdered millions of civilians, in the east, the Germans were therefore scared of the Russians, but not of the Western Allies, who were being deplorably "soft". They had, he claimed, even ordered Russian and Ukrainian slaves to go on working on German estates during the spring sowing.

While agreeing with some of this, Alexandrov still said that Ehrenburg was "oversimplifying" the issue:

At the present stage the Nazis are following their old mischievous policy of sowing distrust among the Allies... They are trying, by means of this political military trick, to achieve what they could not achieve by purely military means. If the Germans, as Ehrenburg says, were only scared of the Russians, they would not, to this day, go on sinking Allied ships, murdering British prisoners, or sending flying bombs over London. "We did not capture Königsberg by telephone," Ehrenburg said. That is quite true; but the explanation he offers for the simple way in which the Allies occupy towns in Western Germany is not the correct one.

This sop to the Allies was no doubt still intended to be in the good Yalta tradition, but it was perhaps not meant to be overwhelmingly convincing. For, although there was to be genuine rejoicing, especially among soldiers and officers on both sides, when, on April 27, the Russian and American forces met at Torgau on the Elbe, and cut the German forces in two, and although there were friendly demonstrations outside the American Embassy on VE-Day in Moscow on May 9, there continued to be considerable distrust of the Western Allies. True, the Allies did not fall for Himmler's (or any other) "separate peace" offer, but no sooner had the Germans capitulated than the Russian press was already full of angry screams about "Churchill's Flensburg Government"*—a government which, they later asserted, was not liquidated until the Russians themselves had taken a very strong line about this "outrageous business."

But that is a different story. The most significant part of Alexandrov's attack on Ehrenburg concerned the new official line on "the German people". Very suddenly the hate propaganda against "the Germans" was stopped. Ehrenburg was no longer allowed to write— at least not on Germany. His hate propaganda had served its purpose in the past, but now it had become inexpedient.

The "no-more-Ehrenburg" blow fell two days before the final Russian offensive against Berlin, which started on April 16, from the bridgeheads on the Oder. A week later, a special communiqué stated:

> The troops of the 1st Belorussian Front under Marshal Zhukov launched their offensive from the bridgeheads on the Oder with the support of artillery and aircraft, and broke through the defences of Berlin. They took Frankfurt-on-the-Oder, Wannlitz, Oranienburg, Birkenwerder, Henningsdorff, Pankow, Köpenick and Karlshorst, and broke into the capital of Germany, Berlin.

At the same time, Konev's troops broke into Berlin from the south, after taking first Cottbus, and then Marienfelde, Teltow and other Berlin suburbs.

On the 25th it was announced that Zhukov and Konev had made their junction north-west of Potsdam, thus completely encircling Berlin. On the same day, Pillau, the last German stronghold in East Prussia was taken.

On May 2, after a week of the most dramatic battles—a week in

---

* The "Government" under Admiral Doenitz—Hitler's "heir"— which continued to function at Flensburg, near the Danish border, as an "administrative organ" for some days after the capitulation. The encouragement allegedly given to it by the British was attributed by the Russians to the most sinister motives on Churchill's part.

the course of which Hitler and Goebbels killed themselves in Berlin —the city surrendered.

Then, on the 7th, the whole German Army capitulated. Jodl signed the capitulation at Reims, and Keitel, the next day, in Berlin. Here the Russian signatory was Marshal Zhukov. To the Russians, the Reims capitulation had been a "preliminary" formality; only a relatively junior Russian officer was present. While Churchill was broadcasting the end of the war on May 8 at 4 p.m., the Russian radio was broadcasting its "Children's Hour"—a pleasant little story about two rabbits and a bird. In Russia, the end of the war was not announced until the early hours of May 9. In Russia VE-Day was a day later than in the West. For one thing, Prague had not yet been liberated. The Western Allies thought this a detail; the Russians did not.

May 9 was an unforgettable day in Moscow. The spontaneous joy of the two or three million people who thronged the Red Square that evening—and the Moscow River embankments, and Gorki Street, all the way up to the Belorussian Station—was of a quality and a depth I had never yet seen in Moscow before. They danced and sang in the streets; every soldier and officer was hugged and kissed; outside the US Embassy the crowds shouted "Hurray for Roosevelt!" (even though he had died a month before)*; they were so happy they did not even have to get drunk, and under the tolerant gaze of the militia, young men even urinated against the walls of the Moskva Hotel, flooding the wide pavement. Nothing like *this* had ever happened in Moscow before. For once, Moscow had thrown all reserve and restraint to the winds. The fireworks display that evening was the most spectacular I have ever seen.

Yet the one-day difference between VE-Day in the West and VE-Day in the East made an unpleasant impression; and at first minor, and then more serious squabbles began between the Allies almost before the ink of Keitel's signature had dried.

* The British Embassy, being on the other side of the Moskva river, some distance from the main scene of mass rejoicing, was given only a few minor friendly demonstrations.

There was the row over the "Flensburg Government"; there were rows over the repatriation of Soviet prisoners and other Soviet citizens, whose return was being delayed. An angry statement on the alleged breaches of the Yalta repatriation agreement was published by General Golikov, head of the Repatriation Commission. Above all, there was more trouble about Poland. Many seeds of unpleasantness were beginning to sprout. . .

Chapter II

YALTA AND AFTER

The Yalta Conference of the Big Three, which was held three months before the collapse of Germany, has been described so often —notably by some of its participants, such as Mr Churchill, Mr James F. Byrnes and Mr Edward Stettinius—that no detailed account of that historic meeting is required here.* Yalta has been described as the "high tide of Big-Three unity" and, at the time, its results were hailed with great praise in most of the American press. It was not until later, when the Cold War was in full swing, that Yalta was described as a "Munich" at which Britain and the United States had "surrendered to Stalin", largely, it was said, because, at the time of Yalta, Roosevelt was a "weary and sick man", who had allowed himself to be bamboozled and outwitted by the wily Russian dictator.

Roosevelt was certainly a sick man. I still remember those truly pathetic newsreels of Yalta showing a terribly emaciated Roosevelt in his wheel-chair. I also remember Fenya, the kindly elderly Russian maid at the Metropole Hotel in Moscow, who was appointed to Yalta as Roosevelt's personal chambermaid and who commented

* The conference took place between February 4 and 11. The delegations were lodged in three of the palaces outside Yalta—the Tsar's palace of Livadia, the Vorontsov Palace and Koreis—which had more or less survived the German occupation. They had to be fitted with new plumbing, and furniture had to be brought from Moscow.

on her return, almost with tears in her eyes: "Such a sweet and kind man, but so terribly, terribly ill." When Roosevelt suddenly died soon afterwards, not only Fenya, but thousands of other Russian women wept.

On the other hand, Stettinius has argued in his book* that the Russians made more concessions at Yalta than they obtained from the Western Allies. His list of "Soviet concessions" includes the following:

The Soviet Union accepted the US formula for voting on the Security Council, thus putting an end to the Dumbarton Oaks *impasse*.

The Soviet Union abandoned her request for all the sixteen Soviet Republics being represented at the UN Assembly, and contented herself with votes for the USSR, the Ukraine and Belorussia only.

The Soviet Union agreed to the Associated Nations, who declared war on Germany by March 1, participating at San Francisco as original members.

The Soviet Union agreed to closer military co-ordination.

She agreed, despite earlier objections, to the French not only having an occupation zone in Germany, but also to their being represented on the Control Commission.

She accepted that the western border of Poland be left for the Peace Conference to settle.

She agreed to a compromise formula on the constitution of the future Polish Government and to "free elections" in Poland.

She bowed to the US view that the figure of twenty billion dollars should be treated by the Reparations Commission in its *initial studies* merely as a *basis of discussion*.

In the case of the Declaration on Liberated Europe the Russians withdrew their two amendments, including that giving a special status to people who had "actively opposed the Nazis".

On the other hand, while appealing to Stalin's "generosity" to Poland, the Western Powers had not felt able to insist on Lwow and the oil areas of Galicia being given to Poland. They had also given way on one or two questions concerning the strict allied supervision of the Polish election but, as Stettinius said in an italicised passage:

* *Roosevelt and The Russians* (London, 1950).

As a result of the military situation [in February 1945] it was not a question of what Great Britain and the United States would permit Russia to do in Poland, but what the two countries could persuade the Soviet Union to accept...

[Our troops] had just recovered ground lost by the Battle of the Bulge and had not yet bridged the Rhine. In Italy our advance was bogged down in the Appennines. The Soviet troops, on the other hand, had swept through almost all Poland and East Prussia and had reached at some points the river Oder... Poland and most of eastern Europe, except for most of Czechoslovakia, was in the hands of the Red Army.*

For all that, Stettinius claims that "the Yalta Agreements were, on the whole, a diplomatic triumph for the United States and Great Britain. The real difficulties with the Soviet Union came *after* Yalta when the agreements were not respected."†

It is clear that Britain and the United States were not negotiating with the Soviet Union from "positions of strength". No doubt both Roosevelt and, especially, Churchill felt very strongly about a number of questions; in the first place Poland. "Poland," Churchill said, "is the most important question before the Conference, and I don't want to leave without its being settled." Eden argued that "the presence of Mikolajczyk in the Polish Government would do more than anything else to add to its authority and convince the British people of its representative nature". Churchill declared himself horrified by the reports that "the Lublin Government had announced its intention of trying members of the Home Army and underground forces as traitors"‡; he also argued against "stuffing the Polish goose so full of German food that it would get indigestion", and particularly against the Western (and not the Eastern) Neisse being taken as part of the western frontier of Poland. Against this, Molotov argued in favour of giving Poland back her ancient frontiers in East

* Stettinius, op. cit., p. 266.   † Ibid., p. 261.
‡ This is precisely what the Soviet authorities were going to do only a few months later.

Prussia and on the Oder. "How long ago were these lands Polish?"
Roosevelt asked. "Very long ago," said Molotov. Roosevelt merely
made a wisecrack in reply: "This might lead the British to ask for a
return of the United States to Great Britain."

But the Russians felt, in their own way, even more strongly about
Poland than Churchill did. In reply to one of Churchill's harangues
about Poland having to remain "captain of her soul", Stalin remarked: "To Britain, Poland is a question of honour; to the Soviet
Union it is a question of *both* honour and security," and, time and
again, he returned to the question of the *Armija Krajowa* constituting a threat to the Red Army in Poland.

The record of Yalta shows that, while agreeing to give the Western
Allies something of a face-saver in the shape of the Harriman-
Molotov-Clark Kerr committee, which would help to "reorganise"
the Polish Government, and thus "prepare" a free Polish election,
Stalin made no secret whatsoever of what he considered to be
Russia's fundamental interests in Poland. A "free and unfettered"
Polish election—even though he reluctantly subscribed to it—was
not one of them.

The same, broadly speaking, applied to other countries in eastern
Europe, notably Rumania and Bulgaria. It is perhaps significant
that, according to Stettinius, Stalin should have remarked several
times at Yalta that he did not give a hang about Greece, and had
every confidence in British policy there. This meant that there was,
in fact, a tacit agreement about "spheres of influence", roughly on
the lines of those already agreed upon in Moscow in October 1944,*
except that, in the case of Poland, Churchill (and, to a lesser extent,
Roosevelt) continued to have serious qualms. But neither could overlook the fact that Poland was in the rear of the Red Army. It is
significant that when, soon after Yalta, the Russians ordered King
Michael of Rumania to dismiss General Radescu and replace him
by the pro-Soviet Petru Groza, Roosevelt thought it inappropriate
to protest because the Red Army's communication and supply lines

---

* See pp. 912–3. This is hotly denied in the post-war Soviet *History*,
which says, in particular, that Churchill's story about the "50–50"
agreement on Yugoslavia is "pure fiction". (IVOVSS, V. p. 134.)

ran through Rumania. The same, in a sense, was also true of Poland.*

The Yalta Conference devoted less time than one might have expected to the problem of Germany. "Closer co-ordination of the three Allies than ever before" was decided upon. The published Report on the Conference said that Nazi Germany was doomed, and that the German people "will only make the cost of their defeat heavier to themsclvcs by attempting to continue a hopeless resistance." The terms of the unconditional surrender were not published:

> These terms will not be made known until the final defeat of Germany... The forces of the Three Powers will each occupy a separate zone of Germany... [There will be] a central Control Commission consisting of the Supreme Commanders of the Three Powers with headquarters in Berlin.†

France, the Report continued, would be invited to take over a zone of occupation and to participate as a fourth member of the Control Commission, if she so desired.

Then followed a passage on the Allies' "inflexible purpose to destroy German militarism and Nazism... to disarm and disband all German armed forces, to break up for all time the German General Staff... to remove or destroy all German military equipment... to bring all war criminals to just and swift punishment and

* Some ten days after Yalta, at the Red Army Day reception that Molotov gave in Moscow on February 23, Vyshinsky, trying to sound rather drunk (which he wasn't) proposed a toast to some of the big shots of the Soviet armaments industries present: "I drink to you," he said, "who are the best and most indispensable auxiliaries of us diplomats. Without you, we should be completely helpless." And he then announced that he was going to leave for Bucharest the next morning, "just to show them where *they* got off." It was not quite clear who "they" were, but it was soon learned that he had had a "very serious" talk with King Michael; that he had banged the royal desk with his fist and that, as a result, the pro-Western General Radescu had been replaced at the head of the Rumanian Government by Mr Peter Groza. Radescu took refuge in the British Legation.

† Berlin, *not* part of the Soviet zone, was to be a distinct zone divided in four.

exact reparation in kind ... wipe out the Nazi Party, Nazi laws, organisations and institutions, remove all Nazi and militarist influence from public offices and from the cultural and economic life of the German people. . . . It is not our purpose to destroy the people of Germany, but only when Nazism and militarism have been extirpated will there be hope for a decent life for Germans, and a place for them in the comity of nations."

In the Protocol of the Yalta Conference (not published at the time) the Surrender Terms for Germany included a provision under which the Big Three would take "any such steps as they deem requisite for future peace and security, including the complete disarmament, demilitarisation and the dismemberment of Germany." The study for the procedure of dismemberment was referred to a committee consisting of Mr Eden, Mr Winant and Mr Gusev (the Foreign Secretary and the US and Soviet Ambassadors in London).*

A Reparations Committee was set up in Moscow under the chairmanship of Mr Maisky which would take "in its initial studies as a basis of discussion" the twenty billion dollars (half of it for the Soviet Union) proposed by the Russians.

The Russians were not particularly pleased with this deliberately non-committal protocol of Reparations, and were later to claim that Roosevelt had agreed to their getting ten billion dollars (from equipment, current production and labour), despite very strong opposition from Churchill, who had kept recalling the fearful reparations muddle after World War I. But there is little doubt that, apart from this Reparations question, the Russians were well satisfied with the

* The post-war *History* claims that at Yalta, the Russians were *against* dismemberment and looked with suspicion at any Western dismemberment plans. (IVOVSS, V, pp. 130–5). If at Teheran Stalin still favoured the dismemberment of Germany, he appears to have changed his mind by the time the Yalta Conference met. The "dismemberment" question was discussed at a number of meetings, particularly between the November 1944 meeting of the European Advisory Commission and Potsdam in July 1945. At the EAC meeting in March 1945 the Russians had clearly changed their minds about the desirability of "dismemberment". In claiming that they had already changed their minds at Yalta, i.e. a month before, the Russians are now stretching a point only slightly.

Protocol on the de-nazification and the demilitarisation of Germany. It is also certain that Stalin took the World Organisation, based on the unity of the Big Three, very seriously—though not quite seriously enough to run any grave risks with Poland, Rumania and the rest of his east-European sphere of influence.

The atom bomb had not yet been exploded, and American military men feared that, unless Russia joined in, the war against Japan might well last till 1947, and cost the United States at least another million casualties. Britain and the USA were therefore anxious, at the time of Yalta, to get Russia to join in the Japanese war. After all the loss of life in the war against Germany, the Russians were not at all keen on another war, and Stalin argued that he would "have to show something for it" before they would readily accept war against Japan. He therefore demanded first, the maintenance of the *status quo* in outer Mongolia; second, the restoration of Russia's former rights violated by Japan in 1904—the return of southern Sakhalin; the restoration (subject to an early agreement with Chiang Kai-shek) of Russian interests in respect of Dairen, Port Arthur and the Chinese Eastern and South-Manchurian railways, to be operated jointly by a Soviet-Chinese Company, with China retaining full sovereignty in Manchuria; and third, the handing over of the Kurile Islands to the Soviet Union (even though these had in effect belonged to Japan for a long time). This was a satisfactory *pourboire* for Russia to receive in the Far East. Stettinius quoted a significant remark of Molotov's, which suggests that the Russians were perfectly content to pursue a Big-Three policy even in China, i.e. to co-exist peacefully with Chiang Kai-shek:

> Molotov told General Patrick Hurley that the Soviet Union was not interested in the Chinese Communists; these weren't really Communists anyway.*

* Stettinius, op. cit., p. 28. One can only wonder whether today Khrushchev agrees with his old friend Molotov! See also p. 1030 for Stalin's remarks on the Chinese Communists to Hopkins in May 1945.

On the whole, Stalin left the British and, even more so, the Americans at Yalta with a rather favourable impression. Byrnes thought him "a very likeable person"; Churchill thought he had "greatly mellowed since the hard days of the war"; while he struck Stettinius as a man "with a fine sense of humour"—

> At the same time one received an impression of power and ruthlessness along with his humour. . . The other members of the Soviet delegation would change their minds perfectly unashamedly whenever Marshal Stalin changed his.*

He appeared as a calm and skilful negotiator, who only showed any strong emotion when he spoke of German reparations and of the fearful devastation caused by the Germans in Russia. On the whole, he was reasonably accommodating, and did not press on his partners demands they thought wholly unreasonable—such as the one that all the sixteen Soviet Republics be represented at UN.† Western observers were impressed by the fact that, throughout the Yalta Conference, Stalin remained in the closest touch with the conduct of the war and did his work as Commander-in-Chief between midnight and 5 a.m.

As one looks closely at the Yalta records, several points stand out clearly. Stalin was all in favour of a United Nations, based on the unity of the Big Three. He was very reluctant to admit France to Germany as a fourth partner, but gave way at Churchill's insistence.

* Ibid., p. 107. This remark is all the more curious in the light of both Stettinius's and Harriman's "theory" that if Stalin "went back on the Yalta decisions" soon afterwards, it was under the pressure of the other members of the Politburo, who were supposed to have criticised him for having been too soft in his dealings with Churchill and Roosevelt.

† Stalin and Molotov started this gambit by explaining that, in 1944, the Soviet Constitution had been amended so as to give all the sixteen Soviet republics the right to conduct their own foreign relations. This was an obvious device to get extra seats at UN. I remember visiting the improvised "Ministry of Foreign Affairs of the Georgian SSR" at Tbilisi in 1946. None of its officials took it in the least seriously. It consisted of only three or four rooms.

He made no secret of his contempt for France's military record or of his personal dislike of de Gaulle, whom, according to Harriman, he described as "an awkward and stubborn man." Kindness, he argued, was the only possible reason for giving France a zone in Germany. According to Stettinius, Stalin called de Gaulle "not a complicated man".

Nor did Stalin make any secret of his mental reservations about Poland. He kept on talking about "agents of the London Government shooting Russian soldiers," and no doubt felt that, so long as Russia was needed as an Ally against Japan, he had little to fear from any Anglo-American protests about Russian policy in either Poland or the Balkans. In the Balkans, moreover, there was a tacit understanding about splitting them into "spheres of influence": just as Stalin "didn't give a hang about Greece", so Churchill had told King Peter of Yugoslavia that he wouldn't sacrifice a single man or a single penny to put any king back on his throne.

The protocol on Germany, and its demilitarisation and denazification, satisfied Stalin, though he thought the agreement on reparations was much too vague. Maisky had spoken of the "astronomical figures" of the damage caused by the Germans to the Soviet Union, and there was one extremely important—and closely-related—point which was raised at Yalta, but apparently dropped almost immediately: the question of a big American reconstruction loan to the Soviet Union.

According to Stettinius's record, this question came up only incidentally when Molotov said to him that Russia expected to receive reparations in kind from Germany, and "also expressed the hope that the Soviet Union would receive long-term credits from the United States."*

Stettinius recalls that Secretary of the Treasury Morgenthau had sent a letter to the President shortly before Yalta advocating "a concrete plan to aid the Russians in the reconstruction period", and suggesting that "this would iron out many of the difficulties we have been having with respect to their problems and policies." But, as Stettinius says: "The Soviet Union did not receive a loan at the close of the war. Whether such a loan would have made her a more

* Op. cit., p. 115.

reasonable and co-operative nation will be one of the great 'if' questions of history."

There is every reason to believe that, at Yalta, Stalin was still hoping that such a loan might materialise; it would have meant the relatively "easy" way of reconstruction for the Russian people, instead of the "hard" way that Stalin had to choose for them despite certain "ideological" objections to the former solution.

It may be possible to read a hint at such a loan into Stalin's toast to Roosevelt at one of the Yalta banquets when he said that the President had been "the chief forger of the instruments which had led to the mobilisation of the world against Hitler." Lend-lease, he said, was "one of the President's most remarkable and vital achievements" which pointed to an exceptionally broad conception of America's national interests.

Although he also paid some glowing compliments to Churchill at the same banquet—"the bravest governmental figure in the world" —all observers are agreed that he was much more anxious to be friendly to Roosevelt than to Churchill. Even so, he said he was sure that Churchill would continue to be at the head of the British Government, and that there would be no Labour victory in the next election. And he seemed to prefer it that way. This, he suggested, was all the more desirable because—

> The difficult task will come after the war, when diverse interests will tend to divide the Allies. I am confident, however, that the present alliance will meet that test and that the peace-time relations of the three Great Powers will be as strong as they were in war-time.*

American writers have made much of Stalin's "betrayal" of Yalta so soon after the conference. Some have attributed it—not at all plausibly—to the criticisms and opposition with which Stalin met from the "revolutionary doctrinaires" in the Politburo. Much more credible are some of the other explanations offered for the "change" in Soviet policy after Yalta. It is probable that Stalin took note of Roosevelt's remark that the United States were unlikely to keep any troops in Europe for more than two years. Secondly, he seems to

* Stettinius, op. cit., p. 198.

have been impressed, soon after Yalta, by the great hostility that the Russians met in Poland, which led to his determination not to take any serious chances, either there or in any of the other east-European countries.

The growing American opposition in March and April, to the idea of a big post-war loan to Russia was also of some importance, in increasing East-West tension. Roosevelt's death caused genuine alarm in Russia*—an alarm which soon proved justified, especially when President Truman made his *début* in his Russian policy by stopping Lend-Lease for Russia immediately after VE-Day—while Russia was still committed to entering the war against Japan, on America's side. As we know from Harry Hopkin's account of his visit to Moscow soon afterwards, Stalin was deeply annoyed and offended by what Stettinius called this "untimely and incredible" step.

Indeed, Yalta, this great manifestation of three-power unity of purpose with victory over Nazi Germany in sight, proved, perhaps inevitably, a watershed in inter-allied relations. Conflicting interests and contrasting ideas that in normal circumstances would have been almost incompatible, had been shelved, while the gigantic struggle was in progress. But now when it came to preparing for peace the working compromises that had been reached proved only too fragile. As we have seen, it was difficult enough to reach these compromises; now they were to be put to the test of being applied in practice and interpreted in detail. Thus it became increasingly difficult to conceal those vital differences of self-interest and outlook between the wartime coalition partners.

Another psychological factor contributed to the tension between Soviet Russia and the Allies towards the very end of the war in Europe. The approach of victory produced in Russia not only waves of relief, hope and indeed, elation, but even extraordinary outbursts of national pride almost bordering on arrogance. There was, not least in the Red Army, a tendency to resent the presence of the

* It made a very deep impression. All Soviet papers appeared with wide black borders on their front pages, and, by a curious instinct, people felt that this was a major tragedy for Russia which had lost "a real friend".

Western Allies in Germany and especially in Berlin—in the capture
of which so many thousands of Russians were to die in the last days
of the war.

On the one hand, Russia was a devastated, almost a ruined,
country, with a formidable task of economic reconstruction ahead
of her. But on the other hand, she was sitting on top of the world,
having won the greatest war in her history. The future seemed bright
as never before. Some soldiers were openly saying: "But for Britain
and America, the whole of Europe would be ours." This "revolutionary romanticism" was not widespread, still less officially
approved, but it had a tiny little corner in many people's hearts. The
future seemed pregnant with all kinds of exciting possibilities. A
revolutionary Europe to a few—a happy, prosperous Russia to most.
Among many of those who now dreamed of such a happy Russia
there also existed the idea that the survival of the Big-Three alliance
after the war would, somehow, tend to liberalise the Soviet régime
(as, in some respects, it had already done during the war). Many
illusions (in either direction) were to be destroyed only a few months
later, with the dropping of the atom bomb on Hiroshima. . .

Chapter III

JUNE, 1945: BERLIN UNDER THE RUSSIANS ONLY

This was very unlike Berlin. There were jasmin bushes round the villa, the garden was full of strong sweet scents, birds were twittering in the trees, and, at the end of the green, sunny alley, the water of the Wannsee was bright blue. "They lived well, the parasites," said the Russian lad, a sentry outside the villa. He was nineteen or twenty, with a little down on his chin, rosy cheeks and laughing blue eyes. On his khaki shirt he wore the Stalingrad Medal and the Bravery Medal. "They lived well, the parasites," he repeated. "Great big farms in East Prussia, and pretty posh houses in the towns that hadn't been burned out or bombed to hell. And look at these *datchas* here! Why did these people who were living so well have to invade *us*?"

This was one of the most common thoughts of Red Army soldiers during that first summer in Germany. They were not impressed by the vestiges of "Western" prosperity, but simply angered at the thought that these "rich" Germans should have wanted to conquer Russia.

"And to think of all our fellows they killed," he went on. "It was tough just outside Berlin. Some of the German youngsters were quite crazy—attacked our tanks with their *faustpatronen*; knocked out quite a few that way. Some of the German girls threw hand grenades out of windows. However, they are all very meek and quiet now. Some of the Germans are really not too bad. They're scared, of course; that's why they are so polite. But I lost a lot of comrades on the way here, and one could never be sure that one would get to Berlin alive. But now I am having a good time. Four of us have a motor-boat and we go out on it at night on the lake. There are a lot of lakes here, all strung together—one can go in the boat for miles. Pretty country round here, don't you think? Now the Germans aren't allowed to come to this place. Wendenschloss it's called."

The "parasite" to whom the villa belonged must have been quite a big local shot in the Nazi Party. In my bedroom there were still some German books—mostly Party literature—*Mein Kampf*, and a volume of Goering speeches, and a biography of Goering, full of idyllic pictures of the brute. Each volume was a presentation copy from the local Party committee.

Wendenschloss was, indeed, roped off from the rest of Berlin. Marshal Zhukov was living in a large villa beside the lake; and in the Yacht Club a "great inter-Allied ceremony" (as the newspapers called it) took place on June 5. Zhukov, Eisenhower, Montgomery and Delattre de Tassigny, sat round a large green table and signed the Four-Power Declaration on the defeat of Germany, the assumption by the Four Powers of the supreme rule over Germany and the establishment of a Control Council.

It was a somewhat disorderly affair. Montgomery arrived at the airport three hours later than the Russians had expected him. There was much unpleasant whispering and hissing: "The Russians want to grab as much as they can."* Although Zhukov was expecting all the signatories to stay for his elaborately-prepared dinner, both Eisenhower and Montgomery excused themselves, and only the French stayed on—the British and Americans leaving almost immediately after the signing ceremony. Why Montgomery had brought ninety-seven people with him nobody could make out. "*Il y a un froid très net*," the French at Wendenschloss remarked. Anyway, the French stayed on for the banquet, and Vyshinsky, Zhukov's

---

* The Western Allies were not at all pleased to have to evacuate very shortly a large territory, including Leipzig, and to hand it to the Russians in accordance with the zonal boundaries previously agreed to. Churchill was much opposed to this evacuation without getting anything in return. He was very angry about the *fait accompli* of the Oder-Neisse Line.

political adviser, made a speech in which (choosing to forget all that Stalin had said about the French at Yalta) he referred to them as "our *real* friends," and General Delattre de Tassigny—who was then in the midst of his flirtation with the French Communists—declared that he wished France to be "a true democratic people's republic"— whatever that meant. Anyway, the Russians were very pleased with the French General, and a few among them perhaps began to think vaguely of Europe in terms of some old-time revolutionary romanticism...

For all that, everything was calculated to show the Germans that the four Allies were monolithically united and that they would continue to be so once Berlin—now under sole Russian occupation— was split into four zones, in terms of the new arrangements made. All the streets of Berlin—even the most devastated ones—were decorated that day with flags of all the four Allies...

At the Wendenschloss ceremony I had a talk with Marshal Sokolovsky, whom I had not seen since the grim days of 1941. I reminded him of how, a fortnight before the all-out German offensive against Moscow, he had explained that the Red Army would gradually *grind down* the might of the German Army. He gave a happy smile, and said he remembered that meeting with the press at Viazma. He told me that he was "quite satisfied" that Hitler was dead, although his remains had not been definitely identified. "But there seems no doubt that he is dead all right," he said. So, he added, was Goebbels, together with his whole family—but that was more common knowledge. Sokolovsky's statement was all the more interesting as the official Russian line at that time—and for a long time afterwards— was that Hitler might have escaped. Sokolovsky's "off-the-record"— or should one say "off-his-guard"?—remark was unique in its own way. Zhukov's statement on the same subject a few days later was "on the record"—and much more cautious.*

* There was a strong suspicion among Western diplomats that there was a shabby political purpose in the innuendo that Hitler had escaped to Spain or South America with certain Western complicities. Stalin persisted in telling Hopkins, about the same time, that Hitler was not dead.

When I mentioned the talk about Russian troops having run wild in Germany, Sokolovsky shrugged his shoulders. "Of course," he said, "a lot of nasty things happened. But what do you expect? *You know what the Germans did* to their Russian war prisoners, how they devastated our country, how they murdered and raped and looted. Have you seen Maidanek or Auschwitz? Every one of our soldiers lost dozens of his comrades. Every one of them had some personal scores to settle with the Germans, and in the first flush of victory our fellows no doubt derived a certain satisfaction from making it hot for those *Herrenvolk* women. However, that stage is over. We have now pretty well clamped down on that sort of thing— not that most German women are vestal virgins. Our main worry," he grinned, "is the awful spread of the clap among our troops."

No one who had known Nazi Germany, and had lived through the war—in France in 1940, in Britain during the Battle of Britain and the London blitz, and the rest of it in Russia—could avoid feeling a pang of *Schadenfreude* at the sight of Berlin. The capital of Hitler's 1,000-year Reich had been turned into a hundred square miles of mostly ruin and rubble. All down the endless Frankfurter Allee not a house—except one, where the commandant of Berlin now had his headquarters—had escaped destruction; Alexanderplatz, Unter den Linden, Friedrichstrasse, Wilhelmstrasse, and then the Potsdamerplatz, and the Kleiststrasse and Tauentzienstrasse and, beyond them, the Kurfürstendamm (here alone a few houses had escaped)—all the old familiar places had been smashed. In the wastes of the Wilhelmstrasse, with Hitler's now shattered Chancellery, there were only ghosts—ghosts of the million people who had bellowed Heil Hitler on the day Hitler became Chancellor, ghosts of the S.A. marching, marching, marching past their Führer in their interminable raucous torchlight procession.

For once, Germany was no longer marching; she had come to the end of the road. Between the ruins, the Wilhelmstrasse was silent now, without a living soul anywhere, and with only a stink of corpses rising from the ruins. The *Tägliche Rundschau*, published under Russian auspices, was printing photographs of Berlin's ruins, and recalling what Hitler had said in 1935: "In ten years' time Berlin will be unrecognisable."

This was Russian Berlin. The Russians were still in sole command. A month had passed since the German capitulation. Early in May Berlin was in a state of complete chaos, with millions milling round the ruins, not knowing what to do, and where to go, or where to find even a scrap of food. On May 4, two days after the capitulation of Berlin, the Russian commandant, General Berzarin, issued his first Order:

1) The Nazi Party and all its organisations are dissolved.

2) Within forty-eight hours all members of the Nazi Party, the Gestapo, the police and members of the public services must register. Within three days, all members of the Wehrmacht and the SS must register, too.

3) All public services in Berlin must be resumed immediately, and food shops and bakeries must open.

4) Within twenty-four hours all food reserves exceeding five days' consumption must be declared.

5) Banks must be closed and all accounts frozen.

6) All arms, ammunition, wireless sets, cameras, cars and petrol must be handed over to the Russian authorities.

7) All printing machinery and typewriters must be registered.

8) No one must leave their dwellings between 10 p.m. and 8 a.m. But theatres, cinemas, restaurants and churches may remain open till 9 p.m.

The entire population, except old people and women with small children was mobilised for work. Men had to return to their regular jobs, or do "heavy work" like repairing bridges and dismantling factories; women had to clear away the rubble, pile up billions of bricks, and bury the thousands of corpses rotting among the ruins. Only those registering for work (apart from the above exceptions) were entitled to a ration card. The distribution of ration cards began on May 8, but the lower-category ration cards were less than adequate. The black market began to flourish right away, and many Russian soldiers swapped food for all kinds of more or less valuable objects. There was real famine among those who had nothing to exchange for food. This was particularly true of Berlin and Dresden.

The dismantling of factories—*Trophäenaktion* ("Operation Booty")—began at once. The Siemens plant near Berlin was completely emptied of machinery during the very first days of the Russian occupation, and the same happened to many other places. It was done under the direction of engineers who had come from Russia, and the military authorities were not too pleased about it.

Within a month of the German capitulation of Berlin, some kind of order had been introduced into the complete chaos. On June 5 the Allied Control Council was formed, and, on June 9 Marshal Zhukov announced the setting up, under his authority, of the SMA, the Soviet Military Administration for Eastern Germany. Even before that, General Berzarin, the commandant of Berlin had set up an administration of sorts in the capital. This was followed, on June 10, by Marshal Zhukov's Order No. 2 permitting the creation of "democratic and anti-Fascist parties" acting, of course, under Russian control. On the very following day the German Communist Party, headed by Pieck and Ulbricht, declared itself in favour of the *Sonderweg*—a "particular German way":

> We believe that it would be wrong to impose the Soviet system on Germany, since this would not correspond to the present development of the country... Instead, we are in favour of a democratic anti-Fascist régime and a parliamentary republic guaranteeing the people democratic rights and freedoms.

A similar line was taken by the SPD, the Socialists, several of whose leaders—notably Fechner, Grotewohl and Gniffke—were shortly to declare themselves in favour of a united Socialist-Communist Party, which, within a year, was to become the SED (*Sozialistische Einheitspartei Deutschlands*). The SMA also permitted the constitution of bourgeois parties—the Catholic CDU and the liberal LDP—provided these entered a united anti-Fascist Front. This anti-Fascist bloc was to be formed on July 14, 1945.

In 1945, not only the bourgeois parties and the Socialists, but also the German Communists were still openly against the *Ostgrenze*, the Oder-Neisse Frontier, and hoped that the Russians would "reconsider" it. It was not till 1948 that the German Communists recognised it as "the Frontier of Peace and Friendship." Nor was it till 1948 that, under the impact of the Stalin-Tito quarrels, the German Communists openly abandoned their *Sonderweg* positions and decided to model their régime, in the main, on the Soviet Union.

There were thousands of Russian soldiers in Berlin during those days. On the ruins of the Reichstag, where deadly fighting had gone on for days, on the pillars of the shattered, battered Brandenburger Tor, on the pedestals of the Siegessäule (Victory Column), of the Bismarck monument, of the smashed equestrian statue of Kaiser Wilhelm I, thousands of Russian names had been scratched, or written or painted: "Sidorov from Tambov", or "Ivanov, all the way from Stalingrad", or "Mikhailov who fought the Fritzes in the Battle of Kursk", or "Petrov, Leningrad to Berlin", and so on. There were Russian soldiers' graves in the Tiergarten, around the Reichstag; and along the main streets, especially in the busier and less devastated streets of East Berlin, notices had been put up everywhere: "HITLERS COME AND GO, BUT THE GERMAN PEOPLE AND THE GERMAN STATE GO ON.—STALIN." The reference to the "German State" made many Germans believe that there would soon be a central German government. There were German policemen with white brassards at street corners, and a few tramcars and a couple of underground lines were running. Water was being pumped out of other underground lines which had been flooded on Hitler's orders and in which a large number of people had been drowned as a result.

There was much army traffic in the main streets and there were also the wheelbarrows—hundreds of them—of Germans moving their belongings from one place to another. There were also lorries packed with D.P.'s. The Germans looked subdued; only once in a while one caught the glimpse of a dirty look. Most of them were busy: they were clearing away rubble and mending pavements.

There was more mateyness between the Russians and the Germans than one would have expected. At street corners soldiers were seen chatting with German men and girls; they were not supposed to sleep with German girls, though they could at their own risk and peril—and they did. Small German boys and elderly women were

the most boisterous of all. The boys would scrounge food and
cigarettes off the Russians, and the elderly women displayed a sort
of motherly familiarity. They waved at Russian lorries for lifts, and
the lorries would often stop.

Colonel-General Berzarin, the commandant of Berlin, was a fine
specimen of a Soviet general.* He was, quite obviously, not at all
pleased at the prospect that Berlin would soon have to be shared
with the British, Americans and French. He felt that as the Russians
had lost thousands in the fierce final battle of the war they *deserved*
Berlin all to themselves. He also felt that he had made as good a job
as possible of Berlin in the incredible circumstances of May 1945,
and that things were beginning to take shape. The arrival of the
others would only cause a lot of rivalry and friction, and undermine
the Russians' authority with the Germans. . .

Anyway, Berzarin was not the kind of man who had much use
for the Allies, least of all the British. The son of a Leningrad steel
worker, and a Party member of long standing, he had joined the
Red Army in 1918 at the age of 14, and, in 1919, he had fought
the British at Archangel. "Yes," he said, "I had to fight there against
our present allies. At first we got it in the neck from them, but later
I realised what good athletes they were—they could certainly *run!*"
In 1939 he had fought at Halkin Gol; in 1941, he commanded a
Russian army at Riga, "and there I got my first knock from the
Germans, and it was a pretty hard knock, I can tell you." Then he
fought on various other fronts—and, finally, "our army was the first
to reach the Oder, and it was we to whom the Germans in Berlin
finally capitulated last month."

"But it was heavy going," he went on. "Our artillery and infantry
won this battle. The allied bombing caused great damage here, but
it was of no direct military value. The allied dropped 65,000 tons of
bombs on Berlin, but it was we who, in a fortnight, fired 40,000 tons

---

* He was to be killed in a car smash only a week later; that, at any
rate, was the official version. Many Russians in Berlin suspected that
he had, in reality, been assassinated by Nazi terrorists.

of shells at it. With tanks and guns we had to smash up whole houses. The Germans were fanatical. Young boys and girls threw hand-grenades at us and attacked our tanks with their infernal near-suicidal *faustpatronen*. There were a lot of barricades all over Berlin. Finally, they capitulated on May 2. A large part of the population and thousands of soldiers were hiding in cellars and shelters. But even after the capitulation some SS-men and Hitler youths continued to fire at us from the ruins. This went on for a few days. Since then, there are still occasionally assassinations of Russian soldiers and especially officers; but, on the whole, everything is quiet. . ."

He admitted that, to put an end to these assassinations, the Russians had had to take hostages from amongst the numerous Nazis.

Berzarin claimed that in May 1945 the Russians had saved Berlin from starvation. He gave figures for the gradual restoration of the underground-railway, tramlines, telephones, gas supply, etc.—and then spoke of the rations. Every person received ¾ lb. of potatoes a day, but the other rations among the five categories varied greatly: bread from 20 oz. to 10 oz., meat from 3 oz. to ⅔ oz., sugar from 1 oz. to ½ oz. Some food even had to be brought from Russia.

"But before long," Berzarin said, "the Red Army, now largely depending on its own supplies, will have to be fed by the Germans, and we are making the peasants grow as much as possible." He was planning to allow a "free market" in Berlin, which would encourage the peasants to bring their produce to the city.

The population of Berlin was already nearly three millions, and more people were coming in all the time. The health services were a major problem: all doctors had been mobilised, and there were 40,000 wounded Germans in Berlin in special hospitals. Housing was, of course, the worst problem of all: forty-five percent of Berlin's houses had been totally destroyed, thirty-five percent partly destroyed, and only some fifteen or twenty percent, mostly in the suburbs, were more or less intact. There was no work for most of the population, who were being used for clearing away rubble.

He also made it clear that it was "well worthwhile" under the Russians to be emphatically anti-Nazi, and all *bona fide* anti-Nazis were being highly favoured.

Anti-Nazis are being used by us for checking all appointments, particularly to the police force. The policemen are carefully chosen; even so, they are allowed to carry only truncheons, not firearms. In smaller jobs we allow nominal, non-active Nazis to remain. All ex-Nazis must report for work.

The cultural side is being developed; there are 200 cinemas in Berlin, and we show them Russian films, such as *Ivan the Terrible*. The centre of musical activity is the Radio Centre; here the German opera orchestra has been reconstituted under the conductor Ludwig. Schools will be restored as soon as possible; but all the Nazi schoolbooks will have to be replaced. The problem of finding enough anti-Nazi teachers will not be easy.

We have organised the municipality, complete with an *Oberbürgermeister*, a Dr Werner and, under him, sixteen departments—food, health, industry, trade, administration, education, etc.

There was both comedy and pathos about the Town Hall of Berlin, in a former Insurance building, which had somehow escaped destruction, somewhere off the Alexanderplatz. The *Oberbürgermeister*, Herr Werner, was a gaunt handsome old man of sixty-eight, wearing a long black frock coat, a stiff butterfly collar and black tie. He was a wealthy *rentier* with a villa at Lichterfelde, and the Russians got hold of him several days before entering Berlin proper, and had appointed him *Oberbürgermeister*.* He said he had lived well till 1942, and had had a large income, but then hard times came, and

* The Berlin City Government was composed of seven *bourgeois*, six Communist Party officials, two Social-Democrats and two non-party members. Two were German communists who had spent years in a Nazi concentration camp, but most of the other communists were "Moscow" Germans. According to Wolfgang Leonhard, at that time a close associate of Ulbricht's, it was the "Ulbricht Group", working in close co-operation with the Russians, who were chiefly responsible for the appointments. It was also Ulbricht who insisted, in June 1945, on the dissolution of the "anti-fascist committees" who had constituted themselves in Berlin spontaneously and "from below", and on their virtual replacement by the political parties, as authorised by Zhukov. It was these parties, especially the Communist Party, which were to provide administrative cadres for the Soviet Zone. (Wolfgang Leonhard, op. cit., pp. 323–35).

he had lost 60 lbs. in weight. The constant bombings of Berlin had got him down. Now he was saying all the right things. General Berzarin had "done him the great honour" of appointing him *Oberbürgermeister* of Berlin. The feeding of Berlin was a terrible problem, since the Nazis had destroyed all the food-stores, saying: "While we are here you'll have food, but when the Bolsheviks take over, you'll starve". But things were not nearly as bad as the Germans—very frightened at first—had expected. The Red Army had presented Berlin with a thousand lorries for clearing the rubble and doing some reconstruction, and they had placed a car at his (Werner's) disposal, since he lived ten miles from his office and also a bodyguard of six soldiers. He also said: "Marshal Stalin gave us twenty-five million marks, and the Marshal's magnanimous gesture has been deeply appreciated by all Berliners." By the end of the summer, schools would be opened, "and when I raised the question of religious tuition with General Berzarin, he said, 'You can educate them in a religious spirit for all I care'. I rejoiced at these words, for I and my family are very devout Lutherans."

There was, he said, even a religious department at the Berlin Town Hall, headed by a Catholic priest, Father Buchholz, who had been locked up in a concentration camp after July 20. At Lichterfelde, Werner said, he had a garden, and some lovely rose-bushes, and he hoped he could soon retire; but now he felt it his duty to do whatever he could to rehabilitate the German people in the eyes of the world. They had fallen so fearfully low.

There was something pathetic about this old-time conservative German. Pathetic in a different way was Herr Geschke, a seedy little man with bloodshot eyes, who seemed in miserable health and almost half-demented. This former German communist deputy had been in a concentration camp for twelve years. He was now head of the Welfare Department at the Berlin Town Hall and, as he told his story of torture and gas-chambers, he suddenly broke down and wept.

Germans released from concentration camps—even broken reeds like Geschke—played an important part during those early weeks in Berlin in selecting personnel for the Russian-sponsored administration, and in doing "democratic" propaganda and denazification work. Before the constitution of the four parties authorised by the Russian authorities, an organisation called ANTIFA was active in purging the administration and in running the "cultural life" of Berlin—and particularly the Berlin radio.

In a sense, the Russians were building on sand; for soon the greater part of Berlin was going to be taken over by "the others". The Russians were invariably bitter about it, claimed that they were building up a coherent anti-Nazi Germany, but that, in Berlin, at any rate, "all this good work would go to pot". I was to remember some of these arguments when, three years later, they attempted their abortive Berlin Blockade.

This was a different Berlin from what it had been. Subdued, frightened, grateful for small mercies, grateful even for a revival of some of the old Berlin frivolity. In one of the surviving buildings of the Kurfürstendamm there was a cabaret attended by well-dressed Germans with furtive looks, by tarts and Russian officers. The whole show was unspeakably vulgar. Some dirty little song about sonny asking Grandpa whether he and Grandma had really made love in their time and granddad replying: "*Olala*", or some such muck. Then a tall boy with a guitar boomed Russian folksongs in broken Russian and a "Song of Transylvania" with the refrain: "*Deine Augen brennen heisser als Paprika*" ("Your eyes burn hotter than paprika"), then there was a tap-dancer, a xylophone player, and a Polish or Jewish female who howled *Parlez-moi d'amour*. There were no anti-Nazi cracks, but the theme-song was a boost for local Berlin patriotism. It was called *Berlin kommt wieder*, and the slimy audience kept joining in with great gusto. At the stall they sold copies of this song, and at the buffet some foul ersatz orangeade. The managers of the cabaret cringed and bowed deeply to the Russian officers.

This was a bit of West Berlin—under the Russians. It almost had a whiff of Isherwood!

*

A few days later, Marshal Zhukov gave his famous press conference on the verandah of his villa overlooking the Wannsee. Vyshinsky was also there. With Zhukov, one felt in the presence of a very great man. Moscow, Leningrad, Stalingrad, and now the offensive which had started on the Vistula on January 12, and had ended here, in Berlin—Zhukov's name was inseparable from them all. But his manner was simple, and full of bonhomie.

He spoke of the Battle of Berlin:

This was not like Moscow or Leningrad, or even Stalingrad... During the first years of the war, we often had to fight against fearful odds; nor did our officers and soldiers have as much experience as they have now. In this Battle of Germany we had great superiority in men, tanks, aircraft, guns and everything. Three-to-one, sometimes even five-to-one. But the important thing was not to take Berlin— that was a foregone conclusion—but to take it in the shortest possible time. The Germans were expecting our blow and we had to think out how to introduce the important element of surprise.

I attacked along the *whole* front, and at night. As prisoners later told us, the great artillery barrage at night was what they had least expected. They had expected night attacks, but not a *general* attack at night. After the artillery barrage, our tanks went into action. We had used 22,000 guns and mortars along the Oder, and 4,000 tanks were now thrown in. We also used 4,000 to 5,000 planes. During the first day alone there were 15,000 sorties.

The great offensive was launched at 4 a.m. on April 16, and we devised some novel features: to help the tanks to find their way, we used searchlights, 200 of them. These powerful searchlights not only helped the tanks, but also blinded the enemy, who could not aim properly at our tanks.

Very soon we broke through the German defences on the Oder along a wide front. Realising this, the German high command threw what reserves it had outside Berlin into the fray, and even some reserves from inside Berlin. But it was no good. These reserves were smashed from the air or by our tanks, and when our troops broke into Berlin, the city was largely denuded of troops. Most of Berlin's anti-aircraft guns had been thrown into the Oder Battle, and the city was defenceless against air attack.

More than half-a-million German soldiers took part in the Berlin operation. 300,000 were taken prisoner even before the capitulation, 150,000 were killed; the rest fled.

And he concluded this brief story in characteristically professional fashion:

It was an interesting and instructive battle, especially as regards tempos and the technique of night-fighting on such a scale.* The main point is that the Germans were smashed on the Oder, and in Berlin itself it was, in fact, just one immense mopping-up operation. It was very, very different from the Battle of Moscow.†

* He said he had had to stay awake for six nights running. He and his officers had only been able to do this by sipping cognac. Vodka, though a good stimulant for the troops, was no good for generals as after a time it had a soporific effect.

† More recent Soviet accounts of the Berlin Operation, notably in vol. V of the official Soviet history of the war (IVOVSS, V, pp. 288–90) published in 1963 show that it was a much more complex affair than Zhukov suggested. In this battle three-and-a-half million people were involved on the two sides, 50,000 guns and mortars, 8,000 tanks and mobile guns, and over 9,000 planes. In this Berlin operation, the Russians smashed seventy German infantry divisions, twelve armoured and eleven motorised divisions. Before the actual capitulation of the Germans on May 8, the Russians captured 480,000 prisoners, besides 1,500 tanks, over 4,000 planes and 10,000 guns. The *History* stresses that the Berlin Operation was carried out not only by the 1st Belorussian Front under Zhukov, but also by two other Fronts, the 1st Ukrainian and the 2nd Belorussian. The Red Army, according to the *History*, had "crushing superiority" in this operation. It also says that the German soldiers and officers, blinded by Nazi propaganda, went on fighting fanatically till the very end and that, between April 16 and May 8, they inflicted very serious losses on the Russians. The three fronts directly concerned with the Berlin operation lost 305,000 men in dead, wounded and missing— chiefly during the breakthrough on the Oder and Neisse and during the fighting inside Berlin. They lost over 2,000 tanks and mobile guns, 1,200 guns, 527 planes. "The Anglo-American casualties during the whole of 1945 were 260,000 men." Several hundred, if not thousand, Russians were killed in the storming of the Reichstag alone. So the fighting inside Berlin was much more serious than merely "a vast mopping-up operation", as Zhukov called it. It seems apparent from the discrepancies between some of the above figures and those quoted by Zhukov that he spoke chiefly of his 1st Belorussian Front, rather than of the more "general" Berlin operation. The rivalry between him and other top generals may have had something to do with it.

Somebody asked what the Russians' relations with the Germans would be. That, he said, depended on how the Germans behaved; the sooner they drew the necessary conclusions from what had happened, the better. He (Zhukov) was certainly in favour of a quick trial of the German war criminals. He thought there was agreement on that point among all the Allies. "And on other points?" somebody asked. "On other points," he said, "there's also *got* to be agreement if we don't want to play into the hands of the Germans."

What rôle, if any, would now be played by the Free German Committee? "It's no longer of any consequence," Zhukov said, and smiled, thus pretty well confirming that it had never been more than a propaganda device. "And the so-called German anti-Fascists?" "Why 'so-called'?" Zhukov said. "There are some genuine ones, though not perhaps very many yet. For twelve years they've had Hitler propaganda pumped into them. . ."

"And what happened to Hitler?"

Zhukov suddenly became very cautious (quite unlike Sokolovsky when he had talked to me only a few days before). For one thing, he had Vyshinsky sitting by his side. "A mysterious business," he said, and then told for the first time the story that was going to be flashed all round the world:

A few days before the fall of Berlin he married Eva Braun. We know this from the diary of one of his A.D.C.'s. But we have not discovered any corpse that could be identified as Hitler's. He may have escaped in a plane at the last moment.

"Wouldn't you say, Marshal, that that was most unlikely?" I asked.

Zhukov ignored the question, and went on:

"Martin Bormann who was in Berlin almost till the very end, appears to have escaped."

"And who *was* Eva Braun?" somebody asked.

Vyshinsky grinned and chipped in: "Maybe a girl, maybe a boy."

Zhukov (laughing): "Somebody said she was a cinema actress, but I don't know."

Vyshinsky: "Maybe a Jewess—". (Laughter.)

After saying that Goebbels and his whole family had been found dead, Zhukov then turned to other things. Now that the war in Europe (he stressed *in Europe*) was at an end, a large part of the Red Army would be demobilised.

Then he talked informally about himself, recalled that he had been born in a village near Moscow in 1896, that, from the age of eleven, he had worked in a fur shop, that, in World War I he had fought first as a private, then as an N.C.O. in the Novgorod Dragoons, and had been awarded two St George's crosses and two St George's medals.

"For personal bravery," Vyshinsky commented.

"For capturing German officers during night reconnaissance," Zhukov explained.

"He was good at night operations even then," Vyshinsky grinned.

Zhukov recalled that he had been a Party member since 1919, and then talked of his experiences in the Far East where he routed the Japanese in the battle of Halkin Gol in 1939.

"The Germans," he said, "are technically better-equipped than the Japanese, and they are very good soldiers—no use denying it— but, taken as a whole, the German army lacks the Japs' real fanaticism."

Then Zhukov spoke of what he called his "principal activities" during the war that had just ended:

> From the very beginning of the war I was engaged on preparing the defence of Moscow. For a time, before the Battle of Moscow, there was also Leningrad to take care of, and then there was the Battle of Moscow itself. After that I had to organise the defence of Stalingrad and then the Stalingrad offensive. I was Deputy Commissar of Defence under Comrade Stalin. Then there was the Ukraine, and Warsaw— and you know the rest.

"And Kursk, and Belorussia?" somebody asked.

"Yes, I had something to do with those too," Zhukov smiled.

Vyshinsky beamed almost obsequiously: "Moscow, Leningrad, Stalingrad, Kursk, Warsaw, and so on, right on to Berlin—pretty wonderful!" he said.

Zhukov added a tribute to Comrade Stalin "and his great under-standing of military affairs"—but this came almost as an afterthought. There were rivalries amongst the Soviet marshals—

none of whom, except himself, he had even mentioned at this press conference—and, moreover, the Party (and Stalin) were conscious of Zhukov's immense popularity in the army and in the country. Very understandably, Zhukov had a very high opinion of himself and, with a curious mixture of modesty and almost boyish boastfulness, he tended to take credit for practically *all* the decisive victories the Red Army had won. Stalin did not like it at all.

That day at Wendenschloss Vyshinsky, while keeping an eye on him, treated him outwardly with the greatest obsequiousness and admiration; but one could vaguely feel that Zhukov did not like Vyshinsky (how could he?) and resented his supervision.*

When, some months later, Marshal Zhukov was recalled from Germany and appointed to the relatively obscure post of Commander of the Odessa Military District, all kinds of explanations were offered for his semi-disgrace. One was that he had proved himself much too independent of the Soviet Party bosses; another, that he had objected to the excessive dismantling of factories in the Soviet Zone, and that he also treated various Party and Trade Union delegations who had come to Berlin with great casualness, sometimes even refusing to see them; it was also said that he had let his troops run wild in Germany, and finally, that he was much too friendly and soft in his relations with the Western Allies, particularly with Eisenhower. In reality, there seems little doubt that Zhukov's eclipse was the most striking manifestation of all of Stalin's and the Party's determination to put the Red Army in its place. Zhukov was too popular in the country.

After Stalin's death, Zhukov made a spectacular come-back; and although he saved Khrushchev in 1957 from what later came to be known as the "anti-Party Group", Khrushchev also decided, before long, that Zhukov was too strong a personality for his taste. The Marshal was accused of looking upon the Army as a distinct political force; he was also accused of immodesty and self-glorification at the expense of the other Russian generals, and of

* When Harry Hopkins saw Zhukov about the same time, he was also unable to talk to him without Vyshinsky always being there, and suggesting to him how to answer questions. (Sherwood, op. cit., p. 904).

having encouraged in the Army his own "personality cult". He was pensioned off at the end of 1957; his great rival, Marshal Konev wrote a disobliging article on him in *Pravda*, and the immense rôle he had played in saving Leningrad and Moscow and in winning so many other victories was deliberately played down in all subsequent accounts of the war published in Russia.

Chapter IV

THE THREE MONTHS' PEACE

The Mood after VE-Day

Although it was generally known that a large number of soldiers were being moved to the Far East during those summer months, very little thought was given to Japan by the Russian people generally. As far as they were concerned, the war—the *real* war—was over with the collapse of Hitler's Germany. The thought that there might yet be another war to fight against Japan was hateful to most; Russia had lost quite enough men as it was.

It is not easy to describe the general mood in the country during that summer of 1945. It was composed of many different things. First of all, perhaps, a feeling of overwhelming relief that the war was over; but this went together with a feeling of immense national pride and a sense of enormous achievement—and every soldier, and nearly every civilian, too, felt that he had done his bit. This feeling of spontaneous joy, pride and relief found perhaps its fullest expression on that unforgettable VE-Day of May 9 in Moscow.

The Army was enormously popular—too popular, indeed, for Stalin's and the Party's taste, though, for a short time after VE-Day, Stalin was determined to cash in on the Army's popularity and, in June, went so far as to assume the title of Generalissimo.

Shortly before, on May 24, he held a great reception at the Kremlin in honour of numerous Soviet marshals, generals and other high-ranking officers, and it was then that he made that strange speech in which he singled out for special praise the *Russian* people, "the most remarkable of all the nations of the Soviet Union"—"the leading nation, remarkable for its clear mind, its patience and its

firm character." The Soviet Government, he said, had made many
mistakes, but even in the desperate moments of 1941-2, the Russian
people had not told its government to go, had not thought of making
peace with Germany, had shown confidence in the Soviet Government and had decided to fight on till final victory, whatever the cost.

A great deal could be read into that speech: a belated *mea culpa*
for many things that had happened before the war and during the
early days of the war; a tribute to the Russians for having fought on
when the Ukraine and so many other parts of the country had been
overrun by the Germans; all sorts of mental reservations not only
about the "disloyal" nationalities like the Crimean Tartars, the
Caucasian mountaineers and probably also the Balts (who were
being punished in varying degrees), but even about the Ukrainians
whose record, in Stalin's suspicious eyes, had been uneven. The Red
Army was rich in Ukrainian generals and Ukrainian Heroes of the
Soviet Union, and yet there were other Ukrainians whose loyalty to
Moscow and the Soviet system had been questionable. In the
Western Ukraine, at that time, Ukrainian nationalists were still
conducting a guerrilla war against the Russians, and this was going
to continue till 1947. Were the Russians, "the leading nation", to be
the Number One citizens in the Soviet Union henceforth? There
were some uneasy reactions in Moscow to this exaltation of Great-
Russian nationalism, especially coming, as it did, from a Georgian
who spoke Russian with a broad Caucasian accent. What strange
mental kink was behind it?

Then, on June 24, came the great apotheosis of the Red Army,
with "Generalissimo" Stalin at its head—the famous Victory Parade
in the Red Square. Marshal Zhukov, by common consent the
greatest of Russia's soldiers, reviewed the troops, and Marshal
Rokossovsky commanded the Parade, in the course of which
hundreds of German banners were flung down, in a torrential rain-
fall, on the steps of the Lenin Mausoleum, and at the feet of
Victorious Stalin. Owing to the downpour—some old women in
Moscow saw in this an evil omen—the civilian parade that was to
follow the military parade was called off; but that night Stalin enter-
tained 2,500 generals, officers and soldiers at the Kremlin. Here he
made another strange speech, in which he paid tribute to the "small

people", to "the little screws and bolts" of the gigantic machine without which the machine, with all its marshals and generals and industrial chiefs could not have worked. This speech also gave rise to some uneasy speculation: was there not here, apart from an extreme anti-egalitarian motif, a warning to the "military caste" that had emerged from the war? During the months that followed Moscow began to buzz with "anecdotes" about marshals' and generals' wives, with their *nouveau-riche* ways and their endless malapropisms.*

There is good reason to suppose that this verbal propaganda, a fairly familiar device in Russia, had been put about on instructions from the Party hierarchy.

Nor was it very long before the official propaganda began to discourage boastfulness on the part of officers and soldiers; the war was declared to be a thing of the past, and the soldiers could not be allowed to rest on their laurels. Very soon after the end of the Japanese war there appeared a poem by one Nedogonov, called *The Flag over the Village Soviet* which was given wide publicity: Its main theme was summed up in the lines: "And if you won't work hard on the *kolkhoz*, we shall spit on all your medals and decorations."

This systematic debunking of the war hero came later, but the first signs of it could already be detected only a couple of months after the victory over Germany.

Economic Hardships Continue

All this was, in a way, ungracious and hurtful; and yet it was understandable. In 1945 Russia was in a serious economic situation; it

* For example, there was the general's wife who kept on talking at the Opera while the overture was being played: "Sh-sh, overture!" her neighbour said. "Overture yourself," she snapped back, thinking *ouvertura* to be some unfamiliar term of abuse. Or else there was the story of the Marshal's wife who had so many silver foxes that she decided to wear only one, but to pin to her chest the tails of the remaining nine, to show that she had ten altogether.

was essential to demobilise as much of the Red Army as possible, and to get down to the hard realities of peace-time reconstruction. Hundreds of towns, tens of thousands of villages had been partly or completely destroyed by the Germans; the industrial areas of Kharkov, Kiev, Stalingrad, Odessa, Rostov, the Donbas, Zaporozhie and Krivoi Rog, besides many others, had been laid waste; millions of Russians and Ukrainians had been deported to Germany and most of them had returned in bad or indifferent health; altogether (though this figure was not to be mentioned until much later) twenty million people had lost their lives—or one-tenth of the entire population, an appalling proportion equalled only by Poland and Yugoslavia. There were also millions of war invalids.

The civilian population of the Soviet Union had not only been underfed, but also grossly overworked during the war years, and many had died under the strain. The whole of the country's agriculture had been run almost entirely by women, and it was the women too who had kept the country's industries going in wartime. *In 1945, fifty-one percent of all industrial workers in the Soviet Union were women.* Many of the other workers were adolescents.

Despite this intensive effort on the part of the Soviet people to keep the war-time industries going—and without this mass-effort Russia could never have won the war—the whole industrial situation was little short of disastrous by the end of the war. With the recovery of some of the industrial areas in 1943–4 and the intensification of production in the east and in central Russia, the production figures for the first half of 1945 showed a slight improvement, compared with the first half of 1944. But this was very little, compared with the not overwhelmingly good pre-war figures:

> During the first half of 1945, the Soviet Union produced only 77% of the coal produced in the first half of 1941; 54% of the oil; 77% of the electric power; 46% of the pig-iron; 52% of the steel; 54% of the coke; 65% of the machine-tools. . .*

Almost everything had had to go into the war industries which in the first half of 1945, had produced nearly 21,000 aircraft, 29,000 aircraft engines, over 9,000 tanks, over 6,000 mobile guns, 62,000

* IVOVSS, vol. V, pp. 376–84.

guns, 873,000 rifles and machine-guns, 82m. shells, bombs and mines, over 3 billion cartridges, etc. The industrial might of the Soviet Union had been practically cut in half since 1941. In 1945 she was producing only *one-eighth* as much steel as the USA. She was faced with the gigantic problem of reconstruction, reconversion and development. Agriculture had to be re-equipped with machinery almost from scratch, and supplied with chemical fertilisers. The production of agricultural machinery and of fertilisers was one of the first things to be stepped up immediately the war in Europe was over.

The number of livestock, very far from enormous in 1940 (when the after-effects of collectivisation were still keenly felt), was much lower still in 1945. In 1945, there were only 47·4 m. head of cattle (which was 3·2 m. more than in 1944). By the end of 1945 the total number of cattle was only 87% of the 1940 figure; cows, 82%; sheep and goats, 70%; pigs, 38%; horses, 51%. In the liberated areas the percentages were lower still (cows, 76%; pigs, 34%; horses, 44%).*

There was also, in 1945, a shortage of high-quality forage; as a result of this and other factors, the state purchases of meat were 61·8 percent of what they had been in 1940, and those of dairy produce, 45 percent. Which, obviously, meant that the civilian population, particularly in the cities, had to continue on short rations—especially those holding clerical-workers', dependents' and children's ration cards. Diplomats and other privileged foreigners in Moscow at that time, who enjoyed higher rations and often attended sumptuous official Soviet receptions, were scarcely aware of the miserable standard of living that continued among "ordinary" Russians. Special efforts were made to give reasonably ample food to industrial workers, and to provide extra meals of sorts for school-children; but most Russians still lived very poorly, their diet consisting almost entirely of bread, potatoes and vegetables, with very little sugar, fats, meat or fish. In 1945, I knew many families with clerical workers' ration-cards who, without actually starving, were having a worse than thin time, and to whom a whole lump of sugar in their tea was almost a luxury. The stopping of Lend-Lease,

* IVOVSS, vol. V, p. 392. Some of the new cattle had been brought from Germany.

which had supplied a substantial amount of food to the Army—
i.e. to about ten million people—caused an appreciable drop in the
total amount of food consumed in Russia.* UNRRA was of some
help in Belorussia and the Ukraine, though it could not be said to
be over-generous; and there was no UNRRA relief at all in the rest
of the Soviet Union.† For a time, the great drought of 1946 was to
make food conditions in very large parts of the Soviet Union even
more difficult.

These hardships at the end of the war, which were, after all, only a
continuation of the war-time hardships, cannot, however, be said
to have undermined Russian morale as a whole, except that a certain
relaxation in war-time discipline was to be reflected, before long, in
intensified black-market activities and in a considerable increase in
crime—a familiar post-war phenomenon in most countries.

But in the summer of 1945 the feeling of elation continued, with
the homecoming of millions of soldiers. In many places, life was
already beginning to rise from the ruins; the Donbas mines were
being rapidly put back into operation; the Kharkov Tractor Plant
was beginning to turn out tractors again; villages in western Russia
and in Belorussia were being rapidly rebuilt—though usually by
only the most rudimentary methods; hundreds of thousands of
people were returning to Leningrad. The reconstruction that had
already begun in the liberated areas in 1944 was being speeded up.

Along with this, there were also millions of personal tragedies—
of women who had now lost all hope of seeing their husbands or
sons return from captivity, and ex-war-prisoners who had survived
the war, but were now being put through the NKVD mill, and of
whom so many were to spend years in camps. There were purges in
which not only real, but also alleged collaborators were to suffer.
These purges were probably heaviest of all in the Baltic Republics

* A small proportion of Lend-Lease food also went to the civilian
population.
† There might have been UNRRA help in the western parts of
Russia proper, but, apparently as a matter of prestige, the Soviet
Government declined it.

and in the western Ukraine. But officially, very little was known about all this at the time, and the full story of the 1944–5 purge still remains to be written—if the real facts ever come to light.

(c) *International Pleasantness and Unpleasantness*

A somewhat uneasy international atmosphere marked those three months of peace "twixt Germany and Japan". It cannot be said that a uniform process of *Gleichschaltung* was yet being applied by the Russians to the whole of eastern Europe. Czechoslovakia was to remain for some time a sort of show-window of East-West co-existence, with the powerful Communist Party under Gottwald apparently co-operating loyally with the "bourgeois" parties. President Benes, though not really trusted by the Russians, was, nevertheless, treated with a great show of respect.* More curious were the friendly gestures made by the Russians to King Michael of Rumania, despite all the unpleasantness of the previous February. Now, in the summer of 1945, it was prominently reported that Marshal Tolbukhin had solemnly conferred on the young King the Order of Victory, the highest Russian military decoration, for the courageous stand he had taken in August 1944 when he broke with Germany. On another occasion it was almost equally prominently reported that some of the most famous Russian singers and musical performers had given a special concert in Bucharest in honour of King Michael and the Dowager Queen Helen and that, after the concert, the artistes, as well as many eminent Soviet scientists who were there, were presented to "Their Majesties".

Among other friendly gestures during that summer was the conferring by Marshal Zhukov of the Order of Victory on Eisenhower and Montgomery; the compliment was returned when Montgomery

* It was at this time that the Czechoslovak premier, Fierlinger, came to Moscow to sign the agreement whereby Ruthenia (the eastern tip of pre-war Czechoslovakia) was "returned" to the Soviet Ukraine.

conferred the G.C.B. on Zhukov, the K.C.B. on Rokossovsky, the O.B.E. on Sokolovsky and Malinin, and so on.

On the other hand, there was a good deal of unpleasantness of one kind or another. The Soviet press showed much indignation over Field-Marshal Alexander's "insolent and insulting" behaviour to the Yugoslavs at Trieste.*

There had also been, as already said, some angry recrimination on the part of the Russians about Churchill's "suspect patronage" of the "Flensburg Government". There were, further, some angry protests over the temporary arrest, in northern Italy, of Nenni and Togliatti, and a good deal of recrimination about British policy in Greece. Much was made, of course, of the leading part played by the communists in both the Italian and the French Resistance, but, for all that, the Russian attitude to the French, Italian and other Western Communist parties remained somewhat vague. Downright revolutionary activities on their part were not encouraged; instead, both while the war lasted and for two years after, they were urged to "co-operate" with the bourgeois parties—and in France, with de Gaulle in particular—and to make their influence felt both in parliament and in the administration.† Only time would show how influential they could become.

* Tito had tried to annex Trieste and Istria, which met with sharp opposition from Churchill and Truman. Although Alexander was at first friendly to the Yugoslavs, he later sharply opposed them on Churchill's instructions, and on one occasion even compared Tito to Hitler and Mussolini, much to Stalin's indignation. (See Churchill, op. cit., vol. IV, pp. 480–8). Later, in 1948, at the time of the Stalin-Tito quarrel, the Russians made a complete about-turn and accused the Yugoslavs of having behaved provocatively and irresponsibly and of nearly having dragged the Soviet Union into an unwanted war with the Western Allies by trying to grab Trieste.

† The most striking example of communist "appeasement" *vis-à-vis* the bourgeoisie was the formal approval that Thorez—just back from Russia—gave on January 21, 1945 to de Gaulle's dissolution of the *gardes patriotiques*, the para-military formations of the pre-dominantly communist part of the Resistance. This approval was given in the name of "national unity", and with the defeat of Germany as No. 1 objective. Thorez's move, obviously taken with

(d) *Poland again—Hopkins—Trial of the Polish Underground*

Poland—always Poland!—continued to be the most acute problem between Russia and the Western Allies in the early summer of 1945. Even before entering Poland proper, that is, in Western Belorussia and Lithuania, the Red Army had met with some armed resistance and sabotage from the "London" Polish underground, the *Armija Krajowa*, and things had gone from bad to worse once the Russians were inside Poland. It was claimed on the Russian side that several hundred Russian soldiers and officers had been assassinated by Poles; the *Armija Krajowa* was also held guilty of many terrorist acts against representatives of the Lublin Government and of sabotaging the recruitment of Poles into the Polish Army fighting side-by-side with the Red Army. The Russians were also impressed by the hostility of a large part of the Polish population, and by the intensive anti-Soviet propaganda conducted in Poland, both by the "London" underground and by the Church.

In January 1945, on instructions from London, the *Armija Krajowa* officially dissolved itself, but was replaced by a secret organisation, called NIE (short for *Niepodleglosc*, i.e. Independence), still with General Okulicki at its head. After the collapse of the Warsaw Rising, Okulicki had been appointed to replace General Bór-Komarowski as head of the *Armija Krajowa*. The new Underground, which had "inherited" the military and radio equipment of the *Armija Krajowa*, continued its activities after the Russians had overrun the whole of Poland. So in March the Soviet Government decided to decapitate this "anti-Russian resistance movement".

Stalin's approval, if not simply on his instructions, annoyed a great part of the communist rank-and-file, and also some leaders like Marty and Tillon (the latter had been highly prominent in the Resistance inside France), both of whom were later to be charged by the communist leadership with irresponsible revolutionary romanticism and *blanquisme*. Similarly, Thorez declared that the Liberation Committees that had emanated from the Resistance must not try to "substitute themselves" for the Governments. (See the author's *France 1940–1955*, p. 244.)

General Okulicki and fifteen others were invited—in two lots—to meet a number of Russian officers, ostensibly with a view to discussing the Yalta decisions on Poland and a *modus vivendi*. The meetings were a trap, Okulicki and the others, among them three members of the "Polish Underground Government" (Jan Jankowski, Adam Ben and Stanislaw Jasiukowicz), and Puzak, socialist president of the "underground parliament", were arrested and taken to Moscow. On April 28 Churchill anxiously inquired, in a letter to Stalin, about the "fifteen Poles" who were rumoured to have been "deported". On May 4, Stalin replied that he had no intention of being silent about the sixteen—not fifteen—Poles. All, or some of them, depending on the outcome of the investigations, would be put on trial.

> [They are] charged with subversive activities behind the lines of the Red Army. This subversion has taken a toll of over a hundred Red Army soldiers and officers; they are also charged with keeping illegal radio transmitters behind our lines... The Red Army is forced to protect its units and rear-lines against saboteurs.

He described Okulicki as a person of "particular odiousness".*

The arrest of these Poles—and the whole Polish question—were right in the centre of the Stalin-Hopkins discussions between May 26 and June 6. These six meetings took place during the "last mission" that Hopkins—a very sick man who was to die only a few months later—was to perform at the request of the new President, Harry Truman. At the very first meeting with Stalin, Hopkins recalled how, on his way back from Yalta, Roosevelt had frequently spoken of "the respect and admiration he had for Marshal Stalin"; but the fact remained that "in the last six weeks deterioration of [American] public opinion had been so serious as to affect adversely the relations between the two countries."

> In a country like ours [Hopkins said] public opinion is affected by specific incidents, and the deterioration... has been centred on our inability to carry into effect the Yalta Agreement on Poland.

Time and again he returned to this question, saying that, in the public view in the United States, "Poland had become a symbol of our ability to work out problems with the Soviet Union." He urged

* *Churchill-Stalin Correspondence*, p. 348.

Stalin to speed up the formation of the "new" Polish Government and also, purely and simply, to release the leaders of the Polish Underground now under arrest.

Stalin would not yield on this point; not only had this Underground committed grave crimes against the Red Army, but these people represented that *cordon sanitaire* policy so dear to Churchill's heart; the British conservatives did not want the new Poland to be friendly to the Soviet Union. In reply to Hopkin's long plea in favour of allowing Poland all the necessary democratic freedoms, as America understood them, Stalin said that (a) in time of war these political freedoms could not be enjoyed to the full extent and (b) nor could they be granted without reservations to Fascist parties trying to overthrow the government. It was obvious that, in Stalin's mind, the word "Fascist" applied to the *Armija Krajowa* and all other Polish elements hostile to Russia.

However, a virtual agreement was reached about including Mikolajczyk and a few others in the Polish Government, and, after his fourth meeting with Stalin, Hopkins was able to report to Truman:

> It looks as though Stalin is prepared to return to and implement the Crimea decision and permit a representative group to come to Moscow to consult with the [Molotov-Harriman-Clark Kerr] commission.

In the course of the six Hopkins-Stalin meetings* several other important questions were, of course, discussed. Hopkins urged Stalin to appoint without delay the Russian member of the Control Council in Germany, since Eisenhower had already been appointed its American member; Stalin said he would appoint Zhukov in the next few days. Stalin persisted in expressing the belief that Hitler was not dead and said he thought that Goebbels and Bormann had also escaped.

Stalin, without objecting to the termination of Lend-Lease, said it had been done in an "unfortunate and brutal" way. "He added that the Russians had intended to make a suitable expression of gratitude to the United States for the Lend-Lease assistance during

---

* Sherwood, op. cit., vol. II, pp. 872–906.

the war, but the way in which the programme had been halted made this impossible now." Hopkins, while deploring certain "technical misunderstandings" which had created this situation, added that the termination of Lend-Lease was not intended as a "pressure weapon" against Russia, as Stalin had suggested. He said "he wished to add that we had never believed that our Lend-Lease help had been the chief factor in the Soviet defeat of Hitler... This had been done by the heroism and blood of the Russian Army."

Another important question discussed by Hopkins and Stalin related to Russia's entry into the war against Japan. Stalin declared that the Soviet Army would be properly deployed in its Manchurian positions by August 8. This part of the Hopkins-Stalin talks will be dealt with later.

The Moscow trial of the Polish Underground opened in the Pillared Hall in Moscow (the very hall where the great Purge Trials of the '30's had taken place) on June 18, and lasted for three days. The presiding judge was the notorious General Ulrich, also of the Purge Trials.

General Okulicki, the principal defendant, a dapper Polish officer, defended himself ably and with courage, pleading guilty to most of the charges (formation of an underground after the dissolution of the *Armija Krajowa*, ignoring the Red Army's orders to surrender arms and radio equipment, secret wireless communications with London, anti-Soviet propaganda amongst the population, etc.) but declined responsibility for the killing of Russian officers and soldiers. Since he had taken command of the *A.K.*, he had been in the part of Poland still under German occupation, and he had had no control over eastern Poland or Lithuania, where the Russians were murdered; when the Russians penetrated into western Poland, nothing like that happened.

When he was asked by the Second Public Prosecutor, General Rudenko, why he had not surrendered the *A.K.*'s armaments, radio transmitters, etc., to the Red Army, the following exchange took place:

Okulicki: I intended to keep them for the future.

Rudenko: For what purpose?
Okulicki: To fight for Poland should she be threatened.
Rudenko: Fight against whom?
Okulicki: Against anyone threatening Poland.
Rudenko: What country did you have in mind?
Okulicki: The Soviet Union.
Rudenko: So what you had in mind was a war against the Soviet Union, with this qualification: "if the Soviet Union threatens the independence of Poland". In such an eventuality what allies, what bloc were you thinking of?
Okulicki: A bloc against the Soviets.
Rudenko: That meant Poland, and who else? What other states?
Okulicki: All other states.
Rudenko: Will you enumerate the states mentioned in your letter to Colonel "Slawbor"? [one of his subordinates].
Okulicki: I mentioned England.
Rudenko: And whom else?
Okulicki: The Germans.
Rudenko: So you were thinking of a bloc with the Germans, with Germany, the enemy of all freedom-loving countries, notorious for its cruelty and barbarity...
Okulicki: I meant a bloc, not with the Germans, but with Europe. (*Laughter*.)*

On the last day of the trial, in his "last words" before the verdict, Okulicki admitted that he had been mistaken in distrusting the Soviet Union and in trusting the Polish Government in London; this had not accepted the Yalta Agreement on Poland, and that was a mistake, which he had recognised at once. Nevertheless, he had maintained the Polish Underground, complete with arms stores and radio equipment, because he had continued to distrust Russia. He remembered that Tsarist Russia had oppressed Poland for 123 years, and he had not been convinced that Poland's independence would be respected by the victorious Russians; he did not know at the time what changes had taken place in Russia. He had fought the Germans, but said that there was nothing in his directives to the *AK* to show that he had ordered acts of terrorism against the Russians, and if these took place without his knowledge (and they *did* take

* *Sudebnyi otchet po delu...polskogo podpoliya* (Report of the Trial of the Polish Underground) (Moscow, 1945), pp. 141–2.

place) it was deeply regrettable. As for his ideas about an alliance with "Europe", including England and Germany, these related to the future and were purely "hypothetical".

That was as far as he would go. But the official Russians were fairly satisfied; in their eyes the trial had shown up the London Government and, indirectly, Churchill, with his *cordon sanitaire*.

As Stalin had already foretold to Hopkins, the sentences were relatively lenient. The Public Prosecutor, no doubt acting on instructions from above, did not demand the death sentence, not even for Okulicki. The latter was given ten years, the three members of the "underground government" between five and eight years, the others much shorter sentences, and three were acquitted.

Even so, there was something distasteful about the whole thing, not only to Western observers, but also to many Russians who remembered the Purge Trials in the late '30's. Just *before* the trial there had also been a particularly nauseating article by Zaslavsky in *Pravda* calling all the accused murderers, bandits, etc., in the worst style of 1937. To many it also seemed a confession of weakness to have these men tried by a Russian, and not a Polish, court. Would there have been too much sympathy for them in Poland? After all, many of them *had* fought for years against the Germans, and the main charge that they were directly responsible for the deaths of many Russian officers and soldiers had not been proved.

Although, on the face of it, the trial looked fair enough, many Russians wondered, as they looked at this same court room and the same sinister Judge Ulrich, whether some pressures had not been brought to bear on the defendants.

Soon afterwards in Poland I found that even pro-Soviet Government Poles were a little embarrassed about the whole thing, and many Poles wondered, of course, what would actually happen to Okulicki and the three other principal prisoners. . .*

* The evidence here is conflicting. According to the US Ambassador in Warsaw, Arthur Bliss Lane (*I Saw Freedom Betrayed*, London, 1947), Okulicki and the others still in Russian prisons were amnestied in 1946, though a few (not Okulicki) were later prosecuted by the Polish authorities. Poles, both in Warsaw and in England, have assured me that Okulicki died in Russian captivity in 1947.

As a result of Harry Hopkins's prodding, the Molotov-Harriman-Clark Kerr Committee at last managed to bring about the formation of a Polish "Government of National Unity". Only a small number of "London Poles", though none of them members of Arciszewski's Polish Government there, entered this government. The most prominent among them was Mikolajczyk, who had resigned from the London Government some months before, and had, albeit reluctantly, accepted the Yalta Agreement on Poland. Despite the great hostility shown him by the "Lublin Poles", Churchill had insisted that he join the new Polish Government. The final negotiations which ended in the formation of this government took place in Moscow between June 17 and 24, thus coinciding, by a grim—and perhaps intentional—irony, with the trial of Okulicki and the other Underground leaders. Both before and after the trial Mikolajczyk had pleaded with the Russians that the Underground leaders be released; he argued with Molotov that such an act of magnanimity on the Russians' part would have a wonderful psychological effect in Poland; but it was of no avail. Bierut, whom Mikolajczyk begged to support his plea, refused to do so, saying it would merely annoy Stalin. "Besides, we don't need these people in Poland just now."*

The Polish Government that was finally formed, and in whose honour Stalin gave a sumptuous banquet at the Kremlin before its members left for Warsaw, was a somewhat lop-sided affair, in which the key positions were held by pro-Soviet Poles; but it was the best the Western Powers could achieve in the circumstances, and they hastened to recognise the new Polish Government. In his speech at the Kremlin that night, Stalin spoke of the harm Poland and Russia had done each other in the past, and admitted that Russia's guilt had been greater than Poland's; he even suggested that a new generation of Poles would have to grow up before all the bitterness disappeared. Germany, he said, would continue to be a threat to both Poland and Russia, and their alliance was essential, but it was not enough in itself, and both countries, therefore, needed the alliance of the United States, Britain and France.†

* Mikolajczyk. *Le viol de la Pologne*, p. 158.
† Ibid., p. 157.

(e) *Close-Up: Civil War Undertones in Poland*

This was for foreign consumption. Stalin and all other Russians knew that an acute struggle was going on in Poland between "East" and "West". When I spent ten days in Poland soon after the formation of the new government, I found there something not unlike a civil war atmosphere. The arrival in Poland of an unusually large group of Western correspondents gave rise to some sharp anti-Russian demonstrations for their benefit. One of them was particularly grim: at Cracow, to show us that the "underground" was active, two unfortunate Russian soldiers were shot outside the hotel where we were staying. Any meetings we had with the "intelligentsia"—whether with writers in Cracow, or with members of the Radio Committee at Katowice—were invariably marked by violent denunciations of the Russians and of their "stooges"— "NKVD" Bierut, Osobka-Morawski, or Gomulka.

Faute de mieux, Mikolajczyk became a symbol of Polish patriotism of the right kind: soon after his arrival in Poland, many thousands staged a tremendous demonstration in his honour at Cracow, which had become like the capital of the old-time and pro-Western Poland, and the stronghold of the Peasant Party, the PSL, and also of all that was most clerical and "reactionary" in the country. The city, with its famous baroque churches, and Pilsudski's tomb—an "anti-Russian" shrine which thousands visited every day —had suffered less damage than most Polish cities. But although the Russians had saved Cracow from destruction, the hostility to them was greater here than anywhere else. The Russian soldiers in Cracow, for their part, were particularly nervous, boorish and defiant, and among those who had come from Germany with all its lawlessness, discipline was far from good, and the Poles wallowed in stories of Russian robbery and rape.

The atmosphere in Warsaw was distinctly better. The city was, of course, a tragic sight. Practically all governmental and other activity was centred in Praga, on the other side of the river, and the Vistula could be crossed only by a temporary wooden bridge. In Warsaw proper, among the few "live" places were the Hotel Polonia and a few blocks of houses behind it; here the Germans had lived till the end, while the rest of Warsaw was burning. Around, for miles, was the desert of burned-out houses and mountains of rubble. There were cigarette vendors outside the Polonia selling mostly UNRRA cigarettes, and the "fourteen flower stalls" of Warsaw were considered a pathetic small beginning of the restoration of life. A few pre-fabricated houses and a few buses and tramcars had been presented to Warsaw by the Soviet Union, and there was much talk that Russia was going to "rebuild half of Warsaw"; but, whether true or not, all this was still in the future. Meantime, most of the workers of Warsaw were busy clearing rubble and patching up houses that could still be made more or less habitable. What was striking in Warsaw, though, was the faith that the city *would* be rebuilt; the "Lublin" Poles had announced that this would be done, and this was psychologically, a great point in their favour. This reconstruction of Warsaw and the Oder-Neisse Line were the two points on which all Poles were agreed.

One day when I was in Warsaw, about 20,000 workers, and some peasant delegations, held a great demonstration in the Krakowskie Przedmescie—all of it in ruins, and from the balcony of the burned-out Opera-house overlooking the street, the members of the government, complete with Mikolajczyk, were there to greet them. There was a great deal of cheering from the demonstrators—but it was not necessarily meant for Mikolajczyk only. Many of these workers, carrying red banners, were PPR and PPS, Communists and Socialists.* "Amazing, amazing," Mikolajczyk was saying, "such vitality among our people, living, as they do, among the ruins, and hungry, very, very hungry..." A girl, in national costume, representing the PSL, the Peasant Party, presented him with a bunch

---

* The pro-Russian Poles, as I noticed particularly at Katowice, the centre of the Silesian black country, were doing their utmost to build up, among the miners, a large trade-union organisation with a strong communist slant, which was expected to be one of the main pillars of the new régime.

of flowers. Mikolajczyk then recalled the "wonderful reception he had been given at Cracow—an ovation, a real ovation." (At this point somebody whispered that it wasn't really a pro-Mikolajczyk ovation, but an anti-Bierut ovation).

In 1945, Poland's "Western Territories" were still a desert. Nearly all the Germans had gone, and the villages were mostly empty. Polish and Russian troops were being used to bring in the harvest. Here and there new settlers were coming in in driblets, some from the Lwow areas, some from tiny "uneconomical" farms in central Poland. Some came without cattle, and although they had been given good German farmhouses—in which they had already installed their holy pictures—they were living on potatoes and little else. Some, between the Oder and the Western Neisse, were saying: "Here we have been given more land than what we had at home, but we have nothing to work it with—we've no horses—and *this isn't our country, anyway.*" Two years later, both the general picture in these parts and the people's mentality had changed completely. By 1947 they looked upon it very much as *their* country. Gomulka, the minister then in charge of the Western Territories, had played a leading part in this process.

A few Germans were still living here in 1945. I remember the local miller's son, a sturdy youngster with turned-up nose and freckles. He looked bewildered. "I don't know where they will send us. We have nowhere to go. I have lived here all my life." On a road we met a procession of several hundred Germans, men, women, children, carrying bundles, and the old folks sitting in horse-carts. Polish soldiers, who were escorting them, bellowed at them when they started telling us some tale of woe. The Germans had had no pity for the Poles; now the Poles had none for the Germans.

Danzig—now Gdansk—was hideous in its destruction. The fighting here had been very heavy, and there were dozens of Russian mass-graves along the coastal road between Gdynia and Danzig. Outside Danzig we saw an experimental factory for making soap out of human corpses, which had been run by a German professor called Spanner. It was a nightmarish sight, with its vats full of human heads and torsoes pickled in some liquid, and its pails full of a flakey substance—human soap. A slow-witted Germanised young Pole, who had worked here as a laboratory assistant, and who now looked very scared, said that the factory had not gone much beyond the experimental stage, though what soap had actually been made was good. It had smelt bad, until some chemical had been added which made it smell of almonds. His mother had liked it. He said that, Professor Spanner had told him that after the war, the Germans would set up a soap factory in each concentration camp, so that the whole thing could be run on a sound industrial basis. Now that the Jews had been wiped out, they could start on millions of Slavs.

Back in Warsaw. I talked to a Russian colonel who said: "There are a lot of AK and NSZ [Polish Fascist] terrorists everywhere, especially in places like Cracow. The PPR [the Polish Communists] are having a very tough time; hundreds of their officials have been bumped off. One has to be very brave to be a Polish communist. In Czechoslovakia there is great enthusiasm for the Red Army, but not here in Poland. The Poles are difficult people; the only good thing is that they hate the Germans even more than they hate us; it may make things easier between us in the long run, especially with the Oder-Neisse frontier, on which they are all very keen. Also, the Red Army is pulling out of Poland, except on the communication lines to Germany, and that may make them feel better and stop all their silly talk about the 'Russian occupation'."

Meanwhile, however, a little civil war was going on in Poland below the surface—and not so very far below. It did not stop until 1947, and not without the help of the Army and a powerful police force, both built up with Russian advice and assistance. Mikolajczyk fled in 1948, Cyrankiewicz replaced Osóbka-Morawski, but, after several years of "Stalinist" terror (though less violent in Poland than elsewhere) a different kind of Poland emerged, with Gomulka at its head—that very Gomulka whom Mikolajczyk regarded in 1945 as a criminal maniac. It was, however, wrong to assume that in 1945 there were no genuine socialists or communists in Poland, except those "sold" to the Russians, or that *all* Poles loved the West; just as there were very many Czechs, so there were also numerous Poles who remembered only too well that their country's alliance with the West had done them no good in 1939.

Not only among the working-class leaders, but also among a part of the intelligentsia there were many who were saying: "With our economy as devastated as it is, and with the Western Territories to settle and organise, only a centrally-controlled socialist economy can cope effectively with all these problems." But this was the "rational" approach and, emotionally, a large number of Poles, starting with the Church, were more or less hostile to Russia.

There were popular rhymes in 1945 on the early return of Lwow to Poland, in which *Lwowa* (the genitive of Lwow) rhymed with *bomba atomowa*.

Chapter V

POTSDAM

At the Potsdam Conference which met on July 17, the Soviet delegation was headed by Stalin and Molotov, the American delegation by the new President, Harry Truman, and the new Secretary of State, James Byrnes, and the British delegation, first by Churchill and Eden and from July 28, i.e. after the Labour victory in the General Election, by Attlee and Bevin, the new Prime Minister and Foreign Secretary.

At the end of the Conference, *Pravda* wrote in its editorial of August 3: "It points to a further strengthening of the co-operation between the Big Three, whose armed alliance brought about victory over the common enemy", and, during the days that followed, it angrily denounced as malicious slander any suggestion, for instance in the Swedish press, that "the seeds of the division of Germany and of Europe into two had been sown at Potsdam."

Yet, unfortunately, that is precisely what happened there, despite the long official communiqué which kept up the semblance of unity among the Big Three. But even this document showed that no agreement had been reached on several questions, and that many decisions had been postponed.

This twenty-page document was divided into the following fifteen sections: 1) Preamble; 2) Establishment of a Council of Foreign Ministers; 3) Germany; 4) German Reparations; 5) German Navy and Merchant Fleet; 6) Königsberg; 7) War Criminals; 8) Austria;

9) Poland; 10) Peace Treaties and Admissions to UNO; 11) Territories under Trusteeship; 12) Revision of the Procedure of the Allied Control Commissions in Rumania, Bulgaria and Hungary; 13) Transfer of German Populations; 14) Military Problems discussed by the Heads of the General Staffs at the Conference; 15) List of Delegates.

It will be seen from this list alone how large a range of subjects was discussed during the thirteen plenary meetings of the Conference, besides the various committee and sub-committee meetings; and even this list is far from exhaustive: it makes no specific mention of Japan, which held a very important place in both the political and military talks at Potsdam, or of such secondary subjects as Trieste and Yugoslavia, or Franco Spain. All three agreed that Spain was not to be admitted to UNO, but neither Britain nor the United States were prepared to break off diplomatic relations with her, as the Russians had urged them to do. Nor was there any mention of Turkey in the communiqué; the Russian demand for bases there was rejected.

One of the most important achievements of Potsdam was the setting up of the Council of Foreign Ministers, whose most urgent task was to draft the peace treaties with Italy, Rumania, Bulgaria, Hungary and Finland. The Council was also to deal, in due course, with a German peace treaty.

The long section on Germany was chiefly concerned with the numerous demilitarisation, denazification and democratisation measures that would be applied to her. There was no mention of any partition of Germany, but the communiqué stated that, for the present, no central German government would be formed. There would, however, be certain central German administrative departments, acting under the guidance of the Allied Control Council.

The disposal of the German Navy and Merchant Fleet was referred to a committee of experts. Britain and the United States agreed, in principle, to the transfer to the Soviet Union of Königsberg and the adjoining territory. Agreement was also reached on the procedure which ultimately led to the constitution of the Nuremberg Tribunal for the trial of the major German war criminals and of other courts dealing with similar cases. The question of recognising the Renner Government set up by the Russians in Austria was postponed until the entry of British and American troops into Vienna. The Russian proposal that the Soviet Union be made a trustee of one of the former Italian colonies met with no favourable response from Britain and America, and the matter was referred to the Council of Foreign Ministers, who were to draft the Italian peace treaty. It was agreed that the transfer of Germans still in Poland, Czechoslovakia and Hungary would henceforth be carried out in an "orderly and humane" manner,

The official Russian line still was that all had gone well at Potsdam. In reality, the whole atmosphere at Potsdam was radically different from that at Teheran and Yalta. There was much angry recrimination on a wide range of subjects. Thus, the British and Americans treated the policy the Russians were pursuing, particularly in Bulgaria and Rumania, as a violation of the Yalta Declaration on Liberated Europe; the Russians counter-attacked by making similar charges about the British in Greece. Truman made great difficulties about recognising the Bulgarian, Hungarian and Rumanian Governments. There was also some recrimination about British and American property—notably oil equipment—in Rumania which had been confiscated by the Germans and had since been taken over by the Russians. The Russians also charged that the Western Powers had set up an "Italian Fascist régime" in Trieste.

But all this, although indicative, was not yet fundamental. The two major differences were focused on Germany and Poland. It is true that all the demilitarisation, denazification, etc., measures were, on the face of it, strictly in accord with previous decisions; on the face of it, too, Germany was placed under the joint control of the Four Powers. The unity of Germany as a political and economic entity was implicitly recognised, and the Russians later claimed great credit for having firmly opposed, as early as March 1945, any Western proposals for the partition of Germany into a western part centred on the Ruhr and Rhineland, a southern part, including Austria, and with Vienna as its capital; and an eastern part, with Berlin as its capital. But while *such* a partition was not brought about, Potsdam undoubtedly laid the foundations for a different kind of partition. All Russian attempts to secure a foothold in the

Ruhr were firmly rejected; but what made the "zonal" division of Germany even more obvious was the agreement that was finally reached on reparations—ostensibly in return for the Western Powers' acceptance of the *fait accompli* of the Oder-Neisse Line as the western boundary of the German territories "under Polish Administration", pending the final German peace settlement. These territories were not to be regarded as part of the Soviet Occupation Zone of Germany.

If, as Stettinius complained, Britain and the United States were not in a strong position at Yalta, Truman and Byrnes thought they were in a very strong position indeed at Potsdam. The American atom test bomb had just been successfully exploded and Truman, in the words of Secretary of War, Henry Stimson, was "immensely pleased" and "tremendously pepped by it". The President said "it gave him an entirely new feeling of confidence" in talking to the Russians.

> He [Truman] stood up to the Russians in the most emphatic and decisive manner, telling them as to certain demands that they absolutely could not have and that the United States was entirely against them... He told the Russians just where they got off and generally bossed the whole meeting.*

Churchill was delighted with the new President, and fully supported his "tough" line with the Russians and what came to be known as his "Open Door" policy in Eastern Europe. He also blew up at the Russians' "effrontery" in wanting to control one of the former Italian colonies on the Mediterranean.

The Russians were glad to see the last of Churchill, but when, after the British General Election, Churchill and Eden were replaced by Attlee and Bevin, they found that they had nothing to congratulate themselves on. According to Mr Byrnes,† Bevin was very "aggressive" indeed in his "forceful opposition" to the new Polish boundaries. Soon after Potsdam, a member of the Russian delegation remarked to me that he had found Mr Bevin an "*ochen*

---

* Stimson, quoted by W. A. Williams, *The Tragedy of American Diplomacy*, New York, 1962, p. 249.
† James F. Byrnes, *Frankly Speaking* (London, 1948), p. 79.

volevoi chelovek"—a "very strong-willed man", which was a polite way of saying that he had found the new Foreign Secretary extremely pigheaded.

The foundations for the real division of Germany, officially still to be under Four-Power control, were laid by the reparations agreement reached at Potsdam. Even before Potsdam the Russians had been helping themselves indiscriminately to reparations—still termed "booty" at the time—from the Soviet Zone. But they continued to hope that the reparations questions would be put on an all-German basis at Potsdam. This was not to be. On July 23, Mr Byrnes declared Stalin's Yalta figure of twenty billion dollars (half of it for the Soviet Union) to be "unpractical", and refused to name any other. He also reiterated the United States Government's opposition to the Russians' meddling in the control of industry in the Ruhr and other parts of Western Germany. And there followed this conversation:

> *Mr Molotov*: I understand that what you have in mind is that each country should take reparations from its own zone. If we fail to reach an agreement, the result will be the same.
> *Mr Byrnes*: Yes.
> *Mr Molotov*: Would not your suggestion mean that each country would have a free hand in its own zone and would act entirely independently of the others?
> *Mr Byrnes*: That is true in substance.*

The Russians fought this proposal for over a week, but, in the end, accepted it, together with the following provisions: they would also have a free hand in collecting German assets throughout Eastern Europe; they would receive a small percentage of the reparations available from Western Germany; and, finally, the Western Powers would "provisionally" recognise the Oder-Neisse Line—rather to Churchill's disgust, as expressed in the final pages of *The Second World War*. What this meant in fact was that the all-German treatment of reparations, for which the Russians had fought so desperately, was down the drain. Even the small face-saver for this "all-German" treatment—the minor reparations deliveries to Russia from Western Germany—was scrapped less than a year later,

---

* Quoted by W. A. Williams, op. cit., p. 251.

apparently on the personal responsibility of General Lucius Clay, the Military Governor of the American Zone.

This reparations settlement was crucial: it started the process whereby Russia was kept strictly outside Western Germany but, at the same time, strengthened her economic—and therefore also political—hold on Eastern Germany and Eastern Europe as a whole. This apparent ratification of a "spheres of influence" policy was, of course, in flat contradiction to Truman's Open Door policy, and American experts have continued to argue on the real significance of this apparent contradiction.

There was a direct connection between the American atom bomb and the singular reparations deal at Potsdam. This was, in fact, symptomatic of the temporary (as Truman thought) division of Germany and of Europe in two. Although appearances were kept up to some extent for the next two or three years, Potsdam marked in the reality the beginning of the end of that "Big-Three Peace" of which the main pillar—as the Russians saw it—was the *joint* control of Germany.

Chapter VI

THE SHORT RUSSO-JAPANESE WAR— HIROSHIMA

There were two periods in the Soviet-German war when the Russians dreaded a Japanese attack on them. First, during the very first months of the war, and indeed, right up to Pearl Harbour; and again during the disastrous summer and autumn of 1942. As a precaution against a Japanese attack, the Russians had to keep substantial forces in the Far East, about forty divisions according to the post-war *History*. Although in extreme emergencies—during the Battle of Moscow and, again, at the time of Stalingrad—the Soviet Supreme Command had to draw on its Far-Eastern forces and bring some particularly tough Siberian troops to the Soviet-German Front, the fact remains that, especially during the first eighteen months of the war, Japan rendered Hitler a great service by tying up with its one-million-strong Kwantung Army important Russian forces which would have been of the greatest value in Europe.

After Stalingrad, and with the war in the Pacific not going quite as well as the Japanese had expected, a Japanese attack on the Soviet Union was "postponed". As the *History* says:

> Stalingrad struck an irreparable blow at the Japanese plans for an invasion of the Soviet Union. Having been bogged down in their war against China, the United States and Britain, the Japanese now had every reason to doubt a successful outcome of their aggressive plans against the Soviet Union... The Japanese Ambassador in Berlin told Ribbentrop on March 6, 1943 that the Japanese Government "considered it wrong to enter the war against the Soviet Union just now."

The subsequent developments of World War II did not change the situation in Japan's favour: by 1943 the strategic initiative in the war in the Pacific passed into the hands of the United States forces... By the spring of 1944 the Japanese General Staff began to elaborate *defensive* plans in the event of a war with the Soviet Union.*

There is good reason to suppose that even if the exact words uttered by the Japanese Ambassador in Berlin after Stalingrad were not known to the Russians at the time, they had an excellent idea of the real position: their espionage service in Japan was exceptionally good. Up till 1942 they enjoyed the invaluable services of Richard Sorge, a German journalist, who had the confidence of Ambassador Ott himself!

The Russians had stored up by then quite a number of grievances against Japan: they had reason to suppose that during the earlier stages of the war the Japanese Embassy in Moscow or Kuibishev had been transmitting much valuable information to the Germans and, at least until Stalingrad, the Japanese had created great difficulties for Soviet shipping in the Pacific, especially for ships bringing supplies from the United States. 178 Soviet ships had been stopped and searched by the Japanese between the beginning of the war and the end of 1944 (mostly during the earlier period), and three Russian cargoes had been sunk by submarines which the Russians later claimed were Japanese.†

For all that, in 1943 and 1944, diplomatic relations between the Soviet Union and Japan remained cool but correct, and the Japanese Ambassador continued to be invited to official receptions. At Teheran and on many other occasions the British and Americans were told that there could be no question of the Soviet Union joining in the war against Japan until after the defeat of Germany. All the same, there were already some curious straws in the wind as early as the middle of 1944; one of them was the publication of a long novel

* IVOVSS, vol. V, p. 526. Note the much greater credit given to the USA and Britain in this 1963 publication than in earlier Soviet histories of the war.

† IVOVSS, vol. V, p. 529. It can, of course, be argued that Japan rendered Russia a great service in *not* attacking her (and many Russians were fully conscious of this at the time), but this was not a point to stress in 1945!

by A. Stepanov called *Port Arthur* which, without actually justifying the Tsarist government's policy of imperialist expansion in the Far East, nevertheless represented the Russo-Japanese War of 1904–5 as a "national" war, and as a humiliating national defeat which called for revenge. Anything less "Leninist" was hard to imagine.

It was not, however, till Yalta, in February 1945, that the Soviet leaders firmly committed themselves to entering the war against Japan; the Soviet Union was to receive Southern Sakhalin lost to the Japanese in 1905 and the Kurile Islands.* The clauses of the Yalta Protocol on the recognition of the *status quo* for Mongolia and on Russian privileges in China were subject to "concurrence" by the Chinese Government, i.e. by Chiang Kai Shek. It was agreed, however, at Yalta that in view of its top-secret nature, the Protocol on Japan could not be communicated to Chiang Kai Shek until after the defeat of Germany.

On April 5, 1945 the Russian people were left in little doubt that they would still have to fight Japan. On that day the Soviet Government denounced its Neutrality Pact with Japan; Molotov informed the Japanese Government that, since the conclusion of the Pact in 1941, the situation had "radically changed"; Germany had attacked the USSR and Japan had helped Germany. Moreover, Japan was fighting a war against Britain and the United States, which were Allies of the Soviet Union. "In virtue of Article 3 . . . allowing the right to denounce the Pact one year before its expiry, the Soviet Union hereby does so, as from April 13, 1945."†

On May 15, 1945 the Japanese Government annulled its alliance

---

* Under a Russo-Japanese agreement of 1855 Sakhalin was to be administered jointly by the two countries, while the Kurile Islands were divided between them. In 1875 Japan abandoned her claims on Sakhalin, but received all the Kurile Islands. Under the 1905 peace treaty, Japan received the southern half of Sakhalin. The Russians now not only demanded the return of Southern Sakhalin, but all the Kurile Islands which they considered as Japanese bases interfering with Russian shipping in the Pacific. Maybe they also suspected even then that the USA had an eye on the Kuriles as a potential air base.
† Juridically, the Five-Year Neutrality Pact was valid till April 13, 1946, despite this repudiation, and Russia's attack on Japan in August 1945 was in fact a violation of the Pact.

with the now non-existent German government and other Fascist governments. The Soviet Government considered this as a preliminary to a new series of peace-feelers the Japanese were about to put out; but there is nothing to show that they intended to respond favourably to them.

While, at the end of May, Harry Hopkins found the Russians extremely sticky on questions like Poland, he found them perfectly co-operative as regards Japan. He cabled to Washington on May 28 saying that, according to Stalin, the Soviet Army would be "properly deployed in the Manchurian positions by August 8"; that Stalin repeated the Yalta statement that the Russian people "must have good reason for going to war", and that this depended on the willingness of the Chinese to agree to the Yalta proposals; he therefore asked that T. V. Soong come to Moscow "not later than July 1", and urged that the USA (as Roosevelt had promised) take up the matter with Chiang Kai-shek.

Stalin's views on China, as reported by Hopkins, are particularly interesting, in the light of what happened later:

> He [Stalin] categorically stated that he would do everything to promote the unification of China under Chiang Kai-shek. His leadership would continue after the war, because no one else was strong enough. He specifically stated that no communist leader was strong enough to unify China. In spite of his reservations about Chiang Kai-shek, he proposed to back him.*

In another message to Washington Hopkins stated that Stalin was all in favour of the Open Door for the USA in China, since she alone was capable of giving large financial aid to that country, Russia having her own reconstruction to take care of. Stalin also intimated that the Soviet Union wanted an occupation zone in Japan.

The full story of the events that led to the capitulation of Japan is one of the most intricate in the whole of World War II. It is clear that, at Yalta, both Roosevelt and Churchill were still extremely

* Sherwood, op. cit., p. 892. None of this is reported in the present-day Soviet *History* which treats the Chinese Communists as the only force in China at the time not defeatist in its attitude to Japan.

anxious that Russia should join in the war against Japan as quickly as possible. The position becomes much less clear after Truman became President. Judging from the Hopkins' mission to Moscow in May, Truman still wanted Russia in the war—which was one of the chief reasons why the new President also wanted to meet Stalin at Potsdam. The Russians now argue, however, that even before he had the atom bomb, Truman was desperately anxious to get Japan— or at least "the Japanese armed forces"—to surrender uncondition- ally before Russia entered the war. They may have suspected this at the time, on the strength of the American broadcasts to that effect, which began as early as May 8,* but consoled themselves with the thought that Japan could not be defeated—at least not within a short time—without the Russians smashing the Kwantung Army in Manchuria. They had understood from Roosevelt at Yalta that, without Russian participation, the war against Japan would have to go on till 1947, and would cost the Americans and British at least another million men.

As early as February-March, the Japanese sought Russian mediation in their desire to end the war with the USA and Britain. The Soviet *History* enumerates several such peace-feelers:

> First of all, two "private" persons approached the Russians on behalf of the Japanese Government—Mr Mijakawa, the Japanese Consul-General in Harbin and Mr Tanakamaru, a fishing mag- nate.
>
> On March 4, the same Tanakamaru called on Mr J. Malik, the Soviet Ambassador in Tokyo, saying that neither Japan nor the United States could start speaking of peace. A "divine outside force" was necessary to bring about a peace settlement, and the Soviet Union could play that rôle.
>
> After the formation of the Suzuki Government, these peace-feelers became even more explicit. Foreign Minister Togo asked Mr Malik on April 20 to arrange for him a meeting with Mr Molotov.
>
> Still anxious to avoid unconditional surrender to the USA, Togo sent ex-premier Hirotake Hirota to see Malik on June 3. He stressed Japan's desire to improve her relations with the USSR. A second

---

* Much is made of these in the Soviet *History*. (IVOVSS, vol. V, p. 536).

meeting took place on the following day, and two further meetings on June 24.*

The *History* dismisses all these Hirota visits to Malik and his offers of large-scale Soviet-Japanese economic co-operation as "a piece of effrontery coming from a gang guilty of so many treacherous acts towards the Soviet Union"; but the fact remains that Malik consented to see Hirota *four times.*

Nevertheless, the Hirota mission failed, and the Japanese Government now tried to establish direct contact with the Soviet Government in Moscow. The Emperor decided to send Prince Konoye to Moscow on July 12, and Mr Sato, the Japanese Ambassador in Moscow was instructed to inform the Soviet Government of the Emperor's desire. But in vain. In the words of the *History*:

> This Japanese proposal was left without an answer by the Soviet Government which was, moreover, preparing to go to the Big-Three Conference at Potsdam. Here the Soviet delegation fully informed its allies of these Japanese "peace" moves. Thus, the Japanese imperialists' attempts to split the Allies failed completely.†

At Potsdam the American military wanted to know when exactly the Russians would attack in the Far East. The Soviet Chief of Staff, General Antonov confirmed that all would be ready by August 8, but much depended on the outcome of the Soviet-Chinese talks which had begun in Moscow shortly before the Potsdam Conference.

As we now know, the Americans were, in fact, no longer interested at the time of Potsdam in Russian participation in the war against Japan. Churchill tells with undisguised glee how he and Harry Truman fooled Stalin.

As Churchill tells the story:

> On July 17 (at Potsdam) world-shaking news arrived. . . "It means", Stimson said, "that the experiment in the Mexican desert has come off. The atomic bomb is a reality".

And almost the first thought that occurred to Churchill was that the Russians could be dispensed with in the war against Japan:

* IVOVSS, vol. V, pp. 536–7.
† IVOVSS, vol. V, p. 538.

We should not need the Russians. The end of the Japanese war no longer depended on the pouring in of their armies... We had no need to ask favours of them... I minuted to Mr Eden: "It is quite clear that the United States do not at the present time desire Russian participation in the war against Japan."

There was no doubt, he wrote, that the bomb would be used.

A more intricate question was what to tell Stalin. The President and I no longer felt we needed his aid to conquer Japan... In our opinion they (the Soviet troops in the Far East) were not likely to be needed, and Stalin's bargaining power, which he had used with such effect upon the Americans at Yalta, was therefore gone.

And then came Churchill's singularly tortuous mental compromise:

Still, he had been a magnificent ally in the war against Hitler, and we both (Churchill and Truman) felt that he must be informed of the great New Fact which now dominated the scene, *but not with any particulars.**

In the end the procedure chosen was this: Nothing was going to be put in writing. Instead, Truman said:

"I think I had best just tell him after one of our meetings that we have an entirely novel form of bomb, something quite out of the ordinary, which we think will have a decisive effect upon the Japanese will to continue the war."

Churchill agreed with this "procedure".† And this is how it was done.

On July 24, after our plenary meeting had ended... I saw the President go up to Stalin, and the two conversed alone, with only their interpreters. I was perhaps five yards away, and I watched with the closest attention their momentous talk. I knew what the President was going to do. What was vital to measure was its effect on Stalin. I can see it all as if it were yesterday. He seemed to be delighted. A new bomb! Of extraordinary power!... What a bit of luck!... I was sure that he had no idea of the significance of what he was being told... If he had had the slightest idea... his reactions would have been obvious... Nothing would have been easier than for him to say:

* Churchill, op. cit., vol. VI, pp. 552–4.   † Ibid., p. 554.

"... May I send my experts to see your experts tomorrow morning?"
But his face remained gay and genial...
   "How did it go?" I asked (Truman). "He never asked a question,"
he replied.*

I must add here a very important historical point which dots the i's
in Churchill's account to an extraordinary degree.

When, in 1946, I privately asked Molotov whether the Soviet
Government had been informed at Potsdam that an atom bomb
would be dropped on Japan, he looked startled, thought for a
moment, and then said: "It's a tricky subject, and the real answer
to your question is both Yes and No. We were told of a 'super-
bomb', of a bomb 'the like of which had never been seen'; but the
word *atom* was not used."

I often wondered afterwards whether Molotov's answer was
strictly true, and I believe it was; had Truman really told Stalin that
the new weapon was not just a "super-bomb", but an *atom bomb*, it
is almost inconceivable that Stalin could have registered the news
as calmly and cheerfully as Churchill said he did, and done nothing
at all about it.

Certainly, there was nothing in the behaviour of either Stalin or
any other Russians at Potsdam after they had been told about the
new weapon to suggest that anything *quite unusual* had happened.
Their plans about Japan were not changed one whit. The
negotiations with the Chinese were resumed in Moscow after Stalin's
and Molotov's return from Potsdam. There was no suggestion of the
Russians being more nervous than before.

If there was anything strange about these negotiations with the
Chinese on something which had already been approved in advance
by both Roosevelt and Churchill, it was the Chinese attempt to draw
out the discussions. What was behind these delaying tactics has since
been explained by Mr Byrnes: "If Stalin and Chiang were still
negotiating, it might delay Soviet entrance and the Japanese might
surrender.† And to drag out the Moscow discussions was precisely

---

* Churchill, op. cit., vol. VI, pp. 579–80. The suggestion that the
Russians already knew all about the bomb from their own intelli-
gence is not borne out by their behaviour after Potsdam.
† J. Byrnes, *All in One Lifetime* (New York, 1958), pp. 291–9.

what on July 23 Chiang Kai-shek had been asked by Washington
to do.

On the face of it, these Soviet-Chinese talks, which went on for a
fortnight (from June 30 to July 14) before Potsdam, and for another
week (August 7 to 14) after Potsdam, should have been little more
than a formality. True, the Yalta Agreement said that "the agreement concerning Outer Mongolia and ports and railroads ... will
require concurrence of Generalissimo Chiang Kai-shek"; but it also
said:

> The President [Roosevelt] will take measures to obtain this con-
> currence... The Heads of the three Great Powers have agreed that
> these claims of the Soviet Union shall be unquestionably fulfilled after
> Japan has been defeated.

Yet the talks on the above questions and on the Friendship and
Alliance Pact with China, also provided for in the Yalta Agreement,
were *not* concluded—as they were expected to be—before the Soviet
Union entered the war on August 8, i.e. two days after the Hiroshima
bomb.

It was the atom bomb that precipitated Russia's entry into the
war. No doubt, after the bomb, Chiang Kai-shek would have liked
to back out of the agreement with Russia, but it was scarcely possible
in view of Roosevelt's and Churchill's firm commitments at Yalta—
and, above all, perhaps, because there was now an enormous
Russian army overrunning Manchuria.

What annoyed the Russians at Potsdam was not the vague news of
some American "super-bomb", but the "Potsdam Ultimatum" to
Japan of July 26 demanding unconditional surrender. They claim
that they had not been consulted about this Anglo-American-
Chinese Ultimatum, and when they asked that its publication be
postponed for two days, they were told that it had already been
released. This may well have made them wonder whether the United
States and Britain were not in a hurry to obtain a Japanese capitulation before the Soviet Union entered the war.

They may have wondered—and yet they did nothing about it,
still assuming that the war could not be won in a short time without

their participation. And they were certainly going to participate, since Stalin thought the spoils promised him at Yalta well worth a major military effort.

There is much conflicting evidence about the Japanese response to the Potsdam Ultimatum. According to both the American official version and the Russian (repeated in the official *History*) the Japanese rejected it; according to certain Japanese sources, the Japanese Government "virtually" accepted it, though it asked for further clarifications.* Be that as it may, it is certain that on August 2 Ambassador Sato paid an urgent visit to Molotov in connection with the Potsdam Ultimatum; he was anxious to obtain the immediate cessation of hostilities and hoped that, with Russian mediation, the absolutely crucial question of the Emperor—not mentioned in the Potsdam Ultimatum—would be settled in an acceptable manner. Molotov was totally unresponsive, obviously unwilling to see Japan capitulate before Russia had joined in the war. When, six days later, he asked Sato to call on him, it was only to inform him of the Soviet Union's declaration of war on Japan. That was two days after the Hiroshima bomb.

The wording of the Soviet declaration of war on Japan was odd. It said that, since the capitulation of Germany, Japan was the only Great Power wanting to continue the war; since Japan had rejected the Potsdam Ultimatum the Japanese Government's proposals that the Soviet Government act as a mediator had "lost all basis". Since Japan had refused to capitulate, the Allies had asked the Soviet Union to join in the war, and so to shorten it.

> The Soviet Government considers that such a policy is the only one that will bring about an early peace, rid peoples of further sacrifices

---

* The German writer Anton Zischka, *Krieg oder Frieden* (War or Peace), Gütersloh, 1961, pp. 61–5 puts forward the view that the Japanese reply to the Ultimatum was either accidentally or, more probably, deliberately mistranslated by certain American officials, Premier Suzuki's "no comment pending further information" being translated as "we are ignoring the ultimatum", the word *mokusatsu* meaning either "ignoring" or "no comment", according to the context.

and sufferings and enable the Japanese people to avert the dangers and destruction that Germany suffered after her refusal to surrender unconditionally.

As from August 9, the Soviet Union would consider herself in a state of war with Japan.

On that night of August 8 Molotov received the press, simply to communicate to it the text of the Soviet declaration of war. He looked even more stony-faced than usual and, after answering only two or three quite innocuous questions, hastened to end this "press conference". Molotov did not mention the Hiroshima bomb; and nor did anyone else.

Yet the Bomb was the one thing everybody in Russia had talked about that whole day. The bomb had been dropped on Hiroshima on the morning of the 6th, but it was not till the morning of the 8th that the Soviet press published, almost at the bottom of the foreign page, a short item—one-third of a column to be exact—which was part of the Truman statement on Hiroshima. The bomb, this statement said, was equal in power to 20,000 tons of TNT.

Although the Russian press played down the Hiroshima bomb, and did not even mention the Nagasaki bomb until much later, the significance of Hiroshima was not lost on the Russian people. The news had an acutely depressing effect on everybody. It was clearly realised that this was a New Fact in the world's power politics, that the bomb constituted a threat to Russia, and some Russian pessimists I talked to that day dismally remarked that Russia's desperately hard victory over Germany was now "as good as wasted".

The news, that same day, that Russia had declared war on Japan aroused no enthusiasm at all. The idea of fighting another war, so soon after all the losses suffered in the war against Germany, had never been popular. Knowing nothing about the Yalta Agreement, most Russians now felt that the new war had been forced on Russia, or at any rate precipitated, by the Hiroshima Bomb. It had, of course, been known for a long time that masses of Russian troops were being sent to the Far East, but everybody felt that there must be some connection between the news about Hiroshima in the morning, and Russia's declaration of war on Japan a few hours later.

On August 7—the day after Hiroshima—Stalin summoned to the Kremlin five of the leading Russian atomic scientists and ordered them to catch up with the United States in the minimum of time, regardless of cost. Beria was placed in charge of all the laboratories and industries which were to produce the atom bomb. Contrary to American expectations, the first Soviet A-bomb was exploded in the Ust-Urt Desert, between the Caspian and the Aral Sea on July 10, 1949; two further A-bombs were exploded within the next week. The Soviet H-bomb followed four years later.

But this was in the future, and the thought that the Americans had a monopoly of the atom bomb had a deeply depressing effect on Russian opinion. The Russian press continued to be silent about it, and the issue of the English weekly *Britansky Soyuznik* which was the first paper inside Russia to give any details on Hiroshima and Nagasaki, sold in the black market for sixty roubles, instead of the official two roubles, or the usual "black-market" price of twenty roubles.

The feeling of resentment against those who had dropped the atom bomb was so acute that any feeling of animosity against Japan was conspicuously absent. I remember that evening of August 8 only too well. There was feverish activity amongst the many Japanese living at the Hotel Metropole in Moscow. They were packing their bags in order to take them to the Japanese Embassy before midnight. They looked morose but dignified, and—partly perhaps because they always tipped well—the hotel staff were very helpful. Nobody else showed any malice either. Shortly before midnight, as they were piling their last trunks on lorries, something of a crowd gathered around, but no hostility was shown and many people even lent a hand with the trunks. It was like a subtle little demonstration of sympathy.

The papers the next day did little more than paraphrase the Note declaring war on Japan, and recall all the evil that Japan had done to Russia and the Soviet Union in the past—starting with the Russo-Japanese war, and going on to Japanese Intervention in 1919, to

Lake Hassan and Halkin Gol, and to all the help Japan had given to Hitler. If, in the past, Marxist writers had said that Japan had stopped the spread of Russian imperialism in the Far East in 1904-5, the papers now spoke of her "perfidious attack on the Russian Navy at Port Arthur", and the "blot of shame" from which Russia had suffered for forty years.

In the next few days, the press reported mass meetings in many factories loudly approving the declaration of war on the "Japanese militarists and imperialists." In reality, the Russians who felt passionately about Germany, had no feelings about Japan at all, and the new war against Japan was distinctly unpopular, except possibly among Russians in the Far East.

The only thing in its favour was that it did not last long. It was clear from the start that the three Russian army groups—the Baikal Front under Marshal Malinovsky, the First Far-Eastern Front under Marshal Meretskov and the Second Far-Eastern Front under General Purkayev, all of them under the general command of Marshal Vassilevsky—had overwhelming superiority over the much-vaunted Kwantung Army. Within a few days they had penetrated deep into Manchuria. The heavy and often fanatical Japanese counter-attacks made little difference; the Russians had more men and incomparably more guns, tanks and planes than the Japanese. On August 16 General Antonov, the Soviet Chief-of-Staff, announced that the declaration of August 14 by the Emperor was "only a general statement on Japan's capitulation", and that no cease-fire order had been given to the Japanese troops fighting the Russians. There had been no actual capitulation by the Japanese armed forces; therefore "the Soviet offensive in the Far East must continue." On August 17 Marshal Vassilevsky sent an ultimatum to the commander of the Kwantung Army, demanding surrender by noon, August 20. The surrender of this Army was, indeed, announced by Stalin in an Order of the Day on August 22. The Russians had used airborne troops extensively in Manchuria, particularly to occupy the ports of Dairen and Port Arthur where they feared an American landing. They also hastened to penetrate into

Northern Korea. The Russian Pacific Navy played an important part in the combined operations that resulted in the occupation of Southern Sakhalin and the Kurile Islands; here, in particular, the Russians met with stiff Japanese resistance—even long after the official capitulation.

In Manchuria, too, even after the official capitulation of the Kwantung Army, numerous Japanese units continued to fight and it was not till September 12 that the final results of the war against Japan were published in a special Sovinformbureau statement. This said that, between August 9 and September 9 the Japanese losses were: 925 planes, 369 tanks, 1,226 guns, 4,836 machine-guns, 300,000 rifles. In relation to the number of prisoners, these figures suggested that the mighty Kwantung Army had been very poorly equipped. 594,000 Japanese prisoners had been taken, including 20,000 wounded. Among the prisoners were 148 generals. The Japanese dead were put at 80,000. The Russian casualties were stated to be extremely low in comparison: 8,000 dead and 22,000 wounded.*

On September 2 the final capitulation of Japan was signed on board the US battleship *Missouri*. The Soviet signatory was a General Derevyanko, totally unknown to the general public in Russia.

Stalin's broadcast that day left people with a strangely unsatisfactory impression. He dwelt, to an extraordinary degree, on the victory over Japan being Russia's revenge for her defeat in the Russo-Japanese war of 1904–5. He recalled that, taking advantage of the weakness of the Tsarist Government, Japan had perfidiously attacked the Russian Navy at Port Arthur, in almost exactly the same way as she was to attack the US Navy at Pearl Harbour thirty-seven years later.

---

* The present-day *History* (IVOVSS, vol. V, p. 581) gives the same figures for the Japanese prisoners, but puts the equipment figures rather higher; it says that the Baikal and 1st Far-Eastern Front alone captured 1,565 guns, 2,169 mortars, 600 tanks, 861 planes, and 13,000 machine-guns. The *History* gives no figures for Russian casualties, which suggests that they were higher than the official 1945 figure.

Russia was defeated in that war. As a result, Japan grabbed Southern Sakhalin and firmly established herself in the Kuriles, thus padlocking our exits to the Pacific. . . This defeat of the Russian troops in 1904 left a bitter memory in the minds of our people. Our people waited and believed that this blot would some day be erased. We, people of the older generation, waited for this day for forty years. Now this day has come.

In conclusion he said that peace had come at last, that the Soviet Union was no longer threatened by either Germany or Japan, and he paid a tribute to the armed forces of the Soviet Union, the United States, China and Great Britain who had won this victory over Japan.

There were fireworks that night to celebrate Victory over Japan; but in and around Red Square there was barely one-tenth of the crowd that had turned out to celebrate the defeat of Germany on May 9.

It was a hollow victory, and everybody was conscious of it. For many years afterwards the official Soviet line was (and still is, though rather less emphatically) that Japan capitulated because of the Soviet Union's entry into the war: if the mighty Kwantung Army had not been defeated, Japan's resistance to America and Britain would have continued for years, and cost them a million lives or more. It was, in fact, precisely the same argument as that Truman, Churchill and others applied to the atom bombs which, they said, had precipitated Japan's unconditional surrender and had so saved untold American and British lives. In reality the best evidence shows that Japan was on the point of surrendering at the time of the Potsdam Ultimatum, and merely wanted assurances concerning the status of the Emperor—the very question Ambassador Sato put to Molotov on August 2, four days before the Hiroshima bomb, and six days before the Soviet declaration of war.*

* How unnecessary it was to drop the atom bomb is shown by Major-General J. F. C. Fuller in *The Second World War* (London, 1948), p. 395: "On the 10th a broadcast from Tokyo announced the acceptance of the Potsdam Ultimatum 'with the understanding that

Even assuming that the Japanese would have continued to resist and that the saving of American lives was all that was at stake, then the dropping of the bomb could still have been held up until September, just before the invasion of Kyushu—which *would* have cost a lot of American lives. If the bomb was dropped in a desperate hurry on August 6, it must have been because Truman was determined to drop it before the Russians had entered the war—which they were expected to do, in accordance with the Yalta Agreement, not much later than the 8th.* But that was not all: the bomb, as is so clearly suggested by Truman, Byrnes, Stimson and others, was dropped very largely in order to impress Russia with America's great might. Ending the war in Japan was incidental (the end of this war was clearly in sight, anyway), but stopping the Russians in Asia and checking them in Eastern Europe was fundamental.

Whether the Russians intended to stick closely to the Yalta Agreement and enter the war on August 8 is not altogether certain; but once the bomb had been dropped, the Russians could not afford to delay; for what if Japan capitulated as a result of the bomb before Russia entered the war? It was essential to enter the war before such a Japanese capitulation, if Russia was to receive her territorial

---

[it] does not comprise any demand which prejudices the prerogatives of the Emperor as a sovereign ruler'. On the following day the Allies replied: 'From the moment of surrender the authority of the Emperor ... shall be subject to the Supreme Commander of the Allied Powers'. [In other words, there was no question of hanging the Emperor as a war criminal.]

"Why was this not made clear in the Declaration of July 26? Had it been, would not [Truman's] 'purpose of God' have been more Christianly followed?" Fuller comments. He also says that the requests made to Russia as early as May to intercede as a mediator must have made it clear to the Western Powers that Japan's position was catastrophic, and that she was completely ripe for surrender. The only obstacle was the question of the Emperor.

* Asked in 1960 whether there was any urgency to end the war in the Pacific before the Russians became too deeply involved, Mr Byrnes replied: "There certainly was on my part. We wanted to get through with the Japanese phase of the war before the Russians came in." (*U.S. News and World Report*, August 15, 1960.)

"reward" and play any part in the occupation of Korea—and Japan.

The real irony of it all is that Japan was ready to capitulate *both without the atom bomb and without Russian intervention.* But this suited neither the USA, nor the Soviet Union, both of which had to strike the "decisive" blow.

It is interesting to note that the present-day *History* does not breathe a word about Stalin's "revenge for 1904", but attributes Russia's entry into the war to three high-minded motives: 1) security against future Japanese aggression; 2) Russia's sacred duty to her Western Allies; and, 3) her moral duty to help, China, Korea and other Asian peoples in their struggle against the Japanese imperialists.

The "new look" of American policy after the dropping of the atom bomb soon became apparent. On August 16 Truman declared that, unlike Germany, Japan would not be divided into occupation zones. Truman firmly rejected the Russian proposal that the Japanese surrender to Russian troops in northern Hokkaido; nor were the Russians to take any part whatsoever in the occupation of Japan. Truman went even further: on August 18 he asked that the Russians let the Americans use one of the Kurile Islands as an air base, a proposal that Stalin rejected with a great show of indignation.*

The uneasiness and anxiety created in Russia by the atom bomb were such that, soon after the capitulation of Japan, Russian correspondents visited Hiroshima and Nagasaki and deliberately reported that the bombs had not been nearly as destructive as the Americans had made out; if there were very heavy casualties, it was because of the inflammable nature of Japanese houses, and any city with stone houses and adequate shelters would not have suffered nearly as

---

* *Correspondence between Stalin and the Presidents of the USA and the Prime Ministers of Great Britain...* (Moscow 1957), vol. II, pp. 267–8.

much. The correspondents said they had interviewed several people who had escaped injury by simply lying down in an ordinary trench!

These stories about the relative innocuousness of the atom bomb were not only intended to reassure the Russian public, but also to support the theory that it was not the atom bomb, but the destruction of the Kwantung Army by the Russians, that had brought Japan to her knees.

They did not make much impression in Russia. Everybody there fully realised that the atom bomb had become an immense factor in the world's power politics, and believed that, although the two bombs had killed or maimed a few hundred thousand Japanese, their real purpose was, first and foremost, to intimidate Russia.

After causing a spell of anxiety and bewilderment, all the bombs did, in effect, was to create on the Russian side a feeling of anger and acute distrust *vis à vis* the West. Far from becoming more amenable, the Soviet Government became more stubborn.* Inside Russia, too, the régime became much harder after the war instead of becoming softer, as so many had hoped it would be.

It was scarcely a coincidence that, ten days after Hiroshima, the Supreme Soviet should have instructed the Gosplan—the State Planning Commission—and the Council of People's Commissars to get busy on a new Five-Year Plan. No breathing-space was to be allowed to the Russian people; the great industrial and economic reconstruction of the country was to start immediately. And, together with it, the making of the Russian atom bomb.

The end of the war was to be followed by years of disappointment and frustration for the Russian people. The wartime hopes of a Big Three Peace gave way to the reality of the Cold War and the "Iron Curtain". The happy illusions of 1944 that the Soviet régime would become more liberal, and life easier and freer after the war, soon went up in smoke. For one thing the Soviet economy was largely in ruins, and to rebuild it a gigantic programme of austerity and hard work was called for. The policy of restoring heavy industry as fast

* The only major exception was Iran, where Moscow yielded to American pressure by evacuating Iranian Azerbaijan.

as possible meant that consumer goods remained scarce for a long time. Housing conditions were bad and food was short. The NKVD, which had shown a certain discretion during the war, came into its own again and a new terror developed which did not come to an end until 1953, after Stalin's death.

Yet despite the disappointments that followed it, the grim but heroic national war of 1941–5 remains both the most fearful and the proudest memory of the Russian people—a war which, for all her losses, turned Russia into the greatest Power of the Old World. Already it almost seems an historical epic of a bygone age—which can never be repeated. To the Russian people the thought of another war is doubly horrifying; for it would be a war without its Sebastopol, Leningrad or Stalingrad; a war in which—everywhere—there would be only victims and no heroes.

THE CHANGED FRONTIERS

Miles
0   100   200

FINLAND

1938

Lake Ladoga

Leningrad

SWEDEN

Baltic Sea

ESTONIA

LATVIA

1938

MOSCOW
150 miles

LITHUANIA

N

EAST
PRUSSIA

BERLIN

Minsk

POLAND

WARSAW

Brest

1938

U S S R

PRAGUE

Lwow

Kiev

CZECHOSLOVAKIA

VIENNA

AUSTRIA

BUDAPEST

RUTHENIA   BUKOVINA

1938

BESSARABIA

Odessa

HUNGARY   RUMANIA

1938
USSR [stippled]   GERMANY [vertical lines]
POLAND [diagonal lines]   CZECHOSLOVAKIA [diagonal lines]
1945 FRONTIERS
USSR [solid]   POLAND [wavy]

BUCHAREST

Danube

SELECTED BIBLIOGRAPHY

The most important single Soviet publication on the war years, not only in terms of sheer bulk, but also for the valuable information it contains is the monumental six-volume (five published to date) *History of the Great Patriotic War of the Soviet Union* (*Istoriya Velikoi Otechestvennoi Voiny Sov. Soyuza*), referred to as IVOVSS. In the Introduction I refer to some of its numerous weaknesses —its stodgy writing, its ever-repeated clichés, its suppression of many awkward facts (for instance the "Moscow panic" of October 16, 1941), the virtual deletion of names of people now out of favour, even though they played an important part during the war years; the magnification of Khruschev's role in the war; the tendentiousness in the treatment of some of the diplomatic episodes just before and during the war; the pooh-poohing of Lend-Lease, and so on. This collective work by dozens of Soviet scholars and various kinds of experts, working under an editorial committee composed of professional historians, leading Party ideologists and a number of generals, and the whole of it published by "The Department of History of the Great Patriotic War of the Institute of Marxism-Leninism attached to the Central Committee of the CPSU" is, of course, a book which has gone through the most careful process of "vetting" at the highest Party level. And yet, despite all this, IVOVSS still contains an immense amount of information most of which was not available in the Stalin days. It contains, for example, a very thorough and, on the whole, convincing explanation of the numerous reasons for the Red Army's disastrous reverses in 1941; it analyses very carefully the reasons, both military and economic, for the relative failure of the second phase of the Russian counter-offensive in the winter of 1941–2; it tells, with masses of new details, the story of the stupendous effort to keep the country's war economy going, with the main armaments production being concentrated in the East. The *History* is based almost entirely on archive material, and this includes such valuable sources as AVP SSR (Foreign Policy Archives), AMO SSSR (Archives of the Ministry of Defence), the war archives of the Institute of Marxism–Leninism (IML); the Central Party

1047

Archives of the same Institute (TsPA IML), the Komsomol and Trade Union Archives, the State Archives of the October Revolution (TsGA-OR), the War History Archives of the Central Committees of the Communist Parties of the Ukrainian, Belorussian and of other Federal Republics of the Soviet Union, and similar archives of the different ministries and of the various *obkoms* (regional party committees)—for instance, those of Smolensk, Briansk, etc. (chiefly on Partisan warfare) or of Sverdlovsk, Cheliabinsk, etc. (chiefly on the war industries). Although these quotations from the various archives are inevitably selective, they still contain much new information. On foreign policy too, the *History* also quotes some revealing documents, for instance some of the dispatches from Astakhov, the Soviet *chargé d'affaires* in Berlin, on his conversations with Weizsäcker and Rib-

bentrop during the summer of 1939—dispatches from which Stalin and Molotov could obviously draw certain conclusions.

I have also, in writing this book, made use of not only a number of general Soviet histories of the war (none of them very satisfactory) but also of a wide range of monographs on various episodes of the war (some, particularly those on Leningrad, are excellent), and an even greater number of personal reminiscences by generals, partisan leaders, etc. Of these books, hundreds of which have appeared, especially since 1958, I give as detailed a list as possible. On the other hand, in listing Western books pertaining to the immediate pre-war period and the war years in Russia, I have confined myself to only some of the most important titles. The same applies to German books on the war in the Soviet Union.

DIPLOMATIC AND OFFICIAL DOCUMENTS

Correspondence between the Chairman of the Council of Ministers of the USSR (Stalin) *and the Presidents of the United States* (Roosevelt and Truman) *and the Prime Ministers of Great Britain* (Churchill and Attlee) *during the Great Patriotic War of 1941–45.* 2 vols. Moscow, 1957.
Documents of British Foreign Policy 1919–39. London, 1947 and after.
Documents of German Foreign Policy. Series D. 1937–45. 10 vols. Washington, 1957.
Dokumenty vneshnei politiki SSR, vols. 1–4. Moscow, 1957, publication continuing.
Dokumenty i materialy kanuna vtoiroi mirovoi voiny. vol. II. *Arkhiv Dircksena.* Moscow, 1948.
Foreign Relations of the United States. Diplomatic Papers. The Conference of Berlin. Washington, 1946.
Le Livre Jaune Français. Documents diplomatiques. Paris, 1939.
Nazi-Soviet Relations 1939–41. Washington, 1948.
Sovetsko-Frantsuskie otnosheniya vo vremia Velikoi Otechestvennoi Voiny. Dokumenty i materialy. Moscow, 1959.
Sovetsko-Chekhoslovatskie otnosheniya vo vremia Velikoi Otechestvennoi Voiny. Dokumenty i materialy. Moscow, 1960.
Soviet Documents on Foreign Policy (1917–41), selected and edited by J. Degras. 3 vols. London, 1948–53.

Vneshnyaya politika Sovetskogo Soyuza v period Otechestvennoi Voiny. 3 vols. Moscow, 1946–7.
Vneshnyaya Politika Sovetskogo Soyuza, 1946 g. Moscow, 1947.
The Trial of German Major War Criminals; Proceedings of the International Military Tribunal sitting at Nuremberg, Germany. 23 vols. (HMSO, London, 1946–51), referred to as TGMWC.

STUDIES AND MEMOIRS CONCERNING DIPLOMATIC RELATIONS WITH THE SOVIET UNION[1]

Beloff, M., *The Foreign Policy of Soviet Russia, 1929–41.* 2 vols. London, 1947.
Bonnet, G., *Fin d'une Europe.* Geneva, 1946.
Byrnes, J. F., *Speaking Frankly.* London, 1947.
Byrnes, J. F., *All in One Lifetime.* New York, 1958.
Carr, E. H., *German-Soviet Relations between the Two Wars.* Baltimore, 1951.
Churchill, W. S., *The Second World War.* 6 vols. London, 1948–54.
Ciano's Diaries. London, 1948.
Coates, W. P. and Z., *A History of Anglo-Soviet Relations.* 2 vols. London, 1945 and 1958.
Coulondre, R., *De Staline à Hitler. Mémoires de deux ambassades.* Paris, 1950.
Dalton, H., *The Fateful Years 1931–45.* London, 1947.
Davies, J., *Mission to Moscow.* London, 1942.
Deane, J. F., *The Strange Alliance.* London, 1947.
Eisenhower, D. D., *Crusade in Europe.* London, 1948.
Feiling, K., *The Life of Neville Chamberlain.* London, 1946.
Gafencu, G., *The Last Days of Europe.* London, 1946.
Gafencu, G., *Preliminaires de la guérre à l'Est.* Paris, 1944.
Gaulle, C. de, *Mémoires.* 3 vols. Paris, 1954–8.
The Memoirs of Cordell Hull. London, 1948.
Ickes, H. L., *The Secret Diary.* New York, 1954.
Izraelyan, V. L., *Diplomaticheskaya istoriya Velikoi Otechestvennoi Voiny 1941–45.* Moscow, 1958.
Kennan, G., *Soviet Foreign Policy 1917–1941.* New York, 1960.
Kennan, G., *Russia and the West under Lenin and Stalin.* New York, 1961.
Leahy, W. D., *I Was There.* London, 1950.
Maisky, I., *Who Helped Hitler?* London, 1964.
Namier, L. B., *Diplomatic Prelude, 1938–39.* London, 1948.
Noel, L., *L'aggression allemande contre la Pologne.* Paris, 1946.
Potemkin, V. P. (ed.), *Istoriya diplomatii,* vol. III (1919–39). Moscow, 1945.
Reynaud, P., *Au coeur de la mêlée.* Paris, 1951.
Reynaud, P., *La France a avésu l'Europe.* 2 vols. 1947.
Schuman, F. L., *Russia since 1917.* New York, 1957.
Scherer, A., *Le problème des "mains libres à l'Est"* (*Rev. d'Histoire de la 2e Guerre Mondiale,* October 1958), Paris, 1958.
Sherwood, R. E., *The White House Papers of Harry L. Hopkins.* 2 vols. London, 1949.
Shirer, W. L., *The Rise and Fall of the Third Reich.* London, 1960.
Stettinius, E. R., *Lend-Lease, Weapon of Victory.* New York, 1944.

---

[1] Including some general works partly dealing with these.

Stettinius, E. R., *Roosevelt and the Russians: The Yalta Conference*. London, 1950.
Taylor, A. J. P., *The Origins of the Second World War*. London, 1961.
Memoirs of Harry Truman. vol. I. New York, 1955.
Williams, W. A., *The Tragedy of American Diplomacy*. New York, 1962.

SOVIET OFFICIAL SPEECHES, ETC.

CPSU Congress reports: 18-yi, 19-yi, 20-yi, 21-yi, 22-oi s'yezd KPSS (Moscow, 1939, 1952, 1956, 1959 and 1961 respectively).
Kalinin, M. I., *Vsyo dlya fronta, vsyo dlya pobedy*. (Articles and speeches.) Moscow, 1942.
Khrushchev, N. A., *The Dethronement of Stalin. (Secret speech at 20th Congress.)* Manchester *Guardian* reprint, Manchester, 1956.

See also February 1946 election speeches by Stalin, Molotov, Voroshilov, Mikoyan, Andreyev, Zhdanov, Khrushchev, Kaganovich, Beria, Malenkov, Vosnesensky and others, all published in pamphlet form (Moscow, 1946).

The Red Army To-day. (Speeches delivered at the 18th Congress of the CPSU(B).) (In English.) Moscow, 1939.
Stalin, I. V., *O Velikoi Otechestvennoi Voine Sovetskogo Soyuza*. 5th ed. Moscow, 1945.
Stalin, I. V., *Voprosy Leninizma*. 11th ed. Moscow, 1940 (contains text of March 10, 1939 speech).

See also *Vneshnyaya politika Sovetskogo Soyuza v gody Otechestvennoi Voiny* for several speeches and statements by V. M. Molotov and others. 3 vols. Moscow, 1946-7.

Zasedaniye Verkhovnogo Soveta SSSR, 1-aya sessiya. 12-19 marta 1946g. Stenograficheskyi otchet. 2 vols. Moscow, 1946 and subsequent Supreme Soviet sessions.

GENERAL SOVIET HISTORIES OF THE WAR

Istoriya Velikoi Otechestvennoi Voiny Sovetskogo Soyuza. 5 vols. Moscow, 1960-3. (See introduction to Bibliography.)
Platonov, Lieut.-Gen. S. P. (and others), *Vtoraya mirovaya voina, 1939-45*. Moscow, 1958.
Telpukhovsky, B. S., *Velikaya Otechestvennaya Voina Sovetskogo Soyuza, 1941-45*. Moscow, 1959. See also German translation of same book with critical German introduction and footnotes:

Telpuchowski, B. S., *Die sowjetische Geschichte des Grossen Vaterländischen Krieges. Kritisch erläutert von Andreas Hillgruber und Hans-Adolf Jakobsen*. Frankfurt a/M., 1961.
Vorobyov F. D. i Kravtsov, V. M., *Velikaya Otechestvennaya Voina Sovetskogo Soyuza, 1941-45*. Moscow, 1961.
Vorobyov, V. F. (and others), *Boyevoi put' sovetskikh vooruzhennykh sil*. Moscow, 1960. (This is a popular history of the Red Army since 1918.)

SPECIAL STUDIES, REMINISCENCES AND DOCUMENTS
ON THE WAR IN RUSSIA, INCLUDING SOME GENERAL
WORKS PARTLY DEVOTED TO THE WAR YEARS

Abbreviations: PR = Partisan and Resistance activity
Mil. = Military
Ec. = Economic and industrial

(a) SOVIET UNION

Ampilov, V. i Smirnov, V., *V malen'kom gorode Lide*. Moscow, 1962. (PR)
Armstrong, J. A., *Ukrainian Nationalism 1939–45*. New York, 1955.
Armstrong, J. A. (ed.). *Soviet Partisans in World War II*. Madison, Wis., 1964.
Azarov, Vice-Adm. I. I., *Osazhdebbaya Odessa*. Moscow, 1962. (1941 defence of Odessa.)
Belov, Gen. I. B., *Za nami Moskva*. Moscow, 1962. (Battle of Moscow.)
Biryuzov, Marshal S. S., *Kogda gremeli pushki*. Moscow, 1961. (Mil.)
Bitva za Tulu. Sbornik materialov i dokumentov. Tula, 1957. (1941 defence of Tula.)
Bitva za Volgu: vospominaniya uchastnikov Stalingradskogo srazheniya. Stalingrad, 1958. (Stalingrad battle.)
Boiko, F. F., *Tsitadel' Chernomoriya*. Moscow, 1963. (Defence of Odessa, 1941.)
Boldin, Gen. I. V., *Stranitsy zhizni*. Moscow, 1961. (Mil., chiefly on 1941.)
Borisov, B., *Podvig Sevastopolya*. Moscow, 1957.
Borisov, B., *Sevastopoltsy ne sdayutsya*. Simferopol, 1961. (Both books on 1941–2 siege of Sebastopol.)
Brinsky, A., *Po tu storonu fronta*. 2 vols. Moscow, 1961. (PR)
Cassidy, H., *Moscow Dateline*. London, 1943.
Chernov, Yu., *Oni oboroniali Moonzund*. Moscow, 1959. (1941 battles on Estonian islands.)
Chuikov, Marshal V. I., *Nachalo puti*. First edition, Moscow, 1959. Second (revised) edition, Moscow, 1962. (Mil., Defence of Stalingrad.) (English translation of second edition, *The Beginning of the Road*. London, 1963.)
Dallin, A., *German Rule in Russia, 1941–45*. London, 1957.
Deborin, A., *O Kharaktere Vtoroi Mirovoi Voiny*. Moscow, 1960.
Deutscher, I., *Stalin: a Political Biography*. London, 1949.
Deviatsot dnei. Sbornik. Leningrad, 1957. (Leningrad blockade symposium.)
Direktivy KPSS i sovetskogo pravitel'stva po khozyalstvennym voprosam. Sbornik dokumentov. Vol. 2, 1929–45. Moscow, 1957. (Ec.)
Djilas, M., *Conversations with Stalin*. London, 1962.
Dorogoi bor'by i slavy. Moscow, 1961. (Symposium including contribution by Marshal K. K. Rokossovsky.)
Dostizheniya sovetskoi vlasti za 40 let v tsifrakh. Moscow, 1957. (Statistical survey for 1917–57.)
Ehrenburg, I., *Voina*. 2 vols. Moscow, 1942–3. (Reprinted articles.)
Ehrenburg, I., *Lyudi, gody, zhizn*. (Series on the war years.) *Novyi Mir*, Moscow, 1962–3.
Erickson, J., *The Soviet High Command . . . 1918–1945*. London, 1962.
Fedorov, A. F., *Podpolnyi obkom deistvuyet*. Moscow, 1958. (PR)

Fedyuninsky, Gen. I. I., *Podnyatuie po trevoge.* Moscow, 1961. (Mil., memoirs on 1941 and later.)
Fischer, G., *Soviet Opposition to Stalin.* Cambridge, Mass., 1951.
Fuller, J. F. C., *The Second World War.* London, 1948.
Garthoff, R. L., *How Russia Makes War: Soviet Military Doctrine.* London, 1954.
Glukhov, V. G., *Narodnyie mstiteli.* Kaluga, 1960. (PR in Kaluga and Briansk areas.)
Goure, L., *The Siege of Leningrad.* London, 1962.
Govorov, Marshal L. A., *V boyakh za gorod Lenina.* Leningrad, 1945. (Mil., battles in Leningrad area.)
Golovko, Adm. A. G., *Vmeste s flotom.* Moscow, 1960. (Naval warfare.)
Grossman, V., *Gody voiny.* Moscow, 1945. (Reprinted war reporting.)
Gvardiya tyla. Moscow, 1960. (Symposium on labour in war-time industry.)
Hindus, M., *Mother Russia.* London, 1943.
Hindus, M., *The Cossacks, the Story of a Warrior People.* London, 1946.
History of the CPSU (in English). Moscow, 1960. (The official Khrushchevite history translated by Andrew Rothstein.)
Inber, V. *Pochti tri goda.* Moscow, 1946. (Leningrad blockade.)
Istoriya VKP(b). Kratkii kurs. Moscow, 1945. (Although this was first published before the war, it continued, throughout the war, to be the standard work on the Party, and was even (wrongly) attributed to Stalin.)
Istoriya Latviiskoi SSR. 3 vols. Riga, 1961. (History of Latvian SSR.)
Iz istorii partizanskogo dvizheniya v Belorussii, 1941–44. Minsk, 1961. (Important symposium on PR in Belorussia.)
Kaftanov, S., *Sovetskaya intelligentsiya v Velikoi Otechestvennoi Voine.* Moscow, 1945.
Kalinin, Gen. S. A., *Razmyshleniya o minuvshem.* Moscow, 1963. (Mil. reminiscenses.)
Kamenetsky, I., *Hitler's Occupation of the Ukraine.* Marquette Univ. Press, 1957.
Karasev, A. V., *Leningradtsy v gody blokady.* Moscow, 1959. (Leningrad blockade.)
Karov, D., *Partizanskoye dvidzeniye v SSSR.* Munich, 1954. (An anti-Soviet account of the Partisan movement.)
Katayev, V., *Katakomby.* Moscow, 1945. (PR in Odessa.)
Klimov, I. D., *Geroicheskaya oborona Tuly.* Moscow, 1961. (1941 defence of Tula.)
Kolarz, W., *Religion in the Soviet Union.* London, 1959.
Kovalev, I. V., *Sovetskyi zheleznodorozhnyi transport 1917–47.* Moscow, 1947. (Ec., railways.)
Kovpak, A., *Ot Putivlya do Karpat.* Moscow, 1949. (PR in Ukraine).
Kozlov, I., *V Krymskom podpolii.* Moscow, 1954. (PR in Crimea.)
Kozlov, V. I., *Lyudi osobogo sklada.* Moscow, 1959. (PR)
KPSS o Vooruzhennykh Silakh Sovetskogo Soyuza. Sbornik dokumentov 1917–1958. Moscow, 1958.
Krasovsky, S. A., *Zhizn v aviatsii.* Moscow, 1960. (Airforce reminiscences.)
Kurskaya Bitva. Iz vospominanii uchastnikov. Kursk, 1958. (Kursk Battle symposium.)
Kuznetsov, Gen. P. G., *Dni boyevyie.* Moscow, 1959. (Mil. reminiscences.)
Leonhard, W., *Child of the Revolution.* London, 1957.

Leningrad v Velikoi Otechestvennoi Voine: Sbornik dokumentov i materialov. Leningrad, 1944.
Liddell Hart, B. H. (ed.), *The Red Army.* New York, 1958.
Liddell Hart, B. H., *The Other Side of the Hill.* London, 1948.
Lin'kov, G. M., *Voina v tylu vraga.* Moscow, 1939. (PR)
Lipalo, P. O., *KPB—organizator i rukovoditel' partizanskogo dvizheniya v Belorussii.* Minsk, 1959. (PR in Belorussia.)
Lipatov, N. P., *Chernaya metallurgiya Urala v gody ... voiny.* Moscow, 1960. (Ec., Urals industry.)
Luknitsky, P., *Na beregakh Nevy.* Moscow, 1961. (Defence of Leningrad.)
Lyashchenko, V., *Karayushchii gorod.* Moscow, 1961. (Mogilev PR)
Magidoff, R., *The Kremlin and the People.* New York, 1953.
Makarov, P. M., *Partizany Tavrii.* Moscow, 1960. (PR in Crimea and north of it.)
Maksimov, S. N., *Oborona Sevastopolya 1941–42.* Moscow, 1959. (1941–2 defence of Sebastopol.)
Medvedev, D. N., *Sil'nyie dukhom.* Moscow, 1957. (PR in West Ukraine.)
Medvedev, D. N., *Eto bylo pod Rovno.* Moscow, 1958. (PR in West Ukraine.)
Mikhailovsky, N. *Tallinskii dnevnik.* Moscow, 1956. (1941 war in Estonia.)
Mirovaya Voina 1939–45. Sbornik statei. Moscow, 1957. (Symposium on Second World War.)
Monastyrskii, Captain F. V., *Zemlya omytaya kroviyu.* Moscow, 1962. (Mil., fighting on Black Sea coast.)
Morozov, V. P., *Zapadneye Voronezha, yanvar-fevral' 1943 g.* Moscow, 1956. (Mil., Spring, 1943.)
Mushnikov, A. N., *Baltiitsy v boyakh za Leningrad, 1941–44.* Moscow, 1955. (Role of Navy in Battles of Leningrad.)
Narodnoye opolcheniye Moskvy. Moscow, 1961. (Moscow "home guard" in Battle of Moscow: symposium.)
Na rzhevskoi zemle. Kalinin, 1963. (PR and German occupation policy in Rzhev area.)
Neustroyev, Lieut.-Col., *Put' k Reichstagu.* Moscow, 1961. (Battle of Berlin.)
Odessa v Velikoi Otechestvennoi Voine Sov. Soyuza. Sbornik. 3 vols. Odessa, 1951. (Symposium on Odessa during the war.)
Orlovskaya Oblast' v gody ... voiny, 1941–45. Sbornik dokumentov i materialov. Orel, 1961. (Documents, etc., on Orel Province during the war.)
Partizanskie byli. Moscow, 1958. (PR)
Pavlov, D. V., *Leningrad v blokade.* Moscow, 1959.
Pavlovsky, Major N. A., *Na ostrovakh.* Moscow, 1963. (1941 war on Estonian islands.)
Popel', Gen. N. K., *V tyazhkuyu poru.* Moscow, 1959. (Mil., on 1941–2.)
Popel', Gen. N. K., *Tanki povernuli na zapad.* Moscow, 1960. (Kursk and after.)
Pravda o religii v Rossii. (Published by Moscow Patriarchate), Moscow, 1942.
Promyshlennost' SSSR. Statisticheskii sbornik. Moscow, 1957. (Book of industrial statistics also relevant to war years.)
Rotmistrov, Gen. P. A., *Tankovoye srazheniye pod Prokhorovkoi.* Moscow, 1960. (Mil., Kursk battle.)
Rozanov, G. L., *Krushenie fashistskoi Germanii.* Moscow, 1953. (Battle of Berlin and end of Nazi Germany.)
Schapiro, L., *The Communist Party of the Soviet Union.* London, 1960.

Shamko, E., *Partizanskoye dvizheniye v Krymu 1941–44*. Simferopol, 1959. (PR in Crimea.)

Sirota, F. I., *Leningrad, gorod-geroi*. Moscow, 1960. (Defence of Leningrad.)

Sobolev, L., *Dorogami pobed*. Moscow, 1945. (Russian advance into Rumania, etc.)

Soobschcheniya Sovetskogo Informburo. 4 vols. Moscow, 1942–4. (Selection of official wartime communications.)

Sovetskie partizany. Moscow, 1960. (PR symposium.)

(anon.) *I. V. Stalin: Kratkaya biografiya*. Moscow, 1942. (Short biography.)

Sokolovsky, Marshal V. D. (ed.), *Military Strategy. Soviet Doctrine and Concepts. Introduction by R. L. Garthoff*. London, 1963.

Sidorov, Col. V. I., *Razgrom nemtsev na Severe*. Moscow, 1945. (Defeat of Germans in N. Finland and N. Norway in 1944.)

Stalingradtsy: rasskazy zhitelei o geroicheskoi oborone. Moscow, 1950. (Defence of Stalingrad symposium.)

Suprunenko, N. I., *Ukraina v Velikoi Otech. Voine Sov. Soyuza, 1941–45*. Kiev, 1956.

Sheverdalkin, P. R., *Geroicheskaya bor'ba leningradskikh partizan*. Leningrad, 1959. (PR in Leningrad province.)

Sputnik Partizana. Moscow, 1942. (Partisan handbook.)

Timokhovich, I. V., *Sovetskaya aviatsiya v bitve pod Kurskom*. Moscow, 1959. (Airforce in Battle of Kursk.)

Treadgold, D. W., *Twentieth-century Russia*. Chicago, 1959.

Tsessarskii, A., *Zapiski partizanskogo vracha*. Moscow, 1956. (Reminiscences of a partisan doctor.)

Tyulenev, Gen. I. V., *Cherez tri voiny*. Moscow, 1960. (Of special interest are his chapters on the Caucasus fighting.)

V boyakh za Orel: Sbornik. Moscow, 1944. (Orel battle 1943.)

Vershigora, P., *Reid na San i Vislu*. Moscow, 1960. (PR in W. Ukraine and Poland.)

Vershigora, P., *Lyudi s chistoi sovestyu*. Moscow, 1948. (PR in Ukraine.)

VLKSM v tsifrakh i faktakh. Moscow, 1949. (Survey of Komsomol activity, particularly during the war.)

Vodolagin, M. A., *Stalingrad v Velokoi Otech. Voine, 1941–43*. Stalingrad, 1949.

V ognennom koltse. Vospominaniya uchastnikov oborony Leningrada. Moscow, 1962. (Symposium on defence of Leningrad.)

Voznenko, V. V. i Utkin, G. M., *Osvobozhdeniye Kieva, osen' 1943 g*. Moscow, 1953. (Liberation of Kiev.)

Voznesensky, N. A., *Voyennaya ekonomika SSSR v period Otech. Voiny*. Moscow, 1948. (Ec., survey of war years.)

Vyshnevsky, V., *Vboyakh 2a Tallin*. Kronstadt, 1944.

V trude kak v boyu: iz istorii komsomolskikh molodezhnykh brigad v gody Velikoi Otech. Voiny. Moscow, 1961. (Komsomol during the war.)

V'yunenko, N. M., *Chernomorski Flot v Velikoi Otech. Voine*. Moscow, 1957. (Black Sea Navy in the war.)

Werth, A., *Leningrad*. London, 1944.

Werth, A., *The Year of Stalingrad*. London, 1946.

Yarkhumov, V. M., *Cherez Nevu (67-ya armiya v boyakh po proryvu blokady Leningrada)*. Moscow, 1960. (The 1943 breaking of the Leningrad blockade.)

Yeremenko, Marshal, A. I., *Na Zapadnom Napravlenii*. Moscow, 1963. (1941 fighting.)
Yeremenko, Marshal A. I., *Stalingrad*. Moscow, 1961.
Yudenkov, A. F., *V ognennom koltse*. Moscow, 1962. (PR in Smolensk province.)
Zamyatin, Col. N. M. (and others), *Bitva pod Kurskom*. Moscow, 1945. (Mil., analysis of Kursk battle.)
Zamyatin, Col. N. M. (and others), *Stalingradskaya bitva*. Moscow, 1943. (Mil., analysis of Stalingrad battle.)

(b) POLAND

Anders, Gen. W., *Katyn*. Paris, 1949.
Bliss Lane, A., *I Saw Freedom Betrayed*. London, 1949.
Bór-Komarowski, Gen. T., *The Secret Army*. London, 1951.
Gomulka, W., *Statyi i rechi*. (Russian translation.) Moscow, 1959.
Istoriya Pol'shi, vol. III. Moscow, 1958.
Mikolajczyk, S., *The Rape of Poland*. London, 1948.
Sudebnyi otchet po delu ob organizatorakh . . . polskogo podpol'ya v tylu Krasnoi Armii . . . rassmotrennomu Voennoi Kollegiei Verkhovnogo Suda Soyuza SSR. (Record of Moscow trial of Polish Underground—General Okulicki and others—June 18 to 21, 1945.) Moscow, 1945.

(c) FINLAND

Kuusaari, N. and Nitemaa, V., *Finlands Krig 1941–45* (in Swedish). Helsinki, 1949.
Lundin, L., *Finland in the Second World War*. Indiana U.P., 1957.
Mannerheim, Maréchal, *Mémoires*. Paris, 1952.
Paasikivi, J. K., *Statyi i rechi, 1944–56*. (Russian translation of articles and speeches.) Moscow, 1958.
Tanner, V., *The Winter War*. New York, 1955.
Wuorinen, J. (ed.), *Finland and World War II*. New York, 1948.

NEWSPAPERS AND PERIODICALS

On ideological, economic and organisational problems during the War much more information is to be found in newspapers and periodicals than in books

PRINCIPAL NEWSPAPERS

Pravda, Izvestiya, Komsomolskaya Pravda, Vechernyaya Moskva: the Army paper *Krasnaya Zvezda* (Red Star) and Navy paper *Krasnyi Flot* Red Navy), besides *Leningradskaya Pravda, Radyanska Ukraina* (Kiev) and others published outside Moscow.

More specialized papers include *Trud* (trade unions), *Gudok* (railwaymen), *Uchitelskaya Gazeta* (teachers), *Literaturnaya Gazeta* (part-literary, part-political), *Sotsialisticheskoye Zemledeliye* (agriculture), *Pionerskaya Pravda* (children), and the official weekly of the Supreme Soviet, *Vedomosti Verkhovnogo Soveta SSSR*. Some of these more specialised papers appeared once,

1056

Selected Bibliography

twice or three times a week. Another bi-weekly was *Moscow News* (in English). During the war the Russians published a paper in London, *Soviet News*, and the British a paper in Moscow, *Britansky Soyuznik* (The British Ally). There were also countless army papers printed locally.

PRINCIPAL PERIODICALS

Bolshevik (renamed *Kommunist* after the war) the principal ideological journal of the Party; *Propagandist* (ceased publication in 1946); *Bloknot Agitatora*; *Bezbozhnik* (the anti-God paper, ceased publication in July 1941); *Kommunisticheskii Internatsional* (Comintern journal, ceased publication in 1943); *Voyennaya Mysl*; *Partiinoye Stroitel'stvo*; *Mirovoye Khoziaistvo i Mirovaya Politika*; *Voprosy Filosofii*; *Voprosy Istorii*; *Planovoye Khoziaistvo*; *Partiinaya Zhizn*; *Voina i Rabochii Klass*, since 1943, renamed after the war *Noyoye Vremya* (*War and the Working Class* and *New Times* respectively), also published in English and other languages; *Literatura i Iskusstvo*, etc. *Ogonyok* was the principal illustrated journal, and *Krokodil* the principal satirical journal.

The principal literary monthlies (though published very irregularly during the war) were *Novyi Mir, Znamya, Oktyabr, Zvezda* (Leningrad); on the theatre: *Teatr*; on the cinema: *Sovetskoye Kino*; on music: *Sovetskaya Muzyka*.

Besides all these, there were, of course, scores of specialized scientific, technical, medical and other journals.

SELECTION OF GERMAN BOOKS ON THE WAR IN RUSSIA

Assmann, K., *Deutsche Schicksalsjahre*. Wiesbaden, 1951.
Conrad, R., *Kampf um den Kaukasus*. Munich, 1955.
Dörr, H., *Pokhod na Stalingrad* (Russian translation). Moscow, 1957.
Einsiedel, H. v., *I Joined the Russians*. Yale U.P., 1953.
Entscheidungsschlachten des zweiten Weltkrieges (Collected articles). Frankfurt a/M., 1960.
Erfurth, N., *Der Finnische Krieg. 1941–44*. Wiesbaden, 1950.
Friessner, Gen. H., *Verratene Schlachten: die Tragödie der Deutschen Wehrmacht in Rumänien und Ungarn*. Hamburg, 1956.
The Goebbels Diaries. London, 1948.
Goerlitz, W., *Der Zweite Weltkrieg*. 2 vols. Stuttgart, 1951.
Goerlitz, W., *Paulus and Stalingrad*. London, 1963.
Greiner, H., *Die Oberste Wehrmachtführung, 1939–43*. Wiesbaden, 1951.
Guderian, H., *Panzer Leader*. London, 1952.
Halder, F., *Hitler als Feldherr*. Munich, 1949.
Halder, F., *Kriegstagebuch*. 3 vols. Stuttgart, 1963.
Heidkamper, O., *Witebsk. Kampf und Untergang der 3. Panzerarmee*. Heidelberg, 1954.
Hillgruber, A., *Die Räumung der Krim*. Berlin, 1959.
Hitler's Secret Conversations 1941–44. New York, 1953.
Hoth, H., *Panzer Operationen*. Heidelberg, 1956.
Koller, K., *Der Letzte Monat* (Luftwaffe). Mannheim, 1949.
Kriegstagebuch des OKW. 4 vols. Frankfurt a/M., 1961.
Lasch, O., *So fiel Königsberg*. Munich, 1959.

Lüdde-Neurath, W., *Regierung Dönitz* ... Göttingen, 1953.
Manstein, E. v., *Verlorene Siege*. Bonn, 1955. (*Lost Victories*.) Chicago, 1958.
Mellenthin, F. v., *Tankovyie srazheniya 1939–45 gg*. (Russian translation.) Moscow, 1957.
Philippi, A. und Heim, F., *Der Feldzug gegen Sowjetrussland*. Stuttgart, 1962.
Pickert, W., *Vom Kuban Brückenkopf bis Sewastopol*. Heidelberg, 1955.
Redelis, V., *Partisanenkrieg*. Heidelberg, 1958.
Rohden, H. v., *Die Luftwaffe ringt um Stalingrad*. Wiesbaden, 1950.
Schröter, H., *Stalingrad "bis zur letzten Patrone"*. Lengerich, 1955.
Schultz, J., *Die letzten 30 Tage*. Stuttgart, 1951.
Tippelskirch, K. v., *Geschichte des zweiten Weltkrieges*. Bonn, 1951.
Vormann, N. v., *Tscherkassy*. Heidelberg, 1954.
Waasen, H. M., *Was geschah in Stalingrad? Wo sind die Schuldigen?* Salzburg, 1950.
Weinert, E., *Das Nationalkomitee "Freies Deutschland", 1943–45*. East Berlin, 1957.

SOME IMPORTANT RUSSIAN LITERARY WORKS WRITTEN DURING OR SOON AFTER THE WAR

PROSE

Bek, A., *Volokolamskoye shosse*. Moscow, 1944.
Fadeyev, A., *Molodaya Gvardiya*. Moscow, 1946.
Gorbatov, B., *Nepokoryonnyie*. Moscow, 1943.
Grossman, V., *Narod bessmerten*. Moscow, 1942.
Kazekevich, E., *Zvezda*. Moscow, 1945.
Kazekevich, E., *Vesna na Odere*. Moscow, 1948.
Korneichuk, A., *Front* (play). Moscow, 1942.
Leonov, L., *V nashi gody. Publitzystika 1941–48*. Moscow, 1949.
Leonov, L., *Pyesy*. Moscow, 1945. (Plays, including *Nashestviye* (The Invasion).)
Nekrasov, V., *V Okopakh Stalingrada*. Moscow, 1946.
Polevoi, B., *Povest o nastoyashchem cheloveke*. Moscow, 1947.
Simonov, K., *Russkie lyudi* (play). Moscow, 1942.
Simonov, K., *Dni i nochi*. Moscow, 1944.
Sholohkov, M., *Nauka nenavisti*. Moscow, 1942.
Sholokhov, M., *Oni srazhalis' za rodinu*. 1959 (reprint).
Tolstoi, A. N., *Polnoye sobraniye sochinenii*, vol. 14. Moscow, 1950.
Tolstoi, A. N., *Ivan Groznyi, Dramaticheskaya povest'*. Moscow, 1945.
Vasilevakaya, V., *Raduga*. Moscow, 1942.

More recent novels on the war years are too numerous to list, but the most important from a documentary standpoint are K. Simonov's *Zhivyie i mertvyie* (Moscow, 1958) and *Soldatami ne rozhdayutsya* (published in Znamya, 1963–4), novels and stories by Yu. Bondarev, Yu. Nagibin, L. Volynsky, V. Grossman, V. Nekrasov, Yu. German, O. Bergholz (*Dnevnyie zvezdy*), B. Polevoi, etc.

WARTIME POETRY

Akhmatova, A., *Izbrannoye*. Tashkent, 1943.
Aliger, M., *Zoya*. Moscow, 1942. (Also in form of a play, Moscow, 1943.)
Bergholz, O., *Stikhi*. Moscow, 1962. (Includes most of her war poems.)
Ehrenburg, I., *Svoboda*. Moscow, 1943.
Inber, V., *O Leningrade, poemy i stikhi*. Leningrad, 1943.
Pasternak, B., *Zemnoi prostor*. Moscow, 1945.
Selvinsky, I., *Krym, Kavkaz, Kuban*. Moscow, 1947.
Simonov, K., *Stikhi*. Moscow, 1942.
Surkov, A., *Stikhi*. Moscow, 1943.
Tikhonov, N., *Kirov s nami*. Moscow, 1942.
Tvardovsky, A., *Vasili Terkin*. Moscow, 1942.

Most of the less conventional poetry on the war was not published until after Stalin's death; see, in particular, *Literaturnaya Moskva* annual, 1955 and 1956, and the *Den' Poezii* annual since 1955, particularly that of 1962. These contain much poetry by "soldier poets" like S. Gudzenko and also many poems, "unpublishable" under Stalin, by older writers like S. Kirsanov, N. Tikhonov, A. Tvardovsky, etc., some of them written during the war.

MUSIC

Music holds an important place in wartime art and propaganda. Of the innumerable symphonies, oratorios, cantatas, etc., directly inspired by the war the most striking are D. Shostakovich's celebrated *7th Symphony* and the even more poignant (though grossly underrated) *8th Symphony*, besides his chamber music, especially his *Piano Trio* of 1944. Important are also a number of wartime compositions by N. Myaskovsky, e.g. his cantata, *Kirov s nami*. Of S. Prokofiev's principal works written during the war, only his opera *War and Peace* has an obvious and direct connection with the War.

There was an enormous output of wartime songs, many included in selections like *Krasnoarmeisky pesennik* (Moscow, 1942), *Pesni* by M. Blanter (Moscow, 1942), *Pesni* by D. and D. Pokrass (Moscow, 1942) and many other later collections.

CINEMA

More important than the feature films produced during the war (mostly historical, including Eisenstein's *Ivan the Terrible*) are the outstanding documentaries on *The German Rout outside Moscow*, on Leningrad, Sebastopol and Stalingrad and *One Day of War*, all produced in 1942. These are not to be confused with the absurd "war films" produced towards the end of the war or soon after (such as *The Third Blow*—reconquest of the Crimea—or *The Fall of Berlin*) the main purpose of which is to demonstrate the military genius of Stalin always coming to the rescue of the flummoxed generals.

CHRONOLOGICAL TABLE

1939
Mar 10 Stalin's survey of international situation since Munich.
     15 Germans invade "post-Munich" Czechoslovakia.
     31 British guarantee to Poland.
Apr 17 "Litvinov Plan", soon rejected by Chamberlain.
     27 Hitler denounces Anglo-German naval agreement and non-aggression
        pact with Poland. No attacks on Russia in his speech.
May 4 Molotov replaces Litvinov as Foreign Commissar.
Jun 12 Strang goes to Moscow.
Jul   9 Churchill again urges immediate military alliance with Russia.
Aug 12 Anglo-French Military Mission arrives in Moscow.
     20 Hitler's telegram to Stalin.
     23 Soviet-German non-aggression pact signed.
     25 Anglo-Polish mutual assistance pact signed.
Sep   1 Germany invades Poland.
      3 Britain and France declare war on Germany.
        Germans sink SS *Athenia* off Ireland.
   1 to 9 Germans overrun western Poland.
     17 Germans reach Brest-Litovsk.
        Russians invade Eastern Poland.
     28 Warsaw surrenders.
Oct 14 HMS *Royal Oak* sunk at Scapa Flow.
Nov 30 Russians invade Finland.
Dec 13 Battle of River Plate; scuttling of *Graf Spee* (17th) 1940.
1940
Feb 11 Russians launch decisive attack on Mannerheim Line.
Mar 12 Soviet-Finnish peace treaty signed.
Apr   9 Germans invade Denmark and Norway. British troops land in Norway.
May 2 Allies evacuate Namsos.
     10 Germans invade Holland, Belgium and Luxemburg.
        Chamberlain resigns. Churchill becomes Prime Minister.
     14 Dutch army surrenders.

1940
May 14 German sweep into France begins.
21 Germans capture Amiens, Arras and Boulogne.
29 to June 3rd Dunkirk evacuation.
Jun 10 Italy declares war on Britain and France.
14 Germans enter Paris.
17 Petain seeks Franco-German armistice, signed 22nd.
17–23 Russians occupy Baltic States.
27–30 Russians occupy Bessarabia and Northern Bukovina.
Jul 15–21 Ninety German bombers shot down over Britain.
Aug 11–18 Peak of Battle of Britain.
Sep 7 First great blitz over London.
13–16 Italians cross Egyptian frontier and take Sidi Barrani.
Oct 7 Germans seize Rumanian oilfields.
Nov 11 Attack on Taranto cripples Italian navy.
12–14 Molotov's visit to Berlin.
Dec 9 Eighth Army opens offensive in North Africa.
18 Hitler finally decides on invasion of Soviet Union (Plan Barbarossa).
1941
Jan 3 Italians surrender Bardia.
30 Eighth Army takes Derna and advances towards Benghazi.
Tobruk captured.
Feb 6 Benghazi captured.
Mar 11 Lend–Lease Bill signed.
28 Battle of Cape Matapan.
31 German counter-offensive in North Africa begins.
Apr 5 Soviet-Yugoslav non-aggression pact signed.
6 Germans invade Greece and Yugoslavia; Britain sends 60,000 men to Greece.
7 British evacuate Benghazi.
13 Germans surround Tobruk and recapture Bardia.
Soviet-Japanese non-aggression pact signed.
22 British evacuation of Greece begins.
May 6 Stalin becomes head of Soviet Government. Molotov remains Foreign Commissar.
10 Rudolf Hess lands in Scotland.
20 German invasion of Crete.
28 to June 2. British evacuate Crete.
Jun 14 Tass communique ambiguously denies danger of German invasion.
22 Germany invades Soviet Union.
28 Germans capture Minsk, capital of Belorussia and large parts of Lithuania, Latvia and Western Ukraine.
Jul 3 Stalin's broadcast to the Russian people.
12 Anglo-Soviet mutual assistance agreement signed.
14 Germans reach Luga river on way to Leningrad.
16 Germans reach Smolensk on way to Moscow.
25 Germans capture Tallinn.
30 Harry Hopkins in Moscow.
Aug — Germans overrun large parts of Ukraine, capturing Dniepropetrovsk on 17th.
30 Germans capture Mga, Leningrad's last railway link.

1941
Sep 8 Germans capture Schülsselburg, thus completing Leningrad's land blockade.
  17 End of "Battle of Kiev" resulting in encirclement of large Russian forces.
  29 German penetration of Donbas begins.
     Beaverbrook and Harriman arrive in Moscow.
  30 German offensive against Moscow begins.
Oct 2 Germans capture Orel.
  6 to 12 Battle of Viazma, ending in encirlement of large Russian forces west of Moscow.
  12 Germans capture Kaluga.
  13 Germans capture Kalinin.
  14–16 Further German advances towards Moscow.
  16 Height of "Moscow panic".
     Germans and Rumanians capture Odessa.
  20 State of siege declared in Moscow.
  24 Germans capture Kharkov.
  25 Failure of first German offensive against Moscow.
  30 Nine-month siege of Sebastopol begins.
Nov 3 Germans capture Kursk.
  9 Germans take Tikhvin, thus almost completely isolating Leningrad.
  12 HMS *Ark Royal* sunk.
  6 and 7 Stalins two "Holy Russia" speeches.
  16 Second German offensive against Moscow begins.
  18 British offensive in Western Desert begins.
  19 Germans take Rostov.
  20 to Dec 25 All-time low in Leningrad rationing.
  22 Germans break into Klin and Istra.
  29 Russians recapture Rostov.
Dec 5 Eden arrives in Moscow.
  6 Russian Moscow counter-offensive begins.
  7 Japanese bomb Pearl Harbour, and raid British Malaya.
  8 Britain and USA declare war on Japan.
     Japanese air-raids on Guam, Midway, Philippines and Hong Kong.
  9 Japanese land on Luzon.
     Russians recapture Tikhvin, thus saving Leningrad.
  11 Hitler declares war on USA.
  10 HMS *Prince of Wales* and HMS *Repulse* sunk by Japanese.
  15 Russians recapture Klin, Istra and relieve Tula.
  19 Penang evacuated.
  24 British recapture Benghazi.
  25 Hong Kong surrenders.
  25–30 Russians establish bridgehead in East Crimea.
  30 Russians recapture Kaluga.
1942
Jan–Mar Russian offensive west of Moscow continues.
Jan 10 Japanese invade Dutch East Indies.
  11 Japanese take Kuala Lumpur.
  21 German counter-offensive in Western Desert begins.
  28 Germans retake Benghazi.

1942
Feb   1 British forces in Malaya withdraw to Singapore.
     15 Singapore surrenders.
     24 US task force raids Wake Island.
     28 Japanese land in Java.
Mar 10 Rangoon falls to Japanese.
     28 Commando raid on St. Nazaire
Apr   9 Surrender of Bataan.
May   1 Japanese take Mandalay.
      6 Corregidor surrenders.
      8 Germans attack in Eastern Crimea.
     12 Russian offensive opens in Kharkov area.
     17 German counter-offensive begins; Russian defeat in Kharkov area.
     20 Germans take Kerch peninsula.
     26 Molotov signs Anglo-Soviet twenty-year Alliance in London, then
        visits Washington.
        Rommel resumes offensive in Western Desert.
     30 Thousand-bomber raid on Cologne.
Jun   3 Battle of Midway Island begins.
      7 Germans and Rumanians launch final attack on Sebastopol.
     11 Publication of the "Second-Front" communique.
     19 British withdraw to Egyptian frontier.
     21 Rommel takes Tobruk.
     28 Eighth Army retreats to El Alamein.
        Beginning of great German offensive in the South.
Jul   3 Fall of Sebastopol.
     19 Germans take Voroshilovgrad.
     28 Germans retake Rostov.
     30 Stalin's "Not another step back" order to the Army.
Aug   3 Germans reach Kotelnikovo.
      7 Americans land in Guadalcanal.
     11 Fall of Maikop and Krasnodar.
  12–15 Churchill, Harriman and Stalin confer in Moscow.
     19 Dieppe raid.
     23 Germans break through to Volga, north of Stalingrad.
        40,000 killed in air-raid on Stalingrad.
     25 Germans held at Mozdok on way to Grozny and Baku.
     31 Battle of Alam Halfa begins.
Sep   3 German breakthrough to Volga south of Stalingrad.
     13 German all-out attack on Stalingrad begins.
     24 Most of central Stalingrad in German hands.
Oct 14–15 Failure of most concentrated German attack on northern Stalingrad
     23 Battle of El Alamein begins.
Nov   4 Rommel in full retreat.
      8 Allied landings in French North Africa.
     13 Sea battle of Guadalcanal.
     19 Russian counter-offensive at Stalingrad begins.
     22 Over 300,000 Germans surrounded at Stalingrad.
Dec 12–23 Manstein's abortive attempt to relieve Stalingrad.
     16–20 Rout of Italians on Don.
     21 Eighth Army reaches Benghazi.

1943

Jan   2 German withdrawal from Caucasus begins.
     23 Eighth Army reaches Tripoli.
     26 Russians liberate Voronezh.
     31 Paulus surrenders at Stalingrad.
Feb   2 Final German surrender at Stalingrad.
      8 Russians take Kursk.
     14 Russians take Rostov.
     16 Russians take Kharkov.
Mar 3–12 Russians liberate Gzhatsk–Viazma–Rzhev triangle.
     15 Germans recapture Kharkov.
     29 Eighth Army takes Mareth Line.
Apr 14 Eighth Army reaches Enfidaville.
     20 Massacre in Warsaw Ghetto.
     26 USSR breaks off relations with London Polish Government following
        Katyn "bombshell".
May   7 Allies take Tunis and Bizerta.
     11 US troops land on Attu, Aleutian Islands.
     12 German Army in Tunisia surrenders.
     22 Comintern dissolved.
Jun 29 US forces land in New Guinea.
Jul   5 Battle of Kursk begins.
     10 Allies land in Sicily.
   12–15 Russian counter-offensive against Orel salient begins.
     26 Mussolini falls from power.
Aug   5 Russians take Orel and Belgorod.
     16 Americans enter Messina.
     23 Russians retake Kharkov.
     27 Japanese evacuate New Georgia Island.
     30 Taganrog recaptured.
     31 Glukhov recaptured.
Sep   3 Allies invade Italy.
      8 Russians liberate Donbas.
     10 Mariupol taken.
     16 Novorossisk taken.
     25 Smolensk taken.
     30 Fifth Army takes Naples.
Oct   7 Russians clear the Taman Peninsula; Dnieper forced.
     13 Italy declares war on Germany.
     14 Zaporozhie recaptured.
     18 Foreign Ministers' conference opens in Moscow.
     19 Germans in Italy retire from Volturno river.
     25 Dniepropetrovsk recaptured.
Nov   1 Americans land on Bouganville in Solomons.
      4 Eighth Army takes Isernia.
      6 Russians recapture Kiev.
     12 Bridgehead established across the Sangro.
        Russians take Zhitomir.
     19 German counter-offensive retakes Zhitomir.
     20 Americans land on Tarawa and Makin Islands.
     28 Teheran conference begins.

1943
Dec   7 Fifth Army take Monte Camino.
      26 *Scharnhorst* sunk.
1944
Jan   4 Fifth Army launches attack east of Cassino.
      27 Leningrad completely relieved.
      15 Americans complete reconquest of Solomon Islands.
Feb 17 German rout in Korsun salient in central Ukraine.
      22 Krivoi Rog taken.
Mar   4 Russian spring offensive opens in Ukraine.
      12 Uman recaptured.
      19 Russians force the Dniester.
Apr   2 Russians enter Rumania.
      11 Liberation of Crimea begins.
      15 Tarnopol liberated.
      22 Allies land at Hollandia, New Guinea.
May   9 Sebastopol taken.
      12 Allies in Italy assault the Gustav Line.
      13 Crimea cleared of Germans.
      18 Cassino taken.
      23 Anzio break-out.
Jun   4 Fifth Army enters Rome.
       6 Allies invade Normandy.
      10 Russians begin offensive against Finland.
      13 First V1 bomb on London.
      15 First super-Fortress raid on Japan.
      19 Americans take Saipan.
      20 Viborg taken by Russians.
      23 Russians begin offensive in Belorussia.
      23–28 Germans encircled at Vitebsk and Bobruisk.
      27 Cherbourg captured.
Jul   3 Russians take Minsk. About 100,000 Germans captured.
       6 Russians take Kovel.
       9 Caen captured.
      13 Vilno captured.
      18 Rokossovsky's troops enter Poland. Pskov liberated.
      20 Attempt to assasinate Hitler.
      23 Lublin taken.
      25 Americans break through at St. Lo.
      28 Brest Litovsk taken.
      31 Russians reach outskirts of Praga, opposite Warsaw.
          Avranches entered.
Aug   1 Beginning of Warsaw Rising.
      11 Eighth Army reaches Florence.
      15 Allies land in south of France.
      16 Americans near Chartres and Dreux.
      20 Russians begin offensive in Bessarabia and Rumania.
      23 King Michael of Rumania interns Antonescu and forms new "peace"
          Government.
      25 Paris liberated.
      26 Eighth Army opens attack in Adriatic sector.

1944
Aug 30 Russians enter Bucharest and Ploesti.
Sep 3 British reach Brussels.
     Americans reach Mons.
     4 Antwerp liberated.
     Cease-fire on Finnish Front.
     5 Russians declare war on Bulgaria.
     8 First V2 lands in Britain.
     9 Russians invade Bulgaria.
    10 Russians capture Praga.
    11 Americans cross German frontier near Trier.
    12 Rumanian armistice signed.
    17 Arnhem battle begins.
    19 Finnish armistice signed.
    28 Calais liberated.
    29 Russians enter Yugoslavia.
Oct 2 Surrender of underground forces in Warsaw.
     9 Churchill arrives in Moscow.
    19 Americans land in Philippines.
    20 Russians and Yugoslavs enter Belgrade.
Nov 1 British land on Walcheren Island.
    12 *Tirpitz* sunk.
    24 Strasbourg captured.
Dec 2 De Gaulle arrives in Moscow.
     5 Allies take Ravenna
    16 German offensive in the Ardennes begins.
    18 North Burma cleared of Japanese.
    27 Russians surround Budapest.
1945
Jan 3 Americans counter-attack Ardennes salient.
    12 Great Russian offensive begins in Poland.
    17 Russians take Warsaw.
    19 Cracow captured.
    20 Tilsit captured.
    Hungarian "Debrecen" Government signs armistice.
    23 Russians reach the Oder.
    29 Russians encircle Poznan.
Feb 3 Allies capture Colmar.
     4 Yalta conference opens.
     5 Americans enter Manila.
    British and Canadians open offensive to reach the Rhine.
     9 Königsberg almost surrounded.
    10 Elbing captured.
    13 Budapest falls.
    19 Americans land on Iwojima.
    23 Poznan taken.
Mar 7 Cologne captured.
    13 Allies command west bank of Rhine.
    23 Rhine crossed.
    29 Russians cross Austrian frontier.
    30 Danzig captured.

1945
Apr 1 Americans invade Okinawa.
     5 Osnabrück captured.
     9 Königsberg surrenders.
     9 Allies begin final offensive in Italy.
    10 Hanover captured.
    12 Death of President Roosevelt.
       Eighth Army cross the Santorno.
    13 Russians take Vienna.
    16 Final Russian Berlin offensive starts.
    19 Americans take Leipzig.
    21 Allies take Bologna.
    23 Russians reach Berlin.
       Allies reach the Po.
    27 Genoa and Verona taken.
       American and Russian forces meet at Torgau.
    30 Hitler's suicide.
May 1 Surrender of German Army on Italian front.
     2 Berlin surrenders to Russians.
     4 Allies reach Trieste.
       Rangoon taken.
     7 Jodl signs unconditional surrender at Eisenhower's H.Q. at Reims.
     8 "V.E." Day. Keitel signs surrender at Zhakov's H.Q. near Berlin.
     9 Russians take Prague. Victory Day in Soviet Union.
    21 Organised resistance ends in Okinawa.
Jul 17 Potsdam conference begins.
Aug 6 Atom bomb dropped on Hiroshima.
     8 Soviet Union declares war on Japan.
     9 Atom bomb dropped on Nagasaki.
       Russian invasion of Manchuria begins.
    14 Japanese agree to surrender.
Sep 2 Japan signs capitulation on board USS *Missouri.*

ACKNOWLEDGEMENTS

Thanks are due to the following publishers for permission to quote from copyright works:

Jonathan Cape Ltd., and Doubleday & Co. Inc., for *Roosevelt and the Russians* by E. R. Stettinius, copyright 1949 by the Stettinius Fund Inc.

Cassell & Co. Ltd., and Houghton Mifflin Co. Inc., for *The Second World War* by Sir Winston Churchill,

Eyre & Spottiswoode Ltd., and Harper & Row, for *The White House Papers of Harry L. Hopkins*, edited by R. E. Sherwood.

Michael Joseph Ltd., and E. P. Dutton & Co. Inc., for *Panzer Leader* by General H. Guderian.

Macmillan & Co. Ltd., and The St. Martin's Press Inc., for *German Rule in Russia* by Alexander Dallin.

INDEX

Abganerovo, 442; Germans halted at, 448; recaptured by Russians, 495; wrecked by bombing, 519
Abyssinia, Italian invasion of, 12
Ackermann, Anton, 735
Adam, Colonel, in Stalingrad Cauldron, 541n.
Adenauer, Konrad, 930
Afghanistan, 292n., 275
AK. See *Armija Krajowa*
Akhmatova, Anna, 410–11; poem on bombing of London, 99
Aktion Kugel, 707
Albania, Italian defeats in, 111
Alexander, Field-Marshal, opposes Tito at Trieste, 1008
Alexander Nevsky, Order of, created, 415
Alexander Nevsky (film), 7, 22, 120
Alexandria, Patriarch of, 432, 437
Alexandrov, G. F., 185; attacks Ehrenburg, 966–7, 968
Alexeanu, Professor, 820, 822, 825
Alexis, Patriarch, 436, 437
Alupka, 831, 832, 836
Alushta, 836
Algiers: French Committee of National Liberation, 920
Ali, Rashid, 124
Aligher, Margarita, 273
All-Slav Committee, 435, 639
Allenstein, 964

Allied Control Council, 988
Allied Military Government in Occupied Countries, 750
Allmedinger, General, 833
American–Soviet Agreement, 480
Amiens, 530n.
Appeasement, 31; British critics of, 5; by Britain and France, 5–6
Anders, General: attack on by Berling, 654; and Katyn massacre, 645, 662, 664, 666n; in Russia, 293, 637–9, 644, 651, 652, 659; in Teheran, 654, 770; leaves Russia, 638–9; meets Churchill, 478, 482
Andreievna, Anna, 337
Andreyev, A. A., 7
Andrusenko, Colonel, 461
Anglo–American–Soviet Agreement, 233
Anglo–American–Soviet Economic Conference, 289–91
Anglo–French Military Mission (1939), 33–41, 42, 43, 50
Anglo–German Naval Agreement, 24
Anglo–Soviet Agreement (1941), 179, 181
Anglo–Soviet Alliance, 377–86, 401, 479–80, 922, 927; first anniversary celebrations, 672–3; Russian press on, 381–2; second anniversary celebrations, 844
Anglo–Soviet co-operation, 286–9
Anglo–Soviet Declaration (1941), 278

1069

Fine works of fiction available from Carroll and Graf.

Bodies and Souls
by John Rechy
"A brilliant novel of modern lives in Southern California."
—*San Francisco Chronicle*
Hardcover $17.95
Trade Paper $8.95

The Diary of a Country Priest
by Georges Bernanos
"This novel is a beautiful and triumphant story." —*New York Times*
$7.95

East River
by Sholem Asch
"A novel of the American spirit ... it makes living an experience of dignity and delight."—*New York Times*
$8.95

The Forty Days of Musa Dagh
by Franz Werfel
"A magnificent novel ... about a stirring episode in history."—*New York Times*
$9.95

The Four Horsemen of the Apocalpyse
by Vincente Blasco Ibanez
The timeless, novel of World War I
$8.95

Gardens of Stone
by Nicholas Proffitt
"A serious war novel, with laughter and tears, comparable to *Mr. Roberts*."—*Washington Post*
$14.95

In the Miro District
by Peter Taylor
"Taylor is one of the best writers America has ever produced."—*New York Times*
Trade Paper $7.95

Kings Row
by Henry Bellamanns
"... a grand yarn, full of the sap of life."—*New York Times Book Review*
$8.95